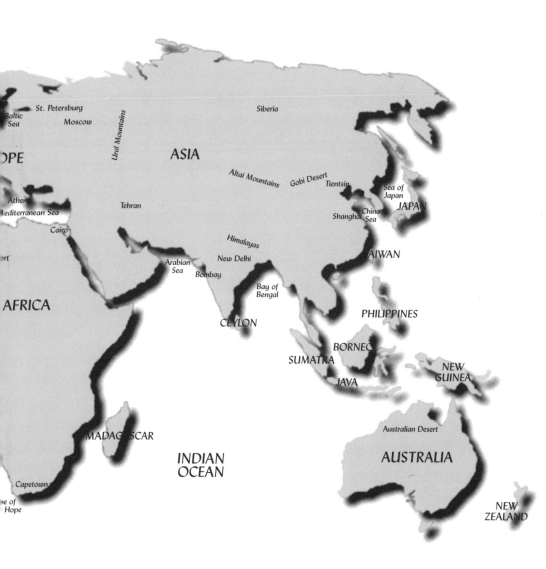

St. Petersburg

Baltic
Sea

Moscow

Ural Mountains

Siberia

PE

ASIA

Altai Mountains

Gobi Desert

Tientsin

Sea of
Japan

JAPAN

Athens

Mediterranean Sea

Tehran

Cairo

Himalayas

Shanghai

China
Sea

ert

Arabian
Sea

New Delhi

Bombay

AIWAN

AFRICA

Bay of
Bengal

CEYLON

PHILIPPINES

BORNEO

SUMATRA

NEW
GUINEA

JAVA

MADAGASCAR

Australian Desert

INDIAN
OCEAN

AUSTRALIA

Capetown

e of
Hope

NEW
ZEALAND

TRAGEDY AND HOPE

"*The powers of financial capitalism had another far-reaching aim, nothing less than to create a world system of financial control in private hands able to dominate the political system of each country and the economy of the world as a whole. This system was to be controlled in a feudalistic fashion by the central banks of the world acting in concert, by secret agreements arrived at in frequent meetings and conferences. The apex of the systems was to be the Bank for International Settlements in Basel, Switzerland, a private bank owned and controlled by the world's central banks which were themselves private corporations. Each central bank...sought to dominate its government by its ability to control Treasury loans, to manipulate foreign exchanges, to influence the level of economic activity in the country, and to influence co-operative politicians by subsequent economic rewards in the business world.*"

Carroll Quigley

BY CARROLL QUIGLEY

The Evolution of Civilizations
Tragedy and Hope: A History of the World in Our Time
The Anglo-American Establishment

TRAGEDY
AND
HOPE

A *History of*
THE WORLD
in Our Time

Carroll Quigley

First published in 1966 by

THE MACMILLAN COMPANY, NEW YORK

COLLIER-MACMILLAN LIMITED, LONDON

Post Office Box 590
San Pedro, California 90733
USA

gsgbooks@earthlink.net

ISBN #0-945001-10-X

TO
ALL WHO CARE
AND SEEK TO HELP

Contents

Preface

The expression "contemporary history" is probably self-contradictory, because what is contemporary is not history, and what is history is not contemporary. Sensible historians usually refrain from writing accounts of very recent events because they realize that the source materials for such events, especially the indispensable official documents, are not available and that, even with the documentation which is available, it is very difficult for anyone to obtain the necessary perspective on the events of one's own mature life. But I must clearly not be a sensible or, at least, an ordinary historian, for, having covered, in an earlier book, the whole of human history in a mere 271 pages, I now use more than 1300 pages for the events of a single lifetime. There is a connection here. It will be evident to any attentive reader that I have devoted long years of study and much original research, even where adequate documentation is not available, but it should be equally evident that whatever value this present work has rests on its broad perspective. I have tried to remedy deficiencies of evidence by perspective, not only by projecting the patterns of past history into the present and the future but also by trying to place the events of the present in their total context by examining all the varied aspects of these events, not merely the political and economic, as is so frequently done, but by my efforts to bring into the picture the military, technological, social, and intellectual elements as well.

The result of all this, I hope, is an interpretation of the present as well as the immediate past and the near future, which is free from the accepted clichés, slogans, and self-justifications which mar so much of "contemporary history." Much of my adult life has been devoted to training undergraduates in techniques of historical analysis which will help them to free their understanding of history from the accepted categories and cognitive classifications of the society in which we live, since these, however necessary they may be for our processes of thought and for the concepts and symbols needed for us to communicate about reality, nevertheless do often serve as barriers which shield us from recognition of the underlying realities themselves. The present work is the result of such an attempt to look at the real situations which lie beneath the conceptual

ix

and verbal symbols. I feel that it does provide, as a consequence of this effort, a fresher, somewhat different, and (I hope) more satisfying explanation of how we arrived at the situation in which we now find ourselves.

More than twenty years have gone into the writing of this work. Although most of it is based on the usual accounts of these events, some portions are based on fairly intensive personal research (including research among manuscript materials). These portions include the following: the nature and techniques of financial capitalism, the economic structure of France under the Third Republic, the social history of the United States, and the membership and activities of the English Establishment. On other subjects, my reading has been as wide as I could make it, and I have tried consistently to view all subjects from as wide and as varied points of view as I am capable. Although I regard myself, for purposes of classification, as a historian, I did a great deal of study in political science at Harvard, have persisted in the private study of modern psychological theory for more than thirty years, and have been a member of the American Anthropological Association, the American Economic Association, and the American Association for the Advancement of Science, as well as the American Historical Association for many years.

Thus my chief justification for writing a lengthy work on contemporary history, despite the necessarily restricted nature of the documentation, must be based on my efforts to remedy this inevitable deficiency by using historical perspective to permit me to project the tendencies of the past into the present and even the future and my efforts to give this attempt a more solid basis by using all the evidence from a wide variety of academic disciplines.

As a consequence of these efforts to use this broad, and perhaps complex, method, this book is almost inexcusably lengthy. For this I must apologize, with the excuse that I did not have time to make it shorter and that an admittedly tentative and interpretative work must necessarily be longer than a more definite or more dogmatic presentation. To those who find the length excessive, I can only say that I omitted chapters, which were already written, on three topics: the agricultural history of Europe, the domestic history of France and Italy, and the intellectual history of the twentieth century in general. To do this I introduced enough on these subjects into other chapters.

Although I project the interpretation into the near future on a number of occasions, the historical narrative ceases in 1964, not because the date of writing caught up with the march of historical events but because the period 1962–1964 seems to me to mark the end of an era of historical development and a period of pause before a quite different era with quite different problems begins. This change is evident in a number of obvious events, such as the fact that the leaders of all the major countries (except

Red China and France) and of many lesser ones (such as Canada, India, West Germany, the Vatican, Brazil, and Israel) were changed in this period. Much more important is the fact that the Cold War, which culminated in the Cuban crisis of October 1962, began to dwindle toward its end during the next two years, a process which was evident in a number of events, such as the rapid replacement of the Cold War by "Competitive Coexistence"; the disintegration of the two superblocs which had faced each other during the Cold War; the rise of neutralism, both within the superblocs and in the buffer fringe of third-bloc powers between them; the swamping of the United Nations General Assembly under a flood of newly independent, sometimes microscopic, pseudopowers; the growing parallelism of the Soviet Union and the United States; and the growing emphasis in all parts of the world on problems of living standards, of social maladjustments, and of mental health, replacing the previous emphasis on armaments, nuclear tensions, and heavy industrialization. At such a period, when one era seems to be ending and a different, if yet indistinct era appearing, it seemed to me as good a time as any to evaluate the past and to seek some explanation of how we arrived where we are.

In any preface such as this, it is customary to conclude with acknowledgment of personal obligations. My sense of these is so broad that I find it invidious to single out some and to omit others. But four must be mentioned. Much of this book was typed, in her usual faultless way, by my wife. This was done originally and in revised versions, in spite of the constant distractions of her domestic obligations, of her own professional career in a different university, and of her own writing and publication. For her cheerful assumption of this great burden, I am very grateful.

Similarly, I am grateful to the patience, enthusiasm, and amazingly wide knowledge of my editor at The Macmillan Company, Peter V. Ritner.

I wish to express my gratitude to the University Grants Committee of Georgetown University, which twice provided funds for summer research.

And, finally, I must say a word of thanks to my students over many years who forced me to keep up with the rapidly changing customs and outlook of our young people and sometimes also compelled me to recognize that my way of looking at the world is not necessarily the only way, or even the best way, to look at it. Many of these students, past, present, and future, are included in the dedication of this book.

CARROLL QUIGLEY

Washington, D.C.
March 8, 1965

I

INTRODUCTION:
WESTERN CIVILIZATION
IN ITS WORLD SETTING

Cultural Evolution in Civilizations

Cultural Diffusion in Western Civilization

Europe's Shift to the Twentieth Century

Cultural Evolution in Civilizations

THERE have always been men who have asked, "Where are we going?" But never, it would seem, have there been so many of them. And surely never before have these myriads of questioners asked their question in such dolorous tones or rephrased their question in such despairing words: "Can man survive?" Even on a less cosmic basis, questioners appear on all sides, seeking "meaning" or "identity," or even, on the most narrowly egocentric basis, "trying to find myself."

One of these persistent questions is typical of the twentieth century rather than of earlier times: Can our way of life survive? Is our civilization doomed to vanish, as did that of the Incas, the Sumerians, and the Romans? From Giovanni Battista Vico in the early eighteenth century to Oswald Spengler in the early twentieth century and Arnold J. Toynbee in our own day, men have been puzzling over the problem whether civilizations have a life cycle and follow a similar pattern of change. From this discussion has emerged a fairly general agreement that men live in separately organized societies, each with its own distinct culture; that some of these societies, having writing and city life, exist on a higher level of culture than the rest, and should be called by the different term "civilizations"; and that these civilizations tend to pass through a common pattern of experience.

From these studies it would seem that civilizations pass through a process of evolution which can be analyzed briefly as follows: each civilization is born in some inexplicable fashion and, after a slow start, enters a period of vigorous expansion, increasing its size and power, both internally and at the expense of its neighbors, until gradually a crisis of organization appears. When this crisis has passed and the civilization has been reorganized, it seems somewhat different. Its vigor and morale have weakened. It becomes stabilized and eventually stagnant. After a Golden Age of peace and prosperity, internal crises again arise. At this point there appears, for the first time, a moral and physical weakness which raises, also for the first time, questions about the civilization's ability to defend itself against external enemies. Racked by internal struggles of a social and constitutional character, weakened by loss of faith in its older

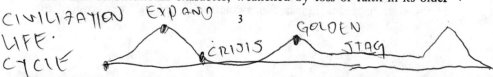

CIVILIZATION EXPAND
LIFE.
CYCLE   CRISIS   GOLDEN
                             STAG

3

ideologies and by the challenge of newer ideas incompatible with its past nature, the civilization grows steadily weaker until it is submerged by outside enemies, and eventually disappears.

When we come to apply this process, even in this rather vague form, to our own civilization, Western Civilization, we can see that certain modifications are needed. Like other civilizations, our civilization began with a period of mixture of cultural elements from other societies, formed these elements into a culture distinctly its own, began to expand with growing rapidity as others had done, and passed from this period of expansion into a period of crisis. But at that point the pattern changed.

In more than a dozen other civilizations the Age of Expansion was followed by an Age of Crisis, and this, in turn, by a period of Universal Empire in which a single political unit ruled the whole extent of the civilization. Western Civilization, on the contrary, did not pass from the Age of Crisis to the Age of Universal Empire, but instead was able to reform itself and entered upon a new period of expansion. Moreover, Western Civilization did this not once, but several times. It was this ability to reform or reorganize itself again and again which made Western Civilization the dominant factor in the world at the beginning of the twentieth century.

As we look at the three ages forming the central portion of the life cycle of a civilization, we can see a common pattern. The Age of Expansion is generally marked by four kinds of expansion: (1) of population, (2) of geographic area, (3) of production, and (4) of knowledge. The expansion of production and the expansion of knowledge give rise to the expansion of population, and the three of these together give rise to the expansion of geographic extent. This geographic expansion is of some importance because it gives the civilization a kind of nuclear structure made up of an older core area (which had existed as part of the civilization even before the period of expansion) and a newer peripheral area (which became part of the civilization only in the period of expansion and later). If we wish, we can make, as an additional refinement, a third, semiperipheral area between the core area and the fully peripheral area.

These various areas are readily discernible in various civilizations of the past, and have played a vital role in historic change in these civilizations. In Mesopotamian Civilization (6000 B.C.–300 B.C.) the core area was the lower valley of Mesopotamia; the semiperipheral area was the middle and upper valley, while the peripheral area included the highlands surrounding this valley, and more remote areas like Iran, Syria, and even Anatolia. The core area of Cretan Civilization (3500 B.C.–1100 B.C.) was the island of Crete, while the peripheral area included the Aegean islands and the Balkan coasts. In Classical Civilization the core area was the shores of the Aegean Sea; the semiperipheral area was the rest of the northern portion of the eastern Mediterranean Sea, while the peripheral area covered the rest of the Mediterranean shores and ultimately Spain, North Africa, and Gaul. In Canaanite Civilization (2200 B.C.–100 B.C.) the core area was the Levant, while the peripheral area was in the western Mediterranean at Tunis, western Sicily, and eastern Spain. The core area of Western Civilization (A.D. 400 to some time in the future) has been the northern half of Italy, France, the extreme western part of Germany, and England; the semiperipheral area has been central, eastern, and southern Europe and the Iberian peninsula, while the peripheral areas have included North and South America, Australia, New Zealand, South Africa, and some other areas.

This distinction of at least two geographic areas in each civilization is of major importance. The process of expansion, which begins in the core area, also begins to slow up in the core at a time when the peripheral area is still expanding. In consequence, by the latter part of the Age of Expansion, the peripheral areas of a civilization tend to become wealthier and more powerful than the core area. Another way of saying this is that the core passes from the Age of Expansion to the Age of Conflict before the periphery does. Eventually, in most civilizations the rate of expansion begins to decline everywhere.

It is this decline in the rate of expansion of a civilization which marks its passage from the Age of Expansion to the Age of Conflict. This latter is the most complex, most interesting, and most critical of all the periods of the life cycle of a civilization. It is marked by four chief characteristics: (a) it is a period of declining rate of expansion; (b) it is a period of growing tensions and class conflicts; (c) it is a period of increasingly frequent and increasingly violent imperialist wars; and (d) it is a period of growing irrationality, pessimism, superstitions, and otherworldliness. All these phenomena appear in the core area of a civilization before they appear in more peripheral portions of the society.

The decreasing rate of expansion of the Age of Conflict gives rise to the other characteristics of the age, in part at least. After the long years of the Age of Expansion, people's minds and their social organizations are adjusted to expansion, and it is a very difficult thing to readjust these to a decreasing rate of expansion. Social classes and political units within the civilization try to compensate for the slowing of expansion through normal growth by the use of violence against other social classes or against other political units. From this come class struggles and imperialist wars. The outcomes of these struggles *within the civilization* are not of vital significance for the future of the civilization itself. What would be of such significance would be the reorganization of the structure of the civilization so that the process of normal growth would be resumed. Because such a reorganization requires the removal of the causes of the civilization's decline, the triumph of one social class over another or of one political unit over another, within the civilization, will not usually have any major influence on the causes of the decline, and will not (except by accident) result in such a reorganization of structure as will give rise to a new period of expansion. Indeed, the class struggles and imperialist wars of the Age of Conflict will probably serve to increase the speed of the civilization's decline because they dissipate capital and divert wealth and energies from productive to nonproductive activities.

In most civilizations the long-drawn agony of the Age of Conflict finally ends in a new period, the Age of the Universal Empire. As a result of the imperialist wars of the Age of Conflict, the number of political units in the civilization are reduced by conquest. Eventually one emerges triumphant. When this occurs we have one political unit for the whole civilization. Just at the core area passes from the Age of Expansion to the Age of Conflict earlier than the peripheral areas, sometimes the core area is conquered by a single state before the whole civilization is conquered by the Universal Empire. When this occurs the core empire is generally a semiperipheral state, while the Universal Empire is generally a peripheral state. Thus, Mesopotamia's core was conquered by semiperipheral Babylonia about 1700 B.C., while the whole of Mesopotamian civilization was conquered by more peripheral Assyria about 725 B.C. (replaced by fully peripheral Persia about 525 B.C.). In Classical Civilization the core area was conquered by semiperipheral Macedonia about 336 B.C., while the whole civilization was conquered by peripheral Rome about 146 B.C. In other civilizations the Universal Empire has consistently been a peripheral state even when there was no earlier conquest of the core area by a semiperipheral state. In Mayan Civilization (1000 B.C.–A.D. 1550) the core area was apparently in Yucatán and Guatemala, but the Universal Empire of the Aztecs centered in the peripheral highlands of central Mexico. In Andean Civilization (1500 B.C.–A.D. 1600) the core areas were on the lower slopes and valleys of the central and northern Andes, but the Universal Empire of the Incas centered in the highest Andes, a peripheral area. The Canaanite Civilization (2200 B.C.–146 B.C.) had its core area in the Levant, but its Universal Empire, the Punic Empire, centered at Carthage in the western Mediterranean. If we turn to the Far East we see no less than three civilizations. Of these the earliest, Sinic Civilization, rose in the valley of the Yellow River after 2000 B.C., culminated in the Chin and Han empires after 200 B.C., and was largely destroyed by Ural-Altaic invaders after A.D. 400. From this Sinic Civilization, in the same way in which Classical Civilization emerged from Cretan Civilization or Western Civilization emerged from Classical Civilization, there emerged two other civilizations: (a) Chinese Civilization, which began about A.D. 400, culminated in the Manchu Empire after 1644, and was disrupted by European invaders in the period 1790–1930, and (b) Japanese Civilization, which began about the time of Christ, culminated in the Tokugawa Empire after 1600, and may have been completely disrupted by invaders from Western Civilization in the century following 1853.

In India, as in China, two civilizations have followed one another. Although we know relatively little about the earlier of the two, the later (as in China) culminated in a Universal Empire ruled by an alien and peripheral people. Indic Civilization, which began about 3500 B.C., was destroyed by Aryan invaders about 1700 B.C. Hindu Civilization, which emerged from Indic Civilization about 1700 B.C., culminated in the Mogul Empire and was destroyed by invaders from Western Civilization in the period 1500–1900.

Turning to the extremely complicated area of the Near East, we can see a similar pattern. Islamic Civilization, which began about A.D. 500, culminated in the Ottoman Empire in the period 1300–1600 and has been in the process of being destroyed by invaders from Western Civilization since about 1750.

Expressed in this way, these patterns in the life cycles of various civilizations may seem confused. But if we tabulate them, the pattern emerges with some simplicity.

From this table a most extraordinary fact emerges. Of approximately twenty civilizations which have existed in all of human history, we have listed sixteen. Of these sixteen, twelve, possibly fourteen, are already dead or dying, their cultures destroyed by outsiders able to come in with sufficient power to disrupt the civilization, destroy its established modes of thought and action, and eventually wipe it out. Of these twelve dead or dying cultures, six have been destroyed by Europeans bearing the culture

CIVILIZATION	ITS DATES	UNIVERSAL EMPIRE	FINAL INVASIONS	THEIR DATES
Mesopotamian	6000 B.C.–300 B.C.	Assyrian} Persian } 725–333 B.C.	Greeks	335 B.C.–300 B.C.
Egyptian	5500 B.C.–300 B.C.	Egyptian	Greeks	334 B.C.–300 B.C.
Cretan	3500 B.C.–1150 B.C.	Minoan-Mycenaean	Dorian Greeks	1200 B.C.–1000 B.C.
Indic	3500 B.C.–1700 B.C.	Harappa?	Aryans	1800 B.C.–1600 B.C.
Canaanite	2200 B.C.–100 B.C.	Punic	Romans	264 B.C.–146 B.C.
Sinic	2000 B.C.–A.D. 400	Chin} Han }	Ural-Altaic	A.D. 200–500
Hittite	1800–1150	Hittite	Indo-European	1200 B.C.–A.D. 1000
Classical	1150 B.C.–A.D. 500	Roman	Germanic	A.D. 350–600
Andean	1500 B.C.–A.D. 1600	Inca	Europeans	1534
Mayan	1000 B.C.–A.D. 1550	Aztec	Europeans	1519
Hindu	1800 B.C.–A.D. 1900	Mogul	Europeans	1500–1900
Chinese	400–1930	Manchu	Europeans	1790–1930
Japanese	850 B.C.–?	Tokugawa	Europeans	1853–
Islamic	500–?	Ottoman	Europeans	1750–
Western	350–?	United States?	future?	?
Orthodox	350–?	Soviet	future?	?

of Western Civilization. When we consider the untold numbers of other societies, simpler than civilizations, which Western Civilization has destroyed or is now destroying, societies such as the Hottentots, the Iroquois, the Tasmanians, the Navahos, the Caribs, and countless others, the full frightening power of Western Civilization becomes obvious.

One cause, although by no means the chief cause, of the ability of Western Civilization to destroy other cultures rests on the fact that it has been expanding for a long time. This fact, in turn, rests on another condition to which we have already alluded, the fact that Western Civilization has passed through three periods of expansion, has entered into an Age of Conflict three times, each time has had its core area conquered almost completely by a single political unit, but has failed to go on to the Age of the Universal Empire because from the confusion of the Age of Conflict there emerged each time a new organization of society capable of expanding by its own organizational powers, with the result that the four phenomena characteristic of the Age of Conflict (decreasing rate of expansion, class conflicts, imperialist wars, irrationality) were gradually replaced once again by the four kinds of expansion typical of an Age of Expansion (demographic, geographic, production, knowledge). From a narrowly technical point of view, this shift from an Age of Conflict to an Age of Expansion is marked by a resumption of the investment of capital and the accumulation of capital on a large scale, just as the earlier shift from the Age of Expansion to the Age of Conflict was marked by a decreasing rate of investment and eventually by a decreasing rate of accumulation of capital.

Western Civilization began, as all civilizations do, in a period of cultural mixture. In this particular case it was a mixture resulting from the barbarian invasions which destroyed Classical Civilization in the period 350–700. By creating a new culture from the various elements offered from the barbarian tribes, the Roman world, the Saracen world, and above all the Jewish world (Christianity), Western Civilization became a new society.

This society became a civilization when it became organized, in the period 700–970, so that there was accumulation of capital and the beginnings of the investment of this capital in new methods of production. These new methods are associated with a change from infantry forces to mounted warriors in defense, from manpower (and thus slavery) to animal power in energy use, from the scratch plow and two-field, fallow agricultural technology of Mediterranean Europe to the eight-oxen, gang plow and three-field system of the Germanic peoples, and from the centralized, state-centered political orientation of the Roman world to the decentralized, private-power feudal network of the medieval world. In the new system a small number of men, equipped and trained to fight, received dues and services from the overwhelming majority of men who were expected to till the soil. From this inequitable but effective defensive system emerged an inequitable distribution of political power and, in turn, an inequitable distribution of the social economic income. This, in time, resulted in an accumulation of capital, which, by giving rise to demand for luxury goods of remote origin, began to shift the whole economic emphasis of the society from its earlier organization in self-sufficient agrarian units (manors) to commercial interchange, economic specialization, and, by the thirteenth century, to an entirely new pattern of society with towns, a bourgeois class, spreading literacy, growing freedom of alternative social choices, and new, often disturbing, thoughts.

From all this came the first period of expansion of Western Civilization, covering the years 970–1270. At the end of this period, the organization of society was becoming a petrified collection of vested interests, investment was decreasing, and the rate of expansion was beginning to fall. Accordingly, Western Civilization, for the first time, entered upon the Age of Conflict. This period, the time of the Hundred Years' War, the Black Death, the great heresies, and severe class conflicts, lasted from about 1270 to 1420. By the end of it, efforts were arising from England and Burgundy to conquer the core of Western Civilization. But, just at that moment, a new Age of Expansion, using a new organization of society which circumvented the old vested interests of the feudal-manorial system, began.

This new Age of Expansion, frequently called the period of commercial capitalism, lasted from about 1440 to about 1680. The real impetus to economic expansion during the period came from efforts to obtain profits by the interchange of goods, especially semiluxury or luxury goods, over long distances. In time, this system of commercial capitalism became petrified into a structure of vested interests in which profits were sought by imposing restrictions on the production or interchange of goods rather than by encouraging these activities. This new vested-interest structure, usually called mercantilism, became such a burden on economic activities that the rate of expansion of economic life declined and even gave rise to a period of economic decline in the decades immediately following 1690. The class struggles and imperialist wars engendered by this Age of Conflict are sometimes called the Second Hundred Years' War. The wars continued until 1815, and the class struggles even later. As a result of the former, France by 1810 had conquered most of the core of Western Civilization. But here, just as had occurred in 1420 when England had also conquered part of the core of the civilization toward the latter portion of an Age of Conflict, the victory was made meaningless because a new period of expansion began. Just as commercial capitalism had circumvented the petrified institution of the feudal-manorial system (chivalry) after 1440, so industrial capitalism circumvented the petrified institution of commercial capitalism (mercantilism) after 1820.

The new Age of Expansion which made Napoleon's military-political victory of 1810 impossible to maintain had begun in England long before. It appeared as the Agricultural Revolution about 1725 and as the Industrial Revolution about 1775, but it did not get started as a great burst of expansion until after 1820. Once started, it moved forward with an impetus such as the world had never seen before, and it looked as if Western Civilization might cover the whole globe. The dates of this third Age of Expansion might be fixed at 1770–1929, following upon the second Age of Conflict of 1690–1815. The social organization which was at the center of this new development might be called "industrial capitalism." In the course of the last decade of the nineteenth century, it began to become a structure of vested interests to which we might give the name "monopoly capitalism." As early, perhaps, as 1890, certain aspects of a new Age of Conflict, the third in Western Civilization, began to appear, especially in the core area, with a revival of imperialism, of class struggle, of violent warfare, and of irrationalities.

By 1930 it was clear that Western Civilization was again in an Age of Conflict; by 1942 a semiperipheral state, Germany, had conquered much of the core of the civilization. That effort was defeated by calling into the fray a peripheral state (the United States) and another, outside civilization (the Soviet society). It is not yet clear whether Western Civilization will continue along the path marked by so many earlier civilizations, or whether it will be able to reorganize itself sufficiently to enter upon a new, fourth, Age of Expansion. If the former occurs, this Age of Conflict will undoubtedly continue with the fourfold characteristics of class struggle, war, irrationality, and declining progress. In this case, we shall undoubtedly get a Universal Empire in which the United States will rule most of Western Civilization. This will be followed, as in other civilizations, by a period of decay and ultimately, as the civilization grows weaker, by invasions and the total destruction of Western culture. On the other hand, if Western Civilization is able to reorganize itself and enters upon a fourth Age of Expansion, the ability of Western Civilization to survive and go on to increasing prosperity and power will be bright. Leaving aside this hypothetical future, it would appear thus that Western Civilization, in approximately fifteen hundred years, has passed through eight periods, thus:

1. Mixture, 350–700
2. Gestation, 700–970
3A. First Expansion, 970–1270
4A. First Conflict, 1270–1440
        Core Empire: England, 1420

3B. Second Expansion, 1440–1690
4B. Second Conflict, 1690–1815
    Core Empire: France, 1810
3C. Third Expansion, 1770–1929
4C. Third Conflict, 1893–
    Core Empire: Germany, 1942

The two possibilities which lie in the future can be listed as follows:

REORGANIZATION	CONTINUATION OF THE PROCESS
3D. Fourth Expansion, 1944–	5. Universal Empire (the United States)
	6. Decay
	7. Invasion (end of the civilization)

From the list of civilizations previously given, it becomes somewhat easier to see how Western Civilization was able to destroy (or is still destroying) the cultures of six other civilizations. In each of these six cases the victim civilization had already passed the period of Universal Empire and was deep in the Age of Decay. In such a situation Western Civilization played a role as invader similar to that played by the Germanic tribes in Classical Civilization, by the Dorians in Cretan Civilization, by the Greeks in Mesopotamian or Egyptian Civilization, by the Romans in Canaanite Civilization, or by the Ayrans in Indic Civilization. The Westerners who burst in upon the Aztecs in 1519, on the Incas in 1534, on the Mogul Empire in the eighteenth century, on the Manchu Empire after 1790, on the Ottoman Empire after 1774, and on the Tokugawa Empire after 1853 were performing the same role as the Visigoths and the other barbarian tribes to the Roman Empire after 377. In each case, the results of the collision of two civilizations, one in the Age of Expansion and the other in the Age of Decay, was a foregone conclusion. Expansion would destroy Decay.

In the course of its various expansions Western Civilization has collided with only one civilization which was not already in the stage of decay. This exception was its half-brother, so to speak, the civilization now represented by the Soviet Empire. It is not clear what stage this "Orthodox" Civilization is in, but it clearly is not in its stage of decay. It would appear that Orthodox Civilization began as a period of mixture (500–1300) and is now in its second period of expansion. The first period of expansion, covering 1500–1900, had just begun to change into an Age of Conflict (1900–1920) when the vested interests of the society were wiped away by the defeat at the hands of Germany in 1917 and replaced by a new organization of society which gave rise to a second Age of Expansion (since 1921). During much of the last four hundred years culminating in the twentieth century, the fringes of Asia have been occupied by a semicircle of old dying civilizations (Islamic, Hindu, Chinese, Japanese). These have been under pressure from Western Civilization coming in from the oceans and from Orthodox Civilization pushing outward from the heart of the Eurasian land mass. The Oceanic pressure began with Vasco da Gama in India in 1498, culminated aboard the battleship *Missouri* in Tokyo Bay in 1945, and still continued with the Anglo-French attack on Suez in 1956. The Russian pressure from the continental heartland was applied to the inner frontiers of China, Iran, and Turkey from the seventeenth century to the present. Much of the world's history in the twentieth century has arisen from the interactions of these three factors (the continental heartland of Russian power, the shattered cultures of the Buffer Fringe of Asia, and the oceanic powers of Western Civilization).

Cultural Diffusion
in Western Civilization

We have said that the culture of a civilization is created in its core area originally and moves outward into peripheral areas which thus become part of the civilization. This movement of cultural elements is called "diffusion" by students of the subject. It is noteworthy that material elements of a culture, such as tools, weapons, vehicles, and such, diffuse more readily and thus more rapidly than do the nonmaterial elements such as ideas, art forms, religious outlook, or patterns of social behavior. For this reason the peripheral portions of a civilization (such as Assyria in Mesopotamian Civilization, Rome or Spain in Classical Civilization, and the United States or Australia in Western Civilization) tend to have a somewhat cruder and more material culture than the core area of the same civilization.

Material elements of a culture also diffuse beyond the boundaries of a civilization into other societies, and do so much more readily than the nonmaterial elements of the culture. For this reason the nonmaterial and spiritual elements of a culture are what give it its distinctive character rather than its tools and weapons which can be so easily exported to entirely different societies. Thus, the distinctive character of Western Civilization rests on its Christian heritage, its scientific outlook, its humanitarian elements, and its distinctive point of view in regard to the rights of the individual and respect for women rather than in such material things as firearms, tractors, plumbing fixtures, or skyscrapers, all of which are exportable commodities.

The export of material elements in a culture, across its peripheral areas and beyond, to the peoples of totally different societies has strange results. As elements of material culture move from core to periphery inside a civilization, they tend, in the long run, to strengthen the periphery at the expense of the core because the core is more hampered in the use of material innovations by the strength of past vested interests and because the core devotes a much greater part of its wealth and energy to nonmaterial culture. Thus, such aspects of the Industrial Revolution as automobiles and radios are European rather than American inventions, but have been developed and utilized to a far greater extent in America because this area was not hampered in their use by surviving elements of feudalism, of church domination, of rigid class distinctions (for example, in education), or by widespread attention to music, poetry, art, or religion such as we find in Europe. A similar contrast can be seen in Classical Civilization between Greek and Roman or in Mesopotamian Civilization between Sumerian and Assyrian or in Mayan Civilization between Mayan and Aztec.

The diffusion of culture elements beyond the boundaries of one society into the culture of another society presents quite a different case. The boundaries between societies present relatively little hindrance to the diffusion of material elements, and relatively greater hindrance to the diffusion of nonmaterial elements. Indeed, it is this fact which determines the boundary of the society, for, if the nonmaterial elements also diffused, the new area into which they flowed would be a peripheral portion of the old society rather than a part of a quite different society.

The diffusion of material elements from one society to another has a complex effect on the importing society. In the short run it is usually benefited by the importation, but in the long run it is frequently disorganized and weakened. When white men first came to North America, material elements from Western Civilization spread rapidly among the different Indian tribes. The Plains Indians, for example, were weak and impoverished before 1543, but in that year the horse began to diffuse northward from the Spaniards in Mexico. Within a century the Plains Indians were raised to a much higher standard of living (because of ability to hunt buffalo from horseback) and were immensely strengthened in their ability to resist Americans coming westward across the continent. In the meantime, the trans-Appalachian Indians who had been very powerful in the sixteenth and early seventeenth centuries began to receive firearms, steel traps, measles, and eventually whiskey from the French and later the English by way of the St. Lawrence. These greatly weakened the woods Indians of the trans-Appalachian area and ultimately weakened the Plains Indians of the trans-Mississippi area, because measles and whiskey were devastating and demoralizing and because the use of traps and guns by certain tribes made them dependent on whites for supplies at the same time that they allowed them to put great physical pressure on the more remote tribes which had not yet received guns or traps. Any united front of reds against whites was impossible, and the Indians were disrupted, demoralized, and destroyed. In general, importation of an element of material culture from one society to another is helpful to the importing society in the long run only if it is *(a)* productive, *(b)* can be made within the society itself, and *(c)* can be fitted into the nonmaterial culture of the importing society without demoralizing it. The destructive impact of Western Civilization upon so many other societies rests on its ability to demoralize their ideological and spiritual culture as much as its ability to destroy them in a material sense with firearms.

When one society is destroyed by the impact of another society, the people are left in a debris of cultural elements derived from their own shattered culture as well as from the invading culture. These elements generally provide the instruments for fulfilling the material needs of these people, but they cannot be organized into a functioning society because of the lack of an ideology and spiritual cohesive. Such people either perish or are incorporated as individuals and small groups into some other culture, whose ideology they adopt for themselves and, above all, for their children. In some cases, however, the people left with the debris of a shattered culture are able to reintegrate the cultural elements into a new society and a new culture. They are able to do this because they obtain a new nonmaterial culture and thus a new idology and morale which serve as a cohesive for the scattered elements of past culture they have at hand. Such a new ideology may be imported or may be indigenous, but in either case it becomes sufficiently integrated with the necessary elements of material culture to form a functioning whole and thus a new society. It is by some such process as this that all new societies, and thus all new civilizations, have been born. In this way, Classical Civilization was born from the wreckage of Cretan Civilization in the period 1150 B.C.—900 B.C., and Western Civilization was born from the wreckage of Classical Civilization in the period A.D. 350—700. It is possible that new civilizations may be born in the debris from the civilizations wrecked by Western Civilization on the fringes of Asia. In this wreckage is debris from Islamic, Hindu, Chinese, and Japanese civilizations. It would appear at the present time that new civilizations may be in the throes of birth in Japan, possibly in China, less likely in India, and dubiously in Turkey or Indonesia. The birth of a powerful civilization at any or several of these points would be of primary significance in world history, since it would serve as a counterbalance to the expansion of Soviet Civilization on the land mass of Eurasia.

Turning from a hypothetical future to a historical past, we can trace the diffusion of cultural elements within Western Civilization from its core area across peripheral areas and outward to other societies. Some of these elements are sufficiently important to command a more detailed examination.

Among the elements of the Western tradition which have diffused only very slowly or not at all are a closely related nexus of ideas at the basis of Western ideology. These include Christianity, the scientific outlook, humanitarianism, and the idea of the unique value and rights of the individual. But from this nexus of ideas have sprung a number of elements of material culture of which the most noteworthy are associated with technology. These have diffused readily, even to other societies. This ability of Western technology to emigrate and the inability of the scientific outlook, with which such technology is fairly closely associated, to do so have created an anomalous situation: societies such as Soviet Russia which have, because of lack of the tradition of scientific method, shown little inventiveness in technology are nevertheless able to threaten Western Civilization by the use, on a gigantic scale, of a technology almost entirely imported from Western Civilization. A similar situation may well develop in any new civilizations which come into existence on the fringes of Asia.

The most important parts of Western technology can be listed under four headings:

1. Ability to kill: development of weapons
2. Ability to preserve life: development of sanitation and medical services
3. Ability to produce both food and industrial goods
4. Improvements in transportation and communications

We have already spoken of the diffusion of Western firearms. The impact which these have had on peripheral areas and other societies, from Cortez's invasion of Mexico in 1519 to the use of the first atom bomb on Japan in 1945, is obvious. Less obvious, but in the long run of much greater significance, is the ability of Western Civilization to conquer disease and to postpone death by sanitation and medical advances. These advances began in the core of Western Civilization before 1500 but have exercised their full impact only since about 1750 with the advent of vaccination, the conquest of plague, and the steady advance in saving lives through the discovery of antisepsis in the nineteenth century and of the antibiotics in the twentieth century. These discoveries and techniques have diffused outward from the core of Western Civilization and have resulted in a fall in the death rate in western Europe and America almost immediately, in southern Europe and eastern Europe somewhat later, and in Asia only in the period since 1900. The world-shaking significance of this diffusion will be discussed in a moment.

Western Civilization's conquest of the techniques of production are so outstanding that they have been honored by the term "revolution" in all history books concerned with the subject. The conquest of the problem of producing food, known as the Agricultural Revolution, began in England as long ago as the early eighteenth century, say about 1725. The conquest of the problem of producing manufactured goods, known as the Industrial Revolution, also began in England, about fifty years after the Agricultural Revolution, say about 1775. The relationship of these two "revolutions" to each other and to the "revolution" in sanitation and public health and the differing rates at which these three "revolutions" diffused is of the greatest importance for understanding both the history of Western Civilization and its impact on other societies.

Agricultural activities, which provide the chief food supply of all civilizations, drain the nutritive elements from the soil. Unless these elements are replaced, the productivity of the soil will be reduced to a dangerously low level. In the medieval and early modern period of European history, these nutritive elements, especially nitrogen, were replaced through the action of the weather by leaving the land fallow either one year in three or even every second year. This had the effect of reducing the arable land by half or one-third. The Agricultural Revolution was an immense step forward, since it replaced the year of fallowing with a leguminous crop whose roots increased the supply of nitrogen in the soil by capturing this gas from the air and fixing it in the soil in a form usable by plant life. Since the leguminous crop which replaced the fallow year of the older agricultural cycle was generally a crop like alfalfa, clover, or sainfoin which provided feed for cattle, this Agricultural Revolution not only increased the nitrogen content of the soil for subsequent crops of grain but also increased the number and quality of farm animals, thus increasing the supply of meat and animal products for food, and also increasing the fertility of the soil by increasing the supply of animal manure for fertilizers. The net result of the whole Agricultural Revolution was an increase in both the quantity and the quality of food. Fewer men were able to produce so much more food that many men were released from the burden of producing it and could devote their attention to other activities, such as government, education, science, or business. It has been said that in 1700 the agricultural labor of twenty persons was required in order to produce enough food for twenty-one persons, while in some areas, by 1900, three persons could produce enough food for twenty-one persons, thus releasing seventeen persons for nonagricultural activities.

This Agricultural Revolution which began in England before 1725 reached France after 1800, but did not reach Germany or northern Italy until after 1830. As late as 1900 it had hardly spread at all into Spain, southern Italy and Sicily, the Balkans, or eastern Europe generally. In Germany, about 1840, this Agricultural Revolution was given a new boost forward by the introduction of the use of chemical fertilizers, and received another boost in the United States after 1880 by the introduction of farm machinery which reduced the need for human labor. These same two areas, with contributions from some other countries, gave another considerable boost to agricultural output after 1900 by the introduction of new seeds and better crops through seed selection and hybridization.

These great agricultural advances after 1725 made possible the advances in industrial production after 1775 by providing the food and thus the labor for the growth of the factory system and the rise of industrial cities. Improvements in sanitation and medical services after 1775 contributed to the same end by reducing the death rate and by making it possible for large numbers of persons to live in cities without the danger of epidemics.

The "Transportation Revolution" also contributed its share to making the modern world. This contribution began, slowly enough, about 1750, with the construction of canals and the building of turnpikes by the new methods of road construction devised by John L. McAdam ("macadamized" roads). Coal came by canal and food by the new roads to the new industrial cities after 1800. After 1825 both were greatly improved by the growth of a network of railroads, while communications were speeded by the use of the telegraph (after 1837) and the cable (after 1850). This "conquest of distance" was unbelievably accelerated in the twentieth century by the use of internal-combustion engines in automobiles, aircraft, and ships and by the advent of telephones and radio communications. The chief result of this tremendous speeding up of communications and transportation was that all parts of the world were brought closer together, and the impact of European culture on the non-European world was greatly intensified. This impact was made even more overwhelming by the fact that the Transportation Revolution spread outward from Europe extremely rapidly, diffusing almost as rapidly as the spread of European weapons, somewhat more rapidly than the spread of European sanitation and medical services, and much more rapidly than the spread of European industrialism, European agricultural techniques, or European ideology. As we shall see in a moment, many of the problems which the world faced at the middle of the twentieth century were rooted in the fact that these different aspects of the European way of life spread outward into the non-European world at such different speeds that the non-European world obtained them in an entirely different order from that in which Europe had obtained them.

One example of this difference can be seen in the fact that in Europe the Industrial Revolution generally took place before the Transportation Revolution, but in the non-European world this sequence was reversed.

This means that Europe was able to produce its own iron, steel, and copper to build its own railroads and telegraph wires, but the non-European world could construct these things only by obtaining the necessary industrial materials from Europe and thus becoming the debtor of Europe. The speed with which the Transportation Revolution spread out from Europe can be seen in the fact that in Europe the railroad began before 1830, the telegraph before 1840, the automobile about 1890, and the wireless about 1900. The transcontinental railroad in the United States opened in 1869; by 1900 the Trans-Siberian Railway and the Cape-to-Cairo railroad were under full construction, and the Berlin-to-Baghdad enterprise was just beginning. By that same date—1900—India, the Balkans, China, and Japan were being covered with a network of railroads, although none of these areas, at that date, was sufficiently developed in an industrial sense to provide itself with the steel or copper to construct or to maintain such a network. Later stages in the Transportation Revolution, such as automobiles or radios, spread even more rapidly and were being used to cross the deserts of the Sahara or of Arabia within a generation of their advent in Europe.

Another important example of this situation can be seen in the fact that in Europe the Agricultural Revolution began before the Industrial Revolution. Because of this, Europe was able to increase its output of food and thus the supply of labor necessary for industrialization. But in the non-European world (except North America) the effort to industrialize generally began before there had been any notable success in obtaining a more productive agricultural system. As a result, the increased supply of food (and thus of labor) needed for the growth of industrial cities in the non-European world has generally been obtained, not from increased output of food so much as from a reduction of the peasants' share of the food produced. In the Soviet Union, especially, the high speed of industrialization in the period 1926–1940 was achieved by a merciless oppression of the rural community in which millions of peasants lost their lives. The effort to copy this Soviet method in Communist China in the 1950's brought that area to the verge of disaster.

The most important example of such differential diffusion rates of two European developments appears in the difference between the spread of the food-producing revolution and the spread of the revolution in sanitation and medical services. This difference became of such world-shaking consequences by the middle of the twentieth century that we must spend considerable time examining it.

In Europe the Agricultural Revolution which served to increase the supply of food began at least fifty years before the beginnings of the revolution in sanitation and medical services which decreased the number of deaths and thus increased the number of the population. The two dates for these two beginnings might be put roughly at 1725 and 1775. As a result of this difference, Europe generally had sufficient food to feed its increased population. When the population reached a point where Europe itself could no longer feed its own people (say about 1850), the outlying areas of the European and non-European worlds were so eager to be industrialized (or to obtain railroads) that Europe was able to obtain non-European food in exchange for European industrial products. This sequence of events was a very happy combination for Europe. But the sequence of events in the non-European world was quite different and much less happy. Not only did the non-European world get industrialization before it got the revolution in food production; it also got the revolution in sanitation and medical services before it got a sufficient increase in food to take care of the resulting increase in population. As a result, the demographic explosion which began in northwestern Europe early in the nineteenth century spread outward to eastern Europe and to Asia with increasingly unhappy consequences as it spread. The result was to create the greatest social problem of the twentieth-century world.

Most stable and primitive societies, such as the American Indians before 1492 or medieval Europe, have no great population problem because the birthrate is balanced by the death rate. In such societies both of these are high, the population is stable, and the major portion of that population is young (below eighteen years of age). This kind of society (frequently called Population Type A) is what existed in Europe in the medieval period (say about 1400) or even in part of the early modern period (say about 1700). As a result of the increased supply of food in Europe after 1725, and of men's increased ability to save lives because of advances in sanitation and medicine after 1775, the death rate began to fall, the birthrate remained high, the population began to increase, and the number of older persons in the society increased. This gave rise to what we have called the demographic explosion (or Population Type B). As a result of it, the population of Europe (beginning in western Europe) increased in the nineteenth century, and the major portion of that population was in the prime of life (ages eighteen to forty-five), the arms-bearing years for men and the childbearing years for women.

At this point the demographic cycle of an expanding population goes into a third stage (Population Type C) in which the birthrate also begins to fall. The reasons for this fall in the birthrate have never been explained in a satisfactory way, but, as a consequence of it, there appears a new demographic condition marked by a falling birthrate, a low death rate, and a stabilizing and aging population whose major part is in the mature years from thirty to sixty. As the population gets older because of the decrease in births and the increase in expectation of life, a larger and larger part of the population has passed the years of bearing children or bearing arms. This causes the birthrate to decline even more rapidly, and eventually gives a population so old that the death rate begins to rise again because of the great increase in deaths from old age or from the casualties of inevitable senility. Accordingly, the society passes into a fourth stage of the demographic cycle (Population Type D). This stage is marked by a declining birthrate, a rising death rate, a decreasing population, and a population in which the major part is over fifty years of age.

It must be confessed that the nature of the fourth stage of this demographic cycle is based on theoretical considerations rather than on empirical observation, because even western Europe, where the cycle is most advanced, has not yet reached this fourth stage. However, it seems quite likely that it will pass into such a stage by the year 2000, and already the increasing number of older persons has given rise to new problems and to a new science called geriatrics both in western Europe and in the eastern United States.

As we have said, Europe has already experienced the first three stages of this demographic cycle as a result of the Agricultural Revolution after 1725 and the Sanitation-Medical Revolution after 1775. As these two revolutions have diffused outward from western Europe to more peripheral areas of the world (the lifesaving revolution passing the food-producing revolution in the process), these more remote areas have entered, one by one, upon the demographic cycle. This means that the demographic explosion (Population Type B) has moved outward from western Europe to Central Europe to eastern Europe and finally to Asia and Africa. By the middle of the twentieth century, India was fully in the grasp of the demographic explosion, with its population shooting upward at a rate of about 5 million a year, while Japan's population rose from 55 million in 1920 to 94 million in 1960. A fine example of the working of this process can be seen in Ceylon where in 1920 the birthrate was 40 per thousand and the death rate was 32 per thousand, but in 1950 the birthrate was still at 40 while the death rate had fallen to 12. Before we examine the impact of this development on world history in the twentieth century let us look at two brief tables which will clarify this process.

The demographic cycle may be divided into four stages which we have designated by the first four letters of the alphabet. These four stages can be distinguished in respect to four traits: the birthrate, the death rate, the number of the population, and its age distribution. The nature of the four stages in these four respects can be seen in the following table:

THE DEMOGRAPHIC CYCLE

STAGE	A	B	C	D
Birthrate	High	High	Falling	Low
Death rate	High	Falling	Low	Rising
Numbers	Stable	Rising	Stable	Falling
Age Distribution	Many young (below 18)	Many in prime (18-45)	Many middle-aged (over 30)	Many old (over 50)

The consequences of this demographic cycle (and the resulting demographic explosion) as it diffuses outward from western Europe to more peripheral areas of the world may be gathered from the following table which sets out the chronology of this movement in the four areas of western Europe, central Europe, eastern Europe, and Asia:

DIFFUSION OF THE DEMOGRAPHIC CYCLE

AREAS

DATES	WESTERN EUROPE	CENTRAL EUROPE	EASTERN EUROPE	ASIA
1700	A	A	A	A
1800	B	A	A	A
1850	B	B	A	A
1900	C	B	B	A
1950	C	C	B	B
2000	D	D	C	B

In this table the line of greatest population pressure (the demographic explosion of Type B population) has been marked by a dotted line. This shows that there has been a sequence, at intervals of about fifty years, of four successive population pressures which might be designated with the following names:

> Anglo-French pressure, about 1850
> Germanic-Italian pressure, about 1900
> Slavic pressure, about 1950
> Asiatic pressure, about 2000

This diffusion of pressure outward from the western European core of Western Civilization can contribute a great deal toward a richer understanding of the period 1850–2000. It helps to explain the Anglo-French rivalry about 1850, the Anglo-French alliance based on fear of Germany after 1900, the free-world alliance based on fear of Soviet Russia after 1950, and the danger to both Western Civilization and Soviet Civilization from Asiatic pressure by 2000.

These examples show how our understanding of the problems of the twentieth century world can be illuminated by a study of the various developments of western Europe and of the varying rates by which they diffused outward to the more peripheral portions of Western Civilization and ultimately to the non-Western world. In a rough fashion we might list these developments in the order in which they appeared in western Europe as well as the order in which they appeared in the more remote non-Western world:

DEVELOPMENTS IN WESTERN EUROPE	DEVELOPMENTS IN ASIA
1. Western ideology	1. Revolution in weapons
2. Revolution in weapons (especially firearms)	2. Revolution in transport and communications
3. Agricultural Revolution	3. Revolution in sanitation and medicine
4. Industrial Revolution	4. Industrial Revolution
5. Revolution in sanitation and medicine	5. Demographic explosion
6. Demographic explosion	6. Agricultural Revolution
7. Revolution in transportation and communications	7. And last (if at all), Western ideology.

Naturally, these two lists are only a rough approximation to the truth. In the European list it should be quite clear that each development is listed in the order of its first beginning and that each of these traits has been a continuing process of development since. In the Asiatic list it should be clear that the order of arrival of the different traits is quite different in different areas and that the order given on this list is merely one which seems to apply to several important areas. Naturally, the problems arising from the advent of these traits in Asiatic areas depend on the order in which the traits arrive, and thus are quite different in areas where this order of arrival is different. The chief difference arises from a reversal of order between items 3 and 4.

The fact that Asia obtained these traits in a different order from that of Europe is of the greatest significance. We shall devote much of the rest of this book to examining this subject. At this point we might point out two aspects of it. In 1830 democracy was growing rapidly in Europe and in America. At that time the development of weapons had reached a point where governments could not get weapons which were much more effective than those which private individuals could get. Moreover, private individuals could obtain good weapons because they had a high enough standard of living to afford it (as a result of the Agricultural Revolution) and such weapons were cheap (as a result of the Industrial Revolution). By 1930 (and even more by 1950) the development of weapons had advanced to the point where governments could obtain more effective weapons (dive-bombers, armored cars, flamethrowers, poisonous gases, and such) than private individuals. Moreover, in Asia, these better weapons arrived before standards of living could be raised by the Agricultural Revolution or costs of weapons reduced sufficiently by the Industrial Revolution. Moreover, standards of living were held down in Asia because the Sanitation-

Medical Revolution and the demographic explosion arrived before the Agricultural Revolution. As a result, governments in Europe in 1830 hardly dared to oppress the people, and democracy was growing; but in the non-European world by 1930 (and even more by 1950) governments did dare to, and could, oppress their peoples, who could do little to prevent it. When we add to this picture the fact that the ideology of Western Europe had strong democratic elements derived from its Christian and scientific traditions, while Asiatic countries had authoritarian traditions in political life, we can see that democracy had a hopeful future in Europe in 1830 but a very dubious future in Asia in 1950.

From another point of view we can see that in Europe the sequence of Agricultural-Industrial-Transportation revolutions made it possible for Europe to have rising standards of living and little rural oppression, since the Agricultural Revolution provided the food and thus the labor for industrialism and for transport facilities. But in Asia, where the sequence of these three revolutions was different (generally: Transportation-Industrial-Agricultural), labor could be obtained from the Sanitary-Medical Revolution, but food for this labor could be obtained only by oppressing the rural population and preventing any real improvements in standards of living. Some countries tried to avoid this by borrowing capital for railroads and steel mills from European countries rather than by raising capital from the savings of their own people, but this meant that these countries became the debtors (and thus to some extent the subordinates) of Europe. Asiatic nationalism usually came to resent this debtor role and to prefer the role of rural oppression of its own people by its own government. The most striking example of this preference for rural oppression over foreign indebtedness was made in the Soviet Union in 1928 with the opening of the Five-Year plans. Somewhat similar but less drastic choices were made even earlier in Japan and much later in China. But we must never forget that these and other difficult choices had to be made by Asiatics because they obtained the diffused traits of Western Civilization in an order different from that in which Europe obtained them.

Europe's Shift
to the Twentieth Century

While Europe's traits were diffusing outward to the non-European world, Europe was also undergoing profound changes and facing difficult choices at home. These choices were associated with drastic changes, in some cases we might say reversals, of Europe's point of view. These changes may be examined under eight headings. The nineteenth century was marked by (1) belief in the innate goodness of man; (2) secularism; (3) belief in progress; (4) liberalism; (5) capitalism; (6) faith in science; (7) democracy; (8) nationalism. In general, these eight factors went along together in the nineteenth century. They were generally regarded as being compatible with one another; the friends of one were generally the friends of the others; and the enemies of one were generally the enemies of the rest. Metternich and De Maistre were generally opposed to all eight; Thomas Jefferson and John Stuart Mill were generally in favor of all eight.

The belief in the innate goodness of man had its roots in the eighteenth century when it appeared to many that man was born good and free but was everywhere distorted, corrupted, and enslaved by bad institutions and conventions. As Rousseau said, "Man is born free yet everywhere he is in chains." Thus arose the belief in the "noble savage," the romantic nostalgia for nature and for the simple nobility and honesty of the inhabitants of a faraway land. If only man could be freed, they felt, freed from the corruption of society and its artificial conventions, freed from the burden of property, of the state, of the clergy, and of the rules of matrimony, then man, it seemed clear, could rise to heights undreamed of before—could, indeed, become a kind of superman, practically a god. It was this spirit which set loose the French Revolution. It was this spirit which prompted the outburst of self-reliance and optimism so characteristic of the whole period from 1770 to 1914.

Obviously, if man is innately good and needs but to be freed from social restrictions, he is capable of tremendous achievements in this world of time, and does not need to postpone his hopes of personal salvation into eternity. Obviously, if man is a godlike creature whose ungodlike actions are due only to the frustrations of social conventions, there is no need to worry about service to God or devotion to any otherworldly end. Man can accomplish most by service to himself and devotion to the goals of this world. Thus came the triumph of secularism.

Closely related to these nineteenth century beliefs that human nature is good, that society is bad, and that optimism and secularism were reasonable attitudes were certain theories about the nature of evil.

To the nineteenth century mind evil, or sin, was a negative conception. It merely indicated a lack or, at most, a distortion of good. Any idea of sin or evil as a malignant positive force opposed to good, and capable of existing by its own nature, was completely lacking in the typical nineteenth-century mind. To such a mind the only evil was frustration and the only sin, repression.

Just as the negative idea of the nature of evil flowed from the belief that human nature was good, so the idea of liberalism flowed from the belief that society was bad. For, if society was bad, the state, which was the organized coercive power of society, was doubly bad, and if man was good, he should be freed, above all, from the coercive power of the state. Liberalism was the crop which emerged from this soil. In its broadest aspect liberalism believed that men should be freed from coercive power as completely as possible. In its narrowest aspect liberalism believed that the economic activities of man should be freed completely from "state interference." This latter belief, summed up in the battle-cry "No government in business," was commonly called "laissez-faire." Liberalism, which included laissez-faire, was a wider term because it would have freed men from the coercive power of any church, army, or other institution, and would have left to society little power beyond that required to prevent the strong from physically oppressing the weak.

From either aspect liberalism was based on an almost universally accepted nineteenth-century superstition known as the "community of interests." This strange, and unexamined, belief held that there really existed, in the long run, a community of interests between the members of a society. It maintained that, in the long run, what was good for one member of society was good for all and that what was bad for one was bad for all. But it went much further than this. The theory of the "community of interests" believed that there did exist a possible social pattern in which each member of society would be secure, free, and prosperous, and that this pattern could be achieved by a process of adjustment so that each person could fall into that place in the pattern to which his innate abilities entitled him. This implied two corollaries which the nineteenth century was prepared to accept: (1) that human abilities are innate and can only be distorted or suppressed by social discipline and (2) that each individual is the best judge of his own self-interest. All these together form the doctrine of the "community of interests," a doctrine which maintained that if each individual does what seems best for himself the result, in the long run, will be best for society as a whole.

Closely related to the idea of the "community of interests" were two other beliefs of the nineteenth century: the belief in progress and in democracy. The average man of 1880 was convinced that he was the culmination of a long process of inevitable progress which had been going on for untold millennia and which would continue indefinitely into the future. This belief in progress was so fixed that it tended to regard progress as both inevitable and automatic. Out of the struggles and conflicts of the universe better things were constantly emerging, and the wishes or plans of the objects themselves had little to do with the process.

The idea of democracy was also accepted as inevitable, although not always as desirable, for the nineteenth century could not completely submerge a lingering feeling that rule by the best or rule by the strong would be better than rule by the majority. But the facts of political development made rule by the majority unavoidable, and it came to be accepted, at least in western Europe, especially since it was compatible with liberalism and with the community of interests.

Liberalism, community of interests, and the belief in progress led almost inevitably to the practice and theory of capitalism. Capitalism was an economic system in which the motivating force was the desire for private profit as determined in a price system. Such a system, it was felt, by seeking the aggrandizement of profits for each individual, would give unprecedented economic progress under liberalism and in accord with the community of interests. In the nineteenth century this system, in association with the unprecedented advance of natural science, had given rise to industrialism (that is, power production) and urbanism (that is, city life), both of which were regarded as inevitable concomitants of progress by most people, but with the greatest suspicion by a persistent and vocal minority.

The nineteenth century was also an age of science. By this term we mean the belief that the universe obeyed rational laws which could be found by observation and could be used to control it. This belief was closely connected with the optimism of the period, with its belief in inevitable progress, and with secularism. The latter appeared as a tendency toward materialism. This could be defined as the belief that all reality is ultimately explicable in terms of the physical and chemical laws which apply to temporal matter.

The last attribute of the nineteenth century is by no means the least: nationalism. It was the great age of nationalism, a movement which has been discussed in many lengthy and inconclusive books but which can be defined for our purposes as "a movement for political unity with those with whom we believe we are akin." As such, nationalism in the nineteenth century had a dynamic force which worked in two directions. On the one side, it served to bind persons of the same nationality together into a tight, emotionally satisfying, unit. On the other side, it served to divide persons of different nationality into antagonistic groups, often to the injury of their real mutual political, economic, or cultural advantages. Thus, in the period to which we refer, nationalism sometimes acted as a cohesive force, creating a united Germany and a united Italy out of a medley of distinct political units. But sometimes, on the other hand, nationalism acted as a disruptive force within such dynastic states as the Habsburg Empire or the Ottoman Empire, splitting these great states into a number of distinctive political units.

These characteristics of the nineteenth century have been so largely modified in the twentieth century that it might appear, at first glance, as if the latter were nothing more than the opposite of the former. This is not completely accurate, but there can be no doubt that most of these characteristics have been drastically modified in the twentieth century. This change has arisen from a series of shattering experiences which have profoundly disturbed patterns of behavior and of belief, of social organizations and human hopes. Of these shattering experiences the chief were the trauma of the First World War, the long-drawn-out agony of the world depression, and the unprecedented violence of destruction of the Second World War. Of these three, the First World War was undoubtedly the most important. To a people who believed in the innate goodness of man, in inevitable progress, in the community of interests, and in evil as merely the absence of good, the First World War, with its millions of persons dead and its billions of dollars wasted, was a blow so terrible as to be beyond human ability to comprehend. As a matter of fact, no real success was achieved in comprehending it. The people of the day regarded it as a temporary and inexplicable aberration to be ended as soon as possible and forgotten as soon as ended. Accordingly, men were almost unanimous, in 1919, in their determination to restore the world of 1913. This effort was a failure. After ten years of effort to conceal the new reality of social life by a facade painted to look like 1913, the facts burst through the pretense, and men were forced, willingly or not, to face the grim reality of the twentieth century. The events which destroyed the pretty dream world of 1919–1929 were the stock-market crash, the world depression, the world financial crisis, and ultimately the martial clamor of rearmament and aggression. Thus depression and war forced men to realize that the old world of the nineteenth century had passed forever, and made them seek to create a new world in accordance with the facts of present-day conditions. This new world, the child of the period of 1914–1945, assumed its recognizable form only as the first half of the century drew to a close.

In contrast with the nineteenth-century belief that human nature is innately good and that society is corrupting, the twentieth century came to believe that human nature is, if not innately bad, at least capable of being very evil. Left to himself, it seems today, man falls very easily to the level of the jungle or even lower, and this result can be prevented only by training and the coercive power of society. Thus, man is capable of great evil, but society can prevent this. Along with this change from good men and bad society to bad men and good society has appeared a reaction from optimism to pessimism and from secularism to religion. At the same time the view that evil is merely the absence of good has been replaced with the idea that evil is a very positive force which must be resisted and overcome. The horrors of Hitler's concentration camps and of Stalin's slave-labor units are chiefly responsible for this change.

Associated with these changes are a number of others. The belief that human abilities are innate and should be left free from social duress in order to display themselves has been replaced by the idea that human abilities are the result of social training and must be directed to socially acceptable ends. Thus liberalism and laissez-faire are to be replaced, apparently, by social discipline and planning. The community of interests which would appear if men were merely left to pursue their own de- sires has been replaced by the idea of the welfare community, which must be created by conscious organizing action. The belief in progress has been replaced by the fear of social retrogression or even human annihilation. The old march of democracy now yields to the insidious advance of authoritarianism, and the individual capitalism of the profit motive seems about to be replaced by the state capitalism of the welfare economy. Science, on all sides, is challenged by mysticisms, some of which march under the banner of science itself; urbanism has passed its peak and is replaced by suburbanism or even "flight to the country"; and nationalism finds its patriotic appeal challenged by appeals to much wider groups of class, ideological, or continental scope.

We have already given some attention to the fashion in which a number of western-European innovations, such as industrialism and the demographic explosion, diffused outward to the peripheral non-European world at such different rates of speed that they arrived in Asia in quite a different order from that in which they had left western Europe. The same phenomenon can be seen within Western Civilization in regard to the nineteenth-century characteristics of Europe which we have enumerated. For example, nationalism was already evident in Eng- land at the time of the defeat of the Spanish Armada in 1588; it raged through France in the period after 1789; it reached Germany and Italy only after 1815, became a potent force in Russia and the Balkans to- ward the end of the nineteenth century, and was noticeable in China, India, and Indonesia, and even Negro Africa, only in the twentieth

century. Somewhat similar patterns of diffusion can be found in regard
to the spread of democracy, of parliamentary government, of liberalism,
and of secularism. The rule, however, is not so general or so simple
as it appears at first glance. The exceptions and the complications appear more numerous as we approach the twentieth century. Even
earlier it was evident that the arrival of the sovereign state did not
follow this pattern, enlightened despotism and the growth of supreme
public authority appearing in Germany, and even in Italy, before it
appeared in France. Universal free education also appeared in central
Europe before it appeared in a western country like England. Socialism also is a product of central Europe rather than of western Europe,
and moved from the former to the latter only in the fifth decade of
the twentieth century. These exceptions to the general rule about the
eastward movement of modern historical developments have various
explanations. Some of these are obvious, but others are very complicated. As an example of such a complication we might mention that in
western Europe nationalism, industrialism, liberalism, and democracy
were generally reached in this order. But in Germany they all appeared
about the same time. To the Germans it appeared that they could
achieve nationalism and industrialism (both of which they wanted)
more rapidly and more successfully if they sacrificed liberalism and
democracy. Thus, in Germany nationalism was achieved in an undemocratic way, by "blood and iron," as Bismarck put it, while industrialism
was achieved under state auspices rather than through liberalism. This
selection of elements and the resulting playing off of elements against
one another was possible in more peripheral areas only because these
areas had the earlier experience of western Europe to study, copy,
avoid, or modify. Sometimes they had to modify these traits as they
developed. This can be seen from the following considerations. When
the Industrial Revolution began in England and France, these countries
were able to raise the necessary capital for new factories because they
already had the Agricultural Revolution and because, as the earliest
producers of industrial goods, they made excessive profits which could
be used to provide capital. But in Germany and in Russia, capital was
much more difficult to find, because they obtained the Industrial Revolution later, when they had to compete with England and France, and
could not earn such large profits and also because they did not already
have an established Agricultural Revolution on which to build their
Industrial Revolution. Accordingly, while western Europe, with plenty
of capital and cheap, democratic weapons, could finance its industrialization with liberalism and democracy, central and eastern Europe had
difficulty financing industrialism, and there the process was delayed to a
period when cheap and simple democratic weapons were being replaced
by expensive and complicated weapons. This meant that the capital for

railroads and factories had to be raised with government assistance; liberalism waned; rising nationalism encouraged this tendency; and the undemocratic nature of existing weapons made it clear that both liberalism and democracy were living a most precarious existence.

As a consequence of situations such as this, some of the traits which arose in western Europe in the nineteenth century moved outward to more peripheral areas of Europe and Asia with great difficulty and for only a brief period. Among these less sturdy traits of western Europe's great century we might mention liberalism, democracy, the parliamentary system, optimism, and the belief in inevitable progress. These were, we might say, flowers of such delicate nature that they could not survive any extended period of stormy weather. That the twentieth century subjected them to long periods of very stormy weather is clear when we consider that it brought a world economic depression sandwiched between two world wars.

II

WESTERN CIVILIZATION
TO 1914

The Pattern of Change

European Economic Developments

COMMERCIAL CAPITALISM

INDUSTRIAL CAPITALISM, 1770–1850

FINANCIAL CAPITALISM, 1850–1931

Domestic Financial Practices

International Financial Practices

THE SITUATION BEFORE 1914

The United States to 1917

The Pattern of Change

I N order to obtain perspective we sometimes divide the culture of a society, in a somewhat arbitrary fashion, into several different aspects. For example, we can divide a society into six aspects: military, political, economic, social, religious, intellectual. Naturally there are very close connections between these various aspects; and in each aspect there are very close connections between what exists today and what existed in an earlier day. For example, we might want to talk about democracy as a fact on the political level (or aspect). In order to talk about it in an intelligent way we would not only have to know what it is today we would also have to see what relationship it has to earlier facts on the political level as well as its relationship to various facts on the other five levels of the society. Naturally we cannot talk intelligently unless we have a fairly clear idea of what we mean by the words we use. For that reason we shall frequently define the terms we use in discussing this subject.

The military level is concerned with the organization of force, the political level with the organization of power, and the economic level with the organization of wealth. By the "organization of power" in a society we mean the ways in which obedience and consent (or acquiescence) are obtained. The close relationships between levels can be seen from the fact that there are three basic ways to win obedience: by force, by buying consent with wealth, and by persuasion. Each of these three leads us to another level (military, economic, or intellectual) outside the political level. At the same time, the organization of power today (that is, of the methods for obtaining obedience in the society) is a development of the methods used to obtain obedience in the society in an earlier period.

These relationships are important because in the twentieth century in Western Civilization all six levels are changing with amazing rapidity, and the relationships between levels are also shifting with great speed. When we add to this confusing picture of Western Civilization the fact that other societies are influencing it or being influenced by it, it would seem that the world in the twentieth century is almost too complicated to understand. This is indeed true, and we shall have to simplify (perhaps even oversimplify) these complexities in order to reach a low level of understanding. When we have reached such a low level perhaps we shall be able to raise the level of our understanding by bringing into our minds, little by little, some of the complexities which do exist in the world itself.

On the military level in Western Civilization in the twentieth century the chief development has been a steady increase in the complexity and the cost of weapons. When weapons are cheap to get and so easy to use that almost anyone can use them after a short period of training, armies are generally made up of large masses of amateur soldiers. Such weapons we call "amateur weapons," and such armies we might call "mass armies of citizen-soldiers." The Age of Pericles in Classical Greece and the nineteenth century in Western Civilization were periods of amateur weapons and citizen-soldiers. But the nineteenth century was preceded (as was the Age of Pericles also) by a period in which weapons were expensive and required long training in their use. Such weapons we call "specialist" weapons. Periods of specialist weapons are generally periods of small armies of professional soldiers (usually mercenaries). In a period of specialist weapons the minority who have such weapons can usually force the majority who lack them to obey; thus a period of specialist weapons tends to give rise to a period of minority rule and authoritarian government. But a period of amateur weapons is a period in which all men are roughly equal in military power, a majority can compel a minority to yield, and majority rule or even democratic government tends to rise. The medieval period in which the best weapon was usually a mounted knight on horseback (clearly a specialist weapon) was a period of minority rule and authoritarian government. Even when the medieval knight was made obsolete (along with his stone castle) by the invention of gunpowder and the appearance of firearms, these new weapons were so expensive and so difficult to use (until 1800) that minority rule and authoritarian government continued even though that government sought to enforce its rule by shifting from mounted knights to professional pikemen and musketeers. But after 1800, guns became cheaper to obtain and easier to use. By 1840 a Colt revolver sold for $27 and a Springfield musket for not much more, and these were about as good weapons as anyone could get at that time. Thus, mass armies of citizens, equipped with these cheap and easily used weapons, began to replace armies of professional soldiers, beginning about 1800 in Europe and even earlier in America. At the same time, democratic government began to replace authoritarian governments (but chiefly in those areas where the cheap new weapons were available and local standards of living were high enough to allow people to obtain them).

The arrival of the mass army of citizen-soldiers in the nineteenth century created a difficult problem of control, because techniques of transportation and of communications had not reached a high-enough level to allow any flexibility of control in a mass army. Such an army could be moved on its own feet or by railroad; the government could communicate with its various units only by letter post or by telegram. The problem of handling a mass army by such techniques was solved partially in the American Civil War of 1861–1865 and completely by Helmuth von Moltke for the Kingdom of Prussia in the Austro-Prussian War of 1866. The solution was a rigid one: a plan of campaign was prepared beforehand against a specific opponent, with an established timetable and detailed instructions for each military unit; communications were prepared and even issued beforehand, to be used according to the timetable. This plan was so inflexible that the signal to mobilize was practically a signal to attack a specified neighboring state because the plan, once initiated, could not be changed and could hardly even be slowed up. With this rigid method Prussia created the German Empire by smashing Austria in 1866 and France in 1871. By 1900 all the states of Europe had adopted the same method and had fixed plans in which the signal for mobilization constituted an attack on some neighbor—a neighbor, in some cases (as in the German invasion of Belgium), with whom the attacker had no real quarrel. Thus, when the signal for mobilization was given in 1914 the states of Europe leaped at each other.

In the twentieth century the military situation was drastically changed in two ways. On the one hand, communications and transportation were so improved by the invention of the radio and the internal-combustion engine that control and movement of troops and even of individual soldiers became very flexible; mobilization ceased to be equivalent to attack, and attack ceased to be equivalent to total war. On the other hand, beginning with the first use of tanks, gas, high-explosive shells, and tactical bombing from the air in 1915–1918, and continuing with all the innovations in weapons leading up to the first atomic bomb in 1945, specialist weapons became superior to amateur weapons. This had a double result which was still working itself out at mid-century: the drafted army of citizen-soldiers began to be replaced by a smaller army of professional specialist soldiers, and authoritarian government began to replace democratic government.

On the political level equally profound changes took place in the twentieth century. These changes were associated with the basis on which an appeal for allegiance could be placed, and especially with the need to find a basis of allegiance which could win loyalty over larger and larger areas from more numerous groups of people. In the early Middle Ages when there had been no state and no public authority, political organization had been the feudal system which was held together by obligations of personal fealty among a small number of people. With the reappearance of the state and of public authority, new patterns of political behavior were organized in what is called the "feudal monarchy." This allowed the state to reappear for the first time since the collapse of Charlemagne's Empire in the ninth century, but with restricted allegiance to a relatively small number of persons over a relatively small area. The development of weapons and the steady improvement in transportation and in communications made it possible to compel obedience over wider and wider areas, and made it necessary to base allegiance on something wider than personal fealty to a feudal monarch. Accordingly, the feudal monarchy was replaced by the dynastic monarchy. In this system subjects owed allegiance to a royal family (dynasty), although the real basis of the dynasty rested on the loyalty of a professional army of pikemen and musketeers.

The shift from the professional army of mercenaries to the mass army of citizen-soldiers, along with other factors acting on other levels of culture, made it necessary to broaden the basis of allegiance once again after 1800. The new basis was nationalism, and gave rise to the national state as the typical political unit of the nineteenth century. This shift was not possible for the larger dynastic states which ruled over many different language and national groups. By the year 1900 three old dynastic monarchies were being threatened with disintegration by the rising tide of nationalistic agitation. These three, the Austro-Hungarian Empire, the Ottoman Empire, and the Russian Empire of the Romanovs, did disintegrate as a consequence of the defeats of the First World War. But the smaller territorial units which replaced them, states like Poland, Czechoslovakia, or Lithuania, organized largely on the basis of language groups, may have reflected adequately enough the nationalistic sentiments of the nineteenth century, but they reflected very inadequately the developments in weapons, in communications, in transportation, and in economics of the twentieth century. By the middle of this latter century these developments were reaching a point where states which could produce the latest instruments of coercion were in a position to compel obedience over areas much larger than those occupied by peoples speaking the same language or otherwise regarding themselves as sharing a common nationality. Even as early as 1940 it began to appear that some new basis more continental in scope than existing nationality groups must be found for the new superstates which were beginning to be born. It became clear that the basis of allegiance for these new superstates of continental scope must be ideological rather than national. Thus the nineteenth century's national state began to be replaced by the twentieth century's ideological bloc. At the same time, the shift from amateur to specialist weapons made it likely that the new form of organization would be authoritarian rather than democratic as the earlier national state had been. However, the prestige of Britain's power and influence in the nineteenth century was so great in the first third of the twentieth century that the British parliamentary system continued to be copied everywhere that people were called upon to set up a new form of government. This happened in Russia in 1917, in Turkey in 1908, in Czechoslovakia and Poland in 1918–1919 and in most of the states of Asia (such as China in 1911).

When we turn to the economic level, we turn to a series of complex developments. It would be pleasant if we could just ignore these, but obviously we cannot, because economic issues have been of paramount importance in the twentieth century, and no one can understand the period without at least a rudimentary grasp of the economic issues. In order to simplify these somewhat, we may divide them into four aspects: (*a*) energy; (*b*) materials; (*c*) organization; and (*d*) control.

It is quite clear that no economic goods can be made without the use of energy and of materials. The history of the former falls into two chief parts each of which is divided into two subparts. The main division, about 1830, separates an earlier period when production used the energy delivered through living bodies and a later period when production used energy from fossil fuels delivered through engines. The first half is subdivided into an earlier period of manpower (and slavery) and a later period using the energy of draft animals. This subdivision occurred roughly about A.D. 1000. The second half (since 1830) is subdivided into a period which used coal in steam engines, and a period which used petroleum in internal-combustion engines. This subdivision occurred about 1900 or a little later.

The development of the use of materials is familiar to everyone. We can speak of an age of iron (before 1830), an age of steel (1830–1910), and an age of alloys, light metals, and synthetics (since 1910). Naturally, all these dates are arbitrary and approximate, since the different periods commenced at different dates in different areas, diffusing outward from their origin in the core area of Western Civilization in northwestern Europe.

When we turn to the developments which took place in economic organization, we approach a subject of great significance. Here again we can see a sequence of several periods. There were six of these periods, each with its own typical form of economic organization. At the beginning, in the early Middle Ages, Western Civilization had an economic system which was almost entirely agricultural, organized in self-sufficient manors, with almost no commerce or industry. To this manorial-agrarian system there was added, after about 1050, a new economic system based on trade in luxury goods of remote origin for the sake of profits. This we might call commercial capitalism. It had two periods of expansion, one in the period 1050–1270, and the other in the period 1440–1690. The typical organization of these two periods was the trading company (in the second we might say the *chartered* trading company, like the Massachusetts Bay Company, the Hudson's Bay Company, or the various East India companies). The next period of economic organization was the stage of industrial capitalism, beginning about 1770, and characterized by owner management through the single-proprietorship or the partnership. The third period we might call financial capitalism. It began about 1850, reached its peak about 1914, and ended about 1932. Its typical forms of economic organization were the limited-liability corporation and the holding company. It was a period of financial or banker management rather than one of owner management as in the earlier period of industrial capitalism. This period of financial capitalism was followed by a period of monopoly capitalism. In this fourth period, typical forms of economic organization were cartels and trade associations. This period began to appear about 1890, took over control of the economic system from the bankers about 1932, and is distinguished as a period of managerial dominance in contrast with the owner management and the financial management of the two periods immediately preceding it. Many of its characteristics continue, even today, but the dramatic events of World War II and the post-war period put it in such a different social and historical context as to create a new, sixth, period of economic organization which might be called "the pluralist economy." The features of this sixth period will be described later.

The approximate relationship of these various stages may be seen in the following table:

Name	Dates	Typical Organization	Management
Manorial	670–	Manor	Custom
Commercial capitalism	a. 1050–1270	Company	Municipal mercantilism
	b. 1440–1690	Chartered company	State mercantilism
Industrial capitalism	1770–1870	Private firm or partnership	Owners
Financial capitalism	1850–1932	Corporation and holding company	Bankers
Monopoly capitalism	1890–1950	Cartels and trade association	Managers
Pluralist economy	1934 to present	Lobbying groups	Technocrats

Two things should be noted. In the first place, these various stages or periods are additive in a sense, and there are many survivals of earlier stages into later ones. As late as 1925 there was a manor still functioning in England, and Cecil Rhodes's chartered company which opened up Rhodesia (the British South Africa Company) was chartered as late as 1889. In the same way owner-managed private firms engaging in industrial activities, or corporations and holding companies engaging in financial activities, could be created today. In the second place all the later periods are called capitalism. This term means "an economic system motivated by the pursuit of profits within a price system." The commercial capitalist sought profits from the exchange of goods; the industrial capitalist sought profits from the manufacture of goods; the financial capitalist sought profits from the manipulation of claims on money; and the monopoly capitalist sought profits from manipulation of the market to make the market price and the amount sold such that his profits would be maximized.

It is interesting to note that, as a consequence of these various stages of economic organization, Western Civilization has passed through four major stages of economic expansion marked by the approximate dates 970–1270, 1440–1690, 1770–1928, and since 1950. Three of these stages of expansion were followed by the outbreak of imperialist wars, as the stage of expansion reached its conclusion. These were the Hundred Years' War and the Italian Wars (1338–1445, 1494–1559), the Second Hundred Years' War (1667–1815), and the world wars (1914–1945). The economic background of the third of these will be examined later in this chapter, but now we must continue our general survey of the conditions of Western Civilization in regard to other aspects of culture. One of these is the fourth and last portion of the economic level, that concerned with economic control.

Economic control has passed through four stages in Western Civilization. Of these the first and third were periods of "automatic control" in the sense that there was no conscious effort at a centralized system of economic control, while the second and fourth stages were periods of conscious efforts at control. These stages, with approximate dates, were as follows:

1. Automatic control: manorial custom, 650–1150
2. Conscious control
   a. municipal mercantilism, 1150–1450
   b. state mercantilism, 1450–1815
3. Automatic control: laissez-faire in the competitive market, 1815–1934
4. Conscious control: planning (both public and private), 1934–

It should be evident that these five stages of economic control are closely associated with the stages previously mentioned in regard to kinds

of weapons on the military level or the forms of government on the political level. The same five stages of economic control have a complex
relationship to the six stages of economic organization already mentioned,
the important stage of industrial capitalism overlapping the transition from
state mercantilism to laissez-faire.

When we turn to the social level of a culture, we can note a number of different phenomena, such as changes in growth of population,
changes in aggregates of this population (such as rise or decline of cities),
and changes in social classes. Most of these things are far too complicated
for us to attempt to treat them in any thorough fashion here. We have
already discussed the various stages in population growth, and shown that
Europe was, about 1900, generally passing from a stage of population
growth with many persons in the prime of life (Type B), to a stage of
population stabilization with a larger percentage of middle-aged persons
(Type C). This shift from Type B to Type C population in Europe can
be placed most roughly at the time that the nineteenth century gave rise
to the twentieth century. At about the same time or shortly after, and
closely associated with the rise of monopoly capitalism (with its emphasis on automobiles, telephones, radio, and such), was a shift in the
aggregation of population. This shift was from the period we might
call "the rise of the city" (in which, year by year, a larger portion of the
population lived in cities) to what we might call "the rise of the suburbs"
or even "the period of megapolis" (in which the growth of residential
concentration moved outward from the city itself into the surrounding
area).

The third aspect of the social level to which we might turn our attention is concerned with changes in social classes. Each of the stages in the
development of economic organization was accompanied by the rise to
prominence of a new social class. The medieval system had provided the
feudal nobility based on the manorial agrarian system. The growth of
commercial capitalism (in two stages) gave a new class of commercial
bourgeoisie. The growth of industrial capitalism gave rise to two new
classes, the industrial bourgeoisie and the industrial workers (or proletariat, as they were sometimes called in Europe). The development of
financial and monopoly capitalism provided a new group of managerial
technicians. The distinction between industrial bourgeoisie and managers
essentially rests on the fact that the former control industry and possess
power because they are owners, while managers control industry (and
also government or labor unions or public opinion) because they are
skilled or trained in certain techniques. As we shall see later, the shift from
one to the other was associated with a separation of control from ownership in economic life. The shift was also associated with what we might
call a change from a two-class society to a middle-class society. Under
industrial capitalism and the early part of financial capitalism, society

began to develop into a polarized two-class society in which an entrenched bourgeoisie stood opposed to a mass proletariat. It was on the basis of this development that Karl Marx, about 1850, formed his ideas of an inevitable class struggle in which the group of owners would become fewer and fewer and richer and richer while the mass of workers became poorer and poorer but more and more numerous, until finally the mass would rise up and take ownership and control from the privileged minority. By 1900 social developments took a direction so different from that expected by Marx that his analysis became almost worthless, and his system had to be imposed by force in a most backward industrial country (Russia) instead of occurring inevitably in the most advanced industrial country as he had expected.

The social developments which made Marx's theories obsolete were the result of technological and economic developments which Marx had not foreseen. The energy for production was derived more and more from inanimate sources of power and less and less from human labor. As a result, mass production required less labor. But mass production required mass consumption so that the products of the new techology had to be distributed to the working groups as well as to others so that rising standards of living for the masses made the proletariat fewer and fewer and richer and richer. At the same time, the need for managerial and white-collar workers of the middle levels of the economic system raised the proletariat into the middle class in large numbers. The spread of the corporate form of industrial enterprise allowed control to be separated from ownership and allowed the latter to be dispersed over a much wider group, so that, in effect, owners became more and more numerous and poorer and poorer. And, finally, control shifted from owners to managers. The result was that the polarized two-class society envisaged by Marx was, after 1900, increasingly replaced by a mass middle-class society, with fewer poor and, if not fewer rich, at least a more numerous group of rich who were relatively less rich than in an earlier period. This process of leveling up the poor and leveling down the rich originated in economic forces but was speeded up and extended by governmental policies in regard to taxation and social welfare, especially after 1945.

When we turn to the higher levels of culture, such as the religious and intellectual aspects, we can discern a sequence of stages similar to those which have been found in the more material levels. We shall make no extended examination of these at this time except to say that the religious level has seen a shift from a basically secularist, materialist, and antireligious outlook in the late nineteenth century to a much more spiritualist and religious point of view in the course of the twentieth century. At the same time a very complex development on the intellectual level has shown a profound shift in outlook from an optimistic and scientific point of view in the period 1860–1890 to a much more pessimistic and irrationalist point of view in the period following 1890. This shift in point of view, which began in a rather restricted group forming an intellectual vanguard about 1890, a group which included such figures as Freud, Sorel, Bergson, and Proust, spread downward to larger and larger sections of Western society in the course of the new century as a result of the devastating experience of two world wars and the great depression. The results of this process can be seen in the striking contrast between the typical outlook of Europe in the nineteenth century and in the twentieth century as outlined in the preceding chapter.

European Economic Developments

COMMERCIAL CAPITALISM

Western Civilization is the richest and most powerful social organization ever made by man. One reason for this success has been its economic organization. This, as we have said, has passed through six successive stages, of which at least four are called "capitalism." Three features are notable about this development as a whole.

In the first place, each stage created the conditions which tended to bring about the next stage; therefore we could say, in a sense, that each stage committed suicide. The original economic organization of self-sufficient agrarian units (manors) was in a society organized so that its upper ranks—the lords, lay and ecclesiastical—found their desires for necessities so well met that they sought to exchange their surpluses of necessities for luxuries of remote origin. This gave rise to a trade in foreign luxuries (spices, fine textiles, fine metals) which was the first evidence of the stage of commercial capitalism. In this second stage, mercantile profits and widening markets created a demand for textiles and other goods which could be met only by application of power to production. This gave the third stage: industrial capitalism. The stage of industrial capitalism soon gave rise to such an insatiable demand for heavy fixed capital, like railroad lines, steel mills, shipyards, and so on, that these investments could not be financed from the profits and private fortunes of individual proprietors. New instruments for financing industry came into existence in the form of limited-liability corporations and investment banks. These were soon in a position to control the chief parts of the industrial system, since they provided capital to it. This gave rise to financial capitalism. The control of financial capitalism was used to integrate the industrial system into ever-larger units with interlinking financial controls. This made possible a reduction of competition with a resulting increase in profits. As a result, the industrial system soon found that it was again able to finance its own expansion from its own profits, and, with this achievement, financial controls were weakened, and the stage of monopoly capitalism arrived. In this fifth stage, great industrial units, working together either directly or through cartels and trade associations, were in a position to exploit the majority of the people. The result was a great economic crisis which soon developed into a struggle for control of the state—the minority hoping to use political power to defend their privileged position, the majority hoping to use the state to curtail the power and privileges of the minority. Both hoped to use the power of the state to find some solution to the economic aspects of the crisis. This dualist struggle dwindled with the rise of economic and social pluralism after 1945.

The second notable feature of this whole development is that the transition of each stage to the next was associated with a period of depression or low economic activity. This was because each stage, after an earlier progressive phase, became later, in its final phase, an organization of vested interests more concerned with protecting its established modes of action than in continuing progressive changes by the application of resources to new, improved methods. This is inevitable in any social organization, but is peculiarly so in regard to capitalism.

The third notable feature of the whole development is closely related to this special nature of capitalism. Capitalism provides very powerful motivations for economic activity because it associates economic motivations so closely with self-interest. But this same feature, which is a source of strength in providing economic motivation through the pursuit of profits, is also a source of weakness owing to the fact that so self-centered a motivation contributes very readily to a loss of economic coordination. Each individual, just because he is so powerfully motivated by self-interest, easily loses sight of the role which his own activities play in the economic system as a whole, and tends to act as if his activities *were* the whole, with inevitable injury to that whole. We could indicate this by pointing out that capitalism, because it seeks profits as its primary goal, is never primarily seeking to achieve prosperity, high production, high consumption, political power, patriotic improvement, or moral uplift. Any of these may be achieved under capitalism, and any (or all) of them may be sacrificed and lost under capitalism, depending on this relationship to the primary goal of capitalist activity—the pursuit of profits. During the nine-hundred-year history of capitalism, it has, at various times, contributed both to the achievement and to the destruction of these other social goals.

The different stages of capitalism have sought to win profits by different kinds of economic activities. The original stage, which we call commercial capitalism, sought profits by moving goods from one place to another. In this effort, goods went from places where they were less valuable to places where they were more valuable, while money, doing the same thing, moved in the opposite direction. This valuation, which determined the movement both of goods and of money and which made them move *in opposite directions,* was measured by the relationship between these two things. Thus the value of goods was expressed in money, and the value of money was expressed in goods. Goods moved from low-price areas to high-price areas, and money moved from high-price areas to low-price areas, because goods were more valuable where prices were high and *money was more valuable where prices were low.*

Thus, clearly, money and goods are not the same thing but are, on the contrary, exactly opposite things. Most confusion in economic thinking arises from failure to recognize this fact. Goods are wealth which you have, while money is *a claim on wealth* which you do not have. Thus goods are an asset; money is a debt. If goods are wealth; money is not-wealth, or negative wealth, or even anti-wealth. They always behave in opposite ways, just as they usually move in opposite directions. If the value of one goes up, the value of the other goes down, and in the same proportion. The value of goods, expressed in money, is called "prices," while the value of money, expressed in goods, is called "value."

Commercial capitalism arose when merchants, carrying goods from one area to another, were able to sell these goods at their destination for a price which covered original cost, all costs of moving the goods, including the merchant's expenses, *and a profit.* This development, which began as the movement of luxury goods, increased wealth because it led to specialization of activities both in crafts and in agriculture, which increased skills and output, and also brought into the market new commodities.

Eventually, this stage of commercial capitalism became institutionalized into a restrictive system, sometimes called "mercantilism," in which merchants sought to gain profits, not from the movements of goods but from restricting the movements of goods. Thus the pursuit of profits, which had earlier led to increased prosperity by increasing trade and production, became a restriction on both trade and production, because profit became an end in itself rather than an accessory mechanism in the economic system as a whole.

The way in which commercial capitalism (an expanding economic organization) was transformed into mercantilism (a restrictive economic organization) twice in our past history is very revealing not only of the nature of economic systems, and of men themselves, but also of the nature of economic crisis and what can be done about it.

Under commercial capitalism, merchants soon discovered that an increasing flow of goods from a low-price area to a high-price area tended to raise prices in the former and to lower prices in the latter. Every time a shipment of spices came into London, the price of spices there began to fall, while the arrival of buyers and ships in Malacca gave prices there an upward spurt. This trend toward equalization of price levels between two areas because of the double, and reciprocal, movement of goods and money jeopardized profits for merchants, however much it may have satisfied producers and consumers at either end. It did this by reducing the price differential between the two areas and thus reducing the margin within which the merchant could make his profit. It did not take shrewd merchants long to realize that they could maintain this price differential, and thus their profits, if they could restrict the flow of goods, so that an equal volume of money flowed for a reduced volume of goods. In this way, shipments were decreased, costs were reduced, but profits were maintained.

Two things are notable in this mercantilist situation. In the first place, the merchant, by his restrictive practices, was, in essence, increasing his own satisfaction by reducing that of the producer at one end and of the consumer at the other end; he was able to do this because he was in the middle between them. In the second place, so long as the merchant, in his home port, was concerned with goods, he was eager that the prices of goods should be, and remain, high.

In the course of time, however, some merchants began to shift their attention from the goods aspect of commercial interchange to the other, monetary, side of the exchange. They began to accumulate the profits of these transactions, and became increasingly concerned, not with the shipment and exchange of goods, but with the shipment and exchange of moneys. In time they became concerned with the lending of money to merchants to finance their ships and their activities, advancing money for both, at high interest rates, secured by claims on ships or goods as collateral for repayment.

In this process the attitudes and interests of these new bankers became totally opposed to those of the merchants (although few of either recognized the situation). Where the merchant had been eager for high prices and was increasingly eager for low interest rates, the banker was eager for a high value of money (that is, low prices) and high interest rates. Each was concerned to maintain or to increase the value of the half of the transaction (goods for money) with which he was directly concerned, with relative neglect of the transaction itself (which was of course the concern of the producers and the consumers).

In sum, specialization of economic activities, by breaking up the economic process, had made it possible for people to concentrate on one portion of the process and, by maximizing that portion, to jeopardize the rest. The process was not only broken up into producers, exchangers, and consumers but there were also two kinds of exchangers (one concerned with goods, the other with money), with almost antithetical, *short-term*, aims. The problems which inevitably arose could be solved and the system reformed only by reference to the system as a whole. Unfortunately, however, three parts of the system, concerned with the production, transfer, and consumption of goods, were concrete and clearly visible so that almost anyone could grasp them simply by examining them, while the operations of banking and finance were concealed, scattered, and abstract so that they appeared to many to be difficult. To add to this, bankers themselves did everything they could to make their activities more secret and more esoteric. Their activities were reflected in mysterious marks in ledgers which were never opened to the curious outsider.

In the course of time the central fact of the developing economic system, the relationship between goods and money, became clear, at least to bankers. This relationship, the price system, depended upon five things: the supply and the demand for goods, the supply and the demand for money, and the speed of exchange between money and goods. An increase in three of these (demand for goods, supply of money, speed of circulation) would move the prices of goods up and the value of money down. This inflation was objectionable to bankers, although desirable to producers and merchants. On the other hand, a decrease in the same three items would be deflationary and would please bankers, worry producers and merchants, and delight consumers (who obtained more goods for less money). The other factors worked in the opposite direction, so that an increase in them (supply of goods, demand for money, and slowness of circulation or exchange) would be deflationary.

Such changes of prices, either inflationary or deflationary, have been major forces in history for the last six centuries at least. Over that long period, their power to modify men's lives and human history has been increasing. This has been reflected in two ways. On the one hand, rises in prices have generally encouraged increased economic activity, especially the production of goods, while, on the other hand, price changes have served to redistribute wealth within the economic system. Inflation, especially a slow steady rise in prices, encourages producers, because it means that they can commit themselves to costs of production on one price level and then, later, offer the finished product for sale at a somewhat higher price level. This situation encourages production because it gives confidence of an almost certain profit margin. On the other hand, production is discouraged in a period of falling prices, unless the producer is in the very unusual situation where his costs are falling more rapidly than the prices of his product.

The redistribution of wealth by changing prices is equally important but attracts much less attention. Rising prices benefit debtors and injure creditors, while falling prices do the opposite. A debtor called upon to pay a debt at a time when prices are higher than when he contracted the debt must yield up less goods and services than he obtained at the earlier date, on a lower price level, when he borrowed the money. A creditor, such as a bank, which has lent money—equivalent to a certain quantity of goods and services—on one price level, gets back the same amount of money—but a smaller quantity of goods and services—when repayment comes at a higher price level, because the money repaid is then less valuable. This is why bankers, as creditors in money terms, have been obsessed with maintaining the value of money, although the reason they have traditionally given for this obsession—that "sound money" maintains "business confidence"—has been propagandist rather than accurate.

Hundreds of years ago, bankers began to specialize, with the richer and more influential ones associated increasingly with foreign trade and foreign-exchange transactions. Since these were richer and more cosmopolitan and increasingly concerned with questions of political significance, such as stability and debasement of currencies, war and peace, dynastic marriages, and worldwide trading monopolies, they became the financiers and financial advisers of governments. Moreover, since their relationships with governments were always in monetary terms and not real terms, and since they were always obsessed with the stability of monetary exchanges between one country's money and another, they used their power and influence to do two things: (1) to get all money and debts expressed in terms of a strictly limited commodity—ultimately gold; and (2) to get all monetary matters out of the control of governments and political authority, on the ground that they would be handled better by private banking interests in terms of such a stable value as gold.

These efforts failed with the shift of commercial capitalism into mercantilism and the destruction of the whole pattern of social organization based on dynastic monarchy, professional mercenary armies, and mercantilism, in the series of wars which shook Europe from the middle of the seventeenth century to 1815. Commercial capitalism passed through two periods of expansion each of which deteriorated into a later phase of war, class struggles, and retrogression. The first stage, associated with the Mediterranean Sea, was dominated by the North Italians and Catalonians but ended in a phase of crisis after 1300, which was not finally ended until 1558. The second stage of commercial capitalism, which was associated with the Atlantic Ocean, was dominated by the West Iberians, the Netherlanders, and the English. It had begun to expand by 1440, was in full swing by 1600, but by the end of the seventeeth century had become entangled in the restrictive struggles of state mercantilism and the series of wars which ravaged Europe from 1667 to 1815.

The commercial capitalism of the 1440–1815 period was marked by the supremacy of the Chartered Companies, such as the Hudson's Bay, the Dutch and British East Indian companies, the Virginia Company, and the Association of Merchant Adventurers (Muscovy Company). England's greatest rivals in all these activities were defeated by England's greater power, and, above all, its greater security derived from its insular position.

INDUSTRIAL CAPITALISM, 1770–1850

Britain's victories over Louis XIV in the period 1667–1715 and over the French Revolutionary governments and Napoleon in 1792–1815 had many causes, such as its insular position, its ability to retain control of the sea, its ability to present itself to the world as the defender of the freedoms and rights of small nations and of diverse social and religious groups. Among these numerous causes, there were a financial one and an economic one. Financially, England had discovered the secret of credit. Economically, England had embarked on the Industrial Revolution.

Credit had been known to the Italians and Netherlanders long before it became one of the instruments of English world supremacy. Nevertheless, the founding of the Bank of England by William Paterson and his friends in 1694 is one of the great dates in world history. For generations men had sought to avoid the one drawback of gold, its heaviness, by using pieces of paper to represent specific pieces of gold. Today we call such pieces of paper gold certificates. Such a certificate entitles its bearer to exchange it for its piece of gold on demand, but in view of the convenience of paper, only a small fraction of certificate holders ever did make such demands. It early became clear that gold need be held on hand only to the amount needed to cover the fraction of certificates likely to be presented for payment; accordingly, the rest of the gold could be used for business purposes, or, what amounts to the same thing, a volume of certificates could be issued greater than the volume of gold reserved for payment of demands against them. Such an excess volume of paper claims against reserves we now call bank notes.

In effect, this creation of paper claims greater than the reserves available means that bankers were creating money out of nothing. The same thing could be done in another way, not by note-issuing banks but by deposit banks. Deposit bankers discovered that orders and checks drawn against deposits by depositors and given to third persons were often not cashed by the latter but were deposited to their own accounts. Thus there were no actual movements of funds, and payments were made simply by bookkeeping transactions on the accounts. Accordingly, it was necessary for the banker to keep on hand in actual money (gold, certificates, and notes) no more than the fraction of deposits likely to be drawn upon *and cashed;* the rest could be used for loans, and if these loans were made by creating a deposit for the borrower, who in turn would draw checks upon it rather than withdraw it in money, such "created deposits" or loans could also be covered adequately by retaining reserves to only a fraction of their value. Such created deposits also were a creation of money out of nothing, although bankers usually refused to express their actions, either note issuing or deposit lending, in these terms. William Paterson, however, on obtaining the charter of the Bank of England in 1694, to use the moneys he had won in privateering, said, "The Bank hath benefit of interest on all moneys which it creates out of nothing." This was repeated by Sir Edward Holden, founder of the Midland Bank, on December 18, 1907, and is, of course, generally admitted today.

This organizational structure for creating means of payment out of nothing, which we call credit, was not invented by England but was developed by her to become one of her chief weapons in the victory over Napoleon in 1815. The emperor, as the last great mercantilist, could not see money in any but concrete terms, and was convinced that his efforts to fight wars on the basis of "sound money," by avoiding the creation of credit, would ultimately win him a victory by bankrupting England. He was wrong, although the lesson has had to be relearned by modern financiers in the twentieth century.

Britain's victory over Napoleon was also helped by two economic innovations: the Agricultural Revolution, which was well established there in 1720, and the Industrial Revolution, which was equally well established there by 1776, when Watt patented his steam engine. The Industrial Revolution, like the Credit Revolution, has been much misunderstood, both at the time and since. This is unfortunate, as each of these has great significance, both to advanced and to underdeveloped countries, in the twentieth century. The Industrial Revolution was accompanied by a number of incidental features, such as growth of cities through the factory system, the rapid growth of an unskilled labor supply (the proletariat), the reduction of labor to the status of a commodity in the competitive market, and the shifting of ownership of tools and equipment from laborers to a new social class of entrepreneurs. None of these constituted the essential feature of industrialism, which was, in fact, the application of nonliving power to the productive process. This application, symbolized in the steam engine and the water wheel, in the long run served to reduce or eliminate the relative significance of unskilled labor and the use of human or animal energy in the productive process (automation) and to disperse the productive process from cities, but did so, throughout, by intensifying the vital feature of the system, the use of energy from sources other than living bodies.

In this continuing process, Britain's early achievement of industrialism gave it such great profits that these, combined with the profits derived earlier from commercial capitalism and the simultaneous profits derived from the unearned rise in land values from new cities and mines, made its early industrial enterprises largely self-financed or at least locally financed. They were organized in proprietorships and partnerships, had contact with local deposit banks for short-term current loans, but had little to do with international bankers, investment banks, central governments, or corporative forms of business organization.

This early stage of industrial capitalism, which lasted in England from about 1770 to about 1850, was shared to some extent with Belgium and even France, but took quite different forms in the United States, Germany, and Italy, and almost totally different forms in Russia or Asia. The chief reason for these differences was the need for raising funds (capital) to pay for the rearrangement of the factors of production (land, labor, materials, skill, equipment, and so on) which industrialism required. Northwestern Europe, and above all England, had large savings for such new enterprises. Central Europe and North America had much less, while eastern and southern Europe had very little in private hands.

The more difficulty an area had in mobilizing capital for industrialization, the more significant was the role of investment bankers and of governments in the industrial process. In fact, the early forms of industrialism based on textiles, iron, coal, and steam spread so slowly from England to Europe that England was itself entering upon the next stage, financial capitalism, by the time Germany and the United States (about 1850) were just beginning to industrialize. This new stage of financial capitalism, which continued to dominate England, France, and the United States as late as 1930, was made necessary by the great mobilizations of capital needed for railroad building after 1830. The capital needed for railroads, with their enormous expenditures on track and equipment, could not be raised from single proprietorships or partnerships or locally, but, instead, required a new form of enterprise—the limited-liability stock corporation—and a new source of funds—the international investment banker who had, until then, concentrated his attention almost entirely on international flotations of government bonds. The demands of railroads for equipment carried this same development, almost at once, into steel manufacturing and coal mining.

FINANCIAL CAPITALISM, 1850–1931

This third stage of capitalism is of such overwhelming significance in the history of the twentieth century, and its ramifications and influences have been so subterranean and even occult, that we may be excused if we devote considerate attention to its organization and methods. Essentially what it did was to take the old disorganized and localized methods of handling money and credit and organize them into an integrated system, on an international basis, which worked with incredible and well-oiled facility for many decades. The center of that system was in London, with major offshoots in New York and Paris, and it has left, as its greatest achievement, an integrated banking system and a heavily capitalized—if now largely obsolescent—framework of heavy industry, reflected in railroads, steel mills, coal mines, and electrical utilities.

This system had its center in London for four chief reasons. First was the great volume of savings in England, resting on England's early successes in commercial and industrial capitalism. Second was England's oligarchic social structure (especially as reflected in its concentrated landownership and limited access to educational opportunities) which provided a very inequitable distribution of incomes with large surpluses coming to the control of a small, energetic upper class. Third was the fact that this upper class was aristocratic but not noble, and thus, based on traditions rather than birth, was quite willing to recruit both money and ability from lower levels of society and even from outside the country, welcoming American heiresses and central-European Jews to its ranks, almost as willingly as it welcomed monied, able, and conformist recruits from the lower classes of Englishmen, whose disabilities from educational deprivation, provincialism, and Nonconformist (that is non-Anglican) religious background generally excluded them from the privileged aristocracy. Fourth (and by no means last) in significance was the skill in financial manipulation, especially on the international scene, which the small group of merchant bankers of London had acquired in the period of commercial and industrial capitalism and which lay ready for use when the need for financial capitalist innovation became urgent.

The merchant bankers of London had already at hand in 1810–1850 the Stock Exchange, the Bank of England, and the London money market when the needs of advancing industrialism called all of these into the industrial world which they had hitherto ignored. In time they brought into their financial network the provincial banking centers, organized as commercial banks and savings banks, as well as insurance companies, to form all of these into a single financial system on an international scale which manipulated the quantity and flow of money so that they were able to influence, if not control, governments on one side and industries on the other. The men who did this, looking backward toward the period of dynastic monarchy in which they had their own roots, aspired to establish dynasties of international bankers and were at least as successful at this as were many of the dynastic political rulers. The greatest of these dynasties, of course, were the descendants of Meyer Amschel Rothschild (1743–1812) of Frankfort, whose male descendants, for at least two generations, generally married first cousins or even nieces. Rothschild's five sons, established at branches in Vienna, London, Naples, and Paris, as well as Frankfort, cooperated together in ways which other international banking dynasties copied but rarely excelled.

In concentrating, as we must, on the financial or economic activities of international bankers, we must not totally ignore their other attributes. They were, especially in later generations, cosmopolitan rather than nationalistic; they were a constant, if weakening, influence for peace, a pattern established in 1830 and 1840 when the Rothschilds threw their whole tremendous influence successfully against European wars. They were usually highly civilized, cultured gentlemen, patrons of education and of the arts, so that today colleges, professorships, opera companies, symphonies, libraries, and museum collections still reflect their munificence. For these purposes they set a pattern of endowed foundations which still surround us today.

The names of some of these banking families are familiar to all of us and should be more so. They include Baring, Lazard, Erlanger, Warburg, Schröder, Seligman, the Speyers, Mirabaud, Mallet, Fould, and above all Rothschild and Morgan. Even after these banking families became fully involved in domestic industry by the emergence of financial capitalism, they remained different from ordinary bankers in distinctive ways: (1) they were cosmopolitan and international; (2) they were close to governments and were particularly concerned with questions of government debts, including foreign government debts, even in areas which seemed, at first glance, poor risks, like Egypt, Persia, Ottoman Turkey, Imperial China, and Latin America; (3) their interests were almost exclusively in bonds and very rarely in goods, since they admired "liquidity" and regarded commitments in commodities or even real estate as the first step toward bankruptcy; (4) they were, accordingly, fanatical devotees of deflation (which they called "sound" money from its close associations with high interest rates and a high value of money) and of the gold standard, which, in their eyes, symbolized and ensured these values; and (5) they were almost equally devoted to secrecy and the secret use of financial influence in political life. These bankers came to be called "international bankers" and, more particularly, were known as "merchant bankers" in England, "private bankers" in France, and "investment bankers" in the United States. In all countries they carried on various kinds of banking and exchange activities, but everywhere they were sharply distinguishable from other, more obvious, kinds of banks, such as savings banks or commercial banks.

One of their less obvious characteristics was that they remained as private unincorporated firms, usually partnerships, until relatively recently, offering no shares, no reports, and usually no advertising to the public. This risky status, which deprived them of limited liability, was retained, in most cases, until modern inheritance taxes made it essential to surround such family wealth with the immortality of corporate status for tax-avoidance purposes. This persistence as private firms continued because it ensured the maximum of anonymity and secrecy to persons of tremendous public power who dreaded public knowledge of their activities as an evil almost as great as inflation. As a consequence, ordinary people had no way of knowing the wealth or areas of operation of such firms, and often were somewhat hazy as to their membership. Thus, people of considerable political knowledge might not associate the names Walter Burns, Clinton Dawkins, Edward Grenfell, Willard Straight, Thomas Lamont, Dwight Morrow, Nelson Perkins, Russell Leffingwell, Elihu Root, John W. Davis, John Foster Dulles, and S. Parker Gilbert with the name "Morgan," yet all these and many others were parts of the system of influence which centered on the J. P. Morgan office at 23 Wall Street. This firm, like others of the international banking fraternity, constantly operated through corporations and governments, yet remained itself an obscure private partnership until international financial capitalism was passing from its deathbed to the grave. J. P. Morgan and Company, originally founded in London as George Peabody and Company in 1838, was not incorporated until March 21, 1940, and went out of existence as a separate entity on April 24, 1959, when it merged with its most important commercial bank subsidiary, the Guaranty Trust Company. The London affiliate, Morgan Grenfell, was incorporated in 1934, and still exists.

The influence of financial capitalism and of the international bankers who created it was exercised both on business and on governments, but could have done neither if it had not been able to persuade both these to accept two "axioms" of its own ideology. Both of these were based on the assumption that politicians were too weak and too subject to temporary popular pressures to be trusted with control of the money system; accordingly, the sanctity of all values and the soundness of money must be protected in two ways: by basing the value of money on gold and by allowing bankers to control the supply of money. To do this it was necessary to conceal, or even to mislead, both governments and people about the nature of money and its methods of operation.

For example, bankers called the process of establishing a monetary system on gold "stabilization," and implied that this covered, as a single consequence, stabilization of exchanges and stabilization of prices. It really achieved only stabilization of exchanges, while its influence on prices were quite independent and incidental, and might be unstabilizing (from its usual tendency to force prices downward by limiting the supply of money). As a consequence, many persons, including financiers and even economists, were astonished to discover, in the twentieth century, that the gold standard gave stable exchanges and unstable prices. It had, however, already contributed to a similar, but less extreme, situation in much of the nineteenth century.

Exchanges were stabilized on the gold standard because by law, in various countries, the monetary unit was made equal to a fixed quantity of gold, and the two were made exchangeable at that legal ratio. In the period before 1914, currency was stabilized in certain countries as follows:

In Britain:	77s. 10½d. equaled a standard ounce (11/12 pure gold).
In the United States:	$20.67 equaled a fine ounce (12/12 pure gold).
In France:	3,447.74 francs equaled a fine kilogram of gold.
In Germany:	2,790 marks equaled a fine kilogram of gold.

These relationships were established by the legal requirement that a person who brought gold, gold coins, or certificates to the public treasury (or other designated places) could convert any one of these into either of the others in unlimited amounts for no cost. As a result, on a full gold standard, gold had a unique position: it was, at the same time, in the sphere of money and in the sphere of wealth. In the sphere of money, the value of all other kinds of money was expressed in terms of gold: and, in the sphere of real wealth, the values of all other kinds of goods were expressed in terms of gold as money. If we regard the relationships between money and goods as a seesaw in which each of these was at opposite ends, so that the value of one rose just as much as the value of the other declined, then we must see gold as the fulcrum of the seesaw on which this relationship balances, but which does not itself go up or down.

Since it is quite impossible to understand the history of the twentieth century without some understanding of the role played by money in domestic affairs and in foreign affairs, as well as the role played by bankers in economic life and in political life, we must take at least a glance at each of these four subjects.

Domestic Financial Practices

In each country the supply of money took the form of an inverted pyramid or cone balanced on its point. In the point was a supply of gold and its equivalent certificates; on the intermediate levels was a much larger supply of notes; and at the top, with an open and expandable upper surface, was an even greater supply of deposits. Each level used the levels below it as its reserves, and, since these lower levels had smaller quantities of money, they were "sounder." A holder of claims on the middle or upper level could increase his confidence in his claims on wealth by reducing them to a lower level, although, of course, if everyone, or any considerable number of persons, tried to do this at the same time the volume of reserves would be totally inadequate. Notes were issued by "banks of emission" or "banks of issue," and were secured by reserves of gold or certificates held in their own coffers or in some central reserve. The fraction of such a note issue held in reserve depended upon custom, banking regulations (including the terms of a bank's charter), or statute law. There were formerly many banks of issue, but this function is now generally restricted to a few or even to a single "central bank" in each country. Such banks, even central banks, were private institutions, owned by shareholders who profited by their operations. In the 1914–1939 period, in the United States, Federal Reserve Notes were covered by gold certificates to 40 percent of their value, but this was reduced to 25 percent in 1945. The Bank of England, by an Act of 1928, had its notes uncovered up to £250 million, and covered by gold for 100 percent value over that amount. The Bank of France, in the same year, set its note cover at 35 percent. These provisions could always be set aside or changed in an emergency, such as war.

Deposits on the upper level of the pyramid were called by this name, with typical bankers' ambiguity, in spite of the fact that they consisted of two utterly different kinds of relationships: (1) "lodged deposits," which were real claims left by a depositor in a bank, on which the depositor might receive interest, since such deposits were debts owed by the bank to the depositor; and (2) "created deposits," which were claims created by the bank out of nothing as loans from the bank to "depositors" who had to pay interest on them, since these represented debt from them to the bank. In both cases, of course, checks could be drawn against such deposits to make payments to third parties, which is why both were called by the same name. Both form part of the money supply. Lodged deposits as a form of savings are deflationary, while created deposits, being an addition to the money supply, are inflationary. The volume of the latter depends on a number of factors of which the chief are the rate of interest and the demand for such credit. These two play a very significant role in determining the volume of money in the community, since a large portion of that volume, in an advanced economic community, is made up of checks drawn against deposits. The volume of deposits banks can create, like the amount of notes they can issue, depends upon the volume of reserves available to pay whatever fraction of checks are cashed rather than deposited. These matters may be regulated by laws, by bankers' rules, or simply by local customs. In the United States deposits were traditionally limited to ten times reserves of notes and gold. In Britain it was usually nearer twenty times such reserves. In all countries the demand for and volume of such credit was larger in time of a boom and less in time of a depression. This to a considerable extent explains the inflationary aspect of a depression, the combination helping to form the so-called "business cycle."

In the course of the nineteenth century, with the full establishment of the gold standard and of the modern banking system, there grew up around the fluctuating inverted pyramid of the money supply a plethora of financial establishments which came to assume the configurations of a solar system; that is, of a central bank surrounded by satellite financial institutions. In most countries the central bank was surrounded closely by the almost invisible private investment banking firms. These, like the planet Mercury, could hardly be seen in the dazzle emitted by the central bank which they, in fact, often dominated. Yet a close observer could hardly fail to notice the close *private* associations between these private, international bankers and the central bank itself. In France, for example, in 1936 when the Bank of France was reformed, its Board of Regents (directors) was still dominated by the names of the families who had originally set it up in 1800; to these had been added a few more recent names, such as Rothschild (added in 1819); in some cases the name might not be readily recognized because it was that of a son-in-law rather than that of a son. Otherwise, in 1914, the names, frequently those of Protestants of Swiss origin (who arrived in the eighteenth century) or of Jews of German origin (who arrived in the nineteenth century), had been much the same for more than a century.

In England a somewhat similar situation existed, so that even in the middle of the twentieth century the Members of the Court of the Bank of England were chiefly associates of the various old "merchant banking" firms such as Baring Brothers, Morgan Grenfell, Lazard Brothers, and others.

In a secondary position, outside the central core, are the commercial banks, called in England the "joint-stock banks," and on the Continent frequently known as "deposit banks." These include such famous names as Midland Bank, Lloyd's Bank, Barclays Bank in England, the National City Bank in the United States, the Crédit Lyonnais in France, and the Darmstädter Bank in Germany.

Outside this secondary ring is a third, more peripheral, assemblage of institutions that have little financial power but do have the very significant function of mobilizing funds from the public. This includes a wide variety of savings banks, insurance firms, and trust companies.

Naturally, these arrangements vary greatly from place to place, especially as the division of banking functions and powers are not the same in all countries. In France and England the private bankers exercised their powers through the central bank and had much more influence on the government and on foreign policy and much less influence on industry, because in these two countries, unlike Germany, Italy, the United States, or Russia, private savings were sufficient to allow much of industry to finance itself without recourse either to bankers or government. In the United States much industry was financed by investment bankers directly, and the power of these both on industry and on government was very great, while the central bank (the New York Federal Reserve Bank) was established late (1913) and became powerful much later (after financial capitalism was passing from the scene). In Germany industry was financed and controlled by the discount banks, while the central bank was of little power or significance before 1914. In Russia the role of the government was dominant in much of economic life, while in Italy the situation was backward and complicated.

We have said that two of the five factors which determined the value of money (and thus the price level of goods) are the supply and the demand for money. The supply of money in a single country was subject to no centralized, responsible control in most countries over recent centuries. Instead, there were a variety of controls of which some could be influenced by bankers, some could be influenced by the government, and some could hardly be influenced by either. Thus, the various parts of the pyramid of money were but loosely related to each other. Moreover, much of this looseness arose from the fact that the controls were compulsive in a deflationary direction and were only permissive in an inflationary direction.

This last point can be seen in the fact that the supply of gold could be decreased but could hardly be increased. If an ounce of gold was added to the point of the pyramid in a system where law and custom allowed 10 percent reserves on each level, it *could permit* an increase of deposits equivalent to $2067 on the uppermost level. If such an ounce of gold were withdrawn from a fully expanded pyramid of money, this *would compel* a reduction of deposits by at least this amount, probably by a refusal to renew loans.

Throughout modern history the influence of the gold standard has been deflationary, because the natural output of gold each year, except in extraordinary times, has not kept pace with the increase in output of goods. Only new supplies of gold, or the suspension of the gold standard in wartime, or the development of new kinds of money (like notes and checks) which economize the use of gold, have saved our civilization from steady price deflation over the last couple of centuries. As it was, we had two long periods of such deflation from 1818 to 1850 and from 1872 to about 1897. The three surrounding periods of inflation (1790–1817, 1850–1872, 1897–1921) were caused by (1) the wars of the French Revolution and Napoleon when most countries were not on gold; (2) the new gold strikes of California and Alaska in 1849–1850, followed by a series of wars, which included the Crimean War of 1854–1856, the Austrian-French War of 1859, the American Civil War of 1861–1865, the Austro-Prussian and Franco-Prussian wars of 1866 and 1870, and even the Russo-Turkish War of 1877; and (3) the Klondike and Transvaal gold strikes of the late 1890's, supplemented by the new cyanide method of refining gold (about 1897) and the series of wars from the Spanish-American War of 1898–1899, the Boer War of 1899–1902, and the Russo-Japanese War of 1904–1905, to the almost uninterrupted series of wars in the decade 1911–1921. In each case, the three great periods of war ended with an extreme deflationary crisis (1819, 1873, 1921) as the influential Money Power persuaded governments to reestablish a deflationary monetary unit with a high gold content.

The obsession of the Money Power with deflation was partly a result of their concern with money rather than with goods, but was also founded on other factors, one of which was paradoxical. The paradox arose from the fact that the basic economic conditions of the nineteenth century were deflationary, with a money system based on gold and an industrial system pouring out increasing supplies of goods, but in spite of falling prices (with its increasing value of money) the interest rate tended to fall rather than to rise. This occurred because the relative limiting of the supply of money in business was not reflected in the world of finance where excess profits of finance made excess funds available for lending. Moreover, the old traditions of merchant banking continued to prevail in financial capitalism even to its end in 1931. It continued to emphasize bonds rather than equity securities (stocks), to favor government issues rather than private offerings, and to look to foreign rather than to domestic investments. Until 1825, government bonds made up almost the whole of securities on the London Stock Exchange. In 1843, such bonds, usually foreign, were 80 percent of the securities registered, and in 1875 they were still 68 percent. The funds available for such loans were so great that there were, in the nineteenth century, sometimes riots by subscribers seeking opportunities to buy security flotations; and offerings from many remote places and obscure activities commanded a ready sale. The excess of savings led to a fall in the price necessary to hire money, so that the interest rate on British government bonds fell from 4.42 percent in 1820 to 3.11 in 1850 to 2.76 in 1900. This tended to drive savings into foreign fields where, on the whole, they continued to seek government issues and fixed interest securities. All this served to strengthen the merchant bankers' obsession both with government influence and with deflation (which would increase value of money and interest rates).

Another paradox of banking practice arose from the fact that bankers, who loved deflation, often acted in an inflationary fashion from their eagerness to lend money at interest. Since they make money out of loans, they are eager to increase the amounts of bank credit on loan. But this is inflationary. The conflict between the deflationary ideas and inflationary practices of bankers had profound repercussions on business. The bankers made loans to business so that the volume of money increased faster than the increase in goods. The result was inflation. When this became clearly noticeable, the bankers would flee to notes or specie by curtailing credit and raising discount rates. This was beneficial to bankers in the short run (since it allowed them to foreclose on collateral held for loans), but it could be disastrous to them in the long run (by forcing the value of the collateral below the amount of the loans it secured). But such bankers' deflation was destructive to business and industry in the short run as well as the long run.

The resulting fluctuation in the supply of money, chiefly deposits, was a prominent aspect of the "business cycle." The quantity of money could be changed by changing reserve requirements or discount (interest) rates. In the United States, for example, an upper limit has been set on deposits by requiring Federal Reserve member banks to keep a certain percentage of their deposits as reserves with the local Federal Reserve Bank. The percentage (usually from 7 to 26 percent) varies with the locality and the decisions of the Board of Governors of the Federal Reserve System.

Central banks can usually vary the amount of money in circulation by "open market operations" or by influencing the discount rates of lesser banks. In open market operations, a central bank buys or sells government bonds in the open market. If it buys, it releases money into the economic system; if it sells it reduces the amount of money in the community. The change is greater than the price paid for the securities. For example, if the Federal Reserve Bank buys government securities in the open market, it pays for these by check which is soon deposited in a bank. It thus increases this bank's reserves with the Federal Reserve Bank. Since banks are permitted to issue loans for several times the value of their reserves with the Federal Reserve Bank, such a transaction permits them to issue loans for a much larger sum.

Central banks can also change the quantity of money by influencing the credit policies of other banks. This can be done by various methods, such as changing the rediscount rate or changing reserve requirements. By changing the rediscount rate we mean the interest rate which central banks charge lesser banks for loans backed by commercial paper or other security which these lesser banks have taken in return for loans. By raising the rediscount rate the central bank *forces* the lesser bank to raise its discount rate in order to operate at a profit; such a raise in interest rates tends to reduce the demand for credit and thus the amount of deposits (money). Lowering the rediscount rate *permits* an opposite result.

Changing the reserve requirements as a method by which central banks can influence the credit policies of other banks is possible only in those places (like the United States) where there is a statutory limit on reserves. Increasing reserve requirements curtails the ability of lesser banks to grant credit, while decreasing it expands that ability.

It is to be noted that the control of the central bank over the credit policies of local banks are permissive in one direction and compulsive in the other. They can compel these local banks to curtail credit and can only permit them to increase credit. This means that they have control powers against inflation and not deflation—a reflection of the old banking idea that inflation was bad and deflation was good.

The powers of governments over the quantity of money are of various kinds, and include (*a*) control over a central bank, (*b*) control over public taxation, and (*c*) control over public spending. The control of governments over central banks varies greatly from one country to another, but on the whole has been increasing. Since most central banks have been (technically) private institutions, this control is frequently based on custom rather than on law. In any case, the control over the supply of money which governments have through central banks is exercised by the regular banking procedures we have discussed. The powers of the government over the quantity of money in the community exercised through taxation and public spending are largely independent of banking control. Taxation tends to reduce the amount of money in a community and is usually a deflationary force; government spending tends to increase the amount of money in a community and is usually an inflationary force. The total effects of a government's policy will depend on which item is greater. An unbalanced budget will be inflationary; a budget with a surplus will be deflationary.

A government can also change the amount of money in a community by other, more drastic, methods. By changing the gold content of the monetary unit they can change the amount of money in the community by a much greater amount. If, for example, the gold content of the dollar is cut in half, the amount of gold certificates will be able to be doubled, and the amount of notes and deposits reared on this basis will be increased manyfold, depending on the customs of the community in respect to reserve requirements. Moreover, if a government goes off the gold standard completely—that is, refuses to exchange certificates and notes for specie—the amount of notes and deposits can be increased indefinitely because these are no longer limited by limited amounts of gold reserves.

In the various actions which increase or decrease the supply of money, governments, bankers, and industrialists have not always seen eye to eye. On the whole, in the period up to 1931, bankers, especially the Money Power controlled by the international investment bankers, were able to dominate both business and government. They could dominate business, especially in activities and in areas where industry could not finance its own needs for capital, because investment bankers had the ability to supply or refuse to supply such capital. Thus, Rothschild interests came to dominate many of the railroads of Europe, while Morgan dominated at least 26,000 miles of American railroads. Such bankers went further than this. In return for flotations of securities of industry, they took seats on the boards of directors of industrial firms, as they had already done on commercial banks, savings banks, insurance firms, and finance companies. From these lesser institutions they funneled capital to enterprises which yielded control and away from those who resisted. These firms were controlled through interlocking directorships, holding companies, and lesser banks. They engineered amalgamations and generally reduced competition, until by the early twentieth century many activities were so monopolized that they could raise their noncompetitive prices above costs to obtain sufficient profits to become self-financing and were thus able to eliminate the control of bankers. But before that stage was reached a relatively small number of bankers were in positions of immense influence in European and American economic life. As early as 1909, Walter Rathenau, who was in a position to know (since he had inherited from his father control of the German General Electric Company and held scores of directorships himself), said, "Three hundred men, all of whom know one another, direct the economic destiny of Europe and choose their successors from among themselves."

The power of investment bankers over governments rests on a number of factors, of which the most significant, perhaps, is the need of governments to issue short-term treasury bills as well as long-term government bonds. Just as businessmen go to commercial banks for current capital advances to smooth over the discrepancies between their irregular and intermittent incomes and their periodic and persistent outgoes (such as monthly rents, annual mortgage payments, and weekly wages), so a government has to go to merchant bankers (or institutions controlled by them) to tide over the shallow places caused by irregular tax receipts. As experts in government bonds, the international bankers not only handled the necessary advances but provided advice to government officials and, on many occasions, placed their own members in official posts for varied periods to deal with special problems. This is so widely accepted even today that in 1961 a Republican investment banker became Secretary of the Treasury in a Democratic Administration in Washington without significant comment from any direction.

Naturally, the influence of bankers over governments during the age of financial capitalism (roughly 1850–1931) was not something about which anyone talked freely, but it has been admitted frequently enough by those on the inside, especially in England. In 1852 Gladstone, chancellor of the Exchequer, declared, "The hinge of the whole situation was this: the government itself was not to be a substantive power in matters of Finance, but was to leave the Money Power supreme and unquestioned." On September 26, 1921, *The Financial Times* wrote, "Half a dozen men at the top of the Big Five Banks could upset the whole fabric of government finance by refraining from renewing Treasury Bills." In 1924 Sir Drummond Fraser, vice-president of the Institute of Bankers, stated, "The Governor of the Bank of England must be the autocrat who dictates the terms upon which alone the Government can obtain borrowed money."

In addition to their power over government based on government financing and personal influence, bankers could steer governments in ways they wished them to go by other pressures. Since most government officials felt ignorant of finance, they sought advice from bankers whom they considered to be experts in the field. The history of the last century shows, as we shall see later, that the advice given to governments by bankers, like the advice they gave to industrialists, was consistently good for bankers, but was often disastrous for governments, businessmen, and the people generally. Such advice could be enforced if necessary by manipulation of exchanges, gold flows, discount rates, and even levels of business activity. Thus Morgan dominated Cleveland's second administration by gold withdrawals, and in 1936–1938 French foreign exchange manipulators paralyzed the Popular Front governments. As we shall see, the powers of these international bankers reached their peak in the last decade of their supremacy, 1919–1931, when Montagu Norman and J. P. Morgan dominated not only the financial world but international relations and other matters as well. On November 11, 1927, the *Wall Street Journal* called Mr. Norman "the currency dictator of Europe." This was admitted by Mr. Norman himself before the Court of the Bank on March 21, 1930, and before the Macmillan Committee of the House of Commons five days later. On one occasion, just before international financial capitalism ran, at full speed, on the rocks which sank it, Mr. Norman is reported to have said, "I hold the hegemony of the world." At the time, some Englishmen spoke of "the second Norman Conquest of England" in reference to the fact that Norman's brother was head of the British Broadcasting Corporation. It might be added that Governor Norman rarely acted in major world problems without consulting with J. P. Morgan's representatives, and as a consequence he was one of the most widely traveled men of his day.

This conflict of interests between bankers and industrialists has resulted in most European countries in the subordination of the former either to the latter or to the government (after 1931). This subordination was accomplished by the adoption of "unorthodox financial policies"— that is, financial policies not in accordance with the short-run interests of bankers. This shift by which bankers were made subordinate reflected a fundamental development in modern economic history—a development which can be described as the growth from financial capitalism to monopoly capitalism. This took place in Germany earlier than in any other country and was well under way by 1926. It came in Britain only after 1931 and in Italy only in 1934. It did not occur in France to a comparable extent at all, and this explains the economic weakness of France in 1938–1940 to a considerable degree.

International Financial Practices

The financial principals which apply to the relationships between different countries are an expansion of those which apply within a single country. When goods are exchanged between countries, they must be paid for by commodities or gold. They cannot be paid for by the notes, certificates, and checks of the purchaser's country, since these are of value only in the country of issue. To avoid shipment of gold with every purchase, bills of exchange are used. These are claims against a person in another country which are sold to a person in the same country. The latter will buy such a claim if he wants to satisfy a claim against himself held by a person in the other country. He can satisfy such a claim by sending to his creditor in the other country the claim which he has bought against another person in that other country, and let his creditor use that claim to satisfy his own claim. Thus, instead of importers in one country sending money to exporters in another country, importers in one country pay their debts to exporters in their own country, and their creditors in the other country receive payment for the goods they have exported from importers in their own country. Thus, payment for goods in an international trade is made by merging single transactions involving two persons into double transactions involving four persons. In many cases, payment is made by involving a multitude of transactions, frequently in several different countries. These transactions were carried on in the so-called foreign-exchange market. An exporter of goods sold bills of exchange into that market and thus drew out of it money in his own country's units. An importer bought such bills of exchange to send to his creditor, and thus he put his own country's monetary units into the market. Since the bills available in any market were drawn in the monetary units of many different foreign countries, there arose exchange relationships between the amounts of money available in the country's own units (put there by importers) and the variety of bills drawn in foreign moneys and put into the market by exporters. The supply and demand for bills (or money) of any country in terms of the supply and demand of the country's own money available in the foreign-exchange market determined the value of the other countries' moneys in relation to domestic money. These values could fluctuate—widely for countries not on the gold standard, but only narrowly (as we shall see) for those on gold.

Under normal conditions a foreign-exchange market served to pay for goods and services of foreigners without any international shipment of money (gold). It also acted as a regulator of international trade. If the imports of any country steadily exceeded exports to another country, more importers would be in the market offering domestic money for bills of exchange drawn in the money of their foreign creditor.

There thus would be an increased supply of domestic money and an increased demand for that foreign money. As a result, importers would have to offer more of their money for these foreign bills, and the value of domestic money would fall, while the value of the foreign money would rise in the foreign-exchange market. This rise (or fall) on a gold relationship would be measured in terms of "par" (the exact gold content equivalent of the two currencies).

As the value of the domestic currency sagged below par in relationship to that of some foreign currency, domestic exporters to that foreign country will increase their activities, because when they receive payment in the form of a bill of exchange they can sell it for more of their own currency than they usually expect and can thus increase their profits. A surplus of imports, by lowering the foreign-exchange value of the importing country's money, will lead eventually to an increase in exports which, by providing more bills of exchange, will tend to restore the relationship of the moneys back toward par. Such a restoration of parity in foreign exchange will reflect a restoration of balance in international obligations, and this in turn will reflect a restored balance in the exchange of goods and services between the two countries. This means, under normal conditions, that a trade disequilibrium will create trade conditions which will tend to restore trade equilibrium.

When countries are not on the gold standard, this foreign-exchange disequilibrium (that is, the decline in the value of one monetary unit in relation to the other unit) can go on to very wide fluctuations—in fact, to whatever degree is necessary to restore the trade equilibrium by encouraging importers to buy in the other country because its money is so low in value that the prices of goods in that country are irresistible to importers in the other country.

But when countries are on the gold standard, the result is quite different. In this case the value of a country's money will never go below the amount equal to the cost of shipping gold between the two countries. An importer who wishes to pay his trade partner in the other country will not offer more and more of his own country's money for foreign-exchange bills, but will bid up the price of such bills only to the point where it becomes cheaper for him to buy gold from a bank and pay the costs of shipping and insurance on the gold as it goes to his foreign creditor. Thus, on the gold standard, foreign-exchange quotations do not fluctuate widely, but move only between the two gold points which are only slightly above (gold export point) and slightly below (gold import point) parity (the legal gold relationship of the two currencies).

Since the cost of packing, shipping and insuring gold used to be about ½ percent of its value, the gold export and import points were about this amount above and below the parity point. In the case of the dollar-pound relationship, when parity was at £1 = $4.866, the gold export point was about $4.885 and the gold import point was about $4.845. Thus:

Gold export point $4.885
  (excess demand for bills by importers)
Parity $4.866
Gold import point $4.845
  (excess supply of bills by exporters)

The situation which we have described is overly simplified. In practice the situation is made more complicated by several factors. Among these are the following: (1) middlemen buy and sell foreign exchange for present or future delivery as a speculative activity; (2) the total supply of foreign exchange available in the market depends on much more than the international exchange of commodities. It depends on the sum total of all international payments, such as interest, payment for services, tourist spending, borrowings, sales of securities, immigrant remittances, and so on; (3) the total exchange balance depends on the total of the relationships of all countries, not merely between two.

The flow of gold from country to country resulting from unbalanced trade tends to create a situation which counteracts the flow. If a country exports more than it imports so that gold flows in to cover the difference, this gold will become the basis for an increased quantity of money, and this will cause a rise of prices within the country sufficient to reduce exports and increase imports. At the same time, the gold by flowing out of some other country will reduce the quantity of money there and will cause a fall in prices within that country. These shifts in prices will cause shifts in the flow of goods because of the obvious fact that goods tend to flow to higher-priced areas and cease to flow to lower-priced areas. These shifts in the flow of goods will counteract the original unbalance in trade which caused the flow of gold. As a result, the flow of gold will cease, and a balanced international trade at slightly different price levels will result. The whole process illustrates the subordination of internal price stability to stability of exchanges. It was this subordination which was rejected by most countries after 1931. This rejection was signified by (a) abandonment of the gold standard at least in part, (b) efforts at control of domestic prices, and (c) efforts at exchange control. All these were done because of a desire to free the economic system from the restricting influence of a gold-dominated financial system.

This wonderful, automatic mechanism of international payments represents one of the greatest social instruments ever devised by man. It requires, however, a very special group of conditions for its effective functioning and, as we shall show, these conditions were disappearing by 1900 and were largely wiped away as a result of the economic changes brought about by the First World War. Because of these changes it became impossible to restore the financial system which had existed before 1914. Efforts to restore it were made with great determination, but by 1933 they had obviously failed, and all major countries had been forced to abandon the gold standard and automatic exchanges.

When the gold standard is abandoned, gold flows between countries like any other commodity, and the value of foreign exchanges (no longer tied to gold) can fluctuate much more widely. In theory an unbalance of international payments can be rectified either through a shift in exchange rates or through a shift in internal price levels. On the gold standard this rectification is made by shifts in exchange rates only between the gold points. When the unbalance is so great that exchanges would be forced beyond the gold points, the rectification is made by means of changing internal prices caused by the fact that gold flows at the gold points, instead of the exchanges passing beyond the gold points. On the other hand, when a currency is off the gold standard, fluctuation of exchanges is not confined between any two points but can go indefinitely in either direction. In such a case, the unbalance of international payments is worked out largely by a shift in exchange rates and only remotely by shifts in internal prices. In the period of 1929–1936, the countries of the world went off gold because they preferred to bring their international balances toward equilibrium by means of fluctuating exchanges rather than by means of fluctuating price levels. They feared these last because changing (especially falling) prices led to declines in business activity and shifts in the utilization of economic resources (such as labor, land, and capital) from one activity to another.

The reestablishment of the balance of international payments when a currency is off gold can be seen from an example. If the value of the pound sterling falls to $4.00 or $3.00, Americans will buy in England increasingly because English prices are cheap for them, but Englishmen will buy in America only with reluctance because they have to pay so much for American money. This will serve to rectify the original excess of exports to England which gave the great supply of pound sterling necessary to drive its value down to $3.00. Such a depreciation in the exchange value of a currency will cause a rise in prices within the country as a result of the increase in demand for the goods of that country.

THE SITUATION BEFORE 1914

The key to the world situation in the period before 1914 is to be found in the dominant position of Great Britain. This position was more real than apparent. In many fields (such as naval or financial) the supremacy of Britain was so complete that it almost never had to be declared by her or admitted by others. It was tacitly assumed by both. As an unchallenged ruler in these fields, Britain could afford to be a benevolent ruler. Sure of herself and of her position, she could be satisfied with substance rather than forms. If others accepted her dominance in fact, she was quite willing to leave to them independence and autonomy in law.

This supremacy of Britain was not an achievement of the nineteenth century alone. Its origins go back to the sixteenth century—to the period in which the discovery of America made the Atlantic more important than the Mediterranean as a route of commerce and a road to wealth. In the Atlantic, Britain's position was unique, not merely because of her westernmost position, but much more because she was an island. This last fact made it possible for her to watch Europe embroil itself in internal squabbles while she retained freedom to exploit the new worlds across the seas. On this basis, Britain had built up a naval supremacy which made her ruler of the seas by 1900. Along with this was her preeminence in merchant shipping which gave her control of the avenues of world transportation and ownership of 39 percent of the world's oceangoing vessels (three times the number of her nearest rival).

To her supremacy in these spheres, won in the period before 1815, Britain added new spheres of dominance in the period after 1815. These arose from her early achievement of the Industrial Revolution. This was applied to transportation and communications as well as to industrial production. In the first it gave the world the railroad and the steamboat; in the second it gave the telegraph, the cable, and the telephone; in the third it gave the factory system.

The Industrial Revolution existed in Britain for almost two generations before it spread elsewhere. It gave a great increase in output of manufactured goods and a great demand for raw materials and food; it also gave a great increase in wealth and savings. As a result of the first two and the improved methods of transportation, Britain developed a world trade of which it was the center and which consisted chiefly of the export of manufactured goods and the import of raw materials and food. At the same time, the savings of Britain tended to flow out to North America, South America, and Asia, seeking to increase the output of raw materials and food in these areas. By 1914 these exports of capital had reached such an amount that they were greater than the foreign investments of all other countries put together. In 1914 British overseas investment was about $20 billion (or about one-quarter of Britain's national wealth, yielding about a tenth of the total national income). The French overseas investment at the same time was about

$9 billion (or one-sixth the French national wealth, yielding 6 percent of the national income), while Germany had about $5 billion invested overseas (one-fifteenth the national wealth, yielding 3 percent of the national income). The United States at that time was a large-scale debtor.

The dominant position of Britain in the world of 1913 was, as I have said, more real than apparent. In all parts of the world people slept more securely, worked more productively, and lived more fully because Britain existed. British naval vessels in the Indian Ocean and the Far East suppressed slave raiders, pirates, and headhunters. Small nations like Portugal, the Netherlands, or Belgium retained their overseas possessions under the protection of the British fleet. Even the United States, without realizing it, remained secure and upheld the Monroe Doctrine behind the shield of the British Navy. Small nations were able to preserve their independence in the gaps between the Great Powers, kept in precarious balance by the Foreign Office's rather diffident balance-of-power tactics. Most of the world's great commercial markets, even in commodities like cotton, rubber, and tin, which she did not produce in quantities herself, were in England, the world price being set from the auction bidding of skilled specialist traders there. If a man in Peru wished to send money to a man in Afghanistan, the final payment, as like as not, would be made by a bookkeeping transaction in London. The English parliamentary system and some aspects of the English judicial system, such as the rule of law, were being copied, as best as could be, in all parts of the world.

The profitability of capital outside Britain—a fact which caused the great export of capital—was matched by a profitability of labor. As a result, the flow of capital from Britain and Europe was matched by a flow of persons. Both of these served to build up non-European areas on a modified European pattern. In export of men, as in export of capital, Britain was easily first (over 20 million persons emigrating from the United Kingdom in the period 1815–1938). As a result of both, Britain became the center of world finance as well as the center of world commerce. The system of international financial relations, which we described earlier, was based on the system of industrial, commercial, and credit relationships which we have just described. The former thus required for its existence a very special group of circumstances—a group which could not be expected to continue forever. In addition, it required a group of secondary characteristics which were also far from permanent. Among these were the following: (1) all the countries concerned must be on the full gold standard; (2) there must be freedom from public or private interference with the domestic economy of any country; that is, prices must be free to rise and fall in accordance with the supply and demand for both goods and money; (3) there must also be free flow of international trade so that both goods and money can go without hindrance to those areas where each is most valuable; (4) the international financial economy must be organized about one center with numerous subordinate centers, so that it would be possible to cancel out international claims against one another in some clearinghouse and thus reduce the flow of gold to a minimum; (5) the flow of goods and funds in international matters should be controlled by economic factors and not be subject to political, psychological, or ideological influences.

These conditions, which made the international financial and commercial system function so beautifully before 1914, had begun to change by 1890. The fundamental economic and commercial conditions changed first, and were noticeably modified by 1910; the group of secondary characteristics of the system were changed by the events of the First World War. As a result, the system of early international financial capitalism is now only a dim memory. Imagine a period without passports or visas, and with almost no immigration or customs restrictions. Certainly the system had many incidental drawbacks, but they *were* incidental. Socialized if not social, civilized if not cultured, the system allowed individuals to breathe freely and develop their individual talents in a way unknown before and in jeopardy since.

The United States to 1917

Just as Classical culture spread westward from the Greeks who created it to the Roman peoples who adopted and changed it, so Europe's culture spread westward to the New World, where it was profoundly modified while still remaining basically European. The central fact of American history is that people of European origin and culture came to occupy and use the immensely rich wilderness between the Atlantic and the Pacific. In this process the wilderness was developed and exploited area by area, the Tidewater, the Piedmont, the trans-Appalachian forest, the trans-Mississippi prairies, the Pacific Coast, and finally the Great Plains. By 1900 the period of occupation which had begun in 1607 was finished, but the era of development continued on an intensive rather than extensive basis. This shift from extensive to intensive development, frequently called the "closing of the frontier," required a readjustment of social outlook and behavior from a largely individualistic to a more cooperative basis and from an emphasis on mere physical prowess to emphasis on other less tangible talents of managerial skills, scientific training, and intellectual capacity able to fill the newly occupied frontiers with a denser population, producing a higher standard of living, and utilizing more extensive leisure.

The ability of the people of the United States to make this readjustment of social outlook and behavior at the "ending of the frontier" about 1900 was hampered by a number of factors from its earlier historical experience. Among these we should mention the growth of sectionalism, past political and constitutional experiences, isolationism, and emphasis on physical prowess and unrealistic idealism.

The occupation of the United States had given rise to three chief geographic sections: a commercial and later financial and industrial East, an agrarian and later industrial West, and an agrarian South. Unfortunately, the two agrarian sections were organized quite differently, the South on the basis of slave labor and the West on the basis of free labor. On this question the East allied with the West to defeat the South in the Civil War (1861–1865) and to subject it to a prolonged military occupation as a conquered territory (1865–1877). Since the war and the occupation were controlled by the new Republican Party, the political organization of the country became split on a sectional basis: the South refused to vote Republican until 1928, and the West refused to vote Democratic until 1932. In the East the older families which inclined toward the Republican Party because of the Civil War were largely submerged by waves of new immigrants from Europe, beginning with Irish and Germans after 1846 and continuing with even greater numbers from eastern Europe and Mediterranean Europe after 1890. These new immigrants of the eastern cities voted Democratic because of religious, economic, and cultural opposition to the upper-class Republicans of the same eastern section. The class basis in voting patterns in the East and the sectional basis in voting in the South and West proved to be of major political significance after 1880.

The Founding Fathers had assumed that the political control of the country would be conducted by men of property and leisure who would generally know each other personally and, facing no need for urgent decisions, would move government to action when they agreed and be able to prevent it from acting, without serious damage, when they could not agree. The American Constitution, with its provisions for division of powers and selection of the chief executive by an electoral college, reflected this point of view. So also did the use of the party caucus of legislative assemblies for nomination to public office and the election of senators by the same assemblies. The arrival of a mass democracy after 1830 changed this situation, establishing the use of party conventions for nominations and the use of entrenched political party machines, supported on the patronage of public office, to mobilize sufficient votes to elect their candidates.

As a result of this situation, the elected official from 1840 to 1880 found himself under pressure from three directions: from the popular electorate which provided him with the votes necessary for election, from the party machine which provided him with the nomination to run for office as well as the patronage appointments by which he could reward his followers, and from the wealthy economic interests which gave him the money for campaign expenses with, perhaps, a certain surplus for his own pocket. This was a fairly workable system, since the three forces were approximately equal, the advantage, if any, resting with the party machine. This advantage became so great in the period 1865–1880 that the forces of finance, commerce, and industry were forced to contribute ever-increasing largesse to the political machines in order to obtain the services from government which they regarded as their due, services such as higher tariffs, land grants to railroads, better postal services, and mining or timber concessions. The fact that these forces of finance and business were themselves growing in wealth and power made them increasingly restive under the need to make constantly larger contributions to party political machines. Moreover, these economic tycoons increasingly felt it to be unseemly that they should be unable to issue orders but instead have to negotiate as equals in order to obtain services or favors from party bosses.

By the late 1870's business leaders determined to make an end to this situation by cutting with one blow the taproot of the system of party machines, namely, the patronage system. This system, which they called by the derogatory term "spoils system," was objectionable to big business not so much because it led to dishonesty or inefficiency but because it made the party machines independent of business control by giving them a source of income (campaign contributions from government employees) which was independent of business control. If this source could be cut off or even sensibly reduced, politicians would be much more dependent upon business contributions for campaign expenses. At a time when the growth of a mass press and of the use of chartered trains for political candidates were greatly increasing the expense of campaigning for office, any reduction in campaign contributions from officeholders would inevitably make politicians more subservient to business. It was with this aim in view that civil service reform began in the Federal government with the Pendleton Bill of 1883. As a result, the government was controlled with varying degrees of completeness by the forces of investment banking and heavy industry from 1884 to 1933.

This period, 1884–1933, was the period of financial capitalism in which investment bankers moving into commercial banking and insurance on one side and into railroading and heavy industry on the other were able to mobilize enormous wealth and wield enormous economic, political, and social power. Popularly known as "Society," or the "400," they lived a life of dazzling splendor. Sailing the ocean in great private yachts or traveling on land by private trains, they moved in a ceremonious round between their spectacular estates and town houses in Palm Beach, Long Island, the Berkshires, Newport, and Bar Harbor; assembling from their fortress-like New York residences to attend the Metropolitan Opera under the critical eye of Mrs. Astor; or gathering for business meetings of the highest strategic level in the awesome presence of J. P. Morgan himself.

The structure of financial controls created by the tycoons of "Big Banking" and "Big Business" in the period 1880–1933 was of extraordinary complexity, one business fief being built on another, both being allied with semi-independent associates, the whole rearing upward into two pinnacles of economic and financial power, of which one, centered in New York, was headed by J. P. Morgan and Company, and the other, in Ohio, was headed by the Rockefeller family. When these two co-operated, as they generally did, they could influence the economic life of the country to a large degree and could almost control its political life, at least on the Federal level. The former point can be illustrated by a few facts. In the United States the number of billion-dollar corporations rose from one in 1909 (United States Steel, controlled by Morgan) to fifteen in 1930. The share of all corporation assets held by the 200 largest corporations rose from 32 percent in 1909 to 49 percent in 1930 and reached 57 percent in 1939. By 1930 these 200 largest corporations held 49.2 percent of the assets of all 40,000 corporations in the country ($81 billion out of $165 billion); they held 38 percent of all business wealth, incorporated or unincorporated (or $81 billion out of $212 billion); and they held 22 percent of all the wealth in the country (or $81 billion out of $367 billion). In fact, in 1930, one corporation (American Telephone and Telegraph, controlled by Morgan) had greater assets than the total wealth in twenty-one states of the Union.

The influence of these business leaders was so great that the Morgan and Rockefeller groups acting together, or even Morgan acting alone, could have wrecked the economic system of the country merely by throwing securities on the stock market for sale, and, having precipitated a stock-market panic, could then have bought back the securities they had sold but at a lower price. Naturally, they were not so foolish as to do this, although Morgan came very close to it in precipitating the "panic of 1907," but they did not hesitate to wreck individual corporations, at the expense of the holders of common stocks, by driving them to bankruptcy. In this way, to take only two examples, Morgan wrecked the New York, New Haven, and Hartford Railroad before 1914 by selling to it, at high prices, the largely valueless securities of myriad New England steamship and trolley lines; and William Rockefeller and his friends wrecked the Chicago, Milwaukee, St. Paul, and Pacific Railroad before

1925 by selling to it, at excessive prices, plans to electrify to the Pacific, copper, electricity, and a worthless branch railroad (the Gary Line). These are but examples of the discovery by financial capitalists that they made money out of issuing and selling securities rather than out of the production, distribution, and consumption of goods and accordingly led them to the point where they discovered that the exploiting of an operating company by excessive issuance of securities or the issuance of bonds rather than equity securities not only was profitable to them but made it possible for them to increase their profits by bankruptcy of the firm, providing fees and commissions of reorganization as well as the opportunity to issue new securities.

When the business interests, led by William C. Whitney, pushed through the first installment of civil service reform in 1883, they expected that they would be able to control both political parties equally. Indeed, some of them intended to contribute to both and to allow an alternation of the two parties in public office in order to conceal their own influence, inhibit any exhibition of independence by politicians, and allow the electorate to believe that they were exercising their own free choice. Such an alternation of the parties on the Federal scene occurred in the period 1880–1896, with business influence (or at least Morgan's influence) as great in Democratic as in Republican administrations. But in 1896 came a shocking experience. The business interests discovered that they could control the Republican Party to a large degree but could not be nearly so confident of controlling the Democratic Party. The reason for this difference lay in the existence of the Solid South as a Democratic section with almost no Republican voters. This section sent delegates to the Republican National Convention as did the rest of the country, but, since these delegates did not represent voters, they came to represent those who were prepared to pay their expenses to the Republican National Convention. In this way these delegates came to represent the business interests of the North, whose money they accepted. Mark Hanna has told us in detail how he spent much of the winter of 1895–1896 in Georgia buying over two hundred delegates for McKinley to the Republican National Convention of 1896. As a result of this system, about a quarter of the votes in a Republican Convention were "controlled" votes from the Solid South, not representing the electorate. After the split in the Republican Party in 1912, this portion of the delegates was reduced to about 17 percent.

The inability of the investment bankers and their industrial allies to control the Democratic Convention of 1896 was a result of the agrarian discontent of the period 1868–1896. This discontent in turn was based, very largely, on the monetary tactics of the banking oligarchy. The bankers were wedded to the gold standard for reasons we have already explained. Accordingly, at the end of the Civil War, they persuaded the

Grant Administration to curb the postwar inflation and go back on the gold standard (crash of 1873 and resumption of specie payments in 1875). This gave the bankers a control of the supply of money which they did not hesitate to use for their own purposes, as Morgan ruthlessly pressurized Cleveland in 1893–1896. The bankers' affection for low prices was not shared by the farmers, since each time prices of farm products went down the burden of farmers' debts (especially mortgages) became greater. Moreover, farm prices, being much more competitive than industrial prices, and not protected by a tariff, fell much faster than industrial prices, and farmers could not reduce costs or modify their production plans nearly so rapidly as industrialists could. The result was a systematic exploitation of the agrarian sectors of the community by the financial and industrial sectors. This exploitation took the form of high industrial prices, high (and discriminatory) railroad rates, high interest charges, low farm prices, and a very low level of farm services by railroads and the government. Unable to resist by economic weapons, the farmers of the West turned to political relief, but were greatly hampered by their reluctance to vote Democratic (because of their memories of the Civil War). Instead, they tried to work on the state political level through local legislation (so-called Granger Laws) and set up third-party movements (like the Greenback Party in 1878 or the Populist Party in 1892). By 1896, however, agrarian discontent rose so high that it began to overcome the memory of the Democratic role in the Civil War. The capture of the Democratic Party by these forces of discontent under William Jennings Bryan in 1896, who was determined to obtain higher prices by increasing the supply of money on a bimetallic rather than a gold basis, presented the electorate with an election on a social and economic issue for the first time in a generation. Though the forces of high finance and of big business were in a state of near panic, by a mighty effort involving large-scale spending they were successful in electing McKinley.

The inability of plutocracy to control the Democratic Party as it had demonstrated it could control the Republican Party, made it advisable for them to adopt a one-party outlook on political affairs, although they continued to contribute to some extent to both parties and did not cease their efforts to control both. In fact on two occasions, in 1904 and in 1924, J. P. Morgan was able to sit back with a feeling of satisfaction to watch a presidential election in which the candidates of both parties were in his sphere of influence. In 1924 the Democratic candidate was one of his chief lawyers, while the Republican candidate was the classmate and handpicked choice of his partner, Dwight Morrow. Usually, Morgan had to share this political influence with other sectors of the business oligarchy, especially with the Rockefeller interest (as was done, for example, by dividing the ticket between them in 1900 and in 1920).

The agrarian discontent, the growth of monopolies, the oppression of labor, and the excesses of Wall Street financiers made the country very restless in the period 1890–1900. All this could have been alleviated merely by increasing the supply of money sufficiently to raise prices somewhat, but the financiers in this period, just as thirty years later, were determined to defend the gold standard no matter what happened. In looking about for some issue which would distract public discontent from domestic economic issues, what better solution than a crisis in foreign affairs? Cleveland had stumbled upon this alternative, more or less accidentally, in 1895 when he stirred up a controversy with Great Britain over Venezuela. The great opportunity, however, came with the Cuban revolt against Spain in 1895. While the "yellow press," led by William Randolph Hearst, roused public opinion, Henry Cabot Lodge and Theodore Roosevelt plotted how they could best get the United States into the fracas. They got the excuse they needed when the American battleship *Maine* was sunk by a mysterious explosion in Havana harbor in February 1898. In two months the United States declared war on Spain to fight for Cuban independence. The resulting victory revealed the United States as a world naval power, established it is an imperialist power with possession of Puerto Rico, Guam, and the Philippines, whetted some appetites for imperialist glory, and covered the transition from the long-drawn age of semidepression to a new period of prosperity. This new period of prosperity was spurred to some extent by the increased demand for industrial products arising from the war, but even more by the new period of rising prices associated with a considerable increase in the world production of gold from South Africa and Alaska after 1895.

America's entrance upon the stage as a world power continued with the annexation of Hawaii in 1898, the intervention in the Boxer uprising in 1900, the seizure of Panama in 1903, the diplomatic intervention in the Russo-Japanese War in 1905, the round-the-world cruise of the American Navy in 1908, the military occupation of Nicaragua in 1912, the opening of the Panama Canal in 1914, and military intervention in Mexico in 1916.

During this same period, there appeared a new movement for economic and political reform known as Progressivism. The Progressive movement resulted from a combination of forces, some new and some old. Its foundation rested on the remains of agrarian and labor discontent which had struggled so vainly before 1897. There was also, as a kind of afterthought on the part of successful business leaders, a weakening of acquisitive selfishness and a revival of the older sense of social obligation and idealism. To some extent this feeling was mixed with a realization that the position and privileges of the very wealthy could be preserved better with superficial concessions and increased opportunity for the discontented to blow off steam than from any policy of blind obstructionism on the part of the rich. As an example of the more idealistic impulse we might mention the creation of the various Carnegie foundations to work for universal peace or to extend scholarly work in science and social studies. As an example of the more practical point of view we might mention the founding of *The New Republic*, a "liberal weekly paper," by an agent of Morgan financed with Whitney money (1914). Somewhat similar to this last point was the growth of a new "liberal press," which found it profitable to print the writings of "muckrakers," and thus expose to the public eye the seamy side of Big Business and of human nature itself. But the great opportunity for the Progressive forces arose from a split within Big Business between the older forces of financial capitalism led by Morgan and the newer forces of monopoly capitalism organized around the Rockefeller bloc. As a consequence, the Republican Party was split between the followers of Theodore Roosevelt and those of William Howard Taft, so that the combined forces of the liberal East and the agrarian West were able to capture the Presidency under Woodrow Wilson in 1912.

Wilson roused a good deal of popular enthusiasm with his talk of "New Freedom" and the rights of the underdog, but his program amounted to little more than an attempt to establish on a Federal basis those reforms which agrarian and labor discontent had been seeking on a state basis for many years. Wilson was by no means a radical (after all, he had been accepting money for his personal income from rich industrialists like Cleveland Dodge and Cyrus Hall McCormick during his professorship at Princeton, and this kind of thing by no means ceased when he entered politics in 1910), and there was a good deal of unconscious hypocrisy in many of his resounding public speeches. Be this as it may, his political and administrative reforms were a good deal more effective than his economic or social reforms. The Clayton Antitrust Act and the Federal Trade Commission Act (1913) were soon tightly wrapped in litigation and futility. On the other hand, the direct election of senators, the establishment of an income tax and of the Federal Reserve System, and the creation of a Federal Farm Loan System (1916) and of rural delivery of mail and parcel post, as well as the first steps toward various laboring enactments, like minimum wages for merchant seamen, restrictions on child labor, and an eight-hour day for railroad workers, justified the support which Progressives had given to Wilson.

The first Administration of Wilson (1913–1917) and the earlier Administration of Theodore Roosevelt (1901–1909) made a substantial contribution to the process by which the United States redirected its aim from extensive expansion of physical frontiers to an intensive exploitation of its natural and moral resources. The earlier Roosevelt used his genius as a showman to publicize the need to conserve the country's natural resources, while Wilson, in his own professorial fashion, did much to extend equality of opportunity to wider groups of the American people. These people were so absorbed in the controversies engendered by these efforts that they hardly noticed the rising international tensions in Europe or even the outbreak of war in August, 1914, until by 1915 the clamorous controversy of the threat of war quite eclipsed the older domestic controversies. By the end of 1915 America was being summoned, in no gentle fashion, to play a role on the world's stage. This is a story to which we must return in a later chapter.

III

THE RUSSIAN EMPIRE
TO 1917

In the nineteenth century most historians regarded Russia as part of Europe but it is now becoming increasingly clear that Russia is another civilization quite separate from Western Civilization. Both of these civilizations are descended from Classical Civilization, but the connection with this predecessor was made so differently that two quite different traditions came into existence. Russian traditions were derived from Byzantium directly; Western traditions were derived from the more moderate Classical Civilization indirectly, having passed through the Dark Ages when there was no state or government in the West.

Russian civilization was created from three sources originally: (1) the Slav people, (2) Viking invaders from the north, and (3) the Byzantine tradition from the south. These three were fused together as the result of a common experience arising from Russia's exposed geographical position on the western edge of a great flatland stretching for thousands of miles to the east. This flatland is divided horizontally into three zones of which the most southern is open plain, while the most northern is open bush and tundra. The middle zone is forest. The southern zone (or steppes) consists of two parts: the southern is a salty plain which is practically useless, while the northern part, next to the forest, is the famous black-earth region of rich agricultural soil. Unfortunately the eastern portion of this great Eurasian plain has been getting steadily drier for thousands of years, with the consequence that the Ural-Altaic-speaking peoples of central and east-central Asia, peoples like the Huns, Bulgars, Magyars, Mongols, and Turks, have pushed westward repeatedly along the steppe corridor between the Urals and the Caspian Sea, making the black-earth steppes dangerous for sedentary agricultural peoples.

The Slavs first appeared more than two thousand years ago as a peaceful, evasive people, with an economy based on hunting and rudimentary agriculture, in the forests of eastern Poland. These people slowly increased in numbers, moving northeastward through the forests, mixing with the scattered Finnish hunting people who were there already. About A.D. 700 or so, the Northmen, whom we know as Vikings, came down from the Baltic Sea, by way of the rivers of eastern Europe, and even-

tually reached the Black Sea and attacked Constantinople. These Northmen were trying to make a way of life out of militarism, seizing booty
and slaves, imposing tribute on conquered peoples, collecting furs, honey,
and wax from the timid Slavs lurking in their forests, and exchanging
these for the colorful products of the Byzantine south. In time the
Northmen set up fortified trading posts along their river highways,
notably at Novgorod in the north, at Smolensk in the center, and at
Kiev in the south. They married Slav women and imposed on the rudimentary agricultural-hunting economy of the Slavs a superstructure of a
tribute-collecting state with an exploitative, militaristic, commercial economy. This created the pattern of a two-class Russian society which has
continued ever since, much intensified by subsequent historical events.

In time the ruling class of Russia became acquainted with Byzantine
culture. They were dazzled by it, and sought to import it into their
wilderness domains in the north. In this way they imposed on the Slav
peoples many of the accessories of the Byzantine Empire, such as Orthodox Christianity, the Byzantine alphabet, the Byzantine calendar, the
used of domed ecclesiastical architecture, the name Czar (Caesar) for
their ruler, and innumerable other traits. Most important of all, they
imported the Byzantine totalitarian autocracy, under which all aspects
of life, including political, economic, intellectual, and religious, were regarded as departments of government, under the control of an autocratic
ruler. These beliefs were part of the Greek tradition, and were based
ultimately on Greek inability to distinguish between state and society.
Since society includes all human activities, the Greeks had assumed that
the state must include all human activities. In the days of Classical Greece
this all-inclusive entity was called the *polis*, a term which meant both
society and state; in the later Roman period this all-inclusive entity was
called the *imperium*. The only difference was that the *polis* was sometimes
(as in Pericles's Athens about 450 B.C.) democratic, while the *imperium*
was always a military autocracy. Both were totalitarian, so that religion
and economic life were regarded as spheres of governmental activity. This
totalitarian autocratic tradition was carried on to the Byzantine Empire
and passed from it to the Russian state in the north and to the later
Ottoman Empire in the south. In the north this Byzantine tradition combined with the experience of the Northmen to intensify the two-class
structure of Slav society. In the new Slav (or Orthodox) Civilization this
fusion, fitting together the Byzantine tradition and the Viking tradition,
created Russia. From Byzantium came autocracy and the idea of the state
as an absolute power and as a totalitarian power, as well as such important applications of these principles as the idea that the state should control
thought and religion, that the Church should be a branch of the government, that law is an enactment of the state, and that the ruler is semi-
divine. From the Vikings came the idea that the state is a foreign

importation, based on militarism and supported by booty and tribute, that economic innovations are the function of the government, that power rather than law is the basis of social life, and that society, with its people and its property, is the private property of a foreign ruler.

These concepts of the Russian system must be emphasized because they are so foreign to our own traditions. In the West, the Roman Empire (which continued in the East as the Byzantine Empire) disappeared in 476; and, although many efforts were made to revive it, there was clearly a period, about 900, when there was no empire, no state, and no public authority in the West. The state disappeared, yet society continued. So also, religious and economic life continued. This clearly showed that the state and society were not the same thing, that society was the basic entity, and that the state was a crowning, but not essential, cap to the social structure. This experience had revolutionary effects. It was discovered that man can live without a state; this became the basis of Western liberalism. It was discovered that the state, if it exists, must serve men and that it is incorrect to believe that the purpose of men is to serve the state. It was discovered that economic life, religious life, law, and private property can all exist and function effectively without a state. From this emerged laissez-faire, separation of Church and State, rule of law, and the sanctity of private property. In Rome, in Byzantium, and in Russia, law was regarded as an enactment of a supreme power. In the West, when no supreme power existed, it was discovered that law still existed as the body of rules which govern social life. Thus law was found by observation in the West, not enacted by autocracy as in the East. This meant that authority was established by law and under the law in the West, while authority was established by power and above the law in the East. The West felt that the rules of economic life were found and not enacted; that individuals had rights independent of, and even opposed to, public authority; that groups could exist, as the Church existed, by right and not by privilege, and without the need to have any charter of incorporation entitling them to exist as a group or act as a group; that groups or individuals could own property as a right and not as a privilege and that such property could not be taken by force but must be taken by established process of law. It was emphasized in the West that the way a thing was done was more important than what was done, while in the East what was done was far more significant than the way in which it was done.

There was also another basic distinction between Western Civilization and Russian Civilization. This was derived from the history of Christianity. This new faith came into Classical Civilization from Semitic society. In its origin it was a this-worldly religion, believing that the world and the flesh were basically good, or at least filled with good potentialities, because both were made by God; the body was made in the image of God; God became Man in this world with a human body, to save men as individuals, and to establish "Peace on earth." The early Christians intensified the "this-worldly" tradition, insisting that salvation was possible only because God lived and died in a human body in this world, that the individual could be saved only through God's help (grace) and by living correctly in this body on this earth (good works), that there would be, some day, a millennium on this earth and that, at that Last Judgment, there would be a resurrection of the body and life everlasting. In this way the world of space and time, which God had made at the beginning with the statement, "It was good" (Book of Genesis), would, at the end, be restored to its original condition.

This optimistic, "this-worldly" religion was taken into Classical Civilization at a time when the philosophic outlook of that society was quite incompatible with the religious outlook of Christianity. The Classical philosophic outlook, which we might call Neoplatonic, was derived from the teachings of Persian Zoroastrianism, Pythagorean rationalism, and Platonism. It was dualistic, dividing the universe into two *opposed* worlds, the world of matter and flesh and the world of spirit and ideas. The former world was changeable, unknowable, illusionary, and evil; the latter world was eternal, knowable, real, and good. Truth, to these people, could be found by the use of reason and logic alone, not by use of the body or the senses, since these were prone to error, and must be spurned. The body, as Plato said, was the "tomb of the soul."

Thus the Classical world into which Christianity came about A.D. 60 believed that the world and the body were unreal, unknowable, corrupt, and hopeless and that no truth or success could be found by the use of the body, the senses, or matter. A small minority, derived from Democritus and the early Ionian scientists through Aristotle, Epicurus, and Lucretius, rejected the Platonic dualism, preferring materialism as an explanation of reality. These materialists were equally incompatible with the new Christian religion. Moreover, even the ordinary citizen of Rome had an outlook whose implications were not compatible with the Christian religion. To give one simple example: while the Christians spoke of a millennium in the future, the average Roman continued to think of a "Golden Age" in the past, just as Homer had.

As a consequence of the fact that Christian religion came into a society with an incompatible philosophic outlook, the Christian religion was ravaged by theological and dogmatic disputes and shot through with "otherworldly" heresies. In general, these heresies felt that God was so perfect and so remote and man was so imperfect and such a worm that the gap between God and man could not be bridged by any act of man, that salvation depended on grace rather than on good works, and that, if God ever did so lower Himself as to occupy a human body, this was not an ordinary body, and that, accordingly, Christ could be either

True God or True Man but could not be both. This point of view was opposed by the Christian Fathers of the Church, not always successfully; but in the decisive battle, at the first Church Council, held at Nicaea in 325, the Christian point of view was enacted into the formal dogma of the Church. Although the Church continued to exist for centuries thereafter in a society whose philosophic outlook was ill adapted to the Christian religion, and obtained a compatible philosophy only in the medieval period, the basic outlook of Christianity reinforced the experience of the Dark Ages to create the outlook of Western Civilization. Some of the elements of this outlook which were of great importance were the following: (1) the importance of the individual, since he alone is saved; (2) the potential goodness of the material world and of the body; (3) the need to seek salvation by use of the body and the senses in this world (good works); (4) faith in the reliability of the senses (which contributed much to Western science); (5) faith in the reality of ideas (which contributed much to Western mathematics); (6) mundane optimism and millennianism (which contributed much to faith in the future and the idea of progress); (7) the belief that God (and not the devil) reigns over this world by a system of established rules (which contributed much to the ideas of natural law, natural science, and the rule of law).

These ideas which became part of the tradition of the West did not become part of the tradition of Russia. The influence of Greek philosophic thought remained strong in the East. The Latin West before 900 used a language which was not, at that time, fitted for abstract discussion, and almost all the dogmatic debates which arose from the incompatibility of Greek philosophy and Christian religion were carried on in the Greek language and fed on the Greek philosophic tradition. In the West the Latin language reflected a quite different tradition, based on the Roman emphasis on administrative procedures and ethical ideas about human behavior to one's fellow man. As a result, the Greek philosophic tradition remained strong in the East, continued to permeate the Greek-speaking Church, and went with that Church into the Slavic north. The schism between the Latin Church and the Greek Church strengthened their different points of view, the former being more this-worldly, more concerned with human behavior, and continuing to believe in the efficacy of good works, while the latter was more otherworldly, more concerned with God's majesty and power, and emphasized the evilness and weakness of the body and the world and the efficacy of God's grace. As a result, the religious outlook and, accordingly, the world outlook of Slav religion and philosophy developed in quite a different direction from that in the West. The body, this world, pain, personal comfort, and even death were of little importance; man could do little to change his lot, which was determined by forces more powerful than he; resignation to Fate, pessimism, and a belief in the overwhelming power of sin and of the devil dominated the East.

To this point we have seen the Slavs formed into Russian civilization as the result of several factors. Before we go on we should, perhaps, recapitulate. The Slavs were subjected at first to the Viking exploitative system. These Vikings copied Byzantine culture, and did it very consciously, in their religion, in their writing, in their state, in their laws, in art, architecture, philosophy, and literature. These rulers were outsiders who innovated all the political, religious, economic, and intellectual life of the new civilization. There was no state: foreigners brought one in. There was no organized religion: one was imported from Byzantium and imposed on the Slavs. The Slav economic life was on a low level, a forest subsistence economy with hunting and rudimentary agriculture: on this the Vikings imposed an international trading system. There was no religious-philosophic outlook: the new State-Church superstructure imposed on the Slavs an outlook derived from Greek dualistic idealism. And, finally, the East never experienced a Dark Ages to show it that society is distinct from the state and more fundamental than the state.

This summary brings Russian society down to about 1200. In the next six hundred years new experiences merely intensified the Russian development. These experiences arose from the fact that the new Russian society found itself caught between the population pressures of the raiders from the steppes to the east and the pressure of the advancing technology of Western Civilization.

The pressure of the Ural-Altaic speakers from the eastern steppes culminated in the Mongol (Tarter) invasions after 1200. The Mongols conquered Russia and established a tribute-gathering system which continued for generations. Thus there continued to be a foreign exploiting system imposed over the Slav people. In time the Mongols made the princes of Moscow their chief tribute collectors for most of Russia. A little later the Mongols made a court of highest appeal in Moscow, so that both money and judicial cases flowed to Moscow. These continued to flow even after the princes of Moscow (1380) led the successful revolt which ejected the Mongols.

As the population pressure from the East decreased, the technological pressure from the West increased (after 1500). By Western technology we mean such things as gunpowder and firearms, better agriculture, counting and public finance, sanitation, printing, and the spread of education. Russia did not get the full impact of these pressures until late, and then from secondary sources, such as Sweden and Poland, rather than from England or France. However, Russia was hammered out between the pressures from the East and those from the West. The result of this hammering was the Russian autocracy, a military, tribute-gathering machine superimposed on the Slav population. The poverty of this population made it impossible for them to get firearms or any other advantages of Western technology. Only the state had these things, but the state could afford them only by draining wealth from the people. This draining of wealth from below upward provided arms and Western technology for the rulers but kept the ruled too poor to obtain these things, so that all power was concentrated at the top. The continued pressure from the West made it impossible for the rulers to use the wealth that accumulated in their hands to finance economic improvements which might have raised the standards of living of the ruled, since this accumulation had to be used to increase Russian power rather than Russian wealth. As a consequence, pressure downward increased and the autocracy became more autocratic. In order to get a bureaucracy for the army and for government service, the landlords were given personal powers over the peasants, creating a system of serfdom in the East just at the time that medieval serfdom was disappearing in the West. Private property, personal freedom, and direct contact with the state (for taxation or for justice) were lost to the Russian serfs. The landlords were given these powers so that the landlords would be free to fight and willing to fight for Moscow or to serve in Moscow's autocracy.

By 1730 the direct pressure of the West upon Russia began to weaken somewhat because of the decline of Sweden, of Poland, and of Turkey, while Prussia was too occupied with Austria and with France to press very forcibly on Russia. Thus, the Slavs, using an adopted Western technology of a rudimentary character, were able to impose their supremacy on the peoples to the East. The peasants of Russia, seeking to escape from the pressures of serfdom in the area west of the Urals, began to flee eastward, and eventually reached the Pacific. The Russian state made every effort to stop this movement because it felt that the peasants must remain to work the land and pay taxes if the landlords were to be able to maintain the military autocracy which was considered necessary. Eventually the autocracy followed the peasants eastward, and Russian society came to occupy the whole of northern Asia.

As the pressure from the East and the pressure from the West declined, the autocracy, inspired perhaps by powerful religious feelings, began to have a bad conscience toward its own people. At the same time it still sought to westernize itself. It became increasingly clear that this process of westernization could not be restricted to the autocracy itself, but must be extended downward to include the Russian people. The autocracy found, in 1812, that it could not defeat Napoleon's army without calling on the Russian people. Its inability to defeat the Western allies in the Crimean War of 1854–1856, and the growing threat of the Central Powers after the Austro-German alliance of 1879, made it clear that Russia must be westernized, in technology if not in ideology, throughout all classes of the society, in order to survive. This meant, very specifically, that Russia had to obtain the Agricultural Revolution and industrialism; but these in turn required that ability to read and write be extended to the peasants and that the rural population be reduced and the urban population be increased. These needs, again, meant that serfdom had to be abolished and that modern sanitation had to be introduced. Thus one need led to another, so that the whole society had to be reformed. In typically Russian fashion all these things were undertaken by government action, but as one reform led to another it became a question whether the autocracy and the landed upper classes would be willing to allow the reform movement to go so far as to jeopardize their power and privileges. For example, the abolition of serfdom made it necessary for the landed nobility to cease to regard the peasants as private property whose only contact with the state was through themselves. Similarly, industrialism and urbanism would create new social classes of bourgeoisie and workers. These new classes inevitably would make political and social demands very distasteful to the autocracy and the landed nobility. If the reforms led to demands for nationalism, how could a dynastic monarchy such as the Romanov autocracy yield to such demands without risking the loss of Finland, Poland, the Ukraine, or Armenia?

As long as the desire to westernize and the bad conscience of the upper classes worked together, reform advanced. But as soon as the lower classes began to make demands, reaction appeared. On this basis the history of Russia was an alternation of reform and reaction from the eighteenth century to the Revolution of 1917. Peter the Great (1689–1725) and Catherine the Great (1762–1796) were supporters of westernization and reform. Paul I (1796–1801) was a reactionary. Alexander I (1801–1825) and Alexander II (1855–1881) were reformers, while Nicholas I (1825–1855) and Alexander III (1881–1894) were reactionaries. As a consequence of these various activities, by 1864 serfdom had been abolished, and a fairly modern system of law, of justice, and of education had been established; local government had been somewhat modernized; a fairly good financial and fiscal system had been established; and an army based on universal military service (but lacking in equipment) had been created. On the other hand, the autocracy continued, with full power in the hands of weak men, subject to all kinds of personal intrigues of the basest kind; the freed serfs had no adequate lands; the newly literate were subject to a ruthless censorship which tried to control their reading, writing, and thinking; the newly freed and newly urbanized were subject to constant police supervision; the non-Russian peoples of the empire were subjected to waves of Russification and Pan-Slavism; the judicial system and the fiscal system were administered with an arbitrary disregard of all personal rights or equity; and, in general, the autocracy was both tyrannical and weak.

The first period of reform in the nineteenth century, that under Alexander I, resulted from a fusion of two factors: the "conscience-stricken gentry" and the westernizing autocracy. Alexander himself represented both factors. As a result of his reforms and those of his grandmother, Catherine the Great, even earlier, there appeared in Russia, for the first time, a new educated class which was wider than the gentry, being recruited from sons of Orthodox priests or of state officials (including army officers) and, in general, from the fringes of the autocracy and the gentry. When the autocracy became reactionary under Nicholas I, this newly educated group, with some support from the conscience-stricken gentry, formed a revolutionary group generally called the "Intelligentsia." At first this new group was pro-Western, but later it became increasingly anti-Western and "Slavophile" because of its disillusionment with the West. In general, the Westernizers argued that Russia was merely a backward and barbaric fringe of Western Civilization, that it had made no cultural contribution of its own in its past, and that it must pass through the same economic, political, and social developments as the West. The Westernizers wished to speed up these developments.

The Slavophiles insisted that Russia was an entirely different civilization from Western Civilization and was much superior because it had a profound spirituality (as contrasted with Western materialism), it had a deep irrationality in intimate touch with vital forces and simple living virtues (in contrast to Western rationality, artificiality, and hypocrisy), it had its own native form of social organization, the peasant village (commune) providing a fully satisfying social and emotional life (in contrast to Western frustration of atomistic individualism in sordid cities); and that a Socialist society could be built in Russia out of the simple self-governing, cooperative peasant commune without any need to pass along the Western route marked by industrialism, bourgeoisie supremacy, or parliamentary democracy.

As industrialism grew in the West, in the period 1830–1850, the Russian Westernizers like P. Y. Chaadayev (1793–1856) and Alexander Herzen (1812–1870) became increasingly disillusioned with the West, especially with its urban slums, factory system, social disorganization, middle-class money-grubbing and pettiness, its absolutist state, and its advanced weapons. Originally the Westernizers in Russia had been inspired by French thinkers, while the Slavophiles had been inspired by German thinkers like Schelling and Hegel, so that the shift from Westernizers to Slavophiles marked a shift from French to Germanic teachers.

The Slavophiles supported orthodoxy and monarchy, although they were very critical of the existing Orthodox Church and of the existing autocracy. They claimed that the latter was a Germanic importation, and that the former, instead of remaining a native organic growth of Slavic spirituality, had become little more than a tool of autocracy. Instead of supporting these institutions, many Slavophiles went out into the villages to get in touch with pure Slavic spirituality and virtue in the shape of the untutored peasant. These missionaries, called "narodniki," were greeted with unconcealed suspicion and distaste by the peasants, because they were city-bred strangers, were educated, and expressed anti-Church and antigovernmental ideas.

Already disillusioned with the West, the Church, and the government, and now rejected by the peasants, the Intelligentsia could find no social group on which to base a reform program. The result was the growth of nihilism and of anarchism.

Nihilism was a rejection of all conventions in the name of individualism, both of these concepts understood in a Russian sense. Since man is a man and not an animal because of his individual development and growth in a society made up of conventions, the nihilist rejection of conventions served to destroy man rather than to liberate him as they expected. The destruction of conventions would not raise man to be an angel, but would lower him to be an animal. Moreover, the individual that the nihilists sought to liberate by this destruction of conventions was not what Western culture understands by the word "individual." Rather it was "humanity." The nihilists had no respect whatever for the concrete individual or for individual personality. Rather, by destroying all conventions and stripping all persons naked of all conventional distinctions, they hoped to sink everyone, and especially themselves, into the amorphous, indistinguishable mass of humanity. The nihilists were completely atheist, materialist, irrational, doctrinaire, despotic, and violent. They rejected all thought of self so long as humanity suffered; they "became atheists because they could not accept a Creator Who made an evil, incomplete world full of suffering"; they rejected all thought, all art, all idealism, all conventions, because these were superficial, unnecessary luxuries and therefore evil; they rejected marriage, because it was conventional bondage on the freedom of love; they rejected private property, because it was a tool of individual oppression; some even rejected clothing as a corruption of natural innocence; they rejected vice and licentiousness as unnecessary upper-class luxuries; as Nikolai Berdyaev put it: "It is Orthodox asceticism turned inside out, and asceticism without Grace. At the base of Russian nihilism, when grasped in its purity and depth, lies the Orthodox rejection of the world . . . , the acknowledgment of the sinfulness of all riches and luxury, of all creative profusion in art and in thought. . . . Nihilism considers as sinful luxury not only art, metaphysics, and spiritual values, but religion also. . . . Nihilism is a demand for nakedness, for the stripping of oneself of all the trappings of culture, for the annihilation of all historical traditions, for the setting free of the natural man. . . . The intellectual asceticism of nihilism found expression in materialism; any more subtle philosophy was proclaimed a sin. . . . Not to be a materialist was to be taken as a moral suspect. If you were not a materialist, then you were in favour of the enslavement of man both intellectually and politically." *

This fantastic philosophy is of great significance because it prepared the ground for Bolshevism. Out of the same spiritual sickness which produced nihilism emerged anarchism. To the anarchist, as revealed by the founder of the movement, Mikhail Bakunin (1814–1876), the chief of all enslaving and needless conventionalities was the state. The discovery that the state was not identical with society, a discovery which the West had made a thousand years earlier than Russia, could have been a liberating discovery to Russia if, like the West, the Russians had been willing to accept both state and society, each in its proper place. But this was quite impossible in the Russian tradition of fanatical totalitarianism. To this tradition the totalitarian state had been found evil and must, accordingly, be competely destroyed, and replaced by the totalitarian society in which the individual could be absorbed. Anarchism was the next step after the disillusionment of the narodniki and the agitations of the nihilists. The revolutionary Intelligentsia, unable to find any social group on which to base a reform program, and convinced of the evil of all conventional establishments and of the latent perfection in the Russian masses, adopted a program of pure political direct action of the simplest kind: assassination. Merely by killing the leaders of states (not only in Russia but throughout the world), governments could be eliminated and the masses freed for social cooperation and agrarian Socialism. From this background came the assassination of Czar Alexander II in 1881, of King Humbert of Italy in 1900, of President McKinley in 1901, as well as many anarchist outrages in Russia, Spain, and Italy in the period 1890–1910. The failure of governments to disappear in the face of this terrorist agitation, especially in Russia, where the oppression of autocracy increased after 1881, led, little by little, to a fading of the Intelligentsia's faith in destructive violence as a constructive action, as well as in the satisfying peasant commune, and in the survival of natural innocence in the unthinking masses.

Just at this point, about 1890, a great change began in Russia. Western industrialism began to grow under governmental and foreign auspices; an urban proletariat began to appear, and Marxist social theory came in from Germany. The growth of industrialism settled the violent academic dispute between Westerners and Slavophiles as to whether Russia must follow the path of Western development or could escape it by falling back on some native Slavic solutions hidden in the peasant commune; the growth of a proletariat gave the revolutionaries once again a social group on which to build; and Marxist theory gave the Intelligentsia an ideology which they could fanatically embrace. These new developments, by lifting Russia from the impasse it had reached in 1885, were generally wel-

* N. Berdyaev, Origin of Russian Communism (London, Geoffrey Bles, 1948), p. 45.

comed. Even the autocracy lifted the censorship to allow Marxist theory to circulate, in the belief that it would alleviate terrorist pressure since it eschewed direct political action, especially assassination, and postponed revolution until after industrialization had proceeded far enough to create a fully developed bourgeois class and a fully developed proletariat. To be sure, the theory created by Marx's mid-nineteenth century Germanic background was (as we shall see) gradually changed by the age-long Russian outlook, at first by the Leninist Bolshevik triumph over the Mensheviks and later by Stalin's Russian nationalist victory over Lenin's more Western rationalism, but in the period 1890–1914 the stalemate of opposed violence was broken, and progress, punctuated by violence and intolerance, appeared.

This period of progress punctuated by violence which lasted from 1890 to 1914 has a number of aspects. Of these, the economic and social development will be discussed first, followed by the political and, lastly, the ideological.

As late as the liberation of the serfs in 1863, Russia was practically untouched by the industrial process, and was indeed more backward by far than Britain and France had been before the invention of the steam engine itself. Owing to lack of roads, transportation was very poor except for the excellent system of rivers, and these were frozen for months each year. Mud tracks, impassable for part of the year and only barely passable for the rest of the time, left villages relatively isolated, with the result that almost all handicraft products and much agricultural produce were locally produced and locally consumed. The serfs were impoverished after liberation, and held at a low standard of living by having a large part of their produce taken from them as rents to landlords and as taxes to the state bureaucracy. This served to drain a considerable fraction of the country's agricultural and mineral production to the cities and to the export market. This fraction provided capital for the growth of a modern economy after 1863, being exported to pay for the import of the necessary machinery and industrial raw materials. This was supplemented by the direct importation of capital from abroad, especially from Belgium and France, while much capital, especially for railroads, was provided by the government. Foreign capital amounted to about one-third of all industrial capital in 1890 and rose to almost one-half by 1900. The proportions varied from one activitiy to another, the foreign portion being, in 1900, at 70 percent in the field of mining, 42 percent in the field of metallurgical industry, but less than 10 percent in textiles. At the same date the entire capital of the railroads amounted to 4,700 million rubles, of which 3,500 belonged to the government. These two sources were of very great importance because, except in textiles, most industrial development was based on the railroads, and the earliest enterprises in heavy industry, apart from the old charcoal metallurgy of the Ural Mountains, were foreign. The first great railroad concession, that of the Main Company for 2,650 miles of line, was given to a French company in 1857. A British corporation opened the exploitation of the great southern iron ore basin at Krivoi Rog, while the German Nobel brothers began the development of the petroleum industry at Baku (both about 1880).

As a consequence of these factors the Russian economy remained largely, but decreasingly, a colonial economy for most of the period 1863–1914. There was a very low standard of living for the Russian people, with excessive exportation of consumers' commodities, even those badly needed by the Russian people themselves, these being used to obtain foreign exchange to buy industrial or luxury commodities of foreign origin to be owned by the very small ruling class. This pattern of Russian economic organization has continued under the Soviet regime since 1917.

The first Russian railroad opened in 1838, but growth was slow until the establishment of a rational plan of development in 1857. This plan sought to penetrate the chief agricultural regions, especially the black-earth region of the south, in order to connect them with the chief cities of the north and the export ports. At that time there were only 663 miles of railroads, but this figure went up over tenfold by 1871, doubled again by 1881 (with 14,000 miles), reached 37,000 by 1901, and 46,600 by 1915. This building took place in two great waves, the first in the decade 1866–1875 and the second in the fifteen years 1891–1905. In these two periods averages of over 1,400 miles of track were constructed annually, while in the intervening fifteen years, from 1876 to 1890, the average construction was only 631 miles per year. The decrease in this middle period resulted from the "great depression" in western Europe in 1873–1893, and culminated, in Russia, in the terrible famine of 1891. After this last date, railroad construction was pushed vigorously by Count Sergei Witte, who advanced from stationmaster to Minister of Finance, holding the latter post from 1892 to 1903. His greatest achievement was the single-tracked Trans-Siberian line, which ran 6,365 miles from the Polish frontier to Vladivostok and was built in the fourteen years 1891–1905. This line, by permitting Russia to increase her political pressure in the Far East, brought Britain into an alliance with Japan (1902) and brought Russia into war with Japan (1904–1905).

The railroads had a most profound effect on Russia from every point of view, binding one-sixth of the earth's surface into a single political unit and transforming that country's economic, political, and social life. New areas, chiefly in the steppes, which had previously been too far from markets to be used for any purpose but pastoral activities, were brought under cultivation (chiefly for grains and cotton), thus competing with the central black-soil area. The drain of wealth from the peasants to the urban and export markets was increased, especially in the period before

1890. This process was assisted by the advent of a money economy to
those rural areas which had previously been closer to a self-sufficient or
a barter basis. This increased agricultural specialization and weakened
handicraft activities. The collection of rural products, which had previously been in the hands of a few large commercial operators who
worked slowly on a long-term basis, largely through Russia's more than
six thousand annual fairs, were, after 1870, thanks to the railroad replaced by a horde of small, quick-turnover middlemen who swarmed
like ants through the countryside, offering the contents of their small
pouches of money for grain, hemp, hides, fats, bristles, and feathers. This
drain of goods from the rural areas was encouraged by the government
through quotas and restrictions, price differentials and different railroad
rates and taxes for the same commodities with different destinations. As
a result, Russian sugar sold in London for about 40 percent of its price in
Russia itself. Russia, with a domestic consumption of 10.5 pounds of sugar
per capita compared to England's 92 pounds per capita, nevertheless exported in 1900 a quarter of its total production of 1,802 million pounds.
In the same year Russia exported almost 12 million pounds of cotton
goods (chiefly to Persia and China), although domestic consumption
of cotton in Russia was only 5.3 pounds per capita compared to England's 39 pounds. In petroleum products, where Russia had 48 percent of
the total world production in 1900, about 13.3 percent was exported,
although Russian consumption was only 12 pounds per capita each year
compared to Germany's 42 pounds. In one of these products, kerosene
(where Russia had the strongest potential domestic demand), almost
60 percent of the domestic production was exported. The full extent of
this drain of wealth from the rural areas can be judged from the export
figures in general. In 1891–1895 rural products formed 75 percent (and
cereals 40 percent) of the total value of all Russian exports. Moreover, it
was the better grains which were exported, a quarter of the wheat crop
compared to one-fifteenth of the rye crop in 1900. That there was a
certain improvement in this respect, as time passed, can be seen from the
fact that the portion of the wheat crop exported fell from half in the
1880's to one-sixth in 1912–1913.

This policy of siphoning wealth into the export market gave Russia a
favorable balance of trade (that is, excess of exports over imports) for the
whole period after 1875, providing gold and foreign exchange which
allowed the country to build up its gold reserve and to provide capital for
its industrial development. In addition, billions of rubles were obtained
by sales of bonds of the Russian government, largely in France as part
of the French effort to build up the Triple Entente. The State Bank,
which had increased its gold reserve from 475 million to 1,095 million
rubles in the period 1890–1897, was made a bank of issue in 1897 and was
required by law to redeem its notes in gold, thus placing Russia on the

international gold standard. The number of corporations in Russia increased from 504 with 912 million rubles capital (of which 215 million was foreign) in 1889 to 1,181 corporations with 1,737 million rubles capital (of which over 800 million was foreign) in 1899. The proportion of industrial concerns among these corporations steadily increased, being 58 percent of the new capital flotations in 1874–1881 as compared to only 11 percent in 1861–1873.

Much of the impetus to industrial advance came from the railroads, since these, in the last decade of the nineteenth century, were by far the chief purchasers of ferrous metals, coal, and petroleum products. As a result, there was a spectacular outburst of economic productivity in this decade, followed by a decade of lower prosperity after 1900. The production of pig iron in the period 1860–1870 ranged about 350 thousand tons a year, rose to 997 thousand tons in 1890, to almost 1.6 million tons in 1895, and reached a peak of 3.3 million tons in 1900. During this period, iron production shifted from the charcoal foundries of the Urals to the modern coke furnaces of the Ukraine, the percentages of the total Russian production being 67 percent from the Urals to 6 percent from the south in 1870 and 20 percent from the Urals with 67 percent from the south in 1913. The production figure for 1900 was not exceeded during the next decade, but rose after 1909 to reach 4.6 million tons in 1913. This compared with 14.4 million tons in Germany, 31.5 million in the United States, or almost 9 million in the United Kingdom.

Coal production presents a somewhat similar picture, except that its growth continued through the decade 1900–1910. Production rose from 750 thousand tons in 1870 to over 3.6 million tons in 1880 and reached almost 7 million in 1890 and almost 17.5 million in 1900. From this point, coal production, unlike pig iron, continued upward to 26.2 million tons in 1908 and to 36 million in 1913. This last figure compares to Germany's production of 190 million tons, American production of 517 million tons, and British production of 287 million tons in that same year of 1913. In coal, as in pig iron, there was a geographic shift of the center of production, one-third of the Russian coal coming from the Donetz area in 1860 while more than two-thirds came from that area in 1900 and 70 percent in 1913.

In petroleum there was a somewhat similar geographic shift in the center of production, Baku having better than 90 percent of the total in every year from 1870 until after 1900 when the new Grozny fields and a steady decline in Baku's output reduced the latter's percentage to 85 in 1910 and to 83 in 1913. Because of this decline in Baku's output, Russian production of petroleum, which soared until 1901, declined after that year. Production was only 35,000 tons in 1870, rose to 600,000 tons in 1880, then leaped to 4.8 million tons in 1890, to 11.3 million in 1900, and reached its peak of over 12 million tons in the following year. For the next twelve years output hovered somewhat below 8.4 million tons.

Because the industrialization of Russia came so late, it was (except in textiles) on a large-scale basis from the beginning and was organized on a basis of financial capitalism after 1870 and of monopoly capitalism after 1902. Although factories employing over 500 workers amounted to only 3 percent of all factories in the 1890's, 4 percent in 1903, and 5 percent in 1910, these factories generally employed over half of all factory workers. This was a far higher percentage than in Germany or the United States, and made it easier for labor agitators to organize the workers in these Russian factories. Moreover, although Russia as a whole was not highly industrialized and output per worker or per unit for Russia as a whole was low (because of the continued existence of older forms of production), the new Russian factories were built with the most advanced technological equipment, sometimes to a degree which the untrained labor supply could not utilize. In 1912 the output of pig iron per furnace in the Ukraine was higher than in western Europe by a large margin, although smaller than in the United States by an equally large margin. Although the quantity of mechanical power available on a per capita basis for the average Russian was low in 1908 compared to western Europe or America (being only 1.6 horsepower per 100 persons in Russia compared to 25 in the United States, 24 in England, and 13 in Germany), the horsepower per industrial worker was higher in Russia than in any other continental country (being 92 horsepower per 100 workers in Russia compared to 85 in France, 73 in Germany, 153 in England, and 282 in the United States). All this made the Russian economy an economy of contradictions. Though the range of technical methods was very wide, advanced techniques were lacking completely in some fields, and even whole fields of necessary industrial activities (such as machine tools or automobiles) were lacking. The economy was poorly integrated, was extremely dependent on foreign trade (both for markets and for essential products), and was very dependent on government assistance, especially on government spending.

While the great mass of the Russian people continued, as late as 1914, to live much as they had lived for generations, a small number lived in a new, and very insecure, world of industrialism, where they were at the mercy of foreign or governmental forces over which they had little control. The managers of this new world sought to improve their positions, not by any effort to create a mass market in the other, more primitive, Russian economic world by improved methods of distribution, by reduction of prices, or by rising standards of living, but rather sought to increase their own profit margins on a narrow market by ruthless reduction of costs, especially wages, and by monopolistic combinations to raise prices. These efforts led to labor agitation on one hand and to monopolistic capitalism on the other. Economic progress, except in some lines, was slowed up for these reasons during the whole decade 1900–1909. Only in 1909, when a largely monopolistic structure of industry had been created, was the increase in output of goods resumed and the struggle with labor somewhat abated. The earliest Russian cartels were formed with the encouragement of the Russian government and in those activities where foreign interests were most prevalent. In 1887 a sugar cartel was formed in order to permit foreign dumping of this commodity. A similar agency was set up for kerosene in 1892, but the great period of formation of such organizations (usually in the form of joint-selling agencies) began after the crisis of 1901. In 1902 a cartel created by a dozen iron and steel firms handled almost three-fourths of all Russian sales of these products. It was controlled by four foreign banking groups. A similar cartel, ruled from Berlin, took over the sales of almost all Russian production of iron pipe. Six Ukraine iron-ore firms in 1908 set up a cartel controlling 80 percent of Russia's ore production. In 1907 a cartel was created to control about three-quarters of Russia's agricultural implements. Others handled 97 percent of railway cars, 94 percent of locomotives, and 94 percent of copper sales. Eighteen Donetz coal firms in 1906 set up a cartel which sold three-quarters of the coal output of that area.

The creation of monopoly was aided by a change in tariff policy. Free trade, which had been established in the tariff of 1857, was curtailed in 1877 and abandoned in 1891. The protective tariff of this latter year resulted in a severe tariff war with Germany as the Germans sought to exclude Russian agricultural products in retaliation for the Russian tariff on manufactured goods. This "war" was settled in 1894 by a series of compromises, but the reopening of the German market to Russian grain led to political agitation for protection on the part of German landlords. They were successful, as we shall see, in 1900 as a result of a deal with the German industrialists to support Tirpitz's naval building program.

On the eve of the First World War, the Russian economy was in a very dubious state of health. As we have said, it was a patchwork affair, very much lacking in integration, very dependent on foreign and government support, racked by labor disturbances, and, what was even more threatening, by labor disturbances based on political rather than on economic motives, and shot through with all kinds of technological weaknesses and discords. As an example of the last, we might mention the fact that over half of Russia's pig iron was made with charcoal as late as 1900 and some of Russia's most promising natural resources were left unused as a result of the restrictive outlook of monopoly capitalists. The failure to develop a domestic market left costs of distribution fantastically high and left the Russian per capita consumption of almost all important commodities fantastically low. Moreover, to make matters worse, Russia as a consequence of these things was losing ground in the race of production with France, Germany, and the United States.

These economic developments had profound political effects under the weak-willed Czar Nicholas II (1894–1917). For about a decade Nicholas tried to combine ruthless civil repression, economic advance, and an imperialist foreign policy in the Balkans and the Far East, with pious worldwide publicity for peace and universal disarmament, domestic distractions like anti-Semitic massacres (pogroms), forged terroristic documents, and faked terroristic attempts on the lives of high officials, including himself. This unlikely mélange collapsed completely in 1905–1908. When Count Witte attempted to begin some kind of constitutional development by getting in touch with the functioning units of local government (the zemstvos, which had been effective in the famine of 1891), he was ousted from his position by an intrigue led by the murderous Minister of Interior Vyacheslav Plehve (1903). The civil head of the Orthodox Church, Konstantin Pobedonostsev (1827–1907) persecuted all dissenting religions, while allowing the Orthodox Church to become enveloped in ignorance and corruption. Most Roman Catholic monasteries in Poland were confiscated, while priests of that religion were forbidden to leave their villages. In Finland construction of Lutheran churches was forbidden, and schools of this religion were taken over by the Moscow government. The Jews were persecuted, restricted to certain provinces (the Pale), excluded from most economic activities, subjected to heavy taxes (even on their religious activities), and allowed to form only ten percent of the pupils in schools (even in villages which were almost completely Jewish and where the schools were supported entirely by Jewish taxes). Hundreds of Jews were massacred and thousands of their buildings wrecked in systematic three-day pogroms tolerated and sometimes encouraged by the police. Marriages (and children) of Roman Catholic Uniates were made illegitimate. The Moslems in Asia and elsewhere were also persecuted.

Every effort was made to Russify non-Russian national groups, especially on the western frontiers. The Finns, Baltic Germans, and Poles were not allowed to use their own languages in public life, and had to use Russian even in private schools and even on the primary level. Administrative autonomy in these areas, even that solemnly promised to Finland long before, was destroyed, and they were dominated by Russian police, Russian education, and the Russian Army. The peoples of these areas were subjected to military conscription more rigorously than the Russians themselves, and were Russified while in the ranks.

Against the Russians themselves, unbelievable extremes of espionage, counterespionage, censorship, provocation, imprisonment without trial, and outright brutality were employed. The revolutionaries responded with similar measures crowned by assassination. No one could trust anyone else, because revolutionaries were in the police, and members of the police were in the highest ranks of the revolutionaries. Georgi Gapon, a priest secretly in the pay of the government, was encouraged to form labor unions and lead workers' agitations in order to increase the employers' dependence on the autocracy, but when, in 1905, Gapon led a mass march of workers to the Winter Palace to present a petition to the czar, they were attacked by the troops and hundreds were shot. Gapon was murdered the following year by the revolutionaries as a traitor. In order to discredit the revolutionaries, the central Police Department in St. Petersburg "printed at the government expense violent appeals to riot" which were circulated all over the country by an organization of reactionaries. In one year (1906) the government exiled 35,000 persons without trial and executed over 600 persons under a new decree which fixed the death penalty for ordinary crimes like robbery or insults to officials. In the three years 1906–1908, 5,140 officials were killed or wounded, and 2,328 arrested persons were executed. In 1909 it was revealed that a police agent, Azeff, had been a member of the Central Committee of the Socialist Revolutionaries for years and had participated in plots to murder high officials, including Plehve and the Grand Duke Sergius, without warning these. The former chief of police who revealed this fact was sent to prison for doing so.

Under conditions such as these no sensible government was possible, and all appeals for moderation were crushed between the extremists from both sides. The defeats of Russian forces in the war with Japan in 1904–1905 brought events to a head. All dissatisfied groups began to agitate, culminating in a successful general strike in October 1905. The emperor began to offer political reforms, although what was extended one day was frequently taken back shortly after. A consultative assembly, the Duma, was established, elected on a broad suffrage but by very complicated procedures designed to reduce the democratic element. In the face of agrarian atrocities, endless strikes, and mutinies in both the army and navy, the censorship was temporarily lifted, and the first Duma met (May 1906). It had a number of able men and was dominated by two hastily organized political parties, the Cadets (somewhat left of Center) and the Octobrists (somewhat right of Center). Plans for wholesale reform were in the wind, and, when the czar's chief minister rejected such plans, he was overwhelmingly censured by the Duma. After weeks of agitation the czar tried to form an Octobrist ministry, but this group refused to govern without Cadet cooperation, and the latter refused to join a coalition government. The czar named Pëtr Stolypin chief minister, dissolved the first Duma, and called for election of a new one. Stolypin was a severe man, willing to move slowly in the direction of economic and political reform but determined to crush without mercy any suspicion of violence or illegal actions. The full power of the government was used to get a second Duma more to its taste, outlawing most of the Cadets, previously the largest party, and preventing certain classes and groups from campaigning or voting. The result was a new Duma of much less ability, much less discipline, and with many unknown faces. The Cadets were reduced from 150 to 123, the Octobrists from about 42 to 32, while there were 46 extreme Right, 54 Marxist Social Democrats, 35 Social Revolutionaries, at least 100 assorted Laborites, and scattered others. This group devoted much of its time to debating whether terrorist violence should be condemned. When Stolypin demanded that the Social Democrats (Marxists) should be kicked out, the Duma referred the matter to a committee; the assembly was immediately dissolved, and new elections were fixed for a third Duma (June, 1908). Under powerful government intimidation, which included sending 31 Social Democrats to Siberia, the third Duma was elected. It was mostly an upper-class and upper-middle-class body, with the largest groups being 154 Octobrists and 54 Cadets. This body was sufficiently docile to remain for five years (1907–1912). During this period both the Duma and the government followed a policy of drift, except for Stolypin. Until 1910 this energetic administrator continued his efforts to combine oppression and reform, especially agrarian reform. Rural credit banks were established; various measures were taken to place larger amounts of land in the hands of peasants; restrictions on the migration of peasants, especially to Siberia, were removed; participation in local government was opened to lower social classes previously excluded; education, especially technical education, was made more accessible; and certain provisions for social insurance were enacted into law. After the Bosnian crisis of 1908 (to be discussed later), foreign affairs became increasingly absorbing, and by 1910 Stolypin had lost his enthusiasm for reform, replacing it by senseless efforts at Russification of the numerous minority groups. He was assassinated in the presence of the czar in 1911.

The fourth Duma (1912–1916) was similar to the third, elected by complicated procedures and on a restricted suffrage. The policy of drift continued, and was more obvious since no energetic figure like Stolypin was to be found. On the contrary, the autocracy sank deeper into a morass of superstition and corruption. The influence of the czarina became more pervasive, and through her was extended the power of a number of religious mystics and charlatans, especially Rasputin. The imperial couple had ardently desired a son from their marriage in 1894. After the births of four daughters, their wish was fulfilled in 1904. Unfortunately, the new czarevich, Alexis, had inherited from his mother an incurable disease, hemophilia. Since his blood would not clot, the slightest cut endangered his life. This weakness merely exaggerated the czarina's fanatical devotion to her son and her determination to see him become czar with the powers of that office undiminished by any constitutional or parliamentary innovations. After 1907 she fell under the influence of a strange wanderer, Rasputin, a man whose personal habits and appearance were both vicious and filthy but who had the power, she believed, to stop the czarevich's bleeding. The czarina fell completely under Rasputin's control and, since the czar was completely under her control, Rasputin became the ruler of Russia, intermittently at first, but then completely. This situation lasted until he was murdered in December 1916. Rasputin used his power to satisfy his personal vices, to accumulate wealth by corruption, and to interfere in every branch of the government, always in a destructive and unprogressive sense. As Sir Bernard Pares put it, speaking of the czarina, "Her letters to Nicholas day by day contain the instructions which Rasputin gave on every detail of administration of the Empire—the Church, the Ministers, finance, railways, food supply, appointments, military operations, and above all the Duma, and a simple comparison of the dates with the events which followed shows that in almost every case they were carried out. In all her recommendations for ministerial posts, most of which are adopted, one of the primary considerations is always the attitude of the given candidate to Rasputin."

As the autocracy became increasingly corrupt and irresponsible in this way, the slow growth toward a constitutional system which might have developed from the zemstvo system of local government and the able membership of the first Duma was destroyed. The resumption of economic expansion after 1909 could not counterbalance the pernicious influence of the political paralysis. This situation was made even more hopeless by the growing importance of foreign affairs after 1908 and the failure of intellectual life to grow in any constructive fashion. The first of these complications will be discussed later; the second deserves a few words here.

The general trend of intellectual development in Russia in the years before 1914 could hardly be regarded as hopeful. To be sure, there were considerable advances in some fields such as literacy, natural science, mathematics, and economic thought, but these contributed little to any growth of moderation or to Russia's greatest intellectual need, a more integrated outlook on life. The influence of the old Orthodox religious attitude continued even in those who most emphatically rejected it. The basic attitude of the Western tradition had grown toward diversity and toleration, based on the belief that every aspect of life and of human experience and every individual has some place in the complex structure of reality if that place can only be found and that, accordingly, unity of the whole of life can be reached by way of diversity rather than by any compulsory uniformity. This idea was entirely foreign to the

Russian mind. Any Russian thinker, and hordes of other Russians with no capacity for thought, were driven by an insatiable thirst to find the "key" to life and to truth. Once this "key" has been found, all other aspects of human experience must be rejected as evil, and all men must be compelled to accept that key as the whole of life in a dreadful unity of uniformity. To make matters worse, many Russian thinkers sought to analyze the complexities of human experience by polarizing these into antitheses of mutually exclusive dualisms: Westerners versus Slavophiles, individualism versus community, freedom versus fate, revolutionary versus reactionary, nature versus conventions, autocracy versus anarchy, and such. There was no logical correlation between these, so that individual thinkers frequently embraced either side of any antithesis, forming an incredible mixture of emotionally held faiths. Moreover, individual thinkers frequently shifted from one side to another, or even oscillated back and forth between the extremes of these dualisms. In the most typical Russian minds both extremes were held simultaneously, regardless of logical compatibility, in some kind of higher mystic unity beyond rational analysis. Thus, Russian thought provides us with striking examples of God-intoxicated atheists, revolutionary reactionaries, violent nonresisters, belligerent pacifists, compulsory liberators, and individualistic totalitarians.

The basic characteristic of Russian thought is its extremism. This took two forms: (1) any portion of human experience to which allegiance was given became the whole truth, demanding total allegiance, all else being evil deception; and (2) every living person was expected to accept this same portion or be damned as a minion of antichrist. Those who embraced the state were expected to embrace it as an autocracy in which the individual had no rights, else their allegiance was not pure; those who denied the state were expected to reject it utterly by adopting anarchism. Those who became materialists had to become complete nihilists without place for any convention, ceremony, or sentiment. Those who questioned some minor aspect of the religious system were expected to become militant atheists, and if they did not take this step themselves, were driven to it by the clergy. Those who were considered to be spiritual or said they were spiritual were forgiven every kind of corruption and lechery (like Rasputin) because such material aspects were irrelevant. Those who sympathized with the oppressed were expected to bury themselves in the masses, living like them, eating like them, dressing like them, and renouncing all culture and thought (if they believed the masses lacked these things).

The extremism of Russian thinkers can be seen in their attitudes toward such basic aspects of human experience as property, reason, the state, art, sex, or power. Always there was a fanatical tendency to eliminate as sinful and evil anything except the one aspect which the thinker considered to be the key to the cosmos. Alexei Khomyakov (1804–1860), a Slavophile, wanted to reject reason completely, regarding it as "the mortal sin of the West," while Fëdor Dostoevski (1821–1881) went so far in this direction that he wished to destroy all logic and all arithmetic, seeking, he said, "to free humanity from the tyranny of two plus two equals four." Many Russian thinkers, long before the Soviets, regarded all property as sinful. Others felt the same way about sex. Leo Tolstoi, the great novelist and essayist (1828–1910), considered all property and all sex to be evil. Western thought, which has usually tried to find a place in the cosmos for everything and has felt that anything is acceptible in its proper place, recoils from such fanaticism. The West, for example, has rarely felt it necessary to justify the existence of art, but many thinkers in Russia (like Plato long ago) have rejected all art as evil. Tolstoi, among others, had moments (as in the essay *What Is Art?* of 1897 or *On Shakespeare and the Drama* of 1903) when he denounced most art and literature, including his own novels, as vain, irrelevant, and satanic. Similarly the West, while it has sometimes looked askance at sex and more frequently has overemphasized it, has generally felt that sex had a proper function in its proper place. In Russia, however, many thinkers, including once again Tolstoi (*The Kreutzer Sonata* of 1889), have insisted that sex was evil in all places and under all circumstances, and most sinful in marriage. The disruptive effects of such ideas upon social or family life can be seen in the later years of Tolstoi's personal life, culminating in his last final hatred of his long-suffering wife whom he came to regard as the instrument of his fall from grace. But while Tolstoi praised marriage without sex, other Russians, with even greater vehemence, praised sex without marriage, regarding this social institution as an unnecessary impediment in the path of pure human impulse.

In some ways we find in Tolstoi the culmination of Russian thought. He rejected all power, all violence, most art, all sex, all public authority, and all property as evil. To him the key of the universe was to be found in Christ's injunction, "Resist not evil." All other aspects of Christ's teachings except those which flow directly from this were rejected, including any belief in Christ's divinity or in a personal God. From this injunction flowed Tolstoi's ideas of nonviolence and nonresistance and his faith that only in this way could man's capacity for a spiritual love so powerful that it could solve all social problems be liberated. This idea of Tolstoi, although based on Christ's injunction, is not so much a reflection of Christianity as it is of the basic Russian assumption that any physical defeat must represent a spiritual victory, and that the latter could be achieved only through the former.

Such a point of view could be held only by persons to whom all prosperity or happiness is not only irrelevant but sinful. And this point of view could be held with such fanaticism only by persons to whom life, family, or any objective gain is worthless. This is a dominant idea in all the Russian Intelligentsia, an idea going back through Plato to ancient Asia: All objective reality is of no importance except as symbols for some subjective truth. This was, of course, the point of view of the Neoplatonic thinkers of the early Christian period. It was generally the point of view of the early Christian heretics and of those Western heretics like the Cathari (Albigenses) who were derived from this Eastern philosophic position. In modern Russian thought it is well represented by Dostoevski, who while chronologically earlier than Tolstoi is spiritually later. To Dostoevski every object and every act is merely a symbol for some elusive spiritual truth. From this point of view comes an outlook which makes his characters almost incomprehensible to the average person in the Western tradition: if such a character obtains a fortune, he cries, "I am ruined!" If he is acquitted on a murder charge, or seems likely to be, he exclaims, "I am condemned," and seeks to incriminate himself in order to ensure the punishment which is so necessary for his own spiritual self-acquittal. If he deliberately misses his opponent in a duel, he has a guilty conscience, and says, "I should not have injured him thus; I should have killed him!" In each case the speaker cares nothing about property, punishment, or life. He cares only about spiritual values: asceticism, guilt, remorse, injury to one's self-respect. In the same way, the early religious thinkers, both Christian and non-Christian, regarded all objects as symbols for spiritual values, all temporal success as an inhibition on spiritual life, and felt that wealth could be obtained only by getting rid of property, life could be found only by dying (a direct quotation from Plato), eternity could be found only if time ended, and the soul could be freed only if the body were enslaved. Thus, as late as 1910 when Tolstoi died, Russia remained true to its Greek-Byzantine intellectual tradition.

We have noted that Dostoevski, who lived slightly before Tolstoi, nevertheless had ideas which were chronologically in advance of Tolstoi's ideas. In fact, in many ways, Dostoevski was a precursor of the Bolsheviks. Concentrating his attention on poverty, crime, and human misery, always seeking the real meaning behind every overt act or word, he eventually reached a position where the distinction between appearance and significance became so wide that these two were in contradiction with each other. This contradiction was really the struggle between God and the Devil in the soul of man. Since this struggle is without end, there is no solution to men's problems except to face suffering resolutely. Such suffering purges men of all artificiality and joins them together in one mass. In this mass the Russian people, because of their greater suffering and their greater spirituality, are the hope of the world and must save the world from the materialism, violence, and selfishness of Western civilization. The Russian people, on the other hand, filled with self-sacrifice, and with no allegiance to luxury or material gain, and purified by suffering which makes them the brothers of all other suffering people, will save the world by taking up the sword of righteousness against the forces of evil stemming from Europe. Constantinople will be seized, all the Slavs will be liberated, and Europe and the world will be forced into freedom by conquest, so that Moscow many become the Third Rome. Before Russia is fit to save the world in this way, however, the Russian intellectuals must merge themselves in the great mass of the suffering Russian people, and the Russian people must adopt Europe's science and technology uncontaminated by any European ideology. The blood spilled in this effort to extend Slav brotherhood to the whole world by force will aid the cause, for suffering shared will make men one.

This mystical Slav imperialism with its apocalyptical overtones was by no means uniquely Dostoevski's. It was held in a vague and implicit fashion by many Russian thinkers, and had a wide appeal to the unthinking masses. It was implied in much of the propaganda of Pan-Slavism, and became semiofficial with the growth of this propaganda after 1908. It was widespread among the Orthodox clergy, who emphasized the reign of righteousness which would follow the millennialist establishment of Moscow as the "Third Rome." It was explicitly stated in a book, *Russia and Europe*, published in 1869 by Nicholas Danilevsky (1822–1885). Such ideas, as we shall see, did not die out with the passing of the Romanov autocracy in 1917, but became even more influential, merging with the Leninist revision of Marxism to provide the ideology of Soviet Russia after 1917.

IV

THE BUFFER FRINGE

I N the first half of the twentieth century the power structure of the
world was entirely transformed. In 1900, European civilization,
led by Britain and followed by other states at varying distances,
was still spreading outward, disrupting the cultures of other societies
unable to resist and frequently without any desire to resist. The European structure which pushed outward formed a hierarchy of power,
wealth, and prestige with Britain at the top, followed by a secondary
rank of other Great Powers, by a tertiary rank of the wealthy secondary
Powers (like Belgium, the Netherlands, and Sweden), and by a qua-
ternary rank of the lesser or decadent Powers (like Portugal or Spain,
whose world positions were sustained by British power).

At the turn of the twentieth century the first cracklings of impending disaster were emitted from this power structure but were generally ignored: in 1896 the Italians were massacred by the Ethiopians at
Adowa; in 1899–1902 the whole might of Britain was held in check by
the small Boer republics in the South African War; and in 1904–1905 Russia was defeated by a resurgent Japan. These omens were generally not
heeded, and European civilization continued on its course to Armaged-
don.

By the second half of the twentieth century, the power structure of
the world presented a quite different picture. In this new situation the
world consisted of three great zones: (1) Orthodox civilization under
the Soviet Empire, occupying the heartland of Eurasia; (2) surrounding
this, a fringe of dying and shattered cultures: Islamic, Hindu, Malayan,
Chinese, Japanese, Indonesian, and others: and (3) outside this fringe,
and chiefly responsible for shattering its cultures, Western Civilization.
Moreover, Western Civilization had been profoundly modified. In
1900 it had consisted of a core area in Europe with peripheral areas in
the Americas, Australia, New Zealand, and the fringes of Africa. By
1950 Western Civilization had its center of power in America, the
fringes in Africa were being lost, and Europe had been so reduced
in power, in wealth, and in prestige that it seemed to many that it must
make a choice between becoming a satellite in an American-dominated

Western Civilization or joining with the buffer fringe to try to create a Third Force able to hold a balance of power between America and the Soviet bloc. This impression was mistaken, and by the late 1950's Europe was in a position, once again, to play an independent role in world affairs.

In previous chapters we have examined the background of Western Civilization and of the Russian Empire to the second decade of the twentieth century. In the present chapter we shall examine the situation in the buffer fringe until about the end of that same decade. At the beginning of the twentieth century the areas which were to become the buff r fringe consisted of (1) the Near East dominated by the Ottoman Empire, (2) the Middle East dominated by the British Empire in India, and (3) the Far East, consisting of two old civilizations, China and Japan. On the outskirts of these were the lesser colonial areas of Africa, Malaysia, and Indonesia. At this point we shall consider the three major areas of the buffer fringe with a brief glance at Africa.

The Near East to 1914

For the space of over a century, from shortly after the end of the Napoleonic Wars in 1815 until 1922, the relationships of the Great Powers were exacerbated by what was known as the "Near East Question." This problem, which arose from the growing weakness of the Ottoman Empire, was concerned with the question of what would become of the lands and peoples left without government by the retreat of Turkish power. The problem was made more complex by the fact that Turkish power did not withdraw but rather decayed right were it was, so that in many areas it continued to exist in law when it had already ceased to function in fact because of the weakness and corruption of the sultan's government. The Turks themselves sought to maintain their position, not by remedying their weakness and corruption by reform, but by playing off one European state against another and by using cruel and arbitrary actions against any of their subject peoples who dared to become restive under their rule.

The Ottoman Empire reached its peak in the period 1526–1533 with the conquest of Hungary and the first siege of Vienna. A second siege, also unsuccessful, came in 1683. From this point Turkish power declined and Turkish sovereignty withdrew, but unfortunately the decline was much more rapid than the withdrawal, with the result that subject peoples were encouraged to revolt and foreign Powers were encouraged to intervene because of the weakness of Turkish power in areas which were still nominally under the sultan's sovereignty.

At its height the Ottoman Empire was larger than any contemporary European state in both area and population. South of the Mediterranean it stretched from the Atlantic Ocean in Morocco to the Persian Gulf; north of the Mediterranean it stretched from the Adriatic Sea to the Caspian Sea, including the Balkans as far north as Poland and the whole northern shore of the Black Sea. This vast empire was divided into twenty-one governments and subdivided into seventy vilayets, each under a pasha. The whole structure was held together as a tribute-gathering military system by the fact that the rulers in all parts were Muslims. The supreme ruler in Constantinople was not only sultan (and thus head of the empire) but was also caliph (and thus defender of the Muslim creed). In most of the empire the mass of the people were Muslims like their rulers, but in much of the empire the masses of the peoples were non-Muslims, being Roman Christians, Orthodox Christians, Jews, or other creeds.

Linguistic variations were even more notable than religious distinctions. Only the peoples of Anatolia generally spoke Turkish, while those of North Africa and the Near East spoke various Semitic and Hamitic dialects of which the most prevalent was Arabic. From Syria to the Caspian Sea across the base of Anatolia were several languages, of which the chief were Kurdish and Armenian. The shores of the Aegean Sea, especially the western, were generally Greek-speaking. The northern shore was a confused mixture of Turkish, Greek, and Bulgarian speaking peoples. The eastern shore of the Adriatic was Greek-speaking up to the 40th parallel, then Albanian for almost three degrees of latitude, merging gradually into various South Slav languages like Croat, Slovene, and (in the interior) Serb. The Dalmatian shore and Istria had many Italian speakers. On the Black Sea shore Thrace itself was a mixture of Turkish, Greek, and Bulgar from the Bosporus to the 42nd parallel where there was a solid mass of Bulgarians. The central Balkans was a confused area, especially in Macedonia where Turkish, Greek, Albanian, Serb, and Bulgar met and mingled. North of the Bulgarian-speaking groups, and generally separated from them by the Danube, were Romanians. North of the Croatians and Serbs, and generally separated from them by the Drava River, were the Hungarians. The district where the Hungarians and Romanians met, Transylvania, was confused, with great blocs of one language being separated from their fellows by blocs of the other, the confusion being compounded by the presence of considerable numbers of Germans and Gypsies.

The religious and linguistic divisions of the Ottoman Empire were complicated by geographic, social, and cultural divisions, especially in the Balkans. This last-named area provided such contrasts as the relatively advanced commercial and mercantile activities of the Greeks; primitive pastoral groups like Albanian goatherders; subsistence farmers scratching a living from small plots of Macedonia's rocky soils; peasant-size farms on the better soils of Serbia and Romania; great rich landed estates producing for a commercial market and worked by serf labor in Hungary and Romania. Such diversity made any hopes of political unity by consent or by federation almost impossible in the Balkans. Indeed, it was almost impossible to draw any political lines which would coincide with geographic and linguistic or religious lines, because linguistic and religious distinctions frequently indicated class distinctions. Thus the upper and lower classes or the commercial and the agricultural groups even in the same district often had different languages or different religions. Such a pattern of diversity could be held together most easily by a simple display of military force. This was what the Turks provided. Militarism and fiscalism were the two keynotes of Turkish rule, and were quite sufficient to hold the empire together as long as both remained effective and the empire was free from outside interference. But in the course of the eighteenth century Turkish administration became ineffective and outside interference became important.

The sultan, who was a completely absolute ruler, became very quickly a completely arbitrary ruler. This characteristic extended to all his activities. He filled his harem with any women who pleased his fancy, without any formal ceremony. Such numerous and temporary liaisons produced numerous children, of whom many were neglected or even forgotten. Accordingly, the succession to the throne never became established and was never based on primogeniture. As a consequence, the sultan came to fear murder from almost any direction. To avoid this, he tended to surround himself with persons who could have no possible chance of succeeding him: women, children, Negroes, eunuchs, and Christians. All the sultans from 1451 onward were born of slave mothers and only one sultan after this date even bothered to contract a formal marriage. Such a way of life isolated the sultan from his subjects completely.

This isolation applied to the process of government as well as to the ruler's personal life. Most of the sultans paid little heed to government, leaving this to their grand viziers and the local pashas. The former had no tenure, being appointed or removed in accordance with the whims of harem intrigue. The pashas tended to become increasingly independent, since they collected local taxes and raised local military forces. The fact that the sultan was also caliph (and thus religious successor to Muhammad), and the religious belief that the government was under divine guidance and should be obeyed, however unjust and tyrannical, made all religious thinking on political or social questions take the form of justification of the *status quo*, and made any kind of reform almost impossible. Reform could come only from the Sultan, but his ignorance and isolation from society made reform unlikely. In consequence the whole system became increasingly weak and corrupt. The administration was chaotic, inefficient, and arbitrary. Almost nothing could be done without gifts and bribes to officials, and it was not always possible to know what official or series of officials were the correct ones to reward.

The chaos and weakness which we have described were in full blossom by the seventeenth century, and grew worse during the next two hundred years. As early as 1699 the sultan lost Hungary, Transylvania, Croatia, and Slavonia to the Habsburgs, parts of the western Balkans to Venice, and districts in the north to Poland. In the course of the eighteenth century, Russia acquired areas north of the Black Sea, notably the Crimea.

During the nineteenth century, the Near East question became increasingly acute. Russia emerged from the Napoleonic Wars as a Great Power, able to increase its pressure on Turkey. This pressure resulted from three motivations. Russian imperialism sought to win an outlet to open waters in the south by dominating the Black Sea and by winning access to the Aegean through the acquisition of the Straits and Constantinople. Later this effort was supplemented by economic and diplomatic pressure on Persia in order to reach the Persian Gulf. At the same time, Russia regarded itself as the protector of the Orthodox Christians in the Ottoman Empire, and as early as 1774 had obtained the sultan's consent to this protective role. Moreover, as the most powerful Slav state, Russia had ambitions to be regarded as the protector of the Slavs in the sultan's domains.

These Russian ambitions could never have been thwarted by the sultan alone, but he did not need to stand alone. He generally found support from Britain and increasingly from France. Britain was obsessed with the need to defend India, which was a manpower pool and military staging area vital to the defense of the whole empire. From 1840 to 1907, it faced the nightmare possibility that Russia might attempt to cross Afghanistan to northwest India, or cross Persia to the Persian Gulf, or penetrate through the Dardanelles and the Aegean onto the British "lifeline to India" by way of the Mediterranean. The opening of the Suez Canal in 1869 increased the importance of this Mediterranean route to the east in British eyes. It was protected by British forces in Gibraltar, Malta (acquired 1800), Cyprus (1878), and Egypt (1882). In general, in spite of English humanitarian sympathy for the peoples subject to the tyranny of the Turk, and in spite of England's regard for the merits of good government, British imperial policy considered that its interests would be safer with a weak, if corrupt, Turkey in the Near East than they would be with any Great

Power in that area or with the area broken up into small independent states which might fall under the influence of the Great Powers.

The French concern with the Near East was parallel to, but weaker than, that of Britain. They had cultural and trade relations with the Levant going back, in some cases, to the Crusades. In addition the French had ancient claims, revived in 1854, to be considered the protectors of Roman Catholics in the Ottoman Empire and of the "holy places" in Jerusalem.

Three other influences which became increasingly strong in the Near East were the growth of nationalism and the growing interests of Austria (after 1866) and of Germany (after 1889). The first stirrings of Balkan nationalism can be seen in the revolt of the Serbs in 1804–1812. By seizing Bessarabia from Turkey in 1812, Russia won the right for local self-government for the Serbs. Unfortunately, these latter began almost immediately to fight one another, the chief split being between a Russophile group led by Milan Obrenovich and a Serb nationalist group led by George Petrović (better known as Karageorge). The Serb state, formally established in 1830, was bounded by the rivers Dvina, Save, Danube, and Timok. With local autonomy under Turkish suzerainty, it continued to pay tribute to the sultan and to support garrisons of Turkish troops. The vicious feud between Obrenovich and Karageorgević continued after Serbia obtained complete independence in 1878. The Obrenovich dynasty ruled in 1817–1842 and 1858–1903, while the Karageorgevic group ruled in 1842–1858 and 1903–1945. The intrigues of these two against each other broadened into a constitutional conflict in which the Obrenovich group supported the somewhat less liberal constitution of 1869, while the Karageorgević group supported the somewhat more liberal constitution of 1889. The former constitution was in effect in 1869–1889 and again in 1894–1903, while the latter was in effect in 1889–1894 and again in 1903–1921. In order to win popular support by an appeal to nationalist sentiments, both groups plotted against Turkey and later against Austria-Hungary.

A second example of Balkan nationalism appeared in the Greek struggle for independence from the sultan (1821–1830). After Greeks and Muslims had massacred each other by the thousands, Greek independence was established with a constitutional monarchy under the guarantee of the three Great Powers. A Bavarian prince was placed on the throne and began to establish a centralized, bureaucratic, constitutional state which was quite unsuited for a country with such unconstitutional traditions, poor transportation and communications, a low level of literacy, and a high level of partisan localism. After thirty turbulent years (1832–1862), Otto of Bavaria was deposed and replaced by a Danish prince and a completely democratic unicameral government which functioned only slightly better. The Danish dynasty continues to rule, although supplanted by a republic in 1924-1935 and by military dictatorships on sundry occasions, notably that of Joannes Metaxas (1936-1941).

The first beginnings of Balkan nationalism must not be overemphasized. While the inhabitants of the area have always been unfriendly to outsiders and resentful of burdensome governments, these sentiments deserve to be regarded as provincialism or localism rather than nationalism. Such feelings are prevalent among all primitive peoples and must not be regarded as nationalism unless they are so wide as to embrace loyalty to all peoples of the same language and culture and are organized in such fashion that this loyalty is directed toward the state as the core of nationalist strivings. Understood in this way, nationalism became a very potent factor in the disruption of the Ottoman Empire only after 1878.

Closely related to the beginnings of Balkan nationalism were the beginnings of Pan-Slavism and the various "pan-movements" in reaction to this, such as Pan-Islamism. These rose to a significant level only at the very end of the nineteenth century. Simply defined, Pan-Slavism was a movement for cultural unity, and, perhaps in the long run, political unity among the Slavs. In practice it came to mean the right of Russia to assume the role of protector of the Slav peoples outside Russia itself. At times it was difficult for some peoples, especially Russia's enemies, to distinguish between Pan-Slavism and Russian imperialism. Equally simply defined, Pan-Islamism was a movement for unity or at least cooperation among all the Muslim peoples in order to resist the encroachments of the European Powers on Muslim territories. In concrete terms it sought to give the caliph a religious leadership, and perhaps in time a political leadership such as he had really never previously possessed. Both of these pan-movements are of no importance until the end of the nineteenth century, while Balkan nationalism was only slightly earlier than they in its rise to importance.

These Balkan nationalists had romantic dreams about uniting peoples of the same language, and generally looked back, with a distorted historical perspective, to some period when their co-linguists had played a more important political role. The Greeks dreamed of a revived Byzantine state or even of a Periclean Athenian Empire. The Serbs dreamed of the days of Stephen Dushan, while the Bulgars went further back to the days of the Bulgarian Empire of Symeon in the early tenth century. However, we must remember that even as late as the beginning of the twentieth century such dreams were found only among the educated minority of Balkan peoples. In the nineteenth century, agitation in the Balkans was much more likely to be caused by Turkish misgovernment than by any stirrings of national feeling. Moreover, when national feeling did appear it was just as likely to appear as a feeling of animosity against neighbors who were different, rather than a feeling of unity with peoples who were the same in culture and religion. And at all times localism and class antagonisms (especially rural hostility against urban groups) remained at a high level.

Russia made war on Turkey five times in the nineteenth century. On the last two occasions the Great Powers intervened to prevent Russia from imposing its will on the sultan. The first intervention led to the Crimean War (1854–1856) and the Congress of Paris (1856), while the second intervention, at the Congress of Berlin in 1878, rewrote a peace treaty which the czar had just imposed on the sultan (Treaty of San Stefano, 1877).

In 1853 the czar, as protector of the Orthodox Christians of the Ottoman Empire, occupied the principalities of Moldavia and Wallachia north of the Danube and east of the Carpathians. Under British pressure the sultan declared war on Russia, and was supported by Britain, France, and Sardinia in the ensuing "Crimean War." Under threat of joining the anti-Russian forces, Austria forced the czar to evacuate the principalities, and occupied them herself, thus exposing an Austro-Russian rivalry in the Balkans which continued for two generations and ultimately precipitated the World War of 1914–1918.

The Congress of Paris of 1856 sought to remove all possibility of any future Russian intervention in Turkish affairs. The integrity of Turkey was guaranteed, Russia gave up its claim as protector of the sultan's Christian subjects, the Black Sea was "neutralized" by prohibiting all naval vessels and naval arsenals on its waters and shores, an International Commission was set up to assure free navigation of the Danube, and in 1862, after several years of indecision, the two principalities of Moldavia and Wallachia, along with Bessarabia, were allowed to form the state of Romania. The new state remained technically under Turkish suzerainty until 1878. It was the most progressive of the successor states of the Ottoman Empire, with advanced educational and judicial systems based on those of Napoleonic France, and a thoroughgoing agrarian reform. This last, which was executed in two stages (1863–1866 and 1918–1921), divided up the great estates of the Church and the nobility, and wiped away all vestiges of manorial dues or serfdom. Under a liberal, but not democratic, constitution, a German prince, Charles of Hohenzollern-Sigmaringen (1866–1914), established a new dynasty which was ended only in 1948. During this whole period the cultural and educational systems of the country continued to be orientated toward France in sharp contrast to the inclinations of the ruling dynasty, which had German sympathies. The Romanian possession of Bessarabia and their general pride in their Latin heritage, as reflected in the name of the country, set up a barrier to good relations with Russia, although the majority of Romanians were members of the Orthodox Church.

The political and military weakness of the Ottoman Empire in the face of Russian pressure and Balkan nationalisms made it obvious that it must westernize and it must reform, if it was going to survive. Broad verbal promises in this direction were made by the sultan in the period 1839–1877, and there were even certain efforts to execute these promises. The army was reorganized on a European basis with the assistance of Prussia. Local government was reorganized and centralized, and the fiscal system greatly improved, chiefly by curtailing the use of tax farmers; government officials were shifted from a fee-paid basis to a salaried basis; the slave market was abolished, although this meant a large reduction in the sultan's income; the religious monopoly in education was curtailed and a considerable impetus given to secular technical education. Finally, in 1856, in an edict forced on the sultan by the Great Powers, an effort was made to establish a secular state in Turkey by abolishing all inequalities based on creed in respect to personal freedom, law, property, taxation, and eligibility for office or military service.

In practice, none of these paper reforms was very effective. It was not possible to change the customs of the Turkish people by paper enactments. Indeed, any attempt to do so aroused the anger of many Muslims to the point where their personal conduct toward non-Muslims became worse. At the same time, these promises led the non-Muslims to expect better treatment, so that relations between the various groups were exacerbated. Even if the sultan had had every intention of carrying out his stated reforms, he would have had extraordinary difficulties in doing so because of the structure of Turkish society and the complete lack of trained administrators or even of literate people. The Turkish state was a theocratic state, and Turkish society was a patriarchal or even a tribal society. Any movement toward secularization or toward social equality could easily result, not in reform, but in complete destruction of the society by dissolving the religious and authoritarian relationships which held both the state and society together. But the movement toward reform lacked the wholehearted support of the sultan; it aroused the opposition of the more conservative, and in some ways more loyal, groups of Muslims; it aroused the opposition of many liberal Turks because it was derived from Western pressure on Turkey; it aroused opposition from many Christian or non-Turkish groups who feared that a successful reform might weaken their chances of breaking up the Ottoman Empire completely; and the efforts at reform, being aimed at the theocratic character of the Turkish state, counteracted the sultan's efforts to make himself the leader of Pan-Islamism and to use his title of caliph to mobilize non-Ottoman Muslims in India, Russia, and the East to support him in his struggles with the European Great Powers.

On the other hand, it was equally clear that Turkey could not meet any European state on a basis of military equality until it was westernized. At the same time, the cheap machinery-made industrial products of the

Western Powers began to pour into Turkey and to destroy the ability of the handicraft artisans of Turkey to make a living. This could not be prevented by tariff protection because the sultan was bound by international agreements to keep his customs duties at a low level. At the same time, the appeal of Western ways of life began to be felt by some of the sultan's subjects who knew them. These began to agitate for industrialism or for railroad construction, for wider opportunities in education, especially technical education, for reforms in the Turkish language, and for new, less formal, kinds of Turkish literature, for honest and impersonal methods of administration in justice and public finance, and for all those things which, by making the Western Powers strong, made them a danger to Turkey.

The sultan made feeble efforts to reform in the period 1838–1875, but by the latter date he was completely disillusioned with these efforts, and shifted over to a policy of ruthless censorship and repression; this repression led, at last, to the so-called "Young Turk" rebellion of 1908.

The shift from feeble reform to merciless repression coincided with a renewal of the Russian attacks on Turkey. These attacks were incited by Turkish butchery of Bulgarian agitators in Macedonia and a successful Turkish war on Serbia. Appealing to the doctrine of Pan-Slavism, Russia came to the rescue of the Bulgars and Serbs, and quickly defeated the Turks, forcing them to accept the Treaty of San Stefano before any of the Western Powers could intervene (1877). Among other provisions, this treaty set up a large state of Bulgaria, including much of Macedonia, independent of Turkey and under Russian military occupation.

This Treaty of San Stefano, especially the provision for a large Bulgarian state, which, it was feared, would be nothing more than a Russian tool, was completely unacceptable to England and Austria. Joining with France, Germany, and Italy, they forced Russia to come to a conference at Berlin where the treaty was completely rewritten (1878). The independence of Serbia, Montenegro, and Romania was accepted, as were the Russian acquisitions of Kars and Batum, east of the Black Sea. Romania had to give Bessarabia to Russia, but received Dobruja from the sultan. Bulgaria itself, the crucial issue of the conference, was divided into three parts: (a) the strip between the Danube and the Balkan mountains was set up as an autonomous and tribute-paying state under Turkish suzerainty; (b) the portion of Bulgaria south of the mountains was restored to the sultan as the province of Eastern Rumelia to be ruled by a Christian governor approved by the Powers; and (c) Macedonia, still farther south, was restored to Turkey in return for promises of administrative reforms. Austria was given the right to occupy Bosnia, Herzegovina, and the Sanjak of Novi-Bazar (a strip between Serbia and Montenegro). The English, by a separate agreement with Turkey, received the island of Cyprus to hold as long as Russia held Batum and Kars. The other states received nothing, although Greece submitted claims to Crete, Thessaly, Epirus, and Macedonia, while France talked about her interest in Tunis, and Italy made no secret of her ambitions in Tripoli and Albania. Only Germany asked for nothing, and received the sultan's thanks and friendship for its moderation.

The Treaty of Berlin of 1878 was a disaster from almost every point of view because it left every state, except Austria, with its appetite whetted and its hunger unsatisfied. The Pan-Slavs, the Romanians, the Bulgars, the South Slavs, the Greeks, and the Turks were all disgruntled with the settlement. The agreement turned the Balkans into an open powder keg from which the spark was kept away only with great difficulty and only for twenty years. It also opened up the prospect of the liquidation of the Turkish possessions in North Africa, thus inciting a rivalry between the Great Powers which was a constant danger to the peace in the period 1878–1912. The Romanian loss of Bessarabia, the Bulgarian loss of Eastern Rumelia, the South Slav loss of its hope of reaching the Adriatic or even of reaching Montenegro (because of the Austrian occupation of Bosnia and Novi-Bazar), the Greek failure to get Thessaly or Crete, and the complete discomfiture of the Turks created an atmosphere of general dissatisfaction. In the midst of this, the promise of reforms to Macedonia without any provision for enforcing this promise called forth hopes and agitations which could neither be satisfied nor quieted. Even Austria, which, on the face of it, had obtained more than she could really have expected, had obtained in Bosnia the instrument which was to lead eventually to the total destruction of the Habsburg Empire. This acquisition had been encouraged by Bismarck as a method of diverting Austrian ambitions southward to the Adriatic and out of Germany. But by placing Austria, in this way, in the position of being the chief obstacle in the path of the South Slav dreams of unity, Bismarck was also creating the occasion for the destruction of the Hohenzollern Empire. It is clear that European diplomatic history from 1878 to 1919 is little more than a commentary on the mistakes of the Congress of Berlin.

To Russia the events of 1878 were a bitter disappointment. Even the small Bulgarian state which emerged from the settlement gave them little satisfaction. With a constitution dictated by Russia and under a prince, Alexander of Battenberg, who was a nephew of the czar, the Bulgarians showed an uncooperative spirit which profoundly distressed the Russians. As a result, when Eastern Rumelia revolted in 1885 and demanded union with Bulgaria, the change was opposed by Russia and encouraged by Austria. Serbia, in its bitterness, went to war with Bulgaria but was defeated and forced to make peace by Austria. The union of Bulgaria and Eastern Rumelia was accepted, on face-saving terms, by the sultan. Russian objections were kept within limits by the power of Austria and

England but were strong enough to force the abdication of Alexander of Battenberg. Prince Ferdinand of Saxe-Coburg-Gotha was elected to succeed Alexander, but was unacceptable to Russia and was recognized by none of the Powers until his reconciliation with Russia in 1896. The state was generally in turmoil during this period, plots and assassinations steadily following one another. A Macedonian revolutionary organization known as IMRO, working for independence for their area, adopted an increasingly terrorist policy, killing any Bulgarian or Romanian statesman who did not work wholeheartedly in cooperation with their efforts. Agitated Bulgarians formed insurgent bands which made raids into Macedonia, and insurrection became endemic in the province, bursting out in full force in 1902. By that date Serb and Greek bands had joined in the confusion. The Powers intervened at that point to inaugurate a program of reform in Macedonia under Austro-Russian supervision.

The Congress of Berlin began the liquidation of the Turkish position in North Africa. France, which had been occupying Algeria since 1830, established a French protectorate over Tunis as well in 1881. This led to the British occupation of Egypt the following year. Not to be outdone, Italy put in a claim for Tripoli but could get no more than an exchange of notes, known as the Mediterranean Agreement of 1887, by which England, Italy, Austria, Spain, and Germany promised to maintain the *status quo* in the Mediterranean, the Adriatic, the Aegean, and the Black seas, unless all parties agreed to changes. The only concrete advantage to Italy in this was a British promise of support in North Africa in return for Italian support of the British position in Egypt. This provided only tenuous satisfaction for the Italian ambitions in Tripoli, but it was reinforced in 1900 by a French-Italian agreement by which Italy gave France a free hand in Morocco in return for a free hand in Tripoli.

By 1900 an entirely new factor began to intrude into the Eastern Question. Under Bismarck (1862–1890) Germany had avoided all non-European adventures. Under William II (1888–1918) any kind of adventure, especially a remote and uncertain one, was welcomed. In the earlier period Germany had concerned itself with the Near East Question only as a member of the European "concert of Powers" and with a few incidental issues such as the use of German officers to train the Turkish Army. After 1889 the situation was different. Economically, the Germans began to invade Anatolia by establishing trading agencies and banking facilities; politically, Germany sought to strengthen Turkey's international position in every way. This effort was symbolized by the German Kaiser's two visits to the sultan in 1889 and 1898. On the latter occasion he solemnly promised his friendship to "the Sultan Abdul Hamid and the three hundred million Muhammadans who revere him as caliph." Most important, perhaps, was the projected "Berlin to Baghdad" railway scheme which completed its main trunk line from the Austro-Hungarian border to Nusaybin in northern Mesopotamia by September 1918. This project was of the greatest economic, strategic, and political importance not only to the Ottoman Empire and the Near East but to the whole of Europe. Economically, it tapped a region of great mineral and agricultural resources, including the world's greatest petroleum reserves. These were brought into contact with Constantinople and, beyond that, with central and northwestern Europe. Germany, which was industrialized late, had a great, unsatisfied demand for food and raw materials and a great capacity to manufacture industrial products which could be exported to pay for such food and raw materials. Efforts had been made and continued to be made by Germany to find a solution to this problem by opening trade relations with South America, the Far East, and North America. Banking facilities and a merchant marine were being established to encourage such trade relations. But the Germans, with their strong strategic sense, knew well that relations with the areas mentioned were at the mercy of the British fleet, which would, almost unquestionably, control the seas during wartime. The Berlin-to-Baghdad Railway solved these crucial problems. It put the German metallurgical industry in touch with the great metal resources of Anatolia; it put the German textile industry in touch with the supplies of wool, cotton, and hemp of the Balkans, Anatolia, and Mesopotamia; in fact, it brought to almost every branch of German industry the possibility of finding a solution for its critical market and raw-material problems. Best of all, these connections, being almost entirely overland, would be within reach of the German Army and beyond the reach of the British Navy.

For Turkey itself the railway was equally significant. Strategically it made it possible, for the first time, for Turkey to mobilize her full power in the Balkans, the Caucasus area, the Persian Gulf, or the Levant. It greatly increased the economic prosperity of the whole country; it could be run (as it was after 1911) on Mesopotamian petroleum; it provided markets and thus incentives for increased production of agricultural and mineral products; it greatly reduced political discontent, public disorder, and banditry in the areas through which it ran; it greatly increased the revenues of the Ottoman treasury in spite of the government's engagement to pay subsidies to the railroad for each mile of track built and for a guaranteed income per mile each year.

The Great Powers showed mild approval of the Baghdad Railway until about 1900. Then, for more than ten years, Russia, Britain, and France showed violent disapproval, and did all they could to obstruct the project. After 1910 this disapproval was largely removed by a series of agreements by which the Ottoman Empire was divided into exclusive spheres of influence. During the period of disapproval the Great Powers concerned issued such a barrage of propaganda against the plan that it is necessary, even today, to warn against its influence. They described the Baghdad

Railway as the entering wedge of German imperialist aggression seeking
to weaken and destroy the Ottoman Empire and the stakes of the other
Powers in the area. The evidence shows quite the contrary. Germany
was the only Great Power which wanted the Ottoman Empire to be
strong and intact. Britain wanted it to be weak and intact. France generally shared the British point of view, although the French, with a
$500,000,000 investment in the area, wanted Turkey to be prosperous as
well. Russia wanted it to be weak and partitioned, a view which was
shared by the Italians and, to some extent, by the Austrians.

The Germans were not only favorably inclined toward Turkey; their
conduct seems to have been completely fair in regard to the administration
of the Baghdad Railway itself. At a time when American and other railways were practicing wholesale discrimination between customers in
regard to rates and freight handling, the Germans had the same rates
and same treatment for all, including Germans and non-Germans. They
worked to make the railroad efficient and profitable, although their
income from it was guaranteed by the Turkish government. In consequence the Turkish payments to the railroad steadily declined, and the
government was able to share in its profits to the extent of almost three
million francs in 1914. Moreover, the Germans did not seek to monopolize control of the railroad, offering to share equally with France and
England and eventually with other Powers. France accepted this offer
in 1899, but Britain continued to refuse, and placed every obstacle in the
path of the project. When the Ottoman government in 1911 sought to
raise their customs duties from 11 to 14 percent in order to finance the
continued construction of the railway, Britain prevented this. In order
to carry on the project, the Germans sold their railroad interests in the
Balkans and gave up the Ottoman building subsidy of $275,000 a kilo-
meter. In striking contrast to this attitude, the Russians forced the Turks
to change the original route of the line from northern Anatolia to southern Anatolia by threatening to take immediate measures to collect all the
arrears, amounting to over 57 million francs, due to the czar from Turkey
under the Treaty of 1878. The Russians regarded the projected railway
as a strategic threat to their Armenian frontier. Ultimately, in 1900, they
forced the sultan to promise to grant no concessions to build railways
in northern Anatolia or Armenia except with Russian approval. The
French government, in spite of the French investments in Turkey of
2.5 billion francs, refused to allow Baghdad Railway securities to be
handled on the Paris Stock Exchange. To block the growth of German
Catholic missionary activities in the Ottoman Empire, the French persuaded the Pope to issue an encyclical ordering all missionaries in that
empire to communicate with the Vatican through the French consulates.
The British opposition became intense only in April, 1903. Early in that
month Prime Minister Arthur Balfour and Foreign Secretary Lord Lans-

downe made an agreement for joint German, French, and British control of the railroad. Within three weeks this agreement was repudiated by the government because of newspaper protests against it, although it would have reduced the Turks and Germans together to only fourteen out of thirty votes on the board of directors of the railway. When the Turkish government in 1910 tried to borrow abroad $30 million, secured by the customs receipts of the country, it was summarily rebuffed in Paris and London, but obtained the sum without hesitation in Berlin. In view of these facts, the growth of German prestige and the decline in favor of the Western Powers at the sultan's court is not surprising, and goes far to explain the Turkish intervention on the side of the Central Powers in the war of 1914–1918.

The Baghdad Railway played no real role in the outbreak of the war of 1914 because the Germans in the period 1910–1914 were able to reduce the Great Powers' objections to the scheme. This was done through a series of agreements which divided Turkey into spheres of foreign influence. In November, 1910, a German-Russian agreement at Potsdam gave Russia a free hand in northern Persia, withdrew all Russian opposition to the Baghdad Railway, and pledged both parties to support equal trade opportunities for all (the "open-door" policy) in their respective areas of influence in the Near East. The French were given 2,000 miles of railway concessions in western and northern Anatolia and in Syria in 1910–1912 and signed a secret agreement with the Germans in February 1914, by which these regions were recognized as French "spheres of influence," while the route of the Baghdad Railway was recognized as a German sphere of influence; both Powers promised to work to increase the Ottoman tax receipts; the French withdrew their opposition to the railway; and the French gave the Germans the 70-million-franc investment which the French already had in the Baghdad Railway in return for an equal amount in the Turkish bond issue of 1911, which France had earlier rebuffed, plus a lucrative discount on a new Ottoman bond issue of 1914. The British drove a much harder bargain with the Germans. By an agreement of June 1914, Britain withdrew her opposition to the Baghdad Railway, allowed Turkey to raise her customs from 11 percent to 15 percent, and accepted a German sphere of interest along the railway route in return for promises (1) that the railway would not be extended to the Persian Gulf but would stop at Basra on the Tigris River, (2) that British capitalists would be given a monopoly on the navigation of the Euphrates and Tigris rivers and exclusive control over irrigation projects based on these rivers, (3) that two British subjects would be given seats on the board of directors of the Baghdad Railway, (4) that Britain would have exclusive control over the commercial activities of Kuwait, the only good port on the upper Persian Gulf; (5) that a monopoly over the oil resources of the area from

Mosul to Baghdad would be given to a new corporation in which British finances would have a half-interest, Royal Dutch Shell Company a quarter-interest, and the Germans a quarter-interest; and (6) that both Powers would support the "open-door" policy in commercial activities in Asiatic Turkey. Unfortunately, this agreement, as well as the earlier ones with other Powers, became worthless with the outbreak of the First World War in 1914. However, it is still important to recognize that the Entente Powers forced upon the Germans a settlement dividing Turkey into "spheres of interest" in place of the projected German settlement based on international cooperation in the economic reconstruction of the area.

These struggles of the Great Powers for profit and influence in the wreckage of the Ottoman Empire could not fail to have profound effects in Turkish domestic affairs. Probably the great mass of the sultan's subjects were still untouched by these events, but an animated minority was deeply stirred. This minority received no encouragement from the despotic Abdul-Hamid II, sultan from 1876 to 1909. While eager for economic improvements, Abdul-Hamid II was opposed to the spread of the Western ideas of liberalism, constitutionalism, nationalism, or democracy, and did all he could to prevent their propagation by censorship, by restrictions on foreign travel or study abroad by Turks, and by an elaborate system of arbitrary police rule and governmental espionage. As a result, the minority of liberal, nationalistic, or progressive Turks had to organize abroad. This they did at Geneva in 1891 in a group which is generally known as the "Young Turks." Their chief difficulty was to reconcile the animosities which existed between the many linguistic groups among the sultan's subjects. This was done in a series of congresses held in Paris, notably in 1902 and in 1907. At the latter meeting were representatives of the Turks, Armenians, Bulgars, Jews, Arabs, and Albanians. In the meantime, this secret organization had penetrated the sultan's army, which was seething with discontent. The plotters were so successful that they were able to revolt in July 1908, and force the sultan to reestablish the Constitution of 1876. At once divisions appeared among the rebel leaders, notably between those who wished a centralized state and those who accepted the subject nationalities' demands for decentralization. Moreover, the orthodox Muslims formed a league to resist secularization, and the army soon saw that its chief demands for better pay and improved living conditions were not going to be met. Abdul-Hamid took advantage of these divisions to organize a violent counter-revolution (April 1909). It was crushed, the sultan was deposed, and the Young Turks began to impose their ideas of a dictatorial Turkish national state with ruthless severity. A wave of resistance arose from the non-Turkish groups and the orthodox Muslims. No settlement of these disputes was achieved by the outbreak of the World War in 1914. Indeed, as we shall see in a later chapter, the Young Turk Revolution of 1908 precipitated a series of international crises of which the outbreak of war in 1914 was the latest and most disastrous.

The British Imperial Crisis: Africa, Ireland, and India to 1926

INTRODUCTION

The old statement that England acquired its empire in a fit of absent-mindedness is amusing but does not explain very much. It does, however, contain an element of truth: much of the empire *was* acquired by private individuals and commercial firms, and was taken over by the British government much later. The motives which impelled the government to annex areas which its citizens had been exploiting were varied, both in time and in place, and were frequently much different from what an outsider might believe.

Britain acquired the world's greatest empire because it possessed certain advantages which other countries lacked. We mention three of these advantages: (1) that it was an island, (2) that it was in the Atlantic, and (3) that its social traditions at home produced the will and the talents for imperial acquisition.

As an island off the coast of Europe, Britain had security as long as it had control of the narrow seas. It had such control from the defeat of the Spanish Armada in 1588 until the creation of new weapons based on air power in the period after 1935. The rise of the German Air Force under Hitler, the invention of the long-range rocket projectiles (V-2 weapon) in 1944, and the development of the atomic and hydrogen bombs in 1945–1955 destroyed England's security by reducing the defensive effectiveness of the English Channel. But in the period 1588–1942, in which Britain controlled the seas, the Channel gave England security and made its international position entirely different from that of any continental Power. Because Britain had security, it had freedom of action. That means it had a choice whether to intervene or to stay out of the various disputes which arose on the Continent of Europe or elsewhere in the world. Moreover, if it intervened, it could do so on a limited commitment, restricting its contribution of men, energy, money, and wealth to whatever amount it wished. If such a limited commitment were exhausted or lost, so long as the British fleet controlled the seas, Britain had security, and thus had freedom to choose if it would break off its intervention or increase its commitment. Moreover, England could make even a small commitment of its resources of decisive importance by using this commitment in support of the second strongest Power on the Continent against the strongest Power, thus hampering the strongest Power and making the second Power temporarily the strongest, as long as it acted in accord with Britain's wishes. In this way, by following balance-of-power tactics, Britain was able to play a decisive role on the Continent, keep the Continent divided and embroiled in its own disputes, and do this with a limited commitment of Britain's own resources, leaving a considerable surplus of energy, manpower, and wealth available for acquiring an empire overseas. In addition, Britain's unique advantage in having security through a limited commitment of resources by control of the sea was one of the contributing factors which allowed Britain to develop its unique social structure, its parliamentary system, its wide range of civil liberties, and its great economic advance.

The Powers on the Continent had none of these advantages. Since each could be invaded by its neighbors at any time, each had security, and thus freedom of action, only on rare and brief occasions. When the security of a continental Power was threatened by a neighbor, it had no freedom of action, but had to defend itself with all its resources. Clearly, it would be impossible for France to say to itself, "We shall oppose German hegemony on the Continent only to the extent of 50,000 men or of $10 million." Yet as late as 1939, Chamberlain informed France that England's commitment on the Continent for this purpose would be no more than two divisions.

Since the continental Powers had neither security nor freedom of action, their position on the Continent always was paramount over their ambitions for world empire, and these latter always had to be sacrificed for the sake of the former whenever a conflict arose. France was unable to hold on to its possessions in India or in North America in the eighteenth century because so much of its resources had to be used to bolster French security against Prussia or Austria. Napoleon sold Louisiana to the United States in 1803 because his primary concern had to be his position on the Continent. Bismarck tried to discourage Germany from embarking on any overseas adventures in the period after 1871 because he saw that Germany must be a continental power or be nothing. Again, France in 1882 had to yield Egypt to Britain, and in 1898 had to yield the Sudan in the same way, because it saw that it could not engage in any colonial dispute with Britain while the German Army stood across the Rhineland. This situation was so clear that all the lesser continental Powers with overseas colonial possessions, such as Portugal, Belgium, or the Netherlands, had to collaborate with Britain, or, at the very least, be carefully neutral. So long as the ocean highway from these countries to their overseas empires was controlled by the British fleet, they could not afford to embark on a policy hostile to Britain, regardless of their personal feelings on the subject. It is no accident that Britain's most constant international backing in the two centuries following the Methuen Treaty of 1703 came from Portugal and that Britain has felt free to negotiate with a third Power, like Germany, regarding the disposition of the Portuguese colonies, as she did in 1898 and tried to do in 1937–1939.

Britain's position on the Atlantic, combined with her naval control of the sea, gave her a great advantage when the new lands to the west of that ocean became one of the chief sources of commercial and naval wealth in the period after 1588. Lumber, tar, and ships were supplied from the American colonies to Britain in the period before the advent of iron, steam-driven ships (after 1860), and these ships helped to establish Britain's mercantile supremacy. At the same time, Britain's insular position deprived her monarchy of any need for a large professional, mercenary army such as the kings on the Continent used as the chief bulwark of royal absolutism. As a result, the kings of England were unable to prevent the landed gentry from taking over the control of the government in the period 1642–1690, and the kings of England became constitutional monarchs. Britain's security behind her navy allowed this struggle to go to a decision without any important outside interference, and permitted a rivalry between monarch and aristocracy which would have been suicidal on the insecure grounds of continental Europe.

Britain's security combined with the political triumph of the landed oligarchy to create a social tradition entirely unlike that on the Continent. One result of these two factors was that England did not obtain a bureaucracy such as appeared on the Continent. This lack of a separate bureaucracy loyal to the monarch can be seen in the weakness of the professional army (already mentioned) and also in the lack of a bureaucratic judicial system. In England, the gentry and the younger sons of the landed oligarchy studied law in the Inns of Court and obtained a feeling for tradition and the sanctity of due process of law while still remaining a part of the landed class. In fact this class became the landed class in England just because they obtained control of the bar and the bench and were, thus, in a position to judge all disputes about real property in their own favor. Control of the courts and of the Parliament made it possible for this ruling group in England to override the rights of the peasants in land, to eject them from the land, to enclose the open fields of the medieval system, to deprive the cultivators of their manorial rights and thus to reduce them to the condition of landless rural laborers or of tenants. This advance of the enclosure movement in England made possible the Agricultural Revolution, greatly depopulated the rural areas of England (as described in *The Deserted Village* of Oliver Goldsmith), and provided a surplus population for the cities, the mercantile and naval marine, and for overseas colonization.

The landed oligarchy which arose in England differed from the landed aristocracy of continental Europe in the three points already mentioned: (1) it got control of the government; (2) it was not opposed by a professional army, a bureaucracy, or a professional judicial system, but, on the contrary, it took over the control of these adjuncts of government itself, generally serving without pay, and making access to these positions difficult for outsiders by making such access expensive; and (3) it obtained complete control of the land as well as political, religious, and social control of the villages. In addition, the landed oligarchy of England was different from that on the Continent because it was not a nobility. This lack was reflected in three important factors. On the Continent a noble was excluded from marrying outside his class or from engaging in commercial enterprise; moreover, access to the nobility by persons of nonnoble birth was very difficult, and could hardly be achieved in much less than three generations. In England, the landed oligarchy could engage in any kind of commerce or business and could marry anyone without question (provided she was rich); moreover, while access to the gentry in England was a slow process which might require generations of effort acquiring landholdings in a single locality, access to the peerage by act of the government took only a moment, and could be achieved on the basis of either wealth or service. As a consequence of all these differences, the landed upper class in England was open to the influx of new talent, new money, and new blood, while the continental nobility was deprived of these valuable acquisitions.

While the landed upper class of England was unable to become a nobility (that is, a caste based on exalted birth), it was able to become an aristocracy (that is, an upper class distinguished by traditions and behavior). The chief attributes of this aristocratic upper class in England were (1) that it should be trained in an expensive, exclusive, masculine, and relatively Spartan educational system centering about the great boys' schools like Eton, Harrow, or Winchester; (2) that it should imbibe from this educational system certain distinctive attitudes of leadership, courage, sportsmanship, team play, self-sacrifice, disdain for physical comforts, and devotion to duty; (3) that it should be prepared in later life to devote a great deal of time and energy to unpaid tasks of public significance, as justices of the peace, on county councils, in the county militia, or in other services. Since all the sons of the upper classes received the same training, while only the oldest, by primogeniture, was entitled to take over the income-yielding property of the family, all the younger sons had to go out into the world to seek their fortunes, and, as likely as not, would do their seeking overseas. At the same time, the uneventful life of the typical English village or county, completely controlled by the upper-class oligarchy, made it necessary for the more ambitious members of the lower classes to seek advancement outside the county and even outside England. From these two sources were recruited the men who acquired Britain's empire and the men who colonized it.

The English have not always been unanimous in regarding the empire as a source of pride and benefit. In fact, the middle generation of the nineteenth century was filled with persons, such as Gladstone, who regarded the empire with profound suspicion. They felt that it was a source of great expense; they were convinced that it involved England in remote strategic problems which could easily lead to wars England had no need to fight; they could see no economic advantage in having an empire, since the existence of free trade (which this generation accepted) would allow commerce to flow no matter who held colonial areas; they were convinced that any colonial areas, no matter at what cost they might be acquired, would eventually separate from the mother country, voluntarily if they were given the rights of Englishmen, or by rebellion, as the American colonies had done, if they were deprived of such rights. In general, the "Little Englanders," as they were called, were averse to colonial expansion on the grounds of cost.

Although upholders of the "Little England" point of view, men like Gladstone or Sir William Harcourt, continued in political prominence until 1895, this point of view was in steady retreat after 1870. In the Liberal Party the Little Englanders were opposed by imperialists like Lord Rosebery even before 1895; after that date, a younger group of imperialists, like Asquith, Grey, and Haldane took over the party. In the Conservative Party, where the anti-imperialist idea had never been strong, moderate imperialists like Lord Salisbury were followed by more active imperialists like Joseph Chamberlain, or Lords Curzon, Selborne, and Milner. There were many factors which led to the growth of imperialism after 1870, and many obvious manifestations of that growth. The Royal Colonial Institute was founded in 1868 to fight the "Little England" idea; Disraeli as prime minister (1874–1880) dramatized the profit and glamour of empire by such acts as the purchase of control of the Suez Canal and by granting Queen Victoria the title of Empress of India; after 1870 it became increasingly evident that, however expensive colonies might be to a government, they could be fantastically profitable to individuals and companies supported by such governments; moreover, with the spread of democracy and the growing influence of the press and the expanding need for campaign contributions, individuals who made fantastic profits in overseas adventures could obtain favorable support from their governments by contributing some part of their profits to politicians' expenses; the efforts of King Leopold II of Belgium, using Henry Stanley, to obtain the Congo area as his own preserve in 1876–1880, started a contagious fever of colony-grabbing in Africa which lasted for more than thirty years; the discovery of diamonds (in 1869) and of gold (in 1886) in South Africa, especially in the Boer Transvaal Republic, intensified this fever.

The new imperialism after 1870 was quite different in tone from that which the Little Englanders had opposed earlier. The chief changes were that it was justified on grounds of moral duty and of social reform and not, as earlier, on grounds of missionary activity and material advantage. The man most responsible for this change was John Ruskin.

Until 1870 there was no professorship of fine arts at Oxford, but in that year, thanks to the Slade bequest, John Ruskin was named to such a chair. He hit Oxford like an earthquake, not so much because he talked about fine arts, but because he talked also about the empire and England's downtrodden masses, and above all because he talked about all three of these things as moral issues. Until the end of the nineteenth century the poverty-stricken masses in the cities of England lived in want, ignorance, and crime very much as they have been described by Charles Dickens. Ruskin spoke to the Oxford undergraduates as members of the privileged, ruling class. He told them that they were the possessors of a magnificent tradition of education, beauty, rule of law, freedom, decency, and self-discipline but that this tradition could not be saved, and did not deserve to be saved, unless it could be extended to the lower classes in England itself and to the non-English masses throughout the world. If this precious tradition were not extended to these two great majorities, the minority of upper-class Englishmen would ultimately be submerged by these majorities and the tradition lost. To prevent this, the tradition must be extended to the masses and to the empire.

Ruskin's message had a sensational impact. His inaugural lecture was copied out in longhand by one undergraduate, Cecil Rhodes, who kept it with him for thirty years. Rhodes (1853–1902) feverishly exploited the diamond and goldfields of South Africa, rose to be prime minister of the Cape Colony (1890–1896), contributed money to political parties, controlled parliamentary seats both in England and in South Africa, and sought to win a strip of British territory across Africa from the Cape of Good Hope to Egypt and to join these two extremes together with a telegraph line and ultimately with a Cape-to-Cairo Railway. Rhodes inspired devoted support for his goals from others in South Africa and in England. With financial support from Lord Rothschild and Alfred Beit, he was able to monopolize the diamond mines of South Africa as De Beers Consolidated Mines and to build up a great gold mining enterprise as Consolidated Gold Fields. In the middle 1890's Rhodes had a personal income of at least a million pounds sterling a year (then about five million dollars) which was spent so freely for his mysterious purposes that he was usually overdrawn on his account. These purposes centered on his desire to federate the English-speaking peoples and to bring all the habitable portions of the world under their control. For this purpose Rhodes left part of his great fortune to found the Rhodes Scholarships at Oxford in order to spread the English ruling class tradition throughout the English-speaking world as Ruskin had wanted.

Among Ruskin's most devoted disciples at Oxford were a group of intimate friends including Arnold Toynbee, Alfred (later Lord) Milner, Arthur Glazebrook, George (later Sir George) Parkin, Philip Lyttelton Gell, and Henry (later Sir Henry) Birchenough. These were so moved by Ruskin that they devoted the rest of their lives to carrying out his ideas. A similar group of Cambridge men including Reginald Baliol Brett (Lord Esher), Sir John B. Seeley, Albert (Lord) Grey, and Edmund Garrett were also aroused by Ruskin's message and devoted their lives to extension of the British Empire and uplift of England's urban masses as two parts of one project which they called "extension of the English-speaking idea." They were remarkably successful in these aims because England's most sensational journalist William T. Stead (1849–1912), an ardent social reformer and imperialist, brought them into association with Rhodes. This association was formally established on February 5, 1891, when Rhodes and Stead organized a secret society of which Rhodes had been dreaming for sixteen years. In this secret society Rhodes was to be leader; Stead, Brett (Lord Esher), and Milner were to form an executive committee; Arthur (Lord) Balfour, (Sir) Harry Johnston, Lord Rothschild, Albert (Lord) Grey, and others were listed as potential members of a "Circle of Initiates"; while there was to be an outer circle known as the "Association of Helpers" (later organized by Milner as the Round Table organization). Brett was invited to join this organization the same day and Milner a couple of weeks later, on his return from Egypt. Both accepted with enthusiasm. Thus the central part of the secret society was established by March 1891. It continued to function as a formal group, although the outer circle was, apparently, not organized until 1909–1913. This group was able to get access to Rhodes's money after his death in 1902 and also to the funds of loyal Rhodes supporters like Alfred Beit (1853–1906) and Sir Abe Bailey (1864–1940). With this backing they sought to extend and execute the ideals that Rhodes had obtained from Ruskin and Stead. Milner was the chief Rhodes Trustee and Parkin was Organizing Secretary of the Rhodes Trust after 1902, while Gell and Birchenough, as well as others with similar ideas, became officials of the British South Africa Company. They were joined in their efforts by other Ruskinite friends of Stead's like Lord Grey, Lord Esher, and Flora Shaw (later Lady Lugard). In 1890, by a stratagem too elaborate to describe here, Miss Shaw became Head of the Colonial Department of *The Times* while still remaining on the payroll of Stead's *Pall Mall Gazette.* In this post she played a major role in the next ten years in carrying into execution the imperial schemes of Cecil Rhodes, to whom Stead had introduced her in 1889.

In the meantime, in 1884, acting under Ruskin's inspiration, a group which included Arnold Toynbee, Milner, Gell, Grey, Seeley, and Michael Glazebrook founded the first "settlement house," an organization by which educated, upper-class people could live in the slums in order to assist, instruct, and guide the poor, with particular emphasis on social welfare and adult education. The new enterprise, set up in East London with P. L. Gell as chairman, was named Toynbee Hall after Arnold Toynbee who died, aged 31, in 1883. This was the original model for the thousands of settlement houses, such as Hull House in Chicago, now found throughout the world, and was one of the seeds from which the modern movement for adult education and university extension grew.

As governor-general and high commissioner of South Africa in the period 1897–1905, Milner recruited a group of young men, chiefly from Oxford and from Toynbee Hall, to assist him in organizing his administration. Through his influence these men were able to win influential posts in government and international finance and became the dominant influence in British imperial and foreign affairs up to 1939. Under Milner in South Africa they were known as Milner's Kindergarten until 1910. In 1909–1913 they organized semisecret groups, known as Round Table Groups, in the chief British dependencies and the United States. These still function in eight countries. They kept in touch with each other by personal correspondence and frequent visits, and through an influential quarterly magazine, *The Round Table*, founded in 1910 and largely supported by Sir Abe Bailey's money. In 1919 they founded the Royal Institute of International Affairs (Chatham House) for which the chief financial supporters were Sir Abe Bailey and the Astor family (owners of *The Times*). Similar Institutes of International Affairs were established in the chief British dominions and in the United States (where it is known as the Council on Foreign Relations) in the period 1919–1927. After 1925 a somewhat similar structure of organizations, known as the Institute of Pacific Relations, was set up in twelve countries holding territory in the Pacific area, the units in each British dominion existing on an interlocking basis with the Round Table Group and the Royal Institute of International Affairs in the same country. In Canada the nucleus of this group consisted of Milner's undergraduate friends at Oxford (such as Arthur Glazebrook and George Parkin), while in South Africa and India the nucleus was made up of former members of Milner's Kindergarten. These included (Sir) Patrick Duncan, B. K. Long, Richard Feetham, and (Sir) Dougal Malcolm in South Africa and (Sir) William Marris, James (Lord) Meston, and their friend Malcolm (Lord) Hailey in India. The groups in Australia and New Zealand had been recruited by Stead (through his magazine *The Review of Reviews*) as early as 1890–1893; by

Parkin, at Milner instigation, in the period 1889–1910, and by Lionel Curtis, also at Milner's request, in 1910–1919. The power and influence of this Rhodes-Milner group in British imperial affairs and in foreign policy since 1889, although not widely recognized, can hardly be exaggerated. We might mention as an example that this group dominated *The Times* from 1890 to 1912 and has controlled it completely since 1912 (except for the years 1919–1922). Because *The Times* has been owned by the Astor family since 1922, this Rhodes-Milner group was sometimes spoken of as the "Cliveden Set," named after the Astor country house where they sometimes assembled. Numerous other papers and journals have been under the control or influence of this group since 1889. They have also established and influenced numerous university and other chairs of imperial affairs and international relations. Some of these are the Beit chairs at Oxford, the Montague Burton chair at Oxford, the Rhodes chair at London, the Stevenson chair at Chatham House, the Wilson chair at Aberystwyth, and others, as well as such important sources of influence as Rhodes House at Oxford.

From 1884 to about 1915 the members of this group worked valiantly to extend the British Empire and to organize it in a federal system. They were constantly harping on the lessons to be learned from the failure of the American Revolution and the success of the Canadian federation of 1867, and hoped to federate the various parts of the empire as seemed feasible, then confederate the whole of it, with the United Kingdom, into a single organization. They also hoped to bring the United States into this organization to whatever degree was possible. Stead was able to get Rhodes to accept, in principle, a solution which might have made Washington the capital of the whole organization or allow parts of the empire to become states of the American Union. The varied character of the British imperial possessions, the backwardness of many of the native peoples involved, the independence of many of the white colonists overseas, and the growing international tension which culminated in the First World War made it impossible to carry out the plan for Imperial Federation, although the five colonies in Australia were joined into the Commonwealth of Australia in 1901 and the four colonies in South Africa were joined into the Union of South Africa in 1910.

EGYPT AND THE SUDAN TO 1922

Disraeli's purchase, with Rothschild money, of 176,602 shares of Suez Canal stock for £3,680,000 from the Khedive of Egypt in 1875 was motivated by concern for the British communications with India, just as the British acquisition of the Cape of Good Hope in 1814 had resulted from the same concern. But in imperial matters one step leads to another, and every acquisition obtained to protect an earlier acquisition requires a new advance at a later date to protect it. This was clearly true in Africa where such motivations gradually extended British control southward from Egypt and northward from the Cape until these were joined in central Africa with the conquest of German Tanganyika in 1916.

The extravagances of the Khedive Ismail (1863–1879), which had compelled the sale of his Suez Canal shares, led ultimately to the creation of an Anglo-French condominium to manage the Egyptian foreign debt and to the deposition of the khedive by his suzerain, the Sultan of Turkey. The condominium led to disputes and finally to open fighting between Egyptian nationalists and Anglo-French forces. When the French refused to join the British in a joint bombardment of Alexandria in 1882, the condominium was broken, and Britain reorganized the country in such a fashion that, while all public positions were held by Egyptians, a British army was in occupation, British "advisers" controlled all the chief governmental posts, and a British "resident," Sir Evelyn Baring (known as Lord Cromer after 1892), controlled all finances and really ruled the country until 1907.

Inspired by fanatical Muslim religious agitators (dervishes), the Mahdi Muhammad Ahmed led a Sudanese revolt against Egyptian control in 1883, massacred a British force under General Charles ("Chinese") Gordon at Khartoum, and maintained an independent Sudan for fifteen years. In 1898 a British force under (Lord) Kitchener, seeking to protect the Nile water supply of Egypt, fought its way southward against fanatical Sudanese tribesmen and won a decisive victory at Omdurman. An Anglo-Egyptian convention established a condominium known as the Anglo-Egyptian Sudan in the area between Egypt and the Congo River. This area, which had lived in disorder for centuries, was gradually pacified, brought under the rule of law, irrigated by extensive hydraulic works, and brought under cultivation, producing, chiefly, long staple cotton.

EAST CENTRAL AFRICA TO 1910

South and east of the Sudan the struggle for a British Africa was largely in the hands of H. H. (Sir Harry) Johnston (1858–1927) and Frederick (later Lord) Lugard (1858–1945). These two, chiefly using private funds but frequently holding official positions, fought all over tropical Africa, ostensibly seeking to pacify it and to wipe out the Arab slave trade, but always possessing a burning desire to extend British rule. Frequently, these ambitions led to rivalries with supporters of French and German ambitions in the same regions. In 1884 Johnston obtained many concessions from native chiefs in the Kenya area, turning these over to the British East Africa Company in 1887. When this company went bankrupt in 1895, most of its rights were taken over by the British government. In the meantime, Johnston had moved south, into a chaos of

Arab slavers' intrigues and native unrest in Nyasaland (1888). Here his exploits were largely financed by Rhodes (1889–1893) in order to prevent the Portuguese Mozambique Company from pushing westward toward the Portuguese West African colony of Angola to block the Cape-to-Cairo route. Lord Salisbury made Nyasaland a British Protectorate after a deal with Rhodes in which the South African promised to pay £10,000 a year toward the cost of the new territory. About the same time Rhodes gave the Liberal Party a substantial financial contribution in return for a promise that they would not abandon Egypt. He had already (1888) given £10,000 to the Irish Home Rule Party on condition that it seek Home Rule for Ireland while keeping Irish members in the British Parliament as a step toward Imperial Federation.

Rhodes's plans received a terrible blow in 1890–1891 when Lord Salisbury sought to end the African disputes with Germany and Portugal by delimiting their territorial claims in South and East Africa. The Portuguese agreement of 1891 was never ratified, but the Anglo-German agreement of 1890 blocked Rhodes's route to Egypt by extending German East Africa (Tanganyika) west to the Belgium Congo. By the same agreement Germany abandoned Nyasaland, Uganda, and Zanzibar to Britain in return for the island of Heligoland in the Baltic Sea and an advantageous boundary in German Southwest Africa.

As soon as the German agreement was published, Lugard was sent by the British East Africa Company to overcome the resistance of native chiefs and slavers in Uganda (1890–1894). The bankruptcy of this company in 1895 seemed likely to lead to the abandonment of Uganda because of the Little Englander sentiment in the Liberal Party (which was in office in 1892–1895). Rhodes offered to take the area over himself and run it for £25,000 a year, but was refused. As a result of complex and secret negotiations in which Lord Rosebery was the chief figure, Britain kept Uganda, Rhodes was made a privy councilor, Rosebery replaced his father-in-law, Lord Rothschild, in Rhodes's secret group and was made a Trustee under Rhodes's next (and last) will. Rosebery tried to obtain a route for Rhodes's railway to the north across the Belgian Congo; Rosebery was informed of Rhodes's plans to finance an uprising of the English within the Transvaal (Boer) Republic and to send Dr. Jameson on a raid into that country "to restore order"; and, finally, Rhodes found the money to finance Kitchener's railway from Egypt to Uganda, using the South African gauge and engines given by Rhodes.

The economic strength which allowed Rhodes to do these things rested in his diamond and gold mines, the latter in the Transvaal, and thus not in British territory. North of Cape Colony, across the Orange River, was a Boer republic, the Orange Free State. Beyond this, and separated by the Vaal River, was another Boer republic, the Transvaal. Beyond this, across the Limpopo River and continuing northward to the Zambezi

River, was the savage native kingdom of the Matabeles. With great personal daring, unscrupulous opportunism, and extravagant expenditure of money, Rhodes obtained an opening to the north, passing west of the Boer republics, by getting British control in Griqualand West (1880), Bechuanaland, and the Bechuanaland Protectorate (1885). In 1888 Rhodes obtained a vague but extensive mining concession from the Matabeles' chief, Lobengula, and gave it to the British South Africa Company organized for the purpose (1889). Rhodes obtained a charter so worded that the company had very extensive powers in an area without any northern limits beyond Bechuanaland Protectorate. Four years later the Matabeles were attacked and destroyed by Dr. Jameson, and their lands taken by the company. The company, however, was not a commercial success, and paid no dividends for thirty-five years (1889–1924) and only 12.5 shillings in forty-six years. This compares with 793.5 percent dividends paid by Rhodes's Consolidated Gold Fields in the five years 1889–1894 and the 125 percent dividend it paid in 1896. Most of the South Africa Company's money was used on public improvements like roads and schools, and no rich mines were found in its territory (known as Rhodesia) compared to those farther south in the Transvaal.

In spite of the terms of the Rhodes wills, Rhodes himself was not a racist. Nor was he a political democrat. He worked as easily and as closely with Jews, black natives, or Boers as he did with English. But he had a passionate belief in the value of a liberal education, and was attached to a restricted suffrage and even to a nonsecret ballot. In South Africa he was a staunch friend of the Dutch and of the blacks, found his chief political support among the Boers, until at least 1895, and wanted restrictions on natives put on an educational rather than on a color basis. These ideas have generally been held by his group since and have played an important role in British imperial history. His greatest weakness rested on the fact that his passionate attachment to his goals made him overly tolerant in regard to methods. He did not hesitate to use either bribery or force to attain his ends if he judged they would be effective. This weakness led to his greatest errors, the Jameson Raid of 1895 and the Boer War of 1899–1902, errors which were disastrous for the future of the empire he loved.

SOUTH AFRICA, 1895–1933

By 1895 the Transvaal Republic presented an acute problem. All political control was in the hands of a rural, backward, Bible-reading, racist minority of Boers, while all economic wealth was in the hands of a violent, aggressive majority of foreigners (Uitlanders), most of whom lived in the new city of Johannesburg. The Uitlanders, who were twice as numerous as the Boers and owned two-thirds of the land and nine-tenths of the wealth of the country, were prevented from participating in political life or from becoming citizens (except after fourteen years' residence) and were irritated by a series of minor pinpricks and extortions (such as tax differentials, a dynamite monopoly, and transportation restrictions) and by rumors that the Transvaal president, Paul Kruger, was intriguing to obtain some kind of German intervention and protection. At this point in 1895, Rhodes made his plans to overthrow Kruger's government by an uprising in Johannesburg, financed by himself and Beit, and led by his brother Frank Rhodes, Abe Bailey, and other supporters, followed by an invasion of the Transvaal by a force led by Jameson from Bechuanaland and Rhodesia. Flora Shaw used *The Times* to prepare public opinion in England, while Albert Grey and others negotiated with Colonial Secretary Joseph Chamberlain for the official support that was necessary. Unfortunately, when the revolt fizzled out in Johannesburg, Jameson raided anyway in an effort to revive it, and was easily captured by the Boers. The public officials involved denounced the plot, loudly proclaimed their surprise at the event, and were able to whitewash most of the participants in the subsequent parliamentary inquiry. A telegram from the German Kaiser to President Kruger of the Transvaal, congratulating him on his success "in preserving the independence of his country without the need to call for aid from his friends," was built up by *The Times* into an example of brazen German interference in British affairs, and almost eclipsed Jameson's aggression.

Rhodes was stopped only temporarily, but he had lost the support of many of the Boers. For almost two years he and his friends stayed quiet, waiting for the storm to blow over. Then they began to act again. Propaganda, most of it true, about the plight of Uitlanders in the Transvaal Republic flooded England and South Africa from Flora Shaw, W. T. Stead, Edmund Garrett, and others; Milner was made high commissioner of South Africa (1897); Brett worked his way into the confidence of the monarchy to become its chief political adviser during a period of more than twenty-five years (he wrote almost daily letters of advice to King Edward during his reign, 1901–1910). By a process whose details are still obscure, a brilliant, young graduate of Cambridge, Jan Smuts, who had been a vigorous supporter of Rhodes and acted as his agent in Kimberley as late as 1895 and who was one of the most important members of the Rhodes-Milner group in the period 1908–1950, went to the Transvaal and, by violent anti-British agitation, became state secretary of that country (although a British subject) and chief political adviser to President Kruger; Milner made provocative troop movements on the Boer frontiers in spite of the vigorous protests of his commanding general in South Africa, who had to be removed; and, finally, war was precipitated when Smuts drew up an ultimatum insisting that the British troop movements cease and when this was rejected by Milner.

The Boer War (1899–1902) was one of the most important events in British imperial history. The ability of 40,000 Boer farmers to hold off ten times as many British for three years, inflicting a series of defeats on them over that period, destroyed faith in British power. Although the Boer republics were defeated and annexed in 1902, Britain's confidence was so shaken that it made a treaty with Japan in the same year providing that if either signer became engaged in war with two enemies in the Far East the other signer would come to the rescue. This treaty, which allowed Japan to attack Russia in 1904, lasted for twenty years, being extended to the Middle East in 1912. At the same time Germany's obvious sympathy with the Boers, combined with the German naval construction program of 1900, alienated the British people from the Germans and contributed greatly toward the Anglo-French entente of 1904.

Milner took over the two defeated Boer republics and administered them as occupied territory until 1905, using a civil service of young men recruited for the purpose. This group, known as "Milner's Kindergarten," reorganized the government and administration of the Transvaal and Orange River Colony and played a major role in South African life generally. When Milner left public life in 1905 to devote himself to international finance and the Rhodes enterprises, Lord Selborne, his successor as high commissioner, took over the Kindergarten and continued to use it. In 1906 a new Liberal government in London granted self-government to the two Boer states. The Kindergarten spent the next four years in a successful effort to create a South African Federation. The task was not an easy one, even with such powerful backing as Selborne, Smuts (who was now the dominant political figure in the Transvaal, although Botha held the position of prime minister), and Jameson (who was the prime minister of the Cape Colony in 1904–1908). The subject was broached through a prearranged public interchange of letters between Jameson and Selborne. Then Selborne published a memorandum, written by Philip Kerr (Lothian) and Lionel Curtis, calling for a union of the four colonies. Kerr founded a periodical (*The State*, financed by Sir Abe Bailey) which advocated federation in every issue; Curtis and others scurried about organizing "Closer Union" societies; Robert H. (Lord) Brand and (Sir) Patrick Duncan laid the groundwork for the new constitution. At the Durban constitutional convention (where Duncan and B. K. Long were legal advisers) the Transvaal delegation was controlled by Smuts and the Kindergarten. This delegation, which was heavily financed, tightly organized, and knew exactly what it wanted, dominated the convention, wrote the constitution for the Union of South Africa, and succeeded in having it ratified (1910). Local animosities were compromised in a series of ingenious arrangements, including one by which the legislative, executive, and judicial branches of the new government were placed in three different cities. The Rhodes-Milner group recognized that Boer nationalism and color intolerance were threats to the future stability and loyalty of South Africa, but they had faith in the political influence of Smuts and Botha, of Rhodes's allies, and of the four members of the Kindergarten who stayed in South Africa to hold off these problems until time could moderate the irreconcilable Boers. In this they were mistaken, because, as men like Jameson (1917), Botha (1919), Duncan (1943), Long (1943), and Smuts (1950) died off, they were not replaced by men of equal loyalty and ability, with the result that the Boer extremists under D. F. Malan came to power in 1948.

The first Cabinet of the Union of South Africa was formed in 1910 by the South African Party, which was largely Boer, with Louis Botha as prime minister. The real master of the government was Smuts, who held three out of nine portfolios, all important ones, and completely dominated Botha. Their policy of reconciliation with the English and of loyal support for the British connection was violently opposed by the Boer Nationalists within the party led by J. B. M. Hertzog. Hertzog was eager to get independence from Britain and to reserve political control in a South African republic to Boers only. He obtained growing support by agitating on the language and educational issues, insisting that all government officials must speak Afrikaans and that it be a compulsory language in schools, with English a voluntary, second language.

The opposition party, known as Unionist, was largely English and was led by Jameson supported by Duncan, Richard Feetham, Hugh Wyndham, and Long. Financed by Milner's allies and the Rhodes Trust, its leaders considered that their chief task was "to support the prime minister against the extremists of his own party." Long, as the best speaker, was ordered to attack Hertzog constantly. When Hertzog struck back with too violent language in 1912, he was dropped from the Cabinet and soon seceded from the South African Party, joining with the irreconcilable Boer republicans like Christiaan De Wet to form the Nationalist Party. The new party adopted an extremist anti-English and anti-native platform.

Jameson's party, under his successor, Sir Thomas Smartt (a paid agent of the Rhodes organization), had dissident elements because of the growth of white labor unions which insisted on anti-native legislation. By 1914 these formed a separate Labour Party under F. H. P. Creswell, and were able to win from Smuts a law excluding natives from most semiskilled or skilled work or any high-paying positions (1911). The natives were compelled to work for wages, however low, by the need to obtain cash for taxes and by the inadequacy of the native reserves to support them from their own agricultural activities. By the Land Act of 1913 about 7 percent of the land area was reserved for future land purchases by natives and the other 93 percent for purchase by whites. At that time the native population exceeded the whites by at least fourfold.

As a result of such discriminations, the wages of natives were about one-tenth those of whites. This discrepancy in remuneration permitted white workers to earn salaries comparable to those earned in North America, although national income was low and productivity per capita was very low (about $125 per year).

The Botha-Smuts government of 1910–1924 did little to cope with the almost insoluble problems which faced South Africa. As it became weaker, and the Hertzog Nationalists grew stronger, it had to rely with increasing frequency on the support of the Unionist party. In 1920 a coalition was formed, and three members of the Unionist party, including Duncan, took seats in Smuts's Cabinet. In the next election in 1924 Cresswell's Labourites and Hertzog's Nationalists formed an agreement which dropped the republican-imperial issue and emphasized the importance of economic and native questions. This alliance defeated Smuts's party and formed a Cabinet which held office for nine years. It was replaced in March 1933 by a Smuts-Hertzog coalition formed to deal with the economic crisis arising from the world depression of 1929–1935.

The defeat of the Smuts group in 1924 resulted from four factors, besides his own imperious personality. These were (1) his violence toward labor unions and strikers; (2) his strong support for the imperial connection, especially during the war of 1914–1918; (3) his refusal to show any enthusiasm for an anti-native program, and (4) the economic hardships of the postwar depression and the droughts of 1919–1923. A miners' strike in 1913 was followed by a general strike in 1914; in both, Smuts used martial law and machine-gun bullets against the strikers and in the latter case illegally deported nine union leaders to England. This problem had hardly subsided before the government entered the war against Germany and actively participated in the conquest of German Africa as well as in the fighting in France. Opposition from Boer extremists to this evidence of the English connection was so violent that it resulted in open revolt against the government and mutiny by various military contingents which sought to join the small German forces in Southwest Africa. The rebels were crushed, and thousands of their supporters lost their political rights for ten years.

Botha and, even more, Smuts played major roles in the Imperial War Cabinet in London and at the Peace Conference of 1919. The former died as soon as he returned home, leaving Smuts, as prime minister, to face the acute postwar problems. The economic collapse of 1920–1923 was especially heavy in South Africa as the ostrich-feather and diamond markets were wiped out, the gold and export markets were badly injured, and years of drought were prevalent. Efforts to reduce costs in the mines by increased use of native labor led to strikes and eventually to a revolution on the Rand (1922). Over 200 rebels were killed. As a result, the popularity of Smuts in his own country reached a low ebb just at the time when he was being praised almost daily in England as one of the world's greatest men.

These political shifts in South Africa's domestic affairs did little to relieve any of the acute economic and social problems which faced that country. On the contrary these grew worse year by year. In 1921 the Union had only 1.5 million whites, 4.7 million natives, 545 thousand mulattoes ("coloured"), and 166 thousand Indians. By 1936 the whites had increased by only half a million, while the number of natives had gone up almost two million. These natives lived on inadequate and eroded reserves or in horrible urban slums, and were drastically restricted in movements, residence, or economic opportunities, and had almost no political or even civil rights. By 1950 most of the native workers of Johannesburg lived in a distant suburb where 90,000 Africans were crowded onto 600 acres of shacks with no sanitation, with almost no running water, and with such inadequate bus service that they had to stand in line for hours to get a bus into the city to work. In this way the natives were steadily "detribalized," abandoning allegiance to their own customs and beliefs (including religion) without assuming the customs or beliefs of the whites. Indeed, they were generally excluded from this because of the obstacles placed in their path to education or property ownership. The result was that the natives were steadily ground downward to the point where they were denied all opportunity except for animal survival and reproduction.

Almost half of the whites and many of the blacks were farmers, but agricultural practices were so deplorable that water shortages and erosion grew with frightening rapidity, and rivers which had flowed steadily in 1880 largely disappeared by 1950. As lands became too dry to farm, they were turned to grazing, especially under the spur of high wool prices during the two great wars, but the soil continued to drift away as dust.

Because of low standards of living for the blacks, there was little domestic market either for farm products or for industrial goods. As a result, most products of both black and white labor were exported, the receipts being used to pay for goods which were locally unavailable or for luxuries for whites. But most of the export trade was precarious. The gold mines and diamond mines had to dig so deeply (below 7,000-foot levels) that costs arose sharply, while the demand for both products fluctuated widely, since neither was a necessity of life. Nonetheless, each year over half of the Union's annual production of all goods was exported, with about one-third of the total represented by gold.

The basic problem was lack of labor, not so much the lack of hands but the low level of productivity of those hands. This in turn resulted from lack of capitalization and from the color bar which refused to allow native labor to become skilled. Moreover, the cheapness of un-skilled labor, especially on the farms, meant that most work was left to blacks, and many whites fell into lazy habits. Unskilled whites, un-willing and unable to compete as labor with the blacks, became indolent "poor whites." Milner's Kindergarten had, at the end of the Boer War, the sum of £3 million provided by the peace treaty to be used to restore Boer families from concentration camps to their farms. They were shocked to discover that one-tenth of the Boers were "poor whites," had no land and wanted none. The Kindergarten decided that this sad condition resulted from the competition of cheap black labor, a con-clusion which was incorporated into the report of a commission estab-lished by Selborne to study the problem.

This famous *Report of the Transvaal Indigency Commission*, pub-lished in 1908, was written by Philip Kerr (Lothian) and republished by the Union government twenty years later. About the same time, the group became convinced that black labor not only demoralized white labor and prevented it from acquiring the physical skills necessary for self-reliance and high personal morale but that blacks were capable of learning such skills as well as whites were. As Curtis expressed it in 1952: "I came to see how the colour bar reacted on Whites and Blacks. Ex-empt from drudgery by custom and law, Whites acquire no skill in crafts, because the school of skill is drudgery. The Blacks, by doing drudgery, acquire skill. All skilled work in mines such as rock-drilling was done by miners imported from Cornwall who worked subject to the colour bar. The heavy drills were fixed and driven under their di-rection by Natives. These Cornish miners earned £1 a day, the Natives about 2s. The Cornish miners struck for higher pay, but the Blacks, who in doing the drudgery had learned how to work the drills, kept the mines running at a lower cost."

Accordingly, the Milner–Round Table group worked out a scheme to reserve the tropical portions of Africa north of the Zambezi River for natives under such attractive conditions that the blacks south of that river would be enticed to migrate northward. As Curtis envisioned this plan, an international state or administrative body "would take over the British, French, Belgian, and Portuguese dependencies in tropical Africa. . . . Its policy would be to found north of the Zambezi a Negro Dominion in which Blacks could own land, enter professions, and stand on a footing of equality with Whites. The inevitable consequence would be that Black laborers south of the Zambezi would rapidly emi-grate from South Africa and leave South African Whites to do their own drudgery which would be the salvation of the Whites." Although this project has not been achieved, it provides the key to Britain's native and central-African policies from 1917 onward. For example, in 1937–1939 Britain made many vain efforts to negotiate a settlement of Germany's colonial claims under which Germany would renounce forever its claims on Tanganyika and be allowed to participate as a member of an international administration of all tropical Africa (including the Belgian Congo and Portuguese Angola as well as British and French territory) as a single unit in which native rights would be paramount.

The British tradition of fair conduct toward natives and nonwhites generally was found most frequently among the best educated of the English upper class and among those lower-class groups, such as missionaries, where religious influences were strongest. This tradition was greatly strengthened by the actions of the Rhodes-Milner group, especially after 1920. Rhodes aroused considerable ill-feeling among the whites of South Africa when he announced that his program included "equal rights for all civilized men south of the Zambezi," and went on to indicate that "civilized men" included ambitious, literate Negroes. When Milner took over the Boer states in 1901, he tried to follow the same policy. The peace treaty of 1902 promised that the native franchise would not be forced on the defeated Boers, but Milner tried to organize the governments of municipalities, beginning with Johannesburg, so that natives could vote. This was blocked by the Kindergarten (led by Curtis who was in charge of municipal reorganization in 1901–1906) because they considered reconciliation with the Boers as a preliminary to a South African Union to be more urgent. Similarly, Smuts as the chief political figure in South Africa after 1910 had to play down native rights in order to win Boer and English labor support for the rest of his program.

The Rhodes-Milner group, however, was in a better position to carry out its plans in the non-self-governing portions of Africa outside the Union. In South Africa the three native protectorates of Swaziland, Bechuanaland, and Basutoland were retained by the imperial authorities as areas where native rights were paramount and where tribal forms of living could be maintained at least partially. However, certain tribal customs, such as those which required a youth to prove his manhood by undergoing inhuman suffering or engaging in warfare or cattle stealing before he could marry or become a full-fledged member of the tribe, had to be curtailed. They were replaced in the twentieth century by the custom of taking work in the mines of South Africa as contract laborers for a period of years. Such labor was as onerous and killing as tribal warfare had been earlier because deaths from disease and accident were very high. But, by undergoing this test for about five years, the survivors obtained sufficient savings to allow them to return to their tribes and buy sufficient cattle and wives to support them as full members of the tribe for the rest of their days. Unfortunately, this procedure did not result in good agricultural practices but rather in overgrazing, growing drought and erosion, and great population pressure in the native reserves. It also left the mines without any assured labor supply so that it became necessary to recruit contract labor farther and farther north. Efforts by the Union government to set northern limits beyond which labor recruiting was forbidden led to controversy with employers, frequent changes in regulations, and widespread evasions. As a consequence of an agreement made by Milner with Portuguese authorities, about a quarter of the natives working in South African mines came from Portuguese East Africa even as late as 1936.

MAKING THE COMMONWEALTH, 1910–1926

As soon as South Africa was united in 1910, the Kindergarten returned to London to try to federate the whole empire by the same methods. They were in a hurry to achieve this before the war with Germany which they believed to be approaching. With Abe Bailey money they founded *The Round Table* under Kerr's (Lothian's) editorship, met in formal conclaves presided over by Milner to decide the fate of the empire, and recruited new members to their group, chiefly from New College, of which Milner was a fellow. The new recruits included a historian, F. S. Oliver, (Sir) Alfred Zimmern, (Sir) Reginald Coupland, Lord Lovat, and Waldorf (Lord) Astor. Curtis and others were sent around the world to organize Round Table groups in the chief British dependencies.

For several years (1910–1916) the Round Table groups worked desperately trying to find an acceptable formula for federating the empire. Three books and many articles emerged from these discussions, but gradually it became clear that federation was not acceptable to the English-speaking dependencies. Gradually, it was decided to dissolve all formal bonds between these dependencies, except, perhaps, allegiance to the Crown, and depend on the common outlook of Englishmen to keep the empire together. This involved changing the name "British Empire" to "Commonwealth of Nations," as in the title of Curtis's book of 1916, giving the chief dependencies, including India and Ireland, their complete independence (but gradually and by free gift rather than under duress), working to bring the United States more closely into this same orientation, and seeking to solidify the intangible links of sentiment by propaganda among financial, educational, and political leaders in each country.

Efforts to bring the dependencies into a closer relationship with the mother country were by no means new in 1910, nor were they supported only by the Rhodes-Milner group. Nevertheless, the actions of this group were all-pervasive. The poor military performance of British forces during the Boer War led to the creation of a commission to investigate the South African War, with Lord Esher (Brett) as chair-

man (1903). Among other items, this commission recommended creation
of a permanent Committee of Imperial Defence. Esher became (unofficial) chairman of this committee, holding the position for the rest of
his life (1905–1930). He was able to establish an Imperial General Staff
in 1907 and to get a complete reorganization of the military forces of
New Zealand, Australia, and South Africa so that they could be incorporated into the imperial forces in an emergency (1909–1912). On the
committee itself he created an able secretariat which cooperated loyally
with the Rhodes-Milner group thereafter. These men included (Sir)
Maurice (later Lord) Hankey and (Sir) Ernest Swinton (who invented
the tank in 1915). When, in 1916–1917, Milner and Esher persuaded the
Cabinet to create a secretariat for the first time, the task was largely
given to this secretariat from the Committee on Imperial Defence. Thus
Hankey was secretary to the committee for thirty years (1908–1938), to
the Cabinet for twenty-two years (1916–1938), clerk to the Privy Council for fifteen years (1923–1938), secretary-general of the five imperial
conferences held between 1921 and 1937, secretary to the British delegation to almost every important international conference held between
the Versailles Conference of 1919 and the Lausanne Conference of 1932,
and one of the leading advisers to the Conservative governments after
1939.

Until 1907 the overseas portions of the Empire (except India) communicated with the imperial government through the secretary of state
for colonies. To supplement this relationship, conferences of the prime
ministers of the self-governing colonies were held in London to discuss
common problems in 1887, 1897, 1902, 1907, 1911, 1917, and 1918. In
1907 it was decided to hold such conferences every four years, to call
the self-governing colonies "Dominions," and to by-pass the Colonial
Secretary by establishing a new Dominion Department. Ruskin's influence, among others, could be seen in the emphasis of the Imperial
Conference of 1911 that the Empire rested on a triple foundation of
(1) rule of law, (2) local autonomy, and (3) trusteeship of the interests and fortunes of those fellow subjects who had not yet attained
self-government.

The Conference of 1915 could not be held because of the war, but
as soon as Milner became one of the four members of the War Cabinet
in 1915 his influence began to be felt everywhere. We have mentioned
that he established a Cabinet secretariat in 1916–1917 consisting of two
protégés of Esher (Hankey and Swinton) and two of his own (his
secretaries, Leopold Amery and W. G. A. Ormsby-Gore, later Lord
Harlech). At the same time he gave the Prime Minister, Lloyd George,
a secretariat from the Round Table, consisting of Kerr (Lothian),
Grigg (Lord Altrincham), W. G. S. Adams (Fellow of All Souls College), and Astor. He created an Imperial War Cabinet by adding

Dominion Prime Ministers (particularly Smuts) to the United Kingdom War Cabinet. He also called the Imperial Conferences of 1917 and 1918 and invited the dominions to establish Resident Ministers in London. As the war drew to a close in 1918, Milner took the office of Colonial Secretary, with Amery as his assistant, negotiated an agreement providing independence for Egypt, set up a new self-government constitution in Malta, sent Curtis to India (where he drew up the chief provisions of the Government of India Act of 1919), appointed Curtis to the post of Adviser on Irish Affairs (where he played an important role in granting dominion status to southern Ireland in 1921), gave Canada permission to establish separate diplomatic relations with the United States (the first minister being the son-in-law of Milner's closest collaborator on the Rhodes Trust), and called the Imperial Conference of 1921.

During this decade 1919–1929 the Rhodes-Milner group gave the chief impetus toward transforming the British Empire into the Commonwealth of Nations and launching India on the road to responsible self-government. The creation of the Round Table groups by Milner's Kindergarten in 1909–1913 opened a new day in both these fields, although the whole group was so secretive that, even today, many close students of the subject are not aware of its significance. These men had formed their intellectual growth at Oxford on Pericle's funeral oration as described in a book by a member of the group, (Sir) Alfred Zimmern's *The Greek Commonwealth* (1911), on Edmund Burke's *On Conciliation with America*, on Sir J. B. Seeley's *Growth of British Policy*, on A. V. Dicey's *The Law and Custom of the Constitution*, and on *The New Testament's* "Sermon on the Mount." The last was especially influential on Lionel Curtis. He had a fanatical conviction that with the proper spirit and the proper organization (local self-government and federalism), the Kingdom of God could be established on earth. He was sure that if people were trusted just a bit beyond what they deserve they would respond by proving worthy of such trust. As he wrote in *The Problem of a Commonwealth* (1916), "if political power is granted to groups before they are fit they will tend to rise to the need." This was the spirit which Milner's group tried to use toward the Boers in 1902–1910, toward India in 1910–1947, and, unfortunately, toward Hitler in 1933–1939. This point of view was reflected in Curtis's three volumes on world history, published as *Civitas Dei* in 1938. In the case of Hitler, at least, these high ideals led to disaster; this seems also to be the case in South Africa; whether this group succeeded in transforming the British Empire into a Commonwealth of Nations or merely succeeded in destroying the British Empire is not yet clear, but one seems as likely as the other.

That these ideas were not solely those of Curtis but were held by the group as a whole will be clear to all who study it. When Lord

Lothian died in Washington in 1940, Curtis published a volume of his speeches and included the obituary which Grigg had written for *The Round Table*. Of Lothian this said, "He held that men should strive to build the Kingdom of Heaven here upon this earth, and that the leadership in that task must fall first and foremost upon the English-speaking peoples." Other attitudes of this influential group can be gathered from some quotations from four books published by Curtis in 1916–1920: "The rule of law as contrasted with the rule of an individual is the distinguishing mark of the Commonwealth. In despotisms government rests on the authority of the ruler or of the invisible and uncontrollable power behind him. In a commonwealth rulers derive their authority from the law, and the law from a public opinion which is competent to change it . . . The idea that the principle of the Commonwealth implies universal suffrage betrays an ignorance of its real nature. That principle simply means that government rests on the duty of the citizens to each other, and is to be vested in those who are capable of setting public interests before their own. . . . The task of preparing for freedom the races which cannot as yet govern themselves is the supreme duty of those who can. It is the spiritual end for which the Commonwealth exists, and material order is nothing except as a means to it. . . . The peoples of India and Egypt, no less than those of the British Isles and Dominions, must be gradually schooled in the management of their national affairs. . . . The whole effect of the war [of 1914–1918] has been to bring movements long gathering to a sudden head. . . . Companionship in arms has fanned . . . long smouldering resentment against the presumption that Europeans are destined to dominate the rest of the world. In every part of Asia and Africa it is bursting into flames. . . . Personally I regard this challenge to the long unquestioned claim of the white man to dominate the world as inevitable and wholesome, especially to ourselves. . . . The world is in the throes which precede creation or death. Our whole race has outgrown the merely national state and, as surely as day follows night or night the day, will pass either to a Commonwealth of Nations or else to an empire of slaves. And the issue of these agonies rests with us."

In this spirit the Rhodes-Milner group tried to draw plans for a federation of the British Empire in 1909–1916. Gradually this project was replaced or postponed in favor of the commonwealth project of free cooperation. Milner seems to have accepted the lesser aim after a meeting, sponsored by the Empire Parliamentary Association, on July 28, 1916, at which he outlined the project for federation with many references to the writings of Curtis, but found that not one Dominion member present would accept it. At the Imperial Conference of 1917, under his guidance, it was resolved that "any readjustment of constitutional relations . . . should be based on a full recognition of the Dominions as

autonomous nations of an Imperial Commonwealth and of India as an
important portion of the same, should recognize the right of the Dominions and India to an adequate voice in foreign policy and in foreign relations, and should provide effective arrangements for continuous
consultation in all important matters of common Imperial concern."
Another resolution called for full representation for India in future Imperial Conferences. This was done in 1918. At this second wartime
Imperial Conference it was resolved that Prime Ministers of Dominions
could communicate directly with the Prime Minister of the United
Kingdom and that each dominion (and India) could establish Resident
Ministers in London who would have seats on the Imperial War Cabinet.
Milner was the chief motivating force in these developments. He hoped
that the Imperial War Cabinet would continue to meet annually after
the war but this did not occur.

During these years 1917–1918, a declaration was drawn up establishing complete independence for the dominions except for allegiance to
the crown. This was not issued until 1926. Instead, on July 9, 1919 Milner
issued an official statement which said, "The United Kingdom and the
Dominions are partner nations; not yet indeed of equal power, but for
good and all of equal status. . . . The only possibility of a continuance
of the British Empire is on a basis of absolute out-and-out equal partnership between the United Kingdom and the Dominions. I say that without any kind of reservation whatsoever." This point of view was re-
stated in the so-called Balfour Declaration of 1926 and was enacted into
law as the Statute of Westminster in 1931. B. K. Long of the South
African Round Table group (who was Colonial Editor of *The Times*
in 1913–1921 and Editor of Rhodes's paper, *The Cape Times*, in South
Africa in 1922–1935) tells us that the provisions of the declaration of
1926 were agreed on in 1917 during the Imperial Conference convoked
by Milner. They were formulated by John W. Dafoe, editor of the
Winnipeg Free Press for 43 years and the most influential journalist
in Canada for much of that period. Dafoe persuaded the Canadian
Prime Minister, Sir Robert Borden, to accept his ideas and then brought
in Long and Dawson (Editor of *The Times*). Dawson negotiated the
agreement with Milner, Smuts, and others. Although Australia and
New Zealand were far from satisfied, the influence of Canada and of
South Africa carried the agreement. Nine years later it was issued
under Balfour's name at a conference convoked by Amery.

EAST AFRICA, 1910–1931

In the dependent empire, especially in tropical Africa north of the
Zambezi River, the Rhodes-Milner group was unable to achieve most of
its desires, but was able to win wide publicity for them, especially for

its views on native questions. It dominated the Colonial Office in London, at least for the decade 1919–1929. There Milner was secretary of state in 1919–1921 and Amery in 1924–1929, while the post of parliamentary under-secretary was held by three members of the group for most of the decade. Publicity for their views on civilizing the natives and training them for eventual self-government received wide dissemination, not only by official sources but also by the academic, scholarly, and journalistic organizations they dominated. As examples of this we might mention the writings of Coupland, Hailey, Curtis, Grigg, Amery, and Lothian, all Round Tablers. In 1938 Lord Hailey edited a gigantic volume of 1,837 pages called *An African Survey*. This work was first suggested by Smuts at Rhodes House, Oxford, in 1929, had a foreword by Lothian, and an editorial board of Lothian, Hailey, Coupland, Curtis, and others. It remains the greatest single book on modern Africa. These people, and others, through *The Times*, *The Round Table*, *The Observer*, Chatham House, and other conduits, became the chief source of ideas on colonial problems in the English-speaking world. Nevertheless, they were unable to achieve their program.

In the course of the 1920's the Round Table program for East Africa was paralyzed by a debate on the priority which should be given to the three aspects of the group's project for a Negro Dominion north of the Zambezi. The three parts were (1) native rights, (2) "Closer Union," and (3) international trusteeship. Generally, the group gave priority to Closer Union (federation of Kenya with Uganda and Tanganyika), but the ambiguity of their ideas on native rights made it possible for Dr. Joseph H. Oldham, spokesman for the organized Nonconformist missionary groups, to organize a successful opposition movement to federation of East Africa. In this effort Oldham found a powerful ally in Lord Lugard, and considerable support from other informed persons, including Margery Perham.

The Round Tablers, who had no firsthand knowledge of native life or even of tropical Africa, were devoted supporters of the English way of life, and could see no greater benefit conferred on natives than to help them to move in that direction. This, however, would inevitably destroy the tribal organization of life, as well as the native systems of land tenure, which were generally based on tribal holding of land. The white settlers were eager to see these things disappear, since they generally wished to bring the native labor force and African lands into the commercial market. Oldham and Lugard opposed this, since they felt it would lead to white ownership of large tracts of land on which detribalized and demoralized natives would subsist as wage slaves. Moreover, to Lugard, economy in colonial administration required that natives be governed under his system of "indirect rule" through tribal chiefs. Closer Union became a controversial target in this dispute because it involved a gradual increase in local self-government which would lead to a greater degree of white settler rule.

The opposition to Closer Union in East Africa was successful in holding up this project in spite of the Round Table domination of the Colonial Office, chiefly because of Prime Minister Baldwin's refusal to move quickly. This delayed change until the Labour government took over in 1929; in this the pro-native, nonconformist (especially Quaker) influence was stronger.

The trusteeship issue came into this controversy because Britain was bound, as a mandate Power, to maintain native rights in Tanganyika to the satisfaction of the Mandates Commission of the League of Nations. This placed a major obstacle in the path of Round Table efforts to join Tanganyika with Kenya and Uganda into a Negro Dominion which would be under quite a different kind of trusteeship of the African colonial Powers. Father south, in the Rhodesias and Nyasaland, the Round Table obsession with federation did not meet this obstacle, and that area was eventually federated, over native protests, in 1953, but this creation, the Central African Federation, broke up again in 1964. Strangely enough, the League of Nations Mandate System which became such an obstacle to the Round Table plans was largely a creation of the Round Table itself.

The Milner Group used the defeat of Germany in 1918 as an opportunity to impose an international obligation on certain Powers to treat the natives fairly in the regions taken from Germany. This opportunity was of great significance because just at that time the earlier impetus in this direction arising from missionaries was beginning to weaken as a consequence of the general weakening of religious feeling in European culture.

The chief problem in East Africa arose from the position of the white settlers of Kenya. Although this colony rests directly on the equator, its interior highlands, 4,000 to 10,000 feet up, were well adapted to white settlement and to European agricultural methods. The situation was dangerous by 1920, and grew steadily worse as the years passed, until by 1950 Kenya had the most critical native problem in Africa. It differed from South Africa in that it lacked self-government, rich mines, or a divided white population, but it had many common problems, such as overcrowded native reserves, soil erosion, and discontented and detribalized blacks working for low wages on lands owned by whites. It had about two million blacks and only 3,000 whites in 1910. Forty years later it had about 4 million blacks, 100,000 Indians, 24,000 Arabs, and only 30,000 whites (of which 40 percent were government employees). But what the whites lacked in numbers they made up in determination. The healthful highlands were reserved for white ownership as early as 1908, although they were not delimited and guaranteed until

1939. They were organized as very large, mostly undeveloped, farms of which there were only 2,000 covering 10,000 square miles in 1940. Many of these farms were of more than 30,000 acres and had been obtained from the government, either by purchase or on very long (999-year) leases for only nominal costs (rents about two cents per year per acre). The native reserves amounted to about 50,000 square miles of generally poorer land, or five times as much land for the blacks, although they had at least 150 times as many people. The Indians, chiefly in commerce and crafts, were so industrious that they gradually came to own most of the commercial areas both in the towns and in the native reserves.

The two great subjects of controversy in Kenya were concerned with the supply of labor and the problem of self-government, although less agitated problems, like agricultural technology, sanitation, and education were of vital significance. The whites tried to increase the pressure on natives to work on white farms rather than to seek to make a living on their own lands within the reserves, by forcing them to pay taxes in cash, by curtailing the size or quality of the reserves, by restricting improvements in native agricultural techniques, and by personal and political pressure and compulsion. The effort to use political compulsion reached a peak in 1919 and was stopped by Milner, although his group, like Rhodes in South Africa, was eager to make natives more industrious and more ambitious by any kinds of social, educational, or economic pressures. The settlers encouraged natives to live off the reserves in various ways: for example, by permitting them to settle as squatters on white estates in return for at least 180 days of work a year at the usual low wage rates. To help both black and white farmers, not only in Kenya but throughout the world, Milner created, as a research organization, an Imperial College of Tropical Agriculture at Trinidad in 1919.

As a consequence of various pressures which we have mentioned, notably the need to pay taxes which averaged, perhaps, one month's wages a year and, in the aggregate, took from the natives a larger sum than that realized from the sale of native products, the percentage of adult males working off the reservations increased from about 35 percent in 1925 to over 80 percent in 1940. This had very deleterious effects on tribal life, family life, native morality, and family discipline, although it seems to have had beneficial effects on native health and general education.

The real crux of controversy before the Mau Mau uprising of 1948–1955 was the problem of self-government. Pointing to South Africa, the settlers in Kenya demanded self-rule which would allow them to enforce restrictions on nonwhites. A local colonial government was organized under the Colonial Office in 1906; as was usual in such cases it consisted of an appointive governor assisted by an appointed Executive Council and advised by a Legislative Council. The latter had, also as usual, a majority of officials and a minority of "unofficial" outsiders.

Only in 1922 did the unofficial portion become elective, and only in 1949 did it become a majority of the whole body. The efforts to establish an elective element in the Legislative Council in 1919–1923 resulted in violent controversy. The draft drawn by the council itself provided for only European members elected by a European electorate. Milner added two Indian members elected by a separate Indian electorate. In the resulting controversy the settlers sought to obtain their original plan, while London sought a single electoral roll restricted in size by educational and property qualifications but without mention of race. To resist this, the settlers organized a Vigilance Committee and planned to seize the colony, abduct the governor, and form a republic federated in some way with South Africa. From this controversy came eventually a compromise, the famous Kenya White Paper of 1923, and the appointment of Sir Edward Grigg as governor for the period of 1925–1931. The compromise gave Kenya a Legislative Council containing representatives of the imperial government, the white settlers, the Indians, the Arabs, and a white missionary to represent the blacks. Except for the settlers and Indians, most of these were nominated rather than elected, but by 1949, as the membership was enlarged, election was extended, and only the official and Negro members (4 out of 41) were nominated.

The Kenya White Paper of 1923 arose from a specific problem in a single colony, but remained the formal statement of imperial policy in tropical Africa. It said: "Primarily Kenya is an African territory, and His Majesty's Government think it necessary definitely to record their considered opinion that the interests of the African natives must be paramount, and that if and when those interests and the interests of the immigrant races should conflict, the former should prevail. . . . In the administration of Kenya His Majesty's Government regard themselves as exercising a trust on behalf of the African population, and they are unable to delegate or share this trust, the object of which may be defined as the protection and advancement of the native races."

As a result of these troubles in Kenya and the continued encroachment of white settlers on native reserves, Amery sent one of the most important members of Milner's group to the colony as governor and commander in chief. This was Sir Edward Grigg (Lord Altrincham), who had been a member of Milner's Kindergarten, an editor of *The Round Table* and of *The Times* (1903–1905, 1908–1913), a secretary to Lloyd George and to the Rhodes Trustees (1923–1925), and a prolific writer on British imperial, colonial, and foreign affairs. In Kenya he tried to protect native reserves while still forcing natives to develop habits of industry by steady work, to shift white attention from political to technical problems such as agriculture, and to work toward a consolidation of tropical Africa into a single territorial unit. He forced through the Colonial Legislature in 1930 the Native Land Trust Ordinance which guaranteed native reserves. But these reserves remained inadequate and were increasingly damaged by bad agricultural practices. Only in 1925 did any sustained effort to improve such practices by natives begin. About the same time efforts were made to extend the use of native courts, native advisory councils, and to train natives for an administrative service. All of these met slow, varied, and (on the whole) indifferent success, chiefly because of natives' reluctance to cooperate and the natives' growing suspicion of white men's motives even when these whites were most eager to help. The chief cause of this growing suspicion (which in some cases reached a psychotic level) would seem to be the native's insatiable hunger for religion and his conviction that the whites were hypocrites who taught a religion that they did not obey, were traitors to Christ's teachings, and were using these to control the natives and to betray their interests, under cover of religious ideas which the whites themselves did not observe in practice.

INDIA TO 1926

In the decade 1910–1920, the two greatest problems to be faced in creating a Commonwealth of Nations were India and Ireland. There can be no doubt that India provided a puzzle infinitely more complex, as it was more remote and less clearly envisioned, than Ireland. When the British East India Company became the dominant power in India about the middle of the eighteenth century, the Mogul Empire was in the last stages of disintegration. Provincial rulers had only nominal titles, sufficient to bring them immense treasure in taxes and rents, but they generally lacked either the will or the strength to maintain order. The more vigorous tried to expand their domains at the expense of the more feeble, oppressing the peace-loving peasantry in the process, while all legal power was challenged by roaming upstart bands and plundering tribes. Of these willful tribes, the most important were the Marathas. These systematically devastated much of south-central India in the last half of the eighteenth century, forcing each village to buy temporary immunity from destruction, but steadily reducing the capacity of the countryside to meet their demands because of the trail of death and economic disorganization they left in their wake. By 1800 only one-fifth of the land in some areas was cultivated.

Although the East India Company was a commercial firm, primarily interested in profits, and thus reluctant to assume a political role in this chaotic countryside, it had to intervene again and again to restore order, replacing one nominal ruler by another and even taking over the government of those areas where it was more immediately concerned. In addition the cupidity of many of its employees led them to intervene as political powers in order to divert to their own pockets some of the fabulous wealth which they saw flowing by. For these two reasons the areas under company rule, although not contiguous, expanded steadily until by 1858 they covered three-fifths of the country. Outside the British areas were over five hundred princely domains, some no larger than a single village but others as extensive as some states of Europe. At this point, in 1857–1858, a sudden, violent insurrection of native forces, known as the Great Mutiny, resulted in the end of the Mogul Empire and of the East India Company, the British government taking over their political activities. From this flowed a number of important consequences. Annexation of native principalities ceased, leaving 562 outside British India, but under British protection and subject to British intervention to ensure good government; within British India itself, good government became increasingly dominant and commercial profit decreasingly so for the whole period 1858–1947; British political prestige rose to new heights from 1858 to 1890 and then began to dwindle, falling precipitously in 1919–1922.

The task of good government in India was not an easy one. In this great subcontinent with a population amounting to almost one-fifth of the human race were to be found an almost unbelievable diversity of cultures, religions, languages, and attitudes. Even in 1950 modern locomotives linked together great cities with advanced industrial production by passing through jungles inhabited by tigers, elephants, and primitive pagan tribes. The population, which increased from 284 million in 1901 to 389 million in 1941 and reached 530 million in 1961, spoke more than a dozen major languages divided into hundreds of dialects, and were members of dozens of antithetical religious beliefs. There were, in 1941, 255 million Hindus, 92 million Muslims, 6.3 million Christians, 5.7 million Sikhs, 1.5 million Jains, and almost 26 million pagan animists of various kinds. In addition, the Hindus and even some of the non-Hindus were divided into four major hereditary castes subdivided into thousands of subcastes, plus a lowest group of outcastes ("untouchables"), amounting to at least 30 million persons in 1900 and twice this number in 1950. These thousands of groups were endogamous, practiced hereditary economic activities, frequently had distinctive marks or garb, and were usually forbidden to marry, eat or drink with, or even to associate with, persons of different caste. Untouchables were generally forbidden to come in contact, even indirectly, with members of other groups and were, accordingly, forbidden to enter many temples or public buildings, to draw water from the public wells, even to allow their shadows to fall on any person of a different group, and were subject to other restrictions, all designed to avoid a personal pollution which could be removed only by religious rituals of varying degrees of elaborateness. Most subcastes were occupational groups covering all kinds of activities, so that there were hereditary groups of carrion collectors, thieves, highway robbers, or murderers (thugs), as well as farmers, fishermen, store-keepers, drug mixers, or copper smelters. For most peoples of India, caste was the most important fact of life, submerging their individuality into a group from which they could never escape, and regulating all their activities from birth to death. As a result, India, even as late as 1900, was a society in which status was dominant, each individual having a place in a group which, in turn, had a place in society. This place, known to all and accepted by all, operated by established procedures in its relationships with other groups so that there was in spite of diversity, a minimum of intergroup friction and a certain peaceful tolerance so long as intergroup etiquette was known and accepted.

The diversity of social groups and beliefs was naturally reflected in an extraordinarily wide range of social behavior from the most degraded and bestial activities based on crude superstitions to even more astounding levels of exalted spiritual self-sacrifice and cooperation. Although the British refrained from interfering with religious practices, in the course of the nineteenth century they abolished or greatly reduced the practice of thuggism (in which a secret caste strangled strangers in honor of the goddess Kali), suttee (in which the widow of a deceased Hindu was expected to destroy herself on his funeral pyre), infanticide, temple prostitution, and child marriages. At the other extreme, most Hindus abstained from all violence; many had such a respect for life that they would eat no meat, not even eggs, while a few carried this belief so far that they would not molest a cobra about to strike, a mosquito about to sting, or even walk about at night, less they unknowingly step on an ant or worm. Hindus, who considered cows so sacred that the worse crime would be to cause the death of one (even by accident), who allowed millions of these beasts to have free run of the country to the great detriment of cleanliness or standards of living, who would not wear shoes of leather, and would rather die than taste beef, ate pork and associated daily with Muslims who ate beef but considered pigs to be polluting. In general, most Indians lived in abject poverty and want; only about one in a hundred could read in 1858, while considerably less could understand the English language. The overwhelming majority at that time were peasants, pressed down by onerous taxes and rents, isolated in small villages unconnected by roads, and decimated at irregular intervals by famine or disease.

British rule in the period 1858–1947 tied India together by railroads, roads, and telegraph lines. It brought the country into contact with the Western world, and especially with world markets, by establishing a uniform system of money, steamboat connections with Europe by the Suez Canal, cable connections throughout the world, and the use of English as the language of government and administration. Best of all, Britain established the rule of law, equality before the law, and a tradition of judicial fairness to replace the older practice of inequality and arbitrary violence. A certain degree of efficiency, and a certain ambitious, if discontented, energy directed toward change replaced the older abject resignation to inevitable fate.

The modern postal, telegraphic, and railroad systems all began in 1854. The first grew to such dimensions that by the outbreak of war in 1939 it handled over a billion pieces of mail and forty million rupees in money orders each year. The railroad grew from 200 miles in 1855 to 9,000 in 1880, to 25,000 in 1901, and to 43,000 in 1939. This, the third largest railroad system in the world, carried 600 million passengers and 90 million tons of freight a year. About the same time, the dirt tracks of 1858 had been partly replaced by over 300,000 miles of highways, of which only about a quarter could be rated as first class. From 1925 onward, these highways were used increasingly by passenger buses, crowded and ramshackle in many cases, but steadily breaking down the isolation of the villages.

Improved communications and public order served to merge the isolated village markets, smoothing out the earlier alternations of scarcity and glut with their accompanying phenomena of waste and of starvation in the midst of plenty. All this led to a great extension of cultivation into more remote areas and the growing of a greater variety of crops. Sparsely settled areas of forests and hills, especially in Assam and the Northwest Provinces, were occupied, without the devastation of deforestation (as in China or in non-Indian Nepal) because of a highly developed forestry conservation service. Migration, permanent and seasonal, became regular features of Indian life, the earnings of the migrants being sent back to their families in the villages they had left. A magnificent system of canals, chiefly for irrigation, was constructed, populating desolate wastes, especially in the northwestern parts of the country, and encouraging whole tribes which had previously been pastoral freebooters to settle down as cultivators. By 1939 almost 60 million acres of land were irrigated. For this and other reasons, the sown area of India increased from 195 to 228 million acres in about forty years (1900–1939). Increases in yields were much less satisfactory because of reluctance to change, lack of knowledge or capital, and organizational problems.

The tax on land traditionally had been the major part of public revenue in India, and remained near 50 percent as late as 1900. Under the Moguls these land revenues had been collected by tax farmers. In many areas, notably Bengal, the British tended to regard these land revenues as rents rather than taxes, and thus regarded the revenue collectors as the owners of the land. Once this was established, these new landlords used their powers to raise rents, to evict cultivators who had been on the same land for years or even generations, and to create an unstable rural proletariat of tenants and laborers unable or unwilling to improve their methods. Numerous legislative enactments sought, without great success, to improve these conditions. Such efforts were counterbalanced by the growth of population, the great rise in the value of land, the inability of industry or commerce to drain surplus population from the land as fast as it increased, the tendency of the government to favor industry or commerce over agriculture by tariffs, taxation, and public expenditures, the growing frequency of famines (from droughts), of malaria (from irrigation projects), and of plague (from trade with the Far East) which wiped out in one year gains made in several years, the growing burden of peasant debt at onerous terms and at high interest rates, and the growing inability to supplement incomes from cultivation by incomes from household crafts because of the growing competition from cheap industrial goods. Although slavery was abolished in 1843, many of the poor were reduced to peonage by contracting debts at unfair terms and binding themselves and their heirs to work for their creditors until the debt was paid. Such a debt could never be paid, in many cases, because the rate at which it was reduced was left to the creditor and could rarely be questioned by the illiterate debtor.

All of these misfortunes culminated in the period 1895–1901. There had been a long period of declining prices in 1873–1896, which increased the burden on debtors and stagnated economic activities. In 1897 the monsoon rains failed, with a loss of 18 million tons of food crops and of one million lives from famine. This disaster was repeated in 1899–1900. Bubonic plague was introduced to Bombay from China in 1895 and killed about two million persons in the next six years.

From this low point in 1901, economic conditions improved fairly steadily, except for a brief period in 1919–1922 and the long burden of the world depression in 1929–1934. The rise in prices in 1900–1914 benefited India more than others, as the prices of her exports rose more rapidly. The war of 1914–1918 gave India a great economic opportunity, especially by increasing the demand for her textiles. Tariffs were raised steadily after 1916, providing protection for industry, especially in metals, textiles, cement, and paper. The customs became the largest single source of revenue, alleviating to some extent the pressure of taxation on cultivators. However, the agrarian problem remained acute, for most of the factors listed above remained in force. In 1931 it was estimated that, in the United Provinces, 30 percent of the cultivators could not make a living from their holdings even in good years, while 52 percent could make a living in good years but not in bad ones.

There was great economic advance in mining, industry, commerce, and finance in the period after 1900. Coal output went up from 6 to 21 million tons in 1900–1924, and petroleum output (chiefly from Burma) went up from 37 to 294 million gallons. Production in the protected industries also improved in the same period until, by 1932, India could produce three-quarters of her cotton cloth, three-quarters of her steel, and most of her cement, matches, and sugar. In one product, jute, India became the chief source for the world's supply, and this became the leading export after 1925.

A notable feature of the growth of manufacturing in India after 1900 lies in the fact that Hindu capital largely replaced British capital, chiefly for political reasons. In spite of India's poverty, there was a considerable volume of saving, arising chiefly from the inequitable distribution of income to the landlord class and to the moneylenders (if these two groups can be separated in this way). Naturally, these groups preferred to invest their incomes back in the activities whence they had been derived, but, after 1919, nationalist agitation and especially Gandhi's influence inclined many Hindus to make contributions to their country's strength by investing in industry.

The growth of industry should not be exaggerated, and its influences were considerably less than one might believe at first glance. There was little growth of an urban proletariat or of a permanent class of factory workers, although this did exist. Increases in output came largely from power production rather than from increases in the labor force. This labor force continued to be rural in its psychological and social orientation, being generally temporary migrants from the villages, living under urban industrial conditions only for a few years, with every intention of returning to the village eventually, and generally sending savings back to their families and visiting them for weeks or even months each year (generally at the harvest season). This class of industrial laborers did not adopt either an urban or a proletarian point of view, were almost wholly illiterate, formed labor organizations only reluctantly (because of refusal to pay dues), and rarely acquired industrial skills. After 1915 labor unions did appear, but membership remained small, and they were organized and controlled by nonlaboring persons, frequently middle-class intellectuals. Moreover, industry remained a widely scattered activity found in a few cities but absent from the rest. Although India had 35 cities of over 100,000 population in 1921, most of these remained commercial and administrative centers and not manufacturing centers. That the chief emphasis remained on rural activities can be seen from the fact that these 35 centers of population had a total of 8.2 million inhabitants compared to 310.7 million outside their limits in 1921. In fact, only 30 million persons lived in the 1,623 centers of over 5,000 persons each, while 289 million lived in centers smaller than 5,000 persons.

One of the chief ways in which the impact of Western culture reached India was by education. The charge has frequently been made that the British neglected education in India or that they made an error in emphasizing education in English for the upper classes rather than education in the vernacular languages for the masses of the people. History does not sustain the justice of these charges. In England itself the government assumed little responsibility for education until 1902, and in general had a more advanced policy in this field in India than in England until well into the present century. Until 1835 the English did try to encourage native traditions of education, but their vernacular schools failed from lack of patronage; the Indians themselves objected to being excluded, as they regarded it, from English education. Accordingly, from 1835 the British offered English-language education on the higher levels in the hope that Western science, technology, and political attitudes could be introduced without disrupting religious or social life and that these innovations would "infiltrate" downward into the population. Because of the expense, government-sponsored education had to be restricted to the higher levels, although encouragement for vernacular schools on the lower levels began (without much financial obligation) in 1854. The "infiltration downward" theory was quite mistaken because those who acquired knowledge of English used it as a passport to advancement in government service or professional life and became renegades from, rather than missionaries to, the lower classes of Indian society. In a sense the use of English on the university level of education did not lead to its spread in Indian society but removed those who acquired it from that society, leaving them in a kind of barren ground which was neither Indian nor Western but hovered uncomfortably between the two. The fact that knowledge of English and possession of a university degree could free one from the physical drudgery of Indian life by opening the door to public service or the professions created a veritable passion to obtain these keys (but only in a minority).

The British had little choice but to use English as the language of government and higher education. In India the languages used in these two fields had been foreign ones for centuries. The language of government and of the courts was Persian until 1837. Advanced and middle-level education had always been foreign, in Sanskrit for the Hindus and in Arabic for the Muslims. Sanskrit, a "dead" language, was that of Hindu religious literature, while Arabic was the language of the Koran, the only writing the ordinary Muslim would wish to read. In fact, the allegiance of the Muslims to the Koran and to Arabic was so intense that they refused to participate in the new English-language educational system and, in consequence, had been excluded from government, the professions, and much of the economic life of the country by 1900.

No vernacular language could have been used to teach the really valuable contributions of the West, such as science, technology, economics, agricultural science, or political science, because the necessary vocabulary was lacking in the vernaculars. When the university of the native state of

Hyderabad tried to translate Western works into Urdu for teaching purposes after 1920, it was necessary to create about 40,000 new words. Moreover, the large number of vernacular languages would have made the choice of any one of them for the purpose of higher education invidious. And, finally, the natives themselves had no desire to learn to read their vernacular languages, at least during the nineteenth century; they wanted to learn English because it provided access to knowledge, to government positions, and to social advancement as no vernacular could. But it must be remembered that it was the exceptional Indian, not the average one, who wanted to learn to read at all. The average native was content to remain illiterate, at least until deep into the twentieth century. Only then did the desire to read spread under the stimulus of growing nationalism, political awareness, and growing concern with political and religious tensions. These fostered the desire to read, in order to read newspapers, but this had adverse effects: each political or religious group had its own press and presented its own biased version of world events so that, by 1940, these different groups had entirely different ideas of reality.

Moreover, the new enthusiasm for the vernacular languages, the influence of extreme Hindu nationalists like B. G. Tilak (1859–1920) or anti-Westerners like M. K. Gandhi (1869–1948), led to a wholesale rejection of all that was best in British or in European culture. At the same time, those who sought power, advancement, or knowledge continued to learn English as the key to these ambitions. Unfortunately, these semi-westernized Indians neglected much of the practical side of the European way of life and tended to be intellectualist and doctrinaire and to despise practical learning and physical labor. They lived, as we have said, in a middle world which was neither Indian nor Western, spoiled for the Indian way of life, but often unable to find a position in Indian society which would allow them to live their own version of a Western way of life. At the university they studied literature, law, and political science, all subjects which emphasized verbal accomplishments. Since India did not provide sufficient jobs for such accomplishments, there was a great deal of "academic unemployment," with resulting discontent and growing radicalism. The career of Gandhi was a result of the efforts of one man to avoid this problem by fusing certain elements of Western teaching with a purified Hinduism to create a nationalist Indian way of life on a basically moral foundation.

It is obvious that one of the chief effects of British educational policy has been to increase the social tensions within India and to give them a political orientation. This change is usually called the "rise of Indian nationalism," but it is considerably more complex than this simple name might imply. It began to rise about 1890, possibly under the influence of the misfortunes at the end of the century, grew steadily until it reached the crisis stage after 1917, and finally emerged in the long-drawn crisis of 1930–1947.

India's outlook was fundamentally religious, just as the British outlook was fundamentally political. The average Indian derived from his religious outlook a profound conviction that the material world and physical comfort were irrelevant and unimportant in contrast with such spiritual matters as the proper preparation for the life to come after the body's death. From his English education the average Indian student derived the conviction that liberty and self-government were the highest goods of life and must be sought by such resistance to authority as had been shown in the Magna Carta, the opposition to Charles I, the "Glorious Revolution" of 1689, the writings of John Locke and of John Stuart Mill, and the general resistance to public authority found in nineteenth century liberalism and laissez-faire. These two points of view tended to merge in the minds of Indian intellectuals into a point of view in which it seemed that English political ideals should be sought by Indian methods of religious fervor, self-sacrifice, and contempt for material welfare or physical comforts. As a result, political and social tensions were acerbated between British and Indians, between Westernizers and Nationalists, between Hindus and Muslims, between Brahmins and lower castes, and between caste members and outcastes.

In the early part of the nineteenth century there had been a revival of interest in Indian languages and literatures. This revival soon revealed that many Hindu ideas and practices had no real support in the earliest evidence. Since these later innovations included some of the most objectionable features of Hindu life, such as suttee, child marriage, female inferiority, image worship, and extreme polytheism, a movement began that sought to free Hinduism from these extraneous elements and to restore it to its earlier "purity" by emphasizing ethics, monotheism, and an abstract idea of deity. This tendency was reinforced by the influence of Christianity and of Islam, so that the revived Hinduism was really a synthesis of these three religions. As a consequence of these influences, the old, and basic, Hindu idea of Karma was played down. This idea maintained that each individual soul reappeared again and again, throughout eternity, in a different physical form and in a different social status, each difference being a reward or punishment for the soul's conduct at its previous appearance. There was no real hope for escape from this cycle, except by a gradual improvement through a long series of successive appearances to the ultimate goal of complete obliteration of personality (*Nirvana*) by ultimate mergence in the soul of the universe (*Brahma*). This release (*moksha*) from the endless cycle of existence could be achieved only by the suppression of all desire, of all individuality, and of all will to live.

The belief in Karma was the key to Hindu ideology and to Hindu society, explaining not only the emphasis on fate and resignation to fate, the idea that man was a part of nature and brother to the beasts, the submergence of individuality and the lack of personal ambition, but also specific social institutions such as caste or even suttee. How could castes be ended if these are God-given gradations for the rewards or punishments earned in an earlier existence? How could suttee be ended if a wife is a wife through all eternity, and must pass from one life to another when her husband does?

The influence of Christianity and of Islam, of Western ideas and of British education, in changing Hindu society was largely a consequence of their ability to reduce the average Hindu's faith in Karma. One of the earliest figures in this growing synthesis of Hinduism, Christianity, and Islam was Ram Mohan Roy (1772-1833), founder of the Brahma Samaj Society in 1828. Another was Keshab Chandra Sen (1841-1884), who hoped to unite Asia and Europe into a common culture on the basis of a synthesis of the common elements of these three religions. There were many reformers of this type. Their most notable feature was that they were universalist rather than nationalist and were Westernizers in their basic inclinations. About 1870 a change began to appear, perhaps from the influence of Rama Krishna (1834-1886) and his disciple Swami Vivekananda (1862-1902), founder of Vedanta. This new tendency emphasized India's spiritual power as a higher value than the material power of the West. It advocated simplicity, asceticism, self-sacrific, cooperation, and India's mission to spread these virtues to the world. One of the disciples of this movement was Gopal Krishna Gokhale (1866-1915), founder of the Servants of India Society (1905). This was a small band of devoted persons who took vows of poverty and obedience, to regard all Indians as brothers irrespective of caste or creed, and to engage in no personal quarrels. The members scattered among the most diverse groups of India to teach, to weld India into a single spiritual unit, and to seek social reform.

In time these movements became increasingly nationalistic and anti-Western, tending to defend orthodox Hinduism rather than to purify it and to oppose Westerners rather than to copy them. This tendency culminated in Bal Gangathar Tilak (1859-1920), a Marathi journalist of Poona, who started his career in mathematics and law but slowly developed a passionte love for Hinduism, even in its most degrading details, and insisted that it must be defended against outsiders, even with violence. He was not opposed to reforms which appeared as spontaneous developments of Indian sentiment, but he was violently opposed to any attempt to legislate reform from above or to bring in foreign influences from European or Christian sources. He first became a political figure in 1891 when he vigorously opposed a government bill which would have curtailed child marriage by fixing the age of consent for girls at twelve years. By 1897 he was using his paper to incite to murder and riots against government officials.

A British official who foresaw this movement toward violent nationalism as early as 1878 sought to divert it into more legal and more constructive channels by establishing the Indian National Congress in 1885. The official in question, Allan Octavian Hume (1829–1912), had the secret support of the viceroy, Lord Dufferin. They hoped to assemble each year an unofficial congress of Indian leaders to discuss Indian political matters in the hope that this experience would provide training in the working of representative institutions and parliamentary government. For twenty years the Congress agitated for extension of Indian participation in the administration, and for the extension of representation and eventually of parliamentary government within the British system. It is notable that this movement renounced violent methods, did not seek separation from Britain, and aspired to form a government based on the British pattern.

Support for the movement grew very slowly at first, even among Hindus, and there was open opposition, led by Sir Saiyid Ahmad Khan, among the Muslims. As the movement gathered momentum, after 1890, many British officials began to oppose it. At the same time, under pressure from Tilak, the Congress itself advanced its demands and began to use economic pressure to obtain these. As a result, after 1900, fewer Muslims joined the Congress: there were 156 Muslims out of 702 delegates in 1890, but only 17 out of 756 in 1905. All these forces came to a head in 1904–1907 when the Congress, for the first time, demanded self-government within the empire for India and approved the use of economic pressures (boycott) against Britain.

The Japanese victory over Russia in 1905, which was regarded as an Asiatic triumph over Europe, the Russian revolt of 1905, the growing power of Tilak over Gokhale in the Indian National Congress, and public agitation over Lord Curzon's efforts to push through an administrative division of the huge province of Bengal (population 78 million) brought matters to a head. There was open agitation by Hindu extremists to spill English blood to satisfy the goddess of destruction, Kali. In the Indian National Congress of 1907, the followers of Tilak stormed the platform and disrupted the meeting. Much impressed with the revolutionary violence in Russia against the czar and in Ireland against the English, this group advocated the use of terrorism rather than of petitions in India. The viceroy, Lord Hardinge, was wounded by a bomb in 1912. For many years, racial intolerance against Indians by English residents in India had been growing, and was increasingly manifested in studied insults and even physical assaults. In 1906 a Muslim League was formed in opposition to the Hindu extremists and in support of the British position, but in 1913 it also demanded self-government. Tilak's group boycotted the Indian National Congress for nine years (1907–1916), and Tilak himself was in prison for sedition for six years (1908–1914).

The constitutional development of India did not stand still during this tumult. In 1861 appointive councils with advisory powers had been created, both at the center to assist the viceroy and in the provinces. These had nonofficial as well as official members, and the provincial ones had certain legislative powers, but all these activities were under strict executive control and veto. In 1892 these powers were widened to allow discussion of administrative questions, and various nongovernmental groups (called "communities") were allowed to suggest individuals for the unofficial seats in the councils.

A third act, of 1909, passed by the Liberal government with John (Lord) Morley as secretary of state and Lord Minto as viceroy, enlarged the councils, making a nonofficial majority in the provincial councils, allowed the councils to vote on all issues, and gave the right to elect the nonofficial members to various communal groups, including Hindus, Muslims, and Sikhs, on a fixed ratio. This last provision was a disaster. By establishing separate electoral lists for various religious groups, it encouraged religious extremism in all groups, made it likely that the more extremist candidates would be successful, and made religious differences the basic and irreconcilable fact of political life. By giving religious minorities more seats than their actual proportions of the electorate entitled them to (a principle known as "weightage"), it made it politically advantageous to be a minority. By emphasizing minority rights (in which they did believe) over majority rule (in which they did not believe) the British made religion a permanently disruptive force in political life, and encouraged the resulting acerbated extremism to work out its rivalries outside the constitutional framework and the scope of legal action in riots rather than at the polls or in political assemblies. Moreover, as soon as the British had given the Muslims this special constitutional position in 1909 they lost the support of the Muslim community in 1911–1919. This loss of Muslim support was the result of several factors. Curzon's division of Bengal, which the Muslims had supported (since it gave them East Bengal as a separate area with a Muslim majority) was countermanded in 1911 without any notice to the Muslims. British foreign policy after 1911 was increasingly anti-Turkish, and thus opposed to the caliph (the religious leader of the Muslims). As a result the Muslim League called for self-government for India for the first time in 1913, and four years later formed an alliance with the Indian National Congress which continued until 1924.

In 1909, while Philip Kerr (Lothian), Lionel Curtis, and (Sir) William Marris were in Canada laying the foundations for the Round Table organization there, Marris persuaded Curtis that "self-government, . . .

however far distant was the only intelligible goal of British policy in India . . . the existence of political unrest in India, so far from being a reason for pessimism, was the surest sign that the British, with all their manifest failings, had not shirked their primary duty of extending western education to India and so preparing Indians to govern themselves." Four years later the Round Table group in London decided to investigate how this could be done. It formed a study group of eight members, under Curtis, adding to the group three officials from the India Office. This group decided, in 1915, to issue a public declaration favoring "the progressive realization of responsible government in India." A declaration to this effect was drawn up by Lord Milner and was issued on August 20, 1917, by Secretary of State for India Edwin S. Montagu. It said that "the policy of His Majesty's Government, with which the Government of India are in complete accord, is that of the increasing association of Indians in every branch of the administration and the gradual development of self-governing institutions with a view to the progressive realisation of responsible government in India as an integral part of the British Empire."

This declaration was revolutionary because, for the first time, it specifically enunciated British hopes for India's future and because it used, for the first time, the words "responsible government." The British had spoken vaguely for over a century about "self-government" for India; they had spoken increasingly about "representative government"; but they had consistently avoided the expression "responsible government." This latter term meant parliamentary government, which most English conservatives regarded as quite unsuited for Indian conditions, since it required, they believed, an educated electorate and a homogeneous social system, both of which were lacking in India. The conservatives had talked for years about ultimate self-government for India on some indigenous Indian model, but had done nothing to find such a model. Then, without any clear conception of where they were going, they had introduced "representative government," in which the executive consulted with public opinion through representatives of the people (either appointed, as in 1861, or elected, as in 1909), but with the executive still autocratic and in no way responsible to these representatives. The use of the expression "responsible government" in the declaration of 1917 went back to the Round Table group and ultimately to the Marris-Curtis conversation in the Canadian Rockies in 1909.

In the meantime, the Round Table study-group had worked for three years (1913–1916) on methods for carrying out this promise. Through the influence of Curtis and F. S. Oliver the federal constitution of the United States contributed a good deal to the drafts which were made, especially to provisions for dividing governmental activities into central and provincial portions, with gradual Indianization of the latter and ultimately of the former. This approach to the problem was named "dyarchy" by Curtis. The Round Table draft was sent to the Governor of New South Wales, Lord Chelmsford, a Fellow of All Souls College, who believed that it came from an official committee of the India Office. After he accepted it in principle he was made Viceroy of India in 1916. Curtis went to India immediately to consult with local authorities there (including Meston, Marris, Hailey, and the retired *Times* Foreign Editor, Sir Valentine Chirol) as well as with Indians. From these conferences emerged a report, written by Marris, which was issued as the Montagu-Chelmsford Report in 1917. The provisions of this report were drawn up as a bill, passed by Parliament (after substantial revision by a Joint Committee under Lord Selborne) and became the Government of India Act of 1919.

The Act of 1919 was the most important law in Indian constitutional history before 1935. It divided governmental activities into "central" and "provincial." The former included defense, foreign affairs, railways and communications, commerce, civil and criminal law and procedures and others; the latter included public order and police, irrigation, forests, education, public health, public works, and other activities. Furthermore, the provincial activities were divided into "transferred" departments and "reserved" departments, the former being entrusted to native ministers who were responsible to provincial assemblies. The central government remained in the hands of the governor-general and viceroy, who was responsible to Britain and not to the Indian Legislature. His Cabinet (Executive Council) usually had three Indian members after 1921. The legislature was bicameral, consisting of a Council of State and a Legistive Assembly. In both, some members were appointed officials, but the majority were elected on a very restricted suffrage. There were, on the electoral lists, no more than 900,000 voters for the lower chamber and only 16,000 for the upper chamber. The provincial unicameral legislatures had a wider, but still limited, franchise, with about a million on the list of voters in Bengal, half as many in Bombay. Moreover, certain seats, on the principle of "weightage," were reserved to Muslims elected by a separate Muslim electoral list. Both legislatures had the power to enact laws, subject to rather extensive powers of veto and of decree in the hands of the governor-general and the appointed provincial governors. Only the "transferred" departments of the provincial governments were responsible to elective assemblies, the "reserved" activities on the provincial level and all activities in the central administration being responsible to the appointed governors and governor-general and ultimately to Britain.

It was hoped that the Act of 1919 would provide opportunities in parliamentary procedures, responsible government, and administration to Indians so that self-government could be extended by successive steps later, but these hopes were destroyed in the disasters of 1919–1922. The violence of British reactionaries collided with the nonviolent refusal to cooperate of Mahatma Gandhi, crushing out the hopes of the Round Table reformers between them.

Mohandas Karamchand Gandhi (1869–1948), known as "Mahatma," or "Great Soul," was the son and grandson of prime ministers of a minute princely state in western India. Of the Vaisya caste (third of the four), he grew up in a very religious and ascetic atmosphere of Hinduism. Married at thirteen and a father at fifteen, Gandhi was sent to England to study law by his older brother when he was seventeen. Such a voyage was forbidden by the rules of his caste, and he was expelled from it for going. Before he left he gave a vow to his family not to touch wine, women, or meat. After three years in England he passed the bar at Inner Temple. Most of his time in Europe was passed in dilettante fads, experimenting with vegetarian diets and self-administered medicines or in religious or ethical discussions with English faddists and Indiophiles. He was much troubled by religious scruples and feelings of guilt. Back in India in 1891, he was a failure as a lawyer because of his inarticulate lack of assurance and his real lack of interest in the law. In 1893 a Muslim firm sent him to Natal, South Africa, on a case. There Gandhi found his vocation.

The population of Natal in 1896 consisted of 50,000 Europeans, mostly English, 400,000 African natives, and 51,000 Indians, chiefly outcastes. The last group had been imported from India, chiefly as indentured workers on three or five-year contracts, to work the humid lowland plantations where the Negroes refused to work. Most of the Indians stayed, after their contracts were fulfilled, and were so industrious and intelligent that they began to rise very rapidly in an economic sense, especially in the retail trades. The whites, who were often indolent, resented such competition from dark-skinned persons and were generally indignant at Indian economic success. As Lionel Curtis told Gandhi in the Transvaal in 1903, "It is not the vices of Indians that Europeans in this country fear but their virtues."

When Gandhi first arrived in Natal in 1893, he found that that country, like most of South Africa, was rent with color hatred and group animosities. All political rights were in the hands of whites, while the nonwhites were subjected to various kinds of social and economic discriminations and segregations. When Gandhi first appeared in court, the judge ordered him to remove his turban (worn with European clothes); Gandhi refused, and left. Later, traveling on business in a first-class railway carriage to the Transvaal, he was ejected from the train at the insistence of a white passenger. He spent a bitterly cold night on the railway platform rather than move to a second- or third-class compartment when he had been sold a first-class ticket. For the rest of his life he traveled only third class. In the Transvaal he was unable to get a room in a hotel because of his color. These episodes gave him his new vocation: to establish that Indians were citizens of the British Empire and therefore entitled to equality under its laws. He was determined to use only peaceful methods of passive mass noncooperation to achieve his goal. His chief weapon would be love and submissiveness, even to those who treated him most brutally. His refusal to fear death or to avoid pain and his efforts to return love to those who tried to inflict injuries upon him made a powerful weapon, especially if it were practiced on a mass basis.

Gandhi's methods were really derived from his own Hindu tradition, but certain elements in this tradition had been reinforced by reading Ruskin, Thoreau, Tolstoi, and the Sermon on the Mount. When he was brutally beaten by whites in Natal in 1897, he refused to prosecute, saying that it was not their fault that they had been taught evil ideas.

These methods gave the Indians of South Africa a temporary respite from the burden of intolerance under Gandhi's leadership in the period 1893–1914. When the Transvaal proposed an ordinance compelling all Indians to register, be fingerprinted, and carry identity cards at all times, Gandhi organized a mass, peaceful refusal to register. Hundreds went to jail. Smuts worked out a compromise with Gandhi: if the Indians would register "voluntarily" the Transvaal would repeal the ordinance. After Gandhi had persuaded his compatriots to register, Smuts failed to carry out his part of the agreement, and the Indians solemnly burned their registration cards at a mass meeting. Then, to test the Transvaal ban on Indian immigration, Gandhi organized mass marches of Indians into the Transvaal from Natal. Others went from the Transvaal to Natal and returned, being arrested for crossing the frontier. At one time 2,500 of the 13,000 Indians in the Transvaal were in jail and 6,000 were in exile.

The struggle was intensified after the creation of the Union of South Africa in 1910 because the Transvaal restrictions on Indians, which forbade them to own land, to live outside segregated districts, or to vote, were not repealed, and a Supreme Court decision of 1913 declared all non-Christian marriages to be legally invalid. This last decision deprived most nonwhite wives and children of all legal protection of their family rights. Mass civil disobedience by Indians increased, including a march by 6,000 from Natal to the Transvaal. Finally, after much controversy, Gandhi and Smuts worked out an elaborate compromise agreement in 1914. This revoked some of the discriminations against Indians in South Africa, recognized Indian marriages, annulled a discriminatory £3 annual tax on Indians, and stopped all importation of indentured labor from India in 1920. Peace was restored in this civil controversy just in time to permit a united front in the external war with Germany. But in South Africa by 1914 Gandhi had worked out the techniques he would use against the British in India after 1919.

Until 1919 Gandhi was very loyal to the British connection. Both in South Africa and in India he had found that the English from England were much more tolerant and understanding than most of the English-speaking whites of middle-class origin in the overseas areas. In the Boer War he was the active leader of an 1,100-man Indian ambulance corps which worked with inspiring courage even under fire on the field of battle. During World War I, he worked constantly on recruiting campaigns for the British forces. On one of these in 1915 he said, "I discovered that the British Empire had certain ideals with which I have fallen in love, and one of these ideals is that every subject of the British Empire has the freest scope possible for his energy and honor and whatever he thinks is due to his conscience." By 1918 this apostle of nonviolence was saying: "We are regarded as a cowardly people. If we want to become free from that reproach, we should learn to use arms. . . . Partnership in the Empire is our definite goal. We should suffer to the utmost of our ability and even lay down our lives to defend the Empire. If the Empire perishes, with it perishes our cherished aspiration."

During this period Gandhi's asceticism and his opposition to all kinds of discrimination were winning him an outstanding moral position among the Indian people. He was opposed to all violence and bloodshed, to alcohol, meat, and tobacco, even to the eating of milk and eggs, and to sex (even in marriage). More than this, he was opposed to Western industrialism, to Western science and medicine, and to the use of Western rather than Indian languages. He demanded that his followers make fixed quotas of homespun cotton each day, wore a minimum of homespun clothing himself, spun on a small wheel throughout all his daily activities, and took the small hand spinning wheel as the symbol of his movement— all this in order to signify the honorable nature of handwork, the need for Indian economic self-sufficiency, and his opposition to Western industrialism. He worked for equality for the untouchables, calling them "God's children" (Harijans), associating with them whenever he could, taking them into his own home, even adopting one as his own daughter. He worked to relieve economic oppression, organizing strikes against low wages or miserable working conditions, supporting the strikers with money he had gathered from India's richest Hindu industrialists. He attacked Western medicine and sanitation, supported all kinds of native medical nostrums and even quackery, yet went to a Western-trained surgeon for an operation when he had appendicitis himself. Similarly he preached against the use of milk, but drank goat's milk for his health much of his life. These inconsistencies he attributed to his own weak sinfulness. Similarly, he permitted handspun cotton to be sewn on Singer sewing machines, and conceded that Western-type factories were necessary to provide such machines.

During this period he discovered that his personal fasts from food,

which he had long practiced, could be used as moral weapons against
those who opposed him while they strengthened his moral hold over
those who supported him. "I fasted," he said, "to reform those who loved
me. You cannot fast against a tyrant." Gandhi never seemed to recognize that his fasting and nonviolent civil disobedience were effective
against the British in India and in South Africa only to the degree
that the British had the qualities of humanity, decency, generosity, and
fair play which he most admired, but that by attacking the British through
these virtues he was weakening Britain and the class which possessed
these virtues and making it more likely that they would be replaced by
nations and by leaders who did not have these virtues. Certainly Hitler
and the Germans who exterminated six million Jews in cold bood during
World War II would not have shared the reluctance of Smuts to imprison a few thousand Indians or Lord Halifax's reluctance to see Gandhi
starve himself to death. This was the fatal weakness of Gandhi's aims and
his methods, but these aims and methods were so dear to Indian hearts
and so selflessly pursued by Gandhi that he rapidly became the spiritual
leader of the Indian National Congress after Gokhale's death in 1915.
In this position Gandhi by his spiritual power succeeded in something
which no earlier Indian leader had achieved and few had hoped for: he
spread political awareness and nationalist feeling from the educated class
down into the great uneducated mass of the Indian people.

This mass and Gandhi expected and demanded a greater degree of self-
government after the end of World War I. The Act of 1919 provided
that, and probably provided as much of it as the political experience
of Indians entitled them to. Moreover, the Act anticipated expansion of
the areas of self-government as Indian political experience increased. But
the Act was largely a failure, because Gandhi had aroused political ambitions in great masses of Indians who lacked experience in political
activities, and these demands gave rise to intense opposition to Indian
self-government in British circles which did not share the ideals of the
Round Table group. Finally, the actions of this British opposition drove
Gandhi from "nonresistance" through complete "noncooperation," to
"civil disobedience," thus destroying the whole purpose of the Act of
1919.

Many British conservatives both at home and in India opposed the
Act of 1919. Lord Ampthill, who had long experience in India and had
valiantly supported Gandhi in South Africa, attacked the Act and
Lionel Curtis for making it. In the House of Lords he said: "The incredible fact is that, but for the chance visit to India of a globe-trotting
doctrinaire with a positive mania for constitution-mongering [Curtis],
nobody in the world would ever have thought of so peculiar a notion as
Dyarchy. And yet the Joint [Selborne] Committee tells us in an airy

manner that no better plan can be conceived." In India men like the governor of the Punjab, Sir Michael O'Dwyer, were even more emphatically opposed to Indian self-government or Indian nationalist agitation. Many Conservatives who were determined to maintain the empire intact could not see how this could be done without India as the major jewel in it, as in the nineteenth century. India not only provided a large share of the manpower in the peacetime imperial army, but this army was largely stationed in India and paid for out of the revenues of the Government of India. Moreover, this self-paying manpower pool was beyond the scrutiny of the British reformer as well as the British taxpayer. The older Tories, with their strong army connections, and others, like Winston Churchill, with an appreciation of military matters, did not see how England could face the military demands of the twentieth century without Indian military manpower, at least in colonial areas.

Instead of getting more freedom at the end of the war in 1918, the Indians got less. The conservative group pushed through the Rowlatt Act in March 1919. This continued most of the wartime restrictions on civil liberties in India, to be used to control nationalist agitations. Gandhi called for civil disobedience and a series of scattered local general strikes (*hartels*) in protest. These actions led to violence, especially to Indian attacks on the British. Gandhi bewailed this violence, and inflicted a seventy-two-hour fast on himself as penance.

In Amritsar an Englishwoman was attacked in the street (April 10, 1919). The Congress Party leaders in the city were deported, and Brigadier R. E. H. Dyer was sent to restore order. On arrival he prohibited all processions and meetings; then, without waiting for the order to be publicized, went with fifty men to disperse with gunfire a meeting already in progress (April 13, 1919). He fired 1,650 bullets into a dense crowd packed in a square with inadequate exits, inflicting 1,516 casualties, of which 379 met death. Leaving the wounded untended on the ground, General Dyer returned to his office and issued an order that all Indians passing through the street where the Englishwoman had been assaulted a week before must do so by crawling on hands and knees. There is no doubt that General Dyer was looking for trouble. In his own words: "I had made up my mind I would do all men to death. . . . It was no longer a question of merely dispersing the crowd, but one of producing a sufficient moral effect from a military point of view not only on those who were present, but more especially throughout the Punjab."

The situation might still have been saved from Dyer's barbarity but the Hunter Committee, which investigated the atrocity, refused to condemn Dyer except for "a grave error of judgment" and "an honest but mistaken conception of duty." A majority of the House of Lords approved his action by refusing to censure him, and, when the government forced him to resign from the army, his admirers in England presented him with a sword and a purse of £20,000.

At this point Gandhi committed a grave error of judgment. In order to solidify the alliance of Hindu and Muslim which had been in existence since 1917, he supported the Khilafat movement of Indian Muslims to obtain a lenient peace treaty for the Turkish sultan (and caliph) following World War I. Gandhi suggested that the Khilafat adopt "noncooperation" against Britain to enforce its demands. This would have involved a boycott of British goods, schools, law courts, offices, honors, and of all goods subject to British taxes (such as alcohol). This was an error of judgment because the sultan was soon overthrown by his own people organized in a Turkish Nationalist movement and seeking a secularized Turkish state, in spite of all Britain was already doing (both in public and in private) to support him. Thus, the Khilafat movement was seeking to force Britain to do something it already wanted to do and was not able to do. Moreover, by bringing up "noncooperation" as a weapon against the British, Gandhi had opened a number of doors he had no desire to open, with very bad consequences for India.

At the Indian National Congress of December, 1919, Tilak and Gandhi were the leading figures. Both were willing to accept the Montagu-Chelmsford Reforms, Tilak because he believed this would be the best way to prove that they were not adequate. But on August 1, 1920, Gandhi proclaimed "noncooperation" in behalf of the Khilafat movement. On the same day Tilak died, leaving Gandhi as undisputed leader of the Congress. At the 1920 meeting he won unanimous approval for "noncooperation," and then moved a resolution for *swaraj* (self-rule) either within or outside the British Empire. The Muslims in Congress, led by Muhammad Ali Jinnah, refused to accept an independent India outside the British Empire because this would subject the Muslims to a Hindu majority without Britain's protecting restraint. As a result, from that point, many Muslims left the Congress.

Noncooperation was a great public success. But it did not get self-rule for India, and made the country less fitted for self-rule by making it impossible for Indians to get experience in government under the Act of 1919. Thousands of Indians gave up medals and honors, gave up the practice of law in British courts, left the British schools, and burned British goods. Gandhi held great mass meetings at which thousands of persons stripped themselves of their foreign clothing to throw it on raging bonfires. This did not, however, give them training in government. It merely roused nationalist violence. On February 1, 1922, Gandhi informed the viceroy that he was about to begin mass civil disobedience, in one district at a time, beginning in Bardoli near Bombay. Civil disobedience, including refusal to pay taxes or obey the laws, was a step beyond noncooperation, since it involved illegal acts rather than legal ones. On February 5, 1922, a Hindu mob attacked twenty-two police constables and killed them by burning the police station down over their heads. In horror Gandhi canceled the campaign against Britain. He was at once arrested and condemned to six years in prison for sedition.

Very great damage had been done by the events of 1919–1922. Britain and India were alienated to the point where they no longer trusted one another. The Congress Party itself had been split, the moderates forming a new group called the Indian Liberal Federation. The Muslims had also left the Congress Party to a large extent and gone to strengthen the Muslim League. From this point onward, Muslim-Hindu riots were annual occurrences in India. And finally the boycott had crippled the Montagu-Chelmsford Reforms, almost two-thirds of the eligible voters refusing to vote in the Councils elections of November, 1920.

IRELAND TO 1939

While the Indian crisis was at its height in 1919–1922, an even more violent crisis was raging in Ireland. Throughout the nineteenth century Ireland had been agitated by grievances of long standing. The three major problems were agrarian, religious, and political. The Cromwellian conquest of Ireland in the seventeenth century had transferred much Irish land, as plunder of war, to absentee English landlords. In consequence high rents, insecure tenure, lack of improvements, and legalized economic exploitation, supported by English judges and English soldiers, gave rise to violent agrarian unrest and rural atrocities against English lives and properties.

Beginning with Gladstone's Land Act of 1870, the agrarian problems were slowly alleviated and, by 1914, were well in hand. The religious problem arose from the fact that Ireland was overwhelmingly Roman Catholic, and resented being ruled by persons of a different religion. Moreover, until the Irish (Episcopal) Church was disestablished in 1869, Irish Catholics had to support a structure of Anglican clergy and bishops, most of whom had few or no parishioners in Ireland and resided in England, supported by incomes from Ireland. Finally, the Act of Union of 1801 had made Ireland a part of the United Kingdom, with representatives in the Parliament at Westminster.

By 1871 those representatives who were opposed to union with England formed the Irish Home Rule Party. It sought to obtain separation by obstructing the functions of Parliament and disrupting its proceedings. At times this group exercised considerable influence in Parliament by holding a balance of power between Liberals and Conservatives. The Gladstone Liberals were willing to give Ireland Home Rule, with no representatives at Westminster; the Conservatives (with the support of a majority of Englishmen) were opposed to Home Rule; the Rhodes-Milner group wanted self-government for the Irish in their home affairs with Irish representatives retained at Westminster for foreign and imperial matters. The Liberal government of 1906–1916 tried to enact a Home Rule bill with continued Irish representation in the House of Commons, but was repeatedly blocked by the opposition of the House of Lords; the bill did not become law until September, 1914.

The chief opposition arose from the fact that Protestant Ulster (Northern Ireland) would be submerged in an overwhelmingly Catholic Ireland. The Ulster opposition, led by Sir Edward (later Lord) Carson, organized a private army, armed it with guns smuggled from Germany, and prepared to seize control of Belfast at a signal from London. Carson was on his way to the telegraph station to send this signal in 1914 when he received a message from the prime minister that war was about to break out with Germany. Accordingly, the Ulster revolt was canceled and the Home Rule Act was suspended until six months after the peace with Germany. As a consequence the revolt with German arms in Ireland was made by the Irish Nationalists in 1916, instead of by their Ulster opponents in 1914. This so-called Easter Revolt of 1916 was crushed and its leaders executed, but discontent continued to simmer in Ireland, with violence only slightly below the surface.

In the parliamentary election of 1918, Ireland elected 6 Nationalists (who wanted Home Rule for all Ireland), 73 Sinn Fein (who wanted an Irish Republic free from England), and 23 Unionists (who wanted to remain part of Britain). Instead of going to Westminster, the Sinn Fein organized their own Parliament in Dublin. Efforts to arrest its members led to open civil war. This was a struggle of assassination, treachery, and reprisal, fought out in back alleys and on moonlit fields. Sixty thousand British troops could not maintain order. Thousands of lives were lost, with brutal inhumanity on both sides, and property damage rose to £50 million in value.

Lionel Curtis, who helped edit *The Round Table* in 1919–1921, advocated in the March 1920 issue that Northern Ireland and Southern Ireland be separated and each given Home Rule as autonomous parts of Great Britain. This was enacted into law eight months later as the Government of Ireland Act of 1920, but was rejected by the Irish Republicans led by Eamon de Valera. The civil war continued. The Round Table group worked valiantly to stop the extremists on both sides, but with only moderate success. Amery's brother-in-law, Hamar (Lord) Greenwood, was appointed chief secretary for Ireland, the last incumbent of that post, while Curtis was appointed adviser on Irish affairs to the Colonial Office (which was headed by Milner and Amery). *The Times* and *The Round Table* condemned British repression in Ireland, the latter saying, "If the British Commonwealth can only be preserved by such means, it would become a negation of the principle for which it has stood." But British violence could not be curtailed until Irish violence could be curtailed. One of the chief leaders of the Irish Republicans was Erskine Childers, an old schoolboy friend of Curtis who had been with him in South Africa, but nothing could be done through him, since he had become fanatically anti-British. Accordingly, Smuts was called in. He wrote a conciliatory speech for King George to deliver at the opening of the Ulster Parliament, and made a secret visit to the rebel hiding place in Ireland to try to persuade the Irish Republican leaders to be reasonable. He contrasted the insecurity of the Transvaal Republic before 1895 with its happy condition under dominion status since 1910, saying: "Make no mistake about it, you have more privilege, more power, more peace, more security in such a sisterhood of equal nations than in a small, nervous republic having all the time to rely on the good will and perhaps the assistance of foreigners. What sort of independence do you call that?"

Smuts arranged an armistice and a conference to negotiate a settlement. From this conference, at which Curtis was secretary, came the Articles of Agreement of December, 1921, which gave Southern Ireland dominion status as the Irish Free State, Northern Ireland continuing under the Act of 1920. The boundary line between the two countries was drawn by a committee of three of which the British member (and chairman) was Richard Feetham of Milner's Kindergarten and the Round Table group, later Supreme Court judge in South Africa.

De Valera's Irish Republicans refused to accept the settlement, and went into insurrection, this time against the moderate Irish leaders, Arthur Griffith and Michael Collins. Collins was assassinated, and Griffith died, exhausted by the strain, but the Irish people themselves were now tired of turmoil. De Valera's forces were driven underground and were defeated in the election of 1922. When De Valera's party, the Fianna Fail, did win an election in 1932 and he became President of Ireland, he abolished the oath of loyalty to the king and the office of governor-general, ended annual payments on seized English lands and appeals to the Privy Council, engaged in a bitter tariff war with Britain, and continued to demand the annexation of Ulster. One of the last links with Britain was ended in 1938, when the British naval bases in Eire were turned over to the Irish, to the great benefit of German submarines in 1939–1945.

The Far East to World War I

THE COLLAPSE OF CHINA TO 1920

The destruction of traditional Chinese culture under the impact of Western Civilization was considerably later than the similar destruction of Indian culture by Europeans. This delay arose from the fact that European pressure on India was applied fairly steadily from the early sixteenth century, while in the Far East, in Japan even more completely than in China, this pressure was relaxed from the early seventeenth century for almost two hundred years, to 1794 in the case of China and to 1854 in the case of Japan. As a result, we can see the process by which European culture was able to destroy the traditional native cultures of Asia more clearly in China than almost anywhere else.

The traditional culture of China, as elsewhere in Asia, consisted of a military and bureaucratic hierarchy superimposed on a great mass of hardworking peasantry. It is customary, in studying this subject, to divide this hierarchy into three levels. Politically, these three levels consisted of the imperial authority at the top, an enormous hierarchy of imperial and provincial officials in the middle, and the myriad of semi-patriarchal, semidemocratic local villages at the bottom. Socially, this hierarchy was similarly divided into the ruling class, the gentry, and the peasants. And, economically, there was a parallel division, the upper-most group deriving its incomes as tribute and taxes from its possession of military and political power, while the middle group derived its incomes from economic sources, as interest on loans, rents from lands, and the profits of commercial enterprise, as well as from the salaries, graft, and other emoluments arising from his middle group's control of the bureaucracy. At the bottom the peasantry, which was the only really productive group in the society, derived its incomes from the sweat of its collective brows, and had to survive on what was left to it after a substantial fraction of its product had gone to the two higher groups in the form of rents, taxes, interest, customary bribes (called "squeeze"), and excessive profits on such purchased "necessities" of life as salt, iron, or opium.

Although the peasants were clearly an exploited group in the traditional society of China, this exploitation was impersonal and traditional and thus more easily borne than if it had been personal or arbitrary. In the course of time, a workable system of customary relationships had come into existence among the three levels of society. Each group knew its established relationships with the others, and used those relationships to avoid any sudden or excessive pressures which might disrupt the established patterns of the society. The political and military force of the imperial regime rarely impinged directly on the peasantry, since the bureaucracy intervened between them as a protecting buffer. This buffer followed a pattern of deliberate amorphous inefficiency so that the military and political force from above had been diffused, dispersed, and blunted by the time it reached down to the peasant villages. The bureaucracy followed this pattern because it recognized that the peasantry was the source of its incomes, and it had no desire to create such discontent as would jeopardize the productive process or the payments of rents, taxes, and interest on which it lived. Furthermore, the inefficiency of the system was both customary and deliberate, since it allowed a large portion of the wealth which was being drained from the peasantry to be diverted and diffused among the middle class of gentry before the remnants of it reached the imperial group at the top.

This imperial group, in its turn, had to accept this system of inefficiency and diversion of incomes and its own basic remoteness from the peasantry because of the great size of China, the ineffectiveness of its systems of transportation and communications, and the impossibility of keeping records of population, or of incomes and taxes except through the indirect mediation of the bureaucracy. The semiautonomous position of the bureaucracy depended, to a considerable extent, on the fact that the Chinese system of writing was so cumbersome, so inefficient, and so difficult to learn that the central government could not possibly have kept any records or have administered tax collection, public order, or justice except through a bureaucracy of trained experts. This bureaucracy was recruited from the gentry because the complex systems of writing, of law, and of administrative traditions could be mastered only by a group possessing leisure based on unearned incomes. To be sure, in time, the training for this bureaucracy and for the examinations admitting to it became quite unrealistic, consisting largely of memorizing of ancient literary texts for examination purposes rather than for any cultural or administrative ends. This was not so bad as it sounds, for many of the memorized texts contained a good deal of ancient wisdom with an ethical or practical slant, and the possession of this store of knowledge engendered in its possessors a respect for moderation and for tradition which was just what the system required. No one regretted that the system of education and of examinations leading to the bureaucracy did not engender a thirst for efficiency, because efficiency was not a quality which anyone desired. The bureaucracy itself did not desire efficiency because this would have reduced its ability to divert the funds flowing upward from the peasantry.

The peasantry surely did not want any increase in efficiency, which would have led to an increase in pressure on it and would have made it less easy to blunt or to avoid the impact of imperial power. The imperial power itself had little desire for any increased efficiency in its bureaucracy, since this might have led to increased independence on the part of the bureaucracy. So long as the imperial superstructure of Chinese society obtained its share of the wealth flowing upward from the peasantry, it was satisfied. The share of this wealth which the imperial group obtained was very large, in absolute figures, although proportionately it was only a small part of the total amount which left the peasant class, the larger part being diverted by the gentry and bureaucracy on its upward flow.

The exploitative nature of this three-class social system was alleviated, as we have seen, by inefficiency, by traditional moderation and accepted ethical ideas, by a sense of social interdependence, and by the power of traditional law and custom which protected the ordinary peasant from arbitrary treatment or the direct impact of force. Most important of all, perhaps, the system was alleviated by the existence of careers open to talent. China never became organized into hereditary groups or castes, being in this respect like England and quite unlike India. The way was open to the top in Chinese society, not for any individual peasant in his own lifetime, but to any individual peasant family over a period of several generations. Thus an individual's position in society depended, not on the efforts of his own youth, but on the efforts of his father and grandfather.

If a Chinese peasant was diligent, shrewd, and lucky, he could expect to accumulate some small surplus beyond the subsistence of his own family and the drain to the upper classes. This surplus could be invested in activities such as iron-making, opium selling, lumber or fuel selling, pig-trading and such. The profits from these activities could then be invested in small bits of land to be rented out to less fortunate peasants or in loans to other peasants. If times remained good, the owner of the surpluses began to receive rents and interest from his neighbors; if times became bad he still had his land or could take over his debtor's land as forfeited collateral on his loan. In good times or bad, the growth of population in China kept the demand for land high, and peasants were able to rise in the social scale from peasantry to gentry by slowly expanding their legal claims over land. Once in the gentry, one's children or grandchildren could be educated to pass the bureaucratic examinations and be admitted to the group of mandarins. A family which had a member or two in this group gained access to the whole system of "squeeze" and of bureaucratic diversion of income flows, so that the family as a whole could continue to rise in the social and economic structure. Eventually some member of the family might move into the imperial center from the provincial level on which this rise began, and might even gain access to the imperial ruling group itself.

In these higher levels of the social structure many families were able to maintain a position for generations, but in general there was a steady, if slow, "circulation of the elite," most families remaining in a high social position for only a couple of generations, after about three generations of climb, to be followed by a couple of generations of decline. Thus, the old American saying that it took only three generations "from shirt-sleeves to shirtsleeves" would, in the old China, have to be extended to allow about six or seven generations from the rice paddy's drudgery back to the rice paddy again. But the hope of such a rise contributed much to increase individual diligence and family solidarity and to reduce peasant discontent. Only in the late nineteenth and early twentieth century did peasants in China come to regard their positions as so hopeless that violence became preferable to diligence or conformity. This change arose from the fact, as we shall see, that the impact of Western culture on China did, in fact, make the peasant's position economically hopeless.

In traditional Chinese society the bureaucrats recruited through examinations from the gentry class were called mandarins. They became, for all practical purposes, the dominant element in Chinese society. Since their social and economic position did not rest on political or military power but on traditions, the legal structure, social stability, accepted ethical teachings, and the rights of property, this middle-level group gave Chinese society a powerful traditionalist orientation. Respect for old traditions, for the accepted modes of thought and action, for the ancestors in society and religion, and for the father in the family became the salient characteristics of Chinese society. That this society was a complex network of vested interests, was unprogressive, and was shot through with corruption was no more objectionable to the average Chinese, on any level, than the fact that it was also shot through with inefficiency.

These things became objectionable only when Chinese society came directly in contact with European culture during the nineteenth century. As these two societies collided, inefficiency, unprogressiveness, corruption, and the whole nexus of vested interests and traditions which constituted Chinese society was unable to survive in contact with the efficiency, the progressiveness, and the instruments of penetration and domination of Europeans. A system could not hope to survive which could not provide itself with firearms in large quantities or with mass armies of loyal soldiers to use such weapons, a system which could not increase its taxes or its output of wealth or which could not keep track of its own population or its own incomes by effective records or which

had no effective methods of communication and transportation over an
area of 3.5 million square miles.

The society of the West which began to impinge on China about
1800 was powerful, efficient, and progressive. It had no respect for the
corruption, the traditions, the property rights, the family solidarity, or
the ethical moderation of traditional Chinese society. As the weapons of
the West, along with its efficient methods of sanitation, of writing, of
transportation and communications, of individual self-interest, and of
corrosive intellectual rationalism came into contact with Chinese society,
they began to dissolve it. On the one hand, Chinese society was too
weak to defend itself against the West. When it tried to do so, as in
the Opium Wars and other struggles of 1841–1861, or in the Boxer uprising of 1900, such Chinese resistance to European penetration was
crushed by the armaments of the Western Powers, and all kinds of concessions to these Powers were imposed on China.

Until 1841 Canton was the only port allowed for foreign imports, and
opium was illegal. As a consequence of Chinese destruction of illegal
Indian opium and the commercial exactions of Cantonese authorities,
Britain imposed on China the treaties of Nanking (1842) and of Tientsin (1858). These forced China to cede Hong Kong to Britain and to
open sixteen ports to foreign trade, to impose a uniform import tariff
of no more than 5 percent, to pay an indemnity of about $100 million,
to permit foreign legations in Peking, to allow a British official to act
as head of the Chinese customs service, and to legalize the import of
opium. Other agreements were imposed by which China lost various
fringe areas such as Burma (to Britain), Indochina (to France), Formosa and the Pescadores (to Japan), and Macao (to Portugal), while
other areas were taken on leases of various durations, from twenty-five
to ninety-nine years. In this way Germany took Kiaochow, Russia took
southern Liaotung (including Port Arthur), France took Kwangcho-
wan, and Britain took Kowloon and Weihaiwei. In this same period
various Powers imposed on China a system of extraterritorial courts
under which foreigners, in judicial cases, could not be tried in Chinese
courts or under Chinese law.

The political impact of Western civilization on China, great as it
was, was overshadowed by the economic impact. We have already indicated that China was a largely agrarian country. Years of cultivation
and the slow growth of population had given rise to a relentless pressure
on the soil and to a destructive exploitation of its vegetative resources.
Most of the country was deforested, resulting in shortage of fuel, rapid
runoff of precipitation, constant danger of floods, and large-scale erosion
of the soil. Cultivation had been extended to remote valleys and up the
slopes of hills by population pressures, with a great increase in the
same destructive consequences, in spite of the fact that many slopes

were rebuilt in terraces. The fact that the southern portion of the country depended on rice cultivation created many problems, since this crop, of relatively low nutritive value, required great expenditure of labor (transplanting and weeding) under conditions which were destructive of good health. Long periods of wading in rice paddies exposed most peasants to various kinds of joint diseases, and to water-borne infections such as malaria or parasitical flukes.

The pressure on the soil was intensified by the fact that 60 percent of China was over 6,000 feet above sea level, too high for cultivation, while more than half the land had inadequate rainfall (below twenty inches a year). Moreover, the rainfall was provided by the erratic monsoon winds which frequently brought floods and occasionally failed completely, causing wholesale famine. In the United States 140 million people were supported by the labor of 6.5 million farmers on 365 million acres of cultivated land in 1945; China, about the same time, had almost 500 million persons supported by the labor of 65 million farmers on only 217 million acres of cultivated land. In China the average farm was only a little over four acres (compared to 157 in the United States) but was divided into five or six separate fields and had, on the average, 6.2 persons living on it (compared to 4.2 persons on the immensely larger American farm). As a result, in China there was only about half an acre of land for each person living on the land, compared to the American figure of 15.7 acres per person.

As a consequence of this pressure on the land, the average Chinese peasant had, even in earlier times, no margin above the subsistence level, especially when we recall that a certain part of his income flowed upward to the upper classes. Since, on his agricultural account alone, the average Chinese peasant was below the subsistence level, he had to use various ingenious devices to get up to that level. All purchases of goods produced off the farm were kept at an absolute minimum. Every wisp of grass, fallen leaf, or crop residue was collected to serve as fuel. All human waste products, including those of the cities, were carefully collected and restored to the soil as fertilizer. For this reason, farmlands around cities, because of the greater supply of such wastes, were more productive than more remote farms which were dependent on local supplies of such human wastes. Collection and sale of such wastes became an important link in the agricultural economics of China. Since the human digestive system extracts only part of the nutritive elements in food, the remaining elements were frequently extracted by feeding such wastes to swine, thus passing them through the pig's digestive system before these wastes returned to the soil to provide nourishment for new crops and, thus, for new food. Every peasant farm had at least one pig which was purchased young, lived in the farm latrine until it was full grown, and then was sold into the city to provide a cash margin for such necessary purchases as salt, sugar, oils, or iron products. In a somewhat similar way the rice paddy was able to contribute to the farmer's supply of proteins by acting as a fishpond and an aquarium for minute freshwater shrimp.

In China, as in Europe, the aims of agricultural efficiency were quite different from the aims of agricultural efficiency in new countries, such as the United States, Canada, Argentina, or Australia. In these newer countries there was a shortage of labor and a surplus of land, while in Europe and Asia there was a shortage of land and a surplus of labor. Accordingly, the aim of agricultural efficiency in newer lands was high output of crops per unit of labor. It was for this reason that American agriculture put such emphasis on labor-saving agricultural machinery and soil-exhausting agricultural practices, while Asiatic agriculture put immense amounts of hand labor on small amounts of land in order to save the soil and to win the maximum crop from the limited amount of land. In America the farmer could afford to spend large sums for farm machinery because the labor such machinery replaced would have been expensive anyway and because the cost of that machinery was spread over such a large acreage that its cost per acre was relatively moderate. In Asia there was no capital for such expenditures on machinery because there was no margin of surplus above subsistence in the hands of the peasantry and because the average farm was so small that the cost of machinery per acre (either to buy or even to operate) would have been prohibitive.

The only surplus in Asia was of labor, and every effort was made, by putting more and more labor on the land, to make the limited amount of land more productive. One result of this investment of labor in land in China can be seen in the fact that about half of the Chinese farm acreage was irrigated while about a quarter of it was terraced. Another result of this excess concentration of labor on land was that such labor was underemployed and semi-idle for about three-quarters of the year, being fully busy only in the planting and harvest seasons. From this semi-idleness of the Asiatic rural population came the most important effort to supplement peasant incomes through rural handicrafts. Before we turn to this crucial point, we should glance at the relative success of China's efforts to achieve high-unit yields in agriculture.

In the United States, about 1940, each acre of wheat required 1.2 man-days of work each year; in China an acre of wheat took 26 man-days of labor. The rewards of such expenditures of labor were quite different. In China the output of grain for each man-year of labor was 3,080 pounds; in the United States the output was 44,000 pounds per man-year of labor. This low productivity of agricultural labor in China would have been perfectly acceptable if China had, instead, achieved high output per acre. Unfortunately, even in this alternative aim China was only moderately successful, more successful than the United States, it is true, but far less successful than European countries which aimed at the same type of agricultural efficiency (high yields per acre) as China did. This can be seen from the following figures:

OUTPUT PER ACRE

IN RICE		IN WHEAT	
United States	47 bushels	United States	14 bushels
China	67 bushels	China	16 bushels
Italy	93 bushels	England	32 bushels

These figures indicate the relative failure of Chinese (and other Asiatic) agriculture even in terms of its own aims. This relative failure was not caused by lack of effort, but by such factors as (1) farms too small for efficient operation; (2) excessive population pressure which forced farming onto less productive soil and which drew more nutritive elements out of the soil than could be replaced, even by wholesale use of human wastes as fertilizer; (3) lack of such scientific agricultural techniques as seed selection or crop rotation; and (4) the erratic character of a monsoon climate on a deforested and semieroded land.

Because of the relatively low productivity of Chinese (and all Asiatic) agriculture, the whole population was close to the margin of subsistence and, at irregular intervals, was forced below that margin into widespread famine. In China the situation was alleviated to some extent by three forces. In the first place, the irregular famines which we have mentioned, and somewhat more frequent onslaughts of plague disease, kept the population within manageable bounds. These two irregular occurrences reduced the population by millions, in both China and India, when they occurred. Even in ordinary years the death rate was high, about 30 per thousand in China compared to 25 in India, 12.3 in England, or 8.7 in Australia. Infant mortality (in the first year of life) was about 159 per thousand in China compared to 240 in India, about 70 in western Europe, and about 32 in New Zealand. At birth an infant could be expected to live less than 27 years in India, less than 35 years in China, about 60 years in England or the United States, and about 66 years in New Zealand (all figures are about 1930). In spite of this "expectation of death" in China, the population was maintained at a high level by a birth rate of about 38 per thousand of the population compared to 34 in India, 18 in the United States or Australia, and 15 in England. The skyrocketing effect which the use of modern sanitary or medical practices might have upon China's population figures can be gathered from the fact that about three-quarters of Chinese deaths are from causes which are preventable (usually easily preventable) in the West. For example, a quarter of all deaths are from diseases spread by human wastes; about 10 percent come from childhood diseases like smallpox, measles, diphtheria, scarlet fever, and whooping cough; about 15 percent arise from tuberculosis; and about 7 percent are in childbirth.

The birthrate was kept up, in traditional Chinese society as a consequence of a group of ideas which are usually known as "ancestor worship." Every Chinese family had, as its most powerful motivation, the conviction that the family line must be continued in order to have descendants to keep up the family shrines, to maintain the ancestral graves, and to support the living members of the family after their productive years had ended. The expense of such shrines, graves, and old persons was a considerable burden on the average Chinese family and a cumulative burden as well, since the diligence of earlier generations frequently left a family with shrines and graves so elaborate that upkeep alone was a heavy expense to later generations. At the same time the urge to have sons kept the birth rate up and led to such undesirable social practices, in traditional Chinese society, as infanticide, abandonment, or sale of female offspring. Another consequence of these ideas was that more well-to-do families in China tended to have more children than poor families. This was the exact opposite of the situation in Western civilization, where a rise in the economic scale resulted in the acquisition of a middle-class outlook which included restriction of the family's offspring.

The pressure of China's population on the level of subsistence was relieved to some extent by wholesale Chinese emigration in the period after 1800. This outward movement was toward the less settled areas of Manchuria, Mongolia, and southwestern China, overseas to America and Europe, and, above all, to the tropical areas of southeastern Asia (especially to Malaya and Indonesia). In these areas, the diligence, frugality, and shrewdness of the Chinese provided them with a good living and in some cases with considerable wealth. They generally acted as a commercial middle class pushing inward between the native Malaysian or Indonesian peasants and the upper group of ruling whites. This movement, which began centuries ago, steadily accelerated after 1900 and gave rise to unfavorable reactions from the non-Chinese residents of these areas. The Malay, Siamese, and Indonesians, for example, came to regard the Chinese as economically oppressive and exploitative, while the white rulers of these areas, especially in Australia and New Zealand, regarded them with suspicion for political and racial reasons. Among the causes of this political suspicion were that emigrant Chinese remained loyal to their families at home and to the homeland itself, that they were generally excluded from citizenship in areas to which they emigrated, and that they continued to be regarded as citizens by successive Chinese governments. The loyalty of emigrant Chinese to their families at home became an important source of economic strength to these families and to China itself, because emigrant Chinese sent very large savings back to their families.

We have already mentioned the important role played by peasant handicrafts in traditional Chinese society. It would, perhaps, not be any real exaggeration to say that peasant handicrafts were the factor which permitted the traditional form of society to continue, not only in China but in all of Asia. This society was based on an inefficient agricultural system in which the political, military, legal, and economic claims of the upper classes drained from the peasantry such a large proportion of their agricultural produce that the peasant was kept pressed down to the subsistence level (and, in much of China, below this level). Only by this process could Asia support its large urban populations and its large numbers of rulers, soldiers, bureaucrats, traders, priests, and scholars (none of whom produced the food, clothing, or shelter they were consuming). In all Asiatic countries the peasants on the land were underemployed in agricultural activities, because of the seasonal nature of their work. In the course of time there had grown up a solution to this social-agrarian problem: in their spare time the peasantry occupied themselves with handicrafts and other nonagricultural activities and then sold the products of their labor to the cities for money to be used to buy necessities. In real terms this meant that the agricultural products which were flowing from the peasantry to the upper classes (and generally from rural areas to the cities) were replaced in part by handicrafts, leaving a somewhat larger share of the peasants' agricultural products in the hands of peasants. It was this arrangement which made it possible for the Chinese peasantry to raise their incomes up to the subsistence level.

The importance of this relationship should be obvious. If it were destroyed, the peasant would be faced with a cruel alternative: either he could perish by falling below the subsistence level or he could turn to violence in order to reduce the claims which the upper classes had on his agricultural products. In the long run every peasant group was driven toward the second of these alternatives. As a result, all Asia by 1940 was in the grip of a profound political and social upheaval because, a generation earlier the demand for the products of peasants' handicrafts had been reduced.

The destruction of this delicately balanced system occurred when cheap, machine-made products of Western manufacture began to flow into Asiatic countries. Native products such as textiles, metal goods, paper, wood carvings, pottery, hats, baskets, and such found it increasingly difficult to compete with Western manufactures in the markets of their own cities. As a result, the peasantry found it increasingly difficult to shift the legal and economic claims which the upper, urban, classes held against them from agricultural products to handicraft products. And, as a consequence of this, the percentage of their agricultural products which was being taken from the peasantry by the claims of other classes began to rise.

This destruction of the local market for native handicrafts could have been prevented if high customs duties had been imposed on European industrial goods. But one point on which the European Powers were agreed was that they would not allow "backward" countries to exclude their products with tariffs. In India, Indonesia, and some of the lesser states of southeastern Asia this was prevented by the European Powers taking over the government of the areas; in China, Egypt, Turkey, Persia, and some Malay states the European Powers took over no more than the financial system or the customs service. As a result, countries like China, Japan, and Turkey had to sign treaties maintaining their tariffs at 5 or 8 percent and allowing Europeans to control these services. Sir Robert Hart was head of the Chinese customs from 1863 to 1906, just as Sir Evelyn Baring (Lord Cromer) was head of the Egyptian financial system from 1879 to 1907, and Sir Edgar Vincent (Lord D'Abernon) was the chief figure in the Turkish financial system from 1882 to 1897.

As a consequence of the factors we have described, the position of the Chinese peasant was desperate by 1900, and became steadily worse. A moderate estimate (published in 1940) showed that 10 percent of the farm population owned 53 percent of the cultivated land, while the other 90 percent had only 47 percent of the land. The majority of Chinese farmers had to rent at least some land, for which they paid, as rent, from one-third to one-half of the crop. Since their incomes were not adequate, more than half of all Chinese farmers had to borrow each year. On borrowed grain the interest rate was 85 percent a year; on money loans the interest rate was variable, being over 20 percent a year on nine-tenths of all loans made and over 50 percent a year on one-eighth of the loans made. Under such conditions of landownership, rental rates, and interest charges, the future was hopeless for the majority of Chinese farmers long before 1940. Yet the social revolution in China did not come until after 1940.

The slow growth of the social revolution in China was the result of many influences. Chinese population pressure was relieved to some extent in the last half of the nineteenth century by the famines of 1877–1879 (which killed about 12 million people), by the political disturbances of the Tai-Ping and other rebellions in 1848–1875 (which depopulated large areas), and by the continued high death rate. The continued influence of traditional ideas, especially Confucianism and respect for ancestral ways, held the lid on this boiling pot until this influence was destroyed in the period after 1900. Hope that some solution might be found by the republican regime after the collapse of the imperial regime in 1911 had a similar effect. And, lastly, the distribution of European weapons in Chinese society was such as to hinder rather than to assist revolution until well into the twentieth century. Then this distribution turned in a direction quite different from that in Western civilization. These last three points are sufficiently important to warrant a closer examination.

We have already mentioned that effective weapons which are difficult to use or expensive to obtain encourage the development of authoritarian regimes in any society. In the late medieval period, in Asia, cavalry provided such a weapon. Since the most effective cavalry was that of the pastoral Ural–Altaic-speaking peoples of central Asia, these peoples were able to conquer the peasant peoples of Russia, of Anatolia, of India, and of China. In the course of time, the alien regimes of three of these areas (not in Russia) were able to strengthen their authority by the acquisition of effective, and expensive, artillery. In Russia, the princes of Moscow, having been the agents of the Mongols, replaced them by becoming their imitators, and made the same transition to a mercenary army, based on cavalry and artillery, as the backbone of the ruling despotism. In Western civilization similar despotisms, but based on infantry and artillery, were controlled by figures like Louis XIV, Frederick the Great, or Gustavus Adolphus. In Western Civilization, however, the Agricultural Revolution after 1725 raised standards of living, while the Industrial Revolution after 1800 so lowered the cost of firearms that the ordinary citizen of western Europe and of North America could acquire the most effective weapon existing (the musket). As a result of this, and other factors, democracy came to these areas, along with mass armies of citizen-soldiers. In central and southern Europe where the Agricultural and Industrial revolutions came late or not at all, the victory of democracy was also late and incomplete.

In Asia generally, the revolution in weapons (meaning muskets and later rifles) came before the Agricultural Revolution or the Industrial Revolution. Indeed, most firearms were not locally made, but were imported and, being imported, came into the possession of the upper class of rulers, bureaucrats, and landlords and not into the hands of peasants or city masses. As a result, these ruling groups were generally able to maintain their position against their own masses even when they could not defend themselves against European Powers. As a consequence of this, any hope of partial reform or of a successful revolution early enough to be a moderate revolution became quite unlikely. In Russia and in Turkey it required defeat in a foreign war with European states to destroy the corrupt imperial regimes (1917–1921). Earlier, the czar had been able to crush the revolt of 1905, because the army remained loyal to the regime, while the sultan, in 1908, had to yield to a reform movement because it was supported by the army. In India, Malaya, and Indonesia the disarmed native peoples offered no threat of revolt to the ruling European Powers before 1940. In Japan the army, as we shall see, remained loyal to the regime and was able to dominate events so that no revolution was conceivable before 1940. But in China the trend of events was much more complex.

In China the people could not get weapons because of their low standards of living and the high cost of imported arms. As a result, power remained in the hands of the army, except for small groups who were financed by emigrant Chinese with relatively high incomes overseas. By 1911 the prestige of the imperial regime had fallen so low that it obtained support from almost no one, and the army refused to sustain it. As a result, the revolutionaries, supported by overseas money, were able to overthrow the imperial regime in an almost bloodless revolution, but were not able to control the army after they had technically come to power. The army, leaving the politicians to squabble over forms of government or areas of jurisdiction, became independent political powers loyal to their own chiefs ("warlords"), and supported themselves and maintained their supply of imported arms by exploiting the peasantry of the provinces. The result was a period of "warlordism" from 1920 to 1941.

In this period the Republican government was in nominal control of the whole country but was actually in control only of the seacoast and river valleys, chiefly in the south, while various warlords, operating as bandits, were in control of the interior and most of the north. In order to restore its control to the whole country, the Republican regime needed money and imported arms. Accordingly, it tried two expedients in sequence. The first expedient, in the period 1920–1927, sought to restore its power in China by obtaining financial and military support from foreign countries (Western countries, Japan, or Soviet Russia). This expedient failed, either because these foreign Powers were unwilling to assist or (in the case of Japan and Soviet Russia) were willing to help only on terms which would have ended China's independent political status. As a consequence, after 1927, the Republican regime underwent a profound change, shifting from a democratic to an authoritarian organization, changing its name from Republican to Nationalist, and seeking the money and arms to restore its control over the country by making an alliance with the landlord, commercial, and banking classes of the eastern Chinese cities. These propertied classes could provide the Republican regime with the money to obtain foreign arms in order to fight the warlords of the west and north, but these groups would not support any Republican effort to deal with the social and economic problems facing the great mass of the Chinese peoples.

While the Republican armies and the warlords were struggling with each other over the prostrate backs of the Chinese masses, the Japanese attacked China in 1931 and 1937. In order to resist the Japanese it became necessary, after 1940, to arm the Chinese masses. This arming of the masses of Chinese in order to defeat Japan in 1941–1945 made it impossible to continue the Republican regime after 1945 so long as it continued to be allied with the upper economic and social groups of China, since the masses regarded these groups as exploiters. At the same time, changes to more expensive and more complex weapons made it impossible either for warlordism to revive or for the Chinese masses to use their weapons to establish a democratic regime. The new weapons, like airplanes and tanks, could not be supported by peasants on a provincial basis nor could they be operated by peasants. The former fact ended warlordism, while the latter fact ended any possibility of democracy. In view of the low productivity of Chinese agriculture and the difficulty of accumulating sufficient capital either to buy or to manufacture such expensive weapons, these weapons (in either way) could be acquired only by a government in control of most of China and could be used only by a professional army loyal to that government. Under such conditions it was to be expected that such a government would be authoritarian and would continue to exploit the peasantry (in order to accumulate capital either to buy such weapons abroad or to industrialize enough to make them at home, or both).

From this point of view the history of China in the twentieth century presents five phases, as follows:

1. The collapse of the imperial regime, to 1911
2. The failure of the Republic, 1911–1920
3. The struggle with warlordism, 1920–1941

   a. Efforts to obtain support abroad, 1920–1927
   b. Efforts to obtain support from the propertied groups, 1927–1941

4. The struggle with Japan, 1931–1945
5. The authoritarian triumph, 1945–

The collapse of the imperial regime has already been discussed as a political and economic development. It was also an ideological development. The authoritarian and traditionalist ideology of the old China, in which social conservatism, Confucianist philosophy, and ancestor worship were intimately blended together, was well fitted to resist the intrusion of new ideas and new patterns of action. The failure of the imperial regime to resist the military, economic, and political penetration of Western Civilization gave a fatal blow to this ideology. New ideas of Western origin were introduced, at first by Christian missionaries and later by Chinese students who had studied abroad. By 1900 there were thousands of such students. They had acquired Western ideas which were completely incompatible with the older Chinese system. In general, such Western ideas were not traditionalist or authoritarian, and were, thus, destructive to the Chinese patriarchal family, to ancestor worship, or to the imperial autocracy. The students brought back from abroad Western ideas of science, of democracy, of parliamentarianism, of empiricism, of self-reliance, of liberalism, of individualism, and of pragmatism. Their possession of such ideas made it impossible for them to fit into their own country. As a result, they attempted to change it, developing a revolutionary fervor which merged with the antidynastic secret societies which had existed in China since the Manchus took over the country in 1644.

Japan's victory over China in 1894–1895 in a war arising from a dispute over Korea, and especially the Japanese victory over Russia in the war of 1904–1905, gave a great impetus to the revolutionary spirit in China because these events seemed to show that an Oriental country could adopt Western techniques successfully. The failure of the Boxer movement in 1900 to expel Westerners without using such Western techniques also increased the revolutionary fervor in China. As a consequence of such events, the supporters of the imperial regime began to lose faith in their own system and in their own ideology. They began to install piecemeal, hesitant, and ineffective reforms which disrupted the imperial system without in any way strengthening it. Marriage between Manchu and Chinese was sanctioned for the first time (1902); Manchuria was opened to settlement by Chinese (1907); the system of imperial examinations based on the old literary scholarship for admission to the civil service and the mandarinate were abolished and a Ministry of Education, copied from Japan, was established (1905); a drafted constitution was published providing for provincial assemblies and a future national parliament (1908); the law was codified (1910).

These concessions did not strengthen the imperial regime, but merely intensified the revolutionary feeling. The death of the emperor and of Dowager Empress Tzu Hsi, who had been the real ruler of the country (1908), brought to the throne a two-year-old child, P'u-I. The reactionary elements made use of the regency to obstruct reform, dismissing the conservative reform minister Yüan Shih-k'ai (1859–1916). Discovery of the headquarters of the revolutionists at Hankow in 1911 precipitated the revolution. While Dr. Sun Yat-sen (1866–1925) hurried back to China from abroad, whence he had directed the revolutionary movement for many years, the tottering imperial regime recalled Yüan Shih-K'ai to take command of the antirevolutionary armies. Instead he cooperated with the revolutionists, forced the abdication of the Manchu dynasty, and plotted to have himself elected as president of the Chinese Republic. Sun Yat-sen who had already been elected provisional president by the

National Assembly at Nanking, accepted this situation, retiring from office, and calling on all Chinese to support President Yüan.

The contrast between Dr. Sun and General Yüan, the first and second presidents of the Chinese Republic, was as sharp as could be. Dr. Sun was a believer in Western ideas, especially in science, democracy, parliamentary government, and socialism, and had lived for most of his life as an exile overseas. He was self-sacrificing, idealistic, and somewhat impractical. General Yüan, on the other hand, was purely Chinese, a product of the imperial bureaucracy, who had no knowledge of Western ideas and no faith in either democracy or parliamentary government. He was vigorous, corrupt, realistic, and ambitious. The real basis of his power rested in the new westernized army which he had built up as governor-general of Chihli in 1901–1907. In this force there were five divisions, well trained and completely loyal to Yüan. The officers of these units had been picked and trained by Yüan, and played principal roles in Chinese politics after 1916.

As president, Yüan opposed almost everything for which Dr. Sun had dreamed. He expanded the army, bribed politicians, and eliminated those who could not be bribed. The chief support of his policies came from a £25 million loan from Britain, France, Russia, and Japan in 1913. This made him independent of the assembly and of Dr. Sun's political party, the Kuomintang, which dominated the assembly. In 1913 one element of Sun's followers revolted against Yüan but were crushed. Yüan dissolved the Kuomintang, arrested its members, dismissed the Parliament, and revised the constitution to give himself dictatorial powers as president for life, with the right to name his own successor. He was arranging to have himself proclaimed emperor when he died in 1916.

As soon as Yüan died, the military leaders stationed in various parts of the country began to consolidate their power on a local basis. One of them even restored the Manchu dynasty, but it was removed again within two weeks. By the end of 1916 China was under the nominal rule of two governments, one at Peking under Feng Kuo-chang (one of Yüan's militarists) and a secession government at Canton under Dr. Sun. Both of these functioned under a series of fluctuating paper constitutions, but the real power of both was based on the loyalty of local armies. Because in both cases the armies of more remote areas were semi-independent, government in those areas was a matter of negotiation rather than of commands from the capital. Even Dr. Sun saw this situation sufficiently clearly to organize the Cantonese government as a military system with himself as generalissimo (1917). Dr. Sun was so unfitted for this military post that on two occasions he had to flee from his own generals to security in the French concession at Shanghai (1918 and 1922). Under such conditions Dr. Sun was unable to achieve any of his pet schemes, such as the vigorous political education of the Chinese people, a widespread network of Chinese railways built with foreign capital, or the industrialization of China on a socialist basis. Instead, by 1920, warlordism was supreme, and the Westernized Chinese found opportunity to exercise their new knowledge only in education and in the diplomatic service. Within China itself, command of a well-drilled army in control of a compact group of local provinces was far more valuable than any Westernized knowledge acquired as a student abroad.

THE RESURGENCE OF JAPAN TO 1918

The history of Japan in the twentieth century is quite distinct from that of the other Asiatic peoples. Among the latter the impact of the West led to the disruption of the social and economic structure, the abandonment of the traditional ideologies, and the revelation of the weakness of native political and military systems. In Japan these events either did not occur or occurred in a quite different fashion. Until 1945 Japan's political and military systems were strengthened by Western influences; the older Japanese ideology was retained, relatively intact, even by those who were most energetic copiers of Western ways; and the changes in the older social and economic structure were kept within manageable limits and were directed in a progressive direction. The real reason for these differences probably rests in the ideological factor—that the Japanese, even the vigorous Westernizers, retained the old Japanese point of view and, as a consequence, were allied with the older Japanese political, economic, and social structure rather than opposed to it (as, for example, Westernizers were in India, in China, or in Turkey). The ability of the Japanese to westernize without going into opposition to the basic core of the older system gave a degree of discipline and a sense of unquestioning direction to their lives which allowed Japan to achieve a phenomenal amount of westernization without weakening the older structure or without disrupting it. In a sense until about 1950, Japan took from Western culture only superficial and material details in an imitative way and amalgamated these newly acquired items around the older ideological, political, military, and social structure to make it more powerful and effective. The essential item which the Japanese retained from their traditional society and did not adopt from Western civilization was the ideology. In time, as we shall see, this was very dangerous to both of the societies concerned, to Japan and to the West.

Originally Japan came into contact with Western civilization in the sixteenth century, about as early as any other Asiatic peoples, but, within a hundred years, Japan was able to eject the West, to exterminate most of its Christian converts, and to slam its doors against the entrance of any Western influences. A very limited amount of trade was permitted on a restricted basis, but only with the Dutch and only through the single port of Nagasaki.

Japan, thus isolated from the world, was dominated by the military dictatorship (or shogunate) of the Tokugawa family. The imperial family had been retired to a largely religious seclusion whence it reigned but did not rule. Beneath the shogun the country was organized in a hereditary hierarchy, headed by local feudal lords. Beneath these lords there were, in descending ranks, armed retainers (samurai), peasants, artisans, and merchants. The whole system was, in theory at least, rigid and unchanging, being based on the double justification of blood and of religion. This was in obvious and sharp contrast with the social organization of China, which was based, in theory, on virtue and on educational training. In Japan virtue and ability were considered to be hereditary rather than acquired characteristics, and, accordingly, each social class had innate differences which had to be maintained by restrictions on intermarriage. The emperor was of the highest level, being descended from the supreme sun goddess, while the lesser lords were descended from lesser gods of varying degrees of remoteness from the sun goddess. Such a point of view discouraged all revolution or social change and all "circulation of the elites," with the result that China's multiplicity of dynasties and rise and fall of families was matched in Japan by a single dynasty whose origins ran back into the remote past, while the dominant individuals of Japanese public life in the twentieth century were members of the same families and clans which were dominating Japanese life centuries ago.

From this basic idea flowed a number of beliefs which continued to be accepted by most Japanese almost to the present. Most fundamental was the belief that all Japanese were members of a single breed consisting of many different branches or clans of superior or inferior status, depending on their degree of relationship to the imperial family. The individual was of no real significance, while the families and the breed were of major significance, for individuals lived but briefly and possessed little beyond what they received from their ancestors to pass on to their descendants. In this fashion it was accepted by all Japanese that society was more important than any individual and could demand any sacrifice from him, that men were by nature unequal and should be prepared to serve loyally in the particular status into which each had been born, that society is nothing but a great patriarchal system, that in this system authority is based on the personal superiority of man over man and not on any rule of law, that, accordingly, all law is little more than some temporary order from some superior being, and that all non-Japanese, lacking divine ancestry, are basically inferior beings, existing only one cut above the level of animals and, accordingly, having no basis on which to claim any consideration, loyalty, or consistency of treatment at the hands of Japanese.

This Japanese ideology was as antithetical to the outlook of the Christian West as any which the West encountered in its contacts with other civilizations. It was also an ideology which was peculiarly fitted to resist the intrusion of Western ideas. As a result, Japan was able to accept and to incorporate into its way of life all kinds of Western techniques and material culture without disorganizing its own outlook or its own basic social structure.

The Tokugawa Shogunate was already long past its prime when, in 1853, the "black ships" of Commodore Matthew Perry sailed into Tokyo Bay. That these vessels could move against the wind, and carried guns more powerful than any the Japanese had ever imagined, was a great shock to the natives of Nippon. The feudal lords who had been growing restive under Tokugawa rule used this event as an excuse to end that rule. These lords, especially the representatives of four western clans, demanded that the emergency be met by abolishing the shogunate and restoring all authority to the hands of the emperor. For more than a decade the decision whether to open Japan to the West or to try to continue the policy of exclusion hung in the balance. In 1863–1866 a series of naval demonstrations and bombardments of Japanese ports by Western Powers forced the opening of Japan and imposed on the country a tariff agreement which restricted import duties to 5 percent until 1899. A new and vigorous emperor came to the throne and accepted the resignation of the last shogun (1867). Japan at once embarked on a policy of rapid Westernization.

The period in Japanese history from the so-called Meiji Restoration of 1867 to the granting of a constitution in 1889 is of the most vital importance. In theory what had occurred had been a restoration of Japan's rule from the hands of the shogun back into the hands of the emperor. In fact what occurred was a shift in power from the shogun to the leaders of four western Japanese clans who proceeded to rule Japan in the emperor's name and from the emperor's shadow. These four clans of Satsuma, Choshu, Hizen, and Tosa won the support of certain nobles of the imperial court (such as Saionji and Konoe) and of the richer mercantile families (such as Mitsui) and were able to overthrow the shogun, crush his supporters (in the Battle of Uemo in 1868), and win control of the government and of the emperor himself. The emperor did not assume control of the government, but remained in a semireligious seclusion, too exalted to concern himself with the functioning of the governmental system except in critical emergencies. In such emergencies the emperor generally did no more than issue a statement or order ("imperial rescript") which had been drawn up by the leaders of the Restoration.

These leaders, organized in a shadowy group known as the Meiji oligarchy, had obtained complete domination of Japan by 1889. To cover this fact with camouflage, they unleashed a vigorous propaganda of revived Shintoism and of abject submission to the emperor which culminated in the extreme emperor worship of 1941–1945. To provide an administrative basis for their rule, the oligarchy created an extensive governmental bureaucracy recruited from their supporters and inferior members. To provide an economic basis for their rule, this oligarchy used their political influence to pay themselves extensive pensions and governmental grants (presumably as compensation for the ending of their feudal incomes) and to engage in corrupt business relationships with their allies in the commercial classes (like Mitsui or Mitsubishi). To provide a military basis for their rule, the oligarchy created a new imperial army and navy and penetrated the upper ranks of these so that they were able to dominate these forces as they dominated the civil bureaucracy. To provide a social basis for their rule, the oligarchy created an entirely new peerage of five ranks of nobility recruited from their own members and supporters.

Having thus assured their dominant position in the administrative, economic, military, and social life of Japan, the oligarchy in 1889 drew up a constitution which would assure, and yet conceal, their political domination of the country. This constitution did not pretend to be a product of the Japanese people or of the Japanese nation; popular sovereignty and democracy had no place in it. Instead this constitution pretended to be an emission from the emperor, setting up a system in which all government would be in his name, and all officials would be personally responsible to him. It provided for a bicameral Diet as a legislature. The House of Peers consisted of the new nobility which had been created in 1884, while the House of Representatives was to be elected "according to the law." All legislation had to pass each house by majority vote and be signed by a minister of state.

These ministers, established as a Council of State in 1885, were responsible to the emperor and not to the Diet. Their tasks were carried out through the bureaucracy which was already established. All money appropriations, like other laws, had to obtain the assent of the Diet, but, if the budget was not accepted by this body, the budget of the preceding year was repeated automatically for the following year. The emperor had extensive powers to issue ordinances which had the force of law and required a minister's signature, as did other laws.

This constitution of 1889 was based on the constitution of Imperial Germany and was forced on Japan by the Meiji oligarchy in order to circumvent and anticipate any future agitation for a more liberal constitution based on British, American, or French models. Basically, the form and functioning of the constitution was of little significance, for the country continued to be run by the Meiji oligarchy through their domination of the army and navy, the bureaucracy, economic and social life, and the opinion-forming agencies such as education and religion. In political life this oligarchy was able to control the emperor, the Privy Council, the House of Peers, the judiciary, and the bureaucracy.

This left only one possible organ of government, the Diet, through which the oligarchy might be challenged. Moreover, the Diet had only one means (its right to pass the annual budget) by which it could strike back at the oligarchy. This right was of little significance so long as the oligarchy did not want to increase the budget, since the budget of the previous year would be repeated if the Diet rejected the budget of the following year. However, the oligarchy could not be satisfied with a repetition of an earlier budget, for the oligarchy's chief aim, after they had ensured their own wealth and power, was to westernize Japan rapidly enough to be able to defend it against the pressure of the Great Powers of the West.

All these things required a constantly growing budget, and thus gave the Diet a more important role than it would otherwise have had. This role, however, was more of a nuisance than a serious restriction on the power of the Meiji oligarchy because the power of the Diet could be overcome in various ways. Originally, the oligarchy planned to give the Imperial Household such a large endowment of property that its income would be sufficient to support the army and navy outside the national budget. This plan was abandoned as impractical, although the Imperial Household and all its rules were put outside the scope of the constitution. Accordingly, an alternative plan was adopted: to control the elections to the Diet so that its membership would be docile to the wishes of the Meiji oligarchy. As we shall see, controlling the elections to the Diet was possible, but ensuring its docility was quite a different matter.

The elections to the Diet could be controlled in three ways: by a restricted suffrage, by campaign contributions, and by bureaucratic manipulation of the elections and the returns. The suffrage was restricted for many years on a property basis, so that, in 1900, only one person in a hundred had the right to vote. The close alliance between the Meiji oligarchy and the richest members of the expanding economic system made it perfectly easy to control the flow of campaign contributions. And if these two methods failed, the Meiji oligarchy controlled both the police and the prefectural bureaucracy which supervised the elections and counted the returns. In case of need, they did not hesitate to use these instruments, censoring opposition papers, prohibiting opposition meetings, using violence, if necessary, to prevent opposition voting, and reporting, through the prefects, as elected candidates who had clearly failed to obtain the largest vote.

These methods were used from the beginning. In the first Diet of 1889, gangsters employed by the oligarchy prevented opposition members from entering the Diet chamber, and at least twenty-eight other members were bribed to shift their votes. In the elections of 1892 violence was used, mostly in districts opposed to the government, so that 25 persons were killed and 388 were injured. The government still lost that election but continued to control the Cabinet. It even dismissed eleven prefectural governors who had been stealing votes, as much for their failure to steal enough as for their action in stealing any. When the resulting Diet refused to appropriate for an enlarged navy, it was sent home for eighteen days, and then reassembled to receive an imperial rescript which gave 1.8 million yen over a six-year period from the Imperial Household for the project and went on to order all public officials to contribute one-tenth of their salaries each year for the duration of the naval building program which the Diet had refused to finance. In this fashion, the Diet's control of increased appropriations was circumvented by the Meiji oligarchy's control of the emperor.

In view of the dominant position of the Meiji oligarchy in Japanese life from 1867 until after 1922, it would be a mistake to interpret such occurrences as unruly Diets, the growth of political parties, or even the establishment of adult manhood suffrage (in 1925) as such events would be interpreted in European history. In the West we are accustomed to narrations about heroic struggles for civil rights and individual liberties, or about the efforts of commercial and industrial capitalists to capture at least a share of political and social power from the hands of the landed aristocracy, the feudal nobility, or the Church. We are acquainted with movements by the masses for political democracy, and with agitations by peasants and workers for economic advantages. All these movements, which fill the pages of European history books, are either absent or have an entirely different significance in Japanese history.

In Japan history presents a basic solidarity of outlook and of purpose, punctuated with brief conflicting outbursts which seem to be contradictory and inexplicable. The explanation of this is to be found in the fact that there was, indeed, a solidarity of outlook but that this solidarity was considerably less solid than it appeared, for, beneath it, Japanese society was filled with fissures and discontents. The solidarity of outlook rested on the ideology which we have mentioned. This ideology, sometimes called Shintoism, was propagated by the upper classes, especially by the Meiji oligarchy but was more sincerely embraced by the lower classes, especially by the rural masses, than it was by the oligarchy which propagated it. This ideology accepted an authoritarian, hierarchical, patriarchal society, based on families, clans, and nation, culminating in respect and subordination to the emperor. In this system there was no place for individualism, self-interest, human liberties, or civil rights.

In general, this system was accepted by the mass of the Japanese peoples. As a consequence, these masses allowed the oligarchy to pursue policies of selfish self-aggrandizement, of ruthless exploitation, and of revolutionary economic and social change with little resistance. The peasants were oppressed by universal military service, by high taxes and high interest rates, by low farm prices and high industrial prices, and by the destruction of the market for peasant handicrafts. They revolted briefly and locally in 1884–1885, but were crushed and never revolted again, although they continued to be exploited. All earlier legislation seeking to protect peasant proprietors or to prevent monopolization of the land was revoked in the 1870's.

In the 1880's there was a drastic reduction in the number of landowners, through heavy taxes, high interest rates, and low prices for farm products. At the same time the growth of urban industry began to destroy the market for peasant handicrafts and the rural "putting-out system" of manufacture. In seven years, 1883–1890, about 360,000 peasant proprietors were dispossessed of 5 million yen worth of land because of total tax arrears of only 114,178 yen (or arrears of only one-third yen, that is, 17 American cents, per person). In the same period, owners were dispossessed of about one hundred times as much land by foreclosure of mortgages. This process continued at varying rates, until, by 1940, three-quarters of Japanese peasants were tenants or part-tenants paying rents of at least half of their annual crop.

In spite of their acceptance of authority and Shinto ideology, the pressures on Japanese peasants would have reached the explosive point if safety valves had not been provided for them. Among these pressures we must take notice of that arising from population increase, a problem arising, as in most Asiatic countries, from the introduction of Western medicine and sanitation. Before the opening of Japan, its population had remained fairly stable at 28–30 million for several centuries. This stability arose from a high death rate supplemented by frequent famines and the practice of infanticide and abortion. By 1870 the population began to grow, rising from 30 million to 56 million in 1920, to 73 million in 1940, and reaching 87 million in 1955.

The safety valve in the Japanese peasant world resided in the fact that opportunities were opened, with increasing rapidity, in nonagricultural activities in the period 1870–1920. These nonagricultural activities were made available from the fact that the exploiting oligarchy used its own growing income to create such activities by investment in shipping, railroads, industry, and services. These activities made it possible to drain the growing peasant population from the rural areas into the cities. A law of 1873 which established primogeniture in the inheritance of peasant property made it evident that the rural population which migrated to the cities would be second and third sons rather than heads of families. This had numerous social and psychological results, of which the chief was that the new urban population consisted of men detached from the discipline of the patriarchal family and thus less under the influence of the general authoritarian Japanese psychology and more under the influence of demoralizing urban forces. As a consequence, this group, after 1920, became a challenge to the stability of Japanese society.

In the cities the working masses of Japanese society continued to be exploited, but now by low wages rather than by high rents, taxes, or interest rates. These urban masses, like the rural masses whence they had been drawn, submitted to such exploitation without resistance for a much longer period than Europeans would have done because they continued to accept the authoritarian, submissive Shintoist ideology. They were excluded from participation in political life until the establishment of adult manhood suffrage in 1925. It was not until after this date that any noticeable weakening of the authoritarian Japanese ideology began to appear among the urban masses.

Resistance of the urban masses to exploitation through economic or social organizations was weakened by the restrictions on workers' organizations of all kinds. The general restrictions on the press, on assemblies, on freedom of speech, and on the establishment of "secret" societies were enforced quite strictly against all groups and doubly so against laboring groups. There were minor socialistic and laborers' agitations in the twenty years 1890–1910. These were brought to a violent end in 1910 by the execution of twelve persons for anarchistic agitations. The labor movement did not raise its head again until the economic crisis of 1919–1922.

The low-wage policy of the Japanese industrial system originated in the self-interest of the early capitalists, but came to be justified with the argument that the only commodity Japan had to offer the world, and the only one on which it would construct a status as a Great Power, was its large supply of cheap labor. Japan's mineral resources, including coal, iron, or petroleum, were poor in both quality and quantity; of textile raw materials it had only silk, and lacked both cotton and wool. It had no natural resources of importance for which there was world demand such as were to be found in the tin of Malaya, the rubber of Indonesia, or the cocoa of West Africa; it had neither the land nor the fodder to produce either dairy or animal products as Argentina, Denmark, New Zealand, or Australia. The only important resources it had which could be used to provide export goods to exchange for imported coal, iron, or oil were silk, forest products, and products of the sea. All these required a considerable expenditure of labor, and these products could be sold abroad only if prices were kept low by keeping wage rates down.

Since these products did not command sufficient foreign exchange to allow Japan to pay for the imports of coal, iron, and oil which a Great Power must have, Japan had to find some method by which it could export its labor and obtain pay for it. This led to the growth of manufacturing industries based on imported raw materials and the development of such service activities as fishing and ocean shipping. At an early date Japan began to develop an industrial system in which raw materials such as coal, wrought iron, raw cotton, or wool were imported, fabricated into more expensive and complex forms, and exported again for a higher price in the form of machinery or finished textiles. Other products which were exported included such forest products as tea, carved woods, or raw silk, or such products of Japanese labor as finished silks, canned fish, or shipping services.

The political and economic decisions which led to these developments and which exploited the rural and urban masses of Japan were made by the Meiji oligarchy and their supporters. The decision-making powers in this oligarchy were concentrated in a surprisingly small group of men, in all, no more than a dozen in number, and made up, chiefly, of the leaders of the four western clans which had led the movement against the shogun in 1867. These leaders came in time to form a formal, if extralegal, group known as the *Genro* (or Council of Elder Statesmen). Of this group Robert Reischauer wrote in 1938: "It is these men who have been the real power behind the Throne. It became customary for their opinion to be asked and, more important still, to be followed in all matters of great significance to the welfare of the state. No Premier was ever appointed except from the recommendation of these men who became known as *Genro*. Until 1922 no important domestic legislation, no important foreign treaty escaped their perusal and sanction before it was signed by the Emperor. These men, in their time, were the actual rulers of Japan."

The importance of this group can be seen from the fact that the Genro had only eight members, yet the office of prime minister was held by a Genro from 1885 to 1916, and the important post of president of the Privy Council was held by a Genro from its creation in 1889 to 1922 (except for the years 1890–1892 when Count Oki of the Hizen clan held it for Okuma). If we list the eight Genro with three of their close associates, we shall be setting down the chief personnel of Japanese history in the period covered by this chapter. To such a list we might add certain other significant facts, such as the social origins of these men, the dates of their deaths, and their dominant connections with the two branches of the defense forces and with the two greatest Japanese industrial monopolies. The significance of these connections will appear in a moment.

THE MEIJ OLIGARCHY

SOCIAL ORIGIN	NAME (GENRO MARKED *)	DATE OF DEATH	DOMINATED	LINKED WITH
Choshu	*Ito *Yamagata *Inoue *Katsura	1909 1922 1915 1913	Army	Mitsui
Satsuma	*Oyama *Matsukata Kuroda Yamamoto	1916 1924	Navy	
Hizen	*Okuma	1922	Progressive Party from 1882	
Tosa	Itagaki	1920	Liberal Party from 1881	Mitsubishi
Noble Court	*Saionji	1940	"Last of the Genro" (1924–1940)	Sumitomo

Japanese history from 1890 to 1940 is largely a commentary on this table. We have said that the Meiji Restoration of 1868 resulted from an alliance of four western clans and some court nobles against the shogunate and that this alliance was financed by commercial groups led by Mitsui. The leaders of this movement who were still alive after 1890 came to form the Genro, the real but unofficial rulers of Japan. As the years passed and the Genro became older and died, their power became weaker, and there arose two claimants to succeed them: the militarists and the political parties. In this struggle the social groups behind the political parties were so diverse and so corrupt that their success was never in the realm of practical politics. In spite of this fact, the struggle between the militarists and the political parties looked fairly even until 1935, not because of any strength or natural ability in the ranks of the latter but simply because Saionji, the "Last of the Genro" and the only non-clan member in that select group, did all he could to delay or to avoid the almost inevitable triumph of the militarists.

All the factors in this struggle and the political events of Japanese history arising from the interplay of these factors go back to their roots in the Genro as it existed before 1900. The political parties and Mitsubishi were built up as Hizen-Tosa weapons to combat the Choshu-

Satsuma domination of the power nexus organized on the civilian-military bureaucracy allied with Mitsui; the army-navy rivalry (which appeared in 1912 and became acute after 1931) had its roots in an old competition between Choshu and Satsuma within the Genro; while the civilian-militarist struggle went back to the personal rivalry between Ito and Yamagata before 1900. Yet, in spite of these fissures and rivalries, the oligarchy as a whole generally presented a united front against outside groups (such as peasants, workers, intellectuals, or Christians) in Japan itself or against non-Japanese.

From 1882 to 1898 Ito was the dominant figure in the Meiji oligarchy, and the most powerful figure in Japan. As minister of the Imperial Household, he was charged with the task of drawing up the constitution of 1889; as president of the Privy Council, he guided the deliberations of the assembly which ratified this constitution; and as first prime minister of the new Japan, he established the foundations on which it would operate. In the process he entrenched the Sat-Cho oligarchy so firmly in power that the supporters of Tosa and Hizen began to agitate against the government, seeking to obtain what they regarded as their proper share of the plums of office.

In order to build up opposition to the government, they organized the first real political parties, the Liberal Party of Itagaki (1881) and the Progressive Party of Okuma (1882). These parties adopted liberal and popular ideologies from bourgeois Europe, but, generally, these were not sincerely held or clearly understood. The real aim of these two groups was to make themselves so much of a nuisance to the prevailing oligarchy that they could obtain, as a price for relaxing their attacks, a share of the patronage of public office and of government contracts. Accordingly, the leaders of these parties, again and again, sold out their party followers in return for these concessions, generally dissolving their parties, to re-create them at some later date when their discontent with the prevailing oligarchy had risen once again. As a result, the opposition parties vanished and reappeared, and their leaders moved into and out of public office in accordance with the whims of satisfied or discontented personal ambitions.

Just as Mitsui became the greatest industrial monopoly of Japan on the basis of its political connections with the prevalent Sat-Cho oligarchy, so Mitsubishi became Japan's second greatest monopoly on the basis of its political connections with the opposition groups of Tosa-Hizen. Indeed, Mitsubishi began its career as the commercial firm of the Tosa clan, and Y. Iwasaki, who had managed it in the latter role, continued to manage it when it blossomed into Mitsubishi. Both of these firms, and a handful of other monopolistic organizations which grew up later, were completely dependent for their profits and growth on political connections.

The task of building Japan into a modern industrial power in a single lifetime required enormous capital and stable markets. In a poor country like Japan, coming late into the industrial era, both of these requirements could be obtained from the government, and in no other way. As a result business enterprise became organized in a few very large monopolistic structures, and these (in spite of their size) never acted as independent powers, even in economic matters, but cooperated in a docile fashion with those who controlled government expenditures and government contracts. Thus they cooperated with the Meiji oligarchy before 1922, with the political party leaders in 1922–1932, and with the militarists after 1932. Taken together, these monopolistic industrial and financial organizations were known as *zaibatsu*. There were eight important organizations of this kind in the period after World War I, but three were so powerful that they dominated the other five, as well as the whole economic system. These three were Mitsui, Mitsubishi, and Sumitomo (controlled by Saionji's relatives). These competed with one another in a halfhearted fashion, but such competition was political rather than economic, and always remained within the rules of a system which they all accepted.

In the period 1885–1901, during which Ito was premier four times, Matsukata twice, and Yamagata twice, it became evident that the oligarchy could not be controlled by the Diet or by the Tosa-Hizen political parties but could always rule Japan through its control of the emperor, the armed forces, and the civil bureaucracy. This victory was hardly established before a rivalry appeared between Ito, supported by the civil bureaucracy, and Yamagata, supported by the armed services. By 1900 Yamagata won a decisive victory over Ito and formed his second Cabinet (1898–1900), from which the Ito group was, for the first time, completely excluded. During this administration Yamagata extended the franchise from half a million to a million voters in order to obtain city support for imposing taxes on rural lands to pay for military expansion. Far more important than this, he established a law that the ministries of the army and the navy must be headed by Cabinet posts held by active generals and admirals of the highest rank. This law made *civilian* rule of Japan impossible thereafter because no prime minister or member of the Cabinet could fill the two defense posts unless they made concessions to the armed services.

In retaliation for this defeat, Ito made an alliance with the Liberal Party of Itagaki (1900) and took office as prime minister for the third time (1900–1901). But he had little freedom of action, since the minister of war, in accordance with the new law, was Yamagata's man, Katsura, and the minister of the navy was Admiral Yamamoto.

In 1903 Yamagata obtained an imperial rescript forcing Ito to retire from active political life to the shelter of the Privy Council. Ito did so, leaving the Liberal Party and the leadership of the civilian forces to his protégé, Saionji. Yamagata had already retired behind the scenes, but still dominated political life through his protégé, Katsura.

The period 1901–1913 saw an alternation of Katsura and Saionji governments, in which the former clearly controlled the government, while the latter, through the Liberal Party, won large and meaningless victories at the polls. Both in 1908 and in 1912 Saionji's party won easy victories in general elections held while he was in office, and in both cases Katsura forced him out of office in spite of his majority in the Diet.

At this point Katsura's ruthless use of the emperor and the militarists to increase the size and power of the army brought a new factor into Japanese political life by leading to a split with the navy. In 1912, when Saionji and Katsura had each headed two governments since 1901, the former refused to increase the army by two divisions (for service in Korea). Katsura at once threw the Saionji government out of office by having the minister of war resign. When Saionji could find no eligible general willing to serve, Katsura formed his third Cabinet (1912–1913) and created the new divisions.

The navy, alienated by the army's high-handed political tactics, tried to keep Katsura out of office in 1912 by refusing to provide an admiral to serve as minister of the navy. They were defeated when Katsura produced an imperial rescript from the new Emperor Taisho (1912–1926) ordering them to provide an admiral. The navy retaliated the following year by forming an alliance with the Liberals and other anti-Katsura forces, on the grounds that his frequent use of imperial intervention in behalf of the lowest partisan politics was an insult to the exalted sanctity of the imperial position. For the first and only time, in 1913, an imperial rescript was refused acceptance, by the Liberal Party; Katsura had to resign, and a new Cabinet, under Admiral Yamamoto, was formed (1913–1914). This alliance of the navy, the Satsuma clan, and the Liberal Party so enraged the Choshu clan that the military and civilian wings of that group came together on an anti-Satsuma basis.

In 1914 it was revealed that several high admirals had accepted bribes from foreign munitions firms such as German Siemens and British Vickers. Choshu used this as a club to force Yamamoto to resign, but since they could not form a government themselves they called Okuma out of retirement to form a temporary government completely dependent on them. The old man was given a majority in the Diet by turning the existing Liberal Party majority out of office and, in a completely corrupt election, providing a majority for a new Constitutional Believers' Party, which Katsura had created in 1913. Okuma was completely dependent on the Choshu oligarchy (which meant on Yamagata, as Ito died in 1909 and Inoue in 1915). He gave them two new army divisions and a strong anti-Chinese policy, but was replaced by General Terauchi, a Choshu militarist and favorite of Yamagata, in 1916. To provide this new government with less obviously corrupt party support, a deal was made with the Liberal Party. In return for seats in the Diet, places in the bureaucracy, and Mitsui money, this old Tosa party sold out to Choshu militarism, and was provided, by the prefectural governors, with a satisfying majority in the general election of 1916.

Under the Terauchi government, Choshu militarism and Yamagata's personal power reached their culmination. By that time every high officer in the army owed his position to Yamagata's patronage. His old civilian rivals, like Ito or Inoue, were dead. Of the four remaining Genro, only Yamagata, aged eighty-one in 1918, still had his hands on the tiller; Matsukata, aged eighty-four, was a weakling; Okuma, aged eighty-one, was an outsider; and Saionji, aged seventy, was a semioutsider. The emperor, as a result of the protests of 1913, no longer intervened in political life. The political parties were demoralized and subservient, prepared to sacrifice any principle for a few jobs. The economic organizations, led by the great *zaibatsu*, were completely dependent on government subsidies and government contracts. In a word, the controls of the Meiji oligarchy had come almost completely into the hands of one man.

It would be difficult to exaggerate the degree of concentration of power in Japan in the period covered by this chapter. In thirty-three years of Cabinet government, there had been eighteen Cabinets but only nine different premiers. Of these nine premiers, only two (Saionji and Okuma) were not of Choshu or Satsuma, while five were military men.

The growing militarization of Japanese life in the period ending in 1918 had ominous implications for the future. Not only did militarists control growing sectors of Japanese life; they had also succeeded in merging loyalty to the emperor and subservience to militarism into a single loyalty which no Japanese could reject without, at the same time, rejecting his country, his family, and his whole tradition. Even more ominous was the growing evidence that Japanese militarism was insanely aggressive, and prone to find the solution for internal problems in foreign wars.

On three occasions in thirty years, against China in 1894–1895, against Russia in 1904–1905, and against China and Germany in 1914–1918, Japan had entered upon warlike action for purely aggressive purposes. As a consequence of the first action, Japan acquired Formosa and the Pescadores and forced China to recognize the independence of Korea (1895). The subsequent Japanese penetration of Korea led to a rivalry with Russia, whose Trans-Siberian Railway was encouraging her to compensate for her rebuffs in the Balkans by increasing her pressure in the Far East.

In order to isolate the approaching conflict with Russia, Japan signed a treaty with Britain (1902). By this treaty each signer could expect support from the other if it became engaged in war with more than one enemy in the Far East. With Russia thus isolated in the area, Japan attacked the czar's forces in 1904. These forces were destroyed on land by Japanese armies under the Satsuma Genro Oyama, while the Russian fleet of thirty-two vessels, coming from Europe, was destroyed by the Satsuma Admiral Togo in Tsushima Straits. By the Treaty of Portsmouth (1905) Russia renounced her influence in Korea, yielded southern Sakhalin and the lease on Liaotung to Japan, and agreed to a joint renunciation of Manchuria (which was to be evacuated by both Powers and restored to China). Korea, which had been made a Japanese protectorate in 1904, was annexed in 1910.

The outbreak of war in 1914 provided a great opportunity for Japanese expansion. While all the Great Powers were busy elsewhere, the Far East was left to Japan. Declaring war on Germany on August 23, 1914, Nipponese troops seized the German holdings on the Shantung Peninsula and the German Pacific islands north of the equator (Marshall Islands, Marianas, and Carolines). This was followed, almost immediately (January 1915), by presentation of "Twenty-one Demands" on China. These demands at once revealed Japan's aggressive ambitions on the continent of Asia, and led to a decisive change in world opinion about Japan, especially in the United States. As preparation for such demands Japan had been able to build up a very pro-Japanese feeling in most of the Great Powers. Formal agreements or notes had been made with these, recognizing, in one way or another, Japan's special concern with East Asia. In respect to Russia a series of agreements had established spheres of influence. These gave northern Manchuria and western Inner Mongolia as spheres to Russia, and southern Manchuria with eastern Inner Mongolia as spheres for Japan.

A number of diplomatic notes between the United States and Japan had arranged a tacit American acceptance of the Japanese position in Manchuria in return for a Japanese acceptance of the "Open-Door" or free-trade policy in China. The Twenty-one Demands broke this agreement with the United States since they sought to create for Japan a special economic position in China. In combination with the injury inflicted on Japanese pride by the rigid American restrictions on Japanese immigration into the United States, this marked a turning point in Japanese-American feeling from the generally favorable tone which it had possessed before 1915 to the growing unfavorable tone it assumed after 1915.

Unfavorable world opinion forced Japan to withdraw the most extreme of her Twenty-one Demands (those which were concerned with the use of Japanese advisers in various Chinese administrative functions), but many of the others were accepted by China under pressure of a Japanese ultimatum. The chief of these permitted Japan to arrange with Germany regarding the disposition of the German concessions in China without interference from China itself. Other demands, which were accepted, gave Japan numerous commercial, mining, and industrial concessions, mostly in eastern Inner Mongolia and southern Manchuria.

In spite of her growing alienation of world opinion in the years of the First World War, the war brought Japan to a peak of prosperity and power it had not previously attained. The demand for Japanese goods by the belligerent countries resulted in a great industrial boom. The increase in the Japanese fleet and in Japanese territories in the northern Pacific, as well as the withdrawal of her European rivals from the area, gave Japan a naval supremacy there which was formally accepted by the other naval Powers in the Washington Agreements of 1922. And the Japanese advances in northern China made her the preeminent Power in East Asian economic and political life. All in all, the successors of the Meiji Restoration of 1868 could look with profound satisfaction on Japan's progress by 1918.

V

THE FIRST WORLD WAR
1914-1918

The Growth of
International Tensions,
1871-1914

INTRODUCTION

THE unification of Germany in the decade before 1871 ended a balance of power in Europe which had existed for 250 or even 300 years. During this long period, covering almost ten generations, Britain had been relatively secure and of growing power. She had found this power challenged only by the states of western Europe. Such a challenge had come from Spain under Philip II, from France under Louis XIV and under Napoleon, and, in an economic sense, from the Netherlands during much of the seventeenth century. Such a challenge could arise because these states were as rich and almost as unified as Britain herself, but, above all, it could arise because the nations of the West could face seaward and challenge England so long as central Europe was disunited and economically backward.

The unification of Germany by Bismarck destroyed this situation politically, while the rapid economic growth of that country after 1871 modified the situation economically. For a long time Britain did not see this change but rather tended to welcome the rise of Germany because it relieved her, to a great extent, from the pressure of France in the political and colonial fields. This failure to see the changed situation continued until after 1890 because of Bismarck's diplomatic genius, and because of the general failure of non-Germans to appreciate the marvelous organizing ability of the Germans in industrial activities. After 1890 Bismarck's masterful grip on the tiller was replaced by the vacillating hands of Kaiser William II and a succession of puppet chancellors. These incompetents alarmed and alienated Britain by challenging her in commercial, colonial, and especially naval affairs. In commercial matters the British found German salesmen and their agents offering better service, better terms, and lower prices on goods of at least equal quality, and in metric rather than Anglo-Saxon sizes and measurements. In the colonial field after 1884, Germany acquired African colonies which threatened to cut across the continent from east to west and thus checkmate the British ambitions to build a railway from the Cape of Good Hope to Cairo. These colonies included East Africa (Tanganyika), South-West Africa, Cameroons, and Togo. The German threat became greater as a result of German intrigues in the Portuguese colonies of Angola and Mozambique, and above all by the German encouragement of the Boers of the Transvaal and the Orange Free State before their war with Britain in 1899–1902. In the Pacific area Germany acquired by 1902 the Caroline, Marshall, and Marianas Islands, parts of New Guinea and Samoa, and a base of naval and commercial importance at Kiaochau on the Shantung Peninsula of China. In naval affairs Germany presented her greatest threat as a result of the German Naval bills of 1898, 1900, and 1902, which were designed to be an instrument of coercion against Britain. Fourteen German battleships were launched between 1900 and 1905. As a consequence of these activities Britain joined the anti-German coalition by 1907, the Powers of Europe became divided into two antagonistic coalitions, and a series of crises began which led, step by step, to the catastrophe of 1914.

International affairs in the period 1871–1914 can be examined under four headings: (1) the creation of the Triple Alliance, 1871–1890; (2) the creation of the Triple Entente, 1890–1907; (3) the efforts to bridge the gap between the two coalitions, 1890–1914; and (4) the series of international crises, 1905–1914. These are the headings under which we shall examine this subject.

THE CREATION OF THE TRIPLE ALLIANCE, 1871–1890

The establishment of a German Empire dominated by the Kingdom of Prussia left Bismarck politically satisfied. He had no desire to annex any additional Germans to the new empire, and the growing ambitions for colonies and a worldwide empire left him cold. As a satisfied diplomat he concentrated on keeping what he had, and realized that France, driven by fear and vengeance, was the chief threat to the situation. His immediate aim, accordingly, was to keep France isolated. This involved the more positive aim to keep Germany in friendly relations with Russia and the Habsburg Empire and to keep Britain friendly by abstaining from colonial or naval adventures. As part of this policy Bismarck made two tripartite agreements with Russia and Austro-Hungary: (a) the Three Emperors' League of 1873 and (b) the Three Emperors' Alliance of 1881. Both of these were disrupted by the rivalry between Austria and Russia in southeastern Europe, especially in Bulgaria. The Three Emperors' League broke down in 1878 at the Congress of Berlin because of Habsburg opposition to Russia's efforts to create a great satellite state in Bulgaria after her victory in the Russo-Turkish War of 1877. The Three Emperors' Alliance of 1881 broke down in the "Bulgarian crisis" of 1885. This crisis arose over the Bulgarian annexation of Eastern Rumelia, a union which was opposed by Russia but favored by Austria, thus reversing the attitude these Powers had displayed at Berlin in 1878.

The rivalry between Russia and Austria in the Balkans made it clear to Bismarck that his efforts to form a diplomatic front of the three great empires were based on weak foundations. Accordingly, he made a second string for his bow. It was this second string which became the Triple Alliance. Forced to choose between Austria and Russia, Bismarck took the former because it was weaker and thus easier to control. He made an Austro-German alliance in 1879, following the disruption of the Three Emperors' League, and in 1882 expanded it into a Triple Alliance of Germany, Austria, and Italy. This alliance, originally made for five years, was renewed at intervals until 1915. After the disruption of the Three Emperors' Alliance in 1885, the Triple Alliance became the chief weapon in Germany's diplomatic armory, although Bismarck, in order to keep France isolated, refused to permit Russia to drift completely out of the German sphere, and tried to bind Germany and Russia together by a secret agreement of friendship and neutrality known as the Reinsurance Treaty (1887). This treaty, which ran for three years, was not renewed in 1890 after the new Emperor, William II, had discharged Bismarck. The Kaiser argued that the Reinsurance Treaty with Russia was not compatible with the Triple Alliance with Austria and Italy, since Austria and Russia were so unfriendly. By failing to renew, William left Russia and France both isolated. From this condition they naturally moved together to form the Dual Alliance of 1894. Subsequently, by antagonizing Britain, the German government helped to transform this Dual Alliance into the Triple Entente. Some of the reasons why Germany made these errors will be examined in a subsequent chapter on Germany's internal history.

THE CREATION OF THE TRIPLE ENTENTE, 1890–1907

The diplomatic isolation of Russia and France combined with a number of more positive factors to bring about the Dual Alliance of 1894. Russian antagonism toward Austria in the Balkans and French fear of Germany along the Rhine were increased by Germany's refusal to renew the Reinsurance Treaty and by the early renewal of the Triple Alliance in 1891. Both powers were alarmed by growing signs of Anglo-German friendship at the time of the Heligoland Treaty (1890) and on the occasion of the Kaiser's visit to London in 1891. Finally, Russia needed foreign loans for railroad building and industrial construction, and these could be obtained most readily in Paris. Accordingly, the agreement was closed during the New Year celebrations of 1894 in the form of a military convention. This provided that Russia would attack Germany if France were attacked by Germany or by Italy supported by Germany, while France would attack Germany if Russia were attacked by Germany or by Austria supported by Germany.

This Dual Alliance of France and Russia became the base of a triangle whose other sides were "ententes," that is, friendly agreements between France and Britain (1904) and between Russia and Britain (1907).

To us looking back on it, the Entente Cordiale between France and Britain seems inevitable, yet to contemporaries, as late as 1898, it must have appeared as a most unlikely event. For many years Britain had followed a policy of diplomatic isolation, maintaining a balance of power on the Continent by shifting her own weight to whatever side of Europe's disputes seemed the weaker. Because of her colonial rivalries with France in Africa and southwest Asia and her disputes with Russia in the Near, Middle, and Far East, Britain was generally friendly to the Triple Alliance and estranged from the Dual Alliance as late as 1902. Her difficulties with the Boers in South Africa, the growing strength of Russia in the Near and Far East, and Germany's obvious sympathy with the Boers led Britain to conclude the Anglo-Japanese Alliance of 1902 in order to obtain support against Russia in China. About the same time, Britain became convinced of the need and the possibility of an agreement with France. The need arose from Germany's direct threat to Britain's most sensitive spot by Tirpitz's naval-building program of 1898. The possibility of agreement with France emerged in the wake of the most acute Anglo-French crisis of modern times, the Fashoda crisis of 1898. At Fashoda on the Nile, a band of French under Colonel Jean Marchand, who had been crossing the Sahara from west to east, came face to face with a force of British under General Kitchener, who had been moving up the Nile from Egypt in order to subdue the tribes of the Sudan. Each ordered the other to withdraw. Passions rose to fever heat while both sides consulted their capitals for instructions. As a consequence of these instructions the French withdrew. As passions cooled and the dust settled, it became clear to both sides that their interests were reconcilable, since France's primary interest was on the Continent, where she faced Germany, while Britain's primary interest was in the colonial field where she increasingly found herself facing Germany. France's refusal to engage in a colonial war with Britain while the German Army sat across the Rhine made it clear that France could arrive at a colonial agreement with Britain. This agreement was made in 1904 by putting all their dis-

putes together on the negotiation table and balancing one against another. The French recognized the British occupation of Egypt in return
for diplomatic support for their ambitions in Morocco. They gave up
ancient rights in Newfoundland in return for new territories in Gabon
and along the Niger River in Africa. Their rights in Madagascar were
recognized in return for accepting a British "sphere of interests" in Siam.
Thus, the ancient Anglo-French enmity was toned down in the face of
the rising power of Germany. This Entente Cordiale was deepened in the
period 1906–1914 by a series of Anglo-French "military conversations,"
providing, at first, for unofficial discussions regarding behavior in a quite
hypothetical war with Germany but hardening imperceptibly through
the years into a morally binding agreement for a British expeditionary
force to cover the French left wing in the event of a French war with
Germany. These "military conversations" were broadened after 1912 by
a naval agreement by which the British undertook to protect France
from the North Sea in order to free the French fleet for action against
the Italian Navy in the Mediterranean.

The British agreement with Russia in 1907 followed a course not dissimilar to that of the British agreement with France in 1904. British suspicions of Russia had been fed for years by their rivalry in the Near
East. By 1904 these suspicions were deepened by a growing Anglo-Russian rivalry in Manchuria and North China, and were brought to a head
by Russian construction of the Trans-Siberian Railway (finished in
1905). A violent crisis arose over the Dogger Bank incident of 1904,
when the Russian fleet, en route from the Baltic Sea to the Far East, fired
on British fishing vessels in the North Sea in the belief that they
were Japanese torpedo boats. The subsequent destruction of that Russian fleet by the Japanese and the ensuing victory of Britain's ally in the
Russo-Japanese War of 1905 made clear to both parties that agreement
between them was possible. German naval rivalry with Britain and the
curtailment of Russian ambitions in Asia as a result of the defeat by
Japan made possible the agreement of 1907. By this agreement Persia
was divided into three zones of influence, of which the northern was
Russian, the southern was British, and the center was neutral. Afghanistan was recognized as under British influence; Tibet was declared to be
under Chinese suzerainty; and Britain expressed her willingness to modify the Straits Agreements in a direction favorable to Russia.

One influence which worked to create and strengthen the Triple
Entente was that of the international banking fraternity. These were
largely excluded from the German economic development, but had
growing links with France and Russia. Prosperous enterprises like the
Suez Canal Company, the Rothschild copper enterprise, Río Tinto, in
Spain, and many newer joint activities in Morocco created numerous
unobtrusive links which both preceded and strengthened the Triple

Entente. The Rothschilds, close friends of Edward VII and of France, were linked to the French investment bank, Banque de Paris et des Pays Bas. This, in turn, was the chief influence in selling nine billion rubles of Russian bonds in France before 1914. The most influential of London bankers, Sir Ernest Cassel, a great and mysterious person (1852–1921), had come from Germany to England at the age of seventeen, built up an immense fortune, which he gave away with a lavish hand, was closely connected with Egypt, Sweden, New York, Paris, and Latin America, became one of King Edward's closest personal friends and employer of the greatest wire-puller of the period, that ubiquitous mole, Lord Esher. These generally anti-Prussian influences around King Edward played a significant part in building up the Triple Entente and in strengthening it when Germany foolishly challenged their projects in Morocco in the 1904–1912 period.

EFFORTS TO BRIDGE THE GAP BETWEEN THE TWO COALITIONS, 1890–1914

At the beginning, and even up to 1913, the two coalitions on the international scene were not rigid or irreconcilably alienated. The links between the members of each group were variable and ambiguous. The Triple Entente was called an entente just because two of its three links were not alliances. The Triple Alliance was by no means solid, especially in respect to Italy, which had joined it originally to obtain support against the Papacy over the Roman question but which soon tried to obtain support for an aggressive Italian policy in the Mediterranean and North Africa. Failure to obtain specific German support in these areas, and continued enmity with Austro-Hungary in the Adriatic, made the Italian link with the Central Powers rather tenuous.

We shall mention at least a dozen efforts to bridge the gap which was slowly forming in the European "concert of the Powers." First in chronological order were the Mediterranean Agreements of 1887. In a series of notes England, Italy, Austria, and Spain agreed to preserve the *status quo* in the Mediterranean and its adjoining seas or to see it modified only by mutual agreement. These agreements were aimed at the French ambitions in Morocco and the Russian ambitions at the Straits.

A second agreement was the Anglo-German Colonial Treaty of 1890 by which German claims in East Africa, especially Zanzibar, were exchanged for the British title to the island of Heligoland in the Baltic Sea. Subsequently, numerous abortive efforts were made by the Kaiser and others on the German side, and by Joseph Chamberlain and others on the British side, to reach some agreement for a common front in world affairs. This resulted in a few minor agreements, such as one of 1898 regarding a possible disposition of the Portuguese colonies in Africa, one of 1899 dividing Samoa, and one of 1900 to maintain the "Open Door" in China, but efforts to create an alliance or even an entente broke down over the German naval program, German colonial ambitions in Africa (especially Morocco), and German economic penetration of the Near East along the route of the Berlin-to-Baghdad Railway. German jealousy of England's world supremacy, especially the Kaiser's resentment toward his uncle, King Edward VII, was ill concealed.

Somewhat similar negotiations were conducted between Germany and Russia, but with meager results. A Commercial Agreement of 1894 ended a long-drawn tariff war, much to the chagrin of the German landlords who enjoyed the previous exclusion of Russian grain, but efforts to achieve any substantial political agreement failed because of the German alliance with Austria (which faced Russia in the Balkans) and the Russian alliance with France (which faced Germany along the Rhine). These obstacles wrecked the so-called Bjorkö Treaty, a personal agreement between the Kaiser and Nicholas made during a visit to each other's yachts in 1905, although the Germans were able to secure Russian consent to the Baghdad Railway by granting the Russians a free hand in northern Persia (1910).

Four other lines of negotiation arose out of the French ambitions to obtain Morocco, the Italian desire to get Tripoli, the Austrian ambition to annex Bosnia, and the Russian determination to open the Straits to their warships. All four of these were associated with the declining power of Turkey, and offered opportunities for the European Powers to support one another's ambitions at the expense of the Ottoman Empire. In 1898 Italy signed a commercial treaty with France, and followed this up, two years later, by a political agreement which promised French support for the Italian ambitions in Tripoli in return for Italian support for the French designs in Morocco. The Italians further weakened the Triple Alliance in 1902 by promising France to remain neutral in the event that France was attacked or had to fight "in defense of her honor or of her security."

In a somewhat similar fashion Russia and Austria tried to reconcile the former's desire to obtain an outlet through the Dardanelles into the Aegean with the latter's desire to control Slav nationalism in the Balkans and reach the Aegean at Saloniki. In 1897 they reached an agreement to maintain the *status quo* in the Balkans or, failing this, to partition the area among the existing Balkan states plus a new state of Albania. In 1903 these two Powers agreed on a program of police and financial reform for the disturbed Turkish province of Macedonia. In 1908 a disagreement over Austrian efforts to construct a railway toward Saloniki was glossed over briefly by an informal agreement between the respective foreign ministers, Aleksandr Izvolski and Lexa von Aehrenthal, to exchange Austrian approval of the right of Russian warships to traverse the Straits for

Russian approval of an Austrian annexation of the Turkish provinces of Bosnia and Herzegovina. All this tentative goodwill evaporated in the heat of the Bosnian crisis of 1908, as we shall see in a moment.

After 1905 the recurrent international crises and the growing solidarity of the coalitions (except for Italy) made the efforts to bridge the gap between the two coalitions less frequent and less fruitful. However, two episodes are worthy of attention. These are the Haldane Mission of 1912 and the Baghdad Railway agreement of 1914. In the former, British Secretary of State for War Lord Haldane went to Berlin to try to restrain Tirpitz's naval program. Although the German Navy had been built in the hope that it would bring England to the conference table, and without any real intention of using it in a war with England, the Germans were not able to grasp the opportunity when it occurred. The Germans wanted a conditional promise of British neutrality in a continental war as a price for suspension of the new naval bill. Since this might lead to German hegemony on the Continent, Haldane could not agree. He returned to London convinced that the Germany of Goethe and Hegel which he had learned to love in his student days was being swallowed up by the German militarists. The last bridge between London and Berlin seemed down, but in June, 1914, the two countries initialed the agreement by which Britain withdrew her opposition to the Baghdad Railway in return for a German promise to remain north of Basra and recognize Britain's preeminence on the Euphrates and Persian Gulf. This solution to a long-standing problem was lost in the outbreak of war six weeks later.

THE INTERNATIONAL CRISES, 1905–1914

The decade from the Entente Cordiale to the outbreak of war witnessed a series of political crises which brought Europe periodically to the brink of war and hastened the growth of armaments, popular hysteria, nationalistic chauvinism, and solidity of alliances to a point where a relatively minor event in 1914 plunged the world into a war of unprecedented range and intensity. There were nine of these crises which must be mentioned here. In chronological order they are:

1905–1906	The First Moroccan Crisis and the Algeciras Conference
1908	The Bosnian Crisis
1911	Agadir and the Second Moroccan Crisis
1911	The Tripolitan War
1912	The First Balkan War
1913	The Second Balkan War

The first Moroccan crisis arose from German opposition to French designs on Morocco. This opposition was voiced by the Kaiser himself in a speech in Tangier, after the French had won Italian, British, and Spanish acquiescence by secret agreements with each of these countries. These agreements were based on French willingness to yield Tripoli to Italy, Egypt to Britain, and the Moroccan coast to Spain. The Germans insisted on an international conference in the hope that their belligerence would disrupt the Triple Entente and isolate France. Instead, when the conference met at Algeciras, near Gilbraltar, in 1906, Germany found herself supported only by Austria. The conference reiterated the integrity of Morocco but set up a state bank and a police force, both dominated by French influence. The crisis reached a very high pitch, but in both France and Germany the leaders of the more belligerent bloc (Théophile Delcassé and Friedrich von Holstein) were removed from office at the critical moment.

The Bosnian crisis of 1908 arose from the Young Turk revolt of the same year. Fearful that the new Ottoman government might be able to strengthen the empire, Austria determined to lose no time in annexing Bosnia and Herzegovina, which had been under Austrian military occupation since the Congress of Berlin (1878). Since the annexation would permanently cut Serbia off from the Adriatic Sea, Aehrenthal, the Austrian foreign minister, consulted with Serbia's protector, Russia. The czar's foreign minister, Izvolski, was agreeable to the Austrian plan if Austria would yield to Izvolski's desire to open the Straits to Russian warships, contrary to the Congress of Berlin. Aehrenthal agreed, subject to Izvolski's success in obtaining the consent of the other Powers. While Izvolski was wending his way from Germany to Rome and Paris in an effort to obtain this consent, Aehrenthal suddenly annexed the two districts, leaving Izvolski without his Straits program (October 6, 1908). It soon became clear that he could not get this program. About the same time, Austria won Turkish consent to its annexation of Bosnia. A war crisis ensued, fanned by the refusal of Serbia to accept the annexation and its readiness to precipitate a general war to prevent it. The danger of such a war was intensified by the eagerness of the military group in Austria, led by Chief of Staff Conrad von Hötzendorff, to settle the Serb irritation once and for all. A stiff German note to Russia insisting that she abandon her support of Serbia and recognize the annexation cleared the air, for Izvolski yielded and Serbia followed, but it created a very bad psychological situation for the future.

The second Moroccan crisis arose (July, 1911) when the Germans sent a gunboat, the *Panther*, to Agadir in order to force the French to evacuate Fez, which they had occupied, in violation of the Algeciras agreement, in order to suppress native disorders. The crisis became acute but subsided when the Germans gave up their opposition to French plans in Morocco in return for the cession of French territory in the Congo area (November 4, 1911).

As soon as Italy saw the French success in Morocco, it seized neighboring Tripoli, leading to the Tripolitan war between Italy and Turkey (September 28, 1911). All the Great Powers had agreements with Italy not to oppose her acquisition of Tripoli, but they disapproved of her methods, and were alarmed to varying degrees by her conquest of the Dodecanese Islands in the Aegean and her bombardment of the Dardanelles (April, 1912).

The Balkan States decided to profit from the weakness of Turkey by driving her out of Europe completely. Accordingly, Serbia, Bulgaria, Greece, and Montenegro attacked Turkey in the First Balkan War and had considerable success (1912). The Triple Alliance opposed the Serbian advance to the Adriatic, and suggested the creation of a new state in Albania to keep Serbia from the sea. A brief war crisis died down when Russia again abandoned the Serbian territorial claims and Austria was able to force Serbia and Montenegro to withdraw from Durazzo and Scutari. By the Treaty of London (1913) Turkey gave up most of her territory in Europe. Serbia, embittered by her failure to obtain the Adriatic coast, attempted to find compensation in Macedonia at the expense of Bulgaria's gains from Turkey. This led to the Second Balkan War, in which Serbia, Greece, Romania, and Turkey attacked Bulgaria. By the ensuing treaties of Bucharest and Constantinople (August–September, 1913), Bulgaria lost most of Macedonia to Serbia and Greece, much of Dobruja to Romania, and parts of Thrace to Turkey. Embittered at the Slavs and their supporters, Bulgaria drifted rapidly toward the Triple Alliance.

Ultimatums from Austria and from Austria and Italy jointly (October, 1913), forced Serbia and Greece to evacuate Albania, and made it possible to organize that country within frontiers agreeable to the Conference of Ambassadors at London. This episode hardly had time to develop into a crisis when it was eclipsed by the Liman von Sanders Affair.

Liman von Sanders was the head of a German military mission invited to the Ottoman Empire to reorganize the Turkish Army, an obvious necessity in view of its record in the Balkan Wars. When it became clear that Liman was to be actual commander of the First Army Corps at Constantinople and practically chief of staff in Turkey, Russia and France protested violently. The crisis subsided in January, 1914, when

Liman gave up his command at Constantinople to become inspector-general of the Turkish Army.

The series of crises from April, 1911, to January, 1914, had been almost uninterrupted. The spring of 1914, on the contrary, was a period of relative peace and calm, on the surface at least. But appearances were misleading. Beneath the surface each power was working to consolidate its own strength and its links with its allies in order to ensure that it would have better, or at least no worse, success in the next crisis, which everyone knew was bound to come. And come it did, with shattering suddenness, when the heir to the Habsburg throne, Archduke Francis Ferdinand, was assassinated by Serb extremists in the Bosnian city of Sarajevo on the 28th of June, 1914. There followed a terrible month of fear, indecision, and hysteria before the World War was begun by an Austrian attack on Serbia on July 28, 1914.

Whole volumes have been written on the crisis of July, 1914, and it is hardly to be expected that the story could be told in a few paragraphs. The facts themselves are woven into a tangled skein, which historians have now unraveled; but more important than the facts, and considerably more elusive, are the psychological conditions surrounding these facts. The atmosphere of nervous exhaustion after ten years of crisis; the physical exhaustion from sleepless nights; the alternating moods of patriotic pride and cold fear; the underlying feeling of horror that nineteenth century optimism and progress were leading to such a disaster; the brief moments of impatient rage at the enemy for starting the whole thing; the nervous determination to avoid war if possible, but not to be caught off guard when it came and, if possible, to catch your opponent off guard instead; and, finally, the deep conviction that the whole experience was only a nightmare and that at the last moment some power would stop it—these were the sentiments which surged to and fro in the minds of millions of Europeans in those five long weeks of mounting tension.

A number of forces made the crises of the period before the outbreak of war more dangerous than they would have been a generation or so earlier. Among these we should mention the influence of the mass army, the influence of the alliance system, the influence of democracy, the effort to obtain diplomatic ends by intimidation, the mood of desperation among politicians, and, lastly, the increasing influence of imperialism.

The influence of the mass army will be discussed more extensively in the next chapter. Briefly, the mass army in a period in which communication was generally by telegraph and travel was by rail was an unwieldy thing which could be handled only in a rather rigid and inflexible fashion. As worked out by the Germans, and used with such success in 1866 and in 1870, this fashion required the creation, long before the war began, of detailed plans executed in sequence from an original signal and organized in such a way that every single person had his fixed role like a part in a great and intricate machine. As used by the Germans in early wars, extended by them and copied by others in the period before 1914, each soldier began to move from his home at a given signal. As they advanced, hour by hour, and day by day, these men assembled their equipment and organized into larger and larger groups, at first in platoons, companies, and regiments, then in divisions and armies. As they assembled they were advancing along lines of strategic attack made long before and, as likely as not, the convergence into armies would not be accomplished until the advance had already penetrated deep into enemy territory. As formulated in theory, the final assembly into a complete fighting machine would take place only a brief period before the whole mass hurled itself on an, as yet, only partially assembled enemy force. The great drawback to this plan of mobilization was its inflexibility and its complexity, these two qualities being so preponderant that, once the original signal was given, it was almost impossible to stop the forward thrust of the whole assemblage anywhere short of its decisive impact on the enemy forces in their own country. This meant that an order to mobilize was almost equivalent to a declaration of war; that no country could allow its opponent to give the original signal much before it gave its own signal; and that the decisions of politicians were necessarily subordinate to the decisions of generals.

The alliance system worsened this situation in two ways. On the one hand, it meant that every local dispute was potentially a world war, because the signal to mobilize given anywhere in Europe would start the machines of war everywhere. On the other hand, it encouraged extremism, because a country with allies would be bolder than a country with no allies, and because allies in the long run did not act to restrain one another, either because they feared that lukewarm support to an ally in his dispute would lead to even cooler support from an ally in one's own dispute later or because a restraining influence in an earlier dispute so weakened an alliance that it was necessary to give unrestrained support in a later dispute in order to save the alliance for the future. There can be little doubt that Russia gave excessive support to Serbia in a bad dispute in 1914 to compensate for the fact that she had let Serbia down in the Albanian disputes of 1913; moreover, Germany gave Austria a larger degree of support in 1914, although lacking sympathy with the issue itself, to compensate for the restraint which Germany had exercised on Austria during the Balkan Wars.

The influence of democracy served to increase the tension of a crisis because elected politicians felt it necessary to pander to the most irrational and crass motivations of the electorate in order to ensure future election, and did this by playing on hatred and fear of powerful neighbors or on such appealing issues as territorial expansion, nationalistic pride, "a place in the sun," "outlets to the sea," and other real or imagined benefits. At the same time, the popular newspaper press, in order to sell papers, played on the same motives and issues, arousing their peoples, driving their own politicians to extremes, and alarming neighboring states to the point where they hurried to adopt similar kinds of action in the name of self-defense. Moreover, democracy made it impossible to examine international disputes on their merits, but instead transformed every petty argument into an affair of honor and national prestige so that no dispute could be examined on its merits or settled as a simple compromise because such a sensible approach would at once be hailed by one's democratic opposition as a loss of face and an unseemly compromise of exalted moral principles.

The success of Bismarck's policy of "blood and iron" tended to justify the use of force and intimidation in international affairs, and to distort the role of diplomacy so that the old type of diplomacy began to disappear. Instead of a discussion between gentlemen to find a workable solution, diplomacy became an effort to show the opposition how strong one was in order to deter him from taking advantage of one's obvious weaknesses. Metternich's old definition, that "a diplomat was a man who never permitted himself the pleasure of a triumph," became lost completely, although it was not until after 1930 that diplomacy became the practice of polishing one's guns in the presence of the enemy.

The mood of desperation among politicians served to make international crises more acute in the period after 1904. This desperation came from most of the factors we have already discussed, especially the pressure of the mass army and the pressure of the newspaper-reading electorate. But it was intensified by a number of other influences. Among these was the belief that war was inevitable. When an important politician, as, for example, Poincaré, decides that war is inevitable, he acts as if it were inevitable, and this makes it inevitable. Another kind of desperation closely related to this is the feeling that war *now* is preferable to war later, since time is on the side of the enemy. Frenchmen, dreaming of the recovery of Alsace and Lorraine, looked at the growing power and population of Germany and felt that war would be better in 1914 than later. Germans, dreaming of "a place in the sun" or fearing an "Entente encirclement," looked at the Russian rearmament program and decided that they would have more hope of victory in 1914 than in 1917 when that rearmament program would be completed. Austria, as a dynastic state, had her own kind of desperation based on the belief that nationalistic agitation by the Slavs doomed her anyway if she did nothing, and that it would be better to die fighting than to disintegrate in peace.

Lastly, the influence of imperialism served to make the crises of 1905–

1914 more acute than those of an earlier period. This is a subject which has given rise to much controversy since 1914 and has, in its crudest form, been presented as the theory that war was a result of the machinations of "international bankers" or of the international armaments merchants, or was an inevitable result of the fact that the European capitalist economic system had reached maturity. All these theories will be examined in another place where it will be shown that they are, at worst, untrue, or, at best, incomplete. However, one fact seems to be beyond dispute. This is the fact that international economic competition was, in the period before 1914, requiring increasing political support. British gold and diamond miners in South Africa, German railroad builders in the Near East, French tin miners in the southwest Pacific, American oil prospectors in Mexico, British oil prospectors in the Near East, even Serbian pork merchants in the Habsburg domains sought and expected to get political support from their home governments. It may be that things were always thus. But before 1914 the number of such foreign entrepreneurs was greater than ever, their demands more urgent, their own politicians more attentive, with the result that international relations were exasperated.

It was in an atmosphere such as this that Vienna received news of the assassination of the heir to the Habsburg throne on June 28, 1914. The Austrians were convinced of the complicity of the Serbian government, although they had no real proof. We now know that high officials of the Serbian government knew of the plot and did little to prevent it. This lack of activity was not caused by the fact that Francis Ferdinand was unfriendly to the Slavs within the Habsburg Empire but, on the contrary, by the fact that he was associated with plans to appease these Slavs by concessions toward political autonomy within the Habsburg domains and had even considered a project for changing the Dual Monarchy of Austrian and Hungarian into a Triple Monarchy of Austrian, Hungarian, and Slav. This project was feared by the Serbs because, by preventing the disintegration of Austria-Hungary, it would force postponement of their dreams of making Serbia the "Prussia of the Balkans." The project was also regarded with distaste by the Hungarians, who had no desire for that demotion associated with a shift from being one of two to being one of three joint rulers. Within the Hapsburg Cabinet there was considerable doubt as to what action to take toward Serbia. Hungary was reluctant to go to war for fear that a victory might lead to the annexation of more Serbs, thus accentuating the Slav problem within the empire and making the establishment of a Triple Monarchy more likely. Ultimately, they were reassured by the promise that no more Slavs would be annexed and that Serbia itself would, after its defeat, be compelled to stop its encouragement of Slav nationalist agitation within the empire and could, if necessary, be weakened by transfer of part of its territory to Bulgaria. On this irresponsible basis, Austria, having received a promise of support from Germany, sent a forty-eight-hour ultimatum to Belgrade. This document, delivered on July 23rd, was far-reaching. It bound Serbia to suppress anti-Habsburg publications, societies, and teaching; to remove from Serbian official positions persons to be named later by Austria; to allow Hapsburg officials to cooperate with the Serbs inside Serbia in apprehending and trying those implicated in the Sarajevo plot; and to offer explanations of various anti-Austrian utterances by Serbian officials.

Serbia, confident of Russian support, answered in a reply which was partly favorable, partly evasive, and in one particular at least (use of Austrian judges on Serbian tribunals) negative. Serbia mobilized before making her reply; Austria mobilized against her as soon as it was received, and, on July 28th, declared war. The Russian czar, under severe pressure from his generals, issued, retracted, modified, and reissued an order for general mobilization. Since the German military timetable for a two-front war provided that France must be defeated before Russian mobilization was completed, France and Germany both ordered mobilization on August 1st, and Germany declared war on Russia. As the German armies began to pour westward, Germany declared war on France (August 3rd) and Belgium (August 4th). Britain could not allow France to be defeated, and in addition was morally entangled by the military conversations of 1906–1914 and by the naval agreement of 1912. Moreover, the German challenge on the high seas, in commercial activities throughout the world, and in colonial activities in Africa could not go unanswered. On August 4th Britain declared war on Germany, emphasizing the iniquity of her attack on Belgium, although in the Cabinet meeting of July 29th it had been agreed that such an attack would not legally obligate Britain to go to war. Although this issue was spread among the people, and endless discussions ensued about Britain's obligation to defend Belgian neutrality under the Treaty of 1839, those who made the decision saw clearly that the real reason for war was that Britain could not allow Germany to defeat France.

Military History, 1914-1918

For the general student of history, the military history of the First World War is not merely the narration of advancing armies, the struggles of men, their deaths, triumphs, or defeats. Rather, it presents an extraordinary discrepancy between the facts of modern warfare and

the ideas on military tactics which dominated the minds of men, especially the minds of military men. This discrepancy existed for many
years before the war and began to disappear only in the course of 1918.
As a result of its existence, the first three years of the war witnessed the
largest military casualties in human history. These occurred as a result
of the efforts of military men to do things which were quite impossible
to do.

The German victories of 1866 and 1870 were the result of theoretical
study, chiefly by the General Staff, and exhaustive detailed training resulting from that study. They were emphatically not based on experience, for the army of 1866 had had no actual fighting experience for two
generations, and was commanded by a leader, Helmuth von Moltke, who
had never commanded a unit so large as a company previously. Moltke's
great contribution was to be found in the fact that, by using the railroad and the telegraph, he was able to merge mobilization and attack
into a single operation so that the final concentration of his forces took
place in the enemy country, practically on the battlefield itself, just
before contact with the main enemy forces took place.

This contribution of Moltke's was accepted and expanded by Count
von Schlieffen, chief of the Great General Staff from 1891 to 1905.
Schlieffen considered it essential to overwhelm the enemy in one great
initial onslaught. He assumed that Germany would be outnumbered and
economically smothered in any fighting of extended duration, and
sought to prevent this by a lightning war of an exclusively offensive
character. He assumed that the next war would be a two-front war
against France and Russia simultaneously and that the former would
have to be annihilated before the latter was completely mobilized. Above
all, he was determined to preserve the existing social structure of Germany, especially the superiority of the Junker class; accordingly, he
rejected either an enormous mass army, in which the Junker control of
the Officers' Corps would be lost by simple lack of numbers, or a long-
drawn war of resources and attrition which would require a reorganized
German economy.

The German emphasis on attack was shared by the French Army
command, but in a much more extreme and even mystical fashion. Under the influence of Ardant Du Picq and Ferdinand Foch, the French
General Staff came to believe that victory depended only on attack and
that the success of any attack depended on morale and not on any physical factors. Du Picq went so far as to insist that victory did not depend
at all on physical assault or on casualties, because the former never occurs and the latter occurs only during flight after the defeat. According
to him, victory was a matter of morale, and went automatically to the
side with the higher morale. The sides charge at each other; there is

never any shock of attack, because one side breaks and flees before impact; this break is not the result of casualties, because the flight occurs
before casualties are suffered and always begins in the rear ranks where
no casualties could be suffered; the casualties are suffered in the flight
and pursuit after the break. Thus the whole problem of war resolved
itself into the problem of how to screw up the morale of one's army to
the point where it is willing to fling itself headlong on the enemy. Technical problems of equipment or maneuvers are of little importance.

These ideas of Du Picq were accepted by an influential group in the
French Army as the only possible explanation of the French defeat in
1870. This group, led by Foch, propagated throughout the army the
doctrine of morale and the *offensive à outrance*. Foch became professor
at the Ecole Supérieure de Guerre in 1894, and his teaching could be
summed up in the four words, "Attaquez! Attaquez! Toujours, attaquez!"

This emphasis on the *offensive à outrance* by both sides led to a concentration of attention on three factors which were obsolete by 1914.
These three were (*a*) cavalry, (*b*) the bayonet, and (*c*) the headlong
infantry assault. These were obsolete in 1914 as the result of three technical innovations: (*a*) rapid-fire guns, especially machine guns; (*b*)
barbed-wire entanglements, and (*c*) trench warfare. The orthodox military leaders generally paid no attention to the three innovations while
concentrating all their attention on the three obsolete factors. Foch,
from his studies of the Russo-Japanese War, decided that machine guns
and barbed wire were of no importance, and ignored completely the
role of trenches. Although cavalry was obsolete for assault by the time
of the Crimean War (a fact indicated in Tennyson's "The Charge of
the Light Brigade"), and although this was clearly demonstrated to be
so in the American Civil War (a fact explicitly recognized in *The Army
and Navy Journal* for October 31, 1868), cavalry and cavalry officers
continued to dominate armies and military preparations. During the War
of 1914–1918 many commanding officers, like John French, Douglas
Haig, and John J. Pershing, were cavalry officers and retained the mentality of such officers. Haig, in his testimony before the Royal Commission on the War in South Africa (1903), testified, "Cavalry will have
a larger sphere of action in future wars." Pershing insisted on the necessity to keep large numbers of horses behind the lines, waiting for the
"breakthrough" which was to be obtained by bayonet charge. In every
army, transportation was one of the weakest points, yet feed for the
horses was the largest item transported, being greater than ammunition
or other supplies. Although transport across the Atlantic was critically
short throughout the war, one-third of all shipping space was in feed
for horses. Time for training recruits was also a critical bottleneck, but

most armies spent more time on bayonet practice than on anything else. Yet casualties inflicted on the enemy by bayonet were so few that they hardly appear in the statistics dealing with the subject.

The belief of military men that an assault made with high morale could roll through wire, machine guns, and trenches was made even more unrealistic by their insistence that such an offensive unit maintain a straight front. This meant that it was not to be permitted to move further in a soft spot, but was to hold back where advance was easy in order to break down the defensive strong points so that the whole front could precede at approximately the same rate. This was done, they explained, in order to avoid exposed flanks and enemy cross fire on advanced salients.

There was some opposition to these unrealistic theories, especially in the German Army, and there were important civilians in all countries who fought with their own military leaders on these issues. Clemenceau in France, and, above all, Lord Esher and the members of the Committee on Imperial Defence in England should be mentioned here.

At the outbreak of war in August 1914, both sides began to put into effect their complicated strategic plans made much earlier. On the German side this plan, known as the Schlieffen Plan, was drawn up in 1905 and modified by the younger Helmuth von Moltke (nephew of the Moltke of 1870) after 1906. On the French side the plan was known as Plan XVII, and was drawn up by Joffre in 1912.

The original Schlieffen Plan proposed to hold the Russians, as best as could be done, with ten divisions, and to face France with a stationary left wing of eight divisions and a great wheeling right and center of fifty-three divisions going through Holland and Belgium and coming down on the flank and rear of the French armies by passing west of Paris. Moltke modified this by adding two divisions to the right wing (one from the Russian front and one new) and eight new divisions to the left. He also cut out the passage through Holland, making it necessary for his right wing to pass through the Liège gap, between the Maastricht appendix of Holland and the forested terrain of the Ardennes.

The French Plan XVII proposed to stop an anticipated German attack into eastern France from Lorraine by an assault of two enlarged French armies on its center, thus driving victoriously into southern Germany whose Catholic and separatist peoples were not expected to rally with much enthusiasm to the Protestant, centralist cause of a Prussianized German Empire. While this was taking place, a force of 800,000 Russians was to invade East Prussia, and 150,000 British were to bolster the French left wing near Belgium.

The execution of these plans did not completely fulfill the expectations of their supporters. The French moved 3,781,000 men in 7,000 trains in 16 days (August 2–18), opening their attack on Lorraine on

August 14th. By August 20th they were shattered, and by August 25th, after eleven days of combat, had suffered 300,000 casualties. This was almost 25 percent of the number of men engaged, and represented the most rapid wastage of the war.

In the meantime the Germans in 7 days (August 6–12) transported 1,500,000 men across the Rhine at the rate of 550 trains a day. These men formed 70 divisions divided into 7 armies and forming a vast arc from northwest to southeast. Within this arc were 49 French divisions organized in 5 armies and the British Expeditionary Force (B.E.F.) of 4 divisions. The relationship of these forces, the commanding generals of the respective armies, and their relative strength can be seen from the following list:

ENTENTE FORCES (NORTH TO SOUTH)			GERMAN FORCES (NORTH TO SOUTH)		
ARMY	COMMANDER	DIVISIONS	DIVISIONS	ARMY	COMMANDER
				I	von Kluck
B.E.F.	Sir John French	4	34	II	von Bülow
V	Lanrezac	10		III	von Hausen
IV	De Langle de Cary			IV	Prince Albrecht of Württemberg
		20	21		
III	Ruffey			V	Crown Prince Frederick
II	Castelnau			VI	Prince Rupprecht of Bavaria
		19	15		
I	Dubail			VII	von Heeringen

The German right wing passed Liège, without reducing that great fortress, on the night of August 5–6 under the instructions of General Erich Ludendorff of the General Staff. The Belgian Army, instead of retreating southwestward before the German wave, moved northwestward to cover Antwerp. This put them ultimately on the rear of the advancing German forces. These forces peeled off eight and a half divisions to reduce the Belgian forts and seven divisions to cover the Belgian force before Antwerp. This reduced the strength of the German right wing, which was increasingly exhausted by the rapidity of its own advance. When the German plan became clear on August 18th, Joffre formed a new Sixth Army, largely from garrison troops, under Michel-Joseph Maunoury but really commanded by Joseph Galliéni, Minitary Governor of Paris. By August 22nd the whole French line west of Verdun was in retreat. Three days later, Moltke, believing victory secure, sent two army corps to Russia from the Second and Third armies. These arrived on the Eastern Front only after the Russian advance into Prussia had been smashed at Tannenberg and around the Masurian Lakes (August 26th–September 15th). In the meantime in the west, Schlieffen's project swept onward toward fiasco. When Lanrezac slowed up Bülow's advance on August 29th, Kluck, who was already a day's march ahead of Bülow, tried to close the gap between the two by turning southeastward. This brought his line of advance east of Paris rather than west of that city as originally planned. Galliéni, bringing the Sixth Army from Paris in any vehicles he could commandeer, threw it at Kluck's exposed right flank. Kluck turned again to face Gallieni, moving northwestward in a brilliant maneuver in order to envelop him within the German arc before resuming his advance southeastward. This operation was accompanied by considerable success except that it opened a gap thirty miles wide between Kluck and Bülow. Opposite this gap was the B.E.F., which was withdrawing southward with even greater speed than the French. On September 5th the French retreat stopped; on the following day they began a general counterattack, ordered by Joffre on the insistence of Galliéni. Thus began the First Battle of the Marne.

Kluck was meeting with considerable success over the Sixth French Army, although Bülow was being badly mauled by Lanrezac, when the B.E.F. began to move into the gap between the First and Second German armies (September 9th). A German staff officer, Lieutenant-Colonel Hentsch, ordered the whole German right to fall back to the Aisne River where a front was formed on September 13th by the arrival of some of the German forces which had been attacking the Belgian forts. The Germans were willing to fall back to the Aisne because they believed the advance could be resumed when they wished to do so. In the next few months the Germans tried to resume their advance, and the French tried to dislodge the Germans from their positions. Neither was able to make any headway against the firepower of the other. A succession of futile efforts to outflank each other's positions merely succeeded in bringing the ends of the front to the English Channel on one extreme and to Switzerland on the other. In spite of millions of casualties, this line, from the sea to the mountains across the fair face of France, remained almost unchanged for over three years.

During these terrible years, the dream of military men was to break through the enemy line by infantry assault, then roll up his flanks and disrupt his rearward communications by pouring cavalry and other reserves through the gap. This was never achieved. The effort to attain it led to one experiment after another. In order these were: (1) bayonet assault, (2) preliminary artillery barrage, (3) use of poison gas, (4) use of the tank, (5) use of infiltration. The last four of these innovations were devised alternately by the Allies and by the Central Powers.

Bayonet assault was a failure by the end of 1914. It merely created mountains of dead and wounded without any real advance, although some officers continued to believe that an assault would be successful if the morale of the attackers could be brought to a sufficiently high pitch to overcome machine-gun fire.

An artillery barrage as a necessary preliminary to infantry assault was used almost from the beginning. It was ineffectual. At first no army had the necessary quantity of munitions. Some armies insisted on ordering shrapnel rather than high-explosive shells for such barrages. This resulted in a violent controversy between Lloyd George and the generals, the former trying to persuade the latter that shrapnel was not effective against defensive forces in ground trenches. In time it should have become clear that high-explosive barrages were not effective either, although they were used in enormous quantities. They failed because: (1) earth and concrete fortifications provided sufficient protection to the defensive forces to allow them to use their own firepower against the infantry assault which followed the barrage; (2) a barrage notified the defense where to expect the following infantry assault, so that reserves could be brought up to strengthen that position; and (3) the doctrine of the continuous front made it impossible to penetrate the enemy positions on a wide-enough front to break through. The efforts to do so, however, resulted in enormous casualties. At Verdun in 1916 the French lost 350,000 and the Germans 300,000. On the Eastern Front the Russian General Aleksei Brusilov lost a million men in an indecisive attack through Galicia (June–August, 1916). On the Somme in the same year the British lost 410,000, the French lost 190,000, and the Germans lost 450,000 for a maximum gain of 7 miles on a front about 25 miles wide (July–November, 1916). The following year the slaughter continued. At Chemin des Dames in April, 1917, the French, under a new commander, Robert Nivelle, fired 11 million shells in a 10-day barrage on a 30-mile front. The attack failed, suffering losses of 118,000 men in a brief period. Many corps mutinied, and large numbers of combatants were shot to enforce discipline. Twenty-three civilian leaders were also executed. Nivelle was replaced by Pétain. Shortly afterward, at Passchendaele (Third Battle of Ypres), Haig used a barrage of 4¼ million shells, almost 5 tons for every yard of an 11-mile front, but lost 400,000 men in the ensuing assault (August–November, 1917).

The failure of the barrage made it necessary to devise new methods, but military men were reluctant to try any innovations. In April, 1915, the Germans were forced by civilian pressure to use poison gas, as had been suggested by the famous chemist Fritz Haber. Accordingly, without any effort at concealment and with no plans to exploit a breakthrough if it came, they sent a wave of chlorine gas at the place where the French and British lines joined. The junction was wiped out, and a great gap was opened through the line. Although it was not closed for five weeks, nothing was done by the Germans to use it. The first use of gas by the Western Powers (the British) in September, 1915, was no more successful. At the terrible Battle of Passchendaele in July 1917, the Germans introduced mustard gas, a weapon which was copied by the British in July 1918. This was the most effective gas used in the war, but it served to strengthen the defense rather than the offense, and was especially valuable to the Germans in their retreat in the autumn of 1918, serving to slow up the pursuit and making difficult any really decisive blow against them.

The tank as an offensive weapon devised to overcome the defensive strength of machine-gun fire was invented by Ernest Swinton in 1915. Only his personal contacts with the members of the Committee of Imperial Defence succeeded in bringing his idea to some kind of realization. The suggestion was resisted by the generals. When continued resistance proved impossible, the new weapon was misused, orders for more were canceled, and all military supporters of the new weapon were removed from responsible positions and replaced by men who were distrustful or at least ignorant of the tanks. Swinton sent detailed instructions to Headquarters, emphasizing that they must be used for the first time in large numbers, in a surprise assault, without any preliminary artillery barrage, and with close support by infantry reserves. Instead they were used quite incorrectly. While Swinton was still training crews for the first 150 tanks, fifty were taken to France, the commander who had been trained in their use was replaced by an inexperienced man, and a mere eighteen were sent against the Germans. This occurred on September 15, 1916, in the waning stages of the Battle of the Somme. An unfavorable report on their performance was sent from General Headquarters to the War Office in London and, as a result, an order for manufacture of a thousand more was canceled without the knowledge of the Cabinet. This was overruled only by direct orders from Lloyd George. Only on November 20, 1917, were tanks used as Swinton had instructed. On that day 381 tanks supported by six infantry divisions struck the Hindenburg Line before Cambrai and burst through into open country. These forces were exhausted by a five-mile gain, and stopped. The gap in the German line was not utilized, for the only available reserves were two divisions of cavalry which were ineffective. Thus the opportunity was lost. Only in 1918 were massed tank attacks used with any success and in the fashion indicated by Swinton.

The year 1917 was a bad one. The French and British suffered through their great disasters at Chemin des Dames and Passchendaele. Romania entered the war and was almost completely overrun, Bucharest being captured on December 5th. Russia suffered a double revolution, and was obliged to surrender to Germany. The Italian Front was completely shattered by a surprise attack at Caporetto and only by a miracle was it reestablished along the Piave (October–December, 1917). The only

bright spots in the year were the British conquests of Palestine and Mesopotamia and the entrance into the war of the United States, but the
former was not important and the latter was a promise for the future
rather than a help to 1917.

Nowhere, perhaps, is the unrealistic character of the thinking of most
high military leaders of World War I revealed more clearly than in the
British commander in chief, Field Marshal Sir Douglas (later Earl) Haig,
scion of a Scottish distillery family. In June, 1917, in spite of a decision
of May 4th by the Inter-Allied Conference at Paris against any British
offensive, and at a time when Russia and Serbia had been knocked out of
the war, French military morale was shattered after the fiasco of the
Nivelle offensive, and American help was almost a year in the future,
Haig determined on a major offensive against the Germans to win the
war. He ignored all discouraging information from his intelligence, wiped
from the record the known figures about German reserves, and deceived
the Cabinet, both in respect to the situation and to his own plans.
Throughout the discussion the civilian political leaders, who were almost
universally despised as ignorant amateurs by the military men, were
proved more correct in their judgments and expectations. Haig obtained
permission for his Passchendaele offensive only because General (later
Field Marshal and Baronet) William Robertson, Chief of the Imperial
General Staff, covered up Haig's falsifications about German reserves
and because First Sea Lord Admiral John Jellicoe told the Cabinet that
unless Haig could capture the submarine bases on the Belgian coast (an
utterly impossible objective) he considered it "improbable that we
could go on with the war next year for lack of shipping." On this basis,
Haig won approval for a "step by step" offensive "not involving heavy
losses." He was so optimistic that he told his generals that "opportunities
for the employment of cavalry in masses are likely to offer." The offensive, opened on July 31st, developed into the most horrible struggle
of the war, fought week after week in a sea of mud, with casualties
mounting to 400,000 men after three months. In October, when the situation had been hopeless for weeks, Haig still insisted that the Germans
were at the point of collapse, that their casualties were double the British (they were considerably less than the British), and that the breakdown of the Germans, and the opportunity for the tanks and cavalry
to rush through them, might come at any moment.

One of the chief reasons for the failure of these offensives was the
doctrine of the continuous front, which led commanders to hold back their
offensives where resistance was weak and to throw their reserves against
the enemy's strong points. This doctrine was completely reversed by
Ludendorff in the spring of 1918 in a new tactic known as "infiltration."
By this method advance was to be made around strong points by penetrat-
ing as quickly as possible and with maximum strength through weak

resistance, leaving the centers of strong resistance surrounded and isolated for later attention. Although Ludendorff did not carry out this plan with sufficient conviction to give it full success, he did achieve amazing results. The great losses by the British and French in 1917, added to the increase in German strength from forces arriving from the defunct Russian and Romanian fronts, made it possible for Ludendorff to strike a series of sledgehammer blows along the Western Front between Douai and Verdun in March and April 1918. Finally, on May 27th, after a brief but overwhelming bombardment, the German flood burst over Chemin des Dames, poured across the Aisne, and moved relentlessly toward Paris. By May 30th it was on the Marne, thirty-seven miles from the capital. There, in the Second Battle of the Marne, were reenacted the events of September 1914. On June 4th the German advance was stopped temporarily by the Second American Division at Château-Thierry. In the next six weeks a series of counterattacks aided by nine American divisions were made on the northern flank of the German penetration. The Germans fell back behind the Vesle River, militarily intact, but so ravaged by influenza that many companies had only thirty men. The crown prince demanded that the war be ended. Before this could be done, on August 8, 1918–"the black day of the German Army," as Ludendorff called it–the British broke the German line at Amiens by a sudden assault with 456 tanks supported by 13 infantry and 3 cavalry divisions. When the Germans rushed up 18 reserve divisions to support the six which were attacked, the Allied Powers repeated their assault at Saint-Quentin (August 31st) and in Flanders (September 2nd). A German Crown Council, meeting at Spa, decided that victory was no longer possible, but neither civil government nor army leaders would assume the responsibility for opening negotiations for peace. The story of these negotiations will be examined in a moment, as the last of a long series of diplomatic conversations which continued throughout the war.

Looking back on the military history of the First World War, it is clear that the whole war was a siege operation against Germany. Once the original German onslaught was stopped on the Marne, victory for Germany became impossible because she could not resume her advance. On the other hand, the Entente Powers could not eject the German spearhead from French soil, although they sacrificed millions of men and billions of dollars in the effort to do so. Any effort to break in on Germany from some other front was regarded as futile, and was made difficult by the continuing German pressure in France. Accordingly, although sporadic attacks were made on the Italian Front, in the Arab areas of the Ottoman Empire, on the Dardanelles directly in 1915, against Bulgaria through Saloniki in 1915–1918, and along the whole Russian Front, both sides continued to regard northeastern France as the vital area. And in that area, clearly no decision could be reached.

To weaken Germany the Entente Powers began a blockade of the Central Powers, controlling the sea directly, in spite of the indecisive German naval challenge at Jutland in 1916, and limiting the imports of neutrals near Germany, like the Netherlands. To resist this blockade, Germany used a four-pronged instrument. On the home front every effort was made to control economic life so that all goods would be used in the most effective fashion possible and so that food, leather, and other necessities would be distributed fairly to all. The success of this struggle on the home front was due to the ability of two German Jews. Haber, the chemist, devised a method for extracting nitrogen from the air, and thus obtained an adequate supply of the most necessary constituent of all fertilizers and all explosives. Before 1914 the chief source of nitrogen had been in the guano deposits of Chile, and, but for Haber, the British blockade would have compelled a German defeat in 1915 from lack of nitrates. Walter Rathenau, director of the German Electric Company and of some five dozen other enterprises, organized the German economic system in a mobilization which made it possible for Germany to fight on with slowly dwindling resources.

On the military side Germany made a threefold reply to the British blockade. It tried to open the blockade by defeating its enemies to the south and east (Russia, Romania, and Italy). In 1917 this effort was largely successful, but it was too late. Simultaneously, Germany tried to wear down her Western foes by a policy of attrition in the trenches and to force Britain out of the war by a retaliatory submarine blockade directed at British shipping. The submarine attack, as a new method of naval warfare, was applied with hesitation and ineffectiveness until 1917. Then it was applied with such ruthless efficiency that almost a million tons of shipping was sunk in the month of April 1917, and Britain was driven within three weeks of exhaustion of her food supply. This danger of a British defeat, dressed in the propaganda clothing of moral outrage at the iniquity of submarine attacks, brought the United States into the war on the side of the Entente in that critical month of April, 1917. In the meantime the Germany policy of military attrition on the Western Front worked well until 1918. By January of that year Germany had been losing men at about half her rate of replacement and at about half the rate at which she was inflicting losses on the Entente Powers. Thus the period 1914–1918 saw a race between the economic attrition of Germany by the blockade and the personal attrition of the Entente by military action. This race was never settled on its merits because three new factors entered the picture in 1917. These were the German counterblockade by submarines on Britain, the increase in German manpower in the West resulting from her victory in the East, and the arrival on the Western Front of new American forces. The first two of these factors were overbalanced in the period March–September, 1918, by the third. By August of 1918 Germany had given her best, and it had not been adequate. The blockade and the rising tide of American manpower gave the German leaders the choice of surrender or complete economic and social upheaval. Without exception, led by the Junker military commanders, they chose surrender.

Diplomatic History, 1914-1918

The beginnings of military action in August 1914 did not mark the end of diplomatic action, even between the chief opponents. Diplomatic activity continued, and was aimed, very largely, at two goals: (*a*) to bring new countries into the military activities or, on the contrary, to keep them out, and (*b*) to attempt to make peace by negotiations. Closely related to the first of these aims were negotiations concerned with the disposition of enemy territories after the fighting ceased.

Back of all the diplomatic activities of the period 1914–1918 was a fact which impressed itself on the belligerents relatively slowly. This was the changed character of modern warfare. With certain exceptions the wars of the eighteenth and early nineteenth centuries had been struggles of limited resources for limited objectives. The growth of political democracy, the rise of nationalism, and the industrialization of war led to total war with total mobilization and unlimited objectives. In the eighteenth century, when rulers were relatively free from popular influences, they could wage wars for limited objectives and could negotiate peace on a compromise basis when these were objectives were attained or appeared unattainable. Using a mercenary army which fought for pay, they could put that army into war or out of war, as seemed necessary, without vitally affecting its morale or its fighting qualities. The arrival of democracy and of the mass army required that the great body of the citizens give wholehearted support for any war effort, and made it impossible to wage wars for limited objectives. Such popular support could be won only in behalf of great moral goals or universal philosophic values or, at the very least, for survival. At the same time the growing industrialization and economic integration of modern society made it impossible to mobilize for war except on a very extensive basis which approached total mobilization. This mobilization could not be directed toward limited objectives. From these factors came total war with total mobilization and unlimited objectives, including the total destruction or unconditional surrender of the enemy. Having adopted such grandiose goals and such gigantic plans, it became almost impossible to allow the continued existence of noncombatants within the belligerent countries or neutrals outside them. It became almost axiomatic that "who is not with me is against me." At the same time, it became almost impossible to compromise sufficiently to obtain the much more limited goals which would permit a negotiated peace. As Charles Seymour put it: "Each side had promised itself a peace of victory. The very phrase 'negotiated peace' became synonymous with treachery." Moreover, the popular basis of modern war required a high morale which might easily be lowered if the news leaked out that the government was negotiating peace in the middle of the fighting. As a consequence of these conditions, efforts to negotiate peace during the First World War were generally very secret and very unsuccessful.

The change from limited wars with limited objectives fought with mercenary troops to unlimited wars of economic attrition with unlimited objectives fought with national armies had far-reaching consequences. The distinction between combatants and noncombatants and between belligerents and neutrals became blurred and ultimately undistinguishable. International law, which had grown up in the period of limited dynastic wars, made a great deal of these distinctions. Noncombatants had extensive rights which sought to protect their ways of life as much as possible during periods of warfare; neutrals had similar rights. In return, strict duties to remain both noncombatant and neutral rested on these "outsiders." All these distinctions broke down in 1914-1915, with the result that both sides indulged in wholesale violations of existing international law. Probably on the whole these violations were more extensive (although less widely publicized) on the part of the Entente than on the part of the Central Powers. The reasons for this were that the Germans still maintained the older traditions of a professional army, and their position, both as an invader and as a "Central Power" with limited manpower and economic resources, made it to their advantage to maintain the distinctions between combatant and noncombatant and between belligerent and neutral. If they could have maintained the former distinction, they would have had to fight the enemy army and not the enemy civilian population, and, once the former was defeated, would have had little to fear from the latter, which could have been controlled by a minimum of troops. If they could have maintained the distinction between belligerent and neutral, it would have been impossible to blockade Germany, since basic supplies could have been imported through neutral countries. It was for this reason that Schlieffen's original plans for an attack on France through Holland and Belgium were changed by Moltke to an attack through Belgium alone. Neutral Holland was to remain as a channel of supply for civilian goods. This was possible because international law made a distinction between war goods, which could be declared contraband, and civilian goods (including food), which could not be so declared. Moreover, the German plans, as we have indicated, called for a short, decisive war against the enemy armed forces, and they neither expected nor desired a total economic mobilization or even a total military mobilization, since these might disrupt the existing social and political structure in Germany. For these reasons, Germany made no plans for industrial or economic mobilization, for a long war, or for withstanding a blockade, and hoped to mobilize a smaller proportion of its manpower than its immediate enemies.

The failure of the Schlieffen plan showed the error of these ideas. Not only did the prospect of a long war make economic mobilization necessary, but the occupation of Belgium showed that national feeling was tending to make the distinction between combatant and noncombatant academic. When Belgian civilians shot at German soldiers, the latter took civilian hostages and practiced reprisals on civilians. These German actions were publicized throughout the world by the British propaganda machine as "atrocities" and violations of international law (which they were), while the Belgian civilian snipers were excused as loyal patriots (although their actions were even more clearly violations of international law and, as such, justified severe German reactions). These "atrocities" were used by the British to justify their own violations of international law. As early as August 20, 1914, they were treating food as contraband and interfering with neutral shipments of food to Europe. On November 5, 1914, they declared the whole sea from Scotland to Iceland a "war zone," covered it with fields of explosive floating mines, and ordered all ships going to the Baltic, Scandinavia, or the Low Countries to go by way of the English Channel, where they were stopped, searched, and much of their cargoes seized, even when these cargoes could not be declared contraband under existing international law. In reprisal the Germans on February 18, 1915, declared the English Channel a "war zone," announced that their submarines would sink shipping in that area, and ordered shipping for the Baltic area to use the route north of Scotland. The United States, which rejected a Scandinavian invitation to protest against the British war zone closed with mines north of Scotland, protested violently against the German war zone closed with submarines on the Narrow Seas, although, as one American senator put it, the "humanity of the submarine was certainly on a higher level that that of the floating mine, which could exercise neither discretion nor judgment."

The United States accepted the British "war zone," and prevented its ships from using it. On the other hand, it refused to accept the German war zone, and insisted that American lives and property were under American protection even when traveling on armed belligerent ships in this war zone. Moroeover, the United States insisted that German submarines must obey the laws of the sea as drawn for surface vessels. These laws provided that merchant ships could be stopped by a war vessel and inspected, and could be sunk, if carrying contraband, after the passengers and the ships' papers were put in a place of safety. A place of safety was not the ships' boats, except in sight of land or of other vessels in a calm sea. The merchant vessel so stopped obtained these rights only if it made no act of hostility against the enemy war vessel. It was not only difficult, or even impossible, for German submarines to meet these conditions; it was often dangerous, since British merchant ships received instructions to attack German submarines at sight, by ramming if possible. It was even dangerous for the German submarines to apply the established law of neutral vessels; for British vessels, with these aggressive orders, frequently flew neutral flags and posed as neutrals as long as possible. Nevertheless, the United States continued to insist that the Germans obey the old laws, while condoning British violations of the same laws to the extent that the distinction between war vessels and merchant ships was blurred. Accordingly, German submarines began to sink British merchant ships with little or no warning. Their attempts to justify this failure to distinguish between combatants and noncombatants on the ground that British floating mines, the British food blockade, and the British instructions to merchant ships to attack submarines made no such distinction were no more successful than their efforts to show that their severity against the civilian population of Belgium was justified by civilian attacks on German troops. They were trying to carry on legal distinctions remaining from an earlier period when conditions were entirely different, and their ultimate abandonment of these distinctions on the grounds that their enemies had already abandoned them merely made matters worse, because if neutrals became belligerents and noncombatants became combatants, Germany and her allies would suffer much more than Britain and her friends. In the final analysis this is why the distinctions were destroyed; but beneath all legal questions was to be found the ominous fact that war, by becoming total, had made both neutrality and negotiated peace almost impossible. We shall now turn our attention to this struggle over neutrality and the struggle over negotiated peace.

So far as legal or diplomatic commitments went, Germany, in July, 1914, had the right to expect that Austria-Hungary, Italy, Romania, and perhaps Turkey would be at her side and that her opponents would consist of Serbia, Montenegro, Russia, and France, with England maintaining neutrality, at the beginning, at least. Instead, Italy and Romania fought against her, a loss which was not balanced by the accession of Bulgaria to her side. In addition, she found her opponents reinforced by England, Belgium, Greece, the United States, China, Japan, the Arabs, and twenty other "Allied and Associated Powers." The process by which the reality turned out to be so different from Germany's legitimate expectations will now take our attention.

Turkey, which had been growing closer to Germany since before 1890, offered Germany an alliance on July 27, 1914, when the Sarajevo crisis was at its height. The document was signed secretly on August 1st, and bound Turkey to enter the war against Russia if Russia attacked Germany or Austria. In the meantime, Turkey deceived the Entente Powers by conducting long negotiations with them regarding its attitude toward the war. On October 29th it removed its mask of neutrality by attacking Russia, thus cutting her off from her Western allies by the southern route. To relieve the pressure on Russia, the British made an ineffectual attack on Gallipoli at the Dardanelles (February–December, 1915). Only at the end of 1916 did any real attack on Turkey begin, this time from Egypt into Mesopotamia, where Baghdad was captured in March 1917, and the way opened up the valley as well as across Palestine to Syria. Jerusalem fell to General Allenby in December 1917, and the chief cities of Syria fell the following October (1918).

Bulgaria, still smarting from the Second Balkan War (1913), in which it had lost territory to Romania, Serbia, Greece, and Turkey, was from the outbreak of war in 1914 inclined toward Germany, and was strengthened in that inclination by the Turkish attack on Russia in October. Both sides tried to buy Bulgaria's allegiance, a process in which the Entente Powers were hampered by the fact that Bulgaria's ambitions could be satisfied only at the expense of Greece, Romania, or Serbia, whose support they also desired. Bulgaria wanted Thrace from the Maritsa River to the Vardar, including Kavalla and Saloniki (which were Greek), most of Macedonia (which was Greek or Serbian), and Dobruja (from Romania). The Entente Powers offered Thrace to the Vardar in November 1914, and added some of Macedonia in May 1915, compensating Serbia with an offer of Bosnia, Herzegovina, and the Dalmatian coast. Germany, on the other hand, gave Bulgaria a strip of Turkish territory along the Maritsa River in July 1915, added to this a loan of 200,000,000 francs six weeks later, and, in September 1915, accepted all Bulgaria's demands provided they were at the expense of belligerent countries. Within a month Bulgaria entered the war by attacking Serbia (October 11, 1915). It had considerable success, driving westward across Serbia into Albania, but exposed its left flank in this process to an attack from Entente forces which were already based on Saloniki. This attack came in September 1918, and within a month forced Bulgaria to ask for an armistice (September 30th). This marked the first break in the united front of the Central Powers.

When war began in 1914, Romania remained neutral, in spite of the fact that it had joined the Triple Alliance in 1883. This adherence had been made because of the Germanic sympathies of the royal family, and was so secret that only a handful of people even knew about it. The Romanian people themselves were sympathetic to France. At that time Romania consisted of three parts (Moldavia, Wallachia, and Dobruja) and had ambitions to acquire Bessarabia from Russia and Transylvania from Hungary. It did not seem possible that Romania could get both of these, yet that is exactly what happened, because Russia was defeated by Germany and ostracized by the Entente Powers after its revolution in 1917, while Hungary was defeated by the Entente Powers in 1918. The Romanians were strongly anti-Russian after 1878, but this feeling decreased in the course of time, while animosities against the Central Powers rose, because of the Hungarian mistreatment of the Romanian minority in Transylvania. As a result, Romania remained neutral in 1914. Efforts by the Entente Powers to win her to their side were vain until after the death of King Carol in October 1914. The Romanians asked, as the price of their intervention on the Entente side, Transylvania, parts of Bukovina and the Banat of Temesvar, 500,000 Entente troops in the Balkans, 200,000 Russian troops in Bessarabia, and equal status with the Great Powers at the Peace Conference. For this they promised to attack the Central Powers and not to make a separate peace. Only the heavy casualties suffered by the Entente Powers in 1916 brought them to the point of accepting these terms. They did so in August of that year, and Romania entered the war ten days later. The Central Powers at once overran the country, capturing Bucharest in December. The Romanians refused to make peace until the German advance to the Marne in the spring of 1918 convinced them that the Central Powers were going to win. Accordingly, they signed the Treaty of Bucharest with Germany (May 7, 1918) by which they gave Dobruja to Bulgaria, but obtained a claim to Bessarabia, which Germany had previously taken from Russia. Germany also obtained a ninety-year lease on the Romanian oil wells.

Though the Entente efforts to get Greece into the war were the most protracted and most unscrupulous of the period, they were unsuccessful so long as King Constantine remained on the throne (to June 1917). Greece was offered Smyrna in Turkey if it would give Kavalla to Bulgaria and support Serbia. Prime Minister Eleutherios Venizelos was favorable, but could not persuade the king, and soon was forced to resign (March 1915). He returned to office in August, after winning a parliamentary election in June. When Serbia asked Greece for the 150,000 men promised in the Serb-Greek treaty of 1913 as protection against a Bulgarian attack on Serbia, Venizelos tried to obtain these forces from the Entente Powers. Four French-British divisions landed at Saloniki (October 1915), but Venizelos was at once forced out of office by King Constantine. The Entente then offered to cede Cyprus to Greece in return for Greek support against Bulgaria but were refused (October 20, 1915). When German and Bulgarian forces began to occupy portions of Greek Macedonia, the Entente Powers blockaded Greece and sent an ultimatum asking for demobilization of the Greek Army and a responsible government in Athens (June, 1916). The Greeks at once accepted, since demobilization made it less likely they could be forced to make war on Bulgaria, and the demand for responsible-government could be met without bringing Venizelos back to office. Thus frustrated, the Entente Powers established a new provisional Greek government under Venizelos at their base at Saloniki. There he declared war on the Central Powers (November 1916). The Entente then demanded that the envoys of the Central Powers be expelled from Athens and that war materials within control of the Athenian government be surrendered. These demands were rejected (November 30, 1916). Entente forces landed at the port of Athens (Piraeus) on the same day, but stayed only overnight, being replaced by an Entente blockade of Greece. The Venizelos government was recognized by Britain (December 1916), but the situation dragged on unchanged. In June 1917, a new ultimatum was sent to Athens demanding the abdication of King Constantine. It was backed up by a seizure of Thessaly and Corinth, and was accepted at once. Venizelos became premier of the Athens government, and declared war on the Central Powers the next day (June 27, 1917). This gave the Entente a sufficient base to drive up the Vardar Valley, under French General Louis Franchet d'Esperey, and force Bulgaria out of the war.

At the outbreak of war in 1914, Italy declared its neutrality on the grounds that the Triple Alliance of 1882, as renewed in 1912, bound it to support the Central Powers only in case of a defensive war and that the Austrian action against Serbia did not fall in this category. To the Italians, the Triple Alliance was still in full force and thus they were entitled, as provided in Article VII, to compensation for any Austrian territorial gains in the Balkans. As a guarantee of this provision, the Italians occupied the Valona district of Albania in November 1914. Efforts of the Central Powers to bribe Italy into the war were difficult because the Italian demands were largely at the expense of Austria. These demands included the South Tyrol, Gorizia, the Dalmatian Islands, and Valona, with Trieste a free city. A great public controversy took place in Italy between those who supported intervention in the war on the Entente side and those who wished to remain neutral. By skillful expenditure of money, the Entente governments were able to win considerable support. Their chief achievement was in splitting the normally pacifiest Socialist Party by large money grants to Benito Mussolini. A rabid Socialist who had been a pacifist leader in the Tripolitan War of 1911 Mussolini was editor of the chief Socialist paper, *Avanti*. He was expelled from the party when he supported intervention on the Entente side, but, using French money, he established his own paper, *Popolo d'Italia*, and embarked upon the unprincipled career which ultimately made him dictator of Italy.

By the secret Treaty of London (April 26, 1915), Italy's demands as listed above were accepted by the Entente Powers and extended to provide that Italy should also obtain Trentino, Trieste, Istria (but not Fiume), South Dalmatia, Albania as a protectorate, the Dodecanese Islands, Adalia in Asia Minor, compensatory areas in Africa if the Entente Powers made any acquisitions on that continent, a loan of £50 million, part of the war indemnity, and exclusion of the Pope from any of the negotiations leading toward peace. For these extensive promises Italy agreed to make war on all the Central Powers within a month. It declared war on Austria-Hungary on May 23, 1915, but on Germany only in August, 1916.

The Treaty of London is of the utmost importance because its ghost haunted the chancelleries of Europe for more than twenty-five years. It was used as an excuse for the Italian attack on Ethiopia in 1935 and on France in 1940.

The Italian war effort was devoted to an attempt to force the Habsburg forces back from the head of the Adriatic Sea. In a series of at least twelve battles on the Isonzo River, on very difficult terrain, the Italians were notably unsuccessful. In the autumn of 1917 Germany gave the Austrians sufficient reinforcements to allow them to break through on to the rear of the Italian lines at Caporetto. The Italian defense collapsed and was reestablished along the Piave River only after losses of over 600,000 men, the majority by desertion. Austria was unable to pursue this advantage because of her war-weariness, her inability to mobilize her domestic economy successfully for war purposes, and, above all, by the growing unrest of the nationalities subject to Habsburg rule. These groups set up governmental committees in Entente capitals and organized "Legions" to fight on the Entente side. Italy organized a great meeting of these peoples at Rome in April 1918. They signed the "Pact of Rome," promising to work for self-determination of subject peoples and agreeing to draw the frontier between the Italians and the South Slavs on nationality lines.

Russia, like Romania, was forced out of the war in 1917, and forced to sign a separate peace by Germany in 1918. The Russian attack on Germany in 1914 had been completely shattered at the battles of Tannenberg and the Masurian Lakes in August and September, but their ability to hold their own against Austrian forces in Galicia made it impossible to bring the war in the east to a conclusion. Russian casualties were very heavy because of inadequate supplies and munitions, while the Austrians lost considerable forces, especially of Slavs, by desertion to the

Russians. This last factor made it possible for Russia to organize a "Czech Legion" of over 100,000 men. German reinforcements to the Austrian front in Galicia in 1915 made possible a great Austro-German offensive which crossed Galicia and by September had taken all of Poland and Lithuania. In these operations the Russians lost about a million men. They lost a million more in the "Brusilov" counterattack in 1916 which reached the Carpathians before it was stopped by the arrival of German reinforcements from France. By this time the prestige of the czarist government had fallen so low that it was easily replaced by a parliamentary government under Kerensky in March 1917. The new government tried to carry on the war, but misjudged the temper of the Russian people. As a result the extreme Communist group, known as Bolsheviks, were able to seize the government in November 1917, and hold it by promising the weary Russian people both peace and land. The German demands, dictated by the German General Staff, were so severe that the Bolsheviks refused to sign a formal peace, but on March 3, 1918, were forced to accept the Treaty of Brest-Litovsk. By this treaty Russia lost Finland, Lithuania, the Baltic Provinces, Poland, the Ukraine and Transcaucasia. German efforts to exploit these areas in an economic sense during the war were not successful.

The Japanese intervention in the war on August 23, 1914, was determined completely by its ambitions in the Far East and the Pacific area. It intended to use the opportunity arising from the Great Powers' concern with Europe to win concessions from China and Russia and to replace Germany, not only in its colonial possessions in the East but also to take over its commercial position so far as possible. The German island colonies north of the equator were seized at once, and the German concession at Kiaochow was captured after a brief siege. In January 1915, "Twenty-one Demands" were presented to China in the form of an ultimatum, and largely accepted. These demands covered accession to the German position in Shantung, extension of Japanese leases in Manchuria, with complete commercial liberty for the Japanese in that area, extensive rights in certain existing iron and steel enterprises of North China, and the closing of China's coast to any future foreign concessions. A demand for the use of Japanese advisers in Chinese political, military, and financial matters was rejected, and withdrawn. On July 3, 1916, Japan won Russian recognition of its new position in China in return for her recognition of the Russian penetration into Outer Mongolia. New concessions were won from China in February 1917, and accepted by the United States in November in the so-called Lansing-Ishii Notes. In these notes the Japanese gave verbal support to the American insistence on the maintenance of China's territorial integrity, political independence, and the "Open Door" policy in commercial matters.

The outbreak of the Bolshevik Revolution in Russia, followed by the

German victory over that country, and the beginning of civil war, gave the Japanese an opportunity in the Far East which they did not hesitate to exploit. With the support of Great Britain and the United States, they landed at Vladivostok in April 1918, and began to move westward along the route of the Trans-Siberian Railway. The Czech Legion on the Russian front had already rebelled against Bolshevik rule and was fighting its way eastward along the same railroad. The Czechs were eventually evacuated to Europe, while the Japanese continued to hold the eastern end of the railroad, and gave support to the anti-Bolshevik factions in the civil war. After a year or more of confused fighting, it became clear that the anti-Bolshevik factions would be defeated and that the Japanese could expect no further concessions from the Bolsheviks. Accordingly, they evacuated Vladivostok in October 1922.

Undoubtedly, the most numerous diplomatic agreements of the war-time period were concerned with the disposition of the Ottoman Empire. As early as February 1915, Russia and France signed an agreement by which Russia was given a free hand in the East in return for giving France a free hand in the West. This meant that Russia could annex Constantinople and block the movement for an independent Poland, while France could take Alsace-Lorraine from Germany and set up a new, independent state under French influence in the Rhineland. A month later, in March 1915, Britain and France agreed to allow Russia to annex the Straits and Constantinople. The immediate activities of the Entente Powers, however, were devoted to plans to encourage the Arabs to rebel against the sultan's authority or at least abstain from supporting his war efforts. The chances of success in these activities were increased by the fact that the Arabian portions of the Ottoman Empire, while nominally subject to the sultan, were already breaking up into numerous petty spheres of authority, some virtually independent. The Arabs, who were a completely separate people from the Turks, speaking a Semitic rather than a Ural-Altaic language and who had remained largely nomadic in their mode of life while the Turks had become almost completely a peasant people, were united to the Ottoman peoples by little more than their common allegiance to the Muslim religion. This connection had been weakened by the efforts to secularize the Ottoman state and by the growth of Turkish nationalism which called forth a spirit of Arabic nationalism as a reaction to it.

In 1915–1916 the British high commissioner in Egypt, Sir Henry McMahon, entered into correspondence with the Sherif Hussein of Mecca. While no binding agreement was signed, the gist of their discussions was that Britain would recognize the independence of the Arabs if they revolted against Turkey. The area covered by the agreement included those parts of the Ottoman Empire south of the 37th degree of latitude except Adana, Alexandretta, and "those portions of

Syria lying to the west of the districts of Damascus, Homs, Hama, and Aleppo, [which] cannot be said to be purely Arab." In addition, Aden was excepted, while Baghdad and Basra were to have a "special administration." The rights of France in the whole area were reserved, the existing British agreements with various local sultans along the shores of the Persian Gulf were to be maintained, and Hussein was to use British advisers exclusively after the war. Extended controversy has risen from this division of areas, the chief point at issue being whether the statement as worded included Palestine in the area which was granted to the Arabs or in the area which was reserved. The interpretation of these terms to exclude Palestine from Arab hands was subsequently made by McMahon on several occasions after 1922 and most explicitly in 1937.

While McMahon was negotiating with Hussein, the Government of India, through Percy Cox, was negotiating with Ibn-Saud of Nejd, and, in an agreement of December 26, 1915, recognized his independence in return for a promise of neutrality in the war. Shortly afterward, on May 16, 1916, an agreement, known as the Sykes-Picot agreement from the names of the chief negotiators, was signed between Russia, France, and Britain. Early in 1917 Italy was added to the settlement. It partitioned the Ottoman Empire in such a way that little was left to the Turks except the area within 200 or 250 miles of Ankara. Russia was to get Constantinople and the Straits, as well as northeastern Anatolia, including the Black Sea coast; Italy was to get the southwestern coast of Anatolia from Smyrna to Adalia; France was to get most of eastern Anatolia, including Mersin, Adana, and Cilicia, as well as Kurdistan, Alexandretta, Syria, and northern Mesopotamia, including Mosul; Britain was to get the Levant from Gaza south to the Red Sea, Transjordan, most of the Syrian Desert, all of Mesopotamia south of Kirkuk (including Baghdad and Basra), and most of the Persian Gulf coast of Arabia. It was also envisaged that western Anatolia around Smyrna would go to Greece. The Holy Land itself was to be internationalized.

The next document concerned with the disposition of the Ottoman Empire was the famous "Balfour Declaration" of November 1917. Probably no document of the wartime period, except Wilson's Fourteen Points, has given rise to more disputes than this brief statement of less than eleven lines. Much of the controversy arises from the belief that it promised something to somebody and that this promise was in conflict with other promises, notably with the "McMahon Pledge" to Sherif Hussein. The Balfour Declaration took the form of a letter from British Foreign Secretary Arthur James Balfour to Lord Rothschild, one of the leading figures in the British Zionist movement. This movement, which was much stronger in Austria and Germany than in Britain, had aspirations for creating in Palestine, or perhaps elsewhere, some territory to which refugees from anti-Semitic persecution or other Jews could go to find "a national home." Balfour's letter said, "His Majesty's Government view with favor the establishment in Palestine of a national home for the Jewish people and will use their best endeavours to facilitate the achievement of this object, it being clearly understood that nothing shall be done which may prejudice the civil and religious rights of existing non-Jewish communities in Palestine, or the rights and political status enjoyed by Jews in any other country." It is to be noted that this was neither an agreement nor a promise but merely a unilateral declaration, that it did not promise a Jewish state in Palestine or even Palestine as a home for the Jews, but merely proposed such a home *in* Palestine, and that it reserved certain rights for the existing groups in the area. Hussein was so distressed when he heard of it that he asked for an explanation, and was assured by D. G. Hogarth, on behalf of the British government, that "Jewish settlement in Palestine would only be allowed in so far as would be consistent with the political and economic freedom of the Arab population." This reassurance apparently was acceptable to Hussein, but doubts continued among other Arab leaders. In answer to a request from seven such leaders, on June 16, 1918, Britain gave a public answer which divided the Arab territories into three parts: (*a*) the Arabian peninsula from Aden to Akabah (at the head of the Red Sea), where the "complete and sovereign independence of the Arabs" was recognized; (*b*) the area under British military occupation, covering southern Palestine and southern Mesopotamia, where Britain accepted the principle that government should be based "on the consent of the governed"; and (*c*) the area still under Turkish control, including Syria and northern Mesopotamia, where Britain assumed the obligation to strive for "freedom and independence." Somewhat similar in tone was a joint Anglo-French Declaration of November 7, 1918, just four days before hostilities ended in the war. It promised "the complete and final liberation of the peoples who have for so long been oppressed by the Turk and the setting up of national governments and administrations that shall derive their authority from the free exercise of the initiative and choice of the indigenous populations."

There have been extended discussions of the compatibility of the various agreements and statements made by the Great Powers regarding the disposition of the Ottoman Empire after the war. This is a difficult problem in view of the inaccuracy and ambiguity of the wording of most of these documents. On the other hand, certain facts are quite evident. There is a sharp contrast between the imperialist avarice to be found in the secret agreements like Sykes-Picot and the altruistic tone of the publicly issued statements; there is also a sharp contrast between the tenor of the British negotiations with the Jews and those with the Arabs regarding the disposition of Palestine, with the result that Jews and Arabs were each justified in believing that Britain would promote their conflicting political ambitions in that area; these beliefs, whether based on misunderstanding or deliberate deception, subsequently served to reduce the stature of Britain in the eyes of both groups, although both had previously held a higher opinion of British fairness and generosity than of any other Power; lastly, the raising of false Arab hopes and the failure to reach any clear and honest understanding regarding Syria led to a long period of conflict between the Syrians and the French government, which held the area as a mandate of the League of Nations after 1923.

As a result of his understanding of the negotiations with McMahon, Hussein began an Arab revolt against Turkey on June 5, 1916. From that point on, he received a subsidy of £225,000 a month from Britain. The famous T. E. Lawrence, known as "Lawrence of Arabia," who had been an archaeologist in the Near East in 1914, had nothing to do with the negotiations with Hussein, and did not join the revolt until October 1916. When Hussein did not obtain the concessions he expected at the Paris Peace Conference of 1919, Lawrence sickened of the whole affair and eventually changed his name to Shaw and tried to vanish from public view.

The Arab territories remained under military occupation until the legal establishment of peace with Turkey in 1923. Arabia itself was under a number of sheiks, of which the chief were Hussein in Hejaz and Ibn-Saud in Nejd. Palestine and Mesopotamia (now called Iraq) were under British military occupation. The coast of Syria was under French military occupation, while the interior of Syria (including the Aleppo-Damascus railway line) and Transjordan were under an Arab force led by Emir Feisal, third son of Hussein of Mecca. Although an American commission of inquiry, known as the King-Crane Commission (1919), and a "General Syrian Congress" of Arabs from the whole Fertile Crescent recommended that France be excluded from the area, that Syria-Palestine be joined to form a single state with Feisal as king, that the Zionists be excluded from Palestine in any political role, as well as other points, a meeting of the Great Powers at San Remo in April 1920 set up two French and two British mandates. Syria and Lebanon went to France, while Iraq and Palestine (including Transjordan) went to Britain. There were Arab uprisings and great local unrest following these decisions. The resistance in Syria was crushed by the French, who then advanced to occupy the interior of Syria and sent Feisal into exile. The British, who by this time were engaged in a rivalry (over petroleum resources and other issues) with the French, set Feisal up as king in Iraq under British protection (1921) and placed his brother Abdullah in a similar position as King of Transjordan (1923). The father of the two new kings, Hussein, was attacked by Ibn-Saud of Nejd and forced to abdicate in 1924. His kingdom of Hejaz was annexed by Ibn-Saud in 1926. After 1932 this whole area was known as Saudi Arabia.

The most important diplomatic event of the latter part of the First World War was the intervention of the United States on the side of the Entente Powers in April 1917. The causes of this event have been analyzed at great length. In general there have been four chief reasons given for the intervention from four quite different points of view. These might be summarized as follows: (1) The German submarine attacks on neutral shipping made it necessary for the United States to go to war to secure "freedom of the seas"; (2) the United States was influenced by subtle British propaganda conducted in drawing rooms, universities, and the press of the eastern part of the country where Anglophilism was rampant among the more influential social groups; (3) the United States was inveigled into the war by a conspiracy of international bankers and munitions manufacturers eager to protect their loans to the Entente Powers or their wartime profits from sales to these Powers; and (4) Balance of Power principles made it impossible for the United States to allow Great Britain to be defeated by Germany. Whatever the weight of these four in the final decision, it is quite clear that neither the government nor the people of the United States were prepared to accept a defeat of the Entente at the hands of the Central Powers. Indeed, in spite of the government's efforts to act with a certain semblance of neutrality, it was clear in 1914 that this was the view of the chief leaders in the government with the single exception of Secretary of State William Jennings Bryan. Without analyzing the four factors mentioned above, it is quite clear that the United States could not allow Britain to be defeated by any other Power. Separated from all other Great Powers by the Atlantic and Pacific oceans, the security of America required either that the control of those oceans be in its own hands or in the hands of a friendly Power. For almost a century before 1917 the United States had been willing to allow British control of the sea to go unchallenged, because it was clear that British control of the sea provided no threat to the United States, but on the contrary, provided security for the United States at a smaller cost in wealth and responsibility than security could have been obtained by any other method. The presence of Canada as a British territory adjacent to the United States, and exposed to invasion by land from the United States, constituted a hostage for British naval behavior acceptable to the United States. The German submarine assault on Britain early in 1917 drove Britain close to the door of starvation by its ruthless sinking of the merchant shipping upon which Britain's existence depended. Defeat of Britain could not be permitted because the United States was not prepared to take over control of the sea itself and could not permit German control of the sea because it had no assurance regarding the nature of such German control. The fact that the German submarines were acting in retaliation for the illegal British blockade of the continent of Europe and British violations of international law and neutral rights on the high seas, the fact that the Anglo-Saxon heritage of the United States and the Anglophilism of its influential classes made it impossible for the average American to see world events except through the spectacles made by British propaganda; the fact that Americans had lent the Entente billions of dollars which would be jeopardized by a German victory, the fact that the enormous Entente purchases of war matériel had created a boom of prosperity and inflation which would collapse the very day that the Entente collapsed— all these factors were able to bring weight to bear on the American decision only because the balance-of-power issue laid a foundation on which they could work. The important fact was that Britain was close to defeat in April 1917, and on that basis the United States entered the war. The unconscious assumption by American leaders that an Entente victory was both necessary and inevitable was at the bottom of their failure to enforce the same rules of neutrality and international law against Britain as against Germany. They constantly assumed that British violations of these rules could be compensated with monetary damages, while German violations of these rules must be resisted, by force if necessary. Since they could not admit this unconscious assumption or publicly defend the legitimate basis of international power politics on which it rested, they finally went to war on an excuse which was legally weak, although emotionally satisfying. As John Bassett Moore, America's most famous international lawyer, put it, "What most decisively contributed to the involvement of the United States in the war was the assertion of a right to protect belligerent ships on which Americans saw fit to travel and the treatment of armed belligerent merchantmen as peaceful vessels. Both assumptions were contrary to reason and to settled law, and no other professed neutral advanced them."

The Germans at first tried to use the established rules of international law regarding destruction of merchant vessels. This proved so dangerous, because of the peculiar character of the submarine itself, British control of the high seas, the British instructions to merchant ships to attack submarines, and the difficulty of distinguishing between British ships and neutral ships, that most German submarines tended to attack without warning. American protests reached a peak when the *Lusitania* was sunk in this way nine miles off the English coast on May 7, 1915. The *Lusitania* was a British merchant vessel "constructed with Government funds as [an] auxiliary cruiser, . . . expressly included in the navy list published by the British Admiralty," with "bases laid for mounting guns of six-inch caliber," carrying a cargo of 2,400 cases of rifle cartridges and 1,250 cases of shrapnel, and with orders to attack German submarines whenever possible. Seven hundred and eighty-five of 1,257 passengers, including 128 of 197 Americans, lost their lives. The incompetence of the acting captain contributed to the heavy loss, as did also a mysterious "second explosion" after the German torpedo struck. The vessel, which had been declared "unsinkable," went down in eighteen minutes. The captain was on a course he had orders to avoid; he was running at reduced speed; he had an inexperienced crew; the portholes had been left open; the lifeboats had not been swung out; and no lifeboat drills had been held.

The propaganda agencies of the Entente Powers made full use of the occasion. *The Times* of London announced that "four-fifths of her passengers were citizens of the United States" (the actual proportion was 15.6 percent); the British manufactured and distributed a medal which they pretended had been awarded to the submarine crew by the German government; a French paper published a picture of the crowds in Berlin at the outbreak of war in 1914 as a picture of Germans "rejoicing" at news of the sinking of the *Lusitania*.

The United States protested violently against the submarine warfare while brushing aside German arguments based on the British blockade. It was so irreconcilable in these protests that Germany sent Wilson a note on May 4, 1916, in which it promised that "in the future merchant vessels within and without the war zone shall not be sunk without warning and without safeguarding human lives, unless these ships attempt to escape or offer resistance." In return the German government hoped that the United States would put pressure on Britain to follow the established rules of international law in regard to blockade and freedom of the sea. Wilson refused to do so. Accordingly, it became clear to the Germans that they would be starved into defeat unless they could defeat Britain first by unrestricted submarine warfare. Since they were aware that resort to this method would probably bring the United States into the war against them, they made another effort to negotiate peace before resorting to it. When their offer to negotiate, made on December 12, 1916, was rejected by the Entente Powers on December 27th, the group in the German government which had been advocating ruthless submarine warfare came into a position to control affairs, and ordered the resumption of unrestricted submarine attacks on February 1, 1917. Wilson was notified of this decision on January 31st. He broke off diplomatic relations with Germany on February 3rd, and, after two months of indecision, asked the Congress for a declaration of war April 3, 1917. The final decision was influenced by the constant pressure of his closest associates, the realization that Britain was reaching the end of her resources of men, money, and ships, and the knowledge that Germany was planning to seek an alliance with Mexico if war began.

While the diplomacy of neutrality and intervention was moving along the lines we have described, a parallel diplomatic effort was being directed toward efforts to negotiate peace. These efforts were a failure but are, nonetheless, of considerable significance because they reveal the motivations and war aims of the belligerents. They were a failure because any negotiated peace requires a willingness on both sides to make those concessions which will permit the continued survival of the enemy. In 1914–1918, however, in order to win public support for total mobilization, each country's propaganda had been directed toward a total victory for itself and total defeat for the enemy. In time, both sides became so enmeshed in their own propaganda that it became impossible to admit publicly one's readiness to accept such lesser aims as any negotiated peace would require. Moreover, as the tide of battle waxed and waned, giving alternate periods of elation and discouragement to both sides, the side which was temporarily elated became increasingly attached to the fetish of total victory and unwilling to accept the lesser aim of a negotiated peace. Accordingly, peace became possible only when war weariness had reached the point where one side concluded that even defeat was preferable to continuation of the war. This point was reached in Russia in 1917 and in Germany and Austria in 1918. In Germany this point of view was greatly reinforced by the realization that military defeat and political change were preferable to the economic revolution and social upheaval which would accompany any effort to continue the war in pursuit of an increasingly unattainable victory.

From the various efforts to negotiate peace it is clear that Britain was unwilling to accept any peace which would not include the restoration of Belgium or which would leave Germany supreme on the Continent or in a position to resume the commercial, naval, and colonial rivalry which had existed before 1914; France was unwilling to accept any solution which did not restore Alsace-Lorraine to her; the German High Command and the German industrialists were determined not to give up all the occupied territory in the west, but were hoping to retain Lorraine, part of Alsace, Luxembourg, part of Belgium, and Longwy in France because of the mineral and industrial resources of these areas. The fact that Germany had an excellent supply of coking coal with an inadequate supply of iron ore, while the occupied areas had plenty of the latter but an inadequate supply of the former, had a great deal to do with the German objections to a negotiated peace and the ambiguous terms in which their war aims were discussed. Austria was, until the death of Emperor Francis Joseph in 1916, unwilling to accept any peace which would leave the Slavs, especially the Serbs, free to continue their nationalistic agitations for the disintegration of the Habsburg Empire. On the other hand, Italy was determined to exclude the Habsburg Empire from the shores of the Adriatic Sea, while the Serbs were even more determined to reach those shores by the acquisition of Habsburg-ruled Slav areas in the western Balkans. After the Russian revolutions of 1917, many of these obstacles to a negotiated peace became weaker. The Vatican, working through Cardinal Pacelli (later Pope Pius XII) sought a negotiated peace which would prevent the destruction of the Habsburg Empire, the last Catholic Great Power in Europe. Prominent men in all countries, like Lord Lansdowne (British foreign secretary before 1914), became so alarmed at the spread of Socialism that they were willing to make almost any concessions to stop the destruction of civilized ways of life by continued warfare. Humanitarians like Henry Ford or Romain Rolland became increasingly alarmed at the continued slaughter. But, for the reasons we have already mentioned, peace remained elusive until the great German offensives of 1918 had been broken.

After what Ludendorff called "the black day of the German Army" (August 8, 1918), a German Crown Council, meeting at Spa, decided victory was no longer possible, and decided to negotiate for an armistice. This was not done because of a controversy between the crown prince and Ludendorff in which the former advised an immediate retreat to the "Hindenburg Line" twenty miles to the rear, while the latter wished to make a slow withdrawal so that the Entente could not organize an attack on the Hindenburg Line before winter. Two Entente victories, at Saint-Quentin (August 31st) and in Flanders (September 2nd) made this dispute moot. The Germans began an involuntary retreat, drenching the ground they evacuated with "mustard gas" in order to slow up the Entente pursuit, especially the tanks. The German High Command removed the chancellor, Hertling, and put in the more democratic Prince Max of Baden with orders to make an immediate armistice or face military disaster (September 29–October 1, 1918). On October 5th a German note to President Wilson asked for an armistice on the basis of the Fourteen Points of January 8, 1918, and his subsequent principles of September 27, 1918. These statements of Wilson had captured the imaginations of idealistic persons and subject peoples everywhere. The Fourteen Points promised the end of secret diplomacy; freedom of the seas; freedom of commerce; disarmament; a fair settlement of colonial claims, with the interests of the native peoples receiving equal weight with the titles of imperialist Powers; the evacuation of Russia; the evacuation and restoration of Belgium; the evacuation of France and the restoration to her of Alsace-Lorraine as in 1870; the readjustment of the Italian frontiers on nationality lines; free and autonomous development for the peoples of the Habsburg Empire; the evacuation, restoration, and guarantee of Romania, Montenegro, and Serbia, with the last-named securing free access to the sea; international guarantees to keep the Straits permanently opened to the ships and commerce of all nations; freedom for the autonomous development of the non-Turkish nationalities of the

Ottoman Empire, along with a secure sovereignty for the Turks themselves; an independent Polish state with free access to the sea and with
international guarantees; a League of Nations to afford "mutual guarantees of political independence and territorial integrity to great and small
states alike"; and no destruction of Germany or even any alteration of
her institutions except those necessary to make it clear when her spokesmen spoke for the Reichstag majority and when they "speak for the
military party and the men whose creed is imperial domination."

In a series of notes between Germany and the United States, Wilson
made it clear that he would grant an armistice only if Germany would
withdraw from all occupied territory, make an end to submarine attacks, accept the Fourteen Points, establish a responsible government,
and accept terms which would preserve the existing Entente military superiority. He was most insistent on the responsible government, warning
that if he had to deal "with military masters or monarchical autocrats"
he would demand "not negotiations but surrender." The German constitution was changed to give all powers to the Reichstag; Ludendorff was
fired; the German Navy at Kiel mutinied, and the Kaiser fled from Berlin (October 29th). In the meantime, the Entente Supreme War Council
refused to accept the Fourteen Points as the basis for peace until Colonel
House threatened that the United States would makes a separate peace
with Germany. They then demanded and received a definition of the
meaning of each term, made a reservation on "the freedom of the seas,"
and expanded the meaning of "restoration of invaded territory" to include compensation to the civilian population for their war losses. On
this basis an armistice commission met German negotiators on November
7th. The German Revolution was spreading, and the Kaiser abdicated
on November 9th. The German negotiators received the Entente military terms and asked for an immediate ending of hostilities and of the
economic blockade and a reduction in the Entente demand for machine
guns from 30,000 to 25,000 on the grounds that the difference of 5,000
was needed to suppress the German Revolution. The last point was conceded, but the other two refused. The armistice was signed on November 11, 1918, at 5:00 A.M. to take effect at 11:00 A.M. It provided that the
Germans must evacuate all occupied territory (including Alsace-
Lorraine) within fourteen days, and the left bank of the Rhine plus
three bridgeheads on the right bank within thirty-one days, that they
surrender huge specified amounts of war equipment, trucks, locomotives,
all submarines, the chief naval vessels, all prisoners of war, and captured
merchant ships, as well as the Baltic fortresses, and all valuables and securities taken in occupied territory, including the Russian and Romanian
gold reserves. The Germans were also required to renounce the treaties
of Brest-Litovsk and of Bucharest, which they had imposed on Russia
and on Romania, and to promise to repair the damage of occupied terri-

tories. This last point was of considerable importance, as the Germans had systematically looted or destroyed the areas they evacuated in the last few months of the war.

The negotiations with Wilson leading up to the Armistice of 1918 are of great significance, since they formed one of the chief factors in subsequent German resentment at the Treaty of Versailles. In these negotiations Wilson had clearly promised that the peace treaty with Germany would be negotiated and would be based on the Fourteen Points; as we shall see, the Treaty of Versailles was imposed without negotiation, and the Fourteen Points fared very poorly in its provisions. An additional factor connected with these events lies in the subsequent claim of the German militarists that the German Army was never defeated but was "stabbed in the back" by the home front through a combination of international Catholics, international Jews, and international Socialists. There is no merit whatever in these contentions. The German Army was clearly beaten in the field; the negotiations for an armistice were commenced by the civilian government at the insistence of the High Command, and the Treaty of Versailles itself was subsequently signed, rather than rejected, at the insistence of the same High Command in order to avoid a military occupation of Germany. By these tactics the German Army was able to escape the military occupation of Germany which they so dreaded. Although the last enemy forces did not leave German soil until 1931, no portions of Germany were occupied beyond those signified in the armistice itself (the Rhineland and the three bridgeheads on the right bank of the Rhine) except for a brief occupation of the Ruhr district in 1923.

The Home Front, 1914-1918

The First World War was a catastrophe of such magnitude that, even today, the imagination has some difficulty grasping it. In the year 1916, in two battles (Verdun and the Somme) casualties of over 1,700,000 were suffered by both sides. In the artillery barrage which opened the French attack on Chemin des Dames in April 1917, 11,000,000 shells were fired on a 30-mile front in 10 days. Three months later, on an 11-mile front at Passchendaele, the British fired 4,250,000 shells costing £22,000,000 in a preliminary barrage, and lost 400,000 men in the ensuing infantry assault. In the German attack of March 1918, 62 divisions with 4,500 heavy guns and 1,000 planes were hurled on a front only 45 miles wide. On all fronts in the whole war almost 13,000,000 men in the various armed forces died from wounds and disease. It has been estimated by the Carnegie Endowment for International Peace that the war destroyed over $400,000,000,000 of property at a time when the value of every object in France and Belgium was not worth over $75,000,000,000.

Obviously, expenditures of men and wealth at rates like these required a tremendous mobilization of resources throughout the world, and could not fail to have far-reaching effects on the patterns of thought and modes of action of people forced to undergo such a strain. Some states were destroyed or permanently crippled. There were profound modifications in finance, in economic life, in social relations, in intellectual outlook, and in emotional patterns. Nevertheless, two facts should be recognized. The war brought nothing really new into the world; rather it sped up processes of change which had been going on for a considerable period and would have continued anyway, with the result that changes which would have taken place over a period of thirty or even fifty years in peacetime were brought about in five years during the war. Also, the changes were much greater in objective facts and in the organization of society than they were in men's ideas of these facts or organization. It was as if the changes were too rapid for men's minds to accept them, or, what is more likely, that men, seeing the great changes which were occurring on all sides, recognized them, but assumed that they were merely temporary wartime aberrations, and that, when peace came, they would pass away and everyone could go back to the slow, pleasant world of 1913. This point of view, which dominated the thinking of the 1920's, was widespread and very dangerous. In their efforts to go back to 1913, men refused to recognize that the wartime changes were more or less permanent, and, instead of trying to solve the problems arising from these changes, set up a false facade of pretense, painted to look like 1913, to cover up the great changes which had taken place. Then, by acting as if this facade were reality, and by neglecting the maladjusted reality which was moving beneath it, the people of the 1920's drifted in a hectic world of unreality until the world depression of 1929–1935, and the international crises which followed, tore away the facade and showed the horrible, long-neglected reality beneath it.

The magnitude of the war and the fact that it might last for more than six months were quite unexpected for both sides and were impressed upon them only gradually. It first became clear in regard to consumption of supplies, especially ammunition, and in the problem of how to pay for these supplies. In July 1914, the military men were confident that a decision would be reached in six months because their military plans and the examples of 1866 and 1870 indicated an immediate decision. This belief was supported by the financial experts who, while greatly underestimating the cost of fighting, were confident that the financial resources of all states would be exhausted in six months. By "financial resources" they meant the gold reserves of the various nations. These were clearly limited; all the Great Powers were on the gold standard under which bank notes and paper money could be converted into gold on demand. However, each country suspended the gold standard at the outbreak of war. This removed the automatic limitation on the supply of paper money. Then each country proceeded to pay for the war by borrowing from the banks. The banks created the money which they lent by merely giving the government a deposit of any size against which the government could draw checks. The banks were no longer limited in the amount of credit they could create because they no longer had to pay out gold for checks on demand. Thus the creation of money in the form of credit by the banks was limited only by the demands of its borrowers. Naturally, as governments borrowed to pay for their needs, private businesses borrowed in order to be able to fill the government's orders. The gold which could no longer be demanded merely rested in the vaults, except where some of it was exported to pay for supplies from neutral countries or from fellow belligerents. As a result, the percentage of outstanding bank notes covered by gold reserves steadily fell, and the percentage of bank credit covered by either gold or bank notes fell even further.

Naturally, when the supply of money was increased in this fashion faster than the supply of goods, prices rose because a larger supply of money was competing for a smaller supply of goods. This effect was made worse by the fact that the supply of goods tended to be reduced by wartime destruction. People received money for making capital goods, consumers' goods, and munitions, but they could spend their money only to buy consumers' goods, since capital goods and munitions were not offered for sale. Since governments tried to reduce the supply of consumers' goods while increasing the supply of the other two products, the problem of rising prices (inflation) became acute. At the same time the problem of public debt became steadily worse because governments were financing such a large part of their activities by bank credit. These two problems, inflation and public debt, continued to grow, even after the fighting stopped, because of the continued disruption of economic life and the need to pay for past activities. Only in the period 1920–1925 did these two stop increasing in most countries, and they remained problems long after that.

Inflation indicates not only an increase in the prices of goods but also a decrease in the value of money (since it will buy less goods). Accordingly, people in an inflation seek to get goods and to get rid of money. Thus inflation increases production and purchases for consumption or hoarding, but it reduces saving or creation of capital. It benefits debtors (by making a fixed-money debt less of a burden) but injures creditors (by reducing the value of their savings and credits). Since the middle classes of European society, with their bank savings, checking deposits, mortgages, insurance, and bond holdings, were the creditor class, they were injured and even ruined by the wartime inflation. In Germany, Poland, Hungary, and Russia, where the inflation went so far that the monetary unit became completely valueless by 1924, the middle classes were largely destroyed, and their members were driven to desperation or at least to an almost psychopathic hatred of the form of government or the social class that they believed to be responsible for their plight. Since the last stages of inflation which dealt the fatal blow to the middle classes occurred after the war rather than during it (in 1923 in Germany), this hatred was directed against the parliamentary governments which were functioning after 1918 rather than against the monarchical governments which functioned in 1914–1918. In France and Italy, where the inflation went so far that the franc or lire was reduced permanently to one-fifth of its prewar value, the hatred of the injured middle classes was directed against the parliamentary regime which had functioned both during and after the war and against the working class which they felt had profited by their misfortunes. These things were not true in Britain or the United States, where the inflation was brought under control and the monetary unit restored to most of its prewar value. Even in these countries, prices rose by 200 to 300 percent, while public debts rose about 1,000 percent.

The economic effects of the war were more complicated. Resources of all kinds, including land, labor, and raw materials, had to be diverted from peacetime purposes to wartime production; or, in some cases, resources previously not used at all had to be brought into the productive system. Before the war, the allotment of resources to production had been made by the automatic processes of the price system; labor and raw materials going, for example, to manufacture those goods which were most profitable rather than to those goods which were most serviceable or socially beneficial, or in best taste. In wartime, however, governments had to have certain specific goods for military purposes; they tried to get these goods produced by making them more profitable than nonmilitary goods using the same resources, but they were not always successful. The excess of purchasing power in the hands of consumers caused a great rise in demand for goods of a semiluxury nature, like white cotton shirts for laborers. This frequently made it more profitable for manufacturers to use cotton for making shirts to sell at high prices than to use it to make explosives.

Situations such as these made it necessary for governments to intervene directly in the economic process to secure those results which could not be obtained by the free price system or to reduce those evil effects which emerged from wartime disruption. They appealed to the patriotism of manufacturers to make things that were needed rather than

things which were profitable, or to the patriotism of consumers to put
their money into government bonds rather than into goods in short supply. They began to build government-owned plants for war production,
either using them for such purposes themselves or leasing them out to
private manufacturers at attractive terms. They began to ration consumers' goods which were in short supply, like articles of food. They
began to monopolize essential raw materials and allot them to manufacturers who had war contracts rather than allow them to flow where
prices were highest. The materials so treated were generally fuels, steel,
rubber, copper, wool, cotton, nitrates, and such, although they varied
from country to country, depending upon the supply. Governments began to regulate imports and exports in order to ensure that necessary
materials stayed in the country and, above all, did not go to enemy states.
This led to the British blockade of Europe, the rationing of exports to
neutrals, and complicated negotiations to see that goods in neutral countries were not reexported to enemy countries. Bribery, bargaining, and
even force came into these negotiations, as when the British set quotas
on the imports of Holland based on the figures for prewar years or cut
down necessary shipments of British coal to Sweden until they obtained
the concessions they wished regarding sales of Swedish goods to Germany. Shipping and railroad transportation had to be taken over almost
completely in most countries in order to ensure that the inadequate space
for cargo and freight would be used as effectively as possible, that load-
ing and unloading would be speeded up, and that goods essential to the
war effort would be shipped earlier and faster than less essential goods.
Labor had to be regulated and directed into essential activities. The rapid
rise in prices led to demands for raises in wages. This led to a growth
and strengthening of labor unions and increasing threats of strikes. There
was no guarantee that the wages of essential workers would go up faster
than the wages of nonessential workers. Certainly the wages of soldiers,
who were the most essential of all, went up very little. Thus there was
no guarantee that labor, if left solely to the influence of wage levels, as
was usual before 1914, would flow to the occupations where it was most
urgently needed. Accordingly, the governments began to intervene in
labor problems, seeking to avoid strikes but also to direct the flow of
labor to more essential activities. There were general registrations of
men in most countries, at first as part of the draft of men for military
service, but later to control services in essential activities. Generally, the
right to leave an essential job was restricted, and eventually people were
directed into essential jobs from nonessential activities. The high wages
and shortage of labor brought into the labor market many persons who
would not have been in it in peacetime, such as old persons, youths,
clergy, and, above all, women. This flow of women from homes into
factories or other services had the most profound effects on social life

and modes of living, revolutionizing the relations of the sexes, bringing women up to a level of social, legal, and political equality closer than previously to that of men, obtaining for them the right to vote in some countries, the right to own or dispose of property in other more backward ones, changing the appearance and costume of women by such innovations as shorter skirts, shorter hair, less frills, and generally a drastic reduction in the amount of clothing they wore.

Because of the large number of enterprises involved and the small size of many of them, direct regulation by the government was less likely in the field of agriculture. Here conditions were generally more competitive than in industry, with the result that farm prices had shown a growing tendency to fluctuate more widely than industrial prices. This continued during the war, as agricultural regulation was left more completely to the influence of price changes than other parts of the economy. As farm prices soared, farmers became more prosperous than they had been in decades, and sought madly to increase their share of the rain of money by bringing larger and larger amounts of land under cultivation. This was not possible in Europe because of the lack of men, equipment, and fertilizers; but in Canada, the United States, Australia, and South America land was brought under the plow which, because of lack of rainfall or its inaccessibility to peacetime markets, should never have been brought under cultivation. In Canada the increase in wheat acreage was from 9.9 million in the years 1909–1913 to 22.1 million in the years 1921–25. In the United States the increase in wheat acreage was from 47.0 million to 58.1 million in the same period. Canada increased her share of the world's wheat crop from 14 percent to 39 percent in this decade. Farmers went into debt to obtain these lands, and by 1920 were buried under a mountain of mortgages which would have been considered unbearable before 1914 but which in the boom of wartime prosperity and high prices was hardly given a second thought.

In Europe such expansion of acreage was not possible, although grasslands were plowed up in Britain and some other countries. In Europe as a whole, acreage under cultivation declined, by 15 percent for cereals in 1913–1919. Livestock numbers were also reduced (swine by 22 percent and cattle by 7 percent in 1913–1920). Woodlands were cut for fuel when importation of coal was stopped from England, Germany, or Poland. Since most of Europe was cut off from Chile, which had been the chief prewar source of nitrates, or from North Africa and Germany, which had produced much of the prewar supply of phosphates, the use of these and other fertilizers was reduced. This resulted in an exhaustion of the soil so great that in some countries, like Germany, the soil had not recovered its fertility by 1930. When the German chemist Haber discovered a method for extracting nitrogen from the air which made it possible for his country to survive the cutting off of Chilean nitrates, the new supply was used almost entirely to produce explosives, with little left over for fertilizers. The declining fertility of the soil and the fact that new lands of lesser natural fertility were brought under cultivation led to drastic declines in agricultural output per acre (in cereals about 15 percent in 1914–1919).

These adverse influences were most evident in Germany, where the number of hogs fell from 25.3 million in 1914 to 5.7 million in 1918; the average weight of slaughtered cattle fell from 250 kilos in 1913 to 130 in 1918; the acreage in sugar beets fell from 592,843 hectares in 1914 to 366,505 in 1919, while the yield of sugar beets per hectare fell from 31,800 kilos in 1914 to 16,350 kilos in 1920. German's prewar imports of about 6½ million tons of cereals each year ceased, and her home production of these fell by 3 million tons per year. Her prewar imports of over 2 million tons of oil concentrates and other feed for farm animals stopped. The results of the blockade were devastating. Continued for nine months after the armistice, it caused the deaths of 800,000 persons, according to Max Sering. In addition, reparations took about 108,000 horses, 205,000 cattle, 426,000 sheep, and 240,000 fowl.

More damaging than the reduction in the number of farm animals (which was made up in six or seven years), or the drain on the fertility of the soil (which could be made up in twelve or fifteen years), was the disruption of Europe's integration of agricultural production (which was never made up). The blockade of the Central Powers tore the heart out of the prewar integration. When the war ended, it was impossible to replace this, because there were many new political boundaries; these boundaries were marked by constantly rising tariff restrictions, and the non-European world had increased both its agricultural and industrial output to a point where it was much less dependent on Europe.

The heavy casualties, the growing shortages, the slow decline in quality of goods, and the gradual growth of the use of substitutes, as well as the constantly increasing pressure of governments on the activities of their citizens—all these placed a great strain on the morale of the various European peoples. The importance of this question was just as great in the autocratic and semidemocratic countries as it was in the ones with fully democratic and parliamentary regimes. The latter did not generally permit any general elections during the war, but both types required the full support of their peoples in order to maintain their battle lines and economic activities at full effectiveness. At the beginning, the fever of patriotism and national enthusiasm was so great that this was no problem. Ancient and deadly political rivals clasped hands, or even sat in the same Cabinet, and pledged a united front to the enemy of their fatherland. But disillusionment was quick, and appeared as early as the winter of 1914. This change was parallel to the growth of the realization that the war was to be a long one and not the lightning stroke of a single campaign and a single battle which all had expected. The inadequacies of the preparations to deal with the heavy casualties or to provide munitions for the needs of modern war, as well as the shortage or disruption of the supply of civilian goods, led to public agitation. Committees were formed, but proved relatively ineffective, and in most activities in most countries were replaced by single-headed agencies equipped with extensive controls. The use of voluntary or semivoluntary methods of control generally vanished with the committees and were replaced by compulsion, however covert. In governments as wholes a somewhat similar shifting of personnel took place until each Cabinet came to be dominated by a single man, endowed with greater energy, or a greater willingness to make quick decisions on scanty information than his fellows. In this way Lloyd George replaced Asquith in England; Clemenceau replaced a series of lesser leaders in France; Wilson strengthened his control on his own government in the United States; and, in a distinctly German way, Ludendorff came to dominate the government of his country. In order to build up the morale of their own peoples and to lower that of their enemies, countries engaged in a variety of activities designed to regulate the flow of information to these peoples. This involved censorship, propaganda, and curtailment of civil liberties. These were established in all countries, without a hitch in the Central Powers and Russia where there were long traditions of extensive police authority, but no less effectively in France and Britain. In France a State of Siege was proclaimed on August 2, 1914. This gave the government the right to rule by decree, established censorship, and placed the police under military control. In general, French censorship was not so severe as the German nor so skillful as the British, while their propaganda was far better than the German but could not compare with the British. The complexities of French political life and the slow movement of its bureaucracy allowed all kinds of delays and evasions of control, especially by influential persons. When Clemenceau was in opposition to the government in the early days of the war, his paper, *L'homme libre*, was suspended; he continued to publish it with impunity under the name *L'homme enchaîné*. The British censorship was established on August 5, 1914, and at once intercepted all cables and private mail which it could reach, including that of neutral countries. These at once became an important source of military and economic intelligence. A Defence of the Realm Act (familiarly known as DORA) was passed giving the government the power to censor all information. A Press Censorship Committee was set up in 1914 and was replaced by the Press Bureau under Frederick E. Smith (later Lord Birkenhead) in 1916. Established in Crewe House, it was able to control all news printed in the press, acting as the direct agent of the Admiralty and War Offices. The censorship of printed books was fairly lenient, and was much more so for books to be read in England than for books for export, with the result that "best sellers" in England were unknown in America. Parallel with the censorship was the War Propaganda Bureau under Sir Charles Masterman, which had an American Bureau of Information under Sir Gilbert Parker at Wellington House. This last agency was able to control almost all information going to the American press, and by 1916 was acting as an international news service itself, distributing European news to about 35 American papers which had no foreign reporters of their own.

The Censorship and the Propaganda bureaus worked together in Britain as well as elsewhere. The former concealed all stories of Entente violations of the laws of war or of the rules of humanity, and reports on their own military mistakes or their own war plans and less altruistic war aims, while the Propaganda Bureau widely publicized the violations and crudities of the Central Powers, their prewar schemes for mobilization, and their agreements regarding war aims. The German violation of Belgian neutrality was constantly bewailed, while nothing was said of the Entente violation of Greek neutrality. A great deal was made of the Austrian ultimatum to Serbia, while the Russian mobilization which had precipitated the war was hardly mentioned. In the Central Powers a great deal was made of the Entente "encirclement," while nothing was said of the Kaiser's demands for "a place in the sun" or the High Command's refusal to renounce annexation of any part of Belgium. In general, manufacture of outright lies by propaganda agencies was infrequent, and the desired picture of the enemy was built up by a process of selection and distortion of evidence until, by 1918, many in the West regarded the Germans as bloodthirsty and sadistic militarists, while the Germans regarded the Russians as "subhuman monsters." A great deal was made, especially by the British, of "atrocity" propaganda; stories of German mutilation of bodies, violation of women, cutting off of children's hands, desecration of churches and shrines, and crucifixions of Belgians were widely believed in the West by 1916. Lord Bryce headed a committee which produced a volume of such stories in 1915, and it is quite evident that this well-educated man, "the greatest English authority on the United States," was completely taken in by his own stories. Here, again, outright manufacture of falsehoods was infrequent, although General Henry Charteris in 1917 created a story that the Germans were cooking human bodies to extract glycerine, and produced pictures to prove it. Again, photographs of mutilated bodies in a Russian anti-Semitic outrage in 1905 were circulated as pictures of Belgians in 1915. There were several reasons for the use of such atrocity stories: (a) to build up the fighting spirit of the mass army; (b) to stiffen civilian morale; (c) to encourage enlistments, especially in England, where volunteers were used for one and a half years; (d) to increase subscriptions for war bonds; (e) to justify one's own breaches of international law or the customs of war; (f) to destroy the chances of negotiating peace (as in December 1916) or to justify a severe final peace (as Germany did in respect to Brest-Litovsk); and (g) to win the support of neutrals. On the whole, the relative innocence and credulity of the average person, who was not yet immunized to propaganda assaults through mediums of mass communication in 1914, made the use of such stories relatively effective. But the discovery, in the period after 1919, that they had been hoaxed gave rise to a skepticism toward all government communications which was especially noticeable in the Second World War.

VI

THE
VERSAILLES SYSTEM
AND THE RETURN
TO "NORMALCY,"
1919-1929

The Peace Settlements, 1919–1923

Security, 1919–1935

Disarmament, 1919–1935

Reparations, 1919–1932

The Peace Settlements,
1919-1923

T H E First World War was ended by dozens of treaties signed in
the period 1919–1923. Of these, the five chief documents were the
five treaties of peace with the defeated Powers, named from the
sites in the neighborhood of Paris where they were signed. These were:

Treaty of Versailles with Germany, June 28, 1919
Treaty of Saint-Germain with Austria, September 10, 1919
Treaty of Neuilly with Bulgaria, November 27, 1919
Treaty of Trianon with Hungary, June 4, 1920
Treaty of Sèvres with Turkey, August 20, 1920

The last of these, the Treaty of Sèvres with Turkey, was never ratified
and was replaced by a new treaty, signed at Lausanne in 1923.

The peace settlements made in this period were subjected to vigorous
and detailed criticism in the two decades 1919–1939. This criticism was as
ardent from the victors as from the vanquished. Although this attack
was largely aimed at the terms of the treaties, the real causes of the attack did not lie in these terms, which were neither unfair nor ruthless,
were far more lenient than any settlement which might have emerged
from a German victory, and which created a new Europe which was, at
least politically, more just than the Europe of 1914. The causes of the
discontent with the settlements of 1919–1923 rested on the procedures
which were used to make these settlements rather than on the terms of
the settlements themselves. Above all, there was discontent at the contrast between the procedures which were used and the procedures which
pretended to be used, as well as between the high-minded principles
which were supposed to be applied and those which really were applied

The peoples of the victorious nations had taken to heart their war-time propaganda about the rights of small nations, making the world safe for democracy, and putting an end both to power politics and to secret diplomacy. These ideals had been given concrete form in Wilson's Fourteen Points. Whether the defeated Powers felt the same enthusiasm for these high ideals is subject to dispute, but they had been promised, on November 5, 1918, that the peace settlements would be negotiated and would be based on the Fourteen Points. When it became clear that the settlements were to be imposed rather than negotiated, that the Four-teen Points had been lost in the confusion, and that the terms of the settlements had been reached by a process of secret negotiations from which the small nations had been excluded and in which power politics played a much larger role than the safety of democracy, there was a revulsion of feeling against the treaties.

In Britain and in Germany, propaganda barrages were aimed against these settlements until, by 1929, most of the Western World had feel-ings of guilt and shame whenever they thought of the Treaty of Ver-sailles. There was a good deal of sincerity in these feelings, especially in England and in the United States, but there was also a great deal of in-sincerity behind them in all countries. In England the same groups, often the same people, who had made the wartime propaganda and the peace settlements were loudest in their complaint that the latter had fallen far below the ideals of the former, while all the while their real aims were to use power politics to the benefit of Britain. Certainly there were grounds for criticism, and, equally certainly, the terms of the peace set-tlements were far from perfect; but criticism should have been directed rather at the hypocrisy and lack of realism in the ideals of the wartime propaganda and at the lack of honesty of the chief negotiators in carry-ing on the pretense that these ideals were still in effect while they vio-lated them daily, and necessarily violated them. The settlements were clearly made by secret negotiations, by the Great Powers exclusively, and by power politics. They had to be. No settlements could ever have been made on any other bases. The failure of the chief negotiators (at least the Anglo-Americans) to admit this is regrettable, but behind their reluctance to admit it is the even more regrettable fact that the lack of political experience and political education of the American and Eng-lish electorates made it dangerous for the negotiators to admit the facts of life in international political relationships.

It is clear that the peace settlements were made by an organization which was chaotic and by a procedure which was fraudulent. None of this was deliberate. It arose rather from weakness and from ignorance, from a failure to decide, before the peace was made, who would make it, how it was to be made, and on what principles it would be based. The normal way to make peace after a war in which the victors form a coalition would be for the victors to hold a conference, agree on the terms they hope to get from the defeated, then have a congress with these latter to impose these terms, either with or without discussion and compromise. It was tacitly assumed in October and November, 1918, that this method was to be used to end the existing war. But this congress method could not be used in 1919 for several reasons. The members of the victorious coalition were so numerous (thirty-two Allied and Associated Powers) that they could have agreed on terms only slowly and after considerable preliminary organization. This preliminary organization never occurred, largely because President Wilson was too busy to participate in the process, was unwilling to delegate any real authority to others, and, with a relatively few, intensely held ideas (like the League of Nations, democracy, and self-determination), had no taste for the details of organization. Wilson was convinced that if he could only get the League of Nations accepted, any undesirable details in the terms of the treaties could be remedied later through the League. Lloyd George and Clemenceau made use of this conviction to obtain numerous provisions in the terms which were undesirable to Wilson but highly desirable to them.

The time necessary for a preliminary conference or preliminary planning was also lacking. Lloyd George wanted to carry out his campaign pledge of immediate demobilization, and Wilson wanted to get back to his duties as President of the United States. Moreover, if the terms had been drawn up at a preliminary conference, they would have resulted from compromises between the many Powers concerned, and these compromises would have broken down as soon as any effort was made to negotiate with the Germans later. Since the Germans had been promised the right to negotiate, it became clear that the terms could not first be made the subject of public compromise in a full preliminary conference. Unfortunately, by the time the victorious Great Powers realized all this, and decided to make the terms by secret negotiations among themselves, invitations had already been sent to all the victorious Powers to come to an Inter-Allied Conference to make preliminary terms. As a solution to this embarrassing situation, the peace was made on two levels. On one level, in the full glare of publicity, the Inter-Allied Conference became the Plenary Peace Conference, and, with considerable fanfare, did nothing. On the other level, the Great Powers worked out their peace terms in secret and, when they were ready, imposed them simultaneously on the conference and on the Germans. This had not been intended. In fact, it was not clear to anyone just what was being done. As late as February 22nd, Balfour, the British foreign secretary, still believed they were working on "preliminary peace terms," and the Germans believed the same on April 15th.

While the Great Powers were negotiating in secret the full conference met several times under rigid rules designed to prevent action. These sessions were governed by the iron hand of Clemenceau, who heard the motions he wanted, jammed through those he desired, and answered protests by outright threats to make peace without any consultation with the Lesser Powers at all and dark references to the millions of men the Great Powers had under arms. On February 14th the conference was given the draft of the Covenant of the League of Nations, and on April 11th the draft of the International Labor Office; both were accepted on April 28th. On May 6th came the text of the Treaty of Versailles, only one day before it was given to the Germans; at the end of May came the draft of the Treaty of Saint-Germain with Austria.

While this futile show was going on in public, the Great Powers were making peace in secret. Their meetings were highly informal. When the military leaders were present the meetings were known as the Supreme War Council; when the military leaders were absent (as they usually were after January 12th) the group was known as the Supreme Council or the Council of Ten. It consisted of the head of the government and the foreign minister of each of the five Great Powers (Britain, the United States, France, Italy, and Japan). This group met forty-six times from January 12th to March 24, 1919. It worked very ineffectively. At the middle of March, because a sharp dispute over the German-Polish frontier leaked to the press, the Council of Ten was reduced to a Council of Four (Lloyd George, Wilson, Clemenceau, Orlando). These four, with Orlando frequently absent, held over two hundred meetings in a period of thirteen weeks (March 27th to June 28th). They put the Treaty of Versailles into form in three weeks and did the preliminary work on the treaty with Austria.

When the treaty with Germany was signed on June 28, 1919, the heads of governments left Paris and the Council of Ten ended. So also did the Plenary Conference. The five foreign ministers (Balfour, Lansing, Pichon, Tittoni, and Makino) were left in Paris as the Council of Heads of Delegations, with full powers to complete the peace settlements. This group finished the treaties with Austria and Bulgaria and had them both signed. They disbanded on January 10, 1920, leaving behind an executive committee, the Conference of Ambassadors. This consisted of the ambassadors of the four Great Powers in Paris plus a French representative. This group held two hundred meetings in the next three years and continued to meet until 1931. It supervised the execution of the three peace treaties already signed, negotiated the peace treaty with Hungary, and performed many purely political acts which had no treaty basis, such as drawing the Albanian frontier in November 1921. In general, in the decade after the Peace Conference, the Conference of Ambassadors was the organization by which the Great Powers ruled Europe. It acted with power, speed, and secrecy in all issues delegated to it. When issues arose which were too important to be treated in this way, the Supreme Council was occasionally reunited. This was done about twenty-five times in the three years 1920–1922, usually in regard to reparations, economic reconstruction, and acute political problems. The most important of these meetings of the Supreme Council were held at Paris, London, San Remo, Boulogne, and Spa in 1920; at Paris and London in 1921; and at Paris, Genoa, The Hague, and London in 1922. This valuable practice was ended by Britain in 1923 in protest against the French determination to use force to compel Germany to fulfill the reparations clauses of the peace treaty.

At all of these meetings, as at the Peace Conference itself, the political leaders were assisted by groups of experts and interested persons, sometimes self-appointed. Many of these "experts" were members or associates of the international-banking fraternity. At the Paris Peace Conference the experts numbered thousands and were organized into official staffs by most countries, even before the war ended. These experts were of the greatest importance. They were formed into committees at Paris and given problem after problem, especially boundary problems, usually without any indication as to what principles should guide their decisions. The importance of these committees of experts can be seen in the fact that in every case but one where a committee of experts submitted a unanimous report, the Supreme Council accepted its recommendation and incorporated it in the treaty. In cases where the report was not unanimous, the problem was generally resubmitted to the experts for further consideration. The one case where a unanimous report was not accepted was concerned with the Polish Corridor, the same issue which had forced the Supreme Council to be cut down to the Council of Four in 1919 and the issue which led to the Second World War twenty years later. In this case, the experts were much harsher on Germany than the final decision of the politicians.

The treaty with Germany was made by the Council of Four assembling the reports of the various committees, fitting the parts together, and ironing out various disagreements. The chief disagreements were over the size and nature of German reparations, the nature of German disarmament, the nature of the League of Nations, and the territorial settlements in six specific areas: the Polish Corridor, Upper Silesia, the Saar, Fiume, the Rhineland, and Shantung. When the dispute over Fiume reached a peak, Wilson appealed to the Italian people over the heads of the Italian delegation at Paris, in the belief that the people were less nationalistic and more favorable to his idealistic principles than their rather hard-boiled delegation. This appeal was a failure, but the Italian delegation left the conference and returned to Rome in protest against Wilson's action. Thus the Italians were absent from Paris at the time that the German colonial territories were being distributed and, accord-

ingly, did not obtain any colonies. Thus Italy failed to obtain compensation in Africa for the French and British gains in territory on that continent, as promised in the Treaty of London in 1915. This disappointment
was given by Mussolini as one of the chief justifications for the Italian
attack on Ethiopia in 1935.

The Treaty of Versailles was presented to the Plenary Conference on
May 6, 1919, and to the German delegation the next day. The conference was supposed to accept it without comment, but General Foch,
commander in chief of the French armies and of the Entente forces in
the war, made a severe attack on the treaty in regard to its provisions for
enforcement. These provisions gave little more than the occupation of
the Rhineland and three bridgeheads on the right bank of the Rhine as
already existed under the Armistice of November 11, 1918. According
to the treaty, these areas were to be occupied for from five to fifteen
years to enforce a treaty whose substantive provisions required Germany
to pay reparations for at least a generation and to remain disarmed forever. Foch insisted that he needed the left bank of the Rhine and the
three bridgeheads on the right bank for at least thirty years. Clemenceau,
as soon as the meeting was over, rebuked Foch for disrupting the harmony of the assembly, but Foch had put his finger on the weakest, yet
most vital, portion of the treaty.

The presentation of the text of the treaty to the Germans the next day
was no happier. Having received the document, the chief of the German delegation, Foreign Minister Count Ulrich von Brockdorff-Rantzau,
made a long speech in which he protested bitterly against the failure to
negotiate and the violation of the prearmistice commitments. As a deliberate insult to his listeners, he spoke from a seated position.

The German delegation sent the victorious Powers short notes of detailed criticism during May and exhaustive counterproposals on May
29th. Running to 443 pages of German text, these counterproposals, criticized the treaty, clause by clause, accused the victors of bad faith in
violating the Fourteen Points, and offered to accept the League of Nations, the disarmament sections, and reparations of 100 thousand million
marks if the Allies would withdraw any statement that Germany had,
alone, caused the war and would readmit Germany to the world's markets. Most of the territorial changes were rejected except where they
could be shown to be based on self-determination (thus adopting Wilson's point of view).

These proposals led to one of the most severe crises of the conference
as Lloyd George, who had been reelected in December on his promise
to the British people to squeeze Germany dry and had done his share in
this direction from December to May, now began to fear that Germany
would refuse to sign and adopt a passive resistance which would require
the Allies to use force. Since the British armies were being disbanded,

such a need of force would fall largely on the French and would be highly welcome to people like Foch who favored duress against Germany. Lloyd George was afraid that any occupation of Germany by French armies would lead to complete French hegemony on the continent of Europe and that these occupation forces might never be withdrawn, having achieved, with British connivance, what Britain had fought so vigorously to prevent at the time of Louis XIV and Napoleon. In other words, the reduction in German's power as a consequence of her defeat was leading Britain back to her old balance-of-power policies under which Britain opposed the strongest Power on the continent by building up the strength of the second strongest. At the same time, Lloyd George was eager to continue the British demobilization in order to satisfy the British people and to reduce the financial burden on Brittain so that the country could balance its budget, deflate, and go back on the gold standard. For these reasons, Lloyd George suggested ₊that the treaty be weakened by reducing the Rhineland occupation from fifteen years to two, that a plebiscite be held in Upper Silesia (which had been given to Poland), that Germany be admitted to the League of Nations at once, and that the reparations burden be reduced. He obtained only the plebiscite in Upper Silesia and certain other disputed areas, Wilson rejecting the other suggestions and upbraiding the prime minister for his sudden change of attitude.

Accordingly, the Allied answer to the German counterproposals (written by Philip Kerr, later Lord Lothian) made only minor modifications in the original terms (chiefly the addition of five plebiscites in Upper Silesia, Allenstein, Marienwerder, North Schleswig, and the Saar, of which the last was to be held in 1935, the others immediately). It also accused the Germans of sole guilt in causing the war and of inhuman practices during it, and gave them a five-day ultimatum for signing the treaty as it stood. The German delegation at once returned to Germany and recommended a refusal to sign. The Cabinet resigned rather than sign, but a new Cabinet was formed of Catholics and Socialists. Both of these groups were fearful that an Allied invasion of Germany would lead to chaos and confusion which would encourage Bolshevism in the east and separatism in the west; they voted to sign if the articles on war guilt and war criminals could be struck from the treaty. When the Allies refused these concessions, the Catholic Center Party voted 64–14 not to sign. At this critical moment, when rejection seemed certain, the High Command of the German Army, through Chief of Staff Wilhelm Groener, ordered the Cabinet to sign in order to prevent a military occupation of Germany. On June 28, 1919, exactly five years after the assassination at Sarajevo, in the Hall of Mirrors at Versailles where the German Empire had been proclaimed in 1871, the Treaty of Versailles was signed by all the delegations except the Chinese. The latter refused, in protest against the disposition of the prewar German concessions in Shantung.

The Austrian Treaty was signed by a delegation headed by Karl Renner but only after the victors had rejected a claim that Austria was a succession state rather than a defeated Power and had forced the country to change its name from the newly adopted "German Austria" to the title "Republic of Austria." The new country was forbidden to make any movement toward union with Germany without the approval of the League of Nations.

The Treaty of Neuilly was signed by a single Bulgarian delegate, the Peasants' Party leader Aleksandr Stamboliski. By this agreement Bulgaria lost western Thrace, her outlet to the Aegean, which had been annexed from Turkey in 1912, as well as certain mountain passes in the west which were ceded from Bulgaria to Yugoslavia for strategic reasons.

The Treaty of Trianon signed in 1920 was the most severe of the peace treaties and the most rigidly enforced. For these and other reasons Hungary was the most active political force for revision of treaties during the period 1924–1934 and was encouraged in this attitude by Italy from 1927 to 1934 in the hope that there might be profitable fishing in such troubled waters. Hungary had good reason to be discontented. The fall of the Habsburg dynasty in 1918 and the uprisings of the subject peoples of Hungary, like the Poles, Slovaks, Romanians, and Croatians, brought to power in Budapest a liberal government under Count Michael Károlyi. This government was at once threatened by a Bolshevik uprising under Béla Kun. In order to protect itself, the Károlyi government asked for an Allied occupation force until after the elections scheduled for April 1919. This request was refused by General Franchet d'Esperey, under the influence of a reactionary Hungarian politician, Count Stephen Bethlen. The Károlyi regime fell before the attacks of Béla Kun and the Romanians in consequence of lack of support from the West. After Béla Kun's reign of Red terrorism, which lasted six months (March–August, 1920), and his flight before a Romanian invasion of Hungary, the reactionaries came to power with Admiral Miklós Horthy as regent and head of the state (1920–1944) and Count Bethlen as prime minister (1921–1931). Count Károlyi, who was pro-Allied, anti-German, pacifist, democratic, and liberal, realized that no progress was possible in Hungary without some solution of the agrarian question and the peasant discontent arising from the monopolization of the land. Because the Allies refused to support this program, Hungary fell into the hands of Horthy and Bethlen, who were anti-Allied, pro-German, undemocratic, militaristic, and unprogressive. This group was persuaded to sign the Treaty of Trianon by a trick and ever afterward repudiated it. Maurice Paléologue, secretary-general of the French Ministry of Foreign Affairs (but acting on behalf of France's greatest industrialist, Eugène Schneider), made a deal with the Hungarians that if they would sign the Treaty of Trianon as it stood and give Schneider control of the Hungarian state railways, the port of Budapest, and the Hungarian General Credit Bank (which had a stranglehold on Hungarian industry) France would eventually make Hungary one of the mainstays of its anti-German bloc in eastern Europe, would sign a military convention with Hungary, and would, at the proper time, obtain a drastic revision of the Treaty of Trianon. The Hungarian side of this complex deal was largely carried out, but British and Italian objections to the extension of French economic control into central Europe disrupted the negotiations and prevented Hungary from obtaining its reward. Paléologue, although forced to resign and replaced at the Quai d'Orsay by the anti-Hungarian and pro-Czech Philippe Berthelot, received his reward from Schneider. He was made a director of Schneider's personal holding company for his central-European interests, the Union européene industrielle et financière.

The Treaty of Sèvres with Turkey was the last one made and the only one never ratified. There were three reasons for the delay: (1) the uncertainty about the role of the United States, which was expected to accept control of the Straits and a mandate for Armenia, thus forming a buffer against Soviet Russia; (2) the instability of the Turkish government, which was threatened by a nationalist uprising led by Mustafa Kemal; and (3) the scandal caused by the Bolshevik publication of the secret treaties regarding the Ottoman Empire, since these treaties contrasted so sharply with the expressed war aims of the Allies. The news that the United States refused to participate in the Near East settlement made it possible to draw up a treaty. This was begun by the Supreme Council at its London Conference of February 1920, and continued at San Remo in April. It was signed by the sultan's government on August 20, 1920, but the Nationalists under Mustafa Kemal refused to accept it and set up an insurgent government at Ankara. The Greeks and Italians, with Allied support, invaded Turkey and attempted to force the treaty on the Nationalists, but they were much weakened by dissension behind the facade of Entente solidarity. The French believed that greater economic concessions could be obtained from the Kemalist government, while the British felt that richer prospects were to be obtained from the sultan. In particular, the French were prepared to support the claims of Standard Oil to such concessions, while the British were prepared to support Royal Dutch Shell. The Nationalist forces made good use of these dissensions. After buying off the Italians and French with economic concessions, they launched a counteroffensive against the Greeks. Although England came to the rescue of the Greeks, it received no support from the other Powers, while the Turks had the support of Soviet Russia. The Turks destroyed the Greeks, burned Smyrna, and came face-to-face with the British at Chanak. At this critical moment, the Dominions, in answer to Curzon's telegraphed appeal, refused to support a war with Turkey. The Treaty of Sèvres, already in tatters, had to be discarded. A new conference at Lausanne in November 1922 produced a moderate and negotiated treaty which was signed by the Kemalist government on July 24, 1923. This act ended, in a formal way, the First World War. It also took a most vital step toward establishing a new Turkey which would serve as a powerful force for peace and stability in the Near East. The decline of Turkey, which had continued for four hundred years, was finally ended.

By this Treaty of Lausanne, Turkey gave up all non-Turkish territory except Kurdistan, losing Arabia, Mesopotamia, the Levant, western Thrace, and some islands of the Aegean. The capitulations were abolished in return for a promise of judicial reform. There were no reparations and no disarmament, except that the Straits were demilitarized and were to be open to all ships except those of belligerents if Turkey was at war. Turkey accepted a minorities treaty and agreed to a compulsory exchange with Greece of Greek and Turkish minorities judged on the basis of membership in the Greek Orthodox or Muslim religions. Under this last provision, over 1,250,000 Greeks were removed from Turkey by 1930. Unfortunately, most of these had been urban shopkeepers in Turkey and were settled as farmers on the unhospitable soil of Macedonia. The Bulgarian peasants who had previously lived in Macedonia were unceremoniously dumped into Bulgaria where they were tinder for the sparks of a revolutionary Bulgarian secret society called the Internal Macedonian Revolutionary Organization (IMRO), whose chief method of political action was assassination.

As a result of the rising tide of aggression in the 1930's, the clause regarding the demilitarization of the Straits was revoked at the Montreux Convention of July 1936. This gave Turkey full sovereignty over the Straits, including the right to fortify them.

All the original peace treaties consisted of five chief parts: (a) the Covenant of the League of Nations; (b) the territorial provisions; (c) the disarmament provision; (d) the reparations provisions; and (e) penalties and guarantees. The first of these must be reserved until later, but the others should be mentioned here.

In theory, the territorial provisions of the treaties were based on "self-determination," but in fact they were usually based on other considerations: strategic, economic, punitive, legal, power, or compensation. By "self-determination" the peacemakers usually meant "nationality," and by "nationality" they usually meant "language," except in the Ottoman Empire where "nationality" usually meant "religion." The six cases where self-determination (that is, plebiscites) was actually used showed that the peoples of these areas were not so nationalistic as the peacemakers believed. Because in Allenstein, where Polish-speaking people were 40 percent of the population, only 2 percent voted to join Poland, the area was returned to Germany; in Upper Silesia, where the comparable figures were 65 percent and 40 percent, the area was split, the more industrial eastern portion going to Poland, while the more rural western part was returned to Germany; in Klagenfurt, where Slovene-speakers formed 68 percent of the population, only 40 percent wanted to join Yugoslavia, so the area was left in Austria. Somewhat similar results occurred in Marienwerder, but not in northern Schleswig, which voted to join Denmark. In each case, the voters, probably for economic reasons, chose to join the economically more prosperous state rather than the one sharing the same language.

In addition to the areas mentioned, Germany had to return Alsace and Lorraine to France, give three small districts to Belgium, and abandon the northern edge of East Prussia around Memel to the Allied Powers. This last area was given to the new state of Lithuania in 1924 by the Conference of Ambassadors.

The chief territorial disputes arose over the Polish Corridor, the Rhineland, and the Saar. The Fourteen Points had promised to establish an independent Poland with access to the Baltic Sea. It had been French policy, since about 1500, to oppose any strong state in central Europe by seeking allies in eastern Europe. With the collapse of Russia in 1917, the French sought a substitute ally in Poland. Accordingly, Foch wanted to give all of East Prussia to Poland. Instead, the experts (who were very pro-Polish) gave Poland access to the sea by severing East Prussia from the rest of Germany by creating a Polish Corridor in the valley of the Vistula. Most of the area was Polish-speaking, and German commerce with East Prussia was largely by sea. However, the city of Danzig, at the mouth of the Vistula, was clearly a German city. Lloyd George refused to give it to Poland. Instead, it was made a Free City under the protection of the League of Nations.

The French wished to detach the whole of Germany west of the Rhine (the so-called Rhineland) to create a separate state and increase French security against Germany. They gave up their separatist agitation in return for Wilson's promise of March 14, 1919 to give a joint Anglo-American guarantee against a German attack. This promise was signed in treaty form on June 28, 1919, but fell through when the United States Senate did not ratify the agreement. Since Clemenceau had been able to persuade Foch and Poincaré to accept the Rhine settlement only because of this guarantee, its failure to materialize ended his political career. The Rhineland settlement as it stood had two quite separate provisions. On the one·hand, the Rhineland and three bridgeheads on the right bank of the Rhine were to be occupied by Allied troops for from five to fifteen years. On the other hand the Rhineland and a zone fifty kilometers wide along the right bank were to be permanently demilitarized and any violation of this could be regarded as a hostile act by the signers of the treaty. This meant that any German troops or fortifications were excluded from this area forever. *This was the most important clause of the Treaty of Versailles.* So long as it remained in effect, the great industrial region of the Ruhr on the right bank of the Rhine, the economic backbone of Germany's ability to wage warfare, was exposed to a quick French military thrust from the west, and Germany could not threaten France or move eastward against Czechoslovakia or Poland if France objected.

Of these two clauses, the military occupation of the Rhineland and the bridgeheads was ended in 1930, five years ahead of schedule. This made it possible for Hitler to destroy the second provision, the demilitarization of western Germany, by remilitarizing the area in March 1936.

The last disputed territorial change of the Treaty of Versailles was concerned with the Saar Basin, rich in industry and coal. Although its population was clearly German, the French claimed most of it in 1919 on the grounds that two-thirds of it had been inside the French frontiers of 1814 and that they should obtain the coal mines as compensation for the French mines destroyed by the Germans in 1918. They did get the mines, but the area was separated politically from both countries to be ruled by the League of Nations for fifteen years and then given a plebiscite. When the plebiscite was held in 1935, after an admirable League administration, only about 2,000 out of about 528,000 voted to join France, while about 90 percent wished to join Germany, the remainder indicating their desire to continue under League rule. The Germans, as a result of this vote, agreed to buy back the coal mines from France for 900 million francs, payable in coal over a five-year period.

The territorial provisions of the treaties of Saint-Germain and Trianon were such as to destroy completely the Austro-Hungarian Empire. Austria was reduced from 115,000 square miles with 30 million inhabitants to 32,000 square miles with 6.5 million inhabitants. To Czechoslovakia went Bohemia, Moravia, parts of Lower Austria, and Austrian Silesia. To Yugoslavia went Bosnia, Herzegovina, and Dalmatia. To Romania went Bukovina. To Italy went South Tyrol, Trentino, Istria, and an extensive area north of the Adriatic, including Trieste.

The Treaty of Trianon reduced Hungary from 125,000 square miles with 21 million inhabitants to 35,000 square miles with 8 million inhabitants. To Czechoslovakia went Slovakia and Ruthenia; to Romania went Transylvania, part of the Hungarian plain, and most of the Banat; to Yugoslavia went the rest of the Banat, Croatia-Slavonia, and some other districts.

The treaties of peace set the boundaries of the defeated states but not those of the new states. These latter were fixed by a number of treaties made in the years following 1918. The process led to disputes and even to violent clashes of arms, and some issues are still subjects of discord to the present time.

The most violent controversies arose in regard to the boundaries of Poland. Of these, only that with Germany was set by the Treaty of Versailles. The Poles refused to accept their other frontiers as suggested by the Allies at Paris, and by 1920 were at war with Lithuania over Vilna, with Russia over the eastern border, with the Ukrainians over Galicia, and with Czechoslovakia over Teschen. The struggle over Vilna began in 1919 when the Poles took the district from the Russians but soon lost it again. The Russians yielded it to the Lithuanians in 1920, and this was accepted by Poland, but within three months it was seized by Polish freebooters. A plebiscite, ordered by the League of Nations, was held in January 1922 under Polish control and gave a Polish majority. The Lithuanians refused to accept the validity of this vote or a decision of the Conference of Ambassadors of March 1923, giving the area to Poland. Instead, Lithuania continued to consider itself at war with Poland until December 1927.

Poland did not fare so well at the other end of its frontier. There fighting broke out between Czech and Polish forces over Teschen in January 1919. The Conference of Ambassadors divided the area between the two claimants, but gave the valuable coal mines to Czechoslovakia (July 1920).

Poland's eastern frontier was settled only after a bloody war with the Soviet Union. The Supreme Council in December 1919 had laid down the so-called "Curzon Line" as the eastern boundary of Polish administration, but within six months the Polish armies had crossed this and advanced beyond Kiev. A Russian counterattack soon drove the Poles back, and Polish territory was invaded in its turn. The Poles appealed in panic to the Supreme Council, which was reluctant to intervene. The French, however, did not hesitate, and sent General Weygand with supplies to defend Warsaw. The Russian offensive was broken on the Vistula, and peace negotiations began. The final settlement, signed at Riga in March 1921, gave Poland a frontier 150 miles farther east than the Curzon Line and brought into Poland many non-Polish peoples, including one million White Russians and four million Ukrainians.

Romania also had a dispute with Russia arising from the Romanian occupation of Bessarabia in 1918. In October 1920, the Conference of Ambassadors recognized Bessarabia as part of Romania. Russia protested, and the United States refused to accept the transfer. In view of these disturbances Poland and Romania signed a defensive alliance against Russia in March 1921.

The most important dispute of this kind arose over the disposition of Fiume. This problem was acute because one of the Great Powers was involved. The Italians had yielded Fiume to Yugoslavia in the Treaty of

London of 1915 and had promised, in November 1918, to draw the Italian-Yugoslav boundary on lines of nationality. Thus they had little claim to Fiume. Nevertheless, at Paris they insisted on it, for political and economic reasons. Having just excluded the Habsburg Empire from the Adriatic Sea, and not wishing to see any new Power rise in its place, they did all they could to hamper Yugoslavia and to curtail its access to the Adriatic. Moreover, the Italian acquisition of Trieste gave them a great seaport with no future, since it was separated by a political boundary from the hinterland whence it could draw its trade. To protect Trieste, Italy wanted to control all the possible competing ports in the area. The city of Fiume itself was largely Italian, but the suburbs and surrounding countryside were overwhelmingly Slav. The experts at Paris wished to give Italy neither Fiume nor Dalmatia, but Colonel House tried to overrule the experts in order to obtain Italian support for the League of Nations in return. Wilson overruled House and issued his famous appeal to the Italian people which resulted in the temporary withdrawal of the Italian delegation from Paris. After their return, the issue was left unsettled. In September 1919 an erratic Italian poet, Gabriele D'Annunzio, with a band of freebooters, seized Fiume and set up an independent government on a comic-opera basis. The dispute between Italy and Yugoslavia continued with decreasing bitterness until November 1920, when they signed a treaty at Rapallo dividing the area but leaving Fiume itself a free city. This settlement was not satisfactory. A group of Fascists from Italy (where this party was not yet in office) seized the city in March 1922 and were removed by the Italian Army three weeks later. The problem was finally settled by the Treaty of Rome of January 1924, by which Fiume was granted to Italy, but the suburb of Port Baros and a fifty-year lease on one of the three harbor basins went to Yugoslavia.

These territorial disputes are of importance because they continued to lacerate relationships between neighboring states until well into the period of World War II and even later. The names of Fiume, Thrace, Bessarabia, Epirus, Transylvania, Memel, Vilna, Teschen, the Saar, Danzig, and Macedonia were still echoing as battlecries of overheated nationalists twenty years after the Peace Conference assembled at Paris. The work of that conference had undoubtedly reduced the numbers of minority peoples, but this had only served to increase the intensity of feeling of the minorities remaining. The numbers of these remained large. There were over 1,000,000 Germans in Poland, 550,000 in Hungary, 3,100,000 in Czechoslovakia, about 700,000 in Romania, 500,000 in Yugoslavia, and 250,000 in Italy. There were 450,000 Magyars in Yugoslavia, 750,000 in Czechoslovakia, and about 1,500,000 in Romania. There were about 5,000,000 White Russians and Ukrainians in Poland and about 1,100,000 of these in Romania. To protect these minorities the Allied and Associated Powers forced the new states of central and eastern Europe to sign minority treaties, by which these minorities were granted a certain minimum of cultural and political rights. These treaties were guaranteed by the League of Nations, but there was no power to enforce observation of their terms. The most that could be done was to issue a public reprimand against the offending government, as was done, more than once, for example, against Poland.

The disarmament provisions of the peace treaties were much easier to draw up than to enforce. It was clearly understood that the disarmament of the defeated Powers was but the first step toward the general disarmament of the victor nations as well. In the case of the Germans this connection was explicitly made in the treaty so that it was necessary, in order to keep Germany legally disarmed, for the other signers of the treaty to work constantly toward general disarmament after 1919 lest the Germans claim that they were no longer bound to remain disarmed.

In all of the treaties, certain weapons like tanks, poisonous gas, airplanes, heavy artillery, and warships over a certain size, as well as all international trade in arms, were forbidden. Germany was allowed a small navy fixed in number and size of vessels, while Austria, Hungary, and Bulgaria were allowed no navy worthy of the name. Each army was restricted in size, Germany to 100,000 men, Austria to 30,000, Hungary to 35,000, and Bulgaria to 20,000. Moreover, these men had to be volunteers on twelve-year enlistments, and all compulsory military training, general staffs, or mobilization plans were forbidden. These training provisions were a mistake, forced through by the Anglo-Americans over the vigorous protests of the French. The Anglo-Americans regarded compulsory military training as "militaristic"; the French considered it the natural concomitant of universal manhood suffrage and had no objections to its use in Germany, since it would provide only a large number of poorly trained men; they did, however, object to the twelve-year enlistment favored by the British, since this would provide Germany with a large number of highly trained men who could be used as officers in any revived German Army. On this, as in so many issues where the French were overruled by the Anglo-Americans, time was to prove that the French position was correct.

The reparations provisions of the treaties caused some of the most violent arguments at the Peace Conference and were a prolific source of controversy for more than a dozen years after the conference ended. The efforts of the Americans to establish some rational basis for reparations, either by an engineering survey of the actual damage to be repaired or an economic survey of Germany's capacity to pay reparations, were shunted aside, largely because of French objections. At the same time, American efforts to restrict reparations to war damages, and not allow them to be extended to cover the much larger total of war costs, were blocked by the British, who would have obtained much less under damages than under costs. By proving to the French that the German capacity to pay was, in fact, limited, and that the French would get a much larger fraction of Germany's payments under "damages" than under "costs," the Americans were able to cut down on the British demands, although the South African delegate, General Smuts, was able to get military pensions inserted as one of the categories for which Germany had to pay. The French were torn between a desire to obtain as large a fraction as possible of Germany's payments and a desire to pile on Germany such a crushing burden of indebtedness that Germany would be ruined beyond the point where it could threaten French security again.

The British delegation was sharply divided. The chief British financial delegates, Lords Cunliffe and Sumner, were so astronomically unrealistic in their estimates of Germany's ability to pay that they were called the "heavenly twins," while many younger members of the delegation led by John Maynard (later Lord) Keynes, either saw important economic limits on Germany's ability to pay or felt that a policy of fellowship and fraternity should incline Britain toward a low estimate of Germany's obligations. Feeling was so high on this issue that it proved impossible to set an exact figure for Germany's reparations in the treaty itself. Instead a compromise, originally suggested by the American John Foster Dulles, was adopted. By this, Germany was forced to admit an unlimited, theoretical obligation to pay but was actually bound to pay for only a limited list of ten categories of obligations. The former admission has gone down in history as the "war-guilt clause" (Article 231 of the treaty). By it Germany accepted "the responsibility of Germany and her allies for causing all the loss and damage to which the Allied and Associated Governments and their nationals have been subjected as a consequence of the war imposed upon them by the aggression of Germany and her allies."

The following clause, Article 232, was concerned with the reparations obligation, listing ten categories of damages of which the tenth, concerned with pensions and inserted by General Smuts, represented a liability larger than the aggregate of the preceding nine categories together. Since a considerable period was needed for the Reparations Commission to discover the value of these categories, the Germans were required to begin immediate delivery to the victors of large quantities of property, chiefly coal and timber. Only in May 1921 was the full reparations obligation presented to the Germans. Amounting to 132 thousand million gold marks (about 32.5 billion dollars), this bill was accepted by Germany under pressure of a six-day ultimatum, which threatened to occupy the Ruhr Valley.

The reparations clauses of the other treaties were of little significance.

Austria was unable to pay any reparations because of the weakened economic condition of that stump of the Habsburg Empire. Bulgaria and Hungary paid only small fractions of their obligations before all reparations were wiped out in the financial debacle of 1931–1932.

The treaties made at Paris had no enforcement provisions worthy of the name except for the highly inadequate Rhineland clauses which we have already mentioned. It is quite clear that the defeated Powers could be made to fulfill the provisions of these treaties only if the coalition which had won the war were to continue to work as a unit. This did not occur. The United States left the coalition as a result of the Republican victory over Wilson in the congressional elections of 1918 and the presidential election of 1920. Italy was alienated by the failure of the treaty to satisfy her ambitions in the Mediterranean and Africa. But these were only details. If the Anglo-French Entente had been maintained, the treaties could have been enforced without either the United States or Italy. It was not maintained. Britain and France saw the world from points of view so different that it was almost impossible to believe that they were looking at the same world. The reason for this was simple, although it had many complex consequences and implications.

Britain, after 1918, felt secure, while France felt completely insecure in the face of Germany. As a consequence of the war, even before the Treaty of Versailles was signed, Britain had obtained all her chief ambitions in respect to Germany. The German Navy was at the bottom of Scapa Flow, scuttled by the Germans themselves; the German merchant fleet was scattered, captured, and destroyed; the German colonial rivalry was ended and its areas occupied; the German commercial rivalry was crippled by the loss of its patents and industrial techniques, the destruction of all its commercial outlets and banking connections throughout the world, and the loss of its rapidly growing prewar markets. Britain had obtained these aims by December 1918 and needed no treaty to retain them.

France, on the other hand, had not obtained the one thing it wanted: security. In population and industrial strength Germany was far stronger than France, and still growing. It was evident that France had been able to defeat Germany only by a narrow margin in 1914–1918 and only because of the help of Britain, Russia, Italy, Belgium, and the United States. France had no guarantee that all these or even any of them would be at its side in any future war with Germany. In fact, it was quite clear that Russia and Italy would not be at its side. The refusal of the United States and Britain to give any guarantee to France against German aggression made it dubious that they would be ready to help either. Even if they were prepared to come to the rescue ultimately, there was no guarantee that France would be able to withstand the initial German assault in any future war as she had withstood, by the barest margin, the assault of

1914. Even if it could be withstood, and if Britain ultimately came to the rescue, France would have to fight, once again, as in the period 1914–1918, with the richest portion of France under enemy military occupation. In such circumstances, what guarantee would there be even of ultimate success? Doubts of this kind gave France a feeling of insecurity which practically became a psychosis, especially as France found its efforts to increase its security blocked at every turn by Britain. It seemed to France that the Treaty of Versailles, which had given Britain everything it could want from Germany, did not give France the one thing it wanted. As a result, it proved impossible to obtain any solution to the two other chief problems of international politics in the period 1919–1929. To these three problems of security, disarmament, and reparations, we now turn.

Security, 1919-1935

France sought security after 1918 by a series of alternatives. As a first choice, it wanted to detach the Rhineland from Germany; this was prevented by the Anglo-Americans. As a second choice, France wanted a "League with teeth," that is, a League of Nations with an international police force empowered to take automatic and immediate action against an aggressor; this was blocked by the Anglo-Americans. As compensation for the loss of these first two choices, France accepted, as a third choice, an Anglo-American treaty of guarantee, but this was lost in 1919 by the refusal of the United States Senate to ratify the agreement and the refusal of Britain to assume the burden alone. In consequence, the French were forced back on a fourth choice—allies to the east of Germany. The chief steps in this were the creation of a "Little Entente" to enforce the Treaty of Trianon against Hungary in 1920–1921 and the bringing of France and Poland into this system to make it a coalition of "satisfied Powers." The Little Entente was formed by a series of bilateral alliances between Romania, Czechoslovakia, and Yugoslavia. This was widened by a French-Polish Treaty (February 1921) and a French-Czechoslovak Treaty (January 1924). This system contributed relatively little to French security because of the weakness of these allies (except Czechoslovakia) and the opposition of Britain to any French pressure against Germany along the Rhine, the only way in which France could guarantee Poland or Czechoslovakia against Germany. In consequence, France continued its agitation both for a British guarantee and to "put teeth" into the League of Nations.

Thus France wanted security, while Britain had security. France needed Britain, while Britain regarded France as a rival outside Europe (especially in the Near East) and the chief challenge to Britain's customary balance-of-power policy in Europe. After 1919 the British, and even some Americans, spoke of "French hegemony" on the Continent of Europe. The first rule of British foreign policy for four centuries had been to oppose *any* hegemony on the Continent and to do so by seeking to strengthen the second strongest Power against the strongest; after 1919 Britain regarded Germany as the second strongest Power and France as the strongest, a quite mistaken view in the light of the population, industrial productivity, and general organizations of the two countries.

Because France lacked security, its chief concern in every issue was political; because Britain had security, its chief concern was economic. The political desires of France required that Germany should be weakened; the economic desires of Britain required that Germany should be strengthened in order to increase the prosperity of all Europe. While the chief political threat to France was Germany, the chief economic and social threat to Britain was Bolshevism. In any struggle with Bolshevist Russia, Britain tended to regard Germany as a potential ally, especially if it were prosperous and powerful. This was the primary concern of Lord D'Abernon, British ambassador in Berlin in the critical years 1920–1926. On the other hand, while France was completely opposed to the economic and social system of the Soviet Union and could not easily forget the immense French investments which had been lost in that country, it still tended to regard the Russians as potential allies against any revival of Germany (although France did not make an alliance with the Soviet Union until 1935).

Because of its insecurity France tended to regard the Treaty of Versailles as a permanent settlement, while Britain regarded it as a temporary arrangement subject to modification. Although dissatisfied with the treaty, France felt that it was the best it could hope to get, especially in view of the narrow margin by which Germany had decided to sign it, even when faced with a worldwide coalition. Britain, which had obtained all of her desires before the treaty was signed, had no reluctance to modify it, although it was only in 1935 (with the Anglo-German naval agreement) that it attempted to modify the colonial, naval, or merchant-marine clauses from which it had benefited. But in 1935 it had, for more than fifteen years, been seeking to modify the clauses from which France had benefited.

The French believed that peace in Europe was indivisible, while the British believed that it was divisible. That means that the French believed that the peace of eastern Europe was a primary concern of the states of western Europe and that the latter states could not allow Germany to move eastward because that would permit her to gain strength to strike back westward. The British believed that the peace of eastern Europe and that of western Europe were quite separate things and that it was their concern to maintain peace in the west but that any effort to extend this to eastern Europe would merely involve the West in "every little squabble" of these continually squabbling "backward" peoples and could, as happened in 1914, make a world war out of a local dispute. The Locarno Pacts of 1925 were the first concrete achievement of this British point of view, as we shall see. To the French argument that Germany would get stronger and thus more able to strike westward if allowed to grow eastward the British usually replied that the Germans were equally likely to become satisfied or get mired down in the great open spaces of the East.

France believed that Germany could be made to keep the peace by duress, while Britain believed that Germany could be persuaded to keep the peace by concessions. The French, especially the political Right in France, could see no difference between the Germans of the empire and the Germans of the Weimar Republic: "Scratch a German and you will find a Hun," they said. The British, especially the political Left, regarded the Germans of the Weimar Republic as totally different from the Germans of the empire, purified by suffering and freed from the tyranny of the imperial autocracy; they were prepared to clasp these new Germans to their hearts and to make any concession to encourage them to proceed on the path of democracy and liberalism. When the British began to talk in this fashion, appealing to high principles of international cooperation and conciliation, the French tended to regard them as hypocrites, pointing out that the British appeal to principles did not appear until British interests had been satisfied and until these principles could be used as obstacles to the satisfaction of French interests. The British tended to reply to the French remarks about the dangers of English hypocrisy with a few remarks of their own about the dangers of French militarism. In this sad fashion, the core of the coalition which had beaten Germany dissolved in a confusion of misunderstandings and recriminations.

This contrast between the French and the British attitudes on foreign policy is an oversimplification of both. About 1935 there appeared a considerable change in both countries, and, long before that date, there were differences between different groups within each country.

In both Britain and France (before 1935) there was a difference of opinion in international politics which followed general political outlooks (and even class lines) rather closely. In Britain, persons who were of the Left tended to believe in revision of the Treaty of Versailles in favor of Germany, collective security, general disarmament, and friendship with the Soviet Union. In the same period, the Right were impatient with policies based on humanitarianism, idealism, or friendship for the Soviet Union, and wanted to pursue a policy of "national interest," by which they meant emphasis on strengthening the empire, conducting an aggressive commercial policy against outsiders, and adopting relative isolationism in general policy with no European political commitments except west of the Rhine (where Britain's interests were immediate). The groups of the Left were in office in Britain for only about two years in the twenty years 1919–1939 and then only as a minority government (1924, 1929–1931); the groups of the Right were in power for eighteen of these twenty years, usually with an absolute majority. However, during these twenty years the people of Britain were generally sympathetic to the point of view of the Left in foreign policy, although they generally voted in elections on the basis of domestic rather than foreign politics. This means that the people were in favor of revision of Versailles, of collective security, of international cooperation, and of disarmament.

Knowing this, the British governments of the Right began to follow a double policy: a public policy in which they spoke loudly in support of what we have called the foreign policy of the Left, and a secret policy in which they acted in support of what we have called the foreign policy of the Right. Thus the stated policy of the government and the policy of the British people were based on support of the League of Nations, of international cooperation, and of disarmament. Yet the real policy was quite different. Lord Curzon, who was foreign secretary for four years (1919–1923) called the League of Nations "a good joke"; Britain rejected every effort of France and Czechoslovakia to strengthen the system of collective security; while openly supporting the Naval Disarmament Conference at Geneva (1927) and the World Disarmament Conference (1926–1935), Britain signed a secret agreement with France which blocked disarmament on land as well as on the sea (July 1928) and signed an agreement with Germany which released her from her naval disarmament (1935). After 1935 the contrast between the public policy and the secret policy became so sharp that the authorized biographer of Lord Halifax (foreign secretary in 1938–1940) coined the name "dyarchy" for it. Also, after 1935, the policies of both Right and Left were changed, the Left becoming antirevisionist as early as 1934, continuing to support disarmament until (in some cases) 1939, and strengthening its insistence on collective security, while the Right became more insistent on revisionism (by that time called "appeasement") and opposition to the Soviet Union.

In France the contrasts between Right and Left were less sharp than in Britain and the exceptions more numerous, not only because of the comparative complexity of French political parties and political ideology, but also because foreign policy in France was not an academic or secondary issue but was an immediate, frightening concern of every

Frenchman. Consequently, differences of opinion, however noisy and intense, were really rather slight. One thing all Frenchmen agreed upon: "It must not happen again." Never again must the Hun be permitted to become strong enough to assault France as in 1870 and in 1914. To prevent this, the Right and the Left agreed, there were two methods: by the collective action of all nations and by France's own military power. The two sides differed in the order in which these two should be used, the Left wanting to use collective action first and France's own power as a supplement or a substitute, the Right wanting to use France's own power first, with support from the League or other allies as a supplement. In addition, the Left tried to distinguish between the old imperial Germany and the new republican Germany, hoping to placate the latter and turn its mind away from revisionism by cooperative friendship and collective action. The Right, on the other hand, found it impossible to distinguish one Germany from another or even one German from another, believing that all were equally incapable of understanding any policy but force. Accordingly, the Right wanted to use force to compel Germany to fulfill the Treaty of Versailles, even if France had to act alone.

The policy of the Right was the policy of Poincaré and Barthou; the policy of the Left was the policy of Briand. The former was used in 1918–1924 and, briefly, in 1934–1935; the latter was used in 1924–1929. The policy of the Right failed in 1924 when Poincaré's occupation of the Ruhr in order to force Germany to pay reparations was ended. This showed that France could not act alone even against a weak Germany because of the opposition of Britain and the danger of alienating world opinion. Accordingly, France turned to a policy of the Left (1924–1929). In this period, which is known as the "Period of Fulfillment," Briand, as foreign minister of France, and Stresemann, as foreign minister of Germany, cooperated in friendly terms. This period ended in 1929, not, as is usually said, because Stresemann died and Briand fell from office, but because of a growing realization that the whole policy of fulfillment (1924–1929) had been based on a misunderstanding. Briand followed a policy of conciliation toward Germany in order to win Germany from any desire to revise Versailles; Stresemann followed his policy of fulfillment toward France in order to win from France a revision of the treaty. It was a relationship of cross-purposes, because on the crucial issue (revision of Versailles) Briand stood adamant, like most Frenchmen, and Stresemann was irreconcilable, like most Germans.

In France, as a result of the failure of the policy of the Right in 1924 and of the policy of the Left in 1929, it became clear that France could not act alone toward Germany. It became clear that France did not have freedom of action in foreign affairs and was dependent on Britain for its security. To win this support, which Britain always held out as a bait but did not give until 1939, Britain forced France to adopt the policy of appeasement of the British Right after 1935. This policy forced France to give away every advantage which it held over Germany: Germany was allowed to rearm (1935); Germany was allowed to remilitarize the Rhineland (1936); Italy was alienated (1935); France lost its last secure land frontier (Spain, 1936–1939); France lost all her allies to the east of Germany, including her one strong ally (Czechoslovakia, 1938–1939); France had to accept the union of Austria with Germany which she had vetoed in 1931 (March 1938); the power and prestige of the League of Nations was broken and the whole system of collective security abandoned (1931–1939); the Soviet Union, which had allied with France and Czechoslovakia against Germany in 1935, was treated as a pariah among nations and lost to the anti-German coalition (1937–1939). And finally, when all these had been lost, public opinion in England forced the British government to abandon the Right's policy of appeasement and adopt the old French policy of resistance. This change was made on a poor issue (Poland, 1939) after the possibility of using the policy of resistance had been destroyed by Britain and after France itself had almost abandoned it.

In France, as in Britain, there were changes in the foreign policies of the Right and the Left after Hitler came to power in Germany (1933). The Left became more anti-German and abandoned Briand's policy of conciliation, while the Right, in some sections, sought to make a virtue of necessity and began to toy with the idea that, if Germany was to become strong anyway, a solution to the French problem of security might be found by turning Germany against the Soviet Union. This idea, which already had adherents in the Right in Britain, was more acceptable to the Right than to the Left in France, because, while the Right was conscious of the political threat from Germany, it was equally conscious of the social and economic threat from Bolshevism. Some members of the Right in France even went so far as to picture France as an ally of Germany in the assault on the Soviet Union. On the other hand, many persons of the Right in France continued to insist that the chief, or even the only, threat to France was from the danger of German aggression.

In France, as in Britain, there appeared a double policy but only after 1935, and, even then, it was more of an attempt to pretend that France was following a policy of her own instead of a policy made in Britain than it was an attempt to pretend it was following a policy of loyalty to collective security and French allies rather than a policy of appeasement. While France continued to talk of her international obligations, of collective security, and of the sanctity of treaties (especially Versailles), this was largely for public consumption, for in fact from the autumn of 1935 to the spring of 1940 France had no policy in Europe independent of Britain's policy of appeasement.

Thus French foreign policy in the whole period 1919–1939 was dominated by the problem of security. These twenty years can be divided into five subperiods as follows:

> 1919–1924, Policy of the Right
> 1924–1929, Policy of the Left
> 1929–1934, Confusion and Transition
> 1934–1935, Policy of the Right
> 1935–1939, Dual Policy of Appeasement

The French feeling that they lacked security was so powerful in 1919 that they were quite willing to sacrifice the sovereignty of the French state and its freedom of action in order to get a League of Nations possessing the powers of a world government. Accordingly, at the first meeting of the League of Nations Committee at the Paris Peace Conference in 1919, the French tried to establish a League with its own army, its own general staff, and its own powers of police action against aggressors without the permission of the member states. The Anglo-Americans were horrified at what they regarded as an inexcusable example of "power politics and militarism." They rode roughshod over the French and drew up their own draft Covenant in which there was no sacrifice of state sovereignty and where the new world organization had no powers of its own and no right to take action without the consent of the parties concerned. War was not outlawed but merely subjected to certain procedural delays in making it, nor were peaceful procedures for settling international disputes made compulsory but instead were merely provided for those who wished to use them. Finally, no real political sanctions were provided to force nations to use peaceful procedures or even to use the delaying procedures of the Covenant itself. Economic sanctions were expected to be used by member nations against aggressor states which violated the delaying procedures of the Covenant, but no military sanctions could be used except as contributed by each state itself. The League was thus far from being a world government, although both its friends and its enemies, for opposite reasons, tried to pretend that it was more powerful, and more important, than it really was. The Covenant, especially the critical articles 10–16, had been worded by a skillful British lawyer, Cecil Hurst, who filled it with loopholes cleverly concealed under a mass of impressive verbiage, so that no state's freedom of action was vitally restricted by the document. The politicians knew this, although it was not widely publicized and, from the beginning, those states which wanted a real international organization began to seek to amend the Covenant, to "plug the loopholes" in it. Any real international political organization needed three things: (1) peaceful procedures for settling all disputes, (2) outlawry of nonpeaceful procedures for this purpose, and (3) effective military sanctions to compel use of the peaceful procedures and to prevent the use of warlike procedures.

The League of Nations consisted of three parts: (1) the Assembly of all members of the League, meeting generally in Septembr of each year; (2) the Council, consisting of the Great Powers with permanent seats and a number of Lesser Powers holding electivc seats for three-year terms; and (3) the Secretariat, consisting of an international bureaucracy devoted to all kinds of international cooperation and having its head-quarters in Geneva. The Assembly, in spite of its large numbers and its infrequent meetings, proved to be a lively and valuable institution, full of hard-working and ingenious members, especially from the secondary Powers, like Spain, Greece, and Czechoslovakia. The Council was less effective, was dominated by the Great Powers, and spent much of its time trying to prevent action without being too obvious about it. Originally, it consisted of four permanent and four nonpermanent members, the former including Britain, France, Italy, and Japan. Germany was added in 1926; Japan and Germany withdrew in 1933; the Soviet Union was admitted in 1934 and was expelled in 1939 after its attack on Finland. Since the number of nonpermanent members was increased during this period, the Council ended up in 1940 with two permanent and eleven nonpermanent members.

The Secretariat was slowly built up and, by 1938, consisted of more than eight hundred persons from fifty-two countries. Most of these were idealistically devoted to the principles of international cooperation, and displayed considerable ability and amazing loyalty during the brief existence of the League. They were concerned with every type of international activity, including disarmament, child welfare, education, the drug traffic, slavery, refugees, minorities, the codification of international law, the protection of wild life and natural resources, cultural cooperation, and many others.

Attached to the League were a number of dependent organizations. Two, the Permanent Court of International Justice and the International Labor Office, were semiautonomous. Others included the Economic and Financial Organization, the Organization for Communications and Transit, the International Health Organization with offices in Paris, and the Intellectual Cooperation Organization with branches in Paris, Geneva, and Rome.

Many efforts were made, chiefly by France and Czechoslovakia, to "plug the gaps in the Covenant." The chief of these were the Draft Treaty of Mutual Assistance (1923), the Geneva Protocol (1924), and the Locarno Pacts (1925). The Draft Treaty bound its signers to renounce aggressive war as an international crime and to bring military assistance to any signer the Council of the League designated to be the victim of an aggression. This project was destroyed in 1924 by the veto of the British Labour government on the grounds that the agreement would increase the burden on the British Empire without increasing its security. The Assembly at once formulated a better agreement known as the Geneva Protocol. This sought to plug all the gaps in the Covenant. It bound its signers to settle international disputes by methods provided in the treaty, defined as aggressor any state which refused to use these peaceful procedures, bound its members to use military sanctions against such aggressors, and ended the "veto" power in the Council by providing that the necessary unanimity for Council decisions could be achieved without counting the votes of the parties to the dispute. This agreement was destroyed by the objections of a newly installed Conservative government in London. The chief British opposition to the Protocol came from the Dominions, especially from Canada, which feared that the agreement might force them, at some time, to apply sanctions against the United States. This was a very remote possibility in view of the fact that the British Commonwealth generally had two seats on the Council and one at least could use its vote to prevent action even if the vote of the other was nullified by being a party to the dispute.

The fact that both the Draft Treaty and the Geneva Protocol had been destroyed by Britain led to an adverse public opinion throughout the world. To counteract this, the British devised a complicated alternative known as the Locarno Pacts. Conceived in the same London circles which had been opposing France, supporting Germany, and sabotaging the League, the Locarno Pacts were the result of a complex international intrigue in which General Smuts played a chief role. On the face of it, these agreements appeared to guarantee the Rhine frontiers, to provide peaceful procedures for all disputes between Germany and her neighbors, and to admit Germany to the League of Nations on a basis of equality with the Great Powers. The Pacts consisted of nine documents of which four were arbitration treaties between Germany and her neighbors (Belgium, France, Poland and Czechoslovakia); two were treaties between France and her eastern allies (Poland and Czechoslovakia); the seventh was a note releasing Germany from any need to apply the sanctions clause of the Covenant against any aggressor nation on the grounds that Germany, being disarmed by the Treaty of Versailles, could not be expected to assume the same obligations as other members of the League; the eighth document was a general introduction to the Pacts; and the ninth document was the "Rhine Pact," the real heart of the agreement. This "Rhine Pact" guaranteed the frontier between Germany and Belgium-France against attack from either side. The guarantee was signed by Britain and Italy, as well as by the three states directly concerned, and covered the demilitarized condition of the Rhineland as established in 1919. This meant that if any one of the three frontier Powers violated the frontier or the demilitarized zone, this violation would bring the four other Powers into action against the violator.

The Locarno Pacts were designed by Britain to give France the security against Germany on the Rhine which France so urgently desired and at the same time (since the guarantee worked both ways) to prevent France from ever occupying the Ruhr or any other part of Germany, as had been done over the violent objections of Britain in 1923–1924. Moreover, by refusing to guarantee Germany's eastern frontier with Poland and Czechoslovakia, Britain established in law the distinction between peace in the east and peace in the west, on which she had been insisting since 1919, and greatly weakened the French alliances with Poland and Czechoslovakia by making it almost impossible for France to honor her alliances with these two countries or to put pressure on Germany in the west if Germany began to put pressure on these French allies in the east, unless Britain consented. Thus, the Locarno Pacts, which were presented at the time throughout the English-speaking world as a sensational contribution to the peace and stability of Europe, really formed the background for the events of 1938 when Czechoslovakia was destroyed at Munich. The only reason why France accepted the Locarno Pacts was that they guaranteed explicitly the demilitarized condition of the Rhineland. So long as this condition continued, France held a complete veto over any movement of Germany either east or west because Germany's chief industrial districts in the Ruhr were unprotected. Unfortunately, as we have indicated, when the guarantee of Locarno became due in March 1936 Britain dishonored its agreement, the Rhine was remilitarized, and the way was opened for Germany to move eastward.

The Locarno Pacts caused considerable alarm in eastern Europe, especially in Poland and Russia. Poland protested violently, issued a long legal justification of her own frontiers, sent her foreign minister to take up residence in Paris, and signed three agreements with Czechoslovakia (ending the dispute over Teschen, as well as a commercial treaty and an arbitration convention). Poland was alarmed by the refusal to guarantee her frontiers, the weakening of her alliance with France, and the special status given to Germany within the League of Nations and on the Council of the League (where Germany could prevent sanctions against Russia, if Russia ever attacked Poland). To assuage this alarm a deal was made with Poland by which this country also received a seat on the Council of the League for the next twelve years (1926–1938).

The Locarno Pacts and the admission of Germany into the League also alarmed the Soviet Union. This country from 1917 had had a feeling of insecurity and isolation which at times assumed the dimensions of mania. For this, there was some justification. Subject to the attacks of propaganda, diplomatic, economic, and even military action, the Soviet Union had struggled for survival for years. By the end of 1921, most of the invading armies had withdrawn (except the Japanese), but Russia continued in isolation and in fear of a worldwide anti-Bolshevik alliance. Germany, at the time, was in similar isolation. The two outcast Powers drifted together and sealed their friendship by a treaty signed at Rapallo in April 1922. This agreement caused great alarm in western Europe, since a union of German technology and organizing ability with Soviet manpower and raw materials would make it impossible to enforce the Treaty of Versailles and might expose much of Europe or even the world to the triumph of Bolshevism. Such a union of Germany and Soviet Russia remained the chief nightmare of much of western Europe from 1919 to 1939. On this last date it was brought into existence by the actions of these same western Powers.

In order to assuage Russia's alarm at Locarno, Stresemann signed a commercial treaty with Russia, promised to obtain a special position for Germany within the League so that it could block any passage of troops as sanctions of the League against Russia, and signed a nonaggression pact with the Soviet Union (April 1926). The Soviet Union, in its turn, as a result of Locarno signed a treaty of friendship and neutrality with Turkey in which the latter country was practically barred from entering the League.

The "Locarno spirit," as it came to be called, gave rise to a feeling of optimism, at least in the western countries. In this favorable atmosphere, on the tenth anniversary of America's entry into the World War, Briand, the foreign minister of France, suggested that the United States and France renounce the use of war between the two countries. This was extended by Frank B. Kellogg, the American secretary of state, into a multilateral agreement by which all countries could "renounce the use of war as an instrument of national policy." France agreed to this extension only after a reservation that the rights of self-defense and of prior obligations were not weakened. The British government reserved certain areas, notably in the Middle East, where it wished to be able to wage wars which could not be termed self-defense in a strict sense. The United States also made a reservation preserving its right to make war under the Monroe Doctrine. None of these reservations was included in the text of the Kellogg-Briand Pact itself, and the British reservation was rejected by Canada, Ireland, Russia, Egypt, and Persia. The net result was that only aggressive war was renounced.

The Kellogg-Briand Pact (1928) was a weak and rather hypocritical document and advanced further toward the destruction of international law as it had existed in 1900. We have seen that the First World War did much to destroy the legal distinctions between belligerents and neutrals and between combatants and noncombatants. The Kellogg-Briand Pact took one of the first steps toward destroying the legal distinction between war and peace, since the Powers, having renounced the use of war, began to wage wars without declaring them, as was done by Japan in China in 1937, by Italy in Spain in 1936–1939, and by everyone in Korea in 1950.

The Kellogg-Briand Pact was signed by fifteen nations which were invited to do so, while forty-eight nations were invited to adhere to its terms. Ultimately, sixty-four nations (all those invited except Argentina and Brazil) signed the pact. The Soviet Union was not invited to sign but only to adhere. It was, however, so enthusiastic about the pact that it was the first country of either group to ratify and, when several months passed with no ratifications by the original signers, it attempted to put the terms of the pact into effect in eastern Europe by a separate agreement. Known as the Litvinoff Protocol after the Soviet foreign minister, this agreement was signed by nine countries (Russia, Poland, Latvia, Estonia, Romania, Lithuania, Turkey, Danzig, and Persia, but not by Finland, which refused), although Poland had no diplomatic relations with Lithuania and the Soviet Union had none with Romania.

The Litvinoff Protocol was one of the first concrete evidences of a shift in Soviet foreign policy which occurred about 1927–1928. Previously, Russia had refused to cooperate with any system of collective security or disarmament on the grounds that these were just "capitalistic tricks." It had regarded foreign relations as a kind of jungle competition and had directed its own foreign policy toward efforts to foment domestic disturbances and revolution in other countries of the world. This was based on the belief that these other Powers were constantly conspiring among themselves to attack the Soviet Union. To the Russians, internal revolution within these countries seemed a kind of self-defense, while the animosity of these countries seemed to them to be a defense against the Soviet plans for world revolution. In 1927 there came a shift in Soviet policy: "world revolution" was replaced by a policy of "Communism in a single country" and a growing support for collective security. This new policy continued for more than a decade and was based on the belief that Communism in a single country could best be secured within a system of collective security. Emphasis on this last point increased after Hitler came to power in Germany in 1933 and reached its peak in the so-called "Popular Front" movement of 1935–1937.

The Kellogg Pact gave rise to a proliferation of efforts to establish peaceful methods for settling international disputes. A "General Act for the Pacific Settlement of International Disputes" was accepted by twenty-three states and came into force in August 1929. About a hundred bilateral agreements for the same purpose were signed in the five years 1924–1929, compared to a dozen or so in the five years 1919–1924. A codification of international law was begun in 1927 and continued for several years, but no portions of it ever came into force because of insufficient ratifications.

The outlawry of war and the establishment of peaceful procedures for settling disputes were relatively meaningless unless some sanctions could be established to compel the use of peaceful methods. Efforts in this direction were nullified by the reluctance of Britain to commit itself to the use of force against some unspecified country at some indefinite date or to allow the establishment of an international police force for this purpose. Even a modest step in this direction in the form of an international agreement providing financial assistance for any state which was a victim of aggression, a suggestion first made by Finland, was destroyed by a British amendment that it was not to go into effect until the achievement of a general disarmament agreement. This reluctance to use sanctions against aggression came to the forefront in the fall of 1931 at the time of the Japanese attack on Manchuria. As a result the "peace structure" based on Versailles, which had been extended by so many well-intended, if usually misdirected, efforts for twelve years, began a process of disintegration which destroyed it completely in eight years (1931–1939).

Disarmament, 1919-1935

The failure to achieve a workable system of collective security in the period 1919–1931 prevented the achievement of any system of general disarmament in the same period. Obviously, countries which feel insecure are not going to disarm. This point, however obvious, was lost on the English-speaking countries, and the disarmament efforts of the whole period 1919–1935 were weakened by the failure of these countries to see this point and their insistence that disarmament must precede security rather than follow it. Thus disarmament efforts, while continuous in this period (in accordance with the promise made to the Germans in 1919), were stultified by disagreements between the "pacifists" and the "realists" on procedural matters. The "pacifists," including the English-speaking nations, argued that armaments cause wars and insecurity and that the proper way to disarm is simply to disarm. They advocated a "direct" or "technical" approach to the problem, and believed that armaments could be measured and reduced by direct international agreement. The "realists," on the other hand, including most of the countries in Europe, led by France and the Little Entente, argued that armaments are caused by war and the fear of war and that the proper way to disarm is to make nations secure. They advocated an "indirect" or "political" approach to the problem, and believed that once security had been achieved disarmament would present no problem.

The reasons for this difference of opinion are to be found in the fact that the nations which advocated the direct method, like Britain, the United States, and Japan, already had security and could proceed directly to the problem of disarmament, while the nations which felt insecure were bound to seek security before they would bind themselves to reduce the armaments they had. Since the nations with security were all naval powers, the use of the direct method proved to be fairly effective in regard to naval disarmament, while the failure to obtain security for those who lacked it made most of the international efforts for disarmament on land or in the air relatively futile.

The history of naval disarmament is marked by four episodes in the period between the wars: (1) the Washington Conference of 1922; (2) the abortive Geneva Conference of 1927; (3) the London Conference of 1930; and (4) the London Conference of 1936.

The Washington Conference was the most successful disarmament conference of the interwar period because such a variety of issues came together at that point that it was possible to bargain successfully. Britain wished (1) to avoid a naval race with the United States because of the financial burden, (2) to get rid of the Anglo-Japanese alliance of 1902, which was no longer needed in view of the collapse of both Germany and Russia, and (3) to reduce the Japanese naval threat in the southwestern Pacific. The United States wished (1) to get Japan out of East Asia and restore the "open door" in China, (2) to prevent the Japanese from fortifying the German-mandated islands which stretched across the American communications from Hawaii to the Philippines, and (3) to reduce the Japanese naval threat to the Philippines. Japan wanted (1) to get out of eastern Siberia without appearing to retreat, (2) to prevent the United States from fortifying Wake Island and Guam, its two bases on the route from Pearl Harbor to Manila, and (3) to reduce American naval power in the extreme western Pacific. By bargaining one of these for another, all three Powers were able to obtain their wishes, although this was possible only because of the goodwill between Britain and the United States and, above all, because at that time, before the use of fleet-tankers and the present techniques of supplying a fleet at sea, the range of any battle fleet was limited by the position of its bases (to which it had to return for supplies at relatively short intervals).

Probably the key to the whole settlement rested in the relative positions of the British and American navies. At the end of 1918, the United States had in its battle line 16 capital ships with 168 guns of 12 to 14 inches; Britain had 42 capital ships with 376 guns of 12 to 15 inches, but the building programs of the two Powers would have given the United States practical equality by 1926. In order to avoid a naval race which would have made it impossible for Britain to balance its budget or get back on the prewar gold standard, that country gave the United States equality in capital ships (with 15 each), while Japan was given 60 percent as much (or 9 capital ships). This small Japanese fleet, however, provided the Japanese with naval supremacy in their home waters, because of an agreement not to build new fortifications or naval bases within striking distance of Japan. The same 10-10-6 ratio of capital ships was also applied to aircraft carriers. France and Italy were brought into the agreements by granting them one-third as much tonnage as the two greatest naval Powers in these two categories of vessels. The two categories themselves were strictly defined and thus limited. Capital ships were combat vessels of from 10,000 to 35,000 tons displacement with guns of not over 16 inches, while carriers were to be limited to 27,000 tons each with guns of no more than 6 inches. The five great naval Powers were to have capital ships and carriers as follows:

Country	Ratio	Tons of Capital Ships	Number of Capital Ships	Tons of Carriers
U.S.A.	5	525,000	15	135,000
Britain	5	525,000	15	135,000
Japan	3	315,000	9	81,000
France	1.67	175,000	not fixed	60,000
Italy	1.67	175,000	not fixed	60,000

These limits were to be achieved by 1931. This required that 76 capital ships, built or projected, be scrapped by that date. Of these the United States scrapped 15 built and 13 building, or 28; the British Empire scrapped 20 built and 4 building, or 24; and Japan scrapped 10 built and 14 building, or 24. The areas in which new fortifications in the Pacific were forbidden included (a) all United States possessions west of Hawaii, (b) all British possessions east of 110° East longitude except Canada, New Zealand, and Australia with its territories, and (c) all Japanese possessions except the "home islands" of Japan.

Among the six treaties and thirteen resolutions made at Washington during the six weeks of the conference (November 1921–February 1922) were a Nine-Power Treaty to maintain the integrity of China, an agreement between China and Japan over Shantung, another between the United States and Japan over the Mandated Pacific Islands, and an agreement regarding the Chinese customs. In consequence of these, the Anglo-Japanese Treaty of 1902 was ended, and Japan evacuated eastern Siberia.

Efforts to limit other categories of vessels at Washington failed because of France. This country had accepted equality with Italy in capital ships only on the understanding that its possession of lesser vessels would not be curtailed. France argued that it needed a larger navy than Italy because it had a world empire (while Italy did not) and required protection of its home coasts both in the Atlantic and in the Mediterranean) (while Italy could concentrate its navy in the Mediterranean). The same objections led both of these Powers to refuse the American invitation to the Geneva Disarmament Conference of 1927.

The Geneva Conference of 1927 tried to limit other categories of vessels beyond capital ships and carriers. It failed because of a violent dispute between Britain and the United States regarding cruisers. The United States, with few offshore bases and a "high-seas" navy, wanted "heavy" cruisers of about 10,000 tons each, carrying 8-inch guns. The British, with many scattered naval bases, wanted many "light" cruisers of 7,500 tons each with 6-inch guns, and were eager to limit "heavy" cruisers in order to increase the naval importance of their million tons of fast merchant ships (which could be armed with 6-inch guns in an emergency). The United States accepted the British division of cruisers into two classes, but asked for limitation of both in accordance with the Washington ratios and with the lowest possible maximum tonnage. Britain wished to limit only "heavy" cruisers, and fixed her own "absolute" cruiser needs at 70 vessels aggregating 562,000 tons, or twice the total suggested by the Americans. The British argued that their cruiser needs had nothing to do with the relative size of the American cruiser fleet, but depended on such "absolute" values as the size of the earth and the miles of shipping lanes to be patroled. On this point Winston Churchill was adamant and was able to force the chief British delegate to the Geneva Conference (Lord Robert Cecil, who wanted to compromise) to resign from the Cabinet.

The conference broke up in a recriminatory atmosphere, to the great joy of the lobbyists of shipbuilding companies and "patriotic" societies. These had harassed the delegates throughout the conference. Three American shipbuilding companies stood to lost contracts worth almost $54 million if the conference had been a success, and they did not hesitate to spend part of that sum to ensure that it would not be a success. Later they were sued for more money by their chief lobbyist at the conference, Mr. William B. Shearer. As a sequel to the conference, Britain signed a secret agreement with France by which France promised to support Britain against the United States on the cruiser and other issues, and Britain promised to support France in preventing limitation of trained infantry reserves at the approaching World Disarmament Conference. This agreement, signed in July 1928, was revealed by pro-American employees of the French Foreign Ministry to William Randolph Hearst and published in his newspapers within two months of its signature. France deported the Hearst reporter in Paris at once, deported Hearst himself on his next visit to France in 1930, and published the text of the agreement with Britain (October 1928).

The London Naval Conference of 1930 was able to reach the agreement which Geneva had failed to achieve. The publicity about Shearer's activities and about the Anglo-French agreement, as well as the arrival of the world depression and the advent of a more pacifist Labour government to office in London, contributed to this success. Cruisers, destroyers, and submarines were defined and limited for the three greatest naval Powers, and certain further limitations were set in the categories fixed at Washington. The agreements were as follows (in tons):

TYPES	U.S.	BRITAIN	JAPAN
Heavy cruisers with guns over 6.1 inches	180,000	146,800	108,400
Light cruisers with guns below 6.1 inches	143,500	192,200	100,450
Destroyers	150,000	150,000	105,500
Submarines	52,700	52,700	52,700

This allowed the United States to have 18 heavy cruisers, Britain 15, and Japan 12, while in light cruisers the three figures would allow about 25, 35, and 18. Destroyers were limited at 1,850 tons each with 5.1-inch guns, and submarines to 2,000 tons each with 5.1-inch guns. This settlement kept the Japanese fleet where it was, forced Britain to reduce, and allowed the United States to build (except in regard to submarines). Such a result could, probably, have been possible only at a time when Japan was in financial stringency and Britain was under a Labour government.

This treaty left unsolved the rivalry in the Mediterranean between Italy and France. Mussolini demanded that Italy have naval equality with France, although his financial straits made it necessary to limit the Italian navy. The claim to equality on such a small basis could not be accepted by France in view of the fact that it had two seacoasts, a worldwide empire, and Germany's new 10,000-ton "pocket battleships" to consider. The Italian demands were purely theoretical, as both Powers, for motives of economy, were under treaty limits and making no effort to catch up. France was willing to concede Italian equality in the Mediterranean only if it could get some kind of British support against the German Navy in the North Sea or could get a general nonaggression agreement in the Mediterranean. These were rejected by Britain. However, Britain succeeded in getting a French-Italian naval agreement as a supplement to the London agreement (March 1931). By this agreement Italy accepted a total strength of 428,000 tons, while France had a strength of 585,000 tons, the French fleet being less modern than the Italian. This agreement broke down, at the last moment, because of the Austro-German customs union and Germany's appropriation for a second pocket battleship (March 1931). No evil effects emerged from the breakdown, for both sides continued to act as if it were in force.

The London Naval Conference of 1936 was of no significance. In 1931 the Japanese invasion of Manchuria violated the Nine-Power Pacific Treaty of 1922. In 1933 the United States, which had fallen considerably below the level provided in the Washington agreement of 1922, authorized the construction of 132 vessels to bring its navy to treaty level by 1942. In 1934 Mussolini decided to abandon orthodox financial policies, and announced a building program to carry the Italian fleet to treaty level by 1939. This decision was justified by a recent French decision to build two battle cruisers to cope with Germany's three pocket battleships.

All these actions were within treaty limitations. In December 1934, however, Japan announced its refusal to renew the existing treaties when they expired in 1936. The Naval Conference called for that date met in a most unfavorable atmosphere. On June 18, 1935, Britain had signed a bilateral agreement with Hitler which allowed Germany to build a navy up to 35 percent of Britain's naval strength in each class and up to 100 percent in submarines. This was a terrible blow to France, which was limited to 33 percent of the British Navy in capital ships and carriers and had to distribute this lesser fleet on two coasts (to deal with Italy as well as Germany) as well as around the world (to protect the French colonial empire). This blow to France was probably the British answer to the French alliance with the Soviet Union (May 2, 1935), the increased German threat on the French northwest coast being intended to deter France from honoring the alliance with the Soviet Union, if Germany struck eastward. Thus France was once again reduced to dependence on Britain. Germany took advantage of this situation to launch twenty-one submarines by October 1935, and two battleships in 1936.

Under these conditions the Naval Conference at London in 1936 achieved nothing of importance. Japan and Italy refused to sign. As a result, the three signers soon were compelled to use the various escape clauses designed to deal with any extensive building by nonsignatory Powers. The maximum size of capital ships was raised to 45,000 tons in 1938, and the whole treaty was renounced in 1939.

The success achieved in naval disarmaments, limited as it was, was much greater than the success achieved in respect to other types of armaments, because these required that nations which felt politically insecure must be included in the negotiations. We have already indicated the controversy between the proponents of the "direct method" and the advocates of the "indirect method" in disarmament. This distinction was so important that the history of the disarmament of land and air forces can be divided into four periods: (*a*) a period of direct action, 1919–1922; (*b*) a period of indirect action, 1922–1926; (*c*) a new period of direct action, 1926–1934; and (*d*) a period of rearmament, 1934–1939.

The first period of direct action was based on the belief that the victories of 1918 and the ensuing peace treaties provided security for the victorious Powers. Accordingly, the task of reaching a disarmament agreement was turned over to a purely technical group, the Permanent Advisory Commission on Disarmament of the League of Nations. This group, which consisted exclusively of officers of the various armed services, was unable to reach agreement on any important issues: it could not find any method of measuring armaments or even of defining them; it could not distinguish actual from potential armaments or defensive from offensive. It gave answers to some of these questions, but they did not win general assent. For example, it decided that rifles in the possession of troops were war materials and so, also, were wood or steel capable of being used to make such rifles, but rifles already made and in storage were not war materials but "inoffensive objects of peace."

As a result of the failure of the Permanent Advisory Commission, the Assembly of the League set up a Temporary Mixed Commission on which only six of twenty-eight members were officers of the armed services. This body attacked the problem of disarmament by the indirect method, seeking to achieve security before asking anyone to disarm. The Draft Treaty of Mutual Guarantee (1922) and the Geneva Protocol (1924) emerged from this commission. Both of these were, as we have said, vetoed by Britain, so that the disarmament portions of the negotiations were never reached. The achievement of the Locarno Pacts, however, provided, in the minds of many, the necessary security to allow a return to the direct method. Accordingly, a Preparatory Commission to the World Disarmament Conference was set up in 1926 to make a draft agreement which was to be completed at a World Disarmament Conference meeting at Geneva in 1932.

The Preparatory Commission had delegates from all the important countries of the world, including the defeated Powers and the chief nonmembers of the League. It held six sessions over three years and drew up three drafts. In general, it encountered the same difficulties as the Permanent Advisory Committee. This latter group, acting as a subcommittee of the Preparatory Commission, used up 3,750,000 sheets of paper in less than six months but still was not able to find answers to the same questions which had baffled it earlier. The chief problems arose from political disputes, chiefly between Britain and France. These two countries produced separate drafts which diverged on almost every point.

The French wanted war potential counted but wanted trained reserves of men excluded from limitation; the British wanted war potential excluded but wanted to count trained reserves; the French wanted supervision by a permanent commission to enforce fulfillment of any agreement, while the Anglo-Americans refused all supervision. Eventually a draft was prepared by including all divergences in parallel columns.

The Preparatory Commission lost more than one full session in denouncing the disarmament suggestions of Litvinoff, the Soviet representative. His first draft, providing for immediate and complete disarmament of every country, was denounced by all. A substitute draft, providing that the most heavily armed states would disarm by 50 percent, the less heavily armed by 33 percent, the lightly armed by 25 percent, and the "disarmed" by 0 percent, with all tanks, airplanes, gas, and heavy artillery completely prohibited, was also rejected without discussion, and Litvinoff was beseeched by the chairman of the commission to show a more "constructive spirit" in the future. After an impressive display of such constructive spirit by other countries, a Draft Convention was drawn up and accepted by a vote which found only Germany and the Soviet Union in the negative (December 1930).

The World Disarmament Conference which considered this draft was in preparation for six years (1926–1932) and was in session for three years (February 1932 to April 1935), yet it achieved nothing notable in the way of disarmament. It was supported by a tremendous wave of public opinion, but the attitudes of the various governments were becoming steadily less favorable. The Japanese were already attacking China; the French and Germans were deadlocked in a violent controversy, the former insisting on security and the latter on arms equality; and the world depression was growing steadily worse, with several governments coming to believe that only a policy of government spending (including spending on arms) could provide the purchasing power needed for economic revival. Once again, the French desire for an international police force was rebuffed, although supported by seventeen states; the British desire to outlaw certain "aggressive" armaments (like gas, submarines, and bombing planes) was rejected by the French, although accepted by thirty states (including the Soviet Union and Italy).

Discussion of these issues was made increasingly difficult by the growing demands of the Germans. When Hitler came to office in January 1933, he demanded immediate equality with France, at least in "defensive" arms. This was refused, and Germany left the conference.

Although Britain tried, for a time, to act as an intermediary between Germany and the Disarmament Conference, nothing came of this, and the conference eventually dispersed. France would make no concessions in regard to armaments unless she obtained increased security, and this was shown to be impossible when Britain, on February 3, 1933 (just four days after Hitler came to office), publicly refused to make any commitments to France beyond membership in the League and the Locarno Pacts. In view of the verbal ambiguities of these documents and the fact that Germany withdrew from both the League and the Disarmament Conference in October 1933, these offered little security to France. The German budget, released in March 1934, showed an appropriation of 210 million marks for the air force (which was forbidden entirely by Versailles) and an increase from 345 million to 574 million marks in the appropriation for the army. A majority of the delegates wished to shift the attention of the Disarmament Conference from disarmament to questions of security, but this was blocked by a group of seven states led by Britain. Disarmament ceased to be a practical issue after 1934, and attention should have been shifted to questions of security. Unfortunately, public opinion, especially in the democratic countries, remained favorable to disarmament and even to pacifism, in Britain until 1938 at least and in the United States until 1940. This gave the aggressor countries, like Japan, Italy, and Germany, an advantage out of all proportion to their real strength. The rearmament efforts of Italy and Germany were by no means great, and the successful aggressions of these countries after 1934 were a result of the lack of will rather than of the lack of strength of the democratic states.

The total failure of the disarmament efforts of 1919–1935 and the Anglo-American feeling that these efforts handicapped them later in their conflicts with Hitler and Japan have combined to make most people impatient with the history of disarmament. It seems a remote and mistaken topic. That it may well be; nevertheless, it has profound lessons today, especially on the relationships among the military, economic, political, and psychological aspects of our lives. It is perfectly clear today that the French and their allies (especially Czechoslovakia) were correct in their insistence that security must precede disarmament and that disarmament agreements must be enforced by inspection rather than by "good faith." That France was correct in these matters as well as in its insistence that the forces of aggression were still alive in Germany, although lying low, is now admitted by all and is supported by all the evidence. Moreover, the Anglo-Americans adopted French emphasis on the priority of security and the need for inspection in their own disarmament discussions with the Soviet Union in the early 1960's. The French idea that political questions (including military) are more fundamental than economic considerations is now also accepted, even in the United States, which opposed it most vigorously in the 1920's and early 1930's. The fact that the secure states could have made errors such as these in that earlier period reveals much about the nature of human thinking, especially its proclivity to regard necessities as unimportant when they are present (like oxygen, food, or security), but to think of nothing else when they are lacking.

Closely related to all this, and another example of the blindness of experts (even in their own areas), is the disastrous influence which economic, and especially financial, considerations played in security, especially rearmament, in the Long Armistice of 1919–1939. This had a double aspect. On the one hand, balanced budgets were given priority over armaments; on the other hand, once it was recognized that security was in acute danger, financial considerations were ruthlessly subordinated to rearmament, giving rise to an economic boom which showed clearly what might have been achieved earlier if financial consideration had been subordinated to the world's economic and social needs earlier; such action would have provided prosperity and rising standards of living which might have made rearming unnecessary.

Reparations, 1919-1932

No subject occupied a larger portion of statesmen's energies than reparations during the decade after the war. For this reason, and because of the impact which reparations had on other issues (such as financial or economic recovery and international amity), the history of reparations demands a certain portion of our attention. This history can be divided into six stages, as follows:

1. The preliminary payments, 1919–1921
2. The London Schedule, May 1921–September 1924
3. The Dawes Plan, September 1924–January 1930
4. The Young Plan, January 1930–June 1931
5. The Hoover Moratorium, June 1931–July 1932
6. The Lausanne Convention, July 1932

The preliminary payments were supposed to amount to a total of 20,000 million marks by May 1921. Although the Entente Powers contended that only about 8,000 million of this had been paid, and sent Germany numerous demands and ultimatums in regard to these payments, even going so far as to threaten to occupy the Ruhr in March 1921 in an effort to enforce payment, the whole matter was dropped in May when the Germans were presented with the total reparations bill of 132,000 million marks. Under pressure of another ultimatum, Germany accepted this bill and gave the victors bonds of indebtedness to this amount. Of these, 82 billions were set aside and forgotten. Germany was to pay on the other 50 billion at a rate of 2.5 billion a year in interest and 0.5 billion a year to reduce the total debt.

Germany could pay these obligations only if two conditions prevailed: (*a*) if it had a budgetary surplus and (*b*) if it sold abroad more than it bought abroad (that is, had a favorable balance of trade). Under the first condition there would accumulate in the hands of the German government a quantity of German currency beyond the amount needed for current expenses. Under the second condition, Germany would receive from abroad an excess of foreign exchange (either gold or foreign money) as payment for the excess of her exports over her imports. By exchanging its budgetary surplus in marks for the foreign-exchange surplus held by her citizens, the German government would be able to acquire this foreign exchange and be able to give it to its creditors as reparations. Since neither of these conditions generally existed in the period 1921–1931, Germany could not, in fact, pay reparations.

The failure to obtain a budgetary surplus was solely the responsibility of the German government, which refused to reduce its own expenditures or the standards of living of its own people or to tax them sufficiently heavily to yield such a surplus. The failure to obtain a favorable balance of trade was the responsibility equally of the Germans and of their creditors, the Germans making little or no effort to reduce their purchases abroad (and thus reduce their own standards of living), while the foreign creditors refused to allow a free flow of German goods into their own countries on the argument that this would destroy their domestic markets for locally produced goods. Thus it can be said that the Germans were unwilling to pay reparations, and the creditors were unwilling to accept payment in the only way in which payments could honestly be made, that is, by accepting German goods and services.

Under these conditions, it is not surprising that the London Schedule of reparations payments was never fulfilled. This failure was regarded by Britain as proof of Germany's inability to pay, but was regarded by France as proof of Germany's unwillingness to pay. Both were correct, but the Anglo-Americans, who refused to allow France to use the duress necessary to overcome German unwillingness to pay, also refused to accept German goods to the amount necessary to overcome German inability to pay. As early as 1921, Britain, for example, placed a 26 percent tax on all imports from Germany. That Germany could have paid in real goods and services if the creditors had been willing to accept such goods and services can be seen in the fact that the real per capita income of the 'German people was about one-sixth higher in the middle 1920's than it had been in the very prosperous year 1913.

Instead of taxing and retrenching, the German government permitted an unbalanced budget to continue year after year, making up the deficits by borrowing from the Reichsbank. The result was an acute inflation. This inflation was not forced on the Germans by the need to pay reparations (as they claimed at the time) but by the method they took to pay reparations (or, more accurately, to avoid payment). The inflation was not injurious to the influential groups in German society, although it was generally ruinous to the middle classes, and thus encouraged the extremist elements. Those groups whose property was in real wealth, either in land or in industrial plant, were benefited by the inflation which increased the value of their properties and wiped away their debts (chiefly mortgages and industrial bonds). The German mark, which at par was worth about 20 to the pound, fell in value from 305 to the pound in August 1921 to 1,020 in November 1921. From that point it dropped to 80,000 to the pound in January 1923, to 20 million to the pound in August 1923, and to 20 billion to the pound in December 1923.

In July 1922, Germany demanded a moratorium on all cash payments of reparations for the next thirty months. Although the British were willing to yield at least part of this, the French under Poincaré pointed out that the Germans had, as yet, made no real effort to pay and that the moratorium would be acceptable to France only if it were accompanied by "productive guarantees." This meant that the creditors should take possession of various forests, mines, and factories of western Germany, as well as the German customs, to obtain incomes which could be applied to reparations. On January 9, 1923, the Reparations Commission voted 3 to 1 (with Britain opposing France, Belgium, and Italy) that Germany was in default of her payments. Armed forces of the three nations began to occupy the Ruhr two days later. Britain denounced this act as illegal, although it had threatened the same thing on less valid grounds in 1921. Germany declared a general strike in the area, ceased all reparations payments, and adopted a program of passive resistance, the government supporting the strikers by printing more paper money.

The area occupied was no more than 60 miles long by 30 miles wide but contained 10 percent of Germany's population and produced 80 percent of Germany's coal, iron, and steel and 70 percent of her freight traffic. Its railway system, operated by 170,000 persons, was the most complex in the world. The occupation forces tried to run this system with only 12,500 troops and 1,380 cooperating Germans. The noncooperating Germans tried to prevent this, not hesitating to use murder for the purpose. Under these conditions it is a miracle that the output of the area was brought up to one-third its capacity by the end of 1923. German reprisals and Allied countermeasures resulted in about 400 killed and over 2,100 wounded—most of the casualties (300 and 2,000 respectively) being inflicted by Germans on Germans. In addition almost 150,000 Germans were deported from the area.

The German resistance in the Ruhr was a great strain on Germany, both economically and financially, and a great psychological strain on the French and Belgians. At the same time that the German mark was being ruined, the occupying countries were not obtaining the reparations they desired. Accordingly, a compromise was reached by which Germany accepted the Dawes Plan for reparations, and the Ruhr was evacuated. The only victors in the episode were the British, who had demonstrated that the French could not use force successfully without British approval.

The Dawes Plan, which was largely a J. P. Morgan production, was drawn up by an international committee of financial experts presided over by the American banker Charles G. Dawes. It was concerned only with Germany's ability to pay, and decided that this would reach a rate of 2.5 billion marks a year after four years of reconstruction. During the first four years Germany would be given a loan of $800 million and would pay a total of only 5.17 billion marks in reparations. This plan did not supersede the German reparations obligation as established in 1921, and the difference between the Dawes payments and the payments due on the London Schedule were added to the total reparations debt. Thus Germany paid reparations for five years under the Dawes Plan (1924–1929) and owed more at the end than it had owed at the beginning.

The Dawes Plan also established guarantees for reparations payments, setting aside various sources of income within Germany to provide funds and shifting the responsibility for changing these funds from marks into foreign exchange from the German government to an agent-general for reparations payments who received marks within Germany. These marks were transferred into foreign exchange only when there was a plentiful supply of such exchange within the German foreign-exchange market. This meant that the value of the German mark in the foreign-exchange market was artifically protected almost as if Germany had exchange control, since every time the value of the mark tended to fall, the agent-general stopped selling marks. This allowed Germany to begin a career of wild financial extravagance without suffering the consequences which would have resulted under a system of free international exchange. Specifically, Germany was able to borrow abroad beyond her ability to pay, without the normal slump in the value of the mark which would have stopped such loans under normal circumstances. It is worthy of note that this system was set up by the international bankers and that the subsequent lending of other people's money to Germany was very profitable to these bankers.

Using these American loans, Germany's industry was largely re-equipped with the most advanced technical facilities, and almost every German municipality was provided with a post office, a swimming pool, sports facilities, or other nonproductive equipment. With these American loans Germany was able to rebuild her industrial system to make it the second best in the world by a wide margin, to keep up her prosperity and her standard of living in spite of the defeat and reparations, and to pay reparations without either a balanced budget or a favorable balance of trade. By these loans Germany's creditors were able to pay their war debts to England and to the United States without sending goods or services. Foreign exchange went to Germany as loans, back to Italy, Belgium, France, and Britain as reparations, and finally back to the United States as payments on war debts. The only things wrong with the system were (a) that it would collapse as soon as the United States ceased to lend, and (b) in the meantime debts were merely being shifted from one account to another and no one was really getting any nearer to solvency. In the period 1924–1931, Germany paid 10.5 billion marks in reparations but borrowed abroad a total of 18.6 billion marks. Nothing was settled by all this, but the international bankers sat in heaven, under a rain of fees and commissions.

The Dawes Plan was replaced by the Young Plan at the beginning of 1930 for a variety of reasons. It was recognized that the Dawes Plan was only a temporary expedient, that Germany's total reparations obligation was increasing even as she paid billions of marks, because the Dawes Plan payments were less than the payments required by the London Schedule; that the German foreign-exchange market had to be freed in order that Germany might face the consequences of her orgy of borrowing, and that Germany "could not pay" the standard Dawes payment of 2.5 billion marks a year which was required in the fifth and following years of the Dawes Plan. In addition, France, which had been forced to pay for the reconstruction of her devastated areas in the period 1919–1926, could not afford to wait for a generation or more for Germany to repay the cost of this reconstruction through reparations payments. France hoped to obtain a larger immediate income by "commercializing" some of Germany's reparations obligations. Until this point all the reparations obligations were owed to governments. By selling bonds (backed by German's promise to pay reparations) for cash to private investors France could reduce the debts she had incurred for reconstruction and could prevent Britain and Germany from making further reductions in the reparations obligations (since debts to private persons would be less likely to be repudiated than obligations between governments).

Britain, which had funded her war debts to the United States at 4.6 billion dollars in 1923, was quite prepared to reduce German reparations to the amount necessary to meet the payments on this war debt. France, which had war debts of 4 billion dollars as well as reconstruction expenses, hoped to commercialize the costs of the latter in order to obtain British support in refusing to reduce reparations below the total of both items. The problem was how to obtain German and British permission to "commercialize" part of the reparations. In order to obtain this permission France made a gross error in tactics: she promised to evacuate all of the Rhineland in 1930, five years before the date fixed in the Treaty of Versailles, in return for permission to commercialize part of the reparations payments.

This deal was embodied in the Young Plan, named after the American Owen D. Young (a Morgan agent), who served as chairman of the committee which drew up the new agreements (February to June 1929). Twenty governments signed these agreements in January 1930. The agreement with Germany provided for reparations to be paid for 59 years at rates rising from 1.7 billion marks in 1931 to a peak of 2.4 billion marks in 1966 and then declining to less than a billion marks in 1988. The earmarked sources of funds in Germany were abolished except for 660 million marks a year which could be "commercialized," and all protection of Germany's foreign-exchange position was ended by placing the responsibility for transferring reparations from marks to foreign currencies squarely on Germany. To assist in this task a new private bank called the Bank for International Settlements was established in Switzerland at Basle. Owned by the chief central banks of the world and holding accounts for each of them, the Bank for International Settlements was to serve as "a Central Bankers' Bank" and allow international payments to be made by merely shifting credits from one country's account to another on the books of the bank.

The Young Plan, which was to have been a final settlement of the reparations question, lasted for less than eighteen months. The crash of the New York stock market in October 1929 marked the end of the decade of reconstruction and opened the decade of destruction between the two wars. This crash ended the American loans to Germany and thus cut off the flow of foreign exchange which made it possible for Germany to appear as if it were paying reparations. In seven years, 1924–1931, the debt of the German federal government went up 6.6 billion marks while the debts of German local governments went up 11.6 billion marks. Germany's net foreign debt, both public and private, was increased in the same period by 18.6 billion marks, exclusive of reparations. Germany could pay reparations only so long as her debts continued to grow because only by increasing debts could the necessary foreign exchange be obtained. Such foreign loans almost ceased in 1930, and by 1931 Germans and others had begun a "flight from the mark," selling this currency for other monies in which they had greater confidence. This created a great drain on the German gold reserve. As the gold reserve dwindled, the volume of money and credit erected on that reserve had to be reduced by raising the interest rate. Prices fell because of the reduced supply of money and the reduced demand, so that it became almost impossible for the banks to sell collateral and other properties in order to obtain funds to meet the growing demand for money.

At this point, in April 1931, Germany announced a customs union with Austria. France protested that such a union was illegal under the

Treaty of Saint-Germain, by which Austria had promised to maintain its independence from Germany. The dispute was referred to the World Court, but in the meantime the French, to discourage such attempts at union, recalled French funds from both Austria and Germany. Both countries were vulnerable. On May 8, 1931, the largest Austrian bank, the Credit-Anstalt (a Rothschild institution), with extensive interests, almost control, in 70 percent of Austria's industry, announced that it had lost 140 million schillings (about $20 million). The true loss was over a billion schillings, and the bank had really been insolvent for years. The Rothschilds and the Austrian government gave the Credit-Anstalt 160 million to cover the loss, but public confidence had been destroyed. A run began on the bank. To meet this run the Austrian banks called in all the funds they had in German banks. The German banks began to collapse. These latter began to call in all their funds in London. The London banks began to fall, and gold flowed outward. On September 21st England was forced off the gold standard. During this crisis the Reichsbank lost 200 million marks of its gold reserve and foreign exchange in the first week of June and about 1,000 million in the second week of June. The discount rate was raised step by step to 15 percent without stopping the loss of reserves but destroying the activities of the German industrial system almost completely.

Germany begged for relief on her reparations payments, but her creditors were reluctant to act unless they obtained similar relief on their war-debt payments to the United States. The United States had an understandable reluctance to become the end of a chain of repudiation, and insisted that there was no connection between war debts and reparations (which was true) and that the European countries should be able to pay war debts if they could find money for armaments (which was not true). When Secretary of the Treasury Mellon, who was in Europe, reported to President Hoover that unless relief was given to Germany immediately on her public obligations, the whole financial system of the country would collapse with very great loss to holders of private claims against Germany, the President suggested a moratorium on intergovernmental debts for one year. Specifically, America offered to postpone all payments owed to it for the year following July 1, 1931, if its debtors would extend the same privilege to their debtors.

Acceptance of this plan by the many nations concerned was delayed until the middle of July by French efforts to protect the payments on commercialized reparations and to secure political concessions in return for accepting the moratorium. It sought a renunciation of the Austro-German customs union, suspension of building on the second pocket battleship, acceptance by Germany of her eastern frontiers, and restrictions on training of "private" military organizations in Germany. These demands were rejected by the United States, Britain, and Germany, but during the delay the German crisis became more acute. The

Reichsbank had its worst run on July 7th; on the following day the North German Wool Company failed with a loss of 200 million marks; this pulled down the Schröder Bank (with a loss of 24 million marks to the city of Bremen where its office was) and the Darmstädter Bank (one of Germany's "Big Four Banks") which lost 20 million in the Wool Company. Except for a credit of 400 million marks from the Bank for International Settlements and a "standstill agreement" to renew all short-term debts as they came due, Germany obtained little assistance. Several committees of international bankers discussed the problem, but the crisis became worse, and spread to London.

By November 1931 all the European Powers except France and her supporters were determined to end reparations. At the Lausanne Conference of June 1932 German reparations were cut to a total of only 3 billion marks, but the agreement was never ratified because of the refusal of the United States Congress to cut war debts equally drastically. Technically this meant that the Young Plan was still in force, but no real effort was made to restore it and, in 1933, Hitler repudiated all reparations. By that date, reparations, which had poisoned international relations for so many years, were being swallowed up in other, more terrible, problems.

Before we turn to the background of these other problems, we should say a few words about the question of how much was paid in reparations or if any reparations were ever paid at all. The question arose because of a dispute regarding the value of the reparations paid before the Dawes Plan of 1924. From 1924 to 1931 the Germans paid about 10.5 billion marks. For the period before 1924 the German estimate of reparations paid is 56,577 billion marks, while the Allied estimate is 10,426 billion. Since the German estimate covers everything that could possibly be put in, including the value of the naval vessels they themselves scuttled in 1918, it cannot be accepted; a fair estimate would be about 30 billion marks for the period before 1924 or about 40 billion marks for reparations as a whole.

It is sometimes argued that the Germans really paid nothing on reparations, since they borrowed abroad just as much as they ever paid on reparations and that these loans were never paid. This is not quite true, since the total of foreign loans was less than 19 billion marks, while the Allies' own estimate of total reparations paid was over 21 billion marks. However, it is quite true that after 1924 Germany borrowed more than it paid in reparations, and thus the real payments on these obligations were all made before 1924. Moreover, the foreign loans which Germany borrowed could never have been made but for the existence of the reparations system. Since these loans greatly strengthened Germany by rebuilding its industrial plant, the burden of reparations as a whole on Germany's economic system was very slight.

VII

FINANCE,
COMMERCIAL POLICY,
AND BUSINESS ACTIVITY,
1897-1947

Reflation and Inflation, 1897–1925

The Period of Stabilization, 1922–1930

The Period of Deflation, 1927–1936

Reflation and Inflation, 1933–1947

Reflation and Inflation,
1897-1925

WE have already seen that valiant efforts were made in the period
1919–1929 to build up an international political order quite different from that which had existed in the nineteenth century.
On the basis of the old order of sovereignty and international law, men
attempted, without complete conviction of purpose, to build a new international order of collective security. We have seen that this effort was
a failure. The causes of this failure are to be found, to some degree, in
the fact that these statesmen had built the new order in a far from
perfect fashion, with inadequate understanding, improper plans, poor materials, and faulty tools. But the failure can be attributed to a much
greater degree to the fact that the resulting political structure was exposed
to the stress of an economic storm which few had foreseen. Collective
security was destroyed by the world economic depression more than by
any other single cause. The economic depression made possible the rise
to power of Hitler, and this made possible the aggressions of Italy and
Japan and made Britain adopt the policy of appeasement. For these reasons, a real understanding of the economic history of twentieth century
Europe is imperative to any understanding of the events of the period.
Such an understanding will require a study of the history of finance,
commerce, and business activity, of industrial organization, and of agriculture. The first three of these will be considered in this chapter from
the beginning of the twentieth century to the establishment of the
pluralist economy about 1947.

The whole of this half-century may be divided into six subdivisions, as
follows:

1. Reflation, 1897–1914
2. Inflation, 1914–1925
3. Stabilization, 1922–1930
4. Deflation, 1927–1936
5. Reflation, 1933–1939
6. Inflation, 1939–1947

These periods have different dates in different countries, and thus overlap if we take the widest periods to include all important countries. But in spite of the difference in dates, these periods occurred in almost every country and in the same order. It should also be pointed out that these periods were interrupted by haphazard secondary movements. Of these secondary movements, the chief were the depression of 1921–1922 and the recession of 1937–1938, both periods of deflation and declining economic activity.

Prices had been rising slowly from about 1897 because of the increased output of gold from South Africa and Alaska, thus alleviating the depressed conditions and agricultural distress which had prevailed, to the benefit of financial capitalists, from 1873. The outbreak of war in 1914 showed these financial capitalists at their worst, narrow in outlook, ignorant, and selfish, while proclaiming, as usual, their total devotion to the social good. They generally agreed that the war could not go on for more than six to ten months because of the "limited financial resources" of the belligerents (by which they meant gold reserves). This idea reveals the fundamental misunderstanding of the nature and role of money on the part of the very persons who were reputed to be experts on the subject. Wars, as events have proved since, are not fought with gold or even with money, but by the proper organization of real resources.

The attitudes of bankers were revealed most clearly in England, where every move was dictated by efforts to protect their own position and to profit from it rather than by considerations of economic mobilization for war or the welfare of the British people. The outbreak of war on August 4, 1914, found the British banking system insolvent in the sense that its funds, created by the banking system for profit and rented out to the economic system to permit it to operate, could not be covered by the existing volume of gold reserves or by collateral which could be liquidated rapidly. Accordingly, the bankers secretly devised a scheme by which their obligations could be met by fiat money (so-called Treasury Notes), but, as soon as that crisis was over, they then insisted that the government must pay for the war without recourse to fiat money (which was always damned by bankers as immoral), but by taxation and by borrowing at high interest rates from bankers. The decision to use Treasury Notes to fulfill the bankers' liabilities was made as early as Saturday, July 25, 1914, by Sir John Bradbury (later Lord Bradbury) and

Sir Frederick Atterbury at the latter's home. The first Treasury Notes were run off the presses at Waterlow and Sons the following Tuesday, July 28th, at a time when most politicians believed that Britain would stay out of the war. The usual Bank Holiday at the beginning of August was extended to three days during which it was announced that the Treasury Notes, instead of gold, would be used for bank payments. The discount rate was raised at the Bank of England from 3 percent to 10 percent to prevent inflation, a figure taken merely because the traditional rule of the bank stated that a 10 percent bank rate would draw gold out of the ground itself, and gold payments need be suspended only when a 10 percent rate failed.

At the outbreak of the war, most of the belligerent countries suspended gold payments and, to varying degrees, accepted their bankers' advice that the proper way to pay for the war was by a combination of bank loans with taxation of consumption. The period within which, according to the experts, the war must cease because of limited financial resources eventually passed, and the fighting continued more vigorously than ever. The governments paid for it in various ways: by taxation, by fiat money, by borrowing from banks (which created credit for the purpose), and by borrowing from the people by selling war bonds to them. Each of these methods of raising money had a different effect upon the two chief financial consequences of the war. These were inflation and public debt. The effects of the four ways of raising money upon these two can be seen from the following table:

 a. Taxation gives no inflation and no debt.
 b. Fiat money gives inflation and no debt.
 c. Bank credit gives inflation and debt.
 d. Sales of bonds give no inflation but give debt.

It would appear from this table that the best way to pay for the war would be by taxation, and the worst way would be by bank credit. However, taxation sufficient to pay for a major war would have such a severe deflationary effect upon prices that economic production would not increase enough or fast enough. Any rapid increase in production is spurred by a small amount of inflation which provides the impetus of unusual profits to the economic system. Increase in public debt, on the other hand, contributes little of value to the effort toward economic mobilization.

From this point of view, it is not easy to say what method of financing a war is best. Probably the best is a combination of the four methods mixed in such a way that at the end there is a minimum of debt and no more inflation than was necessary to obtain complete and rapid economic mobilization. This would probably involve a combination of fiat money and taxation with considerable sales of bonds to individuals, the combination varying at different stages in the mobilization effort.

In the period 1914–1918, the various belligerents used a mixture of these four methods, but it was a mixture dictated by expediency and false theories, so that at the end of the war all countries found themselves with both public debts and inflation in amounts in no wise justified by the degree of economic mobilization which had been achieved. The situation was made worse by the fact that in all countries prices continued to rise, and in most countries public debts continued to rise long after the Armistice of 1918.

The causes of the wartime inflation are to be found in both financial and economic spheres. In the financial sphere, government spending was adding tremendous amounts of money to the financial community, largely to produce goods which would never be offered for sale. In the economic sphere, the situation was different in those countries which were more completely mobilized than in those which were only partly mobilized. In the former, real wealth was reduced by the diversion of economic resources from making such wealth to making goods for destruction. In the others, the total quantity of real wealth may not have been seriously reduced (since much of the resources utilized in making goods for destruction came from resources previously unused, like idle mines, idle factories, idle men, and so on) but the increase in the money supply competing for the limited amounts of real wealth gave drastic rises in prices.

While prices in most countries rose 200 to 300 percent and public debts rose 1,000 percent, the financial leaders tried to keep up the pretense that the money of each country was as valuable as it had ever been and that as soon as the war was ended the situation existing in 1914 would be restored. For this reason they did not openly abandon the gold standard. Instead, they suspended certain attributes of the gold standard and emphasized the other attributes which they tried to maintain. In most countries, payments in gold and export of gold were suspended, but every effort was made to keep gold reserves up to a respectable percentage of notes, and exchanges were controlled to keep them as near parity as possible. These attributes were achieved in some cases by deceptive methods. In Britain, for example, the gold reserve against notes fell from 52 percent to 18 percent in the month July–August 1914; then the situation was concealed, partly by moving assets of local banks into the Bank of England and using them as reserves for both, partly by issuing a new kind of notes (called Currency Notes) which had no real reserve and little gold backing. In the United States the percentage of reserves required by law in commercial banks was reduced in 1914, and the reserve requirements both for notes and deposits were cut in June 1917; a new system of "depositary banks" was set up which required no reserves against government deposits created in them in return for government bonds. Such efforts were made in all countries, but everywhere the ratio of gold reserves to notes fell drastically during the war: in France from 60 percent to 11 percent; in Germany from 59 percent to 10 percent; in Russia from 98 percent to 2 percent; in Italy from 60 percent to 13 percent; in Britain from 52 percent to 32 percent.

The inflation and increase in public debts continued after the war ended. The causes for this were complicated, and varied from country to country. In general, (1) price fixing and rationing regulations were ended too soon, before the output of peacetime goods had risen to a level high enough to absorb the accumulated purchasing power in the hands of consumers from their efforts in war production; thus, the slowness of reconversion from war production to peace production caused a short supply at a time of high demand; (2) the Allied exchanges, which had been controlled during the war, were unpegged in March 1919 and at once fell to levels revealing the great price disequilibrium between countries; (3) purchasing power held back during the war suddenly came into the market; (4) there was an expansion of bank credit because of postwar optimism; (5) budgets remained out of balance because of reconstruction requirements (as in France or Belgium), reparations (as in Germany), demobilization expenses (as in the United States, Italy, and so on); and (6) production of peacetime goods was disrupted by revolutions (as in Hungary, Russia, and so on) or strikes (as in the United States, Italy, France, and so on).

Unfortunately, this postwar inflation, which could have accomplished much good (by increasing output of real wealth) was wasted (by increasing prices of existing goods) and had evil results (by destroying capital accumulations and savings, and overturning economic class lines). This failure was caused by the fact that the inflation, though unwanted everywhere, was uncontrolled because few persons in positions of power had the courage to take the steps necessary to curtail it. In the defeated and revolutionary countries (Russia, Poland, Hungary, Austria, and Germany), the inflation went so far that the former monetary units became valueless, and ceased to exist. In a second group of countries (like France, Belgium, and Italy), the value of the monetary unit was so reduced that it became a different thing, although the same name was still used. In a third group of countries (Britain, the United States, and Japan), the situation was kept under control.

As far as Europe was concerned, the intensity of the inflation increased as one moved geographically from west to east. Of the three groups of countries above, the second (moderate inflation) group was the most fortunate. In the first (extreme inflation) group the inflation wiped out all public debts, all savings, and all claims on wealth, since the monetary unit became valueless. In the moderate-inflation group, the burden of the public debt was reduced, and private debts and savings were reduced by the same proportion. In the United States and Britain the effort to fight inflation took the form of a deliberate movement toward deflation. This preserved savings but increased the burden of the public debt and gave economic depression.

The Period of Stabilization, 1922-1930

As soon as the war was finished, governments began to turn their attention to the problem of restoring the prewar financial system. Since the essential element in that system was believed to be the gold standard with its stable exchanges, this movement was called "stabilization." Because of their eagerness to restore the prewar financial situation, the "experts" closed their eyes to the tremendous changes which had resulted from the war. These changes were so great in production, in commerce, and in financial habits that any effort to restore the prewar conditions or even stabilize on the gold standard was impossible and inadvisable. Instead of seeking a financial system adapted to the new economic and commercial world which had emerged from the war, the experts tried to ignore this world, and established a financial system which looked, superficially, as much like the prewar system as possible. This system, however, was not the prewar system. Neither was it adapted to the new economic conditions. When the experts began to have vague glimmerings of this last fact, they did not begin to modify their goals, but insisted on the same goals, and voiced incantations and exhortations against the existing conditions which made the attainment of their goals impossible.

These changed economic conditions could not be controlled or exorcised by incantations. They were basically not results of the war at all, but normal outcomes of the economic development of the world in the nineteenth century. All that the war had done was to speed up the rate of this development. The economic changes which in 1925 made it so difficult to restore the financial system of 1914 were already discernible in 1890 and clearly evident by 1910.

The chief item in these changes was the decline of Britain. What had happened was that the Industrial Revolution was spreading beyond Britain to Europe and the United States and by 1910 to South America and Asia. As a result, these areas became less dependent on Britain for manufactured goods, less eager to sell their raw materials and food products to her, and became her competitors both in selling to and in buying from those colonial areas to which industrialism had not yet spread. By 1914 Britain's supremacy as financial center, as commercial market, as creditor, and as merchant shipper was being threatened. A less obvious threat arose from long-run shifts in demand—shifts from the products of heavy industry to the products of more highly specialized branches of production (like chemicals), from cereals to fruits and dairy products, from cotton and wool to silk and rayon, from leather to rubber, and so on. These changes presented Britain with a fundamental choice—either to yield her supremacy in the world or reform her industrial and commercial system to cope with the new conditions. The latter was difficult because Britain had allowed her industrial system to become lopsided under the influence of free trade and international division of labor. Over half the employed persons in Britain were engaged in the manufacture of textiles and ferrous metals. Textiles accounted for over one-third of her exports, and textiles, along with iron and steel, for over one-half. At the same time, newer industrial nations (Germany, the United States, and Japan) were growing rapidly with industrial systems better adapted to the trend of the times; and these were also cutting deeply into Britain's supremacy in merchant shipping.

At this critical stage in Britain's development, the World War occurred. This had a double result as far as this subject is concerned. It forced Britain to postpone indefinitely any reform of her industrial system to adjust it to more modern trends; and it speeded up the development of these trends so that what might have occurred in twenty years was done instead in five. In the period 1910–1920, Britain's merchant fleet fell by 6 percent in number of vessels, while that of the United States went up 57 percent, that of Japan up 130 percent, and that of the Netherlands up 58 percent. Her position as the world's greatest creditor was lost to the United States, and a large quantity of good foreign credits was replaced by a smaller amount of poorer risks. In addition, she became a debtor to the United States to the amount of over $4 billion. The change in the positions of the two countries can be summarized briefly. The war changed the position of the United States in respect to the rest of the world from that of a debtor owing about $3 billion to that of a creditor owed $4 billion. This does not include intergovernmental debts of about $10 billion owed to the United States as a result of the war. At the same time, Britain's position changed from a creditor owed about $18 billion to a creditor owed about $13.5 billion. In addition, Britain was owed about $8 billion in war debts from her Allies and an unknown sum in reparations from Germany, and owed to the United States war debts of well over $4 billion. Most of these war debts and reparations were sharply reduced after 1920, but the net result for Britain was a drastic change in her position in respect to the United States.

The basic economic organization of the world was modified in other ways. As a result of the war, the old organization of relatively free commerce among countries specializing in different types of production was replaced by a situation in which a larger number of countries sought economic self-sufficiency by placing restrictions on commerce. In addition, productive capacity in both agriculture and industry had been increased by the artificial demand of the war period to a degree far beyond the ability of normal domestic demand to buy the products of that capacity. And, finally, the more backward areas of Europe and the world had been industrialized to a great degree and were unwilling to fall back to a position in which they would obtain industrial products from Britain, Germany, or the United States in return for their raw materials and food. This refusal was made more painful for both sides by the fact that these backward areas had increased their outputs of raw materials and food so greatly that the total could hardly have been sold even if they had been willing to buy all their industrial products from their prewar sources. These prewar sources in turn had increased their industrial capacity so greatly that the product could hardly have been sold if they had been able to recapture entirely all their prewar markets. The result was a situation where all countries were eager to sell and reluctant to buy, and sought to achieve these mutually irreconcilable ends by setting up subsidies and bounties on exports, tariffs, and restrictions on imports, with disastrous results on world trade. The only sensible solution to this problem of excessive productive capacity would have been a substantial rise in domestic standards of living, but this would have required a fundamental reapportionment of the national income so that claims to the product of the excess capacity would go to those masses eager to consume, rather than continue to go to the minority desiring to save. Such a reform was rejected by the ruling groups in both "advanced" and "backward" countries, so that this solution was reached only to a relatively small degree in a relatively few countries (chiefly the United States and Germany in the period 1925–1929).

Changes in the basic productive and commercial organization of the world in the period 1914–1919 were made more difficult to adjust by other less tangible changes in financial practices and business psychology. The spectacular postwar inflations in eastern Europe had intensified the traditional fear of inflation among bankers. In an effort to stop rises in prices which might become inflationary, bankers after

1919 increasingly sought to "sterilize" gold when it flowed into their country. That is, they sought to set it aside so that it did not become part of the monetary system. As a result, the unbalance of trade which had initiated the flow of gold was not counteracted by price changes. Trade and prices remained unbalanced, and gold continued to flow. Somewhat similar was a spreading fear of decreasing gold reserves, so that when gold began to flow out of a country as a result of an unfavorable balance of international payments, bankers increasingly sought to hinder the flow by restrictions on gold exports. With such actions the unfavorable balance of trade continued, and other countries were inspired to take retaliatory actions. The situation was also disturbed by political fears and by the military ambitions of certain countries, since these frequently resulted in a desire for self-sufficiency (autarchy) such as could be obtained only by use of tariffs, subsidies, quotas, and trade controls. Somewhat related to this was the widespread increase in feelings of economic, political, and social insecurity. This gave rise to "flights of capital"—that is, to panic transfers of holdings seeking a secure spot regardless of economic return. Moreover, the situation was disturbed by the arrival in the foreign-exchange market of a very large number of relatively ignorant speculators. In the period before 1914 speculators in foreign exchange had been a small group of men whose activities were based on long experience with the market and had a stabilizing effect on it. After 1919 large numbers of persons with neither knowledge nor experience began to speculate in foreign exchange. Subject to the influence of rumors, hearsay, and mob panic, their activities had a very disturbing effect on the markets. Finally, within each country, the decline in competition arising from the growth of labor unions, cartels, monopolies, and so on, made prices less responsive to flows of gold or exchange in the international markets, and, as a result, such flows did not set into motion those forces which would equalize prices between countries, curtail flows of gold, and balance flows of goods.

As a result of all these factors, the system of international payments which had worked so beautifully before 1914 worked only haltingly after that date, and practically ceased to work at all after 1930. The chief cause of these factors was that neither goods nor money obeyed purely economic forces and did not move as formerly to the areas in which each was most valuable. The chief result was a complete maldistribution of gold, a condition which became acute after 1928 and which by 1933 had forced most countries off the gold standard.

Modifications of productive and commercial organization and of financial practices made it almost impossible after 1919 to restore the financial system of 1914. Yet this is what was attempted. Instead of seeking to set up a new financial organization adapted to the modified economic organization, bankers and politicians insisted that the old prewar system should be restored. These efforts were concentrated in a determination to restore the gold standard as it had existed in 1914.

In addition to these pragmatic goals, the powers of financial capitalism had another far-reaching aim, nothing less than to create a world system of financial control in private hands able to dominate the political system of each country and the economy of the world as a whole. This system was to be controlled in a feudalist fashion by the central banks of the world acting in concert, by secret agreements arrived at in frequent private meetings and conferences. The apex of the system was to be the Bank for International Settlements in Basle, Switzerland, a private bank owned and controlled by the world's central banks which were themselves private corporations. Each central bank, in the hands of men like Montagu Norman of the Bank of England, Benjamin Strong of the New York Federal Reserve Bank, Charles Rist of the Bank of France, and Hjalmar Schacht of the Reichsbank, sought to dominate its government by its ability to control Treasury loans, to manipulate foreign exchanges, to influence the level of economic activity in the country, and to influence cooperative politicians by subsequent economic rewards in the business world.

In each country the power of the central bank rested largely on its control of credit and money supply. In the world as a whole the power of the central bankers rested very largely on their control of loans and of gold flows. In the final days of the system, these central bankers were able to mobilize resources to assist each other through the B. I. S., where payments between central banks could be made by bookkeeping adjustments between the accounts which the central banks of the world kept there. The B. I. S. as a private institution was owned by the seven chief central banks and was operated by the heads of these, who together formed its governing board. Each of these kept a substantial deposit at the B. I. S., and periodically settled payments among themselves (and thus between the major countries of the world) by bookkeeping in order to avoid shipments of gold. They made agreements on all the major financial problems of the world, as well as on many of the economic and political problems, especially in reference to loans, payments, and the economic future of the chief areas of the globe.

The B. I. S. is generally regarded as the apex of the structure of financial capitalism whose remote origins go back to the creation of the Bank of England in 1694 and the Bank of France in 1803. As a matter of fact its establishment in 1929 was rather an indication that the centralized world financial system of 1914 was in decline. It was set up rather to remedy the decline of London as the world's financial center by providing a mechanism by which a world with three chief financial centers in London, New York, and Paris could still operate as one. The B. I. S. was a vain effort to cope with the problems arising from the growth of a number of centers. It was intended to be the world cartel of ever-growing national financial powers by assembling the nominal heads of these national financial centers.

The commander in chief of the world system of banking control was Montagu Norman, Governor of the Bank of England, who was built up by the private bankers to a position where he was regarded as an oracle in all matters of government and business. In government the power of the Bank of England was a considerable restriction on political action as early as 1819 but an effort to break this power by a modification of the bank's charter in 1844 failed. In 1852, Gladstone, then chancellor of the Exchequer and later prime minister, declared, "The hinge of the whole situation was this: the government itself was not to be a substantive power in matters of Finance, but was to leave the Money Power supreme and unquestioned."

This power of the Bank of England and of its governor was admitted by most qualified observers. In January, 1924, Reginald McKenna, who had been chancellor of the Exchequer in 1915–1916, as chairman of the board of the Midland Bank told its stockholders: "I am afraid the ordinary citizen will not like to be told that the banks can, and do, create money. . . . And they who control the credit of the nation direct the policy of Governments and hold in the hollow of their hands the destiny of the people." In that same year, Sir Drummond Fraser, vice-president of the Institute of Bankers, stated, "The Governor of the Bank of England must be the autocrat who dictates the terms upon which alone the Government can obtain borrowed money." On September 26, 1921, *The Financial Times* wrote, "Half a dozen men at the top of the Big Five Banks could upset the whole fabric of government finance by refraining from renewing Treasury Bills." Vincent Vickers, who had been a director of the bank for nine years, said, "Since 1919 the monetary policy of the Government has been the policy of the Bank of England and the policy of the Bank of England has been the policy of Mr. Montagu Norman." On November 11, 1927, the *Wall Street Journal* called Mr. Norman "the currency dictator of Europe." This fact was admitted by Mr. Norman himself before the court of the bank on March 21, 1930, and before the Macmillan Committee five days later.

Montagu Norman's position may be gathered from the fact that his predecessors in the governorship, almost a hundred of them, had served two-year terms, increased rarely, in time of crisis, to three or even four years. But Norman held the position for twenty-four years (1920–1944), during which he became the chief architect of the liquidation of Britain's global preeminence.

Norman was a strange man whose mental outlook was one of successfully suppressed hysteria or even paranoia. He had no use for governments and feared democracy. Both of these seemed to him to be threats to private banking, and thus to all that was proper and precious in human life. Strong-willed, tireless, and ruthless, he viewed his life as a kind of cloak-and-dagger struggle with the forces of unsound money which were in league with anarchy and Communism. When he rebuilt the Bank of England, he constructed it as a fortress prepared to defend itself against any popular revolt, with the sacred gold reserves hidden in deep vaults below the level of underground waters which could be released to cover them by pressing a button on the governor's desk. For much of his life Norman rushed about the world by fast steamship, covering tens of thousands of miles each year, often traveling incognito, concealed by a black slouch hat and a long black cloak, under the assumed name of "Professor Skinner." His embarkations and debarkations onto and off the fastest ocean liners of the day, sometimes through the freight hatch, were about as unobserved as the somewhat similar passages of Greta Garbo in the same years, and were carried out in a similarly "sincere" effort at self-effacement.

Norman had a devoted colleague in Benjamin Strong, the first governor of the Federal Reserve Bank of New York. Strong owed his career to the favor of the Morgan Bank, especially of Henry P. Davison, who made him secretary of the Bankers Trust Company of New York (in succession to Thomas W. Lamont) in 1904, used him as Morgan's agent in the banking rearrangements following the crash of 1907, and made him vice-president of the Bankers Trust (still in succession to Lamont) in 1909. He became governor of the Federal Reserve Bank of New York as the joint nominee of Morgan and of Kuhn, Loeb, and Company in 1914. Two years later, Strong met Norman for the first time, and they at once made an agreement to work in cooperation for the financial practices they both revered.

These financial practices were explicitly stated many times in the voluminous correspondence between these two men and in many conversations they had, both in their work and at their leisure (they often spent their vacations together for weeks, usually in the south of France).

In the 1920's, they were determined to use the financial power of Britain and of the United States to force all the major countries of the world to go on the gold standard and to operate it through central banks free from all political control, with all questions of international finance to be settled by agreements by such central banks without interference from governments.

It must not be felt that these heads of the world's chief central banks were themselves substantive powers in world finance. They were not.

Rather, they were the technicians and agents of the dominant investment bankers of their own countries, who had raised them up and were perfectly capable of throwing them down. The substantive financial powers of the world were in the hands of these investment bankers (also called "international" or "merchant" bankers) who remained largely behind the scenes in their own unincorporated private banks. These formed a system of international cooperation and national dominance which was more private, more powerful, and more secret than that of their agents in the central banks. This dominance of investment bankers was based on their control over the flows of credit and investment funds in their own countries and throughout the world. They could dominate the financial and industrial systems of their own countries by their influence over the flow of current funds through bank loans, the discount rate, and the rediscounting of commercial debts; they could dominate governments by their control over current government loans and the play of the international exchanges. Almost all of this power was exercised by the personal influence and prestige of men who had demonstrated their ability in the past to bring off successful financial coups, to keep their word, to remain cool in a crisis, and to share their winning opportunities with their associates. In this system the Rothschilds had been preeminent during much of the nineteenth century, but, at the end of that century, they were being replaced by J. P. Morgan whose central office was in New York, although it was always operated as if it were in London (where it had, indeed, originated as George Peabody and Company in 1838). Old J. P. Morgan died in 1913, but was succeeded by his son of the same name (who had been trained in the London branch until 1901), while the chief decisions in the firm were increasingly made by Thomas W. Lamont after 1924. But these relationships can be described better on a national basis later. At the present stage we must follow the efforts of the central bankers to compel the world to return to the gold standard of 1914 in the postwar conditions following 1918.

The bankers' point of view was clearly expressed in a series of government reports and international conferences from 1918 to 1933. Among these were the reports of the Cunliffe Committee of Great Britain (August 1918), that of the Brussels Conference of Experts (September 1920), that of the Genoa Conference of the Supreme Council (January 1922), the First World Economic Conference (at Geneva, May 1927), the report of the Macmillan Committee on Finance and Industry (of 1931), and the various statements released by the World Economic Conference (at London in 1933). These and many other statements and reports called vainly for a free international gold standard, for balanced budgets, for restoration of the exchange rates and reserve ratios customary before 1914, for reductions in taxes and government spending, and for a cessation of all government interference in economic activity either domestic or international. But none of these studies made any effort to assess the fundamental changes in economic, commercial, and political life since 1914. And none gave any indication of a realization that a financial system must adapt itself to such changes. Instead, they all implied that if men would only give up their evil ways and impose the financial system of 1914 on the world, the changes would be compelled to reverse their direction and go back to the conditions of 1914.

Accordingly, the financial efforts of the period after 1918 became concentrated on a very simple (and superficial) goal—to get back to the gold standard—not "a" gold standard but "the" gold standard, by which was meant the identical exchange ratios and gold contents that monetary units had had in 1914.

Restoration of the gold standard was not something which could be done by a mere act of government. It was admitted even by the most ardent advocates of the gold standard that certain financial relationships would require adjustment before the gold standard could be restored. There were three chief relationships involved. These were (1) the problem of inflation, or the relationship between money and goods; (2) the problem of public debts, or the relationship between governmental income and expenditure; and (3) the problem of price parities, or the relationship between price levels of different countries. That these three problems existed was evidence of a fundamental disequilibrium between real wealth and claims on wealth, caused by a relative decrease in the former and increase in the latter.

The problem of public debts arose from the fact that as money (credit) was created during the war period, it was usually made in such a way that it was not in the control of the state or the community but was in the control of private financial institutions which demanded real wealth at some future date for the creation of claims on wealth in the present. The problem of public debt could have been met in one or more of several fashions: (a) by increasing the amount of real wealth in the community so that its price would fall and the value of money would rise. This would restore the old equilibrium (and price level) between real wealth and claims on wealth and, at the same time, would permit payment of the public debt with no increase in the tax rates; (b) by devaluation—that is, reduce the gold content of the monetary unit so that the government's holdings of gold would be worth a greatly increased number of monetary units. These latter could be applied to the public debt; (c) by repudiation—that is, a simple cancellation of the public debt by a refusal to pay it; (d) by taxation—that is, by increasing the tax rate to a level high enough to yield enough income to pay off the public debt; (e) by the issuance of fiat money and the payment of the debt by such money.

These methods were not mutually exclusive, and in some cases overlapped. It might, for example, be argued that devaluation or use of fiat money were forms of partial repudiation. Nor were all these methods equally practical. For example, the first (increase real wealth) was by far the soundest method to achieve a restabilization, but no one saw how to accomplish it. The fourth (taxation) would have put a burden on the economic system so great as to be self-defeating. In Britain, the public debt could have been paid only by a tax of 25 percent for about three hundred years. Such heavy taxes might have had such a depressing effect on production of real wealth that national income would decline faster than tax rates rose, making payment by taxation impossible. Nor were all these alternative methods of paying the public debt of equal practicality in respect to their effects on the two other financial problems occupying the minds of experts and statesmen. These other two problems were inflation and price parities. These problems were just as urgent as the public debt, and the effects upon them of the different methods for paying the public debt could have been completely different. Efforts to pay the public debt by fiat money would have made the inflation problem and perhaps the price-parity problem worse. Taxation and increasing real wealth, on the other hand, would have reduced the inflation problem at the same time as they reduced the public debt, since both would have increased the value of money (that is, they were deflationary). Their effects on the problem of price parity would differ from case to case.

Finally, these methods of paying the public debt were not of equal value in theory. Orthodox theory rejected repudiation, devaluation, and fiat money as solutions to the problem, and, since it showed no way of increasing the production of real wealth, only taxation was left as a possible method of paying public debts. But the theorists, as we have shown, could call taxation a possible way only if they neglected the economic consequences. These consequences in most countries were so disastrous that taxation, if tried, soon had to be supplemented by other, unorthodox, methods. Great Britain and the United States were the only Great Powers which continued to use taxation as the chief method of paying the public debt.

The second problem which had to be faced before stabilization was possible was the problem of inflation. This was caused by the great increase in claims on wealth (money), and showed itself in a drastic increase in prices. There were three possible solutions: (a) to increase the production of real wealth; (b) to decrease the quantity of money; or (c) to devaluate, or make each unit of money equal to a smaller amount of wealth (specifically gold). The first two would have forced prices back to the lower prewar level but would have done it in entirely different ways, one resulting in prosperity and a great rise in standards of living, the second resulting in depression and a great fall in standards of living. The third method (devaluation) was essentially a recognition and acceptance of the existing situation, and would have left prices at the higher postwar level permanently. This would have involved a permanent reduction in the value of money, and also would have given different parities in foreign exchanges (unless there was international agreement that countries devaluate by the same ratio). But it would have made possible prosperity and a rising standard of living and would have accepted as permanent the redistribution of wealth from creditors to debtors brought about by the wartime inflation.

Since the third method (devaluation) was rejected by orthodox theorists, and no one could see how to get the first (increase of real wealth), only the second (deflation) was left as a possible method for dealing with the problem of inflation. To many people it seemed axiomatic that the cure for inflation was deflation, especially since bankers regarded deflation as a good thing in itself. Moreover, deflation as a method for dealing with the problem of inflation went hand in hand with taxation as a method for dealing with the problem of public debts. Theorists did not stop to think what the effects of both would be on the production of real wealth and on the prosperity of the world.

The third financial problem which had to be solved before stabilization became practical was the problem of price parities. This differed because it was primarily an international question while the other two problems were primarily domestic. By suspending the gold standard and establishing artificial control of foreign exchanges at the outbreak of war, the belligerent countries made it possible for prices to rise at different rates in different countries. This can be seen in the fact that prices in Britain rose 200 percent in seven years (1913–1920), while in the United States they rose only 100 percent. The resulting disequilibrium had to be rectified before the two countries went back on the old gold standard, or the currencies would be valued in law in a ratio quite different from their value in goods. By going back on gold at the old ratios, one ounce of fine gold would, by law, become equal to $20.67 in the United States and about 84s. 11½d. in Britain. For the $20.67 in the United States you could get in 1920 about half of what you could have bought with it in 1913; for the 84s. 11½d. in Britain you could get in 1920 only about a third of what it would buy in 1913. The ounce of gold in the United States would be much more valuable than in Britain, so that foreigners (and British) would prefer to buy in the United States rather than in Britain, and gold would tend to flow to the United States from Britain with goods flowing in the opposite direction. In such conditions it would be said that the pound was overvalued and the dollar undervalued. The overvaluation would bring depression to Britain, while the United States would tend to be prosperous. Such disequilibrium of price parities could be adjusted either by a fall of prices in the country whose currency was overvalued or by a rise in prices in the country whose currency was undervalued (or by both). Such an adjustment would be largely automatic, but at the cost of a considerable flow of gold from the country whose currency was overvalued.

Because the problem of price parities would either adjust itself or would require international agreement for its adjustment, no real attention was paid to it when governments turned their attention to the task of stabilization. Instead, they concentrated on the other two problems and, above all, devoted attention to the task of building up sufficient gold reserves to permit them to carry out the methods chosen in respect to these two problems.

Most countries were in a hurry to stabilize their currencies when peace was signed in 1919. The difficulties of the three problems we have mentioned made it necessary to postpone the step for years. The process of stabilization was stretched over more than a decade from 1919 to 1931. Only the United States was able to return to the gold standard at once, and this was the result of a peculiar combination of circumstances which existed only in that country. The United States had a plentiful supply of gold. In addition it had a technological structure quite different from that of any other country, except perhaps Japan. American technology was advancing so rapidly in the period 1922–1928 that even with falling prices there was prosperity, since costs of production fell even faster. This situation was helped by the fact that prices of raw materials and food fell faster than prices of industrial products, so that production of these latter was very profitable. As a result, America achieved to a degree greater than any other country a solution of inflation and public debt which all theorists had recognized as possible, but which none had known how to obtain—the solution to be found in a great increase in real wealth. This increase made it possible simultaneously to pay off the public debt and reduce taxes; it also made it possible to have deflation without depression. A happier solution of the postwar problems could hardly have been found—for a time, at least. In the long run, the situation had its drawbacks, since the fact that costs fell faster than prices and that prices of agricultural products and raw materials fell faster than prices of industrial products meant that in the long run the community would not have sufficient purchasing power to buy the products of the industrial organization. This problem was postponed for a considerable period by the application of easy credit and installment selling to the domestic market and by the extension to foreign countries of huge loans which made it possible for these countries to buy the products of

American industry without sending their own goods into the American market in return. Thus, from a most unusual group of circumstances, the United States obtained an unusual boom of prosperity. These circumstances were, however, in many ways a postponement of difficulties rather than a solution of them, as the theoretical understanding of what was going on was still lacking.

In other countries the stabilization period was not so happy. In Britain, stabilization was reached by orthodox paths—that is, taxation as a cure for public debts and deflation as a cure for inflation. These cures were believed necessary in order to go back on the old gold parity. Since Britain did not have an adequate supply of gold, the policy of deflation had to be pushed ruthlessly in order to reduce the volume of money in circulation to a quantity small enough to be superimposed on the small base of available gold at the old ratios. At the same time, the policy was intended to drive British prices down to the level of world prices. The currency notes which had been used to supplement bank notes were retired, and credit was curtailed by raising the discount rate to panic level. The results were horrible. Business activity fell drastically, and unemployment rose to well over a million and a half. The drastic fall in prices (from 307 in 1920 to 197 in 1921) made production unprofitable unless costs were driven down even faster. This could not be achieved because labor unions were determined that the burden of the deflationary policy should not be pushed onto them by forcing down wages. The outcome was a great wave of strikes and industrial unrest.

The British government could measure the success of their deflation only by comparing their price level with world price levels. This was done by means of the exchange ratio between the pound and the dollar. At that time the dollar was the only important currency on gold. It was expected that the forcing down of prices in Britain would be reflected in an increase in the value of the pound in terms of dollars on the foreign exchange market. Thus as the pound rose gradually upward toward the pre-war rate of $4.86, this rise would measure the fall in British prices downward to the American (or the world) price level. In general terms, this was true, but it failed to take into consideration the speculators who, knowing that the value of the pound was rising, sold dollars to buy pounds, thus pushing the dollar down and the pound upward faster than was justified in terms of the changes in price levels in the two countries. Thus the pound rose to $4.86, while the British price level had not yet fallen to the American price level, but the Chancellor of the Exchequer, Winston Churchill, judging the price level by the exchange rate, believed that it had and went back on the gold standard at that point. As a result, sterling was overvalued and Britain found itself economically isolated on a price plateau above the world market on which she was economically dependent. These higher British prices served to increase imports, decrease exports, and encourage an outflow of gold which made gold reserves dangerously low. To maintain the gold reserve at all, it was necessary to keep the discount rate at a level so high (4½ percent or more) that business activity was discouraged. The only solution which the British government could see to this situation was continued deflation. This effort to drive down prices failed because the unions were able to prevent the drastic cutting of costs (chiefly wages) necessary to permit profitable production on such a deflationary market. Nor could the alternative method of deflation—by heavy taxation—be imposed to the necessary degree on the upper classes who were in control of the' government. The showdown on the deflationary policy came in the General Strike of 1926. The unions lost the strike—that is, they could not prevent the policy of deflation—but they made it impossible for the government to continue the reduction of costs to the extent necessary to restore business profits and the export trade.

As a result of this financial policy, Britain found herself faced with deflation and depression for the whole period 1920–1933. These effects were drastic in 1920–1922, moderate in 1922–1929, and drastic again in 1929–1933. The wholesale price index (1913=100) fell from 307 in 1920 to 197 in 1921, then declined slowly to 137 in 1928. Then it fell rapidly to 120 in 1929 and 90 in 1933. The number of unemployed averaged about 1¾ millions for each of the thirteen years of 1921–1932 and reached 3 million in 1931. At the same time, the inadequacy of the British gold reserve during most of the period placed Britain in financial subjection to France (which had a plentiful supply of gold because of her different financial policy). This subjection served to balance the political subjection of France to Britain arising from French insecurity, and ended only with Britain's abandonment of the gold standard in 1931.

Britain was the only important European country which reached stabilization through deflation. East of her, a second group of countries, including Belgium, France, and Italy, reached stabilization through devaluation. This was a far better method. It was adopted, however, not because of superior intelligence but because of financial weakness. In these countries, the burden of war-damage reconstruction made it impossible to balance a budget, and this made deflation difficult. These countries accepted orthodox financial ideas and tried to deflate in 1920–1921, but, after the depression which resulted, they gave up the task. Belgium stabilized once at 107 francs to the pound sterling, but could not hold this level and had to devaluate further to 175 to the pound (October 1926). France stabilized at 124.21 francs to the pound at the end of 1926, although the stabilization was made *de jure* only in

June 1928. Italy stabilized at 92.46 lire to the pound sterling in December 1927.

The group of countries which reached stabilization through devaluation prospered in contrast with those who reached stabilization through deflation. The prosperity was roughly equal to the degree of devaluation. Of the three Latin countries—Belgium, France, and Italy—Belgium devalued the most and was most prosperous. Her stabilization was at a price level below the world level so that the belga was undervalued by about one-fifth. This served to encourage exports. For an industrial country such as Belgium, this made it possible for her to profit by the misfortunes of Britain. France was in a somewhat similar position. Italy, on the contrary, stabilized at a figure which made the lira considerably overvalued. This was done for purposes of prestige—Mussolini being determined to stabilize the lira at a value higher than that of the French franc. The effects of this overvaluation of the lira on the Italian economy were extremely adverse. Italy was never as prosperous after stabilization as she had been immediately before it.

Not only did the countries which undervalued their money prosper; they decreased the disequilibrium between wealth and money; they were able to use the inflation to increase production; they escaped high taxes; they moderated or escaped the stabilization crisis and the deflationary depression; they improved their positions in the world market in respect to high-cost countries like Britain; and they replenished their gold stocks.

A third group of countries reached stabilization through reconstruction. These were the countries in which the old monetary unit had been wiped out and had to be replaced by a new monetary unit. Among these were Austria, Hungary, Germany, and Russia. The first two of these were stabilized by a program of international assistance worked out through the League of Nations. The last was forced to work out a financial system by herself. Germany had her system reorganized as a consequence of the Dawes Plan. The Dawes Plan, as we have seen in our discussion of reparations, provided the gold reserves necessary for a new currency and provided a control of foreign exchange which served to protect Germany from the accepted principles of orthodox finance. These controls were continued until 1930, and permitted Germany to borrow from foreign sources, especially the United States, the funds necessary to keep her economic system functioning with an unbalanced budget and an unfavorable balance of trade. In the period 1924–1929, by means of these funds, the industrial structure of Germany was largely rebuilt so that, when the depression arrived, Germany had the most efficient industrial machine in Europe and probably the second most efficient in the world (after the United States). The German financial system had inadequate controls over inflation and almost none over deflation because of the Dawes Plan restrictions on the open-market operations of the Reichsbank and the generally slow response of the German economy to changes in the discount rate. Fortunately, such controls were hardly necessary. The price level was at 137 in 1924 and at the same figure in 1929 (1913=100). In that six-year period it had reached as high as 142 (in 1925) and fallen as low as 134 (in 1926). This stability in prices was accompanied by stability in economic conditions. While these conditions were by no means booming, there was only one bad year before 1930. This was 1926, the year in which prices fell to 134 from the 1925 level of 142. In this year unemployment averaged 2 million. The best year was 1925, in which unemployment averaged 636,000. This drop in prosperity from 1925 to 1926 was caused by a lack of credit as a result of the inadequate supplies of domestic credit and a temporary decline in the supplies of foreign credit. It was this short slump in business which led Germany to follow the road to technological reorganization. This permitted Germany to increase output with decreasing employment. The average annual increase in labor productivity in the period 1924–1932 in Germany was about 5 percent. Output per labor hour in industry rose from 87.8 in 1925 to 115.6 in 1930 and 125 in 1932 (1928=100). This increase in output served to intensify the impact of the depression in Germany, so that unemployment, which averaged about three million in the year 1930, reached over six million late in 1932. The implications of this will be examined in detail in our study of the rise to power of Hitler.

The stabilization period did not end until about 1931, although only minor Powers were still stabilizing in the last year or so. The last Great Power to stabilize *de jure* was France in June, 1928, and she had been stabilized *de facto* much earlier. In the whole period, about fifty countries stabilized their currencies on the gold standard. But because of the quantity of gold necessary to maintain the customary reserve ratios (that is, the pre-1914 ratios) at the higher prices generally prevailing during the period of stabilization, no important country was able to go back on the gold standard as the term was understood in 1914. The chief change was the use of the "gold exchange standard" or the "gold bullion standard" in place of the old gold standard. Under the gold exchange standard, foreign exchange of gold standard countries could be used as reserves against notes or deposits in place of reserves in gold. In this way, the world's limited supplies of gold could be used to support a much greater volume of fictitious wealth in the world as a whole since the same quantity of gold could act as bullion reserve for one country and as gold exchange reserve for another. Even those countries which stabilized on a direct gold standard did so in a quite different way from the situation in 1914. In few countries was there free and gratuitous convertibility between notes, coin, and bullion. In Great Britain, for example, by the Gold Standard Act of May 1925, notes could be exchanged for gold only in the form of bullion and only in amounts of at least 400 fine ounces (that is, not less than $8,268 worth at a time). Bullion could be presented to the mint for coinage only by the Bank of England, although the bank was bound to buy all gold offered at 77s. 10½d. per standard ounce. Notes could be converted into coin only at the option of the bank. Thus the gold standard of 1925 was quite different from that of 1914.

This would indicate that even in its most superficial aspects the international gold standard of 1914 was not reestablished by 1930. The legal provisions were different; the financial necessities and practices were quite different; the profound underlying economic and commercial conditions were entirely different, and becoming more so. Yet financiers, businessmen, and politicians tried to pretend to themselves and to the public that they had restored the financial system of 1914. They had created a facade of cardboard and tinsel which had a vague resemblance to the old system, and they hoped that, if they pretended vigorously enough, they could change this facade into the lost reality for which they yearned. At the same time, while pursuing policies (such as tariffs, price controls, production controls, and so on) which drove this underlying reality ever farther from that which had existed in 1914, they besought other governments to do differently. Such a situation, with pretense treated as if it were reality and reality treated as if it were a bad dream, could lead only to disaster. This is what happened. The period of stabilization merged rapidly into a period of deflation and depression.

As we have said, the stage of financial capitalism did not place emphasis on the exchange of goods or the production of goods as the earlier stages of commercial capitalism and industrial capitalism had done. In fact, financial capitalism had little interest in goods at all, but was concerned entirely with claims on wealth—stocks, bonds, mortgages, insurance, deposits, proxies, interest rates, and such.

It invested capital not because it desired to increase the output of goods or services but because it desired to float issues (frequently excess issues) of securities on this productive basis. It built railroads in order to sell securities, not in order to transport goods; it constructed great steel corporations to sell securities, not in order to make steel, and so on. But, incidentally, it greatly increased the transport of goods, the output of steel, and the production of other goods. By the middle of the stage of financial capitalism, however, the organization of financial capitalism had evolved to a highly sophisticated level of security promotion and speculation which did not require any productive investment as a basis. Corporations were built upon corporations in the form of holding companies, so that securities were issued in huge quantities, bringing profitable fees and commissions to financial capitalists without any increase in economic production whatever. Indeed, these financial capitalists discovered that they could not only make killings out of the issuing of such securities, they could also make killings out of the bankruptcy of such corporations, through the fees and commissions of reorganization. A very pleasant cycle of flotation, bankruptcy, flotation, bankruptcy began to be practiced by these financial capitalists. The more excessive the flotation, the greater the profits, and the more imminent the bankruptcy. The more frequent the bankruptcy, the greater the profits of reorganization and the sooner the opportunity of another excessive flotation with its accompanying profits. This excessive stage reached its highest peak only in the United States. In Europe it was achieved only in isolated cases.

The growth of financial capitalism made possible a centralization of world economic control and a use of this power for the direct benefit of financiers and the indirect injury of all other economic groups. This concentration of power, however, could be achieved only by using methods which planted the seeds which grew into monopoly capitalism. Financial control could be exercised only imperfectly through credit control and interlocking directorates. In order to strengthen such control, some measure of stock ownership was necessary. But stock ownership was dangerous to banks because their funds consisted more of deposits (that is, short-term obligations) than of capital (or long-term obligations). This meant that banks which sought economic control through stock ownership were putting short-term obligations into long-term holdings. This was safe only so long as these latter could be liquidated rapidly at a price high enough to pay short-term obligations as they presented themselves. But these holdings of securities were bound to become frozen because both the economic and the financial systems were deflationary. The economic system was deflationary because power production and modern technology gave a great increase in the supply of real wealth. This meant that in the long run the control by banks was doomed by the progress of technology. The financial system was also deflationary because of the bankers' insistence on the gold standard, with all that this implies.

To escape from this dilemma, the financial capitalists acted upon two fronts. On the business side, they sought to sever control from ownership of securities, believing they could hold the former and relinquish the latter. On the industrial side, they sought to advance monopoly and restrict production, thus keeping prices up and their security holdings liquid.

The efforts of financiers to separate ownership from control were aided by the great capital demands of modern industry. Such demands for capital made necessary the corporation form of business organization. This inevitably brings together the capital owned by a large number of persons to create an enterprise controlled by a small number of persons. The financiers did all they could to make the former number as large as possible and the latter number as small as possible. The former was achieved by stock splitting, issuing securities of low par value, and by high-pressure security salesmanship. The latter was achieved by plural-voting stock, nonvoting stock, pyramiding of holding companies, election of directors by cooptation, and similar techniques. The result of this was that larger and larger aggregates of wealth fell into the control of smaller and smaller groups of men.

While financial capitalism was thus weaving the intricate pattern of modern corporation law and practice on one side, it was establishing monopolies and cartels on the other. Both helped to dig the grave of financial capitalism and pass the reins of economic control on to the newer monopoly capitalism. On one side, the financiers freed the controllers of business from the owners of business, but, on the other side, this concentration gave rise to monopoly conditions which freed the controllers from the banks.

The date at which any country shifted to financial capitalism and later shifted to monopoly capitalism depended on the supply of capital available to business. These dates could be hastened or retarded by government action. In the United States the onset of monopoly capitalism was retarded by the government's antimonopoly legislation, while in Germany it was hastened by the cartel laws. The real key to the shift rested on the control of money flows, especially of investment funds. These controls, which were held by investment bankers in 1900, were eclipsed by other sources of funds and capital, such as insurance, retirement and investment funds, and, above all, by those flows resulting from the fiscal policies of governments. Efforts by the older private investment bankers to control these new channels of funds had varying degrees of success, but, in general, financial capitalism was destroyed by two events: (1) the ability of industry to finance its own capital needs because of the increased profits arising from the decreased competition established by financial capitalism, and (2) the economic crisis engendered by the deflationary policies resulting from financial capitalism's obsession with the gold standard.

The Period of Deflation, 1927-1936

The period of stabilization cannot be clearly distinguished from the period of deflation. In most countries, the period of deflation began in 1921 and, after about four or five years, became more rapid in its development, reaching after 1929 a degree which could be called acute.

In the first part of this period (1921–1925), the dangerous economic implications of deflation were concealed by a structure of self-deception which pretended that a great period of economic progress would be inaugurated as soon as the task of stabilization had been accomplished. This psychological optimism was completely unwarranted by the economic facts, even in the United States where these economic facts were (for the short term, at least) more promising than anywhere else. After 1925, when the deflation became more deep-rooted and economic conditions worsened, the danger from these conditions was concealed by a continuation of unwarranted optimism. The chief symptom of the unsoundness of the underlying economic reality—the steady fall in prices —was concealed in the later period (1925–1929) by a steady rise in security prices (which was erroneously regarded as a good sign) and by the excessive lending abroad of the United States (which amounted to almost ten billion dollars in the period 1920-1931, bringing our total foreign investment to almost 27 billion dollars by the end of 1930). This foreign lending of the United States was the chief reason why the maladjusted economic conditions could be kept concealed for so many years. Before the World War, the United States had been a debtor nation and, to pay these debts, had developed an exporting economy. The combination of debtor and exporter is a feasible one. The war made the United States a creditor nation and also made her a greater exporter than ever by building up her acreage of cotton and wheat and her capacity to produce ships, steel, textiles, and so on. The resulting combination of creditor and exporter was not feasible. The United States refused to accept either necessary alternative—to reduce debts owed to her or to increase her imports. Instead, she raised tariffs against imports and temporarily filled the gap with huge foreign loans. But this was hopeless as a permanent solution. As a temporary solution, it permitted the United States to be both creditor and exporter; it permitted Germany to pay reparations with neither a budgetary surplus nor a favorable balance of trade; it permitted dozens of minor countries to adopt a gold standard they could not hold; it permitted France, Britain, Italy, and others to pay war debts to the United States without sending goods. In a word, it permitted the world to live in a fairyland of self-delusions remote from economic realities.

These realities were characterized by (a) fundamental maladjustments, both economic and financial, which made it impossible for the financial system to function as it had in 1914, and (b) the steady deflation.

The fundamental maladjustments were both economic and financial. The economic maladjustments were those which we have already indicated: the industrialization of colonial areas; the overproduction of raw materials and food as a result of wartime high prices, the overexpansion of heavy industry as a result of wartime needs, the obsolescence of much of heavy industry in Europe and in Britain which made it impossible to compete with newer equipment or to cope with the shifts in consumer demand, and the steadily increasing disadvantage of producers of raw materials and food in contrast with producers of industrial goods. To these old factors were added new ones such as the great increase in productive efficiency in Germany and the United States, the return of Russia and Germany to the European economy about 1924, and the return of Europe to the world economy in the period 1925–1927. Many countries sought to resist these factors, both old and new, by adopting political interference with economic life in the form of tariffs, import quotas, export subsidies, and so on.

The financial maladjustments served to create an insufficiency of gold and a maldistribution of gold. The inadequacy of the supply of gold arose from several causes. It has been estimated that the world's stock of gold money needed to increase by 3.1 percent per year in the 1920's to support the world's economic development with stable prices on the gold standard. The production of new gold after 1920 was below this rate.

Moreover, as a result of the activities of the League of Nations and financial advisers like Professor E. W. Kemmerer of Princeton University, every country was encouraged to get on the gold standard. This led to a "gold rush" as each country tried to obtain a supply of gold large enough to provide adequate reserves. Because there were more countries on gold in 1928 than in 1914 and because prices in general were higher, more gold was needed in reserves.

The efforts to get around this by using a gold exchange standard rather than a gold standard were helpful in dealing with the problem of inadequate supplies of gold but increased the difficulty of the problem of maldistribution of gold, since the gold exchange standard did not respond to the flow of gold as readily and thus did not serve so well to stem such flows of gold. The need for gold was made greater by the existence of large floating balances of political or panic funds which might well move from one market to another independent of economic conditions. The need was increased by the fact that in 1920 there were three major financial centers which had to make payments by shipments of gold in contrast to the single financial center of 1914 where payments could be made by bookkeeping transactions. To rectify this problem to some degree, the Bank for International Settlements was created in 1929 but never functioned as its founders had hoped. Finally, the need for gold was increased by the enormous growth in foreign indebtedness, much of it of a political nature such as the war debts and reparations.

On top of this insufficiency of gold was superimposed a drastic maldistribution of gold. This was conclusive proof that the financial system of 1914 had broken down, for the old system would have operated automatically to distribute gold evenly. This maldistribution resulted from the fact that when gold flowed into certain countries the automatic results of such a flow (such as rising prices or falling interest rates) which would have restored equilibrium in 1914 were prevented from acting in 1928. In this period, about four-fifths of the world's gold supply was in five countries, and over half was in two, the United States and France. The gold had been brought to these two for quite different reasons—to the United States because it was the world's greatest creditor and to France because of its devaluation of the franc. Britain, on the other hand, had floating balances of about £800 million, and handled each year £20,000 million in transactions with a gold reserve of only £150 million. Such a situation made it possible for France to use gold as a political weapon against Britain.

As a result of these conditions and the deflationary economic conditions described in Chapter 11, prices began to fall, at first slowly and then with increasing rapidity. The turning point in most countries was in 1925–1926, with Great Britain one of the earliest (January 1925). In the first half of 1929, this slow drift downward began to change to a rapid drop. The following table will show the changes in wholesale prices for five principal countries:

WHOLESALE PRICE INDICES
(1913 = 100)

	UNITED STATES	BRITAIN	FRANCE	ITALY	GERMANY
1924	141	166	489	554	137
1925	148	159	550	646	142
1926	143	148	695	654	134
1927	137	142	642	527	138
1928	139	137	645	491	140
1929	137	120	627	481	137
1930	124	104	554	430	125
1931	105	102	520	376	111
1932	93	90	427	351	97
1933	95	90	398	320	93
1934	108	92	376	313	98
1935	115	93	339	344	102
1936	116	99	411	385	104
1937	124	114	581	449	106

The economic effects of these soft prices after 1925 were adverse, but these effects were concealed for a considerable period because of various influences, especially the liberal credit policies of the United States (both foreign and domestic) and the optimism engendered by the stock-market boom. The facade of prosperity over unsound economic conditions was practically worldwide. Only in France and the United States was it a boom in real wealth, but in the latter it was by no means as great as one might think from a glance at stock prices. In Britain, the boom appeared in the form of the flotation of new stocks of unsound and fraudulent companies and a minor stock-market boom (about one-third as fast a rise in security prices as in the United States). In Germany and in much of Latin America, the boom was based upon foreign borrowing (chiefly from the United States) the proceeds of which were largely put into nonproductive construction. In Italy, held down by the overevaluation of the lira in 1927, the boom was of short duration.

THE CRASH OF 1929

The history of the slump begins about 1927 when France stabilized the franc *de facto* at a level at which it was devalued and undervalued. This led to a great demand for francs. The Bank of France sold francs in return for foreign exchange. The francs were created as credit in France, thus giving an inflationary effect which can be seen in the behavior of French prices in 1926–1928. The foreign exchange which France received for its francs was largely left in that form without being converted into gold. By 1928 the Bank of France found that it held foreign exchange to the value of 32 billion francs (about $1.2 billion). At this point the Bank of France began to transfer its exchange holdings into gold, buying the metal chiefly in London and New York. Because of the inadequate gold reserves in London, a meeting of central bankers in New York decided that the gold purchases of France and Germany should be diverted from London to New York in the future (July 1927). To prevent the resulting outflow of gold from having a deflationary effect which might injure business, the New York Federal Reserve Bank dropped its discount rate from 4 percent to 3½ percent. When the French gold purchases became noticeable in 1928, the Federal Reserve Bank adopted open market operations to counterbalance them, buying securities to a value equal to the French purchases of gold.

As a result there was no reduction in money in the United States. This money, however, was going increasingly into stock-market specu-lation rather than into production of real wealth. This can be seen from the following table of indices of average stock prices for both England and the United States in the years indicated:

INDUSTRIAL SHARES PRICES
(1924 = 100)

YEAR	UNITED KINGDOM	UNITED STATES
1924	100	100
1925	109	126
1926	115	143
1927	124	169
1928	139	220
1929	139	270
1930	112	200
1931	·87	124
1932	84	66
1933	103	95
1934	125	116

The stock-market boom in the United States was really much more drastic than is indicated by these index numbers, because these are yearly averages, and include sluggish stocks as well as market leaders. The boom began as far back as 1924, as can be seen, and reached its peak in the fall of 1929. By the spring of 1929 it had become a frenzy and was having profound effects on business activity, on domestic and international finance, on the domestic affairs of foreign countries, and on the psychology and modes of life of Americans.

Among the financial results of the stock-market boom were the following: In the United States credit was diverted from production to speculation, and increasing amounts of funds were being drained from the economic system into the stock market, where they circulated around and around, building up the prices of securities. In Germany it became increasingly difficult to borrow from the United States, and the foreign loans, which kept the German financial system and the whole system of reparations and war debts functioning, were shifted from long-term loans to precarious short-term credits. The results of this have been examined in the chapter on reparations. In other countries, funds tended to flow to the United States where they could expect to roll up extraordinary earnings in capital gains in a relatively short time. This was especially true of funds from Britain where the stock-market boom ceased after the end of 1928. By that time the fundamentally unsound economic conditions were beginning to break through the facade. The decline in foreign loans by both London and New York began to be noticeable by the last half of 1928 and made it evident that the chief support of the facade was vanishing. But the continued rise of security prices in New York continued to draw money from the rest of the world and from the productive and consumptive systems of the United States itself.

Early in 1929, the board of governors of the Federal Reserve System became alarmed at the stock-market speculation, especially at its draining credit from industrial production. To curtail this, in April 1929, the Federal Reserve authorities called upon the member banks to reduce their loans on stock-exchange collateral. At the same time, it engaged in open-market operations which reduced its holdings of bankers' acceptances from about $300 million to about $150 million. The sterilization of gold was made more drastic. It was hoped in this way to reduce the amount of credit available for speculation. Instead, the available credit went more and more to speculation and decreasingly to productive business. Call money rates in New York which had reached 7 percent at the end of 1928 were at 13 percent by June 1929. In that month, the election of a Labour government in England so alarmed British capital that large amounts flowed to the United States and contributed further to the speculative frenzy. In August, the Federal Reserve discount rate was raised to 6 percent. By this time it was becoming evident that the prices of stocks were far above any value based on earning power and that this earning power was beginning to decline because of the weakening of industrial activity. At this critical moment, on September 26, 1929, a minor financial panic in London (the Hatry Case) caused the Bank of England to raise its bank rate from 4½ percent to 6½ percent. This was enough. British funds began to leave Wall Street, and the overinflated market commenced to sag. By the middle of October, the fall had become a panic. In the week of October 21st on the Stock Exchange and the Curb Exchange in New York, total stocks sold averaged over 9 million a day, and on Thursday, October 24th, almost 19¼ million shares changed hands. The shrinkage in values was measured by several billion dollars a day. Some stocks fell by 100 or even 140 points in a day. Auburn fell 210 points, General Electric 76 points, and U.S. Steel 26 points in 4½ days. By November 6th these three stocks had fallen respectively 55, 78, and 28 points more. It was a financial disaster of unparalleled magnitude.

The stock-market crash reduced the volume of foreign lending from the United States to Europe, and these two events together tore away the facade which until then had concealed the fundamental maladjustments between production and consumption, between debts and ability to pay, between creditors and willingness to receive goods, between the theories of 1914 and the practices of 1928. Not only were these maladjustments revealed but they began to be readjusted with a severity of degree and speed made all the worse by the fact that the adjustments had been so long delayed. Production began to fall to the level of consumption, creating idle men, idle factories, idle money, and idle resources. Debtors were called to account and found deficient. Creditors who had refused repayment now sought it, but in vain. All values of real wealth shrank drastically.

THE CRISIS OF 1931

It was this shrinkage of values which carried the economic crisis into the stage of financial and banking crisis and beyond these to the stage of political crisis. As values declined, production fell rapidly; banks found it increasingly difficult to meet the demands upon their reserves; these demands increased with the decline in confidence; governments found that their tax receipts fell so rapidly that budgets became unbalanced in spite of every effort to prevent it.

The financial and banking crisis began in central Europe early in 1931, reached London by the end of that year, spread to the United States and France in 1932, bringing the United States to the acute stage in 1933, and France in 1934.

The acute stage began early in 1931 in central Europe where the deflationary crisis was producing drastic results. Unable to balance its budget or obtain adequate foreign loans, Germany was unable to meet her reparation obligations. At this critical moment, as we have seen, the largest bank in Austria collapsed because of its inability to liquidate its assets at sufficiently high prices and with enough speed to meet the claims being presented to it. The Austrian debacle soon spread the banking panic to Germany. The Hoover Moratorium on reparations relieved the pressure on Germany in the middle of 1931, but not enough to permit any real financial recovery. Millions of short-term credits lent from London were tied up in frozen accounts in Germany. As a result, in the summer of 1931, the uneasiness spread to London.

The pound sterling was very vulnerable. There were five principal reasons: (1) the pound was overvalued; (2) costs of production in Britain were much more rigid than prices; (3) gold reserves were precariously small; (4) the burden of public debt was too great in a deflationary atmosphere; (5) there were greater liabilities than assets in short-term international holdings in London (about £407 million to £153 million). This last fact was revealed by the publication of the Macmillan Report in June 1931, right at the middle of the crisis in central Europe where most of the short-term assets were frozen. The bank rate was raised from 2½ percent to 4½ percent to encourage capital to stay in Britain. £130 million in credits was obtained from France and the United States in July and August to fight the depreciation of the pound by throwing more dollars and francs into the market. To restore confidence among the wealthy (who were causing the panic) an effort was made to balance the budget by cutting public expenditures drastically. This, by reducing purchasing power, had injurious effects on business activity and increased unrest among ·the masses of the people. Mutiny broke out in the British fleet in protest against pay cuts. Various physical and extralegal restrictions were placed on export of gold (such as issuing gold bars of a low purity unacceptable to the Bank of France). The outflow of gold could not be stopped. It amounted to £200 million in two months. On September 18th New York and Paris refused further credits to the British Treasury, and three days later the gold standard was suspended. The bank rate still stood at 4½ percent. To many experts the most significant aspect of the event was not that Britain went off gold, but that she did so with the bank rate at 4½ percent. It had always been said in Britain that a 10 percent bank rate would pull gold out of the earth. By 1931, the authorities in Britain saw clearly the futility of trying to stay on gold by raising the bank rate. This indicates how conditions had changed. It was realized that the movement of gold was subject to factors which the authorities could not control more than it was under the influence of factors they could control. It also shows—a hopeful sign—that the authorities after twelve years were beginning to realize that conditions had changed. For the first time, people began to realize that the two problems—domestic prosperity and stable exchanges—were quite separate problems and that the old orthodox practice of sacrificing the former to the latter must end. From this point on, one country after another began to seek domestic prosperity by managed prices and stable exchanges by exchange control. That is, the link between the two (the gold standard) was broken, and one problem was made into two.

The British suspension of gold was by necessity, not by choice. It was regarded as an evil, but it was really a blessing. As a result of this mistake, many of the benefits which could have been derived from it were lost by trying to counterbalance the inflationary results of the suspension by other deflationary actions. The discount rate was raised to 6 percent; valiant efforts to balance the budget continued; a protective tariff was established and a program of fairly stiff taxes installed. As a result, prices did not rise enough to give that spur to production which would have been necessary to increase prosperity and reduce unemployment. No system of exchange control was set up. As a result, the depreciation of sterling in respect to gold-standard currencies could not be prevented, and amounted to 30 percent by December 1931. Such a depreciation was regarded by the authorities as an evil—chiefly because of orthodox economic theories which considered parity of exchanges as an end in itself and partly because of the need to pay the £130 million in Franco-American credits—a burden which increased as sterling depreciated in respect to dollars and francs.

As a result of the British abandonment of the gold standard the central core of the world's financial system was disrupted. This core, which in 1914 was exclusively in London, in 1931 was divided among London, New York, and Paris. London's share depended on financial skill and old habits; New York's share depended on her position as the world's great creditor; Paris's share depended on a combination of a creditor position with an undervalued currency which attracted gold. From 1927 to 1931, these three had controlled the world's financial system with payments flowing in to the three, credits flowing out, and stable exchanges between them. The events of September 1931 broke up this triangle. Stable exchanges continued for dollar-franc, leaving dollar-pound and pound-franc to fluctuate. This did not permit an adjustment of the maladjusted exchange rates of 1928–1931. Concretely, the undervaluation of the franc in 1928 and the overvaluation of the pound in 1925 could not be remedied by the events of 1931. A sterling-franc rate which would have eliminated the undervaluation of the franc would have resulted in a sterling-dollar rate which would have over-corrected the overvaluation of sterling. On the other hand, the depreciation of the pound put great pressure on both the dollar and the franc. At the same time, Britain sought to exploit as much as possible her economic relations with her home market, the empire, and that group of other countries known as the "sterling bloc." The home market was set aside by the establishment of customs duties on imports into the United Kingdom (special customs duties November 1931, and a general tariff in February 1932). The empire was brought into closer economic ties by a group of eleven "Imperial Preference" treaties made at Ottawa in August 1932. The sterling bloc was reinforced and enlarged by a series of bilateral trade agreements with various countries, beginning with Norway, Sweden, Denmark, and Argentina.

Thus the world tended to divide into two financial groups—the sterling bloc organized about Britain and the gold bloc organized about the United States, France, Belgium, the Netherlands, and Switzerland.

The depreciation of sterling in relation to gold made the currencies of the gold bloc overvalued, and relieved Britain of that burdensome status for the first time since 1925. As a result, Britain found it easier to export and more difficult to import, and obtained a favorable balance of trade for the first time in almost seven years. On the other hand, the gold countries found their depressions intensified.

As a third result of the British abandonment of the gold standard Britain freed herself from her financial subjection to France. This subjection had resulted from the vulnerable position of the British gold reserves in contrast to the bulging appearance of the French reserves.

After 1931 the financial positions of the two countries were reversed. When Britain was able to add a financial superiority after 1931 to the political superiority she had possessed since 1924, it became possible for Britain to force France to accept the policy of appeasement. Moreover, the financial crisis of 1931 was to bring to power in Britain the national government which was to carry out the policy of appeasement.

As a fourth result, the countries still on gold began to adopt new trade barriers, such as tariffs and quotas, to prevent Britain from using the advantage of depreciated currency to increase her exports to them. The countries already off gold began to see the value in currency depreciation, and the possibility of races in depreciation began to form in the minds of some.

As a fifth result of the abandonment of gold, it became possible to rearm without the resulting unbalancing of the budget leading to financial jeopardy as under a gold standard. Little advantage was taken of this, because pacificism on the Left and appeasement on the Right were regarded as substitutes for arms.

Because of the deflationary policy which accompanied the abandonment of gold in Great Britain, recovery from depression did not result except to a very slight degree. Neither prices nor employment rose until 1933, and, from that year on, the improvement was slow. The depreciation of sterling did result in an improvement in the foreign trade balance, exports rising very slightly and imports falling 12 percent in 1932 in comparison with 1931. This led to a revival of confidence in sterling and a simultaneous decline in confidence in the gold-standard currencies. Foreign funds began to flow to London.

The flow of capital into Britain early in 1932 resulted in an appreciation of sterling in respect to the gold currencies. This was unwelcome to the British government since it would destroy her newly acquired trade advantage. The pound sterling appreciated in respect to the dollar from 3.27 on December 1, 1931, to 3.80 on March 31, 1932. To control this, the government, in May 1932, set up the Exchange Equalization Account with capital of £175 million. This fund was to be used to stabilize the exchange rates by buying and selling foreign exchange against the trend of the market. In this way, the old automatic regulation by the market of the internal credit structure through the international flow of funds was broken. Control of the credit structure was left to the Bank of England, while control of the exchanges went to the Exchange Equalization Fund. This made it possible for Britain to adopt a policy of easy and plentiful credit within the country without being deterred by a flight of capital from the country. Since the Exchange Equalization Fund was not a system of exchange control but merely a government management of the regular exchange market, it was not in a position to handle any very considerable emigration of capital. The easy credit policies of Britain (designed to encourage business activity) had thus to be combined with deflationary prices (designed to prevent any powerful flight of capital). The bank rate was dropped to 2 percent by July 1932, and an embargo was placed on new foreign capital issues to keep this easy money at home. The chief exceptions to this embargo arose from loans to be used in the general policy of binding the sterling bloc to Britain, and the proceeds of these had to be used in Britain.

On this basis, although sterling fell to 3.14 by the end of November 1932, a mild economic revival was built up. Cheap credit permitted a shift of economic activity from the old lines (like coal, steel, textiles) to new lines (like chemicals, motors, electrical products). The tariff permitted a rapid growth of cartels and monopolies whose process of creation provided at least a temporary revival of economic activity. The continued low food prices permitted the income from this increase in activity to be diverted to necessities of a different kind, especially dwelling construction. The budget was balanced, and early in 1934 showed a surplus of £30 million.

The improvement in Britain was not shared by the countries still on gold. As a result of the competition of depreciated sterling, they found their balances of trade pushed toward the unfavorable side and their deflation in prices increased. Tariffs had to be raised, quotas and exchange controls set up. The United States could hardly do the first of these (her tariff of 1930 was already the highest in history), and rejected the others in principle.

THE CRISIS IN THE UNITED STATES, 1933

As a result of the British crisis, the gold countries of Europe sought to modify their financial basis from the gold exchange standard to the gold bullion standard. When Britain abandoned gold in September 1931, France was caught with over £60 million in sterling exchange. This was equal to about 30 percent of her foreign-exchange holdings (7,775 million francs out of 25,194 million). The loss exceeded the total capital and surplus of the Bank of France. To avoid any similar experience in the future, France began to transfer her holdings of exchange into gold, much of it called from the United States. As confidence in the pound rose, that in the dollar fell. It became necessary to raise the New York discount rate from 1½ percent to 3½ percent (October 1932) and to engage in extensive open-market buying of securities to counteract the deflationary effects of this. However, the gold exports and gold hoarding continued, made worse by the fact that the United States was the only gold standard country with gold coins still circulating.

As a result of the decline of confidence and the demand for liquidity, the American banking system began to collapse. The Reconstruction Finance Corporation was set up early in 1932 with $3½ billion in government money to advance to banks and other large corporations. By the end of the year, it had lent over $1½ billion. When the details of these loans were published (in January 1933), runs on the banks were intensified. A bank holiday was declared in Nevada in October 1932, in Iowa in January 1933, in six states during February, and in sixteen states in the first three days of March. From February 1st to March 4th the Federal Reserve Bank in New York lost $756 million in gold; it called in $709 million from the other Federal Reserve Banks, which were also subject to runs.

The banks of the whole United States were closed by executive order on March 4 to be reopened after March 12th if their condition was satisfactory. Export of gold was subjected to license, convertibility of notes into gold was ended, and private holding of gold was made illegal. These orders, completed on April 20, 1933, took the United States off the gold standard. This was done in order that the government could pursue a policy of price inflation in its domestic program. It was not made necessary by the American international financial position, as this continued very favorable. This was quite different from the situation in Britain in 1931. London had left gold unwillingly and had followed an orthodox financial program afterward; Washington left gold in 1933 voluntarily in order to follow an unorthodox financial program of inflation.

As a result of the abandonment of the gold standard by the United States, the central-exchange triangle between London, Paris, and New York was further disrupted. All three exchange rates were able to fluctuate, although the Exchange Equalization Account kept two of them relatively steady. To the worldwide problem of economic distress was now added the problem of exchange stabilization. A dispute ensued among Britain, France, and the United States over which of these two problems should be given priority. France insisted that no economic recovery was possible until exchanges were stabilized. It surely was true that as long as the franc remained on gold at the same valuation, France would suffer from the depreciation of the pound and the dollar. The United States insisted that economic recovery must have priority over stabilization, since the latter would hamper the process of price reflation which the administration considered essential to recovery. Britain, which had supported the priority of recovery over stabilization as long as the pound was the only one of the three currencies which was depreciated, insisted on the importance of stabilization as soon as the advantages of depreciation began to be shared by the dollar. This depreciation of both the dollar and the pound put great strain on the franc. To keep France from being forced off the gold standard, Britain, on April 28, 1933, lent her £30 million to be repaid out of the sterling exchange with which France had been caught in September 1931. Until the middle of 1933, the Exchange Equalization Account was used by Britain to prevent any appreciation of the pound. This was countered in the United States by the inflationary Thomas Amendment to the Agricultural Adjustment Act (May 12, 1933). This Amendment gave the president the power to devaluate the dollar up to 50 percent, to issue up to $3 billion in fiat money, and to engage on an extensive program of public spending.

THE WORLD ECONOMIC CONFERENCE, 1933

This dispute over the priority of stabilization or recovery reached its peak in the World Monetary and Economic Conference held in London from June 12 to July 27, 1933. A Preparatory Commission of Experts drew up a series of preliminary agreements for countries on gold or off, with exchange controls or without, but no agreement could be obtained at the conference itself. Britain and France tried to get the dollar to join them in a temporary *de facto* stabilization in preparation for a real agreement. The franc and pound had already been pegged to each other at 84 francs per pound, which gave a London gold price of 122 shillings. The United States refused to join in any temporary stabilization because of the success of the administration's domestic recovery program. The general price index in the United States rose by 8.7 percent from February to June 1933, and farm products rose by 30.1 percent. The mere hint of a stabilization agreement was sufficient to cause a sharp break in the rise of security and commodity prices (June 14, 1933), so Roosevelt broke off all negotiations toward stabilization (July 3, 1933).

The World Economic Conference, as Professor William Adams Brown wrote, broke up on four great negatives: the countries which had adopted trade restrictions refused to abandon them without currency stabilization; the countries on the gold standard refused to accept price increases as a road to recovery because of fear of inflation; Great Britain wanted price increases but refused to permit an unbalanced budget or a public works program; and the United States, which was seeking recovery through inflation and public works, refused to hamper the program by currency stabilization.

As a result of the failure of the Economic Conference, the countries of the world tended to divide into three groups: a sterling bloc, a gold bloc, and a dollar bloc. The gold and sterling blocs were formally organized, the former on July 3rd and the later on July 8th. A struggle ensued among these three in an effort to shift the economic burdens of past mistakes from one to another.

A great deal has been written since 1933 in an effort to apportion the blame for the failure of the World Economic Conference. It is a futile task. From the point of view of narrow self-interest in the short run, all countries were correct in their actions. From the wider point of view of the world as a whole or of the long-run results, all countries were worthy of blame. By 1933, the day in which any country could follow a policy of short-run self-interest and remain under liberal capitalism was past. For technological and institutional reasons, the economies of the different countries were so intertwined with one another that any policy of self-interest on the part of one would be sure to injure others in the short run and the country itself in the long run. Briefly, the international and the domestic economic systems had developed to a point where the customary methods of thought and procedure in regard to them were obsolete.

The reason why a policy of short-run self-interest on the part of one country was in such sharp conflict with any similar policy pursued by another country does not rest on the fact that the interests of one country were adverse to those of another. That would have been a problem to be treated by simple compromise. The conflicts between economic nationalisms were based on the fact that, viewed superficially, the crisis took entirely different forms in the chief countries of the world. In the United States, the most obvious manifestation of the crisis was low prices, which by 1933 made the whole banking system insolvent. High prices became, thus, for the United States, the chief goal of debtors and creditors alike. In Britain, the most obvious manifestation of the crisis was the outflow of gold which jeopardized the gold standard. A rectification of the international balance of payments rather than a rise in prices thus became the chief immediate aim of British policy. In France, the crisis appeared chiefly as an unbalanced internal budget. The French gold supply was more than adequate, and prices, as a result of the substantial devaluation of 1928, were considered extremely high. But the unbalanced budget created a great problem. If the deficit were filled by borrowing the result would be inflationary and injurious to the creditor classes who had suffered so greatly in the 1920's. If the deficit were filled by taxation, this would lead to deflation (with its decline in business activity) and a flight of capital out of the country. To the French government the only way out of this dilemma was to be found in an increase in business activity, which would increase the tax yield without any rise in rates. It could see no value in the American concern with higher prices or the British concern with trade balances as short-run objectives.

This contrast between the various kinds of impact which the economic and financial crisis made on the various countries could be extended to lesser countries. In Switzerland (where gold reserves were well over 100 percent) the chief problem was "hot money." In Germany, the chief problem was foreign debts, but this soon developed into a combination of all the ailments which were afflicting other countries (low prices, unfavorable balance of trade, unbalanced budget, panicky short-term loans, and so on). In the Netherlands and in the countries of eastern Europe, the chief problem was "segmentation of prices" (that is, that prices of food and raw materials, which they sold, fell faster than prices of manufactured goods which they bought).

As a result of the crisis, regardless of the nature of its primary impact, all countries began to pursue policies of economic nationalism. This took the form of tariff increases, licensing of imports, import quotas, sumptuary laws restricting imports, laws placing national origin, trade-mark, health, or quarantine restrictions on imports, foreign-exchange controls, competitive depreciation of currencies, export subsidies, dumping of exports, and so on. These were first established on an extensive scale in 1931, and spread rapidly as a result of imitation and retaliation.

As a result of such economic nationalism, it soon appeared that the disappearance of the old multilateral system of world finance centering in London would be followed by the breaking of the multilateral system of world trade (also centering in Britain) into a number of partially segregated markets operating on a bilateral basis. International trade declined greatly as the following figures indicate:

VALUE OF TRADE IN MILLIONS OF DOLLARS

	1928	1932	1935	1938
Europe's Trade	58,082	24,426	20,762	24,065
World's Trade	114,429	45,469	40,302	46,865

THE CRISIS IN THE GOLD BLOC, 1934–1936

After the breakup of the World Economic Conference, the United States continued its policy of domestic inflation. As the dollar depreciated, the pressure on the franc increased, while the pound, through the use of the Exchange Equalization Account, tried to follow a middle ground in a depreciated, but stable, relationship to the franc. In this way, by purely artificial means, the pound was kept at about 85 francs. In the late summer of 1933 (September 8th) the United States Treasury began to depreciate the dollar by buying gold at constantly increasing prices (about $30 an ounce, compared to the old stabilization rate of $20.67). This put pressure on the franc as well as on the pound. Deflation became increasingly severe in France, and, in October 1933, a budget deficit of over 40 billion francs gave rise to a Cabinet crisis. By the end of 1933, the gold price in New York reached $34, and the dollar, which had been at 4.40 in relation to the pound in August, fell to 5.50. On February 1, 1934, the United States went back on the gold standard at a considerable devaluation under the old price. The gold content was cut to 59.06 percent of the 1932 amount. At the same time, the Treasury set up a standing offer to buy gold at $35 an ounce. This served to remove much of the uncertainty about the dollar, but stabilized it in regard to the franc at a level which put great pressure on the franc. At this price for gold, the metal flowed to the United States, France losing about 3 billion francs' worth in February 1934.

Thus the world depression and the financial crisis which France had escaped for over three years were extended to her. France had been able to escape because of her drastic devaluation in the 1920's, her well-balanced economy, and her ability to keep down unemployment by placing restrictions on the entrance of seasonal labor from Spain, Italy, and Poland. The crisis of the pound in September 1931 had begun to spread the crisis to France, and the crisis of the dollar in 1933 had made the situation worse. The American actions of 1934, which gave the world a 59-cent dollar and $35 gold, made the position of the gold bloc untenable. They had to suffer a severe deflation, or abandon gold, or devaluate. Most of them (because they feared inflation or because they had foreign debts which would increase in weight if their currency was to depreciate) permitted deflation with all its suffering. Italy even ordered deflation by decree in April 1934, in order to maintain business activity by forcing costs down as much as prices. Eventually, all members of the gold bloc had to abandon gold to some extent because of the pressure from the dollar.

Belgium was the first member of the gold bloc to yield, setting up exchange controls on March 18, 1935, and devaluating the belga to about 72 percent of its former gold content on March 30th. The final blow which forced the change was the British tariff on iron and steel established on March 26, 1935. As a result of this quick and decisive devaluation, Belgium experienced a considerable amount of economic recovery. Almost at once, production and prices rose, while unemployment fell.

The other members of the gold bloc did not profit by the example of Belgium, but determined to defend the gold content of their currencies to the limit. France was the leader in this movement, and by her policy was able to influence the other members of the bloc to resist with the same vigor. This determination of France to defend the franc is to be explained by the fact that the great mass of Frenchmen were creditors in some way or other, and having lost four-fifths of their savings in the inflation of 1914–1926 did not view with any pleasure another dose of the same medicine. In this effort to defend the franc, France was aided greatly by the activity of the British Exchange Equalization Account which bought francs in enormous quantities whenever the currency became very weak. By 1935, the resources of the Account capable of being devoted to this purpose were largely expended, and the franc fell below the gold export point for long periods. The Bank of France raised its discount rate from 2½ percent to 6 percent (May 23-28, 1935) with depressing economic results. Laval in July obtained emergency powers from the Assembly, and adopted a policy of deflation by decree, cutting ordinary public expenditures for the year from 40 billion to 11 billion francs, cutting all public salaries by 10 percent, and also reducing all rents, the cost of public utilities, and the price of bread.

In this way, the strain on the gold reserves (which fell to 16 billion francs during 1935) was relieved at the cost of increased depression. By September, the franc was still overvalued (as far as cost of living was concerned) by about 34 percent as compared to the pound and by about 54 percent as compared to the dollar. The deflation necessary to bring French prices down to parity with the prices in the depreciated-currency countries could not be obtained. By the end of 1935, the government had abandoned the effort, and by borrowing to meet budgetary deficits had turned France toward inflation. Gold began to leave the country again, and this exit became a flood after a government of the Left led by Blum came to power in June 1936.

The Blum "Popular Front" government tried to follow an impossible program: "inflation on gold." It sought inflation to relieve depression and unemployment and sought to remain on gold because this was insisted on by both the Communist and bourgeois supporters of the government. In an effort to restore confidence and slow the "flight from the franc," it became necessary for Blum formally to disavow any intention of installing a Socialist program. The Right thus discovered that it could veto any actions of the Left government merely by exporting capital from France. The flight of such capital continued through the summer of 1936, while Blum negotiated with Britain and the United States regarding devaluation of the franc. On September 24, 1936, the bank rate was raised from 3 percent to 5 percent, and, on the following day, a Three-Power Currency Declaration announced that the franc would be "adjusted," exchange stability would be maintained thereafter (through the stabilization funds), and trade restrictions would be relaxed.

The French devaluation (law of October 2, 1936) provided that the gold content of the franc would be reduced to an amount from 25.2 percent to 34.4 percent of the old figure of 65½ milligrams. From the profits obtained by thus revaluing French gold reserves, an exchange stabilization fund of 10 billion francs was set up.

Although the French devaluation of September 1936 shattered the gold bloc and forced the other members of the bloc to follow suit, it did not end the period of deflation. The reasons for this were chiefly to be found in the complete mismanagement of the French devaluation. This decisive event was delayed too long—at least a year after it should have been done—a year during which gold steadily flowed from France. More-over, when the devaluation came, it was insufficient and left the franc still overvalued in relation to price levels in the other Great Powers. Furthermore, the devaluation was shrouded with uncertainty, since the law permitted the government to devalue to any gold content between 43 and 49 milligrams. By stabilizing at about 46 milligrams, the govern-ment prevented any revival of confidence because of the danger of a further devaluation to 43 milligrams. By the time the government realized that a further devaluation was necessary, the situation had deteriorated so far that a devaluation to 43 milligrams was worthless. Finally, in the devaluation law the government took punitive measures against gold hoarders and speculators, seeking to prevent them from reaping the profits they would obtain by converting their gold back into francs at the new value. As a result, the exported and hoarded gold did not return but stayed in hiding. Thus the financial, budgetary, and economic difficul-ties in France continued. By the middle of 1937, they had become so bad that the only possible solutions were exchange control or a drastic devaluation. The former was rejected because of the pressure from Britain and the United States based on the Tripartite Agreement of 1936 and the support which their stabilization funds afforded the franc; the latter was rejected by all politicians likely to obtain power in France. As a result, the franc passed through a series of depreciations and partial devaluations which benefited no one except the speculators and left France for years torn by industrial unrest and class struggles. Unable to arm or give foreign affairs the attention they needed, the government was subjected to systematic blackmail by the well-to-do of the country because of the ability of these persons to prevent social reform, public spending, arming, or any policy of decision by selling francs. Only in May 1938 was a decisive step made. At that time the franc was drastically depreciated to 179 in the pound, and pegged at that figure. Its gold content (by a law of November 12, 1938) was fixed at about 27.5 milli-grams nine-tenths fine. By that time France had suffered years of economic chaos and governmental weakness. These conditions had en-couraged German aggression, and, when a decisive financial action was made in 1938, it was, because of the rising international crisis, too late to reap any important economic benefits.

We have said that the gold bloc was destroyed by the French de-valuation of September 1936. This was accomplished almost immediately. Switzerland, the Netherlands, and Czechoslovakia devalued their cur-rencies by about 30 percent and Italy by about 40 percent before the end of October. In each case, like Belgium rather than France, the devalua-

tion was large enough in amount and abrupt enough in time to contribute to a noticeable reflation and improvement in business activity.
Each country of the former gold bloc set up a stabilization fund to
control exchange rates, and joined the Tripartite currency agreement of
September 1936.

The historical importance of the banker-engendered deflationary crisis
of 1927–1940 can hardly be overestimated. It gave a blow to democracy
and to the parliamentary system which the later triumphs of these in
World War II and the postwar world were unable to repair fully. It
gave an impetus to aggression by those nations where parliamentary
government collapsed, and thus became a chief cause of World War II. It
so hampered the Powers which remained democratic by its orthodox
economic theories that these were unable to rearm for defense, with the
consequence that World War II was unduly prolonged by the early
defeats of the democratic states. It gave rise to a conflict between the
theorists of orthodox and unorthodox financial methods which led to a
sharp reduction in the power of the bankers. And, finally, it impelled
the whole economic development of the West along the road from financial capitalism to monopoly capitalism and, shortly thereafter, toward the
pluralist economy.

The controversy between the bankers and the theorists of unorthodox
finance arose over the proper way to deal with an economic depression.
We shall analyze this problem later, but here we should say that the
bankers' formula for treating a depression was by clinging to the gold
standard, by raising interest rates and seeking deflation, and by insisting
on a reduction of public spending, a fiscal surplus, or at least a balanced
budget. These ideas were rejected totally, on a point-by-point basis, by
the unorthodox economists (somewhat mistakenly called "Keynesian").
The bankers' formula sought to encourage economic recovery by "restoring confidence in the value of money," that is, their own confidence
in what was the primary concern of bankers. This formula had worked
in the past only when it had, more or less incidentally, reduced costs
(especially wages) faster than wholesale prices so that businessmen regained confidence, not in the value of money but in the possibility of
profits. The unorthodox theorists sought to achieve this latter more
quickly and more directly by restoring purchasing power, and thus
prices, by increasing, instead of reducing, the money supply and by
placing it in the hands of potential consumers rather in the banks or in the
hands of investors.

This change in the accepted theories after 1934 was a slow growth,
and formed part of the eclipse of financial capitalism; in the long run
it meant that banks would be reduced from the masters of the economy
to become its servant in a situation where the major economic decisions
would not be based on the supply of money but on the supply and organi-

zation of real resources. As a matter of fact the whole relationship of money and resources remained a puzzle to many and was still a subject of debate in the 1950's, but at least a great victory had been won by man in his control of his own destiny when the myths of orthodox financial theory were finally challenged in the 1930's.

The end of financial capitalism may well be dated at the collapse of the gold standard in Britain in September 1931, but, on the personal side, it might be dated at the suicide of its most spectacular individual, the "Match King," Ivar Kreuger, in Paris in April 1932.

Ivar Kreuger (1880–1932), after several years' experience as an engineer in America and South Africa, set up in Stockholm in 1911 the contracting firm of Kreuger & Toll. By 1918 this firm was a financial company with a capital of 12 million kronor, and chiefly interested in the Swedish Match Company, a holding company organized by Kreuger. Within a decade, Kreuger had control of over 150 match companies in 43 countries. The securities of these firms were controlled through a Delaware corporation (called International Match Company). This holding company sold millions of dollars of securities with no voting rights, while control was exercised through a small bloc of voting stock held by Kreuger & Toll. By granting loans to the governments of various countries, Kreuger obtained match monopolies which brought in substantial sums. In all, £330 million was lent to governments in this way, including $75 million to France and $125 million to Germany. In return Kreuger obtained control of 80 percent of the world's match industry, most of Europe's paper and wood-pulp production, fourteen telephone and telegraph companies in six countries, a considerable part of the farm-mortgage systems of Sweden, France, and Germany, eight iron-ore mines, and numerous other enterprises, including a considerable group of banks and newspapers in various countries. The whole system was financed in a sumptuous fashion by selling worthless and fraudulent securities to investors through the most prominent investment bankers of the world. In all, about $750 million in such securities was sold, about one-third in the United States. The respected Lee, Higginson, and Company of Boston sold $150 million of these securities to 600 banks and brokers without making any investigation into their value or honesty and received about $6 million in fees for doing so. The money thus raised by Kreuger was used to advance loans to various countries, to pay interest and dividends on securities issued previously, and to finance the further exploits of Mr. Kreuger. As examples of these exploits, we might mention that Kreuger & Toll paid dividends of 25 percent from 1919 to 1928 and 30 percent after 1929, mostly from capital; Swedish Match Company usually paid 15 per cent dividends. This was done in order to persuade the investing public to **buy** more of Kreuger's securities and thus keep the system going. In order to encourage this public, prospectuses were falsified, letters were forged, and the stock market was manipulated at heavy cost. Bonds were issued against the same security several times over. Most brazen of all, bonds were issued against the receipts of the match monopolies of Italy and Spain. Although Kreuger possessed neither of these, he carried them on his books for $80 million and had bonds forged by himself to substantiate the claim. The long-drawn out depression of 1929–1933 made it impossible to keep the system afloat, although Kreuger avoided no degree of corruption and deceit in his efforts to do so. In March 1932 a note for $11 million from International Telephone and Telegraph fell due, and Kreuger, unable to meet it, killed himself. He left claims against his estate of $700 million, while his personal debts were $179 million with assets of $18 million.

The death of Kreuger is merely a symbol of the end of European financial capitalism. For about fifty years before this event, the centralized control made possible by the financial system had been used to develop monopolistic tendencies in industry. These had been furthered by the growth of large combinations, by the formation of cartels and trade associations between units of enterprise, and by the increase of those less tangible restrictions on competition known as imperfect and monopolistic competition. As a result, competition had been declining, control of the market had been increasing, and self-financing by industrial units had been growing. This last development made it possible for industry once more to free itself from financial control as it had been in the owner-management period which preceded financial capitalism. But, unlike this earlier stage, control did not revert from financiers back to the owners of enterprise but instead tended to shift into the hands of a new class of bureaucratic managers whose powers of control were out of all relationship to the extent of their ownership of the enterprises concerned. In France, the bankers, although in retreat when war came in 1939, had been so strengthened by the unorthodox financial policies of the 1920's that they were able to prevent any important victory for monopoly capitalism in the 1930's, with the result that the shift from financial to monoply capitalism did not appear in France until the 1940's. In the United States, also, the transition was not complete when war came in 1939, with the result that the United States, like France, but unlike any other important country, had not shaken off the world depression even as late as 1940.

Reflation and Inflation
1933-1947

The period of reflation began in some countries (like Great Britain and the United States) long before the period of deflation had ended elsewhere (as in France). In most countries the recovery was associated with rising wholesale prices, with abandonment of the gold standard or at least devaluation, and with easy credit. It resulted everywhere in increased demand, rising production, and decreasing unemployment. By the middle of 1932, recovery was discernible among the members of the sterling bloc; by the middle of 1933 it was general except for the members of the gold bloc. This recovery was halting and uncertain. Insofar as it was caused by government actions, these actions were aimed at treatment of the symptoms rather than the causes of the depression, and these actions, by running contrary to orthodox economic ideas, served to slow up recovery by reducing confidence. Insofar as the recovery was caused by the normal working out of the business cycle, the recovery was slowed up by the continuation of emergency measures—such as controls over commerce and finance and by the fact that the economic disequilibriums which the depression had made were frequently intensified by the first feeble movements toward recovery. Finally, the recovery was slowed up by the drastic increase in political insecurity as a result of the aggressions of Japan, of Italy, and of Germany.

Except for Germany and Russia (both of which had isolated their economies from world fluctuations) the recovery continued for no more than three or four years. In most countries the latter half of 1937 and the early part of 1938 experienced a sharp "recession." In no important country had prices reached the 1929 level at the beginning of the recession (although within 10 percent of it), nor had the percentage of persons unemployed fallen to the 1929 level. In many countries (but not the United States or the gold bloc), industrial production had reached 1929 levels.

The recession was marked by a break in wholesale prices, a decline in business activity, and an increase in unemployment. In most countries it began in the spring of 1937 and lasted for about ten months or a year. It was caused by several factors: (1) much of the price rise before 1937 had been caused by speculative buying and by the efforts of "panic money" to seek refuge in commodities, rather than by demand from either consumers or investors; (2) several international commodity cartels created in the period of depression and early recovery broke down with a resulting fall in prices; (3) there was a curtailment of public deficit spending in several countries, especially the United States and France; (4) the replacement of capital goods worn out in the period 1929–1934 had caused much of the revival of 1933–1937 and began to taper off in 1937; (5) the increase in political tension in the Mediterranean and the Far East as a result of the Civil War in Spain and the Japanese attack on North China had an adverse effect; and (6) a "gold scare" occurred. This last was a sudden fall in the demand for gold caused by the fact that the great increase in gold production resulting from the United States Treasury price of $35 an ounce gave rise to rumors that the Treasury would soon cut this price.

As a result of the recession of 1937, the governmental policies of 1933–1935, which had given the first recovery, were intensified and gave rise to a second recovery. Bank rates were lowered—in some cases to 1 percent; deficit spending was resumed or increased; all efforts to get back on a gold standard were postponed indefinitely; in the United States, the sterilization of gold was ended, and all thoughts of reducing the buying price of gold were abandoned. The chief new factor after the recession was one which was of minor but rapidly growing importance. The deficit spending which had been used to pay for public works projects before 1937 was increasingly devoted to rearmament after that date. Britain, for example, spent £186 million on arms in the fiscal year 1936–1937 and £262 million in the year 1937–1938. It is not possible to say to what extent this increase in armaments was caused by the need for deficit spending and to what extent it was the result of the rising political tensions. Similarly, it is not possible to say which is cause and which effect as between political tensions and rearmament. Indeed, the relationships between all three of these factors are mutual reactions of cause and effect. At any rate, after the recession of 1937, armaments, political tensions, and prosperity increased together. For most countries, the political tensions led to the use of arms in open conflict long before full prosperity had been achieved. In most countries, industrial production exceeded the 1929 level by the end of 1937, but because of the increase in population, efficiency, and capital this was achieved without full utilization of resources. In the United States (with Canada as an appendage) and in France (with Belgium as an appendage) production continued low throughout the 1930's, reaching the 1929 level in the first pair only in the late summer of 1939 and never reaching the 1929 level in the second pair. As a result of the failure of most countries (excepting Germany and the Soviet Union) to achieve full utilization of resources, it was possible to devote increasing percentages of these resources to armaments without suffering any decline in the standards of living. In fact, to the surprise of many, the exact opposite resulted—as armaments grew, the standard of living improved because of the fact that the chief obstacle in the way of an improving standard of living—that is, lack of consumers' purchasing power, was remedied by the fact that armament manufacture supplied such purchasing power in the market without turning into the market any equivalent in goods which would use up purchasing power.

The recovery from depression after 1933 did not result in any marked reduction in the restrictions and controls which the depression had brought to commercial and financial activity. Since these controls had been established because of the depression, it might have been expected that such controls would have been relaxed as the depression lifted. Instead, they were maintained and, in some cases, extended. The reasons for this were various. In the first place, as the political crisis became more intense the value of these controls for defense and war was realized. In the second place, powerful bureaucratic vested interests had grown up for enforcing these controls. In the third place, these restrictions, which had been established chiefly for controlling foreign trade, proved very effective in controlling domestic economic activity. In the fourth place, under the protection of these controls the difference in price levels between some countries had grown so great that the ending of controls would have torn their economic structures to pieces. In the fifth place, the demand for protection from foreign competition remained so great that these controls could not be removed. In the sixth place, the debtor-creditor relationships between countries still remained valid and unbalanced and would have required new controls as soon as the old ones were lifted to prevent unbalanced payments and deflationary pressure. In the seventh place, the existence of "imprisoned capital" within national economic systems made it impossible to raise the controls, since the flight of such capital would have been disruptive of the economic system. The chief example of such imprisoned capital was the property of the Jews in Germany, amounting to over 10 billion marks.

For these and other reasons tariffs, quotas, subsidies, exchange controls, and government manipulations of the market continued. The moment at which these controls could have been withdrawn most easily was at the beginning of 1937, because by that time recovery was well developed and the international disequilibriums were less acute because of the disruption of the gold bloc late in 1936. The moment passed without much being accomplished, and, by the end of 1937, the recession and the mounting political crisis made all hopes of relaxing controls utopian.

Such hopes, however, were found both before and after 1937. These included the Oslo Agreements of 1930 and 1937, the Ouchy Convention of 1932, the Hull Reciprocal Trade Program of 1934 and after, the Van Zeeland Mission of 1937, and the constant work of the League of Nations. Of these, only the Hull Program accomplished anything concrete, and the importance of its accomplishment is a subject of dispute.

The Hull Reciprocal Trade Program is of more importance from the political than from the economic point of view. It openly aimed at freer and multilateral trade. The act, as passed in 1934 and renewed at regular intervals since, empowered the executive branch to negotiate with other countries trade agreements in which the United States could reduce tariffs by any amount up to 50 percent. In return for lowering our tariffs in this way, we hoped to obtain trade concessions from the other party to the agreement. Although these agreements were bilateral in form, they were multilateral in effect, because each agreement contained an unconditional most-favored-nation clause by which each party bound itself to extend to the other party concessions at least as great as those it extended to the most favored nation with which it traded. As a result of such clauses any concessions made by either tended to be generalized to other countries. The interest of the United States in removing the restrictions on world trade was to be found in the fact that she had productive capacity beyond that necessary to satisfy articulate domestic demand in almost every field of economic activity. As a result she had to export or find her hands full of surplus goods. The interest of the United States in multilateral trade rather than in bilateral trade was to be found in the fact that her surpluses existed in all types of goods—foodstuffs, raw materials, and industrial products—and the markets for these would have to be sought in all kinds of foreign economies, not in any single type. The United States had excess supplies of food like wheat, pork, and corn; of raw materials like petroleum, cotton, and iron; of specialized industrial products like radios, automobiles, and locomotives. It was not possible to sell all these types to a food-producing country like Denmark, or to a raw-material-producing country like Canada or the Malay States, or to an industrial country like Germany or Britain. Accordingly, the United States became the world's chief defender of freer and multilateral trade. Her chief argument was based on the fact that such trade would contribute to a higher standard of living for all parties. To the United States, whose political security was so sound that it rarely required a moment's thought, a higher standard of living was the chief aim of existence. Accordingly, it was difficult for the United States to comprehend the point of view of a state which, lacking political security, placed a high standard of living in a position second to such security.

In sharp contrast to the United States in its attitude toward the problem of international trade was Nazi Germany. This and other countries were seeking "independence" (that is, political goals in the economic sphere), and they rejected "dependence" even if it did include a higher standard of living. They frequently rejected the argument that autarky was necessarily injurious to the standard of living or to international trade, because by "autarky" they did not mean self-sufficiency in all things, but self-sufficiency in necessities. Once this had been achieved, they stated their willingness to expand the world's trade in nonessentials to an extent as great as any standard of living might require.

The basic key to the new emphasis on autarky is to be found in the fact that the advocates of such economic behavior had a new conception of the meaning of sovereignty. To them sovereignty had not only all the legal and political connotations it had always held, but in addition had to include economic independence. Since such economic independence could, according to the theory, be obtained only by the Great Powers, the lesser states were to be deprived of sovereignty in its fullest sense and be reduced to a kind of vassal or client condition in respect to the Great Powers. The theory was that each Great Power, in order to enjoy full sovereignty, must adopt a policy of autarky. Since no power, however great, could be self-sufficient within its own national boundaries, it must extend this sphere of autarky to include its weaker neighbors, and this sphere would have political as well as economic implications, since it was unthinkable that any Great Power should permit its lesser neighbors to endanger it by suddenly cutting off its supplies or markets. The theory thus led to the conception of "continental blocs" consisting of aggregates of lesser states about the few Great Powers. This theory was entirely in accord with the political development of the late nineteenth and early twentieth century. This development had seen an increasing disparity in the powers of states with a decreasing number of Great Powers. This decline in the number of Great Powers occurred because of the advance of technology, which had progressed to a point where only a few states could follow. The theory of continental blocs was also in accord with the growth of communications, transportation, weapons, and administrative techniques. These made it almost inevitable that the world would be integrated into increasingly large political units. The inevitability of this development can be seen from the fact that the wars of 1914–1945, waged for the preservation of the small states (like Poland, Czechoslovakia, Holland, and Belgium), succeeded in reducing the number of Great Powers from seven to two.

This integration of states into continental or other large blocs was, as we have seen, a quite legitimate and attainable ambition, but it was sought by the aggressor states (like Germany, Japan, and Italy) by quite illegitimate methods. A better method for attaining such integration would have been based on consent and mutual penetration. But this federalist method of integration could have succeeded only if it were honestly offered as an alternative to the authoritarian solution of the aggressor states. This was not done. Instead, the "liberal" states refused to recognize the inevitability of integration and, while resisting the authoritarian solution, sought as well to resist the whole process of integration. They sought to preserve the atomistic world structure of sovereign states which was so out of keeping with technological developments both in politics (new weapons, speedy transportation, and quicker communications) and in economics (mass production and increasing need for exotic materials such as tin, rubber, or uranium found in small and scattered amounts). As a result the liberal Powers resisted the German efforts to cope with the real world developments without putting any realistic or progressive substitute program in its place.

The policy of negativism on the part of the liberal Powers was made worse by the fact that these Powers had put Germany and others into a position (as debtors) where they were driven in the direction of greater integration of the world on a voluntary basis. This appeared in the fact that these Powers had to adopt freer and increased trade in order to pay their debts. Having put the majority of the countries of the world into this position of needing increased integration in order to pay their debts, the liberal countries made it impossible to obtain such integration on a federalist basis by adopting policies of isolationist, economic nationalism for themselves (by high tariffs, ending of long-term loans, and so on). This dog-in-the-manger policy in economic matters was quite similar to their policy in political matters where, after setting up an organization to achieve peace, they declined to permit Germany to be a part of it and, later, when Germany became a part they refused to use the organization for peaceful goals but instead tried to use it to enforce the Treaty of Versailles or to build up a power balance against the Soviet Union.

This failure of the liberal states in the 1920's becomes more obvious when we examine the great increase in restrictive economic and financial policies in the 1930's. It is usually said that the excesses in these were caused by the great increase in nationalism resulting from the depression. This is not true, and the increase in such restrictions cannot be quoted as a proof of increasing nationalism. No country entered upon these policies for nationalistic reasons—that is, for the closer integration of its own people, or to distinguish them more sharply from other people, or for the aggrandizement of its own people over another. The increase in economic nationalism was based on a much more practical cause than that —on the fact that the nation was the only social unit capable of action in the emergency resulting from the depression. And men were demanding action. For this the only available agency was the national state. If a broader agency had been available, it would have been used. Since it was not, the state had to be used—used, not with the purpose of injuring one's neighbors, but solely with the purpose of benefiting oneself. The fact that neighbors were injured was a more or less accidental result, regrettable, but inevitable so long as the largest unit of political organization (that is, the largest unit capable of complete action) was the nation-state. When a theater catches fire, and persons are trampled in the resulting panic, this is not because anyone desired this, but merely because each individual sought to escape from the building as soon as possible. The result is disaster because the individual is the only unit available capable of action. And the individual is too small a unit of action to spare many individuals from tragedy. If a larger unit of organization exists (as, for example, if the persons in the theater are a company of infantry with its officers), or if some cool-headed person can organize the group into a unit of action larger than the individual, all might escape safely. But the chances of forming an organization after the panic has begun are almost nil. In 1929–1934, the panic started before any unit of action larger than the nation-state existed. As a result, all suffered, and the puny efforts to form an organization after the panic began were vain. This is the real tragedy of the 1920's. Because of the conservatism, timidity, and hypocrisy of those who were trying to build an international organization in the period 1919–1929, this organization was so inadequate by 1929 when the emergency began that the organization which had been set up was destroyed rather than strengthened. If the instruments of international cooperation had been further advanced in 1929, the demand for action would have made use of these instruments, and a new era of political progress would have commenced. Instead, the inadequacy of these instruments forced men to fall back on the broadest instrument which was available—the nation-state; and there began a retrogressive movement capable of destroying all Western Civilization.

The economic nationalism which arose from the need to act in a crisis—and to act unilaterally because of the lack of any organ able to act multilaterally (that is, internationally) was intensified after the breakdown in finance and economics of 1931–1933 by several developments. In the first place, it was increased by the discovery, by Germany in 1932, by Italy in 1934, by Japan in 1936, and by the United States in 1938, that deflation could be prevented by rearming. In the second place, it was increased by the realization that political activity was more powerful and more fundamental than economic activity—a realization which became clear when it was found that every step toward a unilateral economic solution resulted in reprisals from other nations which canceled out that step and made necessary another step, which, in its turn, called forth new reprisals; this soon showed that except in a nation capable of self-sufficiency such actions in the economic sphere could accomplish little and that unilateral action, if taken at all, must be accompanied by political steps (which would permit no reprisals). In the third place, economic nationalism was increased, and internationalism reduced, by the great increase in political insecurity, since the preservation of an international economic organization involved entrusting one's economic fate, to some degree, to the hands of another. Rather than this, economic nationalism was increased in the name of autarky, security, economic mobilization, and so on. Self-sufficiency, even if it involved a lower standard of living, was held preferable to international division of labor, on the grounds that political security was more important than a high—and insecure—standard of living.

As a consequence of these three causes, international trade began to suffer a new injury. The old nineteenth century transfer of goods between industrial and colonial areas (producers of food and raw materials) had begun to decline by a purely natural evolution as the result of the industrialization of colonial areas. But now, as a result of the increase in economic nationalism, another kind of transfer was disrupted. This was the transfer among industrial nations resulting from an international division of labor and an uneven distribution of raw materials. An example of this can be seen in the iron and steel industry of western Europe. There British and German coal, French and Belgian low-grade iron ores, Swedish high-grade iron ores were mingled and combined to permit production of high-grade surgical steels in Sweden, of low-grade building steels in Belgium, of heavy machine products in Germany, and of light steel products in France. This transfer of goods began to be disrupted in the onslaught of economic nationalism after 1929. As a result, history turned backward, and the older interchange of colonial for industrial products increased in relative importance.

Economic nationalism also increased the trend toward bilateralism. This received its chief and earliest impetus from Germany, but it was soon followed by other countries until, by 1939, the United States was the only important supporter of multilateral trade. Most countries justified their acceptance of bilateralism on the grounds that they were compelled to accept it because of economic pressure from Germany. In many cases, this was not true. Some states, like Austria or Romania, were compelled to accept bilateralism because that was the only way they could trade with Germany. But other, more important, states, including Britain, did not have this excuse for their actions, although they used it as an excuse. The real reasons for Britain's adoption of bilateralism and protection are to be found in the structure of the British domestic economy, especially the growing rigidity of that economy through the great and rapid increase in monopolies and cartels.

The new trade policy of Britain after 1931 was the complete antithesis of that pursued by the United States, although the more extreme and spectacular methods of Germany concealed this fact from many persons until 1945. The United States sought multilateralism and expansion of world trade. Britain sought debt collection and increase of exports through bilateralism. Without equality of treatment, its trade agreements sought to reduce debts first and to increase exports second, if this second was compatible with the reduction of debts. In some cases, in order to reduce outstanding debts, it made agreements to curtail exports from Britain or to reduce quotas on such goods (Anglo-Italian agreements of April 1936, of November 1936, and of March 1938, as amended March 1939). It established payment agreements and clearings with debtor countries. Current trade was subordinated to liquidation of past debts. This was the direct opposite of the American theory which tended to neglect past debts in order to build up present trade in the hope that eventually past debts could be liquidated because of the increased volume of trade. The British preferred a smaller volume of trade with rapid payments to a larger volume with delayed payments.

These tactics did not work very well. Even with clearings and restricted exports Britain had great difficulty in bringing into existence an unfavorable balance of trade with debtor countries. Its balances generally remained favorable, with exports higher than imports. As a result, payments continued to lag behind (two and a half years in respect to Turkey), and it was necessary to rewrite the commercial agreements embodying the new bilateralism (in the case of Italy, four agreements in three years). In some cases (like Turkey in May 1938), special joint trading organizations were set up to sell products of the clearing country in free-exchange markets so that debts owed to Britain from the clearing country could be paid. This, however, meant that the free-exchange countries had to obtain Turkish products from Britain and could sell none of their own products in Turkey because of lack of exchange.

Because of the failure of Britain's bilateral agreements to achieve what she had hoped, she was driven to replace these agreements by others, always moving in the direction of more control. Clearing agreements which were originally voluntary were later made compulsory; those which were earlier one-ended became later double-ended. Britain made barter agreements with various countries, including one direct swap of rubber for wheat with the United States. In 1939 the Federation of British Industries went so far as to seek an agreement with Germany dividing markets and fixing prices for most economic activities.

As a result of all this, the international commodity markets in which anything could be bought or sold (if the price was right) were disrupted. The center of these (chiefly in Britain) began to disappear, exactly as the international capital market (also centering in Britain) was doing. Both markets were broken up into partial and segregated markets. In fact, one of the chief developments of the period was *the disappear-*

ance of The Market. It is an interesting fact that the history of modern Europe is exactly parallel in time with the existence of the market (from the twelfth century to the twentieth century).

THE PERIOD OF INFLATION, 1938–1945

The period of reflation, which began in most countries in the first half of 1933, merged into the following period of inflation without any sharp line of demarcation between the two. The increase in prices, prosperity, employment, and business activity after 1933 was generally caused by increases in public spending. As the political crisis became worse with the attacks on Ethiopia, on Spain, on China, on Austria, and on Czechoslovakia, this public spending increasingly took the form of spending on armaments. For several years it was possible in most countries to increase the output of armaments without reducing the output of consumers' goods or of capital goods merely by putting to work the resources, men, factories, and capital which had been standing idle in the depression. Only when there were no longer any idle resources and increased armaments had to be obtained by diverting resources to this purpose from the production of consumers' or capital goods did the period of inflation begin. At that point, a competition began between the producers of armaments and the producers of wealth for the limited supply of resources. This competition took the form of price competition, with each side offering higher wages for manpower, higher prices for raw materials. The result was inflation. The money which the community obtained for the production of wealth as well as for the production of arms was available to buy the former only (since arms are not usually offered for sale to the public). This intensified the inflation greatly. In most countries, the transition from reflation to inflation did not occur until after they had entered the war. Germany was the chief exception and possibly also Italy and Russia, since all of these were making fairly full utilization of their resources by 1938. In Britain, such full utilization was not obtained until 1940 or 1941, and in the United States not until 1942 or even 1943. In France and the other countries on the Continent overrun by Germany in 1940 and 1941, such full utilization of resources was not achieved before they were defeated.

The period of inflation 1938–1947 was very similar to the period of inflation 1914–1920. The destruction of property and goods was much greater; the mobilization of resources for such destruction was also greater. As a result, the supply of real wealth, both producers' and consumers', was curtailed much more completely. On the other hand, because of increased knowledge and experience, the output of money and its management was much more skillfully handled. The two factors together gave a degree of inflation which was somewhat less intense in the

Second World War than in the First. Price controls and rationing were better applied and more strictly enforced. Surpluses of money were taken up by new techniques of compulsory or voluntary savings. The financing of the war was more skillful so that a much larger increase in production was obtained from a similar degree of inflation.

Much of the improvement in financing World War II in comparison with World War I arose from the fact that attention was concentrated on real resources rather than on money. This was reflected both in the way in which each country managed its domestic economy and in the relationships between countries. The latter can be seen in the use of Lend-Lease rather than commercial exchange as in World War I to provide America's allies with combat supplies. The use of commercial exchange and orthodox financing in the First World War had left a terrible burden of intergovernmental debts and ill-feeling in the postwar period. In World War II the United States provided Great Britain under Lend-Lease with $27,000 million in supplies, received $6,000 million in return, and wrote off the account with a payment of about $800 million in the postwar settlement.

In domestic economies even more revolutionary techniques were developed under the general category of centralized planning. This went much further in Great Britain than in the United States or Germany, and was chiefly remarkable for the fact that it applied to real resources and not to money flows. The chief of these controls were over manpower and materials. Both of these were allotted where they seemed to be needed, and were not permitted, as in World War I, to be drawn here and there in response to rising wages or prices. Rises in prices were controlled by sopping up excess purchasing power by compulsory or semicompulsory saving and by rationing of specific necessities. Above all, price rises in such necessities were prevented by subsidies to producers, which gave them more payment for production without any increase in the final selling price. As a result, in Britain the cost of living rose from 100 in 1939 to 126 in 1941, but rose no more than to 129 by the war's end in 1945. In the United States wholesale prices of all commodities rose only 26 percent from 1940 to 1945, but were twice as high as in 1940 in 1947. Most of this increase in the United States came after the war's end, and may be attributed to the refusal of the Republican-controlled Congress, led by Senator Taft, to profit from the errors of 1918–1920. As a result, most of the mistakes of that earlier period, such as the ending of price controls and rationing and the delays in reconversion to peacetime production, were repeated, but only after the war itself had been won.

Outside the United States, many of the wartime control mechanisms were continued into the postwar period, and contributed substantially to the creation of a new kind of economic system which we might call the "pluralist economy" because it operates from the shifting alignments of a number of organized interest blocs, such as labor, farmers, heavy industry, consumers, financial groups, and, above all, government. This will be analyzed later. At this point we need only say that the postwar economy was entirely different in character from that of the 1920's following World War I. This was most notable in the absence of a postwar depression, which was widely expected, but which did not arrive because there was no effort to stabilize on a gold standard. The major difference was the eclipse of the bankers, who have been largely reduced in status from the masters to the servants of the economic system. This has been brought about by the new concern with real economic factors instead of with financial counters, as previously. As part of this process, there has been a great reduction in the economic role of gold. From this has flowed two persistent postwar problems which would have been avoided by the gold standard. There are (1) slow worldwide inflation arising from the competing demands for economic resources by consumers, by investors, and by defense and government needs; and (2) the constant recurrence of acute exchange difficulties, such as the "dollar shortage" in world trade, arising from the inability of gold shipments or foreign demand to influence domestic prices sufficiently to reverse these foreign movements. But these inconveniences, associated with the absence of a gold standard and the inadequacies of the financial arrangements in substitute for it, were generally regarded as a small price to pay for the full employment and rising standards of living which advanced industrial countries were able to obtain under planning in the postwar era.

VIII

INTERNATIONAL
SOCIALISM
AND THE
SOVIET CHALLENGE

The International Socialist Movement

The Bolshevik Revolution to 1924

Stalinism, 1924–1939

The
International Socialist Movement

THE international Socialist movement was both a product of the nineteenth century and a revulsion against it. It was rooted in some of the characteristics of the century, such as its industrialism, its optimism, its belief in progress, its humanitarianism, its scientific materialism, and its democracy, but it was in revolt against its laissez faire, its middle-class domination, its nationalism, its urban slums, and its emphasis on the price-profit system as the dominant factor in all human values. This does not mean that all Socialists had the same beliefs or that these beliefs did not change with the passing years. On the contrary, there were almost as many different kinds of Socialism as there were Socialists, and the beliefs categorized under this term changed from year to year and from country to country.

Industrialism, especially in its early years, brought with it social and economic conditions which were admittedly horrible. Human beings were brought together around factories to form great new cities which were sordid and unsanitary. In many cases, these persons were reduced to conditions of animality which shock the imagination. Crowded together in want and disease, with no leisure and no security, completely dependent on a weekly wage which was less than a pittance, they worked twelve to fifteen hours a day for six days in the week among dusty and dangerous machines with no protection against inevitable accidents, disease, or old age, and returned at night to crowded rooms without adequate food and lacking light, fresh air, heat, pure water, or sanitation.

These conditions have been described for us in the writings of novelists such as Dickens in England, Hugo or Zola in France, in the reports of parliamentary committees such as the Sadler Committee of 1832 or Lord Ashley's Committee in 1842, and in numerous private studies like *In*

375

Darkest England by General William Booth of the Salvation Army. Just at the end of the century, private scientific studies of these conditions began to appear in England, led by Charles Booth's *Life and Labour of the People in London* or B. Seebohm Rowntree's *Poverty, a Study of Town Life.*

The Socialist movement was a reaction against these deplorable conditions of the working masses. It has been customary to divide this movement into two parts at the year 1848, the earlier part being called "the period of the Utopian Socialists" while the later part has been called "the period of scientific Socialism." The dividing line between the two parts is marked by the publication in 1848 of *The Communist Manifesto* of Karl Marx and Friedrich Engels. This work, which began with the ominous sentence, "A spectre is haunting Europe—the spectre of Communism," and ended with the trumpet blast, "Workers of the world, unite!" is generally regarded as the seed from which developed, in the twentieth century, Russian Bolshevism and Stalinism. Such a view is undoubtedly an oversimplification, for the development of Socialist ideology is full of twists and turns and might well have grown along quite different paths if the history of the movement itself had been different.

The history of the Socialist movement may be divided into three periods associated with the three Socialist Internationals. The First International lasted from 1864 to 1876 and was as much anarchistic as Socialistic. It was finally disrupted by the controversies of these two groups. The Second International was the Socialist International, founded in 1889. This became increasingly conservative and was disrupted by the Communists during World War I. The Third, or Communist, International was organized in 1919 by dissident elements from the Second International. As a result of the controversies of these three movements, the whole anticapitalist ideology, which began as a confused revolt against the economic and social conditions of industrialism in 1848, became sorted out into four chief schools. These schools became increasingly doctrinaire and increasingly bitter in their relationships.

The basic division within the Socialist movement after 1848 was between those who wished to abolish or reduce the functions of the state and those who wished to increase these functions by giving economic activities to the state. The former division came in time to include the anarchists and the syndicalists, while the latter division came to include the Socialists and the Communists. In general the former division believed that man was innately good and that all coercive power was bad, with public authority the worst form of such coercive power. All of the world's evil, according to the anarchists, arose because man's innate goodness was corrupted and distorted by coercive power. The remedy, they felt, was to destroy the state. This would lead to the disappearance of all other forms of coercive power and to the liberation of the innate goodness of man. The simplest way to destroy the state, they felt, would be to assassinate the chief of the state; this would act as a spark to ignite a wholesale uprising of oppressed humanity against all forms of coercive power. These views led to numerous assassinations of various political leaders, including a king of Italy and a president of the United States, in the period 1895–1905.

Syndicalism was a somewhat more realistic and later version of anarchism. It was equally determined to abolish all public authority, but did not rely on the innate goodness of individuals for the continuance of social life. Rather it aimed to replace public authority by voluntary associations of individuals to supply the companionship and management of social life which, according to these thinkers, the state had so signally failed to provide. The chief of such voluntary associations replacing the state would be labor unions. According to the syndicalists, the state was to be destroyed, not by the assassination of individual heads of states, but by a general strike of the workers organized in labor unions. Such a strike would give the workers a powerful *esprit de corps* based on a sense of their power and solidarity. By making all forms of coercion impossible, the general strike would destroy the state and replace it by a flexible federation of free associations of workers (syndicates).

Anarchism's most vigorous proponent was the Russian exile Michael Bakunin (1814–1876). His doctrines had considerable appeal in Russia itself, but in western Europe they were widely accepted only in Spain, especially Barcelona, and in parts of Italy where economic and psychological conditions were somewhat similar to those in Russia. Syndicalism flourished in the same areas at a later date, although its chief theorists were French, led by Georges Sorel (1847–1922).

The second group of radical social theorists was fundamentally opposed to the anarcho-syndicalists, although this fact was recognized only gradually. This second group wished to widen the power and scope of governments by giving them a dominant role in economic life. In the course of time, the confusions within this second group began to sort themselves out, and the group divided into two chief schools: the Socialists and the Communists. These two schools were further apart in organization and in their activities than they were in their theories, because the Socialists became increasingly moderate and even conservative in their activities, while remaining relatively revolutionary in their theories. However, as their theories gradually followed their activities in the direction of moderation, in the period of the Second International (1889–1919), violent controversies arose between those who pretended to remain loyal to the revolutionary ideas of Karl Marx and those who wished to revise these ideas in a more moderate direction to adapt them to what they considered to be changing social and economic conditions. The strict interpreters of Karl Marx came to be known as Communists, while the more moderate revisionist group came to be known as Socialists. The rivalries of the two groups ultimately disrupted the Second International as well as the labor movement as a whole, so that antilabor regimes were able to come to power in much of Europe in the period 1918–1939. This disruption and failure of the working-class movement is one of the chief factors in European history in the twentieth century and, accordingly, requires at least a brief survey of its nature and background.

The ideas of Karl Marx (1818–1883) and of his associate Friedrich Engels (1820–1895) were published in the *Communist Manifesto* of 1848 and in their three-volume opus, *Das Kapital* (1867–1894). Although they were aroused by the deplorable conditions of the European working classes under industrialism, the chief sources of the ideas themselves were to be found in the idealism of Hegel, the materialism of the ancient Greek atomists (especially Democritus), and the theories of the English classical economists (especially Ricardo). Marx derived from Hegel what has come to be known as the "historical dialectic." This theory maintained that all historical events were the result of a struggle between opposing forces which ultimately merged to create a situation which was different from either. Any existing organization of society or of ideas (*thesis*) calls forth, in time, an opposition (*antithesis*). These two struggle with each other and give rise to the events of history, until finally the two fuse into a new organization (*synthesis*). This synthesis in turn becomes established as a new thesis to a new opposition or antithesis, and the struggle continues, as history continues.

A chief element in Marxist theory was the economic interpretation of history. According to this view, the economic organization of any society was the basic aspect of that society, since all other aspects, such as political, social, intellectual, or religious, reflected the organization and powers of the economic level.

From Ricardo, Marx derived the theory that the value of economic goods was based on the amount of labor put into them. Applying this idea to industrial society where labor obtains wages which reflect only part of the value of the product they are making, Marx decided that labor was being exploited. Such exploitation was possible, he believed, because the working classes did not own the "instruments of production" (that is, factories, land, and tools) but had allowed these, by legal chicanery, to fall into the hands of the possessing classes. In this way, the capitalistic system of production had divided society into two antithetical classes: the bourgeoisie who owned the instruments of production and the proletariat who lived from selling their labor. The proletariat, however, were robbed of part of their product by the fact that their wages represented only a portion of the value of their labor, the "surplus value" of which they were deprived going to the bourgeoisie as profits. The bourgeoisie were able to maintain this exploitative system because the economic, social, intellectual, and religious portions of society reflected the exploitative nature of the economic system. The money which the bourgeoisie took from the proletariat in the economic system made it possible for them to dominate the political system (including the police and the army), the social system (including family life and education), as well as the religious system and the intellectual aspects of society (including the arts, literature, philosophy, and all the avenues of publicity for these).

From these three concepts of the historical dialectic, economic determinism, and the labor theory of value, Marx built up a complicated theory of past and future history. He believed that "all history is the history of class struggles." Just as in antiquity, history was concerned with the struggles of free men and slaves or of plebians and patricians, so, in the Middle Ages, it was concerned with the struggles of serfs and lords, and, in modern times, with the struggles of proletariat and bourgeoisie. Each privileged group arises from opposition to an earlier privileged group, plays its necessary role in historical progress, and is, in time, successfully challenged by those it has been exploiting. Thus the bourgeoisie rose from exploited serfs to challenge successfully the older privileged group of feudal lords and moved into a period of bourgeois supremacy in which it contributed to history a fully capitalized industrial society but will be challenged, in its turn, by the rising power of the laboring masses.

To Marx, the revolution of the proletariat was not only inevitable but would inevitably be successful, and would give rise to an entirely new society with a proletariat system of government, social life, intellectual patterns, and religious organization. The "inevitable revolution" must lead to an "inevitable victory of the proletariat" because the privileged position of the bourgeoisie allowed them to practice a merciless exploitation of the proletariat, pressing these laboring masses downward to a level of bare subsistence, because labor, having become nothing but a commodity for sale for wages in the competitive market, would naturally fall to the level which would just allow the necessary supply of labor to survive. From such exploitation, the bourgeoisie would become richer and richer and fewer and fewer in numbers, and acquire ownership of all property in the society while the proletariat would become poorer and poorer and more and more numerous and be driven closer and closer to desperation. Eventually, the bourgeoisie would become so few and the proletariat would become so numerous that the latter could rise up in their wrath and take over the instruments of production and thus control of the whole society.

According to this theory, the "inevitable revolution" would occur in the most advanced industrial country because only after a long period of industrialism would the revolutionary situation become acute and would the society itself be equipped with factories able to support a Socialist system. Once the revolution has taken place, there will be established a "dictatorship of the proletariat" during which the political, social, military, intellectual, and religious aspects of society will be transformed in a Socialist fashion. At the end of this period, full Socialism will be established, the state will disappear, and a "classless society" will come into existence. At this point history will end. This rather surprising conclusion to the historical process would occur because Marx had defined history as the process of class struggle and had defined the state as the instrument of class exploitation. Since, in the Socialist state, there will be no exploitation and thus no classes, there will be no class struggles and no need for a state.

In 1889, after the First International had been disrupted by the controversies between anarchists and Socialists, a Second International had been formed by the Socialists. This group retained its allegiance to Marxist theory for a considerable period, but even from the beginning Socialist actions did not follow Marxist theory. This divergence arose from the fact that Marxist theory did not provide a realistic or workable picture of social and economic developments. It had no real provision for labor unions, for workers' political parties, for bourgeois reformers, for rising standards of living, or for nationalism, yet these became, after Marx's death, the dominant concerns of the working class. Accordingly, the labor unions and the Social-Democratic political parties which they dominated became reformist rather than revolutionary groups. They were supported by upper-class groups with humanitarian or religious motivations, with the result that the conditions of life and of work among the laboring classes were raised to a higher level, at first slowly and reluctantly, but, in time, with increasing rapidity. So long as industry itself remained competitive, the struggle between industrialists and labor remained intense, because any success which the workers in one factory might achieve in improving their wage levels or their working conditions would raise the costs of their employer and injure his competitive position with respect to other employers. But as industrialists combined together after 1890 to reduce competition among themselves by regulating their prices and production, and as labor unions combined together into associations covering many factories and even whole industries, the struggle between capital and labor became less intense because any concessions made to labor would affect all capitalists in the same activity equally and could be covered simply by raising the price of the product of all factories to the final consumers.

In fact, the picture which Marx had drawn of more and more numerous workers reduced to lower and lower standards of living by fewer and fewer exploitative capitalists proved to be completely erroneous in the more advanced industrial countries in the twentieth century. Instead, what occurred could be pictured as a cooperative effort by unionized workers and monopolized industry to exploit unorganized consumers by raising prices higher and higher to provide both higher wages and higher profits. This whole process was advanced by the actions of governments which imposed such reforms as eight-hour days, minimum-wage laws, or compulsory accident, old age, and retirement insurance on whole industries at once. As a consequence, the workers did not become worse off but became much better off with the advance of industrialism in the twentieth century.

This tendency toward rising standards of living also revealed another Marxist error. Marx had missed the real essence of the Industrial Revolution. He tended to find this in the complete separation of labor from ownership of tools and the reduction of labor to nothing but a commodity in the market. The real essence of industrialism was to be found in the application of nonhuman energy, such as that from coal, oil, or waterpower, to production. This process increased man's ability to make goods, and did so to an amazing degree. But mass production could exist only if it were followed by mass consumption and rising standards of living. Moreover, it must lead, in the long run, to a decreasing demand for hand labor and an increasing demand for highly trained technicians who are managers rather than laborers. And, in the longer run, this process would give rise to a productive system of such a high level of technical complexity that it could no longer be run by the owners but would have to be run by technically trained managers. Moreover, the use of the corporate form of industrial organization as a means for bringing the savings of the many into the control of a few by sales of securities to wider and wider groups of investors (including both managerial and laboring groups) would lead to a separation of management from ownership and to a great increase in the number of owners.

All these developments were quite contrary to the expectations of Karl Marx. Where he had expected impoverishment of the masses and concentration of ownership, with a great increase in the number of workers and a great decrease in the number of owners, with a gradual elimination of the middle class, there occurred instead (in highly industrialized countries) rising standards of living, dispersal of ownership, a relative decrease in the numbers of laborers, and a great increase in the middle classes. In the long run, under the impact of graduated income taxes and inheritance taxes, the rich became poorer and poorer, relatively speaking, and the great problem of advanced industrial societies became, not the exploitation of laborers by capitalists, but the exploitation of unorganized consumers (of the professional and lower-middle-class levels) by unionized labor and monopolized managers acting in concert. The influence of these last two groups on the state in an advanced industrial country also served to increase their ability to obtain what they wished from society as a whole.

As a consequence of all these influences, the revolutionary spirit did not continue to advance with the advance of industrialism, as Marx had expected, but began to decrease, with the result that the more advanced industrial countries became less and less revolutionary. Moreover, what revolutionary spirit did exist in advanced industrial countries was not to be found, as Marx had expected, among the laboring population but among the lower middle class (so-called "petty bourgeoisie"). The average bank clerk, architect's draftsman, or schoolteacher was unorganized, found himself oppressed by organized labor, monopolized industry, and the growing power of the state, and found himself caught in the spiral of rising costs resulting from the efforts of his three oppressors to push the costs of social welfare and steady profits on to the unorganized consumer. The petty bourgeois found that he wore a white collar, had a better education, was expected to maintain more expensive standards of personal appearance and living conditions, but received a lower income than unionized labor. As a consequence of all this, the revolutionary feeling existing in advanced industrial countries appeared among the petty bourgeoisie rather than among the proletariat, and was accompanied by psychopathic overtones arising from the suppressed resentments and social insecurities of this group. But these dangerous and even explosive feelings among the petty bourgeoisie took an antirevolutionary rather than a revolutionary form and appeared as nationalistic, anti-Semitic, antidemocratic, and anti-labor-union movements rather than as antibourgeois or anticapitalist movements such as Marx had expected.

Unfortunately, as economic and social developments in advanced industrial countries moved in the un-Marxian directions we have mentioned, the unionized laborers and their Social Democratic political parties continued to accept the Marxist ideology or at least to utter the old Marxist war cries of "Down with the capitalists!" or "Long live the revolution" or "Workers of the world, unite!" Since the Marxist ideology and the Marxist war cries were more easily observed than the social realities they served to conceal, especially when labor leaders sought all publicity for what they said and profound secrecy for what they did, many capitalists, some workers, and almost all outsiders missed the new developments completely and continued to believe that a workers' revolution was just around the corner. All this served to distort and to confuse people's minds and people's actions in much of the twentieth century. The areas in which such confusions became of great significance were in regard to the class struggle and to nationalism.

We have pointed out that the class struggles between capitalists and the laboring masses were of great importance in the early stages of industrialism. In these early stages the productive process was more dependent on hand labor and less dependent on elaborate equipment than it became later. Moreover, in these early stages, labor was unorganized (and thus competitive), while capitalists were unmonopolized (and thus competitive). As the process of industrialization advanced, however, wages became a decreasing portion of productive costs, and other costs, especially the costs of equipment for mass production, for the technical management required by such equipment, and for the advertising and merchandising costs required for mass consumption, became more and more important. All of these things made planning of increasing significance in the productive process. Such planning made it necessary to reduce the number of uncontrolled factors in the productive process to a minimum while seeking to control as many of these factors as possible. An industry which had hundreds of millions of dollars (or even billions) in equipment and plant, as did the steel industry, automobiles, chemicals, or electrical utilities, had to be able to plan, in advance, the rate and the amount of usage that equipment would receive. This need led to monopoly, which was, essentially, an effort to control both prices and sales by removing competition from the market. Once such competition had been removed from the market, or substantially reduced, it became both possible and helpful for labor to be unionized.

Unionized labor helped planning by providing fixed wages for a fixed period into the future and by providing a better trained as well as a more highly disciplined labor force. Moreover, unionized labor helped planning by establishing the same wages, conditions, hours (and thus costs) on an industrywide basis. In this way unionized labor and monopolized industry ceased to be enemies, and became partners in a planning project centered on a very expensive and complex technological plant. The class struggle in Marxian terms largely disappeared. The one exception was that, in a planned industry, the managerial staff could compare wage costs with fixed capital costs and might decide, to the resentment of labor, to replace a certain amount of labor by a certain amount of new machinery. Labor tended to resent this and to oppose it unless consulted on the problem. The net result was that rationalization of production continued, and advanced industrialized countries continued to advance in spite of the contrary influence of the monopolization of industry which made it possible, to some extent, for obsolete factories to survive because of decreased market competition.

The effects of nationalism on the Socialist movement was of even greater significance. Indeed, it was so important that it disrupted the Second International in 1914–1919. Marx had insisted that all the proletariat had common interests and should form a common front and not fall victim to nationalism, which he tended to regard as capitalistic propaganda, seeking, like religion, to divert the workers from their legitimate aims of opposition to capitalism. The Socialist movement generally accepted Marx's analysis of this situation for a long time, arguing that workers of all countries were brothers and should join together in opposition to the capitalist class and the capitalist state. The Marxian slogans calling on the workers of the world to form a common front continued to be shouted even when modern nationalism had made deep inroads on the outlook of all workers. The spread of universal education in advanced industrial countries tended to spread the nationalist point of view among the working classes. The international Socialist movements could do little to reverse or hamper this development. These movements continued to propagate the internationalist ideology of international Socialism, but it became more and more remote from the lives of the average worker. The Social Democratic parties in most countries continued to embrace the international point of view and to insist that the workers would oppose any war between capitalist states by refusing to pay taxes to support such wars or to bear arms themselves against their "brother workers" in foreign countries.

How unrealistic all this talk was became quite clear in 1914 when the workers of all countries, with a few exceptions, supported their own governments in the First World War. In most countries only a small minority of the Socialists continued to resist the war, to refuse to pay taxes, or to serve in the armed forces, or continued to agitate for social revolution rather than for victory. This minority, chiefly among the Germans and Russians, became the nucleus of the Third, or Communist, International which was formed under Russian leadership in 1919. The Left-wing minority who became the Communists refused to support the war efforts of their various countries, not because they were pacifists as the Socialists were but because they were antinationalist. They were not eager to stop the war as the Socialists were, but wished it to continue in the hope that it would destroy existing economic, social, and political life and provide an opportunity for the rise of revolutionary regimes. Moreover, they did not care who won the war, as the Socialists did, but were willing to see their own countries defeated if such a defeat would serve to bring a Communist regime to power. The leader of this radical group of violent dissident Socialists was a Russian conspirator, Vladimir Ilich Ulyanov, better known as Lenin (1870–1924). Although he expressed his point of view frequently and loudly during the war, it must be confessed that his support, even among extremely violent Socialists, was microscopic. Nevertheless, the fortunes of war served to bring this man to power in Russia in November 1917, as the leader of a Communist regime.

The Bolshevik Revolution to 1924

The corruption, incompetence, and oppression of the czarist regime was forgotten at the outbreak of war in 1914 as most Russians, even those who were sent into battle with inadequate training and inadequate weapons, rallied to the cause of Holy Mother Russia in an outburst of patriotism. This loyalty survived the early disasters of 1914 and 1915 and was able to rally sufficiently to support the great Brusilov offensive against Austria in 1916. But the tremendous losses of men and supplies in this endless warfare, the growing recognition of the complete incompetence and corruption of the government, and the growing rumors of the pernicious influence of the czarina and Rasputin over the czar served to destroy any taste that the Russian masses might have had for the war. This weakening of morale was accelerated by the severe winter and semistarvation of 1916–1917. Public discontent showed itself in March 1917, when strikes and rioting began in Petrograd. Troops in the capital refused to suppress these agitations, and the government soon found itself to be helpless. When it tried to dissolve the Duma, that body refused to be intimidated, and formed a provisional government under Prince Lvov. In this new regime there was only one Socialist, Minister of Justice Alexander Kerensky.

Although the new government forced the abdication of the czar, recognized the independence of Finland and Poland, and established a full system of civil liberties, it postponed any fundamental social and economic changes until the establishment of a future constituent assembly, and it made every effort to continue the war. In this way it failed to satisfy the desires of large numbers of Russians for land, bread, and peace. Powerful public feeling against efforts to continue the war forced the resignation of several of the more moderate members of the government, including Prince Lvov, who was replaced by Kerensky. The more radical Socialists had been released from prison or had returned from exile (in some cases, such as Lenin, by German assistance); their agitations for peace and land won adherents from a much wider group than their own supporters, and especially among the peasantry, who were very remote from Socialist sympathies or ideas but were insisting on an end to the war and a more equitable system of land ownership.

In St. Petersburg and Moscow and in a few other cities, assemblies of workers, soldiers, and peasants, called soviets, were formed by the more radical Socialists in opposition to the Provisional Government. The Bolshevik group, under Lenin's leadership, put on a powerful propaganda campaign to replace the Provisional Government by a nationwide system of soviets and to adopt an immediate program of peace and land distribution. It cannot be said that the Bolshevik group won many converts or increased in size very rapidly, but their constant agitation did serve to neutralize or alienate support for the Provisional Government, especially among the soldiers of the two chief cities. On November 7, 1917, the Bolshevik group seized the centers of government in St. Petersburg and was able to hold them because of the refusal of the local military contingents to support the Provisional Government. Within twenty-four hours this revolutionary group issued a series of decrees which abolished the Provisional Government, ordered the transfer of all public authority in Russia to soviets of workers, soldiers, and peasants, set up a central executive of the Bolshevik leaders, called the "Council of People's Commissars," and ordered the end of the war with Germany and the distribution of large landholdings to the peasants.

The Bolsheviks had no illusions about their position in Russia at the end of 1917. They knew that they formed an infinitesimal group in that vast country and that they had been able to seize power because they were a decisive and ruthless minority among a great mass of persons who had been neutralized by propaganda. There was considerable doubt about how long this neutralized condition would continue. Moreover, the Bolsheviks were convinced, in obedience to Marxist theory, that no real Socialist system could be set up in a country as industrially backward as Russia. And finally, there was grave doubt if the Western Powers would stand idly by and permit the Bolsheviks to take Russia out of the war or attempt to establish a Socialist economic system. To the Bolsheviks it seemed to be quite clear that they must simply try to survive on a day-to-day basis, hope to keep the great mass of Russians neutralized by the achievement of peace, bread, and land, and trust that the rapid advent of a Socialist revolution in industrially advanced Germany would provide Russia with an economic and political ally which could remedy the weaknesses and backwardness of Russia itself.

From 1917 to 1921 Russia passed through a period of almost incredible political and economic chaos. With counterrevolutionary movements and foreign interventionist forces appearing on all sides, the area under Bolshevik control was reduced at one time to little more than the central portions of European Russia. Within the country there was extreme economic and social collapse. Industrial production was disorganized by the disruption of transportation, the inadequate supply of raw materials and credit, and the confusions arising from the war, so that there was an almost complete lack of such products as clothing, shoes, or agricultural tools. By 1920 industrial production in general was about 13 percent of the 1913 figure. At the same time, paper money was printed so freely to pay for the costs of war, civil war, and the operation of the government that prices rose rapidly and the ruble became almost worthless. The general index of prices was only three times the 1913 level in 1917 but rose to more than 16,000 times that level by the end of 1920. Unable to get either industrial products or sound money for their produce the peasants planted only for their own needs or hoarded their surpluses. Acreage under crops was reduced by at least one-third in 1916–1920, while yields fell even more rapidly, from 74 million tons of grain in 1916 to 30 million tons in 1919 and to less than 20 million tons in 1920. The decrease in 1920 resulted from drought; this became so much worse in 1921 that the crops failed completely. Loss of life in these two years of famine reached five million, although the American Relief Administration came into the country and fed as many as ten million persons a day (in August 1922).

In the course of this chaos and tragedy the Bolshevik regime was able to survive, to crush counterrevolutionary movements, and to eliminate foreign interventionists. They were able to do this because their opponents were divided, indecisive, or neutralized, while they were vigorous, decisive, and completely ruthless. The chief sources of Bolshevik strength were to be found in the Red Army and the secret police, the neutrality of the peasants, and the support of the proletariat workers in industry and transportation. The secret police (*Cheka*) was made up of fanatical and ruthless Communists who systematically murdered all real or potential opponents. The Red Army was recruited from the old czarist army but was rewarded by high pay and favorable food rations. Although the economic system collapsed almost completely, and the peasants refused to supply, or even produce, food for the city population, the Bolsheviks established a system of food requisitions from the peasants and distributed this food by a rationing system which rewarded their supporters. The murder of the imperial family by the Bolsheviks in July 1918 removed this possible nucleus for the counterrevolutionary forces, while the general refusal of these forces to accept the revolutionary distribution of agricultural lands kept the peasants neutral in spite of the Bolshevik grain requisitions. Moreover, the peasants were divided among themselves by the Bolshevik success in splitting them so that the poorer peasants banded together to divert much of the burden of grain requisitions onto their more affluent neighbors.

The most acute problem facing the revolutionary regime at the end of 1917 was the war with Germany. At first the Bolsheviks tried to end the fighting without any formal peace, but the Germans continued to advance, and the Bolsheviks were compelled to sign the Treaty of Brest-Litovsk (March 1918). By this treaty Russia lost all the western borderlands, including Poland, the Ukraine, and the Baltic areas. The German forces tried, with little success, to obtain economic resources from the Ukraine, and soon advanced far beyond the boundaries established at Brest-Litovsk to occupy the Don Valley, the Crimea, and the Caucasus.

In various parts of Russia, notably in the south and the east, counter-revolutionary armies called "Whites" took the field to overthrow the Bolsheviks. The Cossacks of the Don under L. G. Kornilov, Anton Denikin, and Pëtr Wrangel occupied the Caucasus, the Crimea, and the Ukraine after the Germans withdrew from these areas. In Siberia a conservative government under Admiral Aleksandr Kolchak was set up at Omsk and announced its intention to take over all of Russia (late 1918). A group of 40,000 armed Czechoslovaks who had deserted from the Habsburg armies to fight for Russia turned against the Bolsheviks and, while being evacuated to the east along the Transsiberian Railway, seized control of that route from the Volga to Vladivostok (summer 1918).

Various outside Powers also intervened in the Russian chaos. An allied expeditionary force invaded northern Russia from Murmansk and Archangel, while a force of Japanese and another of Americans landed at Vladivostok and pushed westward for hundreds of miles. The British seized the oil fields of the Caspian region (late 1918), while the French occupied parts of the Ukraine about Odessa (March 1919).

Against these various forces the Bolsheviks fought with growing success, using the new Red Army and the Cheka, supported by the nationalized industrial and agrarian systems. While these fought to preserve the revolutionary regime within Russia, various sympathizers were organized outside the country. The Third International was organized under Grigori Zinoviev to encourage revolutionary movements in other countries. Its only notable success was in Hungary where a Bolshevik regime under Béla Kun was able to maintain itself for a few months (March–August 1919).

By 1920 Russia was in complete confusion. At this point the new Polish government invaded Russia, occupying much of the Ukraine. A Bolshevik counterattack drove the Poles back to Warsaw where they called upon the Entente Powers for assistance. General Weygand was sent with a military mission and supplies. Thus supported, Poland was able to reinvade Russia and impose the Treaty of Riga (March 1921). This treaty established a Polish-Russian boundary 150 miles east of the tentative "Curzon Line" which had been drawn along the ethnographic frontier by the Western Powers in 1919. By this act Poland took within its boundaries several millions of Ukrainians and White Russians and ensured a high level of Soviet-Polish enmity for the next twenty years.

Much of the burden of this turmoil and conflict was imposed on the Russian peasantry by the agricultural requisitions and the whole system of so-called "war Communism." As part of this system not only were all agricultural crops considered to be government property but all private trade and commerce were also forbidden; the banks were nationalized, while all industrial plants of over five workers and all craft enterprises of over ten workers were nationalized (1920). This system of extreme Communism was far from being a success, and peasant opposition steadily increased in spite of the severe punishments inflicted for violations of the regulations. As counterrevolutionary movements were suppressed and foreign interventionists gradually withdrew, opposition to the system of political oppression and "War Communism" increased. This culminated in peasant uprisings, urban riots, and a mutiny of the sailors at Kronstadt (March 1921). Within a week a turning point was passed; the whole system of "War Communism" and of peasant requisitioning was abandoned in favor of a "New Economic Policy" of free commercial activity in agricultural and other commodities, with the reestablishment of the profit motive and of private ownership in small industries and in small landholding. Requisitioning was replaced by a system of moderate taxation, and the pressures of the secret police, of censorship, and of the government generally were relaxed. As a result of these tactics, there was a dramatic increase in economic prosperity and in political stability. This improvement continued for two years, until, by late 1923, political unrest and economic problems again became acute. At the same time, the approaching death of Lenin complicated these problems with a struggle for power among Lenin's successors.

Because the political organization of the Bolshevik regime in its first few years was on a trial-and-error basis, its chief outlines were not established until about 1923. These outlines had two quite different aspects, the constitutional and the political. Constitutionally the country was organized (in 1922) into a Union of Socialist Soviet Republics (USSR). The number of these republics has changed greatly, rising from four in 1924 and eleven in the 1936–1940 period to fifteen in the 1960's. Of these, the largest and most important was the Russian Soviet Federal Socialist Republic (RSFSR), which covered about three-quarters of the area of the whole Union with about five-eighths of the total population. The constitution of this RSFSR, drawn up in 1918, became the pattern for the governmental systems in other republics as they were created and joined with the RSFSR to form the USSR. In this organization local soviets, in cities and villages, organized on an occupational basis, elected representatives to district, county, regional, and provincial congresses of soviets. As we shall see in a moment, these numerous levels of indirect representation served to weaken any popular influence at the top and to allow the various links in the chain to be controlled by the Communist political party. The city soviets and the provincial congresses of soviets sent representatives to an All-Russian Congress of Soviets which possessed, in theory, full constitutional powers. Since this Congress of Soviets, with one thousand members, met no more than once a year, it delegated its authority to an All-Russian Central Executive Committee of three hundred members. This Executive Committee, meeting only three times a year, entrusted day-to-day administration to a Council of People's Commissars, or Cabinet, of seventeen persons. When the Union of Socialist Soviet Republics was formed in 1923 by adding other republics to the RSFSR, the new republics obtained a somewhat similar constitutional organization, and a similar system was created for the whole Union. The latter possessed a Union Congress of Soviets, large and unwieldy, meeting infrequently, and chosen by the city and provincial soviets. This Union Congress elected an equally unwieldy All-Union Central Executive Committee consisting of two chambers. One of these chambers, the Council of the Union, represented population; the other chamber, the Council of Nationalities, represented the constituent republics and autonomous regions of the Soviet Union. The Council of People's Commissars of the RSFSR was transformed, with slight changes, into a Union Council of Commissars for the whole Union. This ministry had commissars for five fields (foreign affairs, defense, foreign trade, communications, and posts and telegraphs) from which the constituent republics were excluded, as well as numerous commissars for activities which were shared with the republics.

This system had certain notable characteristics. There was no separation of powers, so that the various organs of government could engage in legislative, executive, administrative, and, if necessary, judicial activities. Second, there was no constitution or constitutional law in the sense of a body of rules above or outside the government, since constitutional laws were made by the same process and had the same weight as other laws. Third, there were no guaranteed rights or liberties of individuals, since the accepted theory was that rights and obligations arise from and in the state rather than outside or separate from the state. Last, there were no democratic or parliamentary elements because of the monopoly of political power by the Communist Party.

The Communist Party was organized in a system similar to and parallel to the state, except that it included only a small portion of the population. At the bottom, in every shop or neighborhood, were unions of party members called "cells." Above these, rising level on level, were higher organizations consisting, on each level, of a party congress and an executive committee chosen by the congress of the same level. These were found in districts, in counties, in provinces, in regions, and in the constituent republics. At the top was the Central Party Congress and the Central Executive Committee chosen by it. As years went by, the Central Party Congress met more and more rarely and then merely approved the activities and resolutions of the Central Executive Committee. This committee and its parallel institution in the state (Council of People's Commissars) were dominated, until 1922, by the personality of Lenin. His eloquence, intellectual agility, and capacity for ruthless decision and practical improvisation gave him the paramount position in both party and state. In May 1922, Lenin had a cerebral stroke and, after a series of such strokes, died in January 1924. This long-drawn illness gave rise to a struggle, for control of the party and the state apparatus, within the party itself. This struggle, at first, took the form of a union of the lesser leaders against Trotsky (the second most important leader, after Lenin). But eventually this developed into a struggle of Stalin against Trotsky and, finally, of Stalin against the rest. By 1927 Stalin had won a decisive victory over Trotsky and all opposition.

Stalin's victory was due very largely to his ability to control the administrative machinery of the party behind the scenes and to the reluctance of his opponents, especially Trotsky, to engage in a showdown struggle with Stalin lest this lead to civil war, foreign intervention, and the destruction of the revolutionary achievement. Thus, while Trotsky had the support of the Red Army and of the mass of party members, these were both neutralized by his refusal to use them against Stalin's control of the party machinery.

The party, as we have said, remained a minority of the population, under the theory that quality was more important than quantity. There were 23,000 members in March 1917, and 650,000 in October 1921; at this latter date a purge began which reduced the party rolls by 24 percent. Subsequently, the rolls were reopened, and membership rose to 3.4 million by 1940. The power to admit or to purge, held in the hands of the Central Executive Committee, completely centralized control of the party itself; the fact that there was only one legal party and that elections to positions in the state were by ballots containing only one party, and even one name for each office, gave the party complete control of the state. This control was neither weakened nor threatened by a new constitution, of democratic appearance and form, which came into existence in 1936.

In 1919 the Central Executive Committee of nineteen appointed two subcommittees of five each and a secretariat of three. One of the sub-committees, the Politburo, was concerned with questions of policy, while the other, the Orgburo, was concerned with questions of party organization. Only one man, Stalin, was a member of both of these; in April 1922, a new secretariat of three was named (Stalin, Vyacheslav Molotov, Valerian Kuibyshev) with Stalin as secretary-general. From this central position he was able to build up a party bureaucracy loyal to himself, purge those who would be most opposed to his plans, or transfer to remote positions those party members whose loyalty to himself was not beyond question. At the death of Lenin in January 1924, Stalin was the most influential party member, but still lurked in the background. At first he ruled as one of a triumvirate of Stalin, Grigori Zinoviev, and Lev Kamenev, all united in opposition to Trotsky. The last was removed from his position as war commissar in January 1925, and from the Politburo in October 1926. In 1927, at Stalin's behest, Trotsky and Zinoviev were expelled from the party. Zinoviev was later restored to membership but in 1929 Trotsky was deported to exile in Turkey. By that time Stalin held the reins of government firmly in his own hands.

Stalinism, 1924-1939

As Stalin gradually strengthened his internal control of the Soviet Union after Lenin's death in 1924, it became possible to turn, with increasing energy, to other matters. The New Economic Policy, which Lenin had adopted in 1921, performed so successfully that the Soviet Union experienced a phenomenal recovery from the depths to which "War Communism" had dragged it in 1918–1921.

Unfortunately for the economic theorists of the Soviet Union, the NEP was not really a "policy" at all, and it certainly was not Communism. By reestablishing a new monetary system based on gold, in which one of the new gold rubles was equal to 50,000 of the old, inflated paper rubles, a firm financial basis was provided for recovery. Except for a continuance of government regulation in international trade and in large-scale heavy industry, a regime of freedom was permitted. Agricultural production rose, commercial activities flourished, and the lighter industrial activities devoted to consumers' goods began to recover. Distinctions of wealth reappeared among the peasants, the richer ones (called "kulaks") being regarded with suspicion by the regime and with envy by their less fortunate neighbors. At the same time, those who made their fortunes in commerce (called "nepmen") were sporadically persecuted by the regime as enemies of Socialism. Nonetheless, the economic system flourished. Acreage under cultivation rose from 148 million acres in 1921 to 222 million in 1927; grain collections, after the famine of 1922 had passed, approximately doubled in 1923–1927; coal production doubled in three years, while production of cotton textiles quadrupled. As a consequence of such recovery, the Russian economic system in 1927 was, once again, back to its 1913 level, although, since population had gone up by ten million persons, the per capita income was lower.

In spite of the economic recovery of the NEP, it gave rise to important problems. Just as the free agricultural economy produced kulaks, and the free commercial system produced nepmen, so the mixed industrial system had undesirable consequences. Under this mixed system industries concerned with national defense were under direct state control; heavy industry was controlled by monopolistic trusts, which were owned by the state, but operated under separate budgets and were expected to be profitable; small industry was free. One bad result of this was that small industry was squeezed in its efforts to obtain labor, materials, or credit, and its products were in scarce supply at high prices. Another result was that agricultural prices, being free and competitive, fell lower and lower as agricultural production recovered, but industrial prices, being monopolistic, or in short supply, remained high. The result was a "scissors crisis," as it is called in Europe (or "parity prices," as it is called in America). This meant that the goods farmers sold were at low prices, while the goods they bought were at high prices, and scarce. Thus, in 1923, agricultural prices were at 58 percent of the 1913 level, while industrial prices were at 187 percent of their 1913 level, so that peasants could obtain only one-third as much manufactured goods for their crops as they had been able to obtain in 1913. By withholding credit from industry, the government was able to force factories to liquidate their stocks of goods by lowering prices. As a consequence, by 1924 industrial prices fell to 141 percent of 1913, while agricultural prices rose to 77 percent of 1913. The peasant's position was improved from one-third to one-half of his 1913 position, but at no time did he regain his 1913 parity level. This gave rise to a great deal of agrarian discontent and to numerous peasant disturbances during the latter part of the NEP.

Lenin had insisted that the weakness of the proletariat in Russia made it necessary to maintain an alliance with the peasantry. This had been done during the period of state capitalism (November 1917–June 1918), but the alliance had been largely destroyed in the period of "War Communism" (June 1918–April 1921). Under the NEP this alliance was reestablished, but the "scissors crisis" once again destroyed it. Then it was reestablished only partially. Stalin's victory over Trotsky and his personal inclination for terroristic methods of government led to decisions which marked the end of these cycles of peasant discontent. The decision to build Socialism in a single country made it necessary, it was felt, to emphasize the predominance of heavy industry in order to obtain, as quickly as possible, the basis for the manufacture of armaments (chiefly iron, steel, coal, and electrical power projects). Such projects required great masses of labor to be concentrated together and fed. Both the labor and the food would have to be drawn from the peasantry, but the emphasis on heavy industrial production rather than on light industry meant that there would be few consumers' goods to give to the peasantry in return for the food taken from them. Moreover, the drain of manpower from the peasantry to form urban labor forces would mean that those who continued to be peasants must greatly improve their methods of agricultural production in order to supply, with a smaller proportion of peasants, food for themselves, for the new urban laborers, for the growing party bureaucracy, and for the growing Red Army which was regarded as essential to defend "Socialism in a single country."

The problem of obtaining increasing supplies of food from fewer peasants without offering them consumers' industrial goods in exchange could not, according to Stalin, be worked in a peasant regime based on freedom of commerce, as under the NEP of 1921–1927, or in one based on individual farmers, as in the "War Communism" of 1918–1921; the former of these required that the peasants be given goods in exchange while the latter could be made a failure by peasant refusals to produce more food than was required by their own needs. The NEP could not find a solution to this problem. In spite of the closing of the scissors in 1923–1927, industrial prices remained higher than farm prices, peasants were reluctant to supply food to the cities since they could not get the cities' products they wanted in return, and the amount of peasants' grain which was sold remained about 13 percent of the grain raised in 1927 compared to 26 percent in 1913. Such a system might provide a high standard of living for the peasants, but it could never provide the highly industrialized basis necessary to support "Socialism in a single country."

The new direction which Russia's development took after 1927 and which we call "Stalinism" is a consequence of numerous factors. Three of these factors were (1) the bloodthirsty and paranoiac ambitions of Stalin and his associates, (2) a return of Russia to its older traditions, but on a new level and a new intensity, and (3) a theory of social, political, and economic developments which is included under the phrase "Socialism in a single country." This theory was embraced with such an insane fanaticism by the rulers of the new Russia, and provided such powerful motivations for Soviet foreign and domestic politics, that it must be analyzed at some length.

The rivalry between Stalin and Trotsky in the mid-1920's was fought with slogans as well as with more violent weapons. Trotsky called for "world revolution," while Stalin wanted "Communism in a single country." According to Trotsky, Russia was economically too weak and too backward to be able to establish a Communist system alone. Such a system, all agreed, could not exist except in a fully industrialized country. Russia, which was so far from being industrialized, could obtain the necessary capital only by borrowing it abroad or by accumulating it from its own people. In either case, it would be taken, in the long run, from Russia's peasants by political duress, in the one case being exported to pay for foreign loans and, in the other case, being given, as food and raw materials, to the industrial workers in the city. Both cases would be fraught with dangers; foreign countries, because their own economic systems were capitalistic, would not stand idly by and allow a rival Socialistic system to reach successful achievement in Russia; moreover, in either case, there would be a dangerously high level of peasant discontent, since the necessary food and raw materials would have to be taken from Russia's peasantry by political duress, without economic return. This followed from the Soviet theory that the enmity of foreign capitalist countries would require Russia's new industry to emphasize heavy industrial products able to support the manufacture of armaments rather than light industrial products able to provide consumers' goods which could be given to the peasants in return for their produce.

The Bolsheviks assumed, as an axiom, that capitalistic countries would not allow the Soviet Union to build up a successful Socialistic system which would make all capitalism obsolete. This idea was strengthened by a theory, to which Lenin made a chief contribution, that "imperialism is the last stage of capitalism." According to this theory, a fully industrialized capitalistic country enters upon a period of economic depression which leads it to embrace a program of warlike aggression. The theory insisted that the distribution of income in a capitalistic society would become so inequitable that the masses of the people would not obtain sufficient income to buy the goods being produced by the industrial plants. As such unsold goods accumulated with decreasing profits and deepening depression, there would be a shift toward the production of armaments to provide profits and produce goods which could be sold and there would be an increasingly aggressive foreign policy in order to obtain markets for unsold goods in backward or undeveloped countries. Such aggressive imperialism, it seemed to Soviet thinkers, would inevitably make Russia a target of aggression in order to prevent a successful Communist system there from becoming an attractive model for the discontented proletariat in capitalistic countries. According to Trotsky, all these truths made it quite obvious that "Socialism in a single country" was an impossible idea, especially if that single country was as poor and backward as Russia. To Trotsky and his friends it seemed quite clear that the salvation of the Soviet system must be sought in a world revolution which would bring other countries, especially such an advanced industrial country as Germany, to Russia's side as allies.

While the internal struggle between Trotsky and Stalin was wending its weary way in 1923–1927, it became quite clear not only that world revolution was impossible and that Germany was not going either to a Communist revolution or an alliance with the Soviet, it also became equally clear that "oppressed colonial" areas such as China were not going to ally with the Soviet Union. "Communism in a single country" had to be adopted as Russia's policy simply because there was no alternative.

Communism in Russia alone required, according to Bolshevik thinkers, that the country must be industrialized with breakneck speed, whatever the waste and hardships, and must emphasize heavy industry and armaments rather than rising standards of living. This meant that the goods produced by the peasants must be taken from them, by political duress, without any economic return, and that the ultimate in authoritarian terror must be used to prevent the peasants from reducing their level of production to their own consumption needs, as they had done in the period of "War Communism" in 1918–1921. This meant that the first step toward the industrialization of Russia required that the peasantry be broken by terror and reorganized from a capitalistic basis of private farms to a Socialistic system of collective farms. Moreover, to prevent imperialist capitalistic countries from taking advantage of the inevitable unrest this program would create in Russia, it was necessary to crush all kinds of foreign espionage, resistance to the Bolshevik state, independent thought, or public discontent. These must be crushed by terror so that the whole of Russia could be formed into a monolithic structure of disciplined proletariat who would obey their leaders with such unquestioning obedience that it would strike fear in the hearts of every potential aggressor.

The steps in this theory followed one another like the steps of a geometrical proposition: failure of the revolution in industrially advanced Germany required that Communism be established in backward Russia; this demanded rapid industrialization with emphasis on heavy industry; this meant that the peasants could not obtain consumers' goods for their food and raw materials; this meant that the peasants must be reduced by terroristic duress to collective farms where they could neither resist nor reduce their levels of production: this required that all discontent and independence be crushed under a despotic police state to prevent foreign capitalistic imperialists from exploiting the discontent or social unrest in Russia. To the rulers in the Kremlin the final proof of the truth of this proposition appeared when Germany, which had not gone Communist but had remained capitalistic, attacked Russia in 1941.

A historian, who might question the assumptions or the stages in this theory, would also see that the theory made it possible for Bolshevik Russia to abandon most of the influences of Western ideology in Marxism (such as its humanitarianism, its equality, or its antimilitarist, anti-state bias) and allow it to fall back into the Russian tradition of a despotic police state resting on espionage and terror, in which there was a profound gulf in ideology and manner of living between the rulers and the ruled. It should also be evident that a new regime, such as Bolshevism was in Russia, would have no traditional methods of social recruitment or circulation of elites; these would be based on intrigue and violence and would inevitably bring to the top the most decisive, most merciless, most unprincipled, and most violent of its members. Such a group, forming around Stalin, began the process of establishing "Communism in a single country" in 1927–1929, and continued it until interrupted by the approach of war in 1941. This program of heavy industrialization was organized in a series of "Five-Year Plans," of which the first covered the years 1928–1932.

The chief elements in the First Five-Year Plan were the collectivization of agriculture and the creation of a basic system of heavy industry. In order to increase the supply of food and industrial labor in the cities, Stalin forced the peasants off their own lands (worked by their own animals and their own tools) onto large communal farms, worked cooperatively with lands, tools, and animals owned in common, or onto huge state farms, run as state-owned enterprises by wage-earning employees using lands, tools, and animals owned by the government. In communal farms the crops were owned jointly by the members and were divided, after certain amounts had been set aside for taxes, purchases, and other payments which directed food to the cities. In state farms the crops were owned outright by the state, after the necessary costs had been paid. In time, experience showed that the costs of the state farms were so high and their operations so inefficient that they were hardly worthwhile, although they continued to be created.

The shift to the new system came slowly in 1927–1929 and then was put violently into full operation in 1930. In the space of six weeks

(February–March 1930) collective farms increased from 59,400, with 4,400,000 families, to 110,200 farms, with 14,300,000 families. All peasants who resisted were treated with violence; their property was confiscated, they were beaten or sent into exile in remote areas; many were killed. This process, known as "the liquidation of the kulaks" (since the richer peasantry resisted most vigorously), affected five million kulak families. Rather than give up their animals to the collective farms, many peasants killed them. As a result, the number of cattle was reduced from 30.7 million in 1928 to 19.6 million in 1933, while, in the same five years, sheep and goats fell from 146.7 million to 50.2 million, hogs from 26 to 12.1 million, and horses from 33.5 to 16.6 million. Moreover, the planting season of 1930 was entirely disrupted, and the agricultural activities of later years continued to be disturbed so that food production decreased drastically. Since the government insisted on taking the food needed to support the urban population, the rural areas were left with inadequate food, and at least three million peasants starved in 1931–1933. Twelve years later, in 1945, Stalin told Winston Churchill that twelve million peasants died in this reorganization of agriculture.

To compensate for these setbacks, large areas of previously uncultivated lands, many of them semiarid, were brought under cultivation, mostly in Siberia, as state farms. Considerable research was done on new crop varieties to increase yields, and to utilize the drier lands of the south and the shorter growing season in the north. As a consequence, the area under cultivation increased by 21 percent in 1927–1938. However, the fact that the Soviet population rose, in the same eleven years, from 150 million to 170 million persons, meant that the cultivated acreage per capita rose only from 1.9 to 2.0 acres. The use of semiarid lands required a considerable extension of irrigation; thus there was an increase of about 50 percent in the acreage irrigated in the decade 1928–1938 (from 10.6 million acres to 15.2 million acres). Some of these irrigation projects combined irrigation with the generation of electricity by waterpower, and provided improved water transportation facilities, as in our Tennessee Valley Authority; this was true of the famous project at Dnepropetrovsk on the lower Dnieper River, which had a capacity of half a million kilowatts (1935).

The reduction in farm animals, which was not made up by 1941, combined with the efforts to develop heavy industry, resulted in increased use of tractors and other mechanized equipment in agriculture. The number of tractors rose from 26.7 thousand in 1928 to 483.5 thousand in 1938, while in the same decade the percentage of plowing done by tractors increased from 1 percent to 72 percent. Harvesting was increasingly done by combines, the number of these increasing from almost none in 1928 to 182,000 in 1940. Such complicated machinery was not owned by the collective farms but by independent machine-tractor stations scattered about the country; they had to be hired from these as they were needed. The introduction of mechanized farming of this type was not an unmixed success, as many machines were ruined by inexperienced help and the costs of upkeep and fuel were very high. Nevertheless, the trend toward mechanization continued, partly from a desire to copy the United States and partly from a rather childish enthusiasm for modern technology. These two impulses combined, at times, to produce a "gigantomania," or enthusiasm for large size rather than for efficiency or a satisfactory way of life. In agriculture this gave rise to many enormous state farms of hundreds of thousands of acres which were notoriously inefficient. Moreover, the shift to such large-scale mechanized agriculture, in contrast to the old czarist agriculture organized in scattered peasant plots cultivated in a three-year, fallow-rotation system, greatly increased such problems as spreading drought, losses to insect pests, and decreasing soil fertility, requiring the use of artificial fertilizers. In spite of all these problems, Soviet agriculture, without ever becoming successful or even adequate, provided a steadily expanding base for the growth of Soviet industry, until both were disrupted by the invasion of Hitler's hordes in the summer of 1941.

The industrial portion of the First Five-Year Plan was pursued with the same ruthless drive as the collectivization of agriculture and had similar spectacular results: impressive physical accomplishment, large-scale waste, lack of integration, ruthless disregard of personal comfort and standards of living, constant purges of opposition elements, of scapegoats, and of the inefficient, all to the accompaniment of blasts of propaganda inflating the plan's real achievements to incredible dimensions, attacking opposition groups (sometimes real and frequently imaginary) within the Soviet Union, or mixing scorn with fear in verbal assaults on foreign "capitalist imperialist" countries and their secret "saboteurs" within Russia.

The First Five-Year Plan of 1928–1932 was followed by a Second Plan of 1933–1937 and a Third Plan of 1938–1942. The last of these was completely disrupted by the German invasion of June 1941, and had, from the beginning, undergone periodic modifications which changed its targets in the direction of an increased emphasis on armaments because of the rising international tensions. Because of the inadequacies of the available Soviet statistics, it is not easy to make any definite statements about the success of these plans. There can be no doubt that there was a great increase in the physical output of industrial goods and that this output was very largely in capital equipment rather than in consumers' goods. It is also clear that much of this advance was uncoordinated and spotty and that, while Soviet national income was rising, the standard of living of the Russian peoples was declining from its 1928 level.

The following estimates, made by Alexander Baykov, will give some idea of the magnitude of the achievement of the Soviet economic system in the period 1928–1940:

	1928	1940
Coal (million tons)	35.0	166.0
Oil (million tons)	11.5	31.1
Pig iron (million tons)	3.3	15.0
Steel (million tons)	4.3	18.3
Cement (million tons)	1.8	5.8
Electric power (billion kw.)	5.0	48.3
Cotton textiles (million meters)	2742.0	3700.0
Woolen textiles (million meters)	93.2	120.0
Leather shoes (million pairs)	29.6	220.0
Railroad freight (billion ton-kilometers)	93.4	415.0
Total population (millions)	150.0	173.0
Urban population (estimated percentage)	18.0%	33.0%
Employed persons (millions)	11.2	31.2
Total wage payments (millions of rubles)	8.2	162.0
Grain crops (millions of hectoliters)	92.2	111.2

There can be little doubt that this tremendous achievement in industrialization made it possible for the Soviet system to withstand the German assault in 1941. At the same time the magnitude of the achievement produced great distortions and tensions in Soviet life. Millions of persons moved from villages to cities (some of these entirely new) to find inadequate housing, inadequate food, and violent psychological tensions. On the other hand, the same move opened to them wide opportunities in free education, for themselves and for their children, as well as opportunities to rise in the social, economic, and party structures. As a consequence of such opportunities, class distinctions reappeared in the Soviet Union, the privileged leaders of the secret police and the Red Army, as well as the leaders of the party and certain favored writers, musicians, ballet dancers, and actors, obtaining incomes so far above those of the ordinary Russian that they lived in quite a different world. The ordinary Russian had inadequate food and housing, was subject to extended rationing, having to stand in line for scarce consumers' items or even to go without them for long periods, and was reduced to living, with his family, in a single room, or even, in many cases, to a corner of a single room shared with other families. The privileged rulers and their favorites had the best of everything, including foods and wines, the use of vacation villas in the country or in the Crimea, the use of official cars in the city, the right to live in old czarist palaces and mansions, and the right to obtain tickets to the best seats at the musical or dramatic performances. These privileges of the ruling group, however, were obtained at a terrible price: at the cost of complete insecurity, for even the highest party officials were under constant surveillance by the secret police and inevitably would be purged, sooner or later, to exile or to death.

The growth of inequality was increasingly rapid under the Five-Year plans and was embodied in law. All restrictions on maximum salaries were removed; variations in salaries grew steadily wider and were made greater by the nonmonetary privileges extended to the favored upper ranks. Special stores were established where the privileged could obtain scarce goods at low prices; two or even three restaurants, with entirely different menus, were set up in industrial plants for different levels of employees; housing discrimination became steadily wider; all wages were put on a piecework basis even when this was quite impractical; work quotas and work minimums were steadily raised. Much of this differentiation of wages was justified under a fraudulent propaganda system known as Stakhanovism.

In September 1935, a miner named Stakhanov mined 102 tons of coal in a day, fourteen times the usual output. Similar exploits were arranged in other activities for propaganda purposes and used to justify speedup, raising of production quotas, and wage differences. At the same time, the standard of living of the ordinary worker was steadily reduced not only by raising quotas but also by a systematic policy of segmented inflation. Food was purchased from the collective farms at low prices and then sold to the public at high prices. The gap between these two was steadily widened year by year. At the same time the amount of produce taken from the peasants was gradually increased by one technique or another. When collective farms had to shift to tractors and combines these were taken from the farms themselves and centralized in machine-tractor stations controlled by the government. They had to be hired at rates which approached one-fifth of the total output of the collective farm. One of the chief sources of governmental income was a turnover tax (sales tax) on consumers' goods; this varied from item to item, but was generally about 60 percent or more. It was not imposed on producers' goods, which were, on the contrary, subsidized to the extent of half the government's expenditures. Price segmentation was so great that in the period 1927–1948 consumers' prices went up thirtyfold, wages went up elevenfold, while prices of producers' goods and armaments went up less than threefold. This served to reduce consumption and to falsify the statistical picture of the national income, standards of living, and the breakdown between consumers' goods, capital goods, and armaments.

As public discontent and social tensions grew in the period of the Five-Year plans and the collectivization of agriculture, the use of spying, purges, torture, and murder increased out of all proportion. Every wave of discontent, every discovery of inefficiency, every recognition of some past mistake of the authorities resulted in new waves of police activity. When the meat supplies of the cities almost vanished, after the collectivization of agriculture in the early 1930's, more than a dozen of the high officials in charge of meat supplies in Moscow were arrested and shot, although they were in no way responsible for the shortage. By the middle 1930's the search for "saboteurs" and for "enemies of the state" became an all-enveloping mania which left hardly a family untouched. Hundreds of thousands were killed, frequently on completely false charges, while millions were arrested and exiled to Siberia or put into huge slave-labor camps. In these camps, under conditions of semi-starvation and incredible cruelty, millions toiled in mines, in logging camps in the Arctic, or building new railroads, new canals, or new cities. Estimates of the number of persons in such slave-labor camps in the period just before Hitler's attack in 1941 vary from as low as two million to as high as twenty million. The majority of these prisoners had done nothing against the Soviet state or the Communist system, but consisted of the relatives, associates, and friends of persons who had been arrested on more serious charges. Many of these charges were completely false, having been trumped up to provide labor in remote areas, scapegoats for administrative breakdowns, and to eliminate possible rivals in the control of the Soviet system, or simply because of the constantly growing mass paranoidal suspicion which enveloped the upper levels of the regime. In many cases, incidental events led to large-scale reprisals for personal grudges far beyond any scope justified by the event itself. In most cases these "liquidations" took place in the cells of the secret police, in the middle of the night, with no public announcements except the most laconic. But, in a few cases, spectacular public trials were staged in which the accused, usually famous Soviet leaders, were berated and reviled, volubly confessed their own dastardly activities, and, after conviction, were taken out and shot.

These purges and trials kept the Soviet Union in an uproar and kept the rest of the world in a state of continuous amazement throughout the period of the Five-Year plans. In 1929 a large group of party leaders who objected to the ruthless exploitation of the peasantry (the so-called

"Rightist opposition"), led by the party's most expert theoretician of the Marxist ideology, Nikolai Bukharin, was purged. In 1933 about a third of the members of the party (at least a million names) were expelled from the party. In 1935, following upon the murder of a Stalinist supporter, Serge Kirov, by the secret police, many of the "Old Bolsheviks," including Zinoviev and Kamenev, were tried for treason. The following year, just as the Spanish Civil War was beginning, the same group were tried once more as "Trotskyists" and were shot. A few months later another large group of "Old Bolsheviks," including Karl Radek and Grigori Pyatakov, were tried for treason and executed. Later in that same year (1937) evidence that the Soviet army leaders had been in communication with the German High Command was sent from the German secret police, through Beneš, the president of Czechoslovakia, to Stalin. These communications had been going on since before 1920, were an open secret to careful students of European affairs, and had been approved by both governments as part of a common front against the Western democratic Powers; nevertheless this information was used as an excuse to purge the Red Army of most of its old leaders, while eight of the highest generals, led by Marshal Mikhail Tukhachevski, were executed. Less than a year later, in March 1938, the few remaining Old Bolsheviks were tried, convicted, and executed. These included Bukharin, Aleksei Rykov (who had succeeded Lenin as president of the Soviet Union), and G. Yagoda (who had been head of the secret police).

For every leader who was publicly eliminated by these "Moscow Treason Trials" thousands were eliminated in secret. By 1939 all of the older leaders of Bolshevism had been driven from public life and most had died violent deaths, leaving only Stalin and his younger collaborators, such as Molotov and Voroshilov. All opposition to this group, in action, word, or thought, was regarded as equivalent to counterrevolutionary sabotage and aggressive capitalistic espionage.

Under Stalinism all Russia was dominated by three huge bureaucracies: of the government, of the party, and of the secret police. Of these, the secret police was more powerful than the party and the party more powerful than the government. Every office, factory, university, collective farm, research laboratory, or museum had all three structures. When the management of a factory sought to produce goods, they were constantly interfered with by the party committee (cell) or by the special department (the secret police unit) within the factory. There were two networks of secret-police spies, unknown to each other, one serving the special department of the factory, while the other reported to a high level of the secret police outside. Most of these spies were unpaid and served under threats of blackmail or liquidation. Such "liquidations" could range from wage reductions (which went to the secret police), through beatings or torture, to exile, imprisonment, expulsion from the party (if a member), to murder. The secret police had enormous funds, since it collected wage deductions from large numbers and had millions of slave laborers in its camps to be rented out, like draft animals on a contract basis, for state construction projects. Whenever the secret police needed more money it could sweep large numbers of persons, without trial or notice, into its wage deduction system or into its labor camps to be hired out. It would seem that the secret police, operating in this fashion, were the real rulers of Russia. This was true except at the very top, where Stalin could always liquidate the head of the secret police by having him arrested by his second in command in return for Stalin's promise to promote the arrester to the top position. In this way the chiefs of the secret police were successively eliminated; V. Menzhinsky was replaced by Yagoda in 1934, Yagoda by Nikolai Yezhov in 1936, and Yezhov by Lavrenti Beria in 1938. These rapid shifts sought to cover up the falsifications of evidence which these men had prepared for the great purges of the period, each man's mouth being closed by death as his part in the elimination of Stalin's rivals was concluded. To keep the organization subordinate to the party, none of the leaders of the secret police was a member of the Politburo before Beria, and Beria was completely Stalin's creature until they perished together in 1953.

It would be a grave mistake to believe that the Soviet system of government, with its peculiar amalgam of censorship, mass propaganda, and ruthless terror, was an invention of Stalin and his friends; it would be equally erroneous to believe that this system is a creation of Bolshevism; the truth is that it is a part of the Russian way of life and has a tradition going back through czarism to Byzantianism and to caesarism. In Russia itself it has typical precedents in Ivan the Terrible, Peter the Great, Paul I, or Alexander III. The chief changes were that the system, through the advance of technology, of weapons, of communications, and of transportation, became more pervasive, more constant, more violent, and more irrational. As an example of its irrationality we might point out that policy was subject to sudden reversals, which not only were pursued with ruthless severity, but under which, once policy had shifted, those who had been most active in the earlier official policy were liquidated as saboteurs or enemies of the state for their earlier activities as soon as the policy was changed. In the late 1920's officials in the Ukraine had to speak Ukrainian; in a few years those who did were persecuted for seeking to disrupt the Soviet Union. As leaders were shifted, each demanded 100 percent loyalty, which became an excuse for liquidation by a successor as soon as the leader changed. The reversals in policy toward the peasants created many victims, as did the violent reversals in foreign policy. Soviet-German relations shifted from a basis of friendship in 1922–1927 to one of most violent animosity in 1933–1939, changed to patent friendship and cooperation in 1939–1941, to be followed by violent animosity again in 1941. These reversals of policy were difficult for the heavily censored Russian people to follow; they were almost impossible for Soviet sympathizers or members of Communist parties in foreign countries to follow; and they were very dangerous to the leaders of the Soviet system, who might find themselves under arrest today for having followed a different (but official) policy a year previously.

Yet in spite of all these difficulties, the Soviet Union continued to grow in industrial and military strength in the decade before 1941. In spite of low standards of living, racking internal tensions, devastating purges, economic dislocations, and large-scale waste and inefficiency, the industrial basis of Soviet power continued to expand. Nazi Germans, and the outside world in general, were more aware of the tensions, purges, dislocations, and inefficiency than they were of the growing power, with the result that all were amazed at the Soviet Union's ability to withstand the German assault which began on June 22, 1941.

IX

GERMANY
FROM KAISER
TO HITLER,
1913-1945

Introduction

The Weimar Republic, 1918–1933

The Nazi Regime

COMING TO POWER, 1933–1934

THE RULERS AND THE RULED, 1934–1945

Introduction

THE fate of Germany is one of the most tragic in all human history, for seldom has a people of such talent and accomplishment brought such disasters on themselves and on others. The explanation of how Germany came to such straits cannot be found by examining the history of the twentieth century alone. Germany came to the disaster of 1945 by a path whose beginnings lie in the distant past, in the whole pattern of German history from the days of the Germanic tribes to the present. That Germany had a tribal and not a civilized origin and was outside the boundaries of the Roman Empire and of the Latin language were two of the factors which led Germany ultimately to 1945. The Germanic tribe gave security and meaning to each individual's life to a degree where it almost absorbed the individual in the group, as tribes usually do. It gave security because it protected the individual in a social status of *known* and relatively stable social relationships with his fellows; it gave meaning because it was all-absorbing—totalitarian, if you will, in that it satisfied almost all an individual's needs in a single system.

The shattering of the Germanic tribe in the period of the migrations, fifteen hundred years ago, and the exposure of its members to a higher, but equally total and equally satisfying, social structure—the Roman imperial system; and the subsequent, almost immediately subsequent, shattering of that Roman system caused a double trauma from which the Germans have not recovered even today. The shattering of the tribe left the individual German, as a similar experience today has left many Africans, in a chaos of unfamiliar experiences in which there was neither security nor meaning. When all other relationships had been destroyed, the German was left with only one human relationship on which he turned all his energy—loyalty to his immediate companions. But this could not carry all his life's energy or satisfy all of life's needs—no single human relationship ever can—and the effort to make it do so can

409

only turn it into a monstrosity. But the German tribesman of the sixth century, when all else was shattered, made such an effort and tried to build all security and all meaning on personal loyalty. Any violence, any criminal act, any bestiality was justified for the sake of the allegiance of personal loyalty. The result is to be seen in the earliest work of Germanic literature—the *Niebelungenlied*, a madhouse dominated by this one mood, in a situation not totally unlike the Germany of 1945.

Into the insanity of monomania created by the shattering of the Germanic tribes came the sudden recognition of a better system, which could be, they thought, equally secure, equally meaningful, because equally total. This was symbolized by the word *Rome*. It is almost impossible for us, of the West and of today, imbued as we are with historical perspective and individualism, to see what Classical culture was like, and why it appealed to the Germans. Both may be summed up in the word "total." The Greek *polis*, like the Roman *imperium*, was total. We in the West have escaped the fascination of totalitarianism because we have in our tradition other elements—the refusal of the Hebrews to confuse God with the world, or religion with the state, and the realization that God is transcendental, and, accordingly, all other things must be, in some degree, incomplete and thus imperfect. We also have, in our tradition, Christ, who stood apart from the state and told his followers to "Render to Caesar the things which are Caesar's." And we have in our tradition the church of the catacombs, where clearly human values were neither united nor total, and were opposed to the state. The Germans, as later the Russians, escaped the full influence of these elements in the tradition of the West. The Germans and the Russians knew Rome only in its post-Constantine phase when the Christian emperors were seeking to preserve the totalitarian system of Dioclesian, but in a Christian rather than a pagan totalitarianism. This was the system the detribalized Germans glimpsed just before it also was shattered. They saw it as a greater, larger, more powerful entity than the tribe but with the same elements which they wanted to preserve from their tribal past. They yearned to become part of that imperial totalitarianism. They still yearn for it. Theodoric, the Ostrogoth (Roman Emperor, 489–526), saw himself as a Germanic Constantine. The Germans continued their refusal to accept this second loss, as the Latins and the Celts were prepared to do, and for the next thousand years the Germans made every effort to reconstruct the Christian *imperium*, under Charles V (Holy Roman Emperor, 1519–1555) as under Theodoric. The German continued to dream of that glimpse he had had of the imperial system before it sank—one, universal, total, holy, eternal, imperial, Roman. He refused to accept that it was gone, hating the small group who opposed its revival and despising the great mass who did not care, while regarding himself as the sole defender of values and righteousness who was prepared to sacrifice anything to restore that dream on earth. Only Charlemagne (died 814) came close to achieving that dream, Barbarossa, Charles V, William II, or even Hitler being but pale imitations. After Charlemagne, the state and public authority vanished in the Dark Ages, while society and the Church survived. When the state began to revive at the end of the tenth century, it was obviously a separate entity from the Church or society. The totalitarian *imperium* had been permanently broken *in the West* into two, and later many, allegiances. During the split in the Dark Ages of the single entity which was simultaneously Holy Roman, Catholic, Universal, and Imperial, the adjectives became displaced from the nouns to leave a Universal Catholic Church and a Holy Roman Empire. The former still survives, but the latter was ended by Napoleon in 1806, a thousand years after Charlemagne.

During that thousand years, the West developed a pluralistic system in which the individual was the ultimate good (and the ultimate philosophic reality), faced with the need to choose among many conflicting allegiances. Germany was dragged along in the same process, but unwillingly, and continued to yearn for a single allegiance which would be totally absorbing. This desire appeared in many Germanic traits, of which one was a continued love affair with Greece and Rome. Even today a Classical scholar does more of his reading in German than in any other language, although he rarely recognizes that he does so because the appeal of Classical culture to the Germans rested on its totalitarian nature, recognized by Germans but generally ignored by Westerners.

All the subsequent experiences of the German people, from the failure of Otto the Great in the tenth century to the failure of Hitler in the twentieth century, have served to perpetuate and perhaps to intensify the German thirst for the coziness of a totalitarian way of life. This is the key to German national character: in spite of all their talk of heroic behavior, what they have really wanted has been coziness, freedom from the need to make decisions which require an independent, self-reliant individual constantly exposed to the chilling breeze of numerous alternatives. Franz Grillparzer, the Austrian playwright, spoke like a true German when he said, a century ago, "The most difficult thing in the world is to make up one's mind." Decision, which requires the evaluation of alternatives, drives man to individualism, self-reliance, and rationalism, all hateful qualities to Germanism.

In spite of these desires of the Germans for the coziness of totalitarian oneness, they have been forced as part, even if a relatively peripheral part, of the West to live otherwise. Looking back, it seemed to Wagner that Germany came closest to its desires in the guild-dominated life of late medieval Augsburg; this is why his only happy opera was placed in that setting. But if Wagner is correct, the situation was achieved only briefly. The shift of world trade from Mediterranean and Baltic to the Atlantic destroyed the trans-Germanic commercial basis of German municipal guild life—a fact which Thomas Mann still mourned in our own day. Almost immediately the spiritual unity of the Germans was shattered by the Protestant Reformation. When it became clear that no degree of violence could restore the old religious unity, the Germans, in the settlement of Augsburg (1555), came up with a typically German solution: individuals would be saved from the painful need to make a decision in religious belief by leaving the choice to the prince in each principality. This solution and the almost contemporary reception of the Roman Law were significant indications of the process by which the German municipalism of the late medieval period was replaced by the Germany of principalities (*Länder*) of modern times.

As a result of the loss of religious unity, the Germanies became divided into a Protestant northeast, increasingly dominated by the Hohenzollerns of Brandenburg-Prussia, and a Catholic southwest, increasingly dominated by the Habsburgs of Austria. Significantly enough, both of these began their dynastic rise as "marks," that is, frontier military outposts of Christian Germanism against pagan Slavdom of the East. Even when the Slav East became Christianized and, by copying Byzantium, obtained a society closer to the Germanic heart's desire than the West, the Germans could neither copy nor join the Slavs, because the Slavs, as outlanders from the tribe, were inferiors and hardly human beings at all. Even the Poles, who were more fully part of the West than the Germans, were regarded by the Germans as part of the outer darkness of Slavdom, and thus a threat to the still nonexistent Germanic tribal empire.

Germany's misfortunes culminated in the disasters of the seventeenth century when Richelieu, on behalf of France, used the internal problems of Germany in the Thirty Years' War (1618–1648) to play off one group against another, ensuring that the Habsburgs would never unify Germany, and dooming the Germanies to another two hundred years of disunity. Hitler, Bismarck, and even Kaiser William II could well be regarded as Germany's revenge on France for Richelieu, Louis XIV, and Napoleon. In an exposed position in central Europe, Germany found herself trapped between France, Russia, and the Habsburg dominions and was unable to deal with her basic problems in her own fashion and on their merits. Accordingly, Germany obtained national unity only late and "by blood and iron," and never obtained democracy at all. It might be added that she also failed to achieve laissez faire or liberalism for the same reasons. In most countries democracy was achieved by the middle classes, supported by peasants and workers, in an attack on the monarchy supported by the bureaucracy and landed aristocracy. In Germany this combination never quite came off, because these various groups were reluctant to clash with one another in the face of their threatening neighbors. Instead, Germany's exposed frontiers made it necessary for the various groups to subordinate their mutual antagonisms and obtain unification at the price of a sacrifice of democracy, laissez faire, liberalism, and nonmaterial values. Unification for Germany was achieved in the nineteenth century, not by embracing but by repudiating the typical nineteenth-century values. Starting as a reaction against the assault of Napoleon in 1806, and repudiating the rationalism, cosmopolitanism, and humanitarianism of the Enlightenment, Germany achieved unity only by the following processes:

1. by strengthening the monarchy and its bureaucracy;
2. by strengthening the permanent, professional army;
3. by preserving the landlord class (the Junkers) as a source of personnel for both bureaucracy and army;
4. by strengthening the industrial class through direct and indirect state subsidy, but never giving it a vital voice in state policy;
5. by appeasing the peasants and workers through paternalistic economic and social grants rather than by the extension of political rights which would allow these groups to assist themselves.

The long series of failures by the Germans to obtain the society they wanted served only to intensify their desire for it. They wanted a cozy society with both security and meaning, a totalitarian structure which would be at the same time universal and ultimate, and which would so absorb the individual in its structure that he would never need to make significant decisions for himself. Held in a framework of known, satisfying, personal relationships, such an individual would be safe because he would be surrounded by fellows equally satisfied with their own positions, each feeling important from his membership in the greater whole.

Although this social structure was never achieved in Germany, and never could be achieved, in view of the dynamic nature of Western Civilization in which the Germans were a part, each German over the centuries has tried to create such a situation for himself in his immediate environment (at the minimum in his family or beer garden) or, failing that, has created German literature, music, drama, and art as vehicles of his protests at this lack. This desire has been evident in the Germans' thirst for status (which establishes his relationship with the whole) and for the absolute (which gives *unchanging* meaning to the whole).

The German thirst for status is entirely different from the American desire for status. The American is driven by the desire to get ahead, that is, to change his status; he wants status and status symbols to exist as clear evidence or even measures of the speed with which he is changing his status. The German wants status as a nexus of obvious relationships around himself so there will never be doubt in anyone's mind where he stands, stationary, in the system. He wants status because he dislikes changes, because he abhors the need to make decisions. The American thrives on change, novelty, and decisions. Strangely enough, both react in this opposite fashion for somewhat similar reasons based on the inadequate maturation and integration of the individual's personality. The American seeks change, as the German seeks *external* fixed relationships, as a distraction from the lack of integration, self-sufficiency, and internal resources of the individual himself.

The German wants status reflected in obvious external symbols so that his nexus of personal relationships will be clear to everyone he meets and so that he will be treated accordingly, and almost automatically (without need for painful decisions). He wants titles, uniforms, nameplates, flags, buttons, anything which will make his position clear to all. In every German organization, be it business, school, army, church, social club, or family, there are ranks, gradations, and titles. No German could be satisfied with just his name on a calling card or on the nameplate of his doorway. His calling card must also have his address, his titles, and his educational achievements. The great anthropologist Robert H. Lowie tells of men with two doctorate degrees whose nameplates have "Professor Dr. Dr. So-and-So," for all the world to see their double academic status. The emphasis on minor gradations of rank and class, with titles, is a reflection of Germanic particularism, just as the verbal insistence on the absolute is a reflection of German universalism which must give meaning to the system as a whole.

In this system the German feels it necessary to proclaim his position by verbal loudness which may seem boastful to outsiders, just as his behavior toward his superiors and inferiors in his personal relationships seems to an Englishman to be either fawning or bullying. All three of these are acceptable to his fellow Germans, who are as eager to see these indications of his status as he is to show them. All these reactions, criticized by German thinkers like Kant as craving for precedence, and satirized in German literature for the last two centuries, have been the essential tissue of the personal relationships which make up German life. The correct superscription on an envelope, we are told, would be "Herrn Hofrat Professor Dr. Siegfried Harnischfeger." These pomposities are used in speech as well as in writing, and are applied to the individual's wife as well as to himself.

Such emphasis on position, precedence, titles, gradations, and fixed relationships, especially up and down, are so typically German that the German is most at home in hierarchical situations such as a military, ecclesiastical, or educational organization, and is often ill at ease in business or politics where status is less easy to establish and make obvious.

With this kind of nature and such neurological systems, Germans are

ill at ease with equality, democracy, individualism, freedom, an
features of modern life. Their neurological systems were a con'
of the coziness of German childhood, which, contrary to popular impression, was not a condition of misery and personal cruelty (as it often
is in England), but a warm, affectionate, and externally disciplined
situation of secure relationships. After all, Santa Claus and the child-
centered Christmas is Germanic. This is the situation the adult German,
face to face with what seems an alien world, is constantly seeking to
recapture. To the German it is *Gemütlichkeit*; but to outsiders it may
be suffocating. In any case it gives rise among adult Germans to two
additional traits of German character: the need for external discipline
and the quality of egocentricity.

The Englishman is disciplined from within so that he takes his self-
discipline, embedded in his neurological system, with him wherever
he goes, even to situations where all the external forms of discipline are
lacking. As a consequence the Englishman is the most completely socialized of Europeans, as the Frenchman is the most completely civilized,
the Italian most completely gregarious, or the Spaniard most completely
individualistic. But the German by seeking external discipline shows his
unconscious desire to recapture the externally disciplined world of his
childhood. With such discipline he may be the best behaved of citizens,
but without it he may be a beast.

A second notable carryover from childhood to adult German life
was egocentricity. The whole world seems to any child to revolve around
it, and most societies have provided ways in which the adolescent is
disabused of this error. The German leaves childhood so abruptly that
he rarely learns this fact of the universe, and spends the rest of his life
creating a network of established relationships centering on himself.
Since this is his aim in life, he sees no need to make any effort to see
anything from any point of view other than his own. The consequence
is a most damaging inability to do this. Each class or group is totally
unsympathetic to any point of view except the egocentric one of the
viewer himself. His union, his company, his composer, his poet, his
party, his neighborhood are the best, almost the only acceptable, examples of the class, and all others must be denigrated. As part of this
process a German usually chooses for himself his favorite flower, musical
composition, beer, club, painting, or opera, and sees little value or
merit in any other. Yet at the same time he insists that his myopic or
narrow-angled vision of the universe must be universalized, because no
people are more insistent on the role of the absolute or the universal
as the framework of their own egocentricity. One deplorable consequence of this has been the social animosities rampant in a Germany
which has loudly proclaimed its rigid solidarity.

With an individual personality structure such as this, the German was painfully uncomfortable in the totally different, and to him totally unfriendly, world of nineteenth-century individualism, liberalism, competitive atomism, democratic equality, and self-reliant dynamicism. And the German was doubly uncomfortable and embittered by 1860 to see the power, wealth, and national unity which these nineteenth-century traits had brought to Britain and France. The late arrival of these achievements, especially national unity and industrialism, in Germany left the average German with a feeling of inferiority in respect to England. Few Germans were willing to compete as individuals with British businessmen. Accordingly, the newly unified German government was expected to help German industrialists with tariffs, credit, price and production controls, cheaper labor costs, and such. As a consequence Germany never had a clearly competitive, liberal economy like the Western Powers.

The failure to achieve democracy was reflected in public law. The German Parliament was more of an advisory than a legislative body; the judiciary was not under popular control; and the executive (the chancellor and the Cabinet) were responsible to the emperor rather than to Parliament. Moreover, the constitution, because of a peculiar suffrage system, was weighted to give undue importance to Prussia (which was the stronghold of the army, the landlords, the bureaucracy, and the industrialists). Within Prussia the elections were weighted to give undue influence to these same groups. Above all, the army was subject to no democratic or even governmental control, but was dominated by the Prussian Officers' Corps whose members were recruited by regimental election. This Officers' Corps thus came to resemble a fraternity rather than an administrative or professional organization.

By 1890, when he retired from office, Bismarck had built up an unstable balance of forces within Germany similar to the unstable balance of powers which he had established in Europe as a whole. His cynical and materialistic view of human motivations had driven all idealistic and humanitarian forces from the German political scene and had remodeled the political parties almost completely into economic and social pressure groups which he played off, one against another. The chief of these forces were the landlords (Conservative Party), the industrialists (National Liberal Party), the Catholics (Center Party), and the workers (Social Democratic Party). In addition, the army and the bureaucracy were expected to be politically neutral, but they did not hesitate to exert pressures on the government without the intermediary of any political party. Thus there existed a precarious and dangerous balance of forces which only a genius could manipulate. Bismarck was followed by no genius. The Kaiser, William II (1888-1918), was an incapable neurotic, and the system of recruitment to government service was such as to exclude any but mediocrities. As a result, the precarious structure left by Bismarck was not managed but was merely hidden from public view by a facade of nationalistic, antiforeign, anti-Semitic, imperialistic, and chauvinistic propaganda of which the emperor was the center.

The dichotomy in Germany between appearance and reality, between propaganda and structure, between economic prosperity and political and social weakness was put to the test in World War I, and failed completely. The events of 1914–1919 revealed that Germany was not a democracy in which all men were legally equal. Instead, the ruling groups formed some strange animal lording it over a host of lesser animals. In this strange creature the monarchy represented the body, which was supported by four legs: the army, the landlords, the bureaucracy, and the industrialists.

This glimpse of reality was not welcome to any important group in Germany, with the result that it was covered over, almost at once, by another misleading facade: the "revolution" of 1918 was not really a revolution at all, because it did not radically change this situation; it removed the monarchy, but it left the quartet of legs.

This Quartet was not the creation of a moment, rather it was the result of a long process of development whose last stages were reached only in the twentieth century. In these last stages the industrialists were adopted into the ruling clique by conscious acts of agreement. These acts culminated in the years 1898–1905 in a deal by which the Junkers accepted the industrialists' navy-building program (which they detested) in return for the industrialists' acceptance of the Junkers' high tariff on grains. The Junkers were anti-navy because they, with their few numbers and close alliance with the army, were opposed to any venture into the fields of colonialism or overseas imperialism, and were determined not to jeopardize Germany's continental position by alienating England. In fact, the policy of the Junkers was not only a continental one; on the Continent it was *klein-deutsch*. This expression meant that they were not eager to include the Germans of Austria within Germany because such an increment of Germans would dilute the power of the small group of Junkers inside Germany. Instead, the Junkers would have preferred to annex the non-German areas to the east in order to obtain additional land and a supply of cheap Slav agricultural labor. The Junkers wanted agricultural tariffs to raise the prices of their crops, especially rye and, later, sugar beets. The industrialists objected to tariffs on food because high food prices made necessary high wages, which they opposed. On the other hand, the industrialists wanted high industrial prices and a market for the products of heavy industry. The former they obtained by the creation of cartels after 1888; the latter they obtained by the naval-building program and armaments expansion after 1898. The Junkers agreed to these only in return for a tariff on food which eventually, through "import certificates," became a subsidy for growing rye. This alliance, of which Bülow was the creator, was agreed

on in May 1900, and consummated in December 1902. The tariff of
1902, which gave Germany one of the most protected agricultures in
the world, was the price paid by industry for the Navy bill of 1900,
and, symbolically enough, could be passed through the Reichstag only
after the rules of procedure were violated to gag the opposition.

The Quartet was not Conservative but, potentially at least, revolutionary reactionaries. This is true at least of the landlords and
industrialists, somewhat less true of the bureaucracy, and least true of the
army. The landlords were revolutionary because they were driven to
desperation by the persistent agricultural crisis which made it difficult
for a high-cost area like eastern Germany to compete with a low-cost
area like the Ukraine or high-productivity areas like Canada, Argentina,
or the United States. Even in isolated Germany they had difficulty in
keeping down the wages of German agricultural labor or in obtaining
agricultural credit. The former problem rose from the need to compete
with the industrial wages of West Germany. The credit problem rose
because of the endemic lack of capital in Germany, the need to compete with industry for the available supply of capital, and the impossibility of raising capital by mortgages where estates were entailed. As
a result of these influences, the landlords, overburdened with debts, in
great jeopardy from any price decline, and importers of unorganized
Slav laborers, dreamed of conquests of lands and labor in eastern Europe.
The industrialists were in a similar plight, caught between the high
wages of unionized German labor and the limited market for industrial
products. To increase the supply of both labor and markets, they hoped
for an active foreign policy which would bring into one unit a Pan-
German bloc, if not a Mittel-europa. The bureaucracy, for ideological,
especially nationalist, reasons, shared these dreams of conquest. Only
the army hung back under the influence of the Junkers, who saw how
easily they, as a limited political and social power, could be overwhelmed
in a Mittel-europa or even a Pan-Germania. Accordingly, the Prussian
Officers' Corps had little interest in these Germanic dreams, and looked
with favor on the conquest of Slav areas only if this could be accomplished without undue expansion of the army itself.

The Weimar Republic

The essence of German history from 1918 to 1933 can be found in
the statement *There was no revolution in 1918*. For there to have been
a revolution it would have been necessary to liquidate the Quartet or,
at least, subject them to democratic control. The Quartet represented

the real power in Germany society because they represented the forces of public order (army and bureaucracy) and of economic production (landlords and industrialists). Even without a liquidation of this Quartet, it might have been possible for democracy to function in the interstices between them if they had quarreled among themselves. They did not quarrel, because they had an *esprit de corps* bred by years of service to a common system (the monarchy) and because, in many cases, the same individuals were to be found in two or even more of the four groups. Franz von Papen, for example, was a Westphalian noble, a colonel in the army, an ambassador, and a man with extensive industrial holdings, derived from his wife, in the Saarland.

Although there was no revolution—that is, no real shift in the control of power in Germany in 1919—there was a legal change. In law, a democratic system was set up. As a result, by the late 1920's there had appeared an obvious discrepancy between law and fact—the regime, according to the law, being controlled by the people, while in fact it was controlled by the Quartet. The reasons for this situation are important.

The Quartet, with the monarchy, made the war of 1914–1918, and were incapable of winning it. As a result, they were completely discredited and deserted by the soldiers and workers. Thus, the masses of the people completely renounced the old system in November 1918. The Quartet, however, was not liquidated, for several reasons:

1. They were able to place the blame for the disaster on the monarchy, and jettisoned this to save themselves;
2. most Germans accepted this as an adequate revolution;
3. the Germans hesitated to make a real revolution for fear it would lead to an invasion of Germany by the French, the Poles, or others;
4. many Germans were satisfied with the creation of a government which was democratic in form and made little effort to examine the underlying reality;
5. the only political party capable of directing a real revolution was the Social Democrats, who had opposed the Quartet system and the war itself, at least in theory; but this party was incapable of doing anything in the crisis of 1918 because it was hopelessly divided into doctrinaire cliques, was horrified at the danger of Soviet Bolshevism, and was satisfied that order, trade-unionism, and a "democratic" regime were more important than Socialism, humanitarian welfare, or consistency between theory and action.

Before 1914 there were two parties which stood outside the Quartet system: the Social Democrats and the Center (Catholic) Party. The former was doctrinaire in its attitude, being anticapitalist, pledged to the international brotherhood of labor, pacifist, democratic, and Marxist in an evolutionary, but not revolutionary, sense. The Center Party, like the Catholics who made it up, came from all levels of society and all shades of ideology, but in practice were frequently opposed to the Quartet on specific issues.

These two opposition parties underwent considerable change during the war. The Social Democrats always opposed the war in theory, but supported it on patriotic grounds by voting for credits to finance the war. Its minute Left wing refused to support the war even in this fashion as early as 1914. This extremist group, under Karl Liebknecht and Rosa Luxemburg, became known as the Spartacist Union and (after 1919) as the Communists. These extremists wanted an immediate and complete Socialist revolution with a soviet form of government. More moderate than the Spartacists was another group calling itself Independent Socialists. These voted war credits until 1917 when they refused to continue to do so and broke from the Social Democratic Party. The rest of the Social Democrats supported the war and the old monarchial system until November 1918 in fact, but in theory embraced an extreme type of evolutionary Socialism.

The Center Party was aggressive and nationalist until 1917 when it became pacifist. Under Matthias Erzberger it allied with the Social Democrats to push through the Reichstag Peace Resolution of July 1917. The position of these various groups on the issue of aggressive nationalism was sharply revealed in the voting to ratify the Treaty of Brest-Litovsk imposed by the militarists, Junkers, and industrialists on a prostrate Russia. The Center Party voted to ratify; the Social Democrats abstained from voting; the Independents voted No.

The "revolution" of November 1918 would have been a real revolution except for the opposition of the Social Democrats and the Center Party, for the Quartet in the crucial days of November and December 1918 were discouraged, discredited, and helpless. Outside the Quartet itself there was, at that time and even later, only two small groups which could possibly have been used by the Quartet as rallying points about which could have been formed some mass support for the Quartet. These two small groups were the "indiscriminate nationalists" and the "mercenaries." The indiscriminate nationalists were those men, like Hitler, who were not able to distinguish between the German nation and the old monarchial system. These persons, because of their loyalty to the nation, were eager to rally to the support of the Quartet, which they regarded as identical with the nation. The mercenaries were a larger group who had no particular loyalty to anyone or to any idea but were willing to serve any group which could pay for such service. The only groups able to pay were two of the Quartet—the Officers' Corps and the industrialists—who organized many mercenaries into reactionary armed bands or "Free Corps" in 1918-1923.

Instead of working for a revolution in 1918-1919, the two parties which dominated the situation—the Social Democrats and the Centrists—did all they could to prevent a revolution. They not only left the Quartet in their positions of responsibility and power—the landlords on their estates, the officers in their commands, the industrialists in control of their factories, and the bureaucracy in control of the police, the courts, and the administration—but they increased the influence of these groups because the actions of the Quartet were not restrained under the republic by that sense of honor or loyalty to the system which had restrained the use of their power under the monarchy.

As early as November 10, 1918, Friedrich Ebert, chief figure of the Social Democratic Party, made an agreement with the Officers' Corps in which he promised not to use the power of the new government to democratize the army if the officers would support the new government against the threat of the Independents and the Spartacists to establish a soviet system. As a consequence of this agreement Ebert kept a private telephone line from his office in the Chancellery to General Wilhelm Groener's office at the army's headquarters and consulted with the army on many critical political issues. As another consequence, Ebert and his Minister of War Gustav Noske, also a Social Democrat, used the army under its old monarchist officers to destroy the workers and radicals who sought to challenge the existing situation. This was done in Berlin in December 1918, in January 1919, and again in March 1919, and in other cities at other times. In these assaults the army had the pleasure of killing several thousand of the detested radicals.

A somewhat similar antirevolutionary agreement was made between heavy industry and the Socialist trade unions on November 11, 1918. On that day Hugo Stinnes, Albert Vögler, and Alfred Hugenberg, representing industry, and Carl Legien, Otto Hue, and Hermann Müller representing the unions, signed an agreement to support each other in order to keep the factories functioning. Although this agreement was justified on opportunist grounds, it clearly showed that the so-called Socialists were not interested in economic or social reform but were merely interested in the narrow trade-union objectives of wages, hours, and working conditions. It was this narrow range of interests which ultimately destroyed the average German's faith in the Socialists or their unions.

The history of the period from 1918 to 1933 cannot be understood without some knowledge of the chief political parties. There were almost forty parties, but only seven or eight were important. These were, from extreme Left to extreme Right, as follows:

1. Spartacist Union (or Communist—KPD)
2. Independent Socialist (USPD)
3. Social Democrats (SPD)

4. Democratic
5. Center (including Bavarian People's Party)
6. People's Party
7. Nationalists
8. "Racists" (including Nazis)

Of these parties only the Democrats had any sincere and consistent belief in the democratic Republic. On the other hand the Communists, Independents, and many of the Social Democrats on the Left, as well as the "Racists," Nationalists, and many of the People's Party on the Right, were adverse to the Republic, or at best ambivalent. The Catholic Center Party, being formed on a religious rather than on a social basis, had members from all areas of the political and social spectrum.

The political history of Germany from the armistice of 1918 to the arrival of Hitler to the chancellorship in January 1933 can be divided into three periods, thus:

Period of Turmoil   1918–1924
Period of Fulfillment   1924–1930
Period of Disintegration   1930–1933

During this span of over fourteen years, there were eight elections, in none of which did a single party obtain a majority of the seats in the Reichstag. Accordingly, every German Cabinet of the period was a coalition. The following table gives the results of these eight elections:

PARTY	JAN. 1919	JUNE 1920	MAY 1924	DEC. 1924	MAY 1928	JULY 1930	SEPT. 1932	NOV. 1932	MARCH 1933
Communist	0	4	62	45	54	77	89	100	81
Independent Socialist	22	84							
Social Democrats	163	102	100	131	153	143	133	121	120
Democrats	75	39	28	32	25	20	4	2	5
Center	91	64	65	69	62	68	75	70	74
Bavarian People's		21	16	19	16	19	22	20	18
Economic Party	4	4	10	17	25	23	2	0	0
German People's Party	19	65	45	51	45	30	7	11	2
Nationalists	44	71	95	103	73	41	37	52	52
Nazis	0	0	32	14	12	107	230	196	288

On the basis of these elections Germany had twenty major Cabinet changes from 1919 to 1933. Generally these Cabinets were constructed about the Center and Democratic parties with the addition of representatives from either the Social Democrats or the People's Party. On only two occasions (Gustav Stresemann in 1923 and Hermann Müller in

1928–1930) was it possible to obtain a Cabinet broad enough to include all four of these parties. Moreover, the second of these broadfront Cabinets was the only Cabinet after 1923 to include the Socialists and the only Cabinet after 1925 which did not include the Nationalists. This indicates clearly the drift to the Right in the German government after the resignation of Joseph Wirth in November 1922. This drift, as we shall see, was delayed by only two influences: the need for foreign loans and political concessions from the Western Powers and the recognition that both of these could be obtained better by a government which seemed to be republican and democratic in inclination than by a government which was obviously hand in glove with the Quartet.

At the end of the war in 1918 the Socialists were in control, not because the Germans were Socialistic (for the party was not really Socialist) but because this was the only party which had been traditionally in opposition to the imperial system. A committee of six men was set up: three from the Social Democrats (Ebert, Philip Scheidemann, and Otto Landsberg) and three from the Independent Socialists (Hugo Haase, Wilhelm Dittman, and Emil Barth). This group ruled as a sort of combined emperor and chancellor and had the regular secretaries of state as their subordinates. These men did nothing to consolidate the republic or democracy and were opposed to any effort to take any steps toward Socialism. They even refused to nationalize the coal industry, something which was generally expected. Instead they wasted the opportunity by busying themselves with typical trade-union problems such as the eight-hour day (November 12, 1918) and collective bargaining methods (December 23, 1918).

The critical problem was the form of government, with the choice resting between workers' and peasants' councils (soviets), already widely established, and a national assembly to set up an ordinary parliamentary system. The Socialist group preferred the latter, and were willing to use the regular army to enforce this choice. On this basis a counter-revolutionary agreement was made between Ebert and the General Staff. As a consequence of this agreement, the army attacked a Spartacist parade in Berlin on December 6, 1918, and liquidated the rebellious People's Naval Division on December 24, 1918. In protest at this violence the three Independent members of the government resigned. Their example was followed by other Independents throughout Germany, with the exception of Kurt Eisner in Munich. The next day the Spartacists formed the German Communist Party with a nonrevolutionary program. Their declaration read, in part: "The Spartacist Union will never assume governmental power except in response to the plain and unmistakable wish of the great majority of the proletarian masses in Germany; and only as a result of a definite agreement of these masses with the aims and methods of the Spartacist Union."

This pious expression, however, was the program of the leaders; the masses of the new party, and possibly the members of the Independent Socialist group as well, were enraged at the conservatism of the Social Democrats and began to get out of hand. The issue was joined on the question of councils versus National Assembly. The government, under Noske's direction, used regular troops in a bloody suppression of the Left (January 5-15), ending up with the murder of Rosa Luxemburg and Karl Liebknecht, the Communist leaders. The result was exactly as the Quartet wanted: the Communists and many non-Communist workers were permanently alienated from the Socialists and from the parliamentary republic. The Communist Party, deprived of leaders of its own, became a tool of Russian Communism. As a result of this repression, the army was able to disarm the workers at the very moment when it was beginning to arm reactionary private bands (Free Corps) of the Right. Both of these developments were encouraged by Ebert and Noske.

Only in Bavaria was the alienation of Communist and Socialist and the disarmament of the former not carried out; Kurt Eisner, the Independent Socialist minister-president in Munich, prevented it. Accordingly, Eisner was murdered by Count Anton von Arco-Valley on February 21, 1919. When the workers of Munich revolted, they were crushed by a combination of regular army and Free Corps amid scenes of horrible violence from both sides. Eisner was replaced as premier by a Social Democrat, Adolph Hoffman. Hoffman, on the night of March 13, 1920, was thrown out by a military coup which replaced him by a government of the Right under Gustav von Kahr.

In the meantime, the National Assembly elected on June 19, 1919, drew up a parliamentary constitution under the guidance of Professor Hugo Preuss. This constitution provided for a president elected for seven years to be head of the state, a bicameral legislature, and a Cabinet responsible to the lower house of the legislature. The upper house, or Reichsrat, consisted of representatives of eighteen German states and had, in legislative matters, a suspensive veto which could be overcome by a two-thirds vote of the lower chamber. This lower chamber, or Reichstag, had 608 members, elected by a system of proportional representation on a party basis. The head of the government, to whom the president gave a mandate to form a Cabinet, was called the chancellor. The chief weaknesses of the constitution were the provisions for proportional representation and other provisions, by articles 25 and 48, which allowed the president to suspend constitutional guarantees and rule by decree, in periods of "national emergency." As early as 1925 the parties of the Right were planning to destroy the republic by the use of these powers.

A direct challenge to the republic from the Right came in March 1920, when Captain Ehrhardt's Brigade of the Free Corps marched into Berlin, forced the government to flee to Dresden, and set up a government under Wolfgang Kapp, an ultranationalist. Kapp was supported by the army commander in the Berlin area, Baron Walther von Lüttwitz, who became *Reichswehr* minister in Kapp's government. Since General Hans von Seeckt, chief of staff, refused to support the legal government, it was helpless, and was saved only by a general strike of the workers in Berlin and a great proletarian rising in the industrial regions of western Germany. The Kapp government was unable to function, and collapsed, while the army proceeded to violate the territorial disarmament clauses of the Treaty of Versailles by invading the Ruhr in order to crush the workers' uprising in that area. Seeckt was rewarded for his noncooperation by being appointed commander in chief in May 1920.

As a consequence of these disturbances, the general election of July 1920 went against the "Weimar Coalition." A new government came in which was completely middle-class in its alignment, the Socialists of the Weimar Coalition being replaced by the party of big business, the German People's Party. Noske was replaced as Reichswehr minister by Otto Gessler, a willing tool of the Officers' Corps. Gessler, who held this critical position from March 1920 to January 1928, made no effort to subject the army to democratic, or even civilian, control, but cooperated in every way with Seeckt's secret efforts to evade the disarmament provisions of the peace treaties. German armaments factories were moved to Turkey, Russia, Sweden, the Netherlands, and Switzerland. German officers were drilled in prohibited weapons in Russia and China. Inside Germany, secret armaments were prepared on a considerable scale, and troops in excess of the treaty limits were organized in a "Black Reichswehr" which was supported by secret funds of the regular Reichswehr. The Reichstag had no control over either organization. When the Western Powers in 1920 demanded that the Free Corps be disbanded, these groups went underground and formed a parallel organization to the Black Reichswehr, being supplied with protection, funds, information, and arms from the Reichswehr and Conservatives. In return the Free Corps engaged in large-scale conspiracy and murder on behalf of the Conservatives. According to *The Times* of London, the Free Corps murdered four hundred victims of the Left and Center in one year.

The middle-class Cabinet of Konstantin Fehrenbach resigned on May 4, 1921 and allowed the Weimar Coalition of Socialists, Democrats, and Center to take office to receive the reparations ultimatum of the Allied governments on May 5th. Thus, the democratic regime was further discredited in the eyes of Germans as an instrument of weakness, hardship, and shame. As soon as the job was done, the Socialists were replaced by the People's Party, and the Wirth Cabinet was succeeded by a purely middle-class government under Wilhelm Cuno, general manager of the Hamburg-American Steamship Line. It was this government which "managed" the hyperinflation of 1923 and the passive resistance against the French forces in the Ruhr. The inflation, which was a great benefit to the Quartet, destroyed the economic position of the middle classes and lower middle classes and permanently alienated them from the republic.

The Cuno government was ended by a deal between Stresemann and the Socialists. The former, on behalf of the People's Party, which had hitherto been resolutely anti-republican, accepted the republic; the Socialists agreed to support a Stresemann Cabinet; and a broad coalition was formed for a policy of fulfillment of the Treaty of Versailles. This ended the Period of Turmoil (August 1923).

The Period of Fulfillment (1923–1930) is associated with the name of Gustav Stresemann, who was in every Cabinet until his death in October 1929. A reactionary Pan-German and economic imperialist in the period before 1919, Stresemann was always a supporter of the Quartet, and the chief creator of the German People's Party, the party of heavy industry. In 1923, while still keeping his previous convictions, he decided that it would be good policy to reverse them publicly and adopt a program of support for the republic and fulfillment of treaty obligations. He did this because he realized that Germany was too weak to do anything else and that she could get stronger only by obtaining release from the more stringent treaty restrictions, by foreign loans from sympathetic British and American financiers, and by secret consolidation of the Quartet. All these things could be achieved more easily by a policy of fulfillment than by a policy of resistance like Cuno's.

The Bavarian government of the Right, which had been installed under Gustav von Kahr in 1921, refused to accept Stresemann's decision to readmit the Socialists to the Reich government in Berlin. Instead, Kahr assumed dictatorial powers with the title of state commissioner of Bavaria. In reply the Stresemann Cabinet invested the executive power of the Reich in the Reichswehr minister, an act which had the effect of making von Seeckt the ruler of Germany. In terror of a rightist *coup d'état* (*putsch*), the Communist International decided to allow the German Communist Party to cooperate with the Socialists in an anti-Right front within the parliamentary regime. This was done at once in the states of Saxony and Thuringia. At this the Reichswehr commander in Bavaria, General Otto von Lossow, shifted his allegiance from Seeckt to Kahr. Stresemann-Seeckt in Berlin faced Kahr-Lossow in Munich with the "Red" governments of Saxony and Thuringia in between. The Reichswehr chiefly obeyed Berlin, while the Black Reichswehr and underground Free Corps (especially Ehrhardt's and Rossbach's) obeyed Munich. Kahr-Lossow, with the support of Hitler and Ludendorff, planned to invade Saxony and Thuringia, overthrow the Red governments on the pretext of suppressing Bolshevism, and then continue northward to overthrow the central government in Berlin. The Reich government headed this plot off by an illegal act: The Reichswehr forces of Seeckt overthrew the constitutional Red governments of Saxony and

Thuringia to anticipate Bavaria. As a result, Lossow and Kahr gave up the plans for revolt, while Hitler and Ludendorff refused to do so. By the "Beer-Hall" *Putsch* of November 8, 1923, Hitler and Ludendorff tried to abduct Kahr and Lossow and force them to continue the revolt. They were overcome in a blast of gunfire. Kahr, Lossow, and Ludendorff were never punished; Hermann Göring fled the country; Hitler and Rudolf Hess were given living quarters in a fortress for a year, profiting by the occasion to write the famous volume *Mein Kampf*.

In order to deal with the economic crisis and the inflation, Stresemann's government was granted dictatorial powers overriding all constitutional guarantees, except that the Socialists won a promise not to touch the eight-hour day or the social-insurance system. In this way the inflation was curbed, and a new monetary system was established; incidentally, the eight-hour day was abolished by decree (1923). A reparations agreement (the Dawes Plan) was made with the Allied governments, and the Ruhr was successfully evacuated. In the course of these events the Social Democrats abandoned the Stresemann government in protest at its illegal suppression of the Red government of Saxony, but the Stresemann program continued with the support of the parties of the Center and Right, including, for the first time, the support of the anti-Republican Nationalists. Indeed, the Nationalists with three or four seats in the Cabinet in 1926–1928 were the dominant force in the government, although they continued to protest in public against the policy of fulfillment, and Stresemann continued to pretend that his administration of that policy exposed him to imminent danger of assassination at the hands of the Right extremists.

The German Cabinets from 1923 to 1930, under Wilhelm Marx, Hans Luther, Marx again, and finally Hermann Müller, were chiefly concerned with questions of foreign policy, with reparations, evacuation of the occupied areas, disarmament agitation, Locarno, and the League of Nations. On the domestic front, just as significant events were going on but with much less fanfare. Much of the industrial system, as well as many public buildings, was reconstructed by foreign loans. The Quartet were secretly strengthened and consolidated by reorganization of the tax structure, by utilization of governmental subsidies, and by the training and rearrangement of personnel. Alfred Hugenberg, the most violent and irreconcilable member of the Nationalist Party, built up a propaganda system through his ownership of scores of newspapers and a controlling interest in Ufa, the great motion-picture corporation. By such avenues as this, a pervasive propaganda campaign, based on existing German prejudices and intolerances, was put on to prepare the way for a counter-revolution by the Quartet. This campaign sought to show that all Germany's problems and misfortunes were caused by the democratic and laboring groups, by the internationalists, and by the Jews.

The Center and Left shared this nationalist poison sufficiently to abstain from any effort to give the German people the true story of Germany's responsibility for the war and for her own hardships. Thus the Right was able to spread its own story of the war, that Germany had been overcome by "a stab in the back" from "the three Internationals": the "Gold" International of the Jews, the "Red" International of the Socialists, and the "Black" International of the Catholics, an unholy triple alliance which was symbolized in the gold, red, and black flag of the Weimar Republic. In this fashion every effort was made, and with considerable success, to divert popular animosity at the defeat of 1918 and the Versailles settlement from those who were really responsible to the democratic and republican groups. At the same time, German animosity against economic exploitation was directed away from the landlords and industrialists by racist doctrines which blamed all such problems on bad Jewish international bankers and department store owners.

The general nationalism of the German people, and their willingness to accept the propaganda of the Right, succeeded in making Field Marshal Paul von Hindenburg president of the republic in 1925. On the first ballot none of seven candidates received a majority of the total vote, so the issue went to the polls again. On the second ballot Hindenburg received 14,655,766 votes, Marx (of the Center Party) received 13,751,-615, while the Communist Ernst Thälmann received 1,931,151.

The victory of Hindenburg was a fatal blow to the republic. A mediocre military leader, and already on the verge of senility, the new president was a convinced antidemocrat and antirepublican. To bind his allegiance to the Quartet more closely, the landlords and industrialists took advantage of his eightieth birthday in 1927 to give him a Junker estate, Neudeck, in East Prussia. To avoid the inheritance tax, the deed to this estate was made out to the president's son, Colonel Oskar von Hindenburg. In time this estate came to be known as the "smallest concentration camp" in Germany, as the president spent his last years there cut off from the outside world by his senilities and a coterie of intriguers. These intriguers, who were able to influence the aged presidential mind in any direction they wished, consisted of Colonel Oskar, General Kurt von Schleicher, Dr. Otto Meissner, who remained head of the presidential office under Ebert, Hindenburg, and Hitler; and Elard von Oldenburg-Januschau who owned the estate next to Neudeck. This coterie was able to make and unseat Cabinets from 1930 to 1934, and controlled the use of the presidential power to rule by decree in that critical period.

No sooner did Hindenburg become a landlord in October 1927 than he began to mobilize government assistance for the landlords. This assistance, known as *Osthilfe* (Eastern Help), was organized by a joint session of the Reich and Prussian governments presided over by Hindenburg on December 21, 1927. The stated purpose of this assistance was to increase the economic prosperity of the regions east of the Elbe River in order to stop the migration of Germans from that area to western Germany and their replacement by Polish farm laborers. This assistance soon became a sink of corruption, the money being diverted in one way or another, legally or illegally, to subsidize the bankrupt great estates and the extravagances of the Junker landlords. It was the threat of public revelation of this scandal which was the immediate cause of the death of the Weimar Republic by Hindenburg's hand in 1932.

The combination of all of these events (the real power of the Quartet, the shortsighted and unprincipled opportunism of the Social Democrats and the Center Party, the coterie around Hindenburg, and the *Osthilfe* scandal) made possible the disintegration of the Weimar Republic in the years 1930–1933. The decision of the Quartet to attempt to establish a government satisfactory to themselves was made in 1929. The chief causes of the decision were (1) the realization that industrial plants had been largely rebuilt by foreign loans; (2) the knowledge that these foreign loans were now drying up and that, without them, neither reparations nor internal debts could be met except at a price which the Quartet was unwilling to pay; (3) the knowledge that the policy of fulfillment had accomplished about as much as could be expected from it, the Allied Control Missions having ended, rearmament having progressed as far as possible under the Versailles Treaty, the western frontier having been made secure, and the eastern frontier having been opened to German penetration.

The decision of the Quartet did not result from the economic crisis of 1929, but was made earlier in the year. This can be seen in the alliance of Hugenberg and Hitler to force a referendum on the Young Plan. The Quartet had accepted the much more severe Dawes Plan in 1924 because they were not then ready to destroy the Weimar regime. The challenge to the Young Plan not only indicated that they were ready; it also became an indication of their strength. This test was a disappointment, since they obtained only five million votes adverse to the plan from an electorate of 40 million. As a result, for the first time, the Nazis began a drive to build up a mass following. The moment for which they had been kept alive by the financial contributions of the Quartet had arrived. The effort would never have succeeded, however, were it not for the economic crisis. The intensity of this crisis can be measured by the number of Reichstag seats held by the Nazis:

APRIL 1924	DEC. 1924	1928	1930	JULY 1932	DEC. 1932	MARCH 1933
7	14	12	107	230	196	288

The Nazis were financed by the Black Reichswehr from 1919 to 1923; then this support ceased because of army disgust at the fiasco of the Munich *Putsch*. This lack of enthusiasm for the Nazis by the army continued for years. It was inspired by social snobbery and fears of the Nazi Storm Troops (SA) as a possible rival to itself. This diffidence on the part of the army was compensated by the support of the industrialists, who financed the Nazis from Hitler's exit from prison in 1924 to the end of 1932.

The destruction of the Weimar Republic has five stages:

> Brüning: March 27, 1930–May 30, 1932
> von Papen: May 31, 1932–November 17, 1932
> Schleicher: December 2, 1932–January 28, 1933
> Hitler: January 30, 1933–March 5, 1933
> Gleichschaltung: March 6, 1933–August 2, 1934

When the economic crisis began in 1929, Germany had a democratic government of the Center and Social Democratic parties. The crisis resulted in a decrease in tax receipts and a parallel increase in demands for government welfare services. This brought to a head the latent dispute over orthodox and unorthodox financing of a depression. Big business and big finance were determined to place the burden of the depression on the working classes by forcing the government to adopt a policy of deflation—that is, by wage reductions and curtailment of government expenditures. The Social Democrats wavered in their attitude, but in general were opposed to this policy. Schacht, as president of the Reichsbank, was able to force the Socialist Rudolf Hilferding out of the position of minister of finance by refusing bank credit to the government until this was done. In March 1930, the Center broke the coalition on the issue of reduction of unemployment benefits, the Socialists were thrown out of the government, and Heinrich Brüning, leader of the Center Party, came in as chancellor. Because he did not have a majority in the Reichstag, he had to put the deflationary policy into effect by the use of presidential decree under Article 48. This marked the end of the Weimar Republic, for it had never been intended that this "emergency clause" should be used in the ordinary process of government, although it had been used by Ebert in 1923 to abolish the eight-hour day. When the Reichstag condemned Brüning's method by a vote of 236 to 221 on July 18, 1930, the chancellor dissolved it and called for new elections. The results of these were contrary to his hopes, since he lost seats both to the Right and to the Left. On his Right were 148 seats (107 Nazis and 41 Nationalists); on his Left were 220 seats (77 Communists and 143 Socialists). The Socialists permitted Brüning to remain in office by refusing to vote on a motion of no confidence. Left in office, Brüning continued the deflationary policy by decrees which Hindenburg signed. Thus, in effect, Hindenburg was the ruler of Germany, since he could dismiss or name any chancellor, or could permit one to govern by his own power of decree.

Brüning's policy of deflation was a disaster. The suffering of the people was terrible, with almost eight million unemployed out of twenty-five million employable. To compensate for this unpopular domestic policy, Brüning adopted a more aggressive foreign policy, on such questions as reparations, union with Austria, or the World Disarmament Conference.

In the crisis of 1929–1933, the bourgeois parties tended to dissolve to the profit of the extreme Left and the extreme Right. In this the Nazi Party profited more than the Communists for several reasons: (1) it had the financial support of the industrialists and landlords; (2) it was not internationalist, but nationalist, as any German party had to be; (3) it had never compomised itself by accepting the republic even temporarily, an advantage when most Germans tended to blame the republic for their troubles; (4) it was prepared to use violence, while the parties of the Left, even the Communists, were legalistic and relatively peaceful, because the police and judges were of the Right. The reasons why the Nazis, rather than the Nationalists, profited by the turn from moderation could be explained by the fact that (1) the Nationalists had compromised themselves and vacillated on every issue from 1924 to 1929, and (2) the Nazis had an advantage in that they were not clearly a party of the Right but were ambiguous; in fact, a large group of Germans considered the Nazis a revolutionary Left party differing from the Communists only in being patriotic.

In this polarization of the political spectrum it was the middle classes which became unanchored, driven by desperation and panic. The Social Democrats were sufficiently fortified by trade unionism, and the Center Party members were sufficiently fortified by religion to resist the drift to extremism. Unfortunately, both these relatively stable groups lacked intelligent leadership and were too wedded to old ideas and narrow interests to find any appeal broad enough for a wide range of German voters.

The whole of 1932 was filled with a series of intrigues and distrustful, shifting alliances among the various groups which sought to get into a position to use the presidential power of decree. On October 11, 1931, a great reactionary alliance was made of the Nazis, the Nationalists, the Stahlhelm (a militaristic veterans' organization), and the Junker *Landbund*. This so-called "Harzburg Front" pretended to be a unified opposition to Communism, but really represented part of the intrigue of these various groups to come to power. Of the real rulers of Germany, only the Westphalian industrialists and the army were absent. The industrialists were taken into camp by Hitler during a three-hour speech which he made at the Industrial Club of Düsseldorf at the invitation of Fritz Thyssen (January 27, 1932). The army could not be brought into line, since it was controlled by the presidential coterie, especially Schleicher and Hindenburg himself. Schleicher had political ambitions of his own, and the army traditionally would not commit itself in any open or formal fashion.

In the middle of this crisis came the presidential election of March–April 1932. It offered a fantastic sight of a nominally democratic republic forced to choose its president from among four antidemocratic, antirepublican figures of which one (Hitler) had become a German citizen only a month previously by a legal trick. Since Hindenburg appeared as the least impossible of the four, he was reelected on the second ballot:

	First Ballot	Second Ballot
Hindenburg	18,661,736	19,359,533
Hitler, Nazi	11,338,571	13,418,051
Thälmann, Communist	4,982,079	3,706,655
Düsterberg, Stahlhelm	2,557,876	

Hindenburg continued to support Brüning until the end of May 1932, when he dismissed him and put in Von Papen. This was done at the instigation of Von Schleicher who was hoping to build up some kind of broad-front coalition of nationalists and workers as a facade for the Reichswehr. In this plan Schleicher was able to get Hindenburg to abandon Brüning by persuading him that the chancellor was planning to break up some of the bankrupt large estates east of the Elbe and might even investigate the *Osthilfe* scandals. Schleicher put in Papen as chancellor in the belief that Papen had so little support in the country that he would be completely dependent on Schleicher's ability to control Hindenburg. Instead, the president became so fond of Papen that the new chancellor was able to use Hindenburg's power directly, and even began to undermine the influence of Schleicher in the president's entourage.

Papen's "Cabinet of the barons" was openly a government of the Quartet and had almost no support in the Reichstag and little support in the country. Papen and Schleicher realized that it could not last long. Each began to form a plot to consolidate himself and stop the polarization of political opinion in Germany. Papen's plot was to cut off the financial contributions from industry to Hitler and break down the Nazi Party's independence by a series of expensive elections. The chancellor felt sure that Hitler would be willing to come into a Cabinet of which Papen was head in order to recover the financial contributions from industry and prevent the disruption of his party. Schleicher, on the other hand, hoped to unite the Left wing of the Nazi Party under Otto Strasser with the Christian and Socialist labor unions to support the Reichswehr in a program of nationalism and unorthodox finance. Both plots depended on retaining the favor of Hindenburg in order to retain control of the army and of the presidential power to issue decrees. In this, Papen was more successful than Schleicher, for the aged president had no liking for any unorthodox economic schemes.

Papen's plot developed more rapidly than Schleicher's and appeared more hopeful because of his greater ability to control the president. Having persuaded his close friends, the industrialists, to stop their contributions to the Nazis, Papen called a new election for November 1932. In the balloting the Nazis were reduced from 230 to 196 seats, while the Communists were increased from 89 to 100. The tide had turned. This had three results: (1) Hitler decided to join a coalition government, which he had previously refused; (2) the Quartet decided to overthrow the republic in order to stop the swing to the Communists; and (3) the Quartet, especially the industrialists, decided that Hitler had learned a lesson and could safely be put into office as the figurehead of a Right government because he was growing weaker. The whole deal was arranged by Papen, himself a colonel and an industrialist as well as a Westphalian aristocrat, and was sealed in an agreement made at the home of the Cologne banker Baron Kurt von Schröder, on January 4, 1933.

This agreement came into effect because of Papen's ability to manage Hindenburg. On January 28, 1933, the president forced the resignation of Schleicher by refusing to grant him decree powers. Two days later Hitler came to office as chancellor in a Cabinet which contained only two other Nazis. These were Minister of Air Göring and Frick in the vital Ministry of the Interior. Of the other eight posts, two, the ministries of economics and agriculture, went to Hugenburg; the Ministry of Labor went to Franz Seldte of the Stahlhelm, the Foreign Ministry and the Reichswehr Ministry went to nonparty experts, and most of the remaining posts went to friends of Papen. It would not seem possible for Hitler, thus surrounded, ever to obtain control of Germany, yet within a year and a half he was dictator of the country.

The Nazi Regime

COMING TO POWER, 1933–1934

When Adolf Hitler became chancellor of the German Reich on January 30, 1933, he was not yet forty-four years old. From his birth in Austria in 1889 to the outbreak of war in 1914, his life had been a succession of failures, the seven years 1907–1914 being passed as a social derelict in Vienna and Munich. There he had become a fanatical Pan-German anti-Semite, attributing his own failures to the "intrigues of international Jewry."

The outbreak of war in August 1914 gave Hitler the first real motivation of his life. He became a superpatriot, joined the Sixteenth Volunteer Bavarian Infantry, and served at the front for four years. In his way he was an excellent soldier. Attached to the regimental staff as messenger for the First Company, he was completely happy, always volunteering for the most dangerous tasks. Although his relations with his superiors were excellent and he was decorated with the Iron Cross, second class, in 1914 and with the Iron Cross, first class, in 1918, he was never promoted beyond Private, First Class, because he was incapable of having any real relationships with his fellow soldiers or of taking command of any group of them. He remained on active service at the front for four years. During that period his regiment of 3,500 suffered 3,260 killed in action, and Hitler himself was wounded twice. These were the only two occasions on which he left the front. In October 1918 he was blinded by mustard gas and sent to a hospital at Pasewalk, near Berlin. When he emerged a month later he found the war finished, Germany beaten, and the monarchy overthrown. He refused to become reconciled to this situation. Unable to accept either defeat or the republic, remembering the war as the second great love of his life (the first being his mother), he stayed with the army and eventually became a political spy for the Reichswehr, stationed near Munich. In the course of spying on the numerous political groups in Munich, Hitler became fascinated by the rantings of Gottfried Feder against the "interest slavery of the Jews." At some meetings Hitler himself became a participant, attacking the "Jewish plot to dominate the world" or ranting about the need for Pan-German unity. As a result he was asked to join the German Workers' Party, and did so, becoming one of about sixty regular members and the seventh member of its executive committee.

The German Workers' Party had been founded by a Munich locksmith, Anton Drexler, on January 5, 1919, as a nationalist, Pan-German, workers' group. In a few months Captain Ernst Röhm of Franz von Epp's corps of the Black Reichswehr joined the movement and became the conduit by which secret Reichswehr funds, coming through Epp, were conveyed to the party. He also began to organize a strong-arm militia within the group (the Storm Troops, or SA). When Hitler joined in September 1919, he was put in charge of party publicity. Since this was the chief expense, and since Hitler also became the party's leading orator, public opinion soon came to regard the whole movement as Hitler's, and Röhm paid the Reichswehr's funds to Hitler directly.

During 1920 the party grew from 54 to 3,000 members; it changed its name to National Socialist German Workers' Party, purchased the *Völkischer Beobachter* with 60,000 marks of General von Epp's money, and drew up its "Twenty-five-Point Program."

The party program of 1920 was printed in the party literature for twenty-five years, but its provisions became more remote from attainment as years passed. Even in 1920, many of its clauses were put in to win support from the lower classes rather than because they were sincerely desired by the party leaders. These included (1) Pan-Germanism; (2) German international equality, including the abrogation of the Treaty of Versailles; (3) living space for Germans, including colonial areas; (4) German citizenship to be based on blood only, with no naturalization, no immigration for non-Germans, and all Jews or "other aliens" eliminated; (5) all unearned incomes to be abolished, the state to control all monopolies, to impose an excess-profits tax on corporations, to "communalize" the large department stores, to encourage small business in the allotment of government contracts, to take agricultural land for public purposes without compensation, and to provide old-age pensions; (6) to punish all war profiteers and usurers with death; and (7) to see that the press, education, culture, and religion conform to "the morals and religious sense of the German race."

As the party grew, adding members and spreading out to link up with similar movements in other parts of Germany, Hitler strengthened his control of the group. He could do this because he had control of the party newspaper and of the chief source of money and was its chief public figure. In July 1921, he had the party constitution changed to give the president absolute power. He was elected president; Drexler was made honorary president; while Max Amann, Hitler's sergeant in the war, was made business manager. As a consequence of this event, the SA was reorganized under Röhm, the word "Socialism" in the party name was interpreted to mean nationalism (or a society without class conflicts), and equality in party and state was replaced by the "leadership principle" and the doctrine of the elite. In the next two years the party passed through a series of crises of which the chief was the attempted *Putsch* of November 9, 1923. During this period all kinds of violence and illegality, even murder, were condoned by the Bavarian and Munich authorities. As a result of the failures of this period, especially the abortive *Putsch*, Hitler became convinced that he must come to power by legal methods rather than by force; he broke with Ludendorff and ceased to be supported by the Reichswehr; he began to receive his chief financial support from the industrialists; he made a tacit alliance with the Bavarian People's Party by which Prime Minister Heinrich Held of Bavaria raised the ban on the Nazi Party in return for Hitler's repudiation of Ludendorff's anti-Christian teachings; and Hitler formed a new armed militia (the SS) to protect himself against Röhm's control of the old armed militia (the SA).

In the period 1924–1930 the party continued, without any real growth, as a "lunatic fringe," subsidized by the industrialists. Among the chief contributors to the party in this period were Carl Bechstein (Berlin piano manufacturer), August Borsig (Berlin locomotive manufacturer), Emil Kirdorf (general manager of the Rhenish-Westphalian Coal Syndicate), Fritz Thyssen (owner of the United Steel Works and president of the German Industrial Council) and Albert Vögler (general manager of the Gelsenkirchen Iron and Steel Company and formerly general manager of United Steel Works). During this period neither Hitler nor his supporters were seeking to create a mass movement. That did not come until 1930. But during this earlier period the party itself was steadily centralized, and the Leftish elements (like the Strasser brothers) were weakened or eliminated. In April 1927, Hitler spoke to 400 industrialists in Essen; in April 1928, he addressed a similar group of landlords from east of the Elbe; in January 1932 came one of his greatest triumphs when he spoke for 3 hours to the Industrial Club of Düsseldorf and won support and financial contributions from that powerful group. By that date he was seeking to build his movement into a mass political party capable of sweeping him into office. This project failed. As we have indicated, by the end of 1932 much of the financial support from industry had been cut off by Papen, and party membership was falling away, chiefly to the Communists. To stop this decline, Hitler agreed to become chancellor in a Cabinet in which there would be only three Nazis among eleven members. Papen hoped in this way to control the Nazis and to obtain from them the popular support which Papen had so sorely lacked in his own chancellorship in 1932. But Papen was far too clever for his own good. He, Hugenberg, Hindenburg, and the rest of the intriguers had underestimated Hitler. The latter, in return for Hugenberg's acceptance of new elections on March 5, 1933, promised that there would be no Cabinet changes whatever the outcome of the voting. In spite of the fact that the Nazis obtained only 44 per cent of the ballots in the new election, Hitler became dictator of Germany within eighteen months.

One of the chief reasons for this success rests on the position of Prussia within Germany. Prussia was the greatest of the fourteen states of Germany. Covering almost two-thirds of the country, it included both the great rural areas of the east and the great industrial areas of the west. Thus it included the most conservative as well as the most progressive portions of Germany. While its influence was almost as great under the republic as it had been under the empire, this influence was of quite a different character, having changed from the chief bulwark of conservatism in the earlier period to the chief area of progressivism in the later period. This change was made possible by the large numbers of enlightened groups in the Rhenish areas of Prussia, but chiefly by the fact that the so-called Weimar Coalition of Social Democrats, Center Party, and Liberal Democrats remained unbroken in Prussia from 1918 to 1932. As a consequence of this alliance, a Social Democrat, Otto Braun, held the position of prime minister of Prussia for almost the whole period 1920–1932, and Prussia was the chief obstacle in the path of the Nazis and of reaction in the critical days after 1930. As part of this movement the Prussian Cabinet in 1930 refused to allow either Communists or Nazis to hold municipal offices in Prussia, prohibited Prussian civil servants from holding membership in either of these two parties, and forbade the use of the Nazi uniform.

This obstacle to extremism was removed on July 20, 1932, when Hindenburg, by presidential decree based on Article 48, appointed Papen commissioner for Prussia. Papen at once dismissed the eight members of the Prussian parliamentary Cabinet and granted their governmental functions to men named by himself. The dismissed ministers were removed from their offices by the power of the army, but at once challenged the legality of this action before the German Supreme Court at Leipzig. By its verdict of October 25, 1932, the court decided for the removed officials. In spite of this decision, Hitler, after only a week in the chancellorship, was able to obtain from Hindenburg a new decree which removed the Prussian ministers from office once more and conferred their powers on the federal vice-chancellor, Papen. Control of the police administration was conferred on Hermann Göring. The Nazis already held, through Wilhelm Frick, control of the Reich Ministry of Interior and thus of the national police powers. Thus Hitler, by February 7th, had control of the police powers both of the Reich and of Prussia.

Using this advantage, the Nazis began a twofold assault on the opposition. Göring and Frick worked under a cloak of legality from above, while Captain Röhm in command of the Nazi Party storm troops worked without pretense of legality from below. All uncooperative police officials were retired, removed, or given vacations and were replaced by Nazi substitutes, usually Storm Troop leaders. On February 4, 1933, Hindenburg signed an emergency decree which gave the government the right to prohibit or control any meetings, uniforms, or newspapers. In this way most opposition meetings and newspapers were prevented from reaching the public.

This attack on the opposition from above was accompanied by a violent assault from below, carried out by the SA. In desperate attacks in which eighteen Nazis and fifty-one opposition were killed, all Communist, most Socialist, and many Center Party meetings were disrupted. In spite of all this, it was evident a week before the election that the German people were not convinced. Accordingly, under circumstances which are still mysterious, a plot was worked out to burn the Reichstag building and blame the Communists. Most of the plotters were homosexuals and were able to persuade a degenerate moron from Holland named Van der Lubbe to go with them. After the building was set on fire, Van der Lubbe was left wandering about in it and was arrested by the police. The government at once arrested four Communists, including the party leader in the Reichstag (Ernst Torgler).

The day following the fire (February 28, 1933) Hindenburg signed a decree suspending all civil liberties and giving the government power to invade any personal privacy, including the right to search private homes or confiscate property. At once all Communist members of the Reichstag, as well as thousands of others, were arrested, and all Communist and Social-Democrat papers were suspended for two weeks.

The true story of the Reichstag fire was kept secret only with difficulty. Several persons who knew the truth, including a Nationalist Reichstag member, Dr. Oberfohren, were murdered in March and April to prevent their circulating the true story. Most of the Nazis who were in on the plot were murdered by Göring during the "blood purge" of June 30, 1934. The four Communists who were directly charged with the crime were acquitted by the regular German courts, although Van der Lubbe was convicted.

In spite of these drastic measures, the election of March 5, 1933, was a failure from the Nazi point of view. Hitler's party received only 288 of 647 seats, or 43.9 percent of the total vote. The Nationalists obtained only 8 percent. The Communists obtained 81 seats, a decrease of 19, but the Socialists obtained 125, an increase of 4. The Center Party fell from 89 to 74, and the People's Party from 11 to 2. The Nationalists stayed at 52 seats. In the simultaneous election to the Prussian Diet, the Nazis obtained 211 and the Nationalists 43 out of 474 seats.

The period from the election of March 5, 1933, to the death of Hindenburg on August 2, 1934, is generally called the Period of Coordination (Gleichschaltung). The process was carried on, like the electoral campaign just finished, by illegal actions from below and legalistic actions from above. From below, on March 7th throughout Germany, the SA swept away much of the opposition by violence, driving it into hiding. They marched to most offices of trade unions, periodicals, and local governments, smashing them up, expelling their occupants, and raising the swastika flag. Minister of the Interior Wilhelm Frick condoned these actions by naming Nazis as police presidents in various German states (Baden, Saxony, Württemburg, Bavaria), including General von Epp in Bavaria. These men then proceeded to use their police powers to seize control of the apparatus of state government.

The new Reichstag met on March 23rd at the Kroll Opera House. In order to secure a majority, the Nazis excluded from the session all of the Communist and 30 Socialist members, about 109 in all. The rest were asked to pass an "enabling act" which would give the government for four years the right to legislate by decree, without the need for the presidential signature, as in Article 48, and without constitutional restrictions except in respect to the powers of the Reichstag, the Reichsrat, and the presidency.

Since this law required a two-third majority, it could have been beaten
if only a small group of the Center Party had voted against it. To be sure,
Hitler made it very clear that he was prepared to use violence against
all who refused to cooperate with him, but his power to do so on a
clear-cut constitutional issue in March 1933 was much less than it became later, since violence from him on such a question might well have
arrayed the president and the Reichswehr against him.

In spite of Hitler's intimidating speech, Otto Wels of the Social
Democrats rose to explain why his party refused to support the bill.
He was followed by Monsignor Kaas of the Center Party who explained that his Catholic Group would support it. The vote in favor of
the bill was more than sufficient, being 441-94, with the Social Democrats forming the solid minority. Thus, this weak, timid, doctrinaire, and
ignorant group redeemed themselves by their courage after the eleventh
hour had passed.

Under this "Enabling Act" the government issued a series of revolutionary decrees in the next few months. The diets of all the German
states, except Prussia (which had had its own election on March 5th)
were reconstituted in the proportions of votes in the national election
of March 5th, except that the Communists were thrown out. Each party
was given its quota of members and allowed to name the individual members on a purely party basis. A similar procedure was applied to local
governments. Thus the Nazis received a majority in each body.

A decree of April 7th gave the Reich government the right to name
a governor of each German state. This was a new official empowered
to enforce the policies of the Reich government even to the point of dismissing the state governments, including the prime ministers, diets, and
the hitherto irremovable judges. This right was used in each state to
make a Nazi governor and a Nazi prime minister. In Bavaria, for example, the two were Epp and Röhm, while in Prussia the two were
Hitler and Göring. In many states the governor was the district leader
of the Nazi Party, and where he was not, he was subject to that leader's
orders. By a later law of January 30, 1934, the diets of the states were
abolished; the sovereign powers of the states were transferred to the
Reich; and the governors were made subordinates of the Reich Ministry
of the Interior.

All the political parties except the Nazis were abolished in May, June,
and July 1933. The Communists had been outlawed on February 28th.
The Social Democrats were enjoined from all activities on June 22nd, and
were expelled from various governing bodies on July 7th. The German
State Party (Democratic Party) and the German People's Party were
dissolved on June 28th and July 4th. The Bavarian People's Party was
smashed by the Storm Troopers on June 22nd, and disbanded itself on
July 4th. The Center Party did the same on the following day. A series of
pitched battles between the SA and the Stahlhelm in April–June 1933

ended with the absorption of the latter into the Nazi Party. The Nationalists were smashed by violence on June 21st; Hugenberg was unable to penetrate the SA guard around Hindenburg to protest; and on June 28th his party was dissolved. Finally, on July 14, 1933, the Nazi Party was declared to be the only recognized party in Germany.

The middle classes were coordinated and disappointed. Wholesale and retail trade associations were consolidated into a Reich Corporation of German Trade under the Nazi Dr. von Renteln. On July 22nd the same man became president of the German Industrial and Trade Committee, which was a union of all the chambers of commerce. In Germany these last had been semipublic legal corporations.

The breakup of the great department stores, which had been one of the Nazi promises to the petty bourgeoisie since Gottfried Feder's Twenty-five-Point program of 1920, was abandoned, according to Hess's announcement of July 7th. Moreover, liquidation of the cooperative societies, which had also been a promise of long duration, was abandoned by an announcement of July 19th. This last reversal resulted from the fact that most of the cooperatives had come under Nazi control by being taken over by the Labor Front on May 16, 1933.

Labor was coordinated without resistance, except from the Communists. The government declared May 1st a national holiday, and celebrated it with a speech by Hitler on the dignity of labor before a million persons at Tempelhof. The next day the SA seized all union buildings and offices, arrested all union leaders, and sent most of these to concentration camps. The unions themselves were incorporated into a Nazi German Labor Front under Robert Ley. The new leader, in an article in the *Völkischer Beobachter*, promised employers that henceforth they could be masters in their own houses as long as they served the nation (that is, the Nazi Party). Work was supplied for labor by reducing the work week to forty hours (with a corresponding wage cut), by prohibiting aliens to work, by enforced "labor service" for the government, by grants of loans to married persons, by tax cuts for persons who spent money on repairs, by construction of military automobile roads, and so forth.

Agriculture was coordinated only after Hugenberg left the government on June 29th and was replaced by Richard Darré as Reich minister of food and Prussian minister of agriculture. The various land and peasant associations were merged into a single association of which Darré was president, while the various landlords' associations were united into the German Board of Agriculture of which Darré was president also.

Religion was coordinated in various ways. The Evangelical Church was reorganized. When a non-Nazi, Friedrich von Bodelschwing, was elected Reich bishop in May 1933, he was forcibly removed from office, and the National Synod was forced to elect a Nazi, Ludwig Müller, in his place (September 27th). At the elections for Church assemblies in July 1933, government pressure was so great that a majority of Nazis was chosen in each. In 1935 a Ministry of Church Affairs under Hans Kerrl was set up with power to issue Church ordinances having the force of law and with complete control over Church property and funds. Prominent Protestant leaders, like Martin Niemöller, who objected to these steps, were arrested and sent to concentration camps.

The Catholic Church made every effort to cooperate with the Nazis, but soon found it was impossible. It withdrew its condemnation of Nazism on March 28, 1933, and signed a Concordat with von Papen on July 20th. By this agreement the state recognized freedom of religious belief and of worship, exemption of the clergy from certain civic duties, and the right of the Church to manage its own affairs and to establish denominational schools. Governors of the German states were given a right to object to nominations to the highest clerical posts; bishops were to take an oath of loyalty, and education was to continue to function as it had been doing.

This agreement with the Church began to break down almost at once. Within ten days of the signing of the Concordat, the Nazis began to attack the Catholic Youth League and the Catholic press. Church schools were restricted, and members of the clergy were arrested and tried on charges of evading the monetary foreign-exchange regulations and of immorality. The Church condemned the efforts of Nazis like Rosenberg to replace Christianity by a revived German paganism and such laws as that permitting sterilization of socially objectionable persons. Rosenberg's book, *The Myth of the Twentieth Century*, was put on the *Index*; Catholic scholars exposed its errors in a series of studies in 1934; and finally, on March 14, 1937, Pope Pius XI condemned many of the tenets of Nazism in the encyclical *Mit brennender Sorge*.

Attempts to coordinate the civil service began with the law of April 7, 1933 and continued to the end of the regime without ever being completely successful because of the lack of capable personnel who were loyal Nazis. "Non-Aryans" (Jews) or persons married to "non-Aryans," politically unreliable persons, and "Marxists" were discharged, and loyalty to Nazism was required for appointment and promotion in the civil service.

Of the chief elements in German society, only the presidency, the army, the Catholic Church, and industry were not coordinated by 1934. In addition, the bureaucracy was only partially controlled. The first of these, the presidency, was taken over completely in 1934 as the result of a deal with the army.

By the spring of 1934 the problem of the SA had become acute, since this organization was directly challenging two members of the Quartet, the army and industry. Industry was being challenged by the demand of the SA for the "second revolution"—that is, for the economic reforms which would justify the use of the word "Socialism" in the name "National Socialism." The army was being challenged by the demand of Captain Röhm that his SA be incorporated into the Reichswehr with each officer holding the same rank in the latter as he already held in the former. Since the Reichswehr had only 300,000 men while the SA had three million, this would have swamped the Officers' Corps. Hitler had denounced this project on July 1, 1933, and Frick repeated this ten days later. Nevertheless, Röhm repeated his demand on April 18, 1934, and was echoed by Edmund Heines and Karl Ernst. In full Cabinet meeting Minister of War General von Blomberg refused.

A tense situation developed. If Hindenburg died, the Reichswehr might have liquidated the Nazis and restored the monarchy. On June 21st Hindenburg ordered Blomberg to use the army, if necessary, to restore order in the country. This was regarded as a threat to the SA. Accordingly, Hitler made a deal to destroy the SA in return for a free hand to deal with the presidency when it became vacant. This was done. A meeting of SA leaders was called by Hitler for June 30, 1934, at Bad Wiessee in Bavaria. The SS, under Hitler's personal command, arrested the SA leaders in the middle of the night and shot most of them at once. In Berlin, Göring did the same to the SA leaders there. Both Hitler and Göring also killed most of their personal enemies; the Reichstag incendiaries, Gregor Strasser, General and Mrs. von Schleicher, all of von Papen's close associates, Gustav von Kahr, all those who had known Hitler in the early days of his failure, and many others. Papen escaped only by a narrow margin. In all, several thousands were eliminated in this "blood purge."

Two excuses were given for this violent action: that the murdered men were homosexuals (something which had been known for years) and that they were members of a conspiracy to murder Hitler. That they were in a conspiracy was quite true, but it was by no means mature in June 1934, and it was aimed at the army and heavy industry, and not at Hitler. In fact, Hitler had been wavering until the last moment whether he would throw in his lot with the "second revolution" or with the Quartet. His decision to join the latter and exterminate the former was an event of great significance. It irrevocably made the Nazi movement a counterrevolution of the Right, using the party organization as an instrument for protecting the economic *status quo*.

The supporters of the "second revolution" were driven underground, forming a "Black Front" under the leadership of Otto Strasser. This movement was so ineffectual that the only choice facing the average German was the choice between the reactionary mode of life built about the surviving members of the Quartet (army and industry) and the completely irrational nihilism of the inner clique of the Nazi Party.

Only as the regime approached its end did a third possible way appear: a revived progressive and cooperative Christian humanism which sprang from the reaction engendered within the Quartet by the realization that Nazi nihilism was merely the logical outcome of the Quartet's customary methods of pursuing its customary goals. Many of the persons associated with this new third way were destroyed by the Nazis in the systematic destructiveness which followed the attempt to assassinate Hitler on June 20, 1944.

In return for Hitler's decisive step—the destruction of the SA on June 30, 1934—the army permitted Hitler to become president following Hindenburg's death in August. By combining the offices of president and chancellor, Hitler obtained the president's legal right to rule by decree, and obtained as well the supreme command of the army, a position which he solidified by requiring a personal oath of unconditional obedience from each soldier (Law of August 20, 1934). From this time on, in the minds of the Reichswehr and the bureaucracy, it was both legally and morally impossible to resist Hitler's orders.

THE RULERS AND THE RULED, 1934-1945

Thus, by August 1934, the Nazi movement had reached its goal—the establishment of an authoritarian state in Germany. The word used here is "authoritarian," for, unlike the Fascist regime in Italy, the Nazi regime was not totalitarian. It was not totalitarian because two members of the Quartet were not coordinated, a third member was coordinated only incompletely and, unlike Italy or Soviet Russia, the economic system was not ruled by the state but was subject to "self-rule." All this is not in accord with popular opinion about the nature of the Nazi system either at the time it was flourishing or since. Newspaper men and journalistic writers applied the term "totalitarian" to the Nazi system, and the name has stuck without any real analysis of the facts as they existed. In fact, the Nazi system was not totalitarian either in theory or in practice.

The Nazi movement, in its simplest analysis, was an aggregation of gangsters, neurotics, mercenaries, psychopaths, and merely discontented, with a small intermixture of idealists. This movement was built up by the Quartet as a counterrevolutionary force against, first, the Weimar Republic, internationalism, and democracy, and against, second, the dangers of social revolution, especially Communism, engendered by the world economic depression. This movement, once it came to power at the behest of the Quartet, took on life and goals of its own quite different from, and, indeed, largely inimical to, the life and goals of the Quartet. No showdown or open conflict ever arose between the movement and the Quartet. Instead, a *modus vivendi* was worked out by which the two chief members of the Quartet, industry and the army, obtained their desires, while the Nazis obtained the power and privileges for which they yearned.

The seeds of conflict continued to exist and even to grow between the movement and its creators, especially because of the fact that the movement worked continually to create a substitute industrial system and a substitute army parallel to the old industrial system and the old Reichswehr. Here again the threatening conflict never broke out because the Second World War had the double result that it demonstrated the need for solidarity in the face of the enemy, and it brought great booty and profits to both sides—to the industrialists and Reichswehr on one hand and to the party on the other hand.

Except for the rise of the party, and the profits, power, and prestige which accrued to the leaders (but not to the ordinary members) of the party, the structure of German society was not drastically changed after 1933. It was still sharply divided into two parts—the rulers and the ruled. The three chief changes were: (1) the methods and techniques by which the rulers controlled the ruled were modified and intensified, so that law and legal procedures practically vanished, and power (exercised through force, economic pressures, and propaganda) became much more naked and direct in its application; (2) the Quartet which had held real power from 1919 to 1933 were rearranged and increased to a Quintet, such as existed before 1914; and (3) the line between rulers and ruled was made sharper, with fewer persons in an ambiguous position than earlier in German history; this was made more acceptable to the ruled by creating a new third group of non-citizens (Jews and foreigners) which could be exploited and oppressed even by the second group of the ruled.

The following table shows the approximate relationships of the ruling groups in the three periods of German history in the twentieth century:

THE EMPIRE	THE WEIMAR REPUBLIC	THE THIRD REICH
Emperor		Nazi Party (leaders only)
Army	Army	Industry
Landlords	Bureaucracy	Army
Bureaucracy	Industry	Bureaucracy
Industry	Landlords	Landlords

The ruled groups below these rulers have remained roughly the same. In the Third Reich they included: (1) peasants; (2) laborers; (3) the petty bourgeoisie of clerks, retailers, artisans, small industry, and so on; (4) professional groups, such as doctors, druggists, teachers, engineers, dentists, and so on. Below these was the submerged group of "non-Aryans" and the inhabitants of occupied areas.

A revealing light is cast on Nazi society by examining the positions of the ruling groups. We shall examine each of these in reverse order.

The influence of the landlord group in the earlier period rested on tradition rather than on power. It was supported by a number of factors: (1) the close personal connections of the landlords with the emperor, the army, and the bureaucracy; (2) the peculiar voting rules in Germany which gave the landlords undue influence in Prussia and gave the state of Prussia undue influence in Germany; (3) the economic and social power of the landlords, especially east of the Elbe, a power based on their ability to bring pressure to bear on tenants and agricultural laborers in that area.

All these sources of power were weakening, even under the empire. The republic and the Third Reich merely extended a process already well advanced. The economic power of the landlords was threatened by the agricultural crisis after 1880 and was clearly evident in their demand for tariff protection after 1895. The bankruptcy of the Junker estates was bound to undermine their political influence even if the state was willing to support them with subsidies and *Osthilfe* indefinitely. The departure of the emperor and the change in the position of the army and bureaucracy under the republic weakened these avenues of indirect influence by the landlords. The change in the voting regulations after 1918 and the ending of voting after 1933, combined with the increasing absorbtion of Prussia and the other *Länder* into a unified German state, reduced the political power of the landlord group. Finally, their social influence was weakened by the migration of German farm laborers from eastern to central and western Germany and their replacement by Slav farm labor.

This decrease in the power of the landlord group continued under the Third Reich and was intensified by the fact that this group was the one segment of the Quartet which was successfully coordinated. The landlords lost most of their economic power because the control of their economic life was not left in the hands of the landlords as was done with industry. In both cases economic life was controlled, chiefly by cartels and associations, but in industry these were controlled by industrialists, while in agriculture they were controlled by the state in close cooperation with the party.

Prices, production, conditions of sale, and, in fact, every detail about agriculture was in control of a government corporation called the *Reichsnährstand* which consisted of a complex of groups, associations, and boards. The leader of this complex was the minister of food and agriculture, named by Hitler. This leader appointed the subordinate leaders of all the member organizations of the *Reichsnährstand*, and these, in turn, named their subordinates. This process was continued down to the lowest individual, each leader naming his direct subordinates according to the "leadership principle." Every person engaged in any activity concerned with agriculture, food, or raw-material production, including lumber, fishing, dairying, and grazing belonged to one or several associations in the *Reichsnährstand*. The associations were organized both on a territorial and on a functional basis. On a functional basis they were organized in both vertical and horizontal associations. On a territorial basis were twenty regional "peasantships" (*Landesbauernschaften*) subdivided into 515 local "peasantships" (*Kreisbauernschaften*). On a horizontal basis were associations of persons in the same activity, such as grinding flour, churning butter, growing grain, and so on. On a vertical basis were associations of all persons concerned with the production and processing of any single commodity, such as grain or milk. These organizations, all formed on the "leadership principle," were chiefly concerned with prices and production quotas. These were controlled by the state, but prices were set at a level sufficient to give a profit to most participants, and quotas were based on assessments estimated by the farmers themselves.

While the landlords lost power in this way, they received economic advantages. As befitted a counterrevolutionary movement, the Nazis increased the wealth and privileges of the landlords. The report on the *Osthilfe* scandal, which had been made for Schleicher in 1932, was premanently suppressed. The autarky program gave them a stable market for their products, shielding them from the vicissitudes which they had suffered under liberalism with its unstable markets and fluctuating prices. The prices fixed under Nazism were not high but were adequate, especially in combination with other advantages. By 1937, prices paid to farmers were 23 percent more than in 1933 although still 28 percent below those of 1925. Larger farms which used hired labor were aided by the prevention of unions, strikes, and rising wages. Labor forces were increased by using the labor services of boys and girls in the Nazi Youth Movement and Labor Service. Payments for interest and taxes were both reduced, the former from 950 million marks in 1929–1930 to 630 million marks in 1935–1936, and the latter from 740 million to 460 million marks in the same six years. Farmers were exempt completely from unemployment-insurance contributions which amounted to 19 million marks in 1932–1933. The constant threat of breaking up the bankrupt great estates was removed whether it arose from the state or from private creditors. All farms of over family size were made secure in possession of their owner's family, with no possibility of alienation, by increasing the use of entail on great estates and by the Hereditary Farms Act for lesser units.

These benefits were greater for larger units than for smaller ones, and greatest for the large estates. While small farms (5 to 50 hectares), according to Max Sering, made a net return of 9 marks a hectare in

1925, large ones (over 100 hectares) lost 18 marks a hectare. In 1934 the corresponding figures were 28 and 53, a gain of 19 marks per hectare for small units and of 71 marks per hectare for large units. As a result of this growth in profitability of large units, the concentration of ownership of land in Germany was increased, thus reversing a trend. Both the number and the average size of large units increased.

Thus the landlords won great privileges and rewards in the Third Reich, but at the cost of a drastic reduction in their power. They were coordinated, like the rest of society outside the ruling groups, with the result that they became the least important of these groups.

The bureaucracy was not completely coordinated, but it found its power greatly reduced. The civil service was not, as we have indicated, purged of non-Nazis, although Jews and obvious anti-Nazis were generally retired. Only in the Ministry of Economics, perhaps because of the complete reorganization of the ministry, was there any extensive change at first. But this change did not bring in party members; it brought in men from private business. Outside the Ministry of Economics the chief changes were the ministers themselves and their secretaries of state. The newly created ministries, of course, had new men, but, except on the lowest levels, these were not chosen because they were party members. The old division of the bureaucracy into two classes (academic and nonacademic), with the upper open only to those who passed an academic examination, continued. Only in the lowest, nonskilled ranks did party members overwhelm the service.

By 1939, of 1.5 million civil servants 28.2 percent were party members, 7.2 percent belonged to the SA, and 1.1 percent belonged to the SS. The act of 1933, which expelled non-Ayrans and political unreliables, affected only 1.1 percent (or 25 out of 2,339) of the top civil servants. But new recruits were overwhelmingly party members so that, in time, the bureaucracy would have become almost completely Nazi. The Civil Service Act of 1937 did not require party membership, but the candidate had to be loyal to the Nazi idea. In practice, 99 percent of those appointed to the grade of assessor (the lowest academic rank) were party members from 1933 to 1936. However, a law of December 28, 1939 stated, what had always been understood, that in his civil service work a party member was not subject to party orders but only to the orders of the civil service superior. Here again the lower ranks were more subject to party control by means of the office "party cell" which permitted party members to accomplish their ends by terror. This opens up an important, if nonofficial, aspect of this subject.

A chief change was that where formerly the bureaucracy governed by rational, known rules, under the Nazis it increasingly governed by irrational and even unknown rules. Neither earlier nor later were these rules made by the bureaucracy itself, and to some extent the later rules, because of the bureaucracy's well-known antidemocratic proclivities, may have been more acceptible to the bureaucracy. More important was the influence of party terrorism, through the SA, the SS, and the secret police (Gestapo). Even more important was the growth, outside of the bureaucracy, of a party organization which countermanded and evaded the decisions and actions of the regular bureaucracy. The regular police were circumvented by the party police; the regular avenues of justice were bypassed by the party courts; the regular prisons were eclipsed by the party's concentration camps. As a result, Torgler, acquitted by the regular courts of the charge that he conspired to burn the Reichstag, was immediately thrown into a concentration camp by the secret police; and Niemöller, having served a brief term for violation of the religious regulations, was taken from a regular prison to a concentration camp.

The Reichswehr Officers' Corps was not coordinated, but found itself more subject to the Nazis than it ever was to the Weimar Republic. The republic could never have murdered generals as Hitler did in 1934. This weakening of the power of the army, however, was not in relationship to the party as much as it was in relationship to the state. Previously, the army very largely controlled the State; under the Third Reich the state controlled the army; but the party did not control the army and, for failure to do so, built up its own army (SS). There was a statutory provision which made it illegal for members of the armed services to be simultaneously members of the party. This incompatibility was revoked in the autumn of 1944. However, the army was quite completely subjected to Hitler as chief of the state although not as Führer of the Nazi Party. The army had always been subordinated to the chief of the state. When Hitler obtained this position (with army consent) at the death of Hindenburg on August 2, 1934, he strengthened his position by requiring army officers to take their oath of loyalty to himself personally, and not merely to the German Fatherland as had been done previously. All this was possible because the army, although not coordinated, generally approved of what the Nazis were doing and, where they occasionally disagreed, did so only for tactical reasons. The relations between the two were well stated by Field Marshal Werner von Blomberg, Reich minister of war and commander in chief of the armed forces until February, 1939:

"Before 1938–1939, the German generals were not opposed to Hitler. There was no reason to oppose Hitler since he produced the results which they desired. After this time some generals began to condemn his methods and lost confidence in the power of his judgment. However, they failed as a group to take any definite stand against him, although a few of them tried to do so and, as a result, had to pay for this with their lives or their positions." To this statement it is necessary only to add that the German Officers' Corps maintained its autonomous condition and its control of the army by the destruction of its chief rival, the SA, on June 30, 1934. For this it paid on August 2, 1934. After that, it was too late for it to oppose the movement, even if it had wished to do so.

The position of the industrialists in Nazi society was complex and very important. In general, business had an extraordinary position. In the first place, it was the only one of the Quartet which drastically improved its position in the Third Reich. In the second place, it was the only one of the Quartet which was not coordinated significantly and in which the "leadership principle" was not applied. Instead, industry was left free of government and party control except in the widest terms and except for the exigencies of war, and was subjected instead to a pattern of self-regulation built up, not on the "leadership principle," but on a system where power was proportional to the size of the enterprise.

In these strange exceptions we can find one of the central principles of the Nazi system. It is a principle which is often missed. We have been told that Germany had a corporate state or a totalitarian state. Neither was true. There was no real corporate organization (even fraudulent, as in Italy and Austria), and such an organization, much discussed before and after 1933, was quickly dropped by 1935. The term "totalitarian" cannot be applied to the German system of self-regulation, although it could be applied to the Soviet system.

The Nazi system was dictatorial capitalism—that is, a society organized so that everything was subject to the benefit of capitalism; everything, that is, compatible with two limiting factors: (a) that the Nazi Party, which was not capitalist, was in control of the state, and (b) that war, which is not capitalist, could force curtailment of capitalist benefits (in the short run at least). In this judgment we must define our terms accurately. We define capitalism as "a system of economics in which production is based on profit for those who control the capital." In this definition one point must be noted: the expression "for those who control the capital" does not necessarily mean the owners. In modern economic conditions large-scale enterprise with widely dispersed stockownership has made *management* more important than *ownership*. Accordingly, profits are not the same as dividends, and, in fact, dividends become objectionable to management, since they take profits out of its control.

The traditional capitalist system was a profit system. In its pursuit of profits it was not *primarily* concerned with production, consumption, prosperity, high employment, national welfare, or anything else. As a result, its concentration on profits eventually served to injure profits.

This development got the whole society into such a mess that enemies of the profit system began to rise up on all sides. Fascism was the counterattack of the profit system against these enemies. This counterattack was conducted in such a violent fashion that the whole appearance of society was changed, although, in the short run, the real structure was not greatly modified. In the long run Fascism threatened even the profit system, because the defenders of that system, businessmen rather than politicians, turned over the control of the state to a party of gangsters and lunatics who in the long run might turn to attack businessmen themselves.

In the short run the Nazi movement achieved the aim of its creators. In order to secure profits it sought to avert six possible dangers to the profit system. These dangers were (1) from the state itself; (2) from organized labor; (3) from competition; (4) from depression; (5) from business losses; and (6) from alternative forms of economic production organized on nonprofit bases. These six all merged into one great danger, the danger from any social system in which production was organized on any basis other than profit. The fear of the owners and managers of the profit system for any system organized on any other basis became almost psychopathic.

The danger to the profit system from the state has always existed because the state is not essentially organized on a profit basis. In Germany this danger from the state was averted by the industrialists taking over the state, not directly, but through an agent, the Nazi Party. Hitler indicated his willingness to act as such an agent in various ways: by reassurances, such as his Düsseldorf speech of 1932; by accepting, as a party leader and his chief economic adviser, a representative of heavy industry (Walter Funk) on the very day (December 31, 1931) on which that representative joined the party at the behest of the industrialists; by the purge of those who wanted the "second revolution" or a corporative or totalitarian state (June 30, 1934).

That the industrialists' faith in Hitler on this account was not misplaced was soon demonstrated. As Gustav Krupp, the armaments manufacturer, writing to Hitler as the official representative of the Reich Association of German Industry, put it on April 25, 1933, "The turn of political events is in line with the wishes which I myself and the Board of Directors have cherished for a long time." This was true. The "second revolution" was publicly rejected by Hitler as early as July 1933, and many of its supporters sent to concentration camps, a development which reached its climax in the "blood purge" a year later. The radical Otto Wagener was replaced as chief economic adviser to the Nazi Party by a manufacturer, Wilhelm Keppler. The efforts to coordinate industry were summarily stopped. Many of the economic activities which had come under state control were "reprivatized." The

United Steel Works, which the government had purchased from Ferdinand Flick in 1932, as well as three of the largest banks in Germany, which had been taken over during the crisis of 1931, were restored to private ownership at a loss to the government. Reinmetal-Borsig, one of the greatest corporations in heavy industry, was sold to the Hermann Göring Works. Many other important firms were sold to private investors. At the same time the property in industrial firms still held by the state was shifted from public control to joint public-private control by being subjected to a mixed board of directors. Finally, municipal enterprise was curtailed; its profits were taxed for the first time in 1935, and the law permitting municipal electric-power plants was revoked in the same year.

The danger from labor was not nearly so great as might seem at first glance. It was not labor itself which was dangerous, because labor itself did not come directly and immediately in conflict with the profit system; rather it was with labor getting the wrong ideas, especially Marxist ideas which did seek to put the laborer directly in conflict with the profit system and with private ownership. As a result, the Nazi system sought to control the ideas and the organization of labor, and was quite as eager to control his free time and leisure activities as it was to control his working arrangements. For this reason it was not sufficient merely to smash the existing labor organizations. This would have left labor free and uncontrolled and able to pick up any kind of ideas. Nazism, therefore, did not try to destroy these organizations but to take them over. All the old unions were dissolved into the German Labor Front. This gave an amorphous body of 25 million in which the individual was lost. This Labor Front was a party organization, and its finances were under control of the party treasurer, Franz X. Schwarz.

The Labor Front soon lost all of its economic activities, chiefly to the Ministry of Economics. An elaborate facade of fraudulent organizations which either never existed or never functioned was built up about the Labor Front. They included national and regional chambers of labor and a Federal Labor and Economic Council. In fact, the Labor Front had no economic or political functions and had nothing to do with wages or labor conditions. Its chief functions were (1) to propagandize; (2) to absorb the workers' leisure time, especially by the "Strength Through Joy" organization; (3) to tax workers for the party's profit; (4) to provide jobs for reliable party members within the Labor Front itself; (5) to disrupt working-class solidarity.

This facade was painted with an elaborate ideology based on the idea that the factory or enterprise was a community in which leader and followers cooperated. The Charter of Labor of January 20, 1934, which established this, said, "The leader of the plant decides against the followers in all matters pertaining to the plant in so far as they are regulated by statute." A pretense was made that these regulations merely applied the "leadership principle" to enterprise. It did no such thing. Under the "leadership principle" the leader was appointed from above. In business life the existing owner or manager became, *ipso facto*, leader. Under this system there were no collective agreements, no way in which any group defended the worker in the face of the great power of the employer. One of the chief instruments of duress was the "workbook" carried by the worker, which had to be signed by the employer on entering or leaving any job. If the employer refused to sign, the worker could get no other job.

Wage scales and conditions of labor, previously established by collective agreements, were made by a state employee, the labor trustee, created May 19, 1933. Under this control there was a steady downward reduction of working conditions, the chief change being from a period wage to a piecework payment. All overtime, holiday, night, and Sunday rates were abolished. The labor trustee was ordered to set maximum wage rates in June 1938, and a rigid ceiling was set in October 1939.

In return for this exploitation of labor, enforced by the terroristic activity of the "party cell' in each plant, the worker received certain compensations of which the chief was the fact that he was no longer threatened with the danger of mass unemployment. Employment figures for Germany were 17.8 million persons in 1929, only 12.7 million in 1932, and 20 million by 1939. This increased economic activity went to nonconsumers' goods rather than consumers' goods, as can be seen from the following indices of production:

	1928	1929	1932	1938
PRODUCTION	100	100.9	58.7	124.7
a. Capital goods	100	103.2	45.7	135.9
b. Consumers' goods	100	98.5	78.1	107.8

Business hates competition. Such competition might appear in various forms: (*a*) prices; (*b*) for raw materials; (*c*) for markets; (*d*) potential competition (creation of new enterprises in the same activity); (*e*) for labor. All these make planning difficult, and jeopardize profits. Businessmen prefer to get together with competitors so that they can cooperate to exploit consumers to the benefit of profits instead of competing with each other to the injury of profits. In Germany this was done by three kinds of arrangements: (1) cartels (*Kartelle*), (2) trade associations (*Fachverbände*), and (3) employers' associations (*Spitzenverbände*). The cartels regulated prices, production, and markets. The trade associations were political groups organized as chambers of commerce or agriculture. The employers' associations sought to control labor.

All these existed long before Hitler came to power, an event that had relatively little influence on the cartels, but considerable influence on the other two. The economic power of cartels, left in the hands of businessmen, was greatly extended; the employers' associations were coordinated, subjected to party control through the establishment of the "leadership principle," and merged into the Labor Front, but had little to do, as all relations with labor (wages, hours, working conditions) were controlled by the state (through the Ministry of Economics and the labor trustee) and enforced by the party. The trade associations were also coordinated and subject to the "leadership principle," being organized into an elaborate hierarchy of chambers of economics, commerce, and industry, whose leaders were ultimately named by the Ministry of Economics.

All this was to the taste of businessmen. While they, in theory, lost control of the three types of organizations, in fact they got what they wanted in all three. We have shown that the employers' associations were coordinated. Yet employers got the labor, wage, and working conditions they wanted, and abolished labor unions and collective bargaining, which had been their chief ambition in this field. In the second field (trade associations) activities were largely reduced to social and propaganda actions, but the leaders, even under the "leadership principle," continued to be prominent businessmen. Of 173 leaders throughout Germany, 9 were civil servants, only 21 were party members, 108 were businessmen, and the status of the rest is unknown. Of 17 leaders in provincial economic chambers, all were businessmen, of whom 14 were party members. In the third field, the activities of cartels were so extended that almost all forms of market competition were ended, and these activities were controlled by the biggest enterprises. The Nazis permitted the cartels to destroy all competition by forcing all business into cartels and giving these into the control of the biggest businessmen. At the same time it did all it could to benefit big business, to force mergers, and to destroy smaller businesses. A few examples of this process will suffice.

A law of July 15, 1933, gave the minister of economics the right to make certain cartels compulsory, to regulate capacity of enterprises, and prohibit the creation of new enterprises. Hundreds of decrees were issued under this law. On the same day, the cartel statute of 1923 which prevented cartels from using boycotts against nonmembers was amended to permit this practice. As a result, cartels were able to prohibit new retail outlets, and frequently refused to supply wholesalers or retailers unless they did more than a minimum volume of business or had more than a minimum amount of capital. These actions were taken, for example, by the radio and the cigarette cartels.

Cartels were controlled by big business, since voting power within the cartel was based on output or number of employees. Concentration of enterprise was increased by various expedients, such as granting public contracts only to large enterprises or by "Aryanization" (which forced Jews to sell out to established firms). As a result, on May 7, 1938, the Ministry of Economics reported that 90,448 out of 600,000 one-man firms had been closed in two years. The Corporation Law of 1937 facilitated mergers, refused to permit new corporations of below 500,000 marks capital, ordered all new shares to be issued at a par value of at least 1,000 marks, and ordered the dissolution of all corporations of less than 100,000 marks capital. By this last provision 20 percent of all corporations with 0.3 percent of all corporate capital were condemned. At the same time shareowners lost most of their rights against the board of directors, and on the board the power of the chairman was greatly extended. As an example of a change, the board could refuse information to stockholders on flimsy excuses.

The control of raw materials, which was lacking under the Weimar Republic, was entrusted to the functional trade associations. After August 18, 1939, priority numbers, based on the decisions of the trade associations, were issued by the *Reichstellen* (subordinate offices of the Ministry of Economics). In some critical cases subordinate offices of the *Reichstellen* were set up as public offices to allot raw materials, but in each case these were only existing business organizations with a new name. In some cases, such as coal and paper, they were nothing but the existing cartels.

In this way competition of the old kind was largely eliminated, and that, not by the state but by industrial self-regulation, and not at the expense of profits, but to the benefit of profits, especially of those enterprises which had supported the Nazis—large units in heavy industry.

The threat to industry from depression was eliminated. This can be seen from the following figures:

		1929	1932	1938
National income, 1925-1934 prices billions	RM	70.0	52.0	84.0
Per capita incomes, 1925-1934 prices	RM	1,089.0	998.0	1,226.0
Percentage of national incomes:				
to industry		21.0%	17.4%	26.6%
to workers		68.8%	77.6%	63.1%
to others		10.2%	5.0%	10.3%
Number of corporate bankruptcies		116	134	7
Profit ratios of corporations (heavy industry)		4.06%	−6.94%	6.44%

In the period after 1933 the threat to industry from forms of production based on a nonprofit organization of business largely vanished. Such threats could come from government ownership, from cooperatives, or from syndicalism. The last was destroyed by the destruction of the labor unions. The cooperatives were coordinated by being subjected "irrevocably and unconditionally to the command and administrative authority of the leader of the German Labor Front, Dr. Robert Ley," on May 13, 1933. The threat from public ownership was eliminated under Hitler, as we have indicated.

It would seem, from these facts, that industry was riding the crest of the wave under Nazism. This is quite true. But industry had to share this crest with the party and the army. Of these three it was unquestionably in at least second place, a higher rank than it had ever achieved in any earlier period of German history. Party participation in business activities was not the threat to industry which it might appear to be at first glance. These participations were the efforts of the party to secure an independent economic foundation, and were largely built up of unprofitable activities, or non-Aryan, non-German, or labor-union activities, and were not constructed at the expense of "legitimate" German industry. The Hermann Göring Works arose from government efforts to utilize low-grade iron ore in Brunswick. To this was added various other enterprises: those already in government control (which were thus shifted from a socialized to a profit-seeking basis), those taken from newly annexed areas, and those confiscated from Thyssen when he became a traitor. The Gustloff Works, in complete party control, were made up of non-Aryan properties. The Labor Front, with sixty-five corporations in 1938, was an improvement over the previous situation, since all, except the People's Auto enterprise (Volkswagen), were taken from labor unions. Other party activities were in publishing, a field of little concern to big industry, and largely non-Aryan previously.

The advent of war was contrary to the desires and probably to the interests of industry. Industry wanted to prepare for war, since it was profitable, but they did not like war, since profits, in wartime, took a secondary role to victory. The advent of war was the result of the fact that industry was not ruling Germany directly, but was ruling through an agent. It was not government of, by, and for industry, but government of and by the party and for industry. The interests and desires of these two were not identical. The party was largely paranoid, racist, violently nationalistic, and really believed its own propaganda about Germany's imperial mission through "blood and soil." Industry wanted rearmaments and an aggressive foreign policy to support these, not in order to carry out a paranoid policy but because this was the only kind of program they could see which would combine full employment of labor and equipment with profits. In the period 1936-

1939 the policies of "rearmament for war" and "rearmament for profits" ran parallel courses. From 1939 on they ran parallel only because the two groups shared the booty of conquered areas and were divergent because of the danger of defeat. This danger was regarded as a necessary risk in pursuit of world conquest by the party; it was regarded as an unnecessary risk in pursuit of profits by industry.

This brings us to the new ruling group, the party. The party was a ruling group only if we restrict the meaning of the term "party" to the relatively small group (a few thousand) of party leaders. The four million party members were not part of the ruling group, but merely a mass assembled to get the leaders in control of the state, but annoying and even dangerous once this was done. Accordingly, the period after 1933 saw a double action, a steady growth of power and influence for the *Reichsleiter* in respect to the ruled groups, the Quartet, and the ordinary members of the party itself, and, combined with this, a steady decrease in the influence of the party as a whole in respect to the state. In other words, the leaders controlled the state and the state controlled the party.

At the head of the party was the Führer; then came about twoscore *Reichsleiter;* below these was the party hierarchy, organized by dividing Germany into 40 districts (*Gaue*) each under a *Gauleiter;* each district was subdivided into circles (*Kreise*) of which there were 808, each under a *Kreisleiter;* each *Kreis* was divided into chapters (*Ortsgruppen*), each under an *Ortsgruppenleiter;* these chapters were divided into cells (*Zellen*) and subdivided into blocks under *Zellenleiter* and *Blockleiter*. The *Blockleiter* had to supervise and spy on 40 to 60 families; the *Zellenleiter* had to supervise 4 to 8 blocks (200 to 400 families); and the *Ortsgruppenleiter* had to supervise a town or district of up to 1,500 families through his 4 to 6 *Zellenleiter*.

This party organization became in time a standing threat to the position of the industrialists. The threat became more direct after the outbreak of war in 1939, although, as we have indicated, the issue was suspended for the sake of sharing the booty and for the sake of solidarity in the face of the enemy. The three ruling groups, party, army, and industrialists, remained in precarious balance although secretly struggling for supremacy in the whole period 1934–1945. In general, there was a slow extension of party superiority, although the party was never able to free itself from dependence on the army and business because of their technical competence.

The army was brought partly under party control in 1934 when Hitler became president and obtained the oath of allegiance; this control was extended in 1938 when Hitler became commander in chief. This resulted in the creation of centers of intrigue within the Officers' Corps, but this intrigue, although it penetrated to the highest military level, never succeeded in doing more than wound Hitler once out of a dozen efforts to assassinate him. The power of the army was steadily subjected to Hitler. The old officers were removed from control of the fighting troops after their failure in Russia in December 1941, and by 1945 the Officers' Corps had been so disrupted from within that the army was being guided to defeat after defeat by nothing more tangible than Hitler's "intuition" in spite of the fact that most army officers objected to subjecting themselves and Germany to the jeopardies of such an unpredictable and unproductive authority.

Business was in a somewhat similar but less extreme position. At first, unity of outlook seemed assured, largely because Hitler's mind was able to adopt the colors of an industrialist's mind whenever he made a speech to businessmen. By 1937 businessmen were convinced that armaments were productive, and by 1939 the more unstable elements had even decided that war would be profitable. But once the war began, the urgent need for victory subjected industry to controls which were hardly compatible with the vision of industrial self-government which Hitler had adopted from business. The Four-Year Plan, created as early as 1936, became the entering wedge of outside control. After war began the new Ministry of Munitions under the control of Fritz Todt and Albert Speer (who were Nazis but not businessmen) began to dominate economic life.

Outside its rather specialized area, the organization of the Four-Year Plan, almost completely Nazi, was transformed into a General Economic Council in 1939, and the whole range of economic life was, in 1943, subjected to four Nazis forming the Inner Defense Council. Industry accepted this situation because profits were still protected, promises of material advantages remained bright for years, and the hope did not die that these controls were no more than temporary wartime measures.

Thus the precarious balance of power between party, army, and industry, followed in a secondary role by bureaucracy and landlords, drove themselves and the German people to a catastrophe so gigantic that it threatened for a while to destroy completely all the established institutions and relationships of German society.

X

BRITAIN:
THE BACKGROUND
TO APPEASEMENT,
1900-1939

The Social and Constitutional Background

Political History to 1939

The Social and Constitutional Background

IN the course of the twentieth century Britain experienced a revolution as profound, and considerably more constructive, than those in Russia or Germany. The magnitude of this revolution cannot be judged by the average American because Britain has been, to most Americans, one of the less familiar countries of Europe. This condition is not based on ignorance so much as on misconceptions. Such misconceptions seem to arise from the belief that the English, speaking a similar language, must have similar ideas. These misconceptions are as prevalent among the better-educated classes of Americans as in less well-informed circles, and, as a result, errors and ignorance about Britain are widespread, even in the better books on the subject. In this section, we shall emphasize the ways in which Britain is different from the United States, especially in its constitution and its social structure.

From this political point of view, the greatest difference between Britain and the United States rests in the fact that the former has no constitution. This is not generally recognized. Instead, the statement is usually made that Britain has an unwritten constitution based on customs and conventions. Such a statement seriously misrepresents the facts. The term "constitution" refers to a body of rules concerned with the structure and functioning of a government, and it clearly implies that this body of rules is superior in its force and is formed by a different process than ordinary statute law. In Britain this is not so. The so-called "constitutional law" of England consists either of statutes which differ in no way (either in method of creation or force) from ordinary statutes or it consists of customs and conventions which are *inferior* in force to statutes and which must yield to any statute.

The major practices of the "constitution" of Britain are based on convention rather than on law. The distinction between the two reveals at once the inferiority of the former to the latter. "Laws" (based on statutes and judicial decisions) are enforceable in courts, while "conventions" (based on past practices regarded as proper) are not enforceable in any legal way. The precedents of the British system of government are generally in the nature of conventions which cover the most important parts of the system: the Cabinet and the political parties, the monarchy, the two Houses of Parliament, the relationships between these, and the internal discipline and conduct of all five of these agencies.

The conventions of the system have been highly praised, and described as binding on men's actions. They are largely praiseworthy, but their binding character is much overrated. Certainly they are not sufficiently binding to deserve the name of constitution. This is not to say that a constitution cannot be unwritten. It is perfectly possible to have an unwritten constitution, but no constitution exists unless its unwritten practices are fairly clearly envisaged and are more binding than ordinary law. In Britain neither of these is true. There is no agreement even on fairly clear-cut issues. For example, every textbook asserts that the monarchy no longer has the power to veto legislation because that power has not been used since the reign of Queen Anne. Yet three of the four great authorities on constitutional law in the twentieth century (Sir William Anson, A. V. Dicey, and Arthur Berriedale Keith) were inclined to believe that the royal veto still existed.

The customs of the constitution are admittedly less binding than law; they are not enforceable in the courts; they are not clearly stated anywhere and, accordingly, their nature, binding or not, is left largely to the interpretation of the actor himself. Since so many of the relationships which are covered by conventions are based on precedents which are secret (such as relationships between monarchy and Cabinet, between Cabinet and political parties, between Cabinet and civil service, and all the relationships within the Cabinet) and since, in many cases, the secrecy of these precedents is protected by law under the Official Secrets Act, the binding nature of the conventions has become steadily weaker. Moreover, many of the so-called conventions which have been pointed out by writers on the subject were never true, but were inventions of the writers themselves. Among these was the convention that the monarch was impartial—a convention which accorded not at all with the conduct of Queen Victoria in whose reign the rule was explicitly stated by Walter Bagehot.

Another convention which appeared in textbooks for years was to the effect that Cabinets are overthrown by adverse votes in Parliament. In fact, there have been in the last two generations scores of cases where the Cabinet's desires met with an adverse vote, yet no Cabinet has resigned as a result of such a vote in over sixty years. As early as 1853 the Coalition government was defeated in Commons three times in one week, while as late as 1924 the Labour government was defeated ten times in seven months. It is seriously stated in many books that the Cabinet is responsible to the House of Commons, and controlled by it. This control is supposed to be exercised by the voting of the members of the Parliament with the understanding that the government will resign on an adverse vote and can be compelled to do so by the House of Commons' control over supply. This whole interpretation of the British system of government had little relationship to reality in the nineteenth century and has almost none in the twentieth century. In truth, the Cabinet is not controlled by the Commons, but the reverse.

As W. I. Jennings says in more than one place in his book *Cabinet Government,* "It is the Government that controls the House of Commons." This control is exercised through the Cabinet's control of the political party machinery. This power over the party machinery is exercised through control of party funds and above all by control of nominations to constituencies. The fact that there are no primary elections in Britain and that party candidates are named by the inner clique of the party is of tremendous importance and is the key to the control which the inner clique exercises over the House of Commons, yet it is rarely mentioned in books on the English political system.

In the United States the political parties are very decentralized, with all power flowing from the local districts inward to the central committee. Any man who wins the party nomination in a local primary and in the election can become a party leader. In Britain the situation is entirely different. The party control is almost completely centralized in the hands of a largely self-perpetuating inner clique, and this clique, because of the lack of primary elections, has power of approval over all candidates and can control party discipline by its ability to give the better constituencies to the more docile party members. The statement that the Commons controls the Cabinet, through its control over supply, is not valid, because the Cabinet, if it has a majority in Parliament, can force that majority, by using the party discipline, to pass a supply bill exactly as it forces it to pass other bills. This statement that control of supply provides control of the government was never used to justify the House of Lords' control over the Cabinet, although the Lords could refuse supply as well as the Commons could until 1911.

Another convention, generally stated in most emphatic terms, is concerned with the impartiality of the Speaker of the House of Commons. The validity of this convention can be judged by reading Hansard for 1939 and observing the way in which the Speaker protected the members of the government from adverse questioning. Such questioning of members of the government by the opposition in Parliament has frequently been pointed out as one of the guarantees of free government in Britain. In practice, it has become a guarantee of little value. The government can refuse to answer any question on the grounds of "public interest." To this decision there is no appeal. In addition, when questions are not refused, they are frequently answered in an evasive fashion which provides no enlightenment whatever. This was the regular procedure in answering questions on foreign policy in the period 1935–1940. In that period, questions were even answered by outright falsehoods without any possible redress available to the questioners.

Violation and distortion of the "conventions of the constitution" have steadily increased in the twentieth century. In 1921 a convention of over five hundred years' duration and another of over one hundred years' duration were set aside without a murmur. The former provided that the Convocations of the Church of England be simultaneous with the sessions of Parliament. The latter provided that the Royal Address be approved in council. Even more serious were the distortions of conventions. In 1931 the convention that the leader of the opposition be asked to form a government when the Cabinet resigns was seriously modified. In 1935 the rule regarding Cabinet solidarity was made meaningless. In 1937 the Conservative government even violated a constitutional convention with impunity by having George VI take the coronation oath in a form different from that provided by law.

This process of the weakening and dissolution of the so-called "constitution" went so far in the twentieth century that, by 1932, Sir Austen Chamberlain and Stanley (Lord) Baldwin were agreed that " 'unconstitutional' is a term applied in politics to the other fellow who does something that you do not like." This statement is too sweeping by far. A more accurate estimation of the situation would, perhaps, be worded thus: " 'Unconstitutional' is any action likely to lead to public disorder in the immediate future or likely to affect adversely the government's chances at the polls in any future election."

The kind of act which could lead to such a result would be, in the first place, any open act of repression. More important, it would be, in the second place, any open act of "unfairness." This idea of "unfairness," or, on its positive side, "fair play," is a concept which is very largely Anglo-Saxon and which is largely based on the class structure of England as it existed up to the early twentieth century. This class structure was clearly envisioned in the minds of Englishmen and was so completely accepted that it was assumed without need to be explicitly stated. In this structure, Britain was regarded as divided into two groups the "classes" and the "masses." The "classes" were the ones who had leisure. This meant that they had property and income. On this basis, they did not need to work for a living; they obtained an education in a separate and expensive system; they married within their own class;

they had a distinctive accent; and, above all, they had a distinctive attitude. This attitude was based on the training provided in the special
educational system of the "classes." It might be summed up in the statement that "methods are more important than goals" except that this
group regarded the methods and manners in which they acted as goals
or closely related to goals.

This educational system was based on three great negatives, not easily
understood by Americans. These were (*a*) education must not be voca-
tional—that is, aimed at assisting one to make living; (*b*) education is
not aimed directly at creating or training the intelligence; and (*c*) education is not aimed at finding the "Truth." On its positive side, the
system of education of the "classes" displayed its real nature on the
school level rather than on the university level. It aimed at developing
a moral outlook, a respect for traditions, qualities of leadership and
cooperation, and above all, perhaps, that ability for cooperation in competition summed up in the English idea of "sport" and "playing the
game." Because of the restricted numbers of the upper class in Britain,
these attitudes applied chiefly to one another, and did not necessarily
apply to foreigners or even to the masses. They applied to people who
"belonged," and not to all human beings.

The functioning of the British parliamentary system depended to a
very great extent on the possession by the members of Parliament of
this attitude. Until the end of the nineteenth century, most members
of Parliament, coming from the same class background, had this attitude.
Since then, it has been lost to a considerable extent, in the Conservative
Party by the growing influence of businessmen and the declining influence of the older aristocracy, and in the Labour Party by the fact that
the majority of its members were never subjected to the formative influences, especially educational, which created this attitude. The loss of this
attitude, however, has not been so rapid as one might expect because,
in the first place, plutocracy in England has always been closer to aristocracy than in other countries, there being no sharp divisions between
the two, with the result that the aristocracy of today is merely the plutocracy of yesterday, admission from the latter group to the former
being generally accomplished in one generation through the financial
ability of the first generation of wealth to send its children to the select
schools of the aristocrats. This process is so general that the number
of real aristocrats in Britain is very small, although the number of
nominal aristocrats is quite large. This can be observed in the fact that
in 1938 more than half of the peerage had been created since 1906, the
overwhelming majority for no other reason than recognition of their
ability to acquire a fortune. These new peers have aped the older aristocrats, and this has had the effect of keeping the attitudes which allow
the constitution to function alive, although it must be confessed that

the new businessmen leaders of the Conservative Party (like Baldwin or Chamberlain) displayed a more complete grasp of the forms than of the substance of the old aristocratic attitude.

Within the Labour Party, the majority of whose members have had no opportunity to acquire the attitude necessary to allow the proper functioning of the constitutional system, the problem has been alleviated to a considerable extent by the fact that the members of that party who are of working-class origin have given very wide influence to the small group of party members who were of upper-class origin. The working-class members of the Labour Party have proved very susceptible to what is called the "aristocratic embrace." That is, they have shown a deference to the points of view and above all to the manners and position of the upper classes, and have done so to a degree which would be impossible to find in any country where class lines were not so rigidly drawn as in England. The working-class members of the Labour Party, when they entered Parliament, did not reject the old upper-class methods of action, but on the contrary sought to win upper-class approval and to retain lower-class support by demonstrating that they could run the government as well as the upper class had always done. Thus the business-class leaders of the Conservative Party and the working-class leaders of the Labour Party both consciously sought to imitate the older aristocratic attitude which had given rise to the conventions of parliamentary government. Both failed in essence rather than in appearance, and both failed from lack of real feeling for the aristocratic pattern of thought rather than from any desire to change the conventions.

The chief element in the old attitude which both groups failed to grasp was the one which we have attempted to describe as emphasis on methods rather than on goals. In government, as in tennis or cricket, the old attitude desired to win but desired to win within the rules, and this last feeling was so strong as to lead a casual observer to believe that they lacked a desire to win. In parliamentary life this appeared as a diffidence to the possession of high office or to the achievement of any specific item of legislation. If these could not be obtained within the existing rules, they were gracefully abandoned.

This attitude was based to a very considerable degree on the fact that the members of both government and opposition were, in the time of Queen Victoria, from the same small class, subjected to the same formative influences, and with the same or similar economic interests. Forty out of 69 Cabinet ministers were sons of peers in 1885–1905, while 25 out of 51 were sons of peers in 1906–1916. To resign from office or to withdraw any item of projected legislation did not, at that time, represent any surrender to an adverse group. This was not an attitude which either the new business leaders of the Conservative Party or the working-class leaders of the Labour Party could accept. Their goals were for them of such immediate concrete value to their own interests that they could not regard with equanimity loss of office or defeat of their legislative program. It was this new attitude which made possible at one and the same time the great increase in party discipline and the willingness to cut corners where possible in interpreting the constitutional conventions.

The custom of the constitution thus rests only on public opinion as a sanction, and any British government can do what it wishes so long as it does not enrage public opinion. This sanction is not nearly so effective as might appear at first glance, because of the difficulty which public opinion in England has in obtaining information and also because public opinion in England can express itself only through the ballot, and the people cannot get an election unless the government wishes to give one. All the government needs to do is to prevent an election until public opinion subsides. This can be done by the Conservative much more easily than by the Labour Party because the Conservatives have had a wider control over the avenues of publicity through which public opinion is aroused and because the actions of a Conservative government can be kept secret more easily, since the Conservatives have always controlled the chief other parts of the government which might challenge a government's actions. The first point will be discussed later. The second point can be amplified here.

The Commons and Cabinet are generally controlled by the same party, with the latter controlling the former through the party machinery. This group can do what it wishes with a minimum of publicity or public protest only if the other three parts of the government cooperate. These three parts are the monarchy, the House of Lords, and the civil service. Since all three of these have been traditionally Conservative, a Conservative government could generally count on their cooperation. This meant that a Conservative government, on coming to power, had control of all five parts of the government, while a Labour government had control of only two. This does not necessarily mean that the Conservatives would use their control of the monarchy, the Lords, or the civil service to obstruct a Labour-controlled Commons, since the Conservatives have generally been convinced of the long-run value to be derived from a reluctance to antagonize public opinion. In 1931 they abandoned the gold standard, without any real effort to defend it, as a result of the mutiny in the British fleet; in 1935 they used their control of the British Broadcasting Corporation relatively fairly as a result of public protests at the very unfair way they had used it in 1931.

Nonetheless, the Conservative control of these other parts of the government at a time when they do not control the government have been very helpful to them. In 1914, for example, the army refused to enforce the Irish Home Rule bill which had been passed after two general elections and had been approved three times by the Commons. The army, almost completely Conservative, not only refused to enforce this bill but made it clear that in any showdown on the issue its sympathies would be with the opponents of the bill. This refusal to obey the Liberal government of the day was justified on the grounds that the army's oath of loyalty was to the king and not to the government. This might well be a precedent for a rule that a Conservative minority could refuse to obey the law and could not be forced by the army, a privilege not shared by a Liberal or Labour minority.

Again, in 1931, George V, on the resignation of MacDonald, did not call upon the leader of the opposition to form a government, but encouraged an intrigue which tried to split the Labour Party and did succeed in breaking off 15 out of 289 Labour M.P.'s. MacDonald, who then represented no party, became prime minister on a majority borrowed by the king from another party. That the king would have cooperated in such an intrigue in favor of the Labour Party is very dubious. The only satisfaction which Labour had was in defeating the sessionists in the election of 1935, but this did little to overcome the injury inflicted in 1931.

Or again, in 1929–1931, under the second Labour government, the Conservative House of Lords prevented the enactment of all important legislation, including a Trades Disputes Act, the long-needed democratization of education, and electoral reform. For any Act to pass over the opposition of the Lords, it must, since 1911, be voted in the Commons three times in identical form in not less than two years. This meant that the Conservatives have a suspensive veto over the legislation of opposition governments. The importance of this power can be seen in the fact that very few bills ever became law without the Lords' consent.

Unlike the government of the United States, that of England involves no elements of federalism or separation of powers. The central government can govern in respect to any subject no matter how local or detailed, although in practice it leaves considerable autonomy to counties, boroughs, and other local units. This autonomy is more evident in regard to administration or execution of laws than it is in regard to legislation, the central government usually blocking out its wishes in general legislation, leaving the local authorities to fill in the gaps with administrative regulations and to execute the whole under supervision of the central authorities. However, the needs of local government, as well as the broadening scope of general governmental regulation, have made a congestion of legislation in Parliament so great that no member can be expected to know much about most bills. Fortunately, this is not expected. Voting in Parliament is on strict party lines, and members are expected to vote as their party whips tell them to, and are not expected to understand the contents of the bills for which they are voting.

There is also no separation of powers. The Cabinet is the government and "is expected to govern not only within the law, but, if necessary, without law or even against the law." There is no limit on retroactive legislation, and no Cabinet or Parliament can bind its successors. The Cabinet can enter into war without Parliament's permission or approval. It can expend money without Parliament's approval or knowledge, as was done in 1847 for relief in Ireland or in 1783–1883 in regard to secret-service money. It can authorize violations of the law, as was done in regard to payments of the Bank of England in 1847, in 1857, or in 1931. It can make treaties or other binding international agreements without the consent or knowledge of Parliament, as was done in 1900, 1902, and 1912.

The idea, widely held in the United States, that the Commons is a legislative body and the Cabinet is an executive body is not true. As far as legislation is concerned, Britain has a multicameral system in which the Cabinet is the second chamber, the Commons the third, and the Lords the fourth. Of these three the Conservatives always have control of the Lords, and the same party generally has control of the other two. Legislation originates in the meetings of the inner clique of the party, acting as a first chamber. If accepted by the Cabinet it passes the Commons almost automatically. The Commons, rather than a legislative body, is the public forum in which the party announces the decisions it has made in secret party and Cabinet meetings and allows the opposition to criticize in order to test public reactions. Thus all bills come from the Cabinet, and rejection in Commons is almost unthinkable, unless the Cabinet grants to party members in Commons freedom of action. Even then this freedom usually extends only to the right to abstain from voting, and does not allow the member to vote against a bill. Although machinery for private members' bills exists similar to that in the United States, such bills rarely become law. The only significant one in recent years was an unusual bill of an unusual member from an unusual constituency. It was the divorce law of A. P. Herbert, famous humorist, and Member from Oxford.

This situation is sometimes called "Cabinet dictatorship." It could more accurately be called "party dictatorship." Both the Cabinet and the Commons are controlled by the party, or more accurately by the inner clique of the party. This inner clique may hold seats in the Cabinet, but the two are not the same thing, since members of one may not be members of the other, and the gradations of power are by no means the same in one as in the other. The inner clique of the Conservative Party sometimes meets in the Carlton Club, while the inner clique of the Labour Party meets in a trade-union conclave, frequently in Transport House.

The implication here that the Cabinet controls the Commons, that Commons will never overthrow the Cabinet, and that it will not reject legislation acceptable to the Cabinet is based on the assumption that the party has a majority in Commons. A minority government, usually a coalition government, has no such control over Commons because its powers of party discipline are very weak over any party but its own. With other parties than its own, a government has few powers beyond the threat of dissolution, which, while it does threaten members of all parties with the expenses of an election and the possibility of losing their seats, is a double-edged weapon that may cut both ways. Over its own members the Cabinet has the additional powers arising from control of nominations to constituencies, party funds, and appointment to government offices.

It is not generally recognized that there have been many restrictions on democracy in Britain, most of them in nonpolitical spheres of life, but nonetheless effectively curtailing the exercises of democracy in the political sphere. These restrictions were considerably worse than in the United States, because in the latter country they have been made on a variety of grounds (racial, religious, national, and so on), and because they are recognized as being unjust and are the occasion for feelings of guilt from those whom they benefit and loud protests from others. In Britain the restrictions were almost all based on one criterion, possession of wealth, and have been the occasion for relatively mild objections, because in Britain the idea that wealth entitled its possessor to special privileges and special duties was generally accepted, even by the non-possessing masses. It was this lack of objections from both classes and masses which concealed the fact that Britain, until 1945, was the world's greatest plutocracy.

Plutocracy restricted democracy in Britain to a notable but decreasing degree in the period before 1945. This was more evident in social or economic life than in political life, and in politics it was more evident in local than in national affairs. In political life local government had a restricted suffrage (householders and their wives; in some localities only half as many as in national suffrage). This restricted suffrage elected members of local boards or councils whose activities were unpaid, thus restricting these posts to those who had leisure (that is, wealth). In local government the old English tradition that the best government is government by amateurs (which is equivalent to saying that the best government is government by the well-to-do) still survived. These amateurs were aided by paid secretaries and assistants who had the necessary technical knowledge to handle the problems that arose. These technicians were also of the middle or upper classes because of the expense of the educational system which screened out the poor on the lower levels of schooling. The paid expert who advised the unpaid members of the borough councils was the town clerk. The paid expert who advised the unpaid justice of the peace in the administration of local justice was the clerk of Quarter Sessions.

In national politics the suffrage was wide and practically unrestricted, but the upper classes possessed a right to vote twice because they were allowed to vote at their place of business or their university as well as at their residence. Members of Parliament were, for years, restricted to the well-to-do by the expenses of office and by the fact that Members of Parliament were unpaid. Payment for Members was adopted first in 1911 and fixed at £400 a year. This was raised in 1936 to £500 with an additional £100 for expenses. But the Member's expenses in Commons were so great that a Conservative Member would need at least £1,000 a year additional income and a Labour Member would need about £350 a year additional. Moreover, each candidate for Parliament must post a deposit of £150, which is forfeited if he does not receive over one-eighth of the total vote. This deposit amounted to more than the total annual income of about three-quarters of all English families in 1938, and provided another barrier to the great majority if they aspired to run for Parliament. As a result of these monetary barriers, the overwhelming mass of Englishmen could not participate actively in politics unless they could find an outside source of funds. By finding this source in labor unions in the period after 1890, they created a new political party organized on a class basis, and forced the merger of the two existing parties into a single group also organized on a class basis.

From this point of view the history of English political parties could be divided into three periods at the years of 1915 and 1924. Before 1915 the two major parties were the Liberals and the Unionists (Conservatives); after 1924 the two major parties were the Conservatives and Labour; the decade 1915–1924 represented a period in which the Liberal Party was disrupted and weakened.

Until 1915 the two parties represented the same social class—the small group known as "society." In fact both parties—Conservatives and Liberals—were controlled from at least 1866 by the same small clique of "society." This clique consisted of no more than half-a-dozen chief families, their relatives and allies, reinforced by an occasional recruit from outside. These recruits were generally obtained from the select educational system of "society," being found in Balliol or New College at Oxford or at Trinity College, Cambridge, where they first attracted attention, either by scholarship or in the debates of the Oxford or Cambridge Union. Having attracted attention in this fashion, the new recruits were given opportunities to prove their value to the inner clique of each party, and generally ended by marrying into one of the families which dominated these cliques.

At the beginning of the twentieth century the inner clique of the Conservative Party was made up almost completely of the Cecil family and their relatives. This was a result of the tremendous influence of Lord Salisbury. The only important autonomous powers in the Conservative Party in 1900 were those leaders of the Liberal Party who had come over to the Conservatives as a result of their opposition to Gladstone's project for Home Rule in Ireland. Of these, the most important example was the Cavendish family (dukes of Devonshire and marquesses of Hartington). As a result of this split in the Liberal Party, that party was subjected to a less centralized control, and welcomed into its inner clique many newer industrialists who had the money to support it.

Since 1915 the Liberal Party has almost disappeared, its place being taken by the Labour Party, whose discipline and centralized control bears comparison with that of the Conservative Party. The chief differences between the two existing parties are to be found in methods of recruitment, the inner clique of the Conservative Party being built on the basis of family, social, and educational connections, while that of the Labour Party is derived from the hard school of trade-union politics with a seasoning of upper-class renegades. In either case the ordinary voter in Britain, in 1960 as in 1900, was offered a choice between parties whose programs and candidates were largely the creations of two small self-perpetuating groups over which he (the ordinary voter) had no real control. The chief change from 1900 to 1960 was to be found in the fact that in 1900 the two parties represented a small and exclusive social class remote from the voters' experience, while in 1960 the two parties represented two antithetical social classes which were both remote from the average voter.

Thus, the lack of primary elections and the insufficient payment for Members of Parliament have combined to give Britain two political parties, organized on a class basis, neither of which represents the middle classes. This is quite different from the United States, where both the major parties are middle-class parties, and where geographic, religious, and traditional influences are more important than class influences in determining party membership. In America the prevalent middle-class ideology of the people could easily dominate the parties because both parties are decentralized and undisciplined. In Britain, where both parties are centralized and disciplined and controlled by opposing social extremes, the middle-class voter finds no party which he can regard as representative of himself or responsive to his views. As a result by the 1930's the mass of the middle classes was split: some provided continued support for the Liberal Party, although this was recognized as relatively hopeless; some voted Conservative as the only way to avoid Socialism, although they objected to the proto-Fascism of many Conservatives; others turned to the Labour Party in the hope of broadening it into a real progressive party.

. A study of the two parties is revealing. The Conservative Party represented a small clique of the very wealthy, the one-half percent who had incomes of over £2,000 a year. These knew each other well, were related by marriage, went to the same expensive schools, belonged to the same exclusive clubs, controlled the civil service, the empire, the professions, the army, and big business. Although only one-third of one percent of Englishmen went to Eton or Harrow, 43 percent of Conservative members of Parliament in 1909 had gone to these schools, and in 1938 the figure was still about 32 percent. In this last year (1938) there were 415 Conservative M.P.'s. Of these, 236 had titles and 145 had relatives in the House of Lords. In the Cabinet which made the Munich Agreement were one marquess, three earls, two viscounts, one baron, and one baronet. Of the 415 Conservative M.P.'s at that time, only one had had poor parents, and only four others came from the lower classes. As Duff Cooper (Viscount Norwich) said in March, 1939, "It is as difficult for a poor man, if he be a Conservative, to get into the House of Commons as it is for a camel to get through the eye of a needle." This was caused by the great expenses entailed in holding the position of Conservative M.P. Candidates of that party were expected to make substantial contributions to the party. The cost of an electoral campaign was £400 to £1,200. Those candidates who paid the whole expense and in addition contributed £500 to £1,000 a year to the party fund were given the safest seats. Those who paid about half of these sums were given the right to "stand" in less desirable constituencies.

Once elected, a Conservative M.P. was expected to be a member of one of the exclusive London clubs where many important party decisions were formed. Of these clubs the Carlton, which had over half of the Conservative M.P.'s as members in 1938, cost a £40 entrance fee and 17 guineas annual dues. The City of London Club, with a considerable group of Conservatives on its rolls, had an entrance fee of 100 guineas and annual dues of 15 guineas. Of 33 Conservative M.P.'s who died leaving recorded wills in the period before 1938 all left at least £10,000, while the gross estate of the group was £7,199,151. This gave an average estate of £218,156. Of these 33, 14 left over £100,000 each; 14 more left from £20,000 to £100,000; and only 5 left between £10,000 and £20,000.

Of the 415 M.P.'s on the Conservative side in 1938, 44 percent (or 181) were corporation directors, and these held 775 directorships. As a result, almost every important corporation had a director who was a

Conservative M.P. These M.P.'s did not hesitate to reward themselves, their companies, and their associates with political favors. In eight years (1931–1939) thirteen directors of the "Big Five banks" and two directors of the Bank of England were raised to the peerage by the Conservative government. Of ninety peers created in seven years (1931–1938), thirty-five were directors of insurance companies. In 1935 Walter Runciman, as president of the Board of Trade, introduced a bill to grant a subsidy of £2 million to tramp merchant vessels. He administered this fund, and in two years gave £92,567 to his father's company (Moor Line, Ltd.) in in which he held 21,000 shares of stock himself. When his father died in 1937 he left a fortune of £2,388,453. There is relatively little objection to activities of this kind in England. Once having accepted the fact that politicians are the direct representatives of economic interests, there would be little point in objecting when politicians act in accordance with their economic interests. In 1926 Prime Minister Baldwin had a direct personal interest in the outcome of the coal strike and of the General Strike, since he held 194,526 ordinary shares and 37,591 preferred shares of Baldwin's, Ltd., which owned great collieries.

The situation of 1938 was not much different from the situation of forty years earlier in 1898 except that, at the earlier date, the Conservative Party was subject to an even more centralized control, and the influence of industrial wealth was subordinated to the influence of landed wealth. In 1898 the Conservative Party was little more than a tool of the Cecil family. The prime minister and leader of the party was Robert Arthur Talbot Gascoyne-Cecil (Lord Salisbury), who had been prime minister three times for a total of fourteen years when he retired in 1902. On retirement he handed over the leadership of the party as well as the prime minister's chair to his nephew, protégé, and hand-picked successor, Arthur James Balfour. In the ten years of the Salisbury-Balfour government between 1895 and 1905, the Cabinet was packed with relatives and close associates of the Cecil family. Salisbury himself was prime minister and foreign secretary (1895–1902); his nephew, Arthur Balfour, was first lord of the Treasury and leader in Commons (1895–1902) before becoming prime minister (1902–1905); another nephew, Gerald Balfour (brother of Arthur), was chief secretary of Ireland (1895–1900) and president of the Board of Trade (1900–1905); Lord Salisbury's son and heir, Viscount Cranborne, was undersecretary for foreign affairs (1900–1903) and lord privy seal (1903–1905); Salisbury's son-in-law, Lord Selborne, was undersecretary for the colonies (1895–1900) and first lord of the Admiralty (1900–1905); Walter Long, a protégé of Salisbury, was president of the Board of Agriculture (1895–1900), president of the Local Government Board (1900–1905), and chief secretary for Ireland (1905–1906); George Curzon, another protégé of Salisbury, was undersecretary for foreign affairs (1895–1898) and viceroy of India (1899–1905); Alfred Lyttelton, Arthur Balfour's most intimate friend and the man who would have been his brother-in-law except for his sister's premature death in 1875 (an event which kept Balfour a bachelor for the rest of his life), was secretary of state for the colonies; Neville Lyttelton, brother of Alfred Lyttelton, was commander in chief in South Africa and chief of the General Staff (1902–1908). In addition, a dozen close relatives of Salisbury, including three sons and various nephews, sons-in-law, and grandchildren, and a score or more of protégés and agents were in Parliament or in various administrative positions, either then or later.

The Liberal Party was not so closely controlled as was the Conservative Party, but its chief leaders were on intimate relations of friendship and cooperation with the Cecil crowd. This was especially true of Lord Rosebery, who was prime minister in 1894–1895, and H. H. Asquith, who was prime minister in 1905–1915. Asquith married Margot Tennant, sister-in-law of Alfred Lyttelton, in 1894, and had Balfour as his chief witness at the ceremony. Lyttelton was the nephew of Gladstone as Balfour was the nephew of Salisbury. In later years Balfour was the closest friend of the Asquiths even when they were leaders of two opposing parties. Balfour frequently joked of the fact that he had dinner, with champagne, at Asquith's house before going to the House of Commons to attack his host's policies. On Thursday evenings when Asquith dined at his club, Balfour had dinner with Mrs. Asquith, and the prime minister would stop by to pick her up on his way home. It was on an evening of this kind that Balfour and Mrs. Asquith agreed to persuade Asquith to write his memoirs. Asquith had been almost as friendly with another powerful leader of the Conservative Party, Lord Milner. These two ate their meals together for four years at the scholarship table in Balliol in the 1870's, and had supper together on Sunday evenings in the 1880's. Mrs. Asquith had a romantic interlude with Milner in Egypt in 1892 when she was still Margot Tennant, and later claimed that she got him his appointment as chairman of the Board of Inland Revenue by writing to Balfour from Egypt to ask for this favor. In 1908, according to W. T. Stead, Mrs. Asquith had three portraits over her bed: those of Rosebery, Balfour, and Milner.

After the disruption of the Liberal Party and the beginnings of the rise of the Labour Party, many members of the Liberal Party went over to the Conservatives. Relationships between the two parties became somewhat less close, and the control of the Liberal Party became considerably less centralized.

The Labour Party arose because of the discovery by the masses of the people that their vote did not avail them much so long as the only choice of candidates was, as Bagehot put it, "Which of two rich people will you choose?" The issue came to a head because of a judicial decision. In the

Taff Vale case (1901) the courts decided that labor unions were responsible for damages resulting from their economic actions. To overcome this decision, which would have crippled the unions by making them financially responsible for the damages arising from strikes, the working classes turned to political action by setting up their own candidates in their own party. The funds needed were provided by the labor unions, with the result that the Labour Party became, for all practical purposes, the Trade-Union Party.

The Labour Party is, in theory, somewhat more democratic than the Conservatives, since its annual party conference is the final authority on policies and candidates. But, since unions provide the bulk of the members and the party funds, the unions dominate the party. In 1936, when the party membership was 2,444,357, almost 2 million of these were indirect members through the 73 trade unions which belonged to the party. Between party conferences, administration of the party's work was in the hands of the National Executive Committee, 17 of whose 25 members could be elected by the unions.

Because of its working-class basis, the Labour Party was generally short of funds. In the 1930's it spent on the average £300,000 a year, compared to £600,000 a year for the Conservatives and £400,000 a year for the Liberals. In the election of 1931 the Labour Party spent £181,629 in campaigning, compared to the £472,476 spent by non-Labour candidates. In the election of 1935 the two figures were £196,819 and £526,274.

This shortage of money on the part of the Labour Party was made worse by the fact that the Labour Party, especially when out of office, had difficulty in getting its side of the story to the British people. In 1936 the Labour Party had support from one morning paper with a circulation of two million copies, while the Conservatives had the support of six morning papers with a circulation of over six million copies. Of three evening papers, two supported the Conservatives and one supported the Liberals. Of ten Sunday papers with an aggregate circulation of 13,130,000 copies, seven with a circulation of 6,330,000 supported the Conservatives, one with a circulation of 400,000 supported Labour, and the two largest, with a circulation of 6,300,000, were independent.

The radio, which is the second most important instrument of publicity, is a government monopoly, created by the Conservatives in 1926. In theory it is controlled by an impartial board, but this board was created by Conservatives, is generally manned by Conservative sympathizers, and permits the government to make certain administrative decisions. Sometimes it is run fairly; sometimes it is run very unfairly. In the election of 1931 the government allowed fifteen periods on the B.B.C. for political campaigning; it took eleven periods for the Conservatives, gave three to Labour, and one to the Liberals. In 1935, somewhat more fairly, it permitted twelve periods, taking five for the Conservatives, and giving four to Labour and three to the Liberals.

Since the two chief parties in England do not represent the ordinary Englishman, but instead represent the entrenched economic interests directly, there is relatively little "lobbying," or attempting to influence legislators by political or economic pressure. This is quite different from the United States where lobbyists sometimes seem to be the only objects on a congressman's horizon. In England, where the economic interests are directly represented in Parliament, lobbying comes chiefly from groups influenced by noneconomic issues like divorce, women's suffrage, antivivisection, and so on.

On the whole, if we were to look only at politics Britain would appear at least as democratic as America. It is only when we look outside the sphere of politics to the social or economic spheres that we see that the old division into two classes was maintained relatively rigidly until 1939. The privileged classes were generally able to maintain their grasp on the professions, the educational system, the army, the civil service, and so on, even when they were losing their grasp on the political system. This was possible because training in the expensive educational system of the upper classes continued to be the chief requirement for entrance into these nonpolitical activities. The educational system, as we have said, was divided roughly into two parts: (a) one part for the ruling classes consisted of preparatory schools, the so-called "public schools" and the old universities; and (b) the other for the masses of the people consisted of public elementary schools, the secondary schools, and the newer universities. This division is not absolutely rigid, especially on the university level, but it is quite rigid on the lower level.

As Sir Cyril Norwood, headmaster of Harrow School, said, "The boy of ability from a poor home *may* get to Oxford—it is possible, though not easy—but he has no chance to enter Eton." A private school (called "public school") cost about £300 a year in 1938, a sum which exceeded the annual income of more than 80 percent of English families. The masses of the people obtained free primary schools only after 1870, and secondary schools in 1902 and 1918. These latter, however, were not free, although there were many part-payment places, and less than 10 percent of children entered a secondary school in 1938. On the highest level of education the twelve universities of England and Wales had only 40,000 students in 1938. In the United States, at the same period, the number of students on the university level was 1,350,000, a difference which was only partially compensated by the fact that the population of the United States was four times as numerous as that of Britain.

The educational system of Britain has been the chief bottleneck by which the masses of the people are excluded from positions of power and responsibility. It acts as a restriction because the type of education which leads to such positions is far too expensive for any but an insignificant fraction of Englishmen to be able to afford it. Thus, while Britain had political democracy at a fairly early period it was the last civilized country to obtain a modern system of education. In fact, it is still in process of obtaining such a system. This is in sharp contrast with the situation in France where the amount of education obtainable by a student is limited only by his ability and willingness to work; and positions of importance in the civil service, the professions, and even business are available to those who do best in the educational system. In Britain ability to a considerable degree commands positions for those who pass through the educational system, but the right to do this is based very largely on ability to pay.

The civil service in Britain in 1939 was uniform in all the regular departments of the government, and was divided into three levels. From the bottom up, these were known as "clerical," "executive," and "administrative." Promotion from one level to another was not impossible but was so rare that the vast majority remained in the level they first entered. The most important level—the administrative—was reserved to the well-to-do classes by its method of recruitment. It was open in theory to everyone through a competitive examination. This examination, however, could be taken only by those who were twenty-two or twenty-four years old; it gave 300 out of 1,300 points for the oral part; and the written part was based on liberal subjects as taught in the "public schools" and universities. All this served to restrict admission to the administrative level of the civil service to young men whose families could afford to bring them up in the proper fashion. In 1930, of 56 civil servants in posts commanding salaries of over £2,000 each, only 9 did not have the upper-class background of Oxford, Cambridge, or a "public school." This policy of restricting was most evident in the Foreign Office, where from 1851 to 1919 every person on the administrative level was from Oxford or Cambridge, one-third were from Eton, and one-third had titles. The use of educational restrictions as a method for reserving the upper ranks of the civil service to the well-to-do was clearly deliberate and was, on the whole, successful in achieving the purpose intended. As a result, as H. R. G. Greaves wrote, "The persons to be found in the principal positions of the civil service in 1850, 1900, or 1930 did not differ markedly in type."

A similar situation was to be found elsewhere. In the army in peacetime the officers were almost entirely from the upper class. They obtained commissions by an examination, largely oral, based on study at the universities or at the two military schools (Sandhurst and Woolwich) which cost £300 a year to attend. The pay was small, with heavy deductions for living expenses, so that an officer needed a private income. The navy was somewhat more democratic, although the proportion of officers risen from the ranks decreased from 10.9 percent in 1931 to 3.3 percent in 1936. The naval school (Dartmouth) was very expensive, costing £788 a year.

The clergy of the Established Church represented the same social class, since, until well into the twentieth century, the upper ranks of the clergy were named by the government, and the lower acquired their appointments by purchase. As a consequence, in the 1920's, 71 of 80 bishops were from expensive "public" schools.

The various members of the legal profession were also very likely to be of the upper class, because legal training was long and expensive. This training generally began at one of the older universities. For admission to the bar a man had to be a member of one of the four Inns of Court (Inner Temple, Middle Temple, Lincoln's Inn, Gray's Inn). These are private clubs to which admission was by nomination of members and payment of large admission fees varying from £58 to £208. A member was expected to eat dinners in his inn twenty-four nights a year for three years before being called to the bar. Then he was expected to begin practice by acting as "devil" (clerk) to a barrister for a couple of years. During these years the "devil," even in 1950, paid 100 guineas to the barrister, £130 a year for his share of the rent, 50 guineas a year to the clerk, 30 guineas for his wig and gown, and numerous other "incidental" expenses. Accordingly, it is not surprising to find that sons of wage earners formed less than 1 percent of the admissions to Lincoln's Inn in 1886–1923 and were only 1.8 percent in the period 1923–1927. In effect, then, a member of the bar might well pass five years after receiving the bachelor's degree before he could reach a position where he could begin to earn a living.

As a result, members of the bar have been, until very recently, almost entirely from the well-to-do classes. Since judges are appointed exclusively from barristers with from seven to fifteen years of experience, the judicial system has also been monopolized by the upper classes. In 1926, 139 out of 181 judges were graduates of expensive "public" schools. The same conditions also exist on the lower levels of justice where the justice of the peace, an unpaid official for whom no legal training was required, was the chief figure. These justices of the peace have always been offshoots of the "county families" of well-to-do persons.

With a system of legal administration and justice such as this, the process of obtaining justice has been complex, slow and, above all, expensive. As a result, only the fairly well-to-do can defend their rights in a civil suit and, if the less well-to-do go to court at all, they find themselves in an atmosphere completely dominated by members of the upper classes. Accordingly, the ordinary Englishman (over 90 percent of the total) avoid all litigation even when he has right on his side.

As a result of the conditions just described, the political history of Britain in the twentieth century has been a long struggle for equality. This struggle has appeared in various forms: as an effort to extend educational opportunities, as an effort to extend health and economic security to the lower classes, as an effort to open the upper ranks of the civil services and the defense forces, as well as the House of Commons itself, to those classes which lacked the advantages in leisure and training provided by wealth.

In this struggle for equality the goal has been sought by leveling the upper classes down as well as by leveling the lower classes up. The privileges of the former have been curtailed, especially by taxation and more impersonal methods of recruitment to office, at the same time that the opportunities of the latter have been extended by widening educational advantages and by the practice of granting a living payment for services rendered. In this struggle, revolutionary changes have been made by the Liberal and Conservative parties as well as by the Labour Party, each hoping to be rewarded by the gratitude of the masses of the people at the polls.

Until 1915 the movement toward equality was generally supported by the Liberals and resisted by the Conservatives, although this alignment was not invariable. Since 1923 the movement toward equality has generally been supported by Labour and resisted by the Conservatives. Here, again, the alignment has not been invariable. Both before and after World War I there have been very progressive Conservatives and very reactionary Liberals or Labourites. Moreover, since 1924 the two major parties have, as already mentioned, come to represent two opposing vested economic interests—the interests of entrenched wealth and of entrenched unionism. This has resulted in making the positions of the two parties considerably more antithetical than they were in the period before 1915 when both major parties represented the same segment of society. Moreover, since 1923, as the alienation of the two parties on the political scene has become steadily wider, there has arisen a tendency for each to take on the form of an exploiting group in regard to the great middle class of consumers and unorganized workers.

In the two decades, 1925–1945, it seemed that the efforts of men like Lord Melchett and others would create a situation where monopolized industry and unionized labor would cooperate on a program of restricted output, high wages, high prices, and social protection of both profits and employment to the jeopardy of all economic progress and to the injury of the middle and professional classes who were not members of the phalanxed ranks of cartelized industry and unionized labor. Although this program did succeed to the point where much of Britain's industrial plant was obsolescent, inefficient, and inadequate, this trend was partly ended by the influence of the war but chiefly by the victory of the Labour Party in the election of 1945.

As a result of this victory, the Labour Party began an assault on certain segments of heavy industry in order to nationalize them, and initiated a program of socialized public services (like public medicine, subsidized low food prices, and so on) which broke the tacit understanding with monopolized industry and began to distribute the benefits of the socialized economy outside the ranks of trade-union members to other members of the lower and lower middle classes. The result was to create a new society of privilege which from some points of view looked like an inversion of the society of privilege of 1900. The new privileged were the trade-union elite of the working classes and the older privileged of the upper classes, while the exploited were the middle class of white-collar and professional workers who did not have the unionized strength of the one or the invested wealth of the other.

Political History to 1939

The domestic political history of Britain in the twentieth century could well be divided into three parts by the two great wars with their experience of coalition or "national" government.

In the first period ten years of Conservative government (in which Salisbury was succeeded by Balfour) were followed by ten years of Liberal government (in which Campbell-Bannerman was succeeded by Asquith). The dates of these four governments are as follows:

    A. Conservative
        1. Lord Salisbury, 1895–1902
        2. Arthur J. Balfour, 1902–1905
    B. Liberal
        1. Henry Campbell-Bannerman, 1905–1908
        2. Herbert Henry Asquith, 1908–1915

The government of Balfour was really nothing but a continuation of the Salisbury government, but it was a pale imitation. Balfour was far from being the strong personality his uncle was, and he had to face the consequences of the Salisbury government's mistakes. In addition he had to face the beginnings of all those problems of the twentieth century which had not been dreamed of during the great days of Victoria: problems of imperialist aggressions, of labor agitation, of class animosities, of economic discontents.

The sorry record of the British war administration during the Boer War led to the establishment of a Parliamentary Committee of Investigation under Lord Esher. The report of this group resulted in a whole series of reforms which left Britain far better equipped to stand the shocks of 1914–1918 than she would otherwise have been. Not the least of the consequences of the Committee of Investigation was the creation, in 1904, of the Committee on Imperial Defence. On this latter committee Esher was, for a quarter-century, the chief figure, and as a result of his influence, there emerged from the obscurity of its secretarial staff two able public servants: (Sir) Ernest Swinton, later inventor of the tank, and Maurice (Lord) Hankey, later secretary at the Peace Conference of 1919 and for twenty years secretary to the Cabinet.

The Balfour government was weakened by several other actions. The decision to import Chinese coolies to work the mines of the Transvaal in 1903 led to widespread charges of reviving slavery. The Education Act of 1902, which sought to extend the availability of secondary education by shifting its control from school boards to local government units and by providing local taxes (rates) to support private, church-controlled schools, was denounced by Nonconformists as a scheme to force them to contribute to support Anglican education. The efforts of Joseph Chamberlain, Balfour's secretary of state for the colonies, to abandon the traditional policy of "free trade" for a program of tariff reform based on imperial preference succeeded only in splitting the Cabinet, Chamberlain resigning in 1903 in order to agitate for his chosen goal, while the Duke of Devonshire and three other ministers resigned in protest at Balfour's failure to reject Chamberlain's proposals completely.

Added to these difficulties, Balfour faced a great groundswell of labor discontent from the fact that the wage-earning segment of the population experienced a decline in standards of living in the period 1898–1906 because of the inability of wages to keep up with the rise in prices. This inability arose very largely from the decision of the House of Lords, acting as a Supreme Court, in the Taff Vale case of 1902, that labor unions could be sued for damages arising from the actions of their members in strikes. Deprived in this fashion of their chief economic weapon, the workers fell back on their chief political weapon, the ballot, with the result that the Labour membership of the House of Commons increased from three to forty-three seats in the election of 1906.

This election of 1906 was a Liberal triumph, that party obtaining a plurality of 220 over the Conservatives and a majority of 84 over all other parties. But the triumph was relatively shortlived for the upper-class leaders of that party, like Asquith, Haldane, and Edward Grey. These leaders, who were closer to the Conservative leaders both socially and ideologically than they were to their own followers, for partisan reasons had to give free rein to the more radical members of their own party, like Lloyd George, and after 1910 were unable to govern at all without the support of the Labour Party members and the Irish Nationalists.

The new government started off at full tilt. The Trade Disputes Act of 1906 overturned the Taff Vale decision and restored the strike as a weapon to the armory of the workers. In the same year a Working-men's Compensation Act was put on the books, and in 1909 came an Old Age Pension system. In the meantime the House of Lords, the stronghold of Conservatism, tried to halt the Liberal tide by its veto of an Education bill, of a Licensing bill which would have reduced the number of "public houses," of a bill restricting plural voting, and, as the *coup de grâce*, of Lloyd George's budget of 1909. This budget was aimed directly at Conservative supporters by its taxation of un-earned incomes, especially from landed property. Its rejection by the Lords was denounced by Asquith as a breach of the constitution, which, according to his belief, gave control over money bills to the Lower House.

From this dispute emerged a constitutional crisis which shook Eng-lish society to its foundations. Even after two general elections, in January and in December 1910, had returned the Liberals to power, al-though with a reduced majority, the Lords refused to yield until As-quith threatened to create enough new peers to carry his Parliament bill. This bill, which became law in August 1911, provided that the Lords could not veto a money bill and could not prevent any other bill from becoming law if it was passed in three sessions of the Com-mons over a period of at least two years.

The elections of 1910 had so reduced Asquith's plurality that he became dependent on Irish and Labourite support and, for the next four years, was of necessity compelled to grant to both concessions for which he personally had little taste. In 1909 the Lords, again as a Supreme Court, declared the use of union funds in political campaigns to be illegal, thus destroying the political weapon to which Labour had been driven by the Taff Vale decision of 1902. Asquith was not eager to overthrow this so-called "Osborne Judgement," at least for a while, for as long as union political activities were illegal the Labourite mem-bers of the Commons had to support Asquith in order to avoid a general election they could no longer finance. In order to permit the existing Labour members to live without union funds, the Asquith government in 1911 established payment for members of Parliament for the first time. Labour was also rewarded for its support of the As-quith government by the creation of Health and Unemployment In-surance in 1911, by a Minimum Wage Law in 1912, and by a Trades-Union Act in 1913. This last item made it legal for labor or-ganizations to finance political activities after approval by a majority of their members and from a special fund to be raised from those union members who did not ask to be exempt.

Assaulted by the supporters of women suffrage, dependent on the votes of Labour and the Irish Nationalists, and under steady pressure from Nonconformist Liberals, the Asquith government had an unpleasant period from 1912 to 1915. The unpleasantness culminated in violent controversies over Irish Home Rule and Welsh Disestablishment. Both bills were finally jammed through without the acceptance of the Lords in September 1914, in both cases with provisions which suspended their application until the end of the war with Germany. Thus the weakness and divisions of the Asquith government and the alarming divisions in Britain itself were swallowed up in the greater problems of waging a modern war of unlimited resources.

The problem of waging this war was given eventually to coalition governments, at first (1915–1916) under Asquith and later (1916–1922) under the more vigorous direction of David Lloyd George. The latter coalition was returned to power in the "Khaki Election" of December 1918, on a program promising punishment of German "war criminals," full payment by the defeated powers of the costs of the war, and "homes fit for heroes." Although the Coalition government was made up of Conservatives, Liberals, and Labour, with an ex-Liberal as prime minister, the Conservatives had a majority of seats in Parliament and were in closest contact with Lloyd George so that the coalition government was, except in name, a Conservative government.

The political history of Britain in the years between 1918 and 1945 is a depressing one, chiefly because of Conservative errors in domestic economic policy and in foreign policy. In this period there were seven general elections (1918, 1922, 1923, 1924, 1929, 1931, 1935). In only one (1931) did a party receive a majority of the popular vote, but in four the Conservatives obtained a majority of seats in the House of Commons. On the basis of these elections Britain had ten governments in the period 1918–1945. Of these, three were Conservative-dominated coalitions (1918, 1931, 1940), two were Labour supported by Liberal votes (1924, 1929), and five were Conservatives (1922, 1923, 1924, 1935, 1937), thus:

Lloyd George	December 1918–October 1922
Bonar Law	October 1922–May 1923
Stanley Baldwin	May 1923–January 1924
Ramsey MacDonald	January 1924–November 1924
Second Baldwin	November 1924–June 1929
Second MacDonald	June 1929–August 1931
National Government (MacDonald)	August 1931–June 1935
Third Baldwin	June 1935–May 1937
Neville Chamberlain	May 1937–May 1940
Second National Government (Churchill)	May 1940–July 1945

The Lloyd George coalition was almost a personal government, as Lloyd George had his own supporters and his own political funds and feuds. Although technically a Liberal, Lloyd George had split his own party, so that Asquith was in opposition along with the Labour party and about an equal number of Conservatives. Since the 80 Irish Nationalists and Irish Republicans did not take their seats, the 334 Conservatives in the coalition had a majority of the Commons, but allowed Lloyd George to take the responsibility for handling the postwar problems. They waited four years before throwing him out. During this time domestic affairs were in a turmoil, and foreign affairs were not much better. In the former, the effort to deflate prices in order to go back on the gold standard at the prewar parity was fatal to prosperity and domestic order. Unemployment and strikes increased, especially in the coal mines.

The Conservatives prevented any realistic attack on these problems, and passed the Emergency Powers Act of 1920, which, for the first time in English history, gave a peacetime government the right to proclaim a state of siege (as was done in 1920, 1921, and 1926). Unemployment was dealt with by establishment of a "dole," that is, a payment of 20 shillings a week to those unable to find work. The wave of strikes was dealt with by minor concessions, by vague promises, by dilatory investigations, and by playing one group off against another. The revolt in Ireland was met by a program of strict repression at the hands of a new militarized police known as "Black and Tans." The protectorate over Egypt was ended in 1922, and a reexamination of imperial relations was made necessary by the refusal of the Dominions to support the United Kingdom in the Near East crisis arising from Lloyd George's opposition to Kemal Atatürk.

On October 23, 1923, the Conservatives overthrew Lloyd George and set up their own government under Bonar Law. In the following General Election they obtained 344 of 615 seats, and were able to continue in office. This Conservative government lasted only fifteen months under Bonar Law and Stanley Baldwin. In domestic affairs its chief activities were piecemeal action on unemployment and talk about a protective tariff. On this last issue Baldwin called a General Election in December 1923 and lost his majority, although continuing to have the largest block in Commons, 258 seats to Labour's 191 and the Liberals' 159. Asquith, who held the balance of power, could have thrown his support either way, and decided to throw it to Labour, hoping to give Labour a "fair chance." Thus the first Labour government in history came to office, if not to power.

With an unfriendly House of Lords, an almost completely inexperienced Cabinet, a minority government, a large majority of its members in Commons trade unionists with no parliamentary experience, and a Liberal veto over any effort to carry out a Socialist or even a Labourite program, little could be expected from MacDonald's first government. Little was accomplished, nothing of permanent importance at least, and within three months the prime minister was looking about for an excuse to resign. His government continued the practice of piecemeal solutions for unemployment, began public subsidies for housing, lowered the taxes on necessities (sugar, tea, coffee, cocoa), abolished the corporation tax and the wartime duties of 33⅓ percent on motorcars, watches, clocks, musical instruments, hats, and plate glass, as well as the 1921 duties on "key industries" (optical glass, chemicals, electrical apparatus).

The chief political issue of the day, however, was Communism. This rose to a fever heat when MacDonald recognized Soviet Russia and tried to make a commercial treaty with the same country. MacDonald cooperated with the Liberals with ill-grace and resigned when Parliament decided to investigate the quashing of the prosecution, under the Incitement to Mutiny Act, of the editor of a Communist weekly paper. In the resulting general election the Conservatives played the "red scare" for all it was worth. They were aided greatly when the permanent officials of the Foreign Office issued, four days before the election, the so-called "Zinoviev Letter." This forged document called upon British subjects to support a violent revolution in behalf of the Third International. It undoubtedly played some role in gaining the Conservatives their largest majority in many years, 412 out of 615 seats.

Thus began a Conservative government which was in office under Baldwin for five years. Winston Churchill as chancellor of the Exchequer carried out the stabilization policy which put England on the gold standard with the pound sterling at the prewar rate of parity. As we have indicated in Chapter 7, this policy of deflation drove Britain into an economic depression and a period of labor conflict, and the policy was so bungled in its execution that Britain was doomed to semidepression for almost a decade, was in financial subjection to France until September 1931, and was driven closer to domestic rebellion than she had been at any time since the Chartist movement of 1848. The recognition of Russia and the trade agreement with Russia were abrogated; the import duties were restored; and the income tax was lowered (although the inheritance tax was raised). As deficits grew, they were made up by a series of raids on available special funds. The chief domestic event of the period was the General Strike of May 3–12, 1926.

The General Strike developed from a strike in the coal mines and from the determination of both sides to bring the class struggle to a showdown. The British mines were in bad condition because of the nature of the coal deposits and because of mismanagement which left them with inadequate and obsolete technological equipment. Most of them were high-cost producers compared to the mines of northern France and western Germany. The deflation resulting from the effort to stabilize the pound hit the mines with special impact, since prices could be cut only if costs were cut first, an action which meant, for the mines above all, cutting of wages. The loss of the export trade, resulting from Germany's efforts to pay reparations in coal, and especially the return of the Ruhr mines to full production after the French evacuation of that area in 1924 made the mines the natural focal point for labor troubles in England.

The mines had been under government control during the war. After that conflict ended, many Liberals, Labourites, and the miners themselves wanted nationalization. This attitude was reflected in the report of a royal commission under Lord Sankey which recommended nationalization and higher wages. The government gave the latter but refused the former (1919). In 1921, when government control ended, the owners demanded longer hours and reduced wages. The miners refused, went out on strike for three months (March–June 1921), and won a promise of a government subsidy to raise wages in the worse-paid districts. In 1925, as a result of stabilization, the owners announced new wage cuts. Because the miners objected, the government appointed a new royal commission under Sir Herbert Samuel. This group condemned the subsidy and recommended closing down high-cost mines, selling output collectively, and cutting wages while leaving hours of work the same. Since owners, government, and labor were all willing to force a showdown, the affair drifted into a crisis when the government invoked the Emergency Powers Act of 1920 and the Trades Union Congress answered with an order for a General Strike.

In the General Strike all union labor went out. Upper- and middle-class volunteers sought to keep utilities and other essential economic activities fuctioning. The government issued its own news bulletin (*The British Gazette* under Churchill), used the British Broadcasting Corporation to attack the unions, and had their side supported by the only available newspaper, the antiunion *Daily Mail*, which was printed in Paris and flown over.

The Trades Union Congress had no real heart in the strike, and soon ended it, leaving the striking miners to shift for themselves. The miners stayed out for six months, and then began to drift back to work to escape starvation. They were thoroughly beaten, with the result that many left England. The population of the worst-hit area, South Wales, fell by 250,000 in three years.

Among the results of the failure of the General Strike, two events must be mentioned. The Trades Dispute Act of 1927 forbade sympathy strikes, restricted picketing, prohibited state employees from affiliating with other workers, restored the Taff Vale decision, and changed the basis for collection of labor-union political funds from those who did not refuse to contribute to those who specifically agreed to contribute. The Trades Union Congress, disillusioned with economic weapons of class conflict, discarded the strike from its arsenal, and concentrated its attention on political weapons. In the economic field it became increasingly conservative and began to negotiate with the leaders of industry, like Lord Melchett of Imperial Chemical Industries, on methods by which capital and labor might cooperate to mulct consumers. A National Industrial Council, consisting of the Trades Union Congress, the Federation of British Industries, and the National Conference of Employers, was set up as the instrument of this cooperation.

The last three years of the Conservative government were marked by the creation of a national system of electric-power distribution and of a government-owned monopoly over radio (1926), the extension of the electoral franchise to women between twenty-one and thirty years of age (1928), the Road Transport Act, and the Local Government Act (1929). In these later years the government became increasingly unpopular because of a number of arbitrary acts by the police. As a result, the general election of 1929 was almost a repetition of that of 1923: the Conservatives fell to 260 seats; Labour, with 288 seats, was the largest party but lacked a majority; and the Liberals, with 59 seats, held the balance of power. As in 1923, the Liberals threw their support to Labour, bringing to office the second MacDonald government.

The MacDonald government of 1929–1931 was even less radical than that of 1924. The Labour members were unfriendly to their Liberal supporters and were divided among themselves so that there was petty bickering even within the Cabinet. The Liberal members were more progressive than Labour, and became impatient with Labour's conservative policies. Snowden, as chancellor of the Exchequer, kept the import duties and raised other taxes, including the income tax. Since this was not sufficient to balance the budget, he borrowed from various separate funds and moved forward the date on which income-tax was due.

The Lord Privy Seal, J. H. Thomas, a railroad union leader, was made head of a group seeking a solution to the problem of unemployment. After a few months the task was given up, and he was made secretary of state for the Dominions. This failure appeared worse because both the Liberals and Sir Oswald Mosley (then of the Labour Party) had worked out detailed plans based on public-works projects. Unemployment benefits were increased, with the result that the Insurance Fund had to be replenished by loans. The Coal Mines Act (1930) set up a joint-selling agency, established a subsidy for coal exports and a national wage board for the mines, but left hours of work at seven and a half a day instead of the older seven.

The House of Lords refused to accept an Electoral Reform bill, an Agricultural Land Utilization bill, and Sir Charles Trevelyan's Education bill. The last of these provided free secondary education and raised the school-leaving age to fifteen years; but the Labour government was not insistent on these bills, and Trevelyan resigned in protest at its dilatory attitude. An Agricultural Marketing bill, which benefited the landed group in the House of Lords and raised food prices to the consumer, was passed. Throughout these efforts at legislation it was clear that the Labour Party had difficulty controlling its own members, and the Labour protest vote on most divisions in Commons was quite large.

The problem of the growing budgetary deficit was complicated in 1931 by the export of gold. The National Confederation of Employers and the Federation of British Industries agreed in prescribing wage cuts of one-third. On February 11th a committee under Sir George May, set up on a Liberal motion, brought in its report. It recommended cuts in government expenditures of £96 million, two-thirds to come from unemployment benefits and one-third from employees' wages. This was rejected by the Trades Union Congress and by a majority of the Cabinet.

In June the Macmillan Committee, after two years' study, reported that the whole financial structure of England was unsound and should be remedied by a managed currency, controlled by the Bank of England. Instead of making efforts in any consistent direction, MacDonald, unknown to any of his Cabinet except Snowden and Thomas, resigned but secretly agreed to continue as prime minister supported by the Conservatives and whichever Labour and Liberal members he could get. Throughout the crisis MacDonald consulted with the leaders of the other two parties but not with his own, and he announced the formation of the National government at the same Cabinet meeting at which he told the ministers that they had resigned.

The National government had a Cabinet of ten members, of which four were Labour, four Conservative, and two liberal. The non-Cabinet ministers were Conservative or Liberal. This Cabinet had the support of 243 Conservatives, 52 Liberals, and 12 Labour, and had in opposition 242 Labour and 9 Independents. Only thirteen Labour M.P.'s followed MacDonald, and they were soon expelled from the party.

This crisis was of great significance because it revealed the incapacity of the Labour Party and the power of the bankers. The Labour Party throughout was wracked by petty personal bickering. Its chief members had no understanding of economics. Snowden, the "economic expert" of the Cabinet, had financial views about the same as those of Montagu Norman of the Bank of England. There was no agreed party program except the remote and unrealistic one of "nationalization of industry," and this program was bound to be regarded with mixed enthusiasm by a party whose very structure was based on trade unionism.

As for the bankers they were in control throughout the crisis. While publicly they insisted on a balanced budget, privately they refused to accept balancing by taxation and insisted on balancing by cuts in relief payments. Working in close cooperation with American bankers and Conservative leaders, they were in a position to overthrow any government which was not willing to crush them completely. While they refused cooperation to the Labour government on August 23rd, they were able to obtain a loan of £80 million from the United States and France for the National government when it was only four days old. Although they would not allow the Labour government to tamper with the gold standard in August, they permitted the National government to abandon it in September with bank rates at 4½ percent.

The National government at once attacked the financial crisis with a typical bankers' weapon: deflation. It offered a budget including higher taxes and drastic cuts in unemployment benefits and public salaries. Riots, protests, and mutiny in the navy were the results. These forced Britain off gold on September 21st. A general election was called for October 27th. It was bitterly fought, with MacDonald and Snowden attacking Labour while Conservatives and Liberals fought on the issue of a tariff. Snowden called the Labour Party "Bolshevism run mad." He was later rewarded with a peerage. The government used all the powerful methods of publicity it controlled, including the B.B.C., in a fashion considerably less than fair, while Labour had few avenues of publicity, and was financially weak from the depression and the Trades Disputes Act of 1927. The result was an overwhelming government victory with 458 members supporting it and only 56 in opposition.

The National government lasted four years. Its chief domestic accomplishment was the ending of free trade and the construction of a cartelized economy behind the new trade barriers. The construction of cartels, the revival of the export trade, and the continuance of low food prices gave a mild economic boom, especially in housing. The ending of free trade split the Liberal Party into a government group (under Sir John Simon) and an opposition group (under Sir Herbert Samuel and Sir Archibald Sinclair). This gave three Liberal splinters, for Lloyd George had never supported the government.

The domestic program of the National government was such as to encourage a cartelized economic system, and to curtail the personal freedom of individuals. On this, there was no real protest, for the Labour opposition had a program which, in fact if not in theory, tended in the same direction.

A national system of unemployment insurance was set up in 1933. It required the insurance fund to be kept solvent by varying contributions with needs. With it was a relief program, including a means test, which applied to those not eligible for unemployment insurance. It placed most of the burden on local governments but put all the control in a centralized Unemployment Assistance Board. Unemployed youth were sent to training centers. All educational reform was curtailed, and the project to raise the school-leaving age from fifteen to sixteen was abandoned.

The London Passenger Transport Act of 1933, like the Act creating the B.B.C. seven years earlier, showed that the Conservatives had no real objection to nationalization of public utilities. All the transportation system of the London area, except the railroads, was consolidated under the control of a public corporation. Private owners were bought out by generous exchange of securities, and a governing board was set us of trustees representing various interests.

The Agricultural Marketing Act of 1931, as modified in 1933, provided centralized control of the distribution of certain crops with minimum prices and government subsidies.

The police of London, with jurisdiction over one-sixth the population of England, were reorganized in 1933 to destroy their obvious sympathy with the working classes. This was done by restricting all ranks above inspector to persons with an upper-class education, by training them in a newly created police college, and by forbidding them to join the Police Federation (a kind of union). The results of this were immediately apparent in the contrast between the leniency of the police attitude toward Sir Oswald Mosley's British Union of Fascists (which beat up British subjects with relative impunity) and the violence of police action toward even peaceful anti-Fascist activities. This tolerant attitude toward Fascism was reflected in both the radio and the cinema.

A severe Incitement to Disaffection Act in 1934 threatened to destroy many of the personal guarantees built up over the centuries by making police search of homes less restricted and by making the simple possession of material likely to disaffect the armed forces a crime. It was passed after severe criticism and a Lords' debate which continued until 4:00 A.M. For the first time in three generations, personal freedom and civil rights were restricted in time of peace. This was done by new laws, by the use of old laws like the Official Secrets Acts, and by such ominous innovations as "voluntary" censorship of the press and by judicial extension of the scope of the libel laws. This development reached its most dangerous stage with the Prevention of Violence Act of 1939, which empowers a secretary of state to arrest without warrant and to deport without trial any person, even a British subject, who has not been ordinarily resident in England, if he believes such a person is concerned in the preparation or instigation of acts of violence or is harboring persons so concerned. Fortunately, these new strictions were administered with a certain residue of the old English good-humored tolerances, and were, for political reasons, rarely applied to any persons with strong trade-union support.

The reactionary tendencies of the National government were most evident in its fiscal policies. For these, Neville Chamberlain was chiefly responsible. For the first time in almost a century, there was an increase in the proportion of the total tax paid by the working classes. For the first time since the repeal of the corn laws in 1846, there was a tax on food. For the first time in two generations, there was a reversal in the trend toward more education for the people. The budget was kept balanced, but at a considerable price in human suffering and in wastage of Britain's irreplaceable human resources. By 1939 in the so-called "depressed areas" of Scotland, of South Wales, and of the northeast coast, hundreds of thousands had been unemployed for years, and, as the Pilgrim Fund pointed out, had had their moral fiber completely destroyed by years of living on an inadequate dole. The capitalists of these areas were supported either by government subsidy (as the Runciman family lined their pockets from shipping subsidies) or were bought out by cartels and trade associations from funds assessed on the more active members of the industry (as was done in coal mining, steel, cement, shipbuilding, and so on).

The Derating Act of 1929 of Neville Chamberlain exempted industry from payment of three-quarters of its taxes under certain conditions. In the period 1930–1937 this saved industry £170 million, while many unemployed were allowed to starve. This law was worth about £200,000 a year to Imperial Chemical Industries. On the other hand Chamberlain, as chancellor of the Exchequer, insisted on those appropriations for the air force which ultimately made it possible for the RAF to overcome Göring's attack in the Battle of Britain in 1940.

The General Election of 1935, which gave the Conservatives ten more years in office, was the most shameful of modern times. It was perfectly clear that the English people were wholeheartedly for collective security. In the period November 1934 to June 1935, the League of Nations Union cooperated with other organizations to hold a "Peace Ballot." Five questions were asked, of which the most important were the first (Should Britain remain in the League?) and the fifth (Should Britain use economic or military sanctions against aggressors?). On the first question the answers gave 11,090,387 affirmative and 355,883 negative votes. On the use of economic sanctions, the vote was 10,027,608 affirmative and 635,074 negative. On the use of military sanctions, the vote was 6,784,368 affirmative and 2,351,981 negative.

To add to this, a by-election at East Fulham in the spring of 1935 saw a Labour supporter of collective security defeat a Conservative. The Conservatives resolved to fight a General Election in support of collective security. Baldwin replaced MacDonald as prime minister, and Samuel Hoare replaced the Liberal, Sir John Simon, at the Foreign Office, to make people believe that the past program of appeasement would be reversed. In September, Hoare made a vigorous speech at Geneva in which he pledged Britain's support of collective security to stop the Italian aggression against Ethiopia. The public did not know that he had stopped off in Paris en route to Geneva to arrange a secret deal by which Italy would be given two-thirds of Ethiopia.

The Royal Jubilee was used during the spring of 1935 to build up popular enthusiasm for the Conservative cause. Late in October, a week before the local elections on which Labour had already spent most of its available funds, the Conservatives announced a General Election for November 14th, and asked a popular mandate to support collective security and rearmament. The Labour Party was left without either an issue or funds to support it, and in addition was split on the issue of pacifism, the party leaders in both Lords and Commons refusing to go along with the rest of the party on the issue of rearmament as a support for collective security.

In the election the government lost 83 seats, but the Conservatives still had a majority, with 387 seats to Labour's 154. The Liberal Party was reduced from 34 to 21. This new government was in office for ten years, and had its attention devoted, almost exclusively to foreign affairs. In these, until 1940 as we shall see, it showed the same incapacity and the same bias it had been revealing in its domestic program.

XI

CHANGING ECONOMIC PATTERNS

Introduction

An economic system does not have to be expansive—that is, constantly increasing its production of wealth—and it might well be possible for people to be completely happy in a nonexpansive economic system if they were accustomed to it. In the twentieth century, however, the people of our culture have been living under expansive conditions for generations. Their minds are psychologically adjusted to expansion, and they feel deeply frustrated unless they are better off each year than they were the preceding year. The economic system itself has become organized for expansion, and if it does not expand it tends to collapse.

The basic reason for this maladjustment is that investment has become an essential part of the system, and if investment falls off, consumers have insufficient incomes to buy the consumers' goods which are being produced in another part of the system because part of the flow of purchasing power created by the production of goods was diverted from purchasing the goods it had produced into savings, and all the goods produced could not be sold until those savings came back into the market by being invested. In the system as a whole, everyone sought to improve his own position in the short run, but this jeopardized the functioning of the system in the long run. The contrast here is not merely between the individual and the system, but also between the long run and the short run.

The nineteenth century had accepted as one of its basic faiths the theory of "the harmony of interests." This held that what was good for the individual was good for society as a whole and that the general advancement of society could be achieved best if individuals were left free to seek their own individual advantages. This harmony was assumed to exist between one individual and another, between the individual and the group, and between the short run and the long run. In the nineteenth century, such a theory was perfectly tenable, but in the twentieth century it could be accepted only with considerable modification. As a result of persons seeking their individual advantages, the economic organization of society was so modified that the actions of one such person were very likely to injure his fellows, the society as a whole, and his own long-range advantage. This situation led to such a conflict between theory and practice, between aims and accomplishments, between individuals and groups that a return to fundamentals in economics became necessary. Unfortunately, such a return was made difficult because of the conflict between interests and principles and because of the difficulty of finding principles in the extraordinary complexity of twentieth-century economic life.

The factors necessary to achieve economic progress are supplementary to the factors necessary for production. Production requires the organization of knowledge, time, energy, materials, land, labor, and so on. Economic progress requires three additional factors. These are: innovation, savings, and investment. Unless a society is organized to provide these three, it will not expand economically. "Innovation" means devising new and better ways of performing the tasks of production; "saving" means refraining from consumption of resources so that they can be mobilized for different purposes; and "investment" means the mobilization of resources into the new, better ways of production.

The absence of the third factor (investment) is the most frequent cause of a failure of economic progress. It may be absent even when both of the other factors are working well. In such a case, the savings accumulated are not applied to inventions but are spent on consumption, on ostentatious social prestige, on war, on religion, on other nonproductive purposes, or even left unspent.

Economic progress has always involved shifts in productive resources from old methods to new ones. Such shifts, however beneficial to certain groups and however welcome to people as a whole, were bound to be resisted and resented by other groups who had vested interests in the old ways of doing things and in the old ways of utilizing resources. In a progressive period, these vested interests are unable to defend their vested interests to the point of preventing progress; but, obviously, if the groups in a society who control the savings which are necessary for progress are the same vested interests who benefit by the existing way of doing things, they are in a position to defend these vested interests and prevent progress merely by preventing the use of surpluses to finance new inventions. Such a situation is bound to give rise to an economic crisis. From one narrow point of view, the twentieth century's economic crisis was a situation of this type. To understand how such a situation could arise, we must examine the development in the chief capitalist countries and discover the causes of the crisis.

Great Britain

In Britain, throughout the nineteenth century, the supply of capital was so plentiful from private savings that industry was able to finance itself with little recourse to the banking system. The corporate form was adopted relatively slowly, and because of the benefits to be derived from limited liability rather than because it made it possible to appeal to a widespread public for equity capital. Savings were so plentiful that the surplus had to be exported, and interest rates fell steadily. Promoters and investment bankers were not much interested in domestic industrial securities (except railroads), and for most of the century concentrated their attention on government bonds (both foreign and domestic) and on foreign economic enterprises. Financial capitalism first appeared in foreign securities, and found a fruitful field of operations. The corporation law (as codified in 1862) was very lenient. There were few restrictions on formations of companies, and none on false prospectuses or false financial reports. Holding companies were not legally recognized until 1928, and no consolidated balance sheet was required then. As late as 1933, of 111 British investment trusts only 52 published a record of their holdings.

This element of secrecy is one of the outstanding features of English business and financial life. The weakest "right" an Englishman has is the "right to know," which is about as narrow as it is in American nuclear operations. Most duties, powers, and actions in business are controlled by customary procedures and conventions, not by explicit rules and regulations, and are often carried out by casual remarks between old friends. No record perpetuates such remarks, and they are generally regarded as private affairs which are no concern of others, even when they involve millions of pounds of the public's money. Although this situation is changing slowly, the inner circle of English financial life remains a matter of "whom one knows," rather than "what one knows." Jobs are still obtained by family, marriage, or school connections; character is considered far more important than knowledge or skill; and important positions, on this basis, are given to men who have no training, experience, or knowledge to qualify them.

As part of this system and at the core of English financial life have been seventeen private firms of "merchant bankers" who find money for established and wealthy enterprises on either a long-term (investment) or a short-term ("acceptances") basis. These merchant bankers, with a total of less than a hundred active partners, include the firms of

Baring Brothers, N. M. Rothschild, J. Henry Schroder, Morgan Gren-fell, Hambros, and Lazard Brothers. These merchant bankers in the period of financial capitalism had a dominant position with the Bank of England and, strangely enough, still have retained some of this, de-spite the nationalization of the Bank by the Labour government in 1946. As late as 1961 a Baring (Lord Cromer) was named governor of the bank, and his board of directors, called the "Court" of the bank, included representatives of Lazard, of Hambros, and of Morgan Grenfell, as well as of an industrial firm (English Electric) controlled by these.

The heyday of English financial capitalism is associated with the governorship of Montagu Norman from 1920 to 1944, but it began about a century after the advent of industrial capitalism, with the promotion of Guinness, Ltd., by Barings in 1886, and continued with the creation of Allsopps, Ltd., by the Westminster Bank in 1887. In the latter year, only 10,000 companies were in existence although the creation of companies had been about 1,000 a year in the 1870's and about 2,000 a year in the 1880's. Of the companies registered, about a third fell bankrupt in their first year. This is a very large fraction when we consider that about one-half the companies created were private companies which did not offer securities to the public and presumably already were engaged in a flourishing business. Financial capitalism really took root in Britain only in the 1890's. In two years (1894–1896) E. T. Hooley promoted twenty-six corporations with various noble lords as the directors of each. The total capital of this group was £18.6 million, of which Hooley took £5 million for himself.

From this date onward, financial capitalism grew rapidly in Britain, without ever achieving the heights it did in the United States or Ger-many. Domestic concerns remained small, owner-managed, and relatively unprogressive (especially in the older lines like textiles, iron, coal, ship-building). One chief field of exploitation for British financial capitalism continued to be in foreign countries until the crash of 1931. Only after 1920 did it spread tentatively into newer fields like machinery, electrical goods, and chemicals, and in these it was superseded almost at once by monopoly capitalism. As a result, the period of financial capitalism was relatively weak in Britain. In addition, its rule was relatively honest (in contrast to the United States but similar to Germany). It made little use of holding companies, exercising its influence by interlocking di-rectorates and direct financial controls. It died relatively easily, yielding control of the economic system to the new organizations of monopoly capitalism constructed by men like William H. Lever, Viscount Lever-hulme (1851–1925) or Alfred M. Mond, Lord Melchett (1868–1930). The former created a great international monopoly in vegetable oils centering upon Unilever, while the latter created the British chemical monopoly known as Imperial Chemical Industries.

Financial capitalism in Britain, as elsewhere, was marked not only by a growing financial control of industry but also by an increasing concentration of this control and by an increasing banking control of government. As we have seen, this influence of the Bank of England over the government was an almost unmitigated disaster for Britain. The power of the bank in business circles was never as complete as it was in government, because British businesses remained self-financing to a greater extent than those of other countries. This self-financing power of business in Britain depended on the advantage which it held because of the early arrival of industrialism in England. As other countries became industrialized, reducing Britain's advantage and her extraordinary profits, British business was forced to seek outside financial aid or reduce its creation of capital plant. Both methods were used, with the result that financial capitalism grew at the same time as considerable sections of Britain's capital plant became obsolete.

The control of the Bank of England over business was exercised indirectly through the joint-stock banks. These banks became increasingly concentrated and increasingly powerful in the twentieth century. The number of such banks decreased through amalgamation from 109 in 1866 to 35 in 1919 and to 33 in 1933. This growth of a "money trust" in Britain led to an investigation by a Treasury Committee on Bank Amalgamations. In its report (Colwyn Report, 1919) this committee admitted the danger and called for government action. A bill was drawn up to prevent further concentration but was withdrawn when the bankers made a "gentlemen's agreement" to ask Treasury permission for future amalgamations. The net result was to protect the influence of the Bank of England, since this might have been reduced by complete monopolization of joint-stock banking, and the bank was always in a position to influence the Treasury's attitude on all questions. Of the 33 joint-stock banks existing in 1933, 9 were in Ireland and 8 in Scotland, leaving only 16 for England and Wales. The 33 together had over £2,500 million in deposits in April 1933, of which £1,773 million were in the so-called "Big Five" (Midland, Lloyds, Barclays, Westminster, and National Provincial). The Big Five controlled at least 7 of the other 28 (in one case by ownership of 98 percent of the stock). Although competition among the Big Five was usually keen, all were subject to the powerful influence of the Bank of England, as exercised through the discount rate, interlocking directorships, and above all through the intangible influences of tradition, ambition, and prestige.

In Britain, as elsewhere, the influence of financial capitalism served to create the conditions of monopoly capitalism not only by creating monopoly conditions (which permitted industry to free itself from financial dependency on banks) but also by insisting on those deflationary, orthodox financial policies which eventually alienated industrialists from financiers. Although monopoly capitalism began to grow in Britain as far back as the British Salt Union of 1888 (which controlled 91 percent of the British supply), the victory of monopoly capitalism over financial capitalism did not arrive until 1931. By that year the structure of monopoly capitalism was well organized. The Board of Trade reported in 1918 that Britain had 500 restrictive trade associations. In that same year the Federation of British Industries (FBI) had as members 129 trade associations and 704 firms. It announced that its goals would be the regulation of prices, the curtailment of competition, and the fostering of cooperation in technical matters, in politics, and in publicity. By 1935 it had extended this scope to include (a) elimination of excess productive capacity, (b) restrictions on entry of new firms into a field, and (c) increasing duress on both members and outsiders to obey minimum-price regulations and production quotas. This last ability was steadily strengthened in the period 1931–1940. Probably the greatest achievement in this direction was a decision of the House of Lords, acting as a Supreme Court, which permitted the use of duress against outsiders in order to enforce restrictive economic agreements (the case of Thorne v. Motor Trade Association decided June 4, 1937).

The year 1931 represented for Britain the turning point from financial to monopoly capitalism. In that year financial capitalism, which had held the British economy in semidepression for a decade, achieved its last great victory when the financiers led by Montagu Norman and J. P. Morgan forced the resignation of the British Labour government. But the handwriting was already on the wall. Monopoly had already grown to such a degree that it aspired to make the banking system its servant instead of its master. The deflationary financial policy of the bankers had alienated politicians and industrialists and driven monopolist trade unions to form a united front against the bankers.

This was clearly evident in the Conference on Industrial Reorganization and Relationships of April 1928. This meeting contained representatives of the Trade Union Congress and the Employers' Federation and issued a *Memorandum* to the chancellor of the Exchequer signed by Sir Alfred Mond of Imperial Chemicals and Ben Turner of the trade unions. Similar declarations were issued by other monopolist groups, but the split of monopolist capitalists and of financial capitalists could not become overt until the latter were able to get rid of the Labour government. Once that was achieved, labor and industry were united in opposition to the continuance of the bankers' economic policy with its low prices and high unemployment. The decisive event which caused the end of financial capitalism in Britain was the revolt of the British fleet at Invergordon on September 15, 1931, and not the abandonment of gold six days later. The mutiny made it clear that the policy of deflation must be ended. As a result, no real effort was made to defend the gold standard.

With the abandonment of gold and the adoption of a protective tariff, monopolist capital and labor joined in an effort to raise both wages and profits by a program of higher prices and restrictions on production. The old monopolies and cartels increased in strength and new ones were formed, usually with the blessing of the government. These groups enforced restrictive practices on their members and on outsiders even to the extent of buying up and destroying productive capacity in their own lines. In some cases, as in agricultural products and in coal, these efforts were based on statute law, but in most cases they were purely private ventures. In no case did the government make any real effort to protect consumers against exploitation. In 1942 a capable observer, Hermann Levy, wrote, "Today Britain is the only highly industrialized country in the world where no attempt has yet been made to restrict the domination of quasi-monopolist associations in industry and trade." It is true that the government did not accept the suggestions of Lord Melchett and of the Federation of British Industries that cartels and trade associations be made compulsory, but it gave such free rein to these groups in the use of their economic power that the compulsory aspect became largely unnecessary. By economic and social pressure individuals who refused to adopt the restrictive practices favored by the industry as a whole were forced to yield or were ruined. This, for example, was done to a steel manufacturer who insisted on constructing a continuous-strip steel mill in 1940.

Among the producing groups, social pressures were added to economic duress to enforce restrictive practices. A tradition of inefficiency, high prices, and low output became so entrenched that anyone who questioned it was regarded as socially unacceptable and almost a traitor to Britain. As The Economist, the only important voice in the country which resisted this trend, said (on January 8, 1944) " . . . too few British business men are trying to compete. In these days, to say that a firm has so increased its efficiency that it can sell at low prices is not to give praise for initiative and enterprise, but to criticise it for breaking the rules of 'fair' trading and indulging in the ultimate sin of 'cut-throat' competition."

No detailed analysis of the methods or organization of these restrictive groups can be made here, but a few examples may be indicated. The Coal Mines Act of 1930 set up an organization which allotted production quotas to each colliery and fixed minimum prices. The National Shipbuilders Security, Ltd., was set up in 1930 and began to buy up and destroy shipyards, using funds from a million-pound bond issue whose service charges were met from a 1 percent levy on construction contracts. By 1934 one-quarter of Britain's shipbuilding capacity had been eliminated. The Millers' Mutual Association (1920) entirely suppressed competition among its members, and set up the Purchase Finance Company to buy up and destroy flour mills, using funds secured by a secret levy on the industry. By 1933 over one-sixth of the flour mills in England had been eliminated. In textiles the Lancashire Cotton Corporation acquired 10 million cotton spindles in three years (1934-1937) and scrapped about half of these, while the Spindles Board scrapped about 2 million spindles in one year (1936-1937). In spite of the growing international crisis, these restrictive actions continued unabated until May 1940, but the drive toward total mobilization by the Churchill government brought a fuller utilization of resources in Britain than in any other country.

This wartime experience with full employment made it impossible to return to the semistagnation and partial use of resources which had prevailed under financial capitalism in the 1930's. However, the economic future of Britain in the postwar period was much hampered by the fact that the two opposing political parties represented entrenched economic interests and were not a rather amorphous groupings of diverse interests as in the United States. The Labour Party, which held office from 1945 to 1951 under Clement Attlee, represents the interests of labor unions and, in a more remote fashion, of consumers. The Conservative Party, which held office under Churchill, Eden, Macmillan, and Douglas-Home after 1951 represents the propertied classes, and still continues to show strong banking influence. This has created a kind of balance in which a welfare state has been established, but at the cost of slow inflation and slack use of resources.

Consumption and enjoyment of leisure rather than production have been the marks of the British economy even under the Conservative Party, which has shown more concern for the value of the pound in the foreign exchanges than it has for productive investment. The middle classes and, above all, the professional and educated groups are not directly represented by either party. By their shift from one of these alien parties to the other, they can determine the outcome of elections, but they are not really at home in either and may, ultimately, turn back to the Liberal Party, although they are reluctant to embark upon the period of coalition, and the relatively irresponsible governments this might entail.

The class structure in Britain, which has survived the war in spite of steady attrition, is still being eroded, not by any drastic increase in working-class people rising into the upper class, but by the development of the third class which belongs to neither of the old classes. This new group included the people with "know-how," managers, scientists, professional men, imaginative parvenu entrepreneurs in lines which the older possessing class had ignored. These newly established rich now try to ignore the older upper class, and frequently show surprising resentments toward it. As this new, amorphous, vigorous group, which unfortunately has no common outlook or ideology, increases in numbers, it blurs the outlines of the two older classes. Much of this blurring has been the result of adoption of upper-class characteristics by non-upper-class persons. Increasing numbers of young people are adopting the British Broadcasting Corporation accent, which makes it increasingly difficult to establish the class, educational, and geographic origin of a speaker. Closely related to this is the improved appearance and health of the ordinary Englishman as a consequence of rising standards of living in general and the advent of the National Health service in particular. The loss of these two identifying characteristics leaves clothing as the chief class distinctive mark, but this applies only to men. Many women, as the result of the wide spreading of style magazines and the influence of the cinema, wear similar dresses, use the same cosmetics, and adopt the same hair arrangements. Today, even relatively poor shopgirls are often well dressed and invariably are attractively clean and carefully coiffured.

As in most other countries in the postward world, Britain's economy is increasingly made up of large blocs of interest groups whose shifting alignments determine economic policy within the three-cornered area of consumers' living standards, investment needs, and governmental expenditures (chiefly defense). All these diverse interest groups are increasingly monopolistic in organization, and increasingly convinced of the need for planning for their own interests, but the major factor in the picture is no longer the banking fraternity, as it was before the war, but the government through the Treasury.

This decrease in the power of the bankers, with a corresponding increase in that of other groups, including the government, is not the result of any new laws, such as the nationalization of the Bank of England, but of shifts in the flows of investment funds, which increasingly bypass the banks. Many of the largest industrial enterprises, such as British Imperial Chemicals or Shell Oil, are largely self-financing as a result of monopolistic conditions based on cartels, patent controls, or control of scarce resources. At the same time, the great mass of investment funds come from nonbanking sources. About half of such funds now comes from government and public authorities, such as the National Coal Board, which produces £17 million a year in new money seeking investment. Insurance companies (concerned with nonlife policies) are fairly closely linked with the older banking structure, as they are in most countries, but the banks ignored insurance on lives, which in England developed as a lower-class concern, paid by weekly or monthly premiums through door-to-door collections. These insurance companies in Britain provide £1.5 million a day in money seeking investment (1961), and the largest company, the Prudential, pours out £2 million a week. Much of this goes into industrial shares. In 1953, when the Conservative Party denationalized the steel industry, which

Labour had nationalized in 1948, much of its shares were bought up by funds from insurance companies. These enormous funds create a great danger that the handful of unknown men who handle the investment of such funds could become a centralized power in British economic life. So far they have made no effort to do so, since they supply funds without interfering in the existing management of the corporations in which they invest. They are satisfied with an adequate return on their money, but the possibility of such control exists.

Another source of funds from lower-class sources is the Postal Savings system. This has expanded because the lower classes in England regard banks as alien, upper-class institutions, and prefer to put their savings somewhere else. As a result, Postal Savings at over £6,000 millions are about the same size as the deposits of all the eleven joint-stock banks.

Somewhat similar in character are the investments of pension funds, which reached a total of about £2,000 million at the end of 1960 and are increasing at about £150 million a year.

Two other lower-class nonbanking innovations which have been having revolutionary influences on British life are the building societies (called "building and loan" in the United States) and "hire-purchase" associations (installment-buying organizations) which help the lower classes to acquire homes and to equip them. Together, these have wiped away much of the traditional dinginess of English lower-class life, brightening it up with amenities which have contributed to increase the solidarity of family life. Slum clearance and rebuilding by local government bodies (the so-called Council houses) have added to this. One consequence of the flowing of investment funds outside the control of the banks has been that the traditional controls on consumption and investment by the use of changes of bank rates have become decreasingly effective. This has had the double effect of damping down the movements of the business cycle and shifting such controls to the government, which can regulate consumption by such devices as changes in the terms of installment buying (larger down payments and carrying charges). At the same time, Britain's formerly independent role in all these matters has come increasingly under the influence of outside, uncontrollable influences, such as business conditions in the United States, the competition of the European Common Market, and the pressures of various international agencies, such as the International Monetary Fund. The final result is a complex and increasingly feudalized social-welfare economy in which managers rather than owners share power in a complicated dynamic system whose chief features are still largely unknown even to serious students.

Germany

While Britain passed through the stages of capitalism in this fashion, Germany was passing through the same stages in a different way.

In Germany, capital was scarce when industrialism arrived. Because savings from commerce, overseas trade, or small artisan shops were much less than in Britain, the stage of owner-management was relatively short. Industry found itself dependent upon banks almost at once. These banks were quite different from those in England, since they were "mixed" and not divided into separate establishments for different banking functions. The chief German credit banks, founded in the period 1848–1881, were at the same time savings banks, commercial banks, promotion and investment banks, stockbrokers, safety deposits, and so on. Their relationship to industry was close and intimate from the creation of the Darmstädter Bank in 1853. These banks floated securities for industry by granting credit to the firm, taking securities in return. These securities were then slowly sold to the investing public as the opportunity offered, the bank retaining enough stock to give it control and appointing its men as directors of the enterprise to give that control final form.

The importance of the holding of securities by banks can be seen from the fact that in 1908 the Dresdner Bank was holding 2 billion marks' worth. The importance of interlocking directorates can be seen from the fact that the same bank had its directors on the boards of over two hundred industrial concerns in 1913. In 1929, at the time of the amalgamation of the Deutsche Bank and the Disconto Gesellschaft, the two together had directorships in 660 industrial firms and held the chairmanship of the board in 192 of these. Before 1914, examples of individuals with thirty or even forty directorships were not uncommon.

This banking control of industry was made even closer by the use which the banks made of their positions as brokers and depositories for securities. The German credit banks acted as stockbrokers, and most investors left their securities on deposit with the banks so that they could be available for quick sale if needed. The banks voted all this stock for directorships and other control measures, unless the owners of the stock expressedly forbade it (which was very rare). In 1929 a law was passed preventing the banks from voting stocks deposited with them unless this had been expressedly permitted by the owners. The change was of little significance, since by 1929 financial capitalism was on the wane in Germany. Moreover, permission to vote deposited stock was rarely refused. The banks also voted as a right all stock left as collateral for loans and all stock bought on margin. Unlike the situation in America, stocks bought on margin were considered to be the property of the bank (acting as stockbrokers) until the whole price has been paid. The importance of the stock-brokerage business to German banks may be seen in the fact that in the twenty-four years 1885–1908 one-quarter of the gross profits of the large credit banks came from commissions. This is all the more remarkable when we consider that the brokerage commissions charged by German banks were very small (sometimes as low as one-half per thousand).

By methods such as these, a highly centralized financial capitalism was built up in Germany. The period begins with the founding of the Darmstädter Bank in 1853. This was the first bank to establish a permanent, systematic control of the corporations it floated. It also was the first to use promotion syndicates (in 1859). Other banks followed this example, and the outburst of promotion reached a peak of activity and corruption in the four years 1870–1874. In these four years, 857 stock companies with 3,306,810,000 marks of assets were floated, compared to 295 companies with 2,405,000,000 in assets in the preceeding nineteen years (1851–1870). Of these 857 companies founded in 1870–1874, 123 were in the process of liquidation and 37 were bankrupt as early as September 1874.

These excesses of financial capitalist promotion led to a governmental investigation which resulted in a strict law regulating promotion in 1883. This law made it impossible for German bankers to make fortunes out of promotion and made it necessary for them to seek the same ends by consolidating their control of industrial corporations on a long-term basis. This was quite different from the United States, where the absense of any legal regulation of promotion previous to the SEC Act of 1933 made it more likely that investment bankers would seek to make short-term "killings" from promotions rather than long-term gains from the control of industrial companies. Another result is to be seen in the relatively sounder financing of German corporations through equity capital rather than through the more burdensome (but promoter-favored) method of fixed interest bonds.

The financial capitalism of Germany was at its peak in the years just before 1914. It was controlled by a highly centralized oligarchy. At the center was the Reichsbank whose control over the other banks was relatively weak at all times. This was welcomed by the financial oligarchy, for the Reichsbank, although privately owned, was controlled by the government to a considerable degree. The weakness of the Reichsbank's influence over the banking system arose from the weakness of its influence over the two usual instruments of central-banking control—the rediscount rate and open-market operations. The weakness of the former was based on the fact that the other banks rarely came to the Reichsbank for rediscounts, and usually had a discount rate below that of the Reichsbank. A law of 1899 tried to overcome this weakness by forcing the other banks to adjust their discount rates to that of the Reichsbank, but it was never a very effective instrument of control. Open-market control was also weak because of an official German reluctance "to speculate" in government securities and because the other banks were more responsive to the condition of their portfolios of commercial paper and securities than they were to the size of their gold reserves. In this they were like French rather than British banks. Only in 1909 did the Reichsbank begin a deliberate policy of control through open-market operations, and it was never effective. It was ended completely from 1914 to 1929 by the war, the inflation, and the restrictions of the Dawes Plan.

Because of these weaknesses of the Reichsbank, the control of German financial capitalism rested in the credit banks. This is equivalent to saying that it was largely beyond the control of the government, and rested in private hands.

Of the hundreds of German credit banks, the overwhelming preponderance of power was in the hands of the eight so-called "Great Banks." These were the masters of the German economy from 1865 to 1915. Their overwhelming position can be seen from the fact that of 421 German credit banks in 1907 with 13,204,220,000 marks capital, the eight Great Banks held 44 percent of the total capital of the group. Moreover, the position of the Great Banks was better than this because the Great Banks controlled numerous other banks. In consequence, Robert Franz, editor of *Der Deutsche Oekonomist*, estimated in 1907 that the eight Great Banks controlled 74 percent of the capital assets of all 421 banks.

This power of financial capitalism in Germany was badly shaken by the First World War—in theory more than in fact. It was fatally injured by the postwar inflation, and subjected completely by the depression and by the actions of Hitler after 1933. The turning point from financial to monopoly capitalism was in the year or so following the end of the inflation (1924). In that year the inflation was ended, cartels were given a special legal status with their own Cartel Court to settle disputes, and the greatest creation of financial control ever constructed by German financial capitalism collapsed. The inflation ended in November 1923. The Cartel Decree was November 2, 1923. The great control structure was the Stinnes combine, which began to fall apart at the death of Hugo Stinnes in April 1924. At that time Stinnes had complete control of 107 large enterprises (mostly heavy industry and shipping) and had important interests in about 4,500 other companies. The attempt (and failure) of Stinnes to turn this structure of financial controls into an integrated monopoly marks the end of financial capitalism in Germany.

To be sure, the great need for capital on the part of German industry in the period after 1924 (since so much of German savings was wiped out by the inflation) gave a false afterglow to the setting sun of German financial capitalism. In five years, billions of marks were supplied to German industry through financial channels from loans made outside Germany. But the depression of 1929 to 1934 revealed the falsity of this appearance. As a result of the depression, all the Great Banks but one had to be rescued by the German government, which took over their capital stock in return. In 1937 these banks that had come under government ownership were "reprivatized," but by that time industry had largely escaped from financial control.

The beginnings of monopoly capitalism in Germany goes back at least a generation before the First World War. As early as 1870, the financial capitalists, using direct financial pressure as well as their system of interlocking directors, were working to integrate enterprises and reduce competition. In the older lines of activity, such as coal, iron, and steel, they tended to use cartels. In the newer lines, like electrical supplies and chemicals, they tended to use great monopolistic firms for this purpose. There are no official figures on cartels before 1905 but it is believed that there were 250 cartels in 1896, of which 80 were in iron and steel. The official investigation of cartels made by the Reichstag in 1905 revealed 385, of which 92 were in coal and metals. Shortly after this, the government began to help these cartels, the most famous example of this being a law of 1910 which forced potash manufacturers to become members of the potash cartel.

In 1923 there were 1,500 cartels, according to the Federation of German Industrialists. They were, as we have seen, given a special legal status and a special court the following year. By the time of the financial collapse of 1931 there were 2,500 cartels, and monopoly capitalism had grown to such an extent that it was prepared to take over complete control of the German economic system. As the banks fell under government control, private control of the economic system was assured by releasing it from its subservience to the banks. This was achieved by legislation such as that curtailing interlocking directorates and the new corporation law of 1937, but above all by the economic fact that the growth of large enterprises and of cartels had put industry in a position where it was able to finance itself without seeking help from the banks.

This new privately managed monopoly capitalism was organized in an intricate hierarchy whose details could be unraveled only by a lifetime of study. The size of enterprises had grown so big that in most fields a relatively small number were able to dominate the field. In addition, there was a very considerable amount of interlocking directorates and ownership by one corporation of the capital stock of another. Finally, cartels working between corporations fixed prices, markets, and output quotas for all important industrial products. An example of this—not by any means the worst—could be found in the German coal industry in 1937. There were 260 mining companies. Of the total output, 21 companies had 90 percent, 5 had 50 percent, and 1 had 14 percent. These mines were organized into five cartels of which 1 controlled 81 percent of the output, and 2 controlled 94 percent. And finally, most coal mines (69 percent of total output) were owned subsidiaries of other corporations which used coal, producers either of metals (54 percent of total coal output) or of chemicals (10 percent of total output).

Similar concentration existed in most other lines of economic activity. In ferrous metals in 1929, 3 firms out of 26 accounted for 68.8 percent of all German pig-iron production; 4 out of 49 produced 68.3 percent of all crude steel; 3 out of 59 produced 55.8 percent of all rolling mill products. In 1943, one firm (United Steel Works) produced 40 percent of all German steel production, while 12 firms produced over 90 percent. Competition could never exist with concentration as complete as this, but in addition the steel industry was organized into a series of steel cartels (one for each product). These cartels, which began about 1890, by 1930 had control of 100 percent of the German output of ferrous metal products. Member firm had achieved this figure by buying up the nonmembers in the years before 1930. These cartels managed prices, production, and markets within Germany, enforcing their decisions by means of fines or boycotts. They were also members of the International Steel Cartel, modeled on Germany's steel cartel and dominated by it. The International Cartel controlled two-fifths of the world's steel production and five-sixths of the total foreign trade in steel. The ownership of iron and steel enterprises in Germany is obscure but obviously highly concentrated. In 1932 Friedrich Flick had majority ownership of Gelsen-Kirchner Bergwerke, which had majority control of the United Steel Works. He sold his control to the German government for 167 percent of its value by threatening to sell it to a French firm. After Hitler came into power, this ownership by the government was "reprivatized" so that government ownership was reduced to 25 percent. Four other groups had 41 percent among them, and these were closely interwoven. Flick remained as director of United Steel Works and was chairman of the boards of four other great steel combines. In addition, he was director or chairman of the boards in six iron and coal mines, as well as of numerous other important enterprises. It is very likely that the steel industry of Germany in 1937 was controlled by no more than five men of whom Flick was the most important.

These examples of the growth of monopoly capitalism in Germany are merely picked at random and are by no means exceptional. Another famous example can be found in the growth of I. G. Farbenindustrie, the German chemical organization. This was formed in 1904 of three chief firms, and grew steadily until after its last reorganization in 1926 it controlled about two-thirds of Germany's output of chemicals. It spread into every branch of industry, concentrating chiefly on dyes (in which it had 100 percent monopoly), drugs, plastics, explosives, and light metals. It had been said that Germany could not have fought either of the world wars without I. G. Farben. In the first war, by the Haber process for extracting nitrogen from the air, it provided supplies of explosives and fertilizers when the natural sources in Chile were cut off. In the second war, it provided numerous absolute necessities, of which artificial rubber and synthetic motor fuels were the most important. This company by the Second World War was the largest enterprise in Germany. It had over 2,332.8 million reichsmarks in assets and 1,165 million in capitalization in 1942. It had about 100 important subsidiaries in Germany, and employed 350,000 persons in those in which it was directly concerned. It had interests in about 700 corporations outside Germany and had entered into over 500 restrictive agreements with foreign concerns.

Among these agreements the most significant was the European Dyestuff Cartel. This grew out of a Swiss cartel formed in 1918. When I. G. Farben was reorganized in 1925 and a similar French organization (Kuhlmann group) was set up in 1927, these two formed a French-German cartel. All three countries set up the European Cartel in 1929. Imperial Chemicals, which had won a near monopoly in British territory in 1926, joined the European Cartel in 1931. This British group already had a comprehensive agreement with du Pont in the United States (made in 1929 and revised in 1939). An effort by I. G. Farben to create a joint monopoly with du Pont within the United States broke down after years of negotiation in a dispute over whether division of control should be 50–50 or 51–49. Nevertheless, I. G. Farben made many individual cartel agreements with du Pont and other American corporations, some formal, others "gentlemen's agreements." In its own field of dyestuffs, it set up a series of subsidiaries in the United States which were able to control 40 percent of the American output. To ensure I. G. Farben control of these subsidiaries, a majority of Germans was placed on each board of directors, and Dietrich Schmitz was sent to the United States to become a naturalized American citizen and become the managing head of the chief I. G. Farben subsidiary here. Dietrich Schmitz was a brother of Hermann Schmitz, chairman of the board of I. G. Farben, director of the United Steel Works, of Metallgesellschaft (the German light-metals trust), of the

Bank for International Settlements, and of a score of other important firms. This policy of penetration into the United States was also used in other countries.

While I. G. Farben was the greatest example of concentrated control in German monopoly capitalism, it was by no means untypical. The process of concentration by 1939 had been carried to a degree which can hardly be overemphasized. The Kilgore Committee of the United States Senate in 1945 decided, after a study of captured German records, that I. G. Farben and United Steel Works together could dominate the whole German industrial system. Since so much of this domination was based on personal friendships and relationships, on secret agreements and contracts, on economic pressures and duress as well as on property and other obvious control rights, it is not something which can be demonstrated by statistics. But even the statistics give evidence of a concentration of economic power. In Germany in 1936 there were about 40,000 limited-liability companies, with total nominal capitalization of about 20,000 million reichsmarks. I. G. Farben and United Steel Works had 1,344 million reichsmarks of this capital. A mere 18 companies out of the 40,000 had one-sixth of the total working capital of all companies.

While monopolistic organization of economic life reached its peak in Germany, the differences in this respect between Germany and other countries have been overemphasized. It was a difference of degree only, and, even in degree, Britain, Japan, and a number of smaller countries were not so far behind the German development as one might believe at first glance. The error arose from two causes. On the one hand, German cartels and monopolies were well publicized, while similar organizations in other countries remained in hiding. As the British Committee on Trusts reported in 1929, "What is notable among British consolidations and associations is not their rarity or weakness so much as their unobtrusiveness." It is possible that the British vegetable-oil monopoly around Unilever was as powerful as the German chemical monopoly around I. G. Farben, but, while much has been heard about the latter, very little is heard about the former. After an effort to study the former, *Fortune* magazine wrote, "No other industry, perhaps, is quite so exasperatingly secretive as the soap and shortening industries."

On the other hand, Germany monopolistic organizations have built up disfavor because of their readiness to be used for nationalistic purposes. German cartel managers were patriotic Germans first and businessmen seeking profits and power second. In most other countries (especially the United States), monopoly capitalists are businessmen first and patriots later. As a result, the goals of German cartels were as frequently political as economic. I. G. Farben and others were constantly working to help Germany in its struggle for power, by espionage, by gaining economic advantages for Germany, and by seeking to cripple the ability of other countries to mobilize their resources or to wage war.

This difference in attitude between German and other capitalists became increasingly evident in the 1930's. In that decade the German found his economic and his patriotic motives impelling him in the same direction (to build up the power and wealth of Germany against Russia and the West). The capitalists of France, Britain, and the United States, on the other hand, frequently experienced conflicting motives. Bolshevism presented itself as an economic threat to themselves at the same time that Nazism presented itself as a political threat to their countries. Many persons were willing to neglect or even increase the latter threat in order to use it against the former danger.

This difference in attitude between German and other capitalists arose from many causes. Among these were (a) the contrast between the German tradition of a national economy and the Western tradition of laissez-faire, (b) the fact that world depression caused the threat of social revolution to appear before Nazism rose as a political danger to the West, (c) the fact that cosmopolitan financial capitalism was replaced more rapidly by nationalist monopoly capitalism in Germany than in the West, and (d) the fact that many wealthy and influential persons like Montagu Norman, Ivar Kreuger, Basil Zaharoff, and Henri Deterding directed public attention to the danger of Bolshevism while maintaining a neutral, or favorable, attitude toward Nazism.

The impact of the war on Germany was quite different from its effects on most other countries. In France, Britain, and the United States, the war played a significant role in demonstrating conclusively that economic stagnation and underemployment of resources were not necessary and could be avoided if the financial system were subordinated to the economic system. In Germany this was not necessary, since the Nazis had already made this discovery in the 1930's. On the other hand, the destruction of the war left Germany with a large task to do, the rebuilding of the German industrial plant. But, since Germany could not get to that task until it had its own government, the masses of Germans suffered great hardships in the five years 1945–1950, so that, by the time the proper political conditions arrived to allow the task of rebuilding, these masses of German labor were eager for almost any job and were more concerned with making a living wage than they were with seeking to raise their standards of living. This readiness to accept low wages, which is one of the essential features of the German economic revival, was increased by the influx of surging millions of poverty-stricken refugees from the Soviet-occupied East. Thus a surplus of labor, low wages, experience in unorthodox financial operations, and an immense task to be done all contributed to the German revival.

The signal for this to begin was given by the West German currency reform of 1950, which encouraged investment and offered entrepreneurs the possibility of large profits from the state's tax policies. The whole developed into a great boom when the establishment of the European Common Market of seven western European states offered Germany a mass market for mass production just as the rebuilding of German industry was well organized. The combination of low wages, a docile labor force, new equipment, and a system of low taxes on producers, plus the absence of any need for several years to assume the expense of defense expenditures, all contributed to make German production costs low on the world's markets and allowed Germany to build up a flourishing and profitable export trade. The German example was copied in Japan and in Italy, and, on a different basis, in France, with the result that the Common Market area enjoyed a burst of economic expansion and prosperity which began to transform western European life and to raise most of its countries to a new level of mobility and affluence such as they had never known before. One result of this was the development of what had been backward areas within these countries, most notably in southern Italy, where the boom caught on by 1960. The only area within the Common Market where this did not occur was in Belgium, which was hampered by obsolescent equipment and domestic social animosities, while in France the boom was delayed for several years by the acute political problems associated with the death of the Fourth Republic (1958).

France

Financial capitalism lasted longer in France than in any other major country. The roots of financial capitalism there, like Holland but unlike Germany, go back to the period of commercial capitalism which preceded the Industrial Revolution. These roots grew rapidly in the last half of the eighteenth century and were well established with the founding of the Bank of France in 1800. At that date, financial power was in the hands of about ten or fifteen private banking houses whose founders, in most cases, had come from Switzerland in the second half of the eighteenth century. These bankers, all Protestant, were deeply involved in the agitations leading up to the French Revolution. When the revolutionary violence got out of hand, they were the chief forces behind the rise of Napoleon, whom they regarded as the restorer of order. As a reward for this support, Napoleon in 1800 gave these bankers a monopoly over French financial life by giving them control of the new Bank of France.

By 1811 most of these bankers had gone over to the opposition to Napoleon because they objected to his continuation of a warlike policy. France at that time was still in the stage of commercial capitalism, and constant war was injurious to commercial activity. As a result, this group shifted its allegiance from Bonaparte to Bourbon, and survived the change in regime in 1815. This established a pattern of political agility which was repeated with varying success in subsequent changes of regime. As a result, the Protestant bankers, who had controlled financial life under the First Empire, were still the main figures on the board of regents of the Bank of France until the reform of 1936. Among these figures the chief bore the names Mirabaud, Mallet, Neuflize, and Hottinguer.

In the course of the nineteenth century, a second group was added to French banking circles. This second group, largely Jewish, was also of non-French origin, the majority Germanic (like Rothschild, Heine, Fould, Stern, and Worms) and the minority of Iberian origin (like Pereire and Mirès). A rivalry soon grew up between the older Protestant bankers and the newer Jewish bankers. This rivalry was largely political rather than religious in its basis, and the lines were confused by the fact that some of the Jewish group gave up their religion and moved over to the Protestant group (such as Pereire and Heine).

The rivalry between these two groups steadily increased because of their differing political attitudes toward the July Monarchy (1830–1848), the Second Empire (1852–1870), and the Third Republic (1871–1940). In this rivalry the Protestant group was more conservative than the Jewish group, the former being lukewarm toward the July Monarchy, enthusiastic toward the Second Empire, and opposed to the Third Republic. The Jewish group, on the other hand, warmly supported the July Monarchy and the Third Republic but opposed the Second Empire. In this rivalry the leadership of each group was centered in the richest and more moderate banking family. The leadership of the Protestant group was exercised by Mirabaud, which was on the left wing of the group. The leadership of the Jewish group was held by Rothschild, which was on the right wing of that group. These two wings were so close that Mirabaud and Rothschild (who together dominated the whole financial system, being richer and more powerful than all other private banks combined) frequently cooperated together even when their groups as a whole were in competition.

This simple picture was complicated, after 1838, by the slow rise of a third group of bankers who were Catholics. This group (including such names as Demachy, Seillière, Davillier, de Germiny, Pillet-Will, Gouïn, and de Lubersac) rose slowly and late. It soon split into two halves. One half formed an alliance with the Rothschild group and accepted the Third Republic. The other half formed an alliance with the rising power of heavy industry (largely Catholic) and rose with it, forming under the Second Empire and early Third Republic a powerful industrial-banking group whose chief overt manifestation was the Comité des Forges (the French steel "trust").

Thus there were, in the period 1871–1900, three great groups in France: (a) the alliance of Jews and Catholics dominated by Rothschild; (b) the alliance of Catholic industrialists and Catholic bankers dominated by Schneider, the steel manufacturer; and (c) the group of Protestant bankers dominated by Mirabaud. The first of these accepted the Third Republic, the other two rejected the Third Republic. The first waxed wealthy in the period 1871–1900, chiefly through its control of the greatest French investment bank, the Banque de Paris et des Pays Bas (Paribas). This Paribas bloc by 1906 had a dominant position in French economic and political life.

In opposition to Paribas the Protestant bankers established an investment bank of their own, the Union Parisienne, in 1904. In the course of the period 1904–1919 the Union Parisienne group and the Comité des Forges group formed an alliance based on their common opposition to the Third Republic and the Paribas bloc. This new combination we might call the Union-Comité bloc. The rivalry of these two great powers, the Paribas bloc and the Union-Comité bloc, fills the pages of French history in the period 1884–1940. It paralyzed the French political system, reaching the crisis stage in the Dreyfus case and again in 1934–1938. It also partially paralyzed the French economic system, delaying the development from financial capitalism to monopoly capitalism, and preventing economic recovery from the depression in the period 1935–1940. It contributed much to the French defeat in 1940. At present, we are concerned only with the economic aspects of this struggle.

In France the stage of commercial capitalism continued much longer than in Britain, and did not begin to be followed by industrial capitalism until after 1830. The stage of financial capitalism in turn did not really begin until about 1880, and the stage of monopoly capitalism became evident only about 1925.

During all this period the private bankers continued to exist and grow in power. Founded in commercial capitalism, they were at first chiefly interested in governmental obligations both domestic and foreign. As a result, the greatest private bankers, like the Rothschilds or Mallets, had intimate connections with governments and relatively weak connections with the economic life of the country. It was the advent of the railroad in the period 1830–1870 which changed this situation. The railroads required capital far beyond the ability of any private banker to supply from his own resources. The difficulty was met by establishing investment banks, deposit banks, saving banks, and insurance companies which gathered the small savings of a multitude of persons and made these available for the private banker to direct wherever he thought fitting. Thus, the private banker became a manager of other persons' funds rather than a lender of his own. In the second place, the private banker now became much more influential and must less noticeable. He now controlled billions where formerly he had controlled millions, and he did it unobtrusively, no longer in the open in his own name, but acting from the background, concealed from public view by the plethora of financial and credit institutions which had been set up to tap private savings. The public did not notice that the names of private bankers and their agents still graced the list of directors of the new financial enterprises. In the third place, the advent of the railroad brought into existence new economic powers, especially in ironmaking and coal mining. These new powers, the first powerful economic influences in the state free from private banking control, arose in France from an activity very susceptible to governmental favor and disfavor: the armaments industry.

Industrial capitalism began in France, as elsewhere, in the fields of textiles and ironmaking. The beginning may be discerned before 1830, but the growth was slow at all times. There was no lack of capital, since most Frenchmen were careful savers, but they preferred fixed-interest obligations (usually government bonds) to equity capital, and would rather invest in family enterprises than in securities of other origin. The use of the corporation form of business organization grew very slowly (although it was permitted by French law in 1807, earlier than elsewhere). Private proprietorships and partnerships remained popular, even in the twentieth century. Most of these were financed from profits and family savings (as in England). When these were successful and increased in size, the owners frequently cut off the growth of the existing enterprise and started one or more new enterprises alongside the old one. These sometimes engaged in the identical economic activity but more frequently engaged in a closely related activity. Strong family feeling hampered the growth of large units or publicly owned corporations because of reluctance to give outsiders an influence in family businesses. The preference for fixed-interest obligations over equity securities as investments made it difficult for corporations to grow in size easily and soundly. Finally, the strong feeling against public authority, especially the tax collector, increased the reluctance to embark in public rather than private forms of business organization.

Nonetheless, industry grew, receiving its greatest boost from the advent of the railroad, with its increased demand for steel and coal, and from the government of Napoleon III (1852–1870), which added a new demand for armaments to the industrial market. Napoleon showed special favor to one firm of iron and armaments makers, the firm of Schneider at Le Creusot. Eugène Schneider obtained a monopoly in supplying arms to the French government, sold materials to government-encouraged railway construction, become president of the Chamber of Deputies, and minister of agriculture and commerce. It is hardly surprising that the industrialists looked back on the period of the Second Empire as a kind of golden age.

The loss of political influence by the heavy industrialists after 1871 reduced their profits, and drove them to ally with the Catholic bankers. Thus, the struggle between financial capitalism and monopoly capitalism which appeared in most countries was replaced in France by a clash between two economic blocs, both of which were interested in both industry and banking and neither of which was prepared to accept the unorthodox banking procedures which become one of the chief goals of monopoly capitalism. As a result, monopoly capitalism appeared late in France and, when it did, arose between the two great blocs, with ramifications in both, but largely autonomous from the central control of either. This new autonomous and rather amorphous group which reflected the rise of monopoly capitalism may be called the Lille-Lyons Axis. It rose slowly after 1924, and took over the control of France after the defeat of 1940.

The rise of financial capitalism in France, as elsewhere, was made possible by the demand for capital for railroad building. The establishment of the Crédit Mobilier in 1852 (with 60 million francs in assets) may be taken as the opening date for French financial capitalism. This bank was the model for the credit banks established in Germany later, and, like them, conducted a mixed business of savings accounts, commercial credit, and investment banking. The Crédit Mobilier failed in 1867, but others were founded afterward, some mixed, others more specialized on the British or American pattern.

Once begun, financial capitalism in France displayed the same excesses as elsewhere. In France these were worse than those in Britain or Germany (after the reforms of 1884), although they were not to be compared with the excesses of frenzy and fraud displayed in the United States. In France, as in Britain, the chief exploits of financial capitalism in the nineteenth century were to be found in the foreign field, and in government rather than in business securities. The worst periods of delirium were in the early 1850's, again in the early 1880's, and again in much of the twentieth century. In one year of the first period (July 1, 1854 to July 1, 1855) no less than 457 new companies with combined capital of 1 billion francs were founded in France. The losses to security buyers were so great that on March 9, 1856, the government had to prohibit temporarily any further issue of securities in Paris. Again in the period 1876 to 1882 over 1 billion francs of new stocks were issued, leading to a crash in 1882. And finally, in the whole period 1900–1936, financial capitalism was clearly in control in France. In 1929 a Paris newspaper estimated that in a period of thirty years (from the Humbert embezzlement of 1899) more than 300 billion francs (equivalent to the total public and private debt of France in 1929) had been taken from the French people by worthless securities.

The center of the French economic system in the twentieth century was not to be found, as some have believed, in the Bank of France, but, instead, resided in a group of almost unknown institutions—the private banks. There were over a hundred of these private banks, but only about a score were of significance, and even in this restricted group two (Rothschild and Mirabaud) were more powerful than all the others combined. These private banks were known as the Haute Banque, and acted as the High Command of the French economic system. Their stock was closely held in the hands of about forty families, and they issued no reports on their financial activities. They were, with a few exceptions, the same private banks which had set up the Bank of France. They were divided into a group of seven Jewish banks (Rothschild, Stern, Cahen d'Anvers, Propper, Lazard, Spitzer, and Worms), a group of seven Protestant banks (Mallet, Mirabaud, Heine, Neuflize, Hottinguer, Odier, and Vernes), and a group of five Catholic banks (Davillier, Lubersac, Lehideux, Goudchaux, and Demachy). By the twentieth century the basic fissure to which we have referred had appeared between the Jews and the Protestants, and the Catholic group had split to ally itself either with the Jews or with the forces of monopolistic heavy industry. None the less, the various groups continued to cooperate in the management of the Bank of France.

The Bank of France was not the center of French financial capitalism except nominally, and possessed no autonomous power of its own. It was controlled until 1936, as it had been in 1813, by the handful of private banks which created it, except that in the twentieth century some of these were closely allied with an equally small but more amorphous group of industrialists. In spite of the fissure, the two blocs cooperated with each other in their management of this important instrument of their power.

The Bank of France was controlled by the forty families (not two hundred, as frequently stated) because of the provision in the bank's charter that only the 200 largest stockholders were entitled to vote for the members of the board of regents (the governing board of the bank). There were 182,500 shares of stock outstanding, each with face value of 1,000 francs but usually worth five or ten times that. In the twentieth century there were 30,000 to 40,000 stockholders. Of the 200 who could vote for the twelve elected regents, 78 were corporations or foundations and 122 were individuals. Both classes were dominated by the private banks, and had been for so long that the regents' seats had become practically hereditary. The chief changes in the names of regents were caused by the growth of heavy industry and the transfer of seats through female lines. Three seats were held by the same families for well over a century. In the twentieth century the names of Rothschild, Mallet,

Mirabaud, Neuflize, Davillier, Vernes, Hottinguer, and their relatives were consistently on the board of regents.

The Bank of France acted as a kind of general staff for the forty families which controlled the nineteen chief private banks. Little effort was made to influence affairs by the rediscount rate, and open-market operations were not used until 1938. The state was influenced by the Treasury's need for funds from the Bank of France. Other banks were influenced by methods more exclusively French: by marriage alliances, by indirect bribery (that is, by control of well-paying sinecures in banking and industry), and by the complete dependence of French banks on the Bank of France in any crisis. This last arose from the fact that French banks did not emphasize gold reserves but instead regarded commercial paper as their chief reserve. In any crisis where this paper could not be liquidated fast enough, the banks resorted to the unlimited note-issuing power of the Bank of France.

In the third line of control of the French economy were the investment banks called "banques d'affaires." These were dominated by two banks: the Banque de Paris et des Pays Bas set up by the Rothschild group in 1872 and the Banque de l'Union Parisienne founded by the rival bloc in 1904. These investment banks supplied long-term capital to industry, and took stock and directorships in return. Much of the stock was resold to the public, but the directorships were held indefinitely for control purposes. In 1931, Paribas held the securities of 357 corporations, and its own directors and top managers held 180 directorships in 120 of the more important of these. The control was frequently made easier by the use of nonvoting stock, multiple-voting stock, cooptative directorships, and other refinements of financial capitalism. For example, the General Wireless Company set up by Paribas distributed 200,000 shores of stock worth 500 francs a share. Of these, 181,818 shares, sold to the public, had one-tenth vote each while 18,182 shares, held by the insider group, had one vote each. A similar situation was to be found in Havas stock, also issued by Paribas.

The investment bank of the non-Jewish private banks and their industrial allies was the Union Parisienne. Among its sixteen directors were to be found such names as Mirabaud, Hottinguer, Neuflize, Vernes, Wendel, Lubersac, and Schneider in the period before 1934. The two largest stocksholders in 1935–1937 were Lubersac and Mallet. The directors of this bank held 124 other directorships on 90 important corporations in 1933. At the same time it held stock in 338 corporations. The value of the stock held by the Union Parisienne in 1932 was 482.1 million francs and of that held by Paribas was 548.8 million francs, giving a total for both of 1,030.9 million francs.

In the fourth line of control were five chief commercial banks with 4,416 branches in 1932. At the beginning of the century these had all

been within the "Paribas Consortium," but after the founding of the
Union Parisienne in 1904 they slowly drifted over to the new bloc, the
Comptoir National d'Escompte going over almost at once, with the others following more slowly. As a result, the control of the two great
blocs over the great deposit banks was rather mixed during the twentieth
century, with the old Jewish group of private bankers losing ground
rather steadily. The decline of this group was closely related to the decline of international financial capitalism, and received its worse blow
in the losses in foreign bonds resulting from the First World War.
Regional deposit banks were controlled in varying degrees by one or the
other of the two blocs, the Paribas control being stronger in the north,
west, and south, while the Union-Comité bloc was stronger in the northeast, east, and southeast. Control of savings banks and insurance companies was also shared, especially where they had been founded before
the two blocs achieved their modern form. For example, the largest insurance company in France, with capital and reserves of 2,463 million
francs in 1931, had as directors such names as Mallet, Rothschild, Neuflize,
Hottinguer, and so on.

This cooperation between the two blocs in regard to the lower levels
of the banking system (and the Bank of France itself) did not usually
extend to industrial or commercial activity. There, competition outside
the market was severe, and became a struggle to the death in 1932–
1940. In some activities, spheres of interest were drawn between the
two groups, and thus competition was reduced. Inside France, there was
the basic division between east and west, the Jewish group emphasizing
shipbuilding, transatlantic communications and transportation, and public
utilities in the west, while the Protestant-Catholic group emphasized iron,
steel, and armaments in the east. Outside France, the former group
dominated the colonies, North Africa, and the eastern Mediterranean,
while the latter group emphasized central and eastern Europe (chiefly
through the Union européene industrielle et financière, created in 1920 to
be the economic counterpart of the Little Entente).

In some fields the rivalry of the two groups had worldwide ramifications. In petroleum products, for example, the Jewish bankers, through
the Banque de Paris et des Pays Bas, controlled the Compagnie française
des pétroles, which was allied to Standard Oil and Rockefeller, while the
Catholic-Protestant bankers, through the Union Parisienne, controlled
Petrofina, which was allied to Royal Dutch Shell and Deterding. Jules
Exbrayat, partner of Demachy et Cie. (in which François de Wendel was
majority owner) was a director of Union Parisienne and of Petrofina, and
Alexandre Bungener, partner of Lubersac et Cie., was also a director of
Union Parisienne and of Petrofina. Charles Sergeant, once undersecretary
of the Ministry of Finance and subgovernor of the Bank of France, was for
years chairman of the Union Parisienne, and played a role in one bloc

similar to that played by Horace Finaly in the other bloc. He was a
director of Petrofina and of the Union européene industrielle et financiére.
When he retired for reasons of health in 1938 he was replaced in several positions (including Petrofina and Union Parisienne) by Jean Tan-
nery, honorary governor of the Bank of France. At the same time, Joseph
Courcelle, former inspector of finances, was a director of seventeen
companies including Petrofina and Union Parisienne. On the other
side, Horace Finaly was general manager of Paribas and director of
Standard Franco-Américaine, while his son, Boris, was a director of
Cie. française des pétroles. Former ambassador Jules Cambon and Emile
Oudot, both directors of Parisbas, were respectively directors of Standard
Franco-Américaine and Standard française des pétroles (before these
merged in 1938).

Outside the banking system which we have sketched, the French economy was organized in a series of trade associations, industrial monopolies,
and cartels. These were usually controlled by the Catholic-Protestant bloc
of private bankers, since the Jewish group continued to use the older
methods of financial capitalism while their rivals moved forward to the
more obvious methods of monopoly capitalism. In such cases, individual
companies controlled by the Jewish group frequently jointed the cartels
and associations set up by the rival bloc.

At the center of the system of monopolistic industrial controls was the
Confédération générale du patronat français, which after 1936 (Matignon
agreements) did the collective bargaining for most French industry.
The Confédération was divided into sections for different branches of
industry. Around the Confédération was a series of general trade associations and cartels such as the Comité des Forges, Comité centrale
des Houillères, Union des industries métallurgiques et minières, Société
de l'industrie minérale, and so on. Below these were a large number of
regional associations and local cartels. These were integrated into a single
whole by financial controls, family alliances, and interlocking positions.

In this system the Comité des Forges, trade association of the metallurgical industry, held a key position. In France the iron industry was
originally widely scattered in small enterprises. Of these, the factories
at Le Creusot, acquired by the Schneider family in 1838, were so
favored by Napoleon III that they began to emerge as the chief metal
company in France. As a result of the loss of governmental privileges by
the shift from Second Empire to Third Republic and the blow to
Schneider's prestige from the victory of Krupp steel cannon over Le
Creusot's bronze cannon in 1870, the whole metal industry of France
began to turn toward monopoly and to seek capital from private bankers. The turn toward monopoly appeared almost at once, especially in the
typical French form of the *comptoir* (a joint selling agency).

In 1884, as we have said, the Comité des Forges was formed as an association of all the metallurgical industries of France, using a single *comptoir* to prevent price competition. By the twentieth century, the Comité des Forges consisted of representatives of over 200 companies with nominal capital of about 8 billion francs, but whose securities were worth almost 100 billion francs in 1939. Of the 200 corporations the chief perhaps were Établissements Schneider; Les Forges et Aciéries de la Marine et Homécourt; La Société des Petits-Fils de François de Wendel; Les Aciéries de Longwy, and so on. By the year 1939, 75 percent of French steel production was from six companies. The monopolistic influences, however, were much stronger than these figures would indicate. Of the 200 firms in the Comité des Forges, only 70 were of importance in iron and steel. These 70 had an aggregate capitalization of about 4 billion francs. Of these firms, 51 with 2,727,054,000 francs of capital in 1939 were in the Union-Comité bloc and were controlled by a Schneider-Mirabaud alliance. Eleven corporations with 506 million francs of capital were in the Paribas bloc. Eight firms with 749 million francs of capital were in neither bloc or doubtful.

A somewhat similar development is to be found in the French coal industry. This, perhaps, is not surprising, as the coal industry was largely dominated by the same groups as the steel industry. By 1938, 77 percent of French coal production came from 14 companies. Three of these companies were owned by Wendel, who thus controlled 15.3 percent of French coal output directly, and considerably more indirectly. Parallel to the Comité des Forges in steel, and controlled by the same group, was the Comité-centrale des Houillères in coal. This was supported by taxes on collieries based on output. Voting power within the organization was based on this financial contribution, so that 13 companies controlled over three-fourths of the votes and Wendel over one-sixth. The French coal industry was controlled nearly as completely by the Union-Comité bloc as was the steel industry. Coal in France was found chiefly in two areas—the northwest around Lille and the southeast about Lyons. The latter was controlled almost completely by the Union-Comité bloc, but the Paribas influence was very great in the far richer northern area. It was these Paribas coal mines of the north which gradually drifted away and became one of the chief elements in the monopolistic Lille-Lyons Axis.

The preponderant influence of the Union-Comité bloc in such important fields as iron, steel, and coal was balanced to some extent by the skillful fashion in which the Paribas bloc had taken control of the strategic points in the fields of communications and publicity.

There were only 1,506 corporations registered on the stock exchange in Paris in 1936. Of this number only about 600 were important. If we add to these about 150 or 200 important corporations not registered in Paris, we have a total of about 800 firms. Of these 800, the Paribas bloc controlled, in 1936, almost 400 and the Union-Comité bloc about 300.

The rest were controlled by neither bloc. The superior number of firms controlled by Paribas was counterbalanced by the much heavier capitalization of the Union-Comité firms. This in turn was counterbalanced by the fact that the Parisbas firms were in strategic positions.

The whole Paribas system in the twentieth century was headed by the Baron Edouard de Rothschild, but the active head was René Mayer, manager of the Rothschild bank and nephew by marriage of James Rothschild. The chief center of operations for the system was in the Banque de Paris et des Pays Bas, which was managed, until 1937, by Horace Finaly of a Hungarian-Jewish family brought to France by Rothschild in 1880. From this bank was ruled much of the section of the French economy controlled by this bloc. Included in this section were many foreign and colonial enterprises, utilities, ocean shipping, airlines, shipbuilding and, above all, communications. In this latter group were Cie. générale transatlantique, Cie. générale de télégraphie sans fils, Radio-France, Cie. française de câbles télégraphiques, Cie. internationale des wagon-lits, Havas, and Hachette.

Havas was a great monopolistic news agency, as well as the most important advertising agency in France. It could, and did, suppress or spread both news and advertising. It usually supplied news reports gratis to those papers which would print the advertising copy it also provided. It received secret subsidies from the government for almost a century (a fact first revealed by Balzac), and by the late 1930's these subsidies from the secret funds of the Popular Front had reached a fantastic size. Hachette had a monopoly on the distribution of periodicals and a sizable portion of the distribution of books. This monopoly could be used to kill papers which were regarded as objectionable. This was done in the 1930's to François Coty's reactionary L'Ami du peuple.

After 1934, the Union-Comité bloc was badly injured by the world depression, which fell on heavy industry more severely than on other segments of the economy. After 1937, the Paribas bloc was badly split by the rise of anti-Semitism, the controversy over orthodox and unorthodox financial methods for dealing with depression, and, above all, by the growing foreign crisis. The Rothschild desire to form an alliance with Russia and adopt a policy of resistance to Hitler while supporting Loyalist Spain, continuing orthodox financial policies, and building up the labor unions against the Comité des Forges, collapsed from its own internal contradictions, their own lack of faith in it, and the pressure of Great Britain.

As the two older blocs thus weakened, a new bloc rose rapidly to power between them. This was the Lille-Lyons Axis. It was constructed about two regional groups—one in the north about Lille and the other in the southeast and east about Lyons and in Alsace. The former had a branch running to Brussels in Belgium, while the latter had a branch running to Basle in Switzerland. The Lille end was originally under Rothschild influence, while the Lyons end was originally under Mirabaud influence. The two ends were integrated into a single unit by the activities of several private banks and two deposit banks in Paris. The private banks included Odier, Sautter et Cie., S. Propper et Cie., and Worms et Cie. The credit banks included the Crédit Commercial de France and the Banque française pour le commerce et l'industrie.

This Lille-Lyons Axis was built up about four economic activities: electrical utilities, chemicals, artificial textiles, and light metals. These four were monopolistic and interrelated, chiefly for technological reasons. They were monopolistic either by nature (public utilities) or because they were based on narrowly controlled natural resources (utilities and chemicals), or because they required large-scale operation utilizing by-products and affiliated activities for profitable operation (utilities, chemicals, artificial textiles, and light metals), or because they required use of closely held patents (chemicals, artificial textiles, and light metals).

These activities were interrelated for various reasons. The public utilities of the north were based on coal, while those of the southeast were based on waterpower. The manufacture of light metals concentrated in the southeast because of the available water power. These metals, chiefly aluminum, were made by electrolysis, which provided chemical by-products. Thus the two light-metals firms in France moved into the field of chemicals. The textile industry was already centered in the north (about Lille) and in the southeast (about Lyons). When this textile industry turned to artificial fibers, it had to ally with chemical firms. This was easy because the chemical firms of the southeast were already in close contact with the textile firms of Lyons (chiefly the Gillet family), while the chemical firms of the north were already in close contact with the textile firms of the area (chiefly the Motte family and its relatives). These textile firms of the north already controlled, in cooperation with Paribas, the richest coal mines of the area. These coal mines began to generate electric power at the mine, utilizing all by-products for chemicals and artificial textiles. Since the textile families of the north (like Motte) were already related to the textile families of the southeast (like Gillet) by marriage and by trade associations, it was easy for the Lille-Lyons Axis to grow up along these lines.

As a result of the stalemate between the two great blocs, between financial capitalists and monopoly capitalists, between supporters of the Russian alliance and supporters of appeasement, between orthodox and unorthodox financial measures, between Jews and anti-Semites, France was completely paralyzed and went down to defeat in 1940. This was quite acceptable to the Lille-Lyons Axis. It accepted the defeat with satisfaction, and, with German help, began to take over the whole economy of France. The Paribas bloc was destroyed by the anti-Semite laws, and many of its chief strong points taken over. The Union-Comité bloc was badly crippled by a series of severe blows, including the forced sale of all Schneider's foreign holdings, and of most of Wendel's domestic holdings to the Germans (chiefly to the Hermann Göring Werke), the seizure of the other Lorraine iron properties, and the abolition of the Comité des Forges itself.

At the same time, the Lille-Lyons Axis strengthened itself. The French chemical industry, already largely monopolized by Etablissements Kuhlmann, was forced into a single corporation (Société Francolor) controlled by the Lille-Lyons Axis and I. G. Farben. The light-metals industry, already largely monopolized by Alais, Froges, et Camargue, was centralized almost completely in this firm. The artificial textile industry, already largely monopolized by the Gillet clique, was centralized under a single corporation, France-Rayonne, under joint Gillet-German control. The automobile industry was subjected to a single control—the Comité d'organization d'automobiles—and set up a joint manufacturing company—Société générale française de construction d'automobiles. The whole system was controlled by a small group in Lyons centering about the Gillet family and represented on the political scene chiefly by Pierre Laval.

The struggles between these three great economic power blocs in France are rather difficult for Americans to understand because they were not reflected in price competition in the market where Americans would normally expect economic competition to appear. In the field of price policies, the three blocs generally cooperated. They also cooperated in their attitudes toward labor, although to a lesser degree. Their rivalries appeared in the fields of economic and political power as struggles to control sources of raw materials, supplies of credit and capital, and the instruments of government. Price competition, which to an American always has seemed to be the first, and even the only, method of economic rivalry, has, in Europe, generally been regarded as the last possible method of economic rivalry, a method so mutually destructive as to be tacitly avoided by both sides. In fact, in France, as in most European countries, competing economic groups saw nothing inconsistent in joining together to use the power of the state to enforce joint policies of such groups toward prices and labor.

The French defeat in 1940 shattered the stalemate between the economic power blocs which had paralyzed France in the 1930's and done so much to make the defeat possible. The two older blocs were disrupted under the German occupation and the Vichy regime, the Paribas bloc by the anti-Semitic laws and the Union-Comité bloc because its holdings were desirable to the Germans and their French collaborators. The

Lille-Lyons Axis, led by the associates of the Banque Worms and the
Banque de l'Indochine, sought to take over most of the French economy
as the willing collaborators of the Germans and their old associate,
Pierre Laval, and were fairly successful in doing so, but the economic
confusions of the occupation and the burden of the German occupation
costs made it impossible to win any significant benefits from their position. Moreover, as collaborators with the Nazis the Lille-Lyons Axis
could not expect to survive a German defeat, and did not do so.

The three prewar blocs have played no significant role in France
since 1945, although some of the personnel of Paribas have done so,
notably René Mayer, active head of the Rothschild family interests who
was minister of finance in the early postwar government. Later, in 1962,
De Gaulle made the director of the Rothschild bank, George Pompidou,
prime minister. The rather prominent role played by bankers such as
these did not prevent France from following the pattern of new economic procedures which we have observed in other countries. The
process was delayed by the political paralysis arising from the French
parliamentary system, especially the instability of Cabinets arising from
the multiplicity of parties. The military crisis in Indochina, followed by
the protracted and frustrating civil war in Algeria, prevented France
from establishing any satisfactory economic system until 1958.

The only achievement of the earlier period was, however, a very great
one—the French role in establishing the European Common Market,
which was decisive. This was established by the Treaty of Rome of
1957, with six members (France, West Germany, Belgium, the Netherlands, Italy, and Luxembourg). It planned to remove the internal customs
barriers among its members by stages over at least a dozen years, while
adopting a common external tariff against outsiders. In this way a mass
market would be provided which would allow mass production with
lower costs. France was unable to contribute much to this new market until its political instability was ended by the establishment of the Fifth Republic, on a more authoritarian pattern, in 1958 (constitution of October
4th). In December of that year, the franc was devalued and a program
of fiscal austerity was inaugurated. At once economic activity began
to rise. The rate of growth of industrial production reached 6.3 percent
in 1961 and almost 8.5 percent in 1962. The gold reserves doubled
within two years of the devaluation.

The resulting prosperity, called an "economic miracle" in the 1962
Report of the twenty-nation Organization for Economic Cooperation
and Development (the successor organization to the Marshall Plan),
was unevenly spread in that farmers and government employees obtained less than a fair share of it, and it was accompanied by an undesirable inflation of the cost of living (with 1953 as 100) to 103 in 1956,
up to 138 in 1961, and to 144 in 1962. However, it brought France and

the other Common Market countries to an unprecedented level of prosperity which was in striking contrast to the drab conditions in the unfortunate countries within the Iron Curtain. The British, who had formed a European Free Trade Association of the "Outer Seven" (Austria, Denmark, Norway, Portugal, Sweden, Switzerland) to seek free trade among members but no common external tariff against others, sought to lift its rather lethargic economy by joining the Common Market in 1962, but was rebuffed by De Gaulle, who required as a price that Britain renounce its efforts, going back over decades, to establish a special relationship with the United States.

The United States of America

The United States, which presents the most extreme example of financial capitalism, reached monopoly capitalism only in a partial and distorted fashion and for a very brief period, and has reached the following stage of the pluralist economy only in an unselfconscious and tentative way.

From the beginning, the United States had a shortage of labor in the face of an unprecedented richness of resources. As a result, it sought labor-saving devices and high output per man-day of work, even in agriculture. This means that the amount of capital equipment per man was unusually high throughout American history, even in the earliest period, and this undoubtedly presented a problem in an undeveloped country where private savings were, for many generations, scarce. The accumulation of such savings for investment in labor-saving mechanisms brought an opportunity to financial capitalism at an early date. Accordingly, the United States had financial capitalism over a longer period and in a more extreme form than any other country. Moreover, the size of the country made the problem of transportation so acute that the capital necessary for the early canals, railroads, and iron industry was large and had to be found from sources other than local private persons. Much of it came from government subsidies or from foreign investors. It was observable as early as 1850 and had overseas connections which were still in existence in the 1930's.

By the 1880's the techniques of financial capitalism were well developed in New York and northern New Jersey, and reached levels of corruption which were never approached in any European country. This corruption sought to cheat the ordinary investor by flotations and manipulations of securities for the benefit of "insiders." Success in this was its own justification, and the practitioners of these dishonesties were as socially acceptable as their wealth entitled them to be, without any animadversions on how that wealth had been obtained. Corrupt techniques, associated with the names of Daniel Drew or Jay Gould in the wildest days of railroad financial juggling, were also practiced by Morgan and others who became respectable from longer sustained success which allowed them to build up established firms.

Any reform of Wall Street practices came from pressure from the hinterlands, especially from the farming West, and was long delayed by the close alliance of Wall Street with the two major political parties, which grew up in 1880–1900. In this alliance, by 1900, the influence of Morgan in the Republican Party was dominant, his chief rivalry coming from the influence of a monopoly capitalist, Rockefeller of Ohio. By 1900 Wall Street had largely abandoned the Democratic Party, a shift indicated by the passage of the Whitney family from the Democrats to the Republican inner circles, shortly after they established a family alliance with Morgan. In the same period, the Rockefeller family reversed the ordinary direction of development by shifting from the monopoly fields of petroleum to New York banking circles by way of the Chase National Bank. Soon family as well as financial alliances grew up among the Morgans, Whitneys, and Rockefellers, chiefly through Payne and Aldrich family connections.

For almost fifty years, from 1880 to 1930, financial capitalism approximated a feudal structure in which two great powers, centered in New York, dominated a number of lesser powers, both in New York and in provincial cities. No description of this structure as it existed in the 1920's can be given in a brief compass, since it infiltrated all aspects of American life and especially all branches of economic life.

At the center were a group of less than a dozen investment banks, which were, at the height of their powers, still unincorporated private partnerships. These included J. P. Morgan; the Rockefeller family; Kuhn, Loeb and Company; Dillon, Read and Company; Brown Brothers and Harriman; and others. Each of these was linked in organizational or personal relationships with various banks, insurance companies, railroads, utilities, and industrial firms. The result was to form a number of webs of economic power of which the more important centered in New York, while other provincial groups allied with these were to be found in Pittsburgh, Cleveland, Chicago, and Boston.

J. P. Morgan worked in close relationship to a group of banks and insurance companies, including the First National Bank of New York, the Guaranty Trust Company, the Bankers Trust, the New York Trust Company, and the Metropolitan Life Insurance Company. The whole nexus dominated a network of business firms which included at least one-sixth of the two hundred largest nonfinancial corporations in

American business. Among these were twelve utility companies, five or more railroad systems, thirteen industrial firms, and at least five of the fifty largest banks in the country. The combined assets of these firms were more than $30 billion. They included American Telephone and Telegraph Company, International Telephone and Telegraph, Consolidated Gas of New York, the groups of electrical utilities known as Electric Bond and Share and as the United Corporation Group (which included Commonwealth and Southern, Public Service of New Jersey, and Columbia Gas and Electric), the New York Central railway system, the Van Sweringen railway system (Allegheny) of nine lines (including Chesapeake and Ohio; Erie; Missouri Pacific; the Nickel Plate; and Pere Marquette); the Santa Fe; the Northern system of five great lines (Great Northern; Northern Pacific; Burlington; and others); the Southern Railway; General Electric Company; United States Steel; Phelps Dodge; Montgomery Ward; National Biscuit; Kennecott Copper; American Radiator and Standard Sanitary; Continental Oil; Reading Coal and Iron; Baldwin Locomotive; and others.

The Rockefeller group, which was really a monopoly capitalist organization investing only its own profits, functioned as a financial capitalist unit in close cooperation with Morgan. Allied with the country's largest bank, the Chase National, it was involved as an industrial power in the various Standard Oil firms and the Atlantic Refining Company, but it controlled over half the assets of the oil industry, plus the $2⅓ billion assets in Chase National Bank.

Kuhn, Loeb was chiefly interested in railroads, where it dominated the Pennsylvania, the Union Pacific, the Southern Pacific, the Milwaukee, the Chicago Northwestern, the Katy (Missouri-Kansas-Texas Railroad Company), and the Delaware and Hudson. It also dominated the Bank of Manhattan and the Western Union Telegraph Company for a total of almost $11 billion in assets.

The Mellon group centered in Pittsburgh dominated Gulf Oil, Koppers, Alcoa, Westinghouse Electric, Union Trust Company, the Mellon National Bank, Jones and Laughlin Steel, American Rolling Mill, Crucible Steel, and other firms for total assets of about $3.3 billion.

It has been calculated that the 200 largest nonfinancial corporations in the United States, plus the fifty largest banks, in the mid-1930's, owned 34 percent of the assets of all industrial corporations, 48 percent of the assets of all commercial banks, 75 percent of the assets of all public utilities, and 95 percent of the assets of all railroads. The total assets of all four classes were almost $100 billion, divided almost equally among the four classes. The four economic power blocs which we have mentioned (Morgan; Rockefeller; Kuhn, Loeb and Company; and Mellon) plus du Pont, and three local groups allied with these in Boston, Cleveland, and Chicago, together dominated the following percentages of the

250 corporations considered here: of industrial firms 58 percent of their total assets, of railroads 82 percent, and utilities 58 percent. The aggregate value of the assets controlled by the eight power groups was about $61,205 million of the total assets of $198,351 million in these 250 largest corporations at the end of 1935.

The economic power represented by these figures is almost beyond imagination to grasp, and was increased by the active role which these financial titans took in politics. Morgan and Rockefeller together frequently dominated the national Republican Party, while Morgan occasionally had extensive influence in the national Democratic Party (three of the Morgan partners were usually Democrats). These two were also powerful on the state level, especially Morgan in New York and Rockefeller in Ohio. Mellon was a power in Pennsylvania and du Pont was obviously a political power in Delaware.

In the 1920's this system of economic and political power formed a hierarchy headed by the Morgan interests and played a principal role both in political and business life. Morgan, operating on the international level in cooperation with his allies abroad, especially in England, influenced the events of history to a degree which cannot be specified in detail but which certainly was tremendous. Nevertheless, the slow developments of business life which we have mentioned were making investment bankers like Morgan obsolete, and the deflationary financial policies on which these bankers insisted were laying the foundations of the economic collapse which ended their rule in general social disaster by 1940.

In the United States, however, the demise of financial capitalism was much more protracted than in most foreign countries, and was not followed by a clearly established system of monopoly capitalism. This blurring of the stages was caused by a number of events of which three should be mentioned: (1) the continued personal influence of many financiers and bankers, even after their power had waned; (2) the decentralized condition of the United States itself, especially the federal political system; and (3) the long-sustained political and legal tradition of antimonopoly going back at least to the Sherman Antitrust Act of 1890. As a consequence, the United States did not reach a clearly monopolistic economy, and was unable to adopt a fully unorthodox financial policy capable of providing full use of resources. Unemployment, which had reached 13 million persons in 1933, was still at 10 million in 1940. On the other hand, the United States did take long steps in the direction of balancing interest blocs by greatly strengthening labor and farm groups and by sharply curtailing the influence and privileges of finance and heavy industry.

Of the diverse groups in the American economy, the financiers were most closely related to heavy industry because of the latter's great need for capital for its heavy equipment. The deflationary policies of the bankers were acceptable to heavy industry chiefly because the mass labor of heavy industry in the United States, notably in steel and automobile manufacturing, was not unionized, and the slowly declining prices of the products of heavy industry could continue to be produced profitably if costs could be reduced by large-scale elimination of labor by installing more heavy equipment. Much of this new equipment, which led to assembly-line techniques such as the continuous-strip steel mill, were financed by the bankers. With unorganized labor, the employers of mass labor could rearrange, curtail, or terminate labor without notice on a daily basis and could thus reduce labor costs to meet falls in prices from bankers' deflation. The fact that reductions in wages or large layoffs in mass-employment industries also reduced the volume of purchasing power in the economy as a whole, to the injury of other groups selling consumers' goods, was ignored by the makers of heavy producers' goods. In this way, farmers, light industry, real estate, commercial groups, and other segments of the society were injured by the deflationary policies of the bankers and by the employment policies of heavy industry, closely allied to the bankers. When these policies became unbearable in the depression of 1929–1933, these other interest blocs, who had been traditionally Republican (or at least, like the western farmers, had refused to vote Democratic and had engaged in largely futile third-party movements), deserted the Republican Party, which remained subservient to high finance and heavy industry.

This shift of the farm bloc, light industry, commercial interests (notably department stores), real estate, professional people, and mass, unskilled, labor to the Democratic Party in 1932 resulted in the election of Franklin D. Roosevelt and the New Deal. The new administration sought to curtail the power of the two opposition and exploiting groups (bankers and heavy industry) and to reward and help the groups which had elected it. The farmers were helped by subsidies; labor was helped by government spending to make jobs and provide purchasing power and by encouragement of unionization; while real estate, professional people, and commerical groups were helped by the increasing demand from the increased purchasing power of farmers and labor.

The New Deal's actions against finance and heavy industry were chiefly aimed at preventing these two from ever repeating their actions of the 1920–1933 period. The SEC Act sought to supervise securities issues and stock-exchange practices to protect investors. Railroad legislation sought to reduce the financial exploitation and even the deliberate bankruptcy of railroads by financial interests (as William Rockefeller had done to the Chicago, Milwaukee, and St. Paul or as Morgan had done to the New York, New Haven and Hartford). The Banking Act of 1933 separated investment banking from deposit banking. The whole-sale manipulation of labor by heavy industry was curtailed by the National Labor Relations Act of 1933, which sought to protect labor's rights of collective bargaining. At the same time, with the blessings of the new administration, a drive was made by labor groups allied with it to unionize the masses of unskilled labor employed by heavy industry to prevent the latter from adopting any policy of mass layoffs or sharp and sudden wage reductions in any future period of decreasing de-mand. To this end a Committee for Industrial Organization was set up under the leadership of the one head of a mass labor union in the country, John L. Lewis of the United Mine Workers, and a drive was put on to organize the workers of the steel, automobile, electrical, and other industries which had no unions.

All this served to create more highly organized and more self-con-scious interest blocs in American life, especially among farmers and labor, but it did not represent any victory for unorthodox financing, the real key to either monopoly capitalism or to a managed pluralist economy. The reason for this was that the New Deal, because of President Roosevelt, was fundamentally orthodox in its ideas on the nature of money. Roosevelt was quite willing to unbalance the budget and to spend in a depression in an unorthodox fashion because he had grasped the idea that lack of purchasing power was the cause of the lack of demand which made unsold goods and unemployment, but he had no idea of the causes of the depression and had quite orthodox ideas on the nature of money. As a result, his administration treated the symptoms rather than the causes of the depression and, while spending unorthodoxly to treat these symptoms, did so with money borrowed from the banks in the accepted fashion. The New Deal al-lowed the bankers to create the money, borrowed it from the banks, and spent it. This meant that the New Deal ran up the national debt to the credit of the banks, and spent money in such a limited fashion that no drastic reemployment of idle resources was possible.

One of the most significant facts about the New Deal was its ortho-doxy on money. For the whole twelve years he was in the White House, Roosevelt had statutory power to issue fiat money in the form of greenbacks printed by the government without recourse to the banks. This authority was never used. As a result of such orthodoxy, the depression's symptoms of idle resources were overcome only when the emergency of the war in 1942 made it possible to justify a limitless increase in the national debt by limitless borrowing from private persons and the banks. But the whole episode showed a failure to grasp the nature of money and the function of the monetary system, of which considerable traces remained in the postwar period.

One reason for the New Deal's readiness to continue with an orthodox theory of the nature of money, along with an unorthodox practice in its use, arose from the failure of the Roosevelt administration to recognize the nature of the economic crisis itself. This failure can be seen in Roosevelt's theory of "pump priming." He sincerely believed, as did his secretary of the Treasury, that there was nothing structurally wrong with the economy, that it was simply temporarily stalled, and would keep going of its own powers if it could be restarted. In order to restart it, all that was needed, in New Deal theory, was a relatively moderate amount of government spending on a temporary basis. This would create purchasing power (demand) for consumers' goods, which, in turn, would increase the confidence of investors who would begin to release large unused savings into investment. This would, again, create additional purchasing power and demand, and the economic system would take off of its own power. The curtailment of the powers of finance and heavy industry would then prevent any repetition of the collapse of 1929.

The inadequacy of this theory of the depression was shown in 1937 when the New Deal, after four years of pump priming and a victorious election in 1936, stopped its spending. Instead of taking off, the economy collapsed in the steepest recession in history. The New Deal had to resume its treatment of symptoms but now without hope that the spending program could ever be ended, a hopeless prospect since the administration lacked the knowledge of how to reform the system or even how to escape from borrowing bank credit with its mounting public debt, and the administration lacked the courage to adopt the really large-scale spending necessary to give full employment of resources. The administration was saved from this impasse by the need for the rearmament program followed by the war. Since 1947 the Cold War and the space program have allowed the same situation to continue, so that even today prosperity is not the result of a properly organized economic system but of government spending, and any drastic reduction in such spending would give rise to an acute depression.

The Economic Factors

From an analytical point of view there are a number of important elements in the economic situation of the twentieth century. These elements did not all come into existence at the same time, nor did any single one come into existence everywhere simultaneously. The order in which these elements came into existence is roughly that in which we list them here:

1. rising standards of living
2. industrialism
3. growth of size of enterprises
4. dispersal of ownership of enterprises
5. separation of control from ownership
6. concentration of control
7. decline of competition
8. increasing disparity in the distribution of incomes
9. declining rate of expansion leading to crisis

1. A rise in the general or average standard of living in modern times is obvious and, with intermittent breaks, goes back for a thousand years. Such progress is welcome, but it obviously brings with it certain accompanying factors which must be understood and accepted. A rising standard of living, except in its earliest stages, does not involve any increase in consumption of necessities but instead involves an increase in the consumption of luxuries even to the point of replacing basic necessities by luxuries. As average incomes rise, people do not, after a certain level, eat more and more black bread, potatoes, and cabbage, or wear more and more clothing. Instead, they replace black bread with wheaten bread and add meat to their diet and replace coarse clothing by finer apparel; they shift their emphasis from energy foods to protective foods.

This process can be continued indefinitely. A number of students have divided goods from this point of view into three levels: (*a*) necessities, (*b*) industrial products, and (*c*) luxuries and services. The first would include food and clothing; the second would include railroads, automobiles, and radios; the third would include movies, books, amusements, yachts, leisure, music, philosophy, and so on. Naturally, the dividing lines between the three groups are very vague, and the position of any particular item will vary from society to society and even from person to person.

As standards of living rise, decreasing proportions of attention and resources are devoted to primary or secondary types of products, and increasing proportions to secondary and tertiary types of products. This has very important economic consequences. It means that luxuries tend to become relatively more important than necessities. It also means that attention is constantly being shifted from products for which the demand is relatively inelastic to products for which the demand is relatively elastic (that is, expansible). There are exceptions to this. For example, housing, which is obviously a necessity, is a product for which demand is fairly elastic and might continue to be so until most persons lived in palaces, but, on the whole, the demand for necessities is less elastic than the demand for luxuries.

A rising standard of living also means an increase in savings (or accumulation of surplus) out of all proportion to the rise in incomes. It is a fairly general rule both for societies and for individuals that savings go up faster than incomes as the latter rise, if for no other reason than the fact that a person with an adequate supply of necessities will take time to make up his mind on which luxuries he will expend any increase in income.

Finally, a shift from primary to secondary production usually entails a very great increase in capital investment, while a shift from secondary to tertiary production may not result in any increase in capital investment proportionately as great. Leisure, amusements, music, philosophy, education, and personal services are not likely to require capital investments comparable to those required by the construction of railroads, steel factories, automotive plants, and electrical stations.

As a result of these factors, it may well arise that a society whose rising standards of living have brought it to the point where it is passing from emphasis on secondary to emphasis on tertiary production will be faced with the necessity of adjusting itself to a situation which includes more emphasis on luxuries than on necessities, more attention to products of elastic demand than inelastic, and increased savings with decreasing demands for investment.

2. Industrialization is an obvious element in modern economic development. As used here, it has a very specific meaning, namely, the application of inanimate power to production. For long ages, production was made by using power from animate sources such as human bodies, slaves, or draft animals, with relatively little accomplished by power from such inanimate sources as wind or falling water. The so-called Industrial Revolution began when the energy from coal, released through a nonliving machine—the steam engine—became an important element in the productive process. It continued through improvements in the use of wind power and waterpower to the use of oil in internal-combustion engines and finally to power from atomic sources.

The essential aspect of industrialism has been the great rise in the use of energy per capita of population. No adequate figures are available for most European countries, but in the United States the energy used per capita was:

Year	Energy per Capita	Index
1830	6 million BTU	1
1890	80 million BTU	13
1930	245 million BTU	40

As a result of this increase in the use of energy per capita, industrial output per man-hour rose significantly (in the United States 96 percent from 1899 to 1929). It was this increase in output per man-hour which permitted the rise in standards of living and the increases in investment associated with the process of industrialization.

The Industrial Revolution did not reach all parts of Europe, or even all parts of any single country, at the same moment. In general, it began in England late in the eighteenth century (about 1776) and spread slowly eastward and southward across Europe, reaching France after 1830, Germany after 1850, Italy and Russia after 1890. This eastward movement of industrialism had many significant results, among them the belief on the part of the newer countries that they were at a disadvantage in comparison with England because of the latter's head start. This was untrue, for, from a strictly temporal point of view, these newer countries had an advantage over England, since their newer industrial installations were less obsolescent and less hampered by vested interests. Whatever advantage England had arose from better natural resources, more plentiful supply of capital, and skilled labor.

3. The growth of size of enterprise was a natural result of the process of industrialism. This process required very considerable outlays for fixed capital, especially in the activities most closely associated with the early stages of industrialism, such as railroads, iron foundries, and textile mills. Such great outlays required a new legal structure for enterprise. This was found in the corporation or limited-liability joint-stock company. In this company large capital installations could be constructed and run, with ownership divided into small fractions among a large number of persons.

This increase in size of units was apparent in all countries, but chiefly in the United States, Britain, and Germany. The statistics on this are incomplete and tricky to use, but, in general, they indicate that, while the number of corporations has been increasing, and the average size of all corporations has been falling, the absolute size of the largest corporations has been increasing rapidly in the twentieth century, and the share of total assets or of total output held by the largest corporations has been rising. As a result, the output of certain products, notably chemicals, metals, artificial fibers, electrical equipment, and so on, has been dominated in most countries by a few great firms.

In the United States, where this process has been studied most carefully, it was found that from 1909 to 1930 the number of billion-dollar corporations rose from 1 to 15, and the share of all corporation assets held by the 200 largest rose from 32 percent to over 49 percent. By 1939 this figure reached 57 percent. This meant that the largest 200 corporations were growing faster than other corporations (5.4 percent a year compared to 2.0 percent a year) and faster than total national wealth. As a result, by 1930 these 200 largest corporations had 49.2 percent of all corporate assets (or $81 billion out of $165 billion); they had 38 percent of all business wealth (or $81 billion out of $212 billion); they held 22 percent of all wealth in the country (or $81 billion out of $367 billion). In fact, in 1930, a single corporation (American Telephone and Telegraph) had greater assets than the total wealth in 21 states. No such figures are available for European countries, but there can be no doubt that similar growth was taking place in most of them during this period.

4. Dispersal of ownership of enterprise was a natural result of the growth of size of enterprise, and was made possible by the corporate method of organization. As corporations increased in size, it became less and less possible for any individual or small group to own any important fractions of their stocks. In most countries the number of security holders increased faster than the number of outstanding securities. In the United States the former increased in numbers seven times as fast as the latter from 1900 to 1928. This was a greater spread than in other countries, but elsewhere there was also a considerable spreading out of corporate ownership. This was exactly contrary to the prediction of Karl Marx that the owners of industry would get fewer and fewer as well as richer and richer.

5. The separation of ownership from control has already been mentioned. It was an inevitable counterpart of the advent of the corporate form of business organization; indeed, the corporate form was devised for this very purpose—that is, to mobilize the capital owned by many persons into a single enterprise controlled by a few. As we have seen, this inevitable counterpart was carried to a quite unexpected degree by the devices invented by financial capitalism.

6. The concentration of control was also inevitable in the long run, but here also was carried by special devices to an extraordinary degree. As a result, in highly industrialized countries, the economic systems were dominated by a handful of industrial complexes. The French economy was dominated by three powers (Rothschild, Mirabaud, and Schneider); the German economy was dominated by two (I. G. Farben and Vereinigte Stahl Werke); the United States was dominated by two (Morgan and Rockefeller). Other countries, like Italy or Britain, were dominated by somewhat larger numbers. In no country was the power of these great complexes paramount and exclusive, and in no country were these powers able to control the situation to such a degree that they were able to prevent their own decline under the impact of world political and economic conditions, but their ability to dominate their spheres is undeniable. In France, Rothschild and Schneider were not able to weather the assault of Hitler; in Germany, Thyssen was not able to withstand the attacks of Flick and Göring. In the United

States, Morgan was unable to prevent the economic swing from finan-cial to monopoly capitalism, and yielded quite gracefully to the rising power of du Pont. In Britain, likewise, the masters of financial capital-ism yielded to the masters of chemical products and vegetable oils, once the inevitable writing on the wall had been traced out in a convincing fashion. But all these shifts of power within the individual economic systems indicate merely that individuals or groups are un-able to maintain their positions in the complex flux of modern life, and do not indicate any decentralization of control. On the contrary, even as group succeeds group, the concentration of control becomes greater.

7. A decline in competition is a natural consequence of the con-centration of control. This decline in competition refers, of course, only to price competition in the market, since this was the mechanism which made the economic system function in the nineteenth century. This decline is evident to all students of modern economics, and is one of the most widely discussed aspects of the modern economic system. It is caused not only by the activities of businessmen but also by the actions of labor unions, of governments, of private social welfare or-ganizations, and even of the herdlike behavior of consumers themselves.

8. The increasing disparity in the distribution of income is the most controversial and least well-established characteristic of the system. The available statistical evidence is so inadequate in all European coun-tries that the characteristic itself cannot be proved conclusively. An extensive study of the subject, using the available materials for both Europe and the United States, with a careful analysis of the much bet-ter American materials, will permit the following tentative conclusions. Leaving aside all government action, it would appear that the disparity in the distribution of the national income has been getting wider.

In the United States, for example, according to the National Industrial Conference Board, the richest one-fifth of the population received 46.2 percent of the national income in 1910, 51.3 percent in 1929, and 48.5 percent in 1937. In the same three years, the share of the poorest one-fifth of the population fell from 8.3 percent to 5.4 percent to 3.6 percent. Thus the ratios between the portion obtained by the richest one-fifth and that obtained by the poorest one-fifth increased in these three years from 5.6 to 9.3 to 13.5. If, instead of one-fifths, we examine the ratios between the percentage obtained by the richest one-tenth and that obtained by the poorest one-tenth, we find that in 1910 the ratio was 10; in 1929 it was 21.7; and in 1937 it was 34.4. This means that the rich in the United States were getting richer relatively and probably absolutely while the poor were getting poorer both relatively and absolutely. This last is caused by the fact that the increase in the real national income in the period 1910–1937 was not great enough to compensate for the decrease in percentage going to the poor or for the increase in number of persons in that class.

As a result of such an increase in disparity in the distribution of national income, there will be a tendency for savings to rise and for consumers' purchasing power to decline relative to each other. This is because the savings of a community are largely made by the richer persons in it, and savings increase out of all proportion as incomes rise. On the other hand, the incomes of the poor class are devoted primarily to expenditures for consumption. Thus, if it is correct that there is an increasing disparity in the distribution of the national income of a country, there will be a tendency for savings to rise and consumer purchasing power to decline relative to each other. If this is so, there will be an increasing reluctance on the part of the controllers of savings to invest their savings in new capital equipment, since the existing decline of purchasing power will make it increasingly difficult to sell the products of the existing capital equipment and highly unlikely that the products of any new capital equipment could be sold more easily.

This situation, as we have described it, assumes that the government has not intervened in such a way as to change the distribution of the national income as determined by economic factors. If, however, the government does intervene to disturb this distribution, its actions will either increase the disparity in its distribution or will decrease it. If these actions increase it, the problem of the discrepancy to which we have referred between savings, on one hand, and the level of purchasing power and investment, on the other, will be made worse. If, on the other hand, the government adopts a program which seeks to reduce the disparity in the distribution of the national income, by, for example, adopting a program of taxation which reduces the savings of the rich while increasing the purchasing power of the poor, the same problem of insufficient investment will arise. Such a tax program as we have described would have to be based on a graduated income tax, and, because of the concentration of saving in the upper-income brackets, would have to be carried to such a sharp degree of graduation that the taxes of the very rich would be rapidly approaching the level of confiscation. This would, as the conservatives say, "kill incentive." Of this there can be no doubt, for any person with an income already large enough to satisfy his consumers' wants will be very unlikely to possess any incentive to invest if each dollar of profit made from such investment is to have all but a few cents of its value taken by the government in the form of taxation.

In this way, the problem of increasing disparity in the distribution of national income leads to a single result (decline of investment relative to savings), whether the situation is left subject to purely economic factors or the government takes steps to decrease the disparity. The only difference is that, in the one case, the decline in investment may be attributed to a lack of consumer purchasing power, while, in the other case, it may be attributed to a "killing of incentive" by government action. Thus, we see that the controversy which has raged in both Europe and America since 1932 between progressives and conservatives in regard to the causes of the lack of investment is an artificial one. The progressives, who insisted that the lack of investment was caused by lack of consumer purchasing power, were correct. But the conservatives, who insisted that the lack of investment was caused by a lack of confidence, were also correct. Each was looking at the opposite side of what is a single continuous cycle.

This cycle runs roughly as follows: (*a*) purchasing power creates demand for goods; (*b*) demand for goods creates confidence in the minds of investors; (*c*) confidence creates new investment; and (*d*) new investment creates purchasing power, which then creates demand, and so on. To cut this cycle at any point and to insist that the cycle begins at that point is to falsify the situation. In the 1930's the progressives concentrated attention on stage (*a*), while the conservatives concentrated attention on stage (*c*). The progressives, who sought to increase purchasing power by some redistribution of the national income, undoubtedly did increase purchasing power under stage (*a*), but they lost purchasing power under stage (*c*) by reducing confidence of potential investors. This decrease of confidence was especially noticeable in countries (like France and the United States) which were still deeply involved in the stage of financial capitalism.

It would appear that the economic factors alone affected the distribution of incomes in the direction of increasing disparity. In no major country, however, were the economic factors alone allowed to determine the issue. In all countries government action noticeably influenced the distribution. However, this influence was not usually the result of conscious desire to change the distribution of the national income.

In Italy the economic factors had relatively free rein until after the creation of the corporative state in 1934. The effect of government action was to increase the normal economic tendency toward an increasing disparity in distribution of the national income. This tendency had been allowed to work from an early period until the end of the war in 1918. A drastic effort by Leftish influences in the period 1918–1922 resulted in government action which reversed this tendency. As a result, a counterrevolution brought Mussolini to power in October 1922. The new government suppressed those government actions which had hampered the normal economic tendency, and as a result the trend toward greater disparity in distribution of the national income was resumed. This trend became more drastic after the creation of the dictatorship in 1925, after the stabilization of the lira in 1927, and after the creation of the corporative state in 1934.

In Germany the changes in distribution of the national income were similar to those in Italy, although complicated by the efforts to create a social-service state (an effort going back to Bismarck) and by the hyperinflation. In general, the trend toward increasing disparity in distribution of the national income continued, less rapidly than in Italy, until after 1918. The inflation, by wiping out unemployment for the lower class and by wiping out the savings of the middle class, created a complex situation in which the wealth of the richest class was increased while the poverty of the poorest class was reduced, and the general trend toward increased disparity in income was probably reduced. This reduction became greater under the social-service state of 1924–1930, but was drastically reversed because of the great increase in poverty in the lower classes after 1929. After 1934 the adoption of an unorthodox financial policy and a policy of benefits to monopoly capitalism reinforced the normal trend toward increasing disparity in distribution of income. This was in accord with the desires of the Hitler government, but the full impact of this policy was not apparent on the distribution of incomes until the period of full employment after 1937.

Until 1938 Hitler's policy, although aimed at favoring the high-income classes, raised the standards of living of the lower-income levels even more drastically (by shifting them from unemployment with incomes close to nothing into wage-earning positions in industry) so that the disparity in distribution of income was probably even reduced for a short-run period in 1934–1937. This was not unacceptable to the high-income classes, because it stopped the threat of revolution by the discontented masses and because it was obviously of long-run benefit to them. This long-run benefit began to appear when capacity employment of capital and labor was achieved in 1937. The continuance of the policy of rearmament after 1937 increased the incomes of the high-income groups while decreasing the incomes of the lower-income groups and thus served, from 1937 onward, to reinforce the normal economic tendency toward an increasing disparity in the distribution of incomes. This, of course, is one of the essential features of a Fascist government, and is obvious not only in Germany since 1937, in Italy since 1927, but also in Spain since 1938.

In France and Britain, the trend toward increasing disparity in the distribution of incomes was reversed in recent decades, although in Britain before 1945 and in France before 1936 there was no conscious effort to achieve this result.

In France disparity increased until 1913, then decreased chiefly because of the increasing power of labor unions and actions of the government. The inflation and resulting devaluation badly injured the incomes of the possessing class, so that the disparity became less disperse; but the whole level of living standards was declining, savings were declining, and investment was decreasing more rapidly than either. This process became worse after the depression hit France about 1931 and even worse after the Popular Front adopted its welfare program in 1936. This decline of the general economic level continued quite steadily except for a brief revival after 1938, but the disparity in the distribution of incomes very likely became greater in 1940–1942.

In Britain the disparity became greater, but at a slower rate (because of labor unions), until the First World War, and then almost stabilized, increasing only slightly, because of the severe efforts made in Britain to pay for much of the war's cost by taxation. The decrease in upper-level incomes by taxation, however, was more than overcome by the decrease in lower-level incomes from unemployment. This static condition of the disparity in distribution of the national income doubtless continued until after 1931. Since this last date the situation is confused. The revival of prosperity and the rapid development of new lines of activity combined with the peculiarities of the incidence of British taxation have likely reduced the disparity, but, until 1943, not by anything approaching the degree which one might expect from a first glance at the problem. Since 1943 and especially since 1946 the tax schedule and the government's social welfare program have drastically reduced the disparity in distribution of income and have also cut investment and even savings by private sources to a considerable degree.

It would seem that in the twentieth century the disparity in the distribution of national income, which had been increasing for generations, slowed down and reversed as a result of government activities. This turning point appeared in different countries at different dates, probably earliest in Denmark and France, later in Germany and Italy, latest in Britain and Spain. In France and Britain the tendency was reversed by the action of the government, but in a hesitant fashion which was not able, in any decisive way, to overcome the sag in private enterprise by any upswing in government enterprise. In Germany, Italy, and Spain the governments fell into the hands of the possessing classes, and the desires of the peoples of these countries for a more equitable distribution of incomes were frustrated. In all three types of conditions, there was a decline in real economic progress until after 1950.

9. A declining rate of economic expansion is the last important characteristic of the economic system of Europe in the present century up to 1950. This decline resulted almost inevitably from the other characteristics which we have already discussed. It varied from country to country, the countries of eastern Europe suffering less than those of western Europe on the whole, but chiefly because their previous rate of progress had been so much lower.

The causes of this decline are basically to be found in a relative increase in the power of the vested interests within the community to defend the *status quo* against the efforts of the progressive and enterprising members of the community to change it. This was revealed in the market (the central mechanism of the economic system) as a result of a relative increase in savings in respect to investment. Savings have continued or have increased for several reasons. In the first place, a tradition which placed a high social esteem on savings existed in western Europe from the Protestant Reformation until the 1930's. In the second place, there had grown up established institutionalized savings organizations like insurance companies. In the third place, the rising standards of living increased savings even more rapidly. In the fourth place, the increasing disparity in the distribution of incomes increased savings. In the fifth place, the increase in size of enterprises and the separation of ownership from control acted to increase the amount of corporate savings (undistributed profits).

On the other hand, the inclination to invest did not rise so rapidly as savings, or even decreased. Here, again, the reasons are numerous. In the first place, the shift in advanced industrial countries from secondary to tertiary production reduces the demand for heavy capital investment. In the second place, declining rates of population increase, and geographic expansion may adversely affect the demand for investment. In the third place, the increasing disparity in the distribution of incomes, whether it is counteracted by government action or not, has a tendency to reduce the demand for investment capital. In the fourth place, the decrease in competition has served to reduce the amount of investment by making it possible for the controllers of existing capital to maintain its value by curtailing the investment of new capital which would make the existing capital less valuable. This last point may require additional explanation.

In the past, investment was not only capital-creating but also capital-destroying—that is, it made some existing capital worthless by making it obsolete. The creation by investment, for example, of shipyards for making iron-hull steam vessels not only created this new capital but at the same time destroyed the value of the existing yards equipped to make wooden-hull sailing ships. In the past, new investment was made in only one of two cases: (*a*) if an old investor believed that the new capital would yield sufficient profit to pay for itself and for the old investment now made obsolete, or (*b*) if the new investor was completely free of the old one, so that the latter could do nothing to prevent the destruction of his existing capital holdings by the new investor. Both of these two alternatives, in the twentieth century tended to become less likely (until 1950), the former by the decline in consumer purchasing power and the latter by the decrease in competition.

The way in which the relative decline of investment in respect to savings results in economic crisis is not difficult to see. In the modern economic community, the sum total of goods and services appearing in the market is at one and the same time the income of the community and the aggregate cost of producing the goods and services in question. The sums expended by the entrepreneur on wages, rents, salaries, raw materials, interest, lawyers' fees, and so on, represent costs to him and income to those who receive them. His own profits also enter the picture, since they are his income and the cost of persuading him to produce the wealth in question. The goods are offered for sale at a price which is equal to the sum of all costs (including profits). In the community as a whole, aggregate costs, aggregate incomes, and aggregate prices are the same, since they are merely opposite sides of the identical expenditures.

The purchasing power available in the community is equal to income minus savings. If there are any savings, the available purchasing power will be less than the aggregate prices being asked for the products for sale and by the amount of the savings. Thus, all the goods and services produced cannot be sold as long as savings are held back. In order for all the goods to be sold, it is necessary for the savings to reappear in the market as purchasing power. The usual way in which this is done is by investment. When savings are invested, they are expended into the community and appear as purchasing power. Since the capital good made by the process of investment is not offered for sale to the community, the expenditures made by its creation appear completely as purchasing power. Thus, the disequilibrium between purchasing power and prices which was created by the act of saving is restored completely by the act of investment, and all the goods can be sold at the prices asked. But whenever investment is less than savings, the available supply of purchasing power is inadequate by the same amount to buy the goods being offered. This margin by which purchasing power is inadequate because of an excess of savings over investment may be called the "deflationary gap." This "deflationary gap" is the key to the twentieth century economic crisis and one of the three central cores of the whole tragedy of the century.

The Results of Economic Depression

The deflationary gap arising from a failure of investment to reach the level of savings can be closed either by lowering the supply of goods to the level of the available purchasing power or by raising the supply of purchasing power to a level able to absorb the existing supply of goods, or by a combination of both. The first solution will give a stabilized economy on a low level of economic activity; the second will give a stabilized economy on a high level of economic activity. Left to itself, the economic system under modern conditions would adopt the former procedure. This would work roughly as follows: The existence of the deflationary gap (that is, available purchasing power less than aggregate prices of available goods and services) will result in falling prices, declining economic activity, and rising unemployment. All this will result in a fall in national income, and this in turn will result in an even more rapid decline in the volume of savings. This decline continues until the volume of savings reaches the level of investment, at which point the fall is arrested and the economy becomes stabilized at a low level.

As a matter of fact, this process did not work itself out in any industrial country during the great depression of 1929–1934, because the disparity in the distribution of the national income was so great that a considerable portion of the population would have been driven to zero incomes and absolute want before the savings of the richer segment of the population fell to the level of investment. Moreover, as the depression deepened, the level of investment declined even more rapidly than the level of savings. There can be little doubt that under such conditions the masses of the population would have been driven to revolution before the "automatic economic factors" were able to stabilize the economy, and the stabilization, if reached, would have been on a level so low that a considerable portion of the population would have been in absolute want. Because of this, in every industrial country, governments took steps to arrest the course of the depression before their citizens were driven to desperation.

The methods used to deal with the depression and close the deflationary gap were of many different kinds, but all are reducible to two fundamental types: (a) those which destroy goods and (b) those which produce goods which do not enter the market.

The destruction of goods will close the deflationary gap by reducing the supply of unsold goods through lowering the supply of goods to the level of the supply of purchasing power. It is not generally realized that this method is one of the chief ways in which the gap is closed in a normal business cycle. In such a cycle, goods are destroyed by the simple expedient of not producing the goods which the system is capable of producing. The failure to use the economic system at the 1929 level of output during the years 1930–1934 represented a loss of goods worth $100,000,000,000 in the United States, Britain, and Germany alone. This loss was equivalent to the destruction of such goods. Destruction of goods by failure to gather the harvest is a common phenomenon under modern conditions, especially in respect to fruits, berries, and vegetables. When a farmer leaves his crop of oranges, peaches, or strawberries unharvested because the selling price is too low to cover the expense of harvesting, he is destroying the goods. Outright destruction of goods already produced is not common, and occurred for the first time as a method of combating depression in the years 1930–1934. During this period, stores of coffee, sugar, and bananas were destroyed, corn was plowed under, and young livestock was slaughtered to reduce the supply on the market. The destruction of goods in warfare is another example of this method of overcoming deflationary conditions in the economic system.

The second method of filling the deflationary gap, namely, by producing goods which do not enter the market, accomplishes its purpose by providing purchasing power in the market, since the costs of production of such goods do enter the market as purchasing power, while the goods themselves do not drain funds from the system if they are not offered for sale. New investment was the usual way in which this was accomplished in the normal business cycle, but it is not the normal way of filling the gap under modern conditions of depression. We have already seen the growing reluctance to invest and the unlikely chance that the purchasing power necessary for prosperity will be provided by a constant stream of private investment. If this is so, the funds for producing goods which do not enter the market must be sought in a program of public spending.

Any program of public spending at once runs into the problems of inflation and public debt. These are the same two problems which were mentioned in an earlier chapter in connection with the efforts of governments to pay for the First World War. The methods of paying for a depression are exactly the same as the methods of paying for a war, except that the combination of methods used may be somewhat different because the goals are somewhat different. In financing a war, we should seek to achieve a method which will provide a maximum of output with a minimum of inflation and public debt. In dealing with a depression, since a chief aim is to close the deflationary gap, the goal will be to provide a maximum of output with a necessary degree of inflation and a minimum of public debt. Thus, the use of fiat money is more justifiable in financing a depression than in financing a war. Moreover, the selling of bonds to private persons in wartime might well be aimed at the lower-income groups in order to reduce consumption and release facilities for war production, while in a depression (where low consumption is the chief problem) such sales of bonds to finance public spending would have to be aimed at the savings of the upper-income groups.

These ideas on the role of government spending in combating depression have been formally organized into the "theory of the compensatory economy." This theory advocates that government spending and fiscal policies be organized so that they work exactly contrary to the business cycle, with lower taxes and larger spending in a deflationary period and higher taxes with reduced spending in a boom period, the fiscal deficits of the down cycle being counterbalanced in the national budget by the surpluses of the up cycle.

This compensatory economy has not been applied with much success in any European country except Sweden. In a democratic country, it would take the control of taxing and spending away from the elected representatives of the people and place this precious "power of the purse" at the control of the automatic processes of the business cycle as interpreted by bureaucratic (and unrepresentative) experts. Moreover, all these programs of deficit spending are in jeopardy in a country with a private banking system. In such a system, the creation of money (or credit) is usually reserved for the private banking institutions, and is deprecated as a government action. The argument that the creation of funds by the government is bad while creation of funds by the banks is salutary is very persusasive in a system based on traditional laissez faire and in which the usual avenues of communications (such as newspapers and radio) are under private, or even banker, control.

Public spending as a method of counteracting depression can vary very greatly in character, depending on the purposes of the spending. Spending for destruction of goods or for restriction of output, as under the early New Deal agricultural program, cannot be justified easily in a democratic country with freedom of communications, because it obviously results in a decline in national income and living standards. Spending for nonproductive monuments is somewhat easier to justify but is hardly a long-run solution. Spending for investment in productive equipment (like the TVA) is obviously the best solution, since it leads to an increase in national wealth and standards of living and is a long-run solution, but it marks a permanent departure from a system of private capitalism, and can be easily attacked in a country with a capitalistic ideology and a private banking system. Spending on armaments and national defense is the last method of fighting depression and is the one most readily and most widely adopted in the twentieth century.

A program of public expenditure on armaments is a method for filling the deflationary gap and overcoming depression because it adds purchasing power to the market without drawing it out again later (since the armaments, once produced, are not put up for sale). From an economic point of view, this method of combating depression is not much different from the method listed earlier under destruction of goods, for, in this case also, economic resources are diverted from constructive activities or idleness to production for destruction. The appeal of this method for coping with the problem of depression does not rest on economic grounds at all, for, on such grounds, there is no justification. Its appeal is rather to be found on other, especially political, grounds.

Among these grounds we may list the following: a rearmament program helps heavy industry directly and immediately. Heavy industry is the segment of the economy which suffers earliest and most drastically in a depression, which absorbs manpower most readily (thus reducing unemployment) and which is politically influential in most countries. Such a program is also easily justified to the public on grounds of national defense, especially if other countries are dealing with their economic crises by the same method of treatment.

The adoption of rearmament as a method of combating depression does not have to be conscious. The country which adopts it may honestly feel that it is adopting the policy for good reasons, that it is threatened by aggression, and that a program of rearmament is necessary for political protection. It is very rare for a country consciously to adopt a program of aggression, for, in most wars, both sides are convinced that their actions are defensive. It is almost equally rare for a country to adopt a policy of rearmament as a solution for depression. But, unconsciously, the danger from a neighbor and the advantages to be derived from rearming in the face of such a danger are always more convincing to a country whose economic system is functioning below capacity than it is to a country which is riding a boom. Moreover, if a country adopts rearmament because of fear of another country's arms, and these last are the result of efforts to fill a deflationary gap, it can also be said that the rearmament of the former has a basic economic cause.

As we have mentioned, Fascism is the adoption by the vested interests in a society of an authoritarian form of government in order to maintain their vested interests and prevent the reform of the society. In the twentieth century in Europe, the vested interests usually sought to prevent the reform of the economic system (a reform whose need was made evident by the long-drawn-out depression) by adopting an economic program whose chief element was the effort to fill the deflationary gap by rearmament.

The Pluralist Economy and World Blocs

The economic disasters of two wars, a world depression, and the postwar fluctuations showed clearly by 1960 that a new economic organization of society was both needed and available. The laissez-faire competitive system had destroyed itself, and almost destroyed civilization as well, by its inability to distribute the goods it could produce. The system of monopoly capitalism had helped in this disaster, and clearly showed that its efforts, in Fascist countries, to protect its profits and privileges by authoritarian government and ultimately by war were unsuccessful because it could not combine conservatism in economic and social life with the necessary innovation and freedom in military and intellectual life to win the wars it could start. Moreover, Communism, on the winning side of the war, nonetheless showed that it, like any authoritarian system, failed to produce innovations, flexibility, and freedom; it could make extensive industrial advances only by copying freer peoples, and could not raise its standards of living substantially because it could not combine lack of freedom and force in political life and in the utilization of economic resources with the increased production of food and spiritual or intellectual freedom which were the chief desires of its own peoples.

This almost simultaneous failure of laissez faire, of economic Fascism, and of Communism to satisfy the growing popular demand both for rising standards of living and for spiritual liberty has forced the mid-twentieth century to seek some new economic organization. This demand has been intensified by the arrival on the scene of new peoples, new nations, and new tribes who by their demands for these same goods have shown their growing awareness of the problems, and their determination to do something about them. As this new group of underdeveloped peoples look about, they have been struck by the conflicting claims of the two great super-Powers, the United States and the Soviet Union. The former offered the goods the new peoples wanted (rising standards of living and freedom), while the latter seemed to offer methods of getting these goods (by state accumulation of capital, government direction of the utilization of economic resources, and centralized methods of over-all social planning) which might tend to smother these goals. The net result of all this has been a convergence of all three systems toward a common, if remote, system of the future.

The ultimate nature of that new system of economic and social life is not yet clear, but we might call it the "pluralist economy," and characterize its social structure as one which provides prestige, rewards, and power to managerial groups of experts whose contributions to the system are derived from their expertise and "know-how." These managers and experts, who clearly are a minority in any society, are recruited from the society as a whole, can be selected only by a process of "careers open to talent" on a trial-and-error basis, and require freedom of assembly, discussion, and decision in order to produce the innovations needed for the future success, or even the survival, of the system in which they function. Thus the pluralist economy and the managerial society, from the early 1940's, have forced the growth of a new kind of economic organization which will be totally unlike the four types of pre-1939 (American laissez faire, Stalinist Communism, authoritarian Fascism, and underdeveloped areas).

The chief characteristics of the new pluralist managerial system are five in number:

1. The central problem of decision-making in the new system will be concerned with the allotment of resources among three claimants: (*a*) consumers' goods to provide rising standards of living; (*b*) investment in capital goods to provide the equipment to produce consumers' goods; (*c*) the public sector covering defense, public order, education, social welfare, and all the central care of administrative activities associated with the young, the old, and public welfare as a whole.

2. The process of decision-making among these three claimants will take the form of a complex, multilateral struggle among a number of interested groups. These groups, which differ from one society or area to another, are in constant flux in each society or area. In general, however, the chief blocs or groups involved will be: (*a*) the defense forces, (*b*) labor, (*c*) the farmers, (*d*) heavy industry, (*e*) light industry, (*f*) transport and communication groups, (*g*) finance, fiscal, and banking groups, (*h*) commercial, real-estate, and construction interests, (*i*) scientific, educational, and intellectual groups, (*j*) political party and government workers, and (*k*) consumers in general.

3. The process of decision-making operates by the slow and almost imperceptible shifts of the various blocs, one by one, from support to neutralism to opposition toward the existing division of resources among the three claimant sectors by the central managerial elite. If, for example, there is excess allotment of resources to the defense or governmental sector, the farming groups, consumers, commercial groups, intellectuals, and others will become increasingly dissatisfied with the situation and gradually shift their pressures toward a reduction of the resources for defense and an increase of the resources for the consumer or the capital-investment sectors. Such shifts are complex, gradual, reversible, and continuous.

4. The working out of these shifts of resources to achieve the more concrete goals of the diverse interest blocs in the society will be increasingly dominated by rationalist and scientific methods emphasizing analytical and quantitative techniques. This means that emotional and intuitive forces will play, as always, a considerable role in the shifting of interest blocs which dominate the allotment of resources among the three sectors, but that rational rather than emotional methods, on quantitative rather than qualitative bases, will dominate the ultilization of such resources within each sector for more specific objectives. This will require considerable freedom of discussion in such utilization even where, as in Communist states or in underdeveloped areas, authoritarian and secretive methods are used in reference to the allotments among sectors. And, in general, there will be a very considerable modification of the areas and objectives of freedom in all societies of the world, with gradual reduction of numerous personal freedoms of the past accompanied by

the gradual increase of other fundamental freedoms, especially intellectual, which will provide the technical innovations, the clash of ideas, and the release of personal energy necessary for the success, or even the survival, of modern state systems.

5. The details of the operations of this new system will inevitably differ from area to area and even from state to state. In the Western bloc of states the shifts of public opinion continue to be reflected very largely in shifting political parties. Within the Communist bloc these shifts will take place, as they have in the past, among a smaller group of insiders and on a much more personal basis, so that shifts of targets and direction of policy will be revealed to the public by shifts of personnel in the state's bureaucratic structure. And in the underdeveloped countries, where possession of power is frequently associated with support from the armed forces, the process may be reflected by changes in policy and direction by the existing elite and rulers who retain their power in spite of changing policies.

In the most general way, the period since 1947 has shown that the differences between any two of the three blocs are becoming less; the three methods for achieving policy shifts (just mentioned) are becoming increasingly similar in essence and in fact, however different they continue to be in law. Moreover, in the same years since 1947, the solidarity of both the West and the Communists has become increasingly less, while the unity of outlook, policies, and interests of the uncommitted and underdeveloped peoples of the intermediary zone between the two great Power blocs become increasingly unified.

The method of operation of this newly formed pluralist-managerial system may be called "planning," if it be understood that planning may be both public and private and does not necessarily have to be centralized in either, but is rather concerned with the general method of a scientific and rational utilization of resources, in both time and space, to achieve consciously envisioned future goals.

In this process the greatest achievements have been by western Europe and by Japan. The latter, relieved to a great extent from the need to devote resources to defense, has been able to mobilize these for investment and, to a somewhat lesser degree, for rising standards of living, and has been able to achieve growth rates of gross national product of 7 to 9 percent a year. This has made Japan the only area of the non-Western world and of the underdeveloped countries able to pass into the higher level of industrialization capable of achieving substantial improvements in individual standards of living. These improvements, held back by the emphasis on reconstruction and investment in 1945–1962, have shifted slowly but steadily in the last few years toward consumers' benefits, including such intangibles as increased education, sports, leisure, and entertainment.

Western Europe has had an experience somewhat similar to that of

Japan except that its chief emphasis has been on improved standards of living (collectively known as "welfare"), with more emphasis on defense and less emphasis on investment than Japan. As a result, western Europe, especially West Germany, Italy, France, Scandinavia, and Britain, have, for the first time, come within striking distance of the very high standards of personal consumption found in the United States. In this process these countries have allowed the defensive power of their armed forces to suffer for the sake of their welfare goals, but have felt safe in doing so because of their reliance on American defensive power to deter any Soviet aggression.

In this process western Europe has achieved growth rates in gross national product (GNP) of 4 to 8 percent a year as a consequence of three basic forces. These have been: (1) the skillful (and perhaps lucky) use of financial and fiscal techniques which have encouraged both investment and willingness to consume; (2) the economic and technical aid of the United States, beginning with the Marshall Plan of 1946 and continuing with United States government military aid and investments of savings coming in from the whole Western world; and (3) the growing integration of Europe's economy in the Common Market which has made it feasible to adopt mass-production techniques for a greatly enlarged market.

In this same process the achievements of the United States and of the Soviet bloc have been much less spectacular from a purely economic point of view. In the United States, where the standard of living has reached unprecedented heights of affluence, the burdens of being a super-Power have hampered welfare because of the conflicting claims of defense, governmental expenses, prestige, and other rivalries with the Soviet Union, and the desire to contribute to the growth of the underdeveloped areas of the world. As a result, growth rates of GNP have been from 2 to 5 percent a year, and the burden of the governmental sector, including defense and increasing demands for such welfare items as education, health, and equalization of personal opportunities, have put great pressures on the growth of the consumers' sector.

The Soviet bloc as a whole, apart from the Soviet Union as the dominant member of that bloc, has been ambiguous in its economic growth. The demands of the defense sector and of other reflections of the Cold War, such as the "space race," have combined with the continued failures of Communist agricultural practices and the intrinsic inefficiency of the Communist system as a whole to limit severely the rise in standards of living. To be sure, the standards of living of the Soviet Union itself have reached the highest in Russia's history, while still lagging at only a fraction of those in the United States. But in the Communist bloc as a whole the picture has been far less happy. The non-Russian countries in the bloc have been exploited by the Soviet Union, have been treated as colonial areas (that is, sources of manpower, raw materials, and food based on claims arising from political relations), and have achieved little, if any, increase in GNP beyond that needed to sustain their increasing populations. In the cases of more western areas, such as East Germany, Hungary, and Poland, this has been reflected in absolute declines in living standards. The sharp contrast between this and the visible boom in West Germany has greatly increased the discontent in the European satellites.

The position of the underdeveloped nations has also been generally ambiguous. As a whole, lack of know-how and trained manpower, lack of capital, waste of resources by small privileged elites, absolute shortages of resources in some areas, the rapid growth of populations almost everywhere, and hopelessly unprogressive social structures and ideologies have combined to prevent any considerable improvements in standards of living. These have, in fact, decreased in much of Indonesia, the Near East, and Latin America, and have kept only slightly ahead of the growing population in India, Southeast Asia, and Africa. Only in Japan, as we have said, has there been success from this point of view, while the failure of these desires in China and in Latin America have tended to lead both of these out of their former alignments with the Soviet bloc and the Western bloc toward the more ambivalent political position of the uncommitted nations. In fact, in this process China's enmity toward both the Soviet Union and the United States has tended to place her in a new position, apart from all the pre-1962 alignments of international politics, while Latin America's growing discontent has tended to lead it, from many points of view, toward the position of the Near East countries.

XII

THE POLICY OF
APPEASEMENT,
1931-1936

Introduction

THE structure of collective security, which had been so imperfectly
built after 1919, by the victorious Powers, was destroyed completely in the eight years following 1931 under the assaults of
Japan, Italy, and Germany. These assaults were not really aimed at the
collective security system or even at the peace settlements of which it was
a part. After all, two of the aggressors had been on the winning side in
1919. Moreover, these assaults, although called forth by the world depression, went far beyond any reaction to the economic slump.

From the broadest point of view, the aggressors of 1931–1941 were
attacking the whole nineteenth century way of life and some of the most
fundamental attributes of Western Civilization itself. They were in revolt against democracy, against the parliamentary system, against laissez
faire and the liberal outlook, against nationalism (although in the name
of nationalism), against humanitarianism, against science, and against all
respect for human dignity and human decency. It was an attempt to
brutalize men into a mass of unthinking atoms whose reactions could be
controlled by methods of mass communication and directed to increase the
profits and power of an alliance of militarists, heavy-industrialists, landlords, and psychopathic political organizers recruited from the dregs of
society. That the society which they came to control could have created
such dregs, men who were totally untouched by the traditions of Western
Civilization and who were restrained by no social relationships at all, and
that it could have allowed the militarists and industrialists to use these
dregs as an instrument for seizing control of the state raise profound
doubts about the nature of that society and about its real allegiance to
the traditions to which it paid lip service.

The speed of social change in the nineteenth century, by quickening
transportation and communications and by gathering people in amorphous
multitudes in the cities, had destroyed most of the older social relation-

559

ships of the average man, and by leaving him emotionally unattached to neighborhood, parish, vocation, or even family, had left him isolated and frustrated. The paths which the society of his ancestors had provided for the expression of their gregarious, emotional, and intellectual needs were destroyed by the speed of social change, and the task of creating new paths for expressing these needs was far beyond the ability of the average man. Thus he was left, with his innermost drives unexpressed, willing to follow any charlatan who provided a purpose in life, an emotional stimulus, or a place in a group.

The methods of mass propaganda offered by the press and the radio provided the means by which these individuals could be reached and mobilized; the determination of the militarists, landlords, and industrialists to expand their own power and extend their own interests even to the destruction of society itself provided the motive; the world depression provided the occasion. The materials (frustrated men in the mass), the methods (mass communications), the instrument (the psychopathic political organization), and the occasion (the depression) were all available by 1931. Nevertheless, these men could never have come to power or come within a measurable distance of destroying Western Civilization completely if that civilization had not failed in its efforts to protect its own traditions and if the victors of 1919 had not failed in their efforts to defend themselves.

The nineteenth century had been so successful in organizing techniques that it had almost completely lost any vision of goals. Control of nature by the advance of science, increases in production by the growth of industry, the spread of literacy through universal education, the constant speedup of movement and communications, the extraordinary rise in standards of living—all these had extended man's ability to do things without in any way clarifying his ideas as to what was worth doing. Goals were lost completely or were reduced to the most primitive level of obtaining more power and more wealth. But the constant acquisition of power or wealth, like a narcotic for which the need grows as its use increases without in any way satisfying the user, left man's "higher" nature unsatisfied. From the past of Western Civilization, as a result of the fusion of Classical, Semitic, Christian, and Medieval contributions, there had emerged a system of values and modes of living which received scant respect in the nineteenth century in spite of the fact that the whole basis of the nineteenth century (its science, its humanitarianism, its liberalism, and its belief in human dignity and human freedom) had come from this older system of values and modes of living. The Renaissance and Reformation had rejected the medieval portion of this system; the eighteenth century had rejected the value of social tradition and of social discipline, the nineteenth century rejected the Classical and the Christian portion of this tradition, and gave the final blow to the hierarchical conception of human needs. The twentieth century reaped where these had sown. With its tradition abandoned and only its techniques maintained, Western Civilization by the middle of the twentieth century reached a point where the chief question was "Can it survive?"

Against this background the aggressive Powers rose after 1931 to challenge Western Civilization and the "satisfied" Powers which had neither the will nor the desire to defend it. The weakness of Japan and Italy from the point of view of industrial development or natural resources made it quite impossible for them to have issued any challenge unless they were faced by weak wills among their victims. In fact, it is quite clear that neither Japan nor Italy could have made a successful aggression without the parallel aggression of Germany. What is not so clear, but is equally true, is that Germany could have made no aggression without the acquiescence, and even in some cases the actual encouragement, of the "satisfied" Powers, especially Britain. The German documents captured since 1944 make this quite evident.

The Japanese Assault, 1931-1941

With one notable exception, Japan's background for aggression presented a strong parallel to that of Germany. The exception was the industrial strength of the two Powers. Japan was really a "have not" nation, lacking most of the natural resources to sustain a great industrial system. It lacked much of the necessary basic materials such as coal, iron, petroleum, alloy minerals, waterpower, or even food. In comparison, Germany's claim to be a "have not" nation was merely a propaganda device. Other than this, the similarity of the two countries was striking: each had a completely cartelized industry, a militaristic tradition, a hardworking population which respected authority and loved order, a national obsession with its own unique value and a resentment at the rest of the world for failure to recognize this, and a constitutional structure in which a facade of parliamentary constitutionalism barely concealed the reality of power wielded by an alliance of army, landlords, and industry. The fact that the Japanese constitution of 1889 was copied from the constitution of Bismarck goes far to explain this last similarity.

We have already mentioned the acute problem presented to Japan by the contrast between their limited natural resources and their growing problems. While their resources did not increase, their population grew from 31 million in 1873 to 73 million in 1939, the rate of growth reaching its peak in the period 1925-1930 (8 percent increase in these five years).

With great ingenuity and tireless energy, the Japanese people tried to make ends meet. With foreign exchange earned from merchant shipping or from exports of silk, wood products, or seafoods, raw materials were imported, manufactured into industrial products, and exported to obtain the foreign exchange necessary to pay for imports of raw materials or food. By keeping costs and prices low, the Japanese were able to undersell European exporters of cotton textiles and iron products in the markets of Asia, especially in China and Indonesia.

The possibility of relieving their population pressure by emigration, as Europe had done earlier, was prevented by the fact that the obvious colonial areas had already been taken in hand by Europeans. English-speaking persons, who held the best and yet unfilled areas, slammed the door on Japanese immigration in the period after 1901, justifying their actions on racial and economic arguments. American restrictions on Japanese immigration, originated among laboring groups in California, were a very bitter pill for Japan, and injured its pride greatly.

The steady rise in tariffs against Japanese manufactured goods after 1897, a development which was also led by America, served to increase the difficulties of Japan's position. So also did the slow exhaustion of the Pacific fisheries, the growing (if necessary) restrictions on such fishing by conservationist agreements, the decrease in forestry resources, and political and social unrest in Asia. For a long time, Japan was protected from the full impact of this problem by a series of favorable accidents. The First World War was a splendid windfall. It ended European commercial competition in Asia, Africa, and the Pacific; it increased the demand for Japanese goods and services; and it made Japan an international creditor for the first time. Capital investment in the five years 1915–1920 was eight times as much as in the ten years 1905–1915; laborers employed in factories using over five workers each increased from 948 thousand in 1914 to 1,612 thousand in 1919; ocean shipping rose from 1.5 million tons in 1914 to 3 million tons in 1918, while income from shipping freight rose from 40 million yen in 1914 to 450 million in 1918; the favorable balance of international trade amounted to 1,480 million yen for the four years 1915–1918.

Social life, the economic structure, and the price system, already dislocated by this rapid change, received a terrible jolt in the depression of 1920–1921, but Japan rapidly recovered and was shielded from the full consequences of her large population and limited resources by the boom of the 1920's. Rapid technological advance in the United States, Germany, and Japan itself, demand for Japanese goods (especially textiles) in southern and southeastern Asia, American loans throughout the world, large American purchases of Japanese silk, and the general "boom psychology" of the whole world protected Japan from the full impact of its situation until 1929–1931. Under this protection the older authoritarian and militaristic traditions were weakened, liberalism and democracy grew slowly but steadily, the aping of Germanic traditions in intellectual and political life (which had been going on since about 1880) was largely abandoned, the first party government was established in 1918, universal manhood suffrage was established in 1925, civilian governors replaced military rule for the first time in colonial areas like Formosa, the army was reduced from 21 to 17 divisions in 1924, the navy was reduced by international agreement in 1922 and in 1930, and there was a great expansion of education, especially in the higher levels. This movement toward democracy and liberalism alarmed the militarists and drove them to desperation. At the same time, the growth of unity and public order in China, which these militarists had regarded as a potential victim for their operations, convinced them that they must act quickly before it was too late. The world depression gave this group their great opportunity.

Even before its onset, however, four ominous factors in Japanese political life hung like threatening clouds on the horizon. These were (a) the lack of any constitutional requirement for a government responsible to the Diet, (b) the continued constitutional freedom of the army from civilian control, (c) the growing use of political assassination by the conservatives as a means for removing liberal politicians from public life, as was done against three premiers and many lesser persons in the period 1918–1932, and (d) the growing appeal of revolutionary Socialism in laboring circles.

The world depression and the financial crisis hit Japan a terrible blow. The declining demand for raw silk in competition with synthetic fibers like rayon and the slow decline of such Asiatic markets as China and India because of political disturbances and growing industrialization made this blow harder to bear. Under this impact, the reactionary and aggressive forces in Japanese society were able to solidify their control of the state, intimidate all domestic opposition, and embark on that adventure of aggression and destruction that led ultimately to the disasters of 1945.

These economic storms were severe, but Japan took the road to aggression because of its own past traditions rather than for economic reasons. The militarist traditions of feudal Japan continued into the modern period, and flourished in spite of steady criticism and opposition. The constitutional structure shielded both the military leaders and the civilian politicians from popular control, and justified their actions as being in the emperor's name. But these two branches of government were separated so that the civilians had no control over the generals. The law and custom of the constitution allowed the generals and admirals to approach the emperor directly without the knowledge or consent of the Cabinet, and required that only officers of this rank could serve as ministers for these services in the Cabinet itself. No civilian intervened in the chain of command from emperor to lowly private, and the armed services became a state within the state. Since the officers did not hesitate to use their positions to ensure civilian compliance with their wishes, and constantly resorted to armed force and assassination, the power of the military grew steadily after 1927. All their acts, they said, were in the name of the emperor, for the glory of Japan, to free the nation from corruption, from partisan politicians, and from plutocratic exploitation, and to restore the old Japanese virtues of order, self-sacrifice, and devotion to authority.

Separate from the armed forces, sometimes in opposition to them but generally dependent upon them as the chief purchasers of the products of heavy industry, were the forces of monopoly capitalism. These were led, as we have indicated, by the eight great economic complexes, controlled as family units, known as *zaibatsu*. These eight controlled 75 percent of the nation's corporate wealth by 1930 and were headed by Mitsui, which had 15 per cent of all corporate capital in the country. They engaged in openly corrupt relationships with Japanese politicians and, less frequently, with Japanese militarists. They usually cooperated with each other. For example, in 1927, the efforts of Mitsui and Mitsubishi to smash a smaller competitor, Suzuki Company of Kobe, precipitated a financial panic which closed most of the banks in Japan. While the Showa Bank, operated jointly by the *zaibatsu*, took over many smaller corporations and banks which failed in the crisis and over 180,000 depositors lost their savings, the Cabinet of the militarist General Tanaka granted 1,500 million yen to save the *zaibatsu* themselves from the consequences of their greed.

The militaristic and nationalistic traditions were widely accepted by the Japanese people. These traditions, extolled by the majority of politicians and teachers, and propagated by numerous patriotic societies, both open and secret, were given a free hand, while any opposing voices were crushed out by legal or illegal methods until, by 1930, most such voices were silenced. About the same date, the militarists and the *zaibatsu*, who had previously been in opposition as often as in coalition, came together in their last fateful alliance. They united on a program of heavy industrialization, militarization, and foreign aggression. Eastern Asia, especially northern China and Manchuria, became the designated victim, since these seemed to offer the necessary raw materials and markets for the industrialists and the field of glory and booty for the militarists.

In aiming their attack at Manchuria in 1931 and at northern China in 1937, the Japanese chose a victim who was clearly vulnerable. As we have seen, the Chinese Revolution of 1912 had done little to rejuvenate the country. Partisan bickering, disagreements on goals, struggles for selfish advantages, and the constant threat to good government from military leaders who were not much more than bandits disrupted the country and made rehabilitation very difficult. North of the Yangtze River the war lords fought for supremacy until 1926, while south of the river, at

Canton, the Kuomintang, a political party founded by Sun Yat-sen, and oriented toward the West, set up its own government. Unlike the northern war lords, this party had ideals and a program, although it must be confessed that both of these were embodied in words rather than in deeds.

The Kuomintang ideals were a mixture of Western, native Chinese, and Bolshevik Russian factors. They sought to achieve a unified, independent China with a democratic government and a mixed, cooperative, Socialistic, individualistic economic system. In general, Dr. Sun went to China's own traditions for his cultural ideas, to Western (largely Anglo-American) traditions for his political ideas, and to a mixture, with strong Socialist elements, for his economic ideas. His program envisaged the achievement of these ideals through three successive stages of development of which the first would be a period of military domination to secure unity and independence, the second would be a period of Kuomintang dictatorship to secure the necessary political education of the masses, and only the third would be one of constitutional democracy. This program was followed as far as Stage Two. This presumably was reached in 1927 with the announcement that the Kuomintang would henceforth be the sole legal political party. This had been preceded by eleven years of military domination in which Chiang Kai-shek emerged as the military ruler of most of China in the name of the Kuomintang.

The Kuomintang, under Dr. Sun's influence, accepted the support and some of the ideas of the Communist International, especially in the period 1924–1927. Lenin's theories of the nature of "capitalist imperialism" were quite persuasive to the Chinese and gave them, they thought, the intellectual justification for resisting foreign intervention in Chinese affairs. Russian agents, led by Michael Borodin, came to China after 1923 to assist China in "economic reconstruction," political "education," and resistance to "imperialism." These Russians reorganized the Kuomintang as a totalitarian political party on the Soviet Communist model, and reorganized Chinese military training at the famous Whampoa Military Academy. From these circles emerged Chiang Kai-shek. With German military advisers playing a prominent role in his activities, he launched a series of attacks which extended Kuomintang rule into the territory of the war lords north of the Yangtze River. The chief of these northern warlords, Chang Tso-lin, held his position by cooperation with the Japanese and by resistance to Russian efforts to penetrate Manchuria.

As Chiang Kai-shek achieved military success in these areas after 1926, he became increasingly conservative, and Dr. Sun's program of democracy and Socialism receded further into the future. At the same time, the interference and intrigue of the Communist elements in the Kuomintang camp justified increasingly vigorous repression of their activities. Finally, Chiang's increasing conservatism culminated in 1927 in his marriage to a member of the wealthy Soong family. Of this family, T. V. Soong was an important banker and speculator, his brother-in-law, H. H. Kung, was in a similar economic position, while another sister (alienated from the family by her Communist sympathies) was Mrs. Sun Yat-sen. Soong and Kung between them dominated the Kuomintang government, the former becoming minister of finance while the latter was minister of industry, commerce, and labor.

In 1927 the Communist collaboration was ended by the Kuomintang, the Russians were expelled from China, and the Kuomintang became the only legal party. The native Chinese Communists, under Moscow-trained leaders like Mao Tse-tung, concentrated their strength in the southern rural areas where they established themselves by agrarian re-forms, expropriating landlords, reducing rents, taxes, and interest rates, and building a Communist rural militia manned by the peasants. As soon as the Nationalist forces under Chiang Kai-shek completed the conquest of northern China with the capture of Peking in June 1928, they shifted their attack southward in an effort to destroy the Communist center in Kiangsi. The Communist army, whose growing exactions had disillusioned its peasant supporters, retreated in an orderly withdrawal on a twisting six-thousand-mile route to northwestern China (1934–1935). Even after the Japanese attack on Manchuria in 1931, Chiang continued to fight the Communists, directing five large-scale attacks upon them in the period 1930–1933, although the Communists declared war on Japan in 1932 and continued to demand a united front of all Chinese against this aggressor for the whole period 1931–1937.

Though the Japanese seizure of Manchuria in the autumn of 1931 was an independent action of the Japanese military forces, it had to be condoned by the civilian leaders. The Chinese retaliated by a boycott of Japanese goods which seriously reduced Japan's exports. To force an end to this boycott, Japan landed forces at Shanghai (1932) and, after severe fighting in which much Japanese abuse was inflicted upon Europeans, the Chinese forces were driven from the city and compelled to agree to a termination of the economic boycott against Japan. About the same time, Manchuria was set up as a Japanese protectorate under the rule of Henry P'ui, who had abdicated the Chinese throne in 1912.

As early as January 1932, the United States notified all signers of the Nine-Power treaty of 1922 that it would refuse to accept territorial changes made by force in violation of the Kellogg-Briand Pact to Outlaw War. An appeal to the League of Nations for support, made by China on September 21, 1931, the same day that England went off the gold standard, passed through an interminable series of procedural disputes and finally led to a Commission of Enquiry under the Earl of Lytton. The report of this commission, released in October, 1932, sharply condemned the actions of Japan but recommended no effective joint action to oppose these. The League accepted the Stimson Doctrine of Nonrecognition, and expressed sympathy for the Chinese position.

This whole affair has been rehashed endlessly since 1931 to the accompaniment of claims and counterclaims that effective League action was blocked by the absence of the United States from its councils, or by Stimson's delay in condemning Japanese aggression, or by British refusal to support Stimson's suggestions for action against Japan. All these discussions neglect the vital point that the Japanese army in Manchuria was not under the control of the Japanese civil government, with which negotiations were being conducted, and that these civil authorities, who opposed the Manchurian attack, could not give effective voice to this opposition without risking assassination. Premier Yuko Hamaguchi had been killed as recently as November 1930 for approving the London Naval Agreement to which the militarists objected, and Premier Ki Inukai was dealt with in the same way in May 1932. Throughout, the League discussions were not conducted with the right party.

Except for its violation of nationalist feelings and the completely objectionable means by which it was achieved, the acquisition of Manchuria by Japan possessed many strategic and economic advantages. It gave Japan industrial resources which it vitally needed, and could, in time, have strengthened the Japanese economy. Separation of the area from China, which had not controlled it effectively for many years, would have restricted the sphere of Chiang's government to a more manageable territory. Above all, it could have served as a counterpoise to Soviet power in the Far East and provided a fulcrum to restrain Soviet actions in Europe after the collapse of Germany. Unfortunately, the uncompromising avarice and ignorance of the Japanese militarists made any such solution impossible. This was made quite certain by their two major errors, the attack on China in 1937 and the attack on the United States in 1941. In both cases the militarists bit off more than they could chew, and destroyed any possible advantages they might have gained from the acquisition of Manchuria in 1931.

In the seven years after the first attack on Manchuria in September 1931, Japan sank 2.5 billion yen in capital investments in that area, mostly in mining, iron production, electric power, and petroleum. Year after year this investment increased without returning any immediate yield to Japan, since output from this new investment was immediately reinvested. The only items of much help for Japan itself were iron ore, pig iron, and certain chemical fertilizers. The Manchurian soy-bean crop, although it declined under Japanese rule, was exchanged with Germany for needed commodities obtainable there. For Japan's other urgent material needs, such as raw cotton, rubber, and petroleum, no help could be found in Manchuria. In spite of costly capital investment, it could produce no more than its own needs in petroleum, chiefly from liquefaction of coal.

The failure of Manchuria to provide an answer to Japan's economic problems led the Japanese military leaders toward a new act of aggression, this time directed toward North China itself. As they were preparing their new assault, Chiang Kai-shek was busy preparing a sixth campaign against the Communists, still lurking in the remote northwestern part of China. Neither the growing threat from Japan nor the appeals from the Chinese Communists to form a united Chinese front against Nippon deterred Chiang from his purpose to crush the Communists until, in December 1936, he was suddenly kidnapped by his own northern commander, Chang Hsueh-liang, at Sian, and was forced, under a threat of death, to promise to fight Japan. A Kuomintang-Communist united front was formed in which Chiang promised to fight Japan rather than the Communists and to relax the Kuomintang restrictions on civil liberties, while the Communists promised to abolish their Chinese Soviet Government, become a regional government of the Republic of China, end the expropriation of the landlords, cease their attacks on the Kuomintang, and incorporate their armed forces into the National Army of Chiang Kai-shek on a regional basis.

This agreement had hardly been made, and had not yet been published, when the Japanese opened their attack on North China (July 1937). They were generally successful against a tenacious defense by the National government, driving it successively from Nanking to Hankow (November 1937) and from Hankow to Chungking on the remote upper reaches of the Yangtze River (October 1938). The Japanese, with quite inadequate forces of only seventeen divisions totaling less than 250,000 men in all areas, tried to destroy the Nationalist and Communist armies in China, to cut China off from all foreign supplies by controlling all railroads, ports, and rivers, and to maintain order in Manchuria and occupied China. This was an impossible task. The occupied areas soon took the form of an open lattice in which Japanese troops patroled the rivers and railroads, but the country between was largely in the control of Communist guerrillas. The retreat of the Nationalist government to remote Chungking and its inability to retain the allegiance of the Chinese peasants, especially those behind the Japanese lines, because of its close alliance with the oligarchy of landlords, merchants, and bankers, steadily weakened the Kuomintang and strengthened the Communists.

The rivalry between the Chinese Communists and the Kuomintang broke out intermittently in 1938–1941, but Japan was unable to profit from it in any decisive way because of its economic weakness. The great investment in Manchuria and the adoption of a policy of wholehearted aggression required a reorganization of Japan's own economy from its previous emphasis on light industry for the export market to a new emphasis on heavy industry for armaments and heavy investment. This was carried out so ruthlessly that Japan's production of heavy industry rose from 3 billion yen in 1933 to 8.2 billion yen in 1938, while textile production rose from 2.9 billion yen to no more than 3.7 billion yen in the same five years. By 1938 the products of heavy industry accounted for 53 percent of Japan's industrial output. This increased Japan's need for imports while reducing her ability to provide the exports (previously textiles) to pay for such imports. By 1937 Japan's unfavorable balance of trade with the "non-yen" area amounted to 925 million yen, or almost four times the average of the years before 1937. Income from shipping was reduced by military demands as well, with the result that Japan's unfavorable balance of trade was reflected in a heavy outflow of gold (1,685 million yen in 1937-1938).

By the end of 1938, it was clear that Japan was losing its financial and commercial ability to buy necessary materials of foreign origin. The steps taken by the United States, Australia, and others to restrict export of strategic or military materials to Japan made this problem even more acute. The attack on China had been intended to remedy this situation by removing the Chinese boycott on Japanese goods, by bringing a supply of necessary materials, especially raw cotton, under Japan's direct control, and by creating an extension of the yen area where the use of foreign exchange would not be needed for trading purposes. On the whole, these purposes were not achieved. Guerrilla activities and Japanese inability to control the rural areas made the achievement of a yen area impossible, made trade difficult, and reduced the production of cotton drastically (by about one-third). Export of iron ore from China to Japan fell from 2.3 million tons in 1937 to 0.3 million in 1938, although coal exports rose slightly.

In an effort to increase production, Japan began to pour capital investment into the still-unpacified areas of North China at a rate which rivaled the rate of investment in Manchuria. The Four-Year Plan of 1938 called for 1,420 million yen of such investment by 1942. This project, added to the need for Japan to feed and clothe the inhabitants of North China, made that area a drain on the whole Japanese economy, so that Japanese exports to that area rose from 179 billion yen in 1937 to 312 million in 1938. To make matters worse, the people of this occupied territory refused to accept or use the newly established yen currency because of guerrilla threats to shoot anyone found in possession of it.

All this had an adverse effect on Japan's financial position. In two years of the China war, 1936-1937 to 1938-1939, the Japanese budget rose from 2.3 to 8.4 billion yen, of which 80 percent went for military purposes. Government debt and commodity prices rose steadily, but the Japanese people responded so readily to taxation, government loans, and demands for increased production that the system continued to function. By the end of 1939, however, it was clear that the threefold burden of a conversion to heavy industry, which ruined the export trade, a heavy rate of investment in Manchuria and North China, and an indecisive war with Nationalist China could not be borne forever, especially under the pressure of the growing reluctance of neutral countries to supply Japan with necessary strategic goods. The two most vital needs were in petroleum products and rubber.

To the militarists, who controlled Japan both politically and economically after 1939, it seemed that the occupation of the Dutch Indies and Malaya could do much to alleviate these shortages. The occupation of the Netherlands itself by Hitler's hordes in 1940 and the involvement of England in the European war since 1939 seemed to offer a golden opportunity for Japan to seize these southern regions. To do so would require long lines of communications from Japan to Indonesia. These lines would be exposed to attack from the American bases in the Philippines or from the British base at Singapore. Judging the American psychology as similar to their own, the Japanese militarists were sure that in such circumstances America would not hesitate to attack these vulnerable lines of communication. Thus, it seemed to them that a Japanese attack on the Dutch Indies would inevitably lead to an American war on Japan. Facing this problem, the Japanese militarists reached what seemed to their minds to be an inescapable decision. They decided to attack the United States first. From this decision came the Japanese attack on Pearl Harbor on December 7, 1941.

The Italian Assault, 1934-1936

Although the Fascist government of Benito Mussolini talked in a truculent and vainglorious way from its accession to power in 1922, emphasizing its determination to reestablish the glories of the Roman Empire, to dominate the Mediterranean Sea, and to achieve strategic self-sufficiency by increasing the quantity of home-grown food, its actions were much more modest and did not go far beyond efforts to limit Yugoslav influence in the Adriatic and to overly publicize a modest increase in domestic wheat production. In general, Italy's situation was similar to Japan's. Limited natural resources (especially an almost complete lack of coal or oil) combined with a rapidly falling death rate to create growing pressure of population. This problem, as in Japan, was intensified by restrictions on the emigration of Italians or on the outflow of Italian goods, especially after 1918.

The important dates in modern Italian history are 1922, 1925, 1927 and, above all, 1934. In 1922 the Fascists came to power in a parliamentary system; in 1925 this parliamentary system was replaced by a political dictatorship with nineteenth century Latin-American overtones rather than a twentieth-century totalitarian character, since the economic system remained that of orthodox financial capitalism; in 1927 an orthodox, and restrictive, stabilization of the lira on the international gold standard led to such depressed economic conditions that Mussolini adopted a much more active foreign policy, seeking to create an economic and political entente with the three defeated Powers of central Europe (Austria, Hungary, Bulgaria); in 1934 Italy replaced orthodox economic measures by a totalitarian economy functioning beneath a fraudulent corporative facade and, at the same time, shifted its dynamic foreign policy from central Europe to Africa and the Mediterranean.

The Italian drive to build up a political and economic bloc in central Europe in the period 1927–1934 was both anti-German and anti-Little Entente. This was an impossible combination, for the division of Europe into revisionist and antirevisionist Powers made it impossible for Italy to create a new alignment cutting through this line of conflict. By following an anti-Little Entente and pro-Hungarian policy, Mussolini was anti-French and thus inevitably pro-German, something which Mussolini never was and never wished to be. It took him seven years, however, to realize the illogic of his position.

In these seven years, 1927–1934, Hungary rather than Germany was the most active revisionist force in Europe. By working with Hungary, with the reactionary elements in Austria and Bulgaria, and with dissident Croatian elements in Yugoslavia, Mussolini sought to weaken the Little Entente (especially Yugoslavia) and to create troubled waters for Fascist fishing. He insisted that Italy was a dissatisfied Power because of disappointment over its lack of colonial gains at Versailles in 1919, and the refusal of the League to accede to Tommaso Tittoni's request for a redistribution of the world's resources in accordance with population needs made in 1920. It is true that Italy's population and raw-material problems were acute, but the steps taken by Mussolini offered no hope of alleviating them.

Italy's Danube policy culminated in a treaty of friendship with Austria in 1930 and a series of political and economic agreements with Austria and Hungary known as the "Rome Protocols" in 1934. The Austrian government under Engelbert Dollfuss destroyed the democratic institutions of Austria, wiped out all Socialist and working-class organizations, and established a one-party, dictatorial, corporative state at Mussolini's behest in February—April 1934. Hitler took advantage of this to attempt a Nazi coup in Austria, murdering Dollfuss in July 1934, but he was prevented from moving into the country by a hurried mobilization of Italian troops on the Brenner frontier and a stern warning from Mussolini. This significant event revealed that Italy was the only major Power prepared to fight for Austria's independence and that Mussolini's seven years of work for the revisionist cause had been a mistake. It was, however, a mistake from which the Duce learned nothing. Instead, he condoned an assassination plot by extreme revisionist elements, including the Bulgarian IMRO, Croation separatists, and Hungarian extremists. This resulted in the murder of Alexander, the centralist Serb King of Yugoslavia, and Jean Louis Barthou, the foreign minister of France, at Marseilles in October 1934.

Hitler's ascension to office in Germany in January 1933 found French foreign policy paralyzed by British opposition to any efforts to support collective security or to enforce German observation of its treaty obligations by force. As a result, a suggestion from Poland in April 1933 for joint armed intervention in Germany to remove Hitler from office was rejected by France. Poland at once made a nonaggression pact with Germany and extended a previous nonaggression pact with the Soviet Union (January–May, 1934). This inaugurated a policy of balancing between these two Great Powers which left Poland ripe for the Fourth Partition, which came in 1939.

After the advent to office in France of a new conservative coalition government with Jean Louis Bathou as foreign minister in February 1934, France began to adopt a more active policy against Hitler. This policy sought to encircle Germany by bringing the Soviet Union and Italy into a revived alignment of France, Poland, the Little Entente, Greece, and Turkey. A Balkan Pact of Romania, Yugoslavia, Greece, and Turkey was concluded as early as February 1934; French relations with the Little Entente were tightened as a consequence of visits by Barthou to the various capitals. Russia was brought into the League of Nations in September 1934; a French-Italian agreement was signed in January 1935; a common front against German rearmament (which had been announced in March) was made by France, Italy, and Britain at the Stresa Conference in April 1935, and Germany's action was denounced by the League of Nations the same week; a French-Soviet alliance and a Czech-Soviet alliance were made in May 1935, the latter to be binding on Russia only after the earlier French-Czech alliance went into effect. In the course of building this united front against Germany, but before Italy had been brought into it, Barthou and King Alexander were assassinated at Marseilles, as we have indicated (October 1934). This did not stop the project, for Pierre Laval took Barthou's place and carried out his predecessor's plans, although much less effectively. It was, accordingly, Pierre Laval who brought Italy into this arrangement in January 1935 and the Soviet Union in May 1935.

Laval was convinced that Italy could be brought into the anti-German front only if its long-standing grievances and unfulfilled ambitions in

Africa could be met. Accordingly, Laval gave Mussolini seven percent of the stock of the Djibouti–Addis Ababa Railway (which ran from French Somaliland on the Red Sea to the capital of Ethiopia), a stretch of desert 114,000 square miles in extent but containing only a few hundred persons (sixty-two, according to Mussolini himself) on the border of Libya, a small wedge of territory between French Somaliland and Italian Eritrea, a settlement of the citizenship and education status of Italian immigrants in French Tunisia, and "the right to ask for concessions throughout Ethiopia."

This last point was an important one because, while Laval insisted that he had made no agreement which jeopardized Ethiopia's independence or territorial integrity, he made it equally clear that Italian support against Germany was more important than the integrity of Ethiopia in his eyes. France had been Ethiopia's only real friend for many years. It had engineered a Triparite agreement of Britain, Italy, and France to permit no change in Ethiopia's status without Tripartite consent in 1906, and had brought Ethiopia into the League of Nations over British objections in 1923. Italy, on the other hand, had been prevented from conquering Ethiopia in 1896 only by a decisive defeat of her invading force at the hands of the Ethiopians themselves, while in 1925 Britain and Italy had cut Ethiopia up into economic spheres by an agreement which was annulled by a French appeal to the League of Nations. Laval's renunciation of France's traditional support of Ethiopian independence and integrity was thus of great importance, and brought the three governments concerned (Italy, Britain, and France) into agreement on this issue.

This point of view, however, was not shared by public opinion in these three countries. In France, opinion was too divided to allow us to make any categorical statements about its nature, but it is probable that a majority was in favor of extending collective security to Ethiopia, while an overwhelming majority was convinced that Germany should be the primary object of this instrument of international action. In Italy, it is likely that a majority opposed both Mussolini's war on Ethiopia and the League's efforts to stop this by economic sanctions.

In England, an overwhelming majority was in support of the League of Nations and sanctions against Italy. This was clear from the so-called Peace Ballot of 1935 which, on the basis of a privately conducted straw vote of the English electorate, showed that, of 11½ million polled, over 11 million supported membership in the League, over 10 million supported economic sanctions, and over 6.7 million supported (while only 2.3 million opposed) military sanctions against aggressors. This point of view was opposed by the pacifist Left wing of the Labour Party and by the imperialist Right wing of the Conservative Party. It was also opposed by the British government itself. Sir John Simon (the foreign secretary),

Sir Bolton Eyres-Monsell (the first lord of the Admiralty), and Stanley Baldwin (leader of the party and prime minister) denounced the Peace Ballot and its collective-security basis while the polling was in process, but hastened to give their verbal support as soon as the results became evident. Baldwin, who in November, 1934, had declared that a "collective peace system" was "perfectly impracticable," assured the organizers of the ballot that "the foreign policy of the Government is founded upon the League of Nations," when the results were revealed in July 1935. On this basis was erected one of the most astonishing examples of British "dual" policy in the appeasement period. While publicly supporting collective security and sanctions against Italian aggression, the government privately negotiated to destroy the League and to yield Ethiopia to Italy. They were completely successful in this secret policy.

The Italian aggression against Ethiopia began with an incursion into Ethiopian territory at Wal Wal in December 1934, and broke into full-scale invasion in October 1935. That Italy had no real fear of British military sanctions against them was evident when they put a major part of their military forces, transports, and naval strength in the Red Sea, separated from home by the British-controlled Suez Canal and the massed British fleet at Alexandria. Their use of the Suez Canal to transport munitions and troops naturally revealed their aggressive intentions to Britain at an early stage. The British government's position on Ethiopia was clearly stated in a secret report of an Interdepartmental Committee under Sir John Maffey. The report, presented to the foreign secretary on June 18, 1935, declared that Italian control of Ethiopia would be a "matter of indifference" to Britain. This report was mysteriously and surreptitiously conveyed to the Italians and undiplomatically published by them later. There can be no doubt that it represented the opinion of the British government and that this opinion was shared by the French government.

Unfortunately, public opinion in both countries and throughout most of the world was insisting on collective sanctions against the aggressor. To meet this demand, both governments engaged in a public policy of unenforced or partially enforced sanctions at wide variance with their real intentions. In consequence, they lost both Ethiopia and Italy, the former by their real policy, the latter by their public policy. In the process they gave the League of Nations, the collective-security system, and the political stability of central Europe their death wounds.

Taking advantage of the wave of public support for collective security, Samuel Hoare (now foreign secretary) went to the meeting of the Assembly of the League of Nations in September 1935 and delivered a smashing speech to support of the League, collective security, and sanctions against Italy. The day previously he and Anthony Eden had secretly agreed with Pierre Laval to impose only partial economic sanctions, avoiding all actions, such as blockade or closure of the Suez Canal, which "might lead to war." A number of governments, including Belgium, Czechoslovakia, France, and Britain, had stopped all exports of munitions to Ethiopia as early as May and June 1935, although Ethiopia's appeal to the League of Nations for help had been made on March 17th, while the Italian attack did not come until October 2, 1935. The net result was that Ethiopia was left defenseless in the face of an aggressor who was annoyed, without being sensibly hampered, by incomplete and late economic sanctions. Ethiopia's appeal for neutral observers on June 19th was never acknowledged, and her appeal to the United States for support under the Kellogg-Briand Pact on July 3rd was at once rejected, but Eden found time to offer Mussolini a portion of Ethiopia as part of a deal which would avoid an open Italian aggression (June 24th). The Duce was determined, however, to commit an open aggression as the only method for achieving that modicum of Roman glory for which he thirsted.

Hoare's speech in support of collective security at Geneva in September evoked such applause from the British public that Baldwin decided to hold a general election on that issue. Accordingly, with a ringing pledge to support collective action and collective security and to "take no action in isolation," the National government offered itself at the polls on November 14, 1935, and won an amazing victory. The government's margin of 431 seats out of 615 kept it in power until the next General Election ten years later (July 1945).

Although Article 16 of the League Covenant bound the signers to break off *all* trade and financial relations with an aggressor, France and Britain combined to keep their economic sanctions partial and ineffective. Imposed on November 18, 1935, and accepted by fifty-two nations, these sanctions established an embargo in arms and munitions, on loans and on credit, and on certain key commodities, and established a boycott on purchases of all Italian goods. The embargo did not cover iron ore, coal, or petroleum products, although the last item, of which Italy had less than a two-month supply in October 1935, would have stopped the Italian aggression quickly and completely. The imposition of oil sanctions was postponed time and again until, by the spring of 1936, the conquest of Ethiopia was completed. This was done in spite of the fact that as early as December 12th, ten states, which had been supplying three-quarters of Italy's oil needs, volunteered to support the embargo. The refusal to establish this sanction resulted from a joint British-French refusal on the grounds that an oil sanction would be so effective that Italy would be compelled to break off its war with Ethiopia and would, in desperation, make war on Britain and France. This, at least, was the amazing logic offered by the British government later.

Instead of additional or effective sanctions, Samuel Hoare and Pierre

Laval worked out a secret deal which would have given Italy outright about one-sixth of Ethiopia and have yielded an additional third as a "zone of economic expansion and settlement reserved to Italy." When news of this deal was broken to the public by a French journalist on December 10, 1935, there was a roar of protest from the supporters of collective security, especially in England, on the grounds that this violated the election pledge made but a month previously. To save his government, Baldwin had to sacrifice Hoare, who resigned on December 19th, but returned to the Cabinet on June 5, 1936, as soon as Ethiopia was decently buried. Laval, in France, survived the first parliamentary assault but fell from office in January 1936; he was succeeded at the Quai d'Orsay by Pierre Flandin, who pursued the same policy.

Ethiopia was conquered on May 2, 1936 and annexed to Italy a week later. Sanctions were removed by the various cooperating states and by the League itself in the next two months, just as they were beginning to take effect.

The consequences of the Ethiopian fiasco were of the greatest importance. Mussolini was much strengthened in Italy by his apparent success in acquiring an empire in the face of the economic barrage of fifty-two nations. The Conservative Party in England was entrenched in office for a decade, during which it carried out its policy of appeasement and waged the resulting war. The United States was driven by panic to pass a "Neutrality Act" which encouraged aggression by its provision that the outbreak of a war would cut off supplies of American munitions to both sides, to the aggressor who had armed at his leisure and to the victim yet unarmed. Above all, the Ethiopian crisis destroyed French efforts to encircle Germany. Britain had opposed these efforts from the beginning, and was able to block them with the aid of a number of other factors for which Britain was not primarily responsible. This point is sufficiently important to demand detailed analysis.

Circles and Countercircles, 1935-1939

Laval's agreement of January 1935 with Mussolini had been intended to bring Italy to the side of France in the face of Germany, a goal which seemed perfectly possible in the light of Mussolini's veto on Hitler's coup in Austria in July 1934. This result would have been achieved if Ethiopia could have been taken by Italy without League action. In that case, Mussolini argued, Africa would have been removed from the sphere of League action as North America had been in 1919 (by the Monroe Doctrine amendment to the Covenant) and Asia had been in 1931 (by the failure to take action against Japan). This would have left the League as a purely European organization, according to Mussolini.

This view was regarded with favor in France where the chief, if not the sole, role of the League was to provide security against Germany. This view was completely unacceptable to Britain, which wanted no exclusively European political organization and could not join one herself because of her imperial obligations and her preference for an Atlantic organization (including the Dominions and the United States). Thus, Britain insisted on sanctions against Italy. But the British government never wanted collective security to be a success. As a result, the French desire for no sanctions combined with the British desire for ineffective sanctions to provide ineffective sanctions. Because there were sanctions, France lost Italian support against Germany; because they were ineffective, France lost the League system of collective security against Germany as well. Thus France had neither bread nor cake. Worse than that, the Italian involvement in Africa withdrew Italian political power from central Europe and thus removed the chief force ready to resist the German penetration of Austria. Still worse, the hubbub of the Ethiopian crisis gave Hitler an opportunity to declare the rearmament of Germany and the reestablishment of the German air force in March 1935 and to remilitarize the Rhineland on March 7, 1936.

The remilitarization of the Rhineland in violation of the Versailles Treaty and the Locarno pacts was the most important result of the Ethiopian crisis and the most important event of the period of appeasement. It greatly reduced France's own security and reduced even more the security of France's allies to the east of Germany because, once this zone was fortified, it could decrease greatly France's ability to come to the aid of eastern Europe. The remilitarization of the Rhineland was the essential military prerequisite for any movement of Germany eastward against Austria, Czechoslovakia, Poland, or the Soviet Union. That such a movement was the chief aim of Hitler's policy had been clearly and explicitly stated by him throughout his public life.

German rearmament had proceeded so slowly that Germany had only twenty-five "paper" divisions in 1936, and the German generals demanded and obtained written orders to retreat if France made any move to invade the Rhineland. No such move was made, although Germany had less than 30,000 troops in the area. This failure arose from a combination of two factors: (1) the expense of a French mobilization, which would have required the devaluation of the franc at a time when France was working with desperate energy to preserve the value of the franc;

and (2) the objections of Britain, which refused to allow France to take military action or to impose any sanctions (even economic) against Germany or to use Italy (against whom economic sanctions were still in force) in the field against Germany as provided in the Locarno pacts. In a violent scene with Flandin on March 12th, Neville Chamberlain rejected sanctions, and refused to accept Flandin's argument that "if a firm front is maintained by France and England, Germany will yield without war." Chamberlain's refusal to enforce the Locarno pacts when they fell due was not his personal policy or anything new. It was the policy of the Conservative Party, and had been for years; as early as July 13, 1934, Sir Austen Chamberlain had stated publicly that Britain would not use troops to enforce the Rhineland clauses and would use its veto power in the Council of the League to prevent this by others under the Locarno pacts.

The remilitarization of the Rhineland also detached Belgium from the anti-German circle. Alarmed by the return of German troops to its border and by the failure of the British-Italian guarantee of Locarno, Belgium in October 1936 denounced its alliance with France and adopted a policy of strict neutrality. This made it impossible for France to extend its fortification system, the Maginot Line, which was being built on the French-German border, along the Belgian-German border. Moreover, since France was convinced that Belgium would be on its side in any future war with Germany, the line was not extended along the French-Belgian border either. It was across this unfortified border that Germany attacked France in 1940.

Thus Barthou's efforts to encircle Germany were largely but not completely destroyed in the period 1934–1936 by four events: (1) the loss of Poland in January 1934; (2) the loss of Italy by January 1936; (3) the rearmament of Germany and the remilitarization of the Rhineland by March 1936; and (4) the loss of Belgium by October 1936. The chief items left in the Barthou system were the French and Soviet alliances with Czechoslovakia and with each other. In order to destroy these alliances Britain and Germany sought, on parallel paths, to encircle France and the Soviet Union in order to dissuade France from honoring its alliances with either Czechoslovakia or the Soviet Union. To honor these alliances France required two things as an absolute minimum: (1) that military cooperation against Germany be provided by Britain from the first moment of any French action against Germany and (2) that France have military security on her non-German frontiers. Both of these essentials were destroyed by Britain in the period 1935–1936, and, in consequence, France, finding itself encircled, dishonored its alliance with Czechoslovakia, when it came due in September 1938.

The encirclement of France had six items in it. The first was the British refusal from 1919 to 1939 to give France any promise of support

against Germany in fulfillment of the French alliances with eastern
Europe or to engage in any military commitments in support of such
alliances. On the contrary, Britain made clear to France, at all times,
her opposition to these alliances and that action under them was not
covered by any promises Britain had made to support France against a
German attack westward or by any military discussions which arose
from any Anglo-French efforts to resist such an attack. This distinction
was the motivation of the Locarno pacts, and explains the refusal of
Britain to engage in military conversations with France until the summer of 1938. The British attitude toward eastern Europe was made perfectly clear on many occasions. For example, on July 13, 1934, Foreign
Secretary Sir John Simon denounced Barthou's efforts to create an
"eastern Locarno" and demanded arms equality for Germany.

The other five items in the encirclement of France were: (1) the
Anglo-German Naval Agreement of June 1935; (2) the alienation of
Italy over sanctions; (3) the remilitarization of the Rhineland by Germany with British acquiescence and approval; (4) the neutrality of
Belgium; and (5) the alienation of Spain. We have already discussed all
these except the last, and have indicated the vital role which Britain
played in all of them except Belgium. Taken together, they changed
the French military position so drastically that France, by 1938, found
herself in a position where she could hardly expect to fulfill her military
obligations to Czechoslovakia and the Soviet Union. This was exactly
the position in which the British government wished France to be, a
fact made completely clear by the recently published secret documents.

In May of 1935 France could have acted against Germany with all
her forces, because the Rhineland was unfortified, and there was no
need to worry about the Italian, Spanish, or Belgian frontiers or the
Atlantic coastline. By the end of 1938, and even more by 1939, the
Rhineland was protected by the new German fortified Siegfried Line,
parts of the French Army had to be left on the unfriendly Italian and
Spanish frontiers and along the lengthy neutral Belgian frontier, and
the Atlantic coastline could not be protected against the new German
fleet unless Britain cooperated with France. This need for British cooperation on the sea arose from two facts: (a) the Anglo-German Naval
Agreement of June 1935 allowed Germany to build a navy up to 35
percent of the British Navy, while France was restricted to 33 percent
of Britain's strength in the chief categories of vessels; and (b) the Italian
occupation of the Balearic Islands and parts of Spain itself after the
opening of the Spanish War in July 1936 required much of the French
fleet to stay in the Mediterranean in order to keep open the transportation of troops and food from North Africa to metropolitan France
The details of the Spanish War will be discussed in the next chapter,
but at this point it must be realized that the shift in the control of Spain

from pro-French to anti-French hands was of vital importance to Czechoslovakia and the Soviet Union as a factor in determining whether the French alliances with these two would be fulfilled when the German attack came.

Parallel with the encirclement of France went the encirclement of the Soviet Union and, to a lesser extent, of Czechoslovakia. The encirclement of the Soviet Union was known as the Anti-Comintern Pact. This was a union of Germany and Japan against Communism and the Third International. It was signed in November 1936 and was joined by Italy a year later. Manchukuo and Hungary joined in February 1939, while Spain came in a month after that.

The last countercircle was that against Czechoslovakia. Hungary on the Czechoslovak southern frontier and Germany on its northwestern frontier were both opposed to Czechoslovakia as an "artificial" creation of the Versailles Conference. The German annexation of Austria in March 1938 closed the gap in the anti-Czech circle on the west, while the aggressive designs of Poland after 1932 completed the circle everywhere except on the insignificant Romanian frontier in the extreme east. Although the Czechs offered the Poles a treaty and even a military alliance on three occasions, in 1932–1933, they were ignored, and the Polish-German agreement of January 1934 opened a campaign of vilification of Czechoslovakia by Poland which continued, parallel to the similar German campaign, until the Polish invasion of Czechoslovakia in October 1938.

Of these three countercircles to Barthou's efforts to encircle Germany, the most significant by far was the encirclement of France which alone made the other two possible. In this encirclement of France the most important factor, without which it could never have been achieved, was the encouragement of Britain. Accordingly, we must say a word about the motivations of Britain and the reactions of France.

Any analysis of the motivations of Britain in 1938–1939 is bound to be difficult because different people had different motives, motives changed in the course of time, the motives of the government were clearly not the same as the motives of the people, and in no country has secrecy and anonymity been carried so far or been so well preserved as in Britain. In general, motives become vaguer and less secret as we move our attention from the innermost circles of the government outward. As if we were looking at the layers of an onion, we may discern four points of view: (1) the anti-Bolsheviks at the center, (2) the "three-bloc-world" supporters close to the center, (3) the supporters of "appeasement," and (4) the "peace at any price" group in a peripheral position. The "anti-Bolsheviks," who were also anti-French, were extremely important from 1919 to 1926, but then decreased to little more than a lunatic fringe, rising again in numbers and influence after 1934 to dominate the real policy of the government in 1939. In the earlier period the chief figures in this group were Lord Curzon, Lord D'Abernon, and General Smuts. They did what they could to destroy reparations, permit German rearmament, and tear down what they called "French militarism."

This point of view was supported by the second group, which was known in those days as the Round Table Group, and came later to be called, somewhat inaccurately, the Cliveden Set, after the country estate of Lord and Lady Astor. It included Lord Milner, Leopold Amery, and Edward Grigg (Lord Altrincham), as well as Lord Lothian, Smuts, Lord Astor, Lord Brand (brother-in-law of Lady Astor and managing director of Lazard Brothers, the international bankers), Lionel Curtis, Geoffrey Dawson (editor of *The Times*), and their associates. This group wielded great influence because it controlled the Rhodes Trust, the Beit Trust, *The Times* of London, *The Observer*, the influential and highly anonymous quarterly review known as *The Round Table* (founded in 1910 with money supplied by Sir Abe Bailey and the Rhodes Trust, and with Lothian as editor), and it dominated the Royal Institute of International Affairs, called "Chatham House" (of which Sir Abe Bailey and the Astors were the chief financial supporters, while Lionel Curtis was the actual founder), the Carnegie United Kingdom Trust, and All Souls College, Oxford. This Round Table Group formed the core of the three-bloc-world supporters, and differed from the anti-Bolsheviks like D'Abernon in that they sought to contain the Soviet Union between a German-dominated Europe and an English-speaking bloc rather than to destroy it as the anti-Bolsheviks wanted. Relationships between the two groups were very close and friendly, and some people, like Smuts, were in both.

The anti-Bolsheviks, including D'Abernon, Smuts, Sir John Simon, and H. A. L. Fisher (Warden of All Souls College), were willing to go to any extreme to tear down France and build up Germany. Their point of view can be found in many places, and most emphatically in a letter of August 11, 1920, from D'Abernon to Sir Maurice (later Lord) Hankey, a protégé of Lord Esher who wielded great influence in the interwar period as secretary to the Cabinet and secretary to almost every international conference on reparations from Genoa (1922) to Lausanne (1932). D'Abernon advocated a secret alliance of Britain "with the German military leaders in cooperating against the Soviet." As ambassador of Great Britain in Berlin in 1920–1926, D'Abernon carried on this policy and blocked all efforts by the Disarmament Commission to disarm, or even inspect, Germany (according to Brigadier J. H. Morgan of the commission).

The point of view of this group was presented by General Smuts in a speech of October 23, 1923 (made after luncheon with H. A. L.

Fisher). From these two groups came the Dawes Plan and the Locarno pacts. It was Smuts, according to Stresemann, who first suggested the Locarno policy, and it was D'Abernon who became its chief supporter. H. A. L. Fisher and John Simon in the House of Commons, and Lothian, Dawson, and their friends on *The Round Table* and on *The Times* prepared the ground among the British governing class for both the Dawes Plan and Locarno as early as 1923 (*The Round Table* for March 1923; the speeches of Fisher and Simon in the House of Commons on February 19, 1923, Fisher's speech of March 6th and Simon's speech of March 13th in the same place, *The Round Table* for June 1923; and Smuts's speech of October 23rd).

The more moderate Round Table group, including Lionel Curtis, Leopold Amery (who was the shadow of Lord Milner), Lord Lothian, Lord Brand, and Lord Astor, sought to weaken the League of Nations and destroy all possibility of collective security in order to strengthen Germany in respect to both France and the Soviet Union, and above all to free Britain from Europe in order to build up an "Atlantic bloc" of Great Britain, the British Dominions, and the United States. They prepared the way for this "Union" through the Rhodes Scholarship organization (of which Lord Milner was the head in 1905–1925 and Lord Lothian was secretary in 1925–1940), through the Round Table groups (which had been set up in the United States, India, and the British Dominions in 1910–1917), through the Chatham House organization, which set up Royal Institutes of International Affairs in all the dominions and a Council on Foreign Relations in New York, as well as through "Unofficial Commonwealth Relations Conferences" held irregularly, and the Institutes of Pacific Relations set up in various countries as autonomous branches of the Royal Institutes of International Affairs. This influential group sought to change the League of Nations from an instrument of collective security to an international conference center for "nonpolitical" matters like drug control or international postal services, to rebuild Germany as a buffer against the Soviet Union and a counterpoise to France, and to build up an Atlantic bloc of Britain, the Dominions, the United States, and, if possible, the Scandinavian countries.

One of the effusions of this group was the project called Union Now, and later Union Now with Great Britain, propagated in the United States in 1938–1945 by Clarence Streit on behalf of Lord Lothian and the Rhodes Trust. Ultimately, the inner circle of this group arrived at the idea of the "three-bloc world." It was believed that this system could force Germany to keep the peace (after it absorbed Europe) because it would be squeezed between the Atlantic bloc and the Soviet Union, while the Soviet Union could be forced to keep the peace because it would be squeezed between Japan and Germany. This plan would work only if Germany and the Soviet Union could be brought into contact with each other by abandoning to Germany Austria, Czechoslovakia, and the Polish Corridor. This became the aim of both the anti-Bolsheviks and the three-bloc people from the early part of 1937 to the end of 1939 (or even early 1940). These two cooperated and dominated the government in that period. They split in the period 1939–1940, with the "three-bloc" people, like Amery, Lord Halifax, and Lord Lothian, becoming increasingly anti-German, while the anti-Bolshevik crowd, like Chamberlain, Horace Wilson, and John Simon, tried to adopt a policy based on a declared but unfought war against Germany combined with an undeclared fighting war against the Soviet Union. The split between these two groups appeared openly in public and led to Chamberlain's fall from office when Amery cried to Chamberlain, across the floor of the House of Commons, on May 10, 1940, "In the name of God, go!"

Outside these two groups, and much more numerous (but much more remote from the real instruments of government), were the appeasers and the "peace at any price" people. These were both used by the two inner groups to command public support for their quite different policies. Of the two the appeasers were much more important than the "peace at any price" people. The appeasers swallowed the steady propaganda (much of it emanating from Chatham House, *The Times*, the Round Table groups, or Rhodes circles) that the Germans had been deceived and brutally treated in 1919. For example, it was under pressure from seven persons, including General Smuts and H. A. L. Fisher, as well as Lord Milner himself, that Lloyd George made his belated demand on June 2, 1919, that the German reparations be reduced and the Rhineland occupation be cut from fifteen years to two. The memorandum from which Lloyd George read these demands was apparently drawn up by Philip Kerr (Lord Lothian), while the minutes of the Council of Four, from which we get the record of those demands, were taken down by Sir Maurice Hankey (as secretary to the Supreme Council, a position obtained through Lord Esher). It was Kerr (Lothian) who served as British member of the Committee of Five which drew up the answer to the Germans' protest of May, 1919. General Smuts was still refusing to sign the treaty because it was too severe as late as June 23, 1919.

As a result of these attacks and a barrage of similar attacks on the treaty which continued year after year, British public opinion acquired a guilty conscience about the Treaty of Versailles, and was quite unprepared to take any steps to enforce it by 1930. On this feeling, which owed so much to the British idea of sportsmanlike conduct toward a beaten opponent, was built the movement for appeasement. This movement had two basic assumptions: (*a*) that reparation must be made for Britain's treatment of Germany in 1919 and (*b*) that if Germany's most obvious demands, such as arms equality, remilitarization of the Rhineland, and perhaps union with Austria, were met, Germany would become satisfied and peaceful. The trouble with this argument was that once Germany reached this point, it would be very difficult to prevent Germany from going further (such as taking the Sudetenland and the Polish Corridor). Accordingly, many of the appeasers, when this point was reached in March 1938 went over to the anti-Bolshevik or "three-bloc" point of view, while some even went into the "peace at any price" group. It is likely that Chamberlain, Sir John Simon, and Sir Samuel Hoare went by this road from appeasement to anti-Bolshevism. At any rate, few influential people were still in the appeasement group by 1939 in the sense that they believed that Germany could ever be satisfied. Once this was realized, it seemed to many that the only solution was to bring Germany into contact with, or even collision with, the Soviet Union.

The "peace at any price" people were both few and lacking in influence in Britain, while the contrary, as we shall see, was true in France. However, in the period August 1935 to March 1939 and especially in September 1938, the government built upon the fears of this group by steadily exaggerating Germany's armed might and belittling their own, by calculated indiscretions (like the statement in September 1938 that there were no real antiaircraft defenses in London), by constant hammering at the danger of an overwhelming air attack without warning, by building ostentatious and quite useless air-raid trenches in the streets and parks of London, and by insisting through daily warnings that everyone must be fitted with a gas mask immediately (although the danger of a gas attack was nil).

In this way, the government put London into a panic in 1938 for the first time since 1804 or even 1678. And by this panic, Chamberlain was able to get the British people to accept the destruction of Czechoslovakia, wrapping it up in a piece of paper, marked "peace in our time," which he obtained from Hitler, as he confided to that ruthless dictator, "for British public opinion." Once this panic passed, Chamberlain found it impossible to get the British public to follow his program, although he himself never wavered, even in 1940. He worked on the appeasement and the "peace at any price" groups throughout 1939, but their numbers dwindled rapidly, and since he could not openly appeal for support on either the anti-Bolshevik or the "three-bloc" basis, he had to adopt the dangerous expedient of pretending to resist (in order to satisfy the British public) while really continuing to make every possible concession to Hitler which would bring Germany to a common frontier with the Soviet Union, all the while putting every pressure on Poland to negotiate and on Germany to refrain from using force in order to gain time to wear Poland down and in order to avoid the necessity of backing up by action his pretense of resistance to Germany. This policy went completely astray in the period from August 1939 to April 1940.

Chamberlain's motives were not bad ones; he wanted peace so that he could devote Britain's "limited resources" to social welfare; but he was narrow and totally ignorant of the realities of power, convinced that international politics could be conducted in terms of secret deals, as business was, and he was quite ruthless in carrying out his aims, especially in his readiness to sacrifice non-English persons, who, in his eyes, did not count.

In the meantime, both the people and the government were more demoralized in France than in England. The policy of the Right which would have used force against Germany even in the face of British disapproval ended in 1924. When Barthou, who had been one of the chief figures in the 1924 effort, tried to revive it in 1934, it was quite a different thing, and he had constantly to give at least verbal support to Britain's efforts to modify his encirclement of Germany into a Four-Power Pact (of Britain, France, Italy, Germany). This Four-Power Pact, which was the ultimate goal of the anti-Bolshevik group in England, was really an effort to form a united front of Europe against the Soviet Union and, in the eyes of this group, would have been a capstone to unite in one system the encirclement of France (which was the British answer to Barthou's encirclement of Germany) and the Anti-Comintern Pact (which was the German response to the same project).

The Four-Power Pact reached its fruition at the Munich Conference of September 1938, where these four Powers destroyed Czechoslovakia without consulting Czechoslovakia's ally, the Soviet Union. But the scorn the dictators had for Britain and France as decadent democracies had by this time reached such a pass that the dictators no longer had even that minimum of respect without which the Four-Power Pact could not function. As a consequence, Hitler in 1939 spurned all Chamberlain's frantic efforts to restore the Four-Power Pact along with his equally frantic and even more secret efforts to win Hitler's attention by offers of colonies in Africa and economic support in eastern Europe.

As a result of the failure of the policy of the French Right against Germany in 1924 and the failure of the "policy of fulfillment" of the French Left in 1929-1930, France was left with no policy. Convinced that French security depended on British military and naval support in the field before action began (in order to avoid a German wartime occupation of the richest part of France such as existed in 1914-1918), depressed by the growing unbalance of the German population over the French population, and shot through with pacifism and antiwar feeling, the French Army under Pétain's influence adopted a purely defensive strategy and built up defensive tactics to support it.

In spite of the agitations of Charles de Gaulle (then a colonel) and his parliamentary spokesman, Paul Reynaud, to build up an armored striking force as an offensive weapon, France built a great, and purely defensive, fortified barrier from Montmédy to the Swiss frontier, and retrained many of its tactical units into purely defensive duties within this barrier. It was clear to many that the defensive tactics of this Maginot Line were inconsistent with France's obligations to her allies in eastern Europe, but everyone was too paralyzed by domestic political partisanship, by British pressure for a purely western European policy, and by general intellectual confusion and crisis weariness to do anything about bringing France's strategic plans and its political obligations into a consistent pattern.

It was the purely defensive nature of these strategic plans, added to Chamberlain's veto on sanctions, which prevented Flandin from acting against Germany at the time of the remilitarization of the Rhineland in March 1936. By 1938 and 1939, these influences had spread demoralization and panic into most parts of French society, with the result that the only feasible plan for France seemed to be to cooperate with Britain in a purely defensive policy in the west behind the Maginot Line, with a free hand for Hitler in the east. The steps which brought France to this destination are clear: they are marked by the Anglo-German Naval Agreement of June 1935; the Ethiopian crisis of September 1935; the remilitarization of the Rhineland in March 1936; the neutralization of Belgium in 1936; the Spanish Civil War of 1936–1939; the destruction of Austria in March 1938; and the Czechoslovak crisis leading up to Munich in September 1938. Along these steps we must continue our story.

The Spanish Tragedy, 1931-1939

From the summer of 1936 to the spring of 1939, Spain was the scene of a bitter conflict of arms, ideologies, and interests. This conflict was both a civil war and an international struggle. It was a controversial problem at the time and has remained a controversial problem since. For twenty or more years, the bitter feelings raised by the struggle remained so intense that it was difficult to determine the facts of the dispute, and anyone who tried to make an objective study of the facts was subjected to abuse from both sides.

The historical past of Spain has been so different from that of the rest of Western Civilization that it sometimes seems doubtful if it should be regarded as part of Western Civilization. This difference is increased by the fact that, since the late fifteenth century, Spain has refused to share in the experiences of Western Civilization and, if many powerful groups could have had their wish, would have remained in its fifteenth- or sixteenth-century condition.

From the invasion of the Arabs in 711 to their final ejection in 1492, Spanish life was dominated by the struggle against this foreign intruder. From 1525 to 1648, Spain was in a struggle with the new religious movements aroused by Luther. Since 1648 it has been, except for brief intervals and for exceptional personalities, at war with modern rationalism and modern science, with the Enlightenment, the French Revolution, and Napoleon, with modern democracy, modern secularism, modern liberalism, modern constitutionalism, and the bourgeois conception of modern society as a whole. As a result of more than a thousand years of such struggles, almost all elements of Spanish society, even those which were not, in theory, opposed to the new movements in Western culture, have developed a fanatical intolerance, an uncompromising individualism, and a fatal belief that physical force is a solution to all problems, however spiritual.

The impact of the bourgeois, liberal, scientific, and industrialized West of the nineteenth century upon Spain was similar to its impact on other backward political units such as Japan, China, Turkey, or Russia. In each case, some elements of these societies wished to resist the political expansion of the West by adopting its industry, science, military organization, and constitutional structures. Other elements wished to resist all westernization, by passive opposition if nothing more effective could be found, to the death if necessary, and to keep secreted in their hearts and minds the older native attitudes even if their bodies were compelled to yield to alien, Western, patterns of action.

In Spain, Russia, and China this attitude of resistance was sufficiently successful to delay the process of westernization to a date when Western Civilization was beginning to lose its own tradition (or at least its faith in it) and to shift its allegiance (or at least its behavior) to patterns of thought and action which were quite foreign to the main line of Western tradition. This shift, to which we have referred in the first section of this present chapter, was marked by a loss of the basic element of moderation to be found in the real tradition of the West. As ideological intolerance or totalitarian authoritarianism, for example, grew in the West, this was bound to have an adverse effect upon efforts to carry Western democracy, liberalism, or parliamentary constitutionalism to areas like Japan, China, Russia, or, the case in point, Spain.

During the nineteenth century, the elements willing at least to compromise with the Western way of life were not completely unsuccessful in Spain, probably because they received a certain amount of support from the army, which realized its inability to fight effectively without a largely westernized society to support it. This, however, was destroyed by the efforts of the "Restoration Monarchy" of 1875–1931 to find support among the opponents of modernization and by the Spanish defeat at the hands of the United States in 1898. Alfonso XII (1874–1885) came to the throne as a military reaction after a long period of revolutionary confusion. The defeat by the United States, like the Chinese defeat by Japan in 1894, or the Turkish defeat by Russia in 1877, widened the gap between the "progressive" and "reactionary" groups in Spain (if we may use these terms to indicate a willingness or a refusal to westernize).

Moreover, the war of 1898, by depriving Spain of much of its empire, left its oversized army with little to do and with a reduced area on which to batten. Like a vampire octopus, the Spanish Army settled down to drain the lifeblood of Spain and, above all, Morocco. This brought the army (meaning the officers) into alignment with the other conservative forces in Spain against the scanty forces of bourgeois liberalism and the rapidly growing forces of proletarian discontent. These conservative forces consisted of the Church (meaning the upper clergy), the landlords, and the monarchists. The forces of proletarian discontent consisted of the urban workers and the much larger mass of exploited peasants. These latter groups, which had no real acquaintance with the Western liberal tradition and found it of little hope when they did, were fertile soil for the agitators of proletarian revolution who were already challenging the bourgeois liberalism of the West.

To be sure, Spanish individualism, provincialism, and suspicions of the state as an instrument of the possessing classes made any appeal to the totalitarian authoritarianism of Communism relatively weak in Spain. On the other hand, the appeal of anarchism, which was both individualist and antistate, was stronger in Spain than anywhere else on earth (stronger even than in Russia where anarchism received its most complete verbal formulation at the hands of men like Bakunin).

Finally, the appeal of Socialism was almost as strong as anarchism, and much more effectively organized. Socialism to many discontented Spaniards (including many bourgeois intellectuals and professional men) seemed to offer a combination of social reform, economic progress, and a democratic secular state which was better fitted to Spanish needs than anarchism, Bolshevism, or laissez-faire constitutionalism. The weak link in this Socialist program was that the democratic, nontotalitarian state envisaged by the Socialist intellectuals in Spain was quite compatible with Spanish individualism (and basic democracy) but quite at variance with Spanish intolerance. There was a legitimate ground for doubt that any such Socialist state, if it came to power in Spain, would be tolerant enough to permit that intellectual disagreement which is so necessary for a democratic society, even one directing a Socialist economic system.

The bourgeoisie of Spain, relatively few in numbers because of Spain's economic backwardness, were in a difficult position. While the bourgeoisie of England and France had attacked the forces of feudalism, bureaucratic monarchy, militarism, and clericalism, and had created a liberal, secular state and a bourgeois society before they were themselves attacked by the rising forces of proletarian discontent on their Left, the bourgeoisie of Spain could see the proletarian threat from the Left before they were able to overcome the vested interests of the Right. As a result of this, the bourgeoisie tended to split into two parts. On the one hand were industrial and commercial bourgeoisie who supported the liberal ideas of laissez-faire, consitutional parliamentarianism, private property, antimilitarism, antibureaucratic freedom, anticlericalism, and a limited state authority. On the other hand were the intellectual and professional bourgeoisie who would have added to this program a sufficient degree of social reform, democracy, economic interventionism, and nationalization of property to put them into the Socialist camp. Both these divisions of the bourgeois group tended to move further to the Right after 1931 as the growing pressure of proletarian revolution threatened both private property and liberal democracy. The bourgeois liberals feared the loss of private property and, to save it, hastily abandoned their earlier antimilitarism, anticlericalism, and such; the bourgeois Socialists feared the loss of liberal democracy, but they found nowhere to go because liberal democracy could find no real basis in the fanatical intolerance of Spain, a feature as prevalent on the Right as on the Left. In truth, both bourgeois groups were largely crushed out, and their members practically exterminated, by the Right because of their earlier allegiance to antimilitarism, anticlericalism, and antimonarchism, and by the Left because of their continued allegiance to private property.

Strangely enough, the only defenders these bourgeois found outside their own group was in the small but well-organized body of Stalinist Communists, whose ideological preconceptions of the natural course of social development were so strong that they insisted that Spain must pass through a period of bourgeois liberal capitalism and industrialization before it would be ripe for the later stage of totalitarian Communism. This point of view, explicitly stated in Stalin's letter to the Spanish Left-wing Socialist leader, Largo Caballero, on September 21, 1936, warned against premature efforts toward social and economic reforms for which Spain's degree of industrial development made it quite unready, and called for general "anti-fascist" support for a liberal state against the "reactionaries" of the Right. In consequence of this point of view, the Communists in Spain were almost as willing to exterminate the revolutionaries of the Left (especially the anarchists, "Trotskyist" Communists, and left-wing Socialists) as they were to eliminate the reactionaries of the Right.

This complex and confused situation in Spain was made even more involved by the struggle between Castilian centralization (which was frequently unenlightened and reactionary) and the supporters of local autonomy and separatism (which were frequently progressive or even revolutionary) in Catalonia, the Basque country, Galicia, and elsewhere. This struggle was intensified by the fact that industrialism had grown up only in Catalonia and the Basque provinces, and, accordingly, the strength of the revolutionary proletariat was strongest in the areas where separatism was strongest.

Opposed to all these forces was that alignment of officers, upper clergy, landlords, and monarchists which came into existence after 1898 and especially after 1918. The army was the poorest in Europe and relatively the most expensive. There was a commissioned officer for every six men and a general for every 250 men. The men were miserably underpaid and mistreated, while the officers squandered fortunes. The Ministry of War took about a third of the national budget, and most of that went to the officers. Money was wasted or stolen, especially in Morocco, in lumps of millions at a time for the benefit of officers and monarchist politicians. Everything was done on a lavish scale. For example, there were no less than five military academies. But the army remained so inefficient that it lost 13,000 men a year for ten years fighting the Riffs in Morocco, and in July 1921 lost 12,000 killed out of 20,000 engaged in one battle. The army had the right, incredible as it may seem, to court-martial civilians, and did not hesitate to use this power to prevent criticism of its depredations. Nevertheless, the outcry against corruption and defeats in Morocco resulted in a parliamentary investigation. To prevent this, a military coup under General Primo de Rivera, with the acquiescence of King Alfonso XIII, took over the government, dissolved the Cortes, and ended civil liberties, with martial law and a strict censorship throughout Spain (1923).

The landlords not only monopolized the land but, more important than that, squandered their incomes with little effort to increase the productivity of their estates or to reduce the violent discontent of their peasant tenants and agricultural workers. Of the 125 million acres of arable land in Spain, about 60 percent was not cultivated, while another 10 percent was left fallow. The need for irrigation, fertilizers, and new methods was acute, but very little was done to achieve them. On the contrary, while the Spanish grandees wasted millions of pesetas in the gambling casinos of the French Riviera, the technical equipment of their estates steadily deteriorated. Making use of the surplus agricultural population, they sought to increase rents and to decrease agricultural wages. To permit this they made every effort to make leases shorter in duration (not over a year) and revocable at the landlord's will and to break up every effort of agricultural workers to seek government or unionized action to raise wages, reduce hours, or improve working conditions.

While all this was going on, and while most of Spain was suffering from malnutrition, most of the land was untilled, and the owners refused to use irrigation facilities which had been built by the government. As a result, agricultural yields were the poorest in western Europe. While 15 men owned about a million acres, and 15,000 men owned about half of all taxed land, almost 2 million owned the other half, frequently in plots too small for subsistence. About 2 million more, who were completely landless, worked 10 to 14 hours a day for about 2.5 pesetas (35 cents) a day for only six months in the year or paid exorbitant rents without any security of tenure.

In the Church, while the ordinary priests, especially in the villages, shared the poverty and tribulations of the people, and did so with pious devotion, the upper clergy were closely allied with the government and the forces of reaction. The bishops and archbishops were named by the monarchy and were partly supported by an annual grant from the government as a result of the Concordat of 1851. Moreover, the clergy and the government were inextricably intertwined, the upper clergy having seats in the upper chamber, control of education, censorship, marriage, and the willing ear of the king. In consequence of this alliance of the upper clergy with the government and the forces of reaction, all the animosities built up against the latter came to be directed against the former also. Although the Spanish people remained universally and profoundly Catholic, and found no attraction whatever in Protestantism and very little attraction in rational skepticism of the French sort, they also became indelibly anticlerical. This attitude was reflected in the notable reluctance of Spanish men to go to church or receive the sacraments during the interval between confirmation at the age of thirteen and extreme unction on their deathbeds. It was also reflected in the proclivity of the Spanish people for burning churches. While other peoples expressed turbulent outbursts of antigovernmental feeling in attacks on prisons, post offices, banks, or radio stations, the Spaniards invariably burn churches, and have done so for at least a century. There were great outbursts of this strange custom in 1808, 1835, 1874, 1909, 1931, and 1936, and it was indulged in by the Right as well as by the Left.

The monarchists were divided into at least two groups. One of these, the Renovación Española, supported the dynasty of Isabella II (1833-1868), while the other, the Comunión Tradicionalista, supported the claims of Isabella's uncle, Don Carlos. The Renovation group was a clique of wealthy landowners who used their contacts with the government to evade taxes, and to obtain concessions and sinecures for themselves and their friends. The Carlists were a fanatically intolerant and murderous group from remote rural regions of Spain, and were almost entirely clerical and reactionary in their aims.

All these groups, the landlords, officers, higher clergy, and monarchists (except the Carlists), were interest groups seeking to utilize Spain for their own power and profit. The threat to their positions following the First World War and the defeats in Morocco led them to support Primo de Rivera's dictatorship. However, the general's personal instability and his efforts to appease the industrialists of Catalonia, as well as his unbalanced budgets and his efforts to build up a popular following by cooperating with laboring groups, led to a shift of support, and he was forced to resign in 1930, following an unsuccessful officers' revolt in 1929.

Realizing the danger to his dynasty from his association with an unpopular dictatorship, Alfonso XIII tried to restore the constitutional government. As a first step, he ordered municipal elections for April 12, 1931. Such elections had been managed successfully by wholesale electoral corruption before 1923, and it was believed that this control could be maintained. It was maintained in the rural areas, but, in 46 out of 50 provincial capitals, the antimonarchical forces were victorious. When these forces demanded Alfonso's abdication, he called upon General Sanjurjo, commander of the Civil Guard, for support. It was refused, and Alfonso fled to France (April 14, 1931).

The republicans at once began to organize their victory, electing a Constituent Assembly in June 1931, and establishing an ultramodern unicameral, parliamentary government with universal suffrage, separation of Church and State, secularization of education, local autonomy for separatist areas, and power to socialize the great estates or the public utilities. Such a government, especially the provisions for a parliamentary regime with universal suffrage, was quite unfitted for Spain with its high illiteracy, its weak middle class, and its great inequalities of economic power.

The republic lasted only five years before the Civil War began on July 18, 1936. During that period it was challenged constantly from the Right and from the extreme Left, the former offering the greatest test because it commanded economic, military, and ideological power through the landlords, the army, and the Church. During this time the nation was ruled by coalition governments: first by a coalition of the Left from December 1931 to September, 1933; then by the Center from September 1933 to October 1934; third, by a coalition of the Right from October 1934 to the Popular Front election of February 1936; and, last, by the Left after February 1936. These shifts of government resulted from changes in alignments of the multitude of political parties. The Right formed a coalition under José María Gil Robles in February 1933, while the Left formed a coalition under Manuel Azaña in February 1936. As a result, the Right coalition won the second parliamentary election in November 1933, while the Left won the third, or Popular Front, election of February 1936.

Because of this shifting of governments, the liberal program which was enacted into law in 1931–1933 was annulled or unenforced in 1933–

1936. This program included educational reform, army reform, separation of Church and State, agrarian reform, and social assistance for peasants and workers.

In an effort to reduce illiteracy (which was over 45 percent in 1930), the republic created thousands of new schools and new teachers, raised teachers' salaries to a minimum of about $450 a year (this affected 21,500 out of 37,500 teachers), founded over a thousand new libraries, and encouraged adult education.

Efforts were made to obtain a smaller, better paid, more efficient army. The 23,000 officers (including 258 generals) were reduced to 9,500 officers (including 86 generals), the surplus being retired on full pay. The number of enlisted men was reduced to about 100,000 with higher pay. Organization was completely reformed. As a result, over $14 million was saved on the cost of the army in the first year (1931–1932). Unfortunately, nothing was done to make the army loyal to the new regime. Since the choice to retire or stay on active duty was purely voluntary, the republican officers tended to retire, the monarchists to stay on, with the result that the army of the republic was more monarchist in its sympathies than the army had been before 1931. Although the officers, disgruntled at their narrowing opportunities for enriching themselves, were openly disrespectful and insubordinate toward the republic, almost nothing was done to remedy this.

The Church was subjected to laws establishing complete separation of Church and State. The government gave up its right to nominate the upper clergy, ended the annual grant to the Church, took ownership (but not possession) of Church property, forbade teaching in public schools by the clergy, established religious toleration and civil divorce, and required that all corporations (including religious orders and trade unions) must register with the government and publish financial accounts.

To assist the peasants and workers, mixed juries were established to hear rural rent disputes; importation of labor from one district to another for wage-breaking purposes was forbidden; and credit was provided for peasants to obtain land, seed, or fertilizers on favorable terms. Manorial lands, those of monarchists who had fled with Alfonso, and customarily uncultivated lands were expropriated with compensation, to provide farms for a new class of peasant proprietors.

Most of these reforms went into effect only partially or not at all. The annual contribution to the Church could not be ended, because the Spanish people refused to contribute voluntarily to the Church, and an alternative system of ecclesiastical taxation enforced by the state had to be set up. Few of the abandoned or poorly cultivated estates could be expropriated because of lack of money for compensation. The clergy could not be excluded from teaching because of the lack of trained teachers. Most expropriated ecclesiastical property was left in the control of the Church either because it was necessary for religious and social services or because it could not be tracked down.

The conservative groups reacted violently against the republic almost as soon as it began. In fact, the monarchists criticized Alfonso for leaving without a struggle, while the upper clergy and landlords ostracized the papal legate for his efforts to make the former adopt a neutral attitude toward the new regime. As a result, three plots began to be formed against the republic, the one monarchist led by Calvo Sotelo in parliament and by Antonio Goicoechea behind the scenes; the second a parliamentary alliance of landlords and clericals under José María Gil Robles; and the last a conspiracy of officers under Generals Emilio Barrera and José Sanjurjo. Sanjurjo led an unsuccessful rebellion at Seville in August 1932. When it collapsed from lack of public support, he was arrested, condemned to death, reprieved, and finally released (with all his back pay) in 1934. Barrera was arrested but released by the courts. Both generals began to prepare for the rebellion of 1936.

In the meantime, the monarchist conspiracy was organized by former King Alfonso from abroad as early as May 1931. As part of this movement a new political party was founded under Sotelo, a "research" organization known as Spanish Action was set up "to publish texts from great thinkers on the legality of revolution," a war chest of 1.5 million pesetas was created, and an underground conspiracy was drawn up under the leadership of Antonio Goicoechea. This last action was taken at a meeting in Paris presided over by Alfonso himself (September 29, 1932).

Goicoechea performed his task with great skill, under the eyes of a government which refused to take preventive action because of its own liberal and legalistic scruples. He organized an alliance of the officers, the Carlists, and his own Alfonsist party. Four men from these three groups then signed an agreement with Mussolini on March 31, 1934. By this agreement the Duce of Fascism promised arms, money, and diplomatic support to the revolutionary movement and gave the conspirators a first-installment payment of 1,500,000 pesetas, 10,000 rifles, 10,000 grenades, and 200 machine guns. In return the signers, Lieutenant General Emilio Barrera, Antonio Lizarza, Rafael de Olazabal, and Antonio Goicoechea, promised when they came to power to denounce the existing French-Spanish "secret treaty," and to sign with Mussolini an agreement establishing a joint export policy between Spain and Italy, as well as an agreement to maintain the *status quo* in the western Mediterranean.

In the meantime, Gil Robles's coalition, known as CEDA (Spanish Confederation of Autonomous Right Parties), along with his own clerical party (Popular Action) and the Agrarian Party of the big landlords, was able to replace the Left Republican Manuel Azaña by the Right Republican Alejandro Lerroux as prime minister (September 1933). It then called new elections in November 1934, and won a victory with 213 seats for the Right, 139 for the Center, and 121 for the Left. The Center Cabinet continued in office, supported by the votes of the Right. It revoked many of the reforms of 1931-1933, allowed most of the rest to go unenforced, released all the Rightist conspirators from prison (including Sanjurjo), gave an amnesty to thousands of monarchist plotters and exiles, and restored their expropriated estates. By a process of consolidating portfolios and abolishing Cabinet seats, Gil Robles slowly reduced the Cabinet from thirteen ministers at the end of 1933 to nine two years later. Of these CEDA took three in October 1934 and five in March 1935.

The advent to office of CEDA in October 1934 led to a violent agitation which burst into open revolt in the two separatist centers of the Basque country and Catalonia. The latter, led by the bourgeois Left, received little support from the workers, and collapsed at once; the uprising in Asturias, however, spearheaded by anarchist miners hurling dynamite from slings, lasted for nine days. The government used the Foreign Legion and Moors, brought from Morocco by sea, and crushed the rebels without mercy. The latter suffered at least 5,000 casualties, of which a third were dead. After the uprising was quelled, all the Socialist press was silenced and 25,000 suspects were thrown into prison.

This uprising of October 1934, although crushed, served to split the oligarchy. The fact that the government had sent Moors to the most Catholic part of Spain (where they had never penetrated during the Saracen invasions) and the demands of the army, monarchists, and the biggest landlords for a ruthless dictatorship alarmed the leaders of the Church and the president of the republic, Alcalá Zamora. This ultimately blocked Gil Robles's road to power by parliamentary methods. After March 1935 he controlled the portfolios of Justice, Industry and Commerce, Labor, and Communications, but could not get the Interior (which controlled the police). This was held by Portela Valladares, a moderate close to Zamora. Gil Robles as minister of war encouraged reactionary control of the army and even put General Franco in as his undersecretary for war, but he could not get rid of Portela Valladares. Finally, he demanded that the police be transferred from the Ministry of Interior to his own Ministry of War. When this was refused, he upset the Cabinet, but, instead of getting more from this action, he got less, for Alcalá Zamora handed the premier's seat over to moderates (Joaquin Chapaprieta, a businessman, followed by Portela Valladares) and ordered new elections.

For these elections of February 1936, the parties of the Left formed a coalition, the Popular Front, with a published program and plan of action. The program was of a moderate Left character, promising a full restoration of the constitution, amnesty for political crimes committed after

November 1933, civil liberties, an independent judiciary, minimum wages, protection for tenants, reform of taxation, credit, banking, and the police, and public works. It repudiated the Socialist program for nationalization of the land, the banks, and industry.

The plan of action provided that while all the Popular Front parties would support the government by their votes in the Cortes, only the bourgeois parties would hold seats in the Cabinet, while the workers' parties, such as the Socialists, would remain outside.

The election of February 16, 1936 followed a campaign of violence and terrorism in which the worst offenders were the members of a microscopic new political party calling itself the Falange. Openly Fascist on the Italian model, and consisting largely of a small number of rich and irresponsible youths, this group was led by Primo de Rivera the younger. In the election, the Popular Front captured 266 out of 473 seats, while the Right had 153 and the Center only 54; CEDA had 96, the Socialists 87, Azaña's Republican Left 81, the Communists 14.

The defeated forces of the Right refused to accept the results of this election. As soon as the results were known, Sotelo tried to persuade Portela Valladares to hand over the government to General Franco. That was rebuffed. The same day the Falange attacked workers who were celebrating. On February 20th the conspirators met and decided their plans were not yet ripe. The new government heard of this meeting and at once transferred General Franco to the Canary Islands, General Manuel Goded to the Balearics, and General Emilio Mola from his command in Morocco to be governor-general of Navarre (the Carlist stronghold). The day before Franco left Madrid, he met the chief conspirators at the home of the monarchist deputy Serrano Delgado. They completed their plans for a military revolt but fixed no date.

In the meantime, provocation, assassination, and retaliation grew steadily, with the verbal encouragement of the Right. Property was seized or destroyed, and churches were burned on all sides. On March 12th the Socialist lawyer who had drafted the constitution of 1931 was fired at from an automobile, and his companion was killed. Five men were brought to trial; the judge was assassinated (April 13th). The next day a bomb exploded beneath a platform from which the new Cabinet was reviewing the troops, and a police lieutenant was killed (April 14th). The mob retaliated by assaults on monarchists and by burning churches. On March 15th there was an attempt to assassinate Largo Caballero. By May the monarchist assassins were beginning to concentrate on the officers of the Assault Guards, the only branch of the police which was completely loyal to the republic. In May the captain of this force, Faraudo, was killed by shots from a speeding automobile; on July 12th Lieutenant Castillo of the same force was killed in the same way. That night a group of men in the uniform of the Assault Guards took Sotelo from his bed, and shot him. The uprising, however, was already beginning in England and in Italy, and broke out in Morocco on July 18th.

One of the chief figures in the conspiracy in England was Douglas Jerrold, a well-known editor, who has revealed some details in his auto-biography. At the end of May 1936, he obtained "50 machine guns and a half million rounds of S.A. ammunition" for the cause. In June he persuaded Major Hugh Pollard to fly to the Canary Islands in order to transport General Franco by plane to Morocco. Pollard took off on July 11th with his nineteen-year-old daughter Diana and her friend Dorothy Watson. Louis Bolín, who was Jerrold's chief contact with the conspirators, went at once to Rome. On July 15th orders were issued by the Italian Air Force to certain units to prepare to fly to Spanish Morocco. The Italian insignia on these planes were roughly painted over on July 20th and thereafter, but otherwise they were fully equipped. These planes went into action in support of the revolt as early as July 27th; on July 30th four such planes, still carrying their orders of July 15th, landed in French Algeria, and were interned.

German intervention was less carefully planned. It would appear that Sanjurjo went to Berlin on February 4, 1936, but could get no commitment beyond a promise to provide the necessary transport planes to move the Moroccan forces to Spain if the Spanish fleet made transport by sea dangerous by remaining loyal to the government. As soon as Franco reached Morocco from the Canaries on July 18th, he appealed for these planes through a personal emissary to Hitler and through the German consul at Tetuan. The former met Hitler on July 24th, and was promised assistance. The plans to intervene were drawn up the same night by Hitler, Göring, and General Werner von Blomberg. Thirty planes with German crews were sent to Spain by August 8th, and the first one was captured by the Loyalist government the next day.

In the meantime, the revolt was a failure. The navy remained loyal because the crews overthrew their officers; the air force generally remained loyal; the army revolted, along with much of the police, but, except in isolated areas, these rebellious units were overcome. At the first news of the revolt, the people, led by the labor unions and the militia of the workers' political parties, demanded arms. The government was reluctant because of fear of revolution from the Left as well as the Right, and delayed for several days. Two Cabinets resigned on July 18th and July 19th rather than arm the Left, but a new Cabinet under José Giral was willing to do so. However, because arms were lacking, orders were sent at once to France. The recognized government in Madrid had the right to buy arms abroad and was even bound to do so to some degree by the existing commercial treaty with France.

As a result of the failure of the revolt, the generals found themselves isolated in several different parts of Spain with no mass popular support and with control of none of the three chief industrial areas. The rebels held the extreme northwest (Galicia and León), the north (Navarre), and the south (western Andalusia) as well as Morocco and the islands. They had the unlimited support of Italy and Portugal, as well as unlimited sympathy and tentative support from Germany. But the rebel position was desperate by the end of July. On July 25th the German ambassador informed his government that the revolt could not succeed "unless something unforeseen happens." By August 25th the acting state secretary of foreign affairs in Germany, Hans Dieckhoff, wrote, "it is not to be expected that the Franco Government can hold out for long, even after outward successes, without large-scale support from outside."

In the meantime, Italian and Portuguese aid kept the rebellion going. The French and British, whose only desire at first was to avoid an open clash arising from the Great Powers' supplying arms and men to opposite sides in the conflict were prepared to sacrifice any interests of their countries to avoid this. Impelled by pacifist sentiments, and a desire to avoid war at any cost, French Premier Léon Blum and French Foreign Minister Yvon Delbos suggested on August 1, 1936, that an agreement not to intervene in Spain should be signed by the chief Powers concerned. This idea was eagerly taken up by Britain and was acceptable to the Popular Front government of France, since it was clear that if there was no intervention, the Spanish government could suppress the rebels. Great Britain accepted the French offer at once, but efforts to get Portugal, Italy, Germany, and Russia into the agreement were difficult because of the delays made by Portugal and Italy, both of which were helping the rebels. By August 24th all six Powers had agreed, and by August 28th the agreement went into effect.

Efforts to establish some kind of supervision by the Nonintervention Committee or by neutral forces were rejected by the rebels and by Portugal, while Britain refused to permit any restrictions to be placed on war matériel going to Portugal at the very moment when it was putting all kinds of pressure on France to restrict any flow of supplies across the Pyrenees to the recognized government of Spain (November 30, 1936). Britain also put pressure on Portugal to stop assistance to the rebels but with little success, as Portugal was determined to see a rebel victory. Along with Italy and Germany, Portugal delayed joining the nonintervention agreement until it decided that such an agreement would hurt the Loyalist forces more than the rebels. Even then there was no intention of observing the agreement or permitting any steps to enforce it if such actions would hamper the rebels.

On the other hand, France did little to help the Madrid government, while Britain was positively hostile to it. Both governments stopped all shipments of war matériel to Spain in the middle of August. By its insistence on enforcing nonintervention against the Loyalists, while ignoring the systematic and large-scale evasions of the agreement in behalf of the rebels, Britain was neither fair nor neutral, and had to engage in large-scale violations of international law. Britain refused to permit any restrictions to be placed on war matériel going to Portugal (in spite of its protests to Portugal for transshipping these to the rebels). It refused to allow the Loyalist Spanish Navy to blockade the seaports held by the rebels, and took immediate action against efforts by the Madrid government to interfere with any kind of shipments to rebel areas, while wholesale assaults by the rebels on British and other neutral ships going to Loyalist areas drew little more than feeble protests from Britain. In August 1936, when a Loyalist cruiser intercepted a British freighter carrying supplies to Morocco, the British battle cruiser *Repulse* went after the Spanish cruiser cleared for action. On the other hand, the British refusal to recognize the rebel government, or to grant it belligerent status, placed interference with shipping by these forces in the category of piracy; yet Britain did almost nothing when in one year (June 1937–June 1938) 10 British ships were sunk, 10 were captured and held, 28 more were seriously damaged, and at least 12 others were damaged by the rebels out of a total of 140 British ships which went to Spain in that year. By the beginning of 1937 Britain was clearly seeking a rebel victory, and, instead of trying to enforce nonintervention or to protect British rights on the seas, was actively supporting the rebel blockade of Loyalist Spain. This was clearly evident when the British Navy after May 1937 began to intercept British ships headed for Loyalist ports and on some pretext, or simply by force, made them go elsewhere, such as Bordeaux or Gibraltar. These tactics were admitted by the First Lord of the Admiralty in the House of Commons on June 29, 1938.

The rebel forces were fewer in numbers than the Loyalists, and fought with less vigor and under poor leadership, according to German secret reports from Spain at the time, but were eventually successful because of their great superiority in artillery, aviation, and tanks, as a result of the one-sided enforcement of the nonintervention agreement. This was admitted by the governments concerned as soon as the war was over, and by General Franco on April 13, 1939. We have seen that Italian intervention began even before the revolt broke out and that Portuguese intervention on behalf of the rebels followed soon after. German intervention was somewhat slower, although all their sympathies were with the rebels. At the end of July, a German citizen in Morocco organized a Spanish corporation called Hisma to obtain German supplies and assistance for the rebels. This firm began to transport the rebel troops from Morocco to Spain on August 2nd. It soon obtained a monopoly on all German goods sold to rebel Spain and set up a central purchasing office for this purpose in Lisbon, Portugal. By August all important units of the German Navy were in Spanish waters, and their ranking admiral paid a state visit to Franco in his headquarters in Morocco as early as August 3rd. These units gave naval support to the rebellion from then on.

Early in October, General Göring established a corporation called Rowak, with three million reichsmarks credit provided by the German government. This was given a monopoly on the export of goods to Spain, and orders were issued to the German Navy to protect these goods in transit.

The failure of the Franco forces to capture Madrid led to a joint Italian-German meeting in Berlin on October 20, 1936. There it was decided to embark on a policy of extensive support for Franco. As part of this policy both Powers recognized the Franco government and withdraw their recognition from Madrid on November 18, 1936, and Italy signed a secret alliance with the rebel government ten days later. Japan recognized the Franco regime early in December, following the signature of the German-Japanese Anti-Comintern Pact of November 25, 1936.

As a result of all these actions, Franco received the full support of the aggressor states, while the Loyalist government was obstructed in every way by the "peace-loving" Powers. While the Axis assistance to the rebels was chiefly in the form of supplies and technical assistance, it was also necessary to send a large number of men to work some of this equipment or even to fight as infantry. In all, Italy sent about 100,-000 men and suffered about 50,000 casualties (of which 6,000 were killed). Germany sent about 20,000 men, although this figure is less certain. The value of the supplies sent to General Franco was estimated by the countries concerned as 500 million reichsmarks by Germany and 14 billion lire by Italy. Together this amounts to over three-quarters of a billion dollars.

On the other side, the Loyalists were cut off from foreign supplies almost at once because of the embargoes of the Great Powers, and obtained only limited amounts, chiefly from Mexico, Russia, and the United States, before the Nonintervention agreement cut these off. On January 18, 1937, the American Neutrality Act was revised to apply to civil as well as international wars, and was invoked against Spain immediately, but "unofficial" pressure from the American government prevented exports of this kind to Spain even earlier. As a result of such actions, shortages of supplies for the Madrid government were evident at the end of August and became acute a few weeks later, while supplies for the rebels were steadily increasing.

The Madrid government made violent protests against the Axis intervention, both before the Nonintervention Committee in London and before the League of Nations. These were denied by the Axis Powers.

An investigation of these charges was made under Soviet pressure, but the committee reported on November 10th that these charges were unproved. Indeed, Anthony Eden, nine days later, went so far as to say in the House of Commons that so far as nonintervention was concerned, "there were other Governments more to blame than either Germany or Italy."

Since we have captured large quantities of secret German and Italian documents and have not captured any Soviet documents, it is not possible to fix the date or the degree of Soviet intervention in Spain, but it is conclusively established that it was much later in date and immensely less in quantity than that of either Italy or Germany. On October 7, 1936, the Soviet representative informed the Nonintervention Committee that it could not be bound by the nonintervention agreement to a greater extent than the other participants. Soviet intervention appears to have begun at this time, three and a half years after Italian intervention and almost three months after both Italian and German units were fighting with the rebels. Russian military equipment went into action before Madrid in the period October 29–November 11, 1936.

As late as September 28, 1936, the German chargé d'affaires in the Soviet Union reported that he could find no reliable proof of violation of the arms embargo by the Soviet government, and on November 16th he reported no evidence of the transport of troops from Odessa. Food shipments were being sent by September 19th, and extensive shipments of military supplies began to be reported a month later. Earlier, but unsubstantiated, reports had arrived from German agents in Spain itself. The amount of Soviet aid to Madrid is not known. Estimates of the number of technical advisers and assistants vary from 700 to 5,000, and were probably not over 2,000; no infantry forces were sent. In addition, the Third International recruited volunteers throughout the world to fight in Spain. These went into action early in November 1936 before Madrid, and were disbanded in October 1938.

This Soviet intervention in support of the Madrid government at a time when it could find support almost nowhere else served to increase Communist influence in the government very greatly, although the number of Communists in Spain itself were few and they had elected only 14 of 473 deputies in February 1936. Communists came into the Cabinet for the first time September 4, 1936. In general, they acted to maintain the Popular Front, to concentrate on winning the war, and to prevent all efforts toward social revolution by the extreme Left. For this reason, they overthrew Largo Caballero's government in May 1937, and set up Juan Negrín, a more conservative Socialist, as premier in a Cabinet which continued on the same general lines until after the war ended.

The small number of Russian or other "volunteers" on the Loyalist side, in spite of the extravagant statement of Franco's supporters at the time and since, is evident from the inability of the rebel forces to capture any important numbers of "foreign Reds" in spite of their great desire to do so. After the Battle of Teruel, at which such "foreign Reds" were supposed to be very active, Franco had to report to Germany that he had found "very few" among the 14,500 captives taken; this fact had to be kept "strictly confidential," he said (December 1937).

As a matter of fact, intervention in Spain by the Soviet Union was not only limited in quantity; it was also of brief duration, chiefly between October 1936 and January 1937. The road to Spain was, for the Soviet Union, a difficult one, as the Italian submarine fleet was waiting for Russian shipping in the Mediterranean, and did not hesitate to sink it. This was done in the last few months of 1936. Moreover, the Anti-Comintern Pact of November 1936 and the Japanese attack on North China in 1937 made it seem that all Russian supplies were needed at home. Furthermore, the Soviet Union was more concerned with reopening supplies to Loyalist Spain from France, Britain, or elsewhere, because, in a competition of supplies and troops in Spain, the Soviet Union could not match Italy alone and certainly not Italy, Germany, and Portugal together. Finally, the German government in 1936 gave the Czechoslovak leader Edward Beneš documents indicating that various Soviet Army officers were in contact with German Army officers. When Beneš sent these documents on to Stalin, they gave rise to a series of purges and treason trials in the Soviet Union, which largely eclipsed the Spanish Civil War and served to put a stop to the major part of the Soviet contribution to the Loyalist government. Efforts to compensate for this decrease in Soviet support by an increase in support by the Third International were not effective, since the latter organization could get men to go to Spain but could not obtain military supplies, which were what the Loyalist government needed for their own manpower.

Although the evidence for Axis intervention in Spain was overwhelming and was admitted by the Powers themselves early in 1937, the British refused to admit it and refused to modify the nonintervention policy, although France did relax its restrictions on its frontier sometimes, notably in April–June 1938. Britain's attitude was so devious that it can hardly be untangled, although the results are clear enough. The chief result was that in Spain a Left government friendly to France was replaced by a Right government unfriendly to France and deeply obligated to Italy and Germany. The evidence is clear that the real sympathies of the London government favored the rebels, although it had to conceal the fact from public opinion in Britain (since this opinion favored the Loyalists over Franco by 57 percent to 7 percent, according to a public-opinion poll of March 1938). It held this view in spite of the fact that such a change could not fail to be adverse to British interests, for it meant that Gibraltar at one end of the middle passage to India could be neutralized by Italy just as Aden at the other end had been neutralized by the conquest of Ethiopia. That fear of war was a powerful motive is clear, but such fear was more prevalent outside the government than inside. On December 18, 1936, Eden admitted that the government had exaggerated the danger of war four months earlier to get the nonintervention agreement accepted, and when Britain wanted to use force to achieve its aims, as it did against the piracy of Italian submarines in the Mediterranean in the autumn of 1937, it did so without risk of war. The nonintervention agreement, as practiced, was neither an aid to peace nor an example of neutrality, but was clearly enforced in such a way as to give aid to the rebels and place all possible obstacles in the way of the Loyalist government suppressing the rebellion.

This attitude of the British government could not be admitted publicly, and every effort was made to picture the actions of the Nonintervention Committee as one of evenhanded neutrality. In fact, the activities of this committee were used to throw dust in the eyes of the world, and especially in the eyes of the British public. On September 9, 1936, Count Bismarck, the German member of the committee, notified his government that France and Britain's aim in establishing the committee was "not so much a question of taking actual steps immediately as of pacifying the aroused feelings of the Leftist parties in both countries by the very establishment of such a committee—[and] to ease the domestic political situation of the French Premier. . . ."

For months the meaningless debates of this committee were reported in detail to the world, and charges, countercharges, proposals, counter-proposals, investigations, and inconclusive conclusions were offered to a confused world, thus successfully increasing its confusion. In February 1937, an agreement was made to prohibit the enlistment or dispatch of volunteers to fight on either side in Spain, and on April 30th patrols were established on the Portuguese and French borders of Spain as well as on the seacoasts of Spain. At the end of a month, Portugal ended the supervision on her land frontier, while Italy and Germany abandoned the sea patrol.

Constant efforts by Portugal, Italy, and Germany to win recognition for the rebels as "belligerents" under international law were blocked by Britain, France, and Russia. Such recognition would have allowed the rebel forces those rights on the high seas which the recognized government of Madrid was in practice being denied. Russia wished to extend belligerent rights to Franco only if all foreign volunteers were withdrawn first. While debating and quibbling went on about issues like belligerency, supervision by patrols, withdrawal of volunteers, and such before the Nonintervention Committee in London, the Franco rebel forces, with their foreign contingents of Moors, Italians, and Germans, slowly crushed the Loyalist forces.

As a result of the nonintervention policy, the military preponderance of the rebels was very large except in respect to morale. The rebels generally had about 500 or even more planes while the government had at one time as many as 150. It has been estimated that the greatest concentration of Loyalist artillery was 180 pieces at the Battle of Teruel in December 1937, while the greatest concentration of rebel artillery was 1,400 pieces against 120 on the Loyalist side at the battle on the Ebro in July 1938. The Italian Air Force was very active, with 1,000 planes making over 86,000 flights in 5,318 separate operations during which it dropped 11,584 tons of bombs during the war. With this advantage the "Nationalist" forces were able to join their southwestern and northwestern contingents during 1936, to crush the Basques and form a continuous territory between Galicia and Navarre across northern Spain in 1937, to drive eastward across Spain to the east coast in 1938, thus cutting Loyalist Spain in two; to capture most of Catalonia, including Barcelona, in January 1939; and to close in on Madrid in 1939. The Loyalist capital surrendered on March 28th. England and France recognized the Franco government on February 27, 1939, and the Axis troops were evacuated from Spain after a triumphal march through Madrid in June 1939.

When the war ended, much of Spain was wrecked, at least 450,000 Spaniards had been killed (of which 130,000 were rebels, the rest Loyalists), and an unpopular military dictatorship had been imposed on Spain as a result of the actions of non-Spanish forces. About 400,000 Spaniards were in prisons, and large numbers were hungry and destitute. Germany recognized this problem, and tried to get France to follow a path of conciliation, humanitarian reform, and social, agricultural, and economic reform. This advice was rejected, with the result that Spain has remained weak, apathetic, war-weary, and discontented ever since.

XIII

THE DISRUPTION OF
EUROPE, 1937-1939

Austria infelix, *1933–1938*

The Czechoslovak Crisis, 1937–1938

The Year of Dupes, 1939

Austria *Infelix*, 1933-1938

THE Austria which was left after the Treaty of Saint-Germain was so weak economically that its life was maintained only by financial aid from the League of Nations and the Western democratic states. Its area of population had been so reduced that it consisted of little more than the great city of Vienna surrounded by a huge but inadequate suburb. The city, with a population of two millions in a country whose population had been reduced from 52 to 6.6 millions, had been the center of a great empire, and now was a burden on a small principality. Moreover, the economic nationalism of the Succession States like Czechslovakia cut this area off from the lower Danube and the Balkans whence it had drawn its food supply in the prewar period.

Worse than this, the city and the surrounding countryside were antithetical in their outlooks on every political, social, or ideological issue. The city was Socialist, democratic, anticlerical if not antireligious, pacifist, and progressive in the nineteenth-century meaning of the word "progress"; the country was Catholic if not clerical, ignorant, intolerant, belligerent, and backward.

Each area had its own political party, the Christian Socialists in the country and the Social Democrats in the city. These were so evenly balanced that in none of the five elections from 1919 to 1930 did the vote polled for either party fall below 35 percent or rise above 49 percent of the total vote cast. This meant that the balance of power in Parliament fell to the insignificant minor parties like the Pan-Germans or the Agrarian League. Since these minor groups threw in their lot with the Christian Socialists from 1920 onward, the dichotomy between the city and the country was transformed into a division between the government of the capital city (dominated by the Social

Democrats) and that of the federal government (dominated by the Christian Socialists).

The Social Democrats, although very radical and Marxist in word, were very democratic and moderate in deed. In control of the whole country from 1918 to 1920, they were able to make peace, to crush out the threat of Bolshevism from Hungary to the east or from Bavaria to the north, to establish an effective democratic constitution with considerable autonomy for the local states (formerly provinces), and to give the new country a good impetus toward becoming a twentieth-century welfare state. The measure of their success may be seen in the fact that the Communists never were able to get established after 1919 or to elect a member to Parliament. On the other hand, the Social Democrats were unable to reconcile their desire for union with Germany (called *Anschluss*) with the need for financial aid from the Entente Powers who opposed this.

An agreement between the Pan-Germans and the Christian Socialists to put *Anschluss* on the shelf and concentrate on getting financial aid from the victorious Entente made it possible to overthrow the coalition Cabinet of Michael Mayr in June 1921, and replace it by a Pan-German-Christian Socialist alliance under the Pan-German Johann Schober. In May 1922, this alliance was reversed when the Christian Socialist leader, Monsignor Ignaz Seipel, a Catholic priest, became chancellor. Seipel dominated the federal government of Austria until his death in August 1932, and his policies were carried on after that by his disciples, Dollfuss and Schuschnigg. Seipel was able to achieve a certain amount of financial reconstruction by wringing international loans from the victorious Powers of 1918. He achieved this, in spite of Austria's poor credit status, by insisting that he would be unable to prevent *Anschluss* if Austria reached a stage of financial collapse.

In the meantime the Social Democrats in control of the city and state of Vienna embarked upon an amazing program of social welfare. The old monarchical system of indirect taxes was replaced by a system of direct taxes which bore heavily on the well-to-do. With an honest, efficient administration and a balanced budget, the living conditions of the poor were transformed. This was especially notable in regard to housing. Before 1914 this had been deplorable. A census of 1917 showed that 73 percent of all apartments were "one room" (with over 90 percent of workers' apartments in this class), and of these, 92 had no sanitary facilities, 95 percent had no running water, and 77 percent had no electricity or gas; many had no outside ventilation. Although this one room was smaller than 12 feet by 15 feet in size, 17 percent had a lodger, usually sharing a bed. As a result of the housing shortage, disease (especially tuberculosis) and crime were rampant, and real-estate values rose over 2,500 percent in the fifteen years

1885–1900. These economic conditions had been maintained by a very undemocratic political system under which only 83,000 persons, on a property basis, were allowed to vote and 5,500 of the richest were allowed to choose one-third of all seats on the city council.

Into this situation the Social Democrats came in 1918. By 1933 they had built almost 60,000 dwellings, mostly in huge apartment houses. These were constructed with hardwood floors, outside windows, gas, electricity, and sanitary facilities. In these large apartment buildings more than half the ground space was left free for parks and playgrounds, and central laundries, kindergartens, libraries, clinics, post offices, and other conveniences were provided. One of the largest of these buildings, the Karl Marx Hof, covered only 18 percent of its lot, yet held 1,400 apartments with 5,000 inhabitants. These were built so efficiently that the average cost per apartment was only about $1,650 each; since rent was expected to cover only upkeep and not construction cost (which came from taxes), the average rent was less than $2.00 a month. Thus the poor of Vienna spend only a fraction of their income for rent, less than 3 percent, compared to 25 percent in Berlin and about 20 percent in Vienna before the war. In addition, all kinds of free or cheap medical care, dental care, education, libraries, amusements, sports, school lunches, and maternity care were provided by the city.

While this was going on in Vienna, the Christian Socialist–Pan-German federal government was sinking deeper into corruption. The diversion of public funds to banks and industries controlled by Seipel's supporters was revealed by parliamentary investigations in spite of the government's efforts to conceal the facts. When the federal government struck back with its own investigation of the finances of the city of Vienna, it had to report that they were in admirable condition. All this served to increase the appeal of the Social Democrats throughout Austria, in spite of their antireligious and materialist orientation. This can be seen from the fact that the Socialist electoral vote increased steadily, rising from 35 percent of the total vote in 1920 to 39.6 percent in 1923 to 42 percent in 1927. At the same time, the number of Christian Socialist seats in Parliament fell from 85 in 1920 to 82 in 1923 to 73 in 1927 to 66 in 1930.

In 1927 Monsignor Seipel formed a "Unity List" of all the anti-Socialist groups he could muster, but he could not turn the tide. The election gave his party only 73 seats compared to 71 for the Social Democrats, 12 for the Pan-Germans, and 9 for the Agrarian League. Accordingly, Seipel embarked on a very dangerous project. He sought to change the Austrian constitution into a presidential dictatorship as the first step on the road to a Habsburg restoration within a corporative Fascist state. Since any change in the constitution required a two-thirds vote in a Parliament where the Social-Democratic opposition held 43 percent of the seats, Monsignor Seipel sought to break this opposition by encouraging the growth of an armed reactionary militia, the *Heimwehr* (Home Guard). This project failed in 1929, when Seipel's constitutional changes were largely rejected by the Parliament. As a result, it became necessary to use illegal methods, a task which was carried out by Seipel's successor, Engelbert Dollfuss, in 1932–1934.

The Heimwehr first appeared in 1918–1919 as bands of armed peasants and soldiers formed on the fringes of Austrian territory to resist incursions of Italians, South Slavs, and Bolsheviks. After this danger passed, it continued in existence as a loose organization of armed reactionary bands, financed at first by the same German Army groups which were financing the Nazis in Bavaria at the same time (1919–1924). Later these bands were financed by industrialists and bankers as a weapon against the trade unions, and after 1927 by Mussolini as part of his projects of revisionism in the Danube area. At first, these Heimwehr units were fairly independent with their own leaders in different provinces. After 1927 they tended to coalesce, although rivalry between leaders remained bitter. These leaders were members of the Christian Socialist or Pan-German parties and sometimes had Habsburg sympathies. The leaders were Anton Rintelen and Walter Pfrimer in Styria, Richard Steidle in Tyrol, Prince Ernst Rüdiger von Starhemberg in Upper Austria, and Emil Fey in Vienna. The "chief of the general staff" of the movement as it became unified was a multi-murderer fugitive from German justice, Waldemar Pabst, who had been involved in numerous political murders ordered by the nationalists in Germany in the period 1919–1923.

These organizations openly drilled in military formations, made weekly provocative marches into industrial areas of the cities, openly declared their determination to destroy democracy, labor unions, and the Socialists and to change the constitution by force, and assaulted and murdered their critics.

Seipel's efforts to amend the constitution by using Heimwehr pressure against the Social Democrats failed in 1929, although he did succeed in increasing the powers of the Christian Democratic President Wilhelm Miklas somewhat. About the same time, Seipel rejected an offer from the Social Democrats to disarm and disband both the Heimwehr and the Social Democratic militia, the *Schutzbund*.

Seipel's tactics alienated his supporters in the Pan-German and Agrarian League so that his party no longer commanded a majority in the chamber. It resigned in September 1930. Using the new constitutional reforms which had been passed the year before, Seipel formed a "presidential" Cabinet, a minority government, of Christian Socialists and Heimwehr. For the first time this latter group obtained Cabinet posts, and these the most threatening, since Starhemberg became minister of interior (which controlled the police), and Franz Hüber, another Heimwehr leader, became minister of justice. This was done in spite of the fact that the Heimwehr had just introduced into its organization an oath which bound its members to reject parliamentary democracy in favor of the one-party, cooperative, "leadership" state. From this point on, the constitution was steadily violated by the Christian Socialists.

New elections were called for November 1930. Starhemberg promised Pfrimer that they would carry out a *Putsch* to prevent the elections, and Starhemberg publicly announced, "Now we are here, and we will not drop the reins, whatever the result of the elections." Chancellor Karl Vaugoin, however, was convinced his group would win the elections; accordingly he vetoed the *Putsch*. Minister of Justice Hüber confiscated the papers of the Pan-Germans, the Agrarians, and dissident Christian Socialists, as well as of the Social Democrats, during the campaign on the ground that they were "Bolshevik." In this confusion of cross-purposes the election was held, the last election held in prewar Austria. The Christian Socialists lost 7 seats, while the Social Democrats gained 1. The former had 66, the latter 72, the Heimwehr had 8, and the Pan-German–Agrarian bloc had 19. The minority Seipel government tamely resigned, replaced by a more moderate Christian Socialist government under Otto Ender with Pan-German–Agrarian support.

In June 1931, though Seipel tried again to form a government, he could not obtain sufficient support, and the weak coalitions of moderate Christian Socialists and Pan-Germans continued in spite of a Heimwehr revolt led by Pfrimer in September 1931. Pfrimer and his followers were brought to trial for treason, and acquitted. No effort was made to collect their arms, and it soon became clear that the Christian Socialist coalition, moved by their own sympathies and fear of Heimwehr violence, were opening an attack on the Social Democrats and the labor unions. These attacks were intensified after May 1932, when a new Cabinet, with Dollfuss as chancellor and Kurt Schuschnigg as minister of justice, took office. This Cabinet had only a one-vote majority in the Parliament, 83 for and 82 against, and was completely dependent on the 8 Heimwehr deputies which provided its majority. It would not call an election, because the Christian Socialists knew they would be overwhelmed. Since they were determined to rule, they continued to rule, illegally and eventually unconstitutionally.

Although the Nazis in Austria were growing stronger and more violent every day, the Christian-Socialist–Heimwehr coalition passed its time destroying the Social Democrats. The Heimwehr militia would attack the Socialists in the industrial parts of the cities, coming in by train from the rural areas for the purpose, and the Christian Socialist government would then suppress the Social Democrats for these "disorders." After one such affair, in October 1932, Dollfuss appointed the Heimwehr leader, Ernst Fey, as state secretary (later minister) for public security with command of all the police in Austria. This gave the Heimwehr, with 8 seats in Parliament, 3 seats in the Cabinet. Fey at once prohibited all meetings except by the Heimwehr. From that point on, the police systematically raided and destroyed Social Democrat and labor-union property—"searching for arms," they said. On March 4, 1933, the Dollfuss government was beaten in Parliament by one vote, 81–80. It threw out one vote on a technicality and used the resulting uproar as an excuse to prevent by force any more meetings of parliament.

Dollfuss ruled by decree, using a law of the Habsburg Empire of 1917. This law allowed the government to issue emergency economic decrees during the war if they were approved by parliament within a stated period subsequently. The Habsburg Empire and the war were both finished, and the decrees of Dollfuss were not concerned with economic matters nor were they accepted by Parliament within the stated period, but the government used this method to rule for years. The first decrees ended all meetings, censored the press, suspended local elections, created concentration camps, wrecked the finances of the city of Vienna by arbitrary interference with tax collections and expenditures, wrecked the supreme constitutional court to prevent it from reviewing the government's acts, and reestablished the death penalty. These decrees were generally enforced only against the Social Democrats and not against either the Nazis or the Heimwehr, who were reducing the country to chaos. When the Socialist mayor of Vienna disbanded the Heimwehr unit of that city, he was at once overruled by Dollfuss.

In May the Christian Socialist Party conference failed to elect Dollfuss as head of the party. He at once announced that parliament would never be restored and that all political parties would be absorbed gradually into a single new party, the "Fatherland Front." From this time on, Dollfuss and his successor Schuschnigg worked little by little to build up a personal dictatorship. This was not easy, as the effort was opposed by the Social Democrats (who insisted on a restoration of the constitution), by the Pan-Germans and their Nazi successors (who wanted union with Hitler's Germany), and by the Heimwehr (who were supported by Italy and wanted a Fascist state to dominate the Danube area).

While Dollfuss continued his attacks on the workers, the Nazis began to attack him and the Heimwehr. The Nazi movement in Austria was under direct orders from Germany and was financed from there. It engaged in wholesale attacks, parades, bombings, and murderous assaults on the government's supporters. In May 1933, Hitler crippled Austria financially by putting a 1,000-mark tax on all German tourists going to Austria. On June 19 Dollfuss outlawed the Nazis, arrested their leaders, and deported Hitler's "Inspector General for Austria." The Nazi Party went underground but continued its outrages, especially hundreds of bombings and thousands of acts of vandalism. In June 1933 they tried to murder Steidle and Rintelen, and in October they succeeded in wounding Dollfuss.

In the face of these Nazi atrocities, Dollfuss continued his methodical destruction of the Socialists. Since 1930, and probably since 1927, Mussolini had been arming Hungary and the Heimwehr in Austria. The Social Democrats, supported by Czechoslovakia and France, opposed this. In January 1933, the Socialist railway union revealed that a trainload of 50,000 rifles and 200 machine guns was en route from Mussolini to the Heimwehr and to Hungary. In the resulting controversy a joint Anglo-French note protesting this violation of the peace treaties and ordering the arms to be either returned to Italy or destroyed was rejected by Dollfuss. Instead, Dollfuss made an agreement with Mussolini for support against the Nazis through the Heimwehr and for destroying the Socialists in Austria. In March 1933, Dollfuss outlawed the Republican Defense Corps, the militia of the Socialist party, took the Heimwehr into his Cabinet, and ended Parliament.

Because the continued agitations of the Nazis in 1933 made necessary more support for Dollfuss from Mussolini and the Heimwehr, the government began to take steps to abolish the Socialist movement completely. At the end of January 1934, orders were issued to the Heimwehr, and they began to occupy union headquarters, Socialist buildings, and the city halls of various provincial cities. On February 10th Fey arrested most of the leaders of the Socialist militia, and the following day made a speech to the Heimwehr in which he said, "Chancellor Dollfuss is our man; tomorrow we shall go to work, and we shall make a thorough job of it."

Bloodshed had already occurred in the provinces, and, when on February 12th Fey attacked the workers in Vienna in their union centers, their Socialist headquarters, and their apartment houses, full-scale fighting broke out. The government had an overwhelming advantage, using the regular army, as well as the Heimwehr and police, and bringing up field artillery to smash the great apartment houses. By February 15th the fighting was finished, the Socialist party and their labor unions were outlawed, their newspapers declared illegal, hundreds were dead, thousands were in concentration camps and prisons, thousands more were reduced to economic want, the elective government of Vienna was replaced by a "federal commissar," all the workers' welfare, sports, and educational movements were wrecked, and the valuable properties of these organizations had been turned over to more favored organizations such as the Heimwehr and the Catholic groups. Soon afterward, rents were raised in the Socialist apartment houses, tenants were forced to pay for facilities which had previously been free (including garbage collection), workers were forced, in one way or another, to join the Fatherland Front, and even the Socialist workers were forced to seek jobs through the employment exchanges of the Catholic unions.

A new constitution was declared, under the emergency economic decree power of 1917, on April 24, 1934. It changed Austria from a "democratic republic" to a "Christian, German, corporative, federal state." This constitution was both fraudulent and illegal, and Dollfuss's efforts to make it more legal, if not less fraudulent, had the opposite result. Dollfuss had signed a concordant with the Vatican in June 1933. Since the Holy See wanted this agreement to be approved by Parliament, Dollfuss decided to kill several birds with one stone by convoking a rump of the old Parliament to accept this document, to terminate the disrupted sesssion of March 4, 1933, and to accept the 471 decrees he had issued since that date. Among these decrees was the new constitution of 1934. Since the government insisted that the old constitution had never been suspended or even violated, the new one had to be accepted either by a plebiscite or by a two-thirds vote of the old Parliament with at least half its members present. This was done on April 30, 1934, the various acts being accepted by a fraction of the old Parliament. Because the Socialists were prevented from attending, and the Pan-Germans refused to attend, only 76 out of 165 were present, and some of these voted against the acts proposed.

The new constitution was of no importance because the government continued to rule by decree, and violated it as it pleased. For example, a decree of June 19, 1934, deprived the courts of their constitutional power to rule on the constitutionality of all the government's acts before July 1, 1934.

The corporative aspect of the new constitution was a complete fraud. In many activities no corporations were set up; where they were set up, members were appointed and not elected as provided in law; and, in any case, they did nothing. Instead, the whole banking and industrial system was filled with the petty bureaucrats of the Fatherland Front. Because of mismanagement and the world depression, the banks of Austria collapsed in 1931–1933, precipitating the world banking crisis. The Austrian government took over these banks and gradually replaced their personnel, especially Jewish personnel, by party hacks. Since the banks controlled about 90 percent of the country's industrial corporations, these party hacks were able to place their friends throughout the economic system. By 1934 almost nothing could be done in the business world without "friends" in the government, and anything could be done with "friends." Such "friendship" was best obtained by bribery, with the result that periodical payments were being made from business to political figures. Early in 1936 the scandal broke when it was revealed that the Phoenix Insurance Company (of which Vaugoin, ex-chancellor and leader of the Christian Socialist party, was now president), had lost 250 million in gifts and "loans" corruptly given. The government had to admit this, and published a list of political groups and politicians who had received a total of less than 3 million schillings. This left most of the loss unexplained. It remained unexplained to the end. Legal proceedings were begun against twenty-seven persons, but the Schuschnigg government never brought any of them to trial.

This corruption spread through the government until finally a point was reached where, as Starhemberg put it, "No one knew whom he could trust, and there was justification for habouring the most amazing suspicions." Outrages by the Nazis increased in May and June 1934, to the point where bombings were averaging fifteen a day. On July 12th, by decree, the government fixed the death penalty for such bombings. The Nazis threatened a *Putsch* at the first such sentence. This first sentence was carried out on July 24th, but against a twenty-two-year-old *Socialist* after a summary trial. The same day the police and the Fatherland Front were notified by their spies that the Nazis were going to attack the next day. All the details were given to Fey, but he and Dollfuss spent the evening discussing a possible Socialist uprising. The Cabinet meeting of July 25th was postponed because of the warning, but no effort was made to protect the ministers. About 1:00 P.M. 154 Nazis in eight trucks rushed into the chancellory without a shot being fired. They at once murdered Dollfuss and locked themselves in. Another group of Nazis seized the radio station of Vienna and announced a new government with Rintelen as chancellor. There were also sporadic Nazi uprisings in which scores were killed in the provinces. The Nazi "Austrian Legion" in Germany and the German government did not dare to move because of a stern warning from Mussolini that he would invade Austria from the south if they did.

After six hours of negotiations in which Fey and the German minister acted as intermediaries, the besieged men in the chancellery were removed to be deported to Germany. When Dollfuss was found to be dead, thirteen were executed and a large number imprisoned; all the Nazi organizations were closed and their activities suspended. At the same time, those who had tried to warn the government against the plot or to prevent it were arrested and some were killed (including the police spy who had sent the specific details the day before the crime).

Schuschnigg and the Heimwehr split the government between them after Dollfuss's death. Each took four seats in the Cabinet. Schuschnigg was chancellor in the government and vice-leader of the Fatherland Front, while Starhemberg was leader of the Fatherland Front and vice-chancellor of the government.

From July 1934 on, Schuschnigg sought to get rid of the Heimwehr, especially Starhemberg, to create a purely personal dictatorship with only one party, one trade union, and one policy, to satisfy the Nazis without yielding any essential power or positions, to keep the Socialists crushed, and to get as much support from Mussolini as he could.

We have said that Dollfuss and Schuschnigg were faced by three opponents in 1932: the Socialists, the Nazis, and the Heimwehr. They sought to destroy these in this order by mobilizing against each the power of the ones not yet destroyed, plus the Christian Socialists. As the effort progressed, they tried to destroy the Christian Socialists as well, by driving all groups into a single amorphous and meaningless political party, the Fatherland Front. This party's purpose was to mobilize support for these two leaders personally. It had no real political principles and was completely undemocratic, being bound to accept the decisions of the "leader." All persons, no matter what their political beliefs, even Nazis, Catholics, Communists, and Socialists, were forced to join by political, social, and economic pressure. The result was that all political morale was destroyed, public integrity was wrecked, and many among the politically active portions of the population were driven to the two underground extremist groups, the Nazis and the Communists, to the former in much larger numbers than to the latter. Even the Socialists, in order to prevent the loss of their angry members to the Communists, had to adopt a more revolutionary attitude. Because everything was driven underground, and the field was left to meaningless slogans, crass materialist advantages, and pious expressions of righteousness, no one knew what anyone's real thoughts were or whom they could trust.

The loss of Italian support for the Heimwehr and for an independent Austria after the Ethiopian affair made it possible for Schuschnigg to get rid of Starhemberg and his militia and made it necessary to conciliate the Nazis. Fey was dropped from the government in October 1935. A political supplement to the Rome Protocols was signed by Austria, Italy, and Hungary on March 23, 1936; it provided that no signer would enter an agreement with a nonsignatory state to change the political situation of the Danube area without consultation with the other signers. In April Austria copied Germany, and further alienated France and the Little Entente, by decreeing the establishment of general military service. In the same month, Schuschnigg ordered the disarmament of the Catholic militia. In May 1936 three Heimwehr members, including Starhemberg, were dropped from the Cabinet, and Starhemberg was removed as leader of the Fatherland Front. A week later a series of decrees ordered the disarmament of the Heimwehr, created an armed militia for the Fatherland Front as the sole armed militia in the country, ordered that in the future the leader of the Front and the chancellor must be the same person, gave the chancellor the right to appoint the heads of all local political units and to approve their appointments, prohibited all parades and assemblies until September 30th, and declared that the Fatherland Front was "an authoritarian foundation," a legal person, and "the sole instrument for the formation of political will in the state."

Thus "strengthened" in Austria, and under pressure from Mussolini to make peace with Hitler, Schuschnigg signed an agreement of July 11, 1936, with Franz von Papen, the German minister. According to the published portion of this agreement, Germany recognized Austrian independence and sovereignty; each country promised not to interfere in the domestic politics of the other; Austria admitted it was a German state; and additional agreements to relieve the existing tension were promised. In secret agreements made at the same time, Austria promised an amnesty for political prisoners, promised to take Nazis into positions of "political responsibility," to allow them the same political rights as other Austrians, and to allow Germans in Austria the same rights to use their national symbols and music as citizens of third states. Both states revoked financial and other restrictions on tourists. Mutual prohibition on each other's newspapers were lifted to the extent that five specifically named German papers could enter Austria and five named Austrian papers could enter Germany. Other paragraphs promised mutual concessions in regard to economic and cultural relations.

Austro-German relations for the next eighteen months were dominated by this agreement, Germany, through Papen, trying to extend it bit by bit, while Schuschnigg sought to hold Germany to its recognition of Austrian sovereignty and its promise not to interfere in Austria's domestic political affairs. By the end of that period Germany was insisting that, since the Austrian Nazis were Germans, their desires and activities were not an Austrian, but a German, domestic problem.

The secret documents published since 1945 make it quite clear that Germany had no carefully laid plans to annex Austria, and was not encouraging violence by the Nazis in Austria. Instead, every effort was made to restrict the Austrian Nazis to propaganda in order to win places in the Cabinet and a gradual peaceful extension of Nazi influence. At the same time, military measures were held in reserve, prepared for use if necessary. To be sure, wild men on the lower levels of the Nazi Party in Germany were encouraging all kinds of violence in Austria, but this was not true of the real leaders. These ordered von Papen to try to get at least two years of peace in 1936, and they removed the Austrian Nazi wild men who opposed this from their positions of leadership. In this way the violent Tavs Plan of the Austrian Nazis was replaced by the Keppler Plan of peaceful and gradual penetration through Papen and the Austrian politician Artur von Seyss-Inquart.

The invasion of Austria as early as March 12, 1938, and the immediate annexation of Austria were a pleasant surprise, even for the Nazi leaders in Germany, and arose from several unexpectedly favorable circumstances. Accordingly, the decision to invade was not made before March 10, 1938, and even then was conditional, while the decision to annex was not made until noon on March 12th by Hitler personally and was unknown to both Ribbentrop and Göring as late as 10:30 P.M. on March 12th. The circumstances which brought this unexpected speedup in the German plans were based on two facts: (1) the international situation and (2) the events in Austria. We shall discuss these in order.

As far as obvious political events are concerned, 1937 was the only quiet year after 1933. But the capture and release of various secret documents now make it clear that 1937 was a critical turning point because in that year the German government and the British government made secret decisions which sealed the fate of Austria and Czechoslovakia and dominated the history of the next three years.

The decision made by the German government (that is, by Hitler) was to prepare for open military aggression against Czechoslovakia and Austria and to carry this out before 1943–1945, probably in 1938. This decision was announced by Hitler to a secret meeting of seven persons on November 5, 1937. Among those present, besides Hitler and his aide, Colonel Hossback, were the minister of war (Werner von Blomberg), the commanders in chief of the army (Werner von Fritsch), the navy (Erich Raeder), and the air force (Hermann Göring), and the foreign minister (Konstantin von Neurath). It is evident from some of Hitler's statements that he had already received certain information about the secret decisions being made by Chamberlain on the British side; for example, he said flatly that Britain wanted to satisfy the colonial ambitions of Germany by giving it non-British areas like Portuguese Angola, something which we now know was in Chamberlain's mind. Hitler further assured his listeners that "almost certainly Britain, and probably France as well, had already tacitly written off the Czechs and were reconciled to the fact that this question would be cleared up in due course by Germany. . . . An attack by France without British support, and with the prospect of the offensive being brought to a standstill on our western fortifications, was hardly probable. Nor was a French march through Belgium and Holland without British support to be expected."

Hitler thought that, by reducing German support for Franco in Spain, the war there could be extended, and, by encouraging Italy to stay in Spain, especially in the Balearic Islands, the French African troops could be kept from crossing the Mediterranean Sea for use in Europe, and in general that France and Britain would be so tied down in the Mediterranean by Italy that they would take no action against Germany over Czechoslovakia and Austria. In fact, Hitler was so sure of an Anglo-French war against Italy in 1938 that he was confident Czechoslovakia and Austria could be conquered by Germany in that year.

These ideas were completely unacceptable to Blomberg, Fritsch, and Neurath. They objected that German rearmament was so backward that they did not have a single motorized division capable of movement, that there was no reason to expect an Anglo-French–Italian war in 1938, that Italy, in such a war, could tie down only twenty French divisions, leaving more than enough to attack Germany, and that such an attack would be very dangerous because Germany's fortifications on her western frontier were "insignificant." Hitler brushed these objections aside. He "repeated his previous statements that he was convinced of Britain's non-participation, and, therefore, he did not believe in the probability of belligerent action by France against Germany."

As a result of the opposition from Blomberg, Fritsch, and Neurath in this conference of November 1937, Hitler replaced these three by more amenable subordinates in a sudden coup on February 4, 1938. Hitler himself took the posts of minister of war and commander in chief, with General Wilhelm Keitel as chief of staff for all the armed forces of the Reich. Neurath was replaced in the Foreign Ministry by the fanatical Ribbentrop. The very able Dirksen was sent to London as ambassador, but his ability was wasted, as Ribbentrop paid no attention to his reports and his well-founded warnings.

In the meantime the British government, especially the small group controlling foreign policy, had reached a seven-point decision regarding their attitude toward Germany:

1. Hitler Germany was the front-line bulwark against the spread of Communism in Europe.

2. A four-Power pact of Britain, France, Italy, and Germany to exclude all Russian influence from Europe was the ultimate aim; accordingly, Britain had no desire to weaken the Rome-Berlin Axis, but regarded it and the Anglo-French Entente as the foundation of a stable Europe.

3. Britain had no objection to German acquisition of Austria, Czechoslovakia, and Danzig.

4. Germany must not use force to achieve its aims in Europe, as this would precipitate a war in which Britain would have to intervene because of the pressure of public opinion in Britain and the French system of alliances; with patience, Germany could get its aims without using force.

5. Britain wanted an agreement with Germany restricting the numbers and the use of bombing planes.

6. Britain was prepared to give Germany colonial areas in south-central Africa, including the Belgian Congo and Portuguese Angola if Germany would renounce its desire to recover Tanganyika, which had been taken from Germany in 1919, and if Germany would sign an international agreement to govern these areas with due regard for the rights of the natives, an "open-door" commerical policy, and under some mechanism of international supervision like the mandates.

7. Britain would use pressure on Czechoslovakia and Poland to negotiate with Germany and to be conciliatory to Germany's desires.

To these seven points we should add an eighth: Britain must rearm in order to maintain its position in a "three-bloc world" and to deter Germany from using force in creating its bloc in Europe. This point was supported by Chamberlain, who built up the air force which saved Britain in 1940, and by the Round Table Group led by Lord Lothian, Edward Grigg, and Leopold Amery, who put on a campaign to establish compulsory military service.

The first seven points were reiterated to Germany by various spokesmen from 1937 onward. They are also to be found in many recently published documents, including the captured archives of the German Foreign Ministry, the documents of the British Foreign Office, and various extracts from diaries and other private papers, especially extracts from Neville Chamberlain's diary and his letters to his sister. Among numerous other occasions these points were covered in the following cases: (a) in a conversation between Lord Halifax and Hitler at Berchtesgaden on November 17, 1938; (b) in a letter from Neville Chamberlain to his sister on November 26, 1937; (c) in a conversation between Hitler, Ribbentrop, and the British Ambassador (Sir Nevile Henderson) in Berlin on March 3, 1938; (d) in a series of conversations involving Lord Halifax, Ribbentrop, Sir Thomas Inskip (British minister of defense), Erich Kordt (Ribbentrop's assistant), and Sir Horace Wilson (Chamberlain's personal representative) in London on March 10–11, 1938; and (e) in a conference of Neville Chamberlain with various North American journalists held at Lord Astor's house on May 10, 1938. In addition, portions of these seven points were mentioned or discussed in scores of conversations and documents which are now available.

Certain significant features of these should be pointed out. In the first place, in spite of persistent British efforts lasting for more than two years, Hitler rejected Angola or the Congo and insisted on the return of the German colonies which had been lost in 1919. During 1939 Germany steadily refused to negotiate on this issue and finally refused even to acknowledge the British efforts to discuss it. In the second place, the British throughout these discussions made a sharp distinction between Germany's aims and Germany's methods. They had no objections to Germany's aims in Europe, but they insisted that Germany must not use force to achieve these aims because of the danger of war. This distinction was accepted by the German professional diplomats and by the German professional soldiers, who were quite willing to obtain Germany's aims by peaceful means, but this distinction was not accepted by the leaders of the Nazi Party, especially Hitler, Ribbentrop, and Himmler, who were too impatient and who wanted to prove to themselves and the world that Germany was powerful enough to take what it wanted without waiting for anybody's permission.

These wild men were encouraged in this attitude by their belief that Britain and France were so "decadent" that they would stand for anything, and by their failure to see the role played by public opinion in England. Convinced that the governing group in England wanted Germany to get Austria, Czechoslovakia, and Danzig, they could not understand why there was such an emphasis on using peaceful methods, and they could not see how British public opinion could force the British government to go to war over the methods used when the British government made it perfectly clear that the last thing that they wanted was a war. This error was based on the fact that these Nazis had no idea of how a democratic government works, had no respect for public opinion or a free press, and were encouraged in their error by the weakness of the British ambassador in Berlin (Henderson) and by Rippentrop's associations with the "Cliveden Set" in England while he had been ambassador there in 1936-1938.

In the third place, the British government could not publicly admit to its own people these "seven points" because they were not acceptable to British public opinion. Accordingly, these points had to remain secret, except for various "trial balloons" issued through *The Times*, in speeches in the House of Commons or in Chatham House, in articles in *The Round Table* and by calculated indiscretions to prepare the ground for what was being done. In order to persuade the British people to accept these points, one by one, as they were achieved, the British government spread the tale that Germany was armed to the teeth and that the opposition to Germany was insignificant.

This propaganda first appeared in the effusions of the Round Table Group whose leader, Lord Lothian, has visited Hitler in January 1935, and had been pushing this seven-point program in *The Times*, in *The Round Table*, at Chatham House and All Souls, and with Lord Halifax. In the December 1937 issue of *The Round Table*, where most of the seven points which Halifax had just discussed with Hitler were mentioned, a war to prevent Germany's ambitions in Europe was rejected on the grounds that its "outcome is uncertain" and that it "would entail objectionable domestic disasters." In adding up the balance of military forces in such a war, it gave a preponderance to Germany, by omitting both Russia and Czechoslovakia and by estimating the French Army at only two-thirds the size of the German and placing the British Army at less than three divisions. By the spring of 1938 this completely erroneous view of the situation was being propagated by the government itself.

For years before June 1938, the government insisted that British rearming was progressing in a satisfactory fashion. Churchill and others questioned this, and produced figures on German rearmament to prove that Britain's own progress in this field was inadequate. These figures (which were not correct) were denied by the government, and their own rearmament defended. As late as March 1938, Chamberlain said that British armament were such as to make Britain an "almost terrifying power . . . on the opinion of the world." But, as the year went on, the government adopted a quite different attitude. In order to persuade public opinion that it was necessary to yield to Germany, the government and its supporters pretended that its armaments were quite inadequate in comparison with Germany.

We now know, thanks to the captured papers of the German Ministry of War, that this was a gross exaggeration. From 1936 to the outbreak of war in 1939, German aircraft production was not raised, but averaged 425 planes a month of all types (including commercial). Its tank production was low, and even in 1939 was less than Britain's. In the first nine months of 1939 Germany produced only 50 tanks a month; in the last four months of 1939, in wartime, Germany produced 247 "tanks and self-propelled guns," compared to British production of 314 tanks in the same period. At the time of the Munich Crisis in 1938, Germany had 35 infantry and 4 motorized divisions none of them fully manned or equipped. At that time Czechoslovakia could mobilize at least 33 divisions. Moreover, the Czech Army was better trained, had far better equipment, and had better morale and better fortifications. At that time Germany's tanks were all below 10 tons and were armed with machine guns, except for a handful of 18-ton tanks (Mark III) armed with a 37-mm. gun. The Czechs had hundreds of 38-ton tanks armed with 75-mm. cannon. In March 1939, when Germany overran Czechoslovakia, it captured 469 of these superior tanks along with 1,500 planes, 43,000 machine guns, and over 1 million rifles. From every point of view this was little less than Germany had at Munich, and, at Munich, if the British government had desired it, Germany's 39 divisions with the possible assistance of Poland and Hungary, would have been opposed by Czechoslovakia's 34 divisions supported by France, Britain, and Russia.

Before leaving this subject it should perhaps be mentioned that Germany in 1939 brought into production a Mark IV tank of 23 tons armed with a 75-mm. cannon but obtained only 300 of the Mark III and Mark IV together before the outbreak of war in September, 1939. In addition, it had obtained by the same date 2,700 of the inferior Mark I and Mark II tanks which suffered breakdowns of as much as 25 percent a week. At this same date (September 1939) Germany had an air force of 1,000 bombers and 1,050 fighters. In contrast with this, the British air program of March 1934, which emphasized fighter planes, was to provide a first-line force of 900 planes. This was stepped up, under the urging of Chamberlain, and the program of May 1938 was planned to provide a first-line force of 2,370 planes. This was raised again in 1939. Under it, Britain produced almost 3,000 "military" planes in 1938 and about 8,000 in 1939 compared to 3,350 "combat" planes produced in Germany in 1938 and 4,733 in 1939. Moreover, the quality of British planes was superior to that of Germany's. It was this margin which made it possible for Britain to defeat Germany in the Battle of Britain in September 1940.

From these facts it is quite clear that Britain did not yield to superior force in 1938, as was stated at the time and has been stated since by many writers, including Winston Churchill, whose war memoirs were written two years after the Reichswehr archives were captured. We have evidence that the Chamberlain government knew these facts but consistently gave a contrary impression and that Lord Halifax went so far in this direction as to call forth protests from the British military attachés in Prague and Paris.

The Chamberlain government made it clear to Germany both publicly and privately that they would not oppose Germany's projects. As Dirksen wrote to Ribbentrop on June 8, 1938, "Anything which can be got without a shot being fired can count upon the agreement of the British." Accordingly, it was clear that Britain would not oppose the annexation of Austria, although they continued to warn vigorously against any effort to use force. In February 1938, Sir John Simon and Chamberlain announced in the House of Commons that neither the League of Nations nor Great Britain could be expected to support Austrian independence; on February 12th Hitler told Schuschnigg that Lord Halifax agreed "with everything he [Hitler] did with respect to Austria and the Sudeten Germans." On March 3rd Nevile Henderson told Hitler that changes in Europe were acceptable if accomplished without "the free play of force" and that he personally "had often expressed himself in favor of the Anschluss." Finally, on March 7th, when the crisis was at its height, Chamberlain in the House of Commons refused to guarantee Austria or any small nation. This statement was made to the cheers of the government supporters. The following day the Foreign Office sent a message to its missions in Europe in which it stated its "inability to guarantee protection" to Austria. This made it so clear to Hitler that Britain would not move that his orders to invade Austria also ordered no precautions to be taken by the defense forces on Germany's other frontiers (March 11, 1938). In fact, Hitler was considerably more worried about Italy than he was about Britain and France, in spite of Mussolini's agreement of September 1937 to support Germany's ambitions in Austria in return for German support of his ambitions in the Mediterranean.

Although the international stage had been set, the invasion and annexation would not have come about in March had it not been for conditions in Austria, especially Schuschnigg's determination to prevent the execution of the Keppler Plan for Nazi penetration of the Austrian government. As soon as he extended one concession, he took away another, so that the Nazi position became a bitter joke. At last Papen persuaded Schuschnigg to visit Hitler at Berchtesgaden on February 12, 1938. There the Austrian chancellor was upbraided by an enraged Hitler and forced to sign a new agreement which did much to fulfill the Keppler Plan. Although no ultimatum was given to Schuschnigg, it was made quite clear that, if peaceful methods did not work, warlike ones would be used. Schuschnigg promised (1) to appoint Seyss-Inquart, a Nazi, as minister of security with unlimited control of the police in Austria; (2) to release from prison and to restore to their positions all Nazis who were being held, including the rebels of July 1934; (3) to exchange one hundred army officers with Germany; (4) to permit Nazis in Austria to profess their creed and join the Fatherland Front with the same rights as others, the Nazi Party to remain illegal. In return, Hitler repeated the agreement of July 11, 1936.

On his return to Austria, Schuschnigg put these concessions into effect piecemeal without any public statement, but he was still determined to resist. On March 2nd he began to negotiate with the long-outlawed Socialist groups, and on March 9th he suddenly announced a plebiscite for Sunday, March 13th. This plebiscite, as planned, was completely unfair. There was only one question, which asked the voter, "Are you for a free and German, independent and social, Christian and united Austria, for peace and work, for the equality of all those who affirm themselves for the people and the Fatherland?" There were no voting lists; only *yes* ballots were to be provided by the government; anyone wishing to vote *no* had to provide his own ballot, the same size as the *yes* ballots, with nothing on it but the word *no*.

The Nazis were outraged. Through Seyss-Inquart, Hitler sent an ultimatum that the plebiscite must be postponed and replaced by one in which the opposite point of view (union with Germany) could be expressed as well. As the day passed (March 11th), these German demands were increased. In the afternoon, as the German Army was marching toward the frontier, came the demand for Schuschnigg to resign and for Seyss-Inquart to become chancellor. If an affirmative answer came before 7:30 P.M. the invasion was to be stopped. Schuschnigg resigned, but

President Miklas refused to name Seyss-Inquart chancellor until 11:00 P.M. By that time the Germany forces were crossing the border, and their advance could not be stopped. Orders had been given to the Austrians not to resist, and the Germans were generally welcomed. Göring demanded a telegram from Seyss-Inquart asking for German troops to restore order and thus justify the invasion. He never got it, so he wrote one himself.

The lack of resistance, the welcome from the Austrians, and the inaction of Italy and the Western Powers encouraged the Germans to increase their ambitions. During most of March 12th they were talking about an early withdrawal after the Seyss-Inquart government was established, but the uproarious welcome given Hitler at Linz on that day, the need for such Austrian products as wood, the manpower available in Austria's half-million unemployed, the opportunity to plunder the Jews, and the complete lack of opposition decided Hitler to annex Austria. This was done on March 13th, and a plebiscite was ordered for April 10th to approve the action. In the meantime, those who had opposed the Nazis were murdered or enslaved, the Jews were plundered and abused, and extravagant honors were paid to the Nazi gangsters who had been disturbing Austria for years. The plebiscite of April 10th, under great pressure from the Nazis, showed over 99 percent of the Germans in favor of the Anschluss.

The Czechoslovak Crisis, 1937-1938

Czechoslovakia was the most prosperous, most democratic, most powerful, and best administered of the states which arose on the ruins of the Habsburg Empire. As created in 1919, this country was shaped like a tadpole and was made up of four main portions. These were, from west to east, Bohemia, Moravia, Slovakia, and Ruthenia. It had a population of 15,000,000 of which 3,400,000 were Germans, 6,000,000 were Czechs, 3,000,000 were Slovaks, 750,000 were Hungarians, 100,000 were Poles, and 500,000 were Ruthenians. In general, these people lived on a higher level of education, culture, economic life, and progressiveness as we move from east to west, the Germans and Czechs being on a high level, while the Slovaks and Ruthenians were on a lower level.

The large number of minorities, and especially the large number of Germans, arose from the need to give the country defensible and viable frontiers. On the northwest the obvious strategic frontier was along the Sudeten Mountains, and, to secure this, it was necessary to put into Czechoslovakia the large number of Germans on the south side of these mountains. These Germans objected to this, although they had never been part of Germany itself, because they regarded all Slavs as inferior people and because their economic position was threatened. The Sudeten area had been the most industrialized portion of the Habsburg Empire, and found its markets restricted by the new territorial divisions. Moreover, the agrarian reforms of the new republic, while not aimed at the Germans, injured them more than others just because they had formed an upper class. This economic discontent became stronger after the onset of the world depression in 1929 and especially after Hitler demonstrated that his policies could bring prosperity to Germany. On the other hand, the minorities of Czechoslovakia were the best-treated minorities in Europe, and their agitations were noticeable precisely because they were living in a democratic liberal state which gave them freedom to agitate.

Among the Germans of the Sudetenland, only part were Nazis, but these were noisy, well organized, and financed from Berlin. Their numbers grew steadily, especially after the Austrian *Anschluss*. The Nazi Party in Czechoslovakia was banned in 1934 but, under Konrad Henlein, merely changed its name to the Sudeten German Party. With 600,000 members, it polled 1,200,000 votes in the election of May 1935 and obtained 44 seats in the Parliament, only one less than the largest party. As soon as Edward Beneš succeeded Tomáš Masaryk as president of Czechoslovakia in 1935, he took steps to conciliate the Sudetens, offering them, for example, places in the administration proportionate to their percentage of the total population. This was not acceptable to the Germans because it would have given them only one-fifth of the places in their own area, where they were over 90 percent of the population, as well as one-fifth in Slovakia, where they had no interest at all.

In 1937 the prime minister, Milan Hodža, offered to transfer all the Germans in the national administration to the Sudeten areas and to train others until the whole bureaucracy in these areas was German. None of these suggestions was acceptable to Konrad Henlein for the simple reason that he wanted no concessions within Czechoslovakia, however extensive; his real desire was to destroy the Czechoslovak state. Since he could not admit this publicly, although he did admit it in his letters to Hitler in 1937, he had to continue to negotiate, raising his demands as the government made larger concessions. These concessions were a danger to the state because the fortified zone against Germany ran along the mountains and thus right through the Sudetenland. Every concession to the Sudetens thus weakened the country's ability to defend itself against attack. These two facts made all efforts to compromise with Henlein futile from the beginning, and made the constant British pressure on the

Czech government to give additional concessions worse than futile. It is worthy to note that no public demand was made by either Henlein or Germany to detach the Sudetenland from Czechoslovakia until after September 12, 1938, although influential persons in the British government were advocating this, both in public and private, for months before this date.

The Czech strength rested on its army of approximately thirty-three divisions, which was the best in Europe in quality, the excellent fortification system, and its alliances with France, the Soviet Union, and the Little Entente. The annexation of Austria surrounded Bohemia with German territory on three sides, but its position, from a military point of view, was still strong. A line drawn from Berlin to Vienna would pass by Prague, but the German Army could not safely invade Bohemia across its weakly fortified southern frontier with Austria because of the danger of a Czech counterattack from its fortified base into Bavaria.

Within two weeks of Hitler's annexation of Austria, Britain was moving. It was decided to put pressure on the Czechs to make concessions to the Germans; to encourage France and eventually Germany to do the same; to insist that Germany must not use force to reach a decision, but to have patience enough to allow negotiations to achieve the same result; and to exclude Russia, although it was allied to Czechoslovakia, from the negotiations completely. All this was justified by the arguments that Czechoslovakia, in a war with Germany, would be smashed immediately, that Russia was of no military value whatever and would not honor its alliance with the Czechs anyway, and that Germany would be satisfied if it obtained the Sudetenland and the Polish Corridor. All these assumptions were very dubious, but they were assiduously propagated both in public and in private and may, at times, even have convinced the speakers themselves.

The group which spread this version of the situation included Chamberlain, Lord Halifax, John Simon, Samuel Hoare, Horace Wilson, the Cliveden Set, the British ambassador in Berlin (Sir Nevile Henderson), and the British minister in Prague (Basil Newton). To make their aims more appealing they emphasized the virtues of "autonomy" and "self-determination" and the contribution to European peace which would arise if Germany were satisfied and if Czechoslovakia were "neutralized like Switzerland" and "guaranteed like Belgium." By "neutralization" they meant that Czechoslovakia must renounce its alliances with the Soviet Union and with France. By "guaranteed" they meant that the rump of Czechoslovakia which was left after the Sudetenland went to Germany would be guaranteed by France and Germany but emphatically not by Britain.

How Czechoslovakia could be guaranteed against Germany by France alone after its defenses had been destroyed, when it could not, according to Britain, be defended in 1938 when its defenses were intact, and when it would be supported by France, the Soviet Union, and Britain, is only one of the numerous British illogicalities displayed in this crisis. Nevertheless, Britain was able to win support for these plans, especially in France where Foreign Minister Georges Bonnet and Prime Minister Edouard Daladier reluctantly accepted them.

In France, fear of war was rampant. Moreover, in France, even more obviously than in England, fear of Bolshevism was a powerful factor, especially in influential circles of the Right. The ending of the Soviet Alliance, the achievement of a four-Power pact, and the termination of Czechoslovakia as "a spearhead of Bolshevism in central Europe" had considerable appeal to those conservative circles which regarded the Popular Front government of Léon Blum as "a spearhead of Bolshevism" in France itself. To this group, as to a less vociferous group in Britain, even a victory over Hitler in war to save Czechoslovakia would have been a defeat for their aims, not so much because they disliked democracy and admired authoritarian reaction (which was true) as because they were convinced that the defeat of Hitler would expose all of central, and perhaps western, Europe to Bolshevism and chaos. The slogan of these people, "Better Hitler than Blum," became increasingly prevalent in the course of 1938 and, although nothing quite like this was heard in Britain, the idea behind it was not absent from that country. In this dilemma the "three-bloc world" of the Cliveden Set or even the German-Soviet war of the antiBolsheviks seemed to be the only solution. Because both required the elimination of Czechoslovakia from the European power system, Czechoslovakia was eliminated with the help of German aggression, French indecision and war-weariness, and British public appeasement and merciless secret pressure.

There is no need to follow the interminable negotiations between Henlein and the Czech government, negotiations in which Britain took an active role from March 1938 to the end. Plan after plan for minority rights, economic concessions, cultural and administrative autonomy, and even political federalism were produced by the Czechs, submitted to Britain and Germany, and eventually brushed aside as inadequate by Henlein. The latter's "Karlsbad Demands," enunciated on April 24th after Henlein's conference with Hitler, were extreme. They began with an introduction denouncing the Czechs and the Czechoslovak state, insisting that the country must abandon its foreign policy and cease to be an obstacle to the German "Drive to the East." They then enumerated eight demands. Among these we find (1) complete equality between Czechs and Germans, (2) recognition of the German group as a corporation with legal personality, (3) demarcation of the German areas, (4) full self-government in those areas, (5) legal protection for citizens outside those areas, (6) reparation for damages inflicted by the Czechs on the Sudetens since 1918, (7) German officials in German areas, and (8) full freedom to profess German nationality and German political philosophy. There is here no hint of revision of the frontiers, yet when, after long weeks of negotiations, the Czech government substantially conceded these points under severe pressure from Britain, Henlein broke off the negotiations and fled to Germany (September 7-12, 1938).

As early as March 17, 1938, five days after the *Anschluss*, the Soviet government called for consultations looking toward collective actions to stop aggression and to eliminate the increased danger of a new world slaughter. This was summarily rejected by Lord Halifax. Instead, on March 24th, Chamberlain announced in the House of Commons Britain's refusal to pledge aid to the Czechs if they were attacked or to France if it came to their rescue. When the Soviet request was repeated in September 1938, it was ignored.

The French prime minister and the French foreign minister went to London at the end of April and tried to get Britain to agree to three things: (1) naval conversations aiming to ensure France's ability to transport its African troops to France in a crisis; (2) economic support for the Little Entente to save them from German economic pressure; and (3) a promise that if Anglo-French pressure on Czechoslovakia resulted in extensive concessions to the Sudetens and Germany then refused these concessions and tried to destroy the Czech state, an Anglo-French guarantee would then be given to Czechoslovakia. The first two of these were postponed and the third was refused. It was also made clear to the French that, in the event of any British-French war against Germany, Britain's contribution to this joint effort would be restricted to the air, since this was the only way in which Britain itself could be attacked, although it might be possible at some time to send two divisions to France. When the French tried to obtain assurance that these two divisions would be motorized, it was reiterated that these units were not being promised but were merely a possible future contribution and that no assurance could be given that they would be motorized. The violence of these Anglo-French discussions is not reflected in the minutes published by the British government in 1949. The day after they ended, Chamberlain wrote to his sister, "Fortunately the papers have had no hint of how near we came to a break [with the French] over Czechoslovakia."

It is clear from the evidence that Chamberlain was determined to write off the Sudetenland and not to go to war with Germany unless public opinion in England compelled it. In fact, he felt that Germany could impose its will upon Czechoslovakia by economic pressure alone, although he did not go so far as to say, with Sir Nevile Henderson and Lord Halifax, that this method could be successful "in a short time." "If Germany adopted this course," according to Chamberlain, "no *casus belli* would then arise under the terms of the Franco-Czechoslovak treaty, and Germany would be able to accomplish everything she required without moving a single soldier." If Germany did decide to destroy Czechoslovakia, he did not see how this could be prevented. But he "did not believe that Germany wanted to destroy Czechoslovakia." Accordingly, by putting Anglo-French pressure on the Czechs to negotiate, it would be possible "to save something of Czechoslovakia and in particular to save the existence of the Czechoslovak State." In any case, he was determined not to go to war over it, because nothing could prevent Germany from achieving immediate victory over the Czechs and, even if the Germans were subsequently defeated after a long war, there was no guarantee that Czechoslovakia could be reestablished in its existing form.

Chamberlain's point of view (which was the decisive force in this whole crisis) was presented in more positive terms to a group of North American journalists at a luncheon at Lady Astor's house on May 10, 1938: he wanted a four-Power pact, the exclusion of Russia from Europe, and frontier revisions of Czechoslovakia in favor of Germany. Since these things could not be obtained immediately, he kept up the intense diplomatic pressure on Czechoslovakia to make concessions to the Sudeten Germans. Under French pressure he also asked Germany what it wanted in this problem, but, until September, obtained no answer, on the grounds that this was a question to be settled by the Sudetens and the Czechs.

In the meantime, the German occupation of Austria changed the strategic situation for Germany so that it was necessary for Hitler to modify his general order to the armed forces for operational plans against France, Czechoslovakia, and Austria. These orders had been issued on June 24, 1937. The new directive, as drafted by General Keitel on May 20, 1938, and submitted for Hitler's signature, began, "It is not my intention to smash Czechoslovakia by military action in the immediate future without provocation, unless an unavoidable development of the political conditions *within* Czechoslovakia forces the issue, or political events in Europe create a particularly favorable opportunity which may perhaps never recur."

This draft was entirely rewritten by Hitler and signed on May 30, 1938. Its opening sentence then read, "It is my unalterable decision to smash Czechoslovakia by military action in the near future." It then went on to say that in case of war with Czechoslovakia, whether France intervened or not, all forces would be concentrated on the Czechs in order to achieve an impressive success in the first three days. The general strategic plan based on this order provided that forces would be transferred to the French frontier only after a "decisive" blow against Czechoslovakia. No provision was made for war against the Soviet Union (except for naval activity in the Baltic), and all regular forces were to be withdrawn from East Prussia in order to speed up the defeat of the Czechs. X-day was set for October 1st, with deployment of troops to begin on September 28th.

These orders were so unrealistic that the German military leaders were aghast. They realized that the reality was so different from Hitler's picture of it that Germany would be defeated fairly readily in any war likely to arise over Czechoslovakia. All their efforts to make Hitler see the reality were completely unsuccessful and, as the crisis continued, they became more and more desperate until, by the end of August, they were in a panic. This feeling was shared by the whole Foreign Ministry except Ribbentrop himself. Hitler was isolated in his mountain retreat, living in a dream world and very short-tempered. He was cut off from outside contacts by Ribbentrop, Himmler, and Hess, who told him that Russia, France, and Britain would not fight and that the Czechs were bluffing. One of the mysteries yet remaining is why Ribbentrop was so sure that Britain would not fight. He was right.

The German generals tried to dissuade Hitler from his project, and, when they found that they had no influence over him, they persuaded various important people who saw him to intervene for the same purpose. Thus, they were able to get Admiral Miklós Horthy, Regent of Hungary, to try to influence the Führer during his visit of August 21-26, 1938. Hitler interrupted by shouting, "Nonsense! Shut up!" The generals and several important civil leaders then formed a conspiracy led by General Ludwig Beck (chief of the General Staff). All the important generals were in it, including General Erwin Witzleben (governor of Berlin) and General Georg Thomas (chief of supply). Among the civil leaders were Baron Ernst von Weizsäcker (state secretary in the Foreign Ministry), Erich Kordt (head of Ribbentrop's office), and Ulrich von Hassell (ambassador to Rome, 1932–1938). Their plot had three stages in it: (1) to exert every effort to make Hitler see the truth; (2) to inform the British of their efforts and beg them to stand firm on the Czechoslovak issue and to tell the German government that Britain would fight if Hitler made war on Czechoslovakia; (3) to assassinate Hitler if he nevertheless issued the order to attack Czechoslovakia. Although message after message was sent to Britain in the first two weeks of September, by Weizsäcker, by Kordt, by the generals, and by others in separate missions, the British refused to cooperate. As a result, the plan was made to assassinate Hitler as soon as the attack was ordered. This project was canceled at noon on September 28, 1938, when news reached Berlin that Chamberlain was going to Munich to yield. The attack order was to have been given by Hitler at 2:00 P.M. that day.

In the meantime the Czechs were negotiating with Konrad Henlein in an effort to reach some compromise less radical than his Karlsbad demands. Pressure was exercised on the Czechs by Britain and France.

From May 31st onward, Lord Halifax tried to force France to threaten the Czechs that their alliance would be revoked or at least weakened if they did not make concessions to the Sudetens. This threat was finally made on September 21, 1938.

The pressure on the Czechs was greatly increased by the sending of a British mission under Lord Runciman to Czechoslovakia at the beginning of August. This mission was presented to the public as being sent to mediate between Henlein and the government at the request of the Czech government. In fact, it was imposed on the Czech government, and its chief function was to increase the pressure on that government to make concessions. It was publicly announced that the members of this mission went as private persons and that the British government was not bound by anything which they did. Under this pressure the Czechs yielded little by little and, as already stated, conceded the essence of the Karlsbad Demands on September 6th. Since the Sudeten leaders did not want any settlement which would not ensure the destruction of Czechoslovakia, they instigated a street riot and broke off negotiations. The official British investigation reported that the riot in question was entirely the fault of the Sudeten leaders (who had attacked a policeman).

In the meantime the British had been working out a plan of their own. It involved, as we have said, (1) separation of the Sudetenland from Czechoslovakia, probably through the use of a plebiscite or even by outright partition; (2) neutralization of the rest of Czechoslovakia by revising her treaties with Russia and France, and (3) guarantee of this rump of Czechoslovakia (but not by Britain). This plan was outlined to the Czech ambassador in London by Lord Halifax on May 25th, and was worked out in some detail by one of Lord Halifax's subordinates, William (now Lord) Strang, during a visit to Prague and to Berlin in the following week. This was the plan which was picked up by Lord Runciman and presented as his recommendation in his report of September 21, 1938.

It is worthy of note that on September 2nd Lord Runciman sent a personal message by Henlein to Hitler in which he said that he would have a settlement drawn up by September 15th. What is, perhaps, surprising is that Lord Runciman made no use whatever of the Karlsbad Demands or the extensive concessions to meet them which the Czechs had made during these negotiations, but instead recommended to the British Cabinet on September 16th, and in his written report five days later, the same mélange of partition, plebiscites, neutralization, and guarantee which had been in the mind of the British Foreign Office for weeks. It was this plan which was imposed on the Czechs by the Four-Power Conference at Munich on September 30th.

It was also necessary to impose this plan on the French government and on the public opinion of the world, especially on the public opinion of England. This was done by means of the slowly mounting war scare, which reached the level of absolute panic on September 28th. The mounting horror of the relentless German mobilization was built up day by day, while Britain and France ordered the Czechs not to mobilize in order "not to provoke Germany." The word was assiduously spread on all sides that Russia was worthless and would not fight, that Britain certainly would not go to war to prevent the Sudetens from exercising the democratic right of self-determination, that Germany could overwhelm the Czechs in a few days and could wipe out Prague, Paris, and London from the air in the first day, that these air attacks would be accompanied by gas attacks on the civilian population from the air, and that, even if Germany could be defeated after years of war, Czechoslovakia would never be reconstructed because it was an artificial monstrosity, an aberration of 1919.

We now know that all these statements and rumors were not true; the documentary evidence indicates that the British government knew that they were not true at the time. Germany had 22 partly trained divisions on the Czech frontier, while the Czechs had 17 first-line and 11 other divisions which were superior from every point of view except air support. In addition, they had excellent fortifications and higher morale. These facts were known to the British government. On September 3rd the British military attaché in Prague wrote to London that "there are no shortcomings in the Czech army, as far as I have been able to observe, which are of sufficient consequence to warrant a belief that it cannot give a good account of itself [even fighting alone.] . . . In my view, therefore, there is no material reason why they should not put up a really protracted resistance single-handed. It all depends on their morale."

The fact that the Germans were going to attack with only 22 divisions was reported to London by the military attaché on September 21st. The fact that Russia had at least 97 divisions and over 5,000 planes had been reported by the attaché in Moscow, although he had a very low opinion of both. The fact that Russia sold 36 of their latest-model fighting planes to Czechoslovakia was also known. That Russia would fight if France fought was denied at the time, but it is now clear that Russia had assured everyone that it would stand by its treaty obligations. In 1950 it was revealed by President Beneš that Russia had put every pressure on him to resist the German demands in September 1938. Similar pressure was put on France, a fact which was reported to London at the time.

By the third week of September, Czechoslovakia had 1,000,000 men and 34 divisions under arms. The Germans in the course of September increased their mobilization to 31 and ultimately to 36 divisions, but this probably represented a smaller force than that of the Czechs as many of the 19 first-line divisions were at only two-thirds strength, the other one-third having been used as a nucleus to form the reserve divisions. Of the 19 first-line divisions 3 were armored and 4 were motorized. Only 5 divisions were left on the French frontier in order to overcome Czechoslovakia as quickly as possible. France, which did not completely mobilize, had the Maginot Line completely manned on a war basis, plus more than 20 infantry divisions. Moreover, France had available 10 motorized divisions. In air power the Germans had a slight edge in average quality, but in numbers of planes it was far inferior. Germany had 1,500 planes while Czechoslovakia had less than 1,000; France and England together had over 1,000; Russia is reported to have had 5,000. Moreover, Russia had about 100 divisions. While these could not be used against Germany, because Poland and Romania would not allow them to pass over their territory, they would have been a threat to persuade Poland to remain neutral and to bring Romania to support Czechoslovakia in keeping the Little Entente intact and thus keeping Hungary neutral. With Poland and Hungary both neutral, there is no doubt that Germany would have been isolated. The neutrality of Poland and Romania would not have prevented the Russian Air Force from helping Czechoslovakia and, if worse came to worst, Russia could have overrun East Prussia across the Baltic States and from the Baltic Sea, since it had been almost completely denuded of regular German Army forces. It is quite clear that Italy would not have fought for Germany.

The evidence shows that the Chamberlain government knew these facts but consistently gave a contrary impression. Lord Halifax particularly distorted the facts. Although all reports indicated that the morale of the Czech Army was high, he took an isolated sentence from a poorly written report from the British military attaché in Berlin as authority for stating that the morale of the Czechoslovak Army was poor and the country would be overrun. Although General Maurice Gamelin, the French commander in chief, gave a very encouraging report on the Czech Army, and was quoted to this effect by Chamberlain in a Cabinet meeting of September 26th, Halifax the next day quoted him as saying that the Czech resistance would be of extremely brief duration. The military attaché in Prague protested about the statement in reference to Czech morale, pointing out that it was made in reference to the frontier police, which were not military. The military attaché in Paris questioned Lord Halifax's statement about Gamelin's views, and quoted contrary views from Gamelin's closest associates in the French Army. The falsehood that Gamelin was defeatist was spread in the newspapers, and is still widely current.

Just when the crisis was reaching the boiling point in September, the British ambassador in Paris reported to London that Colonel Charles A. Lindbergh had just emerged from Germany with a report that Germany had 8,000 military airplanes and could manufacture 1,500 a month. We now know that Germany had about 1,500 planes, manufactured 280 a month in 1938, and had abandoned all plans to bomb London even in a war because of lack of planes and distance from the target. Lindbergh repeated his tale of woe daily both in Paris and in London during the crisis. The British government began to fit the people of London with gas masks; the prime minister and the king called on the people to dig trenches in the parks and squares; schoolchildren began to be evacuated from the city; the Czechs were allowed to mobilize on September 24th; and three days later it was announced that the British fleet was at its war stations. In general, every report or rumor which could add to the panic and defeatism was played up, and everything that might contribute to a strong or a united resistance to Germany was played down. By the middle of September, Bonnet was broken, and Daladier was bending, while the British people were completely confused. By September 27th Daladier had caved in, and so had the British people.

In the meantime, on September 13th, without consulting his Cabinet, Chamberlain asked Hitler by telegraph for an interview. They met on September 15th at Berchtesgaden. Chamberlain tried to reopen at once the discussions toward a general Anglo-German settlement which Halifax had opened in November 1937, but which had been broken off since Nevile Henderson's conference with Hitler on March 3rd. Hitler interrupted to say that he must have self-determination for the Sudeten Germans at once and that the Czech-Soviet treaty must be abolished. If he did not get these, there would be an immediate war. Chamberlain asked to be allowed to return to London to confer with the French and Lord Runciman.

The Anglo-French conference of September 18, 1938, saw the last glimmering of French resistance to Britain's plans, chiefly from Daladier. Chamberlain blamed Beneš for Czechoslovakia's plight, while Lord Halifax repeated all the mistaken arguments about the hopelessness of resistance and the improbability of Czechoslovakia being revived with its present boundaries even after a costly victory. Chamberlain excluded all possible solutions from discussion except partition. To him the problem was "to discover some means of preventing France from being forced into war as a result of her obligations and at the same time to preserve Czechoslovakia and save as much of that country as was humanly possible." Daladier feebly tried to get the discussion to the real problem, German aggression. Eventually he accepted the British solution of partition of all areas of Czechoslovakia with over 50 percent Germans, and a guarantee for the rest.

As he yielded on the main issue, Daladier tried to get certain concessions: (1) that the Czechs must be consulted; (2) that the rump of Czechoslovakia should be guaranteed by Britain as well as others; (3) that economic aid should be extended to this rump. The last was rejected; the second was accepted on the understanding that Czechoslovakia give up its alliances and generally do what Britain wanted "in issues involving war and peace"; the first was accepted.

The way in which Chamberlain applied "consultation with the Czechs" before partition was imposed is an interesting example of his mind at work. The British, French, and Czechs were agreed in opposition to the use of a plebiscite in this dispute, although the Entente suggested it to put pressure on the Czechs. Chamberlain said: "The idea of territorial cession would be likely to have a more favorable reception from the British public if it could be represented as the choice of the Czechoslovak Government themselves and it could be made clear that they had been offered the choice of a plebiscite or of territorial cession and had preferred the latter. This would dispose of any idea that we were ourselves carving up Czechoslovak territory." He felt it particularly important to show that the Czechoslovak government preferred cession because they were so definitely opposed to a plebiscite that they would fight rather than accept a plebiscite.

This Anglo-French decision was presented to the Czechoslovak government at 2:00 A.M. on September 19th, to be accepted at once. The terms leaked to the press in Paris the same day. After vigorous protests, the Czechoslovaks rejected the Anglo-French solution and appealed to the procedures of the German-Czechoslovak Arbitration Treaty of 1926. The Czechs argued that they had not been consulted, that their constitution required that their Parliament be consulted, that partition would be ineffective in maintaining peace because the minorities would rise again, and that the balance of power in Europe would be destroyed. Beneš refused to believe that new guarantees could be more effective, when Czechoslovakia would be weaker, than those which were now proving inadequate. London and Paris rejected the Czech refusal. Pressure was increased on the Czechs. The French threatened to revoke the French-Czechoslovak alliance and to abandon the whole country to Germany if the Anglo-French solution was not accepted. The British added that the Sudetenland would not be returned to Czechoslovakia even after a successful war against Germany. The British minister in Prague threatened to order all British subjects from the country if he did not receive an immediate acceptance. The Czechoslovak government accepted at 5:00 P.M. on September 21st. Lord Halifax at once ordered the Czech police to be withdrawn from the Sudeten districts, and expressed his wish that the German troops move in at once.

The next day, September 22nd, Chamberlain took the Czech acceptance to Hitler at Godesberg on the Rhine. He found the Führer in a vile temper, receiving messages every few minutes about the atrocities being inflicted on the Sudetens by the Czechs. Hitler now demanded self-determination for the Hungarians, Poles, and Slovaks in Czechoslovakia, as well as for the Sudetens. He insisted that he must have the

Sudeten areas at once. After that, if the Czechs challenged his choice of a frontier, he would hold a plebiscite and prove how wrong they were. An international commission could supervise the vote. At any rate, he must have the German areas before October 1st, for on that day the German forces would move in, war or no war. At Chamberlain's request he embodied his demands in a memorandum which proved to be an ultimatum. This ultimatum was at once carried to Prague to be presented to the Czechs by the British military attaché.

Back in London, the Cabinet agreed to reject the Godesberg Demands and to support France if it had to go to war as a result. The French Cabinet also rejected these demands. So did a new Czech Cabinet under General Jan Syrový. The Soviet Union explicitly recognized its commitments to Czechoslovakia, and even promised to come to the aid of the Czechs without the necessary preliminary action by France if the case were submitted to the League of Nations (this was to prevent Britain and France from charging Russia with aggression in any action it might take in behalf of Czechoslovakia). On the same day (September 23rd) Russia warned Poland that it would denounce their Nonaggression Treaty if Poland attacked Czechoslovakia.

Apparently a united front had been formed against Hitler's aggression—but only apparently. Mr. Chamberlain was already beginning to undermine the unity and resolution of this front, and he now received considerable assistance from Bonnet in Paris. This culminated on September 27th when he made a speech on the radio in which he said, "How horrible, fantastic, incredible it is that we should be digging trenches and trying on gas masks here because of a quarrel in a far-away country between people of whom we know nothing . . . a quarrel that has already been settled in principle. . . ." The same day he sent a telegram to Beneš that if he did not accept the German demands by 2:00 P.M. the following day (September 28th) Czechoslovakia would be overrun by the German Army, and nothing could save it. This was immediately followed by another message that in such a case Czechoslovakia could not be reconstituted in its frontiers whatever the outcome of the war. Lastly, he sent another note to Hitler. In this he suggested a four-Power conference, and guaranteed that France and Britain would force Czechoslovakia to carry out any agreement if Hitler would only abstain from going to war.

At 3:00 P.M. on Wednesday, September 28th, Chamberlain met Parliament for the first time during the crisis to inform it of what had been done. The whole city of London was in a panic. The Honorable Members sat hunched on their benches, waiting for Göring's bombs to come through the roof. As Chamberlain drew to the end of his long speech, a message was brought to him. He announced that it was an invitation to a four-Power conference at Munich on Thursday. There was a roar of joy and relief as Chamberlain hurried from the building without any formal ending to the session.

At Munich, Hitler, Chamberlain, Mussolini, and Daladier carved up Czechoslovakia without consulting anyone, least of all the Czechs. The conference lasted from 12:30 P.M. on September 29th to 2:30 A.M. when the agreement of the four Powers was handed to the Czech minister in Berlin, who had been waiting outside the door for over ten hours. The agreement reached Prague only eighteen hours before the German occupation was to begin.

The Munich agreement provided that certain designated areas of Czechoslovakia would be occupied by the German Army in four stages from October 1st to October 7th. A fifth area, to be designated by an international commission, would be occupied by October 10th. No property was to be withdrawn from these areas. The international commission would order plebiscites which must be held before the end of November, the areas designated being occupied by an international force during the interval. The same international commission was to supervise the occupation and draw the final frontier. For six months the populations concerned would have the right of option into and out of the areas transferred under the supervision of a German-Czechoslovak commission. The rump of Czechoslovakia was to be guaranteed by France and Britain. Germany and Italy would join this guarantee as soon as the Polish and Hungarian minority problems in that state had been settled. If they were not settled in three months, the four Powers would meet again to consider the problem.

The Munich agreement was violated on every point in favor of Germany, so that ultimately the German Army merely occupied the places it wanted. As a result, the Czech economic system was destroyed, and every important railroad or highway was cut or crippled. This was done by the International Commission, consisting of German Secretary of State Weizsäcker and the French, British, Italian, and Czech diplomatic representatives in Berlin. Under dictation of the German General Staff, this group, by a 4 to 1 vote, accepted every German demand and canceled the plebiscites. In addition, the guarantee of the rump of Czechoslovakia was never given, although Poland seized areas in which the majority of the population was not Polish on October 2nd and Hungary was given southern Slovakia on November 2nd. The final frontier with Germany was dictated by Germany alone to the Czechs, the other three members of the commission having withdrawn.

Beneš resigned as president of Czechoslovakia under the threat of a German ultimatum on October 5th and was replaced by Emil Hácha. Slovakia and Ruthenia were given complete autonomy at once. The Soviet alliance was ended, and the Communist Party outlawed. The anti-Nazi refugees from the Sudetenland were rounded up by the Prague government and handed over to the Germans to be destroyed. All these events showed very clearly the chief result of Munich: Germany was supreme in central Europe, and any possibility of curtailing that power either by a joint policy of the Western Powers with the Soviet Union and Italy or by finding any openly anti-German resistance in central Europe itself was ended. Since this was exactly what Chamberlain and his friends had wanted, they should have been satisfied.

The Year of Dupes, 1939

Plans for appeasement by Chamberlain and plans for aggression by Hitler did not end with Munich. Within three weeks of this agreement (October 21, 1938), Hitler issued orders to his generals to prepare plans to destroy the rump of Czechoslovakia and to annex Memel from Lithuania. A month later he added Danzig to this list, although he signified his desire to achieve this through a revolutionary action without a war against Poland. This reluctance for war against Poland did not arise from any affection for peace but from the fact that he had not made up his mind whether to attack France or Poland. He was inclined at first to attack westward, and did not change his mind and decide to deal first with Poland until April 1, 1939. The plans to attack France and the Low Countries soon were reported to London and Paris and had a good deal to do with building up the war spirit in those areas.

In addition, Italian demands for territorial concessions from France in November 1938 aroused the fighting spirit of that country from the level to which it had sagged in September. Mussolini was seeking his share in the booty of appeasement but lacked the strength to do much more than make a nuisance of himself. His followers staged a great demonstration in the Italian Chamber of Corporations on November 30, 1938, in which there were loud demands for Nice, Corsica, and Tunis from France. In December the old Laval-Mussolini agreement of January, 1935, was denounced as inadequate, and a violent anti-French campaign was waged in the Italian press. These disturbances were encouraged by Chamberlain when he pointedly announced in the House of Commons on December 12th that Britain was not bound to come to the aid of France or its possessions if they were attacked by Italy.

Bonnet at once tried to repair this damage by asking Chamberlain to make a reference to the fact that Italy had bound itself to preserve the *status quo* in the Mediterranean in the Anglo-Italian ("Ciano-Perth") Agreement of April 1938. Chamberlain refused. Bonnet at once pointed out to London that France had bound itself on December 4, 1936, to come to the assistance of Britain if it were attacked and that this promise was still completely valid. Nonetheless, it was only on February 6th, when Hitler's plans to attack Holland and France "almost immediately" were reported in London, that Chamberlain could persuade himself to state in Commons that "any threat to the vital interests of France, from whatever quarter it came, must evoke the immediate cooperation of this country."

The Italian demands on France had two important results. The fighting spirits of the French people were revived by being threatened by such a weak Power as Italy, and Bonnet was driven to a new appeasement of Germany. On December 6th Ribbentrop came to Paris, signed a treaty of friendship and neutrality, and opened a series of economic discussions. On this occasion the German foreign minister received from Bonnet the impression that France would give Germany a free hand in eastern Europe. French fears that Britain would seek to detach Mussolini from Hitler by making concessions to Italy at the expense of France did not end until February 1939, and reached their peak in January, when Chamberlain and Halifax made a formal visit to Rome to recognize the King of Italy as Emperor of Ethiopia. This had been agreed between the two Powers in the Ciano-Perth Agreement of April 1938, and was carried into effect in November, although the conditions originally set by Britain, the withdrawal of Italian troops from Spain, had not been fulfilled.

Before Hitler could carry on any further aggressions, he had to dispose of the carcass of Czechoslovakia. He and Ribbentrop were outraged that they had been cheated out of a war in September, and immediately made up their minds to wipe the rest of Czechoslovakia off the map as soon as possible and proceed to a war. The next time, said Hitler, he hoped no "dirty pig" would suggest a conference.

Orders to plan an invasion of the rump of Czechoslovakia were issued on October 21st, as we have said. Keitel's plans, presented on December 17th, provided that the task would be done by the peacetime army without mobilization. Any possibility of opposition from Britain or France was effectively disposed of by Lord Halifax's insistence that the guarantee to Czechoslovakia be worded so as to be binding on all four of the Munich Powers jointly (or at least on three of them) and would not be accepted by Britain if worded in such a way as to bind the signers individually. This made any guarantee meaningless, and this distasteful project was indefinitely postponed by a German note to Lord Halifax on March 3, 1939.

By this last date Hitler was ready to strike at the rump of Czechoslovakia. Hungary was invited to join in this operation, and eagerly accepted on March 13th. In the meantime the projected victim was a nest of intrigue. Sudeten Nazis were everywhere, seeking to make trouble. Poland and Hungary were working to get a common frontier by obtaining Slovakia as a protectorate for Poland and Ruthenia as a province of Hungary. They hoped in this way to block Germany's movement to the east and to keep Russian influence out of central Europe. Within the two autonomous provinces, Slovakia and Ruthenia, and to a much lesser degree in Bohemia-Moravia, there was turmoil as various reactionary and semi-Fascist groups angled for power and German favor.

The degree of political maturity in Slovakia may be judged from the fact that the members of Monsignor Tiso's Cabinet personally took bombs from the Nazis to stir up trouble in their own province. Their efforts to break away from Prague completely were hampered by the financial insolvency of Slovakia. When they appealed to Prague for financial assistance on March 9, 1939, President Hácha deposed the Slovak premier and three of his ministers. Seyss-Inquart, accompanied by several German generals, forced the Slovak Cabinet to issue a declaration of independence from Prague. Tiso, summoned to Hitler's presence in Berlin on March 13th, was "persuaded" to approve this action. The declaration was received with profound apathy by the Slovak people, although the German radio filled the air with stories of riots and disturbances, and various Nazi bands within both Slovakia and Bohemia did their best to make the facts fit this description.

On March 14th, Hácha, the president of Czechoslovakia, was forced to go to Berlin. Although he was sixty-six years old, and not in the best of health, Hácha was subjected to a brutal three-hour long tonguelashing by Hitler during which he had to be revived from a fainting spell by an injection administered by Hitler's physician. He was forced to sign documents handing Czechoslovakia over to Hitler and ordering all resistance to the invading German forces to cease. Ruthenia had already proclaimed its independence (March 14th). Within a week, Bohemia-Moravia and Slovakia were declared German protectorates, and the former was taken within the German economic system. Ruthenia was annexed by Hungary after one day of independence.

Europe had not yet recovered from the shock of March 15th when Germany seized Memel from Lithuania on March 22nd, and Italy obtained its crumb of satisfaction by seizing Albania on April 7, 1939.

It is usually said that the events of March 1939 revealed Hitler's real nature and real ambitions, and marked the end of appeasement. This is certainly not true as stated. It may have opened the eyes of the average man to the fact that appeasement was merely a kind of slow suicide, and quite incapable of satisfying the appetites of aggressors who were insatiable. It also made clear that Hitler was not really concerned with self-determination or with a desire to bring all Germans "back to the Reich." The annexation of territories containing millions of Slavs showed

that Hitler's real aim was power and wealth and eventually world domination. Thus, from March onward, it became almost impossible to sell
appeasement to the public, especially to the British public, who were
sufficiently sturdy and sensible to know when they had had enough.

But the British public and the British government were two different
things, and it is quite untrue to say that the latter learned Hitler's real
ambitions in March 1939 and determined to oppose them. Above all, it
is completely wrong to say this of Chamberlain, who, more and more,
was running foreign policy as his own personal business. Hitler's real
ambitions were quite clear to most men in the government even before
Munich, and were made evident to the rest during that crisis, especially
by the way in which the German High Command seized hundreds of
villages in Czechoslovakia with overwhelming Czech populations and
only small German minorities, and did so for strategic and economic
reasons in the period October 1–10, 1938. But for the members of the
government, the real turning point took place in January 1939, when
British diplomatic agents in Europe began to bombard London with
rumors of a forthcoming attack on the Netherlands and France. At that
moment, appeasement in the strict sense ceased. To the government the
seizure of Czechoslovakia in March was of little significance except for
the shock it gave to British opinion. The government had already written off the rump of Czechoslovakia completely, a fact which is clear as
much from their direct statements as by their refusal to guarantee that
rump, and the attention given to other matters even when the seizure
was known (as it was after March 11th). For example, Lord Halifax
sent President Roosevelt a long letter analyzing the international situation on January 24th; it is completely realistic about Hitler's outlook and
projects, but Czechoslovakia is not mentioned; neither is appeasement.

Nevertheless, concessions to Germany continued. But now parallel
with concessions went a real effort to build up a strong front against
Hitler for the day when concessions would break down. Moreover, concessions were different after March 17th because now they had to be
secret. They had to be secret because public opinion refused any longer
to accept any actions resembling appeasement, but they were continued
for several reasons. In the first place British rearmament was slow, and
concessions were given to win time. In the second place the projects of
the anti-Bolsheviks and "three-bloc-world" supporters demanded continued concessions. In the third place, Chamberlain continued to work
to achieve his seven-point settlement with Hitler in the hope that he
could suddenly present it to the British electorate as a prelude to a
triumphant General Election which he planned for the winter of 1939–
1940. Of these three causes, the first, to gain time for rearmament, was
the least important, although it was the one most readily used to justify
secret concessions when they were found out. This is clear from the na-

ture of the concessions. These were frequently such as to strengthen Germany rather than to gain time for Britain.

The projects of the anti-Bolsheviks and the "three-bloc-world" supporters were too dangerous to admit publicly, but they were sufficiently well known in Berlin to lead to the belief, even in moderate circles, that Britain would never go to war for Poland. For example, Weizsäcker, the German secretary of state, chided Nevile Henderson in June 1939 for abandoning his often-repeated statement that "England desired to retain the sea; the European Continent could be left to Germany." However, these two groups, although still active in 1939, and even in 1940, had not originally envisaged the complete destruction of Czechoslovakia or Poland. They had expected that Hitler would get the Sudentenland, Danzig, and perhaps the Polish Corridor and that he would then be stabilized between the "oceanic bloc" and the Soviet Union, with contact with the latter across the Baltic States. It was expected that a rump Czechoslovakia and a rump Poland would be able to survive between Germany and Russia, as Holland or Switzerland could survive between the oceanic bloc and Germany. Moreover, the "three-bloc-world" supporters never wanted Hitler to drive southward either to the Adriatic or to the Aegean. Accordingly, although divided in respect to Romania and the Black Sea, they were determined to support Turkey and Greece against both Germany and Italy.

As a consequence of these hidden and conflicting forces, the history of international relations from September 1938 to September 1939 or even later is neither simple nor consistent. In general, the key to everything was the position of Britain, for the aims of the other countries concerned were relatively simple. As a result of the dualistic or, as Lord Halifax's biographer calls it, "dyarchic" policy of Britain, there were not only two policies but two groups carrying them out. The Foreign Office under Lord Halifax tried to satisfy the public demand for an end to appeasement and the construction of a united front against Germany. Chamberlain with his own personal group, including Sir Horace Wilson, Sir John Simon, and Sir Samuel Hoare, sought to make secret concessions to Hitler in order to achieve a general Anglo-German settlement on the basis of the seven points. The one policy was public; the other was secret. Since the Foreign Office knew of both, it tried to build up the "peace front" against Germany so that it would look sufficiently imposing to satisfy public opinion in England and to drive Hitler to seek his desires by negotiation rather than by force so that public opinion in England would not force the government to declare a war that they did not want in order to remain in office. This complex plan broke down because Hitler was determined to have a war merely for the personal emotional thrill of wielding great power, while the effort to make a "peace front" sufficiently collapsible so that it could be cast aside if Hitler either obtained his goals by negotiation or made a general settlement with Chamberlain merely resulted in making a "peace front" which was so weak it could neither maintain peace by the threat of force nor win a war when peace was lost. Above all, these involved maneuvers drove the Soviet Union into the arms of Hitler.

This complex scheme meant that the British government accepted the events of March 15th except for feeble protests. These were directed less against the deed itself than against the risk of agitating public opinion by the deed. On March 15th Chamberlain told the Commons that he accepted the seizure of Czechoslovakia, and refused to accuse Hitler of bad faith. But two days later, when the howls of rage from the British public showed that he had misjudged the electorate, he went to his constituency in Birmingham on March 17th and denounced the seizure. However, nothing was done except to recall Henderson from Berlin "for consultations" and cancel a visit to Berlin by the president of the Board of Trade planned for March 17-20. The seizure was declared illegal but was recognized in fact at once, and efforts were made to recognize it in law by establishing a British consulate general accredited to Germany at Prague. Moreover, £6,000,000 in Czech gold reserves in London were turned over to Germany with the puny, and untrue, excuse that the British government could not give orders to the Bank of England (May 1939).

The German acquisition of the Czech gold in London was but one episode in an extensive, and largely secret, plan for economic concessions to Germany. For Chamberlain and his friends, the Czechoslovak crisis of March 1939 was merely an annoying interruption to their efforts to make a general agreement with Germany in terms of the seven points we have already mentioned. These efforts had been interrupted after March 3, 1938 by the Czechoslovak crisis of that year, but they remained the chief item in Chamberlain's plans, and he tried to get Hitler to discuss these projects when the two leaders came face to face on September 15th at Berchtesgaden. Hitler interrupted, and turned the discussion at once to the crisis. Again, after the Munich agreement was signed on September 30th, Chamberlain tried to get Der Führer to discuss a general settlement, but he was evaded. This process was continued for a year, Chamberlain and his friends proposing concessions and Hitler either evading or ignoring them. There was a slight change, however, after September 1938: Chamberlain's project was widened to include economic concessions, and the efforts to achieve it became increasingly secret, especially after the events of March 1939.

After September, 1938, the seven-point project was broadened by adding an eighth point: economic support for Germany, especially in exploiting eastern Europe. The German economic situation was critical at the end of 1938 because of the speed of rearmament, the expense and economic disruption arising from the mobilization of 1938, and the great shortage of foreign exchange, which hampered the importation of necessary commodities. Göring, as commissioner of the Four-Year Economic Plan, presented these facts at a secret conference on October 14, 1938. In the course of his speech he spoke roughly as follows:

"I am faced with unheard-of difficulties. The Treasury is empty; industrial capacity is crammed with orders for many years. In spite of these difficulties, I am going to go ahead under all circumstances. Memoranda are no help; I want only positive proposals. If necessary, I am going to convert the economy with brutal methods to achieve this aim. The time has come for private enterprise to show if it has a right to continued existence. If it fails, I am going over to state enterprise regardless. I am going to make barbaric use of the full powers given me by the Führer. All the aims and plans of the state, the party, and other agencies which are not along this line must be rejected pitilessly. Ideological problems cannot be solved now, there will be time for them later. I warn against making promises to labor which I cannot keep. The desires of the Labor Front must sink into the background. Industry must be fully converted. An immediate investigation of productive plants is to be started to determine whether they can be converted for armaments or export, or whether they are to be closed down. The problem of the machine-tool industry comes first in this. . . . It remains now to decide who is going to carry out this task—the state or self-administered industry."

The Entente governments were aware of these German problems, but, instead of seeking to increase them, they sought to alleviate them. When economic and political duress was put by Germany on the countries of southeastern Europe in October and November 1938, Chamberlain defended Germany's right to do so in the House of Commons. No economic support was granted to these countries to help them to resist, except for a loan to Turkey. On the contrary, the British government, through the Federation of British Industries, began to negotiate with Germany to create a complete system of industrial cooperation, with cartels dividing the world's markets and fixing prices for over fifty industrial groups. A coal agreement was signed, at Britain's request, at the end of January 1939, and a general agreement was signed between the Federation of British Industries and the Reichsgruppe Industrie on March 16, 1939.

In his speech of January 30, 1939, Hitler had said, "We must export or die." Two weeks later the British government sent Frank Ashton-Gwatkin to Berlin "to find out, if possible, what roads are still open to economic recovery and reconstruction and might, therefore, be worth pursuing, and what roads are closed." On March 5th he reported that Germany's critical economic situation was caused by its political actions in 1938 and that it must now turn to economic actions for 1939. This, he felt, "implies though it does not necessitate, some limitation of the armaments race; secondly, it means that Germany must look towards the United Kingdom for assistance or cooperation in the economic sphere." He listed the concessions that the Germans wanted, and concluded, "We should not ignore the possibilities of a more peaceful development; and we should not put Hitler in a position to say that once again he made an offer of cooperation to England and that that offer was pushed aside." Accordingly, the discussions continued and the British government announced that the president of the Board of Trade, Oliver Stanley, would go to Berlin on March 17th.

The British military attaché in Berlin protested as violently as he dared against this economic appeasement in a letter of February 27th, saying: "We can only reduce the speed and scope of the universal armaments race by forcing a reduction of tempo on Germany. Germany is apparently now in dire economic straits. We have not applied the economic screw—Germany has tightened it down herself—and it is surely unsound for us to ease it before Germany has made an effort to do so herself. From the military point of view, concessions made by us to the present regime in Germany are generally to be deplored. The opposition in Germany and our potential allies in a possible war—above all, America, are becoming more and more convinced of our weakness and lack of will or power to stand up to Germany."

When the Bohemian crisis broke on March 15, 1939, Chamberlain announced that Oliver Stanley's visit to Berlin that weekend would be postponed but that the economic conversations between the British and German industrial associations were continuing. Public outcry continued so high that on March 28th it was announced that these negotiations were being broken off because of disturbed public opinion. However, on April 2nd, only five days later, the German commercial attaché in London was secretly informed that the British were ready to reopen the discussions. The amazing fact is that the British unilateral guarantee to Poland was given on March 31st, exactly halfway between the public breaking off and the secret resumption of the economic negotiations. It should perhaps be mentioned that France throughout this period was also negotiating trade agreements to send raw materials to Germany as a result of a preliminary agreement signed during Ribbentrop's visit to Paris early in December 1938. Although the documentation is not complete, we know that this French-German agreement was in final draft by March 11th.

In spite of these concessions Hitler was thirsting for war, and replied to every concession with a new bombshell which disturbed British public opinion once more. In November 1938 the Germans engaged in several days of sustained atrocities against the Jews, destroying their property, razing their temples, assaulting their persons, and concluded by imposing on the Jews of Germany a collective fine or assessment of one billion reichsmarks. This was followed by a series of laws excluding the Jews from the economic life of Germany.

Public outrage at these actions was still high when, in December, 1938, the Germans announced that they were increasing their submarine fleet from 45 percent to 100 percent of Britain's, as provided in the Treaty of 1935, and were remodeling two cruisers under construction from 6-inch-gun to 8-inch-gun vessels. Every effort by Britain to persuade Germany not to do so or even to word their announcement in a way which would allay public opinion was rebuffed by Germany. Finally, in March came the complete destruction of Czechoslovakia. At the same time pressure began to be applied to Poland.

Germany opened its negotiations with Poland in a fairly friendly way on October 24, 1938. It asked for Danzig and a strip a kilometer wide across the Polish Corridor to provide a highway and four-track railroad under German sovereignty. Poland's economic and harbor rights in Danzig were to be guaranteed and the "corridor across the Corridor" was to be isolated from Polish communication facilities by bridging or tunneling. Germany also wanted Poland to join an anti-Russian bloc. If these three things were granted, Germany was prepared to make certain concessions to Poland, to guarantee the country's existing frontiers, to extend the Nonaggression Pact of 1934 for twenty-five years, to guarantee the independence of Slovakia, and to dispose of Ruthenia as Poland wished. These suggestions were generally rejected by Poland. They were repeated by Germany with increased emphasis on March 21st. About the same time, the Germans were using pressure on Romania to obtain an economic agreement, which was signed on March 23rd.

On March 17th London received a false report of a German ultimatum to Romania. Lord Halifax lost his head and, without checking his information, sent telegrams to Greece, Turkey, Poland, Bulgaria, and the Soviet Union asking what each country was prepared to do in the event of a German aggression against Romania. Four replied by asking London what *it* was prepared to do, but Moscow suggested an immediate conference in Bucharest of France, Britain, Poland, Romania, and the Soviet Union to try to form a united front against aggression (March 18, 1939). This was rebuffed by Lord Halifax, who wanted nothing more than an agreement among these states to consult in a crisis, as if they would not do so anyway. Poland was reluctant to sign any agreement involving Russia. However, when news reached London of Hitler's demands on Poland, Britain suddenly issued a unilateral guarantee of the latter state (March 31st). This was extended to Romania and Greece after Italy's attack on Albania (April 13th).

The text of Chamberlain's guarantee to Poland is of extreme importance. He said: "Certain consultations are now proceeding with other governments. In order to make perfectly clear the position of His Majesty's Government in the meantime, before those consultations are concluded, I now have to inform the House [of Commons] that during that period, in the event of any action which clearly threatened Polish independence and which the Polish Government accordingly considered it vital to resist with their national forces, His Majesty's Government would feel themselves bound at once to lend the Polish Government all support in their power."

This was an extraordinary assurance. The British government since 1918 had resolutely refused any bilateral agreement guaranteeing any state in western Europe. Now they were making a *unilateral* declaration in which they obtained nothing but in which they guaranteed a state in *eastern* Europe, and they were giving that state the responsibility of deciding when that guarantee would take effect, something quite unprecedented. A little thought will show that all these strange features really stultify the guarantee, and the net result was to leave the situation exactly where it had been before, except that a very severe warning had been conveyed in this fashion to Germany to use negotiation and not force. If Germany used force against Poland, public opinion in Britain would force Britain to declare war whether there was a guarantee or not.

The fact that Chamberlain's guarantee was temporary and unilateral left the British free to cancel it when necessary. The fact that it guaranteed Poland's "independence" and not its territorial integrity left the way open for Germany to get Danzig or the Corridor by negotiation, and the fact that it came into effect when Poland wished made it impossible for Britain or British public opinion to refuse to accept any change which Poland worked out in negotiation with Hitler. Most of these points were recognized by the German government. They were pointed out in *The Times* of April 1st and accepted by Chamberlain.

The guarantee was accepted by Bonnet, who, as long ago as November, had said that he wanted to get rid of both the Franco-Polish and the Franco-Soviet alliances.

If the chief purpose of the unilateral guarantee to Poland was to frighten Germany, it had precisely the opposite effect. On hearing of it, Hitler made his decision: to attack Poland by September 1. Orders to this effect were issued to the German Army on April 3, and the plans for Operation White, as it was called, were ready on April 11. On April 28, in a public speech to the Reichstag, Hitler denounced the Anglo-German Naval Agreement of 1935 and the German-Polish

Nonaggression Pact of 1934. He also announced the terms he had offered Poland which had been rejected. As a result, negotiations broke off between the two Powers and were never really resumed. Instead, the crisis was intensified by provocative acts on both sides.

On May 22 a German-Italian alliance was signed, the "Pact of Steel," as Mussolini called it. Here, again, the wording was important. It was a clearly aggressive alliance, since the parties promised to support each other, not against "unprovoked attack," as was customary, but in all cases. At the signing, Germany was told flatly that Italy could not make war before 1943 and that the approaching war would be a "war of exhaustion." The very next day, May 23, 1939, Hitler held a secret conference with his generals. In the course of a lengthy speech he said:

"Danzig is not the subject of this dispute at all. It is a question of expanding our living space in the East and of securing our food supplies, and the settlement of the Baltic problems. Food supplies can be expected only from thinly populated areas. Over and above the natural fertility, thoroughgoing German exploitation will increase production enormously. There is no other possibility in Europe. Beware of gifts of colonial territory. These do not solve the food problem. Remember—blockade. If fate brings us into conflict with the West, possession of extensive areas in the East will be advantageous. We shall be able to expect excellent harvests even less in wartime than in time of peace. The population of these non-German areas will perform no military service and will be available as a source of labor. The Polish problem is inseparable from conflict with the West. . . . Poland sees danger in a German victory in the West and will attempt to rob us of a victory there. There is, therefore, no question of sparing Poland, and we are left with the decision: *To attack Poland at the first suitable opportunity*. We cannot expect a repetition of the Czech affair. There will be war. Our job is to isolate Poland. The success of this isolation will be the decisive factor. Therefore, the Führer must reserve the decision to give the final order to attack. There must be no simultaneous conflict with the Western Powers [France and England]. . . . If there were an alliance of France, England, and Russia, I would have to attack England and France with a few annihilating blows. I doubt the possibility of a peaceful settlement with England. We must prepare ourselves for the conflict. England sees in our development the foundation of a hegemony which would weaken England. England is therefore our enemy, and the conflict with England will be a life-and-death struggle."

In the face of this misunderstanding and hatred on the part of Hitler, and in the full knowledge that he had every intention of attacking Poland, Britain made no real effort to build up a peace front, and continued to try to make concessions to Hitler. Although the British unilateral guarantee to Poland was made into a mutual guarantee on April 6, Poland guaranteed Britain's "independence" in exactly the same terms as Britain had guaranteed that of Poland on March 31st. No British-Polish alliance was signed until August 25th, the same day on which Hitler ordered the attack on Poland to begin on August 26th. Worse than this, no military agreements were made as to how Britain and Poland would cooperate in war. A British military mission did manage to get to Warsaw on July 19th, but it did nothing. Furthermore, economic support to rearm Poland was given late, in inadequate amounts, and in an unworkable form. There was talk of a British loan to Poland of £100 million in May; on August 1st Poland finally got a credit for $8,163,300 at a time when all London was buzzing about a secret loan of £1,000,000,000 from Britain to Germany.

The effects of such actions on Germany can be seen in the minutes of a secret conference between Hitler and his generals held on August 22nd. The Führer said: "The following is characteristic of England. Poland wanted a loan from England for rearmament. England, however, gave only a credit to make sure that Poland buys in England, although England cannot deliver. This means that England does not really want to support Poland."

Perhaps even more surprising is the fact that France, which had had an alliance with Poland since 1921, had no military conversations with Poland after 1925, except that in August 1936 Poland was given 2,000,000,000 francs as a rearmament loan (Rambouillet Agreement), and on May 19, 1939, the Polish minister of war signed an agreement in Paris by which France promised full air support to Poland on the first day of war, local skirmishing by the third day, and a full-scale offensive on the sixteenth day. On August 23rd General Gamelin informed his government that no military support could be given to Poland in the event of war until the spring of 1940 and that a full-scale offensive could not be made by France before 1941–1942. Poland was never informed of this change, and seems to have entered the war on September 1st in the belief that a full-scale offensive would be made against Germany in the west during September.

The failure to support Poland by binding political, economic, and military obligations in the period before August 23rd was probably deliberate, in the hope that this would force Poland to negotiate with Hitler. If so, it was a complete failure. Poland was so encouraged by the British guarantee that it not only refused to make concessions but also prevented the reopening of negotiations by one excuse after another until the last day of peace. This was quite agreeable to Hitler and Ribbentrop. When Count Ciano, the Italian foreign minister, who had been kept completely in the dark by the Germans, visited Ribbentrop on August 11th he asked his host: "What do you want? The Corridor or Danzig? . . . 'Not any longer.' And he fixed on me those cold . . . eyes of his. 'We want war.' " Ciano was shocked, and spent two days trying, quite vainly, to persuade Ribbentrop and Hitler that war was impossible for several years.

In the light of these facts the British efforts to reach a settlement with Hitler, and their reluctance to make an alliance with Russia, were very unrealistic. Nevertheless, they continued to exhort the Poles to reopen negotiations with Hitler, and continued to inform the German government that the justice of their claims to Danzig and the Corridor were recognized but that these claims must be fulfilled by peaceful means and that force would be inevitably be met by force. On the other hand, they argued, a German agreement to use negotiation would ultimately bring them the possibility of a disarmament agreement, colonial acquisitions, and economic concessions in a settlement with England.

The same point of view had been clearly put by Lord Halifax at Chatham House on June 29th. The key was "no use of force, but negotiations," then a chance to settle "the colonial problem, the questions of raw materials, trade barriers, *Lebensraum*, the limitations of armaments," and other issues. This emphasis on methods, with the accompanying neglect of the balance of power, the rights of small nations, or the danger of German hegemony in Europe, was maintained throughout. Moreover, the British continued to emphasize that the controversy was over Danzig, when everyone else knew that Danzig was merely a detail, and an almost indefensible detail. The real issue was Germany's plan to destroy Poland as one more step on the way to the complete domination of Europe.

Danzig was no issue on which to fight a world war, but it was an issue on which negotiation was almost mandatory. This may have been why Britain insisted that it was the chief issue. But because it was not the chief issue, Poland refused to negotiate because it feared that if negotiation began it would lead to another Munich in which all the Powers would join together to partition Poland. Danzig was a poor issue for a war because it was a free city under the supervision of the League of Nations, and, while it was within the Polish customs and under Polish economic control, it was already controlled politically by the local Nazi Party under a German *Gauleiter*, and would at any moment vote to join Germany if Hitler consented.

In the midst of all these confusions, the British opened negotiations to get Russia to join the "Peace Front." Although the documents probably never will be published on the Soviet side, the course of the discussions is fairly clear. Both sides thoroughly distrusted each other, and it is highly doubtful if either wanted an agreement except on terms which were unacceptable to the other. Chamberlain was very anti-Bolshevik, and the Russians, who had seen him perform in regard to Ethiopia, Spain, and Czechoslovakia, were not convinced that he had finally decided to stand up to Hitler. In fact, he had not. A few words on this last point are relevant here.

We have mentioned that the economic discussions between Britain and Germany, which were publicly broken off on March 28th, were secretly reopened five days later. We do not know what became of these, but, about July 20th, Helmuth Wohlthat, Reich commissioner for the Four-Year Plan, who was in London at an international whaling conference, was approached with an amazing proposition by R. S. Hudson, secretary to the Department of Overseas Trade. Although Wohlthat had no powers, he listened to Hudson and later to Sir Horace Wilson, Chamberlain's personal representative, but rejected their suggestion that he meet Chamberlain. Wilson offered (1) a nonaggression pact with Germany, (2) a delimitation of spheres of interest, (3) colonial concessions in Africa along the lines already mentioned, (4) an economic agreement, and (5) a disarmament agreement. One sentence of Dirksen's report on this matter is significant. It says, "Sir Horace Wilson definitely told Herr Wohlthat that the conclusion of a nonaggression pact would enable Britain to rid herself of her commitments vis-à-vis Poland." That Chamberlain wanted a nonaggression pact with Germany was stated by him publicly on May 3rd, only five days after Hitler denounced his nonaggression pact with Poland.

Dirksen's report of July 21st continued: "Sir Horace Wilson further said that it was contemplated holding new elections in Britain this autumn. From the point of view of purely domestic political tactics, it was all one to the Government whether the elections were held under the cry 'Be Ready for a Coming War!' or under the cry 'A Lasting Understanding with Germany in Prospect and Achievable!' It could obtain the backing of the electors for either of these cries and assure its rule for another five years. Naturally, it preferred the peaceful cry."

News of these negotiations leaked out, apparently from the French, who wished to break them off, but the rumor was that the discussions were concerned with Chamberlain's efforts to give Germany a loan of £1,000,000,000. This is not supported by the documents. This outcry, however, made it difficult to carry on the discussions, especially as Hitler and Ribbentrop were not interested. But Chamberlain kept Lord Runciman busy training to be the chief economic negotiator in the great settlement he envisaged. On July 29th, Kordt, the German chargé d'affaires in London, had a long talk with Charles Roden Buxton, acting, he believed, on behalf of Chamberlain. It was along the same lines. These offers were repeated in a highly secret conversation between Dirksen and Wilson in the latter's residence on August 3rd. Wilson wanted a four-Power pact, a free hand for Germany in eastern Europe, a colonial agreement, an economic agreement, and so forth. Dirksen's record of this conversation then reads:

"After recapitulating his conversation with Wohlthat, Sir Horace Wilson expatiated at length on the great risk Chamberlain would incur by starting confidential negotiations with the German government. If anything about them were to leak out, there would be a grand scandal and Chamberlain would probably be forced to resign." Dirksen did not see how any binding agreement could be reached under conditions such as this, "for example, owing to Hudson's indiscretion, another visit of Herr Wohlthat to London was out of the question." To this, Wilson suggested that "the two emissaries could meet in Switzerland or elsewhere." It was pointed out by Wilson that if Britain could get a nonaggression pact with Germany, it would adopt a nonintervention policy in respect to Greater Germany. This would embrace the Danzig question, for example.

It is clear that these negotiations were not a purely personal policy of Chamberlain's but were known to the Foreign Office. For example, on August 9th Lord Halifax repeated much of the political portion of these conversations. After Munich, he said, he had looked forward to fifty years of peace, with "Germany the dominant power on the continent, with predominant rights in southeastern Europe, particularly in the field of commercial policy; Britain would engage only in moderate trade in that area; in Western Europe, Britain and France protected from conflicts with Germany by the lines of fortification on both sides and endeavoring to retain and develop their possessions by defensive means; friendship with America; friendship with Portugal; Spain for the time being an indefinite factor which for the next few years at least would necessarily have to hold aloof from all combinations of powers; Russia an out-of-the-way, vast and scarcely surveyable territory; Britain bent on safeguarding her Mediterranean communications with the dominions and the Far East." This was "three-bloc-world" talk straight from All Souls College or Cliveden.

It was almost impossible to keep negotiations such as these, or rather proposed negotiations, secret. There can be no doubt that rumors about them reached the Russians in July 1939 and, by strengthening their ancient suspicions of Britain, made them decide to avoid any agreement with Britain and to take instead the nonaggression pact offered by Hitler. The outburst of public rage at Russia for doing this by Britain and America now seems singularly inappropriate in view of the fact that the British government was trying to do the same thing at the same time and the fact that France had signed what Russia regarded as a nonaggression pact with Germany on December 6, 1938. Indeed, Sir Nevile Henderson, who undoubtedly was more extreme than some of his associates, went so far as to condone an *alliance* between Britain and Germany on

August 28, 1939. Obviously, such an alliance could be aimed only at Russia. The relevant portion of his report to Lord Halifax reads:

"At the end Herr von Ribbentrop asked me whether I could guarantee that the Prime Minister could carry the country with him in a policy of friendship with Germany. I said there was no possible doubt whatever that he could and would, provided Germany cooperated with him. Herr Hitler asked whether England would be willing to accept an alliance with Germany. I said, speaking personally, I did not exclude such a possibility provided the development of events justified it."

The theory that Russia learned of these British approaches to Germany in July 1939 is supported by the fact that the obstacles and delays in the path of a British-Russian agreement were made by Britain from the middle of April to the second week of July, but were made by Russia from the second week in July to the end on August 21st. This is supported by other evidence, such as the fact that discussions for a commercial agreement between Germany and Russia, which were broken off on January 30, 1939, were resumed on July 23rd and this agreement was signed on August 19th.

The negotiations for an Anglo-Russian agreement were opened by Britain on April 15th, probably with the double purpose of satisfying the demand in Britain and warning Hitler not to use force against Poland. The first British suggestion was that the Soviet Union should give unilateral guarantees to Poland and Romania similar to those given by Britain. The Russians probably regarded this as a trap to get them into a war with Germany in which Britain would do little or nothing or even give aid to Germany. That this last possibility was not completely beyond reality is clear from the fact that Britain did prepare an expeditionary force to attack Russia in March 1940, when Britain was technically at war with Germany but was doing nothing to fight her.

The Russians did not reject the British suggestion of April 1939, but agreed to guarantee Poland and Romania if the guarantee were extended to all the states on their western frontier, including Finland, Estonia, Latvia, Lithuania, Poland, and Romania, and if it were accompanied by a mutual-assistance pact of Britain, France, and Russia and by a military convention in which each state specified what it would do if the pact came into effect. This offer was a much greater concession than the British seemed to appreciate, since it meant that Russia was guaranteeing its renunciation of all the territory in these six states which it had lost to them since 1917.

Instead of accepting the offer, the British began to quibble. They refused to guarantee the Baltic States on the ground that these states did not want to be guaranteed, although they had guaranteed Poland on March 31st when Józef Beck did not want it and had just asked the Soviet Union to guarantee Poland and Romania, neither of whom wanted a Soviet guarantee. When the Russians insisted, the British countered by insisting that Greece, Turkey, Holland, Belgium, and Switzerland must also be guaranteed. In place of the alliance which Russia wanted, to protect itself against having to fight Germany alone, Britain suggested that the Russian guarantee would become valid only if Britain and France took action to fulfill their own guarantee first.

France and Russia were both pushing Britain to form a Triple Alliance, but Britain was reluctant. Churchill and Lloyd George were pushing in the same direction, but Chamberlain fought back on the floor of the House, refusing to "help to form or to join any opposing blocs." He also refused to send a cabinet minister to negotiate in Moscow, and refused Eden's offer to go. Instead, he sent William (later Lord) Strang, a second-rank Foreign Office official, and only on June 14th. Moreover, the British delayed the discussions to the great irritation of the Soviet leaders, although verbally they were always insisting on speed.

To show its displeasure, the Soviet Union on May 3rd replaced Litvinov with Molotov as foreign minister. This should have been a warning. Litvinov knew the West and was favorable to democracy, to collective security, and to the Western Powers. As a Jew, he was anti-Hitler. Molotov was a contrast from every point of view, and could not have been impressed with British sincerity when he had to negotiate with Strang rather than with Halifax or Eden. The conversations continued, with Molotov still in insisting on the three essentials: (1) mutual assistance in a triple alliance, (2) guarantees to all the border states, and (3) specific obligations as to the amount of assistance by a military convention.

On May 19th Chamberlain in Commons refused "an alliance between ourselves and other countries," and pointed with satisfaction to "that great, virile nation on the borders of Germany which under this agreement [of April 6th] is bound to give us all the aid and assistance it can." He was talking about Poland! He seemed not to realize that Poland was much weaker than the Czechoslovakia he had wrecked in 1938, but he should have known better, because the French clearly knew better. Poland, indeed, was opposed to any agreement of the Western Powers with the Soviet Union, and refused either to be guaranteed by the latter or to accept military assistance from her, even if attacked by Germany. Poland feared that if Russian troops ever entered the areas which it had taken from Russia in 1920, they could never be persuaded to leave. When Russia suggested in May that the Polish-Romanian Alliance of 1926, which was directed exclusively against Russia, should now be extended to oppose Germany as well, Poland refused, although Romania was willing.

In the same month, Romania agreed to allow Russian troops to cross the country to oppose Germany if needed, and Romania's position was more delicate than Poland's regarding territory previously taken from

Russia because Russia had never recognized the Romanian acquisition of Bessarabia. On June 6th Latvia, Estonia, and Finland sent a flat refusal to be guaranteed by Russia. The next day Estonia and Latvia signed non-aggression treaties with Germany, and probably secret military agreements as well, since General Franz Halder, the German chief of staff, went at once to these countries to inspect their fortifications which were being constructed by Germany.

Strang arrived in Moscow only on June 14th, almost two months after Britain had opened these discussions. By July new difficulties arose because of the Russian insistence on a military convention as an integral part of any treaty. Britain demurred but finally reluctantly agreed to conduct the military negotiations at the same time as the political negotiations. However, the members of the military mission took a slow ship, chartered for the occasion (speed thirteen knots), and did not reach Moscow until August 11th. They were again negotiators of the second rank: an admiral who had never been on the Admiralty staff, a purely combat army general, and an air marshal who was an outstanding flyer but not a strategist. To negotiate with these three the Soviet Union named the commander in chief of the Russian Army, the commander in chief of the Russian Navy, and the chief of the Russian General Staff. In London, according to rumor, neither side wanted an agreement, and the military mission had been sent to Moscow to spy out Russia's defenses. From this time on, the obstacles to an agreement were clearly coming from the Russian side, although, considering Chamberlain's secret efforts to make a settlement with Germany, there is no reason to believe that he wanted an agreement with Russia. But perhaps his negotiators in Moscow did; certainly the French did.

From August 10th on, the Russians demanded specific answers, and raised their own demands with every answer. They wanted an exact military commitment as to what forces would be used against Germany in the west so that she would not be free to hurl her whole force against the east; they wanted guarantees whether the states concerned accepted or not; they wanted specific permission to fight across territory, such as Poland, between Russia and Germany. These demands were flatly rejected by Poland on August 19th. On the same day, Russia signed the commercial treaty with Germany. Two days later France ordered its negotiators to sign the documents offered by Russia, including the right to cross Poland, but the Soviet Union refused to accept this signature until Poland consented as well.

On the same day, it was announced that Ribbentrop was coming to Moscow to sign a nonaggression pact. He arrived with a staff of thirty-two persons in a Condor plane on August 23rd and signed the agreement with Molotov late that night. The published portion of the agreement provided that neither signer would take any aggressive action against the other signer or give any support to a third Power in such action. The secret protocol which was added delimited spheres of interest in eastern Europe. The line followed the northern boundary of Lithuania and the Narew, Vistula, and San rivers in Poland, and Germany gave Russia a free hand in Bessarabia.

This agreement was greeted as a stunning surprise in the Entente countries. There was no reason why it should have been, as they had been warned of the possibility on numerous occasions by responsible persons, including Germans like Kordt and Weizsäcker. It was also stated that the negotiations leading up to the agreement had been going on for months and that the Anglo-Soviet discussions accordingly were always a blind. The evidence seems to indicate that the first tentative approaches were made in May 1939, and were reported to Paris at once by the French ambassador, Robert Coulondre, from Berlin. These approaches were distrustfully received by both sides and were broken off completely at Hitler's order on June 29th. They were reopened by the Germans on July 3rd. Only on August 15th did Molotov announce his conviction that the Germans were really sincere, and the negotiations proceeded rapidly from that point.

While it is untrue to say that the German-Soviet Nonaggression Pact made the war inevitable, it certainly made it possible for Hitler to start his war with an easier mind. On August 25th he gave the order to attack on August 26th, but canceled it within a few hours, as word arrived that the British had signed an alliance with Poland that same day. Now began a week of complete chaos in which scores of people ran about Europe trying to avoid the war or to make it more favorable to their side. The British begged the Poles and the Germans to negotiate; the Italians tried to arrange another four-Power conference; various outsiders issued public and private appeals for peace; secret emissaries flew back and forth between London and Germany.

All this was in vain, because Hitler was determined on war. Most of his attention in the last few days was devoted to manufacturing incidents to justify his approaching attack. Political prisoners were taken from concentration camps, dressed in German uniforms, and killed on the Polish frontier as "evidence" of Polish aggression. A fraudulent ultimatum with sixteen superficially reasonable demands on Poland was drawn up by Ribbentrop and presented to the British ambassador when the time limit had already elapsed. It was not presented to the Poles, perhaps because they were so afraid of a second Munich that they hardly dared to talk with anyone. Indeed, the Polish ambassador in Berlin had been ordered by Beck not to accept any document from the Germans.

The German invasion of Poland at 4:45 A.M. on September 1, 1939, did not by any means end the negotiations to make peace, nor, for that matter, did the complete collapse of Polish resistance on September 16– 17. Since these efforts were futile, little need be said of them except that France and Britain did not declare war on Germany until more than two days had elapsed. During this time no ultimatums were sent to Germany, but she was begged to withdraw her forces from Poland and open negotiations. While Poland shuddered under the impact of the first *Blitzkreig*, British public opinion began to grumble, and even the government's supporters in Parliament became restive. Finally, at 9:00 A.M. on September 3rd, Henderson presented to Schmidt, Hitler's interpreter, an ultimatum which expired at 11:00 A.M. In a similar fashion France entered the war at 6:00 P.M. on September 3rd.

XIV

WORLD WAR II:
THE TIDE OF
AGGRESSION, 1939-1941

Introduction

THE history of the Second World War is a very complex one. Even now, after hundreds of volumes and thousands of documents have been published, many points are not clear, and interpretations of numerous events are hotly disputed. The magnitude of the war itself would contribute to such disputes. It lasted exactly six years, from the German invasion of Poland on September 1, 1939 to the Japanese surrender on September 2, 1945. During that period it was fought on every continent and on every sea, in the heights of the atmosphere and beneath the surface of the ocean, and fought with such destruction of property and lives as had never been witnessed before.

The total nature of the Second World War can be seen from the fact that deaths of civilians exceeded deaths of combatants and that many of both were killed without any military justification, as victims of sheer sadism and brutality, largely through cold-blooded savagery by Germans, and, to a lesser extent, by Japanese and Russians, although British and American attacks from the air on civilian populations and on nonmilitary targets contributed to the total. The distinctions between civilians and military personnel and between neutrals and combatants, which had been blurred in the First World War, were almost completely lost in the second. This is clear from a few figures. The number of civilians killed reached 17 millions, of which 5,400,000 were Polish; while Poland had less than 100,000 soldiers killed or missing in the Battle of Poland in 1939, Polish civilians to the number of 3,900,000 were executed, or murdered in the ghetto, subsequently.

The armies which began to move in September 1939 had no new weapons which had not been possessed by the armies of 1918. They still used infiltration tactics, with columns of tanks, strafing airplanes, and infantrymen moving in trucks, but the proportions of these and the ways in which they cooperated with one another had been greatly modified. Weapons for defense were also much as they had been at the end of the previous war, but, as we shall see, they were not prepared in proper amounts nor were they used in proper fashions. These defensive weapons included antitank guns, antiaircraft guns with controlled fire, minefields, mobile artillery on caterpillar tracks, trenches, and defense in depth.

Germany used the offensive weapons we have mentioned in the new fashion, while Poland in 1939, Norway, the Low Countries, and France in 1940, the Balkan countries and the Soviet Union in 1941 did not use the available defensive tactics properly. As a result, Hitler advanced from one astounding victory to another. In the course of 1942 and 1943, new weapons created by democratic science and new tactics learned in Russia, in North Africa, and on the oceans of the world made it possible to stop the authoritarian advance and to reverse the direction of the tide. In 1944 and 1945 the returning tide of Anglo-American and Soviet power overwhelmed Italy, Germany, and Japan with the superior quality and the superior quantities of their equipment and men. Thus the war divides itself, quite naturally, into three parts: (1) the Axis advance covering 1939, 1940, and 1941; (2) the balance of forces in 1942; and (3) the Axis retreat in 1943, 1944, and 1945.

The Germans were able to advance in the period 1939–1941 because they had sufficient military resources, and used them in an effective way. The chief reason they had sufficient military resources was not based, as is so often believed, on the fact that Germany was highly mobilized for war, but on other factors. In the first place, Hitler's economic revolution in Germany had reduced financial considerations to a point where they played no role in economic or political decisions. When decisions were made, on other grounds, money was provided, through completely unorthodox methods of finance, to carry them out. In France and England, on the other hand, orthodox financial principles, especially balanced budgets and stable exchange rates, played a major role in all decisions and was one of the chief reasons why these countries did not mobilize in March 1936 or in September 1938 or why, having mobilized in 1939 and 1940, they had totally inadequate numbers of airplanes, tanks, antitank guns, and motorized transportation.

There was another reason for the military inadequacy of the Western Powers in 1939. This, of even greater significance than the influence of orthodox finance, arose from conflicts of military theories in the period 1919–1939. Several violently conflicting theories held the stage during the twenty years of armistice, and paralyzed the minds of military men to the point where they were unable to provide consistent advice on which politicians could base their decisions. In Germany, on the other hand, decisions (not necessarily correct ones) were made, and action could go on.

One theoretical dispute raged around the role of tanks in combat. The tank had been invented to protect advancing infantry against machine-gun fire by its ability to put machine guns out of action. Accordingly, tanks were originally scattered among the infantry, to advance with it, both moving at a rate of speed no greater than that of a man on foot, consolidating the ground, yard by yard, as both moved forward. This view of the tactical function of tanks continued to be held in high military circles in France and England until too late in 1940. It was sharply challenged, even a decade earlier, by those who insisted that tanks should be organized in distinct units (armored brigades or divisions) and should be used, without close infantry support, moving as perpendicular columns rather than in parallel lines against the defensive formations, and should seek to penetrate through these formations at high speed and without consolidating the ground covered, in order to fan out on the rear of the defensive formations to disrupt their supplies, communications, and reserves. According to these new ideas, the breakthrough made by such an armored column could be exploited and the ground consolidated by motorized infantry, following the armored division in trucks and dismounting to occupy areas where this would be most useful.

In France, the new theory of armored warfare was advocated most vigorously by Colonel Charles de Gaulle. It was generally rejected by his superior officers, so that De Gaulle was still a colonel in 1940. This theory was, however, accepted in the German Army, notably by Heinz Guderian in 1934, and was used very effectively against the Poles in 1939 and against the Western Front in 1940.

At full strength a German *panzer* (armored) division had two regiments of tanks and two regiments of motorized infantry plus various specialized companies. This gave it a total of 14,000 men with 250 tanks and about 3,000 motorized vehicles. In September 1939, Germany had six of these panzer divisions with a total of 1,650 tanks of which one-third were 18-ton models with a 37-mm. gun (Mark III), while two-thirds were 10-ton models (Mark II). By May 1940, when the attack was made in the west, there were 10 armored divisions with a total of 2,000 tanks, some of which were the new Mark IV model, a 23-ton conveyance carrying a 75-mm. gun. No major increase occurred in the next year, but the number of armored divisions was doubled by splitting the ten which existed in May 1940. Thus in June 1941, when Germany attacked Russia, it had 20 armored divisions with a total of 3,000 tanks, of which several hundred were Mark IV but 1,000 were still Mark II. In opposition to these, Poland had only a handful of tanks in 1939, France had over 3,000 in May 1940, and the Soviet Union had, in June 1941, about 15,000 scattered tanks, almost all light or obsolescent models.

A second theory which paralyzed the Western Powers in the years before World War II was concerned with the superiority of defensive over offensive tactics. This defensive theory, of which the Englishman Basil Liddell Hart was the most voluble proponent, assumed that attack would be made in lines, as the Western Powers themselves were trained to attack, and that such an attack would be very unlikely to succeed because of the great increase in firepower of modern weapons. It was argued, on the basis of the experience of World War I, that machine guns could hold up advancing infantry indefinitely and that artillery fire, carefully placed and ranged so that it could cover the field, could prevent tanks from silencing the defensive machine guns to allow infantry to advance.

The Maginot Line was based on these theories. As such, it was not a defense in depth (which would seek to break up offensive columns by allowing them to penetrate to varying depths, thus separating tanks, infantry, and artillery so that each could be dealt with by proper weapons as impetus was dispersed), but was a rigid line (which sought to stop the offensive lines in front of it, as a whole).

The theory of defensive superiority left the military forces of the Western states with inadequate offensive training, poor offensive morale, and unable to come to the help of distant allies (like Poland); it put a premium on a passive, indecisive, inactive military outlook (such as shown by Pétain or Gamelin in the years leading up to 1940) and left them unable to handle any real offensive when it came against them. The theory of continuous defensive lines, which must be kept intact or instantly reestablished whenever they are breached, created a psychology which was incapable of dealing with an assault which came at it in columns and inevitably must breach any defensive line at the point of impact. When this occurred in 1940, French military units threw down their arms or tried to make a precipitous retreat to some point where a new continuous line could be established. As a consequence, the Poles in 1939 and, to a greater extent, the French in 1940, were constantly abandoning positions from which they had not been driven, until units were too broken up to allow hope of reestablishing any continuous line, and France proved to be too small to permit continued retreat. The only alternative seemed to be surrender. As we shall see later, another, highly effective, alternative was discovered, mostly in Russia, by 1942.

In the interwar period there was a third theory, violently disputed, about the effectiveness of air power. In its most extreme form, this theory held that the chief cities of Europe could be destroyed almost completely in the first twenty-four hours of a war, devastated by high-explosive bombs and rendered uninhabitable by gas attacks from the air. This theory, frequently associated with the name of the Italian General Giulio Douhet, was much more prevalent in civilian circles than in military ones, and played an important role in persuading the British and French peoples to accept the Munich Agreement. Like most farfetched ideas, it was supported more frequently by slogans than by logic or by facts, in this case by mottoes like, "The bombers will always get through." The chief facts to support the theory were to be found in the Spanish Civil War, notably in the German destruction of Guernica in 1937 and the ruthless Italian bombardment of Barcelona in 1938. No one paid much attention to the fact that, in both of these cases, the targets were totally undefended.

The military advocates of such air bombardment, most of them considerably more moderate than General Douhet, concentrated their attention on what was called "strategic bombing," that is, on the construction of long-range bombing planes for use against industrial targets and other civilian objectives and on very fast fighter planes for defense against such bombers. They generally belittled the effectiveness of anti-aircraft artillery and were generally warm advocates of an air force separately organized and commanded and thus not under the direct control of army or naval commanders. These advocates were very influential in Britain and in the United States.

The upholders of strategic bombing received little encouragement in Germany, in Russia, or even in France, because of the dominant position held by traditional army officers in all three of these countries. In France, all kinds of air power were generally neglected, while in the other two countries strategic bombing against civilian objectives was completely subordinated in favor of tactical bombing of military objectives immediately on the fighting front. Such tactical bombing demanded planes of a more flexible character, with shorter range than strategic bombers and less speed than defensive fighters, and under the closest control by the local commanders of ground forces so that their bombing efforts could be directed, like a kind of mobile and long-range artillery, at those points of resistance, of supply, or of reserves which would help the ground offensive most effectively. Such "dive-bombers," or Stukas, played a major role in the early German victories of 1939–1941. Here, again, this superiority was based on quality and method of usage and not on numbers. In the three major campaigns of 1939–1941 Germany had a first-line air force of about 2,000 planes, of which half were fighters and half were tactical bombers. On the other side, Poland had 377 military aircraft in 1939; France and Britain had about 3,500 in 1940; while the Soviet Union had at least 8,000 of very varying quality in 1941.

At the outbreak of war in 1939, ideas about sea power were so generally held and with such firm conviction that they were questioned only occasionally. One of these ideas was that sea power was dominated by big-gun capital ships, all other vessels serving simply as accessories to this backbone of the fleet. A related idea assumed that the area in which a fleet could function effectively was limited by the positions of its major bases, such as Pearl Harbor, Gibraltar, Singapore, Toulon, or Kiel. Another idea, rarely disputed, stated that no landing could be made from the sea on a defended shore. These ideas on the nature and limits of sea power had received only minor challenges in the interwar period, except from the extreme advocates of air power like General William Mitchell of the United States Army Air Force. Such extremists, who insisted that land-based planes could make all battleships (or even all navies) obsolete, did not succeed in convincing the admirals or politicians. In the United States Mitchell was subjected to a court-martial and forced to resign. Although the experiences of the Second World War did not support the extreme advocates of air power, either in respect to the navy or to strategic bombing, the ideas of land warfare and especially of sea warfare which were prevalent in 1939 had to be drastically modified by 1945.

The Battle of Poland, September 1939

The German invasion of Poland began with powerful air attacks at 4:40 A.M. on September 1. These attacks, aimed at airfields, assembly points, and railroads, wiped out the Polish air force of 377 planes, mostly on the ground, and, in combination with the rapidly advancing German armored spearheads of tank divisions, made it impossible for Poland to mobilize completely, crippled Polish reconnaissance, destroyed any centralized system of communications, and reduced Polish resistance to numerous fragments of uncoordinated fighting units. The Poles had 30 infantry divisions, a motorized brigade, 38 companies of tanks, and large masses of cavalry, but could bring only a portion of these into action.

Germany struck at Poland with 2,000 planes (of which 400 were dive-bombers) supporting 44 divisions (of which 6 were armored or panzer divisions and 6 were motorized). These forces were organized into 5 armies. The Fourth Army drove down from Pomerania in the northwest while the Eighth and Tenth armies drove upward from Saxony, the three converging in a pincers movement at a point west of Warsaw. At the same time, a much larger pincer converging on the Bug River, a hundred miles east of Warsaw, was formed by the German Third Army, advancing from the Polish Corridor and East Prussia, and the German Fourteenth Army driving northeastward from Galicia and Slovakia. The armored divisions, supported by dive-bombers, raced ahead of their supporting infantry and disrupted all Polish plans, communications, and supplies. The Polish forces, caught in too advanced positions, vainly tried to fight their way eastward to the Vistula and the Bug rivers but were broken up, isolated, and destroyed. Violent but hopeless fighting continued in the pockets, but by September 15th, when Guderian's tanks entered Brest-Litovsk in eastern Poland, the country had been destroyed.

Although Britain and France declared war on Germany on September 3rd, it cannot be said that they made war during the next two weeks in which fighting raged in Poland. British airplanes roamed over Germany, dropping leaflets for propaganda purposes, and French patrols ventured into the space between the Maginot Line and the German Westwall, but no support was given to Poland. Although France had three million men under arms and Hitler had left only eight regular divisions on his western border, no attack was made by France. Strict orders were issued to the British Air Force not to bomb any German land forces, and these orders were not modified until April 1940; similar orders by Hitler to the *Luftwaffe* were maintained for part of this same period. When some British Members of Parliament, led by Amery, put pressure on the government to drop bombs on German munition stores in the Black Forest, the air minister, Sir H. Kingsley Wood, rejected the suggestion with asperity, declaring: "Are you aware it is private property? Why, you will be asking me to bomb Essen next!" Essen was the home of the Krupp munitions factories.

Similar efforts to force the French to take some action against Germany were rejected on the ground that this might irritate the Germans so that they would strike back at the Western Powers. To quiet the English parliamentary group which was demanding action, its leading figure, Winston Churchill, was made first lord of the Admiralty, but the British Navy went into action so slowly that the German "pocket" battleships were able to escape from their ports and from the North Sea out on to the high seas where they could become commerce raiders. Blockade of Germany was established in such a perfunctory fashion that large quantities of French iron ore, as well as other commodities, continued to go to Germany through the neutral Low Countries in return for German coal coming by the same route. These exchanges continued for weeks. On his part Hitler issued orders to his air force not to cross the Western frontier except for reconnaissance, to his navy not to fight the French, and to his submarines not to molest passenger vessels and to treat unarmed merchant ships according to the established rules of international prize law. In open disobedience to these orders, a German submarine sank the liner *Athenia*, westward bound in the Atlantic, without warning and with a loss of 112 lives, on September 3rd.

As Poland was collapsing without a hand being raised to help it, the Soviet Union was invited by Hitler to invade Poland from the east and occupy the areas which had been granted to it in the Soviet-German agreement of August 23rd. The Russians were eager to move, in order to ensure that the Germans stop as far as possible from the Soviet frontiers, but they were desperately afraid that if they did enter Poland the Western Powers might declare war on Russia in support of their guarantee to Poland and would then wage war against the Soviet Union while not fighting Germany or even while allowing economic and military aid to go to Germany.

Accordingly, the Kremlin held up its invasion of Poland until September 17th. On that day the Polish government petitioned Romania to be allowed to seek refuge in that state. The Soviet Union felt that it could not be accused of aggression against Poland if no Polish government still existed on Polish soil. The Soviet leaders sought to justify their advance into Polish territory with the excuse that they must restore order and provide protection for the Ruthenian and White Russian peoples of eastern Poland. The Soviet and Nazi armies met without incidents. On September 28th a new agreement was made between Molotov and Ribbentrop, dividing Poland. Accordingly, Lithuania was shifted into the Soviet sphere, while in Poland itself the German sphere was extended eastward from the Vistula to the Bug River along the old Curzon Line because Russia wanted to follow the nationality boundary.

The Sitzkrieg,
September 1939-May 1940

The period from the end of the Polish campaign to the German attack on Denmark and Norway on April 9, 1940, is frequently called the *Sitzkrieg* (sitting war) or even the "phony war," because the Western Powers made no real effort to fight Germany. These Powers were eager to use the slow process of economic blockade as their chief weapon, in order to avoid casualties. So long as he remained in office, Chamberlain was convinced that no military decision could be reached and that Germany could be beaten only by economic measures. Even after the fall of France, the British chiefs of staff declared, "Upon the economic factor depends our only hope of bringing about the downfall of Germany."

Early in October, Hitler made a tentative offer to negotiate peace with the Western Powers, on the grounds that the cause of the fighting, Poland, no longer existed. This offer was rejected by the Western Powers with the public declaration that they were determined to destroy Hitler's regime. This meant that the war must continue. The British answer to Hitler's offer, and possibly the French answer as well, was not based so much on a desire to continue with the war as it was on the belief that Hitler's rule in Germany was insecure and that the best way to reach peace would be to encourage some anti-Hitler movement within Germany itself. Chamberlain had a passionate personal hatred of Hitler for having destroyed his plans for appeasement. He hoped that a long economic blockade would give rise to such discontent inside Germany that Hitler would be removed and peace made.

GERMAN MOBILIZATION AND
THE ALLIED ECONOMICAL BLOCKADE

Germany was extremely vulnerable to a blockade, but its effects were indecisive. In spite of some casual threats by Hitler that Germany was prepared for a war of any duration, no plans had been made for a long war, and there was no real effort toward economic mobilization by Germany before 1943. The country's industrial plant for making armaments was increased only slightly in the five years 1937–1942, so that, contrary to general opinion, Germany was neither armed to the teeth nor fully mobilized in this period.

In each of the four years 1939–1942, Britain's production of tanks, self-propelled guns, and planes was higher than Germany's. In the first four months of the war (September–December 1939), for example, England produced 314 tanks, while Germany produced 247. The Germans expected each military campaign to be of such brief duration that no real economic mobilization would be necessary. This policy was successful until Hitler bogged down in Russia in 1941, but, even there, the Führer's conviction that Russia would collapse after just one more attack delayed economic mobilization for months.

As late as September 1941, Hitler issued an order for a substantial reduction in armaments production, and the counterorder calling for full mobilization of the German economic system was not issued until the last day of that year. Even then the mobilization was never total or anything like it. The captured records of the German War Ministry for the year 1944, the year of the big effort, show that only about 33 percent of Germany's output in that year went for direct war purposes compared to 40 percent in the United States, and almost 45 percent in Britain. The results of this effort in airplane production can be seen in the fact that Germany produced almost 40,000 aircraft of all kinds in that year 1944, while England produced almost 30,000 and the United States produced over 96,000 military aircraft in the same year.

Germany's economic mobilization which began in 1942 was to have been carried out by Fritz Todt, the engineer who had been in charge of the construction of the Westwall. Todt, however, was killed in an airplane crash on February 12, 1942. His successor, Albert Speer, was an organizer of great ability, but he had to share his functions with several other offices, including Göring's Four-Year-Plan organization, and he spent most of his time negotiating agreements to obtain needed resources from these. A Central Planning Board, on which Speer was one of four men, had powers of top allocation of material resources, but no control over labor. On September 2, 1943, Speer's office was amalgamated with the raw-materials department of the Ministry of Economics to form a Ministry of Armaments and War Production. This new organization obtained control of more and more of the production program without ever obtaining important parts of it. It took eighteen months to get control of naval construction, including submarines and guns (July 1943 to December 1944), while Speer took over production of fighter planes only in March 1944, and of all other planes except "jets" in June 1944. At the same time, more and more war production was getting into the hands of the S.S. because its control of concentration camps gave it the largest available supply of labor. As a result, Speer's office never had anything like complete control of economic mobilization. It is amazing that Germany could have carried on such a great war effort with such a ramshackle organization of its economic life.

When Germany began the war in September 1939, less than a third of its oil, rubber, and iron ore were of domestic origin; it had only two months' supply of gasoline at the peacetime rate of consumption and about three months' supply of aviation fuel. Germany expended less than 100,000 tons of gasoline and oil in Poland and less than 500,000 tons in the conquest of Denmark, Norway, the Low Countries, and France in the period April–June 1940, but captured in the process about two million tons, mostly in France.

At first the British economic warfare against Germany was quantitative rather than qualitative, seeking to reduce the supply of all war matériel rather than concentrating attention, as was done later, on interrupting the supply of a few vital commodities such as ball bearings or aviation fuel. The blockade, with little real effort, was able to cut off immediately over half of Germany's supply of petroleum products and almost half of its iron ore, but, in general, the blockade was established slowly. There was very poor Anglo-French coordination for the whole period before the fall of France in June 1940, and there was a general agreement not to use aerial bombardment, preemptive buying, export control of enemy products, or rationing of neutral purchases. These special techniques of economic warfare began to be applied only in the spring of 1940, just before they were disrupted by the fall of France.

The early British efforts to control contraband and to obtain a quantitative restriction on German imports placed a burden on the navy which it was unable to bear, particularly because of the demand for naval vessels for convoy duty. In this last respect Britain was very fortunate, for here, also, Germany was woefully unprepared for a major war. In the whole period from the launching of the first German submarine in 1935 to the outbreak of war, the German Navy built only 57 submarines. Only 26 of these were equipped for service in the Atlantic. These were subject to such limitations, especially in regard to their cruising range, that less than ten could be kept in the shipping zone at any one time. British minefields in the English Channel, which destroyed three U-boats immediately, made it necessary for these vessels to go out by the route north of Scotland, with the result that they could not operate, by reason of limited cruising range, farther west than 12° 30′ W. (about 80 miles west of Ireland), so that the British Navy did not have to convoy farther west than this line.

As far as the U-boats were concerned, there was no improvement in this situation until the latter half of 1941. The number of U-boat sinkings reached seven a month, and Germany's replacement capacity for building these weapons reached 15 a month (compared to 25 a month in the First World War). This production margin made it possible to raise the number of German submarines at sea, by steady steps, from 15 in April 1941 to 60 at the end of the year. This improvement, from the German point of view, was counterbalanced by an improvement in the British antisubmarine defense tactics, as we shall see, but the struggle became so severe that it is deservedly known as the Battle of the Atlantic. Our present concern with this subject lies in the fact that the inadequacy of the German submarine attack in 1939–1941 made it considerably easier for the British Navy to cope with the blockade problem.

In contraband control work, suspicious merchant vessels were forced to put into a control harbor for search of their cargoes. Control points were placed in Canada, in the Mediterranean, in the north of Scotland, and elsewhere, but the United States would not permit one in the Caribbean Sea area. When vessels being detained began to clog up these ports, whole categories of vessels were exempt from control. This applied, for example, to American ships after January 1940. In order to reduce congestion and delay, vessels which certified that they had no contraband and gave detailed reports of their lading were issued commercial passports, called navicerts, by British representatives in their ports of departure and were generally exempt from search or delay. This use of navicerts, voluntary at first, was made compulsory in July 1940. At the same time, the use of British credit, repair facilities, insurance, refueling stations, charts, and all kinds of shipping aids were denied to vessels which did not have a British "ship-warrant." This system, with the unofficial support of the United States, gradually made it possible to control most of the shipping of the world. The United States and other countries also cooperated from 1940 in rerouting passengers and mails through points like Bermuda or Gibraltar where they could be searched by the British. This gave Britain control of information and enemy funds for blockade purposes.

In order to reduce the enemy's ability to buy abroad, financial connections were cut, his funds abroad were frozen, and his exports were blocked. The United States cooperated in these efforts as well, freezing the financial assets of various nations as they were conquered by the aggressor Powers and finally the assets of the aggressors themselves in June–July 1941. One of the chief steps in this effort was the interruption of the export of German coal by sea from the Baltic to Italy on March 5, 1940, three months before Italy itself became a belligerent. This disrupted the Italian economy. Efforts to supply only half of Italy's needs from Germany by rail almost disrupted the German transportation system (since it required the use of 15,000 railroad cars). At the same time, curtailment of Italian exports and the need to buy British coal reduced the Italian gold reserve, almost at once, from 2.3 to 1.3 billion lire.

Because the British Navy lacked ships to enforce any complete control of contraband by stopping vessels for search, various devices were adopted. Beginning in December 1939, agreements were signed with neutrals by which these latter agreed not to reexport their imports to Britain's enemies. Compulsory rationing of neutral imports was established at the end of July 1940. At the same time, preemptive buying of vital commodities at their source to prevent Germany and its allies from obtaining them began. Because of limited British funds, most of this task of preemptive buying was taken over by the United States, almost completely so by February 1941.

After 1941, the blockade became increasingly effective, especially by the elimination of neutrals (like the Soviet Union, Japan, and the United States) and by the shift from quantitative to qualitative controls. Under this new system the blockade concentrated on a few vital materials and commodities, trying to increase the rate of German usage of these or to reduce their stocks by bombardment or sabotage, and seeking out such materials (like industrial diamonds) at their sources, frequently in remote regions of the earth, then following them by economic-intelligence information to a point where Britain could get them by seizure or by preemptive purchase.

The blockade was enforced by Britain with little regard for international law or for neutral rights, but there was relatively little protest from the neutrals, because the most influential neutrals were already so deeply committed to one side or to the other that they could hardly be regarded as neutrals and were not prepared to defend such a status. The United States openly favored Britain, while Italy and Japan equally openly favored Germany. The Soviet Union favored neither side but was very fearful of attack from both; until April 1940, it was more fearful of Britain and France, while after the fall of Norway and France it became increasingly fearful of Germany. Both of these fears, through geographic and political circumstances, inclined it to a wholehearted economic support of Germany. This continued to the day of the German attack on the Soviet Union on June 22, 1941.

The Nazi-Soviet Trade Agreement of August 19, 1939, promised that Germany would provide 200 million marks' credit to be used for machinery and industrial installations for Russia in return for Russian raw materials to the value of 180 million marks. On February 11, 1940, a new agreement increased these exchanges to 750 million marks' value and provided that Russian deliveries should be made in 18 months and be paid for by German deliveries covering 27 months, the accounts to be balanced in this 2:3 ratio at six-month intervals. At the same time, Russia promised to facilitate transshipment of goods to Germany from Iran, Afghanistan, and the Far East, across Siberia.

This Trans-Siberian leak in the blockade of Germany could have been of great significance because it allowed Germany to keep contact with allied Japan and provided a route to the tin, rubber, and oil of the Netherlands Indies and southeast Asia. However, transportation difficulties, lack of full cooperation by the Russians and Japanese, as well as payment problems, kept the 1940 total for Trans-Siberian freightage to Germany down to about 166,000 tons, of which 58,000 were soybeans and 45,000 were whale oil. In the five months of 1941, before the outbreak of war in Russia, this transit of goods to Germany reached 212,000 tons with soybeans and whale oil accounting for 142,000 tons of the total. Such essential items as rubber, tin, copper, wool, or lubricating oils amounted to only a small fraction of the total.

Germany did much better in obtaining goods from the Soviet Union itself, for the total on this score reached 4,541,202 tons over the 22 months from September 1, 1939 to June 22, 1941. The largest items in this figure were 1,594,530 tons of grain, 777,691 tons of wood and timber, 641,604 tons of petroleum products, 165,157 tons of manganese ore, and 139,460 tons of cotton, but, once again, there were relatively small amounts of vital defense materials which Germany urgently needed. On the other hand, the items Germany did obtain were very profitable to it because Germany was far behind on its repayments to Russia, a situation which became worse as June 1941 approached. The materials Germany had promised in payment were industrial products of great value to the Soviet defense, and Germany delayed in its shipments as much as possible because of Hitler's plans to attack eastward. The Soviet demands that the Germans should catch up on their arrears of payment became one of the irritants which hastened the Nazi attack on Russia in 1941.

On the whole, the blockade had no decisive effect on Germany's ability to wage war until 1945. After examining the evidence on this problem, the chiefs of the blockade of the Foreign Economic Administration in Washington wrote, "Germany's war production and military operations were never seriously hampered by a shortage of any essential raw materials or industrial products, with the single exception of petroleum—and even that shortage resulted from the combined effect of the Soviet

Army's capture of Romanian oil fields and the concentrated bombing of Germany's synthetic production rather than directly from economic warfare." The same writers point out that Germany's food supply, in calories per capita, was at the prewar level until the very last months of the war.

The ability of the Germans to cope with the blockade was largely due to their high level of engineering skill and their ruthless exploitation of conquered Europe, especially of the manpower of dominated areas. German engineering ability made it possible to get around material shortages or to repair industrial plants damaged by air raids, but these efforts required more and more manpower, which Germany lacked. An increase in the labor supply was obtained by enslaving the captured peoples of Poland, Czechoslovakia, Russia, and other countries. In the same way, the German food supply was kept up by starving these enslaved peoples.

In the early part of the war, the blockade was not effective because of the low level of German mobilization, the slow and faulty fashion in which the blockade was (perhaps necessarily) applied, the large number of neutral and nonbelligerent countries, the leaks to Germany across Soviet Russia and Vichy France, the ineffectiveness of quantitative controls under a limited naval patrol, and the succession of German conquests which brought such valuable assets as the Norwegian iron-ore route, the French iron mines and aluminum industry, the Romanian oil wells, or the Yugoslav copper mines under direct German control.

THE SOVIET BORDERLANDS, SEPTEMBER 1939–APRIL 1940

During the "phony war" from September 1939 to April 1940, there were persons in Britain, France, and Germany who were willing to fight to the bitter end and other persons who were eager to make peace. Such persons engaged in extensive intrigues and cross-intrigues in order to negotiate peace or to prevent it. One of the most publicized of these efforts gave rise to the so-called "Venlo incident" of November 1939. On October 9th Hitler ordered his commanding generals to prepare for an immediate attack on the Low Countries and France. Shortly afterward, two members of British military Intelligence in the Netherlands, who were officially attached to the British diplomatic mission at The Hague, were approached by a man whom they believed to be an agent of discontented generals of the German General Staff. This man, who may have been a "double agent" working for both sides, wished to discuss the possibility of negotiating peace if the German generals removed Hitler and his chief associates by a *coup d'état*. The proposal sounded authentic because the British leaders had been approached with similar offers, which were known to be authentic, since August 1938, and there was, at that very moment, late in 1939, a member of the German General Staff who was passing information (including the date of Hitler's projected attack on Holland) to the Netherlands military attaché in Berlin.

With Lord Halifax's permission, the two British officers, Major Richard Henry Stevens and Captain Sigismund Payne-Best, with an observer from the Netherlands government, Lieutenant Klop, held five meetings on Dutch territory with the German negotiators. At the fifth meeting, at Venlo on November 9th, the negotiators, who were really members of the Security Police of the S.S., shot Lieutenant Klop, and escaped into Germany with his body, the two British agents, a Dutch chauffeur, and the automobile in which they had been traveling. The incident aroused great notoriety at the time and, in some circles, was taken to indicate that Britain was really eager to find some way out of the conflict, in spite of its proclaimed determination to fight to a finish.

The Venlo incident was but one, and on the whole a rather unimportant one, of a number of unsuccessful efforts to make peace between the Western Powers and Germany in the six months following the defeat of Poland. These efforts combined with the lack of fighting in the "phony war" to convince the leaders of the Soviet Union that the Western Powers had little heart in fighting Germany and would prefer to be fighting Russia. As we shall see, this was probably true of Chamberlain and his close associates and of Daladier and his successor as prime minister of France, Paul Reynaud. To avoid or at least postpone an attack, from either the Western Powers or Germany, became the chief aim of Soviet policy, and every effort was made to strengthen Russia's military, strategic, and political position. It was felt in the Kremlin, in the period from September to May, that the danger of attack was greater from the Western Powers than it was from Germany, since Germany was in such great need of Russian raw materials that it would probably keep the peace if the Soviet Union made serious efforts to fulfill the economic agreements it had signed with Germany. Moreover, the political agreements of August 23rd and September 28th, by giving the Soviet Union a free hand east of a specified line, made it possible for Russia to strengthen its defenses against Germany by advancing its frontiers and military bases up to that line. Furthermore, the Soviet leaders believed that full economic cooperation with Germany might persuade Hitler to bring pressure on Japan to reduce its pressure on the Soviet Far Eastern frontier.

The Japanese pressure on the Soviet Far East reached its peak in the years 1938 and 1939 with two attacks by the Japanese Army on Soviet territory. The second of these attacks, at Nomonhan on the Manchurian-Mongolian frontier, resulted in a major Japanese defeat in which Nippon suffered 52,000 casualties; it was ended by a truce signed on September 16, 1939, only one day before Russian forces began to move into Poland. From the diplomatic point of view the Soviet Far Eastern policy was a success, for Hitler, in the years 1939–1941, put pressure on Japan to relax its efforts to expand on the northern part of the Asiatic mainland and to replace this with a movement against British Malaya and the Netherlands East Indies. The Japanese defeat at Nomonhan and the fact that the raw materials which Japan needed were to be found in the south rather than in Mongolia, Siberia, or even northern China, persuaded Japan to accept the change of direction. A Soviet ambassador returned to Tokyo in November 1939, for the first time since June 1938.

During the period 1929 to October 1941, the Soviet Union had excellent information about Japanese affairs from its "master spy" in the Far East, Richard Sorge. Sorge, a member of the Nazi Party from 1933, representative of many German newspapers in Tokyo from the same year, and press attaché in the German Embassy in Tokyo in 1939–1941, had an excellent knowledge of the most secret matters in the Far East because of his own intimate relations with the German ambassador and because of his secret agents (including Saionji, adopted son of the "last Genro," and Ozaki, adviser to Prince Konoye) in Japanese governing circles. By reporting to Moscow on the condition of the Japanese military forces and the gradual triumph, within the Japanese government, of the anti-British over the anti-Russian influence, Sorge made it possible for the Soviet Union to weaken its defenses in the Far East in order to strengthen them in Europe.

In Europe, after the occupation of Poland (which shielded the Russian center), the Soviet leaders were worried about two areas. In the south, including the Balkans, the Dardanelles, or the Caspian oil fields, they were very fearful of an Anglo-French attack, while in the Baltic they were fearful of both the Western Powers and Germany.

The Soviet fears of the Western Powers in the south appear quite unfounded to us, but seemed very real to them in 1939. The information which has been released since 1945 shows that there was some basis for this fear but that the Anglo-French threat to Russia was much greater in the Baltic than it was in the south. In the latter area the Kremlin was suspicious of the French Army of the Orient in Syria. The Russians believed that General Maxime Weygand had a force of several hundred thousand men which he wished to use across Iran or Turkey in an attack on the Russian oil fields in the Caspian region. In January 1940, Germany obtained reports from Paris that Weygand proposed to attack the Soviet Union from Romania. As a matter of fact, Weygand had only three poorly equipped divisions totaling about 40,000 men, and his plans were largely defensive. He hoped to support the Allied guarantees to Turkey, Greece, and Romania (given in April 1939), and to protect the Romanian oil fields by moving northward from Salonika if Germany, Hungary, or Bulgaria made any warlike move in the Balkans.

The political situation in the Balkans was of such precarious stability that the Western Powers did not dare to make a move in the area for fear everything would collapse. Turkey, Greece, Romania, and Yugoslavia were joined in a Balkan Entente aimed at preventing any Bulgarian aggression. Since these four states could mobilize over a hundred divisions, although lacking all modern or heavy equipment, they could keep Bulgaria quiet. Unfortunately, the Balkan Entente was not designed for protection against Italy or Germany, where the real danger lay.

Italy had various projects to attack Greece from the Albanian territory it had seized in April 1939. It also had fully matured plans to disrupt Yugoslavia by subsidizing and supporting a Croat revolt, under Ante Pavelić, against the dominant Serb majority in that state. During the "phony war" the Italians hoped that the Western Powers would allow Italy to carry out its project against Yugoslavia in order to block any German movement into that area. Such permission seemed possible from the fact that the democratic states had not guaranteed Yugoslavia as they had the other three states of the Balkan Entente. Italy's project was set for early June 1940, but was interrupted by Hitler's attack in the West, which was made, without notifying his Italian partner, on May 10th.

Another element of instability in southeastern Europe was the position of Hungary, which aspired to detach Transylvania from Romania. Since Hungary could not take this area by its own power, it sought support from Italy rather than from Germany (which the Hungarians feared). With Italian support, Hungary refused to allow German troops to cross its territory to attack Poland in September 1939, and began to negotiate an agreement with Italy by which the Duke of Aosta would be offered the crown of Hungary, as an anti-German solution to Hungary's ambiguous constitutional position. This project, like the one in Croatia, was upset by the growing rivalry of Germany and Russia in the Balkans.

During the period from September 1939 to June 1940, Hitler had no political ambitions with respect to the Balkans or the Soviet Union. From both he wanted nothing more than the maximum supply of raw materials and a political peace which would permit these goods to flow to Germany. Both areas cooperated fully with Germany in economic matters, but fear of Germany was so great that both areas also sought political changes which might strengthen their ability to resist Germany at a later date. Hungarian efforts to obtain support from Italy were not successful, as we have seen, because Italy wavered between fear of Germany and recognition of the fact that its own ambitions in the Balkans, the Mediterranean, or Africa could be obtained only with German support. The Balkan Entente sought support and military supplies from the Western Powers but could obtain little, since these Powers believed that they did not have the equipment to defend themselves. The only important step they took was a military alliance with Turkey. This was signed with France and England on October 19, 1939 in the form of a mutual-assistance pact, except that Turkey could not be compelled to take up arms against Russia. This last clause was inserted on Turkish insistence but was kept secret and, in consequence, the Soviet Union was not reassured by the agreement.

In the meantime the Soviet Union took steps to defend itself against any attack from the Baltic. In the period September 29–October 10, 1939, three of the Baltic states, Estonia, Latvia, and Lithuania, were forced to sign military-assistance pacts with Russia. Estonia and Latvia provided naval and air bases for Russian forces, while the city of Vilna was given to Lithuania by Russia. About 25,000 Russian troops were stationed in each of the three countries. Appeals from these countries to Germany for support against Russia were summarily rejected, and they were advised to yield to the Soviet demands. As part of the reorganization of this area, Hitler on September 27th ordered that the so-called "Balts" (German-speaking residents of the Baltic states) should be moved to Germany as quickly as possible. This was done within a month.

From the Soviet point of view Finland provided a much more important problem than any of the Baltic states. The city of Leningrad, one of Russia's greatest industrial centers with a population of 3,191,000 persons, was joined to the Baltic Sea by the Gulf of Finland. This gulf, about 150 miles long and 50 miles wide, ran west to east, with its northern and eastern shores occupied by Finland and its southern shore largely Estonian. Leningrad, at the extreme southeastern corner of the gulf, was at the southern end of the Karelian Isthmus, a neck of land running north and south between the gulf and Lake Ladoga, some 20 miles farther east. The Finnish frontier crossed this isthmus from the gulf to Lake Ladoga only 20 miles north of Leningrad.

On October 14th the Soviet Union demanded that the Finnish frontier north of Leningrad be pushed back along the shore of the gulf so that the frontier would run westward from Lake Ladoga instead of southward as formerly. This would put the Finnish frontier about 50 miles from Leningrad, leaving Finland about half of the Karelian Isthmus. In addition, the Bolsheviks demanded a 30-year lease on the Finnish naval base at Hangö at the entrance to the Gulf of Finland, a strip about 100 miles long and 10 miles wide in central Finland (where the Finnish frontier came closest to the railroad line between Leningrad and Russia's ice-free port of Murmansk on the Arctic Sea), and a small area of about 25 square miles where the Finnish frontier reached the Arctic Ocean west of Murmansk. In return for these concessions Moscow offered a nonaggression pact, about 2,100 square miles of wooded area in central Finland, and permission to Finland to fortify the Aaland Islands between Finland and Sweden, something which had been forbidden since 1921.

It is not yet clear why Finland rejected the Russian demands of October 1939. The Germans and Russians believed that it was done under British influence, but the evidence is not available. At any rate, the Finns asked for German support and were rebuffed as early as October 6–7 1939 (before the Russian demands were received); they ordered mobilization of their armed forces against the Soviet Union on October 9th, and were reported by the German minister to be "completely mobilized" ten days later. In the negotiations Stalin abandoned the Soviet demand for Hangö if he could get the Island of Russarö nearby and the island of Suursaari farther up the gulf, but insisted on most of the Karelian demand; the Finns offered about a third of the Karelian demand but refused to grant any naval bases in the gulf. On November 9th the discussions broke down; four days later the Finnish negotiators went home. For some unexplained reason, the Finns seem to have felt that the Russians would not attack their country, but the Soviets attacked at several points on November 29th.

If the Finns had misinterpreted the Soviet determination to attack, the Soviets misinterpreted the Finnish determination to resist. Although attacked at five major points by large forces with heavy equipment, the Finns made very skillful use of the terrain and the winter weather. In the first two months (December–January) a half-dozen or more Soviet divisions were torn to pieces. Only in February 1940 did the Soviet offensive begin to move, and by the end of the month Finland's forces were so exhausted by superior numbers that they accepted the Soviet terms. Peace was signed on March 12, 1940.

As soon as Finland realized that Russia seriously intended to attack, it set up a new Cabinet under Risto Ryti to wage the war and simultaneously seek peace by negotiation. This latter proved to be difficult because on December 2nd, Moscow set up a puppet Finnish government under a minor and discredited Finnish Communist in exile, V. Kuusinen; a mutual-aid pact was signed with this puppet state at once. The existence of this regime discouraged Germany from offering any mediation seeking peace, in spite of its eagerness to see the end of the fighting in Finland, but on March 12th, when peace was made with the authentic Finnish government, Kuusinen was simply left in the lurch by Moscow.

The Soviet attack on Finland provided the leaders in the Entente countries with a heaven-sent opportunity to change the declared but unfought war with Germany, which they did not want, into an undeclared but fighting war against the Soviet Union. The fact that a Russian war would be hundreds of miles away, while the war with Germany was on their doorstep, was an added advantage, especially in Paris, which had been steadily resisting British suggestions for any unfriendly action against Germany along the Rhine. Accordingly, Britain and France resurrected the moribund League of Nations, violated the Covenant to put Finland, Egypt, and South Africa on the Council, and illegally (according to the

American Journal of International Law) expelled Russia from the League as an aggressor.

That Russia was an unprovoked aggressor is beyond question, but there was at least a surface inconsistency between the violence of the Anglo-French reaction against Russian aggression in 1939 and the complacency with which they had viewed other aggressions in 1931–1939. This last act of the League of Nations was its most efficient. Although the League's consideration of the Japanese aggression in China had required fifteen months and resulted in no punishment, Russia was condemned in eleven days in December 1939. The German aggressions of 1936–1939 had not even been submitted to the League of Nations, and the Italian seizure of Albania had been recognized by Britain with unseemly haste earlier in 1939, but the Anglo-French leaders now prepared to attack the Soviet Union both from Finland and from Syria.

In the north, every effort was made by France and Britain to turn the Soviet attack on Finland into a general war against Russia. On December 19, 1939, the Supreme War Council decided to provide Finland with "all indirect assistance in their power" and to use diplomatic pressure on Norway and Sweden to aid Finland against Russia. The Scandinavian countries were informed of this on December 27th. On February 5, 1940, the Supreme War Council decided to send to Finland an expeditionary force of 100,000 heavily armed troops to fight the Soviet hordes. Germany at once warned Norway and Sweden that it would take action against them if the two Scandinavian countries permitted passage of this force.

Germany and Russia were both eager to end the Finnish fighting before any Anglo-French intervention could begin, the former because it feared that Anglo-French forces in Scandinavia would be able to stop shipments of Swedish iron ore across Norway to Germany through the seaport of Narvik, the Russians because they were convinced of an Anglo-French desire to attack them. The evidence supports both of these fears.

Because of its very high quality, Swedish iron ore was essential to the German steel industry. In 1938 Germany imported almost 22 million tons of ore, of which almost nine million tons came from Sweden and over five million came from France. A German-Swedish trade agreement of December 22, 1939, promised that Sweden would ship ten million tons of ore in 1940, of which two or three million would go by way of Narvik. As early as September 1939, the British were discussing a project to interrupt the Narvik shipments either by an invasion of Norway or by mining Norwegian territorial waters. When Germany heard of the Anglo-French expeditionary force being prepared to cross Norway to Finland, it assumed that this was merely an excuse to cut off the ore shipments. Accordingly, Germany began to prepare its own plans to seize Norway first.

As a matter of fact, the Anglo-French expeditionary force was really intended to attack Russia, but it was unable to arrive on time, although Britain and France did all they could to force Finland to continue to fight until they could arrive on the scene. In February word was sent that if Finland made peace the two Western Powers would not be bound to support Finnish independence after the great war ended. On January 3rd the British ambassador was withdrawn from Moscow. On February 26th Lord Halifax rejected a Soviet request that Britain convey its peace terms to Finland; they had to be sent through Sweden instead. On March 4th Daladier and Lord Ironsides formally promised Finland an expeditionary force of 57,000 men. The Scandinavian countries put pressure on Finland not to ask for troops, and informed Britain that they would tear up their railroad tracks if the expeditionary force tried to cross.

When the request from the Finns did not arrive, Daladier, on March 8th, sent them a threatening message which said: "I assure you once more, we are ready to give our help immediately. The airplanes are ready to take off. The operational force is ready. If Finland does not now make her appeal to the Western Powers, it is obvious that at the end of the war the Western Powers cannot assume the slightest responsibility for the final settlement regarding Finnish territory."

According to the Finnish foreign minister, V. Tanner, Daladier at this time told the Finnish military attaché in Paris that if Finland stopped fighting Russia, the Western Powers would make peace with Germany. According to the same authority, Anglo-French agents did all they could, up to the final moment, to prevent or to disrupt the Soviet-Finnish peace negotiations, and had made plans to cross Scandinavia, even without permission, and to use any Finnish appeal for an expeditionary force as a weapon to arouse the Scandinavian people to overthrow their own governments. The Swedish prime minister, in return, threatened to fight on the side of Russia against any Entente effort to force a transit. When the Finnish request did not come, Britain, on March 12th, informed Norway and Sweden that it *had* arrived, and made a formal request for transit across the two countries. This was refused, and Finland made peace the same day.

The Soviet-Finnish Peach Treaty of March 12, 1940 was made at the insistence of the Finnish commander in chief, Baron Mannerheim, although it was much more severe than the Russian demands of October. In addition to the areas in the north and the naval base at Hangö, the Soviet aggressors took many of the islands of the Gulf of Finland and the whole of the Karelian Isthmus, including all the shores of Lake Ladoga. These gains made it possible for Russia to bring both official and unofficial pressure on Finland to influence its foreign and domestic policy. To resist this steady pressure, Finland began, in August 1940, secret military conversations with Germany.

The failure of the Anglo-French expeditionary force to reach Finland does not mean that no aid reached the Finns. Germany refused all aid, and intercepted most of Italy's aid, releasing it again once peace had been made. The Western Powers, however, encouraged volunteers to go and sent much valuable equipment. Early in March, Chamberlain wrote to his sister about Finnish aid as follows: "They began by asking for fighter planes, and we sent all the surplus we could lay hands on. They asked for AA guns, and again we stripped our own imperfectly-armed home defences to help them. They asked for small arms ammunition, and we gave them priority over our own army. They asked for later types of planes, and we sent them 12 Hurricanes, against the will and advice of our Air Staff. They said that men were no good now, but that they would want 30,000 in the spring."

The Soviet-Finnish treaty of March 12th did not put an end to the Anglo-French projects to attack Russia or to cross Scandinavia. Anger against both the Soviet Union and the Scandinavian countries remained high in Paris and London. The Finnish expeditionary force was kept together in England, where its existence gave a powerful incentive to the German project to invade Norway before Britain did so. On April 5th, only four days before the German attack on Norway, Lord Halifax sent a note to Norway and Sweden threatenting these countries with dire, if unstated, consequences at the hands of Britain if they refused to cooperate with the Western Powers in sending aid to Finland "in whatever manner they may see fit" in any future Soviet attack on Finland.

Six days later, two days *after* Germany's aggression against Denmark and Norway, General Weygand was ordered to attack the Soviet Union from Syria. This project had been initiated on January 19, 1940, when Daladier ordered General Gamelin and Admiral Jean Darlan to draw up plans to bomb Russia's Caucasian oil fields from Syria. These plans were submitted on February 22nd but were held up in favor of the Finnish project; on April 11th, a month after the Soviet-Finnish peace, the new French premier, Reynaud, ordered General Weygand to carry out the raid on the Soviet oil wells of the Caucasus as soon as possible. Weygand was unable to do this before the end of June. By that time France had been defeated by Germany, and Britain was in no position to attack any new enemies.

THE GERMAN ATTACK ON DENMARK AND NORWAY, APRIL 1940

Hitler's orders to attack France through the Netherlands and Belgium were issued on October 9, 1939, and the date of the attack was set for

November 8th. This was postponed on November 7th; between that date and May 10th, the order to attack was given and revoked a half-dozen times because of adverse weather conditions and lack of munitions. Each of these order was reported to the West through the Dutch military attaché in Berlin, but, as no attack eventuated, it is probable that faith in this informant declined.

Information also came from other sources. One order to attack was reported to the West by Count Ciano, the Italian foreign minister, but the Italians were dependent on their own spies, since they could get no information from Hitler, and did not know of the date which was finally used on May 10th. In January a German plane with operational orders for the attack made an emergency landing in Belgium; the orders were captured before they could be destroyed completely. This caused great alarm in the West, but no one could be sure if the captured documents were authentic or part of a Nazi false alarm.

In the meantime, from December 1939, onward, plans to invade Norway were prepared at the insistence of the German admirals. These plans were made in cooperation with Major Vidkun Quisling, a former Norwegian minister of war and leader of the insignificant Nazi Party in Norway. Formal orders were issued by Hitler on March 1, 1940 to occupy both Denmark and Norway. Violations of Norwegian neutrality by both sides in the early months of 1940 influenced these plans very little. In February the British Navy intercepted the German prison ship *Altmark* in Norwegian waters and released about three hundred British sailors who had been captured by the German commerce raider *Graf Spee*; on April 7th the British placed a minefield in Norwegian waters to interrupt the flow of Swedish iron ore down the western coast of Norway from Narvik to Germany. But by that time the German operations had begun.

Denmark yielded to a German ultimatum on April 9th as German divisions overran the country; and seaborne forces landed in Copenhagen harbor. The same morning secret German agents inside Norway and troops smuggled into Norwegian harbors in merchant vessels seized Norwegian airfields, radio stations, and docks. They were supported at once by airborne infantry in Oslo and Stavanger and by seaborne forces at Oslo, Trondheim, Bergen, and Narvik. Although German naval losses were large, including three cruisers and eleven destroyers, the operation was a complete success. Oslo was captured in its sleep the first day, and the Luftwaffe had air supremacy over most of Norway by the end of that day.

The Allied expeditionary force which had been prepared for Finland, with some additional forces from France, was committed to Norway in a scattered and piecemeal fashion, chiefly around Trondheim and Narvik. The Trondheim expedition was badly bungled and had to be evacuated to sea on May 1st; the Narvik expedition captured that city on May 27th but began to evacuate, taking the Norwegian royal family with it, a week later. In the operation, British naval losses were heavy, and included the aircraft carrier *Glorious*.

The Norwegian fiasco brought Britain's increasingly restive public opinion to the boiling point. In the parliamentary debate of May 7-10, Chamberlain feebly defended his policies, but was subjected to a devastating attack from all sides. The high point was reached when Leopold Amery, repeating Cromwell's words to the Long Parliament, cried at Chamberlain: "You have sat too long here for any good you have been doing. Depart, I say—let us have done with you. In the name of God, go!" In the following vote of confidence Chamberlain was victorious, 281–200, but his nominal majority of 200 had fallen to 81, equivalent to a defeat. The next day, May 9, 1940, the Speaker was very busy preventing the Honorable Members from continuing their attack on Chamberlain. On May 10th, at dawn, the German armies struck westward against the Netherlands, Belgium, Luxembourg, and France. Chamberlain resigned, and was replaced by a national government under Winston Churchill.

After forty years of parliamentary life, during much of which he had been the best-hated man in the House of Commons, Churchill's arrival to the highest political office was received by Englishmen with a sigh of relief. Right or wrong, fairly or unfairly, Churchill had always been a fighter and, in May 1940, as the German armies swept westward, what the forces of decency and democracy needed was a fighter, to provide a nucleus about which those who wished to resist tyranny and horror could rally. In his first speech, the new prime minister provided such a nucleus: all he had to offer was "blood, toil, tears and sweat. . . . Our only aim is victory," he said, "for without victory there is no survival."

The Fall of France
(May-June 1940)
and the Vichy Regime

In the next six months neither victory nor survival seemed very likely for the West. The German forces which attacked on May 10th were inferior in manpower to the forces which faced them but were much more unified, used their equipment in an effective fashion, and had a single plan which they proceeded to carry out. Amounting to about 136 divisions, they were opposed by 156 divisions, but the defenders were divided into four different national armies, were arranged improperly, were given tasks too difficult for their size and equipment and, in general, were so managed that their weakest points coincided completely with the most powerful German attacks.

The French plan of campaign was dominated by two factors: the Maginot Line and Plan D. The Maginot Line, an elaborate and expensive system of permanent fortifications, ran from Switzerland to Montmédy. Behind this line, where they could not be used in the great battle drawing near, were stationed 62 of 102 French divisions on this frontier. From Montmédy to the sea, France had 40 divisions, plus the British Expeditionary Force of 10 divisions. According to Plan D, the anticipated German attack on the Low Countries was to be met by the Allied forces north of Montmédy advancing as rapidly as possible to meet the enemy. If the Belgian Army of 20 divisions were successful in holding up the German advance, it was hoped that a new Belgian-British-French line could be formed along the Dyle River or even forty miles farther north along the Albert Canal; if the Belgian defense were less successful, the new line was to be formed along the Scheldt River, fifty miles behind the Dyle. To carry out this rapid movement as soon as the German attack was announced, the French placed their best and fastest divisions on the extreme left (in Henri Giraud's Seventh Army) and their poorest divisions close to the end of the Maginot Line (in André Corap's Ninth Army), where they were expected to make a relatively short advance to take a position between Sedan and Namur along the Meuse River. Once this Plan D advance into the Low Countries had been achieved, it was expected that the new line, from the sea to Longwy (deep in the Maginot Line), would stand as follows:

Netherlands forces—10 divisions
Giraud's Seventh Army—7 divisions
Belgian forces—20 divisions
Lord Gort's British Expeditionary Force—10 divisions
Jean Blanchard's First Army—6 divisions
Corap's Ninth Army—9 divisions
Charles Huntziger's Second Army—7 divisions

Originally the German plans were, as the French anticipated, a modified version of the Schlieffen Plan of 1905, involving a wide sweep through the Low Countries. The false alarms of a German attack in the winter of 1939-1940 revealed to the Germans, however, that the Allies would meet this attack by a rapid advance into Belgium. Accordingly, at the suggestion of General Erich von Manstein, the Germans modified their plans to encourage the Allied advance into Belgium while the Germans planned to strike with their greatest strength at Sedan, the pivot of the Allied turning movement. Such an assault at Sedan made it necessary for the German forces to pass over the narrow, winding roads of the Ardennes Forest, then to cross the deep and swift Meuse River, and to break between Corap's and Huntziger's forces, but, if this could be done and Sedan taken, excellent roads and a railroad ran from Sedan westward across France to the sea.

Under the "Manstein Plan" the German attack from the North Sea to Sedan was organized in four armies. In the north, the Netherlands was attacked by the German Eighteenth Army (one panzer and four infantry divisions); in the middle, Belgium was attacked by the German Sixth Army (two panzer and 15 infantry divisions) and the German Fourth Army (two panzer and 12 infantry divisions); farther south, in the Ardennes area, France was attacked by the German Twelfth Army (five panzer and four other divisions); from Sedan to Switzerland, although Germany had about 30 divisions, all were infantry formations and no major offensive was made.

The "Manstein Plan" was a total surprise to the French. They were so convinced that the Ardennes were impassable for large forces, especially for tanks, that everything was done to make the German task easier: Corap and Huntziger placed their poorest forces (six Series B divisions, undermanned, with little training) on either side of Sedan and their best forces on their fronts most remote from the Ardennes (that is, from Sedan). In Huntziger's case these better divisions were *behind* the Maginot Line itself. Because of the Ardennes, Corap gave his four poor divisions near Sedan no antitank guns, no antiaircraft guns, and no air support (reserving these for his high-quality divisions forty miles farther north), and expected them to defend a front of ten miles per division (while the French Third Army, deep behind the Maginot Line, had a front of 1.8 miles per division). Moreover, Corap's poor divisions were not stationed on the Meuse, but two days' march to the west of it, and were required, once the German attack began, to race the Germans to the intervening river.

The German attack began at 5:35 on May 10th. Two days later the panzer division with the German Eighteenth Army broke through the Dutch defenses and began to join up with parachute and airborne forces which had been dropped behind these; the Netherlands collapsed. The Dutch field forces surrendered on May 14th, after much of the center of Rotterdam had been destroyed in a twenty-minute air attack. The Netherlands royal family and the government moved to England to continue the war.

The great mass of the German attack fell on Belgium, and was greatly aided by the failure of many ordinary defensive precautions. Vital bridges over the Meuse and the Albert Canal were destroyed only partly or not at all. The defenders on the Albert Canal were attacked from the rear by parachutists and glider forces which had been landed behind them. The powerful fort of Eben Emael, covering the canal bridges, was captured by airborne volunteers who landed on its roof and destroyed its gun apertures with explosives. Belgium's forces fell backward toward the Dyle as the French and British units, according to Plan D, wheeled northeastward, on Sedan as a pivot, to meet them. As the Belgian forces withdrew northwest, while the German attack swung southwest, the main burden of the German assault now fell on the French First Army, to pin it down and thus prevent it from reinforcing Corap farther south. In this the Germans were successful; on May 15th, as news of the breakthrough at Sedan became known, Gamelin ordered all forces in Belgium to fall backward from the Dyle Line toward the Scheldt.

The attack through the Ardennes on Corap's Ninth Army was made by a special German force of five panzer and three motorized divisions under General Paul von Kleist. These passed through the forest and crossed the Meuse to fling themselves on the right side of Corap's inexperienced divisions. By the evening of May 15th, Corap's army had been "volatilized," and the German spearhead was racing forward thirty-five miles west of Sedan. The misplaced French Sixth Army, in reserve 300 miles south near Lyon, began to move toward the breach, while General Giraud, with three divisions from the Seventh Army, was ordered from the extreme northwest, and seven other divisions were taken from the forces behind the Maginot Line. All these arrived too late, because von Kleist's advance units crossed France and reached the sea at Abbeville on May 20th, having covered 220 miles in eleven days. No coordinated attack was ever made on this thin extended line, although orders were issued for it to be attacked both from the north and the south.

The Allied forces retreating southward from Belgium were greatly hampered by masses of refugees clogging the roads, were constantly harassed by Stukas, and had lost communication between units. There was almost no contact or cooperation between the French, British, and Belgians in the north, or between these and the French forces south of Kleist's breakthrough. Panic swept Paris. On May 16th sixteen French generals, including Gamelin, were dismissed, and the command given to Weygand, who did not arrive from Syria until May 20th. During this period, evacuation of the government to Tours was ordered, and the secret archives of the Foreign Ministry were burned in bonfires on the lawns of the Quai d'Orsay.

On May 17th Reynaud replaced Daladier as minister of national defense and generally shook up the government, replacing many weak men by defeatists, appeasers, and Fascist sympathizers. The chief new face was that of Marshal Pétain, eighty-three years old, the man chiefly responsible for the inadequacy of French military planning in the interwar period. Pétain was recalled from the ambassadorship in Madrid to be vice-premier in the new Cabinet. Certain French politicians, including Pierre Laval, hoped that Pétain might play a role in French domestic politics such as Hindenburg had played in Germany: to protect the organized vested interests of industry and business from changes by the Left in a period of defeat.

Weygand spent five days (May 20th-25th) in an unsuccessful effort to get a coordinated attack on Kleist's salient. On May 25th-26th, Kleist, moving up the coast from the Somme, on the rear of the northern Allied forces, captured Boulogne and Calais, leaving Dunkerque as the only major port on the Allied rear. Withdrawal to this port was threatened by a German break through the Belgian Army toward Ypres. On May 27th, King Leopold of Belgium made an unconditional surrender of his armies to the Germans, over the objections of the Belgian civil government and without making certain that the Allied Command had been informed. The British Expeditionary Force at once began to evacuate the Continent through Dunkerque.

In seven days, using 887 water craft of all types and sizes, 337,131 men were taken off the beaches at Dunkerque under relentless air bombardment (May 28th–June 4th). By Hitler's direct order, no intensive ground attack was made on the Allied forces within the Dunkerque perimeter, as Hitler was convinced that Britain would make peace as soon as France was defeated, and wished to save his dwindling armored forces and munitions for the attack on the rest of France. In the interval before this new attack, Weygand tried to form a new line along the Somme and Aisne rivers from the sea to the Maginot Line and to eliminate three bridgeheads the Germans already held south of the Somme.

The Battle of France began on June 5th with German attacks on the western and eastern ends of the "Weygand Line." By June 8th the western end had been broken, and German forces began to move to the rear of the Somme defenses. As the line collapsed and the military forces fell back, they disintegrated among packed masses of civilian refugees, hurried onward by German dive-bombers. Paris and later all cities of France were declared open cities, not to be defended. Just as in Kleist's original breakthrough, no effort was made to hold up the Germans by road obstacles, civilian resistance, house-to-house fighting, destruction of supplies, or (above all) destruction of abandoned gasoline. The German armored units roamed at will on captured fuel.

On June 12th Weygand requested the French government to seek an armistice; Reynaud refused to permit any civilian surrender, since this was forbidden by an Anglo-French agreement of March 12, 1940. Instead, he gave permission for a military capitulation, if the civil government continued the war from French North Africa or from overseas bases, as Norway, the Netherlands, and Belgium were doing. Pétain,

Weygand, and their supporters refused to leave France. They also flatly rejected any military capitulation, for they wanted to end the fighting with an armistice which would allow France to maintain a French Army as a guarantee against any economic or social changes in France.

There was also considerable pressure behind the scenes from anti-democratic French industrialists in monopolistic lines such as chemicals, light metals, synthetic fibers, and electrical utilities. These industrialists, together with politicians like Laval and private or commercial banks, like the Banque Worms, or the Banque de l'Indochine, had been negotiating cartel and other agreements with Germany for ten years, and felt an armistice would offer a splendid opportunity to complete and enforce these agreements.

As the military collapse continued, piteous appeals for help were sent to London and to Washington. Reynaud sent eighteen messages to Churchill asking for more air support, but could obtain none, as the British War Cabinet wished to save all the planes it still had for the defense of Britain after the French collapse. Appeals to Roosevelt were no more successful; 150 planes and 2,000 75-mm. cannons were sent, but they sailed from Halifax only on June 17th and were at sea when the fighting ceased.

The chief concern in London and Washington was over the fate of the French fleet and of French North and West Africa, especially Dakar. If Hitler obtained the French fleet or any considerable portion of it, British and American security would be in acute jeopardy. The French fleet was of high quality and included two new battleships (*Richelieu* and *Jean Bart*) which had just been built but were not yet in service. Such a navy, in combination with the German and Italian navies, might destroy Britain's sea defenses and force a British surrender. This would place America in great danger, as American security in the Atlantic had been preserved by the British fleet since 1818 and, by 1940, the whole American battle fleet had to be kept in the Pacific to face Japan.

Only less immediate than these dangers was the threat to both British and American security from a German occupation of French North and West Africa. This would close the British route through the Mediterranean immediately and allow the Italian forces in Libya to invade Egypt with relative impunity. The possession of Dakar by German forces would provide a base from which submarines could attack the British route to the East by way of South Africa and might permit an attack on Brazil, only 1,700 miles west of Dakar.

With these considerations in mind, Washington and London did all they could to dissuade Mussolini from attacking France and to persuade the French to avoid any armistice which might yield either French Africa or the French fleet to Hitler. Eventually Britain gave permission to France to seek an armistice if the fleet sailed to British ports. This was rejected by the French military and naval authorities. As a final effort, Churchill, on June 16th, offered France a political union with Britain, involving joint Anglo-French citizenship and a joint Cabinet. This was never considered by the French.

As the military debacle continued to grow and Reynaud would not make a separate peace and could not get a Cabinet agreement to withdraw overseas, he resigned (June 16th) and was replaced by a new government headed by Marshal Pétain. The old man, surrounded by defeatists and appeasers who had been intriguing for deals with the Nazis for years, at once asked for an armistice, and issued an ambiguous public statement which led some French units to cease fighting immediately. On June 10th Italy had declared war, but was unable to make any important military advances against French resistance. On June 14th the Germans entered Paris, the French government having moved to Tours on June 11th and continuing to Bordeaux on June 15th.

The armistice negotiations were conducted in the same railway carriage at Compiègne in the forest of Rethondes where Germany had surrendered in 1918; they took three days, and went into effect on June 25th. Hitler was so convinced that Britain would also make peace that he gave surprisingly lenient terms to France. In spite of Mussolini's demands, France did not have to give up any overseas territory or any ports on the Mediterranean, no naval vessels or any airplanes or armaments to be used against England. Northern France and all the western coast to the Pyrenees came under occupation, but the rest was left unoccupied, ruled by a government free from direct German control and policed by French armed forces. The chief burden of the surrender came from three provisions: (1) the division of the country into two zones, with about two-thirds of French productive capacity in the occupied zone; (2) all French prisoners of war, amounting to almost two million men, were to remain in German hands until the final peace treaty, while German prisoners were to be released at once; and (3) all the expenses of the German occupation were to be paid by unoccupied France. The two zones were sealed off so completely that even postal communication was reduced to a minimum; this crippled the economy of the unoccupied part. The expenses of the army of occupation were set at the outrageous sum of 400 million francs a day. Moreover, by fixing the exchange rate at one reichsmark for 20 francs, in place of the prewar rate of one for eleven francs, it becaame possible for the occupying forces to buy goods very cheaply in France, thus draining wealth to Germany.

The governmental system of Vichy France was a kind of bureaucratic tyranny. Pierre Laval pushed through a series of constitutional laws which ended the Third Republic and the parliamentary system, combining in the hands of Marshal Pétain the joint functions of head of the state (formerly held by the president) and head of the government (formerly held by the prime minister), with the right to legislate by decree. Laval was designated as Pétain's successor in holding these powers, and the parliamentary chambers were dismissed.

In spite of this appearance of centralized authority, the government as a whole operated on the basis of whim and intrigue, the various ministers following mutually inconsistent policies and seeking to extend these by increasing their influence over Pétain. The procrastinations, suspicions, ambiguities, and secrecies of the marshal himself make it difficult to determine what his own policy was, or even if he had one. It seems likely that he followed various policies simultaneously, allowing his legal powers to be exercised by quite dissimilar subordinates in an effort to achieve a few clearly defined aims. These aims seem to have been four in number, in decreasing importance: (1) to maintain, at all costs, the independence of unoccupied France; (2) to secure the release, as rapidly as possible, of the prisoners of war; (3) to reduce the financial charges of the occupation forces; and (4) to reduce, bit by bit, the barriers between the occupied and unoccupied zones.

The ideology of Vichy was a typical Fascist mélange of nationalism, social-solidarity, anti-Semitism, antidemocracy, anti-Communism, opposion to class conflicts, to liberalism, or to secularism, with resounding blasts on the virtues of discipline, self-sacrifice, authority, and repentance; but all these things meant very little either to the rulers or the ruled of the new regime. In general, corruption and intrigue, idealism and self-sacrifice were about as prevalent under Vichy as they had been under the Third Republic, but secrecy was more successful, civil liberties were absent, the distance between propaganda and behavior was, if anything, wider, and hypocrisy replaced cynicism as the chief vice of politicians. The two strongest characteristics of the regime, which made it sufficiently solid to continue to function, were negative ones: hatred of the Third Republic and hatred of England. But these ideas were too negative and too remote from the problems of day-to-day existence to provide very satisfactory guides to Vichy policy. As a result, there was complete confusion of policy.

Some leaders, and these the less influential, like Weygand, were resolutely anti-German, and were patiently awaiting the day when Vichy could turn against the German conquerors. Others, and these the more influential, like Laval or Admiral Darlan, had faith in a final German victory over Britain, and felt that France must accept the inevitable hegemony of Germany but try to secure for itself a privileged position as "favorite satellite." While Pétain's personal views were probably closer to those of Weygand, his pessimistic and defeatist personality led him to embrace the other point of view as a necessary evil. Accordingly, under German pressure he removed Weygand from all participation in public life (November 1941) and accepted Laval and later Darlan as his chief advisers and designated successors. In this situation Darland had an advantage over Laval, in view of Pétain's personal inclinations, for Laval was a wholehearted and frank advocate of collaboration with Hitler, while Darlan was a much more devious and ambiguous personality, and thus closer to Pétain's own character and policy. Accordingly, Laval was named foreign minister and successor in July 1940, but was removed from office, as unduly pro-German, on December 13, 1940. Darlan, who had been minister of the navy, became foreign minister, vice-premier, minister of the interior, successor-designate and chief adviser to Pétain in February 1941 and held these positions until April 1942; at that date Hitler forced Pétain to make Laval head of the government with full powers in both internal and external affairs.

The policy of Vichy France can hardly be called a success under Pétain, Darlan, or Laval. Some of the basic assumptions on which the regime had been founded proved to be false. Britain did not surrender. Efforts to collaborate with Hitler did not succeed in releasing the prisoners of war, in reducing the costs of occupation, or in lowering the barriers between the two zones of France. More than a million prisoners were still in German hands in January 1944. In addition, large numbers of French civilians were forced to go to labor in Germany. In spite of all kinds of resistance, the number of these reached 650,000 by late 1943. The occupation payments were reduced from 400 million to 300 million francs a day in May 1942, but were increased again, to 500 million in November 1942, and finally to 700 million a day in July 1944. In forty-five months (to April 1944) France paid 536,000 million francs of these charges. Such payments resulted in a completely unbalanced budget and extreme inflation. Futile efforts to control this inflation by price-fixing, wage-fixing, and rationing gave rise to enormous black-market transactions and widespread corruption, to the great profit of both German and Vichy officials. The latter did not even retain the satisfaction of believing that the armistice had preserved the integrity of France and of its empire, for Alsace-Lorraine was, in fact if not in law, annexed to Germany, and most of the overseas empire fell out of Vichy control in 1942. Lorraine was Germanized, and those inhabitants who remained loyal to France or to French culture were persecuted and exiled, hundreds of thousands coming as refugees to unoccupied France.

The continued resistance of Britain, the treatment of Alsace-Lorraine, the growing economic strain, and, above all, Hitler's attack on the Soviet Union in June 1941 led to the growth of an anti-German underground resistance in France. Russia's involvement in the war shifted the Communists throughout the world, as if by magic, from a pro-German, antiwar policy to an anti-German, prowar policy. Their discipline and fanaticism gradually made them the dominant influence in the resistance, in France, and elsewhere in Europe.

British and American policies toward Vichy France, as toward Franco Spain or neutral Russia, were parallel but far from identical. London, which broke off diplomatic relations with the new French regime in June 1940, followed a severe policy but at the same time sought to win France back into some kind of anti-Nazi resistance. Vichy weakness made this a hopeless task. At the same time, London tried to build up General de Gaulle, as leader of the "Free French," into a diluted French government-in-exile, although De Gaulle's uncooperative personality and arrogant pride made this a difficult and unpalatable task. De Gaulle obtained little support in the French Empire and almost none in France itself, but continued to enjoy a certain measure of British support.

In Washington, on the other hand, De Gaulle obtained almost no support. The United States continued to recognize the Vichy regime, with Roosevelt sending Admiral Leahy as his personal representative to Pétain and Robert Murphy as his special agent in North Africa. In general the United States encouraged France, offered certain economic concessions, especially in North Africa, and sought little more than steadfast adherence to the armistice terms and continued withholding of the fleet and empire from Nazi hands. Both the United States and Britain made numerous secret and special agreements with various representatives of the Vichy government but achieved very little. An agreement of February 26, 1941, between Robert Murphy and General Weygand did allow the United States, in return for certain commercial promises, to maintain consular "observers" in North Africa. These observers obtained large amounts of valuable military and economic information for the United States and Britain during the months preceding the Allied invasion of North Africa on November 8, 1942.

The Battle of Britain, July-October 1940

The collapse of France was one of the most astonishing events in European history. For weeks, or even months, millions of persons in all parts of the world were stunned, walking about in a painful fog. Equally important, although not recognized at the time, was the determination of Britain to go on fighting. Hitler, who had won a victory surpassing his expectations, could not end the war, and was left without plans for continuing it. He began to improvise such plans without adequate information to make them good and without adequate preparation for carrying them out. If Germany had concentrated on building submarines, the newly acquired U-boat bases in Norway, in the Low Countries, and in France might have made it possible to blockade Britain into surrender, but Hitler rejected this plan. Instead he ordered an invasion of Britain (Operation Sealion), a project in which no German, not even Hitler himself, had much confidence.

At the same time, Britain's refusal to make peace revealed to the full the inadequacies of the French armistice. Hitler sought to remedy these by a project to capture Gibraltar (Operation Felix). Sealion and Felix required Hitler's active attention from July to November 1940. In the first half of December, Hitler put Sealion and Felix aside and replaced them with two new projects. The new projects sought to conquer all the Balkans (Operation Marita) and to attack the Soviet Union (Operation Barbarossa). These went into operation in April–June 1941.

Hitler's change of plans in December 1940 was a consequence of four influences: (1) it was, by that time, clear that Sealion could not be carried out; (2) Franco's refusal to cooperate had made Felix impractical; (3) Mussolini's foolish attempts to conquer Egypt and Greece had opened a hornets' nest in the eastern Mediterranean; and (4) there was growing tension, much of it in Hitler's own mind, between Germany and the Soviet Union.

Operation Sealion was beyond Germany's strength, but no one saw this at the time. It required, as a first necessity, air supremacy for the Luftwaffe over southern England. Following this, the invasion would require a large flotilla of invasion craft to carry men and supplies across a lengthy stretch of water and to assemble these forces in combat formation in England. The German Navy was in no position to defend such a flotilla against the British Navy with minefields and to preserve both the invasion flotilla and the minefields by German air superiority.

Britain had adequate manpower, including the men evacuated from France and thousands of anti-Nazi refugees from overrun countries, but had little heavy equipment and certainly had only a fraction of the thirty-nine divisions the Germans estimated to be the size of the defensive forces. These forces were hurriedly prepared; barbed wire and mines were placed on all the landing beaches; watchers were stationed everywhere; all road signs which might guide the invaders were removed; and all able-bodied men, many armed only with fowling guns, were drilled for defense against parachutists. Fortunately, none of these defensive measures ever had to be tested, because Germany was unable to win air superiority over England.

Although air superiority had not yet been achieved by Germany, orders for the invasion were issued at the middle of July, the date was finally fixed at September 21st, but it was postponed, temporarily on September 17th and indefinitely on October 12th. The attacks of the Luftwaffe were directed successively, from July 10th to the end of October, at coastal defenses, at R.A.F. installations, and at London itself. Very heavy damage was inflicted on England, but the losses to the German Air Force were more significant, reaching 1,733 planes with their pilots in three and a half months. In the same period, the British dead reached 375 pilots and over 14,000 civilians. The greatest loss for the Germans in one day was 76 planes on August 15th, but the turning point of the battle came on September 15th when 56 invading planes were shot down.

The counterattack of the R.A.F. on German bases was also very successful; hundreds of invasion craft, in some cases loaded with German soldiers under training, were destroyed. As the Battle of Britain drew to its close in October 1940, the Germans shifted to night bombing of British cities. This practice continued, night after night, with fearful destruction and great loss of life, until Hitler's attack on the Soviet Union in June 1941. During that time, millions of city dwellers, deprived of their sleep, night after night, or crowded into ill-ventilated underground shelters, emerged each morning into scenes of conflagration and ruin to resume their daily work at the war effort.

The calm courage and methodical devotion to duty of the average Englishman ended Hitler's sequence of diplomatic and military victories, and inflicted on Nazi Germany its first and decisive defeat. The successful defense of Britain, forcing Hitler to give up the project for invading England, was the turning point of the European war. Coming as the first year of war was ending, a year in which Hitler had achieved unprecedented conquests, it ended any possibility of a short war, and forced the Germans into a long struggle for which they had neither plans nor resources.

The defenders were victorious in the Battle of Britain for six chief reasons: (1) the indomitable spirit of the English people put surrender out of the question; (2) British planes were equal in numbers and superior in quality to the German planes; (3) British pilots were of better quality and with better fighting spirit; (4) the British operational organization was far superior; (5) fighting over their own land, British pilots could usually be saved by parachuting; and (6) British scientific inventions were far ahead of those of Germany. This sixth point is of vital significance.

Radar was used in scientific experiments in Britain as early as 1924. Adapted for defense against air attack in 1935, a chain of radar stations had been laid out in 1937 and began continuous operation in April 1939. Before war began in September, these stations could detect most aircraft at distances up to 100 miles. Eventually a very elaborate centralized system could report on all enemy planes over or near Britain. After the fall of France, special night-fighter planes with their own individual radar detectors with a three-mile range were being provided. When they began to shoot down German bombers in total darkness in December 1940, the Luftwaffe did not know what was happening. By March 1940, effective radar-aiming devices were being attached to antiaircraft guns on the ground. These increased the effectiveness of such guns in shooting down enemy bombers by fivefold. These new devices were so helpful that over 100 bombers were shot down by night fighters in the winter of 1940–1941, and an equal number by radar antiaircraft guns.

Science was also applied to the British night bombing raids on Germany, but at a much later date. In 1940 and 1941 almost 45,000 tons of bombs were dropped on German targets, but 90 percent fell harmlessly in fields. In 1941 new navigational techniques, using intersecting radio beams from three stations in England, were used to provide greater accuracy in navigation for more planes. Using this method, Britain launched a thousand-bomber raid on Cologne in May 1942. By the end of that year an entirely new method was introduced; this had an accuracy of about one yard per mile of distance from base, and could place over half of the bombs dropped from 30,000 feet within 150 yards of the target at 250 miles' distance. About the same time (early 1943) radar was adapted to allow bombers to see the target through night or clouds. As we have already indicated, bomb damage, however great, had no decisive effects on Germany's ability to wage war, but the growing effectiveness of British and American bombing made it necessary for Germany to devote increasing amounts of its resources and manpower to air defense and to production of fighter planes, and, by drawing German planes back to western Europe from Russia, aided the Russian defense very considerably.

The Mediterranean
and Eastern Europe,
June 1940-June 1941

The collapse of France had a shattering effect along the Soviet-German borderlands, from the Baltic to the Aegean Sea. In the week following June 15, 1940, the Soviet Union sent peremptory notes to Lithuania, Latvia, and Estonia, demanding that their governments be reorganized to include persons more acceptable to the Kremlin. Since Soviet armed forces were already within these states, and no hand of assistance was raised anywhere, least of all in Berlin, the Baltic countries yielded to the Soviet demands. In the first week of August, the three new governments held elections, in typical Soviet fashion, with only a single list of candidates; the newly elected parliaments at once sought, and obtained, union with Soviet Russia as Socialist Soviet Republics.

Farther south, Romania's hopes that the Anglo-French guarantee of April 1939 might bring support from Weygand's forces in Syria were dashed by Weygand's defeat in France. On May 29, 1940, at a Romanian Crown Council, King Carol insisted that protection must be sought elsewhere and that only an alignment with Germany would permit Romania to resist any possible Soviet pressure. It was felt that Germany's need for Romanian oil would make it very unwilling to allow the war to spread to that area. Accordingly, Romania abandoned its policy of neutrality and aligned itself with Germany, the foreign minister, Grigore Gafencu, resigning in protest at the new policy.

Romania did not obtain the benefits it had hoped from its change in policy. On June 26, 1940, having previously notified Germany, the Soviet Union demanded Bessarabia and northern Bukovina from Romania within twenty-four hours. Germany protested against the demand for Bukovina, since this had not been granted to Russia in the Nazi-Soviet Agreement of August 1939. Otherwise Germany made no objection, although Hitler was personally disturbed and had to be reassured by Ribbentrop that he had actually agreed to give Bessarabia to the Soviet Union.

The loss of Bessarabia was a severe blow to the more moderate leaders in Romania. But worse was yet to come. On August 26th Hitler summoned Romanian leaders to Vienna and, in the presence of Count Ciano and representatives of Hungary, forced Romania to give two-thirds of Transylvania to Hungary. In return, Germany gave Romania a guarantee of its new, reduced frontiers.

The "Vienna Award" destroyed the forces of moderation within Romania. Riots and assassinations became the regular method of domestic political activity. These were instigated very largely by the "Iron Guard," a reactionary anti-Semitic political group which had been in a quasi-civil war with 'the Romanian government since 1933, but had been suppressed by the strong-arm tactics of King Carol. On September 5, 1940, an Iron Guard government under Ion Antonescu took office in Bucharest. Its first act was to depose the king and chase him into exile, replacing him on the throne by his son Michael. Two days later, under indirect German pressure, southern Dobruja was yielded to Bulgaria. Thus, in the space of a week, the territorial gains Romania had made at the expense of three of her neighbors in 1919 were largely canceled.

Moscow protested against the Vienna Award on the grounds that it had not been consulted and that no guarantee of Romania by Germany was necessary. These protests were rejected on the basis that Berlin had been informed of various Soviet activities with equally small notice and that the guarantee was necessary to forestall any possible British attack on the Romanian oil fields. Shortly thereafter German military units began to move into Romania, while Soviet units began to seize the uninhabited islands in the mouths of the Danube. At the same time a German military occupation of Finland began under the pretext that the forces in question were en route to Norway (September 19th).

The confusion following the defeat of France spread quickly to the Mediterranean area. This was dominated by two factors: (1) Mussolini's jealous determination to obtain some glorious conquest in the Mediterranean to match Hitler's impressive victories in the north, and (2) the complete inadequacy, from Germany's point of view, of the terms of the French armistice. By these terms neither Germany nor Italy obtained any units of the French fleet, any naval bases in the Mediterranean, or any parts of the French overseas territories. On June 24th, when the armistice was made, Hitler had been so convinced that Britain would make peace that he had neglected these items and had rebuffed Mussolini's efforts to include them. Within a month, Hitler recognized his error and demanded from France extensive military and naval bases and transport facilities in North Africa (July 15, 1940). These demands were rejected by Pétain at once.

Hitler had little real interest in the Mediterranean area at any time, and simply hoped that it would remain quiet. His personal belief, as soon as the invasion of Britain became remote, was that Britain wished to hold out until the Soviet Union became strong enough to attack Germany from the east. There is no evidence that the Soviet Union had any plans to do so, or that it was in communication with Britain in any such project, however remote, or that Hitler was afraid of Russia. On the contrary, the Soviet Union became, if anything, increasingly cooperative toward Germany, especially in the economic sphere, and by May 1941, was almost obsequious; all efforts for improved Anglo-Soviet understanding were rejected until after June 22, 1941; and Hitler, far from being fearful of the Soviet Union, despised it completely, and was convinced that he could conquer it in a few weeks. His decision to attack Russia, first stated on July 29, 1940, and issued as a formal directive (Operation Barbarossa) on December 18th, was based on two considerations: (1) only by destroying Russia and all Britain's hopes based on Russia could Britain be forced to ask for peace, and (2) Soviet cooperation with Germany was Stalin's personal policy and depended on his life, a factor regarded as too undependable to allow Germany to place any long-range expectations on it.

In spite of Hitler's desires, the Mediterranean area could not be kept quiet. The inadequacy of the French armistice, Mussolini's demands for a more active Mediterranean policy, British naval successes against the Italian Navy, Admiral Raeder's warning that some defensive measures must be taken to avert any American intervention in French Africa—

all these kept calling the Mediterranean to Hitler's attention at a time when he wanted to concentrate on the problem of how to attack the Soviet Union.

In order to deter the United States from any intervention in West Africa, and in the belief that it would aid the anti-Roosevelt isolationists in the presidential election of 1940, Germany, Italy, and Japan signed a military alliance on September 27, 1940. This Tripartite Pact, announced with great propagandist fanfare, provided that the signers would aid one another in every way if one of them was attacked by a Power not already involved in the European war or in the Sino-Japanese conflict. To aim this agreement more specifically at the United States, and to allay the natural anxieties of the Soviet Union, one clause provided that the new pact would not change the existing relationships of the signers with Russia. As we shall see in a moment, Ribbentrop's efforts, in November 1940, to obtain Soviet adherence to the Tripartite Pact led to a turning point in the Nazi-Soviet collaboration.

As France was falling in June 1940, Spain assured Hitler that it would enter the war on Germany's side as soon as it had accumulated sufficient supplies, especially grain, to be able to resist the British blockade. This assurance was repeated by Ramón Serrano Suñer, the Spanish foreign minister, brother-in-law of Señora Franco, in Berlin on September 17th. About the same time, Admiral Raeder spoke to Hitler about the need to exclude Britain from the Mediterranean by capturing Gibraltar and Suez. To these possible objectives Hitler added the idea of seizing some of the Canary or Cape Verde islands, or even one of the Azores, to be used as defensive points against any American attempt to land in French West Africa.

About the same time, in September 1940, under pressure from pro-German collaborators led by Laval, Marshal Pétain removed Weygand from his post as minister of national defense and sent him to Africa as coordinator and commander in chief of the French colonial possessions there. Fearful that Weygand might cooperate with an American landing, Hitler at the middle of October began serious efforts to settle the western Mediterranean situation, once for all, in cooperation with Vichy France and Franco Spain.

In anticipation of such an attempt, Britain in July 1940 had attacked and largely destroyed the major vessels of the French fleet at anchor at Mers-el-Kebir (near Oran, Algeria) and at Dakar (West Africa). With somewhat greater skill the French units at Alexandria, Egypt, were demobilized by agreement. These British attacks on French vessels and subsequent De Gaullist attacks with British support on Dakar (September 23rd) and elsewhere were probably unnecessary and served to drive the Vichy regime into the arms of the Germans. On June 24, 1940, the French Navy had been ordered to scuttle its vessels if there was any chance of their falling into control of foreigners (be they German, Italian, or British). The fact that Britain killed 1,400 French seamen by bombardment of anchored vessels greatly increased the normally anti-British bias of the Vichy regime and made it possible for the most anti-British members, such as Laval or Admiral Darlan, to eliminate the more moderate ones like General Weygand.

Hitler's efforts to coordinate Fascist Italy, Franco Spain, and Vichy France in a single policy in the western Mediterranean was not an easy one, as Italy and Spain expected to satisfy their shameless ambitions at French expense, while Hitler trusted neither France nor Spain. On October 22, 1940, Hitler traveled by train to the Spanish frontier to confer with Franco and obtain a commitment to attack Gibraltar. Franco's demands were not modest. He wanted French Morocco, parts of Algeria and French West Africa, about half a million tons of grain, and the motor fuel and armaments necessary for the capture of Gibraltar. For this, as Hitler bitterly told Mussolini, Franco offered Germany his "friendship." Hitler also obtained Franco's promise to enter the war on Germany's side at some indefinite date in the future and to join the Tripartite Pact at once, if this could be kept secret.

Disappointed in the south, Hitler's train returned northward across France. The following day, October 24, 1940, Hitler and Ribbentrop met Pétain and Laval at Montoire-sur-le-Loire and drew up a rather ambiguous agreement. This document proclaimed the signers' joint interest in the speedy defeat of Britain and promised that France, in return for a favorable attitude toward the territorial ambitions of Italy and Spain, would be allowed to share in the booty of the disrupted British Empire at the end of the war so that the total overseas possessions of France would not be reduced in that area. Four days later, Laval was made foreign minister of the Vichy regime.

At this point Hitler's disappointments began to flow over. Having just concluded unsatisfactory agreements with Spain and France, he received at Montoire a delayed message from Mussolini, forwarded from Berlin, announcing that Italy was about to attack Greece. Since Hitler and Ribbentrop had vetoed any attack on either Greece or Yugoslavia as early as July 7th, and had repeated this warning several times since, Hitler at once ordered his train from France to Florence to dissuade Mussolini from his projected attack on Greece. When the two leaders met in Florence, October 28, 1940, the Italian attack on Greece had already begun, so they restricted their discussion to other topics, such as the ingratitude of General Franco.

During the summer of 1940, Mussolini's irascible disposition had not been improved by the failure of Italian ground forces against France, the meager results of the French-Italian armistice, the failure of the Italian Navy to disrupt British convoys to Malta and Alexandria, the complete collapse of the Italian Air Force, and a series of German vetoes against any Italian movement against Yugoslavia or Greece. The Duce's efforts to attack Egypt overland from Libya were resisted by his generals for months. When Rodolfo Graziani finally attacked on September 13th, he advanced, without difficulty, a distance of seventy miles in five days, to Sidi Barrâni in Egypt. There he stopped, and refused to go on.

Thirsty for some success to console his wounded ego, the Duce of Fascism decided to attack Greece. The German military occupation of Romania was the final straw which broke his imperious patience. "Hitler always faces me with a *fait accompli*," he told Count Ciano. "This time I am going to pay him back in his own coin. He will find out from the newspapers that I have occupied Greece. In this way the equilibrium will be reestablished." The Italian generals were unanimously against the project, and had to be driven to it. In an outburst to Ciano, Mussolini threatened to go personally to Greece "to see the incredible shame of Italians who are afraid of Greeks."

Unfortunately for Mussolini, his generals had better judgment than he had. The attack, which began from Albania on October 28th, was stopped completely within three weeks; the subsequent Greek counterattack carried deep into Albania, and Greek pressure continued throughout the winer.

As promised in the guarantee of April 1939, Britain joined Greece against Italy at once, but its own weakness did not allow any substantial increase in its forces in the area. On November 11, 1940, twenty-one British planes made a torpedo attack on the chief units of the Italian fleet in Taranto harbor and sank three out of six battleships at a cost of two planes and one pilot killed. A month later, on December 7, 1940, Graziani's forces of 80,000 men in Egypt were suddenly attacked by General Archibald Wavell with 31,000 men and 225 tanks. In two months, at a cost of only 500 killed, Wavell captured 130,000 Italians with 400 tanks and 1,300 cannon, and advanced westward 600 miles to El Agheila. Shortly thereafter, in an equally brief period (February 11–April 6, 1941), Italian East Africa and Ethiopia were conquered and 100,000 Italian troops destroyed by a British imperial force which suffered only 135 killed.

The Italian failures in Greece and Africa, along with Franco's refusal to attack Gibraltar, forced a considerable rearrangement of Hitler's plans. In the space of two weeks (December 7–21, 1940), Franco flatly refused to execute Operation Felix (December 7th), and, accordingly, this project was canceled (December 11th); Italy decided to ask for German and Bulgarian aid against Greece; the Nazi-Soviet rivalry in Bulgaria and Finland came to a head; and three new war directives were ordered by Hitler, operations Attila, Marita, and Barbarossa.

Operation Attila (December 10th) sought partial compensation for the abandonment of Operation Felix by ordering an immediate occupation of all Vichy France, with a special effort to capture elements of the French fleet in Toulon, if French North Africa rebelled against the Vichy government. This plan was carried out when the Western Powers invaded North Africa in November 1942.

The Italian appeal to Germany for aid against Greece (December 7th) led to a transformation of the relationship between the two Powers: Italy's status changed from that of an ally to that of a satellite. On December 19th Hitler promised to attack Greece from Bulgaria, but not before March 1941, at the earliest. He rejected a detailed Italian request for raw materials, on the ground that he had no way of knowing how these would be used; instead he suggested that large numbers of Italian laborers should be sent to Germany and there work up the raw materials into finished products which could then be sent to Italy to be used according to the advice of German "experts" stationed in Italy. For the immediate relief of Italy's military problems, Hitler refused to send any forces to Albania to fight Greece, but instead offered an armored force, under General Rommel, to fight in Libya, and a German air fleet (of about 500 planes) to be stationed in Sicily to protect Fascist convoys to Libya and to disrupt British convoys through the Mediterranean.

The German intervention in the central Mediterranean in the early months of 1941 was a great success on the ground and in the air, but was not able to prevent the British from strengthening their position on the water. The first Malta convoy of 1941 was badly battered by the first intervention of the Luftwaffe; Britain's sole aircraft carrier in the eastern Mediterranean, *Illustrious*, was damaged so badly that it had to limp to the United States (by way of Suez and around Africa) for repairs; no other British convoy got through the Mediterranean for four months. On the other hand, Rommel's force was transported to Libya without loss.

These two blows to Britain were somewhat balanced by a British naval victory over the Italians off Cape Matapan on March 28-29, 1941. With the loss of one man in one plane, Britain sank three cruisers and two destroyers and damaged a battleship. This battle is notable for the first use of radar-controlled gunnery at sea. With this innovation, at night, the opening salvo of six 15-inch guns by *Warspite* scored five hits; earlier in the engagement, in the daylight, the Italian battleship *Vittorio Veneto* fired more than ninety 15-inch shells without a hit. As a consequence of this battle, Mussolini ordered the Italian fleet not to operate beyond the range of Italian land-based fighter planes until an aircraft carrier could be built. Accordingly, the Italian Navy played no role in the subsequent struggle for Libya, Greece, and Crete.

Rommel's arrival in Libya reversed the situation in North Africa. He had tanks and good air support against British forces which had been largely depleted by sending an armored division to Greece (landed at Piraeus on March 7th). This division and three infantry divisions were sent to Greece over the objections of the very able Greek commander in chief, General Alexander Papagos, who "thought that withdrawal of troops from success in Africa to certain failure in Europe was a strategic error." Striking at El Agheila with a German armored division supported by two Italian divisions on March 31, 1941, Rommel reached the Egyptian frontier on April 11th.

In the meantime, Ribbentrop was engaged in involved diplomatic maneuvers. The Tripartite Pact of September 1940, in spite of Russia's suspicions, was really intended to frighten the United States to abstain from interference in the tumults of Eurasia. To strengthen this threat, Ribbentrop sought to obtain Russia's adherence to the Tripartite Pact and a Soviet-Japanese nonaggression pact which would free Japan in Asia to allow it to strike southward against Singapore. These maneuvers were a disaster for Germany. Futile efforts to obtain Soviet adherence to the Tripartite Pact merely succeeded in revealing the bitter German-Soviet rivalry in Bulgaria and Finland, while the successful Soviet-Japanese Nonaggression Pact of April 13, 1941 made it possible to withdraw Soviet troops from the Far East in sufficient numbers to save Moscow from Hitler's attack on that city in November.

During Molotov's visit to Berlin on November 12-15, 1940, Germany offered the Soviet Union a worldwide division of spheres of influence among the aggressor states: Italy would take North and East Africa; Germany would take western Europe, western and central Africa; Japan could have Malaya and Indonesia; while the Soviet Union could have Iran and India; Germany, Italy, and the Soviet Union would pursue a cooperative policy in the Near East to free Turkey from its British connections and obtain for Russia freer access to the Mediterranean through the Dardanelles. Hitler offered Molotov a picture of a brilliant, if remote, future:

"After the conquest of England the British Empire would be apportioned as a gigantic world-wide estate in bankruptcy of 40 million square kilometers. In this bankrupt estate there would be for Russia access to the ice-free and really open ocean. Thus far, a minority of 45 million Englishmen had ruled 600 million inhabitants of the British Empire. He [Hitler] was about to crush this minority. Even the United States was actually doing nothing but picking out of this bankrupt estate a few items particularly suitable to the United States. . . . He wanted to create a world coalition of interested powers which would consist of Spain, France, Italy, Germany, Soviet Russia, and Japan and, would to a certain degree represent a coalition—extending from North Africa to

Eastern Asia—of all those who wanted to be satisfied out of the British bankrupt estate."

Molotov was only mildly interested in these grandiose schemes about spheres of interest, and seemed to have no ambitions in respect to the British Empire. Instead he wanted detailed answers to specific questions: Why were German troops stationed in Finland? Could not an accurate demarcation between Soviet and Nazi interests be drawn in Finland? Why could not the Nazi guarantee of Romania be balanced by a Soviet guarantee of Bulgaria, or, failing in this, the Romanian guarantee be canceled? What were the exact limits of Germany's New Order in Europe and of Japan's East Asian Sphere?

After hours of discussion, during which the Germans evaded Molotov's questions about Finland and Bulgaria, Ribbentrop offered Russia a protocol covering five points: (1) the Soviet Union would join the Tripartite Pact; (2) the four Powers would "respect each other's natural spheres of influence"; (3) they would "undertake to join no combination of Powers and to support no combination of Powers which is directed against one of the Four Powers"; (4) the four respective spheres of influence would follow the vague German suggestions; and (5) the three European Powers would seek to detach Turkey from British influence and to open the Dardanelles to the free passage of Soviet warships.

Molotov immediately presented Germany with additional proposals drawn up in a formal draft protocol. These added to the German suggestions five other points: (1) that German troops be withdrawn from Finland immediately, (2) that Bulgaria sign a mutual-assistance pact with the Soviet Union and hand over to it a base from which Russian naval and air forces could defend the Dardanelles, (3) that the area from Batum and Baku to the Persian Gulf be recognized as "a center of Soviet aspirations," (4) that Japan yield to the Soviet Union its oil and coal concessions in northern Sakhalin, and (5) that the prospective agreement with Turkey be expanded to include a Soviet military and naval base "on the Bosporus and Dardanelles" and a guarantee of Turkish independence and territorial integrity by all three Powers.

Molotov's conditions for joining the Tripartite Pact enraged Hitler. Four weeks later he issued orders for Operation Barbarossa, a joint Finnish-German-Romanian attack on the Soviet Union. Before this could be carried out, however, the ambiguous situation on the German right flank, in the Balkans, had to be cleared up by Operation Marita. The chief aims of this operation were to drive from the area British forces which had entered Greece in consequence of the Italian attack, and to prevent them from bombing the Romanian oil fields while Germany was occupied with Russia. The original plan called for a pincers movement into Greece from Bulgaria and Yugoslavia after these two countries had been brought into the Axis system by diplomatic activity.

German forces moved steadily into Romania beginning in October 1940; four months later, Moscow was informed by Hitler that these occupying forces had reached "almost 700,000" men. On March 1st Bulgaria joined the Tripartite Pact, and these German forces began to occupy that country the same day.

Yugoslavia did not succumb so easily. For almost six weeks, because of strong opposition in the country and in the Cabinet, Regent Prince Paul resisted the German demands. When Yugoslavia accepted and signed the Tripartite Pact at Vienna on March 25th, it was able to obtain promises of substantial concessions in return: freedom from any German military occupation, release from any promise of military support to Germany under the pact, and a promise of German support for Yugoslavia's desire for an outlet on the Aegean at Salonika.

Soviet opposition to these German advances was somewhat indirect. There were vigorous protests against the movement of German troops into Romania and Bulgaria. Turkey was informed that Russia would abide fully by the Soviet-Turkish Nonaggression Pact of 1925, if Turkey became involved in hostilities with a third Power (meaning Germany). Most significant of all, a military *coup d'état* in Yugoslavia overthrew the Yugoslav regency and government on the night of March 26th-27th, replacing the regent, Prince Paul, as head of the state by the young King Peter and installing a less pliant Cabinet under General Dŭsan Simović. This new government signed a treaty of friendship and nonaggression with the Soviet Union on the night of April 5th-6th. Less than six hours later, Belgrade was subjected to a violent bombardment from the Luftwaffe, and thirty-three German divisions began to invade Yugoslavia and Greece. Both countries were overrun within three weeks and were divided up among the jackal collaborators of Nazi Germany.

From Bulgaria and Hungary, Yugoslavia was invaded by three German columns. The two satellite states followed along behind to occupy the areas allotted to them. Greek forces, overextended, into Albania in the west and outflanked by the German capture of Salonika in the east, fell back southward, but were soon cut off from 68,000 British troops in Thessaly. On April 20th the Greek government advised the British to evacuate because the situation was hopeless, but the almost total destruction of the Piraeus from the air and the sudden capture of the Corinth Canal by German paratroopers made this operation very difficult. Without air protection, the British Navy evacuated 44,000 British troops from various beaches, landing 27,000 of them on the island of Crete.

After a week of bitter mountain fighting, much of it hand-to-hand, with the German Air Force supreme in the sky, the British began to evacuate Crete. When the operation was over on May 1st, Britain had lost 55,000 men in Greece and Crete and had had one battleship, seven cruisers, and thirteen destroyers sunk or damaged; it had lost all North Africa except Egypt itself, and had seen two more countries overrun by Germany. The only possible consolation was to be found in the fact that Yugoslav and Greek resistance had delayed Hitler's attack on the Soviet Union by three weeks, and the heavy German losses in Crete (over 30 percent casualties) persuaded Hitler to renounce all airborne operations in the future. A somewhat more remote benefit rested in the fact that German brutality and Balkan stubbornness gave rise to extensive guerrilla operations which drained Axis strength in the mountains of Yugoslavia, Crete, and Greece.

The loss of Crete gravely threatened the British position in the Near East. In Iraq, on April 3rd, a group of army officers led by Rashid Ali el-Gailani overthrew the government and seized power; a month later this new regime made an attack on British treaty installations in Mesopotamia. Admiral Darlan provided bases in Syria for German and Italian planes going to aid the rebels, and on May 28th signed "Paris Protocols" which almost took France into the war on the side of Germany. These agreements promised to the Iraqi rebels most French military supplies in Syria, and to provide Germany with air bases in Syria and at Dakar, to hand over transport facilities, including ports and railroads in Syria, the port of Bizerte in Tunisia, the railroad from Bizerte to Gabès, French munitions for Germany, French ships for transporting supplies across the Mediterranean, French naval vessels for protecting such shipments, and a submarine base at Dakar. The violent objections of Weygand and other officers against these agreements and the vigorous protests of the United States persuaded Marshal Pétain to overrule Darlan and to cancel the agreements (June 6th).

The rebellion in Iraq was overthrown in May, and a joint force of British and Free French supporters of De Gaulle conquered Syria and Lebanon in June. About the same time, by a tenacious defense of Malta and relentless attacks on Axis convoys to Libya, the British Navy sought to restore its control of the surface of the Mediterranean Sea. This made it necessary for the Axis, in spite of the growing demands of the Battle of the Atlantic and the Battle of Russia, to increase its air and underseas forces in the Mediterranean. In November 1941, 70 percent of Axis supplies for Libya were sunk. In September, Hitler sent the first German submarines (only six of them) to the Mediterranean, and in December he sent the Second Air Fleet of 500 planes under Marshal Albert Kesselring to Sicily. In November the British lost an aircraft carrier and a battleship to U-boats; the following month, in a daring personal exploit, the Italians sent three two-man human torpedoes into Alexandria harbor and sank the two British battleships left in the eastern Mediterranean.

By June 1941, the attrition of British seapower was becoming almost unbearable. With only a handful of operational U-boats, plus some support from surface raiders and land-based planes, the Axis sank, in the period from September 1939 to June 1941, a total of 1,738 merchant ships of a total tonnage of 7,118,112; in addition almost 3,000,000 tons were left damaged in ports. In buying supplies, chiefly from the United States, Britain had used up, by June 1941, almost two-thirds of its dollar assets, gold stocks, and marketable United States securities.

American Neutrality
and Aid to Britain

When the European war began in September 1939, American public opinion was united in its determination to stay out. The isolationist reaction following American intervention in the First World War and the Paris Peace Conference in 1917–1919 had, if anything, become stronger in the 1930's. Historians and publicists were writing extensively to show that Germany had not been solely guilty of beginning the war in 1914 and that the Entente Powers had made more than their share of secret treaties seeking selfish territorial aims, both before the war and during the fighting.

In 1934 a committee of the United States Senate investigated the role played by foreign loans and munition sales to belligerents in getting the United States involved in World War I. Through the carelessness of the Roosevelt Administration, this committee fell under the control of isolationists led by the chairman, Republican Senator Gerald P. Nye of North Dakota. As a result, the evidence before the committee was mobilized to show that American intervention in World War I had been pushed by bankers and munitions manufacturers ("merchants of death") to protect their profits and their interests in an Entente victory in the early years of the war. Under these influences American public opinion in the late 1930's had an uncomfortable feeling that American youths had been sent to die in 1917–1918 for selfish purposes concealed behind propaganda slogans about "the rights of small nations," "freedom of the seas," or "making the world safe for democracy." These feelings were reinforced in the late 1930's by growing disillusionment with the cynicism of authoritarian aggression and the weakness of British appeasement. All this helped to create a widespread determination to keep out of Europe's constant quarrels in the future and, above all, to avoid any repetition of what was regarded as the "error of 1917."

The isolationist point of view had been enacted into American statute law, not only in the 1920's by restrictions on contact with the League of Nations and other international organizations but also later, in the Roosevelt administrations, in the so-called Neutrality Acts. These misnamed laws sought to avoid any repetition of the events of 1914–1917 by curtailing loans and munition sales to belligerent countries. Originally enacted in 1935, and revised in the next two years, these laws provided that export of arms and munitions to belligerents would cease whenever the President proclaimed a state to be a participant in a war outside the Americas. Any materials, including munitions, named by the President had to be sold on a "cash-and-carry" basis, with full payment and transfer of title before leaving the United States, and had to be transported on foreign ships. The "cash" but not the "carry" provision also applied to all other trade with belligerents. In addition, loans to belligerents were forbidden, and American citizens could be warned not to travel on belligerents' ships.

An early statute, the Johnson Act of 1934, prevented loans to most European Powers by forbidding such loans to countries whose payments were in arrears on their war debts of World War I. Moreover, by a so-called "moral embargo" the Roosevelt Administration sought to restrict export of war materials on ethical or humanitarian grounds where no legal basis existed for doing so. Under this provision, for example, airplane manufacturers were asked not to sell planes to countries which had bombed civilians, as Italy had done in Ethiopia, Japan had done in China, or the Soviet Union had done in Finland.

In the years 1935–1939 the neutrality laws proved to be quite unneutral in practice, and a considerable encouragement to aggressors. The Italian attack on Ethiopia showed that an aggressor could arm at his leisure and then, by making an attack, prevent his victim from purchasing from the United States the means to defend himself. These laws gave a great advantage to a state like Italy, which had ships to carry supplies from the United States or which had cash to buy them here, in contrast with a country like Ethiopia which had no ships and little cash. By special legislation the Neutrality Acts had been extended to civil wars to cover the Spanish uprising of 1936 and had cut the recognized government of Spain off from purchasing munitions while the rebel regime continued to obtain such munitions from the Axis Powers.

The obvious unfairness of these laws in the Sino-Japanese crisis of 1937 persuaded President Roosevelt to refrain from proclaiming a state of war in East Asia, although in fact it was clear to everyone that a war was going on there. Above all, by 1939, it was obvious that the Neutrality Acts were encouraging Nazi aggression, since Germany, by making war on Britain and France, could cut them off from American armaments. For this reason, the Roosevelt Administration tried to get the Congress to repeal the embargo provision of the Neutrality Acts but was unable to overcome isolationist opposition led by Senator William E. Borah of Idaho (July 1939).

As soon as the war began in Europe, Roosevelt called a special session of Congress to revise the neutrality laws so that the Entente Powers could obtain supplies in the United States. Under the resulting revision of these acts, in November 1939, the embargo on munitions was repealed and all purchases by belligerents were placed on a "cash-and-carry" basis; loans to belligerent Powers were forbidden, Americans were excluded from travel on belligerent ships, and American ships were not to be armed, to carry munitions, or to go to any areas the President had proclaimed as combat areas. Under this last provision, all European ports on the Baltic or the Atlantic from Bergen south to the Pyrenees were closed to American ships. As the war spread, these areas were extended by proclamation.

The collapse of France in June 1940, combined with the arrogant Japanese demands on the Netherlands East Indies and French Indochina (August–September 1940) and the signing of the Tripartite Pact, gave rise to a severe crisis in American foreign affairs. We have already indicated the danger to American security which could arise from the French fleet or Dakar falling into German hands or from a successful Nazi invasion of Britain. This danger raised the controversy over American foreign policy to a feverish pitch and widened the extremes of public opinion. These extremes ranged from the advocates of immediate intervention into the war on the side of Britain on the one hand to the defenders of extreme isolationism on the other. The extreme interventionists insisted that Britain could be saved only by an immediate American declaration of war on Germany, not because of America's ability to fight at once, which was recognized to be small, but because British morale needed such a declaration to provide it with the strength to go on fighting. The isolationists, on the other hand, argued that it was no concern of the United States whether Britain collapsed or survived, since Hitler had no desire to attack America, and, even if he did, the Western Hemisphere could withdraw into itself and survive with security and prosperity. Most American opinion, in the summer of 1940, was undecided or confused but tended to incline to a point of view somewhere between the two extremes.

In order to unify America's political front, Roosevelt took two outstanding leaders of the Republican Party (both interventionists) into his Cabinet as secretaries of war and of the navy. Henry L. Stimson had been secretary of war in the Taft administration and secretary of state in the Hoover Administration, and Frank Knox had been the Republican candidate for Vice-President in 1936; both were promptly repudiated by the Republican leaders, but played a major role in the Roosevelt Administration thereafter. In combination with the secretary of the treasury (Henry Morgenthau), the secretary of state (Cordell Hull), and the secretary of the interior (Harold Ickes), this gave Roosevelt a preponderantly interventionist Cabinet. Roosevelt himself was sympathetic to this point of view, but his strong sense of political realism made him aware of the powerful currents of isolationism in American public opinion, especially in the Midwest. As a consequence, Roosevelt, who seemed to the outside public to be an advanced inter-ventionist, was definitely a restraining influence inside the Administra-tion. In his own mind his role clearly was to act as a brake on his Cabinet colleagues while he used the prestige and publicity of his office to educate American public opinion in the belief that America could not stand alone, isolated, in the world and could not allow Britain to be defeated if any acts of ours could prevent it.

Outside the Administration, American public opinion was being bom-barded by paid and volunteer agitators of all shades of opinion from inside the country and from abroad. Many of these were organized into lobbying and pressure groups of which the most notable were, on the interventionist side, the Committee to Defend America by Aiding the Allies and, on the isolationst side, the America First movement. The controversy reached its peak during the presidential campaign of 1940 and subsequently, as Congress enacted into law the vital defensive measures desired by the third Roosevelt Administration.

The international crisis led Roosevelt to violate the constitutional precedent against a third term. In spite of the fact that the Republican candidate, Wendell Willkie, was in general agreement with Roosevelt's position on foreign affairs, his desire to win the election had led him to indulge in what he subsequently called "campaign oratory" and to make violent accusations against his opponent. Among others, he as-sured the American people that Roosevelt's reelection meant that "we will be at war." To counteract these charges and to win back antiwar voters who might have been attracted by the generally isolationist outlook of the Republican Party, especially of its senior congressional leaders, Roosevelt replied with some campaign oratory of his own. Some of his assurances were thrown back in his face later: in New York he said, "We will not send our army, navy or air forces to fight in foreign lands outside of the Americas, except in case of attack"; and in Boston he said most emphatically, "I have said this before, but I shall say it again and again and again: Your boys are not going to be sent into any foreign wars."

This "campaign oratory" on both sides was based on the general recognition that the overwhelming majority of Americans were deter-mined to stay out of war, but the confusion in the minds of this majority was revealed on numerous occasions, as on October 5, 1940, when a Gallup Poll of public opinion showed that 70 percent of Americans felt it was more important to defeat Hitler than to keep out of war. This poll was close enough to Roosevelt's own sentiments for him to feel justified in taking any actions which would increase the chances of a Hitler defeat and improve the ability of America to defend itself.

The fall of France raised the problem of American defense in an acute form. The American army and air force were pathetically weak, while the navy was adequate to its tasks only in the Pacific. To remedy these deficiencies it was agreed, in July 1940, to seek an army of 1,400,000 men and an air force of 18,000 planes by April 1942, and a "two-ocean" navy increased by 1,325,000 tons of ships as soon as possible. These objectives could not be achieved, in view of the slowness of American mobilization, both economic and military, and were made even more unattainable by the constant demands of Britain, China, Greece, and others for military equipment as soon as it came off the production line. Two months after these goals had been set, an official memorandum estimated that the United States had no more than 55,000 men in its army and 189 planes in its air force ready for immediate action (September 25, 1940).

As the military forces of the country slowly grew, a series of strategic plans were drawn up to fix the way in which these forces would be used. All these plans decided that Germany was the major danger, with Japan of secondary importance, and, accordingly, that every effort, including actual warfare, should be used to defeat Germany and that, until this goal was achieved, every effort must be made to postpone any showdown of strength with Japan. The priority of a German defeat over a Japanese defeat was so firmly entrenched in American strategic thinking that, as early as November, 1940, it was seriously considered that it might be necessary, if Japan attacked the United States, for the United States to make war on Germany in order to retain this order of priority. As events turned out, Germany's declaration of war on the United States four days after the Japanese attack saved the United States from the need to attempt something which American public opinion would never have condoned—an attack on Germany after we had been attacked by Japan.

Although $17.7 billion had been appropriated by the American government for rearmaments by October 1940, the actual production of armaments remained insignificant until 1942. There were several reasons for this slow progress. In the first place, the governmental side of the rearmament effort was not centralized because of Roosevelt's ingrained distaste for all unified, centralized administration. Instead, similar and conflicting powers were scattered about among various administrators or were granted to unwieldy committees made up of conflicting personalities, while the really vital powers of duress over labor, industry, or material priorities were largely nonexistent. In the second place, industry was very reluctant, in view of the recent economic depression with its great volume of unused capital equipment, to build new plant or new equipment for defense manufacture, unless the government gave them such concessions in regard to prices, taxes, or plant depreciation that the new equipment would cost the corporation little or nothing. Even then the more monopolistic corporations (which formed the overwhelming majority of the corporations with defense contracts) were reluctant to expand production facilities, since this would jeopardize price and market relationships in the postwar period.

Accordingly, most industrialists, especially the largest ones, who were in closest contact with the government, rejected the Administration's plans for defense production as grandiose and impossible. This was most emphatic following Roosevelt's statement in May 1940 that America's goal was to produce 50,000 planes a year. Although the industry was almost unanimous in calling this a "fantastic" figure, issued only as a "New Deal propagandist trick," America's plane production in the next five years was about six times this figure, and reached 96,000 in 1944. These results were achieved because the government paid for nine-tenths of the new factories and compelled modern mass-production methods to be adopted by what was still, even in 1941, a handicraft industry.

In addition to the reluctance to expand capacity, both industry and labor were reluctant to convert existing equipment from peacetime production to war production at a time when government spending was creating a level of peacetime demand and peacetime profits such as had not been known in many years. Businessmen accepted war contracts but continued to allocate capacity, materials, and labor forces to civilian products because these were more profitable, satisfied old customers who were expected to remain customers in the postwar period, and required no conversion of capacity or disruption of distribution facilities.

This was particularly true of the automobile industry, which refused to convert or even to give up the unnecessary luxury of annual model changeovers until, in January 1942, the government ended pleasure-car manufacture for the duration of the war. But as a result of reluctance to do this earlier, about two years of wartime production by the automobile industry was lost and more pleasure cars were manufactured in 1941 than in almost any year in history. In December 1940, Walter P. Reuther, head of the United Automobile Workers, suggested that the unused capacity of the automobile industry (which he estimated at 50 percent) be used to produce airplanes; this was rejected by both airplane and automobile manufacturers. The latter insisted that only 10 or 15 percent of their machine tools could be used in the manufacture of munitions. After the forced conversion of 1942, 66 percent of these machine tools were used in this way, and the automobile industry eventually built two-thirds of all the combat airplane engines produced in the United States between July 1940 and August 1945.

In most industries the government had little or no authority to compel defense contracts to be carried out before civilian contracts, with the result that the latter were generally given preference until 1942. Even in such a vital product as machine tools, no effective system of compulsory priorities for defense was set up until May 1942. This was so typical of the war mobilization that it can be said with assurance that no real mobilization was established until after June 1942. A year later, by July 1943, there had been an astonishing increase. We produced only 16 light tanks in March 1941, and these were too light for service in Europe; our first medium tank (the General Grant) was finished in April 1941, but thirty months later, late in 1943, we were turning out 3,000 tanks a month. In July 1940, the United States produced 350 combat planes, and in March 1941, could do no better than 506 such planes, but by December 1942, we produced 5,400 planes a month, and in August 1943, reached 7,500. A similar situation existed in shipbuilding. In all of 1939 the United States built only 28 ships totaling 342,000 tons, and in 1940 could raise this to no more than 53 ships of 641,000 tons. In September 1941, when the German U-boats were aiming to sink 700,000 tons a month, the United States completed only 7 ships of 64,450 tons. But among those seven ships of September 1941 was the first "Liberty ship," a mass-production model largely based on a British design. Two years later, in September 1943, the United States launched 155 ships, aggregating 1,700,000 tons, and was in a position to continue at this rate of five ships a day, or 19 million tons a year, indefinitely.

It must always be remembered that these impressive figures were reached almost two years after the attack on Pearl Harbor at the end of 1941, and that for two years after the fall of France the United States faced a critical diplomatic crisis with almost no military resources to fall back on or to meet the piteous appeals for aid which came from Britain, China, Greece, Turkey, Sweden, and dozens of other countries. Except for Britain, most of these appeals received little satisfaction. China, for example, received only 48 planes in the first eight months of 1940 and only $9 million worth of all kinds of arms and munitions in the whole year 1940. Of the 2,251 combat planes produced in the United States from July 7, 1940, to February 1, 1941, 1,512 went to Britain and 607 went to our own army and navy.

Boxed in between the steady advance of authoritarian aggression, the inadequacy of American war production, the appeals of the aggressors' potential victims, and the outraged howls of American isolationists, the Roosevelt Administration improvised a policy which consisted, in almost equal measure, of propagandist public statements, tactical subterfuges, and hesitant half-steps. In September 1940, in spite of the adverse effect it might have on Roosevelt's chances in the November election, the Administration persuaded the Congress to enact a Selective Service Act to build up the manpower of the armed forces through compulsion. It provided for one year' of training for 900,000 men, and stipulated that they must not be used outside the Western Hemisphere.

In the same month, September 1940, Roosevelt proclaimed a limited National Emergency and, by executive fiat, gave fifty old destroyers of World War I to Britain in return for ninety-nine-year leases of naval and air bases in British possessions in this hemisphere from Newfoundland to Trinidad.

The opening of a new session of Congress in January 1941 gave Roosevelt an opportunity to state the aims of America's foreign policy. He did so in the famous "Four Freedoms" speech: America was looking forward to a world founded upon four essential human freedoms: freedom of speech and expression, freedom of every person to worship God in his own way, freedom from want, and freedom from fear. In casting about for some way in which America could contribute to these ends while still remaining out of the war, and without enraging the isolationists completely, the Roosevelt Administration, in the early months of 1941, came up with a number of procedures which they summed up in the phrases "America as the Arsenal of Democracy" and "Lend-Lease."

The Arsenal of Democracy idea meant that America would do all it could to supply armaments and essential supplies to countries resisting aggressors, especially to Britain. The British side of this idea was reflected in a public statement of Winston Churchill's: "Give us the tools and we'll finish the job." These statements are of historical significance because, even as they were being made, the military experts in both America and Britain were trying to persuade the political leaders that material contributions from the United States to Britain, no matter how large, would not be sufficient: American fighting men would also be needed.

The Arsenal of Democracy project, even if not adequate to defeat Hitler by itself, faced the tremendous obstacles of Britain's inability to pay and Britain's inability to ensure that war materials from the United States could be delivered in England. These two problems occupied much of Roosevelt's attention in 1941, the one in the months January to March and the other in the months March to December.

At the outbreak of war in September 1939, Britain had about $4,500,-000,000 in assets which could be converted readily into dollars to buy supplies in the United States (gold, dollar exchange, or American securities). In the first sixteen months of the war, Britain earned another $2,000,000,000 of dollars from sales of gold or of those goods, like Scotch whiskey or English woolens, which America was willing to buy. But in that sixteen months, Britain paid out nearly $4,500,000,000 for American goods and placed orders for about $2,500,000,000 more, so that the year 1941 opened with Britain's uncommitted dollar reserves down to about $500,000,000. In the first few months of that year 1941, Britain was selling United States securities (which had been taken over from British subjects) at a rate of $10,000,000 a week. It was clear that Britain's ability to pay in dollars for urgently needed supplies was reaching the end. This end could not be postponed by means of loans, since they were forbidden by the Neutrality Acts and the Johnson Act. Moreover, the experience of the First World War had shown that loans left a most unhappy postwar legacy.

To Roosevelt's realistic mind it seemed foolish to allow monetary considerations to stand as an obstacle in the way of self-defense (as he regarded the survival of Britain). Rather, he felt that the resources of war should be pooled between the United States and Britain so that each could use what it needed from a common store. He emphasized that Englishmen were already dying in our defense and that the British had already given us hundreds of millions of dollars to build factories and machines to manufacture planes, engines, ships, or tanks; they were also giving us, without cost, vital secrets in radar and submarine detection, our first successful liquid-cooled airplane engine (the Rolls-Royce "Merlin," built by Packard in a factory constructed with British money and used in our best escort fighter plane, the P-51 Mustang), many secret features incorporated in the engines of our B-24 (Liberator) bombers, and the Whittle jet engine (which was later adapted to produce the General Electric Company's jet engine used in the P-80 Shooting Star).

As early as December 17, 1940, Roosevelt expressed his point of view to the American people in the following characteristic statement: "Suppose my neighbor's house catches fire, and I have a length of garden hose four or five hundred feet away. If he can take my garden hose and connect it up with his hydrant, I may help him put out the fire. Now what do I do? I don't say to him before that operation, 'Neighbor, my garden hose cost me $15; you have to pay me $15 for it.' What is the transaction that goes on? I don't want $15—I want my garden hose back after the fire is over. . . ." A bill embodying these ideas was introduced in the Congress on January 10, 1941 as H.R. 1776, and became law two months later as the Lend-Lease Act.

During these two months, debate raged both on Capitol Hill and throughout the nation, with the isolationists using every possible argument against it. Senator Burton K. Wheeler, who had been vice-presidential nominee on a third-party ticket in 1924 and had become increasingly isolationist and reactionary with the passing years, said that the bill would "plow under every fourth American boy." Other opponents argued that Britain had tens of billions in concealed dollar assets and that Lend-Lease was merely a clever trick for foisting the costs of Britain's war onto the backs of American taxpayers. Still others insisted that Lend-Lease was an unneutral act which would arouse German rage and eventually involve the American people in a war they had no need to get in. The bill finally passed by a largely party-line vote; in the House of Representatives this vote was 260–161, with only 25 Democrats voting against it and only 24 Republicans voting for it. It provided that the President could "sell, transfer title to, exchange, lease, lend, or otherwise dispose of . . . any defense article" to any nation whose defense he found vital to the defense of the United States; the payment could be made to the United States by any "payment or repayment in kind or property or any other direct or indirect benefit which the President deems satisfactory." By November 1941, $14.3 billion had been provided for carrying out these provisions.

The Lend-Lease Act was to expire in two years. The change in American public opinion can be judged from the fact that it was renewed in March 1943 by a vote of 476–6 in the House and 82–0 in the Senate.

In spite of the large appropriations for Lend-Lease provided in 1941, it moved little additional supplies to any fighting nation before 1942. The American productive system was almost completely clogged up with unfilled orders which had been placed previously by either the British or the American governments. When the Soviet Union came into the war in consequence of Germany's attack in June 1941, no additional outlet was provided for Lend-Lease goods by this event, because American public opinion was too strongly anti-Communist to allow the Soviet Union to partake of Lend-Lease benefits. Only at the end of the year was Russia admitted to these benefits.

Shortly afterward the productive log jam in war industries was broken by the so-called Victory Program of August 1941. This program ended the attempt to build a war-productive system out of the surplus capacity of the peacetime civilian industrial system, and courageously faced the issue that adequate economic mobilization for war could be achieved only if it were based on three fundamental principles: (1) civilian production must be curtailed to provide labor, materials, and capital for war industry; (2) any adequate war industry requires a great increase in investment in new industrial capacity; and (3) economic mobilization is impossible unless there is some degree of centralized control by the government and some degree of duress on business, labor, and consumers.

As part of this effort, Roosevelt at the end of August 1941 set up a new agency of the government, the Supply Priorities and Allocations Board, which, while it had all the weaknesses of a committee organization in contrast with a single executive organization, began, for the first time, to face the fact that there could be no real economic mobilization without a single over-all plan of priorities and allocations among the many different groups demanding access to economic resources. Behind this whole effort toward economic mobilization was a secret decision of Roosevelt's military advisers, made in the summer of 1941, that the war could not be won unless the United States planned eventually to raise the number of men in its armed forces to 8,000,000.

An 8,000,000-man army looked very remote in the summer of 1941 as the 900,000 draftees provided by the Selective Service Act of 1940 approached the end of their year of training and eagerly began to prepare to disperse to their civilian activities again. To have permitted this would undoubtedly have inflicted a dangerous blow to the preparedness program. Accordingly, the Roosevelt Administration asked the Congress to extend the terms of service of these men. At once the isolationists were in full cry, and this time they found a greater response in American public opinion. It seemed to many to be very unfair to keep in service for several years men who, when they reported for service, had been assured that they need serve for only one year. The supporters of the extension argued that America's preparedness and security must take precedence over any such mistaken assurances. An Act extending the period of selective-service training by an additional eighteen months passed the Congress on August 12, 1941, by the narrow margin of one vote, 203–202. Once again, the Republicans were solidly opposed to the Act, only 21 voting for it, while 133 voted against it.

As the voting on the extension of selective service was being counted, the historic Atlantic Conference of Roosevelt and Churchill was being held on the battleship *Prince of Wales* in a small harbor in Newfoundland. After four days of conferences (August 9-12, 1941), the chiefs of government of the United States and Britain issued the so-called Atlantic Charter as their first formal enunciation of war aims. According to this document they renounced all ambitions toward territorial aggrandizement for themselves and, for others, hoped to obtain territorial settlements and forms of government in accord with the freely expressed wishes of the peoples concerned. They also aspired to see equal access to trade and raw materials for all states, international economic collaboration, freedom of the seas, and postwar disarmament.

Certain differences of outlook which emerged from the discussions between the British and Americans were either omitted or compromised in the public announcement. The British were still in favor of imperial preference and a certain measure of bilateralism, commercial discrimination, and economic autarchy in international trade, while Secretary Hull's influence set the American delegation solidly in opposition to these and in favor of multilateral, nondiscriminatory trade relations on most-favored-nations principles. A second difference, which was soon pushed into the background, rested in the contrast between Churchill's desire for some statement of preference for a long-range postwar plan for an international organization to replace the League of Nations, and Roosevelt's preference for an immediate postwar system based on police action by the few Great Powers, or even by a simple Anglo-American partnership. At any rate, Roosevelt was too reluctant to rouse the unsleeping dogs of isolationism to allow the Atlantic Conference to issue any public statement on international organization.

The Atlantic Charter was issued to the world as soon as the conference ended; at least equal in importance were the simultaneous military and strategic conversations which were kept secret. Once again, these decided that the defeat of Germany must have priority over the defeat of Japan, but there was a wide difference of opinion on how Germany could be defeated. The British had no plans or expectations for making any large-scale invasion of Europe with ground forces. Instead, they hoped that Germany could be worn down to defeat, after a very long war, by blockade, aerial bombardment, subversive activity, and propaganda. They wanted large numbers of heavy bombers, and hoped for American intervention in the war, as soon as possible, largely for its propaganda value against German morale. Apparently, no one pointed out that a German defeat by British methods would leave the Soviet armies supreme in all Europe, with no Axis, Anglo-American, or local forces to oppose them.

On military grounds alone, the Americans at the Atlantic Conference rejected the British theories. They rejected any immediate American intervention into the war on the grounds that the United States was not sufficiently armed to be effective. The only immediate contribution which the United States could add by intervention, they felt, would be in escorting convoys of British supply vessels to Europe. The American military experts rejected the idea that Germany could be defeated by blockade, propaganda, air attacks, or by anything less than a large-scale invasion by ground forces. For this purpose the War Department in Washington was planning an army of 8,000,000 men.

An additional difference of opinion between the British and Americans emerged from the discussions regarding Japanese aggression. The British wanted a joint or parallel message to Japan, accompanied, if possible, by threatening naval movements, to demand a cessation of aggressive Japanese actions. The Americans were reluctant, fearing to take any steps which might speed up Japanese aggression and thus distract attention from the German problem; Roosevelt even said that continued peace with Japan was so essential that "he would turn a deaf ear if Japan went into Thailand, but not if they went into the Dutch East Indies." In the latter case he envisaged nothing more than economic warfare for a considerable period.

Immediately following the Atlantic Conference, Roosevelt was concerned with two major European problems, leaving the rising tension with Japan in Hull's hands. The two problems were naval escort of convoys to Britain and military supplies for the Soviet Union.

During the spring, summer, and autumn of 1941, Roosevelt was under constant pressure from many of his Cabinet to grab the bull by the horns and establish American naval escort of supply ships to Britain. At first he yielded to this pressure, but by July he became convinced that American public opinion would not accept convoy escort all the way to Britain, and substituted for this escort to the meridian of Iceland, with the argument that this was still within the Western Hemisphere. Orders to organize convoy escorts all the way to Britain had been issued on February 26th. To protect these, an Atlantic Fleet, under Admiral King, had been created on February 1st. This was reinforced by three battleships, an aircraft carrier, four cruisers, and numerous destroyers, transferred from the Pacific in May. In March, Roosevelt ordered two destroyer bases and two seaplane bases to be constructed with Lend-Lease funds in northern Ireland and Scotland. At the same time, he gave Britain ten Coast Guard cutters to be based in Iceland, and seized possession of sixty-five Axis and Danish ships anchored in American harbors. A month later, Greenland was declared to be in the Western Hemisphere, and the United States took over its protection and began to construct bases.

The Red Sea was declared not to be a combat area, thus reopening it to American merchant ships carrying supplies to Egypt (April 10, 1941). The financial assets of the Axis Powers and of all occupied and belligerent countries in Europe were frozen, and Axis consulates in the United States were closed (June 14-16, 1941). American flying schools were made available to train British aviators. Four thousand marines who had been ordered to occupy the Azores in anticipation of a Nazi move toward Gibraltar or the Atlantic islands were released from this assignment when Hitler moved eastward in June. Accordingly, they were reassigned to occupy Iceland, which they did, in agreement with the Icelandic government, in July.

In the meantime, by presidential proclamation, the American Neutrality Zone which had been defined in September 1939 as west of 60° W. longitude was extended to 26° W. longitude, the meridian of Iceland. The United States Navy was ordered to follow all Axis raiders or submarines west of this meridian, broadcasting their positions to the British. On July 19, 1941, American naval convoys were ordered as far eastward as this meridian. The first such convoy left on September 16, 1941. In practice, American escort vessels covered about 1,200 miles of distance in the mid-Atlantic between 52° W. and 26° W., picking up from Canadian escorts south of Newfoundland and delivering their charges to British escorts south of Iceland. This gave the Canadians and British routes of about 650 miles to cover on either end. By this time, Axis submarines had moved from the waters off the British Isles to the mid-Atlantic, where they were operating by a "wolf-pack" technique. Under this method, as soon as a convoy was discovered, a dozen or more submarines would assemble in its path and attack on the surface at night. This proved to be a very effective method, especially against inexperienced American escorts, which maintained too rigid stations too close to their convoys. But this method had the great weakness that it required extensive radio communication with Germany for orders; this revealed the locations of the U-boats, and eventually became a fatal weakness.

American naval escort of British convoys could not fail to lead to a "shooting war" with Germany. The Roosevelt Administration did not shrink from this probability. The growing tension with Japan combined with the American strategic decision that Germany must be defeated before Japan to compel an increasingly active policy in the Atlantic in order to avoid a situation where we would be at war in the Pacific while still at peace with Germany. Fortunately for the Administration's plans, Hitler played into its hands by declaring war on the United States on December 11, 1941. By that date "incidents'" were becoming more frequent.

On October 17th the United States destroyer *Kearney* suffered casualties when it was torpedoed; two weeks later the destroyer *Reuben James* was blown to pieces, with great loss of life, by a chain of explosives from a German torpedo, its own forward magazine, and its own depth charges. On November 10th an American escort of eleven vessels, including the carrier *Ranger*, picked up a convoy of six vessels, including America's three largest ocean liners, the *America*, the *Washington*, and the *Manhattan*, with 20,000 British troops, and guarded them from off Halifax to India and Singapore. Pearl Harbor was attacked as this convoy was passing South Africa, and the *Washington* eventually reached home by crossing the Pacific to California.

Many of the activities of the American Navy in the summer of 1941 were known not at all or were known only very imperfectly to the American public, but it would seem that public opinion generally supported the Administration's actions. In September, Roosevelt sought congressional action to repeal the section of the Neutrality Acts forbidding the arming of merchant vessels. This was done on October 17th, the vote in the House going 259–138, with only 21 Democrats opposing the change and only 39 Republicans supporting it. On that same day the *Kearney* was torpedoed. Two weeks later all the essential portions of the Neutrality Acts were repealed (November 13th). The vote in the

House, 212–194, once again showed the partisan nature of the Administration's foreign policy, for only 22 of 159 Republican votes were for repeal. By this vote the United States "resumed its traditional right to send its ships wherever it pleased and to arm and protect them in every way possible." This meant that open naval warfare with Germany was in the immediate future.

During this period, from June to December 1941, Roosevelt was also kept occupied by the problem of military aid for the Soviet Union. The Nazi forces which flung themselves on Russia, on June 22, 1941, were at the peak of their powers, and the Soviet Union was soon in grave need of any aid it could get. Churchill, although filled with suspicions of the Soviet regime, or the good faith of its leaders, was willing to accept anyone, "even the devil," as he put it himself, as an ally against the Nazi menace, and to extend whatever aid was available to such an ally. Roosevelt shared these ideas to a considerable extent, but the American people were suspicious of Bolshevism, and American military experts were generally agreed that the Soviet Union could not hold out against Hitler long enough for any aid to be effective. Accordingly, it was several months before Roosevelt was in a position to make Lend-Lease supplies available to the Kremlin.

The Nazi Attack on Soviet Russia, 1941-1942

In planning his attack on Soviet Russia, Hitler used the customary German strategic concepts; these gave priority to the destruction of enemy armies over the seizure and occupation of enemy territory and resources. This destruction was to be achieved (and quickly achieved, according to Hitler), in a series of gigantic pincers movements of the double-arm type which had worked so well against Poland in 1939. In these operations a huge outer pincers of armored-division spearheads and a simultaneous but smaller inner pincers of infantry-division columns would enclose a mass of enemy troops, the armored pincers cutting a large segment of these off from their supplies and communications while the infantry columns would slice up the enclosed mass of enemy forces into smaller masses willing to surrender. This method was used, again and again, with extraordinary success against the Soviet armies, after June 1941, enclosing, and frequently capturing, hundreds of thousands of Russians at a time, but the very size of the operations used up Nazi men, materials, and (above all) time without inflicting any fatal blow on the Soviet capacity to resist.

Because of these German strategic ideas, no geographical objectives were given primary priority in the German plans. Secondary priority was given, at Hitler's insistence, to the capture of Leningrad in the north and to the capture of Kiev and the Caucasus to the south. These geographical objectives were set in order to link up with the Finns and cut the Murmansk railway in the north, and to capture, or at least cut off from Russian armies, the Soviet oil centers in the south. The capture of Moscow was, by Hitler's direct orders, given only tertiary priority in the German strategic plans.

The German generals disagreed with Hitler's geographic conceptions, and insisted that Moscow be made the chief geographic goal of the German advance because it was the vital railroad center of European Russia; it was also an important industrial center, and contained the heart and brain of the whole Soviet autocracy. Its capture would, according to the generals, cripple Russia's ability to shift troops and supplies north and south and would thus make it possible to isolate, for easier conquest, the Leningrad or the Kiev fronts. Moreover, its capture would paralyze the overcentralized system of Soviet tyranny, and strike such a blow to Bolshevik prestige that it would probably be unable to survive.

In the first three months of the campaign of 1941 and for all of the campaign of 1942, Hitler resisted the pressure from his generals and insisted that the maximum German effort should be devoted to the two areas originally set in the north and the south. Only in September 1941, when it was too late for a successful assault on Moscow, did Hitler recognize that his own geographic objectives could not be achieved, with the result that he fell back on his generals' advice for an attack on Moscow. This dispersal and shifting of geographic objectives, combined with German inability to destroy the Soviet armies completely, brought Germany to the point which Hitler had always insisted must be avoided above all else: a two-front war of attrition by a Germany which was nowhere near total economic mobilization.

German authorities estimated that Russia had over 200 divisions (of which 30 to 35 were in the Far East), with 8,000 aircraft of diverse quality, and 15,000 tanks, mostly light or obsolescent. On the European front they expected to encounter 125 infantry, 25 cavalry, 25 motorized, and at least 5 armored divisions. Against these Russian forces, Hitler planned to hurl 141 German and 33 satellite (Finnish, Romanian, Italian, Hungarian, Slovak, and Croat) divisions. The German forces included 19 (half-size) armored divisions with 3,200 tanks, 14 motorized divisions, and 3 air fleets with 2,000 planes. These forces were organized into three army groups (northern, central, and southern) aiming in the general direction of Leningrad (500 miles away), Moscow (750 miles), and the lower Volga (Stalingrad, 800 miles away). Each army group consisted of infantry and panzer armies placed alternately across the front, in order to operate the double-clawed pincer movements we have mentioned. The whole German front, from north to south, had seven infantry armies and four panzer armies organized in this alternating fashion, with two infantry armies forming each end of the line, and the satellite forces on the extreme flanks (Finns to the north, the others to the south).

The Soviet Union was warned of the impending Nazi attack from Washington and London, as well as by its own spies, and had the exact date of the assault almost as soon as it was set in Berlin. An anti-Nazi German in Berlin gave a copy of Hitler's secret directive for Operation Barbarossa to the American commercial attaché within three weeks of its formulation; this was sent to the Kremlin by Secretary of State Hull early in March 1941. All these helpful moves were received with ill grace by the Soviet leaders, and those who offered them were treated as troublemakers. Moscow made no effort to escape the Nazi pincers by withdrawing its forces from their exposed frontier positions, but continued to hope that its abject economic collaboration with Hitler would lead him to cancel the attack orders, in recognition of the fact that he could obtain more, in an economic sense, from collaborating in peace than from conquest in war. This hope was futile, because Hitler had such a gigantic disrespect for Russia's fighting powers that he expected a complete German victory in about six weeks. So convinced was Hitler on this point that he flatly rejected, in June, again in July, and once again in August, suggestions from the chief of the Great General Staff that any preparations be made for fighting in winter. For this refusal Germany was to suffer bitterly.

Hitler's estimates about the weakness of the Soviet armies and the brevity of the approaching campaign were generally shared by military men throughout the world. In the United States, Chief of Staff General George C. Marshall believed that Germany would be victorious in six weeks.

The Nazi armies sprang forward at dawn on Sunday, June 22, 1941. At the end of five days two envelopments had been closed and on the following day a third was completed. In these pockets there were such large Russian forces that the perimeters could not be closed completely, and broken Russian units escaped through the German lines. Nevertheless, from these pockets were taken 289,874 prisoners, 2,585 tanks, and 1,149 cannon. By July 25th several more encirclements had been completed on the central front (yielding 185,487 more prisoners with 2,030 tanks and 1,918 guns).

At this point a crisis arose in the German High Command. All the great successes we have mentioned were on the central front, while the northern and southern fronts, which Hitler wanted emphasized, were advancing much more slowly. This resulted from the fact that Hitler's generals did not share the Führer's strategic ideas, and had disposed the German forces so that, in effect, they overruled his directives and gave preponderance to their own goal, the capture of Moscow. For this reason they had given two of their four panzer armies to Field Marshal Fedor von Bock's Army Group Center, and one to each of the other army groups. Since the Russians had massed their strength in the south, German Army Group South, under Gerd von Rundstedt, had only 800 tanks, while his Soviet opponent, Marshal S. M. Budënny had 2,000.

The brilliant success of the German Army Group Center led the German General Staff and Hitler to change their minds, but in opposite directions. The weakness of the Soviet defense persuaded Bock to adopt a plan, advanced by Guderian, that Army Group Center abandon further efforts at pincers encirclements and send its armored units on a straight all-out drive to Moscow, one hundred miles away. About the same time, Hitler decided to strengthen the advance of Army Groups North and South, by directing the efforts of the two panzer armies of Army Group Center away from their own front and onto the fronts of the two flanking army groups. This would have left Army Group Center with infantry forces only, thus slowing its advance and restricting its operations to tactical mopping-up activities, but it would have increased the ability of the flanking army groups to close pincer envelopments by giving each of them the use of two panzer armies. By Directive No. 33, on July 19th, Hitler issued orders for this change. Although the generals resisted and stalled in carrying out these instructions, the advance on Moscow was broken.

General Franz Halder wrote in his diary on July 26th: "The Führer's analysis, which at many points is unjustly critical of the Field Command, indicates a complete break with the strategy of large operational conceptions. You cannot beat the Russians with operational successes, he argues, because they simply do not know when they are defeated. On that account it will be necessary to destroy them bit by bit, in small encircling actions of a purely tactical character." Against these ideas of Hitler's his generals argued for weeks, in vain. On August 21st, Hitler issued Directive No. 34. It began: "The proposals of the Army High Command for the continuance of the operations in the east, dated August 18, do not conform to my intentions. . . . The principal object is not the capture of Moscow." In place of this, it set the following objectives: to seize the Crimea and the Dombas coal mines, to cut off the Caucasian oil supplies, to isolate Leningrad, and to make direct contact with the Finns.

As a consequence of the shift of emphasis to the south, German Army Group South completed a colossal envelopment east of Kiev (August 24–September 21). In a great bag 200 miles wide, the Germans captured 665,000 prisoners with 3,718 cannon and 884 tanks. Hitler called this "the greatest battle in the history of the world"; his chief of staff called it "the greatest strategic blunder of the Eastern Campaign."

At this point in the campaign a curious phenomenon appeared: large numbers of anti-Stalinist Russians began to surrender to the Nazis. Most of these were Ukrainians, and the majority were eager to fight with the Nazis against the Stalinist regime of the Soviet Union. If the Nazis had been willing to cooperate with this movement, and to treat these deserters in a decent fashion, it is extremely likely that the flood of Russian deserters would have become an overwhelming torrent and the Moscow regime would have collapsed. Instead, the Nazis, led by Hitler, resolutely refused to adopt the role of "Liberator of the Slavs," and instead insisted on playing the role of "Annihilator of the Slavs." The arrogance, sadism, and racism of the Nazi system soon presented itself in a form as hateful to the average Slav as Stalinism itself.

As soon as the conquering German armies seized Soviet territory, various Nazi and satellite organizations of exploitation, of enslavement, and of extermination moved in, led by the SS. Prisoners of war and civilians were rounded up by the millions and deported to German slave-labor camps where they were starved, frozen, and beaten into subhuman derelicts at the very time that they were expected to work, fifteen or more hours a day, on Nazi war production. Those inhabitants of conquered areas who escaped deportation or imprisonment generally were deprived of most of their possessions, especially of their food stores and livestock. All industrial equipment which had not been removed by the retreating Soviet armies was stolen or destroyed by the Nazis. The deserters who wished to fight with the Nazis against Stalin would have been welcomed by many German Army officers, but their use in this fashion was generally discouraged and frequently forbidden by the Nazi political leaders such as Hitler or Himmler. In spite of this, some Russian units in the Nazi armies were formed, although generally they were used only for guard or garrison duties. The size of this movement of anti-Stalinist deserters can be judged from the fact that, in spite of the obstacles we have mentioned, the number of such deserters serving in the Nazi armed forces reached 900,000 in June 1944. These were nominally under the leadership of a renegade Soviet general, A. A. Vlasov, who had served as Soviet military adviser to Chiang Kai-shek in China in 1938, with the rank of major general, and had been captured by the Nazis when serving as deputy commander of the Volkhov front, in June 1942. Nothing effective could be done with "Vlasov formations" because of the opposition of Hitler and Himmler. When Germany was clearly on the road to defeat in November 1944, Himmler withdrew his opposition, and allowed Vlasov to issue a call for an anti-Stalinist liberation army of Russians. In six weeks this organization received a million applications for membership, but could obtain almost no equipment and could organize combat units of no more than 50,000 men. At the end of the war, hundreds of thousands of Vlasov's supporters fled westward to the American and British armies for refuge from Stalin's vengeance, but were handed over to the Soviet Union to be murdered out of hand or sent to slave-labor camps in Siberia. The dimensions of human suffering involved in this whole situation is beyond the human imagination. The number of Soviet prisoners captured by the Nazis, according to the records of the German Army, reached over 2,000,000 by November 1, 1941, and reached 3,060,000 by March 1, 1942. Over 500,000 of these died of starvation, typhus, or froze to death in prison camps in the winter of 1941–1942. In the whole Eastern campaign up to January 1944 the Nazis captured 5,553,000 prisoners.

On September 6, 1941, in Directive No. 35, Hitler suddenly accepted the suggestions of his generals, and ordered an attack on Moscow. After two weeks of reorganization of forces, this attack began. About the same time, Leningrad was encircled, thus commencing an unsuccessful siege which continued until the city was relieved twenty-eight months later.

By October 8, 1941, two great encirclements west of Moscow closed on 663,000 Soviet prisoners with 5,412 cannon and 1,242 tanks. Mopping up took two weeks. By that time, the weather had broken, and the Germans were advancing through pouring rain, sleet, and mud. They suffered their first cases of frostbite on November 7th, but, with Moscow only thirty-eight miles away, the attack continued. A week later, Siberian divisions, moved from the Far East, in consequence of the Japanese-Soviet Nonaggression Pact and Richard Sorge's information that the Japanese had decided to attack Singapore rather than Siberia, appeared before Moscow. The first Soviet counteroffensive came on November 28th, just as the 2nd German Armored Division caught sight of the towers of the Kremlin from a distance of fourteen miles. The next night the temperature fell to 22° below zero Fahrenheit. The Germans, without any preparation for a winter campaign, began to suffer horribly. Yet when Field Marshal von Rundstedt, commander of Army Group South, allowed some of his units to withdraw, he was removed by Hitler.

On December 19th the commander in chief, Field Marshal Walther von Brauchitsch was relieved and his post taken by Hitler himself. The Führer issued an order which said: "The army is not to withdraw a single step. Every man must fight where he stands." A few days later, Guderian was removed for violation of this order. In spite of Hitler's attitude, Russian pressure throughout the winter made necessary one German withdrawal after another. By the spring of 1942, many units had fallen back a hundred or more miles. During this period the Luftwaffe generally could not operate for lack of winter lubricants, and when its planes did take to the air they had to be used to carry supplies to ground forces which were cut off by Russians. Tanks could be used only after their engines had been warmed up for twelve hours. Frostbite casualties in the German Army ran about a thousand a day, and by February 28, 1942, the total German casualties in the Russian offensive reached over a million (31 percent).

We have mentioned that military assistance to the Soviet Union from the United States was held up by the slowness of American economic mobilization, the anti-Bolshevism of American public opinion, and the general lack of confidence in Soviet ability to withstand the Nazi attack. These obstacles were not decisive with Churchill or Roosevelt. On July 12, 1941, Britain signed an alliance with Russia. Four weeks later Harry Hopkins returned from a hurried visit to Moscow to report to the Atlantic Conference his conviction that the Soviet Union would be able to hold out against the Nazi attack. He also brought a completely unreasonable demand from Stalin for an immediate British invasion of western Europe to relieve the German pressure on Russia. Unable to grant any hopes of such an invasion in 1941 or even in 1942, Roosevelt and Churchill decided to send a full-scale economic mission to Moscow to determine Russia's material needs. This mission, headed by Averell Harriman and Lord Beaverbrook, was in Moscow for three days at the end of September 1941, and signed an agreement for Soviet aid to June 30, 1942.

In the postwar period it was frequently stated that the Roosevelt Administration should have taken advantage of Stalin's urgent need for supplies in September 1941, by forcing him to sign agreements to recognize the independence and territorial integrity of various countries in eastern Europe. Strangely enough, during the discussions in Moscow at the time, Stalin was eager to obtain a formal statement on war aims and on specific territorial boundaries, but the United States was reluctant: it objected to any "secret accords" which might hamper freedom of action later, and was unwilling either to abandon the peoples of eastern Europe to Russia or to insist on their rights vigorously enough to drive the Soviet Union to make a separate peace with Hitler. Such a separate peace was quite out of the realm of possibility, but no agreements about boundaries and governments made in 1941 could have been enforced against the Soviet Union four years later after these areas had fallen under Soviet military occupation.

The agreement of September 30, 1941, provided that, in the next nine months, the Anglo-Americans would send to the Soviet Union 1,050,000 tons of supplies, including 300 fighting planes, 100 bombers, and 500 tanks a month. Up to that moment Russia had purchased about $100,000,-000 of supplies in the United States with its own money, had obtained $29,000,000 in supplies from United States loans to be repaid in future deliveries of gold bullion, and had obtained from Britain considerable supplies, including 450 planes, 3,000,000 pairs of boots, and 22,000 tons of rubber. But financing the new Moscow agreement was quite a different task, and could be done only under Lend-Lease. By the end of November, Roosevelt was able to get American public opinion, and especially American Catholic opinion, to reduce its objections to such a step sufficiently to allow him to establish it.

As with Lend-Lease aid to Britain, such aid to Soviet Russia raised the problem of how supplies could be delivered. In the first two years of Lend-Lease, 46 percent of the total shipped went across the Pacific to Siberia in Soviet ships; 23 percent took the 76-day route to the Persian Gulf to go north over the completely inadequate trans-Iranian route; 41 percent took the 12-day sea route to Murmansk or Archangel. The dangers of this last route can be seen from the fact that 21 percent of the cargoes on it were lost by German attack, partly by submarines and surface raiders, but chiefly by air attacks from Finnish and Norwegian bases. The horrors of this northern route to Russia are almost beyond description. In the summer, twenty-four hours of light each day allowed attacks to be continuous; in the winter water temperature was so low that torpedoed seamen could survive no more than a few minutes in it. And in both seasons there was no relief at the end of the voyage, for the Russian ports were within easy bombing range of German air bases under conditions of visibility (notably surrounding hills and poor Soviet cooperation) which allowed only a few seconds' warning before any attack.

XV

WORLD WAR II:
THE EBB OF
AGGRESSION, 1941-1945

The Rising Sun
in the Pacific, to 1942

TRADITIONALLY, American policy in the Far East had sought to preserve the territorial integrity and political independence of China and to maintain an "Open Door" for China's foreign trade. These goals became increasingly difficult to achieve in the course of the twentieth century because of the growing weakness of China itself, the steady growth of aggression in Japan, and the deepening involvement of other Powers with Far Eastern interests in a life-or-death struggle with Germany. After the fall of France and the Low Countries in the summer of 1940, Britain could offer the United States little more than sympathy and some degree of diplomatic support in the Far East, while the Netherlands and France, with rich colonial possessions within reach of Japan's avid grasp, could provide no real opposition to Japan's demands. After Hitler's attack on Russia in June 1941, the Soviet Union, which had actually fought Japanese forces in the Far East in 1938 and again in 1939, could exert no pressure on Japan to deter further Nipponese aggression. Thus, by the summer of 1941, Japan was ready for new advances in the Far East, and only the United States was in a position to resist.

This situation was complicated by the domestic political divisions within the United States and Japan. In general, these divisions tended to postpone any showdown between the two Powers. On the one hand, the American government had developed a fissure between its military strategic plans and its diplomatic activities, just at the time when isolationist opinion within the country was making its most vociferous objections to the Administration's policies in both these fields. On the other hand, the Japanese government was by no means united, either on the direction or on the timing of its next moves.

The divisions in public opinion within the United States and even within the Roosevelt Administration are obvious enough to Americans, but the equally great divisions in Japan are largely ignored. It should be recognized by Americans today, as it was recognized by the Japanese leaders at the time, that the Japanese aggressions of 1941 which culminated in the attack on Pearl Harbor on December 7th were based on fear and weakness and not on arrogance and strength. To be sure, the earlier aggressions which began in Manchuria in 1931 and in North China in 1937 had been arrogant enough. The Japanese had been supremely confident of their ability to conquer all China, if necessary, even as late as 1939. As a consequence, their advance had been accompanied by brutality against the Chinese, by various actions to drive all Europeans and all European economic enterprises out of China, and by insults and humiliations to Europeans found in China, especially in Shanghai.

By 1939 all of this was beginning to change. The attack on China had bogged down completely. The Japanese economy was beginning to totter under a combination of circumstances, including the exhausting effort to strangle China and to administer a fatal blow to the retreating Chinese government by octopus tactics, the reorganization of Japan's home industry from a light basis to a heavy industrial plant (for which Japan lacked the necessary resources), the gigantic capital investment in Manchuria and North China, the growing restrictions on Japanese trade imposed by Western countries, and, finally, the combination of a rapidly growing population with acute material shortages. Problems such as these might have driven many nations, even in the West, to desperate action. In Japan the situation was made more critical by the large-scale diversion of manpower and resources from consumption to capital-formation at a very high rate. And, finally, all this was taking place in a country which placed a high esteem on military arrogance.

In theory, of course, Japan might have sought to remedy its material shortages in a peaceful way, by seeking to increase Japan's foreign trade, exporting increasing amounts of Japanese goods to pay for rising Japanese imports. In fact, such a policy had obvious weaknesses. The world depression after 1929 and the growth of economic autarchy in all countries, including the United States, made it very difficult to increase Japanese exports. The excessively high American Smoot-Hawley tariff of 1930, although not so intended, seemed to the Japanese to be an aggressive restriction on their ability to live. The "imperial preference" regulations of the British Commonwealth had a similar consequence. Since Japan could not defend itself against such economic measures, it resorted to political measures. To do otherwise would have been contrary to Japanese traditions. But, by embarking on this course, Japan was heading in a direction which could hardly have a favorable outcome. If Japan adopted political measures to defend itself against economic restrictions, the Western Powers would inevitably defend themselves with even greater economic restrictions on Japan, driving Japan, by a series of such stages, to open war. And, in such a war, in view of its economic weakness, Japan could hardly hope to win. These stages were confused and delayed over a full decade of years (1931–1941), by indecision and divided counsels in both Japan and the Western Powers. In the process Japan found a considerable advantage in the parallel aggressions of Italy and Germany. It also found a considerable disadvantage in the fact that Japan's imports were vital necessities to her, while her exports were vital necessities to no one. This meant that Japan's trade could be cut off or reduced by anyone, to Japan's great injury, but at much smaller cost to the other nation.

The steps leading to open war between Japan and the Western Powers were delayed by the long-drawn indecision of the Sino-Japanese War. For years Japan hoped to find a solution for its economic and social problems in a decisive victory over China, while in the same years the Western Powers hoped for an end to Japanese aggression by a Japanese defeat in China. Instead, the struggle in that area dragged on without a decision. The Western Powers were too divided at home and among themselves, too filled with pacifism and mistaken political and economic ideas to do anything decisive about China, especially when open war was impossible and anything less than war would injure China as well as Japan. Thus, no sanctions were imposed on Japan for its aggression on Manchuria in 1931 or for its attack on North China in 1937. The American Neutrality Act was not applied to this conflict because President Roosevelt adopted the simple legalistic expedient of failing to "find" a war in the Far East. But the mere existence of laws which might have imposed economic sanctions or economic retaliation on Japan revealed to that country the basic weakness of its own position.

In 1937 Japan received a series of lessons in the precarious state of its strategic-economic position. In the first half of that year, as background for its growing military pressure on China, Japan bought a record amount of American scrap iron and steel, 1.3 million metric tons in six months. Agitation to curtail this supply, either by applying the Neutrality Act to the Sino-Japanese conflict or by some lesser action, was growing in the United States. Early in October 1937, President Roosevelt caused a controversy by a speech suggesting a "quarantine" of aggressor nations. Isolationist sentiment in the United States, especially in the Midwest, was too strong to allow the administration to take any important steps toward such a "quarantine." Nevertheless, Stimson, who had been American secretary of state at the time of the Manchurian crisis in 1931, made a public appeal for an embargo on the shipment of war materials to Japan. A month later, November 3-24, 1937, a conference of the signers of the Nine-Power Treaty of 1922, which guaranteed the integrity of China, met at Brussels to discuss what steps might be taken to end Japan's aggression in China. There was considerable talk of economic sanctions, but no Great Power was willing to light the fuse on that stick of dynamite, so the occasion lapsed, and nothing was done. But the lesson was not wasted on Japan; it intensified its efforts to build up Japanese power to a position where it could use political action to defend itself against any economic reprisals. Naturally, the political actions it took in this direction served only to hasten economic reprisals against itself, especially by the United States, the world's most devoted defender of the *status quo* in the Far East and the only Great Power in any position, especially after Hitler's attacks, to adopt an active policy against Japan.

Japan could have achieved little toward a political solution of its problems if it had not been for the aggressions of Italy and Germany on the other side of the world. A full year before the Brussels Conference, on November 25, 1936, Japan had joined the league of aggressors known as the Anti-Comintern Pact. Discussions seeking to strengthen this arrangement into a full German-Japanese alliance went on for years, but were not concluded until September 1940.

Hitler was not sure whether he wanted Japanese support against the Western democracies or against the Soviet Union, and, accordingly, sought an agreement which could be swung either way, while Japan was interested in a German alliance only if it ran against the Soviet Union. At the same time, Germany objected to the Japanese war on China, since this prevented Japan's strength from being directed against either of Germany's possible foes, and jeopardized German economic interests in China. All these difficulties continued, although Ribbentrop's advent to the post of foreign minister in Berlin in February 1938 inaugurated a period of wholehearted cooperation with Japan in China, replacing Neurath's earlier efforts to maintain some kind of neutral balance in the Sino-Japanese War. The German military advisers with Chiang Kai-shek were withdrawn, although some of them had been in their positions for ten years and were likely to be replaced by Soviet advisers; the German ambassador was withdrawn from China, and the protection of German interests was generally left to lesser officials, using Japanese officials in areas under Japanese occupation; the Japanese regime in Manchukuo was explicitly recognized (20 February 1938); all shipments of German war materials to China (which reached a value of almost 83 million marks in 1937) were ended, and incompleted contracts totaling 282 million marks were canceled; the Japanese claim that their attack on Nationalist China was really an anti-Communist action, although recognized as a fraud in Berlin, was tacitly accepted; and the earlier German efforts to mediate peace between China and Japan ceased.

In spite of these concessions, Japan continued its efforts to curtail German economic enterprises in China, along with those of other Western nations. The alienation of these two aggressor countries by the summer of 1939 can be judged by the fact that the Nazi-Soviet Nonaggression Pact of August 1939 was made in flagrant violation of the German-Japanese Anti-Comintern Agreement of November 1936, since this latter document bound the signers to make no political agreements with the Soviet Union without the previous consent of the other signatory state. This was regarded in Tokyo as such a blow to the prestige of the Japanese government that the prime minister resigned.

In the meantime the American government began to tighten the economic pincers on Japan just as Japan was seeking to tighten its military pincers on China. In the course of 1939 Japan was able to close all the routes from the outside into China except through Hong Kong, across French Indochina, and along the rocky and undeveloped route from Burma to Chungking. The American government retaliated with economic warfare. In June 1938 it established a "moral embargo" on the shipment of aircraft or their parts and bombs to Japan by simply requesting American citizens to refuse to sell these articles. Early in 1939 large American and British loans to China sought to strengthen that country's collapsing financial system. In September 1939 Washington gave the necessary six-month notice to cancel the 1911 commercial treaty with Japan; this opened the door to all kinds of economic pressure against Japan. At the same time, the "moral embargo" was extended to eleven named raw materials which were vital to Japan's war machine. In December this embargo was extended to cover light metals and all machinery or plans for making aviation gasoline.

In general, there was considerable pressure in the United States, both inside the administration and elsewhere, to increase American economic sanctions against Japan. Such a policy was opposed by the isolationists in the country, by our diplomatic agents in Tokyo, and by our quasi-allies, Britain, France, and the Netherlands. These diverse opinions agreed that economic sanctions could be enforced, in the long run, only by war. To put it bluntly, if Japan could not get petroleum, bauxite, rubber, and tin by trade, it could be prevented from seizing areas producing these products only by force. To avoid this obvious inference, Cordell Hull sought to make America's economic policy ambiguous so that Japan might be deterred from evil actions by fear of sanctions not yet imposed and won to conciliatory actions by hopes of concessions not yet granted. Such a policy was a mistake, but it obtained President Roosevelt's explicit approval in December 1939. It was a mistake, since it paralyzed the less aggressive elements in Japanese affairs, allowing the more aggressive elements to take control, because the uncertainty it engendered became so unbearable to many, even of the less aggressive, that any drastic action seeking to end the strain became welcome; there was no real faith in America's intentions, with the result that the period of sustained uncertainty came to be interpreted in Japan as a period of American rearmament preliminary to an attack on Japan, and the ambiguity of American commercial policy toward Japan was, over the months of 1940–1941, slowly resolved in the direction of increasing economic sanctions. There was a steady increase in America's economic pressure on Japan by extensions of the "moral embargo," by the growth of financial obstacles, and by increasing purchasing difficulties, presumably based on America's rearmament program.

Japan continued to advance in China with brusque disregard of Western interests, citizens, or property. By the end of 1939, Japan controlled all the chief cities, river valleys, and railroad lines of eastern China, but faced constant guerrilla opposition in rural areas and had no control over the deep interior of China, which remained loyal to Chiang Kai-shek's government in far-off Chungking on the Upper Yangtze in southwestern China. In March 1940 the Japanese set up a puppet Chinese government at Nanking, but the reality of its power deceived no one.

In the winter of 1939–1940, Japan began to make vigorous commercial demands on the Netherlands East Indies. These demands, chiefly concerned with petroleum and bauxite, were increased after the German victories in France and the Low Countries. From these victories and from Hull's doctrinaire refusal to encourage any Japanese hope that they could win worthwhile American concessions from a more moderate policy, the advocates of extremism in Japan gained influence. A Japanese demand was made on France, following the latter's defeat by Germany, to allow Japanese troops to enter northern Indochina, in order to cut off supplies going to China. This was conceded at once by the Vichy government. At the same time (June 1940), Britain received a demand to withdraw its troops from Shanghai and close the Burma Road to Chinese imports. When Hull refused to cooperate with Britain, either in forcing Japan to desist or in any policy aiming to win better Japanese behavior by concessions, Britain withdrew from Shanghai and closed the Burma Road for three months.

Just at that moment a powerful new weapon against Japan was added to the American arsenal, by an amendment to the National Defense Act giving the President authority to embargo the export of supplies which he judged to be necessary to the defense of the United States. The first presidential order under this new authority required licenses for many goods which Japan needed, including aluminum, airplane parts, all arms or munitions, optical supplies, and various "strategic" materials, but left petroleum and scrap iron unhindered.

As France was falling in June 1940, Roosevelt, for reasons of domestic policy, added to his Cabinet two leaders of the Republican Party, Henry L. Stimson and Frank C. Knox; both of these were interventionists in behalf of Britain, while Stimson, for years, had been demanding economic sanctions against Japan, assuring the more cautious of his audience that such a policy would bring about a Japanese retreat rather than any war. The error in this point of view was clearly revealed at Pearl Harbor in December 1941, but the exact nature of the error is not always recognized.

The real error in the American negotiations with Japan in 1940–1941 was a double one. On the one hand, there was no correlation between our demands on Japan and our actual power in the Pacific, since our demands were vastly more extensive than our strength. On the other hand, there was no correlation between our strategic plans and our diplomatic activity, with the consequence that there was no correlation between our German policy and our Japanese policy. The American strategic plans were based on the premise that Germany must be defeated before Japan. From this perfectly correct premise followed several corollaries which were not fully grasped by American leaders, especially by the nonmilitary leaders. One of these corollaries provided that America must not get into war with Japan before it got into war with Germany, for, if it did so, it would either have to abandon its strategic plans and proceed to fight Japan or declare war on Germany itself. The much greater danger from Germany, and especially from a German victory over either Britain or the Soviet Union, made the first of these unacceptable, while American public opinion would never have accepted an American declaration of war against Germany when we were already in a state of war with Japan. A second corollary from all these conditions was that American diplomatic pressure on Japan must be timed in terms of American-German relations and not in terms of American-Japanese relations in order to avoid pushing Japan into desperate action before American-German relations had passed the breaking point.

As we shall see, American diplomatic pressure on Japan was increased on the basis of moral outrage, high-flown principles, incidental retaliation, and an unrealistic conception of international legality, without any attempt to coordinate this pressure either with our relations to Germany or, what was even worse, with our actual power in the Pacific. Hull was able to do this because his attitudes were generally shared by the civilian heads of the two service departments, by Stimson as secretary of war, and by Knox as secretary of the navy; thus the more realistic views of the military and naval leaders, and their better appreciation of the implications of America's strategic plans, did not have their proper weight on America's policy-making on the Cabinet level or even at the White House. Fortunately, America was saved from many of the consequences of these errors when Hitler made his greatest mistake by declaring war on the United States.

By the beginning of 1941, the Japanese attack on China had bogged down and was in such imminent danger of collapse that something drastic had to be done. But there was no agreement within Japan as to what direction such drastic action should take. A timid majority existed, even within the Japanese government itself, which would have been willing to withdraw from the Chinese "incident" if this could have been done without too great "loss of face." On the whole, this group was timid and ineffectual because of the danger of assassination by the extreme militarists and hypernationalist groups within Japan. Moreover, it was impossible to reach any agreement with the Chinese Nationalist government which would allow Japan to retain its "face" by covering a real withdrawal from China with an apparent diplomatic triumph of some sort.

The advocates of an aggressive policy in Japan were divided among the insignificant group who still believed that an all-out assault on China could be brought to a successful conclusion and the more influential groups who would have sought to redeem the stalemate in China by shifting the offensive against either Soviet Siberia or the rich Anglo-Dutch possessions of Malaysia and Indonesia. In the long run, the group which advocated a drive to the south was bound to prevail, because Malaysia and Indonesia were obviously weak and rich, while Soviet Siberia lacked those items (such as petroleum, rubber, or tin) which Japan most urgently needed, and it had demonstrated its power in the battles of 1938–1939. Germany, which originally encouraged the Japanese to move southward against British Malaysia and then, when it was too late, sought to redirect the Japanese blow against Siberia, played an insignificant role in Japan's policy. The decision to move southward, where the defense was weaker and the prizes so much greater, was made in an ambiguous and halfhearted way in the summer of 1941. The critical turning point was probably during the last week in July.

During the six-week period, March 12–April 22, Matsuoka, the fire-eating foreign minister, was absent from Tokyo on a visit to Berlin and to Moscow. In the German capital he was advised to make no political agreements with the Soviet Union, because of the imminent approach of war between that country and Germany. Matsuoka at once went to Moscow, where he signed a Soviet-Japanese Neutrality Pact on April 13, 1941. In the meantime, in March, Japanese diplomats won special economic concessions in Siam, while in June the nine-month-old trade discussions with the Netherlands East Indies broke down without Nippon obtaining any of the concessions it desired. These agreements, if obtained, might have put Japan in a position where it could have withstood a total American petroleum embargo. Failure to obtain these meant that Japan's large oil reserves would continue to decrease to the point where Japan would be militarily helpless from total lack of oil. America could accelerate this process either by curtailing the supply of oil or by forcing Japan into actions which would increase the rate of its consumption. Japanese oil production in 1941 was only three million barrels a year compared to a consumption rate of about 32 million barrels a year.

Reserves, which had been 55 million barrels in December 1939, were below 50 million in September 1941, and fell to about 43 million by Pearl Harbor.

On July 21, 1941, Japan's threats won from Vichy France the right to move troops into southern Indochina. This was a threat to British Malaya rather than to the Burma Road in China. Within a week, on July 26, 1941, the United States froze all Japanese financial assets in the United States, virtually ending trade between the two countries. The members of the British Commonwealth issued similar orders, while the Netherlands Indies established special licenses for all exports to Japan. No licenses were issued for vital commodities like oil or bauxite. In the same week, an American military mission went to China, and the Philippine Army was incorporated into the American Army.

As a result of these pressures, Japan found itself in a position where its oil reserves would be exhausted in two years, its aluminum reserves in seven months. The chief of the General Staff of the Japanese Navy told the emperor that if Japan resorted to a war to break this blockade it would be very doubtful that it could win. The president of the Japanese Planning Board confirmed this gloomy opinion. The armed forces insisted that Japan had a choice between a slow decline to extinction under economic pressure or war which might allow it to break out of its predicament. The navy had little hope of victory in such a war, but agreed with this analysis. It was also agreed that war, if it came, must begin before the middle of December, when weather conditions would become too adverse to permit amphibious belligerent operations; it was clear that economic pressure was too damaging to allow Japan to postpone such operations until the resumption of good weather in 1942. Accordingly, the decision was made to make war in 1941, but to continue negotiations with the United States until late October. If an agreement could be reached by that date, the preparations for war could be suspended; otherwise the negotiations would be ended and the advance to open war continued. Matsuoka, the foreign minister, who was opposed to continuing the negotiations with the United States, was dropped from the Cabinet on July 16th; from that date on, the civilian portion of the Cabinet desperately sought to reach an agreement in Washington, while the military portion calmly prepared for war.

In the course of 1941, Japan's preparations for war were gradually expanded from a project to close the southern routes into China by an attack on Malaya, to an attack on the United States. The decision to close the Burma Road by force meant that Japan must move into French Indochina and Siam, and cross British Malaya, after neutralizing the British naval base at Singapore. Such a movement had numerous disadvantages. It would mean war with Britain; it would leave the Japanese lines of communication southward open to a flank attack from American bases in the Philippines; it was doubtful if China could be defeated even when all Western supplies were cut off (after all, these supplies were so insignificant that in 1940 American arms and munitions to China were worth only $9 million); even a total defeat of China would leave Japan's material shortages acute, especially in respect to the greatest material need, petroleum products. In view of these disadvantages, under which Japan would expend so much to gain so little, it seemed to many Japanese leaders that very considerable gains could be obtained with only a slight additional effort if an attack on the rich Netherlands Indies were combined with the attack on Malaya and the Burma Road. Such an advance to the tin and bauxite of Malaya and to the oil of the Dutch Indies had every advantage over any alternative possibility, such as an attack on eastern Siberia, especially as the Japanese Army (but not the Navy) had a higher opinion of Soviet power than they had of Anglo-American strength.

Having given the attack on Malaya and Indonesia the preference over any possible attack on Siberia, the Japanese leaders accepted the fact that this would mean war with Britain and the United States. In this they were probably not wrong, although some Americans have claimed that America would not have gone to war if Japan had passed by the Philippines and left other American territories untouched on its road to the south. It is certainly true that such actions would have touched off a violent controversy within the United States between the isolationists and the interventionists, but it seems almost certain that the policies of the Roosevelt Administration would have been carried out, and these policies included plans for war against Japan's southern movement even if American areas were not attacked. In any case, judging American reactions in terms of their own, the Japanese decided that an American flank attack from an untouched Philippines on their extended communications to the southward would be too great a risk to run; accordingly, an attack on the Philippines to prevent this was included in the Japanese plans for their southern movement.

This decision led at once to the next step, the project to attack the American fleet at Pearl Harbor on the grounds that an inevitable war with the United States could be commenced most effectively with a surprise attack on the American Navy rather than by waiting for an intact American fleet to come to seek out the Japanese in their zones of active operations in the southwestern Pacific. It must be recognized that one of the chief factors impelling the Japanese to make the attack on Pearl Harbor was that few Japanese (and these mostly in the army) had any hope that Japan could defeat the United States in any war carried to a decisive conclusion. Rather, it was hoped that, by crippling the American fleet at Pearl Harbor, Japan could conquer such a large area of the southwestern Pacific and southeastern Asia that peace could be negotiated on favorable terms. Here, once again, the Japanese misjudged American psychology.

The negotiations in Washington between Kichisaburo Nomura and Secretary Hull were among the strangest diplomatic discussions ever carried on. Although Nomura probably was not informed of the Japanese plans to make war, he could not have failed to infer them because he had received instructions that he must reach an agreement by late October if peace were to be preserved. He found it impossible to reach such an agreement because Hull's demands were extreme, and his own superiors in Tokyo were unwilling to make any political concessions to win a relaxation of economic restrictions.

The Americans had a clear view of the situation because they had broken the secret Japanese codes and generally had Nomura's instructions from Tokyo before he did. Thus the Americans knew that Nomura had no powers to yield on any vital political issue, that he had been given a deadline in October, and that war would begin if he failed to obtain relaxation of the economic embargo before that deadline. They did not, however, have any details on the Japanese military plans, since these were not communicated by radio, and they did not realize that these plans included an attack on Pearl Harbor. In the course of November American Naval Intelligence knew that Japanese armed forces were mobilizing and moving southward; by November 20th it became clear that a task force of the navy, including four of the largest Japanese aircraft carriers, had vanished. At the end of November intercepted Japanese messages showed clearly that the negotiations were no longer of significance. In early December these showed that the Japanese Embassy in Washington had been ordered to destroy all its codes and to prepare its staff for departure.

The negotiations between Hull and Nomura were lengthy, technical, and hopeless. In essence they boiled down to the conclusion that America would not relax its economic restrictions on Japan unless (1) Japan promised to refrain from acts of force in the southwest Pacific area; (2) Japan agreed to violate its treaty with Germany to permit the United States to support Britain even to the point of war with Germany without any Japanese intervention on the side of Germany; and (3) that Japan would agree to withdraw its armed forces from Indochina and from China and restore equality of economic opportunity in the latter country on a schedule to be worked out later.

When it became clear on October 15, 1941, that agreement was impossible, Hideki Tojo, leader of the activist military group in Japan, forced Prince Fumimaro Konoye to resign. The new Cabinet had General Tojo as Premier, Minister of the Army, and Minister of Home Affairs (controlling domestic police). This was clearly a war government, but the negotiations continued in Washington.

On November 10th operations orders were issued to the Japanese Navy to destroy the American fleet in Pearl Harbor on December 7th. Orders had already been issued to conquer Thailand, Malaya, the Philippines, Borneo, and Sumatra; the rest of the Netherlands East Indies were to be taken in a second movement and all the conquered areas enclosed in a defensive perimeter to run from the Japanese Kurile Islands, through Wake Island and the Marshall Islands, along the southern and western edges of Timor, Java, and Sumatra, to the Burma-India border. By November 20th the American defensive forces knew that Japan was about to strike but still felt that the blow would be southward.

On November 27th a war warning was sent from Washington to Pearl Harbor, but no changes were made there for increased precautions or a higher level of alertness. Fortunately, the three carriers of the American Pacific Fleet were not in Pearl Harbor on the morning of the attack, but the Japanese had detailed anchorage sites for the vessels which were there, including seven battleships and seven cruisers. The Japanese attack force consisted of six carriers with 450 planes escorted by two battleships, two cruisers, eleven destroyers, twenty regular submarines, and five midget submarines. This force, in complete radio silence and without encountering any other vessels, sailed in 11 days in a great northward circle from the Kuriles to a point 275 miles north of Pearl Harbor. From that point, at 6:00 A.M. on December 7, 1941, was launched an air strike of 360 planes, including 40 torpedo planes, 100 bombers, 130 dive-bombers, and 90 fighters. The five midget submarines, dropped from larger submarines, were already operating at Pearl Harbor and were able to enter because the antitorpedo net was carelessly left open after 4:58 A.M. on December 7th. These submarines were detected at 3:42 before they entered the harbor, but no warning was sent until 6:54 after one had been attacked and sunk.

About the same time, an army enlisted man, using radar, detected a group of strange planes coming down from the north 132 miles away, but his report was disregarded. At 7:30 an enlisted sailor noticed two dozen planes about a mile over his ship but did not report it. In the next half-hour these early arrivals from the Japanese carriers were joined by others, and at 7:55 the attack began. Within thirty minutes the Battle Line of the Pacific Fleet had been wiped out. The American losses included 2,400 men killed, almost 1,200 wounded, four battleships sunk with three others badly damaged, many other vessels sunk or damaged, and hundreds of planes destroyed on the grounds. The greatest damage was inflicted by special shallow-water torpedos launched from planes which came in below the 100-foot altitude. In all, the Japanese losses were small, amounting to no more than a couple of dozen planes, because the surprise was so great. The Japanese fleet was not found after the attack, because the search order was issued 180 degrees off direction through an error in interpretation.

Pearl Harbor was but one of several attacks made by the Japanese in their opening assaults on December 7th-10th. Air attacks on Wake Island, Midway Island, Guam, the Philippines, and Malaya destroyed hundreds of planes, mostly on the ground, and set fire to large stores of supplies. Lack of antiaircraft facilities, inadequate air power and fields, and carelessness by higher officers transformed the defenders' situations from critical to hopeless, although personal bravery and resourcefulness made the Japanese pay heavily for their gains.

Midway Island, 1,300 miles northwest of Honolulu and linked to it by a very important cable, survived a hit-and-run attack of December 8, 1941, and by 1942 was America's westernmost base, especially valuable for planes, submarines, and reconnaissance. Wake Island, 1,200 miles southwest of Midway, was struck on December 8th and surrendered on December 23rd after a heavy two-day assault. Guam, 1,500 miles west of Wake and in the midst of the Japanese-mandated Mariana Islands, was invaded at the beginning and gave up on December 10th. The Philippines, 3,000 miles west of Wake, were attacked by landings at nine points in the seventeen days before Christmas; by December 27th the Japanese had compelled the American ground forces to evacuate Manila and to retire into their last defense areas, the rocky caves of the island of Corregidor and the forests of the Bataan Peninsula. Savage fighting continued until May 6, 1942, when the last American forces on Corregidor surrendered. The commanding officers, General Douglas MacArthur and Admiral Thomas Hart, had already withdrawn to Australia.

Fifteen hundred miles west of the Philippines, a Japanese army invaded Thailand from Indochina, and on December 9th captured Bangkok without a struggle. About the same time Japanese landings were made on the Malay Peninsula north of Singapore. When the British battle cruiser *Repulse* and the new battleship *Prince of Wales* ventured north without air cover (since their accompanying carrier, *Indomitable*, ran aground), they were sunk by Japanese land-based planes (December 10th). These were the only Allied capital ships west of Pearl Harbor. But the event had much more significance than this. It showed that the capital ship was no longer the mistress of the seas, as it had been for at least two generations, and, by doing so, it showed that the American losses at Pearl Harbor, concentrated as they were on battleships, were not nearly so important as they had seemed to be. But, even more significant, these sinkings off the east coast of Malaya marked the end of British supremacy on the seas which had begun with the destruction of the Spanish Armada in 1588. For the next two years supremacy on the seas was in dispute, but at the end of that time the decision was falling clearly in favor of a new champion, the United States.

Fanning outward as they spread over the southwestern Pacific and southeastern Asia, the Japanese forces captured Hong Kong on December 25, 1941 and advanced on Singapore across the swamps on its landward side. This great naval base, the bastion of all British power in the Far East, had to surrender on February 15, 1942, without even being able to defend itself, its great guns, aimed seaward at an army which never came, being completely useless against the Japanese who crept up on it from the landward side.

Lying north of Australia in a great curve from Singapore to New Guinea was the Malay Barrier, originally intended to form the southern perimeter of the Japanese defense area. Like beads on a necklace across a distance of 3,500 miles were stretched dozens of islands: Sumatra, Java, Bali, Lumbok, Flores, Timor, New Guinea, and others. These were taken so rapidly by the Japanese octopus that the straits between the various islands were closed before some Allied ships could escape through to the south. Five Allied cruisers and many destroyers were caught in this way and sunk in the week of February 26, 1942; Sumatra, Java, and Timor surrendered by March 9th; and Netherlands forces were wiped out, British forces withdrew to Ceylon, and the few surviving American vessels limped home for repairs. Rangoon, the Burmese capital, surrendered on March 8th, and exactly a month later the triumphant Japanese naval forces swept westward to strike at Ceylon. In the first week of April, Holy Week of 1942, Japanese Admiral Chuichi Nagumo, who had led the attack on Pearl Harbor, made a similar attack on Ceylon, sinking the British carrier *Hermes*, two heavy cruisers, and many lesser vessels (including 136,000 tons of merchant ships).

At this dark moment, mid-April of 1942, the tide of battle in the Pacific began to turn. The three American aircraft carriers which had been spared at Pearl Harbor (*Lexington, Enterprise,* and *Saratoga*) were joined by one of the two carriers from the Atlantic (*Yorktown*). These, with cruisers, destroyers, submarines, and supply ships, became nuclei for "task forces" which relentlessly prowled the Pacific. On April 2, 1942, the new carrier *Hornet*, with sixteen United States Army Mitchell bombers (B-25's) wedged on its deck, sailed from San Francisco with a message for Tokyo. Escorted by the *Enterprise* Task Force to a point 850 miles from the Japanese capital (and thus 2,100 miles from their assigned landing fields in China) the sixteen B-25's were taken off the plunging deck of the carrier by their army crews of eighty men led by Lieutenant Colonel James H. Doolittle. Four hours later they dumped sixteen tons of bombs on the Japanese capital, and continued westward to China. Fifteen planes crashed in China after running out of gasoline, while the sixteenth found internment in Siberia. With Chinese help, seventy-one of eighty crew members returned to America. The whole episode was more spectacular than fruitful, but it did give a great boost to American morale, and frightened the Japanese so badly that they kept four Japanese air groups in Japan for defense.

During this period of the war the United States had amazingly correct information regarding Japanese war plans. Some of this came from our control over the Japanese codes, but much of the most critical intelligence came from other sources which have never been revealed. Through these channels, while Admiral William Halsey was still en route back from the Tokyo raid with two carriers, American naval authorities learned of two Japanese projects. The first of these planned to send an invasion force from Rabaul in New Britain, north of New Guinea, to capture Port Moresby on the southern shore of New Guinea. The second plan hoped to extend the Japanese defense perimeter eastward by seizing the Aleutian Islands and Midway Island in the northern Pacific. The former project was frustrated in the Battle of the Coral Sea, May 7-8, 1942, while the second project was disastrously defeated in the decisive Battle of Midway, June 4, 1942.

The Coral Sea, brilliantly blue and white, forms a rectangle more than 1,000 miles wide from east to west and slightly longer from north to south. Open on the south, it is boxed in on the other three sides with Australia to the west, the New Hebrides and New Caledonia to the east, and New Guinea and the Solomon Islands to the north. On May 8th, as the Japanese invasion force for Port Moresby came into this area from the northwest, it was intercepted by an American task force, including the carriers *Lexington* and *Yorktown*. The invasion force was turned back, a small Japanese carrier was sunk, and a large carrier severely damaged, while fires on both American carriers were extinguished. After the battle, however, the *Lexington* blew apart from gasoline fires ignited by an electric-motor spark deep within its hull.

The Turning Tide, 1942-1943: Midway, El Alamein, French Africa, and Stalingrad

The Second World War was a gigantic conflict because it was an agglomeration of several wars. Each of these wars had a different turning point, but all of these occurred in the year following the surrender of Corregidor on May 6, 1942. The first turning point to be reached, in the war between the United States and Japan, occurred at Midway on June 4, 1942, while the second was reached in the defeat of the Italo-German attack on Egypt on November 2, 1942. The American war on Germany took a turn for the better with the successful American invasion of French North Africa on November 8, 1942, while, at the same time, the crucial struggle between Nazi Germany and the Soviet Union reached its turn in the long agony at Stalingrad from November 1942 to February 1943. Needless to say, long and bitter exertions were needed to push the three aggressor states back from their points of farthest advance.

The Battle of Midway arose from a Japanese trap which was supposed to destroy the rest of the Pacific Fleet but resulted quite differently. Whatever illusions the Japanese Army may have had, the Japanese Navy fully recognized that it could not possibly win in the Pacific until the American fleet was totally destroyed. To achieve this, a trap was set to draw the fleet out from Pearl Harbor by the threat of a Japanese amphibious invasion of Midway Island from the southwest. When the Americans hurried out to attack this invasion fleet at Midway, they were to have been destroyed by the planes from four Japanese carriers lying in ambush 200 miles northwest of Midway. The ambush was reversed because Admiral Chester Nimitz at Pearl Harbor had a clear picture of the Japanese plans and sent his own carriers out to spring on the Japanese carriers from a point 200 miles northeast of their position.

The American counterambush worked because of a most extraordinary series of fortunate chances. The four Japanese carriers expected the American counterattack to come from Pearl Harbor after several days' delay, and accordingly felt free to use their own carrier planes to bombard the Midway defenses, softening them up for the benefit of the invading force coming up on Midway from the southwest. These bombardment planes had returned from Midway to their carriers and were still feverishly refueling on the flight decks when the American carrier "strike" came in: 116 planes from *Enterprise* and *Hornet* were followed shortly after by 35 planes from *Yorktown*.

Caught in a horrible tactical position, the Japanese defended so skillfully that 37 out of 41 American torpedo-bombers were lost, but, as wave after wage of dive-bombers continued to come in, the Japanese defense was "saturated," and soon all four carriers were sinking in flames. Before the fourth Japanese carrier went down, it sent off 40 planes which torpedoed the *Yorktown*. The American carrier was incapacitated and mistakenly abandoned, so that it was easily sunk by a Japanese submarine two days later. This loss, even in combination with the loss of the *Lexington* in the Coral Sea a month earlier, was a cheap price to pay for the destruction of five Japanese carriers in these two areas in the space of five weeks, since the United States had the industrial capacity to replace its losses, while Japan did not.

Two events of November 1942, the British victory at El Alamein and the Anglo-American invasion of French North Africa, provided tactical lessons and strategic reversals fully as great as those provided in the

Pacific five months earlier. During most of 1942, the British clung to their lifeline across the Mediterranean from Gibraltar to Malta and Egypt by no more than a fingernail's margin. Italo-German submarine and air attacks were steadily intensified. While the whole northern shore of the Mediterranean from Gibraltar to the Aegean was under Axis control or sympathetic to it, the Italian foothold on the southern shore of the Mediterranean in Libya was steadily strengthened, largely by German reinforcements, and German pressure was brought to bear on Vichy France to increase Nazi influence in French North Africa.

As long as the British were opposed only by Italian forces in the Mediterranean, they were able to keep convoys moving, but on January 10, 1941, the German Air Force intervened in the central Mediterranean with devastating effect. From that point onward, for a period of two years (until May 1943) it was impossible to get a merchant convoy through the Mediterranean from Gibraltar to Alexandria; accordingly, the British imperial forces in Egypt had to be supplied by the longer route around Africa. Even British naval vessels found it difficult to pass through the Mediterranean; in the course of 1941 all the British capital ships and carriers in the central and eastern Mediterranean were sunk or damaged so badly that they had to be withdrawn.

The island of Malta, situated in the middle of the Axis supply line from Italy to Africa, was pulverized from the air for more than nineteen months (until October 1942), and all vessels, even submarines, had to be withdrawn from its harbors. Efforts to replenish its supplies of food and ammunition became suicidal, but had to be continued, as its civilian population stood up magnificently under the pounding and could not be left without supplies by the fighting services. For months at a time, no convoys could get through, but each time supplies approached exhaustion, fragments of a convoy arrived with enough to keep the island fighting a little longer. In June 1941 ten merchant ships from Alexandria and six from Gibraltar were sent simultaneously in order to divide the enemy; although protected by a battleship, two carriers, twelve cruisers and forty-four destroyers, only two of the sixteen cargo vessels arrived at Malta, at a cost of three destroyers and a cruiser sunk and many others damaged. Two months later, when Malta had only a week's supplies left, fourteen very fast merchant vessels were sent from Gibraltar with an escort of two battleships, four carriers, seven cruisers, and twenty-five destroyers. Five badly damaged merchant ships reached Malta with a naval loss of a carrier, two cruisers, and a destroyer sunk, another carrier and two cruisers badly damaged.

This severe fighting in the central Mediterranean arose from the vital need, by both sides, to control the communications of that area. The northern shore of the Mediterranean Sea, from west to east, was controlled by Franco Spain, by Vichy France, by the Axis, and by Turkey.

Spain was pro-Axis but unable, through economic weakness, to inter-vene in the war until Britain was thoroughly beaten; Vichy France remained ambiguous and a major leak in the economic blockade of Europe until November 1942; Turkey was pro-British but unable to offer anything more than benevolent neutrality. On the southern shore of the Mediterranean, Libya (consisting of Tripolitania in the west and Cyrenaica in the east) was in between Egypt and French North Africa, and could be used as a base to attack either, because of the Axis supply lines from Italy and Sicily. These lines were greatly strengthened by the Axis conquest of Greece and Crete in May and June 1941.

From this base in Libya the Axis struck at Egypt three times, and were answered by three British counterattacks. These provide the historian with an amazing sequence of movements in which the battle lines surged across Africa between Egypt and French Tunis, a distance of 1,200 miles. The real struggle was for control of Cyrenaica, and especially for its sea-ports strung like beads from Benghazi eastward 270 miles by way of Derna and Tobruk to Sollum on the Egyptian frontier. If the Germans could control this stretch, they could use Tobruk as a supply port free from interference from Malta, while, if the British could control it, they could provide air cover for Malta from African fields.

The first Axis advance, by the Italians under Graziani, went no farther than Sidi Barrâni in Egypt, 50 miles east of Sollum (September 1940). This was repulsed by an amazing British advance of 500 miles from Sidi Barrâni to El Agheila, 150 miles beyond Benghazi (December 1940– February 1941). It was to stop this Italian retreat, early in 1941, that the Nazis intervened with an air fleet of 500 planes, under Kesselring, and the famous Afrika Korps, under Field Marshal Erwin Rommel. Rommel, a tactical genius, had three German divisions (two armored and one motorized) supported by seven Italian divisions (six infantry and one armored). By a series of smashing blows, Rommel advanced eastward to Egypt, destroying most of the British armor on the way, but his advance stopped at Sollum in April 1941. Hitler held up most of the supplies going to Rommel because he needed them in Greece, Crete and, later, in Russia. The supply routes to Rommel were very precarious because of British naval attacks out of Alexandria, only 250 miles to the east, and because of an Australian division left in Tobruk, that, although surrounded by Rommel and besieged for months, denied him the use of its port.

While Rommel's supplies were dwindling and the British Navy was being driven from the central Mediterranean by Axis air power and submarines, the defense of Egypt was being built up by the circum-Africa supply line. Over this 10,000-mile route came 951 light tanks and 13,000 trucks, many of these under Lend-Lease, by the end of 1941. With this equipment General Claude Auchinleck attacked Rommel in November 1941 and in two months relieved Tobruk and forced the Ger-

mans back to El Agheila (January 1942). Within a week Rommel counterattacked and advanced eastward, being stopped forty miles west of
Tobruk (mid-February 1942). Both sides rested there, while the Western
Powers feverishly built up their supplies in Egypt. At the end of May
1942, Rommel struck again; this time he captured Tobruk and was finally
stopped at El Alamein, only sixty miles short of Alexandria, after five
days of furious fighting at that point (July 1-5, 1942).

In August, General Bernard L. Montgomery, later Field Marshal and
First Viscount Montgomery of Alamein, replaced General Auchinleck.
His forces were equipped with every piece of armament that could be
spared from the United States, including 700 two-engine bombers, 1,000
fighting planes, over 400 M-4 Sherman tanks, 90 new American self-
propelled guns, and 25,000 trucks and other vehicles. On October 23rd,
while Rommel was absent in Germany, Montgomery attacked the Axis
forces at their strongest point, along the coast road, and after twelve days
of violent combat broke through the German position. Rommel returned,
but could not stop the rout. By November 20th he had lost Benghazi
and was still retreating. Worse than that, on November 8th, only four
days after El Alamein, Rommel heard that a large-scale American invasion of French North Africa had already landed at three points. These
had to be hurled backward, for the German forces could be cut off if the
Americans passed Tunis.

The American invasion of North Africa on November 8, 1942 (Operation Torch) arose as a compromise of quite dissimilar strategic ideas in
Moscow, London, and Washington. Stalin was insistent that the Anglo-
Americans must open a "second front" in western Europe in 1942
in order to reduce the Nazi pressure on Russia. He was completely unreasonable in his attitude, going so far as to taunt Churchill with cowardice at the Moscow Conference in August 1942. In London there was,
indeed, great lack of faith in any possible invasion of Europe; instead,
there was hope that the Germans could be brought to terms by air attacks and economic blockade after perhaps ten years; Churchill went
a little further by speaking of a possible invasion of the Continent from
the Mediterranean through what he mistakenly called the "soft under-
belly of the Axis." In Washington the military leaders were convinced,
from the earliest stages of the war, that Hitler could not be beaten without a full-scale invasion of western Europe. As early as April 1942, Harry
Hopkins and General Marshall appeared in London with plans for an
invasion of western Europe by thirty American and eighteen British
divisions. The British were very reluctant, but, as Stalin kept insisting on
a "second front" in 1942, Roosevelt, on July 25th, obtained, as a compromise, an agreement to invade French North Africa in the autumn of
1942.

There was hardly time for adequate planning, and no time for adequate training, before the landings were made on November 8th. Although the operation was a joint British-American venture, the British role was little publicized to avoid antagonizing French—especially French naval—feelings, which were still hostile because of the British attacks on Dakar, Oran, and Syria. In addition, a difficult problem arose about the question of political cooperation with the French authorities in North Africa. The British had placed most of their faith in General de Gaulle, but it soon became clear that he had very little support in North Africa, and was too difficult and uncooperative personally to be made part of the invasion plans.

The Americans, who had maintained diplomatic relations with Vichy, believed it would be necessary to replace the local Vichy leaders as soon as North Africa had been conquered; they pinned their faith on the heroic General Henri Giraud, who had obtained considerable publicity by his spectacular escapes from German prisons in both world wars. Unfortunately, as the invasion proceeded, it was discovered that Giraud had even less influence in North Africa than De Gaulle, especially in the French Navy, which was providing the chief combat resistance to the invasion. Accordingly, in order to stop the fighting, it became necessary to make a deal with Admiral Darlan, who was in North Africa at the time; this deal, which recognized Darlan as the chief political authority in all French North Africa, with Giraud as his commander in chief, has given rise to much controversy. It was argued that the high principles enunciated in our declared war aims, especially in the Atlantic Charter, were being unnecessarily sacrified by making a deal with an unprincipled Nazi collaborator such as Darlan.

The deal was justified by its makers, General Mark Clark on behalf of General Eisenhower and Ambassador Robert Murphy on behalf of President Roosevelt, on grounds of military urgency. This argument is rather weak, since Darlan's cease-fire order, made at noon on November 8th, was not obeyed in two combat areas (Morocco and Oran) and obeyed only partially in the third area (Algiers), and by the time the formal deal was made on November 11th, organized fighting by the French forces had ceased everywhere. The additional justification made, to the effect that some kind of legal continuity with the Vichy regime had to be established to avoid French guerrilla resistance, involves too many unknown factors to permit any convincing judgment of its value. It seems weak, since the German reaction to the Allied invasion of North Africa took an anti-French direction which was so drastic that any French resistance to the Americans or British would have been clearly pro-German, and thus most unlikely behavior for any patriotic Frenchmen. In any case, the Darlan deal was soon swallowed up in the swift pace of events, and was personally ended when Darlan was assassinated by his French enemies on December 24th.

The Anglo-American invasion of North Africa, known as Operation Torch and under the over-all command of General Eisenhower, involved landings at three points: on the Atlantic coast of Morocco near Casablanca by a force coming from North America, and at two points on the Mediterranean coast in Algeria by forces coming from England. The Morocco attack was almost foolhardy, since it involved carrying 35,000 completely inexperienced and inadequately trained troops with 250 tanks, all in 102 vessels, a distance of 4,000 miles across the ocean to make a night landing on a hostile coast. In spite of these obstacles and tenacious French resistance at certain points, the operation was a success, and fighting ceased in three days. The other portion of Operation Torch, the landings in Algeria, were on a larger scale, since they involved 49,000 American and 23,000 British troops, and were equally successful. By November 14th the Allies were moving eastward into Tunisia to cut off Rommel's retreat from the east, and by November 29th they were only twelve miles from Tunis. From that point they were hurled backward by the Germans.

Hitler's reactions to Torch were vigorous. All France was occupied by Nazi forces; his efforts to capture the French fleet at Toulon were frustrated when most of the vessels were scuttled at their anchorages or were sunk trying to escape from the harbor; as early as November 10th, German airborne troops, with Laval's blessings, were occupying Tunisia. These German forces held up the Allied advance from the west, inflicting a bitter defeat on the American forces at the Kasserine Pass in February 1943. In this way Rommel, who had been forced out of El Agheila by Montgomery on December 13th, was able to withdraw westward into Tunisia and take a stand along the Mareth Line below Gabès in southeastern Tunisia in February.

During the third week in January 1943, Roosevelt, Churchill, and their staffs met in secret conference at Casablanca. Once again the Americans had to struggle against English reluctance to commit themselves to any "cross-Channel" invasion of Europe, to any offensive against Japan or, indeed, to any long-range planning. From the compromises of the conference emerged agreement to postpone any cross-Channel operation, to keep up pressure on Germany in Europe by air attacks, and to allow the United States to take any offensive actions against Japan which would not jeopardize the priority still given to the defeat of Germany. Two other decisions were to proceed to the military occupation of Sicily and to demand the "unconditional surrender" of the three totalitarian Powers. Naturally, the military decision on Sicily was kept secret, but the political decision on unconditional surrender was published with great fanfare, and at once initiated a controversy which still continues.

The controversy over unconditional surrender is based on the belief that the expression itself is largely meaningless and had an adverse influence by discouraging any hopes within the Axis countries that they could find a way out by slackening their efforts, by revolting against their governments, or by negotiations seeking some kind of "conditional" surrender. There seems to be little doubt that the demand for unconditional surrender was incompatible with earlier statements that we were fighting the German, Japanese, and Italian governments rather than the German, Japanese, and Italian peoples and that this demand, by destroying this distinction, to some extent solidified our enemies and prolonged their resistance, especially in Italy and Japan, where opposition to the war was widespread and active. Even in Germany the demand for unconditional surrender discouraged those more moderate and peace-loving Germans upon which our postwar policy toward Germany must be based and, in fact, has been based. But in 1943, and for most of the duration of the war, the Allied Powers had neither time nor inclination to look ahead toward any postwar policy with respect to Germany, and issued the demand for unconditional surrender without any analysis of its possible effects on the enemy peoples, either during the war or after it was over. The demand for unconditional surrender was made, rather, as a morale booster for the Allied Powers themselves, and in this function it may well have had some slight influence at the time.

As the Allied leaders were conferring in Casablanca after turning back the German assault in Africa, Soviet forces were inflicting an even greater defeat on Hitler in eastern Europe. Hitler's Russian campaign of 1942 was very similar to that of 1941 except that his original plan was restricted to a single aim: to capture the oil fields of the Caucasus. The German forces, consisting of 44 infantry, 10 armored, and 6 motorized divisions, along with 43 satellite divisions and 700 planes, were to drive along the north shore of the Black Sea, pass through a congested bottleneck at Rostov, and capture the Soviet oil fields (the chief of which, at Baku, was 700 miles beyond Rostov). To protect the long northern flank of this drive, other German attacks were ordered farther north toward Voronezh and toward Stalingrad on the Volga River. The German offensive did reach the Caucasus, advancing almost as far as Grozny (400 miles beyond Rostov), but did not capture the chief oil fields. As in the 1941 offensive, scores of Soviet divisions were destroyed and hundreds of thousands of Soviet prisoners were captured, but no vital injury was inflicted on the Soviet Union.

Suddenly, on July 18th, after seven weeks of advance, Hitler ordered the capture of Stalingrad. Since all the available armored forces had been put into the Caucasus offensive, where they uselessly clogged up Rostov, the attack on Stalingrad could not begin until September 12th. After two months of savage house-to-house fighting, the Germans had possession of almost all the city, but it had been completely demolished. In late November, Russian counteroffensives north and south of Stalingrad broke through Romanian armies on either side of the German Sixth Army and joined together on its rear. Hitler forbade any retreat or any effort by the Sixth Army to fight its way westward out of the trap. Instead he undertook to supply the Sixth Army from the air until new German forces could break in to relieve it. The surrounded Sixth Army consisted of 20 divisions, about 270,000 men, including 3 armored and 3 motorized divisions. Although a force of this size required about 1,500 tons of supplies each day, the Luftwaffe was never able to deliver as much as 200 tons a day, and lost about 300 planes in the effort. Nor could the German forces to the west, although only 40 miles away, fight their way in to the Sixth Army.

While this was going on at Stalingrad from December 1942 through January 1943, another Soviet offensive, striking down from the northeast toward Rostov, was trying to cut off the whole German force in the Caucasus by capturing the city of Rostov and thus closing the bottleneck north of the Sea of Azov. The German withdrawal from the Caucasus began on the first day of 1943. With extraordinary skill the Germans succeeded in keeping the Rostov passage open, although by January 23rd it was no more than 30 miles wide. The German Sixth Army at Stalingrad, although frozen, starved, and hardly able to fight for lack of supplies, was not permitted to surrender because, as soon as it did so, the three Soviet armies which had surrounded it would be freed to drive west and close the Rostov passage. On January 23rd General Friedrich von Paulus, commanding the Sixth Army, accepted Hitler's radio order to fight to the last man in order to gain time. A week later Hitler promoted him to field marshal, and two days later he surrendered. Of 270,000 Germans originally surrounded, over 100,000 were dead, 34,000 had been evacuated by air, and 93,000 surrendered. Ten days after Paulus's surrender, the Germans abandoned Rostov. For the next two weeks it looked as if a new Soviet offensive from Voronezh might cut off the whole of German Army Group South, but Field Marshal von Manstein succeeded in reestablishing a stable defensive line by April 1st, just about at the line where the German offensive of 1942 had begun eleven months earlier. But, in that eleven months, Hitler had lost about 38 German divisions, an equal number of satellite divisions, had reduced all German divisions from nine battalions to six, had failed to capture the Caucasus oil fields, Moscow, or Leningrad, and had not been able to cut the Murmansk railway.

Over that railway, and by other routes, a growing flood of American supplies was flowing to the Soviet armies. By October 1942, 85,000 trucks had arrived, with the result that the Soviet Army from that date to the end of the war had greater mobility than the Germans. Luftwaffe forces on the eastern front had 2,000 planes in the campaign of 1941, 1,300 at the opening of the campaign of 1942, and could hardly be kept at 1,000 after the end of that campaign. Allied pressure in the west made it necessary to reduce the portion of the German Air Force allotted to the east, with the result that Germany had only 265 operational planes on the Russian front on May 1, 1944. At the same time, American supplies, including planes, flowed into the Soviet Union in an amazing flood. The German U-boats were unable to prevent this flow of goods, although they did sink 77 out of 2,660 vessels loaded with Lend-Lease supplies. Many of these sinkings occurred on the frightful Murmansk route.

In 1941 and 1942 the Allies sent the Soviet Union almost 2,000,000 tons of supplies. This was followed by over 4,500,000 tons in 1943 and a total of over 15,000,000 tons worth $10,000,000,000 before the end of the struggle. Included in the final total were 375,000 trucks, 52,000 jeeps, 7,056 tanks, 6,300 other combat vehicles, 2,328 artillery vehicles, 14,795 aircraft, 8,212 antiaircraft guns, 1,900 steam locomotives, 66 diesel locomotives, 11,075 railway cars, 415,000 telephones, 3,786,000 vehicle tires, 15,000,000 pairs of military boots, 4,478,116 tons of food, and 2,670,371 tons of petroleum products. In contrast with this, the German armored divisions were kept idle for lack of fuel for weeks at a time as early as 1942, and both operational and training flights of the Luftwaffe were drastically curtailed from 1942 onward. The lack of fuel was so acute that Hitler decided, late in 1942, to decommission most of the surface vessels of the German Navy. When Grand Admiral Raeder protested too vigorously, he was removed from his position as head of the navy, and replaced by the U-boat specialist Admiral Karl Doenitz, in January, 1943.

All these events should have made it clear that Germany could not possibly win the war, but for the next two years Hitler and his immediate associates became increasingly fanatical, increasingly merciless, and increasingly remote from reality. Anyone who audibly doubted their insane vision of the world was speedily liquidated.

Closing in on Germany, 1943-1945

The year 1943 represented the turning point in the European struggle as the year 1942 had seen the turning point in the Pacific. In 1943 North Africa was freed from the Nazi grasp in May, Sicily was overrun in July and August, the southern part of Italy was occupied, and the German armies were pushed backward from eastern Europe. As a consequence, the Mediterranean was opened to Allied traffic, and Italy was forced to surrender in September 1943.

These were the obvious events of this critical year 1943, open to public view and hopeful in their implications for the future. But the role of this year as a turning point in the conflict with Germany was much greater than this, for, behind the scenes, the military successes of the year forced decisions on strategic plans and postwar projects whose implications are still being worked out today. And still very much behind the scenes, these strategic and postwar plans revealed deep fissures and rivalries among the three Allied Powers.

Rivalries among the members of a coalition are always to be expected and are usually, and necessarily, kept secret during the war itself. In the Second World War they were most significant in the year 1943. In the years before 1943 these disputes were more concerned with strategic decisions than with postwar planning, while in the later years, when strategy had been set, postwar plans were the chief causes of disputes. The year 1943, however, had its full share of both, since the major strategic decisions were made in that year, and these decisions, in themselves, played a major role in determining the nature of the postwar world.

In the years 1941–1943 the chief strategic questions were concerned with two problems: (1) Should the European war against Germany continue to receive priority over the Pacific war against Japan? and (2) Should Germany be attacked, indirectly, by aerial bombardment, blockade, and guerrilla forces or should Europe be invaded with large infantry forces, either from England directly across the Channel to western Europe or from the Mediterranean through southern Europe? The answers given to these strategic questions, especially the last one, played a major role in establishing the postwar political settlement in Europe.

In the earlier years a certain direction was given to postwar planning by Roosevelt's proclamation of the Four Freedoms in January 1941, and the Anglo-American publication of the Atlantic Charter in August 1941. When the stunning news of Pearl Harbor reached London on December 7, 1941, Foreign Minister Eden was just leaving for Moscow. It was decided that he should go anyway but that Prime Minister Churchill should go simultaneously to Washington to do all he could to prevent popular, anti-Japanese feeling in the United States from reversing the agreement that the military defeat of Germany must have priority over the defeat of Japan. In Washington, at what was called the Arcadia Conference (December 22, 1941–January 14, 1942), the exuberant prime minister found no desire to change the agreed military priorities, and was able to plan intensified military activity along the lines already established. At the same time Roosevelt presented him with a draft for a public "Declaration of the United Nations." This document declared that the twenty-six signatory states were fighting "to defend life, liberty, independence, and religious freedom and to preserve human rights and justice in their own lands as well as in other lands, and that they are now engaged in a common struggle against savage and brutal forces seeking to subjugate the world." Each signer promised "to employ its full resources and to make no separate armistice or peace" in the struggle for victory over Hitlerism.

Most of the secret discussions leading up to the publication of this declaration on January 1, 1942 were concerned with verbal or procedural issues, but some of these were symbolic of future problems. There was considerable discussion as to the order in which the signatures should be affixed to the document; the decision to rank them in two groups, with the four "Great Powers" of the United States, the United Kingdom, the Soviet Union, and China followed by twenty-two lesser states in alphabetical order, was an early indication of the similar division which still exists in the United Nations today. The inclusion of China, in spite of its obvious weakness, among the Great Powers was a concession made to the United States by the other Powers. The American leaders, from Roosevelt down, insisted that China was, or at least should be, a Great Power, although the only evidence they could find to support this argument was its larger population. The Americans seemed to hope that by encouragement and reiteration, or perhaps even by invocation, China could be made into a Great Power, able to dominate the Far East after the defeat of Japan.

Other notable features of this United Nations Declaration were: (1) the fact that De Gaullist France was excluded from the signers in order not to recognize it as a government, (2) the fact that the United States was ranked first among the Great Powers, and (3) the difficulty in wording the declaration so that Japan, with which the Soviet Union was not at war, should not specifically be included among the enemy and yet, at the same time, should not be excluded from the "brutal forces" which were condemned.

In the meantime, in Moscow, Anthony Eden was being faced with Soviet demands for a specific delimitation of the postwar boundaries of eastern Europe. In the north, the Bolshevik leaders wanted explicit British recognition that Latvia, Estonia, and Lithuania were parts of the Soviet Union and that the Soviet-Finnish frontier should be as it had existed after the "winter war" of 1939–1940; in the center, the Soviets demanded a frontier with Poland along the so-called Curzon Line, which followed, it was true, the linguistic frontier, but was 150 miles west of the Polish-Soviet frontier of the 1921–1939 period; in the south, Stalin wanted Eden to agree to a Soviet-Romanian border which would have allowed Russia to have Bessarabia and Bukovina. These demands sought recognition of the Soviet Union's western boundary as it existed between the Nazi-Soviet Pact of September 1939 and Hitler's attack in June 1941, except that the Curzon Line was, in some places, slightly to the east of the 1940 line.

Although these Soviet demands were clearly in conflict with the high purposes of the Atlantic Charter, Churchill was not averse to accepting them on grounds of physical necessity, but American objections to any settlement of territorial questions while the war was still going on forced him to refuse Stalin's requests. In general, the British found themselves in a difficult position between the high and proclaimed principles of the Americans and the low and secret interests of the Russians. Because of American pressure, Eden avoided any territorial commitments, and persuaded Stalin to accept a twenty-year treaty of alliance with Britain. This Anglo-Soviet Treaty of May 26, 1942 had no territorial provisions, and included a statement that the signers would "act in accordance with the two principles of not seeking territorial aggrandizement for themselves and of non-interference in the internal affairs of other States."

Although the Soviet Union accepted the terms of the British alliance, in 1942 their suspicions of the West were still high, and their relations with Britain became increasingly unfriendly, reaching a critical stage by 1943. In Moscow there was fear that the West wished to protract the war in order to bleed both Germany and the Soviet Union to death. It was feared that this end could be obtained if American supplies to Russia were placed at a level sufficiently high to keep Russia fighting but insufficiently high to allow her to defeat Hitler. To avoid this, Moscow continued to insist, with unreasonable repetition, on the need to increase Lend-Lease supplies to it and, above all, on the need to open a second front on the Continent by an immediate Anglo-American invasion of Europe from England. Judging, perhaps, that American psychology would work along the same lines of "power politics" as their own, a mistake which the Japanese, with considerably greater reason, had made in the months before Pearl Harbor, the Russians could not conceive that the United States would grant sufficient aid to Russia to permit a speedy defeat of Hitler, since such a policy, almost inevitably, would leave the victorious Soviet armies supreme in eastern, and probably also in central, Europe.

As a matter of fact, while some Americans unquestionably did think in terms of "power politics" and may, in a few cases, have gone so far as to prefer a Hitler victory over Stalin to a Stalin victory over Hitler, such people were very remote from the centers of power in the American government. At those centers of power there was complete conviction in the value of unrestricted aid to Russia, the speediest possible defeat of Germany, and a full "cross-Channel" invasion of Europe as soon as possible. In fact, these aims were so firmly embraced by those Americans with whom the Russians had relationships, men like Harry Hopkins, General Marshall, or Roosevelt himself, that these men sometimes misled the Russians by expressing their hopes rather than their expectations, with the consequence that Russian suspicions were roused again, at a later date, when these hopes were not fulfilled. Immediately after the signing of the Anglo-Soviet alliance, Soviet Foreign Commissar Molotov came to Washington to urge the need for an immediate second front in Europe. Although such a project would have been unwise, if not impossible, in 1942, the White House communiqué of June 11, 1942 sought to satisfy the Russians and to frighten the Germans by saying that "full understanding was reached with regard to the urgent tasks of creating a second front in Europe in 1942."

In the early summer of 1942 Soviet messages to Washington and to London continued to insist on the need for an immediate second front in Western Europe in order to reduce the Nazi military pressure on the Soviet forces. Recognizing the impossibility of such a venture in 1942, the Anglo-Americans sought to relieve the pressure on Russia by landing at a place where the German defense would not be so strong. It was this desire which resulted in the decision of July 25, 1942 to invade North Africa in November. Having made the decision to substitute this project for any possible cross-Channel attack in 1942, it was necessary to convey the news to the Soviet Union. Churchill undertook this delicate task on his first meeting with Stalin in Moscow in August 1942. The result was a most unpleasant explosion by Stalin. The Soviet leader charged that Molotov had obtained a definite promise for a second front in 1942, that failure to carry out this promise would jeopardize Soviet military plans, and that Churchill was opposed to such a venture from cowardice!

The strategic disputes among the three Allied Powers were sharp and based on very different outlooks, but in no case did cowardice play any role. The Soviet insistence on an immediate, all-out cross-Channel attack to relieve Nazi pressure on Russia was perfectly understandable, although insistence on such an attack in 1942 was unrealistic. Equally understandable was Russia's fear that the Anglo-Americans might divert their power from Germany in order to avoid a Soviet-dominated post-war Europe, although this fear showed no realistic appreciation of the American outlook. On the other hand, the British reluctance to attempt the cross-Channel attack was perfectly clear. Sir Alan Brooke, the chief of the Imperial General Staff, opposed all plans for such an assault, while others, like Churchill, wanted to postpone such an attack indefinitely or reduce it to no more than a series of small raids to establish permanent anti-German bridgeheads in western Europe. The difficulties of such raids were shown on August 19, 1942 when a force of 5,000 men, mostly Canadians, landed at Dieppe and suffered 3,350 casualties in a few hours.

The Americans, especially General Marshall, were convinced that Germany could be defeated only by a cross-Channel attack, and advocated one on the largest possible scale at the earliest possible date.

These differences of strategic opinion reflected basic differences of outlook. The American outlook was largely military. They were eager

to defeat Germany and end the war as soon as possible and had little time
or energy for political problems or postwar planning. The British, on
the other hand, were much concerned with political issues and the way
in which the postwar situation would be influenced by strategic and
military actions earlier. The Soviet leaders, to some extent, represented
a combination of the two other points of view and could do so because
there was no such divergence between their military and political or between their wartime and postwar aims. The more deeply the Anglo-
Americans could be involved in the struggle with Germany, the sooner
Germany could be defeated, and such a defeat, especially if it arose from
a cross-Channel attack, would deliver all of eastern Europe into the
power of the Red armies, which would find no rivals in that area.

Churchill and other British leaders could not forget the terrible casualties Britain had suffered in the trench warfare of 1916. They felt that
these casualties had injured Britain permanently by wiping out a whole
generation of Britain's young people, especially among the better-educated
class, and they were determined not to repeat this error in 1944. These
leaders wanted a Balkan or Aegean offensive which, they believed, would,
with fewer casualties, leave the English-speaking Powers dominant in the
Mediterranean and in the Near East, would make it possible to balance
Soviet power in eastern Europe, and would cut the Soviet Union off from
the Balkans and some of central Europe. The possibility of Britain obtaining American consent to such an Aegean offensive was so remote that little effort was made to get it by direct persuasion. On the contrary,
efforts to move toward it, step by step, were persistent. These efforts
sought to postpone, or to reduce the emphasis on, the cross-Channel invasion, since this would, inevitably, have compelled the end of Britain's
Mediterranean projects. But here, again, American insistence on the cross-
Channel invasion was so emphatic that the British could not challenge
this directly, just as they could not advocate an Aegean invasion directly.
Instead, while accepting the cross-Channel invasion explicitly, the British
offered, one after another, alternative projects which would postpone or
distract from the cross-Channel invasion.

The North African invasion was the first of these distractions, followed
by the Sicilian campaign, and then by the Italian invasion. These were
accepted by the Americans, since they felt it was urgent to do something
to meet the Soviet demands for Anglo-American action against Hitler.
Some kind of Balkan intervention was the next British proposal, but
there was no hope of obtaining American consent to such a project. It
was formally rejected by the Combined Chiefs of Staff on September
9, 1943. Churchill did not give up, but continued to push these peripheral
schemes as best he could. He ordered General Wilson, British commander
in the Near East, "to be bold, even rash" in attacking the Germans in the
Aegean and he also tried to persuade Eisenhower to shift forces from Italy

to the Aegean or to persuade Turkey to declare war on Germany. The only success Churchill had in these efforts was to persuade the Americans to engage in an amphibious attack on Italy at Anzio after the Americans had canceled plans for such an attack and had decided to choke off the Italian offensive in order to concentrate on the cross-Channel attack.

In the long run Churchill had to accept the American strategic plans because America would provide most of the supplies and even a majority of the men for any direct attack on Europe. The American ability to compel British acquiescence in strategic decisions was a very real element in the conduct of the war. It arose from the great British need for American manpower and supplies, and it functioned through the mechanism of the Combined Chiefs of Staff.

When Churchill came to the Arcadia Conference in Washington at the end of 1941, his chief aim was to retain the established priority of "Germany first." He obtained this very easily on its own intrinsic merits, but at the same time he had to accept something he did not want—a Combined Chiefs of Staff organization to control strategy on a worldwide basis. This new committee developed more power than Churchill, or anyone else, expected, because it had control of the supply of weapons. This power was decisive. Since no military operation could be conducted without weapons or supplies, control over these gave the Combined Chiefs of Staff control over all operations and, thus, over the strategic conduct of the war and over all local commanders. The Combined Chiefs of Staff operated through weekly meetings within the framework of the general policy decisions made by Roosevelt and Churchill at their periodic conferences. In this way Britain's dependence on the United States for its implements of war gave the United States control of British strategic decisions and military operations, even in those areas (such as southeast Asia or the Near East) where a British commander was nominally in charge. In the same way, the United States had indirect control over much of Britain's postwar planning.

In spite of the fact that the Anglo-Americans had agreed in ambiguous terms with Molotov's insistence on the need for a direct attack on Hitler in Europe in 1942, it was perfectly clear that no such assault could be made that early in the war, so the attack on North Africa was offered as a substitute. In the course of the North African fighting it became clear that the cross-Channel attack could not be mounted before the spring of 1944. Accordingly, when the Germans in North Africa surrendered in May 1943, it was necessary to open a new front against Hitler quickly, since it would have been very dangerous to leave Hitler free to throw most of his forces against Russia for a full year. Plans for attacks on Sardinia or Sicily had been prepared, and on January 23, 1943, orders were issued to invade the latter island during the "favorable July moon." This was not regarded by the Russians as a major effort, and their resentment rose to the boiling point. As Secretary of State Hull put it in his memoirs, the atmosphere in Anglo-Russian relations became reminiscent of what it had been exactly four years earlier, just before the Nazi-Soviet Treaty of August 1939. It was at this time, apparently, that two fateful, and mutually incompatible, decisions were made on the highest levels of authority in Washington and Moscow.

The decision made in Washington is one we have already mentioned— the decision to try to win Soviet cooperation in the postwar world by doing everything possible to win her trust and cooperation in the wartime period. This decision was probably based on the belief that it was not possible to control Russia's postwar behavior by any policy of force against her during the war itself, since such an effort would benefit Hitler without winning any enforceable agreements from Stalin.

At this time, it would appear, Stalin made his decision to seek Russian security in the postwar world, not through any scheme for friendly cooperation in some idealistic international organization, as Roosevelt hoped, but by setting up, on the Soviet Union's western frontiers, a buffer area of satellite states under governments friendly to Moscow. Such governments, probably in Communist control, would replace the *Cordon sanitaire* which the Western Powers had created to isolate Russia following the First World War, with what might be called a *Cordon "insanitaire"* which could serve to isolate the Soviet Union from the outside world following World War II. Washington was informed of this possibility by the American ambassador in Moscow on April 28, 1943, but paid little attention to the warning, probably because of the near-impossibility of finding any alternative policy toward the Soviet Union.

In spite of Soviet scorn, the military operations in Africa and the Mediterranean were major efforts for the inexperienced forces of unmilitarized nations, although they obviously could not compare to the Nazi-Soviet deathlock involving hundreds of divisions on the plains and in the forests of eastern Europe. The victory in North Africa was completed in May 1943. Two months later came the invasion of Sicily. The attack on this strategic island was the greatest landing-assault of the war, eight divisions coming ashore simultaneously side by side. The island is almost a right-angle triangle, with its right angle in the extreme northeast, separated from the Italian mainland by the Strait of Messina, only three miles wide. The landings were made on the opposite side of the island, on the hypotenuse of the triangle, where the coast faces southwestward toward Tunisia. The British Eighth Army, under General Montgomery, with 250,000 men in 818 ships and escort vessels, landed on the southeastern point of the Sicilian triangle, while the American Seventh Army (General George Patton), with 228,000 men and 580 vessels, landed on the British left on either side of Gela.

The defensive forces of four Italian divisions and two German panzer divisions were widely scattered on the island, and the Allied landings were skillfully executed against light resistance (July 10, 1943). Once ashore, however, the campaign was ineptly carried on because occupation of territory was given precedence over destruction of enemy forces: Patton drove northwestward to seize Palermo (July 22nd), and then followed the enemy forces eastward to Messina along the northern coast; Montgomery, moving slowly northward parallel to the eastern coast, made a detour to the west of Mount Etna.

No efforts were made to close the Straits of Messina; as a result, the Germans were able to send almost two divisions as reinforcements from Italy and, later, when the island had to be abandoned, they were equally free to evacuate it, carrying almost 40,000 troops with 9,650 vehicles and 17,000 tons of stores over the Straits of Messina to Italy in seven days without loss of a man. At the same time, in a separate operation, 62,000 Italian troops also escaped to the mainland. By August 17th Sicily had been conquered, but the evacuated enemy forces were reorganizing to defend Italy itself.

The Italians had no taste for the defense of Italy. They had been dragged into the war by Mussolini's action and against their own desires, in June 1940, and by 1943 they were heartily sick of the whole thing. This discontent was fully developed long before the attack on Sicily in June. In February the Duce had dismissed Count Ciano, his son-in-law, and Count Dino Grandi from their posts as ministers of foreign affairs and of justice because of their defeatism and opposition. But these qualities continued to spread, even in the innermost circles of the government. The invasion of Sicily gave the final spurt to this development. On July 24th the Fascist Grand Council passed a motion calling for the restoration of the constitutional functions of all agencies of the government and the restoration to the king of full command of the armed forces. This motion, carried 18–8, was essentially a vote of no-confidence in Mussolini. The following morning the king demanded the Duce's resignation and, as he was leaving the palace, had him arrested.

The fall of Mussolini, on July 25, 1943, after being in power for over twenty years, did nothing to improve Italy's position. The king, who was opposed to the establishment of a parliamentary regime or a responsible government, put Marshal Pietro Badoglio, the conqueror of Ethiopia, in as head of the government but would not allow him to establish a Cabinet of non-Fascist leaders. The Fascist Party was abolished and the Fascist Militia was incorporated into the regular army, but it was impossible to get rid of Fascist sympathizers from either the administrative system or from the armed services. On the whole, the fall of Mussolini was welcomed by the Italian people, not because of any political ideas but simply because they believed that it would lead to the end of the war and the end of food rationing. It achieved neither of these, because the powers of contending forces were too evenly balanced in Italy to allow any decisive outcome to be reached.

The history of Italy in 1943 is a history of lost opportunities, perhaps necessarily lost, but, nevertheless, a disappointment to everyone concerned. If events had turned out favorably, Italy might have got out of the war in the summer of that year and the Germans might have been ejected from the peninsula shortly afterward. Instead, Italy was torn to pieces; its peoples and the invading Allied troops suffered great hardships; and the country got out of the war so slowly that Germans were still fighting on Italian soil at the final surrender in 1945.

These general misfortunes of Italy were the result of a number of forces working together. One was the military weakness of Italy in respect to Germany; this made it impossible for Italy to end the war, or even to surrender to the Allies, because any effort to do so would lead to an immediate German seizure of the whole country and of its leaders, the exploitation and devastation of the one and the massacre of the others. Italy was far too weak to hold the Germans back long enough to permit an Allied occupation of Italy. A second factor was the weakness of the Allies because of the diversion of their power to Britain in preparation for Overlord: this meant that the Allies lacked the strength to move quickly into Italy to protect it from complete German occupation, even if Italy could surrender secretly to the Allies and cooperate with their entrance. A third factor was the complete mistrust of the Italians both by the Germans and by the Allies. This mistrust, for which the political conduct of the Italians, both foreign and domestic, over at least two generations, was responsible, provided the key to the whole situation. The only way in which the fighting in Italy could have been ended quickly would have been for Italy to surrender secretly to the Allies and cooperate with them in an immediate large-scale invasion of northern Italy, but the Allies were too distrustful of the Italians to cooperate with them in a project such as this or even to accept a secret surrender. And, finally, a fourth obstacle was the wooden and inflexible Allied insistence on unconditional surrender which, meaningless as it might have been, nevertheless made it impossible for the Badoglio government either to cooperate with the Allies as co-belligerents against the Germans (as it wished to do) or to keep the surrender secret from the Germans long enough to forestall their violent reactions. Not only did unconditional surrender exclude both co-belligerency and secrecy; it also left the Italians helpless to resist the Germans. Above all, these four factors made it impossible to prevent a German seizure of Rome, which was, in some ways, the center of the whole problem.

The Germans, who had eight divisions in Italy, doubled this number as soon as they heard of the fall of Mussolini. They refused a request from the Badoglio government to allow any of the fifty-three Italian divisions in the Balkans and Russia to return home, thus holding them as hostages. When the Badoglio government made contact with the Allies through Madrid on August 16th and offered to join them in fighting Germany, all it could obtain was a demand for unconditional surrender. After days of discussion, an armistice accepting the Allied terms was signed on September 3rd, with the understanding that it would be kept secret until the Allies had troops ready to land in force on the mainland. Three days later, the Italian government discovered that the Allied landing operation, already in progress, was only a small force and was headed for Salerno, south of Naples, where it would be no help to the Italians in resisting any German efforts to take over most of Italy. They insisted that the publication of the armistice and a tentative Allied paratrooper "drop" in Rome must be put off until sufficient Allied forces were within striking distance of Rome to protect the city from the German troops near it. Eisenhower refused, and published the Italian surrender on September 8th, one day before the American Seventh Army landed at Salerno.

The Germans reacted to the news of the Italian "betrayal" and of the Allied invasion of southern Italy with characteristic speed. While the available forces in central Italy converged on the Salerno beachhead, an armored division fought its way into Rome, Italian troops were disarmed or intimidated everywhere, and the Badoglio government, with King Victor Emmanuel, had to flee to the British-controlled area around Brindisi. Much of the Italian fleet escaped to Allied control in the Mediterranean, but numerous vessels were sunk by the Germans or were scuttled to escape falling into their hands. In most of Italy, there was political paralysis and confusion; at some places Italians fought one another, or simply murdered one another, while opinion ranged the whole gamut from complete indifference on one extreme to violent fanaticism on the other.

In order to have some legal excuse for controlling Italy, the Germans sent parachutists to rescue Mussolini from his "prison" in a summer hotel in the mountains of the Gran Sasso, escaping with him by air to northern Italy where he was presented with a German-picked government of "neo-Fascists" under the name Italian Social Republic (September 13-15, 1943). Broken and weary, the ex-Duce of Fascism became a pliant tool of German ruthlessness and of the corrupt and criminal neo-Fascists who surrounded him. In this group the most influential were the family of Mussolini's mistress, Clara Petacci, which Count Ciano called "that circle of prostitutes and white slavers which for some years have plagued Italian political life."

In Allied hands, the king and Badoglio were forced, on September 29, 1943, to sign another, much longer, armistice; by its provisions "the Italian Government were bound hand and foot, and made completely subject to the will of the Allied Governments as expressed through the Allied Commander-in-Chief." In conformity to this will, on October 13th the king's government declared war against Germany.

As the Allied forces slowly recovered Italian territory from the tenacious grasp of the Germans, the royal government remained subservient to its conquerors. Civilian affairs immediately behind the advancing battle lines were completely in military hands under an organization known as Allied Military Government of Occupied Territory, or AMGOT; farther back, civilian affairs were under an Allied Control Commission. The creation of these organizations, on a purely Anglo-American basis, to rule the first Axis territory to be "liberated" became a very important precedent for Soviet behavior when their armies began to occupy enemy territory in eastern Europe: The Russians were able to argue that they could exclude the Anglo-Americans from active participation in military government in the east since they had earlier been excluded from such participation in the west.

While these political events were taking place, the military advance was moving like a snail. The Allied invasion of Italy, at American insistence, was given very limited resources for a very large task. This limitation of resources in Italy sought to prevent the British from using the Italian campaign as an excuse for delaying or postponing the cross-Channel attack on Europe scheduled for the spring of 1944. It was only under such limitations of resources, explicitly stated, that the Americans had accepted the British suggestion for any invasion of mainland Italy at all. In May 1943, at a plenary meeting in Washington, the Combined Chiefs of Staff had set May 1944 as target date for a cross-Channel invasion of Europe with 29 divisions, had ordered a full-scale aerial offensive on Germany with 2,700 heavy and 800 medium bombers, had given the American Joint Chiefs of Staff complete control over the Pacific war against Japan, and had asked General Eisenhower to draw up plans for an invasion of Italy using no forces beyond what he had on hand. This last limitation was repeated on July 26th when the general was ordered to carry out his plans.

The invasion of Italy was a two-pronged effort. On September 3rd two British divisions under General Montgomery crossed the Straits of Messina and began to move northward against little opposition. Six days later a British airborne division from Bizerte was landed at Taranto and began to move up the Adriatic coast. On the same day, September 9th, the Fifth Army of two American and two British divisions under Lieutenant General Mark W. Clark landed at Salerno. The landing site was in the next bay south of the famous Bay of Naples, and separated from it by the rugged Sorrento Peninsula. There was no preliminary bombardment by naval guns, in order to retain tactical surprise, and the American units came over the heavily mined and barbwired beaches right into the face of the German 16th Panzer Division. Within three days, six German divisions, four of them motorized, were around the Salerno beachhead, with six hundred tanks. In fierce fighting, the area was slowly expanded, although at one point the German counterattacks almost broke through to the beach. Naval gunfire against the German tanks was the decisive factor in a seesaw struggle.

On September 13th the American 82nd Airborne Division was dropped behind the beachhead. About the same time, Rommel, in command in northern Italy, refused to release reinforcements to Kessel-ring in the south. On September 16th the latter commander authorized a withdrawal from the area in order to get beyond the range of naval gunfire. On the same day, Montgomery's Eighth Army made contact with Clark's Fifth Army, and an Allied line was stretched across Italy to the Adriatic. This line moved slowly northward, capturing Naples on the first day of October 1943. The city was a shambles, filled with wreckage and heavily booby-trapped; the water supply had been delib-erately polluted, and all food stores and government records had been destroyed; the harbor area, completely in flames, was filled with sunken ships, locomotives, and other large objects to make it unusable. This was the kind of situation where American energy, humanitarianism, and ingenuity excelled; sanitation and order were restored at once, food was provided for the hungry Italians, and the harbor was cleaned up so successfully that it was handling tonnage beyond its prewar rated ca-pacity within three months.

By October 7th the Allied advance had been stopped on the Volturno River line twenty miles north of Naples. Two months later, when Gen-eral Eisenhower was transferred to take over the Supreme Command for the approaching invasion of western Europe, the Allied lines had moved northward no farther than the German Gustav Line. This line, eighty miles south of Rome and following, roughly, the Rapido River in the west and the lower Garigliano in the east, took every advantage of the rugged terrain, and allowed the enemy to inflict heavy casualties on the attackers, especially by artillery fire from the greatly feared German 88-mm. guns. To outflank this position, an amphibious landing was ordered beyond the German rear at Anzio, just north of the Pontine Marshes, thirty miles south of Rome. Originally the landing was to have been made in one operation, leaving the Allied forces on a beach with supplies for eight days and no provision for any reinforcements or re-plenishment from the sea. This was based on the expectation that the main Allied forces would come up from the south in time to relieve the new beachhead. When it became clear that the Allied forces could not advance up the peninsula, the plan was canceled on December 22nd. Three days later, at a hurriedly summoned conference at Tunis, Church-ill was able to have the plan reinstated, offering a British division to go with the single American division originally planned.

On January 20, 1944, General Clark tried to cross the flooded Rapido River at the foot of the great hill on which stood the ancient Benedictine Monastery of Monte Cassino. His aim was to advance northward toward Anzio. After two days of bloody fighting, the crossing had to be abandoned; that same day (January 22nd) the two Allied divisions landed at Anzio, hoping to cut the German communications going southward toward Monte Cassino. The landing was easy, but within a week Marshal Kesselring was able to shift sufficient forces from the subsiding Rapido front to seal off the Anzio beachhead. Although the Allies committed four more divisions to the Anzio operation, giving six in all, they could not break out of the German vise. The result was a stalemate in which the Germans could hold both the Rapido line and the Anzio line by shifting forces rapidly from one to the other as seemed necessary.

As is usual in a stalemate, there was much of criticism of these operations, especially from the Allied side. It was suggested that the German success in holding the Rapido was due to the accuracy of their artillery fire and that this was being spotted from the ancient monastery (founded by St. Benedict in A.D. 529) on the top of Monte Cassino. It was further suggested that General Clark should have obliterated the monastery with aerial bombardment but had failed to do so because he was a Catholic. After February 15, 1944, General Clark did destroy the site completely by Air Force bombs without helping the situation a bit. We now know that the Germans had not been using the monastery; but, once it was destroyed by us, they dug into the rubble to make a stronger defense.

The stalemate on the Gustav Line was broken in the latter half of May 1944. By that time French, Polish, and Italian units were fighting on the Allied side, giving twenty-seven Allied divisions against twenty German. On May 16th a French corps crossed the Garigliano River, and three days later, after terrible casualties, a Polish division captured Monte Cassino. Kesselring sullenly withdrew northward, followed by the Allied forces. The latter were greeted with hysterical enthusiasm by the liberated Italians. On May 25th contact was made with the Anzio forces, and, on June 4, 1944, the American 88th Division, an all-selective-service unit, entered Rome.

As the liberating forces came in and the Germans hurriedly withdrew, Rome was little short of a madhouse. Hundreds of prisoners held by the Germans and neo-Fascist secret police were murdered in their cells, and helpless civilians were murdered as hostages or in reprisal by the retreating German forces. Guerrilla bands behind the German lines performed good services to the Allied cause, harassing communications, assisting Allied intelligence, and helping escaping prisoners. Many of these guerrillas were fighting for social revolution as well as for the liberation of Italy, and there was a good deal of rivalry and even of violent conflict among them. The dominant influence was that of the

Communists, who were more highly disciplined and more closely controlled than the non-Communist units.

The fall of Mussolini gave a considerable impetus to postwar planning within the Allied camps. There had been a certain amount of this during the dark days from 1939 to 1943, but on the whole the Allied leaders were reluctant to commit themselves to any projects which might restrict their freedom of action in conducting the war or in manipulating its diplomatic and propagandist background. The collapse of one of the enemy states, however, made it necessary to devote some serious attention to postwar plans. At the same time, experiences in Italy showed that the problems of the postwar era would be much broader than merely political or diplomatic, and would include social, economic, and ideological problems on a scale never experienced previously. It was clear that the poverty, confusion, and human suffering found by our advancing armies in Italy would be increased tenfold when the much more bitter resistance of Germany had been overcome.

In order to avoid any repetition of the widespread Allied "deals" with Darlan and other "Vichyites," the occupied areas of Italy were subjected to a completely military Allied government, although, to obtain legal continuity and legal justification for this government, the various agreements were signed by Badoglio. Even this small amount of contact with ex-Fascist leaders aroused adverse comment in certain circles in the United States, although at the same time and, usually, in the same circles, there was objection to the use of a purely military administration as an alternative. The only other possibility would have been to turn the newly liberated areas over to the local anti-Fascist native groups. This last solution was out of the question, for these groups were generally so determined on social and economic revolution that they would have created conflicts and disturbances which would have jeopardized the position of our armies of occupation and would certainly have increased the social and economic problems which most Americans were eager to reduce. These social and economic problems were mostly of a very practical nature and were concerned with starvation, disease, public order, and the care of displaced persons.

All these problems were drastically increased by the ruthless destructiveness of the German forces as they withdrew toward Germany itself. Food supplies were taken away or were destroyed; millions were left homeless, many of them far from their homes and in pitiful conditions of semistarvation and disease. These conditions, which became steadily worse as the war drew to its close, made a great appeal to the humanitarian feelings of Americans, and presented problems with which American generosity and organizational efficiency were well able to deal. On the other hand, Americans had weak political interests and narrow ideological training and were eager to avoid problems such as forms of government, patterns of property distribution, or nationalistic disputes. It is, then, not surprising that American postwar planning and the behavior of American administrators neglected the latter kinds of problems to devote their energies to the more practical tasks of material survival. On the political, legal, or ideological problems the American "liberators" had little to offer beyond rather vague and idealistic praise of democracy, private ownership, and freedom.

While the military efforts of the Anglo-Americans were, in full public view, passing from victory to victory in the early months of 1943, a very ominous situation had arisen behind the scenes in respect to their relations with the Soviet Union. We have already mentioned the evidence that quite incompatible decisions about the postwar world had been made in Washington and Moscow at this time. The decision in Washington seems to have been that every effort would be made, through wartime concessions to the Soviet Union, to obtain Russian cooperation in a postwar international organization and that all territorial problems should be left to the postwar period. The decision in Moscow seems to have been that the Anglo-American Powers could not be trusted and that the Soviet Union must seek to ensure its postwar security by creation of a series of satellite and buffer states on its western frontier. The incompatibility of these points of view gave rise to the Polish crisis of May 1943.

After the Nazi-Soviet division of Poland in September 1939, a Polish government-in-exile was established in France and later in London, with General Wladyslaw Sikorski as prime minister. This government, although recognized as the successor to the defeated Polish government by most of the world, was not recognized by the Axis Powers or by the Soviet Union. These pretended that Poland had ceased to exist. Russia, which had received half of Poland, with 13.2 million of Poland's 35 million inhabitants, incorporated these areas into the Soviet Union, imposing Soviet citizenship on the inhabitants, and forced over a million of them to go to other parts of Russia to work in mines, in factories, or on farms. Most educated or professional persons among the Poles were arrested and put into concentration camps with the captured officers of the Polish armies. In the meantime the portions of Poland taken by Germany had been divided into two parts, of which the western (with 10.5 million inhabitants) was incorporated into Germany, and the rest (with 11.5 million inhabitants, and including Warsaw) was organized as the government-general of Poland under German administration. The Nazis sought to force all ethnic Poles into the government-general; to exterminate, either directly or through the exhaustion and malnutrition of slave labor, all the educated elements among the Polish people; and to murder without compunction the country's large Jewish population.

The German attack on the Soviet Union on June 22, 1941 led to a brief reversal of the Kremlin's attitude toward Poland. In an apparent effort to obtain Polish support in the struggle with Germany, the Soviet Union reestablished diplomatic relations with the Polish government-in-exile in London, and signed an agreement on July 30, 1941 by which the Soviet-German partition treaties of 1939 were canceled, a general amnesty was granted Polish citizens imprisoned in the Soviet Union, and General Wladyslaw Anders was allowed to organize a new Polish army from the Poles in the Soviet Union. Efforts to create this army were hampered by the fact that about 10,000 Polish officers along with about 5,000 Polish intellectuals and professional persons, all of whom had been held in three camps in western Russia, could not be found. In addition at least 100,000 Polish prisoners of war, out of the 230,000 captured by Soviet forces in September 1939, had been exterminated in Soviet labor camps from starvation and overwork, and over a million Polish civilians were being similarly treated.

Constant obstacles were offered by the Soviet authorities to the efforts of General Anders to reconstruct a Polish army in the east. When rations were cut to 26,000 to feed a force of 70,000 soldiers and many thousands of Polish civilian refugees, Anders obtained permission to evacuate his force to Iran (March 1942). It was this group which fought so well the following years in Italy and in western Europe.

As soon as Anders's forces left Russia, the Soviet leaders began to organize a group of Polish and Russian Communists into a so-called Union of Polish Patriots which sponsored a Polish-language radio station and a new Communist-controlled Polish army in Russia. In January 1943, Moscow informed the Sikorski government in London that all Poles originating from the provinces occupied by Soviet forces in September 1939 would be regarded as Soviet subjects.

While Soviet-Polish relations were deteriorating, the German radio suddenly announced, on April 13, 1943, that German forces in occupied Russia had discovered, at Katyn near Smolensk, Russia, mass graves containing the bodies of 5,000 Polish officers who had been murdered by the Soviet authorities in the spring of 1940. Moscow called this a Nazi propaganda trick and declared that the Polish officers had been murdered and buried by the Nazis themselves when they captured the officers and the locality by overrunning this Soviet territory and its concentration camps in August 1941. When the Polish government in London requested an investigation of this crime at the site by the International Red Cross, the Soviet government broke off diplomatic relations with the Sikorski government on the grounds that it had fallen victim to Nazi propaganda because of anti-Soviet feeling.

The Katyn massacres were a subject of controversy for years. Today there is no doubt that the great mass of evidence indicates that these victims, numbering 4,243, met their deaths by being shot through the back of the neck in the early spring of 1940 and not August 1941 (or later), when the area was in German possession. This evidence, which clearly indicates Soviet guilt, includes the following points: (1) the victims were wearing the uniforms and boots issued to them at the outbreak of war in 1939, and these were in good condition, showing a minimum of wear as might be the case in April 1940, but could not have been true in August 1941; (2) all letters, journals, or documents on the bodies had dates previous to May 1940, and in no case later; (3) the victims were arranged in the graves in groups in the same order in which they had been removed from the Soviet concentration camp at Kozielski in March and April 1940; (4) the victims wrote letters to their families at home up to April 1940, but not later; (5) letters to victims from their families were delivered by Soviet authorities up to April 1940, but were returned to the senders as undeliverable after that date; (6) in private conversations various Soviet authorities at various times admitted the murders. There is much other evidence showing Soviet guilt in this affair, but it must not be forgotten that both Soviet Russia and Nazi Germany were determined to exterminate all Polish leaders and the Polish nation by reducing the leaderless Poles to the status of slave laborers and that Germany also would have killed these Polish officers if they had captured them, since the Germans did exterminate 4,000,000 Poles in this way during the war. Although the number of bodies at Katyn was less than 5,000, the number of officers murdered was almost twice this figure, the rest, apparently, having been drowned in the White Sea.

The crisis in Soviet-Polish relations in the spring of 1943 marks a turning point in the relations of the three Great Powers fighting Germany, although every effort was made to conceal this fact at that time. From March 1943 onward, the Soviet authorities did all they could to build up the Union of Polish Patriots as the center of aspirations of the Poles still suffering in their own country, while, at the same time, Washington began to pay the Polish government-in-exile an annual subsidy of $12.5 million to finance its underground organizations in Poland and its diplomatic relations with Latin-American countries. Within Poland itself, the London government soon had a secret army and a secret underground government, including a parliament, schools, and a system of courts. This government met in secret, made decisions, and executed sentences on disloyal Poles, especially on collaborators with the Nazis.

Nazi plans aimed at the eventual extermination of the Poles and the Polish nation. In the winter of 1939–1940, all Poles were deported, street by street with only a few hours' notice, from the western areas annexed to Germany into the government-general. In the latter areas, under the rule of Hans Frank and Arthur Seyss-Inquart, all wealth which could be used by Germany was confiscated and removed; all Polish institutions of higher learning or culture were abolished, so that only elementary schools (and these conducted in the German language) were allowed; all outstanding persons were murdered; millions were deported westward to work as slave laborers in German factories; the food consumption of those who remained was reduced by German seizure of food supplies to a quarter of the daily need (to 600 calories); and various measures, such as separation of the sexes, were taken to prevent the reproduction of Poles. Under these circumstances it is remarkable that Polish spirit could not be broken, that hundreds of thousands of Poles continued to resist in guerrilla bands, in the underground "Home Army" under Generals "Grot" (Stefan Rowecki) and "Bor" (Thaddeus Komorowski), and that sabotage, propaganda, spying, and communication with the Polish government in London continued to flourish.

At the time these events were taking place, the people of the English-speaking world were almost totally ignorant of the diplomatic controversies behind the scenes and almost equally ignorant of the conditions of life in German-occupied Europe. On the other hand, they were fully aware of the victory in North Africa, of the conquest of Sicily, and of the invasion of Italy. The strategic decisions involved in these campaigns and, above all, the decision of September 1943 to reject Churchill's plans for a Balkan campaign in order to concentrate on the cross-Channel offensive for 1944, were of vital importance in setting the form that postwar Europe would take. If the strategic decision of 1943 had been made differently, to postpone the cross-Channel attack and, instead, to concentrate on an assault from the Aegean across Bulgaria and Romania toward Poland and Slovakia, the postwar situation would have been quite different. This we can say with assurance even though we cannot say with any certainty what the difference would have been.

In the course of 1943, while Roosevelt, Churchill, and Stalin were still devoting their chief attention to the conduct of the war, their foreign ministers, Cordell Hull, Anthony Eden, and Vyachislav Molotov, were giving increasing attention to planning for postwar problems. The chief of these problems which were discussed were: (1) the economic demobilization of the victor Powers, (2) the relief and rehabilitation of the defeated countries and of the liberated areas, (3) problems involving refugees and displaced persons, (4) problems of finance and of international monetary exchanges, (5) the punishment of "war criminals" in the defeated states, (6) the forms of government of these states and of the liberated states, (7) territorial questions such as the boundaries of Germany, of Hungary, or of Poland, (8) the disposition of the colonial possessions, or, as they were called, the "dependent areas," of both victors and vanquished, (9) the problem of the postwar political relationships of the victorious states and of the world as a whole.

It is evident that many of these problems were of an explosive nature and could lead to disputes among the Allies and possibly even to a weakening of their joint anti-German efforts. As a consequence, the foreign ministers' discussions of many of these problems were tentative and hesitant and were frequently interrupted to confer with the three heads of governments. Even on this higher level, agreement could not be reached in some cases, and these problems were generally put aside lest efforts to reach an agreement alienate the Allies to the detriment of their war efforts against Germany. This was most emphatically true of questions involving the possible postwar situation in eastern Europe where the frontiers of Germany, of Poland, and of the Soviet Union or the status of Poland and of the Baltic states were far too controversial to be raised except in a most tentative way.

It has frequently been argued in recent years that failure to reach any agreement on the territorial and governmental settlement of eastern Europe while the war was still in progress meant that these questions would tend to be settled by the military situation in existence at the end of the war with little consideration for questions of legality, humanity, freedom, nationalism, the rights of small states, or other factors which were mentioned so frequently in the Allied wartime propaganda. Specifically, this meant that the Soviet armies would undoubtedly dominate eastern Europe once Germany was defeated and that these armies could make a settlement based on force unless the Soviet Union had been compelled, before the complete defeat of Germany, to make agreements with its fellow Allies for some more desirable settlement in eastern Europe. These arguments usually assume that the Soviet Union was reluctant to make an early agreement on this subject and that it could have been forced to do so because of its need for American supplies during the fighting. This assumption implies that America should have threatened to reduce or to cut off Lend-Lease supplies going to the Soviet Union unless we could obtain Soviet agreement to the kind of eastern European settlement we wanted. These arguments are based on hindsight and not on any realistic understanding of the historical facts as they developed.

It is now clear, from the published documents, that the Soviet Union was eager to obtain some early agreement on the eastern European postwar settlement and that both the United States and Britain were reluctant to make such an agreement, apparently because of the fear that we could do so only at the price of extensive concessions to Russia at the expense of the smaller eastern European states. We were unwilling to use our control of Lend-Lease supplies to force concessions from Russia because any reduction of such supplies, by weakening the Soviet Union's resistance to Germany, would increase Germany's ability to fight the Anglo-Americans and would lengthen the war. Moreover, Soviet ideas on the Baltic states and the eastern frontiers of Poland were so rigidly uncompromising that no concessions could have been obtained on these points except, perhaps, by reducing Lend-Lease shipments to a degree which the Anglo-Americans, in their own interests, were unwilling to do. It was feared that any drastic Anglo-American pressure on Russia in this form would lead to violent protests from the electorate in Britain and in the United States, since the citizens of the two democratic Powers were much more concerned with getting on with the war than they were with the postwar situation of the Poles or of the Baltic states. Moreover, the Anglo-American leaders were fearful that, if Russia's ability to fight Germany was reduced by any curtailing of supplies, the Soviet leaders might make a separate peace with Hitler, allowing the Nazis to turn the full brunt of their fury westward. Rumors of possible Soviet-Nazi discussions looking toward a separate peace were circulating in London and Washington at various times, particularly in the latter part of 1943, and the Anglo-American leaders were too clearly aware of the sudden Nazi-Soviet agreement of August 1939 to push the Russians so hard that they might make another, more fateful, agreement of a similar character.

The blunt truth which was faced by the Anglo-American leaders throughout the war was that full-scale Soviet resistance to Germany seemed essential if the Nazis were ever to be beaten and that what seemed, at the time, to be lesser or more remote considerations had to yield to that fundamental fact. Winston Churchill, in June 1941, had welcomed the Russians as allies against Hitler with the statement that he would be ready to ally with the devil in hell if the devil was ready to fight Hitler. Naturally, this point of view became less extreme as the defeat of Hitler became less remote, but the Germans fought so well, up to the very end of the war, that it never became possible to force any Soviet concessions in regard to the postwar political settlement in eastern Europe. Instead, the tactic was adopted, wholeheartedly by President Roosevelt, more reluctantly by Prime Minister Churchill, of trying to win the Soviet leaders, especially Stalin, to a less suspicious and more conciliatory mood by full-scale cooperation in the war and by friendly concessions to Soviet sensibilities on wider issues. This alternative policy was by no means an easy one, for Soviet suspicions were so close to the surface and Soviet sensibilities were so touchy that cooperation with these people proved to be a very delicate and unpleasant business. It was, however, a business at which Roosevelt was personally adept, and it worked, adequately enough, until the war with Germany and Roosevelt's life drew to their close together in the spring of 1945.

The various postwar problems we have mentioned were discussed at a series of high-level conferences during the war years. At a conference in Washington in March 1943, Eden and Roosevelt agreed that

Germany should be broken up into three or four states after its defeat, but did not see eye to eye on many other matters. Roosevelt felt that only the four Great Powers would need to be armed in the postwar world and could keep the peace for all other states if they could agree among themselves. Other states, relieved of the burden of armaments, could devote all their resources to economic reconstruction. The four Great Powers would be helped in the task of keeping the peace for all by their joint possession of various strategic points throughout the world, like Dakar or Formosa, and could work together to instruct the public opinion of the world by a joint sponsorship of informational centers scattered about the globe. In such a system, in which lesser states did not have to defend themselves, there could be no objection, in Roosevelt's thinking, to separating peoples, like the Serbs and Croats, who could not agree, or in providing independence for dependent areas, such as Hong Kong. Most of this made little sense to Eden, who was not prepared to give up Hong Kong or other portions of the British colonial possessions or to see the Soviet Union on the borders of a Europe in which all other states were disarmed. The chief areas of agreement at this conference were that Germany should be dismembered after the war and that Poland could obtain East Prussia.

Two months later, at the so-called "Trident" Conference in Washington, Churchill and Roosevelt went over the same matters (May 1943). The cross-Channel attack, *Overlord*, was set for May 1944, and an intensified aerial bombardment of Germany ordered as a preliminary. No important decisions could be made on postwar problems, although the atmosphere was brightened by a Soviet announcement of the abolition of the Communist International and an Anglo-American announcement renouncing extraterritorial rights in China.

The next conference, held in May and June 1943 at Hot Springs, Virginia, was of a technical nature, and discussed postwar food and agricultural problems. From this conference there emerged a United Nations Food and Agriculture Organization (FAO), an advisory body to collect and disseminate agricultural information, as had been done previously by the League of Nations affiliate, the International Institute of Agriculture in Rome.

Closely related to FAO, but of a temporary rather than permanent character and possessing administrative rather than simply advisory powers, was the United Nations Relief and Rehabilitation Administration (UNRRA). At the first meeting of this international organization, at Atlantic City, New Jersey, in November 1943, forty-four nations agreed to contribute 1 percent of their national incomes to purchase relief supplies for war-devastated peoples. Herbert Lehman, former governor of New York, was elected director-general of the new organization.

In the meantime, in August 1943 at Quebec, in what is sometimes called the "Quadrant" Conference, Churchill and Roosevelt found some time for discussion of postwar policy, although their chief concern was with Italy, with *Overlord*, and with a new supplement to *Overlord* consisting of an invasion of southern France from the Mediterranean Sea and up the Rhone Valley. This new invasion, known as *Anvil*, was to be launched in the summer of 1944.

At Quebec, Churchill accepted Roosevelt's postwar projects with considerable reluctance. The prime minister felt strongly that the United States and the Soviet Union would be the two giants of the postwar world and that Britain's best interests lay in building some kind of British sphere of influence in Europe and in Asia as a balance against these two giants. He wished to see two regional associations for these two areas, with Britain in both, the two forming part, if necessary, of some larger, worldwide association. It soon became clear that the United States would accept no regional associations of this character, and insisted on a worldwide association of individual countries. The American insistence on no spheres of influence and no settlement of frontiers while the war was on, like the American insistence that China was a Great Power, was regarded by the other two Allies as childishly unrealistic and even hypocritical, especially as both Britain and Russia were convinced that the United States was aiming to create American spheres of interest, if not regional associations, in its areas of chief concern, Latin America and the Far East.

Churchill had to accept Roosevelt's projects for a postwar international organization for fear that resistance to these might lead to a revival of American isolationism following the Second World War, as had happened after 1919. This, above all, Churchill had to prevent, since it would leave Britain facing the Soviet Union with no Great Power companionship. Accordingly, at Quebec in August 1943, Churchill accepted Hull's draft for a postwar United Nations Organization, consisting of four Great Powers and associated lesser Powers on a worldwide basis. This meant that Britain was committed to seek support against the Soviet Union from the United States within the United Nations organization rather than through some tripartite balance-of-power system with spheres of influence.

One important consequence of this British commitment to the American point of view appeared in 1943 with respect to the explosive problem of the Polish frontiers. Britain and Russia reached a tentative agreement to move the whole Polish state westward by wholesale transfers of population, drawing its eastern boundary along the Curzon Line and compensating for this loss of territory in the east by moving its western boundary to the Oder and Neisse rivers. Churchill sincerely felt that this shift would greatly strengthen Poland, since the areas lost in the east to Russia were largely swamps and pine barrens, while the areas to be acquired from Germany in the west were rich in agricultural and mineral resources. This project had to be abandoned, however, when it was rejected by both the United States and Poland. The only agreement which could be reached was an informal one that Poland should obtain East Prussia.

In preparation for the forthcoming first meeting of the Big Three (Roosevelt, Churchill, and Stalin) in Teheran, their foreign ministers met in Moscow in October 1943. Russian suggestions to force Turkey into the war or to demand air bases in Sweden were rejected, and it was generally agreed not to dismember Germany after the war but to force Germans to pay reparations for damages and to undergo punishment for crimes against humanity or international law. It was agreed that a disarmed Germany should be ruled jointly under an Inter-Allied Commission and that Austria should be reestablished as an independent country.

The chief achievement of the conference was the signature of a Four-Nation Declaration on the United Nations. This document stated that the signers would continue to cooperate after the war "for the organization and maintenance of peace and security." It further promised to create "a general international organization based on the principle of the sovereign equality of all peace-loving states and open to membership by all such states." The four Powers also promised not to use their armies in the postwar period in the territories of other states "except for the purposes envisaged in this declaration and after joint consultation" and to cooperate together to regulate postwar armaments. This declaration was significant because of the American promise not to relapse into isolation again and because of the American success in having China accepted, admittedly with reluctance, as a Great Power.

In reporting to a joint session of Congress on the significance of this agreement, Secretary of State Hull voiced that kind of naïve idealism which made Churchill squirm. He said, "As the provisions of the Four-Nation Declaration are carried into effect, there will no longer be need for spheres of influence, for alliances, for balancing of power, or any other kind of special arrangements through which, in the unhappy past, the nations strove to safeguard their security or to promote their interests." He went on to point out, as a desirable fact, that questions of boundaries had been left in abeyance until the end of hostilities, as the United States had desired.

Just at this time considerable efforts were being made in the United States to obtain popular commitments against any postwar return to isolationism. On September 7, 1943, a conference of leaders of the Republican Party at Mackinac Island, Michigan, endorsed the hopes for a postwar international organization. Two weeks later, the Fulbright Resolution favoring such an organization passed the House of Representatives by a vote of 360 to 29, and in November a similar expression, the Connally Resolution, was accepted in the United States Senate by a vote of 85 to 5.

The Moscow Conference of Foreign Ministers was followed, within a month, by the first meeting of the Big Three, held at Teheran from November 28 to December 1, 1943. Since Russia was not at war with Japan, there were no Chinese representatives at Teheran, and the Anglo-Americans met with these at two separate conferences in Cairo before and after the sessions in Teheran (November 22-26 and December 3-6, 1943). Although the war against China was being fought quite independently from the war against Germany, the Cairo discussions formed a background for the Teheran negotiations, and undoubtedly influenced them. Once again, this influence was exerted through strategic discussions.

Originally, American strategy against Japan had, under General MacArthur's influence, given a major role to the army with supporting roles for the navy and air force. This earlier strategy had taken a form known as "island-hopping" and had envisaged a major role for China and the Chinese Army. This strategy intended to approach Japan from Australia, island by island, landing on each and wiping out the Japanese garrisons on each before going on to the next. Eventually this method would have brought the American Army into contact with China, both across Burma into the southwestern provinces and also along the southeastern coast at the traditional points of entry to China, at Hong Kong and Canton. Once contact with China had been made in this way, the final assault on Japan would be made by using Chinese forces and Chinese bases as major elements in this final assault.

Just as the Teheran Conference was meeting, this Far East strategy was being modified as a result of three factors. In the first place, the success of the United States Navy with carrier-based planes and with amphibious landing operations was showing that an attack on Japan could be made directly from the open Pacific without any need to recapture many of Japan's island bases beyond those which were needed as bases for our own air-force attacks on Japan and that this could be done without any preliminary contact with the Chinese mainland. At the same time, it was becoming increasingly clear that the Chinese regime of Chiang Kai-shek was hopelessly corrupt and noncombative and could contribute little or nothing to the final assault on Japan's home islands or even to the elimination of the large Japanese forces on the Asiatic mainland. It was just at this moment that Stalin indicated his willingness to intervene in the war on Japan and to provide Soviet forces for the elimination of the Japanese troops in Asia as soon as the war with Germany was finished. As American faith in China's ability to overcome the Japanese forces on the Asiatic mainland steadily dwindled and their faith in America's ability to strike a fatal blow at Japan itself from the open Pacific grew, it became increasingly a part of America's aims to obtain a Soviet commitment to enter the war against Japan in order to overcome the Japanese troops in Asia. This desire, forced on Roosevelt by his military leaders, greatly weakened the President in his negotiations with Stalin, since Roosevelt could not be adamant on Russia's position in eastern Europe, or even in eastern Asia, if he was seeking to obtain a Soviet commitment to go to war with Japan.

At Teheran, Stalin was chiefly motivated by an intense fear of Germany and a desire to strengthen the Soviet Union along its western border as protection against Germany. Apparently, this fear was so great that Stalin did not want Germany to go Communist after the war, possibly from fear that such a change would strengthen it. Instead, he demanded, and obtained, Polish frontiers on the Curzon Line and the Oder-Neisse Line and won acquiescence for his rather moderate plans for Finland. The latter included the 1940 frontier, a Soviet naval base at Hangö or Petsamo, reparations to Russia, and a complete break with Germany.

The British were generally unsuccessful in obtaining their desires at Teheran. They hoped to postpone *Overlord* and the projected campaign to reopen the Burma Road, shifting the Burma equipment instead to the Aegean, but were forced to accept a May 1944 target date for *Overlord*, while Stalin emphatically vetoed any Turkish, Aegean, or Balkan projects. Stalin and Roosevelt did authorize Churchill to negotiate with Turkey in an effort to persuade that country to go to war on Germany, but no one had much hope that these efforts would be successful, and Roosevelt and Stalin generally opposed them for fear they might delay *Overlord*.

Roosevelt was mostly concerned with military questions at Teheran. Having fixed a date for *Overlord*, he announced his decision to give the supreme command of that operation to Eisenhower. On the same day, as a result of Stalin's announcement that the Soviet Union would go to war with Japan as soon as Germany was beaten, he made the decisive shift in Far East strategy from the Chinese approach to the Pacific approach to Japan, leaving the Japanese Asiatic forces to Russia rather than to the Chinese, and decided to allow the Burma campaign to languish. At the same time, he asked Stalin for the use of heavy-bomber bases in European Russia and in the Siberian Maritime Provinces. The Siberian bases were to be used against Japan, but never came into action because Stalin was reluctant and because the rapid American advance across the Pacific gave the United States substitute bases, especially on Okinawa. The bases in European Russia were to have been used for a "shuttle-bombing" technique by which American heavy bombers would fly from England to Russia, and return, bombing Germany on both trips. The technique was used several times but could not be continued because the Russians did not provide sufficient antiaircraft protection for the eastern bases, with the result that the German Air Force bombed American planes on the ground with relative impunity and heavy losses.

The Teheran Conference reached important conclusions regarding Iran and Yugoslavia. A joint declaration was signed and issued by which the three Powers agreed to maintain the independence, sovereignty, and territorial integrity of Iran. This was regarded as a victory for the Anglo-American cause, since Russian intrigues in Persia had been threatening its independence and integrity since the days of the czars and had been particularly objectionable since the Anglo-Soviet military occupation of the country in August 1941. This occupation had been undertaken to force the expulsion of about seven hundred German agents and technicians, and was justified under the Soviet-Persian Treaty of 1921. That treaty permitted Russia to send troops into Persia if it were ever threatened by other forces. As the Russians occupied the northern portion of the country, the British occupied the south. Iranian public opinion was sullenly submissive. The assembly accepted an Allied demand that the German, Italian, Romanian, and Hungarian legations be expelled, and a week later the shah abdicated in favor of his son, Muhammad Riza Pahlavi. On January 29, 1942, Britain, the Soviet Union, and Iran signed an alliance by which the first two promised to respect and protect Iran's integrity, sovereignty, and independence, while Iran gave the two Powers military control over the trans-Iranian trade route until six months after the war ended, and promised as well to sever diplomatic relations with all countries which had broken with the other two signers.

Reorganization and reequipment of the trans-Iranian route under American guidance made it possible to ship to the Soviet Union over this route 5.5 million tons of supplies during the war. These efforts carried a considerable disruption of Iranian life, especially by price inflation and acute food shortages, but the chief disturbance arose from Soviet political actions in northern Iran. The Russians excluded most Iranian officials, and encouraged local separatist and revolutionary forces. On several occasions the United States secretary of state sent inquiries to Moscow about these activities, but never received a satisfactory reply. Thus, the Declaration of Teheran of December 1, 1943 was a diplomatic victory for the West, for in it Stalin joined with Roosevelt and Churchill in guaranteeing Iran's independence and integrity.

The Teheran agreement about Yugoslavia was even more significant than the one about Iran, and could not, in any honesty, be called a victory for the West. The South Slav state had been suffering under a brutal Axis occupation since the spring of 1941 and was also split by a civil war between two underground movements which spent more energy fighting each other than they used to fight the Axis. The earlier of these undergrounds, that of the Chetniks, supported the Yugoslav legitimate government now in exile in London; it was led by General Draža Mihajlović, minister of war in the exiled government. The second underground movement, known as the Partisans, was Leftish and republican in its sympathies and was dominated by the Communists led by Moscow-trained Josip Broz, known as Tito.

The contrast between these two underground movements was a sharp one, but to Churchill and Roosevelt these differences were largely ignored in favor of the more immediate question of which was more willing to fight the Axis. The answer to that question, in Churchill's opinion was Tito. For this reason Churchill at Teheran made the fateful suggestion that the Allied supplies going to Yugoslavia be shifted from Mihajlović to Tito and that Russia should send a military mission to Tito to join the British military mission already there. These suggestions were accepted by the Big Three apparently without any clear idea of what this change in policy meant, but it was a change filled with significance since it meant that the Communists would control Yugoslavia in the postwar period. This outcome was certainly not intended by at least two of the Big Three, but they were willing to overlook obvious facts in their eagerness to defeat Germany. Among these obvious items was the fact that Mihajlović represented the forces of royalism, of Serb centralism, and of social conservatism, while the Partisans represented the forces of republicanism, of South Slav federalism, and of social revolution.

Mihajlović's reluctance to continue guerrilla attacks on the Axis forces lost him British support but was, from his point of view, the only possible tactic. Every guerrilla attack on the Germans was answered by German reprisals on the Serbs in which thousands were massacred, undefended villages were destroyed, and hundreds of peasants had to flee to the mountains where they were recruited into Partisan bands. Tito, who had no desire to maintain the previous social, economic, or ideological structure of Yugoslavia, had no desire to avoid German reprisals which simultaneously destroyed the old social structure and provided recruits for his Partisan forces. Accordingly, Tito was more willing to fight Germans, and thus won the right to Allied support at Teheran. But Tito's willingness to fight Germans was only slightly more eager than that of Mihajlović, since the chief aim of each was to keep his forces strong enough to take over Yugoslavia when the Axis was driven out. Moreover, neither group, even with Allied supplies, was sufficiently strong to drive the Axis out of the country or to take over control of any significant parts of the country. The Italian forces in Yugoslavia were defeated by the Anglo-American victory in Italy itself, while the German forces were ultimately expelled by the advance of Soviet and Bulgarian forces from the east in the winter of 1944-1945. Nevertheless, the Teheran decision to shift Allied supplies from the Chetniks to the Partisans was of major significance in forming postwar Europe.

The Allied leaders parted after the Cairo and Teheran conferences in hopeful moods and proceeded to direct their full energies to military matters. Thus, there was no other important meeting until the Second Quebec Conference in September 1944, and no other meeting of the Big Three until Yalta in February 1945. The nine months following Teheran were devoted to military matters of which the chief was *Overlord*, begun on D-Day, June 6, 1944.

The preparations for *Overlord* were among the most elaborate in military history. The planning, under British General Frederick E. Morgan, occupied almost a year before Eisenhower came to England to take command in January 1944. The preparatory work involved the accumulation of enormous manpower and supplies in England, extensive intelligence work and retraining of troops, detailed planning on a very large scale, the accumulation of much special equipment, including over 5,000 escort vessels and landing craft, two artificial floating harbors, numerous block ships and caissons for emergency piers, and strenuous exertions to overcome the German Air Force and submarine fleet before the project began.

The Eighth American Air Force had been established in England in August 1942, but had not delivered the full impact of its attack because of constant diversion of men and planes to North Africa and the Mediterranean. At Casablanca in January 1943, the divergent British and American ideas on aerial bombardment were reconciled in what was called the "Combined Bomber Offensive." The Americans believed that Germany could be crippled to the point of paralysis by precision daylight bombing on strategically chosen plants of German industry; the British, who felt that daylight bombing would be too costly, placed their hopes in nighttime saturation bombing of whole areas, thus destroying civilian morale and exhausting German manpower as well as destroying military facilities. The Combined Bomber Offensive sought "round-the-clock" bombing of Germany by allowing each Ally to concentrate on its special type of attack. Gradually the very heavy casualties suffered by the Americans in daylight raids, along with recognition that "precision bombing" was far too inaccurate to fulfill the goals set for it, plus technical advances such as radar and radio-locating which improved the precision of night bombing brought the Americans to some extent to the British point of view.

The Combined Bomber Offensive shifted its targets several times, and at the beginning of 1944 concentrated on the elimination of German fighting planes. This was achieved by killing off German pilots faster than they could be trained, a goal which was greatly assisted by the fact that fuel supplies in Germany were not sufficient to permit adequate training flights. In spite of Allied bombing on factories, German production of fighter planes rose steadily in 1944 and was at 2,500 a month just before D-Day. But pilot training, from lack of gasoline, had been cut from 260 to 100 hours and even in some cases to 50 hours. As a result, losses of planes from accidents were almost as high as losses from Allied action and, in February 1944, reached the extraordinarily high figure of 1,300 planes, half of the month's production of new planes. In the meantime, losses of American bombing planes on raids over Germany were approaching 10 percent, and in one case, over the ball-bearing factory at Schweinfurt, reached 25 percent of the planes sent. In the early months of 1944 a series of raids on Berlin was launched with the deliberate purpose of provoking the German fighter forces into combat so that they could be destroyed. This was a complete success. On the last of these raids the Allied bombers were not attacked by German fighters at all, and by June the Allies had won complete aerial supremacy over Germany.

A similar result, somewhat earlier and not so conclusive, was reached in the antisubmarine warfare. In this effort, thanks to radar and combined air and sea attacks, the U-boats were driven completely from the North Atlantic. The turning point occured in May 1943, when 30 percent of the German submarines which put to sea failed to return. The number of Allied ships torpedoed fell from 141 in March 1943 to 19 in June 1944 and only 3 in August 1944. At the same time the Allied shipbuilding program was growing so rapidly that even in 1943, after losses had been subtracted, it increased by almost 11 million tons.

The Germans were poorly prepared to cope with any Allied landing in the west. Two-thirds of their forces were fighting in Russia and eastern Europe, and the rest had to be spread from the Aegean to the Pyrenees and thence north to Norway and Finland. The drain on German manpower and vital materials was so great that the country grew steadily weaker. Still it fought on, the leaders becoming more and more ruthless and more and more remote from reality until finally they were living in an insane frenzy of hatred, suspicion, and frustration. Lack of manpower, particularly of trained hands, and lack of materials, even of such ordinary commodities as concrete or steel, made it impossible to strengthen the German defenses to the necessary degree. Above all, lack of gasoline made it impossible even to withdraw equipment before the advancing Russians. In the last two months of 1943, the German armies lost almost a thousand tanks and half as many self-propelled guns to Soviet forces. Repairs became as difficult to achieve as new construction. In June 1943 the Germans had 2,569 operational tanks and 463 under repair; in February 1944 the corresponding figures were 1,519 and 1,534.

In the west the German defenses had, necessarily, been allowed to run down in order to strengthen the Russian front. While there were a few good divisions in the west, the majority of the German forces there were in units not prepared for combat, and totally lacking in mobility. The men were over-age or very young, physically unfit or convalescing, prepared to serve as occupation police and beach-watchers but quite unfit for real fighting. There was even one division made up almost entirely of men with digestive disorders. Most divisions in the west were only two regiments, and, because they were totally lacking in transport, they were classified as "static" (not fully combatant) units.

Although Hitler had ordered the coast to be fortified, this was done almost nowhere, for lack of concrete and manpower. Allied aerial bombardment increased these lacks; almost a million men were engaged in air defense in Germany itself. Disruption of railway transportation made it difficult to get the supplies that were available to the shore area. In May, for example, with a daily need of 240 carloads of cement for one area, the arrival was 16 a day. When Rommel took over the active defense in the west, he ordered a continuous belt of land mines to be laid, requiring, at a minimum, 50 million mines. Only 6 million were laid. Similarly, sea mines were ordered laid off the coast, plus a renewal of the mid-Channel mines which had been put down in 1943 and were now too old to function properly. The last could not be done at all, while the coastal mines were put down in the wrong area.

The chief German defensive forces were the Fifteenth Army defending the Pas-de-Calais and the Seventh Army farther southwest in Normandy and Brittany. The Germans expected the attack to come in the Pas-de-Calais, since it was closer to England. They continued to believe this, even after D-Day, since they thought that the Normandy landings were merely a diversion preliminary to the main attack farther north. Moreover, the Germans were convinced that the attacks would come just before high tide in order to minimize the width of beach to cross and, accordingly, constructed their obstacles and laid mines down to the half-tide mark only.

Although the Allied cross-Channel attack was not a large one, being only five attack divisions preceded by parts of three airborne divisions, it was beautifully planned, competently carried out, and encountered a number of very lucky chances, especially from the weather.

The desired landing conditions were low tide, just after dawn, following a moonlit night. These occurred only once a month and lasted for only three days. In June 1944 these days were the 5th, 6th, and 7th. Bad weather, making air operations difficult, and impossibly heavy surf forced Eisenhower to postpose the attack on June 5th; but because better weather information, expertly interpreted, showed the Allies that the weather would improve suddenly, the supreme commander ordered the attack to take place on June 6th, at a time when the Germans expected the adverse weather to continue. The two American divisions went ashore on either side of the Vire River near Carentan with "Utah Beach" to the west and "Omaha Beach" (between the Vire and the Drôme rivers) to the east. A Canadian and two British divisions went ashore between the Drôme and the Orne rivers, in front of Bayeux and Caen. Airborne divisions were dropped inland on either flank of the attack area to hold up any German counterthrust, and another airborne division was dropped inside Utah Beach to sieze the causeways which crossed the lagoons inside the beach. Tactical surprise was achieved at all points, so completely, in fact, that at Omaha Beach the strongest German coastal battery in the west was found unmanned and unguarded. Except at Omaha Beach, where high bluffs had to be scaled under fire, the landings were immediately successful. At Omaha the issue hung on the balance into the second day. As a result, 2,000 casualties were suffered at Omaha compared to 200 at Utah Beach.

As soon as the landings were established, men and equipment were poured into the beachheads. A great gale of June 19th-23rd stopped all unloading for two days and destroyed the American artificial harbor at Omaha, but, by the time the gale began, there had been put ashore 629,000 men, 95,000 vehicles, and 218,000 tons of supplies. The millionth man landed on July 6th, just a month after the first.

In spite of this success, the Allied forces were hemmed in in Normandy for two months. On the left, the British forces under the cautious Montgomery were unable to take Caen; the American forces under General Bradley were stopped in the center before Saint-Lô. Only on the right was movement possible, to cross the peninsula (June 18th) and turn westward to storm and capture Cherbourg. This great seaport, taken with its 40,000 German troops on June 27th, was so devastated that it could not be brought into service until late in August, and Allied supplies continued to come in over the Normandy beaches.

In the first 18 days of July, Caen and Saint-Lô were taken after severe fighting initiated by a terrific aerial bombardment by over 2,200 planes which dropped 7,000 tons of explosives on one town and 4,000 on the other. Both towns were wrecked, but the Allied forces were still unable to move, meeting furious resistance from German forces as they fought their way across field after field, each bordered by an impenetrable hedgerow.

As the Allies crept forward in this way, two sensational events occurred elsewhere in western Europe. On June 15th the first of Hitler's "vengeance weapons," the V-1, was fired from Pas-de-Calais on London. This was a small jet-propelled, pilotless, and automatically guided plane, moving at 400 miles per hour and carrying a one-ton explosive charge. About 8,000 of these were fired in 80 days, but the defense was steadily improved so that, late in August, 90 percent were being stopped before they reached London. Nevertheless, 2,300 reached their targets, inflicting over 20,000 casualties, one-quarter of them fatal, and forcing a million women and children to evacuate the city.

On September 8, 1944, the V-1 was replaced by the much superior V-2, a rocket which could not be intercepted because it moved faster than sound. A total of 1,050 of these weapons fell on England before the end of the war, killing over 2,700 persons and injuring three times that number. On the whole these weapons, while frightening, used up large German resources and energies but achieved no military results.

Equally spectacular was the attempt to assassinate Hitler by exploding a bomb concealed in a briefcase beside his chair at his headquarters in East Prussia. This was the last of several attempts of this kind, made by the same group which had tried in vain to negotiate with Chamberlain, Halifax, and Churchill in September 1938. The conspirators, mostly from the conservative upper classes, consisted chiefly of army officers, with a minority of civilian and diplomatic leaders. The chief military figures were Generals Ludwig Beck, Georg Thomas, Erwin von Witzleben, Karl von Stuelpnagel, and others; the chief civilian leader was Carl Goerdeler, one-time mayor of Leipzig; the chief intellectual figure was Count Helmut von Moltke, son of the German commander in chief of 1914; the leading diplomatic figures were the brothers Kordt, Theodor and Erich, the first in the London Embassy, while the second headed Ribbentrop's office in the Foreign Ministry; among those linked with the conspiracies in an ambiguous fashion were Admiral Wilhelm Canaris, chief of Military Counterintelligence, and Paul Schmidt, Hitler's personal interpreter.

This group for years discussed ways of getting rid of Hitler and what should be done with Germany afterward. Sporadically they made attempts to kill the Führer. All of these were unsuccessful because of a combination of bad luck, lack of resolution, and Hitler's extraordinary intuition.

On July 20, 1944, however, success seemed near when Colonel Count Klaus Schenk von Stauffenberg, chief of staff of the Home Army, made his daily report to Hitler, and left the conference without picking up his briefcase, which rested against the leg of Der Führer's chair. In the briefcase was an English-made bomb with a ten-minute fuse. When the bomb exploded, Stauffenberg gave the signal for the military units in Berlin, Paris, and elsewhere to seize control of these areas from the fanatical Nazi SS units.

Unfortunately, Hitler's conference on July 20th, because of the heat, was held in a wooden shed instead of the usual concrete bunker. This allowed the explosion to dissipate itself. Moreover, a few seconds before the bomb went off, Hitler left his chair to go to a map on the most distant wall of the conference room. As a result, some in the room were killed or badly injured, but Hitler escaped relatively unscathed. This was broadcast on the radio at once by the Nazis, and, by contradicting Stauffenberg's signal, threw the conspirators into sufficient confusion and irresolution to enable the SS and loyal Nazis to disrupt the plot.

About 7,000 suspects were arrested and about 5,000 were killed, usually after weeks or even months of horrible tortures. A few, like Field Marshal Rommel, were allowed to commit suicide, as a special reward for their past services to the Nazis. As a consequence of this fiasco, the anti-Hitler opposition was destroyed, the most fanatical and least sane Nazis increased their power within Germany, any chance of negotiating peace—admittedly a remote possibility at all times—became impossible, and the inner administration of the Nazi regime became a complete madhouse.

In the meantime, in the west, the main strength of the German forces was concentrated against the British near Caen. As the latter slowly inched southward toward Calais, a newly formed American Third Army, mostly armored, under General George S. Patton, drove southward from Saint-Lô to Avranches (July 18–August 1). While some units turned westward from Avranches into Brittany in an effort to capture additional seaports at Saint-Malo, Brest, and Saint-Nazaire, the armored units swung eastward to Le Mans (August 11th) and then northward to Argentan, leaving only a narrow gap (Calais-Argentan) between American and British forces, as an escape route through which eight shattered German divisions might escape eastward (August 19-12, 1944). Many broke through, but 25,000 men were captured in this pocket, and the German defensive forces in France were completely disrupted. From Le Mans units of the American Third Army, moving at speeds up to forty miles a day, drove eastward south of Paris, passing the city to reach the Seine at Fontainebleau. On their left, the American First Army reached the river below Paris on the same day, while farther west British and Canadian armies swung left toward the lower Seine.

In the midst of this excitement the American Seventh Army, with strong French forces, landed on the Mediterranean coast of France (August 15th) and began to drive northward up the Rhône Valley. The landings, made between Toulon and Cannes against negligible resistance, quickly captured Marseille. At the end of two days, the German High Command ordered all German forces to withdraw from the French Atlantic and Mediterranean coasts except from seaports and fortresses. At the end of eight days, the Seventh Army had advanced 140 miles up the Rhône and had taken 57,000 prisoners. Both Lyon and Dijon were taken without a fight, and contact was made with the United States Third Army near Châtillon-sur-Seine on September 12th.

In the meantime, on August 19, 1944, the citizens of Paris rose in revolt, led by 50,000 armed members of the French Forces of the Interior (FFI), as the underground resistance armies were called. Here, as elsewhere in Europe, these forces were dominated by Communists. General Jean Leclerc, with the French 2nd Armored Division, burst into the city on August 24th and accepted the surrender of the German garrison of 10,000 men eager to escape from the FFI. By this time the resistance forces were rising in much of France, attacking German forces and wreaking vengeance on Frenchmen who had collaborated with the Germans. On August 26th De Gaulle entered Paris and immediately was made president of a provisional government formed by a coalition of returning exiles and underground leaders. General Eisenhower reviewed a triumphal march of Allied forces down the Champs Elysées, but the main Allied armies swept by both sides of Paris toward the German frontiers.

During the autumn of 1944, the Allied advance in the west was slowed up, as much by its own problems of transport and supply as it was by German opposition. This advance had to cross a series of famous rivers, the Seine, the Somme, the Aisne, and the Meuse. All were crossed without difficulty because of weak German resistance. But the big problem looming ahead was the Rhine, where German resistance would inevitably be tenacious. On an Allied front over two hundred miles wide, the American Third Army, on the right, captured Verdun as early as August 3rd; the American First Army, in the center, took Sedan and entered Belgium (August 31st); on the left the British Second Army passed Amiens heading for Lille (August 31st), while on the extreme left the Canadian First Army had the unrewarding task of sealing off the entrenched German garrisons in the Channel ports. These were taken, one by one, after very bitter fighting, but in most cases the harbors could not be used at once because of damage or other causes. Antwerp, taken on September 4th, could not be used for two months because the Germans continued to hold the river banks nearer the sea.

On September 11th the United States First Army crossed the German frontier near Trier and headed for the Rhine. When Aachen, the first German city to be reached, refused to surrender, it was almost completely destroyed by bombardment and taken by bitter street fighting. Most German cities subsequently preferred to surrender.

At this point, a sharp difference of opinion arose between Eisenhower and Montgomery. The former wished to continue the broad-front assault on Germany, while the latter wished to put every hope on a single lightning thrust across the lower Rhine and into the essential industrial area of the Ruhr. The lower Rhine splits into a number of small rivers as it approaches the sea; in order to pass several of these in one rush Montgomery offered a daring plan: three airborne divisions were to be dropped at step-intervals ahead of the British Second Army to capture the river crossings and open the way for a sixty-mile advance by the Second Army. On August 15th, this attempt was made. The American 82nd Airborne Division dropped at Eindhoven to cover the Meuse River; the American 101st Airborne Division dropped near Nijmegen to cover the Waal crossing; and the British 1st Airborne Division was dropped near Arnhem to cover the northernmost branch of the Rhine, the Neder Rijn, above Rotterdam. German resistance to the advance of the Second

Army was so great that it was unable to reach Arnhem, and after a week of furious fighting, the remnants of this heroic group, less than a quarter of those dropped, were evacuated. This failure doomed the hopes for one vital thrust across the Rhine to the Ruhr.

By mid-December the Allied armies were struggling eastward toward the Rhine, in fog and rain, with short days and long nights. Conditions were particularly bad in the thick forests of the Ardennes. There the Germans determined to make their last counteroffensive. Secretly concentrating 25 divisions in weather too bad for air reconnaissance, the Germans struck westward, chiefly with armored forces, into General Omar Bradley's Twelfth Army Group, splitting it wide open and threatening to break through over the Meuse. Although the First and Third American armies were separated by a German advance of over 60 miles, no vital points were reached largely because of the stubborn American resistance, even when surrounded, as at Bastogne. By December 26th the German drive had stopped, and three weeks later most of the lost ground had been recovered. In the attack the Germans inflicted casualties of about 76,000 on the Americans, but suffered casualties of about 90,000 themselves and used up irreplaceable supplies and equipment. Before this Battle of the Bulge could be finished, Hitler had to withdraw from it many of the forces which had made the original attack, in order to send them hurriedly to the east in a vain attempt to slow down the Soviet winter offensive which began on January 12, 1945.

The Battle of the Bulge was hardly over before the German defenses in the west had to sustain a series of shifting hammerlike blows preparatory to the Allied invasion of Germany. Plans for the spring offensives showed 85 Allied divisions attacking 80 understrength German divisions. In the east the Germans were already reeling before the Soviet winter offensive of 155 divisions. On March 7, 1945, the American 9th Armored Division captured the Ludendorff Railway Bridge across the Rhine at Remagen a few minutes before it was to have been blown up by the Germans. In spite of desperate Nazi efforts to destroy it, this could not be done for ten days. By that time it was too late, for other crossings had been established, and many Allied divisions were across. By the end of March 1945, German strength in the west amounted to no more than 46 divisions heavily pressed by 85 Allied divisions. As the official *History of the United States Army* put it, "The German Army could no longer be considered a major obstacle." But the German military leaders, under the fanatical insistence of Hitler and Himmler, were not permitted to surrender.

The Allied advance in the west was regarded with mixed feelings in Moscow, where there was real concern that the Germans might shift all their strength to the east to oppose Russia while admitting the Anglo-American forces in the west. The Germans regarded the Russians as subhumans aroused to frenzy by German atrocities on Soviet soil, and had every reason to fear Russian occupation and retaliation, while everyone knew that any American occupation would be motivated by humanitarian considerations rather than by retaliation. The Nazi leaders were too much absorbed in their own irrationalities to adopt such tactics as these, however, although the Soviet leaders continued to dread the possibility and convinced themselves, in spite of the contradictory evidence, that it was likely. Accordingly, the Soviet advance became a race with the Western Powers, even though these Powers, by Eisenhower's orders, held back their advance at many points (such as Prague) to allow the Russians to occupy areas the Americans could easily have taken first.

From midsummer of 1943 until the war's end in May 1945, the Soviet offensive in the east was almost continuous. In January 1944, Russian forces crossed the old border into Poland; in February they pushed the Germans back from besieged Leningrad, and, in the following month, they began a southern offensive which crossed the Prut into Romania. In July 1944, the Soviet armies reached the Vistula River, across from Warsaw, and began an offensive to overrun Romania. These events raised in acute form the problem of who would rule over the liberated areas of eastern Europe.

In general, the Anglo-Americans recognized the Russian need for security along their western frontier, but felt that this could be obtained if independent states with constitutional governments (in which the Communist Party played a role) could be established in Poland, Romania, Bulgaria, Greece, and Yugoslavia. They saw no hope of liberating the Baltic states from Russia, and paid little attention to Finland. It was generally felt that Russian security in eastern Europe could be assured if the victorious Powers, including Russia, could retain their unity in the postwar period and operate together in a United Nations organization in peacetime as they had done in war. While the Western Powers recognized that the Russians had a justifiable suspicion of international organizations based on their unhappy experiences with the League of Nations, it was felt that this could be overcome by the English-speaking Powers giving evidence of their new spirit of cooperation and by the existence of regional arrangements, such as the Anglo-Soviet twenty-year alliance of May 26, 1942, or the French-Soviet agreement of December 10, 1944. All efforts to achieve some arrangement with Russia over the lesser states was deeply involved with the indecisive negotiations about the fate of Germany.

There was general agreement about Germany to the extent that the errors of October 1918 would not be repeated: German military leaders would be forced to sign a total capitulation without any legal restrictions on the victors' future behavior toward Germany; Germany would then fall under the victors' rule directly through military government; considerable portions of eastern Germany, possibly as far west as the western Neisse River (the line of the Oder), would be taken from Germany; Germany would be completely disarmed and industrially crippled; and considerable reparations in kind would be taken from her. The apparent conflict between the desire to reduce Germany's industrial level and the desire to obtain reparations from her was glossed over temporarily by a plan to dismantle German industrial plants as reparations for Russia.

These agreements about Germany left unsettled at least three major questions and, in consequence, left Stalin with a strong feeling of insecurity about Germany's future: there was no agreement whether Germany would be dismembered or be treated as a unity, even under military occupation; there was no agreement about the nature of the future German government; and there was no agreement about methods for permanent enforcement of German disarmament and restricted industrial development.

We need not narrate the continuous series of negotiations, temporary agreements, misunderstandings, and reinterpretations which went on for years among the Allied Powers regarding the fate of Germany and of the liberated countries. The idea that the Soviet Union and the Anglo-American Powers could continue to cooperate in peace as they had done in war, either by diplomacy and conference of their leaders or within some structure of international organization, was naïve. Such a possibility was foreclosed by two factors: the fundamental underlying suspicions on both sides, even in wartime, and the very nature of the political power of modern states.

For these two reasons, both sides, in the midst of reassuring public statements about their solidarity of outlook and plans for postwar cooperation, began to work toward another, more realistic arrangement of spheres of interest and power balances. This alternative, and ultimately inevitable, path was adopted earlier by Stalin and Churchill than by Roosevelt, not because the latter was naïve or ill but because he wanted to smother the naked opposition of power balances by a chaotic blanket of legal restrictions, conflicting public opinion, and alternative institutional arrangements which would hamper the outright operation of power conflicts and which would allow men like himself to divert and postpone crises from day to day, while they improvised better economic and social arrangements for their peoples in the successive intervals of peace won from the postponement of forcible solutions to power conflicts. None of this could be achieved, in Roosevelt's view, unless Stalin's mania of suspicion of capitalist Powers could be reduced by granting him as concessions things he could not be prevented from taking anyway. In the last resort Roosevelt's sense of the realities of power were quite as acute as Churchill's or Stalin's, but he concealed that sense much more deliberately and much more completely under a screen of high-sounding moral principles and idealistic statements of popular appeal. It is unlikely that Roosevelt had any alternative plan based on power politics to fall back upon if his stated aims of postwar cooperation and United Nations failed. Churchill, on the other hand, while sincerely pursuing cooperative goals, had a secondary outline based on power balance and spheres of interest. Stalin reversed Churchill's priorities, giving primary position to spheres of power and secondary, rather ironic, acceptance of cooperation and international organizations.

So far as eastern Europe was concerned, the Stalin priorities made quite impossible any mechanism of cooperation or international agreement. There can be little doubt that Stalin was determined to achieve security on the Soviet western frontier by establishing a buffer of states under complete Communist control. This covered Poland, Romania, and Bulgaria necessarily and any others he might get incidentally. He was not concerned with Greece, Albania, or Austria, had little hope of getting Czechoslovakia, hoped to retain Yugoslavia, and had considerable, but unspecified, fears over Iran. The technique to be used to get Communist control over these states was similar to that used by Hitler in Austria: (1) to establish a coalition government containing Communists; (2) to get in Communist hands the ministries of Defense (the army), Interior (the police), and, if possible, Justice (the courts); (3) to use administrative decrees to take over education and the press and to cripple opposition political parties; and (4) to establish, finally, a completely Communist regime, under the protection of Soviet military forces if necessary.

.The success of these steps in Poland, Bulgaria, and Romania was assured, while the war was still going on, by the Western Powers' acceptance of coalition governments containing Communists as a necessary price for Soviet security locally and for Soviet cooperation elsewhere (especially the Far East) and by the fact that Russian armies were in occupation of the areas concerned.

One of the first evidences of Churchill's alternative policy based on spheres of power was Eden's suggestion to the Soviet ambassador in London on May 5, 1944 that Britain would permit Russia to take the lead in policy about Romania in return for Russian support for Britain's policies in Greece. This was defended as being based on "military realities," was opposed by Secretary of State Hull, but was accepted by Roosevelt "for a three months' trial." It led to an agreement between Churchill and Stalin, at the Moscow Conference of October 9-18, 1944, that Anglo-Soviet interests in the Balkans might be divided on a percentage basis, with Russia predominant in Romania and Bulgaria, with England predominant in Greece, and with Hungary and Yugoslavia divided fifty-fifty. No one had any idea what these percentages meant, but the agreement was put down on paper and signed. At Stalin's insistence, the gist of the arrangement had already been sent to Washington, where Roosevelt initialed it during Hull's absence on vacation (June 12, 1944).

This agreement had little influence on Churchill's actions. He continued to work for cooperative constitutional arrangements in eastern Europe and elsewhere. When Belgian Foreign Minister Paul Henri Spaak, in the summer of 1944, sought to obtain a Western defense bloc, extending from Norway to the Iberian Peninsula and including Britain, Churchill and Eden both rebuffed the plan on the grounds that it would divide Europe into two blocs, Western and Soviet, which would outbid each other for German support in the postwar world. The British chiefs of staff, however, in the autumn of 1944, sought to establish, as an alternative policy, the dismemberment of Germany and the incorporation of industrialized west Germany into Western defense plans in the event of Russian hostility in postwar eastern or central Europe. The British civil leaders, led by Eden, in September and again in October, rejected these General Staff suggestions and reiterated their determination to pursue a policy of unity and cooperation within the United Nations and to renounce any efforts to form any anti-Soviet bloc, least of all with Germany. The chiefs of staff yielded, unconvinced, and warned of the need to prepare an alternative policy if the United Nations broke down owing to differences with Russia and the need then arose to face a united Germany dominated by, or in collaboration with, Russia.

In the meantime the Soviet Union, in 1944, under cover of the continued violence of war and the negotiations to establish a united postwar world organization, took steps to establish its western buffer of Communized satellite states.

In August 1944, Finland, Romania, and Bulgaria sought to get out of the war. King Michael of Romania overthrew the pro-Nazi government of General Antonescu and sent a delegation, led by a Communist, to Moscow to sign a formal armistice. The surrender, signed on September 12th, was to the United Nations, but its enforcement was left to the Soviet High Command, with the Anglo-British members of the Allied Control Commission relegated to the status of observers. A similiar armistice was signed with Finland on September 19th.

The Bulgarian surrender was more complicated, since that country was not at war with Russia. A new Bulgarian government, formed on September 4th, proclaimed its neutrality, and requested withdrawal of all German forces. Russia declared war the next day, marched unopposed into Sofia on September 16th and supported a *coup d'état* which established a Communist-dominated government. The new regime at once declared war on Germany and was occupied by Russian forces. Churchill and Eden, from Quebec, vetoed an armistice like the Romanian one, but the final Bulgarian armistice of October 28, 1944 was little different.

Soviet forces meanwhile had crossed Bulgaria and invaded Yugoslavia, liberating Belgrade on October 15th. They then swung north into Hungary, reached Budapest on November 11th, and surrounded it by the end of the month. The Germans prevented a Hungarian surrender by seizing control of the government on October 15, 1944, and as a result Budapest was largely destroyed in fierce fighting during November and December. Only on January 20, 1945, was the provisional government of General Miklos able to conclude an armistice with the Russians, although fighting continued in the country for several months longer. The agreement left Hungary largely under Soviet military control (signed January 20, 1945).

Vain efforts extending over several years were made by the Western Powers, especially Britain, to prevent Yugoslavia and Poland from falling under complete Communist influence. In the course of 1943, rather futile efforts were made, through control of supplies of weapons and the work of British liaison officers, to get the Chetniks and Partisans to fight Germans rather than each other. Growing evidence that the pro-Serb Chetniks under royalist General Mihajlović were collaborating with the Germans inclined the British to shift their support to Tito, but it proved as difficult to get the royal Yugoslav government-in-exile in London to accept Tito as it was to get the latter to accept the royal government. A successful German attack on Tito, which forced him to flee to the Adriatic islands, brought both sides to terms, and, in October 1944, royal Prime Minister Ivan Subasic agreed to join a Tito government in which the Partisans would hold an overwhelming majority of the posts. The agreement promised free elections for a constituent assembly within three months of total liberation and the return of King Peter only after he had been accepted by a plebiscite. The king refused to accept this agreement until Churchill threatened to expel him from England. The new government, accepted by the Powers at Yalta, was established in Belgrade on March 4, 1945.

As might be inferred, the Polish settlement was even less happy than the Yugoslav one, since the Poles were under the full weight of the Soviet armies, and inaccessible to Western power. As early as 1943, the Polish Cabinet in London, which operated an underground army and underground government in Poland, was threatened by Russian demands that the Polish eastern frontier be moved westward to the Curzon Line and that anti-Soviet members of the government be removed. Futile negotiations dragged on for months. In July 1944, when the Soviet armies were approaching the Vistula, a Communist "Polish Committee of National Liberation" was set up under Soviet protection in Russia. It claimed full legal sovereignty over Poland under the Constitution of 1921 and denounced the Polish government in London as illegal.

Polish ministers hurried from London to Moscow to negotiate. While they were still talking there, and when the Soviet Army was only six miles from Warsaw, the Polish underground forces in the city, at a

Soviet invitation, rose up against the Germans. A force of 40,000 responded to the suggestion, but the Russian armies stopped their advance and obstructed supplies to the rebels, in spite of appeals from all parts of the world. On October 3, 1944, after sixty-three days of hopeless fighting, the Polish Home Army had to surrender to the Germans. This Soviet treachery removed the chief obstacle to Communist rule in Poland, and the London government accordingly was ignored. On January 5, 1945, Russia recognized the Committee of National Liberation as the government of Poland, while the Western Powers continued to recognize the government in London.

Only in Greece was it possible to save a Balkan state from Communist domination; this was achieved because the country was accessible to British forces arriving by sea. The guerrillas resisting the Germans in Greece were controlled by two groups: a Communist one was known from its initials as ELAS, while a smaller local group of anti-Communist resistance fighters in Epirus was known as EDES (under pro-English Colonel Zervas). British efforts to unite the two groups under a common government and program were frustrated by the extreme unpopularity of the king. Finally, such a government was formed under a liberal republican, George Papandreou, with British General R. M. Scobie as commander in chief of all guerrilla fighters. In mid-October 1944, British forces returned to Athens with this government, but armed ELAS groups prowled Athens as a constant threat to public order. A decision to disarm these led to an armed uprising in the city. Defeated by the British, they took to the hills, but received no support from Russia, and, on February 13, 1945, accepted disarmament and amnesty under the regency of Archbishop Damaskinos, with General Nicholas Plastiras as prime minister in a non-Communist government.

In spite of these conflicts with Communist elements in eastern Europe, the Western Powers continued to cooperate with the Soviet Union in the military subjugation of Germany and the diplomatic negotiations to establish a general postwar arrangement. In the latter negotiations the problem of a European, particularly a German, postwar settlement was inextricably mingled with the establishment of a world security organization. The central core of both was the hope that the three Great Powers would be able to cooperate in peace as they had done in war, but this rather tenuous hope was concealed under a mass of other considerations.

We have already seen the dominant role played in Soviet operations by Russia's insistence on security along its western frontier. Britain had equally forceful aspirations, of which the chief were to prevent an American reversion into postwar isolationism as in 1921 and to maintain the unity of the Commonwealth. The Roosevelt Administration in Washington was equally fearful of any resurgence of American isolationism, and hoped to avoid it by a symphonic appeal to mingled notes of American idealism and interests: The United States would be the greatest Power in a world security organization which would prevent future wars but, at the same time, would be unable to impose any decisions on the United States. Under that peace the world would be reconstructed economically to satisfy the basic needs of all human beings, end poverty and disease by American technical skill and science, and raise standards of living everywhere to the simultaneous satisfaction of American idealism and American industry's need for profitable markets.

The outlines of this American postwar paradise were sketched as goals by such proclamations as the Four Freedoms speech of January 1941, the Atlantic Charter of August 14, 1941, and the United Nations Declaration of January 2, 1942. Differences of view among the Big Three in drawing up the latter document were concealed in its final wording, but are of some significance. They included American insistence on excluding France and including China as Great Powers, British efforts to include social security and to protect imperial preference, and Soviet objections to the importance of religious freedom.

The organizational structures to secure these goals in the postwar period were sketched out in a number of international conferences on various governmental levels. These included the major summit conferences of heads of governments already mentioned and subsequent ones at Second Quebec (September 1944), Moscow (October 1944), Malta (January 1945), Yalta (February 1945), and Potsdam (July 1945), and a number of specialists' conferences. The latter included: (1) a conference on postwar economic problems at London in September 1941; (2) another on food and agriculture at Hot Springs, Virginia, in May–June 1943; (3) one on refugees and emergency postwar relief held at Atlantic City, New Jersey, in November 1943; (4) a conference on international monetary problems at Bretton Woods, New Hampshire, in July 1944; (5) the Conference of Ministers of Education of the Allied Governments, held in London in April 1944; and (6) the two conferences to establish an international security organization at Dumbarton Oaks, Washington, in October 1944, and at San Francisco in April–June 1945.

These conferences were surrounded with preliminary and subsequent negotiations and gave rise to the basic international organizations of the postwar period. Among these were the Food and Agriculture Organization (FAO), now stationed in Rome; the United Nations Relief and Rehabilitation Administration (UNRRA); the International Monetary Fund and the International Bank for Reconstruction and Development (World Bank), now in Washington; the United Nations Educational, Scientific, and Cultural Organization (UNESCO), now in Paris; and the United Nations security organization now operating out of its glittering glass buildings along the East River, New York City. The arguments and conflicts whose compromises and resolutions provided these postwar organizations of "one world" idealism will be discussed later; during the war itself they were largely lost under the din of world conflict.

While the Western Powers were thus laying the foundations for their constructive, humanitarian, and rational approach to the postwar world during 1943–1945, the basically destructive, pathological, and irrational character of Nazism was turning Germany and occupied Europe into a madhouse. By September 1943, no objective person in Germany could expect a German victory; by September 1944, every German military leader saw that defeat was imminent. Yet the Nazi hierarchy and its jackal collaborators, isolated from reality by their obsessive delusions, only increased the violence of their insane frenzies. This violence was turned increasingly inward in a determination to destroy everything in one vast holocaust if Hitler's New Order could not be achieved. Efforts to destroy entirely those peoples, such as Jews, gypsies, Slavs, and the "politically unreliable," who were special targets of the Nazi psychosis, were accelerated as the Western and Soviet armies slashed deeper into the Reich. Eager subordinates worked overtime to slaughter the emaciated prisoners in concentration camps before the whole system collapsed. More significantly, persons held as resisters and opponents in crowded prisons were condemned to destruction by shooting or hanging before they could be released by the invading armies.

In many places within Germany the uproar of the war itself was almost lost in the crackle of the executioners' guns, the screams of the tortured, the acrid smell of the gas chambers, the moans of millions of victims of avarice and hate, the stench of burning bodies, and the scurrying around of the bestial Nazis seeking to hide or destroy documentary evidence, to conceal the treasures looted from centuries of Europe's earlier culture in the days of Hitler's victories; to secrete the jewels and precious metals (including gold yanked from the teeth of murdered Jews), and to satisfy their last impulses of avarice and spite. Hundreds of millions of dollars of such hidden loot were uncovered by the armies in their final stages of victory.

When these victorious armies broke into Germany, late in 1944, the Nazis were still holding the survivors of 8,000,000 enslaved civilian workers, 10,000,000 Jews, 5,750,000 Russian prisoners of war, and millions of prisoners from other armies. Over half of the Jews and Russians and several millions of the others, possibly 12,000,000 in all, were killed by murder, overwork, or deliberate neglect before final victory in the spring of 1945. The work of these enslaved and exploited millions allowed the great majority of Germans to escape the economic stringencies of the war. While the standards of living of the British were pushed downward by rationing and shortages to levels where energy and work were hampered, and at a time when German-occupied countries were frequently forced below the subsistence level, German standards of living were, on the average, higher than they had been since 1928, and the mobilization of Germans for work or war service was less stringent than in any other major combatant country. This was especially true of women and nonessential workers. By mid-1943, for example, the number of persons in domestic service in Germany was only about 8 percent less than four years earlier, while in Britain over the same four years the reduction was 67 percent. Over the same period the number of workers in heavy industry increased 68.5 percent in Britain, but only 18.8 percent in Germany. In August 1944, Albert Speer, minister of armaments and war production and one of the few rational figures in high position in Germany, estimated that there were still 7.7 million unproductive employees in Germany, including 1.4 million in domestic service. The number of women mobilized for war production in the first four years of the conflict was 2.25 million in Britain compared to 182,000 in Germany.

This relative ease of the Germans in the midst of history's most destructive war was possible because of the convergence of a number of factors of which the most significant were the slowness of industrial mobilization, the ruthless looting of occupied areas, and the working to death of millions of enslaved peoples. As one consequence of this situation, recognition that the war was lost came to the Germans, as it came to Hitler, relatively late and with surprising suddenness, but the leaders of the armed forces recognized their hopeless position a year, or even two years, before the end. Fear of Hitler's terror prevented them from taking any steps to end the war or even from mentioning it to Hitler, from fear of his rage; and their efforts to kill Hitler, though persistent, were pathetically incompetent.

Thus Hitler's fanatical devotion to destruction made surrender impossible and drove the war on to its bitter end. This bitterness was carried to the majority of Germans by the Combined Bomber Offensive, approved by the Combined Chiefs of Staff on June 10, 1943. Before this offensive the bombardment of Germany from the air was of little significance. In the whole war almost 1.5 million tons of bombs were dropped on Germany, but only 15,000 of this fell in 1940, and about 46,000 in 1941. The 1942 figure, even with the help of the United States Eighth Air Force, was only 7,000 tons higher than that for 1941. Thus 95 percent of the total bombs dropped on Germany in the war fell after January 1943.

The Combined Bomber Offensive was an effort to carry out the largely erroneous ideas of an Italian general, Giulio Douhet, whose most significant achievement was a book, *The Command of the Air: An Essay on the Art of Aerial Warfare*, published in Italian in 1921. In this and other works, Douhet made a series of claims and assumptions which were almost totally wrong and had a pernicious influence on subsequent history.

These included the following: (1) that the defensive supremacy prevailing in land warfare in 1916 would continue, and, accordingly, no decision could be reached by ground combat; (2) that air forces, on the contrary, had an offensive supremacy against which no defense was possible; (3) that decision in war, accordingly, could be reached by air forces alone and could be reached, on that basis, within the first twenty-four hours of a future war; (4) that all air power must be devoted to such strategic purposes (immediate total defeat of the enemy) and must not allow themselves to become involved, on a tactical basis, with ground or naval forces; (5) that aerial victory would be achieved by the immediate and total collapse of civilian morale under minimal bombardment; (6) accordingly, that attack by air must be directed at civilians in enemy cities, with poison gas as the chief weapon supplemented by incendiary bombs but with high-explosive bombs unnecessary beyond a minimum and token amount of about twenty tons. (Any city, he felt, would be destroyed totally by 500 tons of bombs, mostly gas.)

To this nonsense Douhet added a number of subsidiary ideas, including the following: (1) war must begin with a preemptive (first) strike from the air on enemy cities without any formal declaration of war; (2) since antiaircraft guns are totally ineffective and fighter planes are almost equally futile, bombers do not need high speed and will never need escort by fighter planes; and (3) since whole cities will collapse immediately, there is no problem of target selection, no need for economic warfare or economic mobilization, and little need for concern for replacements or reserves of planes or other equipment.

On their face these ideas seem so unconvincing that it is almost inconceivable that they played a major role in twentieth-century history, but they did play such a role, and made a substantial contribution toward forming the new age in which we live. These ideas were almost wholly ignored in the Soviet Union and were largely rejected in Germany; they created great controversy in France; and were accepted to a large extent among airmen in Britain and the United States. Wherever they were accepted they led airmen to struggle to escape from tactical operations by getting free from the other services (land or sea) by the creation of a third service, the independent air force.

Acceptance of Douhetism by civilian leaders in France and England was one of the chief factors in appeasement and especially in the Munich surrender of September 1938. Baldwin reflected these ideas in November 1932, when he said: "I think it is well also for the man in the street to realise that there is no power on earth that can protect him from being bombed. Whatever people may tell him, the bomber will always get through. . . . When the next war comes, and European civilization is wiped out, as it will be, and by no force more than that force, then do not let them lay blame on the old men." In September 1938, the Chamberlain government reflected these ideas and prepared the way to Munich by issuing 35 million gas masks to city dwellers.

And as a consequence of Douhetism among British and American airmen, the strategic bombing of Germany was mishandled from the beginning until almost the end of the war. Correctly, such strategic bombing should have been based on careful analysis of the German war economy to pick out the one or two critical items which were essential to the war effort. These items were probably ball bearings, aviation fuels, and chemicals, all of them essential and all of them concentrated. After the war German General Gotthard Heinrici said that the war would have ended a year earlier if Allied bombing had been concentrated on ammonia plants. Whether this is correct or not, the fact remains that strategic bombing was largely a failure, and was so from poor choice of targets and from long intervals between repeated attacks. Relentless daily bombardment, with heavy fighter escort, day after day, in spite of losses, with absolute refusal to be distracted to area or city bombing because of losses or shifting ideas might have made a weighty contribution to the defeat of Germany and shortened the war substantially. As it was, the contribution by strategic bombing to the defeat of Germany was relatively incidental, in spite of the terrible losses suffered in the effort.

The shift to city bombing was more or less accidental. In spite of the erroneous ideas of Chamberlain, Baldwin, Churchill, and the rest, the war opened and continued for months with no city bombing at all, for the simple reason that the Germans had no intentions, no plans, and no equipment for strategic bombing. The British, who had the intentions but still lacked the plans and equipment, also held back. After the fall of France, where almost all German bombardment was tactical or psychological with the major exception of the attack on Rotterdam, the Battle of Britain was fought and lost by tactical bombing on shipping and occasional airdromes or airplane factories.

The attack on cities began by accident when a group of German planes which were lost dumped their bomb loads, contrary to orders, on London on August 24, 1940. The RAF retaliated by bombing Berlin the next night. On September 2, 1940, as counterretaliation, Göring announced the beginning of city bombardment for September 7th, but the policy had already begun with a series of attacks on Liverpool after August 28th. The British efforts to counterattack by daylight raids on military objectives in Germany resulted in such losses that the air offensive was shifted to night attacks. This entailed also a shift from industrial targets to indiscriminate bombing of urban areas. This was justified with the wholly mistaken argument that civilian morale was a German weak point and that the destruction of workers' housing would break this morale. The evidence shows that the German war effort was not weakened in any way by lowering of civilian morale, in spite of the horrors heaped upon it. In 1942 an effort was was made to begin "thousand-bomber" raids against a single target in one night, and three of these were carried out, the first at Cologne on May 30th. This was a terrible shock to the Germans, but had little impact on their ability to wage war. Since the British Bomber Command had about 450 first-line bombers, a raid as large as that on Cologne required use of all reserves and training planes, with instructors flying about a quarter of the planes. Of 1,046 planes sent off, 898 reached the target and dropped 1,455 tons of bombs, with 40 planes lost in action and 12 more damaged beyond repair. In the city 474 persons were killed, 565 hospitalized, over 5,000 injured, 45,000 made homeless, and hundreds of factories destroyed, yet the life of the city was back to normal in two weeks, with war production in the city back to normal in about six weeks. The next thousand-plane raid (really 956), on Essen two days after the attack on Cologne, was so ineffective, partly from cloudy weather, that the German air defense did not even report an attack on Essen that night, while reporting attacks on three other Ruhr cities.

Improvements in finding their targets, heavier attacks, and the arrival of the American Eighth Air Force (which inaugurated "round-the-clock bombing" in 1943) increased the damage from strategic bombing of Germany, without reducing the scale of the German war effort. This failure resulted from a number of factors which should be understood. The chief one was that the Western governments had, from 1933 on, entirely misconceived the nature and amount of German munitions production. It was overestimated by a wide margin (twofold or threefold) in 1933-1943, and was underestimated by an equal margin in 1943-1945. The British assumed that there was full industrial mobilization for war in Germany as early as 1938; but this was never achieved and was not even attempted until December 1943.

Consequently, Germany, until the winter of 1944-1945, had a cushion of unmobilized resources which allowed an astonishingly rapid repair of bomb damage and an even more astonishing increase in production of war goods as late as January 1945.

Failure by the Western Powers to analyze the German war economy led to changeable and misguided efforts to attack it. When successful attacks were made on vital objects, such as ball-bearing or chemical plants, they were not followed up, thus giving the Germans time to repair or even to disperse these facilities. Much effort was expended on bombing almost wholly unrewarding targets, such as airfields, submarine pens, ports, railroad yards, tank factories, and others. For a variety of reasons, these targets could not be damaged sufficiently to make substitution or repair impossible. The original decision for the Combined Bomber Offensive in January 1943 gave highest target priority to submarine construction yards. A fraction of the planes and crews used in this unremunerative task could have contributed greatly to defeat the submarine if they had been used in night searches for the submarines themselves on the Atlantic.

As early as June 10, 1943, the Combined Bomber Offensive top priority was shifted from submarine yards to German fighter-plane production, but here the error was made of concentrating on body and assembly plants (of which there were many) instead of on engine factories, which were few and more vulnerable. By April 1944, with production of German fighter planes increasing rapidly, this effort had failed, and the Bomber Offensive at last turned, in May 1944, toward a vulnerable target: air-plane-fuel production. To this was added, in October 1944, an attack on the general rail and canal transport system. The fuel attack incidentally disrupted the chemical industry, and this combination, along with trans-portation, brought the German economic base for war to its knees in February 1945. The delay was partly caused by the lack of determination in concentrating on the targets selected and the constant attraction of the mirage of city bombing. Even after May 1944, when the chief target was fuel factories, only 16 percent of the bombs dropped were aimed at these, and 27 percent were still being thrown away on bombing civilian residences in cities. The importance of choosing the correct target in strategic bombing may be seen from one incidental, and probably ac-cidental, success. The Germans had only one factory producing the Maybach heavy HL engine used in their Tiger and Panther tanks. This was destroyed by an aerial bomb in 1944. This immobilized hundreds of these heavy tanks on the Russian front and contributed substantially to a successful Russian breakthrough.

The British effort to break German civilian morale by area night bomb-ing was an almost complete failure. In fact, one of the inspiring and amaz-ing events of the war was the unflinching spirit under unbearable attack shown by ordinary working people in industrial cities. This was as true in Russia (in Moscow and above all in Leningrad) as it was in Germany or Britain (above all in the dock areas of East London). Attacks on these peoples had a greater influence on the morale of their soldiers fighting on the front than it did on the suffering peoples themselves.

The most extraordinary example of this suffering occurred in the British fire raids on Hamburg in 1943. For more than a week, beginning on July 24th, Hamburg was attacked with a mixture of high-explosive and incendiary bombs so heavily and persistently that entirely new condi-tions of destruction known as "fire storms" appeared. The air in the city, heated to over a thousand degrees, began to rise rapidly, with the result that ground-level winds of gale or even hurricane force rushed into the city. These winds were so strong as to knock people off their feet or to move flaming beams and walls through the air. The heat was so intense that normally nonflammable substances burned, and fires were ignited yards from any flame. The water supply was destroyed on July 27th, but the flames were too hot for water to be effective: it turned to steam before it could reach flaming objects, and all ordinary methods of quenching flames by depriving them of oxygen were made impossible by the storm of fresh air roaring in from the suburbs. Nevertheless, the supply of oxygen could not keep up with the combustion, and great layers of carbon monoxide settled in the shelters and basements, killing the people huddled there. Those who tried to escape through the streets were enveloped in flames as if they were walking through the searing jet of a blowtorch. Some who wrapped themselves in blankets dipped in water from a canal were scalded as the water turned suddenly to steam. Hundreds were cremated, and their ashes dispersed by the winds. No final figures for the destruction were possible until 1951, when they were set by German authorities at 40,000 dead (including 5,000 children), 250,000 houses destroyed (about half the city), with over 1,000,000 persons made homeless. This was the greatest destruction by air attacks on a city until the fire raid on Tokyo of March 9, 1945, which still stands today as the most devastating air attack in human history.

The arrival of the American strategic air forces and the beginning of the Combined Bomber Offensive in the summer of 1943 gave a new turn to the air attack on Germany. The first great American effort, against Schweinfurt, a city which produced 80 percent of German ball bearings, showed the difficulty of the American aim of precision daylight bombing of military targets (October 14, 1943). A force of 228 heavy bombers dropped 450 tons of explosives on the target, but 62 planes and 599 men failed to return. Such losses could not be sustained, and resulted from the fact that escorting fighter planes were of such short range that they had to turn back at the German border. As a result, Schweinfurt was not bombed again for four months, during which most of its ball-bearing production was dispersed to five small nearby towns. A series of well-aimed attacks after February 21, 1944, cut production about a quarter in the next eight weeks, but this had little influence on Germany's fighting power.

The figures on German munitions production are revealing. In 1944, when Germany had armed forces of about 150 full divisions of 12,000 men each, it manufactured sufficient armaments to equip completely 250 infantry and 40 panzer divisions. In some cases, full expansion continued into 1945. The total production of munitions in Germany in January 1945 was a quarter larger than in January 1943. Aircraft production in January 1945 was the same as January 1944, and both were almost 40 percent over January 1943. Production of weapons in January 1945 was 4 percent more than the same month of 1944. Production of tanks, with January–February 1942 taken as 100, was up 54 percent in January 1943; up 338 percent in January 1944; and up 457 percent in January 1945. The following figures for actual production of specific items will help to put the strategic bombing of Germany into perspective:

ITEMS	YEAR	GERMANY	UNITED KINGDOM
Military aircraft	1942	14,200	23,600
	1944	39,600	26,500
Tanks	1942	6,300	8,600
	1944	19,000	4,600
Heavy trucks	1942	81,000	109,000
	1944	89,000	91,000
Heavy antitank guns	1942	2,100	500
	1944	13,800	1,900
Antiaircraft guns	1942	4,200	2,100
	1944	8,200	200
Machine guns	1942	320,000	1,510,000
	1944	790,000	730,000
Small-arms ammunition (rounds)	1942	1,340 million	2,190 million
	1944	5,370 million	2,460 million

It would probably not be unfair to say that Germany in January 1945, after two years of heavy air bombardment from the Western Powers, was not only outproducing the United Kingdom on most significant items of military equipment but had also improved its relative position. Some of this, of course, can be attributed to the fact that the United States was taking over production of some items, but the chief cause was the unbelievable economic mobilization of Germany in the year from December 1943 to December 1944. The relative costs of the strategic bombing effort may be shown in figures. The Americans and British together lost 40,000 planes and 158,906 airmen, almost equally divided between them. The Germans suffered about 330,000 civilians killed, almost 1,000,000 injured, and about 8,000,000 made homeless; for the last year and a half of the war over 1,000,000 Germans were employed clearing and repairing bomb damage. All these things contributed indirectly to hamper the German war effort.

The direct contribution of strategic bombing to the war effort came chiefly after September 1944, and was to be found mainly in the disruption of fuel and transportation. Even this could have been avoided if Hitler had been willing to take the advice of his subordinates and adopt proper defensive measures against the Western air attacks. Hitler himself insisted on priority of flak (antiaircraft guns) over fighter planes and of retaliatory bombing of England over defense by German fighter planes, both mistaken decisions. If the men and materials which Germany devoted to its efforts to bomb England had been entirely used for defensive fighter planes, the influence of Allied strategic bombing on the outcome of the war would have been insignificant.

Germany would still have been defeated, because in the long run its position was hopeless, once Hitler attacked Russia while Britain was still undefeated. This defeat arose from the destruction of the German armies in battle, and was made inevitable from the economic point of view by the loss of the Romanian oil supply in August 1944, and the loss of the Ruhr industrial region in April 1945.

One unforeseen (and still largely unrecognized) event in the defeat of Germany's ground armies was Hitler's greater resistance to Western than to Soviet advances. It had been assumed, especially in the Kremlin, that Hitler's hatred of Communism would lead him to weaken his defenses in the west in order to resist more effectively the advance of Russia. He did exactly the opposite. In the late summer of 1944, two-thirds of Germany's fighting men were resisting the Russians in the east (2,000,000 in all), with 300,000 in Italy and 700,000 elsewhere in the west. By the time of Yalta (February 1, 1945), Germany had 106 divisions in the west (of which 27 were in Italy) facing an equal number of slightly larger divisions of the Western Powers, while they had 133 in the east (24 less than on June 1, 1944), of which only 75 (including 4 armored) faced Russia's 100 divisions (with 80 more in reserve) along the 600-mile front from the Carpathian Mountains to the Baltic.

This shift in German forces can be explained on military grounds, but the real causes were much deeper and were embedded in the distorted recesses of Hitler's brain and in the very nature of Nazism. In spite of Hitler's verbal attacks on Communism, his real hatred was directed at the values and traditions of Western Civilization and at Christian and middle-class ways of life. This hatred impelled him to overrule the objections of his military commanders in order to mobilize all his dwindling reserves of manpower and supplies (especially truck transport and gasoline) to hurl his final offensive effort against the Western Powers on December 16, 1944. This futile effort stopped the Western attack on Germany for two months, but opened the east to annihilating Soviet blows which began on January 12, 1945.

The Western ground attack on Germany was not resumed after the Battle of the Bulge until February 8, 1945. Two months later a pincers was extending eastward, north and south of the Ruhr. On April 1st this closed to complete the encirclement of the great industrial area; seventeen days later Field Marshall Walter Model surrendered his 325,000 Germans and at once killed himself. Ten days later again, the German-Italian forces in Italy, trapped in Lombardy between Army Group C and impassable swamps, sea, and rivers, began to surrender a force about three times as large. On April 28th, Mussolini, on his way to the Swiss frontier with extensive treasure, was captured and killed by Italian guerrillas; his body was taken back to Milan, scene of his earliest triumphs, to hang by the heels in a public square alongside that of his mistress, Clara Petacci.

The long-drawn Italian campaign, which had served its purpose by tying down dozens of German divisions in the peninsula, ended with a total of 536,000 German and 312,000 Allied casualties.

Meanwhile, General Eisenhower, following the victory in the Ruhr, ignored Berlin to the northeast and drove directly eastward toward Dresden. He was unduly disturbed by rumors that the Germans had prepared a final defensive "redoubt" in southeastern Germany. Churchill and others, for political bargaining purposes, wanted the American advance redirected to Berlin, but the Joint Chiefs of Staff in Washington refused to interfere with Eisenhower's decisions in the field. These decisions, based on military considerations only, and ignoring political factors, permitted the Soviet forces to "liberate" all of the capital cities of central Europe. Budapest fell to the Russians on February 13th, followed by Vienna on April 13th. On April 25th Russian forces encircled Berlin and made contact with American troops seventy miles to the south, at Torgau on the Elbe. The previous day, Eisenhower, advancing on Prague, had been warned by the Soviet General Staff that Russian forces would occupy the Moldau Valley (which included the Czech capital). As late as May 4th, when the American forces were sixty miles from Prague and the Soviet armies more than a hundred miles from the city, an effort by the former to advance to the city was stopped at the request of the Soviet commander, despite a last vain message from Churchill to Eisenhower to take the Czech capital for political bargaining purposes.

In the meantime, the Russian troops, screaming, looting, and raping, were smashing into Berlin. On April 20th, following Hitler's fifty-sixth birthday celebration, which most of the Nazi Party and military leaders attended, the Führer refused to leave the doomed city. Most of the rest escaped that night through the last narrow corridor to central Germany. For another nine days Hitler continued to telephone orders from his bunker in the garden of the new Chancellery building, but few paid any attention to these. His former lieutenants were scattered throughout central Germany, intriguing to take over as Leader or planning to vanish from sight. Only Goebbels, with his wife and six young children, and Hitler's mistress, Eva Braun, planned to remain to the end. The Führer experienced a complete mental breakdown on April 22nd. A week later only a few subordinates remained to carry out his last wishes. With Russian shells falling all about the Chancellery, he married Eva Braun, ordered Göring and Himmler arrested for treachery, and drew up a "Political Testament" which blamed the war and all Germany's misfortunes on the Jews, and told the nation, "The aim must still be to win territory in the East for the German people." On the afternoon of April 30, 1945, with the Russian soldiers only a block away, Eva Braun took poison and Hitler shot himself through the mouth. Subordinates, in accord with their instructions, flooded the bodies with gasoline and burned them in a Russian shellhole in the Chancellery garden.

At Hitler's death, leadership of the wreckage of Germany was bequeathed to Admiral Karl Doenitz. His efforts to surrender to the Western Powers while continuing the war against the Soviet Union were rebuffed on May 4th, and three days later all German forces were surrendered unconditionally to all the victor Powers. The latter's armies continued to advance, overrunning concentration and prison camps with the ovens still hot, finding thousands of bodies of murdered inmates stacked up like cordwood, with other thousands, staggering out, like walking skeletons in filthy rags, to meet the incredulous gaze of well-fed, softhearted American youths.

Soon the names Buchenwald, Dachau, and Belsen were being repeated with horror throughout the world. At Belsen 35,000 dead bodies and 30,000 still breathing were found. The world was surprised and shocked. There was no excuse for the surprise, for Hitler's aims and these methods, including the genocide of any peoples or groups his twisted mind condemned, had been common knowledge among students of Nazism long before 1939 and had been explicitly advocated in *Mein Kampf*, a book which sold 227,000 copies before Hitler came to power and over a million copies in 1933, his first year as chancellor. That Hitler's government in practice was making every effort to carry out all the vile purposes which it embraced in theory had been made explicitly clear to all informed persons by 1939, most notably, perhaps, in *The Revolution of Nihilism* by Hermann Rauschning, former Nazi leader in Danzig, or in *The Brown Book of the Hitler Terror*, based on evidence from refugees, and published in 1933. There was no excuse for the world's press to be surprised at Nazi bestiality in 1945, since the evidence had been fully available in 1938. By V-E Day, May 8, 1945, this bestiality had brought death to more than 30,000,000 human beings as sacrifices to mystic Germanic tribalism.

Closing in on Japan, 1943-1945

When Germany surrendered on May 8, 1945, Japan was already defeated, but could not make itself accept unconditional surrender and was trying to stave off that inevitable end by suicide tactics. In the thirty-five months from the Battle of Midway to the German surrender, the Japanese Navy and merchant marine had been swept from the western Pacific and largely destroyed in the process, cutting the home islands off from vital overseas supplies and leaving millions of their armed forces isolated in southeast Asia, China, New Guinea, the Phillippines, and other island pockets.

The war against Germany and the war against Japan were separate wars, although involving the same victorious nations. Weapons, strategy, and tactics were quite different, chiefly because one was a war of air and land, while the other was a struggle of naval and air forces over an immense ocean. Even American strategic bombing was different in the Pacific, using B-29's, unknown in Europe, for area bombing of civilians in cities, something we disapproved in Europe. The great weapons against Japan were the aircraft carriers, which relentlessly prowled the ocean and provided the necessary protection for amphibious assaults on the island steppingstones which led to Japan. The total destruction of the Japanese Navy and Air Force were almost incidental to this process of protecting landing forces of marines and army units.

Even where the same weapons were used in the European and Pacific struggles, the outcomes were different. In the former, the German submarines were hunted down and destroyed, while in the Pacific, American submarines made a great contribution to victory by the almost total annihilation of the Japanese merchant fleet. Japan's minimal need for merchant shipping to keep its civilian population from starvation was about 2 million tons. It had started the war with 6 million tons, added 3.5 million tons during the war from building and capture of foreign vessels, but had 8.2 million tons sunk during the war and finally surrendered with only 231 vessels of 860,936 tons still able to operate. Of the loss, 5.1 million tons were sunk by submarines, 2.3 million by aircraft, and 0.3 million by mines. By the spring of 1945 Japanese merchant shipping was already below its minimum civilian-survival level.

Immediately after Midway, the vital issue for the United States became the need to stop the Japanese advance against Australia in the southwestern Pacific. At that time the southern edge of the Japanese defense perimeter ran east and west through New Guinea just north of Australia. Its advanced base was Rabaul on New Britain Island, taken from Australia in January 1942. This base, a magnificent but remote harbor 3,000 miles from Tokyo, was linked to the Japanese capital by two fortified bases which had been constructed illegally in the Japanese Mandated Islands. About 800 miles north of Rabaul was Truk in the Caroline Islands, and almost 700 miles north of Truk was Saipan, in the Marianas Islands. From Saipan, later a B-29 base for bombing Tokyo, it was almost 1,600 miles to the Japanese capital. Just before Midway the Japanese extended their threat 600 miles farther south from Rabaul, southwest to New Guinea (thus threatening Australia) and southeast to Guadalcanal, the southernmost of the Solomon Islands (2,375 miles north of Wellington, New Zealand).

The American counterattack to this Japanese southward push took the form of two parallel thrusts northward, passing to the east and west of Rabaul and Truk. The western thrust, under General MacArthur, aimed to reconquer New Guinea and move northward through the Admiralty

Islands and the Philippines to the China Sea. The eastern American thrust, under naval control, sought to go northward through the Solomon Islands, then bypass Rabaul and Truk far to the east through the Marshall Islands, returning to the Tokyo road by attacking the Marianas from the Marshall Islands (700 miles east of Truk). This double movement is usually referred to as a "ladder" in which alternative advances on either side by the Americans led to Japanese counterattacks from Rabaul and Truk between the two legs.

At first much of the fighting was piecemeal, with inadequate supplies for both sides, but American supplies continued to come, while Japanese support was much more intermittent. This eventually became the story of the Pacific war, as American supplies, delivered from 6,000 or more miles away, buried the Japanese beneath water and earth. This struggle northward from Australia and New Zealand was to have been accompanied by a third thrust, under General Joseph W. Stilwell and Lord Louis Mountbatten from India, across Burma, to reestablish connections with southwestern China. For some time it was expected that MacArthur and Stilwell, converging on China from the Philippines and Burma, would establish a mainland base from which the final assault on Japan could be made. The Burma Campaign, held up by the difficulties of the terrain and constant diversion of men and supplies to other theaters, did not reach China, over the hand-built Burma Road, until February 1945. MacArthur was held up for two years (1942-1944) in the New Guinea area. Thus we must focus our attention on the eastern drive from New Zealand northward through the Solomons.

This eastern drive began on August 7, 1942, when Guadalcanal was invaded by naval and marine forces from Wellington, New Zealand, 2,375 miles farther south. By February 8, 1943, after six months of horrible jungle combat, often without either air or sea support, the Solomons were conquered. Six drawn naval battles during the struggle greatly weakened the enemy surface forces, while his air forces were crippled. In the same period, Japanese advance bases were expelled from the Aleutian Islands, and at least 135,000 enemy ground forces were left isolated in New Guinea and Rabaul.

By the autumn of 1943, the Allied forces had reached the great barrier of the Japanese Mandated Islands in the central Pacific. These were passed in a series of amphibious operations called "island hopping." The first of these, Tarawa, in the Gilbert archipelago, was a small operation in comparison with subsequent "landings," but its name still brings horror to those who remember it. In four days 3,100 marines were torn to pieces (a third fatally) to capture a small coral island defended by 2,700 Japanese with 2,000 civilian laborers. The fanaticism of the Japanese was a revelation, and may be measured by the fact that 4,500 were killed. We learned a great deal about amphibious warfare at Tarawa, especially the need for thorough preliminary naval bombardment and for detailed knowledge and planning in regard to tides, winds, reefs, and local fire support.

In February 1943, this experience was applied at Kwajalein, the world's largest atoll, 560 miles north of Tarawa, and at Eniwetok, 340 miles west of Kwajalein, in the Marshall Islands. In these landings Americans had their first large-scale experience of the irrationalities of fighting Japanese. Officers of the Mikado attacked tanks with ornamental swords, while privates sometimes killed themselves when they had Americans at their mercy. But usually they fought skillfully and tenaciously until the outcome was hopeless, when they made suicidal "Banzai!" charges. These two landings cost 695 American dead to kill 11,556 Japanese. During these operations Admiral Raymond Spruance led a carrier task force in a strike on Truk which destroyed over 200 Japanese planes and a dozen naval vessels at a cost of 17 American aircraft.

In the course of 1943 the American advance up the right leg of the Pacific "ladder" to Tokyo got so far ahead of schedule that several projected landings were eliminated, all future landings were advanced in date by a couple of months, and the whole weight of the advance was shifted from its original project of a final assault on Japan from Formosa or the Asiatic mainland to an undated and unspecified amphibious attack from Pacific bases. This left three major problems: (1) the need for an island close enough to Japan for preliminary bombardment by land-based planes; (2) the possibility of very large American casualties when the Japanese invasion came off (possibly in 1946); and (3) what could be done about the millions of Japanese ground forces in northern China and in Manchuria. The last two of these problems led to efforts to obtain Soviet intervention in the war against Japan; they meant, almost certainly, that considerable concessions must be made to the Russians in the Far East and that the final assault on Japan must be left until several months after the final defeat of Germany, to allow Soviet forces to be shifted from Europe to the Far East. In the meantime, the need for an air base for land-based bombers within range of Japan resulted in the conquest of the Marianas Islands.

The Marianas were 700 miles north of Truk, over 1,000 miles northwest of Eniwetok, and almost 1,600 miles from Tokyo. The conquest of Saipan in the middle of this archipelago in June and July 1944 was the second great amphibious landing that summer, two marine divisions, under Lieutenant General Holland M. Smith, hitting the beach at Saipan on June 15th, only nine days after D-Day in Normandy. The Japanese had 29,000 men on Saipan, 7,000 on Tinian, and 18,000 on Guam. All three were eliminated by the end of July. Japanese resistance was so intense on Saipan that an American Army division, held in reserve at sea for the other islands, had to be thrown ashore at Saipan on the second day. That island was conquered by July 9th, with 27,000 of the Japanese garrison of

32,000 killed to 3,400 Americans dead and 13,000 wounded. Over 24,000 Japanese and 2,214 Americans were killed on the other two islands.

Efforts by the Japanese fleet to disrupt the Marianas attack led to the Battle of the Philippine Sea (June 19-20, 1944). This was another "naval" battle in which no surface vessels fired upon, or even saw, each other, since it was fought entirely in the air and under the surface. On the opening day the Japanese lost 402 planes, while destroying 26 American planes, and two of their carriers were sunk by American submarines. As the Japanese fleet, denuded of air protection, fled westward, Spruance's planes pursued and sank a carrier and several lesser vessels at a cost of 20 planes. This engagement shattered the Japanese naval air support and left the Philippines open to American assault.

In September 1944, another amphibious attack landed in the Palau group of the western Caroline Islands, 1,175 miles directly west of Truk and only 610 miles directly east of Mindanao, the large southern island of the Philippines. Feverish haste was made to conquer this group and to prepare Ulithi Atoll, the best harbor in the area, as a base for American surface vessels, since the invasion of Leyte in the Philippines had been moved up from December 20th to October 20th, only four weeks after the occupation of Ulithi on September 23rd. The invasion forces of two divisions had left Hawaii on September 15th with their original destination at Yap, just south of Ulithi, but were diverted to rendezvous with two divisions from MacArthur at sea, 450 miles east of Leyte. In the meantime, in the first half of 1944, the Japanese fleet shifted from the Inland Sea of Japan to Lingga Roads, off Singapore, in order to be closer to a supply of fuel oil; and the Japanese Army on the mainland of China drove southward from Hankow to Hanoi (Indochina), cutting Chiang Kai-shek off from all eastern China and overrunning the American strategic bombing bases in the area.

On July 27th President Roosevelt, Admiral Chester Nimitz, and General MacArthur, meeting at Pearl Harbor, decided to speed up the assault on Japan, to recapture the Philippines without awaiting the defeat of Germany, and to force Japan "to accept our terms of surrender by the use of sea and air power without an invasion of the Japanese homeland." On September 13th Admiral William F. Halsey suggested cancellation of four projected intermediate landings and use of these troops for the immediate seizure of Leyte. The suggestion, conveyed to Roosevelt and Churchill at the Second Quebec ("Octagon") Conference, was approved and ordered within ninety minutes (September 15, 1944). The Palau landing began the same day.

Both the time and place of the American landing at Leyte were anticipated in Tokyo, but the Japanese were unable to reinforce the single division on the spot. To cover the landing Admiral Halsey led the Third Fleet of 9 fleet carriers, 8 escort carriers, 6 battleships, 14 cruisers, and 58 destroyers to pound the Ryukyu Islands, Formosa, and Luzon (October 10-17, 1944). With over 1,000 American planes in the air at a time, this force destroyed 915 enemy planes and hundreds of naval vessels. Since Japanese naval planes had been critically reduced in the Battle of the Philippine Sea and since most of these destroyed in Halsey's sweep were land-based, the Japanese were critically short of trained pilots after October 17th, and began to adopt *kamikaze* (suicide) tactics. In these tactics half-trained pilots dived their planes, loaded with bombs, onto the decks of American ships. These new tactics inflicted severe losses on the Americans in the next few months.

In the week of October 17-24, Halsey's Third Fleet was back off Leyte to cover the invasion force of 732 ships. In five days 132,400 men and 200,000 tons of supplies were landed against only moderate opposition. To destroy this landing the Japanese gave orders which resulted in the Battle of Leyte, the largest naval conflict in history.

The eastern shore of the Philippines may be regarded as two very large islands, Luzon on the north and Mindanao to the south, separated by a cluster of smaller islands (the Visayas) which include almost contiguous Samar and Leyte on the eastern shore. Between Luzon and Samar was San Bernardino Strait, while, farther south, Leyte and Mindanao are separated by Surigao Strait. The Japanese plan was to send a small force as bait from Japan to entice Halsey's Third Fleet northeast from Luzon, while three other Japanese forces (one from Japan and two from Sinpapore) would secretly approach from the west, with the Center Force under Admiral Takao Kurita passing through San Bernardino Strait, and the Southern Force under Admirals Kiyohide Shima and Shoji Nishimura passing through Surigao Strait to converge on Admiral Frederick C. Sherman's Seventh Fleet to destroy both it and the Leyte beachhead before Halsey could return from his northern pursuit of Admiral Jisaburo Ozawa's sacrificial "bait."

These plans, requiring precise timing and ruthless execution, failed only because the quality of American fighting men was so superior to that of Japanese admirals that it overcame Japanese superiority in guns and ships in actual combat. The resulting Battle of Leyte ended the Japanese Navy as an effective fighting force. On one side were 216 American and 2 Australian ships, with 143,668 men, plus many auxiliary vessels, while the enemy had 64 major ships manned by 42,800 Japanese.

The Japanese Northern Force was made up of 2 heavy, 1 large, and 3 small carriers, which could no longer be used as carriers because of lack of naval aviators. These 6 vessels, escorted by 3 light cruisers and 8 destroyers, sailed down from Japan to entice "Bull" Halsey's Third Fleet, with almost all the American heavy striking power, northward away from the Leyte landing. Unexpectedly it escaped observation until October 24th, a day later than expected, and had to sail in circles waiting for Halsey to come north.

In the meantime, Kurita's Center Force, which hoped to remain undetected, had been intercepted by American submarines, and reported. This Japanese force, headed for San Bernardino Strait, had 7 battleships (including the two largest in the world of 68,000 tons, with 18.1-inch guns), 11 heavy cruisers, 2 light cruisers, and 19 destroyers. All these major vessels were faster and heavier than comparable American ships but had little air cover, poor fire control, and inferior morale. On October 23rd the American submarines *Darter* and *Dace* torpedoed three of Kurita's heavy cruisers, sinking two (including Kurita's flagship). While Kurita was being rescued from the water and dried out, Halsey, warned by *Darter*, sent an air strike over the top of the Philippines and sank the 68,000-ton battleship *Musashi* with 19 torpedoes and 17 bomb hits, and also knocked out a heavy cruiser. Hours earlier, Japanese land planes from Luzon made a strike at Halsey and were mostly destroyed, but a single bomb, exploding in the carrier *Princeton*'s bakery, set a fire which ignited its torpedoes and aviation gasoline and blew it apart, inflicting heavy casualties on the cruiser *Birmingham* which had come to the rescue. When Halsey's planes, returning from west of the Philippines, gave exaggerated reports on the damage to Kurita and announced that he had turned westward, Halsey took off with 65 ships (including all his heavy vessels) northward to where Ozawa's "bait" of 17 ships was patiently circling. Kurita, seven hours behind schedule, resumed his course to San Bernardino Strait and Leyte Gulf.

In the meantime, two other Japanese forces were converging on Surigao Strait, far to the south. Together they had 2 battleships, 3 heavy cruisers, a light cruiser, and 8 destroyers. Their approach was reported to the American Seventh Fleet off Leyte. This moved southward to meet the threat at Surigao Strait, assuming that Halsey would continue to cover San Bernardino Strait. The intercepting force of Admiral Thomas Kinkaid's Seventh Fleet had 6 battleships, 4 heavy cruisers, 4 light cruisers, and 28 destroyers.

As the Japanese Southern Force plowed through Surigao Strait in the long, dark night of October 24-25, it was attacked by 30 PT boats; these were dispersed after great confusion. Then came more than 100 torpedoes from American destroyers, scoring 9 hits, which sank 3 Japanese destroyers and a battleship. Gunfire from the American heavy ships then sank most of the Southern Force; damaged vessels were pursued by air and submarine, until, by November 5th, only one cruiser and 5 destroyers of the whole force were still afloat.

As the Seventh Feet disengaged from the remnants of the Southern Force at 5:00 A.M. on October 25th, the main Japanese force, under Kurita, 175 miles to the north, had emerged from San Bernardino Strait and was bearing down on Leyte, which was protected by a flotilla of 6 escort carriers with a screen of 7 destroyers under Rear Admiral Clifton Sprague. These small vessels were off Samar Island with about 25 planes each and were backed by two similar flotillas farther south. Surprise was complete on both sides, at 6:47 A.M., when a patrol plane discovered Kurita's presence. The news had hardly registered, when the Japanese big guns opened fire. Fortunately, Kurita was completely disconcerted by the encounter, and believed he had run into Halsey's fleet.

Sprague, under cover of smokescreens and rain squalls, tried to escape the heavy Japanese gunfire, while holding the enemy out of Leyte Gulf by vigorous air strikes from his "baby flat-tops" and torpedo attacks from his destroyers. The Japanese shells, of 5- to 16-inch caliber, were all armor-piercing and went through the thin plates of Sprague's vessels without exploding; but, with up to forty holes each, these ships were soon leaking freely. They attacked so vigorously, however, using their 5-inch guns when all torpedoes were gone, that Kurita's fleet was scattered, and he decided to withdraw to regroup his forces. He had sunk two American destroyers, an escort carrier, and a destroyer escort, but lost three heavy cruisers in return. By this time (9:15 A.M.) air attacks were beginning to come in from all over the Philippines, and Kurita had received news that only one destroyer had survived the Southern Force's defeat at Surigao. He began to withdraw through San Bernardino Strait. Sprague's escort carriers were much cut up, and still under heavy pounding from the earliest kamikaze attacks. These sank St. Lô, an escort carrier, about 11:30.

At 8:45 A.M. urgent appeals to Admiral Halsey had detached a force of five fast carriers with escort vessels to pursue Kurita. Two hours later, while still 335 miles away, these launched a series of air strikes, 147 planes in all, of which 14 were lost without significant damage to the Japanese. The following day strikes of 257 planes sank another of Kurita's cruisers.

During this same eventful October 25th, Admiral Ozawa's Northern Force, the "bait," had been swallowed. In five air attacks, totaling 527 planes, Halsey's carriers, commanded by Admiral Mitscher, sank four Japanese carriers and a destroyer. Among these was the last of the six carriers which had attacked Pearl Harbor in 1941.

The Battle of Leyte, strategically ill-advised from the Japanese point of view, ended its navy as a significant force in the Pacific. From that date, the American advance was held up chiefly by suicide tactics (the kamikaze attacks). Leyte is of great historical significance as the last naval battle in which battleships participated and played a role, admittedly minor. The Third Fleet's Battle Line of six great ships did not even fire its heavy guns.

While General MacArthur and the army were clearing up the Philippines, capturing Manila after fierce house-to-house combat on March 14, 1945, the navy and air arms pressed on toward Japan. By October 1, 1944, two intermediate targets had been set: one was to capture Iwo

Jima in the Bonin Islands, about halfway from Saipan to Tokyo, to be used as an emergency landing area and fighter-plane base for the B-29's attacking Tokyo from Saipan. The other was to capture Okinawa and other islands in the Ryukyus as bases for land forces to invade Japan itself.

Iwo Jima was invaded on February 19th and secured by March 26th. Bitter fighting which involved flushing Japanese, one by one, out of caves yielded 20,703 Japanese killed and only 216 prisoners by March 26th; 2,469 more (of which a third were killed) were disposed of in the next two months. The Americans lost about 5,000 killed, but three divisions suffered over two-thirds casualties in the struggle to capture this island of 4.5 by 2.5 miles. The dead on both sides thus amounted to 2,400 per square mile.

Iwo will always be remembered for the famous raising of the American flag on the top of 550-foot Mount Suribachi at the southern tip of the island on February 23rd, while fighting was still severe. On April 7th the value of the island was shown when, for the first time, B-29's returning from Tokyo jolted down onto Iwo for relief; fifty-four landed that day. These big planes, flying the round trip from Saipan to Tokyo in about seven hours, were already engaged in the systematic destruction of all Japanese cities. The flimsy houses of these crowded urban areas made them very vulnerable to incendiary bombs, but the distance was so great that only moderate-sized bomb loads could be carried. On March 9, 1945, the Air Force tried a daring experiment. The defensive armament was removed from 279 B-29's, releasing weight for additional incendiaries, and these planes, without guns but carrying 1,900 tons of fire bombs, were sent on a low-level attack on Tokyo. The result was the most devastating air attack in all history. With a loss of only 3 planes, 16 square miles of central Tokyo were burned out; 250,000 houses were destroyed, over a million persons were made homeless and 84,793 were killed. This was more destructive than the first atomic bomb over Hiroshima five months later.

The conquest of Okinawa was a much bigger task than Iwo Jima; 760 miles west of Iwo, it was only 360 miles from the Chinese mainland, and almost the same distance from both Formosa and Japan. It was 830 miles southwest of Tokyo Bay, a full 900 miles north of Leyte, and over 1,200 from the United States Navy's refuge in Ulithi Atoll. The size of the island, almost 500 square miles, made it a possible staging area for an invasion of Japan.

The magnitude of the assault on heavily populated Okinawa is almost beyond belief. The fighting navy of 110 combat vessels with over 100 supply ships protected an amphibious attack of 1,213 vessels carrying 182,113 assault troops. The preliminary bombardment by naval guns fired 40,412 rounds in 16- to 5-inch calibers. The assault, on a perfect

Easter morning, April 1, 1945, hit the coral reef, with four divisions on a front five miles wide. The size of the whole operation may be judged from the fact that the supply tankers in eight weeks (to May 27th) delivered 8¾ million barrels of fuel oil and 21½ million gallons of aviation gasoline; in five of these weeks the same tankers delivered over 24 million letters to men engaged in the attack.

The Okinawa campaign was the most severe of the Pacific War. It required three months of intense combat to secure the island against the 77,000 Japanese defenders, most of whom had to be killed or committed suicide. The invasion force had 40,000 casualties, of which almost one-fifth were killed. The naval and air support suffered intensely from 1,900 kamikaze attacks which sank 30 and damaged 368 naval vessels, with the loss of 763 fleet aircraft, and with 10,000 naval casualties (of which half were killed).

The degree and kind of resistance from the Japanese at Okinawa raised grave questions regarding the final defeat of Japan. By May 1945, a major part of the Japanese population was completely disillusioned with the war and eager to find a way out of it. These sentiments were shared by most of the civilian leaders and by a good portion of the naval leaders. Some of the army, however, still believed that they could make the costs of an American invasion of Japan too high to be acceptable to American opinion. Somewhat similar ideas occurred to some of the American leaders. These Japanese fanatics believed that they could get a major part of Japan's fighter-plane construction dispersed and placed underground by mid-September 1945. If these facilities were used to build cheap, uninstrumented kamikaze planes manned by untrained suicide volunteers (who were available in large numbers) and supplemented by human torpedoes, it might be possible to inflict unbearable losses on any American invasion of Japan itself.

As part of this project the Japanese had perfected a manned glider bomb, called *Baka* (foolish) by the Americans, which carried a man and 2,645 pounds of trinitroanisol in a 20-foot fuselage with 16.5-foot wing-span. Without any engine, but carrying three thrust rockets, this weapon was dropped from a conventional plane and came in on its target at over 600 miles per hour. Even with air cover and using proximity fuses, American ship defenses could be "saturated" and exhausted if enough of these came in over sufficiently extended periods. Several incidents in the Okinawa campaign raised fears of this nature. On April 16th the destroyer *Laffey* sustained 22 attacks in 80 minutes and destroyed all of them, but 6 kamikazes hit the ship, knocking it out. On May 11th, the picket ship *Hadley* was attacked by 10 planes simultaneously; all were destroyed but the vessel was hit by a *Baka*, a kamikaze, and a bomb, and was knocked out.

Neither of these ships was sunk, but casualties were so heavy that

American leaders shuddered to think of the results if such attacks were hurled at troop transports coming in on amphibious attack. In June 1945, American estimates of their casualties in such an attack were over half a million. It is true that Japan could have offered such resistance, for at mid-August 1945, when 2,550 kamikaze planes had been expended, the Japanese still had 5,350 left, with adequate pilots ready, and had about 5,000 planes for orthodox bombing attacks, plus about 7,000 more in storage or under repair. These, with bombs and gasoline, were being saved for the American invasion. These considerations form the background to the Yalta and Potsdam conferences and the decision to use the atom bomb on Japan.

The conference of Roosevelt, Churchill, and Stalin held at Yalta, in the Crimea, on February 4-12, 1945, sought to reach agreement on most of the issues of the war and of the immediate postwar period. The nature of this conference and its decisions has been so much distorted by partisan propaganda in recent years that it is difficult for any historian today to reconstruct the situation as it seemed at the time. In general, the conference seems to have been cordial, cooperative, and optimistic, and it is incorrect to project subsequent animosities and conflicts backward into the conference itself. As the discussions proceeded, the victorious armies were pressing forward rapidly into Germany in the Soviet offensive which began on January 12, 1945, and Eisenhower's attack which had begun on February 8, 1945. Victory could clearly be foreseen in the European war, but in the Far East the future was much more clouded.

In Europe the attitude of mutual trust seems to have been high, probably higher than the actual relationships of the three Powers justified, but this was so prevalent that no efforts were made to establish limits of demarcation for the advancing armies within Germany. There was rapid agreement on joint postwar administration of Germany, with a four-Power control commission (to include France) and three separate zones of military occupation (any zone for France to be taken out of the area assigned to the Western Powers). Berlin, outside any zone, was to be governed jointly by a *Kommandatura* of commandants assigned by the respective zone commanders in chief. Access to Berlin, as a military question and on the advice of the United States War Department, was left to subsequent military arrangements with "freedom of transit" as the guiding principle.

Differences regarding the rules of the United Nations Organization were settled with surprising ease. Stalin accepted Roosevelt's suggestion that the members of the Security Council be unable to veto discussion of disputes involving themselves within the Council, and the Anglo-Americans, in turn, accepted the Soviet demand for extra seats in the Assembly by offering them two, for the Ukraine and White Russia.

The crucial problem of Poland was subject to agreements which gave the Russians much of what they wanted. The Curzon Line of 1919 was accepted as its eastern frontier, but the western border was left indefinite, since Stalin would have placed it farther to the west (involving deportation of additional millions of German residents) than either Roosevelt or Churchill considered acceptable. It was no longer possible to find a government for Poland by fusion of the London group with the Communist-dominated Lublin Committee, since the former, after the resignation of Mikolájczyk, had become openly anti-Soviet and the latter, on December 31, 1944, had been recognized by Moscow as the government of Poland. Compromise was reached by agreement to expand the Lublin group by the addition of "democratic leaders from Poland abroad" and that this expanded government would be recognized when it had been "pledged to the holding of free and unfettered elections as soon as possible on the basis of universal suffrage and secret ballot." No form of supervision of these elections, even by their ambassadors, could be obtained by the English-speaking countries.

Much of the Yalta Conference was concerned with the Far East. It would be a mistake to regard these discussions as revolving about payments to Soviet Russia in the Far East in return for its intervention in the war with Japan. All three Powers were agreed that Japanese imperialist gains at the expense of Russia and China since 1854 should be undone, and Stalin was as ready to enter the war against Japan after the defeat of Germany as Roosevelt was eager to have Russia do so. The talk was concerned rather with the terms and details of both of these actions.

The First Cairo Conference of Roosevelt, Churchill, and Chiang Kai-shek on December 1, 1943 had agreed to a "Declaration" which promised that "Japan will be expelled from all territories which she has taken by violence and greed." At Yalta this declaration was extended and specified. It was agreed to undo the results of the Russo-Japanese War of 1904 as follows:

Southern Sakhalin would be granted to the Soviet Union along with a lease on the Port Arthur naval base and a dominant position in the "internationalized" port of Dairen; the Chinese Eastern Railroad and the South Manchurian Railroad which serves Dairen would be operated jointly by a Soviet-Chinese company in which Soviet interests would be dominant, although full sovereignty over Manchuria would be retained by China. In addition the Kurile Islands would be ceded to the Soviet Union; and Outer Mongolia, which had been free of Chinese power for decades, would be granted autonomy permanently.

These agreements, drawn up in a formal document at Yalta and specified as the price of Soviet intervention in the war on Japan, were kept secret, although it was agreed that they should be conveyed to Chiang

Kai-shek. This could not be done much before the Soviet intervention in the war, because security was so poor in Chungking that there were no secrets from the Japanese there; accordingly, the Chinese were not informed of the secret Yalta agreements until President Truman told the Chinese prime minister and foreign minister, T. V. Soong, about June 10, 1945.

During this period, the Great Powers were thoroughly disillusioned with China. A generation of almost constant warfare under a government lacking in energy or principles had brought the whole organization to the verge of dissolution. Trade had reached a point of semicollapse; inflation was rampant; capital of the most fundamental kinds, such as farm tools, roads, and communications, was worn out; 90 percent of the railroads were out of operation; and the chief concern of almost all Chinese was survival. The existing political divisions offered little hope of remedying any of China's ills even after Japan had been defeated. The dominant Kuomintang Party was shot through with corruption and complacency and seemed to have few concerns except remaining in office. Its chief aim seemed to be to maintain its armed blockade of the Communist forces operating out of Yenan in northwestern China. There the highly disciplined Communist armies had taken over the area and appeared to have gained some degree of local support.

American hopes of fusing the two parties into a common and energetic Chinese government, however, broke down on the refusals of the Kuomintang and the remoteness of the Communists. The Russians seemed to have little interest in these matters, and Stalin made it clear, in his conversations with his Western colleagues, that he had little concern with the situation beyond his rigid determination to secure the specific and strictly limited goals established by his vision of Russian national interests. He had little sympathy for the Chinese Communists or for the Chinese in general, regarded Chiang Kai-shek as the best of a poor lot, and seemed fully prepared to allow the United States to try its own independent hand in working out any agreements it wished in respect to the governing of China.

As became clear even in 1944, however, the United States was not going to get its wishes in China even when it could decide what those wishes were. As early as September 1944, Roosevelt was so completely disillusioned with the Chinese war effort, especially with Chiang's lack of energy in fighting the Japanese, that he suggested that General Stilwell should be given command of all Chinese forces. This demand, sent to Chiang on September 16th, was answered within ten days by a blunt demand from Chiang that Stilwell be removed from China.

These circumstances made it inevitable at the time that American leaders, especially the military, should welcome possible intervention of Soviet forces against Japan on the mainland of Asia and should doubly welcome the addition of the first atomic bombs to their arsenal of weapons.

The making of the first atomic bombs is surely the most amazing story of World War II. It is a long, complex, and technical study which most historians would like to omit, but it is not possible to understand the history of the mid-twentieth century without some understanding of how this almost unbelievable weapon was achieved and especially why the Western Powers were able to achieve it and the Fascist Powers were not. The gist of this story will be told in the next chapter. Here we need only record that the United States obtained its first three atom bombs over a three-week period from July 15 to August 10, 1945.

The theory on which the nuclear explosions were based was known to the scientists of all countries before April 1939, and the direction in which practical efforts to achieve a bomb must go were established and equally known before worldwide secrecy descended a year later, in April 1940, just before the fall of France. Scientific ignorance, however, was so universal among political and military leaders throughout the world that the use of the existing scientific knowledge would not have been achieved anywhere but for two factors: (1) many of the world's greatest nuclear scientists had fled as refugees from Fascism to England and the United States, and (2) Franklin Roosevelt was quite willing to listen to unconventional suggestions if his attention could be obtained.

In the years 1939–1941 the refugee scientists in the United States were so fearful that Hitler would obtain the atomic bomb that they were able to prevail upon the best known among them, Einstein, to allow his name to be used to catch Roosevelt's attention. Once this had been done, the urging of these same scientists and the growing urgency of the war itself made it possible for the administrative talents of American scientists to utilize the enormous resources made available to them to reach the goal they sought. After September 1942, Brigadier General Leslie R. Groves, U.S.A., was in charge of the whole project and, in an atmosphere of fanatical secrecy, brought it to a successful conclusion with an expenditure of about $2 billion and the work of about 150,000 persons.

In this, as in other matters, the sudden death of President Roosevelt on April 12, 1945 had a great and incalculable effect. Vice-President Truman knew nothing of the atomic-research program until he was told of it by Secretary of War Henry Stimson, briefly on April 12th and at greater length two weeks later. In fact, Truman had been kept so far outside the whole war effort that his first few months as President required an almost superhuman effort of absorbed attention to get the major lines of policy into his hands. To avoid a repetition of this situation in case of his own death, he decided to place James F. Byrnes, perhaps the most widely experienced man in American government, into the office of secretary of state, since at that time the incumbent of this first

Cabinet post was designated as second in line of succession, after the Vice-President, to the Presidency. The new secretary of state, however, had been serving as "Assistant President" largely concerned with domestic questions, and he was almost as unfamiliar with the main problems of foreign policy as Truman himself.

The problems which Truman, Byrnes, and their advisers faced in reestablishing the peace of the world were greatly intensified by the obstructionism of the Soviet government and by the fact that Winston Churchill had set an election in England, the first in ten years, for July 5, 1945, to renew his government's mandate. The result was not clear until July 27, 1945, because of the need to count absentee ballots from soldiers overseas, but these eventually showed a smashing two-to-one victory of the Labour Party over Churchill's Conservatives.

Thus Byrnes became secretary of state only on June 30th. He went with President Truman to the Potsdam Conference, which opened on July 17th and lasted until August 2nd, but on July 28, 1945, Clement Attlee and Ernest Bevin, the new prime minister and foreign secretary of Britain, replaced Churchill and Eden as delegates at Potsdam. The transition was made somewhere easier by the fact that Attlee had been deputy prime minister since 1942 and had been on the British delegation to Potsdam from the opening of the conference. Nevertheless, the fact that Stalin was the sole survivor of the Big Three heads of government who had conferred so often during the war undoubtedly weakened the West in this last, "Terminal," conference.

In general, the American delegation seemed to regard as its chief aims to seek to continue the Big Three cooperation into the postwar world within the structure of the United Nations whose charter had been adopted at San Francisco on June 25th. The American delegation felt that Europe was falling very rapidly into two antithetical parts in which Britain would seek to balance a Soviet-dominated eastern Europe by a British-dominated western Europe. The Americans wished to avoid this and particularly to prevent two possible consequences of this: a revival of Germany by Britain to help serve as a shield against Soviet power in the east and the jeopardizing of western Europe's and the world's economic revival by the splitting of Europe into opposed blocs. As one evidence of this American attitude, we might mention President Truman's refusal to confer separately with Churchill before the main conference at Potsdam and his refusal to allow the State Department and the Foreign Office to make any advance agreement on joint policies.

On July 16th, while Truman was surveying the devastation of Berlin, the atomic scientists were gathered on the desolate open plain of Alamogordo, New Mexico, 125 miles southeast of Albuquerque. There an implosion-type plutonium bomb at the top of a steel tower one hundred feet high was detonated at 5:30 A.M. The result was an explosion beyond all expectations: a burst of blinding light far brighter than the sun expanded into a ball of fire two miles high, which lasted, second after second, as a great mushrooming pillar of radioactive smoke and dust surging upward to a height of almost eight miles. Almost a minute later, as if the door of a hot oven had been opened, the blast reached "base camp," ten miles from the bomb point, with sufficient force to push some people backward. The light was seen 180 miles away by early risers, and the sound, by some freak, split windows at that distance. At the scene, General Thomas F. Farrell said to General Groves, "The war is over," but the scientists, stricken with horror at their success in releasing a force equivalent to 17,500 tons of TNT from about 12 pounds of plutonium, had had a glimpse of hell. In that instant, many of them became politicians, convinced of the social responsibilities of science, especially to avoid war and to direct the unlimited power of science to human welfare. It was soon established that the steel bomb tower had been volatilized, as was a 4-inch iron pipe, 16 feet high, deeply set in concrete 1,500 feet away. Another forty-ton steel tower, 70 feet high and a half-mile away, had been torn to pieces.

The first message of the great event in New Mexico reached Secretary of War Stimson at Potsdam on July 17th. It had only three words: "Babies satisfactorily born." More details followed, and General Groves's detailed account arrived by courier on July 21st. All this information was given to Churchill as it arrived. It was agreed to give the Russians no information, but merely to mention the success of the new bomb as casually as possible to prevent any later accusations of withholding information when the story became public. The prime minister at once saw the significance of the event, but his chief of staff, Field Marshal Lord Alanbrooke, belittled Churchill's excitement, and wrote in his diary:

"He had absorbed all the minor American exaggerations and, as a result, was completely carried away. It was now no longer necessary for the Russians to come into the Japanese war; the new explosive alone was sufficient to settle the matter. Furthermore, we now had something in our hands which would redress the balance with the Russians."

Lord Alanbrooke's ignorance, based on his illiteracy in scientific matters, was shared by almost all military men of all armies in the world and by the overwhelming mass of politicians as well. Among the latter group was Stalin, but fortunately not Truman. The President on July 18th ordered the second bomb to be dropped on Japan as soon as it was ready, and on July 24th he chose the list of possible targets: Hiroshima, Kokura, Nigata, and Nagasaki. Secretary Stimson, moved by the tears of Professor Edwin O. Reischauer and his own memories of the place, persuaded the President to drop from the list Kyoto, a city of temples, shrines, and artistic treasures. These cities were already being spared from B-29 air raids to reserve them for the test of the atom bomb.

On this same day Truman told Stalin of the successful test. There is no doubt that the President, in order to discourage any questions from Stalin, overdid the casualness of his communication. Moreover, he spoke to him aside, using a Russian interpreter whose English was limited. Truman's own account shows that Stalin either did not understand or was ignorant of the fact that an atomic explosion was a significant event. The President wrote:

"I casually mentioned to Stalin that we had a new weapon of unusual destructive force. The Russian Premier showed no special interest. All he said was that he was glad to hear it and hoped we would make good use of it against the Japanese."

It seems likely that Stalin's personal interest in atomic fission in July 1945 was about the same as that of Lord Alanbrooke, although, as we shall see in the next chapter, lesser men in the Soviet system were more aware of the significance of the subject.

The atom bomb thus seems to have played no role at Potsdam. General Marshall and Secretary Stimson, as well as Churchill, realized that Soviet assistance was no longer needed to defeat Japan, but no move was made to avoid such intervention. It is, however, extremely likely that the frantic and otherwise inexplicable haste to use the second and third bombs, twenty-one and twenty-four days after Alamogordo, arose from the desire to force a Japanese surrender before any effective Soviet intervention.

The chief task of Potsdam was to lay the basis for a peace settlement. This was to be worked out, in each case, by a council of foreign ministers of the Big Three, France and China, using general principles agreed on at Potsdam. These principles were vague and were interpreted or violated subsequently so that, on the whole, the Soviet Union achieved what it wished east of the Oder River and Adriatic and north of Greece, while the Western Powers obtained their general desires west and south of these boundaries. As usual, the chief problem was Germany. There the Soviet Union still wanted some kind of partition in order to dominate the fragments, while, in the west, only France, from continued fear of Germany, sought to fragment and weaken that country, while the English-speaking countries wanted as unified an administration as feasible and a level of economic revival sufficient to make American economic aid unnecessary. In addition, the United States was determined to avoid any repetition of the 1920's when German reparations had been paid to the other victors from resources borrowed from the United States.

The chief principles for postwar Germany, as established at Potsdam, were: (1) permanent and total disarmament and dispersal of all military forces; (2) complete de-Nazification of public and private life; (3) nullification of all Nazi discriminatory laws; (4) punishment of individuals guilty of war crimes and atrocities; (5) indefinite postponement of any central German government (and thus of any German peace treaty), but maintenance of a central, national, administrative machine to be used by the Control Council for economic activities of national scope; (6) decentralization and democratization of political life and of the judicial system; (7) a multiparty system with only Nazi groups forbidden; (8) democratization and westernization of German education; (9) establishment of basic Western freedoms of speech, press, religion, and labor-union activities.

On the economic side, it was agreed that Germany should be treated as a single economic unit, with uniform control measures in all zones, aimed at establishing a consumer-oriented economy, under German control, and able to ensure maintenance of occupying forces and refugees, with a standard of living for the Germans themselves no higher than that of non-Russian continental Europe. This somewhat modified version of the Morgenthau scheme (which had sought the complete ruralization of German economic life to an agrarian basis) was modified almost at once by a number of factors.

The first modifying factor was the desire for reparations. The Americans insisted that reparations must be taken, as far as possible, from existing stocks and plants rather than from future production (a complete reversal of the American position of 1919) in order to avoid the error of the 1919–1933 period, the overbuilding of German capital equipment and American financing of German reparation payments into the indefinite future. No total and no division of reparation benefits were set, but it was provided that all reparations come from Germany as a whole and be credited to the victors on a percentage basis. To administer this, to escape from Polish reparation claims, and to get the Russians out of the Italian question (so that that country could become a partner of the Western Powers), Secretary Byrnes worked out a complicated deal.

The central basis for this deal was that Germany had an industrialized west and an agricultural east. The Soviet Union wanted reparations from the industrial plants of the west, while the United States and Britain wanted agricultural products (not reparations) from eastern Germany to feed the western Germans and the millions of German refugees and repatriates who were pouring westward from all Communist-dominated areas of the east and from the lands lost to Poles, Czechs, and others. In simple terms, Byrnes's compromise was that each country take reparations from its own zone, but that Russia would get 40 percent of the heavy war industrial equipment of western Germany for which it would pay for only 25 percent in food, coal, and other basic needs from the east. From this total the Soviet Union would pay the reparation claims of Poland, release Italy from all Russian reparation claims, and agree to the immediate admission of Italy into the United Nations.

One of the critical events of this period was the Soviet refusal to supply food or coal to the areas of Berlin occupied by the democratic Powers. This and the millions of Germans streaming westward to seek refuge beyond the reach of vengeful Russians, Poles, and Czechs played a great role in arousing sympathy for Germans in the west and in establishing a common front of cooperative work and mutual dependence in that area.

On July 26, 1945, Truman, Attlee, and Chiang Kai-shek issued an ambiguous ultimatum to Japan, warning the latter that it must accept immediate unconditional surrender or suffer complete and utter destruction. This was regarded by the three leaders as a threat of atomic holocaust unless Japan laid down its arms, but the atomic threat was unspecified and, to the Japanese, meaningless, while their chief concern, whether "unconditional surrender" meant removal of the emperor, was equally unspecified. The Japanese premier, Admiral Kantaro Suzuki, who had been put into office to find a way out of the war, was caught in a trap. If he made any serious effort to surrender, he could be murdered by the militarists, while his secret efforts had been rebuffed by the West as too vague. To ward off the former, he made a public statement that the Potsdam Declaration was "unworthy of notice."

On July 26th the heavy cruiser *Indianapolis*, topheavy with new antiaircraft and radar equipment and still unequipped with underwater submarine detection devices, unloaded the bomb without its last essential part of Uranium-235 on Tinian. It put to sea at once and, in the night of July 29th, between Guam and Leyte, was practically blown apart by torpedoes from Japanese submarine I-58. In fourteen minutes, with all communications knocked out, the great ship rolled over and dived to the bottom. One-third of her 1,200 men were already dead; the rest were left struggling in the water. Four days passed without anyone in the American armed forces asking a question about the *Indianapolis*. Then an American plane spotted survivors in a large oil patch; 316 were picked up in the next few days. But the bomb was safe on Tinian.

While the I-58 was stalking the *Indianapolis* in the Pacific, the heavy cruiser *Augusta* was in mid-Atlantic, bringing President Truman and his assistants back from Potsdam. From midocean the President sent the signal to Washington and Tinian to drop the bomb on Japan. By August 5th all was ready, and at 2:45 A.M. the following morning the modified B-29 *Enola Gay*, Colonel Paul W. Tibbets, Jr., in command, went roaring down the long Tinian runway on its 7-hour flight to Hiroshima. Only one man aboard, a scientist commissioned as a navy captain, William S. Parsons, knew exactly what the strange new bomb was or why Colonel Tibbets had been given such unorthodox orders regarding bombing technique. These orders were to dive for maximum speed and turn 150 degrees the moment the bomb was released. Parsons directly violated his orders to arm the bomb before it was loaded in the plane, because he had seen several B-29's en route to Japan crash on takeoff, and he realized that an atomic accident might destroy Tinian airfield with its hundreds of million-dollar planes and its tens of thousands of trained men. Just before takeoff, Captain Parsons borrowed a loaded revolver to use on himself if the *Enola Gay* landed in Japanese territory.

Six and a half hours later, 1,700 miles north of Tinian, the *Enola Gay* came in sight of its target. The doomed city lay quiet in flooding early-morning sunshine. At 9:15, precisely on schedule, the giant plane went into its bombing run at 31,600 feet, speed 328 mph. As the bomb was released, the plane twisted violently away to get as far as possible from the blast. Seconds ticked off as the bomb fell almost five miles to 2,000 feet; then the two masses of uranium came together at lightning speed and turned to energy. The fireball expanded outward, enveloping the center of the city, its intense heat and blast driving outward to shatter buildings and ignite the debris. Fifteen miles away, the *Enola Gay* was slapped twice by the concussion. An hour and a half later, from 360 miles away, the crew could look back and still see the mushroom cloud rearing up to 40,000 feet. Under that cloud, at least 40,000 Japanese were killed instantly; an additional 12,000 died in the next few days; and eventually 60,175 perished, with an equal number injured. The city was over half destroyed, with the area of devastation extending out a mile from ground zero.

News of this great disaster was released at once in Washington, but in Japan communications were disrupted, and there was no agreement on what had happened. The emperor sent word to Premier Suzuki to accept the Potsdam Declaration, but the militarists insisted on three conditions: (1) Japan would disarm its own troops, (2) the occupation of Japan would be limited, and (3) war criminals would be tried by Japanese courts. All assumed that the emperor's position was beyond discussion. The stalemate continued, as the Soviet Union declared war on Japan (late on August 8th). The Japanese Supreme War Council remained deadlocked day after day, in spite of a second, plutonium, bomb dropped on Nagasaki with about 100,000 casualties, of which one-third were dead (August 9, 1945).

Early on the morning of August 10th, when the War Council had been in continuous session for sixteen hours, Emperor Hirohito personally ordered it to make peace. A message accepting the Potsdam terms, with reservation of the emperor's position, was sent the same day. This was accepted by an American note which provided that the Supreme Commander of the Allied Powers (SCAP) would issue orders to the emperor and government of Japan. A military coup was attempted in Japan but was suppressed on August 15th. Seven Japanese generals and admirals committed hara-kari. The emperor then, for the first time in history, spoke on the radio, asking his people to accept the peace. Many listeners expected him to ask them to fight to the death. All were stunned, and remained in this strange condition for weeks. They had been so misled by their own propaganda that many had believed they were about to win the war. A cease-fire was issued late on August 16th. On September 2nd the final surrender was signed on the deck of the battleship *Missouri* in the shadow of the great 16-inch guns and under the thirty-one-star flag which Perry had flown at the same anchorage ninety-two years before.

Thus ended six years of world war in which 70 million men had been mobilized and 17 million killed in battle. At least 18 million civilians had been killed. The Soviet Union and Germany had lost most heavily. The former had 6.1 million soldiers killed and 14 million wounded, but lost over 10 million civilian dead. Germany lost 6.6 million servicemen killed or died in service, with 7.2 million wounded and 1.3 million missing. Japan's armed forces had 1.9 million dead. Britain's war dead were 357,000, while America's were 294,000.

All this personal tragedy and material damage of untold billions of dollars was needed to demonstrate to the irrational minds of the Nazis, Fascists, and Japanese militarists that the Western Powers and the Soviet Union were stronger than the three aggressor states and, accordingly, that Germany could not establish a Nazi continental bloc in Europe nor could Japan dominate an East-Asian Co-Prosperity Sphere. This is the chief function of war: to demonstrate as conclusively as possible to mistaken minds that they are mistaken in regard to power relationships. But, as we shall see, in demonstrating these objective facts in order to change mistaken subjective pictures of these facts, war also changes most drastically the objective facts themselves.

XVI

THE NEW AGE

Introduction

Rationalization and Science

The Twentieth-Century Pattern

Introduction

ANY war performs two rather contradictory services for the social context in which it occurs. On the one hand, it changes the minds of men, especially the defeated, about the factual power relationship between the combatants. And, on the other hand, it alters the factual situation itself, so that changes which in peacetime might have occurred over decades are brought about in a few years.

This has been true of all wars, but never has it been truer than in respect to World War II. The age which began in 1945 was a new age from almost every point of view. Looking back, it is now clear that the first generation of the twentieth century, from about 1895 to 1939, was a long period of transition from the nineteenth-century world to a totally different world of the twentieth century. Some of these changes are obvious: a shift from a period of democracy to an age of experts; from a world dominated by Europe, and even by Britain, to a world divided into three great blocs; from a world in which man still lived, as he had for a million years, surrounded by nature, to a situation where nature is dominated, transformed and, in a sense, totally destroyed by man; from a system where man's greatest problems were the material ones of man's helplessness in the face of the natural threats of disease, starvation, and the unpredictability of natural catastrophes to the totally different system of the 1960's and 1970's where the greatest threat to man is man himself, and where his greatest problems are the social (and nonmaterial) ones of what his true goals of existence are and what use he should make of his immense power over the universe, including his fellowmen.

For thousands of years, some men had viewed themselves as creatures a little lower than the angels, or even God, and a little higher than the beasts. Now, in the twentieth century, man has acquired almost divine powers, and it has become increasingly clear that he can no longer regard himself as an animal (as the leading thinkers of the nineteenth century did), but must regard himself as at least a man (if he cannot bring himself to break so completely with his nineteenth-century pred-

831

ecessors as to come to regard himself as obligated to act like an angel or even a god).

The whole trend of the nineteenth century had been to emphasize man's animal nature, and in doing so, to seek to increase his supply of material necessities, his indulgence in creature comforts, his experiences of food, movement, sex, and emotion. This effort had resulted in the sharp curtailment or almost total neglect of the conventions of man's earlier history, conventions which had been, on the whole, based on a conception of man as a dualistic creature in which an eternal spiritual soul was encased, temporarily, in an ephemeral, material body. This older conception had been embodied, in the form in which the nineteenth century challenged it, largely in the seventeenth century, and had been reflected in that earlier period in the widespread influence of Puritanism, of Jansenism, and of other, basically pessimistic, inhibiting, masochistic, and self-disciplining ideologies. The eighteenth century had been a long age of struggle to get free of this older, seventeenth-century outlook, and had been so prolonged largely because those who turned away from the seventeenth century could neither envisage, nor agree upon, the newer ideology they wanted to put in the place of the older one they wished to reject.

This newer ideology was found in the nineteenth century, and may be regarded as one which emphasized man's freedom to indulge his more animal-like aspects: to obtain freedom, for his body, from disease, death, hunger, discomfort, and drudgery. This movement eventually gave us modern surgery and medical science, modern technology, mass production of food and other consumers' goods, central heating, indoor plumbing, domestic lighting, air conditioning, and the plethora of so-called labor-saving devices. The outlook behind these achievements may be symbolized by Charles Darwin, whose writings came to stand for proof of the animal nature of man, and of Sigmund Freud, whose writings were taken to show that sex was the dominant, if not the sole, human motivation and that inhibitions were the great bane of human life. This latter point of view came to be accepted on the most pervasive level of human experience in the attacks on inhibitions and discipline which we call "progressive" education as represented in the outpourings of such semipopular thinkers as Rousseau in the earliest stage of the movement (in *Emile*) or John Dewey in the latest stage.

We who enter the twentieth century must not assume, as earlier ages so often did, that our immediate predecessors were wrong and that we should seek a point of view which appears true largely because it is opposed to them. This mistaken method of human progress has led men in the past to oscillate over the centuries from one extreme point of view to its opposite, and then, a few generations later, back again. Thus, the humanism of the sixteenth century had reacted against the scholasticism of the medieval period and was reacted against in turn by the Puritanism of the seventeenth century, the materialism of the nineteenth century, and the reaction against this latest outlook by the "flight from freedom" and blind mass discipline of reactionary totalitarianism in the Fascist and Nazi aberrations.

It should be evident by now that truth is a remote goal which man approaches by walking, a process in which one foot is always behind the other foot. The true and final goal of man as we know him must be a synthesis of varied elements, because man is so obviously a creature of varied nature. And our imperfect vision, both of man's nature and of the universe in which he operates, must be a consensus of divergent points of view, since man's obviously limited vision permits each individual, group, or age to see the truth in a partial fashion only. Any consensus, however temporary, must be a reconciliation of such divergent and partial views to provide a more adequate (but still temporary) total view.

This can be seen most essentially in the fact that the great achievements of the nineteenth century and the great crisis of the twentieth century are both related to the Puritan tradition of the seventeenth century. The Puritan point of view regarded the body and the material world as sinful and dangerous and, as such, something which must be sternly controlled by the individual's will. God's grace, it was felt, would give the individual the strength to curb both his body and his feelings, to control their tendencies toward laziness, the distractions of pleasure, and the diversions of enjoyment, and make it possible for the individual, by total application to work, to demonstrate that he was among the chosen recipients of God's grace.

This Puritan outlook, rejected outwardly in the nineteenth century's vision of the truth, was, nevertheless, still an influential element in the nineteenth century's behavior, especially among those who contributed most to the nineteenth century's achievement of its own goals. The Puritan point of view contributed elements of self-discipline, self-denial, masochism, glorification of work, emphasis on the restrictions of enjoyment of consumption, and subordination both of the present to the future and of oneself to a larger whole. These became significant elements in the bourgeois, middle-class pattern of behavior which dominated the nineteenth century. The middle classes were themselves largely products of the seventeenth century, and had adopted this point of view as one of the features which distinguished them from the more self-indulgent attitudes of the other two social classes—the peasants below them or the aristocracy and nobility above them.

In the nineteenth century the elements of the Puritan point of view were quite detached from the other-worldly goals they had served in the seventeenth century (God and personal salvation) and were attached to individualistic and largely selfish, this-worldy, goals, but they carried over attitudes and patterns of behavior which remained largely detached from the nineteenth century's stated goals, and these, by a combination of seventeenth-century methods with nineteenth-century goals, produced the immense physical achievements of the nineteenth century.

These methods appeared in a number of essential ways, notably in an emphasis on self-discipline for future benefits, on restricted consumption and on saving, which provided the capital accumulation of the nineteenth century's industrial development; in a devotion to work, and in a postponement of enjoyment to a future which never arrived. A typical example might be John D. Rockefeller: great saver, great worker, and great postponer of any self-centered action, even death. To such people, and to the prevalent middle-class ideology of the nineteenth century, the most adverse comments which could be made about a "failure," to distinguish him from a "successful" man, were that he was a "wastrel," a "loafer," a "sensualist," and "self-indulgent." These terms reflected the value that the middle classes placed on work, saving, self-denial, and social conformity. All these values were carried over from seventeenth-century Puritanism, and were found most frequently among the religious groups rooted in that century, the Quakers, Presbyterians, Nonconformists (so called in England), and Jansenist survivals, and were less evident among religious groups with older orientations, such as Roman Catholics, High Anglicans, or orthodox Christians. These older creeds were more prevalent among the lower and the upper classes and in southern and eastern Europe rather than in northern or western Europe. This explains why the energy, self-discipline, and saving which made the world of 1900 was middle class, Protestant, and northwestern European. As we shall see later, in discussion of the American crisis of the twentieth century, these outlooks, values, and groups are now being superseded by quite different outlooks, values, and groups. In America today, those who wish to preserve them frequently show a tendency to embrace fanatical Right-wing political groups to implement that effort, and often speak among themselves of their efforts to preserve the values of WASPS (white Anglo-Saxon Protestants).

We shall speak later of these essential features of the nineteenth-century point of view, because their disappearance in the twentieth century, associated as it is with the crisis of the middle classes, is an essential part of the crisis of the twentieth century, where it is to be seen most clearly in the English-speaking and Scandinavian countries. We shall call these features, as a single bundle, "future preference," and understand that it includes the gospel of saving, of work, and of postponed enjoyment, consumption, and leisure. Closely related to it is a somewhat different idea, based on a constant and irremedial dissatisfaction with one's present position and present possessions. This is associated with the nineteenth century's emphasis on acquisitive behavior, on achievement, and on infinitely expansible demand, and is equally associated with the middle-class outlook. Both of these together (future preference and expansible material demands) were basic features in nineteenth-century middle-class society, and indispensable foundations for its great material achievements. They are inevitably lacking in backward, tribal, underdeveloped peasant societies and groups, not only in Africa and Asia but also in many peripheral areas and groups of Western Civilization, including much of the Mediterranean, Latin America, central France, or in the Mennonite communities of southern Pennsylvania and elsewhere. The lack of future preference and expansible material demands in other areas, and the weakening of them in middle-class Western Civilization, are essential features of the twentieth-century crisis.

Though this crisis, which has appeared as a breakdown, disruption, and rejection of the nineteenth century's way of doing things, was fully evident by the year 1900, it was brought to an acute stage by the two world wars and the world depression. If we may be permitted to oversimplify, two antithetical ways of dealing with this crisis appeared. One way, going back to men like Georges Sorel (*Reflections on Violence*, 1908), sought a solution of this crisis in irrationalism, in action for its own sake, in submergence of the individual into the mass of his tribe, community, or nation, in simple, intense concrete feelings and acts. The other tendency, based on nineteenth century's science, sought a solution of the crisis in rationalization, science, universality, cosmopolitanism, and the continued pursuit of eternal—if rapidly retreating—truth. While the great mass of people in Western Civilization either ignored the problem and the antithetical character of the two proffered solutions, drifting unconsciously toward the one or struggling confusedly toward the other, two smaller groups were quite aware of the antithesis and rivalry of the two. From the crisis itself and the myriad individual events which led through it, came World War II. Although few were consciously aware of it, this war became a struggle between the forces of irrationality, represented by Fascism, and the forces of Western science and rationalization, represented by the Allied nations.

The Allied nations won this fearful struggle because they represented the forces of the ancient traditions of the West which had made Western Civilization the most powerful and most prosperous civilization that had ever existed in the past six thousand years of experience of this form of human organization. This ability to use the Western tradition appeared in a capacity to use rationalization, science, diversity, freedom, and voluntary cooperation—all long-existent attributes of Western Civilization.

Rationalization and Science

The application of rationalization and science to World War II is one of the basic reasons (although not necessarily the most important reason) for the victory of the West in the war. As a consequence of that victory, these two methods survived the challenge from reactionary, totalitarian, authoritarian Fascism, and expanded from the limited areas of human experience where they had previously operated to become dominant factors in the twentieth-century world. The two are obviously not identical; and neither is equivalent to rationalism (although both use rationalism as a prominent element in their operations). Rationalism, strictly speaking, is a rather unconvincing ideology. It assumes that reality is rational and logical, and, accordingly, is comprehensible to man's conscious mental processes, and can be grasped by human reason and logic alone. It assumes that what is rational and logical is real, that what is not rational and logical is dubious, unknowable, and unimportant, and that the observations of the human senses are unreliable or even illusory.

Rationalization and science differ from rationalism in two chief ways: (1) they are more empirical, in that they are willing to use sense observations, and (2) they are more practical, in that they are more concerned with getting things done in the temporal world than they are with discovering the nature of ultimate truth. They do not necessarily deny the existence of such an ultimate truth, but they agree that any conclusions reached about its nature, using their methods, are proximate rather than ultimate. Both methods, thus, are analytical, tentative, proximate, modest, and relatively practical. The chief difference between them is that science is a somewhat narrower subdivision of rationalization, because it has a more rigid and self-conscious methodology.

Taken together, these two have played significant roles in Western Civilization for centuries, but have always remained somewhat peripheral to the experience of ordinary men. One of the chief consequences of World War II is that they are no longer peripheral. Of course, it must be recognized that rationalization and science are not yet, by any means, central to the experience of ordinary men, or even to the majority of men. But now they almost certainly must become matters of firsthand experience for the majority of men if Western Civilization is to survive. As the novelist of these matters, Sir Charles P. Snow, has said, scientists increasingly play a vital role in those crucial, secret decisions "which determine in the crudest sense whether we live or die."

Before World War II, science was recognized by all to be a significant element in life, but few had firsthand contact with it, and very few had any real appreciation of its nature and achievements. It was reserved largely for academic people, and for a small minority of these, and it touched the lives of most men only indirectly, by its influence on technology, especially on medical practice, transportation, and communications. There was very clearly, before 1939, what Sir Charles Snow has called "Two Societies" in our one civilization. This meant that most men lived in an ignorance of science almost as great as that of a Hottentot and almost equally great among highly educated professors of literature at Harvard, Oxford, and Princeton. It also meant that scientists were quite out of touch with the major realities of the world in which they lived, and were smitten by the impacts of war, depression, and political disturbances under conditions of ignorance, naïveté, and general bafflement at least as great as that of the uneducated ordinary man. World War II brought science into government, and especially into war, and brought politics, economics, and social responsibility into science in a way which must be beneficial to both but which was almost unimaginably shocking to both. Reading, for example, the interchange of questions and answers which go on between scientists and politicians before congressional committees concerned with outer space, atomic energy, or medical research is a revelation of the almost total lack of communication which takes place behind that prolific interchange of words.

The impact of rationalization is almost as great, although much less recognized. It had always existed in an incidental and minor way in men's experiences, but hardly justified a special name until it became a conscious and deliberate technique. It is a method of dealing with problems and processes in an established sequence of steps, thus: (1) isolate the problem; (2) separate it into its most obvious stages or areas; (3) enumerate the factors which determine the outcome desired in each stage or area; (4) vary the factors in a conscious, systematic, and (if possible) quantitative way to maximize the outcome desired in the stage or area concerned; and (5) reassemble the stages or areas and check to see if the whole problem or process has been acceptably improved in the direction desired.

Such rationalization is analytical and quantitative (even numerical). It was first used on an extensive scale at the end of the nineteenth century to solve problems of mass production, and led, step by step, to assembly-line techniques in which regulated quantities of materials (parts), power, labor, and supervision were delivered in a rational arrangement of space and time to produce a continuous outflow of some final product. All elements in the process were applied to measurable units to a system operated in accord with a dominant plan to achieve a desired result. Naturally, such a process serves to dehumanize the productive process and, since it also seeks to reduce every element in the process to a repetitive action, it leads eventually to an automation in which even supervision is electronic and mechanical.

From the basically engineering problem of production, rationalization gradually spread into the more dominant problem of business. From maximizing production, it shifted to maximizing profits. This gave rise to "efficiency experts" such as Frederick Winslow Taylor (whose *The Principles of Scientific Management* appeared in 1911) and, eventually, to management consultants, like Arthur D. Little, Inc.

This point had been reached by 1939, when rationalization was still remote from ordinary life and very remote from politics and war. As in so many other innovations, the introduction of rationalization into war was begun by the British and then taken over, on an enormous scale, by the Americans. Its origin is usually attributed to the efforts of Professor P. M. S. Blackett (Nobel Prize, 1948) to apply radar to antiaircraft guns. From there Blackett took the technique into antisubmarine defense, whence it spread, under the name "Operational Research" (OP), into many aspects of the war effort. In its original form, the Anti-Aircraft Command Research Group, known as "Blackett's circus," included three physiologists, two mathematical physicists, one astrophysicist, a surveyor, a general physicist, two mathematicians, and an army officer. It was a mixed-team approach to operational problems, emphasizing an objective, analytical, and quantitative method. As Blackett wrote in 1941, "The scientist can encourage numerical thinking on operational matters, and so can help to avoid running the war on gusts of emotion."

Operational research, unlike science, made its greatest contribution in regard to the use of existing equipment rather than to the effort to invent new equipment. It often gave specific recommendations, reached through the techniques of mathematical probability, which directly contradicted the established military procedures. A simple case concerned the problem of air attack on enemy submarines: For what depth should the bomb fuse be set? In 1940 the RAF Coastal Command set its fuses at 100 feet. This was based on estimates of three factors: (1) the time interval between the moments the submarine sighted the plane and the plane sighted the submarine; (2) the speed of approach of the plane; and (3) the speed of submergence of the submarine. One fixed factor was that the submarine was unlikely to be sunk if the bomb exploded more than 20 feet away. Operational Research added an additional factor: How near was the bomber to judging the exact spot where the submarine went down? Since this error increased rapidly with the distance of the original sighting, a submarine which had time to submerge deeply would almost inevitably be missed by the bomb in position if not in depth; but, with 100-foot fuses, submarines which had little time to submerge were missed because the fuse was too deep even when the position was correct. OP recommended setting fuses at 25 feet to sink the near sightings, and practically conceded the escape of all the distant sightings. When fuses were set at 35 feet, successful attacks on submarines increased 400 percent with the same equipment.

The British applied OP to many similar problems: (1) With an inadequate number of A.A. guns, is it better to concentrate them to protect part of a city thoroughly or to disperse them to protect all of the city inadequately? (The former is better.) (2) Repainting night bombers from black to white when used on submarine patrol increased sightings of submarines 30 percent. (3) Are small convoys safer for merchant ships than large ones? (No, by a large margin.) (4) With an inadequate number of patrol planes, was it better to search the whole patrol area some days (as was the practice) or to search part of it every day with whatever planes were available? (Calculations of a mathematician, S. D. Poisson, who died in 1840, showed that the latter was better.)

Some of OP's improvements were very simple. For example, a statistical study of sightings of German submarines by patrol planes showed that twice as many were seen on the left side of the plane as on the right side. Investigation showed this was because the plane flew on automatic pilot, allowing the pilot (on the left side) almost full time to watch the sea, while the copilot on the right side was busy much of the time. Assignment of another crewman to the right side when the copilot was busy increased sightings about 30 percent. Until late 1941 the RAF bombed German cities as they were able. Then OP, using the German bombing of Britain as a base, calculated the number of people killed per ton of bombs dropped, and applied this to Germany to show that the casualties inflicted on Germany were about 400 civilians killed per month—about half the German automobile-accident death rate—while 200 RAF crewmen were killed per month in doing the bombing. Such bombing could never influence the outcome of the war. Later it was discovered that the raids were really killing only 200 German civilians (almost all noncombatants contributing little to the war effort) at the cost of the 200 RAF fighting men each month, and thus were a contribution to a German victory! These estimates made it advisable to shift planes from bombing Germany to U-boat patrol, so that the German submarine war, which was really strangling Britain, could be brought under control. A bomber, in its average life of 30 missions, dropped 100 tons of bombs on Germany, killing 20 Germans and destroying a few houses. The same plane in thirty missions of submarine patrol saved, on the average, 6 loaded merchant vessels and their crews from submarines. As might be expected, this discovery was violently resisted by the head of the RAF Bomber Command, Chief Marshal Sir Arthur ("Bomber") Harris.

Closely linked with this was the question whether it was better to use Britain's shipbuilding capacity to construct escort vessels or merchant ships. This involved the choice between saving existing merchant ships or outbuilding the losses from submarines. It required a statistical study of the effectiveness of escort vessels. At the time, the Admiralty regarded small convoys as safer and large ones as dangerous, and had forbidden convoys of over sixty ships. They assigned escort vessels to each convoy at the rate of three plus one-tenth of the number of ships protected. OP was able to show that this assignment rule was inconsistent with the prejudice against large convoys. Studying past losses, they showed that convoys of under 40 ships (averaging 32 each) suffered losses of 2.5 percent, while large convoys of over 40 ships (averaging 54 ships each) were twice as safe, with losses of only 1.1 percent. Using information from rescued German U-boat crews, OP was able to show that U-boat success depended on the density of escort vessels around the perimeter of the convoy and that the percentage of ships sunk was inversely proportional to the size of the convoy. By 1944 a convoy of 187 ships arrived without loss. If the shift to large convoys had been made in the spring of 1942, rather than in the spring of 1943, a million tons of merchant shipping (or 200 ships) could have been saved. The combination of larger convoys, and the shift of some planes from bombing Germany to submarine patrol, turned the corner on the U-boat menace in the summer of 1943 and helped save many ships which were used in the Allied amphibious landings, especially on D-Day in 1944.

The shock of the fall of France in June 1940 marked a turning point in the relations between universities and government in the United States. At that time, the chief contacts between the two were the National Academy of Sciences, founded in 1863, and the National Advisory Committee for Aeronautics (NACA), founded in 1915. The former was a nongovernmental body electing its own members from American scientists and bound to advise the government, upon request, in scientific or technical matters. A dependent body, the National Research Council, had members from the government at large and representatives of over a hundred scientific societies to act as liaison between the academy and the scientific community. The NACA was a government agency which performed a similar function in aeronautics and did extensive research in its field with government funds. In 1938 Vannevar Bush, professor of electrical engineering and vice-president of Massachusetts Institute of Technology, an outstanding figure in applied mathematics and electronics, best known as the inventor of the differential analyzer (for mechanical solution of differential equations in calculus), became a member of NACA. The following year he became president of the Carnegie Institution of Washington and chairman of NACA.

As France fell, Bush persuaded President Roosevelt to create a National Defense Research Committee with Bush as chairman. The twelve members served without pay, and consisted of two each from the army, the navy, and the National Academy of Sciences, with six others. Bush named Frank B. Jewett, president of Bell Telephone Laboratories and the NAS; Karl T. Compton, president of MIT; James B. Conant, president of Harvard; Richard C. Tolman, of California Institute of Technology; and others. They set up headquarters at the Carnegie Institution and Dumbarton Oaks, a Harvard Byzantine research center in Washington.

The NDRC in its first year gave over two hundred contracts to various universities, and thus established the pattern of relations between government and the universities which still exists. In that first year it spent only $6.5 million, but in the six years 1940–1946 it spent almost $454 million. During that whole period, there was only one shift in the civilian personnel of the NDRC. In May 1941 a higher and wider organization was created, the Office of Scientific Research and Development (OSRD), with Bush as chairman and Conant as his deputy. Conant took Bush's place as chairman of NDRC, and Roger Adams, professor of chemistry at the University of Illinois, was added to NDRC. These groups were the supreme influence in America in introducing rationalization and science into government and war in 1940–1946, fostering hundreds of new technical developments and inventions, including the atom bomb. One of their earliest acts was to make a census of research facilities and a National Roster of Scientific and Specialized Personnel (with 690,000 names); they did not hesitate to call upon the services of both as needed. When money ran short, they found it from private sources, as in June 1941, when, simply by asking, they obtained half a million dollars from MIT and an equal sum from John D. Rockefeller, Jr., to pay salaries when congressional appropriations ran short.

Somewhat similar organizations grew up in Britain, in the Soviet Union, and in the enemy countries, but none worked so successfully as that of the Americans, who, here, as elsewhere, showed a genius for improvised large-scale organization. On the whole, the British were more fertile in new ideas than the Americans (probably because they were less conventional in their thinking processes), but the Americans were superior in development and production. The Soviet Union, which was very lacking in new ideas, was fairly successful (considering its obvious handicaps, such as enemy invasion and industrial backwardness) in development. Its organization was somewhat like that in the United States but much more centralized, since its Academy of Sciences controlled government funds and allotted both tasks and funds to university and special research groups. Germany, which had a high degree of innovation (comparable to that in the United States) was paralyzed by myriad conflicting and overlapping authorities in control of development and production and by the fact that the whole chaotic mess was under the tyranny of vacillating autocrats. Japan, almost lacking in innovation, achieved a surprising degree of production under a system of conflicting autocratic authorities almost as bad as that of Germany.

Rationalization of behavior, as represented in Operations Research, and the application of science to new weapons, as practiced by the English-speaking countries, were in sharp contrast with the methods of waging war used by the Tripartite aggressors. Hitler fought the war by basing his hopes on inspiration (his own) and willpower (usually, refusal to retreat an inch); Mussolini tried to fight his war on rhetoric and slogans; the Japanese tried to gain victory by self-sacrifice and willingness to die. All three irrational methods were obsolete as compared with the Anglo-American method of rationalization and science.

First news of the success of Operations Research in Britain was brought to the United States by President Conant in 1940 and was formally introduced by Vannevar Bush, as chairman of the New Weapons Committee of the Joint Chiefs of Staff, in 1942. By the end of the war, the technique had spread extensively through the American war effort, and, with the arrival of peace, became an established civilian profession. The best-known example of this is the Rand Corporation, a private research and development firm, under contract to the United States Air Force, but numerous lesser organizations and enterprises are now concerned with rationalization techniques in political life, the study of war and strategy, in economic analysis, and elsewhere. Similar groups arose in Britain. One of the most complex applications of the technique has been Operation Bootstrap, by which the Puerto Rican Industrial Development Corporation, advised by Arthur D. Little, Inc., has sought to transform the Puerto Rican economy. Persons interested in OP have organized societies in England (1948) and the United States (1949) which publish a quarterly and a journal.

A great impetus has been given to the rationalization of society in the postwar world by the application of mathematical methods to society to an unprecedented degree. Much of this used the tremendous advances in mathematics of the nineteenth century, but a good deal came from new developments. Among these have been applications of game theory, information theory, symbolic logic, cybernetics, and electronic computing. The newest of these was probably game theory, worked out by a Hungarian refugee mathematician, John von Neumann, at the Institute for Advanced Study. This applied mathematical techniques to situations in which persons sought conflicting goals in a nexus of relationships governed by rules. Closely related to this were new mathematical methods for dealing with decision-making. The basic work in the new field was the book *Theory of Games and Economic Behavior*, by John von Neumann and Oskar Morgenstern (Princeton, 1944).

Similar impetus to this whole development was provided by two other fields of mathematics in which the significant books in America were

C. E. Shannon and W. Weaver, *The Mathematical Theory of Communication* (University of Illinois, 1949), and Norbert Wiener, *Cybernetics, or Control and Communication in the Animal and the Machine* (Massachusetts Institute of Technology, 1949). A flood of books have amplified and modified these basic works, all seeking to apply mathematical methods to information, communications, and control systems. Closely related to this have been increased use of symbolic logic (as in Willard von Orman Quine, *Mathematical Logic*, Harvard, 1951), and the application of all these to electronic computers, involving large-scale storage of information with speedy retrieval of it and fantastically rapid operations of complex calculations. These, and related techniques, are now transforming methods of operation and behavior in all aspects of life and bringing on a large-scale rationalization of human life which is becoming one of the most significant characteristics of Western Civilization in the twentieth century.

Closely related to all this, both in the war and in the postwar period, have been advances in science. Here, also, the great impetus came from the struggle for victory in the war and the subsequent permeation of all aspects of life by attitudes and methods (in this case science) which had been peripheral to the experience of most people in the prewar period. The consequences of this revolution now surround us on all sides and are obvious, even to the most uncomprehending, in television and electronics, in biology and medical science, in space exploration, in automation of credit, billing, payroll, and personnel practices, in atomic energy, and above all in the constant threat of nuclear incineration which now faces all of us. In much of this the fundamental innovations were British, or at least European, but their full exploitation and production processes have been American.

The mobilization of these processes under the OSRD and NDRC by those two Massachusetts Yankees, Bush and Conant, is one of the miracles of the war. In sharp contrast with the OSS, it achieved its goals with a minimum of administrative friction, by the use of existing agencies, except in the few cases, such as the atom bomb, where no agency had existed previously. Probably no new group in the history of American government achieved so much with such a high degree of helpful cooperation. Most of this was the result of Bush's broad vision, tact, and total lack of desire for personal celebrity. Much of it was done quietly in individual discussions and unpublicized committee meetings. For example, as chairman of the Joint Committee on New Weapons and Equipment (JNW) of the Joint Chiefs of Staff from its founding in May 1942 to the end of the war, Bush achieved wonders, not only in persuading military men to use new weapons and new techniques but also in persuading the different services to integrate their introduction of new methods and their future plans.

The impetus to the use of science in many fields came from the British. This began in World War I when men like (Sir) Henry T. Tizard, (Sir) Robert A. Watson-Watt, and Professor Frederick A. Lindemann (Lord Cherwell after 1956) studied aviation problems scientifically. This link between government and science in aviation was maintained in Britain, as it was in the United States, during the Long Armistice. After Hitler came to power, Dr. H. E. Wimperis, Director of Scientific Research at the Air Ministry, and his colleague A. P. Rowe, set up a Committee on Research on Air Defence, with Tizard as chairman and Rowe as secretary, with Professors A. V. Hill and P. M. S. Blackett as members, and Watson-Watt as consultant. Professor Hill, physiologist, had won the Nobel Prize in 1922, while Blackett, ex-naval officer and nuclear physicist, was the initiator of Operational Research and won a Nobel Prize in physics in 1948. Watson-Watt may be regarded as the chief discoverer of radar.

In sharp contrast with OSRD and NDRC in America, this committee had a stormy life. In 1908, while studying physics in Berlin with Walther Nernst (Nobel Prize, 1920), Tizard met a fellow student, F. A. Lindemann, who was born and educated as a German, but held a British passport from his wealthy father's naturalization in England before his birth. Lindemann became a moody, driving, uncompromising, and erratically trained amateur scientist who devoted his best hours and energy to upper-class English social life, and combined intermittent flashes of scientific brilliance with total lack of objectivity and consistently poor judgment. Tizard, a fairly typical English civil servant, was, nonetheless, attracted to Lindemann, and in 1919 helped secure for him an appointment as professor of experimental philosophy at Oxford. At the time, science was at a low ebb at Oxford, and Lindemann, over the next two decades, built up its Clarendon Laboratory toward the high level which the Cavendish Laboratory at Cambridge University had achieved under Lord Rutherford. During this period Lindemann became the close friend and scientific adviser of Winston Churchill. Through Churchill's influence, Lindemann was forced on Tizard's Committee for the Scientific Survey of Air Defence, where he acted as a disruptive influence from July 1935, until the three scientific members (Hill, Blackett, and Wimperis) forced him off in September 1936 by resigning together. The whole committee was then dissolved and reappointed under Tizard without Lindemann. The latter reversed the tables four years later when Churchill became prime minister with Lindemann as almost his only scientific adviser. Tizard was dropped from the committee in June 1940. But by that time the great work in radar was done.

The Tizard Committee, with only £10,000 for research, held its first meeting on January 28, 1935, and by June 16th (before Lindemann joined) had a radar set on which they followed a plane 40 miles. On

March 13, 1936, they identified a plane flying at 1,500 feet 75 miles away. In September 1938, five stations southeast of London followed Chamberlain's plane flying to the Munich Conference, and on Good Friday 1939, as Mussolini was invading Albania, a chain of twenty stations began continuous operations along the eastern coast.

One of the chief advances here was Watson-Watt's use of a cathode vacuum tube (such as we now use in television) to watch the returning radio signal. This signal, sent out from a radio vacuum tube in pulses, returned through a crystal detector to appear as a "blip," or spot, on the cathode tube's fluorescent screen. The shorter the wavelength of the sending wave, the sharper and more accurate the returning signal, the shorter the necessary aerial, and the lower the transmitting tower; but vacuum tubes could not broadcast waves less than 10 meters in length (300,000 kilocycles). Just as the war began, Professor John T. Randall, at the University of Birmingham, invented the resonant-cavity magnetron, an object no bigger than a fist, which broadcasts high-power, very short, radio waves. This ended interference from ground reflections or reflections from the ionosphere, and allowed sharp discrimination of objects without need for long antennae or high towers. By the time the magnetron came into use (1941), broadcasting from tubes had been improved to allow use of 1.5 meter waves, but the magnetron was developed for 0.1 meter waves. All subsequent radar development was based on it. At the same time, great advances were being made in crystals for detectors. This later grew into the use of artificial crystals (transistors) for amplification in receivers as well as for detection.

In August 1940, Sir Henry Tizard, ousted from his committee by Lindemann, led a British scientific mission to Washington. He brought a large box of blueprints and reports on British scientific work, including radar, a new explosive (RDX, half again as powerful as TNT), studies on gaseous diffusion of uranium isotopes for an atom bomb, and much else. This visit gave a great impetus to American scientific work. As one consequence of it, 350 men from the United States were working in the radar net stations in England by November 1941 (a month before Pearl Harbor).

Of the many inventions which emerged from science in World War II, we have space here to mention only a few: shaped charges, proximity fuses, medical advances, and the atom bomb.

Six hundred years of ordnance research on artillery had brought guns to a high state of excellence long before World War II, but artillery, with all its advantages of range and accuracy, had three intrinsic disadvantages: the backward thrust of the explosive gases of propulsion gave it a violent recoil; the same gases corroded and wore down the inside of the barrel very rapidly; and the projectile, on hitting the target, dispersed its explosive force, sending most of it backward into the air from the resistance of the target itself. A rocket avoids the first two of these problems because it directs the recoil forward to push the rocket, and needs no container barrel at all. The Russians, who had greatly developed the use of rockets, used them in large numbers against the Germans in 1941. Since rockets need no barrel to shoot through but merely require a holder until they can fully ignite, rockets allow an infantryman to supply his own artillery support, especially against tanks. By the end of the war, American rockets were delivered for use in individual, disposable plastic launchers which were thrown away after the rocket inside had been fired.

The great disadvantages of rockets were their inaccuracy and short range, both of which came from the weak and uneven burning of the propellant. Great improvements were made in the study of propellants by the Germans, especially from the work of Hermann Oberth, Walter Dornberger, and Werner von Braun at Peenemünde Rocket Research Institute on the Baltic Sea. These men, working on the basis of earlier studies by the American professor, Robert H. Goddard (*A Method of Reaching Extreme Altitudes*, 1929), and by a Polish high school teacher in Russia, K. E. Ziolkovsky (1857–1935), greatly advanced rocketry during the war and developed the V-2, which devastated London and Antwerp from September 8, 1944 until the war's end. The English had been expecting this attack, since a German test rocket had gone astray in June 1944, and had exploded over Sweden. The pieces from it, which were handed over to the Allies, made it possible to reconstruct the characteristics of the rocket, but left them in dread that it was being held back until the Germans could perfect an atomic-bomb warhead. From this point of view, the first V-2 on England at 6:43 P.M., September 8, 1944, followed by another, sixteen seconds later, was a relief: they carried warheads of conventional explosives. But that warhead of 1,654 pounds came in on a 46-foot rocket traveling at three times the speed of sound, coming down from an altitude of 60 miles from a launching site 200 miles away. More than 1,100 of these rockets killed 3,000 British before they were stopped.

Just as a rocket reversed the recoil of a gun, directing it forward, so a shaped charge reversed the shape of the projectile. An artillery projectile is bullet-shaped, with its forward end pointed or convex. In 1888 C. E. Munroe had shown that if the explosive charge were made concave, with the cavity at its forward end against the target, the explosive force would be directed forward toward the target (as rays of light go forward from a concave headlight cavity) instead of backward. The American bazooka of 1942 combined this shaped charge with a rocket to provide an infantry weapon with which a single man could knock out a tank. A relatively small charge carried to a tank with an impetus no greater than a well-hit baseball exploded most of its power forward in a narrow pencil of explosive force which sometimes penetrated six inches of armor or six feet of masonry. A hole less than an inch wide on a tank could destroy its crew by spraying them with molten metal forced inward from the shaped charge. In a few cases, this occurred through eight-inch armor without the armor being fully penetrated. Thus the tank, triumphant in 1940, was brought under control, and by 1945 was used largely as mobile artillery.

An even more remarkable advance was the proximity fuse. This was a fuse containing a tiny radar set which measured the distance to the target and could be adjusted to explode at a fixed distance. First used to explode A.A. shells within lethal distance of enemy planes, it soon was adapted to explode just over the heads of ground forces. The latter use, however, was not permitted for more than two years, for fear the enemy would obtain a dud and be able to copy it.

The proximity VT fuse was, after the atom bomb, the second greatest scientific achievement of the war, although the magnetron contributed more than either to an Allied victory. Producing the fuse seemed impossible: It would be necessary to make a radar sending and receiving set to fit in a space smaller than an ice-cream cone; to make it strong enough to withstand 20,000 times the force of gravity in original acceleration and the spin in flight of 475 rotations per minute; to have it detonate at a precise instant in time with no chance of exploding earlier to endanger the gunner; and to be sure that it would explode entirely if it missed its target zone so that there would never be a dud. These problems were solved, and production began in 1942. By the end of the war, Sylvania had made over 130 million minute radio tubes, of which five were needed in each fuse.

First used in action by the U.S.S. *Helena* against a Japanese dive-bombing plane on January 5, 1943, it destroyed the attacker on the second salvo. An order of the Combined Chiefs of Staff prohibited use of the fuse except over water, where the enemy could not recover duds, but late in 1943 secret intelligence obtained plans of the V-1 robot plane which Hitler was preparing to bomb London. The CCS released proximity fuses to be used over England against this new threat. The first V-1 came over on June 12, 1944, the last, 80 days later, the VT fuses being used only during the final four weeks. In the last week, VT fuses destroyed 79 percent of the V-1's that came over. On the final day only 4 out of 104 reached London. They were being destroyed by three machines developed by NDRC and made in the United States: detected by SCR-584 radar, their courses predicated by M-9 computers, and shot down by VT fuses. General Sir F. A. Pile, Chief of British A.A. Command, sent Bush a copy of his report on this operation, inscribed, "With my compliments to OSRD who made the victory possible."

The VT fuse was released by CCS for general use on land at the end of October 1944, and was first used against German ground forces in the Battle of the Bulge. The results were devastating. In thick fog the Germans massed their men together, believing they were safe since the range could not be measured for orthodox artillery time fuses; they were massacred by VT shells exploding over their heads, and even those who crouched in foxholes were hit. On another evening, near Bastogne, German tanks were observed entering a wood for the night. After they were settled, the area was blasted with VT shells. In the morning seventeen German tanks surrounded by their dead crews were found in the area.

One of the greatest victories of science in the war was in the treatment of the wounded. Ninety-seven percent of the casualties who reached the front-line dressing stations were saved, a success which had never been approached in earlier wars. The techniques which made this possible, involving blood transfusions, surgical techniques, and antibiotics, have all been continued and amplified in the postwar world, although the destruction of man's natural environment by advancing technology has created new hazards and new causes of death by advancing cancer, disintegrating circulatory systems, and increasing mental breakdowns.

The greatest achievement of science during the war, and, indeed, in all human history, was the atom bomb. Its contribution to victory was secondary, since it had nothing to do with the victory over Germany and at most, shortened the war with the Japanese only by weeks. But this greatest example of the power of cooperating human minds has changed the whole environment in which men live. The only human discovery which can compare with it was man's invention of the techniques of farming almost nine thousand years earlier, but this earlier advance was slow and empirical. The advance to the atom bomb was swift and theoretical, in which men, by mathematical calculations, were able to anticipate, measure, judge, and control events which had never happened previously in human experience. It is not possible to understand the history of the twentieth century without some comprehension of how this almost unbelievable goal was achieved and especially why the Western Powers were able to achieve it, and the Fascist Powers were not.

As late as the fall of France in 1940, all countries were equal in their scientific knowledge, because science was then freely communicable, as it must be, by its very nature. Much of that knowledge, in physical science, rested on the theories of three Nobel Prize winners of 1918–1922. These were Max Planck (1858–1947), who said that energy did not move in a continuous flow like water but in discrete units, called *quanta*, like bullets; Albert Einstein (1879–1955), whose theory of relativity indicated that matter and energy were interchangeable according to the formula $E = mc^2$; and Niels Bohr (1885–1962), who offered a picture of the atom as a planetary structure with a heavy, complex nucleus, and circumrotating electrons in fixed orbits established by their energy levels according to Planck's quantum theory. At that time (1940) all scientists knew that some of the heavier elements naturally disintegrated and were reduced to somewhat lighter elements by radioactive emission of negatively charged electrons or of positively charged alpha particles (helium nuclei, consisting of two positively charged protons with two uncharged neutrons).

As early as 1934, in Rome, Enrico Fermi (Nobel Prize, 1938) and Emilio Segre (Nobel Prize, 1959), without realizing what they had done, had split uranium atoms into lighter elements (chiefly barium and krypton) by shooting neutrons into the uranium nucleus. (Such neutrons had been isolated and identified in 1932, by Sir James Chadwick, Nobel Prize winner in 1935.) Although Ida Noddack at once suggested that Fermi had split the atom, the suggestion was generally ignored until Otto Hahn, Lise Meitner, and Fritz Strassmann in Germany, in 1937–1939, repeated Fermi's experiments and sought to identify the bewildering assortment of lighter radioactive elements which emerged when uranium was bombarded with a stream of neutrons.

By February 1939, it was established that the heaviest element, 92 uranium, could be split in various ways into lighter elements nearer the middle of the atomic table and that large amounts of energy were released in the process. For example, 92 uranium might be split into 56 barium and 36 krypton. The reason for the release of energy was that the nuclear particles (protons and neutrons) had smaller masses in the nucleus of elements near the middle of the atomic table than they had in the nuclei of elements nearer the top or the bottom of the table or than the particles had alone outside any nucleus. This meant that the nuclear particles had the least mass in the elements near 26 iron and that energy would be released if heavier elements could be broken into lighter ones nearer iron or if lighter elements could be built up into heavier elements nearer iron. Now that scientists can do both of these things, at least at the very top (hydrogen) and the very bottom (uranium) of the table, we call the splitting process "fission" and the building-up process "fusion" of nuclei. As explosive forces, they are now represented by the "atomic" bomb and the "hydrogen," thermonuclear, bomb. The amount of energy released by either process can be calculated by Einstein's equation, $E = mc^2$, where c is the speed of light (30 billion centimeters, or about 186,000 miles a second). By this equation, if only an ounce of matter is destroyed, 5,600,000 kilowatt hours of energy would be released. In 1939, of course, no one could conceive how lighter elements could be fused into heavier ones, as scientists had just revealed uranium could be fissured.

To the historian of these events, the months of January and February 1939 are of crucial significance. On January 2nd, Fermi, self-exiled from

Mussolini's Italy, reached New York with his wife and children, from Stockholm, where he had just received the Nobel Prize. Four days later the Hahn-Strassmann report on uranium fission was published in Germany, and Otto Frisch, sent by his aunt, Lise Meitner, from Sweden (where they were both refugees from Hitler's Germany), dashed to Copenhagen to confer with Bohr on the real meaning of Hahn's report. Bohr left the next day, January 7th, to join Einstein at the Institute for Advanced Study in Princeton, while Frisch and Meitner, in Sweden, repeated Hahn's fissure of uranium and reported on the results in quantitative terms, in the English journal *Nature* on February 11 and 18, 1939. These reports, which first used the word "fission," introduced the "Atomic Age," and showed that, weight for weight, uranium fission would be twenty million times more explosive than TNT.

Such a burst of energy would, of course, not be noticed in nature if only a few atoms of uranium split; moreover, no large number would split unless the uranium was so pure that its atoms were massed together and unless the stream of splitting neutrons continued to hit their nuclei. Immediately, in February 1939, a number of scientists thought that these two conditions, which do not exist in nature, might be created in the laboratory. It took only a few minutes to realize that this process would become an almost instantaneous chain reaction if extra neutrons, to serve as fission bullets, were issued by the splitting process. Since the uranium nucleus has 146 neutrons, while barium and krypton together have only 82 plus 47, or 129, it is obvious that each split uranium atom must release 17 neutrons capable of splitting other uranium atoms if they hit their nuclei with the right momentum.

This idea was tested at once by Frédéric Joliot-Curie (Nobel Prize, 1935) in Paris, and by Fermi and another refugee, Leo Szilard, with their associates, at Columbia University, New York. The three teams submitted their reports to publication in March 1939. Bohr and others had already suggested that large-scale uranium fission does not occur in nature because natural uranium was widely dispersed atomically by being overwhelmingly diluted in chemical combination and mixture with other substances in its ores; they pointed out also that even pure natural uranium would probably not explode because it was a mixture of three different kinds, or isotopes, of uranium, all with the same atomic number 92 (and thus with the same chemical reactions, since these are based on the electrical charge of the nucleus as a whole) but with quite different atomic weights of 234, 235, and 238. These isotopes could not be separated by chemical means, since their identical atomic numbers (or nuclear electrical charges) meant that they had the same chemical reactions in joining to form different compounds. They could be separated only by physical methods based on their slightly different mass weights.

As uranium is extracted only with great difficulty, and in small amounts, from its ores, 99.28 percent of it is U-238, 0.71 percent of it is U-235, and only a trace is U-234. Thus, natural uranium has 140 times as much U-238 as U-235. It was soon discovered that U-235 was split by slow or very fast neutrons, but, when it split, it emitted very energetic neutrons traveling at high speeds. These fast neutrons would have to be slowed down to split any more U-235, but since U-238 gobbles up all neutrons which come by at intermediate speeds, chain-reaction fission in uranium cannot occur in nature, where each atom of U-235 is surrounded by atoms of U-238 as well as by other neutron-absorbing impurities.

From this it was clear that a chain reaction could be continued in either of two cases: (1) if very pure natural uranium could be mixed with a substance (called a "moderator") which would slow down neutrons without absorbing them or (2) if a mass of U-235 alone could be obtained so large that the fast neutrons emitted by fission would slow down to splitting speed before they escaped from the mass. The former reaction could probably be controlled, but the latter mass of U-235 would almost certainly explode spontaneously, since there are always a few slow neutrons floating around in space to start the chain reaction. Even in 1939 scientists guessed that ordinary water, heavy water (made of hydrogen with a nucleus of a neutron and a proton instead of only one proton), or carbon would make good moderators for a controlled reaction. They also knew at least four ways in which, by physical methods, U-235 could be separated from U-238.

At the very end of 1939, scientists had worked out what happened when U-238 gobbled up intermediate speed neutrons. It would change from 92 U-238 to 92 U-239, but almost at once the U-239, which is unstable, would shoot out a negative charge (beta ray or electron) from one of the 147 neutrons in its nucleus, turning that neutron into a proton, and leaving the weight at 239 while raising its positive charges (atomic number) to 93. This would be a new element, one number beyond uranium, and therefore named neptunium after the planet Neptune, one planet beyond Uranus as we move outward in the solar system. Theory seemed to show that the new "transuraniac" element 93 Np-239 would not be stable, but would soon (it turned out to be about two days) shoot out another electron from a neutron along with energy in the form of gamma rays. This would give a new transuraniac element number 94 with mass of 239. This second transuraniac element was called plutonium, with symbol 94 Pu-239. At the very end of 1939 theory seemed to indicate that this plutonium, like U-235, would be fissured by slow neutrons, if a sufficiently large lump of it could be made. Moreover, since it would be a different element, with 94 positive charges, it could be separated from the 92 U-238, in which it was created, by chemical methods (usually much easier than the physical methods of separation required for isotopes of the same element).

Theory reached this far by the spring of 1940. At that time, in the space of the months April to June, several things happened: (1) the Nazis overran Denmark and Norway, capturing Bohr in one country and the world's only heavy-water factory in the other country; (2) news reached America that the Nazis had forbidden all further sales of Czechoslovakia's uranium ores and had taken over the greater part of Germany's major physical research laboratory, the Kaiser Wilhelm Institute in Berlin, for uranium research; (3) a blanket of secrecy was dropped throughout the world on scientific research on nuclear fission; and (4) the Nazis overran the Netherlands, Belgium, and France, capturing, among others, Joliot-Curie. At that time uranium was a largely worthless commodity of which a few tons a year was used for coloring ceramics; it was produced only incidentally as a byproduct of efforts to produce other minerals such as cobalt or radium. Just before war began, Edgar Sengier, managing director of Union Minière of Katanga, Belgian Congo, learned from Joliot-Curie his discovery of chain fission of Uranium-235. Accordingly, after the fall of France, Sengier ordered all available uranium ore, 1,250 tons of it, shipped to New York. This ore was 65 percent uranium oxide, compared to marketable North American ores of 0.2 percent, and the full-scale postwar exploitation of South African ores of .03 percent! For more than two years Sengier could find no one in the United States interested in his ores, which lay in a warehouse on Staten Island until the end of 1942.

Just before the curtain of secrecy on atomic research fell in the spring of 1940, astounding information on the subject was published in Soviet Russia, but, like most Russian-language publications, was ignored in the outer world. In 1939 the Soviet Academy of Sciences set up, under the chairmanship of V. I. Vernadsky, director and founder (1922) of the Leningrad Radium Institute, an "Isotopes Committee" to work on the separation of uranium isotopes and the production of heavy water. The first cyclotron in Europe, an atom smasher of four million electron volts (4 MeV) which had been operational since 1937, went into full experimental use in April 1940, and, at the same time, the Academy of Sciences ordered immediate construction of a cyclotron of 11 MeV, comparable to the world's largest, the 60-inch cyclotron at the University of California, operated by Ernest O. Lawrence, the inventor of these machines (Nobel Prize, 1939).

In this same fatal spring of 1940, a conference on isotope separation in Moscow publicly discussed the problem of separation of U-235; subsequently, Y. B. Khariton and Y. B. Zeldovich published a paper on the problem of the critical mass for spontaneous explosion of this isotope ("The Kinetics of Chain Decomposition of Uranium," in *Zhurnal Eksperimentalnoi i teoreticheskoi*, X, 1940, 477). This was followed by publication of similar papers, some even in 1941, which might have shown clearly to anyone who wished to see that the Soviet Union was further developed than the United States at that time. No one, unfortunately, did wish to see. About the same time, Edwin A. McMillan (Nobel Prize, 1951) and Philip H. Abelson, using E. O. Lawrence's great cyclotron at Berkeley, California, had studied the results arising from neutron bombardment of Uranium-238, and indicated the nature of 93 neptunium and the fissionable possibilities of 94 plutonium (*Physical Review*, June 15, 1940). Bohr, as well as Louis A. Turner of Princeton, had already indicated some of the characteristics, including fissionability, of plutonium.

The Soviet position in atomic research in 1940 is astonishing in view of the depredations inflicted on Soviet scientists by Stalin in the purges of 1937–1939. In June 1940, Soviet science in this subject was about on a level with that of the German scientists who remained in Nazi Germany, although both were far behind the refugee scientists who were still making their ways westward to the English-speaking world. The Soviet scientists were, apparently, interested in atomic research only for industrial power purposes, and were not much concerned with achieving atomic explosives. Accordingly, they concentrated on atomic piles of mixed uranium isotopes, rather than on uranium separation, and most of their work was suspended after the Nazi invasion in 1941. In a similar way the remaining German scientists, although seeking the bomb, decided in February 1942 that large-scale separation of isotopes was too expensive to be practical, and spent the rest of the war years on the hopeless task of trying to devise an atomic pile which could be used as a bomb. The great German error was their failure to reach the conception of "critical mass," the point which had been published in Russia in 1940.

In the United States and Britain the impact of the events of 1940 was much more intense among the refugee scientists than among the Americans. On the whole, the refugees had a higher level both of scientific training and of political awareness than the native scientists, and most of the outstanding American scientists had acquired their specialized knowledge in Europe, chiefly at Göttingen or elsewhere in Germany. As early as April 1939, a group of Hungarian refugees, led by Leo Szilard and including Eugen Wigner, Edward Teller, and John von Neumann, tried to establish a voluntary censorship of research information and to arouse the American government to the significance of the possible atom bomb. On March 17, 1939, Fermi visited the admiral in charge of the Technical Division of Navy Operations but could arouse no interest. In July Szilard, driven once by Wigner and a second time by Teller, made two visits to Einstein and persuaded him to send a letter and memorandum to President Roosevelt through the banker Alexander Sachs. The President read the material on October 11, 1939, and the wheels of government began to move, but very slowly. Only on December 6, 1941, the day before

Pearl Harbor, was the decision taken to make an all-out effort to unlock atomic energy.

When the curtain of secrecy fell in June 1940, all the theory needed for the task was known by all capable physicists; what was not known was (1) that their theories would work, and (2) how the immense resources needed for the task could be mobilized. As late as 1939, less than an ounce of uranium metal had ever been made in the United States. Now it was necessary to make tons of it in extremely refined form. To build an atomic pile for a controlled nuclear reaction, hundreds of tons of heavy water or of graphite refined to a degree hitherto unknown were also needed. This task, entrusted to the direction of Arthur H. Compton (Nobel Prize, 1927), with Fermi doing the actual work, was set up at the University of Chicago. The pile of purified graphite with lumps of uranium all through it was built in a squash court under the West Stands of Stagg Field, where football had been discontinued. The pile of graphite, shaped as a roughly flattened sphere about 24 feet in diameter, had 12,400 pounds of uranium in small scattered lumps distributed in a cube at its center. Neutron counters, thermometers, and other instruments kept track of the fission rate going on inside it. Before the top layers could be added, these indicators began to rise increasingly rapidly to danger levels; therefore rods of cadmium steel were inserted through the graphite lattice. Cadmium, which absorbs large quantities of neutrons without being changed, could be used to hold back the fission process until the pile was finished. On December 2, 1942, before a team of scientists, these cadmium rods were slowly withdrawn to the point where a chain nuclear reaction took off. It could be damped down or speeded up to explosive level simply by pushing the rods in or pulling them out. This first sustained nuclear reactor was a great success, but it contributed little toward an atom bomb. Within it, at full operation, plutonium was made at a rate which would require 70,000 years to obtain enough for a bomb. This pile operated on purified natural uranium in which the U-238 was 140 times the U-235.

To separate U-235 from U-238 by physical methods, four techniques were attempted on parallel paths. Two of these ceased to be significant after the end of 1943. The two survivors were gas diffusion and electromagnetic separation. In the latter, gaseous compounds of uranium were electrically charged so that they would move along a vacuum tube and pass through a powerful magnet which made them swerve. The heavier U-238 compounds would swerve less than the slightly lighter U-235 compounds, and the two could be separated. Using the gigantic new cyclotron magnet at the University of California, which was 184 inches across, Ernest O. Lawrence and Emilio Segre showed that it would require about 45,000 such units to separate a pound of U-235 a day.

The electromagnetic separator plant (called Y-12) as set up at Oak

Ridge in 1943 covered 825 acres and was housed in 8 large buildings (two of which were 543 feet by 312 feet). Several thousand magnets, most of which were 20 feet by 20 feet by 2 feet, consumed astronomical quantities of electricity in separating uranium isotopes into gigantic tanks. These tanks, weighing fourteen tons each, were pulled out of line by as much as three inches by the magnetic attractions created, straining the pipes carrying uranium compound, and eventually they had to be fastened to the floor. Since copper for electrical connections was in such short supply, 14,000 tons of silver from the Treasury reserve of American paper money was secretly taken from the Treasury vaults (although still carried publicly on the Treasury balance sheets) and made into wiring for the Y-12 plant. From this plant came much of the U-235 used in the Hiroshima A-bomb.

The gaseous-diffusion method, which had been carried fairly far by the British before America took it over, took advantage of the fact that atoms of lighter U-235 gas move more rapidly than the heavier U-238 and thus pass more rapidly through a porous barrier. If a mixture of the two isotopes, in the only available gaseous form of the unstable and violently corrosive uranium hexafluoride, were pumped thus through 4,000 successive barriers, with billions of holes, each not over 4 ten-millionths of an inch, the mixture after the last barrier would be largely the U-235 form of the compound (90 percent pure).

By the end of April 1943, in three adjacent valleys near Oak Ridge, Tennessee, three plants were under construction for gaseous diffusion and electromagnetic separation of U-235 and for a large uranium pile to make plutonium out of U-238. By the end of the war, Oak Ridge, covering 70 square miles, had a population of 78,000 persons and was the fifth largest community in Tennessee. Because the plutonium plant was so dangerous, owing to its enormous generation of heat and radioactivity, a larger and more isolated plant was begun on a tract of 670 square miles near Hanford, Washington. A construction camp of 60,000 workers was set up there in April 1943; construction of the first fission pile was begun in June; and it began to operate in January 1945. It is interesting to note that the two sites at Oak Ridge and Hanford were chosen for their proximity to the hydroelectric power plants of the Tennessee Valley Authority and Grand Coulee which had been built by Roosevelt's New Deal. By the end of the war, nuclear production was using a large fraction of the total electricity produced in the United States, and would have been impossible without these great electrical-generating constructions of the New Deal (which were still regarded with intense hatred by American conservatives).

A third site, for research on the bomb itself and its final assembly, was built on a flat mesa near Los Alamos, New Mexico, twenty miles from Santa Fe. Robert Oppenheimer of the University of California, with the world's greatest assemblage of working scientists (including almost a dozen Nobel laureates), planned and constructed the earliest bombs at that isolated spot.

Until May 1, 1943, these complex projects were operated by committees and subcommittees of scientists of which the chief chairmen were James B. Conant, Vannevar Bush, E. O. Lawrence, Harold Urey, and A. O. Compton. The actual construction work was delegated to the United States Army Corps of Engineers in charge of Leslie R. Groves, an expert on constructing buildings, whose chief achievement was the Pentagon Building in Washington. From his graduation at West Point, Groves had held only desk jobs, had been a lieutenant for seventeen years, and was still a major when war began. He was raised to brigadier general on his appointment as head of the Manhattan District, in charge of the physical administration of the atom-bomb project in September 1942. On May 1, 1943, he took over total charge of the whole project.

An earnest, hard-working man, Groves had little imagination, no sense of humor, and not much familiarity with science or scientists (whom he regarded as irresponsible "longhairs"). Although he drove himself and his associates relentlessly, he greatly hampered the progress of the task by his fanatical obsession with secrecy. This obsession was based on his belief that the project involved fundamental scientific secrets (there were no such secrets). His efforts were quite in vain, as the only real secrets, the technological ones regarding isotope separation, critical mass, and trigger mechanisms of the bombs, were revealed to the Soviet Union, almost as soon as they were achieved, by British scientists. The secrecy, thus, was secrecy for the American public rather than for the Germans or the Russians (neither of whom were actually seeking the information, since, like General Groves himself, they had little faith in the feasibility of the project).

For security reasons General Groves "compartmentalized" the work, and allowed only about a dozen persons to see the project as a whole. Consequently, the vast majority of those working on the project were not allowed to know what they were really doing or why, and this lack of perspective greatly delayed the solution of problems. The whole project of about 150,000 persons were segregated from their fellow citizens; all communications were cut off or censored; and the project was overrun with guards and security officials who did not hesitate to eavesdrop, read mail, monitor telephones, record conversations, and isolate individuals. These activities significantly delayed American achievement of the atom bomb without achieving their ostensible purpose, since there is no evidence either that the three enemy Powers could have made the bomb or that Russia's making of the bomb was significantly delayed by General Groves's extreme degree of secrecy.

General Groves's personal position was paradoxical. He took the assignment with disappointment and reluctance, had no real faith that the project would be successful until it actually was, carried secrecy to the nth degree, yet was convinced that the engineering problems were so colossal that the Soviet Union, even if it had the knowledge of how we did it, would be unable to repeat the achievement in less than twenty years, if ever. I myself heard General Groves make these statements in 1945. On the other hand, General Groves was a tireless and driving manager and an expert manipulator of the personal, political, and military arrangements which made the bomb possible.

In the last two years of the project (July 1943–July 1945), it passed through crisis after crisis in a frenzied sequence which made it appear, every alternative month, that it would be a $2 billion fiasco. In January 1944, when the enormous gaseous-diffusion plant at Oak Ridge was under full construction but without the diffusion barriers, since no effective ones could be made, it became necessary to junk the barriers on which tests had been made for almost two years and to turn to mass production of millions of square feet of a new barrier which had scarcely been tested. When this plant began to operate, section by section, at the end of the year, it worked so ineffectively that it seemed almost impossible that the concentration of U-235 could ever be raised over 15 or 20 percent without the construction of miles of additional barrier which would delay the bomb by months and use up fantastic quantities of uranium hexafluoride gas just to fill the chambers. Similarly, the electromagnetic separator plants suffered breakdown after breakdown, and operated at a level which made it seem impossible to raise the U-235 content over 50 percent.

By April 1944, it seemed clear that 95 percent U-235 could not be obtained before 1946 even if the gas-diffusion and electromagnetic plants were run in series instead of parallel, with the latter starting off with 20 percent U-235 from the former instead of both trying to process natural uranium from scratch. At that point, Oppenheimer discovered that Philip Abelson (who had originally discovered how to make uranium hexafluoride) had been working for the navy, trying to make enriched U-235 to be used to propel a nuclear submarine. He was using thermal separation, one of the two methods (the other was centrifuge) that the Manhattan District had rejected in 1942. Thermal separation was based on the fact that a liquid mixture in a container with a hot wall and an opposite cold wall will tend to separate; the heavier liquid will tend to accumulate near the cold wall, will cool, and sink, while the lighter liquid will tend to gather near the hot wall, get warmer, and rise. Abelson, who knew nothing of the work of the Manhattan District, or of the successful nuclear pile at Chicago, was working at the Philadelphia Navy Yard where he had 102 vertical, double concentric pipes, each 48 feet long, in which the inner pipe was heated by steam, the outer pipe was kept cool, and the ring-shaped space between the two was filled with a uranium liquid mixture whose two isotopes tended to separate from each other. From the top of these pipes he hoped to be able to draw one-fifth ounce a day of 5 percent U-235 by July 1, 1944.

Groves grasped at this straw, and on June 27, 1944 signed a contract for a thermal-diffusion plant at Oak Ridge to be ready in ninety days. The new plant, which eventually cost over $15 million, was 522 feet long, 82 feet wide, and 75 feet high, and was to contain twenty-one exact copies of Abelson's plant (2,142 tubes in all); it would yield U-235 enriched to a few percentage points to be fed into the inadequate gas-diffusion plant. It began to produce in March 1945. By placing the three separation methods in sequence and working night and day to improve the efficiency of all three, it began to look as if U-235 for one bomb might be available in the second half of 1945.

These disappointments with U-235 naturally turned men's hopes to the plutonium being made at Hanford. When the first giant pile went "critical" there on September 27, 1944, it shut itself down after a day and then restarted itself again after another day. Frenzied study and consultation with the smaller piles at Oak Ridge and at Chicago finally revealed the unexpected production, within the pile, of a neutron-absorbing isotope, Xenon 135, with a half-life of 9 hours; the pile started itself again when this decayed, and thus stopped draining neutrons from the uranium fission process. This problem was eventually solved by greatly increasing the uranium tubes in the pile.

All through this worry, Los Alamos was having problems with the trigger mechanisms. Experiment and calculations eventually showed that the critical mass of U-235 was less than 11 pounds, about the size of a small grapefruit, if it were properly compressed and in spherical shape. To achieve this, two mechanisms were conceived, known as the "gun" and "implosion." The "gun" was designed to create a critical mass by shooting a lump of U-235 at high velocity into a subcritical mass so that the combination would be over the critical mass. The resulting shape, however, was so unspherical that it was calculated that the whole amount of U-235 necessary for the gun trigger bomb would be almost twice the ideal critical mass. This increase from about 11 to about 21 pounds of U-235 per bomb would extend the date on which the bomb was ready by weeks, since the output of U-235 was so small.

The second trigger, called "implosion," planned to make a hollow sphere of U-235 or plutonium which was critical in total amount but kept subcritical by the hole in the center. This metallic sphere would be crushed together into the space in its center to make a critical mass there by the explosion of twenty or more crescent-shaped pieces of TNT which surrounded the sphere. The difficulty was that all the surrounding TNT had to explode at the same instant in order to ram the nuclear material together at the center; any lag would simply bulge the nuclear material erratically and prevent the achievement of critical mass. All the ordnance experts, including Captain Parsons, of the United States Navy, in charge of this part of the work at Los Alamos, were convinced that such accurate timing of TNT explosion, with two dozen pieces exploded within a millionth of a second, would be impossible.

This brought up another crisis because Glenn Seaborg (Nobel Prize, 1951) and Segre predicted and then demonstrated that the Plutonium-238 which they were seeking from the Hanford piles spontaneously changed itself, at a slow rate, into its isotope Plutonium-240. Since Pu-240 was a spontaneous fissioner, this impurity would prematurely explode the target mass of plutonium in the gun-type trigger, since the inefficiency of the gun mechanism made it necessary to have the target mass so large (perfectly safe with U-235, but suicide with Pu-238 if there was Pu-240 in it also). The plutonium, therefore, had to be used with an implosion trigger, and, if that could not be devised, the \$400 million cost of the Hanford plant had been practically thrown away.

Fortunately, George Kistiakowsky, chemistry professor from Harvard and a great authority on explosives, came to Los Alamos, and by the spring of 1945 had worked out an ignition by which all the TNT would explode within a few millionths of a second. This saved the plutonium scheme, but it was clear that this material would hardly be available in a bomb amount until late summer of 1945 and that there would not be enough to test the implosion trigger on it, if it were to be used in the war.

By July 1945, everyone concerned with the bomb was working around the clock, and a few had begun to fear that the war would be over before the bomb would be ready. On the other hand, a group of the scientists, led by Szilard who had instigated the project, were beginning to agitate that the bomb should not be used against Japan. Their motives have been questioned since, but were both simple and honorable. They had pressed for the atom bomb in 1939 because they feared that Germany was working on one and might get it first. Once the defeat of Germany ended that danger, many scientists regarded continued work on the bomb as immoral and no longer defensive (since there was no chance of Japan's developing one). No one in July 1945 realized that all the significant information about making the bomb, notably the relative merits of different kinds of uranium, methods of plutonium separation, and the two kinds of trigger mechanisms, had been sent on to the Soviet Union, chiefly from Klaus Fuchs and David Greenglass by way of Harry Gold and Anatoli A. Yakovlev in June 1945. Even today American "security" agents are trying to keep secret these facts which have been fully explained in easily available technical publications.

For many years after 1945 the American people were kept in a state of alarm by stories of "networks" of "atomic spy rings," made up of Communist Party members or sympathizers, who were prowling the country to obtain by espionage what the Soviet Union was unable to achieve by its own efforts in scientific research and industrial development. These stories have been spread largely by partisan conservatives and Right-wing neo-isolationists, by the periodical press and other entertainment media who make money out of sensationalism, and by the publicity agencies of the Federal Bureau of Investigation (whose chief purpose, for more than a quarter-century, has been to depict J. Edgar Hoover as the chief, if not the sole, defense of our country against subversion).

An early and fairly typical example of these efforts was a semidocumentary film called the *House on 92nd Street*, which was made by Louis de Rochemont, in collaboration with the FBI, and was widely and favorably viewed by the American people in 1946. It showed that the FBI, *before the war*, had infiltrated the Nazi espionage network in this country and successfully frustrated its large-scale efforts to communicate to Germany atomic secrets which it had obtained from an employee in an atomic plant under military control. At the end of the picture the commentator's voice announced that the efforts of the FBI had successfully frustrated all efforts by foreign agents to penetrate our atomic secrets during the war, and would continue to do so.

The falsehoods in this motion picture, as in most of the subsequent publicity on atomic spying, are too numerous to be refuted completely; but it might be pointed out that atomic security was guarded by military Intelligence exclusively, and the FBI knew nothing of the project until April 1943, when Army Intelligence, G-2, asked the FBI *to stop* its surveillance of a Manhattan District employee whom the FBI had been watching because he was a suspected Communist (not because he was in the atomic project, of which the FBI knew nothing official until April 5, 1943). G-2 continued as the sole agency in Manhattan District security until after the war, although it used the resources of FBI (such as fingerprint files), as of other government agencies on a cooperative basis.

As for the tale of FBI exploits in the *House on 92nd Street*, as late as 1962 General Groves knew of no German efforts at atomic espionage. As to the final boast of that movie that no atomic secrets had been stolen during the war owing to FBI efforts, we now know that the information which was "stolen" went to the crowd that the FBI was watching, the Communists.

Most of the stories of atomic espionage which are now accepted as gospel by most Americans are similar to the *House on 92nd Street*. These stories were spread by partisan groups to discredit the Democratic administrations which had been in office in Washington from 1933 to 1953, by fanatical neo-isolationist conservatives who wished to discredit foreigners (including our Allies, such as England), scientists, the United

Nations, and all persons whose political sympathies were anywhere to the left of Warren G. Harding, and by various government agencies, such as the FBI and the air force, who could use such stories to obtain increased appropriations from the Congress. Some of the details of these struggles will be mentioned later.

When we speak of atomic secrets and spying, we must distinguish three quite different types of information: (1) scientific principles, (2) questions of general production tactics (such as, which methods are workable or unworkable), and (3) detailed information of engineering construction. No secrets of Group 1 existed; and secrets of Group 3 would usually have required elaborate blueprints and formulas which could not be passed by spying methods of communication. There remains information of Group 2, which could be extremely helpful in saving wasted time and effort. In most cases information of this type would have little meaning to anyone without a minimum of scientific training. This kind of information, so far as present information allows a judgment, would seem to have been passed to the Russians from two English scientists, Alan Nunn May and Klaus Fuchs, and an American Army enlisted man, David Greenglass, in the period to September 1945. Nunn May had little directly to do with the A-bomb, but he had worked on the heavy-water nuclear pile in Canada and had visited the graphite pile in Chicago several times. He gave Soviet agents Lieutenant Angelov and Colonel Zabotin, in Canada, considerable information about atomic piles, as well as the daily output of U-235 and plutonium at Oak Ridge (400 and 800 grams, respectively), and handed over a trace of the uranium isotope U-233.

The information from Fuchs, which was much more valuable, culminated about the same period (June 1945) and gave information on gaseous diffusion, the two trigger devices, and the fact that work had been done without much success toward a fusion H-bomb. Greenglass, at the same time, gave the same Russian contact, Harry Gold, a rough sketch of part of the "implosion trigger" for the A-bomb. There may have been other spying episodes of which we are not now aware, but the information passed to the Russians of which we are now aware probably did not contribute much significant aid to their achievement of the A-bomb. The H-bomb will be considered later. Statements frequently made that the Russians could not have made the A-bomb without information obtained from espionage, or statements that such information speeded up their acquisition of the bomb by years (or even by eighteen months) are most unlikely, although here again we cannot be sure. They must have been saved from trying some unremunerative lines of endeavor, but the real problems in making the bomb were engineering and fiscal problems, which Russia could overcome, on a crash basis, once it was known that we had such a bomb. This knowledge was given to the world by the destruction of Hiroshima.

The Twentieth-Century Pattern

The decision to use the bomb against Japan marks one of the critical turning points in the history of our times. We cannot now say that the world would have been better, but we can surely say that it would have been different. We can also say, with complete assurance, that no one involved in the decision had a complete or adequate picture of the situation. The scientists who were consulted had no information on the status of the war itself, had no idea how close to the end Japan already was, and had no experience to make judgments on this matter. The politicians and military men had no real conception of the nature of the new weapon or of the drastic revolution it offered to human life. To them it was simply a "bigger bomb," even a "much bigger bomb," and, by that fact alone, they welcomed it.

Some people, like General Groves, wanted it to be used to justify the $2 billion they had spent. A large group sided with him because the Democratic leaders in the Congress had authorized these expenditures outside proper congressional procedures and had cooperated in keeping them from almost all members of both houses by concealing them under misleading appropriation headings. Majority Leader John W. McCormack (later Speaker) once told me, half joking, that if the bomb had not worked he expected to face penal charges. Some Republicans, notably Congressman Albert J. Engel of Michigan, had already shown signs of a desire to use congressional investigations and newspaper publicity to raise questions about misuse of public funds. During one War Department discussion of this problem, a skilled engineer, Jack Madigan, said: "If the project succeeds, there won't be any investigation. If it doesn't, they won't investigate anything else." Moreover, some air-force officers were eager to protect the relative position of their service in the postwar demobilization and drastic reduction of financial appropriations by using a successful A-bomb drop as an argument that Japan had been defeated by air power rather than by naval or ground forces.

After it was all over, Director of Military Intelligence for the Pacific Theater of War Alfred McCormack, who was probably in as good position as anyone for judging the situation, felt that the Japanese surrender could have been obtained in a few weeks by blockade alone: "The Japanese had no longer enough food in stock, and their fuel reserves were practically exhausted. We had begun a secret process of mining all their harbors, which was steadily isolating them from the rest of the world.

If we had brought this operation to its logical conclusion, the destruction of Japan's cities with incendiary and other bombs would have been quite unnecessary. But General Norstad declared at Washington that this blockading action was a cowardly proceeding unworthy of the Air Force. It was therefore discontinued."

Even now it is impossible to make any final and impartial judgment of the merits of this decision. The degree to which it has since been distorted for partisan purposes may be seen from the contradictory charges that the efforts to get a bomb slowed down after the defeat of Germany and the opposite charge that they speeded up in that period. The former charge, aimed at the scientists, especially the refugees at Chicago who had given America the bomb by providing the original impetus toward it, was that these scientists, led by Szilard, were anti-Nazi, pro-Soviet, and un-American, and worked desperately for the bomb so long as Hitler was a threat, but on his demise opposed all further work for fear it would make the United States too strong against the Soviet Union. The opposite charge was that the Manhattan District worked with increasing frenzy after Germany's defeat, because General Groves was anti-Soviet. A variant of this last charge is that Groves was a racist and was willing to use the bomb on nonwhites like the Japanese but unwilling to use it against the Germans. It is true that Groves in his report of April 23, 1945, which was presented to President Truman by Secretary Stimson two days later, said that Japan had always been the target. The word "always" here probably goes back only to the date on which it was realized that the bomb would be so heavy that it could not be handled by any American plane in the European theater and, if used there, would have to be dropped from a British Lancaster, while in the Pacific the B-29 could handle it.

It seems clear that no one involved in making the decision in 1945 had any adequate picture of the situation. The original decision to make the bomb had been a correct one based on fear that Germany would get it first. On this basis the project might have been stopped as soon as it was clear that Germany was defeated without it. By that time other forces had come into the situation, forces too powerful to stop the project. It is equally clear that the defeat of Japan did not require the A-bomb, just as it did not require Russian entry into the war or an American invasion of the Japanese home islands. But, again, other factors involving interests and nonrational considerations were too powerful. However, if the United States had not finished the bomb project or had not used it, it seems most unlikely that the Soviet Union would have made its postwar efforts to get the bomb.

There are several reasons for this: (1) the bomb's true significance was even more remote from Soviet political and military leaders than from our own, and would have been too remote to make the effort to get it worthwhile if the bomb had never been demonstrated; (2) Soviet strategy had no interest in strategic bombing, and their final decision to make the bomb, based on our possession of it, involved changes in strategic ideas, and the effort, almost from scratch, to obtain a strategic bombing plane (the Tu-4) able to carry it; and (3) the strain on Soviet economic resources from making the bomb was very large, in view of the Russian war damage. Without the knowledge of the actual bomb which the Russian leaders obtained from our demonstration of its power, they would almost certainly not have made the effort to get the bomb if we had not used it on Japan.

On the other hand, if we had not used the bomb on Japan, we would have been quite incapable of preventing the Soviet ground forces from expanding wherever they were ordered in Eurasia in 1946 and later. We do not know where they might have been ordered because we do not know if the Kremlin is insatiable for conquest, as some "experts" claim, or is only seeking buffer security zones, as other "experts" believe, but it is clear that Soviet orders to advance were prevented by American possession of the A-bomb after 1945. It does seem clear that ultimately Soviet forces would have taken all of Germany, much of the Balkans, probably Manchuria, and possibly other fringe areas across central Asia, including Iran. Such an advance of Soviet power to the Rhine, the Adriatic, and the Aegean would have been totally unacceptable to the United States, but, without the atom bomb, we could hardly have stopped it. Moreover, such advance would have led to Communist or Communist-dominated coalition governments in Italy and France. If the Soviet forces had advanced to the Persian Gulf across Iran, this might have led to such Communist-elected governments in India and much of Africa.

From these considerations it seems likely that American suspension of the atomic project after the defeat of Germany or failure to use the bomb against Japan would have led eventually to American possession of the bomb in an otherwise intolerable position of inferiority to Russia or even to war in order to avoid such a position (but with little hope, from war, to avoid such inferiority). This would have occurred even if we assume the more optimistic of two assumptions about Russia: (1) that they would not themselves proceed to make the bomb and (2) that they are not themselves insatiably expansionist. On the whole, then, it seems that the stalemate of mutual nuclear terror without war in which the world now exists is preferable to what might have occurred if the United States had made the decision either to suspend the atomic project after the defeat of Germany or to refuse to use it on Japan. Any other possible decisions (such as an open demonstration of its power before an international audience in order to obtain an international organization able to control the new power) would probably have led to one of the two outcomes already described. But it must be clearly recognized that the particular stalemate of nuclear terror in which the world now lives derives directly from the two decisions made in 1945 to continue the project after the defeat of Germany and to use the bomb on Japan.

This nuclear stalemate, in turn, leads to pervasive consequences in all aspects of the world in the twentieth century. It gives rise to a frenzied race between the two super-Powers to outstrip each other in the application of science and rationality to life, beginning with weapons. This effort provides such expensive equipment and requires such skill from the operators of this equipment that it makes obsolete the army of temporarily drafted citizen-soldiers of the nineteenth century and of "the armed hordes" of World War I and even of World War II, and requires the use of highly trained, professional, mercenary fighting men.

The growth of the army of specialists, foretold by General de Gaulle in 1934 and foreseen by others, destroys one of the three basic foundations of political democracy. These three bases are (1) that men are relatively equal in factual power; (2) that men have relatively equal access to the information needed to make a government's decisions; and (3) that men have a psychological readiness to accept majority rule in return for those civil rights which will allow any minority to work to build itself up to become a majority.

Just as weapons development has destroyed the first of these bases, so secrecy, security considerations, and the growing complexity of the issues have served to undermine the second of these. The third, which was always the weakest of the three, is still in the stage of relative vitality and relative acceptability that it had in the nineteenth century, but is in much greater danger from the threat of outside forces, notably the changes in the other two bases, plus the greater danger today from external war or from domestic economic breakdown.

One great danger in regard to the second of these basic foundations (availability of information necessary for decision-making) is the impact upon it of the expansion of rationalization. While this has led to automatic and mechanical storage and retrieval of information, it has also led to efforts to establish automatic electronic decision-making on the basis of the growing volume and complexity of such information. This renunciation of the basic feature of being human—judgment and decision-making—is very dangerous and is a renunciation of the very faculty which gave man his success in the evolutionary struggle with other living creatures. If this whole process of human evolution is now to be abandoned in favor of some other, unconscious and mechanical, method of decision-making, in which the individual's flexibility and awareness are to be subordinated to a rigid group process, then man must yield to those forms of life, such as the social insects, which have already carried this method to a high degree of perfection.

This whole process has been made the central focus of a recent novel, *Fail-Safe*, by Eugene Burdick and Harvey Wheeler. The reduction of men to automatons in a complicated nexus of expensive machines is well shown in that book. To its picture must be added two points: (1) It does not require a blown condenser, as in the book, to unleash the full dangers of the situation; it is a situation which is dangerous in itself even if it functions perfectly; and (2) the avoidance of the ultimate total catastrophe in the book, because a few men, at and near the top, were able to resume the human functions of decision, self-sacrifice, love of their fellowmen, and hope for the future, should not conceal the fact that the whole world in that story came within minutes of handing its resources over to the insects.

Regardless of the outcome of the situation, it is increasingly clear that, in the twentieth century, the expert will replace the industrial tycoon in control of the economic system even as he will replace the democratic voter in control of the political system. This is because planning will inevitably replace laissez faire in the relationships between the two systems. This planning may not be single or unified, but it will be *planning*, in which the main framework and operational forces of the system will be established and limited by the experts on the governmental side; then the experts within the big units on the economic side will do their planning within these established limitations. Hopefully, the elements of choice and freedom may survive for the ordinary individual in that he may be free to make a choice between two opposing political groups (even if these groups have little policy choice within the parameters of policy established by the experts) and he may have the choice to switch his economic support from one large unit to another. But, in general, his freedom and choice will be controlled within very narrow alternatives by the fact that he will be numbered from birth and followed, as a number, through his educational training, his required military or other public service, his tax contributions, his health and medical requirements, and his final retirement and death benefits.

Eventually, in two or three generations, as the ordinary individual who is not an expert or a skilled professional soldier or a prominent industrial executive becomes of less personal concern to the government, his contacts with the government will become less direct and will take place increasingly through intermediaries. Some movement in this direction may be seen already in those cases where taxpayers whose incomes are entirely from wages or salaries find that their whole tax is already paid by their employer or in the decreasing need for the military draftee to be called to serve by a letter from the President. The development of such a situation, a kind of neofeudalism, in which the relationships of ordinary people to government cease to be direct and are increasingly through intermediaries (who are private rather than public authorities), is a long way in the future.

One consequence of the nuclear rivalry has been the almost total destruction of international law and the international community as they existed from the middle of the seventeenth century to the end of the nineteenth. That old international law was based on a number of sharp rational distinctions which no longer exist; these include the distinction between war and peace, the rights of neutrals, the distinction between combatants and noncombatants, the nature of the state, and the distinction between public and private authority. These are now either destroyed or in great confusion. We have already seen the obliteration of the distinctions between combatants and noncombatants and between neutrals and belligerents brought on by British actions in World War I. These began with the blockade of neutrals, like the Netherlands, and the use of floating mines in navigational waters. The Germans retaliated with acts against Belgian civilians and with indiscriminate submarine warfare. These kinds of actions continued in World War II with the British night-bombing effort aimed at destroying civilian morale by the destruction of workers' housing (Lord Cherwell's favorite tactic) and the American fire raids against Tokyo. It is generally stated in American accounts of the use of the first atom bomb that target planning was based on selection of military targets, and it is not generally known even today that the official orders from Cabinet level on this matter specifically said "military objectives surrounded by workers' housing." The postwar balance of terror reached its peak of total disregard both of noncombatants and of neutrals in the policies of John Foster Dulles, who combined sanctimonious religion with "massive retaliation wherever and whenever we judge fit" to the complete destruction of any noncombatant or neutral status.

Most other aspects of traditional international law have also been destroyed. The Cold War has left little to the old distinction between war and peace in which wars had to be formally declared and formally concluded. Hitler's attacks without warning; the Korean War, which was not a "war" in international law or in American constitutional law (since it was not "declared" by Congress); and the fact that no peace treaty has been signed with Germany to end World War II, while we are already engaged in all kinds of undeclared warlike activities against the Soviet Union, have combined to wipe out many of the distinctions between war and peace which were so painfully established in the five hundred years before Grotius died (in 1645).

Most of these losses are obvious but there are others, equally significant but not yet widely recognized. The growth of international law in the late medieval and Renaissance periods not only sought to make the distinctions we have indicated, as a reaction against "feudal disorder"; it also sought to make a sharp distinction between public and private authority (in order to get rid of the feudal doctrine of *dominia*) and to set up sharp criteria of public authority involving the new doc-trine of sovereignty. One of the chief criteria of such sovereignty was ability to maintain the peace and to enforce both law and order over a definite territory; one of its greatest achievements was the elimination of arbitrary nonsovereign private powers such as robber barons on land or piracy on the sea. Under this conception, ability to maintain law and order became the chief evidence of sovereignty, and the possession of sovereignty became the sole mark of public authority and the existence of a state. All this has now been destroyed. The Stimson Doctrine of 1931, now carried to its extreme conclusion in the American refusal to recognize Red China, shifted recognition from the objective criterion of ability to maintain order to the subjective criterion of approval of the form of government or liking of a government's domestic behavior.

The destruction of international law, like the destruction of inter-national order, has gone much further than this. As long as the chief criterion for a state's sovereignty, and hence of recognition, was ability to maintain order, states in international law were regarded as equal. This concept is still recognized in theory in such organizations as the Assembly of the United Nations. But the achievement of nuclear weap-ons, by creating two super-Powers in a Cold War, destroyed the fact of the equality of states. This had the obvious result of creating Powers on two levels: ordinary and super; but it had the less obvious, and more significant, consequence of permitting the existence of states of lower levels of power, far below the level of ordinary Powers. This arose be-cause the nuclear stalemate of the two super-Powers created an umbrella of fear of precipitating nuclear war which falsified their abilities to act at all.

As a result, all kinds of groups and individuals could do all kinds of actions to destroy law and order without suffering the consequences of forcible retaliation by ordinary powers or by the super-Powers, and could become recognized as states when they were still totally lacking in the traditional attributes of statehood. For example, the Léopoldsville group were recognized as the real government of the whole Congo in spite of the fact that they were incapable of maintaining law and order over the area (or even in Léopoldsville itself). In a similar way a gang of rebels in Yemen in 1962 were instantly recognized before they gave any evidence whatever of ability to maintain control or of readiness to assume the existing international obligations of the Yemen state, and before it was established that their claims to have killed the king were true. In Togo in the following year a band of disgruntled soldiers killed the president, Sylvanus Olympio, and replaced him with a recalled polit-ical exile.

Under the umbrella of nuclear stalemate, the boundaries of old states are shattered by guerrillas in conflict, supported by outsiders; outside governments subsidize murders or revolts, as the Russians did in Iraq in July 1958, or as Nasser of Egypt did in Jordan, Syria, Yemen, and elsewhere in the whole period after 1953, and as the American CIA did in several places, successfully in Iran in August 1953, and in Guatemala in May 1954, or very unsuccessfully, as in the Cuban invasion of April 1961. Under the Cold War umbrella, small groups or areas can obtain recognition as states without any need to demonstrate the traditional characteristics of statehood, namely, the ability to maintain their frontiers against their neighbors by force and the ability to maintain order within these frontiers. They can do this either by securing the intervention (usually secret) of some outside Power or even by preventing the intervention of a recognized Power fearful of precipitating nuclear or lesser conflict. In this way areas with a few states (such as southeast Asia) were shattered into many; states went out of existence or appeared (as Syria did in 1958 and 1961); and so-called new states came into existence by scores without reference to any traditional realities of political power or to the established procedures of international law.

The number of separate states registered as members in the United Nations rose steadily from 51 in 1945 to 82 in 1958 to 104 in 1961, and continued to rise. The difference in power between the strongest and the weakest became astronomical, and the whole mechanism of international relations, outside the UN organization as well as within it, became more and more remote from power considerations or even from reality, and became enmeshed in subjective considerations of symbols, prestige, personal pride, and petty spites. By 1963 single tribes in Africa were looking toward recognition of statehood through membership in the UN even when they lacked the financial resources to support a delegation at UN heaquarters in New York City or in the capitals of any major country and were, indeed, incapable of controlling police forces to maintain order in their own tribal areas.

In this way the existence of nuclear stalemate within the Cold War carried on the total destruction of traditional international law and the gradual loss of meaning of the established concepts of state and public authority, and opened the door to a feudalization of authority somewhat similar to that which the founders of the modern state system and of international law had sought to overcome in the period from the twelfth century to the seventeenth.

XVII

NUCLEAR RIVALRY AND THE COLD WAR: AMERICAN ATOMIC SUPREMACY, 1945-1950

The Factors
The Origins of the Cold War, 1945–1949
The Crisis in China, 1945–1950
American Confusions, 1945–1950

The Factors

HISTORICALLY, the period 1945 to early 1963 forms a unity. During this period a number of factors interacted upon one another to present a very complicated and extraordinarily dangerous series of events. That mankind and civilized life got through the period of almost two decades may be attributed to a number of lucky chances rather than to any particular skill among the two opposing political blocs or among the neutrals.

The period as a whole is so complex that no successful effort has been made by any historian to present it as a unity. Instead, it is usually treated as a series of separate, relatively isolated, developments, such as events in the Far East, United States domestic history, Soviet domestic history, developments in science and technology, the rise of the neutrals, and other developments. Such a presentation is not adequate because it falsifies the historical fact that these (and other) developments occurred simultaneously, and constantly reacted upon one another. Moreover, the central fact of the whole period, and the one which dominated all the others, was the scientific and technological rivalry between the United States and the Soviet Union, because this rivalry formed the very foundation and core of the Cold War, which was recognized by everyone to be the dominant political factor of the period.

Unfortunately, the Cold War is almost always described in terms which put minor emphasis on, or which may even neglect, the role of Soviet-American technological rivalry. This is done because most historians do not feel competent to discuss it; but chiefly it is done because much of the evidence is secret. Because of such secrecy, the story of this Soviet-American technological rivalry falls into two quite distinct, and even contradictory, parts: (1) what the real situation was and (2) what prevalent public opinion believed the situation to be. For example, in 1954-1955 the Soviet Union had a thermonuclear so-called H-bomb many months before we did, when public opinion believed the opposite; again, in late 1960 there was a widespread belief throughout the world in a so-called "missile gap," or American inferiority in nuclear missile weapons, when no such inferiority existed; and finally, for a period of several years, from 1957 to about 1960, the Russians were in advance of the United States and the free world generally in missile technology and in missile-guidance mechanisms, although this was not reflected, then or later, in any superiority in nuclear missile weapons, because of their simultaneous inferiority in nuclear warheads for missiles, an inferiority by a wide margin both in numbers and in variety of such explosive weapons.

In dealing with this central factor of the world situation, the historian is prevented by secrecy on both sides from making any assured or final judgments, and must simply make a judicious estimate of the situation on the basis of available information. Unfortunately, the influence of this factor is so central, and thus so all-pervasive, that inability to be sure of the facts on this matter brings a fair amount of uncertainty into many other areas, such as, for example, the foreign policy of John Foster Dulles or the real significance of the so-called "atomic espionage cases." Such uncertainty, however, is always present in historical analysis of the recent past, and most historians, knowing that the documents and thus the facts are unavailable for contemporary history (say, the last twenty years), usually leave the most recent past to others, to political scientists, journalists, or biographers.

In the history of the period 1945-1963 there are six chief factors: (1) the Cold War and the nuclear balance; (2) demobilization and remobilization, with special emphasis on interservice rivalries and the pressures from industrial complexes; (3) partisan political struggles in the United States, centering on the rise and decline of unilateralism; (4) personal political struggles in the Soviet Union, centering on the succession to Stalin; (5) intrabloc discords, centering on the relations between the United States and its allies on one side and the relations between the Soviet Union and its satellites on the other side; and (6) the role of neutralism, revolving around backward nationalisms and anticolonialism. The history of the period can be understood only in terms of the interplay of these six factors, in all their complexities, treated simultaneously, but before we attempt to do this we must make a brief examination of each factor separately in order to define our terms and to establish secondary chronological sequences.

The Cold War, as we shall see in the next chapter, was an inevitable consequence of the defeats of Germany, Japan, France, and Italy, and the collapse of Nationalist China, but it was raised to an acute and sustained crisis by the existence of nuclear weapons and the development of rocket missiles. The combination threatened the survival of man as a civilized being, although it probably did not threaten his continued existence, after a nuclear holocaust, on a degraded social level as a distinct species of living being. The fear of human extermination was spread by many well-intentioned, mistaken, or mercenary people, and reached its peak, perhaps, in the commercial success of Nevil Shute's *On the Beach*, both as novel and as motion picture. The annihilation of man, as shown in such works, is technically possible, but will certainly not result from the weapons which would be used in total thermonuclear war. However, there is always a remote possibility that a madman such as Hitler might decide to destroy the human race as revenge for the frustration of his insane ambitions. This could be done in a number of ways, of which the simplest would be to encase a large number of thermonuclear bombs in thick layers of cobalt; the ensuing fallout of radioactive cobalt 60 could extinguish all *animal* life on earth (excluding most plants, insects, and other invertebrates). No sane policy would use such a bomb, since cobalt 60 is 320 times as radioactive as radium, and it would require at least four hundred such bombs, each at least one ton in weight, to release enough radioactivity to extinguish all animal life on earth.

However, even without a cobalt bomb, any extensive nuclear war would kill hundreds of millions of human beings and would release sufficient radioactivity to inflict such extensive genetic damage that subsequent generations of human beings would produce a substantial percentage of monsters; this fact, added to the genetic damage to birdlife, might create a situation where men would be unable to compete successfully with insects (who are much more immune to genetic damage from radioactivity).

The balance of nuclear weapons is a central factor in the Cold War, since no agreement on cessation of nuclear testing, nuclear disarmament, conventional disarmament, or relaxation of tension can occur until both sides recognize that a nuclear balance of equilibrium (the so-called "nuclear stalemate") has been achieved. This came close to achievement early in 1950, when both sides had atomic weapons, but was destroyed at that time by President Truman's order to proceed with the development of the hydrogen bomb. It was not achieved again until the end of 1962, because when both sides had achieved the H-bomb by 1956, that balance was disturbed by the missile race, which reached its widest disequilibrium with the Soviet success with "Sputnik" in October 1957. This led to the subsequent race to obtain an intercontinental ballistic missile with nuclear warhead (ICBM) in 1957-1962.

By 1963, when both sides had these weapons, the balance of terror was established and negotiation was possible. As a matter of fact, the balance was not equal, since the American total capability in nuclear war was far superior to that of the Soviet Union in 1963, but weapons development had reached approximately the same point; the United States was more vulnerable to Russia's fewer weapons because a larger part of its population was industrial and urban, and the Soviet Union had growing problems in other areas, notably its alienation from Communist China. At the same time, gross fissures began to appear in the Western bloc from

De Gaulle's efforts to turn Europe out of the American camp and into a Third ("neutralist") Force. About the same time, the Cuban Crisis of October 1962, somewhat like the Fashoda Crisis of 1898, by bringing the United States and the Soviet Union to the edge of a war that neither wanted, revealed to both the mutual balance of error and the need to do something about it. All this marked the end of the historical period which began in 1945.

The chief subdivisions of the history of nuclear balance over the period 1945–1963 are as follows:

1. The American Atomic Monopoly from Alamogordo in June 1945 to the first Soviet atom bomb ("Joe I") in August 1949.
2. A brief nuclear balance from 1949 to 1950.
3. The Race for the Hydrogen Bomb from January 1950 through the first American hydrogen fusion at Eniwetok in November 1952 and the first Soviet H-bomb explosion of August 1953 to the American achievement of a practical thermonuclear weapon in March 1954. This contest continued for two more years as each side tried to perfect the new weapon as an aerial bomb. The United States made its first successful air drop of a fusion bomb on May 21, 1956—almost certainly later than the comparable Soviet test.
4. The Race for the ICBM from 1956 to 1962 has been widely misunderstood because propaganda falsehoods from both sides sought to conceal the true situation and often confused even themselves. Basically the problem was, at the beginning, how to combine the American Nagasaki bomb, which weighed 9,000 pounds, with the German V-2 rocket, which carried a warhead of 1,700 pounds only 200 miles. The Soviet government sought to close the gap between rocket power and nuclear payload by working toward a more powerful rocket, while the Americans, over the opposition of the air force and the aviation industry, sought to close the gap by getting smaller bombs. The result of the race was that the Soviet government acquired a series of very powerful rocket boosters ranging in thrust from 800,000 pounds to 1.5 million pounds, and capable of hurling capsules from one to over seven tons in weight. These were demonstrated to an astonished world from October 1957 onward.

These Soviet successes in space made the American effort in rocket boosters look very second-rate, but this impression was rather misleading. It was perfectly true that the United States in 1957–1960 had no powerful rocket boosters capable of hurling large space vehicles into orbit or past the moon (as was done with the 3,245-pound Soviet Lunik I in January 1959), but the United States in this period had a large number of fission and fusion warheads in a great variety of sizes, and was rapidly developing moderately powerful rockets able to carry these great distances. In fact, the first American ICBM was fired from Cape Canaveral in December 1957, two months after Sputnik I, and went full range in November 1958.

By 1961 the United States had a varied assortment of missiles, both solid- and liquid-fueled, some able to be fired in minutes, and capable of carrying nuclear warheads, whose explosive power was equivalent to as little as 750,000 tons of TNT (thus forty-three times the force of the Hiroshima A-bomb) to 5,000,000 or more tons of TNT. These could be delivered distances from 1,000 to over 6,000 miles and with such accuracy that at least half could be landed in a circle within 3 miles of a target.

These developments left the Soviet Union with a much smaller number of giant rockets able to carry 20-megaton (20,000,000 tons of TNT) warheads, but so large that their locations were soon spied out by American high-flying U-2 photographic planes. To remedy this overemphasis on size, the Soviet Union, in October 1961, broke the moratorium on nuclear explosive testing which had existed since October 1958, and exploded a great variety of small bombs from 1 to 5 megatons, as well as a gigantic one of 25 megatons and a colossal one of 58 megatons; the latter, the largest bomb ever exploded, was equal to one-third the total of all previous nuclear explosions from 1945 to the end of previous testing in December 1958.

Even before these final tests, in 1960 elaborate calculations on the giant electronic computers in the Pentagon were estimating the consequences of a hypothetical total nuclear war in June 1963. Two answers were: (1) If the Soviet Union struck first and the United States retaliated, the war would be over in a single day with a Russian victory in which they lost 40 million of their 220 million population dead and 40 percent of their industrial capacity, while America would have 150 million of its 195 million people dead and 60 percent of its industry destroyed. (2) If the United States struck first with a nuclear attack, in reply to a Soviet advance of ground troops into Germany, 75 million Russians and 110 million Americans would be killed, half the industry of both would be destroyed, and neither could win. On this basis, some relaxation of tension became imperative, as soon as the Soviets could .be satisfied they had achieved stalemate by their 1961–1962 nuclear tests.

Closely related to this four-stage sequence of nuclear capability is the quite different four-stage sequence of strategic planning. This is concerned with what we plan to do as distinct from what we are able to do. From the American side it has four stages, as follows:

1. "Great Power Cooperation" within the United Nations Organization, 1945–1946.

2. "Containment of" Soviet expansion by all means available, including economic aid to others (the Marshall Plan), conventional forces (as in NATO), and nuclear weapons, 1946–1953.

3. "Liberation," "Massive Retaliation," and the "New Look," 1953–1960. This period, associated with the influence of Secretary of State John Foster Dulles, sought to deal with foreign crisis by the use of slogans and quite unrealistic policies which could never have been used. Our allies, the neutrals, and even the Russians were ignored and often despised, while the State Department engaged in what Dulles himself called, in January 1956, "going to the brink" of war. This policy sought to reduce government spending and balance the budget by reducing expenditures for all local or conventional wars and to base our strategy and our foreign policy on the threat that any Soviet advance of any kind anywhere of which we disapproved would be stopped by our "massive retaliation" with all-out nuclear attack anywhere we judged appropriate, on a unilateral (without consultation with our allies) and on a "first-strike" basis (that is, we would do this even if the Soviet Union had not attacked us and had not used nuclear weapons). This policy was hopelessly irresponsible and not only alienated allies (such as France) and neutrals (such as India), but could not be used, since we would never adopt such suicidal and ineffective tactics to reply to a Communist local advance in Korea, southeast Asia, Tibet, Afghanistan, Iran, Egypt, Yugoslavia, or most other places on the periphery of the Soviet bloc. This policy abandoned NATO, in fact if not in theory, and meant that we had publicly adopted a policy we would never carry out; because even if we were willing to accept the full consequences of the Soviet nuclear counterblow to our "massive retaliation" we could not ever win in such a war, since Soviet ground forces, with their 125 divisions in Europe, could easily overrun NATO's 25 divisions and would occupy all Europe except Britain and Spain. The Kremlin leaders, moving to Paris or Rome (perhaps in the Vatican) would be beyond our reach and could hold London under nuclear threat, while both the United States and the Soviet Union were devastated. The Dulles doctrine was not a doctrine of action but solely a doctrine of threats, since it expected that the threat alone would stop Soviet advances and that it would never be necessary to carry out the threat. The policy worked, in the sense that the world and the United States lived through it, only because the Soviet Union, at the same time, was in the "interregnum" between the death of Stalin (March 5, 1952) and the accession to full power of Khrushchev (July 4, 1957 to March 27, 1958). The last two years were occupied by the Eisenhower administration's efforts to get back to a more workable defense policy based on a variety of responses to Soviet actions and to do so without either repudiating Dulles or excessively unbalancing the budget.

4. "Graduated deterrence," from 1960 onward, was really an effort to get back to the polices of 1950 as advocated by the National Security Council paper NSC 58 of March 1950, and generally to the advice given by Robert Oppenheimer before his public career had been destroyed by the "massive retaliation" advocates in 1953. This revived doctrine called for a graduated and varied strategic response to Soviet aggression combined with cooperation with our allies, recognition of the rights of neutrals to be neutral, increased economic and cultural aid to both groups, and relaxation of tension with the Soviet Union by cultural and scientific cooperation. This broad and varied program had at its core development of at least four levels of possible war: (1) war with conventional weapons; (2) addition of tactical nuclear weapons; (3) strategic nuclear attack on a "no cities" basis (with attacks aimed only at Soviet military bases and installations); and (4) the "total-devastation response." Each of these had subgradations and gave rise to unsolved problems such as "escalation," that is, the possibility that one level would develop gradually into a more intense level in the heat of combat. Moreover, such complex responses required immense outlays of money, even if the achievement of the whole was spread over many years. But this cost, it was felt, would be worthwhile, since nuclear warfare on a "no cities" basis would save about 100 million American lives in the first week of war in comparison with war on the "total-devastation" level. One element in this whole strategic shift was the shift of the emphasis of our response from Strategic Air Command (SAC) nuclear bombing to conventional army forces and to the navy's nuclear submarines with Polaris missiles. The former would reduce the temptation to the Soviet Union to instigate local "brush-fire" wars, while the latter would be even more successful in preventing any Soviet nuclear "first strike," since such an attack would be much less able to find and destroy Polaris submarines than it would be to wipe out fixed SAC bases.

The next great aspect of postwar history was the partisan political struggles within the United States, centering on the rise and decline of unilateralism and neo-isolationism. As we shall see in a later chapter, the party struggle in the United States took the form of a struggle between the party of the middle classes, the Republicans, and the party of the fringes, the Democrats. This lineup, with its multitude of exceptional cases, found the intellectuals (including the scientists), the internationalists, the minorities, and the cosmopolitans in the Democratic Party, with the businessmen, bankers, and clerks in the Republican Party. The isolationism of the latter, combined with their inability to cope with the world depression or with the international crisis arising from Hitler, kept the Democrats in the White House for twenty years (1933-1953). The defeat of Dewey by Truman in 1948 was a particularly bitter pill, and the Republican partisans after that event were ready to adopt any weapon which could be used to discredit the Democratic administration. They found such a weapon ready at hand in the neo-isolationist forces within the Republican Party which were entrenched in the Congress by the seniority system of committee controls which operated there. Since either party in the United States wins a presidential election on a national (and not on a local) basis and by appealing to the moderate middle-group people who are willing to shift their vote and to consider the issues presented, a party which is long out of the White House will be reduced to the control of its local, narrow, ignorant, and extremist core which is unwilling to consider issues or the national welfare, or to shift their party stand and votes. For these reasons, the Republican Party had fallen into congressional control (represented by Senate figures such as Senators Robert Taft, Kenneth Wherry, Styles Bridges, and William Jenner) of those who were most ignorant of the real issues and were most remote from any conceptions of national political responsibility.

This group, to whom we often give the name "neo-isolationist," knew nothing of the world outside the United States, and generally despised it. Thus, they gave no consideration to our allies or neutrals, and saw no reason to know or to study Russia, since it could be hated completely without need for accurate knowledge. All foreigners were regarded as unprincipled, weak, poor, ignorant, and evil, with only one aim in life, namely, to prey on the United States. These neo-isolationists and uni-lateralists were equally filled with suspicion or hatred of any American intellectuals, including scientists, because they had no conception of any man who placed objective truth higher than subjective interests, since such an attitude was a complete challenge to the American businessman's assumption that all men are and should be concerned with the pursuit of self-interest and profit.

At the end of the war, it was but natural that many Americans should seek to return from foreign and incomprehensible matters, including countries, peoples, and problems which were a standing refutation of the American neo-isolationist's ideas of human nature, of social structure, and of proper motivations.

Neo-isolationism had a series of assumptions which explain their statements and actions and which could not possibly be held by anyone who had any knowledge of the world outside American lower-middle-class business circles. These beliefs were at least seven in number:

1. Unilateralism: the belief that the United States should and could act by itself without need to consider allies, neutrals, or the Soviet Union.
2. National omnipotence: the belief that the United States is so rich and powerful that no one else counts and that there is, accordingly, no need to study foreign areas, customs, or policies, since America's

policies can be based exclusively on its own power and its own high moral principles (which have no real meaning to anyone else).

3. Unlimited goals (or utopianism): the belief that there are final solutions to the world's problems. This assumes that American power permits it to do what it wishes and that demonstration of this power to troublemaking foreigners will make them leave the United States alone and secure forever. This idea was reflected in its crudest form in the belief that America's power could be applied to the world in one final smash after which everything would be settled forever. Upholders of this view refused to accept that America's security in the nineteenth century had been an untypical and temporary condition and that constant danger and constant problems were a perpetual condition of human life except in brief and unusual circumstances. This kind of impatience with foreign problems and danger was clearly stated by Dulles in his article "A Policy of Boldness" in *Life* magazine, May 19, 1952. There he insisted that the Truman policy of containment must be replaced by a policy of "liberation," since the former was based on "treadmill policies which at best might perhaps keep us in the same place until we drop exhausted." These policies, he argued, would lead to financial collapse and loss of civil liberties, were "not designed to win victory conclusively," and did not seek to solve the problem of the Soviet Union but to live with it, "presumably forever." His solution was to refuse to recognize Communist control either in the European satellites or in China, to deny the existence of the Iron Curtain, and to free millions enslaved by Communism. Although the only way these millions could be freed was by war, Dulles refused to advocate preventive war, and established no method of achieving his goals except his belief that, if he refused to face reality, reality would change. However, he did accept preventive war in the form of massive retaliation if the Communists made any further advances, and he established the argument that the Truman policy of containing the Communists was a policy of refusing to defeat them, from softness or fear or sympathy. This became the basis for future partisan Republican charges that Democratic administrations were "soft on Communism" and pursued "no-win" policies.

4. The neo-isolationist belief in American omnipotence and foreign inferiority led, almost at once, to the conclusion that continuance of the Soviet threat arose from internal treason within America and that the Russian nuclear successes must be based on treason and espionage and could not possibly be based on foreign science or Soviet industrial capability. The neo-isolationists were convinced that the only threat to America came from internal subversion, from Communist sympathizers and "fellow travelers," since no foreign threat could harm our omnipotence. All opposition to neo-isolationist views was branded

as "un-American," and was traced to low motivations or corruption of American life by such non-American innovations as economic planning, social welfare, or concern for foreigners. Henry Wallace and Mrs. Roosevelt, who were the special targets of these isolationists, were accused of conspiring to give away America's wealth (in order to weaken it): "a quart of milk to every Hottentot."

5. Since the chief "high moral principle" which motivated the neo-isolationists was their own economic self-interest, they were especially agitated by high taxes, and insisted that Soviet Russia and the Democrats were engaged in a joint tacit conspiracy to destroy America by high taxes by using Cold War crisis to tax America into bankruptcy.

6. Since the neo-isolationists rejected all partial solutions or limited goals, and were unwilling to pay to increase America's military power (since they insisted it was already overwhelmingly powerful), there was little they could do in foreign affairs except to talk loudly and sign anti-Communist pacts and manifestos. This explains Dulles's verbal bluster and "missile rattling" and his pactomania which kept him running about the world signing documents which bound people to pursue anti-Communist policies.

7. The unrealistic and unhistoric nature of neo-isolationism meant that it could not actually be pursued as a policy. It was pursued by John Foster Dulles, with permanent injury to our allies, the neutrals, and the personnel of American government, but it was not followed in the Pentagon and was followed only halfheartedly by Eisenhower in the White House. The President sought to keep the moderate middle group of voters in his camp by radiating his personal charm around the country, but the Pentagon refused to follow Dulles's tactics of appeasing the neo-isolationists by refusing to defend their departmental employees. When Senator McCarthy turned his extravagant charges of subversion and treason from the State Department to the army, the employees of the latter were defended by Secretary Robert Stevens, and McCarthy's downfall began. The neo-isolationist forces, although defeated at the ballot box in 1960 and 1962, still continue in an increasingly irresponsible form under a variety of names, including John Birch Society members, or, more generally, as the "Radical Right."

Much less obvious to the public eye than neo-isolationism, but equally influential in creating the history of 1945–1963, was the struggle within the American defense services as to what use would be made of the nuclear weapon. In 1945 the atom bomb was at once hailed as the "absolute weapon" against which there was "no defense." If true, this would have meant the end of the army and navy, since the existing bomb, shaped like a hen's egg, 10 feet 8 inches long, 5 feet in diameter, and weighing 10,000 pounds, could be handled in the B-29 only by modifying its bomb drop to widen the opening, and could not be handled by the ground forces or by navy guns or carrier planes. Morever, the range and intensity of its destruction gave rise to immediate claims from the advocates of air power that massed ground forces, slow-moving armored equipment, and all naval vessels, especially the expensive carriers and capital ships, were made obsolete by the new weapon. These extravagant claims were made more critical in their impact by the Strategic Bombing Surveys of World War II and the demobilization problems at the war's end.

The advocates of air power from at least 1908 had made extravagant claims, usually based on future rather than on presently available equipment, that the airplane provided the final supreme weapon which made all other methods of warfare unnecessary. This was seen in the arguments of General Giulio Douhet of Italy, General "Billy" Mitchell of the United States, and the refugee Russian airplane designer Alexander de Seversky. Douhet as early as 1921 preached that the next war would be ended in the first twenty-four hours by the total destruction of all enemy cities from the air; Mitchell in the mid-1920's raised a great furor with his claims that land-based planes had made battleships and lesser naval vessels obsolete; and Seversky, before, during, and after World War II, claimed that air power had made other arms needless. We have seen how these claims had a considerable and pernicious influence on men's actions before and during World War II. Many airmen who did not believe these claims nevertheless felt that they had to support them in order to obtain a large slice of their country's defense funds from civilian politicians who were in no position to judge the merits of such claims.

The experience of World War II did not, at first glance, support the claims of the advocates of air power. On November 3, 1944, the United States Secretary of War, on order of the President, set up a committee of twelve to conduct a Strategic Bombing Survey to examine the contribution of strategic bombing to final victory by evaluating bomb damage, assessing captured German and Japanese documents, and interviewing the leaders of the defeated countries. The German survey, which came out in 208 parts over several years, beginning in 1945, did not, on the whole, support the claims of the air enthusiasts, but rather showed that the air-force contribution was much less than had been anticipated or hoped and had become substantial, chiefly in transportation and in gasoline supplies, only after October 1944, when Germany was already beaten (with tactical air-force help) on the ground.

These conclusions were very unwelcome to the army air-force officers devoted to strategic bombing, and especially to the airplane-manufacturing industry, which had reached the multibillion-dollar size and hoped to retain at least some of its market after the war's end. In the last few months of the war against Japan, at least $400 million worth of Boeing

B-29's and parts were in action in the Pacific. Loss of faith in strategic bombing would expose air-force officers and the air-force industry to a grim and poverty-stricken postwar world. Accordingly, it became necessary to both groups to persuade the country that Japan had been defeated by strategic air power. The Strategic Bombing Survey of Japan did not support this contention, although by concentrating on strategic bombing it helped to cover up the vital role played by submarines in the destruction of the Japanese merchant marine, the equally vital role played by the early Marine Corps work in amphibious warfare, and, above all, in the magnificent job done by naval supply forces for all arms, including the strategic bombing bases themselves. The protection and supply of these bases in the Marianas was in sharp contrast with the loss of B-29 bases in continental China to Japanese ground forces, and showed to any unbiased outsider the need for a balanced distribution of all arms in any effective defense system. In such a balanced system the role of strategic bombing and of large long-range planes in general (as contrasted with tactical planes and fighters) would obviously be less than either the air-force officers or the airplane industrialists considered satisfactory.

Accordingly, it became urgent for these two groups and their supporters to convince the country (1) that the atom bomb was not "just another" weapon but was the final, "absolute," weapon; (2) that the atom bomb had been the decisive factor in the Japanese surrender; and (3) that nuclear weapons were fitted only for air-force use and could not be, or should not be, adapted for naval or ground-force use. The first two of these points were fairly well established in American public opinion in 1945–1947, but the third, because of atomic secrecy, had largely to be argued out behind the scenes. All three points were largely untrue (or true only if hedged about with reservations which would largely destroy their value as air-force propaganda), but those who used them were defending interests, not truth, even when they insisted that the interests they were defending were those of the United States and not merely those of the air force. In this controversy, the scientists, most of whom were naïvely defending truth, were bound to be crushed. On the other hand, any dissident scientist could obtain access to money and support by making an alliance with the air force.

At the center of this problem was the struggle for control of nuclear reactions within the United States, but the ultimate objective of the struggle was the right to exercise influence on the subdividing of the national defense budget. Thus, the struggle centered on the personnel of the Atomic Energy Commission (AEC) and especially of its scientific advisory panel of outstanding scientists, the so-called General Advisory Committee (GAC) of the AEC. And at the center of the whole struggle was Robert Oppenheimer.

Robert Oppenheimer, wartime director of the Los Alamos laboratory which made the A-bombs, was not a great scientist of the class including Einstein, Bohr, or Fermi, but his knowledge of the subject was profound, and wider than most. He was very well educated in cultural matters, especially literature and music, and could quote Homer in Greek and the Bhagavad-Gita in Sanskrit at appropriate occasions. His social and, to a greater extent, his political education did not begin until about 1935, when he was thirty-one and already a full professor at California Institute of Technology and at the University of California. His political naïveté continued until after the war. He had always been a persuasive talker, got along very well with a wide diversity of people, and during the war he discovered he was an excellent administrator. By 1947 he was the chief scientific adviser to most of the important agencies of the government, informally, if not formally, since other scientists frequently consulted with him before giving their decisions on problems. From 1947 on, he was chairman of the GAC, as well as a member of the Atomic Energy Committee of the Defense Department's Research and Development Board; of the National Science Foundation; of the President's Scientific Advisory Board; chairman of the board of the *Bulletin of Atomic Scientists*; and consultant on atomic energy to the CIA, to the State Department, to the National Security Council, to the American delegation to the United Nations, and to the Joint Congressional Committee on Atomic Energy (the congressional watchdog over the AEC)—in all, he was on a total of thirty-five government committees.

In spite of Oppenheimer's exalted positions in 1947–1953, which included the directorship of the great Institute for Advanced Study in Princeton (American copy of All Souls College at Oxford), there was a shadow on Oppenheimer's past. In his younger and more naïve days he had been closely associated with Communists. Certainly never a Communist himself, and never, at any time, disloyal to the United States, he had, nonetheless, had long associations with Communists. Partly this arose from his political inexperience, partly from the prevalence of Communists among the intellectual circles of the San Francisco Bay region where he spent the years 1929–1942 as a professor, and partly from his sudden and belated realization of the terrible tragedy of the world depression and of Hitler about 1936. At any rate, his brother, Frank Oppenheimer, and the latter's wife were Communist Party workers in San Francisco at least from 1937 to 1941, while Oppenheimer's own wife, whom he married in 1940, was an ex-Communist, widow of a Communist who had been killed fighting Fascism in Spain in 1937.

The Oppenheimers continued to have friends who were Communists, and Oppenheimer contributed money until the end of 1941, through Communist channels, to Spanish Refugee Relief and to aid for migratory farm workers in California. As late as 1943 he had some kind of remote emotional relationship with a girl, daughter of a fellow professor, who was a Communist. All of this "derogatory" information was known to General Groves and to Army Intelligence, G-2, before Oppenheimer was made head of Los Alamos in 1942. The appointment was made because his talents were urgently needed, and there was no reason to feel that he was a Communist himself or that he had ever been, or would ever be, disloyal to the United States.

For the next four years Oppenheimer was kept under constant surveillance by M-2; his conversations secretly recorded, telephone calls and letters monitored, and all his movements shadowed. In 1954, under oath, General Groves testified to his belief in Oppenheimer's discretion and loyalty, and he repeated this in his memoirs, published in 1962. The significance of all this is that this ancient evidence, plus Oppenheimer's alleged opposition to efforts to make the H-bomb in 1946–1949, was used by the advocates of air power, the neo-isolationists, the exponents of massive retaliation, and the professional anti-Communists in 1953–1954 to destroy Oppenheimer's public reputation, to end his opportunity for continued public service, and to discredit the preceding Democratic administration in Washington. It was an essential element in the massive-retaliation, neo-isolationist, McCarthyite, Dulles interregnum of 1953–1957, which ran almost exactly parallel to the post-Stalin interregnum in the Soviet Union during the same years.

The last significant factor in this postwar period of eighteen years was provided by the events in the Far East. In this factor also there are three subperiods, of which the most significant was the middle one from "the loss of China" to the Communists late in 1949 to the Geneva "Summit Conference" of July 1955. In this period the Far East was in confusion over the Chinese victory in mainland China; the outbreak of war in Korea in June 1950; the Korean armistice of July 1953; the Indo-Chinese war and armistice in 1953–1954; and the threatened Chinese Communist attack on Quemoy, if not on Formosa, in the winter of 1954–1955. The earlier period of Far Eastern history saw the slow decay of the Nationalist Chinese regime of Chiang Kai-shek and the revival of Japan, while the later, third, period centered upon the growing strength and dangerous pugnacity of "Red" China. This third period ended with the Chinese attack on India in October 1962 and the break between Communist China and the Soviet Union at the end of 1962.

The interweaving of these six factors makes up a major part of the history of the period 1945–1963. In each case we can discern three stages, of which the middle one is the most critical. The dates of these stages are not, of course, the same for all six factors, but they are close enough so that the whole eighteen years can be examined successfully as three consecutive subperiods organized around the central core of the nuclear rivalry between the United States and the Soviet Union. Accordingly, we can examine this whole period in the three stages: (1) American atomic supremacy, 1945–1950; (2) the race for the H-bomb, 1950–1957; and (3) the race for the Intercontinental Ballistic Missile (IBM) from 1957 to early 1963.

The Origins of the Cold War, 1945-1949

The surrender of Japan left much of the world balanced between the mass armies of the Soviet Union and the American nuclear monopoly. It was an unequal balance, because the United States would not have used its atomic weapon against the Russians for anything Russia was likely to do. Stalin realized this, and largely ignored the atom bomb, although his designer, Andrei Tupolev, successfully copied four B-29's captured by the Russians in the Far East in 1944 and brought these to production (as Tu-4's) in 1947. Otherwise, the Kremlin's assessment of the situation was quite mistaken.

Stalin assumed that the United States would soon relapse into isolationism, as it had done after World War I, and would be fully occupied with a postwar economic collapse like that of 1921. Accordingly, he regarded Britain as the chief obstacle to his plans, and, seeing that it was both small and weak, with most unpromising economic prospects, he proceeded to carry out his designs with relatively little attention to the reactions of either English-speaking Power. These plans involved the creation of a Soviet-controlled buffer fringe of satellite states on the Soviet frontiers in all areas occupied by Soviet armies, and Communist coalition governments beyond these areas. In both cases the local Communists would be controlled by leaders of their own nationality who had been trained under Comintern auspices in the Soviet Union. In some cases, these Communist leaders had been exiles in Russia for more than twenty years.

The chief error in Stalin's postwar strategy was his total misjudgment of President Truman and, on a wider stage, of the American people as a whole. Some of this error undoubtedly arose from Stalin's ignorance of the world outside Russia and from the fact that his terrorist tactics in Russia in the 1930's had made it difficult for him to get reliable foreign information from his diplomatic corps, which was shielded from contact with foreigners and was more concerned with sending Stalin the information he expected than with that derived from independent observations. In any case, the Kremlin misjudged both Truman and the American people.

Truman, in spite of a natural suspicion of the Russians, ended the war with every intention of trying to carry out Roosevelt's original plans for postwar cooperation with the Soviet Union. In addition, having learned much from the 1920's, he intended to make every effort to avoid either a postwar economic depression or a relapse into isolationism. His success in avoiding these events made it possible to reverse his inherited policy of cooperation with Russia when Stalin's actions in 1946–1947 made it clear that cooperation was the last thing the Kremlin wanted. These actions appeared most clearly in regard to Germany.

We have already noted the Soviet subversion of Poland, Romania, and Bulgaria by native Communists returning from Russia under the protection of the Soviet armies. The same thing occurred, but more gradually, in eastern Germany. There the Communists at first pretended to cooperate with any "anti-Fascist" groups, but their unwillingness to cooperate with the Western Powers in the administration of Germany appeared almost at once. They gradually closed off their occupation zone and refused to carry out the earlier agreements to treat Germany as a single administrative and economic unit. This meant that the usual economic exchange within Germany of food from the agricultural eastern portion of the country for the industrial products of western Germany was broken. Instead, East German food was drained to the Soviet Union. To prevent starvation of the West Germans, the United States and Britain had to send in hundreds of millions of dollars' worth of food and other supplies. On May 3, 1946, General Lucius D. Clay, head of the American Military Government in Germany, informed the Russians that no future agreements would be made to ship West German industrial equipment as reparations to Russia until the Russians agreed to treat Germany as an economic unit and to give some accounting of their reparations plundering of East Germany. Both points referred to open violations of the Potsdam Agreement regarding the treatment of Germany.

The Soviet Union justified these and other violations of earlier agreements on the urgent need for their own economic rehabilitation. There can be no doubt that the Soviet Union had suffered great economic damage from the war, possibly the loss of a quarter of its prewar wealth, more than all the other victor countries combined, but the Kremlin could have obtained much more by continued cooperation with the United States than it did from its postwar policy of studied enmity. This enmity was based on a number of factors: In the first place, Stalin was misled by the false ideology of Marx and Lenin which spoke of the inevitable struggle of capitalism and Communism, of the inevitable economic breakdown of the capitalist system, and of the capitalist endeavor to avoid such a breakdown by militarist aggression. On this basis, Stalin could not believe that the United States was prepared to be generous and cooperative toward the Soviet Union.

Moreover, Stalin was worried by the weakness in depth of the Soviet system from economic damage and from ideological dissent. The war had been fought on an ideology of patriotism and nationalism, not as a Communist ideological struggle, and the Kremlin by 1946 was eager to get back to its Communist ideology, partly as justification of the new hardships of reconstruction under the fourth Five-Year Plan (March 13, 1946) and partly to overcome the Russian soldiers' admiration for what they had seen of the West. These soldiers, for example, were amazed to discover that the "exploited" German workers of whom they had heard so much had standards of living several times higher than those of the ordinary Russian. The discovery that ordinary Germans had watches, even wristwatches, was an astounding revelation to the Russian soldiers, who proceeded to seize these wherever they saw them.

A third factor guiding Soviet behavior was the discovery that there was no mass support for Russia or for Communist ideology in eastern and central Europe, especially among the peasants, and that the buffer of Communist states along Russia's western border would have to be built on force and not on consent. The governments of these states could be recruited from men of the respective nations who had been living in the Soviet Union for years under endless Communist indoctrination, but the unindoctrinated masses in each country would have to be held in bondage by Soviet military forces, at least until local Communist parties and local secret-police organizations subservient to Moscow's orders could be built up. The urgent need for this, from the Kremlin's point of view, was shown, when Austria and Hungary, although under Soviet military occupation, were permitted relatively free elections in November 1945. Both resulted in sharp defeats for the local Communist parties. Because such an outcome could not be permitted in the buffer satellites farther east, elections there had to be postponed until the local governments were sufficiently communized and entrenched to be able to guarantee a favorable outcome to any election.

It was this situation which made it impossible, in Russia's view, to carry out the promises made at Yalta and elsewhere about free elections in Poland or other countries neighboring on Russia. The United States, through Secretary of State Byrnes, assured the Kremlin that it wanted these neighboring states to have "democratic" governments "friendly" to the Soviet Union. The Kremlin knew, although Byrnes apparently did not, that these were mutually exclusive terms. They insisted these governments must be "friendly," while he insisted that they must be "free" and "democratic" in the Western sense. Since the Kremlin assumed that Byrnes knew as well as they did of the contradiction in terms here, they assumed that his insistence on "democratic" governments in eastern Europe indicated that he really wanted governments unfriendly to the Soviet Union. They were willing to call any governments which were friendly "free" and "democratic," but Byrnes refused to accept this reversal of the ordinary American meaning of these words.

These disputes over Germany and eastern Europe, which were regarded in the West as Soviet violations of their earlier agreements at Yalta and Potsdam, were regarded in Moscow as evidence for Stalin's conviction of the secret aggressive designs of the West. By the winter of 1945–1946, the Russian peoples were being warned of the dangers from the West. This began in 1945 with attacks on "cosmopolitanism" and prohibitions of Soviet soldiers "fraternizing" with aliens, especially soldiers of the United States or Britain, in the course of their occupation duties. Early in November 1945, Molotov warned the Moscow Soviet that Fascism and imperialist aggression were still loose in the world. Similar speeches were made by other Soviet leaders, including Stalin. By the spring of 1946, xenophobia, one of the oldest of Russian culture traits, was rampant again. In September 1946, and again in September 1947, Andrei Zhdanov, the Kremlin's leader of the international Communist movement, made speeches which were simply declarations of ideological war on the West. They presented the Soviet Union as the last best hope of man, surrounded by prowling, capitalist beasts of prey seeking to destroy it.

On this basis the Soviet Union found it impossible to cooperate with the West or to accept the American economic assistance in reconstruction which was offered. The American Congress in the last renewal of the Lend-Lease Act in 1945 had forbidden use of these funds for postwar rehabilitation, but other funds were made available. For the transitional period these amounted to about $9 billion. These transitional funds were made available on a humanitarian and economic basis and not on political or ideological grounds. Accordingly, they were available to the Soviet Union and other areas under Communist control in accordance with the provisions of each fund. For example, the United Nations Relief and Rehabilitation Administration (UNRRA), was an international organization which handled goods worth $3,683 million, of which 65 percent was provided from the United States, 15 percent from Britain, and 3.5 percent from Canada. Its grants went to 17 countries with China first ($518 million), Poland next ($478 million), Italy with $418 million, Yugoslavia with $416 million, and the Ukraine, seventh, with $188 million.

Beyond the primary, humanitarian aim of most United States assistance was the desire to get local economies functioning, and efforts to further America's basic conviction of the value of a high level of international trade on a multilateral basis. The United States was opposed to all restrictive trade measures such as autarchy, bilateralism, or quotas, and had as its ultimate aim the restoration of multilateral trade at the highest possible level, with freely convertible international monetary exchanges. It was convinced that such a system would be advantageous for all peoples, and did not see that it was anathema to the Soviet system, which had restrictions and quotas on economic life, even within the country, so that, while most Russians lived in poverty, a privileged minority, buying in special stores with special funds and special ration cards, had access to luxuries undreamed of by the ordinary person.

In the American plans for economic recovery, Great Britain, as the world's greatest trader, had a special role. The United Kingdom could not exist without very large imports, but it could not pay for these without large exports. Such exports had to be much larger than before the war, even to pay for the prewar level of imports, because many of Britain's prewar sources of overseas incomes from investments, shipping, insurance, and so on, had been drastically reduced by the war. In 1945 the British balance-of-payments deficit was about 875 million pounds sterling, and in 1946 it was still 344 million pounds. To tide over this deficit until British exports could recover, the United States in July 1946 provided Britain with a credit of $3,750 million, with interest at 2 percent and repayment in fifty annual installments to begin on December 31, 1951. The interest was to be waived whenever the British trade balance would not pay for imports on her 1936–1938 level. In return for this, Britain gave rather indefinite promises to work to reduce its bilateralism in trade, especially imperial preference, and to release, as soon as feasible, its blocked sterling accounts.

Lend-Lease was ended in September 1945, with the Japanese surrender, and all claims were settled with Britain under an agreement of December 1945. This canceled the American grants under Lend-Lease of over $30,000 million and gave Britain permanent establishments on British soil, with supplies in Britain or en route, for a settlement of $650 million payable on the same terms as the British loan just mentioned.

Assistance similar to these was available to the Soviet Union but was generally rebuffed. Even in 1945, efforts to establish international emergency committees for coal, transportation, and economic recovery in Europe were boycotted by the Soviet Union, with the exception of the one on transportation, which was necessary to supply the Russian troops. Little cooperation could be obtained from Soviet authorities for handling or aiding refugees, except for their demands for the return, to concentration camps or slave labor, of those who had fled from eastern Europe. On October 15, 1945, Moscow signed an agreement similar to Britain's by which they agreed to pay, after July 1954, for the quarter-billion dollars' worth of goods on their final Lend-Lease demands yet unfilled when Lend-Lease ended; but they refused to discuss any general Lend-Lease settlement and they refused to negotiate for a general loan, similar to that made to Britain, although Stalin had asked for one of $6 billion as early as January 1945. An American offer to discuss such a credit was rejected by Russia as "financial aggression" in March 1946. The offer was renewed

in April and again in September 1946, but the American aims of multilateral trade free of artificial restraints except tariffs, like the American
insistence on free elections, were regarded in Moscow as clear evidence
of America's aggressive aims.

One significant, but perhaps not essential, factor in the deterioration
of the relations of the Big Three in 1945 and 1946 lies in the provincial
ignorance of the three foreign ministers, Byrnes, Bevan, and Molotov,
who conducted the negotiations. All three were men of limited background and narrow outlook who saw the world from a narrow nationalistic point of view and were incapable of appreciating the outlook of
different cultures or the different values and verbal meanings to be found
in alien minds. Nevertheless, it does seem clear that the postwar breakdown of cooperation was inevitable in view of the conceptions of public
authority, state power, and political security to be found in all three
countries.

On the whole, if blame must be allotted, it may well be placed at the
door of Stalin's office in the Kremlin. American willingness to cooperate
continued until 1947, as is evident from the fact that the Marshall Plan
offer of American aid for a cooperative European recovery effort was
opened to the Soviet Union, but it now seems clear that Stalin had decided to close the door on cooperation and adopted a unilateral policy of
limited aggression about February or March of 1946. The beginning of
the Cold War may be placed at the date of this inferred decision or may
be placed at the later and more obvious date of the Soviet refusal to
accept Marshall Plan aid in July 1947. The significance of the latter date
is revealed by the fact that Czechoslovakia, which accepted on July 7th,
was forced by Stalin's direct order to Prime Minister Gottwald to reverse this decision on July 10th.

One significant encouragement to Soviet aggression came from the
almost total demobilization of the American war effort. Pressure from
special-interest groups such as business, labor unions, and cattlemen,
aroused public opinion for the ending of price controls and rationing and
obtained cooperation from an anti–New Deal coalition in Congress to
end most of the nation's economic controls in 1946. At the same time
came almost total military demobilization. In spite of Ambassador Harriman's explicit warnings from Moscow in April 1945, and Stalin's declaration of cold warfare in February 1946, the American government carried out the demobilization plan of September 1943, which was based on
individual rather than on unit discharges. This destroyed the combat effectiveness of all units by the end of 1945, when almost half the men
had been demobilized, and every unit, as a result, was at 50 percent. The
army's 8 million men in August 1945 was at 4¼ million by the end of
the year and reached 1.9 million by July 1946. The air force fell from
218 combat groups to 109 groups in the last four months of 1945. The

navy fell from 3.4 million men in August 1945 to 1.6 million in March 1946.

The most critical example of the Soviet refusal to cooperate and of its insistence on relapsing into isolation, secrecy, and terrorism is to be found in its refusal to join in American efforts to harness the dangerous powers of nuclear fission. Long before the test at Alamogordo, some of the nuclear scientists, spurred on once again by Szilard, were trying to warn American political leaders of the unique character of the dangers from this source. Centered in the Chicago Argonne Laboratories, this group wished to prevent the use of the bomb on Japan, slow up bomb (but not general nuclear) research, establish some kind of international control of the bomb, and reduce secrecy to a minimum. Early in April 1945, Szilard wrote to President Roosevelt to this effect, and, on the latter's death, sought out Byrnes and repeated his views verbally. The future secretary of state found difficulty in grasping Szilard's arguments, especially as they were delivered in a Hungarian accent, but the new President Truman soon set up an "Interim" Committee to give advice on nuclear problems. This committee, led by Secretary of War Stimson, was dependent on its scientific members, Bush, Conant, and Karl T. Compton, for relevant facts or could call on its "scientific panel" of Oppenheimer, Fermi, Arthur H. Compton, and E. O. Lawrence for advice. All these scientists except Fermi were "official" scientists, deeply involved in governmental administrative problems involving large budgets and possible grants to their pet projects and universities, and were regarded with some suspicion by the agitated, largely refugee, scientists in the Manhattan District laboratories. These suspicions deepened as the "official" scientists recommended use of the bomb on Japan "near workers' houses."

At Chicago seven of the agitated scientists, led by James Franck of Göttingen (Nobel Prize, 1925) and including Szilard and Eugene Rabinowitch, sent another warning letter to Washington. They forecast the terror of a nuclear arms race which would follow use of the bomb against Japan. Later, in July 1945, they presented a petition seeking an international demonstration and international control of the new weapon. Szilard obtained sixty-seven signatures to this petition before it was blocked by General Groves and Arthur Compton, using military secrecy as an excuse. After Hiroshima this group formed the Association of Atomic Scientists, later reorganized as the Federation of Atomic Scientists, whose Bulletin (BAS) has been the greatest influence and source of information on all matters concerned with the political and social impact of nuclear weapons. The editor of this amazing new periodical was Eugene Rabinowitch.

The energetic lobbying of this group of atomic scientists had a considerable influence on subsequent atomic history. When the "official scientists," late in 1945, supported the administration's May-Johnson bill, which would have shared domestic control of atomic matters with the armed services, the BAS group mobilized public opinion behind the junior senator from Connecticut, Brian McMahon, and pushed through the McMahon bill to presidential signature in August 1946. The McMahon bill set up an Atomic Energy Commission (AEC) of five full-time civilian commissioners, named by the President, with David Lilienthal, former TVA czar, as chairman. This commission, from August 1946, had ownership and control of all fissionable materials (uranium and thorium) from the mine to the final disposal of atomic wastes, including control of all plants and process patents, with the right to license private nuclear enterprises free of danger to society.

The AEC as it functioned was a disappointment to the BAS scientists. They had sought freedom from military influence and reduced emphasis on the military uses of nuclear fission, free dissemination of theoretical research, and a diminution of the influence of the official scientists. They failed on all these points, as the AEC operated largely in terms of weapons research and production, remained extravagantly secretive even on purely theoretical matters, and was, because of the scientific ignorance of most of the commissioners, inevitably dominated by its scientific advisory committee of "official" scientists led by Oppenheimer.

To the BAS group and to a wider circle of nonscientists, the AEC was a more or less temporary organization within the United States, whose work would be taken over eventually by a somewhat similar international organization. As a first step in this direction, the United Nations, at the suggestion of Bush and Conant and on the joint invitation of three heads of English-speaking governments (President Truman, Prime Minister Attlee, and Prime Minister Mackenzie King of Canada), set up a United Nations Atomic Energy Commission (UNAEC) of all members of the Security Council plus Canada (January 1946). A State Department committee led by Undersecretary Dean Acheson and David Lilienthal and a second committee of citizens led by Bernard Baruch spent much of 1946 in the monstrous task of trying to work out some system of international control of nuclear energy. The task of educating the nonscientists generally fell on Oppenheimer, who gave dozens of his brilliant, extemporaneous, chalk-dusted lectures on nuclear physics. The final plan, presented to the UN by Baruch on June 14, 1946, provided an international control body similar to the AEC. It would own, control, or license all uranium from the mine through processing and use, with operation of its own nuclear facilities throughout the world, inspection of all other such facilities, absolute prohibition of nuclear bombs or diversion of nuclear materials to nonpeaceful purposes, and punishment for evasion or violation of its regulations free from the Great Power veto which normally operated in the Security Council of UN. The vital point in Baruch's plan was that it would go into effect by stages so that inspection and monopoly of nuclear materials would be operative before the American atomic plants were handed over to the new international agency and before the American stockpile of nuclear bombs was dismantled.

This extraordinary offer, an offer to give up the American nuclear monopoly, technical secrets, and weapons to an international agency, in return for a possibly ineffective system of international inspection, was brusquely rejected by Andrei Gromyko on behalf of the Soviet Union within five days. The Soviet spokesman demanded instead a reverse sequence of stages covering (1) immediate outlawing and destruction of all nuclear weapons, with prohibition of their manufacture, possession, or use; (2) a subsequent agreement for exchange of information, peaceful use of atomic energy, and enforcement of regulations; and (3) no tampering whatever with the Great Power veto in the UN. Since only the United States had the atom bomb at the time, the adoption of this sequence could require the United States to give up the bomb without any assurance that anyone else would do anything, least of all adopt any subsequent control methods, methods which might allow the Soviet Union to make its own bombs in secret after the United States had destroyed its in public. The nature of this Soviet suggestion shows clearly that the Soviet Union had no real desire for international control, probably because it was unwilling to open the secret life of the Soviet Union, including bomb-making, to international inspection.

The Soviet refusal of the American efforts at international nuclear control, like their refusal of American loans and economic cooperation, provides some of the evidence of the Kremlin's state of mind in 1946. This evidence became overwhelming in 1947 and 1948, when Soviet aggression appeared along the whole crescent from Germany, across Asia, to the Far East.

In Germany, as we have seen, the area under Soviet occupation was increasingly isolated from the West and increasingly communized internally. The Soviet military forces encouraged the formation of a dominant German Socialist Unity Party (SED) under Communist control. Local provincial elections in the winter of 1946-1947 gave victory to the SED in the Soviet zone and to democratic parties, the Christian Democrats and Social Democrats, in the provinces of the three Western zones.

Austria was also divided into four areas of military occupation, except that it had a single central government of its own under the old Social Democrat leader, Karl Renner, who had also been chancellor in 1919. While the Anglo-Americans supported the Austrians against starvation by the use of UNRRA assistance, the Soviet zone was systematically ransacked. This destroyed all Communist influence in the country, as was clear when the election of November 1945, reduced them to four seats in an assembly of 165 members. Only in May 1955, two years after Stalin's death, was it possible to get Soviet consent to a peace treaty and withdrawal of all four occupying forces (October 1955).

Even the friends of Russia suffered from Stalin's pressure and his insistence that the Kremlin must remain the center for Communist decisions throughout the world. In Yugoslavia, where Tito was originally as anti-Western as Stalin himself, Moscow's efforts to dominate Yugoslavia alienated Tito completely by a combination of economic, diplomatic, and propaganda pressure. The rivalry between the two Slavs came to a head at the end of 1947 when Tito tried to build up a non-Russian Communist bloc by signing friendship treaties with Bulgaria, Hungary, and Romania. By March 1948, a complete break between Belgrade and Moscow was reached. Tito took his place next to Trotsky in Stalin's list of the damned, and the next few years were filled with efforts to overthrow Tito, and the purging of Tito sympathizers by Stalin's cooperative jackals in the other Communist satellites.

Farther east, strong Soviet pressure had been put on Greece, Turkey, and Iran since 1945. On Greece this pressure came through the Communist regimes in Albania, Yugoslavia, and Bulgaria, but in Turkey and Iran it came from the Soviet Union directly. These pressures were probably designed to bring into power in the three countries governments relatively favorably inclined toward the Soviet Union to the extent that the latter could obtain a veto power over any collaboration of the three with the Western Powers, especially with Great Britain. This was an effort in which Stalin had few good cards and which showed his ignorance of political conditions in countries outside his own. In these three, as in other countries, most people desired two things: political independence and economic aid. Neither of these could be or would be obtainable from Stalin, the first because it violated his imperious nature and the second because of economic scarcity in the Soviet Union itself.

Nevertheless, the effort was made. In Greece the election of March 31, 1946 gave the Popular Party (which supported the king) 231 out of 354 seats in the Chamber. The following September a plebiscite on the return of the monarchy gave 69 percent favorable votes. The Communist groups refused to accept these results and by 1946 were carrying on guerrilla warfare in the mountains, using the three adjacent Communist states as bases for supplies, training, and rest areas. A commission of the Security Council of the UN studied the situation in the early months of 1947 and condemned Greece's three northern neighbors, but a Soviet veto stopped any further action by the UN.

Instead, the guerrilla leader "General Markos" set up a Greek Provisional government in the mountains, but alienated much support among Greece's impoverished peasants by the banditry of his guerrillas and especially by their kidnapping of thousands of peasant children who were

smuggled into the three Communist countries for Communist indoctrination. Many of these children did not return for eight or ten years, and
hundreds vanished forever. Large groups returned from Albania as late
as 1963.

The Soviet pressure on Turkey was uncalled for and totally unremunerative. We have already noted that the Soviet-German accords of
1940–1941 showed Soviet ambitions for bases "on the Bosporus and the
Dardanelles" and for a sphere of political influence "south of Batum and
Baku in the general direction of the Persian Gulf." Thus in this area, as
in the Far East, Stalin resumed the expansionist aims of czarist Russia.
At Potsdam, Stalin had looked even farther afield by asking for a trusteeship in the former Italian colony of Libya and a less definite influence in
Eritrea on the western shore of the Red Sea. These aims were formally
demanded by Moscow in September 1945 and in April 1946 (Conference
of Foreign Ministers in Paris).

As early as March 19, 1945, Russia denounced its treaty of friendship
with Turkey and within a few months made demands, both official and
unofficial, for Kars, Trebizond, and other areas of northeastern Turkey.
Anti-Turkish agitation was encouraged among the Kurds (a non-Turkish
people living at the base of the Anatolian peninsula and divided among
Turkey, Iran, and Iraq), and the Georgia Socialist Soviet Republic demanded eight Turkish provinces covering much of the Black Sea coast
and Kurdistan. On August 8, 1946, Molotov demanded a joint Soviet-
Turkish defense of the Straits. Only after Stalin's death, on May 30, 1953,
did the Kremlin renounce the earlier territorial demands on Turkey, but
by that time the alienation was complete: Turkey had been driven into
the Western camp, soon allied with Greece and Yugoslavia in a defensive
alignment against the north Balkan Soviet satellites (August 1954), and
became the eastern pillar of NATO.

The Soviet aggressions on Iran began in 1945 when Soviet-sponsored
Communists, under the protection of the Russian armies occupying
northern Iran, set up "independent" Communist governments at Tabriz
and in Iranian Kurdistan. These were apparently intended to be incorporated into Soviet Azerbaidzhan with the Kurdish areas to be taken
from Turkey, but the failure of the latter scheme made this impossible.
Nevertheless, the Russian Army refused to evacuate northern Iran in
March 1946, as it was bound to do by the agreement of January 29, 1941,
which had admitted it. Only in May did Iran win Soviet evacuation of
its forces by agreeing to form a joint Soviet-Iranian oil company to exploit the petroleum resources of northern Iran (a project which never
was fulfilled).

By the end of 1946 Britain found the burden of providing military
and economic aid to Greece and Turkey too heavy for its overstrained
resources. It was, moreover, eager to overcome the American aloofness

in the Near East, where it felt it was bearing much of the Soviet pressure alone. Accordingly, in February 1947, it threatened to withdraw completely from Greece and Turkey by April 1st. On March 12th the American President enunciated the "Truman Doctrine" to a joint session of Congress. This stated that "it must be the policy of the United States to support free peoples who are resisting attempted subjugation by armed minorities or by outside pressures." He asked for financial assistance to "free peoples to work out their own destinies in their own way." His request for $400 million for aid to Greece and Turkey was granted, after considerable debate, in May 1947. Two weeks later, at Harvard's commencement, Secretary of State General George C. Marshall enunciated the "Marshall Plan," which offered American economic support for a European Recovery Program which would include the Soviet Union and other Communist states. Once again Stalin's ignorance committed him to an unrewarding path. He rejected this offer, and forced Czechoslovakia, which had previously accepted, to do the same.

The path Stalin was following took a more aggressive turn in 1947 and 1948. This involved complete Soviet domination of the area already under Communist control, the shift of Communist parties from coalition to opposition in other areas, the instigation of Communist outbreaks in "colonial" areas (especially in the Far East), and the expulsion of the Western Powers from their enclave in Berlin. All this was to be achieved while avoiding an open clash with the United States. As part of this process, which was badly bungled everywhere except in Czechoslovakia, the Communists withdrew from the "bourgeois" coalition governments which they had joined in 1944-1945: in Belgium in March 1947, in France and Italy in May, and in Austria in the autumn. At the same time, agitation from Communist-dominated trade unions was increased, and the first postwar large-scale strikes began at the end of the year. As part of this same harassment, the Soviet Union in the UN vetoed applications for membership by Italy and Finland.

In the states already under Communist control, the Soviet influence was intensified by efforts to establish a system in which the local parties and secret police were controlled by Soviet agents in the Russian embassies. As part of this effort, the Third International, or Comintern, which had been dissolved in theory by Stalin in December 1943 (but had continued to operate secretly out of Moscow), was reestablished under the new name "Cominform." This was done under Zhdanov's direction at a meeting of representatives of the Communist parties of France, Italy, Poland, Bulgaria, Romania, Yugoslavia, Hungary, and Czechoslovakia held in Poland in September 1947. The delegates were told by Zhdanov and Georgi Malenkov of the Soviet Union that the world was now divided into two antithetical forces—the "imperialist group" headed by the United States and the "peace-loving" group headed by the Soviet

Union—and that it was necessary to reestablish direct operational control of the Communist parties.

The Soviet effort to obtain operational control of the party in Yugoslavia was vigorously resisted by Tito. As a final effort in this direction, Stalin in February 1948 tried to force Yugoslavia into a federation with more docile Bulgaria. Tito flatly refused. As a result, Yugoslavia was expelled from the Cominform in June 1948, and all-out economic, propaganda, ideological, and political warfare was begun by the Soviet bloc against Tito. The conflict was used by Stalin as an excuse to purge all oppositionist Communists within the bloc as "Titoists." As part of this struggle, Tito closed the Yugoslav border to the Greek guerrillas, with the result that they, with General Markos, ended their disturbances in 1949, and Tito became a recipient of American economic aid which eventually reached $700 million. This process reached its climax with the achievement of a Greek-Yugoslav alliance in 1954.

A parallel effort by Stalin to take Czechoslovakia completely into the Communist camp was more successful, and was, in fact, the most successful of his numerous efforts to increase his power in the last six years of his life. In Czechoslovakia the Russian-trained Communist Klement Gottwald had become prime minister in a coalition government in July 1946. In February 1948, the Communist minister of the interior replaced eight Prague police officials by Communists, was overruled by the Cabinet, but refused to back down, calling out into the streets the workers' militia, armed factory workers, and the police (all three under Communist control) to sustain his refusal. When the non-Communist ministers protested and some threatened to resign, Gottwald threatened the ill President Beneš with civil war if he did not dismiss twelve non-Communist ministers. Beneš, who had been determined to seek support from Russia and not from the Western Powers since his unhappy disillusionment with the latter at Munich in September 1938, yielded to Gottwald's demands on February 25, 1948; he himself resigned on May 4th and died in September 1948. His friend, Foreign Minister Jan Masaryk, son of the founder of Czechoslovakia, and the chief Czech advocate of a pro-Western policy, died mysteriously by a fall from a window on May 10th. The Communist control of Czechoslovakia was then complete.

Stalin's victory in Czechoslovakia was followed by an even more dramatic defeat, in an effort to eject the United States, France, and Britain from their sectors in West Berlin. Apparently he believed that the United States was considering a withdrawal from Berlin and that a Soviet push would hasten that event. The former belief may have been based on good evidence, but the latter inference from it was quite mistaken.

American policy in Germany for almost three years (April 1945–April 1948) was a confusion of conflicting and ambiguous objectives. The basic idea, going back to 1942, was to make it impossible for Germany to wage aggressive war again, but no plans had been made, even on a tentative basis, as to how this goal should be sought. Two decisions left unsolved were whether Germany would be broken up and how reparations might be obtained from her without building the country up economically to provide these. Efforts by the State Department to settle these questions were blocked by other departments, notably by the Civil Affairs Division of the War Department, which wanted them left unsettled, and by the Treasury Department, which had totally different aims from State.

In a farsighted message from London in August 1944, Ambassador John Winant warned that lack of an agreed reparations policy would inevitably lead to a breakdown of joint Allied control of Germany and to a struggle with Russia for control of Germany. These wise words were ignored, and President Roosevelt, to stop the bickering, postponed all decisions. Secretary of the Treasury Morgenthau took advantage of this lacuna and of his close personal friendship with Roosevelt to push forward his own pet scheme to reduce Germany to a purely agricultural state by almost total destruction of her industry, the millions of surplus population to be, if necessary, deported to Africa! The secretary, supported by his assistant secretary, Harry Dexter White, was deeply disturbed by Germany's history of aggression and by her efforts to annihilate other "races," and was fairly certain that an American relapse into isolationism would make it possible for Germany to try again. The only way to prevent such an attempt, he felt, was to reduce Germany's industry, and thus her warmaking capacity, as close to nothing as possible. The resulting chaos, inflation, and misery would be but slight repayment for the horrors Germany had inflicted on others over many years.

By personal influence Morgenthau obtained acceptance of a somewhat modified version of this plan by both Roosevelt and Churchill at the Quebec Conference of September 1944. There is little doubt that Churchill's approval had been won by his scientific adviser, Lord Cherwell, who had personal animosities against Germany and had been the chief civilian advocate of indiscriminate bombing of German cities.

The error at Quebec was quickly repudiated, but no real planning was done, and the Morgenthau Plan played a considerable role in JCS 1067, the directive set up to guide the American military occupation of Germany. In the same context the vague and unsettled reparations discussions at Yalta proposed that reparations of $20,000 million, of which half to go to Russia, be obtained by the dismantling of German industry. The JCS 1067 directive ordered that Germany be treated as a defeated enemy and not as a liberated country, with the chief objective that of preventing future German aggression; no steps were to be taken to secure its economic recovery. At the Potsdam Conference it was agreed that the German economy should not be permitted to recover higher than a level which would sustain the occupation forces and displaced refugee persons, with standards of living for the German people themselves no higher than the average standards of living of other European countries. This rather ambiguous level was subsequently defined as equal to the German standard of living of 1932, at the bottom of the depression, the level, in fact, which had brought Hitler to power in January 1933.

It took more than two years of misery for Germany and frustrating relations with the Soviet occupation forces to secure any change in these American objectives. During these two years, lack of equipment, of fertilizers, and of encouragement to enterprise made German economic and social conditions worsen until the end of 1947. Much of the country was still in ruins, housing was lacking, production of food and coal were in almost total collapse, unemployment was very high, inflation was rampant, crime (especially from bands of displaced persons, ex-Nazis, and juvenile delinquents) was widespread, and the black market, using cigarettes as a monetary standard, was flourishing. Hunger and cold in the winter took a considerable toll, and the Germans, for two years, experienced some of the misery they had inflicted on others in the preceding dozen or more years.

Without a revival of industry, which was hampered by disarmament, reparations, and war damage, it was impossible to resume the two vital necessities of recovery, increased mining of coal and export of industrial products to pay for food imports. By the end of 1947, the Americans and British were thoroughly tired of paying astronomical sums each year to keep food flowing to western Germany. All efforts to make an economic reunion with eastern Germany failed because of Soviet insistence that such a reestablishment of interchange of food for industrial products between the two halves of Germany must be tied in with recognition of renewed Soviet claims for $10 billion in reparation payments to be taken from current production, two points which had been unsettled by the wartime agreements.

To revive German industry so that it could pay for imports of food, the Anglo-Americans devised a reform of the German currency. The Soviet government objected violently to this, because it might work but also because it would inevitably bind West Germany economically to the West: if the products of a revived West German industry could not be exchanged for eastern European food, they would have to be exchanged for food and raw materials from the West.

The German currency reform of 1948 is the fiscal miracle of the postwar world. From it came (1) an explosion of industrial expansion and economic prosperity for West Germany; (2) the tying of the West German economy to the West; (3) an example and model for other western European countries (and for Japan) in economic expansion; and (4) a wave of prosperity for western Europe as a whole which continued year after year and refuted completely the claims of Communists (or even Socialists) and, to a lesser extent, the claims of American businessmen that they held the sole key to prosperity. The reform, which went into effect on June 1, 1948, drastically reduced the volume of money in western Germany by exchanging new Deutschemarks for the current Reichsmarks on a one-to-one basis for the first 60 but on a 6.5-to-100 basis for all over 60. The new marks were blocked in banking accounts in complicated ways which encouraged their use for production.

The Soviet Union used the monetary reform in West Germany as an excuse for its blockade of Berlin which lasted in extreme form from June 24, 1948, to May 12, 1949 (although it had begun, on a partial basis, on March 31st). It began in an atmosphere of rapidly rising East-West tension. In December 1947, the King of Romania was forced into abdication and exile. Shortly after the new year, the SED in East Germany was purged of any leaders likely to show independence toward Stalin. The Czech takeover in February 1948 was preceded by Soviet invitations to Bulgaria, Romania, Hungary, and Finland to sign military alliances with Russia. All did so, but the Finnish delegates (in February) flatly refused Stalin's demand that the Soviet have the right to move troops into Finland on its own decision. In Italy, on April 18, 1948, desperate Communist efforts to get a strong foothold in the Italian government were defeated in the first general elections under the new Republican constitution. This election marks the turning point in postwar Italian history just as the simultaneous Berlin crisis and monetary reform mark the turning point in postwar German history. The Communists had participated in all three of Italy's postwar governments, under the Christian Democrat Prime Minister Alcide De Gasperi, but went into opposition in his fourth government, set up on May 31, 1947 (as they did in all countries of western Europe about the same time). The new constitution of January 1, 1948, required a new election during which the fate of newly democratic Italy hung in the balance. The results were a great defeat for the Communists, who obtained only 182 seats in their Popular Front alliance with the Left-wing Socialists, compared to 307 Christian Democrat members in the Assembly of 570 seats.

The Soviet decision to push the Western Powers out of their occupation sectors in western Berlin was part of this general Soviet movement. It was accompanied by claims that the whole city was an integral part of the Soviet occupation zone of eastern Germany and that the Western Powers were present there only on sufferance. To this the Western Powers answered that their presence in Berlin was on exactly the same basis as that of the Russians—the right of conquest. The Kremlin at no time admitted that it was establishing a blockade or that its aim was to eject the Western Powers. Its aims, rather, were to close access to smugglers, criminals, and eventually to the new "illegal" marks introduced by the monetary reform.

As we have seen, through the neglect of General Lucius Clay, as Eisen-hower's deputy in 1945, the Western Powers had obtained no Soviet recognition of their access rights to Berlin from the western occupation zones of Germany. Rail, canal, road, and air traffic to the west were un-der Soviet control and were constantly harassed by shifting regulations, delays, and open obstacles. By the early months of 1948, rail and road routes were tied in knots, and air traffic along the recognized corridor was jeopardized by trespassing Soviet fighter planes, intruding barrage balloons, and unannounced aircraft gunfire. On May 5th a Russian fighter pilot, buzzing a British transport plane as it approached Berlin, collided with it and killed himself and the fifteen persons on the British plane. On June 24th all traffic by ground to Berlin from the west was closed, on a variety of excuses, and only the harassed air corridor was open. Hopes of supplying the 2,000,000 persons in the western sectors of the city by air were dim, as the population's need for food was over 2,000 tons a day and the need for coal for power would be about 5,000 tons a day, excluding home heating. Nevertheless, the attempt began.

Day after day the operation became more intense and more efficient, with planes landing, originally at two, later at three, airports, as fast as they could get in. This continued night and day, reached 3,000 tons in 362 planes on July 5th and erratically crept upward, in spite of deterio-rating weather conditions and lengthening darkness, through the winter.

In September the city government, broken up by Communist mobs, moved from the Soviet sector to the western part of the city, but was replaced by a new, completely Communist city government in the east-ern sector. The Western Powers stopped all goods flowing between zones to the east and began to merge the three zones of the Western Powers and took steps to create a Western German government to rule over them in succession to the military occupation regime. To indicate the temporary nature of the new system, until the reunion of eastern Germany could permit establishment of a permanent government, the new regula-tions were called a Basic Law rather than a constitution, and were drawn up by a council of delegates from the provincial assemblies rather than by an elected constituent assembly. The new West German regime be-gan to operate in May 1949, in the same month as the ending of the Berlin blockade.

The Berlin blockade was won by the West because of the tireless efficiency of the airlift and the resolute determination of the Berliners themselves to undergo any personal hardships or death rather than to submit to another despotic government. Food was scarce, other supplies nonexistent, and heat almost totally lacking through the winter of 1948–1949. Some starved, and many froze, but the resistance did not waver, and the airlift went on. Night and day, in spite of weather, weariness, and accidents (which killed 61 airmen), the planes roared in and out again. Soviet harassment of the airlift, by night flying on instrument in the air corridor, was never sufficient to stop it, as the Soviet clearly feared to push the dispute to open conflict. By September, planes were landing, around the clock, every three minutes. Daily tonnage crept slowly upward, passed 5,000 tons a day as the New Year opened, and by April passed 8,000 tons a day. One day that month, 1,398 planes, landing every 62 seconds, delivered 12,941 tons of supplies. The Soviet blockade had been defeated.

On May 12th, after elaborate negotiations, the ground routes to the city were reopened. In eleven months the American airlift had landed more than 1.6 million tons of freight in about 200,000 flights, a demonstration which undoubtedly awed even the Russians. And, in the interval, West Germany had been united from three zones to one and had obtained its own German government. The West German elections of August 14, 1949, gave the Christian Democrats 31 percent of the vote, with 139 seats in the Parliament. The chief opposition party, the Social Democratic, had 29 percent, with 131 seats. The Communists, with 5 percent and 15 seats, were in fifth place, after two other minority groups, the conservative, centralist Free Democrats with 52 seats, and the moderate, anti-Prussian, federalist German Party with 17 seats. Though the first chancellor, Konrad Adenauer, an anti-Nazi who had been imprisoned by Hitler, won his post by only a single vote, he kept it until 1963.

The Crisis in China, 1945-1950

The critical year 1949, which showed so clearly that the Kremlin's influence in Europe was severely limited within the area of control of the Soviet armies, saw also a shift of Stalin's activity to the Far East, where he tried new tactics in new circumstances. In Europe, outside the area of Soviet military occupation, even in West Berlin, Stalin had met a series of defeats in Austria, Germany, Yugoslavia, Greece, Turkey, Iran, and even Finland. In the Far East, where there was no extensive area of Soviet military control, different tactics were both necessary and possible. There also Stalin was largely defeated, although it took many years to demonstrate this fact. His defeat arose from his failure to recognize that Communism could advance in backward areas only so long as it was anticolonial rather than Communist and worked to further local interests rather than those of Moscow. Stalin did not recognize these truths, and Soviet success in adopting tactics based on them was largely reserved for his successors after 1953.

At first glance the Communist success in ejecting the Nationalist government of Chiang Kai-shek from China does not seem to support these remarks, but it must be recognized that the Communist victory in China was not a victory for Stalin and was not regarded as one by Stalin himself. In fact, the victory of Mao Tse-tung in China was not encouraged, expected, or notably assisted by Moscow.

Stalin was like a shrewd old wolf of the north Siberian forest. Understanding nothing outside his own experience, he never forgot what had happened to himself. Stalin had been involved once before, in 1927, in an effort to communize China, and had failed disastrously in the attempt. Now, in the wake of World War II, he had no desire to repeat that fiasco. What he wanted in the Far East is not clear, but it seems evident that he wanted a weak China surrounded by small states in which American influence was minimal. Such a weak China could be guaranteed by continued rule under the Nationalist government, possibly with the Communists playing a role in a coalition, as the United States seemed to wish. Through such a weak and divided China, Stalin could anticipate no threat to himself either from American efforts or from China itself. To reduce the danger of either of these alternatives, Stalin would have welcomed Communist or largely Communist regimes in Japan, Korea, southeast Asia, and Indonesia, with an autonomous or independent Communist Chinese regime in control of northwestern China, and possibly even Manchuria, as a buffer to the Soviet Union's own territory.

At the end of the war in the Far East in 1945, it was clear to most observers that Roosevelt's pretense that Nationalist China was a great Power, like his equally confused pretense that France was not a significant Power, was mistaken. China's war effort against Japan weakened fairly steadily from Pearl Harbor to the end. This decline resulted, very largely, from the almost total corruption of the regime, which left the Chinese peasant in sullen discontent and roused open disfavor among many urban groups, notably students. Many portions of the huge area of China were only nominally subject to Chiang Kai-shek's rule, and a very considerable extent in the western and northwestern far interior were subjected to the Communist regime of Mao Tse-tung and Chou En-lai, operating out of Yenan, in barren northern Shensi Province.

Chiang Kai-shek was a man of considerable ability and experience, and may not himself have been involved in the corruption of his regime, but he was deeply involved personally with cliques and gangs of persons whose chief aims were to profit from their public positions and from their close associations with Chiang and to resist, by any means, efforts to reform or strengthen China which might reduce their opportunities for corruption. These relationships, in 1945, in some cases had continued for almost twenty years. American aid and the contributions of the Chinese themselves disappeared in the network of corrupt and mutually beneficial relationships which were spread throughout the system and which made it impossible for the Chiang regime to provide a decent living for the people of China or even to defend itself against possible enemies, internal or external. Arms and supplies from abroad were dissipated, vanishing in one way or another, sometimes forever; but on other occasions they turned up subsequently in the hands of guerrillas or of the Communist enemies of Chiang's regime. An enormous and incompetent army drained from the peasants, at low prices, large requisitions which were sold, usually for private profit, at high prices into urban black markets. In the two years following the defeat of Japan, $1,432 million in American assistance to China vanished in one way or another, and at the end the Chinese Army and the Chiang regime was weaker than ever.

In spite of this weakness and waste, the Nationalist government refused to obey American advice either to reform or simply to consolidate itself in the parts of China it still controlled. It was determined to destroy the Communist regime, especially when Mao began to take steps to consolidate the buffer area which he and Stalin wished to establish in northwestern and northern China. This determination became a panic to prevent the Russian forces in Manchuria from turning over that rich area to the Communist units. The Soviet forces there, after looting the area under the guise of reparations from Japan, began to withdraw early in 1946. By a simple process of informing Mao and not informing Chiang of their withdrawal schedules, they ensured that the abandoned areas should be occupied immediately by Communist forces. The United States, which had been engaged in evacuating three million Japanese from China, moved fourteen Nationalist Chinese armies, most of which had been trained and equipped by the United States, to North China and Manchuria to block the Communist takeover. After the defeat of the Communist forces in the north, however, the Nationalists, contrary to American advice, attempted to crush the Communist forces everywhere. They did succeed in capturing the Communist capital of Yenan in March 1947, but, as the effort continued, their own forces were dispersed and defeated, while the Chinese forces, supported by disgruntled peasants, took over much of rural China.

General Marshall, on a mission from President Truman, spent much of 1946 in China. At first he hoped to work out some kind of coalition regime which would stop the civil war by taking Communists into the Chiang government in a minority role. Because this was not acceptable to either side, Marshall, and later (1947) General Wedemeyer, tried to get Chiang to reform and to consolidate in the areas he still controlled. Promises were free, but efforts to carry them out were insignificant. In an attempt to force the Nationalist government to stop the civil war and carry out the American program of reform, consolidation, and coalition with the Communists, an American embargo on arms shipments to China existed for eleven months, from August 1946 to July 1947. Unfortunately, this was just the period in which the Communists were expanding their forces with captured Japanese arms obtained from the Russians and with large acquisition of earlier American arms shipments to the Nationalists which were corruptly allowed to go to the Reds. To stop this and to stop the wastage of Nationalist troops by incompetent leadership, it would have been necessary to allot at least 10,000 American officers to Chiang's forces, attached to every unit down to company level. Neither side wanted to do this, as the problems of language translation, of inability to enforce recommendations, or to overcome personal Chinese resentment against such interference by foreigners were almost insuperable.

Marshall, in 1946, became convinced that the Nationalist regime was hopeless and that it could overcome the Communists only if the United States took actual control by American personnel and fought the Communists with American troops. He was unwilling to do this because he felt that the Chinese would resent it themselves, and it would make impossible any American effort to save Europe from direct Soviet control. Since there could be no question that Europe was more significant by an immense margin, he made the choice, represented by the Marshall Plan, to save Europe. He did not regard the Chinese position as total loss because he was convinced that any Chinese regime, Nationalist or Communist, would find it almost impossible to create a strong and properous China. General Wedemeyer, whose report was submitted to Washington in 1949, agreed with General Marshall about the corruption and incompetence of the Chiang regime and the hopeless state of its future prospects, but felt that large American aid and control should be extended, as a method of delaying the Communist advance. However, Wedemeyer, unlike Marshall, gave less consideration either to Europe or to political possibilities in Washington.

The policy adopted in the Truman Administration was something of a compromise between the Marshall and Wedemeyer recommendations. On the whole, the administration secretly adjusted its outlook to the hopelessness of the Chiang regime and its future, but it did continue assistance by appropriating $400 million in Chinese aid in 1948. The inability of the Chiang government to make any substantial use of such aid continued to be revealed in 1947–1949. The printing of paper money for the government's expenses continued until the Chinese paper dollar became almost valueless. In August 1948, a new yuan currency replaced the previous Chinese dollar at a rate of one yuan to $3 million, but the new money was decreased in value by deflation as the old had been.

The abuse of the Chinese people continued, under guise of a general mobilization against the Communists, and the war efforts against the latter were used as a cover for terroristic elimination of any groups who showed less than wholehearted support of the Chiang regime and its corrupt procedures, regardless of how anti-Communist such groups might be. American military advice and training was continually disregarded or ignored, the best troops being thrown piecemeal, under incompetent and corrupt generals, against Communist forces. In this way 300,000 men, including the best of the American-trained divisions, were wasted in Manchuria and North China in September to November 1948.

On November 6th the American military mission decided unanimously that the situation could not be saved without the use of American ground forces and that "no amount of military assistance would save the present situation." At mid-January 1949, the main field armies north of the Yangtze were destroyed by Communist forces. By that time, Mao's successes were going far beyond the limits expected or hoped for by Stalin, but the latter's efforts to slow up the Communist advances were disregarded. Soviet agents from central Asia took over Sinkiang Province, but in China itself Mao's advance was quite independent of Russian control, since it could be financed from Chinese areas already controlled and could be fought with weapons captured from National forces to add to the captured Japanese weapons obtained from Soviet sources earlier.

The Communist victories were carried to conclusion in 1949. In January, Peiping was captured from the Nationalists and, three months later, the Yangtze River was crossed, and Nanking fell (April 23rd). In the course of the summer, all the south fell, and the Nationalist government, eight years to the day after Pearl Harbor, fled from the mainland to Taiwan (Formosa), where they were protected from Communist pursuit by the United States Seventh Fleet.

In December 1949 Mao Tse-tung and Stalin met in Moscow for their first and last meeting. These led to a mutual-assistance treaty signed on February 14, 1950. By this agreement Mao sought economic and technical assistance which he needed to build up China, while Stalin sought to use these needs to turn China's unexpected developments in directions he desired. Most of the agreements remained secret, but the chief included a defensive military alliance, detailed agreements by which most of the railways and ports controlled by the Russians in the north would be turned over to the Red Chinese by the end of 1952 (these included Port Arthur), and a loan to China of $60 million a year for five years at 1 percent interest (much less in total than China had sought). Less tangible agreements left Outer Mongolia and Chinese Tannu-Tuva in Soviet control, set up a condominium in Sinkiang, left North Korea in the area of Soviet control, and turned China's expansionist ambitions southward. At the same time, a secret agreement may have been made to support the projected North Korean attack on South Korea, as 50,000 Koreans in the Chinese Communist forces were weeded out and transferred to the North Korean Army in the next five months.

One consequence of the Sino-Soviet agreements of February 1950 was a mass influx of Soviet advisers and technicians into China to guide their allies in use of the new equipment and methods made possible by the Soviet loan. These rose to scores of thousands, of which about half were military. At the same time, about 6,000 Chinese students were admitted to university study in Russia. All this cooperation ended in the shattering collapse of this alliance exactly ten years after it was established (1960).

American Confusions, 1945-1950

The American response to the Soviet refusal of postwar cooperation was confused and tentative. For months after the Truman Administration recognized the situation, it was reluctant to make any public announcement of this fact because our military demobilization could not be reversed until it had run its course in 1947 and until a new strategic system and consequent military organization could be reached. For this reason, the first announcement came from Winston Churchill in his speech in Fulton, Missouri, in June 1946. In this he spoke of the "Iron Curtain" which Stalin was lowering between the Soviet bloc and the West. It was also British initiative over Greece and Turkey at the end of the year which led to the "Truman Doctrine" of March 1947.

Truman could not get any constructive help from the leaders of the armed forces in establishing a new strategy (they were much too busy fighting each other in protection of the vested interests surviving from World War II), so he was forced to fall back on other forms of resistance, particularly economic, diplomatic, and ideological. The resulting strategy is known as "containment." It lasted from early 1947 to 1953, and was resumed gradually after 1958. Its chief characteristics were economic and financial aid to other nations, to eliminate the misery and ignorance which fosters Communism, and acceptance of the rights of neutrals and allies to follow their own policies and to be consulted on our policies, without *primary* reliance on our military force.

As early as August 1945, Truman asked the Joint Chiefs of Staff (JCS) to draw up recommendations for America's postwar security needs. The bitter rivalries among the three services made it impossible for the JCS to agree on a common strategy, and thus they could not ascertain the country's weapons needs. At the time, the air force was convinced that the next war would be very brief and would be settled by the Strategic Air Command dropping atom bombs on enemy cities. In its view the army and navy's roles would be restricted to mopping up after SAC had defeated the enemy. Accordingly, it wanted 70 air groups of the new 6-engine, propellered B-36 bombers (Convair), which flew in prototype in 1946 after six years' work but which would not be available in quantity until 1949 (when jet propulsion made them obsolete).

The navy in 1945 was much larger than all other navies of the world combined—"a five-ocean navy to fight a no-ocean opponent," said the air force—but its future had been placed in great jeopardy by the atombomb tests staged at Bikini Atoll in the Pacific in 1946. These tests showed that a fleet would suffer very great damage, unless widely dispersed, from atomic explosions in the air, while a blast under water would drench it with almost irradicable radioactivity. Nonetheless, the navy had to seek a role in the growing rivalry with Russia, and pinned its hopes on its ability to reach the enemy with atom-armed planes flown from the deck of a 65,000 ton "supercarrier" of astronomical cost.

The army, almost eclipsed by the plans of its more glamorous rivals, wanted Universal Military Training (UMT) leading to highly trained reserve units, in spite of the air force's insistence that World War III would be over before ground forces could be mobilized.

These disagreements between services made it impossible for the JCS to achieve any agreement on strategy or on weapons needs in answer to Truman's request of 1945. Accordingly, in June 1946, they informed the President that a unified strategy could be reached only after achievement of a unification of the three services into a single organization. For this reason, it was not until April 1950, that the United States obtained a strategic military policy to underlie Truman's policy of containment, which was then three years old. The new strategic policy was embodied in NSC 68, which, despite its code identification, did not come from the National Security Council, but was the child of the Policy Planning Staff of the State Department, led by Paul Nitze.

The inability of the armed services to provide the country with a defense policy, because of interservice rivalries, is a consequence of the fact that military leaders are specialists and technicians, concerned with means rather than with goals, and, like all technicians, need guidance (or goals) set by other persons with larger perspectives. This weakness is more obvious in peacetime than in war, and is more common among Americans than among some others. Americans work together best when the organization's goal is explicitly established. In this they differ from the British, who can work together perfectly well in organizations without any apparent goals and are, indeed, suspicious of any desire to establish explicit goals or overriding policy. Americans, when goals are established (as they are in business in peacetime by the balance sheet or as they are in war by the desire for victory) work together very effectively, but political work in peacetime, with its ambiguous goals, is relegated to rivalry, bickering, and total inability to relate means to goals. As a result, the means themselves tend to become goals.

It was the emphasis upon means rather than goals, and the compromises between conflicting means, which led to the National Security Act of 1947. This sought to evade the need for clear hard thinking about goals and the subordination of means to goals by reorganization of the top levels of governmental operation concerned with security. It set up a system based on secrecy and anonymity which may, in time, revolutionize the whole American system of government. In this reorganization there were at least three major parts: (1) unification of the armed services; (2) creation of the National Security Council as an advisory board to the President; and (3) reorganization of the whole system of intelligence and spying, through the Central Intelligence Agency (CIA) and the code-breaking National Security Agency (NSA).

Basically, rivalry among the American armed services was a rivalry for congressional appropriations, a struggle over slicing the annual budget. In this struggle each service sought to convince congressmen that its particular weapons provided the best defense for the United States. The air force, which in 1946 was still a branch of the army, touted the claims of the manned bomber; the navy, only recently disillusioned with its old love, the battleship, had now shifted its affections to the aircraft carrier; the army had to stick with the humble foot soldier but almost concealed him from view with its insistence on trucks, tanks, and cannon. As a matter of fact, the manned bomber, the aircraft carrier, and the tank were all obsolescent in 1946, but their supporters were unwilling to concede this, since such a concession would, they thought, shift appropriations to the other services. The manned bomber was threatened by rockets with homing devices which would bring such rockets, at speeds higher than manned bombers could ever reach, in for the kill by seeking out the plane's engine exhaust heat or by use of radar and electronic-eye devices. The aircraft carrier was threatened by atomic bombs, since it was too vulnerable to these to justify its cost of over $100 million. The tank was threatened by shaped charges, and, in general, the whole tactical outlook of ground forces, with their traditional emphasis on mass and concentration, was challenged by nuclear, biological, and chemical weapons which put great value on dispersal.

In these struggles between the services, the clashes are particularly bitter in a period of demobilization, and this bitterness is accentuated by the fact that each service has alliances with the industrial complexes which supply their equipment. These complexes not only supply funds, such as advertising, for each service to carry its message to the Congress and the people, but also exert every influence to retain equipment and tactics in obsolescent modes and types (but newer models) by dangling, before the high officers who can influence contracts, offers of future well-paying consultant positions with the industrial firms concerned. Most high officers of the American armed forces in the war and postwar period retired before the fixed age of sixty-two, often on a disability basis (which exempted retirement pay from income taxes), and then took consultant jobs with industrial firms whose chief business was in war contracts.

Thus, four-star general Brehon B. Somervell, chief of Army Service Forces in World War II, retired on a disability salary of $16,000 a year at the age of fifty-four to join a number of industrial firms, including Koppers, which paid him $125,000 a year; three-star general L. H. Campbell, chief of ordnance in World War II, retired on disability at $9,000 a year at age fifty-nine and became an executive, at $50,000 a year, of firms from whom he had previously purchased $3 billion in armaments. Four-star General Clay retired at fifty-two on $16,000 a year, but signed up at once with General Motors and Continental Can at over $100,000 a year. Three-star air-force General Ira C. Eaker left the service at age fifty with $9,000 a year and joined Hughes Tool Company at $50,000. Another three-star air-force general, Harold C. George, went with Eaker to Hughes, at $40,000. General Joseph T. McNarney, in 1952, took his four stars, and $16,000 a year, to join Consolidated Vultee at $100,000.

These are but a few of more than a hundred general officers whose postretirement alliances with industrial firms encouraged their successors, still on active service, to remain on friendly terms with such appreciative business corporations. These connections undoubtedly inhibit officers of the armed services in their efforts to obtain fresh ideas, fresh tactics, and fresh equipment for America's defense.

In this struggle there occurs rivalry between the services to secure larger shares of existing budgets, but there also occurs cooperation to increase the total joint budget. The best way to do the latter is by war scares, which undoubtedly increase appropriations for all services. The spectacular increase in the joint defense budget of the United States from about $14 billion in the late 1940's to about $60 billion in the early 1960's is partly caused by a real Soviet threat to the United States, but it is also partly caused by a scare engendered by the armed services. If the Soviet Union has been deterred from aggression by those expenditures, the money was well spent, but, since the Soviet Union never has had any intention of engaging the United States in open war, it is legitimate to believe that many of the billions spent could have been used to fight the Soviet Union in more remunerative ways than by the purchase of manned bombers, aircraft carriers, or tanks.

The struggles between the services in the United States after 1945 have been vigorous and often unscrupulous. They have involved putting pressure on administrators in the executive branch from the President down, and especially on the high civilian heads in the Pentagon, of misleading congressmen, and of propagandizing the public.

The air force, for a variety of reasons, was the most successful of the three services in this propaganda war. After all, flyers had plenty of experience, since they had been propagandizing the world since about

1908, five years after the first plane flew, without benefit of publicity, in 1903. The air force was interested only in strategic bombing, and had little interest in tactical work under command of ground forces which, the flyers insisted, hampered their special genius. To get free of the army and become a separate service, coequal with the navy and army, the army air forces in 1946 put their full pressure behind legislation to "unify" the armed services. "Unify" here really meant change two into three. This was done by reducing the two Cabinet posts for war and navy to a single post for defense, with three equal secretaries for army, navy, and air outside the Cabinet. The "unity" presumably was to be obtained from the secretary of defense's control over the three service secretaries, but this was impossible since they were named by the President, not by the secretary of defense, and they had little influence over their services, each of which looked to its chief commander on the Joint Chiefs of Staff.

The fact that the Joint Chiefs had operational command of their departments meant that they had to defend the diverse interests of these, and could contribute little to unity or to any general ideas, even strategic ones; while if they had been separated from their actual commands in order to be free to reach a general consensus on strategic ideas they would have retained no control over their services. The only real lines of authority in the whole system were those in the hands of the President himself and those lines of command going downward from the Joint Chiefs to their own services. There were only very weak lines between the secretary of defense and the Joint Chiefs or to his service secretaries, or between the latter and the services for which they were responsible. As a result, very little unification was achieved, even after amendments to the Act, and in 1949 the interservice rivalries reached their most intense peak. By the end of that year UMT, the supercarrier, and the 70-group air force were all dead, killed off by interservice rivalries, in spite of the fact that all public-opinion polls showed strong support for all of them.

James Forrestal, who had been secretary of the navy since 1944, and who, on behalf of the navy, had emasculated the unification bill, was made first secretary of defense, and was called upon to administer it in 1947. Within a year he had reversed his opinions and was demanding amendments to strengthen the Act, especially the powers of his own post. His mind collapsed under the strain, and he resigned in 1949, committing suicide shortly afterward. Although public-opinion polls showed that two-thirds of Americans approved UMT and only a quarter or less opposed it, the air force in 1948 was able to persuade the Congress that there was a necessary choice between UMT and the 70-group air force; accordingly, the air-force budget was raised $822 million and UMT was buried in committee.

Forrestal was replaced as secretary of defense by Louis Johnson, one-time national commander of the American Legion, who favored the air force, as Forrestal had favored the navy, in these intramural battles. Al-though the supercarrier had been authorized and appropriated for, and although construction had begun under Forrestal, Johnson used a vote of two to one in JCS against it (Admiral Louis Denfeld in the minority) as excuse for canceling the contract. The subsequent "Admirals' Revolt" took the form of anonymous letters to Congress charging corruption on the B-36 contract, as well as public charges, which were quite correct, that the plane was already obsolete. The whole scandal received a full-scale congressional investigation, the "B-36 affair," as a result of which the B-36 was discredited, Admiral Denfeld was removed from the JCS, and Johnson, having alienated everyone by his efforts to save money, was replaced by General Marshall (1950).

The Unification Act had excluded retired officers from the post of secretary of defense, but this clause was made unapplicable to General Marshall so that he could succeed Johnson in 1950. Thus, the supporters of each of the three services held the position successively in less than a two-year period. Marshall said that he took the job to get UMT, but the act, as passed in 1951, was in a form which allowed the Administration to prevent its execution, and it never went into effect. In its place, troops were raised for the services, chiefly the army, by successive extensions of the wholly unsatisfactory Selective Service Acts.

The interservice battles of 1945–1950 were largely a victory for the air force, which got rid of the supercarrier and UMT, and thus obtained the biggest bite from the budget. Much of this bite went to SAC, which had been created in March 1946, and was taken over from General George Kenney by General Curtis E. LeMay in October 1948. At the time, SAC was really SAD. Starting in 1946 with only a single group able to deliver the atom bomb, for most of this period it struggled along with the 300-mph B-29. "It lacked planes, bases, equipment, and trained men." Above all, it still operated on the old premise that the outbreak of war would be preceded by negotiations and mobilization. LeMay changed all that. He was not a desk soldier, nor was he a paper pusher. Ruthless, efficient, and singleminded, he flitted about from base to base in a self-piloted plane, a big cigar clamped at a belligerent angle in his set jaw. He gave SAC a single purpose ("mission"), isolated it from every-thing else in the defense chaos by moving its headquarters from Wash-ington to Nebraska, and demanded immediate and efficient war readiness.

With sufficient funds LeMay would have kept a third of SAC in the air at all times, ready to go; another third at "war readiness" for quick takeoff; and the final third on call within a few hours. Until 1952, when he began to get the new eight-jet intercontinental B-52's, he bridged the gap with modified B-36's and medium-range, six-jet, B-47's. With the support of Air Secretary Thomas K. Finletter, he established bases within range of the Soviet Union, in Europe, Greenland, North Africa, and Okinawa. By 1955 he had a force of remarkable efficiency and high morale, a success resulting from three factors which provide a lesson for all organizational success: a clear-cut mission, leadership, and continuity. The last quality was achieved by retaining LeMay in command of SAC for eight years, in violation of the established armed services practice of three- to four-year periods of rotation of duty.

In all this turmoil of controversy in 1947–1950, the army had not been idle. Its struggles for promotions, pay increases, perquisites, and assignments were ensured success to some extent by creating a new kind of army, an army topheavy with officers and paper pushers who worked from 8:00 A.M. to 4:00 P.M., five days a week, and had very little fighting effectiveness. This was done by setting up a structure of officers and auxiliary activities which absorbed almost the total budget of the department in noncombat lines and filled the combat units with a small number of short-term draftees of very little combat value. In January 1952, for example, the Department of Defense had 5 million employees, of which 3.7 million were in uniform and 1.3 million were civilians. Those in uniform used up $37 billion for pay, food, housing, and clothing—that is, $10,000 per head—in a total defense budget of $46 billion. The 1.3 million civilians cost $5.2 billion, or $4,000 a year each, leaving only $3 billion in the total defense budget for equipment, research, and other costs which contribute directly to defense. The army's share of the 3.7 million uniformed personnel was 2 million, but that provided only 12 divisions, at most 150,000 men, for combat.

In spite of these enormous expeditures, the puny combat effectiveness of the "standing army" was shown in the Korean War when nine-tenths of the officers in combat were Reserves who had to be called from their peacetime activities to fight. The army solution to the disappointments of Korea was more of the same; in June 1951, the Selective Service Act of 1948 was amended to drop the draft age from 19 to 18 and raise the authorized limit on the men in active service from over 2 million to 5 million. That is, the qualitative deficiencies of Korea were to be solved by quantitative increases of the same inadequate quality, a step which might not improve America's defense position but could justify increasingly rapid promotion for officers.

The last few months of 1949 include the major turning points in the whole period 1947–1963. Three events which marked this were the well-publicized B-36 crisis, the loss of China, and the secret H-bomb crisis which followed the explosion of the Soviet Union's first A-bomb in August. Another significant event of the period was the organization of NATO (North Atlantic Treaty Organization) following the treaty of April 4, 1949, signed in Washington. This mutual defense pact "to safeguard the freedom, common heritage, and civilization of their peoples, founded on the principles of democracy, individual liberty, and the rule of law," had, as signers, the United States, Canada, and ten West European countries (Iceland, Norway, Denmark, the Netherlands, Belgium, Luxembourg, France, the United Kingdom, Portugal, and Italy). In February 1952, Greece and Turkey joined the pact, and in May 1955 the West German Federal Republic became a member. The agreement was largely anchored on Germany: it flowed out of the threat provided by the Berlin blockade, and directly implied the merging of West Germany into the Western camp. As the chief step in this process, the three western zones of Germany were merged into one, and, in September 1949, the military rule of Germany was replaced by the Adenauer regime.

Throughout this period, fear of communism was growing within the United States. The real threat, if any, behind this fear is still uncertain. The Soviet and Communist hatred of the American way of life is well established, and the existence of the American Communist Party as a willing tool of an international Communist conspiracy directed from Moscow is also beyond dispute. Such Communists were undoubtedly engaged in subversion and espionage, and were assisted in these efforts by "fellow travelers" and other sympathizers. Moreover, some Communists and fellow travelers were undoubtedly present in government and, to a greater degree, in some other areas, notably certain labor unions, higher education, and especially in the more creative end of the entertainment field, such as the theater, writing, and Hollywood scenario production. On the other hand, the number of Communists in the United States, according to the FBI, was only about 75,000 in 1945 and fell steadily to 50,000 in 1950 and to 3,000 in 1960.

It is still impossible to make any real assessment of the influence of Communists, either in government or out of it, in the period of 1949–1950 with which we are now concerned; this is equally true of the earlier years, going back to 1933, with which most of the charges and countercharges made in 1949 were concerned. The chief reason for this is that secrecy, which still prevails, was used by both sides to portray, by selective publicity, a false picture. Falsehood, manipulation, selection, and distortion of evidence were prevalent on both sides, and were used especially by the anti-Communists, not because they were less addicted to the truth than Communists, but because they, on the offensive, were the ones who were raising the issues, and exposing the evidence. Apparently, these anti-Communists, including the press, the House Committee on Un-American Activities (HUAC), and the Federal Bureau of Investigation (FBI), felt that a good cause justified shoddy or misleading methods.

The Communist Party of the United States (CPUS), like others throughout the world, was always, from its founding in 1919, a tightly disciplined body of conspirators whose primary allegiance was to the Soviet Union and whose secondary aim, after the preservation of the Soviet Union itself, was to establish a similar regime in the United States. Tactics varied from year to year, and the party line shifted with changing political and world conditions without, however, ever abandoning these two goals. In 1935, with the threat of Fascism spreading through the world, the Communist International (Comintern) adopted a "Popular Front" tactic which was, essentially, a temporary alliance of all non-Fascist groups to oppose Nazi aggression and to support the Soviet Union against German attack. In this period the Communist Party of the United States was a relatively open group, with openly available headquarters and telephone numbers, and with a good deal of cooperation and free exchange through a broad spectrum of political and social activities, and cooperation from the political Center to the extreme political Left. There was, at that time, widespread disillusionment with the existing structure of society because of enormous unemployment, pervasive poverty, and bourgeois paralysis in the face of economic stagnation and Fascist aggression. Communist insistence that something be done about these things won widespread sympathy, even in circles which were totally non-Communist. The Communists themselves took full advantage of this atmosphere by establishing Communist front and fellow-traveler organizations of all kinds, and the distinction between party members and fellow travelers became very free, confused, and blurred. The Communist command system, however, remained fully aware of who were devoted to their permanent goals and who were not, and retained general control, under cover, of all organizations they regarded as important.

This ambiguous situation of Left-wing fellowship began to break down in 1938–1940 as the complete dominance of Soviet national selfishness within Communist parties everywhere became evident, at first in Spain, later in the Nazi-Soviet Pact of August 1939, and in the Soviet-Finnish War the following winter.

For the American Communist Party the chief turning point here was the enactment of the Foreign Agents Registration Act in 1940. The United States Communist Party broke its affiliation with the Comintern and instead established a secret link between the Comintern and the United States party, chiefly through Gerhart Eisler (who was finally deported in 1949 and became an official of the East German Communist regime). In 1943 the Comintern itself was officially dissolved by the Soviet Government, although secretly it continued to exist. As part of this same process, in a sort of wartime common front, the United States party itself was dissolved in 1944 and reappeared at once as the Communist Political Association. Earl Browder, who personified the Popular Front tactic of the 1930's, continued as the head of the Political Association and the common-front tactic until July 1945, when he was removed as a traitor to the Marxist-Leninist ideology and replaced by William Z. Foster. At the same time, the Communist Party of the United States was reestablished to pursue a more aggressive and narrower policy.

The abandonment of the United Front approach in 1945 was a gross tactical error which almost totally destroyed the party in the next fifteen years. It had been ordered from Moscow through the French Communist leader, Jacques Duclos, and was, like other mistakes of the Kremlin at the same time, based on a totally mistaken conception of what the postwar world would be like. This misconception was firmly rooted in the greater misconceptions of Marxist-Leninist doctrine, and assumed (1) that there would be a postwar economic depression; (2) that the United States would relapse into isolationism; and (3) that the United States and Europe, especially Britain, would engage in an imperialist rivalry for markets and economic advantages. Just as the new Soviet foreign policy prepared to exploit this anticipated chaos, so the CPUS was reorganized to profit from the same chaos. Instead, it committed suicide.

This collapse of the CPUS from 75,000 members with ample funds in 1945 to less than 3,000 members with hardly a dime fifteen years later was assisted by the actions of the United States government, the attacks of party members who were leaving it in droves, and the efforts of ex-members, political leaders, and intellectual bellwethers to strike at the CPUS in substitute for their inability to strike at the USSR. Many of these virtuous warriors were fighting for their convictions, but at least an equally large number were fighting for their personal profit or their personal partisan advantage. In this effort to win personal advantage from a worthy struggle, leadership was taken by some of the ex-Communists, the FBI, and the House Committee on Un-American Activities.

These anti-Communists, some of them professionsals, tried to demonstrate that the CPUS, by its penetration into the Federal government under the New Deal, into labor unions or education, and into entertainment, especially Hollywood, had gravely endangered the nation. On the whole, from the perspective of decades, these charges, concerned with the period before 1945, seem grossly exaggerated. On the other hand, the making of these charges in the period 1947-1955 was very damaging to the country. The influence of Communists, within or outside government, had been slight. It is, for example, almost impossible to find a single motion picture, book, or play which can be identified as having had influence in leading Americans to feel favorably toward a Communist system for this country. It is even difficult to find examples of such an effort. On the other hand, it is possible to find examples of books which gave a too favorable impression of the Soviet Union, just as it is possible to find favorable books on any country, including Tibet, Perón's Argentina, Castro's Cuba, or Trujillo's Dominican Republic. Some of these favorable books on the USSR, such as Lord and Lady Passfield's *Soviet Communism: A New Civilization?* (1935) or Albert Rhys Williams's *The Soviets* (A Book-of-the-Month Club recommendation in 1937), undoubtedly had influence in establishing an unduly favorable picture of

Soviet life, but their influence could not in any way compare, in strengthening Communism in the United States, with the influence in that direction exercised by the breakdown of the capitalist laissez-faire economy in 1929-1939, or with the failure of the democratic countries to stand up to Fascist aggression in Germany, Italy, and Spain in that same decade.

Espionage is another matter, but this is more from the nature of espionage than the nature of Communism, except for the very significant fact that the ideological appeal of Communism to the half educated makes it possible for the Soviet Union to obtain secrets without financial payments. In general, the nature of espionage is totally ignored by most people, and this ignorance was only increased by the activities of the anti-Communist spy agitations of the 1949-1954 period. All past history shows that *espionage* has been generally successful and *intelligence* has been generally a failure. By this I mean that no country had much success in keeping secrets, in the twentieth as in all earlier centuries, but neither has any other country had much success in evaluating or in interpreting the secrets it obtained. The so-called "surprises" of history have emerged not because other countries did not have the information but because they refused to believe it. The date of Hitler's attack on the West in May 1940 had been given to the Netherlands by the German Counterintelligence Office as soon as it was decided; the Western countries refused to believe it. The same was true of every one of Hitler's surprises. Stalin was given the date of the German attack on the Soviet Union by a number of informants, including the United States Department of State, but he refused to believe. Both the Germans and the Russians had the date of D-Day, but ignored it. The United States had available all the Japanese coded messages, knew that war was about to begin, and that a Japanese fleet with at least four large carriers was loose (and lost) in the Pacific, yet Pearl Harbor was a total surprise. This last point was so hard to believe, once the evidence was available, that the same groups who were howling about Soviet espionage in 1948-1955 were also claiming that President Roosevelt expected and wanted Pearl Harbor. Both these beliefs, if they were believed, were based on gigantic ignorance and misconceptions about the nature of intelligence.

The whole purpose of secrecy in government should not be to keep information from other states (this is almost impossible) but to make it as difficult as possible for other states to get certain information, so that, when they do get such restricted information, it will be so intermingled with other information and misinformation that it cannot be evaluated promptly enough to do them much good. Any espionage system gets more information than it can handle rapidly. Any country should assume that the enemy has *all* its own secret information. The lessons of past history fully support this assumption. Following every war the discovery is made that the enemy, during the war, had every other state's most cherished secrets. In fact, the most successful kind of counterespionage work is achieved, not by preventing access to secrets, but by permitting access to information which is not true. This was done most successfully in 1943 in preparing the American invasion of Sicily, which was a surprise to the Germans because they had been provided, through their espionage in Spain, with false information about an invasion of the Balkans. The Germans had a somewhat similar success through their Operation North Pole by which the Germans successfully took over and operated the French Underground and the associated British espionage net in a large part of France for about a year. Finally, it is not generally recognized by outsiders that almost all the information gathered by any espionage net is nonsecret material fully available to anyone as public information. Even in work against a supersecret area like the Soviet Union or in nuclear "secrets" this is true. Allen Dulles said that more than 90 percent of the information which the CIA gathers on the Soviet Union is nonsecret. Soviet espionage reports on the United States must contain *at least* 97 percent nonsecret material.

Many, if not most, of the "spies" and "atomic spies" apprehended, with high-powered publicity, by the FBI and the Un-American Activities Committee in 1948–1954 (to the great alarm of the American people) were not concerned with secrets, while some of them were not engaged in espionage at all, and almost none of them had anything to do with nuclear secrets (contrary to the publicity releases of the agencies who accused them). There was nuclear espionage, and it was successful, but almost nothing was achieved by any spy chasers in the United States either to reveal the culprits or to punish them. Fuchs and Nunn May were real nuclear spies for the Soviet, but others at least equally important are hardly ever mentioned. For example, Frédéric Joliot-Curie, the greatest French nuclear physicist (Nobel Prize, 1935) and an admitted member of the Communist Party, knew as much about our nuclear work as anyone in Europe, Britain, or Canada. His chief associates fled from France (he did not) in 1940 and worked on the nuclear project in England and Canada until they returned to France after that country's liberation. Some of these associates, notably Hans von Halban and Lew Kowarski, certainly knew as much as Nunn May and may have known as much as Fuchs, and unquestionably told all they knew to Joliot-Curie, a Communist, in 1944. Or again, as an example of numerous unexplored paths by which nuclear information went to Russia, an outstanding Polish nuclear physicist who studied with Joliot-Curie was Ignace Zlotowski. He was in the United States in the critical years during the Soviet race to make the atom bomb as a member of the Polish Embassy staff and Poland's representative on the UN Atomic Energy Commission. He sent large quantities of nuclear information behind the Iron Curtain and was present as an observer at the Bikini bomb tests in 1946.

Finally, it is evident that a great deal of nuclear information (whether secret or not is unknown), as well as uranium metal, went to the Soviet Union as part of Lend-Lease in 1943. Major George Racey Jordan, USAAF, tried in vain to disrupt these shipments at the time. While most of Jordan's evidence is unreliable, the shipment of uranium to Russia is corroborated from other sources. The significance of such shipments is still unknown, since the export license permitting them was granted at the request of General Groves. Jordan's other evidence, most of which was very discreditable to the New Deal (since he testified that he, Groves, and others were under direct pressure from Harry Hopkins and Vice-President Henry Wallace to allow export of nuclear materials, radar, and other secrets to Russia) was subsequently shown to be false, yet all his statements were given nationwide publicity by news commentators like Fulton Lewis, Jr., by *Life* magazine, and by the House Un-American Activities Committee, and are still widely believed.

Most of the "atomic spy" cases are similar to this. The earliest of these was the arrest of Soviet naval Lieutenant Redin by the FBI on March 26, 1946, on charges that a Seattle naval engineer, Herbert Kennedy, had sold Redin "secrets" about the Bikini test ship *Yellowstone* for $250. This case was a forerunner of others in respect to two false assertions in news releases: (1) claims by the FBI that information leading to the apprehension of Redin had come from the Gouzenko "atomic spy" case in Canada (February 1946) and (2) claims by the HUAC that it had unearthed this significant case. Redin was eventually acquitted when his defense showed that Kennedy had been paid for research he did for Redin in the Seattle Public Library. Neither Gouzenko nor HUAC had anything to do with it.

The change in the climate of American opinion (and thus in the attitudes of American juries) over four years may be observed in the contrast between the acquittal of Redin in 1946 and the conviction of Abraham Brothman in 1950. The FBI publicity and the universal belief of the American press, both at Brothman's arrest in July 1950 and at his trial in November 1950, was that he was "part of a Soviet spy apparatus under a Russian trade organization chief working to ferret out atomic secrets" (*The New York Times*, July 30, 1950) or that the trial was an "ATOMIC SPY CASE" (all New York newspaper headlines, November 8-23, 1950). In fact, Brothman and his secretary (Miss Moskowitz) were the only defendants in a trial for conspiracy to persuade a third person, not on trial (Harry Gold), to commit perjury in July 1947. Undoubtedly, Brothman and his secretary had discussed together what they could do about the testimony to be given by the semimoronic Gold before a grand jury. Their purpose, in which they clearly failed, was to keep Brothman from being involved in any charges of giving secrets to Communists. Technically they were guilty of conspiracy, were so found, and were sentenced to a total of nine years' imprisonment. In spite of the fact that the trial clearly showed that Brothman had nothing to do with espionage, secrets, or atomic research, the mistaken impression that he did was never removed by the press, and remained in the public mind as an established truth, so that United States Attorney Irving Saypol, who prosecuted this case in November 1950, referred to Brothman as convicted of "*espionage*" when he prosecuted the Rosenberg case before the same judge in April 1951. The true story, as far as Brothman was concerned, seems to be quite different.

Brothman was an industrial chemist and chemical inventor who owned a number of chemical laboratories and factories held as subsidiaries of his Pennsylvania Sugar Company. His chief concern was in industrial solvents in which he held patents on processes and equipment. In 1940, when Brothman was seeking orders for his products, he was approached by a Russian, Jacob Golos, then proprietor of World Tourists, a Communist-front travel agency but previously employed by the Soviet Trade Commission (AMTORG) and its Purchasing Commission. Brothman offered Golos 10 percent commission on any orders he could place with either agency for Brothman's products or processes. We now know that Golos was a high official in the Soviet secret police, a major Soviet spy, and one of the three-man Control Commission of the American Communist Party. Brothman knew none of this and was not himself a Communist, although in 1940 he regarded the Soviet Union as the chief obstacle to world Fascism.

For several months in 1940, Brothman gave to Golos, both directly and through Golos's mistress, Elizabeth Bentley, blueprints and descriptions of the chemical processes he had for sale. All of these were available to any prospective purchaser and had been written up and advertised by Brothman in the regular chemical journals, and many were his own inventions. When Brothman objected to talking to Golos or Miss Bentley on the ground that they knew no chemistry, Golos sent him another agent, a chemist, Harry Gold, who had been doing industrial research (which gradually developed into industrial espionage) for AMTORG for several years. Although Brothman got little or no business from the Russians, he hired Gold as a chemist in one of his laboratories in 1943. Four years later, after Gold, unknown to Brothman, had become an atomic spy contact with Fuchs, Brothman discussed with his secretary how Gold's testimony before a grand jury might be given to prevent unfavorable inferences regarding Brothman's contacts with Golos in 1940. In view of the changed American attitude toward such Russian contacts from 1940 to 1947, this is not, perhaps, a surprising reaction, but in the increasingly tense situation of 1950 it won Brothman a seven-year prison sentence for conspiring with his secretary to persuade Gold to commit perjury. (Gold was not tried either for the conspiracy or for perjury.)

The changed atmosphere of American public opinion from 1947 on was greatly intensified by the increasingly strained world conditions, and by the growing public knowledge of the nature of the Communist movement, its connections with Soviet Russia, and their joint conspiracy against the West. Much of this evidence came from ex-Communists, such as Elizabeth Bentley, Louis Budenz, Whittaker Chambers, John Lautner, and others. All of these undoubtedly were ex-Communists and, equally undoubtedly, revealed much valuable information about the Communist conspiracy and properly roused the American public to the danger of this conspiracy. But it is equally true that the first three names mentioned are known and remembered because they dramatized, distorted, and manipulated, (consciously or unconsciously) evidence for their own private purposes. This is particularly true of Elizabeth Bentley and Louis Budenz, both of whom exaggerated their previous roles in the Communist Party, were very ignorant of the real nature and significance of their own evidence (or of any evidence), knew very little that was not based on hearsay (often at second or third hand), and undoubtedly embroidered and manipulated their evidence for their private profit. Budenz, who was "managing editor" (really copy editor) of the Communist newspaper the *Daily Worker* from 1941 to 1945, carefully planned his withdrawal from the party to protect his own interests. His decision was made early in 1945; he arranged for a position on the faculty of Notre Dame University at the end of September, obtained his weekly pay in advance from the *Daily Worker* for the second week of October, left the paper and the party on October 11th, and joined the Notre Dame faculty two days later. In the next eight years, in addition to his salary, he received gross earnings of $70,000 as a professional ex-Communist lecturer and writer.

This is certainly legitimate, but it is obvious that Budenz, in order to retain his value in this specialized market, had to continue to produce new evidence if not new sensations. Much of this evidence, released over the years, became more remote from his personal knowledge or even from the facts. This is, for example, very clear in his efforts to show that American foreign policy in China was controlled, determined, or influenced by persons whom he called "Communists."

Miss Bentley's profiting from her role of ex-Communist was much less legitimate, as can be seen from one example. Early in 1950, when Miss Bentley's position was, in money and reputation, precarious, and her eighteen months of successful notoriety as an informer seemed to be approaching eclipse, she signed a contract with Devin-Adair for an autobiography to be written with the editorial assistance of John Brunini, who would also share in the royalties. At the time a libel suit against Miss Bentley by William Remington whom she had called a "Communist" had been settled by an out-of-court payment of $9,000 to Remington on Miss Bentley's behalf by the radio network and program sponsor for whom she had made the charges. John Brunini, who was to share the profits of Miss Bentley's book, was foreman of the grand jury which indicted Remington for perjury a few weeks later (May 1950) for testifying he had not been a Communist. The evidence that he was, given before the grand jury headed by Brunini, came from Miss Bentley. Perjury, however, requires two witnesses. Brunini obtained the second witness by browbeating Mrs. Remington into a statement that her former husband had told her that he paid dues to the Communist Party. To obtain this corroboration from the former Mrs. Remington, Brunini threatened her with contempt proceedings, by making her believe, contrary to the truth, that the privilege against use of a wife's evidence did not apply to her after her separation from Remington in January 1947. This disgraceful procedure, which eventually led to Remington's conviction for perjury and to his death in prison by the hand of another prisoner, is indicative of Miss Bentley's attitude toward truth. To cover up her financial relationship with Brunini when she was preparing to cooperate with him in the indictment of Remington, the book contract was redrawn, omitting Brunini's name. This was done apparently as a consequence of statements of two employees of Devin-Adair who knew of the contract with Brunini's name (one was the woman who typed it). A new contract was drawn which did not contain Brunini's name, and the two employees left Devin-Adair's employment. The book, published under the title *Out of Bondage*, in 1951, pretended to be Miss Bentley's memoirs, but two years later, when an effort was made to use it against her in another judicial proceeding, she called it "fiction."

In addition to the distorting influence of profit, the story of the Communist threat to the United States was also confused and manipulated for partisan motivations. When the wholesale revelations of ex-Communists began in 1947, the New Deal and its successor had been in the White House for more than fourteen years. The Republicans, especially the congressional delegations, were prepared to do almost anything to destroy the reputation of President Truman and the memory of Franklin Roosevelt in order to win the presidential election of 1948. They were offered a great opportunity to do so when the Republicans won control of both Houses of Congress in the congressional elections of 1946. This effort was spearheaded, in 1947 and 1948, by the House Committee on Un-American Activities, whose antics over previous years had already shown large-scale disregard of the rules of good procedure, fair treatment, and unbiased investigation.

The HUAC in 1947–1948 had nine members of which the chief were J. Parnell Thomas, of New Jersey (Chairman); Karl E. Mundt, of South Dakota; and Richard M. Nixon, of California, on the Republican side, and four southern democrats, led by John S. Wood, of Georgia, and John E. Rankin, of Mississippi, on the Democratic side. The value of the publicity gained by the committee in these two years may be judged from the fact that it carried both Mundt and Nixon to the Senate in 1948 and 1950 and the latter to the Vice-Presidency and close to the Presidency itself in 1952 and 1960. There can be no doubt that the Republican members of the Committee realized the value of the publicity to be gained by membership on it and that their actions were consistently aimed more at partisan advantage for themselves and the discrediting of previous Democratic incumbents in the White House than they were directed to ascertaining the nature and functioning of the Communist conspiracy in the United States. Other legislative committees occasionally copied these tactics. It was this partisan, rather than investigatory, bias in the behavior of such committees which reduced so much of this investigation of Communism into personal vendettas such as those between Hiss and Chambers, between Remington and Bentley, and between Lattimore and Budenz. In these battles of personalities, charges and countercharges flew about so freely at hearings, in the press, over the airwaves, and occasionally in judicial proceedings, that the truth cannot now be ascertained. There can be no doubt that falsehood and even perjury were to be found on both sides. What is equally regrettable is that numerous other accused Communists, both in government and out, whose names were given to these committees on the same basis, and sometimes in the same breath, as Hiss, Remington, or Lattimore were almost totally ignored and lost in the personal controversies aroused over these three, largely because of the partisan handling of the investigatory committees.

These revelations began in January and February 1947, when Budenz identified Gerhart Eisler as a Communist leader in the United States. Within a few weeks President Truman gave the investigators a prime weapon when he issued an order (March 21, 1947) requiring a loyalty oath from all government workers. The significance of this was that any Communists in the government could be prosecuted for perjury unless they had admitted the fact.

In the course of the summer the FBI arrested a half-dozen individuals at various times and announced that they "had stolen vital atomic bomb secrets from the heart of the atomic bomb project at Los Alamos." This alarming news was reinforced by a number of press releases from the HUAC. When the accused were brought to trial, however, it developed that they had been guilty of insignificant and technical infractions of the law, such as taking snapshots of each other while serving as soldiers at Los Alamos or pilfering of government property there. Eventually two were given suspended sentences, one was sentenced to eighteen months, a fourth got six months, and a fifth paid a fine of $250. The original charges of atomic espionage were in headlines; the final disposition of the cases, if recorded at all, appeared as insignificant items on a back page, unconnected with "atomic espionage."

In February 1948, Representative Thomas, chairman of the HUAC, was seeking from the Congress the largest appropriations his committee had ever obtained. Apparently to bolster this request, on the last day of the month, from his hospital bed he issued a six-page report on Dr. Edward U. Condon, Director of the National Bureau of Standards. Condon, one of the world's great authorities on quantum mechanics, had been attacked by Thomas for about a year, chiefly in press releases and in two articles in national magazines, apparently because of animosity over Condon's opposition to the Johnson-Mays bill for atomic-energy control. The report of February 1948 said flatly, "Dr. Condon is one of the weakest links in our atomic security." This charge was based on a mishmash of falsehoods, irrelevancies, and incorrect inferences. It was charged that Condon had obtained his job from the favor of Henry Wallace, then secretary of commerce, with the implication that Condon must be a Left-winger if Wallace was. In fact, Wallace did not even know Condon, and appointed him only for the administrative reason that the Bureau of Standards was a part of the Commerce Department. Or again, the HUAC report quoted from a letter of J. Edgar Hoover to W. Averell Harriman when the latter was secretary of commerce in May 1947. This letter had been stolen from the FBI loyalty report on Condon and was merely a history of unevaluated reports of Condon's actions as reported to the FBI. As published in the HUAC report it was edited to cut out (without any indication) sentences favorable to Condon. It was charged that Condon's passport was taken up by the State Department when he planned to go to Russia in 1946. The fact was that this plan was a government-sponsored project to fly about two dozen American scientists to Russia in an army plane, and Condon's participation was canceled by the army because it regarded him as too valuable a nuclear physicist to be risked behind the Iron Curtain, where he might be kidnapped. The HUAC report said that Condon recruited members to join an organization listed as "subversive" by the attorney general, the American-Soviet Science Society. It later developed that this organization, which existed for the purpose of translating scientific reports from Russian to English, using funds from the Rockefeller Foundation, had never been listed as subversive by the attorney general, but on the contrary had been encouraged by the United States government as a method of finding out what the Russians were doing in science. The HUAC had simply confused this society with an entirely different organization, which the attorney general had listed.

On this kind of evidence the HUAC demanded Condon's removal from the government and ominously reported that "the situation as regards Dr. Condon is not an isolated one . . . there are other Government

officials in strategic positions who are playing Stalin's game to the detriment of the United States." Condon's repeated requests for an opportunity to appear before the committee to refute its charges under oath
were ignored. The committee, especially its chairman, continued to
harass Condon so that it was impossible for him to do his work in the
Bureau of Standards. This was done by subjecting him to one loyalty
investigation after another (each takes a great deal of work, by the FBI
and the accused, and requires months). These investigations, one after
another, cleared Dr. Condon, but each clearance was followed by new
charges and a new investigation. After the fourth clearance, and the
opening of a fifth investigation, Condon resigned from the government
in 1954. This fifth investigation was demanded by Vice-President Nixon,
who seems to have felt that his original participation in the unjustified
smearing of Condon six years before had to be sustained by continued
persecution. By that time Chairman Thomas, who was the director of
this persecution in 1947-1949, had been sent to prison as a common
criminal for making the employees in his congressional office, paid from
government funds, secretly give back substantial parts of their salaries
to him. Thomas should have restricted his efforts for additional money
to smearing innocent scientists in paid articles in national magazines.

The Condon case was still in its early full publicity in July and August
1948, when the Thomas committee hit the headlines for weeks, day after
day, with the testimony of Louis Budenz, Elizabeth Bentley, Whittaker
Chambers, and other "experts" on Communists. They listed several dozen
names of Communists in government in the 1930's, organized in formal
groups or cells, and generally paying dues and sending information
through "couriers" like Miss Bentley. Most of those named ignored the
charges or simply made a denial to the press, but a few, such as Hiss,
who sought to refute the charges, were met by new ones. Eventually,
as we have seen, Remington and Hiss were both jailed for perjury, the
former for denying he had been a Communist and the latter for denying
he gave government documents to Chambers. Both cases required two
trials before convictions were obtained.

Others of these named were called before the committee and refused
to give evidence under the Fifth Amendment to the Constitution, which
protects against self-incrimination. Little was done about these, but it
is clear that many of them were in fact Communists and that Bentley
and Chambers knew them as such, by hearsay at least. Bentley's original
evidence in 1948 gave a score of names of Communists she had "known"
in the government. More than two years passed before it became clear
that she did not "know" them at all, had never met them, and could not
identify them by sight, but had merely gathered their names from her
contacts with the few Communists who reported directly to her and
whom she knew well. Similarly, she indicated in her original evidence

that she broke with the Communists and went to the FBI, for patriotic reasons, in August 1945. Only in 1953, when the Eisenhower Administration was still trying to make a major issue of the Communists in the New Deal, did Attorney General Brownell, in publishing a letter of J. Edgar Hoover, inadvertently reveal that Miss Bentley's revelations to it did not begin until November 8, 1945, the day after the newspapers revealed that Budenz had been giving names. Miss Bentley's earlier visit to the FBI in New Haven in August 1945 had nothing to do with her desire to give information or with Communists, but was simply her desire to find out if a man who had dated her was an employee of the FBI.

The most sensational evidence from the HUAC was released in the late summer of 1948 just in time to influence the presidential election in November. Apparently it did not have the influence expected, since Truman was elected. The controversy from its revelations continued for years, and the charges, both from HUAC and from other sources, increased in violence. Few of the revelations after 1948 were ever sustained in court. For example, two separate "atomic espionage" cases involving Clarence F. Hiskey at Argonne Laboratory in Chicago and Joseph W. Weinberg at Berkeley Radiation Laboratory were played up by HUAC in 1949. Eventually Hiskey refused to answer questions before HUAC, was prosecuted for contempt, and was acquitted in 1951. Weinberg, accused by HUAC of giving "atomic secrets" to a well-known Communist, Steven Nelson, eventually was prosecuted for perjury at the committee's insistence, and was acquitted in 1953. Both scientists found their careers injured by the committee's charges. There were many similar cases.

The revelation of Communist influence in the United States was undoubtedly valuable, but the cost, in damage to the reputations of innocent persons and in the total confusion of the American people, was a very high and largely unnecessary cost. Eventually some agencies of the government, such as the Bureau of Standards, the army and, above all, the State Department were severely injured by loss of morale, disruption of work, and refusal of valuable personnel to work for the government under such conditions.

Much of this damage came from the efforts of Senator Joseph R. McCarthy, Republican, of Wisconsin to prove that the State Department and the army were widely infiltrated with Communists and from the efforts of the neo-isolationists and the "China lobby" to demonstrate that the Mao conquest of China was entirely due to the treasonable acts of Communists and fellow travelers in the State Department and the White House.

McCarthy was not a conservative, still less a reactionary. He was a fragment of elemental force, a throwback to primeval chaos. He was the enemy of all order and of all authority, with no respect, or even understanding, for principles, laws, regulations, or rules. As such, he had nothing to do with rationality or generality. Concepts, logic, distinctions of categories were completely outside his world. It is, for example, perfectly clear that he did not have any idea of what a Communist was, still less of Communism itself, and he did not care. This was simply a term he used in his game of personal power. Most of the terms which have been applied to him, such as "truculent," "brutal," "ignorant," "sadistic," "foul-mouthed," "brash," are quite correct but not quite in the sense that his enemies applied them, because they assumed that these qualities and distinctions had meaning in his world as they did in their own. They did not, because his behavior was all an act, the things he did to gain the experience he wanted, that is, the feeling of power, of creating fear, of destroying the rules, and of winning attention and admiration for doing so. His act was that of Peck's Bad Boy, but on a colossal scale, as the total rejection of everything he had come from in his first twenty years of life. He sought fame and acclaim by showing an admiring world of schoolmates what a tough guy he was, defying all the rules, even the rules of decency and ordinary civilized behavior. But like the bad boy of the schoolyard, he had no conception of time or anything established, and once he had found his act, it was necessary to demonstrate it every day. His thirst for power, the power of mass acclaim and of publicity, reached the public scene at the same moment as television, and he was the first to realize what could be done by using the new instrument for reaching millions.

His thirst for power was insatiable because, like hunger, it was a daily need. It had nothing to do with the power of authority or regulated discipline, but the personal power of a sadist. All his destructive instincts were against anything established, the wealthy, the educated, the well mannered, the rules of the Senate, the American party system, the rules of fair play. As such, he had no conception of truth or the distinction between it and falsehood, just as he had no conception of yesterday, today, tomorrow as distinct entities. He simply said whatever would satisfy, momentarily, his yearning to be the center of the stage surrounded by admiring, fearful, shocked, amazed people. He did not even care if their reaction was admiration, fear, shock, or amazement, and he did not care if they, as persons, had the same reaction or a different one the next day or even a moment later. He was exactly like an actor in a drama, one in which he made the script as he went along, full of falsehoods and inconsistencies, and he was genuinely surprised and hurt if a person whom he had abused and insulted for hours at a hearing did not walk out with him to a bar or even to dinner the moment the hearing session was over. He knew it was an act; he expected you to know it was an act. There really was no hypocrisy about it, no cynicism, no falsehood, as far as he was concerned, because he was convinced that this was the way the world was. Everyone, he was convinced, had a racket; this just happened to be his, and he expected people to realize this and to understand it.

Of course, to the observant outsider who did not share his total amorality, it was all false, invented as he went along, and constantly changed, everything substantiated by documents pulled from his bulging briefcase and waved about too rapidly to be read. Mostly these documents had nothing to do with what he was saying; mostly he had never looked at them himself; they were merely props for the performance, and, to him, it was as silly for his audience to expect such documents to be relevant as it would be for the audience in a theater to expect the food that is being eaten, the whiskey that is being drunk, or the documents which are read *in that play* to be relevant to what the actor is saying.

Like any actor who might be charged with inconsistency or with lying because what he says in one play is not compatible with what he says in another play, McCarthy was puzzled, offended, hurt, or amused. With him every day, every hour, was a different play. As a result, to the audience nothing was consistent with anything else. He gave several different dates for his birth, and after 1945, never the correct one (November 14, 1908). Every time he spoke or wrote of his war experiences, the story was a different one, and with each version he became a larger, more nonchalant hero. Eventually, in 1952, when his power in Washington was at its height, and most of the government feared to draw his wrath (or even his attention), he intimidated the Air Force into awarding him the Distinguished Flying Cross (given for twenty-five combat missions), although he had been a grounded intelligence officer, who took occasional rides in planes.

Since laws and regulations were, for McCarthy, nonexistent, his business and financial affairs are, like his life, a chaos of illegalities. From 1935 to 1942 his gross income was less than $25,000, yet during the seven years he put more than twice that into the stock market. When he was elected judge in 1939, one of his earliest decisions was appealed by the state to its supreme court, where it was found that McCarthy had destroyed those portions of the record in which he had justified dismissing the state's complaints. Shortly after he arrived in Washington, as a new senator in 1947, he heard of Pepsi-Cola's difficulties with sugar rationing, accepted a $10,000 unsecured loan from Pepsi-Cola's lobbyist, and, the next day, opened an attack on sugar rationing. When this attack was successful, the same lobbyist endorsed a note for $20,000 which McCarthy used to cover his overextended bank account in Wisconsin. A year later, as the most active member of a joint congressional committee on housing, he gutted the public housing features out of the Taft-Ellender-

Waggoner housing bill in return for thousands of dollars in favors from the private housing lobby. One of these favors was $10,000 from Lustron Corporation in return for putting his name, as author, on one of its publicity releases. And so it went, most of his ill-gotten gains being dissipated on horse-racing bets, gambling, or parties for his friends. When the Senate Subcommittee on Privileges and Elections, late in 1951, began to study one of his bank accounts, it found unexplained deposits of almost $173,000 and others of almost $97,000 funneled through the administrative assistant in his office.

Until early 1950, Communism meant little to McCarthy. He had been elected to the Senate over the incumbent, La Follette, in 1946, as a result of Communist-controlled votes in the labor unions of Milwaukee. As senator he collaborated in a joint Nazi and Communist plot to injure the United States and its army by reversing the convictions of German S.S. troops for atrocities committed on American prisoners of war captured in the Battle of the Bulge. But by January 1950, McCarthy was looking for an issue to be used for his reelection in 1952. At dinner with three men, two of them associates of mine, in the Colony Restaurant in Washington (January 7, 1950) he asked what issue he should use. After several suggestions, he seized upon Communism: "That's it," he said. "The government is full of Communists. We can hammer away at them."

To obtain an audience for this hammering, he requested bookings for Lincoln's Birthday speeches from the Senate Republican Campaign Committee and was given assignments at Wheeling, West Virginia, Salt Lake City, and Reno. Without any real conception of what he was doing, and without any research or knowledge of the subject, at Wheeling on February 9th, McCarthy waved a piece of paper (copy of a four-year-old letter from Byrnes to Representative Adolph Sabath) and said, "While I cannot take the time to name all of the men in the State Department who have been named as members of the Communist Party and members of a spy ring, I have here in my hand a list of 205 that were known to the Secretary of State as being members of the Communist Party and who nevertheless are still working and shaping the policy of the State Department." The letter in fact named no names, had nothing to do with spying or even with Communists, but simply reported that 3,000 employees of abolished war agencies, who were being shifted to the State Department budget, had been screened and 284 had been listed as undesirable (of which 79 had been already separated from service, 26 of these because they were aliens). Every time McCarthy repeated the charge, the numbers and the categories changed; for example, the following night, he told his Salt Lake City audience, "Last night . . . I stated that I had the names of 57 card-carrying members of the Communist Party."

Out of the controversy raised by these charges emerged McCarthy the accuser, known to every American and praised or reviled by millions. He loved it. On February 20th, in an incoherent speech of more than six hours in the Senate, he announced that he had penetrated "Truman's iron curtain of secrecy" and that he was going to give 81 cases, identified by numbers without names. What ensued in the next six hours was bedlam, as case after case was presented, filled with contradictions and irrelevancies. There were 81 numbers but only 66 cases, for cases were left out, some were repeated with different numbers, many had never been employed by the State Department or even by the government, and one, "primarily a morals case," had been discharged from it because he was "anti-Communist," while another, Case 72, was "a high type of man, a Democratic American who . . . opposed Communism." It was, according to the Senate Republican leader, Senator Taft, "a perfectly reckless performance." Nevertheless, Taft and his colleagues determined to accept and support these charges, since they would injure the Administration. Accordingly, Taft told McCarthy, "If one case doesn't work, try another." The public, informed only of the charges, without the cynical details, gathered from the newspaper headlines that the State Department was full of Communist spies. Even today few people realize that McCarthy, in five years of accusations, never turned up a Communist in the State Department, although undoubtedly there must have been some there.

McCarthy repeated this performance before a Senate subcommittee chaired by Senator Millard Tydings of Maryland, a few weeks later. From March 7th through early July, this subcommittee of the Senate Foreign Relations Committee took 1,500 printed pages of testimony plus more than 1,000 pages of documentation. McCarthy's testimony, it soon developed, was based entirely on evidence turned up by House of Representative committees of the previous Congress. He gave names to the 66 cases (he called it 81 cases) he had mentioned in his Senate speech and 35 new names. In few cases was there any evidence. When asked for evidence, he airily told Senator Tydings that that was *his* job: the evidence was in the State Department, and it was up to the committee to get it. After the files in question were obtained by the committee and found to contain no evidence to support McCarthy's charges, McCarthy called them "phony files" and insisted they had been "raped and rifled" of the FBI reports which had been in them. J. Edgar Hoover was called in, had the files examined, and reported that "the State Department files were intact."

McCarthy ignored this rebuff. New charges followed. Eventually he announced that he would base his whole reputation on one case. For more than a week he tantalized the world and the committee by withholding the name: "the top Russian espionage agent" in the United States, "Alger Hiss's boss in the espionage ring in the State Department," "the chief architect of our Far Eastern policy." At last the name was released: Professor Owen Lattimore, of the Johns Hopkins University, the English-speaking world's greatest authority on Mongolia. The only trouble was that Lattimore was not a Communist, not a spy, and not employed by the State Department.

The Tydings subcommittee report, issued in July, condemned McCarthy for "a fraud and a hoax" on the Senate: "Starting with nothing, Senator McCarthy plunged headlong forward, desperately seeking to develop some information." McCarthy should have been finished. He was not. And for a very simple reason: in politics truth is not so important as power, and McCarthy soon showed that he had the power—the power of an inflamed and misled public opinion. In the election of November 1950, several members of the Senate who had been most outspoken against McCarthy, including some of the most influential leaders of that august body, were defeated—by McCarthyism, if not by McCarthy. Tydings was beaten in Maryland in 1950, and Scott Lucas, the Democratic leader in the Senate, who had harassed McCarthy during his performance on February 20th, went down with him. William Benton, senator from Connecticut, who introduced a resolution to expel McCarthy from the Senate in 1951 and whose charges were fully supported by the Senate's investigation of McCarthy's private finances, was defeated in 1952. With him went down to defeat Lucas's successor as Democratic leader, Senator McFarland of Arizona. From 1950 to 1954 most of his fellow senators, and many in the executive branch, were terrorized by McCarthy's power with the electorate, and opposed him on nothing they could possibly concede. During this period he violated more laws and regulations than any previous senator in history. Thousands of his secret supporters in the Administration sent him information and misinformation, classified secrets, spite letters, anonymous notes. The Eisenhower Administration at one time considered charging McCarthy himself with espionage but did not have the courage. Much of this material was read by McCarthy over nationwide television broadcasts. When a reporter once said to him, "Isn't that a classified document?" McCarthy said, "It *was*. I just declassified it."

It may be doubted that McCarthy's power to defeat his enemies was as great as they thought, but he encouraged these thoughts. Certainly he defeated Tydings.

Senator Tydings, from an old and wealthy Maryland family, with a brilliant combat record in World War I, was too conservative for Franklin Roosevelt, who tried to "purge" him in the primary campaign of 1938, but had been soundly rebuffed. McCarthy did it differently. Using the large sums of money which came to him from real anti-Communists throughout the country, McCarthy hired a group of shady characters, led by an ex-FBI agent (fired for immorality during enforcement of the Mann "white-slave" Law), and sent them, well equipped with funds, into Maryland to fight Tydings as a "pro-Communist." The state election laws were violated on a wholesale basis, including excess expenditures, forgery, use of out-of-state paid campaigners, and numerous other violations. The *coup de grâce* was administered to Tydings by wide circulation of a faked photograph of Tydings and Communist leader Earl Browder cozily together, a concoction of McCarthy's staff. After Tydings was defeated, several of his victorious opponent's staff, including his campaign manager, were tried and sentenced to jail or to pay fines, for electoral-law violations, but that did not change the result of the election, and few other senators wanted to risk the same ordeal by opposing McCarthy in the Senate.

The Republicans were as scared as the Democrats, and with good reason, for party lines, like all other distinctions, meant nothing to McCarthy, and he continued his charges in 1953-1954 with his own party in control of both houses of Congress and Eisenhower in the White House. The chief change was that he stopped talking of "twenty years of treason" in the White House and talked of "twenty-one years of treason." The new President, in an effort to divert these attacks, continued to yield to him, as he had yielded to him during the campaign. The Administration was soon boasting that 1,456 Federal workers had been "separated" in the first four months of the "Eisenhower security program." At the end of the first year the President raised this total to 2,200. It took some weeks for the Democrats to discover that these figures did not apply to subversives or even to security risks, but to anyone who left the government service. By the end of its first year, the new Administration adopted completely McCarthy's refusal to be hampered by categories. Vice-President Nixon said, "We're kicking the Communists and fellow travelers and security risks out of the Government . . . by the thousands." It was soon clear that no known Communists were kicked out and that "security risks" included all kinds of persons, such as those who imbibed too freely at Washington's endless cocktail parties. A Communist in the State Department would have been a prize among this motley group, but none was announced.

For a while, the new Administration tried to outdo McCarthy, chiefly by demonstrating in committee hearings that China had been "lost" to the Communists because of the careful planning and intrigue of Communists in the State Department. The chief effort in this direction was done by a well-organized and well-financed "China Lobby" radiating from the activities of Alfred Kohlberg, a wealthy exporter who had had business interests in China. This group, with its allies, such as McCarthy, mobilized a good deal of evidence that Communists had infiltrated into various academic, journalistic, and research groups concerned with the Far East. But they failed to prove their contention that a conspiracy of these

Communists and fellow travelers, acting through the State Department, had given China to Mao. Mao won out in China because of the incompetence and corruption of the Chiang Kai-shek regime, and he won out in spite of any aid the United States gave, or could give, to Chiang, because the latter's regime was incapable of holding out against Mao, without drastic reforms, whatever the scale of American aid (without American military intervention to make war on Mao, which very few desired). The China Lobby's version was based on two contentions: (1) that there were Communists in significant positions close to the agencies which helped to form American academic and public opinion on the Far East and (2) that there were frequent agreements between known Communists and known formulators of American policy and opinion on China. This whole subject is too complex for adequate discussion here, but the situation must be outlined.

There is considerable truth in the China Lobby's contention that the American experts on China were organized into a single interlocking group which had a general consensus of a Leftish character. It is also true that this group, from its control of funds, academic recommendations, and research or publication opportunities, could favor persons who accepted the established consensus and could injure, financially or in professional advancement, persons who did not accept it. It is also true that the established group, by its influence on book reviewing in *The New York Times*, the *Herald Tribune*, the *Saturday Review*, a few magazines, including the "liberal weeklies," and in the professional journals, could advance or hamper any specialist's career. It is also true that these things were done in the United States in regard to the Far East by the Institute of Pacific Relations, that this organization had been infiltrated by Communists, and by Communist sympathizers, and that much of this group's influence arose from its access to and control over the flow of funds from financial foundations to scholarly activities. All these things were true, but they would have been true of many other areas of American scholarly research and academic administration in the United States, such as Near East studies or anthropology or educational theory or political science. They were more obvious in regard to the Far East because of the few persons and the bigger issues involved in that area.

On the other hand, the charges of the China Lobby, accepted and proliferated by the neo-isolationists in the 1950's and by the radical Right in the 1960's, that China was "lost" because of this group, or that the members of this group were disloyal to the United States, or engaged in espionage, or were participants in a conscious plot, or that the whole group was controlled by Soviet agents or even by Communists, is not true. Yet the whole subject is of major importance in understanding the twentieth century.

In the first place, because of language barriers, the number of people who could be "experts" on the Far East was limited. Most of these, like Pearl Buck, Professor Fairbank of Harvard, or Professors Latourette and Rowe of Yale, and many others, were children or relatives of people who originally became concerned with China as missionaries. This gave them a double character: they learned the language and they had a feeling of spiritual mission about China. When we add to this that they were, until after 1950, few in numbers and had access, because of the commercial importance of the Far East, to relatively large amounts of research, travel, and publication funds on Far East matters, they almost inevitably came to form a small group who knew each other personally, met fairly regularly, had a fairly established consensus (based on conversations and reading each other's books) on Far East questions, and generally had certain characteristics of a clique.

Lattimore, for example, because he knew Mongolian and the others did not, tended to become everybody's expert on Mongolia, was rarely challenged on Mongolia or northwest interior China, and inevitably became rather opinionated, if not conceited, on the subject. Moreover, many of these experts, and those the ones which were favored by the Far East "establishment" in the Institute of Pacific Relations, were captured by Communist ideology. Under its influence they propagandized, as experts, erroneous ideas and sought to influence policy in mistaken directions. For example, they sought to establish, in 1943-1950, that the Chinese Communists were simple agrarian reformers, rather like the third-party groups of the American Mid-west; or that Japan was evil and must be totally crushed, the monarchy removed, and (later) that American policy in Japan, under General MacArthur, was a failure; they even accepted, on occasion, the Stalinist line that Communist regimes were "democratic and peace-loving," while capitalist ones were "warlike and aggressive." For example, as late as 1951 the John Day Company (Richard J. Walsh, president) published an indictment of MacArthur's policies in Japan by Robert Textor. The book, called *Failure in Japan*, had an introduction by Lattimore and sought to show that our occupation policy led to "failure for democratic values in Japan and a situation of strategic weakness for the West." This childish libel was propagated by the IPR, which mailed out 2,300 postcards advertising the book.

Behind this unfortunate situation lies another, more profound, relationship, which influences matters much broader than Far Eastern policy. It involves the organization of tax-exempt fortunes of international financiers into foundations to be used for educational, scientific, "and other public purposes." Sixty or more years ago, public life in the West was dominated by the influence of "Wall Street." This term has nothing to do with its use by the Communists to mean monopolistic industrialism, but, on the contrary, refers to international financial capitalism deeply involved in the gold standard, foreign-exchange fluctuations, floating of fixed-interest securities and, to a lesser extent, flotation of industrial shares for stock-exchange markets. This group, which in the United States, was completely dominated by J. P. Morgan and Company from the 1880's to the 1930's was cosmopolitan, Anglophile, internationalist, Ivy League, eastern seaboard, high Episcopalian, and European-culture conscious. Their connection with the Ivy League colleges rested on the fact that the large endowments of these institutions required constant consultation with the financiers of Wall Street (or its lesser branches on State Street, Boston, and elsewhere) and was reflected in the fact that these endowments, even in 1930, were largely in bonds rather than in real estate or common stocks. As a consequence of these influences, as late as the 1930's, J. P. Morgan and his associates were the most significant figures in policy making at Harvard, Columbia, and to a lesser extent Yale, while the Whitneys were significant at Yale, and the Prudential Insurance Company (through Edward D. Duffield) dominated Princeton.

The names of these Wall Street luminaries still adorn these Ivy League campuses, with Harkness colleges and a Payne Whitney gymnasium at Yale, a Pyne dormitory at Princeton, a Dillon Field House and Lamont Library at Harvard. The chief officials of these universities were beholden to these financial powers and usually owed their jobs to them. Morgan himself helped make Nicholas Murray Butler president of Columbia; his chief Boston agent, Thomas Nelson Perkins of the First National Bank of that city, gave Conant his boost from the chemical laboratory to University Hall at Harvard; Duffield of Prudential, caught unprepared when the incumbent president of Princeton was killed in an automobile in 1932, made himself president for a year before he chose Harold Dodds for the post in 1933. At Yale, Thomas Lamont, managing partner of the Morgan firm, was able to swing Charles Seymour into the presidency of that university in 1937.

The significant influence of "Wall Street" (meaning Morgan) both in the Ivy League and in Washington, in the period of sixty or more years following 1880, explains the constant interchange between the Ivy League and the Federal government, an interchange which undoubtedly aroused a good deal of resentment in less-favored circles, who were more than satiated with the accents, tweeds, and High Episcopal Anglophilia of these peoples. Poor Dean Acheson, in spite of (or perhaps because of) his remarkable qualities of intellect and character, took the full brunt of this resentment from McCarthy and his allies in 1948–1954. The same feeling did no good to pseudo-Ivy League figures like Alger Hiss.

Because of its dominant position in Wall Street, the Morgan firm came also to dominate other Wall Street powers, such as Carnegie, Whitney, Vanderbilt, Brown-Harriman, or Dillon-Reed. Close alliances were made with Rockefeller, Mellon, and Duke interests but not nearly so intimate ones with the great industrial powers like du Pont and Ford. In spite of the great influence of this "Wall Street" alignment, an influence great enough to merit the name of the "American Establishment," this group could not control the Federal government and, in consequence, had to adjust to a good many government actions thoroughly distasteful to the group. The chief of these were in taxation law, beginning with the graduated income tax in 1913, but culminating, above all else, in the inheritance tax. These tax laws drove the great private fortunes dominated by Wall Street into tax-exempt foundations, which became a major link in the Establishment network between Wall Street, the Ivy League, and the Federal government. Dean Rusk, Secretary of State after 1961, formerly president of the Rockefeller Foundation and Rhodes Scholar at Oxford (1931–1933), is as much a member of this nexus as Alger Hiss, the Dulles brothers, Jerome Greene, James T. Shotwell, John W. Davis, Elihu Root, or Philip Jessup.

More than fifty years ago the Morgan firm decided to infiltrate the Left-wing political movements in the United States. This was relatively easy to do, since these groups were starved for funds and eager for a voice to reach the people. Wall Street supplied both. The purpose was not to destroy, dominate, or take over but was really threefold: (1) to keep informed about the thinking of Left-wing or liberal groups; (2) to provide them with a mouthpiece so that they could "blow off steam," and (3) to have a final veto on their publicity and possibly on their actions, if they ever went "radical." There was nothing really new about this decision, since other financiers had talked about it and even attempted it earlier. What made it decisively important this time was the combination of its adoption by the dominant Wall Street financier, at a time when tax policy was driving all financiers to seek tax-exempt refuges for their fortunes, and at a time when the ultimate in Left-wing radicalism was about to appear under the banner of the Third International.

The best example of this alliance of Wall Street and Left-wing publication was *The New Republic*, a magazine founded by Willard Straight, using Payne Whitney money, in 1914. Straight, who had been assistant to Sir Robert Hart (Director of the Chinese Imperial Customs Service and the head of the European imperialist penetration of China) and had remained in the Far East from 1901 to 1912, became a Morgan partner and the firm's chief expert on the Far East. He married Dorothy Payne Whitney whose names indicate the family alliance of two of America's greatest fortunes. She was the daughter of William C. Whitney, New York utility millionaire and the sister and co-heiress of Oliver

Payne, of the Standard Oil "trust." One of her brothers married Gertrude Vanderbilt, while the other, Payne Whitney, married the daughter of Secretary of State John Hay, who enunciated the American policy of the "Open Door" in China. In the next generation, three first cousins, John Hay ("Jock") Whitney, Cornelius Vanderbilt ("Sonny") Whitney, and Michael Whitney ("Mike") Straight, were allied in numerous public policy enterprises of a propagandist nature, and all three served in varied roles in the late New Deal and Truman administrations. In these they were closely allied with other "Wall Street liberals," such as Nelson Rockefeller.

The New Republic was founded by Willard and Dorothy Straight, using her money, in 1914, and continued to be supported by her financial contributions until March 23, 1953. The original purpose for establishing the paper was to provide an outlet for the progressive Left and to guide it quietly in an Anglophile direction. This latter task was entrusted to a young man, only four years out of Harvard, but already a member of the mysterious Round Table group, which has played a major role in directing England's foreign policy since its formal establishment in 1909. This new recruit, Walter Lippmann, has been, from 1914 to the present, the authentic spokesman in American journalism for the Establishments on both sides of the Atlantic in international affairs. His biweekly columns, which appear in hundreds of American papers, are copyrighted by the New York Herald Tribune which is now owned by J. H. Whitney. It was these connections, as a link between Wall Street and the Round Table Group, which gave Lippmann the opportunity in 1918, while still in his twenties, to be the official interpreter of the meaning of Woodrow Wilson's Fourteen Points to the British government.

Willard Straight, like many Morgan agents, was present at the Paris Peace Conference but died there of pneumonia before it began. Six years later, in 1925, when his widow married a second time and became Lady Elmhirst of Dartington Hall, she took her three small children from America to England, where they were brought up as English. She herself renounced her American citizenship in 1935. Shortly afterward her younger son, "Mike," unsuccessfully "stood" for Parliament on the Labour Party ticket for the constituency of Cambridge University, an act which required, under the law, that he be a British subject. This proved no obstacle, in 1938, when Mike, age twenty-two, returned to the United States, after thirteen years in England, and was at once appointed to the State Department as Adviser on International Economic Affairs. In 1937, apparently in preparation for her son's return to America, Lady Elmhirst, sole owner of The New Republic, shifted this ownership to Westrim, Ltd., a dummy corporation created for the purpose in Montreal, Canada, and set up in New York, with a grant of $1.5 million, the William C. Whitney Foundation of which Mike became president. This helped finance the family's interest in modern art and dramatic theater, including sister Beatrix's tours as a Shakespearean actress.

Mike Straight served in the Air Force in 1943-1945, but this did not in any way hamper his career with *The New Republic*. He became Washington correspondent in May 1941; editor in June 1943; and publisher in December 1946 (when he made Henry Wallace editor). During these shifts he changed completely the control of *The New Republic*, and its companion magazine *Asia*, removing known liberals (such as Robert Morss Lovett, Malcolm Cowley, and George Soule), centralizing the control, and taking it into his own hands. This control by Whitney money had, of course, always existed, but it had been in abeyance for the twenty-five years following Willard Straight's death.

The first editor of *The New Republic*, the well-known "liberal" Herbert Croly, was always aware of the situation. After ten years in the job, he explained the relationship in the "official" biography of Willard Straight which he wrote for a payment of $25,000. "Of course they [the Straights] could always withdraw their financial support if they ceased to approve of the policy of the paper; and, in that event, it would go out of existence as a consequence of their disapproval." Croly's biography of Straight, published in 1924, makes perfectly clear that Straight was in no sense a liberal or a progressive, but was, indeed, a typical international banker and that *The New Republic* was simply a medium for advancing certain designs of such international bankers, notably to blunt the isolationism and anti-British sentiments so prevalent among many America progressives, while providing them with a vehicle for expression of their progressive views in literature, art, music, social reform, and even domestic politics. In 1916, when the editorial board wanted to support Wilson for a second term in the Presidency, Willard Straight took two pages of the magazine to express his own support for Hughes. The chief achievement of *The New Republic*, however, in 1914-1918 and again in 1938-1948, was for interventionism in Europe and support of Great Britain.

The role of "Mike" Straight in this situation in 1938-1948 is clear. He took charge of this family fief, abolished the editorial board, and carried on his father's aims, in close cooperation with labor and Left-wing groups in American politics. In these efforts he was in close contact with his inherited Wall Street connections, especially his Whitney cousins and certain family agents like Bruce Bliven, Milton C. Rose, and Richard J. Walsh. They handled a variety of enterprises, including publications, corporations, and foundations, which operated out of the law office of Baldwin, Todd, and Lefferts of 120 Broadway, New York City. In this nexus were *The New Republic*, *Asia*, *Theatre Arts*, the Museum of Modern Art, and others, all supported by a handful of foundations, including the William C. Whitney Foundation, the Gertrude Vanderbilt Whitney Foundation, the J. H. Whitney Foundation, and others. An interesting addition was made to these enterprises in 1947 when Straight founded a new magazine, the *United Nations World*, to be devoted to the support of the UN. Its owners of record were *The New Republic* itself (under its corporate name), Nelson Rockefeller, J. H. Whitney, Max Ascoli (an anti-Fascist Italian who had married American wealth and used it to support a magazine of his own, *The Reporter*), and Beatrice S. Dolivet. The last lady, Mike Straight's sister, made her husband, Louis Dolivet, "International Editor" of the new magazine.

An important element in this nexus was *Asia* magazine, which had been established by Morgan's associates as the journal of the American Asiatic Society in 1898, had been closely associated with Willard Straight during his lifetime, and was owned outright by him from January 1917. In the 1930's it was operated for the Whitneys by Richard J. Walsh and his wife, known to the world as Pearl Buck. Walsh, who acted as editor of *Asia*, was also president of the holding corporation of *The New Republic* for several years and president of the John Day publishing company. In 1942, after Nelson Rockefeller and Jock Whitney joined the government to take charge of American propaganda in Latin America in the Office of the Coordinator of Inter-American Affairs, *Asia* magazine changed its name to *Asia and the Americas*. In 1947, when Mike Straight began a drive to "sell" the United Nations, it was completely reorganized into *United Nations World*.

Mike Straight was deeply anti-Communist, but he frequently was found associated with them, sometimes as a collaborator, frequently as an opponent. The opposition was seen most clearly in his efforts as one of the founders of the American Veterans Committee (AVC) and its political sequel, the Americans for Democratic Action (ADA). The collaboration may be seen in Straight's fundamental role in Henry Wallace's third-party campaign for the Presidency in 1948.

The relationship between Straight and the Communists in pushing Wallace into his 1948 adventure may be misjudged very easily. The anti-Communist Right had a very simple explanation of it: Wallace and Straight were Communists and hoped to elect Wallace President. Nothing could be further from the truth. All three—Straight, Wallace, and the Communists, joined in the attempt merely as a means of defeating Truman. Straight was the chief force in getting the campaign started in 1947 and was largely instrumental in bringing some of the Communists into it, but when he had them all aboard the Wallace train, he jumped off himself, leaving both Wallace and the Communists gliding swiftly, without guidance or hope, on the downhill track to oblivion. It was a brilliantly done piece of work.

The Communists wanted a third party in 1948 because it seemed the only way to beat Truman and destroy the Marshall Plan. They hated the President for the "Truman Doctrine" and his general opposition to the Soviet Union, but, above all, because he had prevented the postwar economic collapse and the American relapse into isolationism, both of which the Communists had not only expected but critically needed. It was obvious to everyone that a two-party campaign in 1948 would give the vote of the Right to the Republicans and the vote of the Left to the Democrats, with the victory decided by where the division came in the Center. In such a situation neither Straight nor the Communists could influence the outcome in any way. But a third party on the Left, by taking labor and other Left-wing votes from Truman, could reduce the Democratic totals in the major states enough to throw those states and the election to the Republicans. Why Straight wanted to do this in the critical months from September 1946 to April 1948 is unknown, but he clearly changed his mind in the spring of 1948, abandoning poor, naïve Henry Wallace to the Communists at that time. A possible explanation of these actions will be given later.

What is clear is that Mike Straight had a great deal to do with Wallace in the autumn of 1946 when the former Vice-President broke with Truman and was fired from the Cabinet. The break came over a Wallace speech, very critical of American policy toward Russia, given before a wildly biased pro-Soviet audience in Madison Square Garden on September 12, 1946. At the time Truman told reporters he had approved the speech before delivery (a version which Wallace still upholds), but, within a few days, Secretary of State Byrnes forced the President to make a choice between him or Wallace, and the latter was dismissed from the Cabinet.

Out of the government, without a platform from which to address the public, Wallace's political future looked dim in the early autumn of 1946. Straight provided the platform, by giving him his own editorial chair at *The New Republic* (announced October 12, 1946). For the next fifteen months the Wallace campaign was a Straight campaign. The latter supplied speechwriters, research assistants, editorial writers, office space, money, and *The New Republic* itself. Technically Wallace was editor, but the magazine staff and expenditures steadily increased in directions which had little to do with the magazine and everything to do with Wallace's presidential campaign, although this effort was not announced to the public until a year later, in December 1947.

In the meantime, from the spring of 1947 onward, the Communists came in. It would not be strictly true to say that Straight "brought them in," but I believe it is fair to say that he "let them in." For example, one of the first to arrive was Lew Frank, Jr., brought in by Straight, who later insisted that he did not realize that Frank was a Communist. As a matter of fact, there was no evidence that Frank was a member of the Communist Party, but Straight knew exactly where Frank stood politically since they had engaged, on opposite sides, in a bitter struggle between Communists and anti-Communists for control of AVC. In this, Frank had been a member of the Communist caucus within AVC's national planning committee (as Straight told David A. Shannon in 1956), and followed every twist of the party line in this whole period. This party line became the pattern for Wallace's formal speeches, since Frank was his most important speechwriter over a period of eighteen months from early 1947 to October 1948. More than this, Frank accompanied Wallace on his endless travels during this period. In the autumn of 1947 these three, Wallace, Frank, and Straight, made a trip to the Mediterranean and were given an audience together by the Pope on November 4, 1947. On his return from this journey, Wallace was a changed man; his mind was made up, to run against Truman on a third-party ticket. The announcement was made public in *The New Republic* in December.

Straight continued to work for Wallace for President, and *The New Republic* remained the center of the movement for almost four more months, but something had changed. While he was still working for Wallace as President and allowing the Communists into the project, he was simultaneously doing two other things: working openly, and desperately, to prevent the new third party from campaigning on any level other than the presidential, by blocking everywhere he could Communist efforts to run third-party candidates for state or congressional offices in competition with the Democrats; much less publicly, he worked with his anti-Communist friends in labor, veteran, and liberal groups to prevent endorsement of the Wallace candidacy. As a consequence, the Communists were destroyed and eventually driven out of such organizations, notably from the CIO-PAC (the great political alignment of labor and progressive groups). As David Shannon wrote in *The Decline of American Communism* (1959), "The Communists' support of Wallace shattered the 'left-center' coalition in the CIO; for the Communist unions, the Wallace movement was the beginning of the end. The coalition began to dissolve almost immediately after Wallace's announcement." What this means is that Wallace's campaign to defeat Truman destroyed completely the remaining vestiges of the Popular Front movement of the 1930's, drove the Communists out of the unions and all progressive political groups, and drove the Communist unions out of the labor movement of the country. This ended Communism as a significant political force in the United States, and the end was reached by December 1948, long before McCarthy or J. Edgar Hoover or HUAC did their work. The men who achieved this feat were Wallace and Straight, although it is still not completely clear if they recognized what they were doing.

During the winter of 1947–1948, Lew Frank recognized that he was incapable of handling the complex issues raised in Wallace's many speeches. Accordingly, he joined a "Communist research group" which met in the Manhattan home of the wealthy "Wall Street Red," Frederick Vanderbilt Field. The chief members of this group, probably all Communists, were Victor Perlo and David Ramsay. This pair drew up for Wallace an attack on the Marshall Plan and an alternative Communist plan for European reconstruction, which was published in *The New Republic* on January 12, 1948, was presented by Wallace to the Marshall Plan "Hearings" of the House Foreign Affairs Committee on February 24th, but was subsequently repudiated by Straight. In the three months following the Perlo article, Straight was busy sawing off the limb on which Wallace now sat with the Communists. He discharged from *The New Republic* payroll all those who were working for the campaign rather than for the magazine, and the office on East Forty-ninth Street once again settled down to publishing a "liberal" weekly. In protest at this reversal, his managing editor, Edd Johnson, resigned.

If Mike Straight planned to do what he did do to the Communists in 1946–1948, that is, to get them out of progressive movements and unions, he pulled off the most skillful political coup in twentieth century American politics. It is not clear that he did plan it or intend it. But as a very able and informed man, he must have had some motivation when he began, in 1947, the effort which he knew might defeat Truman in 1948. While the evidence is not conclusive, there are hints that another, more personal, motive might have been involved, at least partly, in building up the Wallace threat to Truman's political future. It concerns the Whitney family interest in overseas airlines.

The Whitney family were deeply involved in airlines. Sonny Whitney was a founder of Pan-American Airlines and chairman of its board of directors from its establishment in 1928 until he went to military service in 1941. Mike's brother, Air Commodore Whitney Willard Straight, C.B.E., was even more deeply involved on the British side. Big brother Whitney (born in 1912) had been in civil aviation in England from the age of twenty-two, and by 1946–1949, was not only a director of the Midland Bank, one of the world's greatest financial institutions, but was also a director of Rolls-Royce and of BOAC, as well as chairman of the board of directors of BEA (British European Airways). In the years following the end of the war, a violent struggle was going on, within aviation circles and the United States government, over the future of American transocean air services. Before the war, these had been a monopoly of Pan-Am; now, at the end of the war, the struggle was over how the CAB would divide up this monopoly and what disposition would be made of the enormous air-force investment in overseas bases. Apparently the White House was not cooperative in these matters at first, but late in 1947 C. V. Whitney was made, by presidential interim appointment,

Assistant Secretary of the new Department of the Air Force and, eighteen months later, after Truman's inauguration, was made Assistant Secretary of Commerce for Aeronautics. This was the most important post concerned with civil aviation in any Federal department. The connection, if any, between these appointments and Mike Straight's original support and later abandonment of Wallace has never been revealed.

The associations between Wall Street and the Left, of which Mike Straight is a fair example, are really survivals of the associations between the Morgan Bank and the Left. To Morgan all political parties were simply organizations to be used, and the firm always was careful to keep a foot in all camps. Morgan himself, Dwight Morrow, and other partners were allied with Republicans; Russell C. Leffingwell was allied with the Democrats; Grayson Murphy was allied with the extreme Right; and Thomas W. Lamont was allied with the Left. Like the Morgan interest in libraries, museums, and art, its inability to distinguish between loyalty to the United States and loyalty to England, its recognition of the need for social work among the poor, the multipartisan political views of the Morgan firm in domestic politics went back to the original founder of the firm, George Peabody (1795–1869). To this same seminal figure may be attributed the use of tax-exempt foundations for controlling these activities, as may be observed in many parts of America to this day, in the use of Peabody foundations to support Peabody libraries and museums. Unfortunately, we do not have space here for this great and untold story, but it must be remembered that what we do say is part of a much larger picture.

Our concern at the moment is with the links between Wall Street and the Left, especially the Communists. Here the chief link was the Thomas W. Lamont family. This family was in many ways parallel to the Straight family. Tom Lamont had been brought into the Morgan firm, as Straight was several years later, by Henry P. Davison, a Morgan partner from 1909. Lamont became a partner in 1910, as Straight did in 1913. Each had a wife who became a patroness of Leftish causes, and two sons, of which the elder was a conventional banker, and the younger was a Left-wing sympathizer and sponsor. In fact, all the evidence would indicate that Tom Lamont was simply Morgan's apostle to the Left in succession to Straight, a change made necessary by the latter's premature death in 1918. Both were financial supporters of liberal publications, in Lamont's case *The Saturday Review of Literature*, which he supported throughout the 1920's and 1930's, and the *New York Post*, which he owned from 1918 to 1924.

The chief evidence, however, can be found in the files of the HUAC which show Tom Lamont, his wife Flora, and his son Corliss as sponsors and financial angels to almost a score of extreme Left organizations, including the Communist Party itself. Among these we need mention only two. One of these was a Communist-front organization, the Trade Union Services, Incorporated, of New York City, which in 1947 published fifteen trade-union papers for various CIO unions. Among its officers were Corliss Lamont and Frederick Vanderbilt Field (another link between Wall Street and the Communists). The latter was on the editorial boards of the official Communist newspaper in New York, the *Daily Worker*, as well as its magazine, *The New Masses*, and was the chief link between the Communists and the Institute of Pacific Relations in 1928–1947. Corliss Lamont was the leading light in another Communist organization, which started life in the 1920's as the Friends of the Soviet Union, but in 1943 was reorganized, with Lamont as chairman of the board and chief incorporator, as the National Council of American-Soviet Friendship.

During this whole period of over two decades, Corliss Lamont, with the full support of his parents, was one of the chief figures in "fellow traveler" circles and one of the chief spokesmen for the Soviet point of view both in these organizations and also in connections which came to him either as son of the most influential man in Wall Street or as professor of philosophy at Columbia University. His relationship with his parents may be reflected in a few events of this period.

In January 1946, Corliss Lamont was called before HUAC to give testimony on the National Council of American-Soviet Friendship. He refused to produce records, was subpoenaed, refused, was charged with contempt of Congress, and was so cited by the House of Representatives on June 26, 1946. In the midst of this controversy, in May, Corliss Lamont and his mother, Mrs. Thomas Lamont, presented their valuable collection of the works of Spinoza to Columbia University. The adverse publicity continued, yet when Thomas Lamont rewrote his will, on January 6, 1948, Corliss Lamont remained in it as co-heir to his father's fortune of scores of millions of dollars.

In 1951 the Subcommittee on Internal Security of the Senate Judiciary Committee, the so-called McCarran Committee, sought to show that China had been lost to the Communists by the deliberate actions of a group of academic experts on the Far East and Communist fellow travelers whose work in that direction was controlled and coordinated by the Institute of Pacific Relations (IPR). The influence of the Communists in IPR is well established, but the patronage of Wall Street is less well known.

The IPR was a private association of ten independent national councils in ten countries concerned with affairs in the Pacific. The headquarters of the IPR and of the American Council of IPR were both in New York and were closely associated on an interlocking basis. Each spent about $2.5 million dollars over the quarter-century from 1925 to 1950, of which about half, in each case, came from the Carnegie Foundation and the Rockefeller Foundation (which were themselves interlocking groups controlled by an alliance of Morgan and Rockefeller interests in Wall Street). Much of the rest, especially of the American Council, came from firms closely allied to these two Wall Street interests, such as Standard Oil, International Telephone and Telegraph, International General Electric, the National City Bank, and the Chase National Bank. In each case, about 10 percent of income came from sales of publications and, of course, a certain amount came from ordinary members who paid $15 a year and received the periodicals of the IPR and its American Council, *Pacific Affairs* and *Far Eastern Survey*.

The financial deficits which occurred each year were picked up by financial angels, almost all with close Wall Street connections. The chief identifiable contributions here were about $60,000 from Frederick Vanderbilt Field over eighteen years, $14,700 from Thomas Lamont over fourteen years, $800 from Corliss Lamont (only after 1947), and $18,000 from a member of Lee, Higginson in Boston who seems to have been Jerome D. Greene. In addition, large sums of money each year were directed to private individuals for research and travel expenses from similar sources, chiefly the great financial foundations.

Most of these awards for work in the Far Eastern area required approval or recommendation from members of IPR. Moreover, access to publication and recommendations to academic positions in the handful of great American universities concerned with the Far East required similar sponsorship. And, finally, there can be little doubt that consultant jobs on Far Eastern matters in the State Department or other government agencies were largely restricted to IPR-approved people. The individuals who published, who had money, found jobs, were consulted, and who were appointed intermittently to government missions were those who were tolerant of the IPR line. The fact that all these lines of communication passed through the Ivy League universities or their scattered equivalents west of the Appalachians, such as Chicago, Stanford, or California, unquestionably went back to Morgan's influence in handling large academic endowments.

There can be little doubt that the more active academic members of IPR, the professors and publicists who became members of its governing board (such as Owen Lattimore, Joseph P. Chamberlain, and Philip C. Jessup of Columbia, William W. Lockwood of Princeton, John K. Fairbank of Harvard, and others) and the administrative staff (which became, in time, the most significant influence in its policies) developed an IPR party line. It is, furthermore, fairly clear that this IPR line had many points in common both with the Kremlin's party line on the Far East and with the State Department's policy line in the same area. The interrelations among these, or the influence of one on another, is highly disputed. Certainly no final conclusions can be drawn. Clearly there were some Communists, even party members, involved (such as Frederick Vanderbilt Field), but it is much less clear that there was any disloyalty to the United States. Furthermore, there was a great deal of intrigue both to help those who agreed with the IPR line and to influence United States government policy in this direction, but there is no evidence of which I am aware of any explicit plot or conspiracy to direct American policy in a direction favorable either to the Soviet Union or to international Communism. Efforts of the radical Right to support their convictions about these last points undoubtedly did great, lasting, and unfair damage to the reputations and interests of many people.

The true explanation of what happened is not yet completely known and, as far as it is known, is too complicated to elucidate here. It is, however, clear that many persons who were born in the period 1900–1920 and came to maturity in the period 1928–1940 were so influenced by their experiences of war, depression, and insecurity that they adopted, more or less unconsciously, certain aspects of the Communist ideology (such as the economic interpretation of history, the role of a dualistic class struggle in human events, or the exploitative interpretation of the role of capital in the productive system and of the possessing groups in any society). Many of these ideas were nonsense, even in terms of their own experiences, but they were facile interpretative guides for people who, whatever their expert knowledge of their special areas, were lacking in total perspective on society as a whole or human experience as a whole. Moreover, many of these people felt an unconscious obligation to "help the underdog." This favorable attitude toward the downtrodden and the oppressed was rooted in our Western Christian heritage, especially in nineteenth-century humanitarianism, and in the older Christian idea that all persons are redeemable and will prove trustworthy if they are but trusted. This outlook was, for example, prevalent in that ubiquitous intriguer, Lionel Curtis, who was the original guide and parent of the IPR and of many similar organizations. As children of missionaries, many of the organizers and members of the IPR obtained this spirit from their family background along with their knowledge of the Far Eastern languages which made them "experts."

It must be confessed that the IPR had many of the marks of a fellow-traveler or Communist "captive" organization. But this does not, in any way, mean that the radical Right or the professional ex-Communist version of these events is accurate. For example, Elizabeth Bentley and, above all, Louis Budenz testified before the McCarran Committee on the IPR. The latter identified almost every person associated with the organization as a Communist or "under Communist discipline" by his personal knowledge. In the most famous case, that of Owen Lattimore, Budenz's emphatic testimony that Lattimore was a Communist and that his orders were issued by small Communist Party conclaves of Earl Browder,

Budenz, F. V. Field, and others was totally refuted, not only by the direct contradictory testimony of Browder and Field, but by subsequent evidence from more reliable witnesses and from Budenz himself. Questioning eventually made it clear that Budenz did not know Lattimore or his work or any of his books (including one which he quoted as proof of Lattimore's adherence to the party line). Moreover, Budenz gave direct testimony that the 1944 mission to China of Vice-President Henry Wallace, accompanied by Lattimore and John Carter Vincent (a State Department expert on the Far East who has been accused of Communism), drew up recommendations which were pro-Communist. This was shown to be the exact contrary of the truth and a mere figment of Budenz's active imagination. Budenz testified that the replacement of General Stilwell (who was anti-Chiang and relatively favorable to Mao) by General Wedemeyer was the consequence of the influence of Lattimore and Vincent on Wallace. Joseph Alsop, who was present at all the discussions in question and drafted the recommendations, later testified that he himself was the author of all the "pro-Communist" passages which Budenz attributed to Lattimore and that he himself had suggested the relatively pro-Chiang General Wedemeyer as Stilwell's successor in order to block Wallace's suggestion of General Chennault for the position.

The radical Right version of these events as written up by John T. Flynn, Freda Utley, and others, was even more remote from the truth than were Budenz's or Bentley's versions, although it had a tremendous impact on American opinion and American relations with other countries in the years 1947–1955. This radical Right fairy tale, which is now an accepted folk myth in many groups in America, pictured the recent history of the United States, in regard to domestic reform and in foreign affairs, as a well-organized plot by extreme Left-wing elements, operating from the White House itself and controlling all the chief avenues of publicity in the United States, to destroy the American way of life, based on private enterprise, laissez faire, and isolationism, in behalf of alien ideologies of Russian Socialism and British cosmopolitanism (or internationalism). This plot, if we are to believe the myth, worked through such avenues of publicity as *The New York Times* and the *Herald Tribune*, the *Christian Science Monitor* and the *Washington Post*, the *Atlantic Monthly* and *Harper's Magazine* and had at its core the wild-eyed and bushy-haired theoreticians of Socialist Harvard and the London School of Economics. It was determined to bring the United States into World War II on the side of England (Roosevelt's first love) and Soviet Russia (his second love) in order to destroy every finer element of American life and, as part of this consciously planned scheme, invited Japan to attack Pearl Harbor, and destroyed Chiang Kai-shek, all the while undermining America's real strength by excessive spending and unbalanced budgets.

This myth, like all fables, does in fact have a modicum of truth. There does exist, and has existed for a generation, an international Anglophile network which operates, to some extent, in the way the radical Right believes the Communists act. In fact, this network, which we may identify as the Round Table Groups, has no aversion to cooperating with the Communists, or any other groups, and frequently does so. I know of the operations of this network because I have studied it for twenty years and was permitted for two years, in the early 1960's, to examine its papers and secret records. I have no aversion to it or to most of its aims and have, for much of my life, been close to it and to many of its instruments. I have objected, both in the past and recently, to a few of its policies (notably to its belief that England was an Atlantic rather than a European Power and must be allied, or even federated, with the United States and must remain isolated from Europe), but in general my chief difference of opinion is that it wishes to remain unknown, and I believe its role in history is significant enough to be known.

The Round Table Groups have already been mentioned in this book several times, notably in connection with the formation of the British Commonwealth in chapter 4 and in the discussion of appeasement in chapter 12 ("the Cliveden Set"). At the risk of some repetition, the story will be summarized here, because the American branch of this organization (sometimes called the "Eastern Establishment") has played a very significant role in the history of the United States in the last generation.

The Round Table Groups were semi-secret discussion and lobbying groups organized by Lionel Curtis, Philip H. Kerr (Lord Lothian), and (Sir) William S. Marris in 1908-1911. This was done on behalf of Lord Milner, the dominant Trustee of the Rhodes Trust in the two decades 1905-1925. The original purpose of these groups was to seek to federate the English-speaking world along lines laid down by Cecil Rhodes (1853–1902) and William T. Stead (1849-1912), and the money for the organizational work came originally from the Rhodes Trust. By 1915 Round Table groups existed in seven countries, including England, South Africa, Canada, Australia, New Zealand, India, and a rather loosely organized group in the United States (George Louis Beer, Walter Lippmann, Frank Aydelotte, Whitney Shepardson, Thomas W. Lamont, Jerome D. Greene, Erwin D. Canham of the *Christian Science Monitor*, and others). The attitudes of the various groups were coordinated by frequent visits and discussions and by a well-informed and totally anonymous quarterly magazine, *The Round Table*, whose first issue, largely written by Philip Kerr, appeared in November 1910.

The leaders of this group were: Milner, until his death in 1925, followed by Curtis (1872-1955), Robert H. (Lord) Brand (brother-in-law of Lady Astor) until his death in 1963, and now Adam D. Marris, son of Sir William and Brand's successor as managing director of Lazard

Brothers bank. The original intention had been to have collegial leadership, but Milner was too secretive and headstrong to share the role. He did so only in the period 1913-1919 when he held regular meetings with some of his closest friends to coordinate their activities as a pressure group in the struggle with Wilhelmine Germany. This they called their "Ginger Group." After Milner's death in 1925, the leadership was largely shared by the survivors of Milner's "Kindergarten," that is, the group of young Oxford men whom he used as civil servants in his reconstruction of South Africa in 1901-1910. Brand was the last survivor of the "Kindergarten"; since his death, the greatly reduced activities of the organization have been exercised largely through the Editorial Committee of *The Round Table* magazine under Adam Marris.

Money for the widely ramified activities of this organization came originally from the associates and followers of Cecil Rhodes, chiefly from the Rhodes Trust itself, and from wealthy associates such as the Beit brothers, from Sir Abe Bailey, and (after 1915) from the Astor family. Since 1925 there have been substantial contributions from wealthy individuals and from foundations and firms associated with the international banking fraternity, especially the Carnegie United Kingdom Trust, and other organizations associated with J. P. Morgan, the Rockefeller and Whitney families, and the associates of Lazard Brothers and of Morgan, Grenfell, and Company.

The chief backbone of this organization grew up along the already existing financial cooperation running from the Morgan Bank in New York to a group of international financiers in London led by Lazard Brothers. Milner himself in 1901 had refused a fabulous offer, worth up to $100,000 a year, to become one of the three partners of the Morgan Bank in London, in succession to the younger J. P. Morgan who moved from London to join his father in New York (eventually the vacancy went to E. C. Grenfell, so that the London affiliate of Morgan became known as Morgan, Grenfell, and Company). Instead, Milner became director of a number of public banks, chiefly the London Joint Stock Bank, corporate precursor of the Midland Bank. He became one of the greatest political and financial powers in England, with his disciples strategically placed throughout England in significant places, such as the editorship of *The Times*, the editorship of *The Observer*, the managing directorship of Lazard Brothers, various administrative posts, and even Cabinet positions. Ramifications were established in politics, high finance, Oxford and London universities, periodicals, the civil service, and tax-exempt foundations.

At the end of the war of 1914, it became clear that the organization of this system had to be greatly extended. Once again the task was entrusted to Lionel Curtis who established, in England and each dominion, a front organization to the existing local Round Table Group. This front organization, called the Royal Institute of International Affairs, had as its nucleus in each area the existing submerged Round Table Group. In New York it was known as the Council on Foreign Relations, and was a front for J. P. Morgan and Company in association with the very small American Round Table Group. The American organizers were dominated by the large number of Morgan "experts," including Lamont and Beer, who had gone to the Paris Peace Conference and there became close friends with the similar group of English "experts" which had been recruited by the Milner group. In fact, the original plans for the Royal Institute of International Affairs and the Council on Foreign Relations were drawn up at Paris. The Council of the RIIA (which, by Curtis's energy came to be housed in Chatham House, across St. James's Square from the Astors, and was soon known by the name of this headquarters) and the board of the Council on Foreign Relations have carried ever since the marks of their origin. Until 1960 the council at Chatham House was dominated by the dwindling group of Milner's associates, while the paid staff members were largely the agents of Lionel Curtis. *The Round Table* for years (until 1961) was edited from the back door of Chatham House grounds in Ormond Yard, and its telephone came through the Chatham House switchboard.

The New York branch was dominated by the associates of the Morgan Bank. For example, in 1928 the Council on Foreign Relations had John W. Davis as president, Paul Cravath as vice-president, and a council of thirteen others, which included Owen D. Young, Russell C. Leffingwell, Norman Davis, Allen Dulles, George W. Wickersham, Frank L. Polk, Whitney Shepardson, Isaiah Bowman, Stephen P. Duggan, and Otto Kahn. Throughout its history the council has been associated with the American Round Tablers, such as Beer, Lippmann, Shepardson, and Jerome Greene.

The academic figures have been those linked to Morgan, such as James T. Shotwell, Charles Seymour, Joseph P. Chamberlain, Philip Jessup, Isaiah Bowman and, more recently, Philip Moseley, Grayson L. Kirk, and Henry M. Wriston. The Wall Street contacts with these were created originally from Morgan's influence in handling large academic endowments. In the case of the largest of these endowments, that at Harvard, the influence was usually exercised indirectly through "State Street," Boston, which, for much of the twentieth century, came through the Boston banker Thomas Nelson Perkins.

Closely allied with this Morgan influence were a small group of Wall Street law firms, whose chief figures were Elihu Root, John W. Davis, Paul D. Cravath, Russell Leffingwell, the Dulles brothers and, more recently, Arthur H. Dean, Philip D. Reed, and John J. McCloy. Other nonlegal agents of Morgan included men like Owen D. Young and Norman H. Davis.

On this basis, which was originally financial and goes back to George Peabody, there grew up in the twentieth century a power structure between London and New York which penetrated deeply into university life, the press, and the practice of foreign policy. In England the center was the Round Table Group, while in the United States it was J. P. Morgan and Company or its local branches in Boston, Philadelphia, and Cleveland. Some rather incidental examples of the operations of this structure are very revealing, just because they are incidental. For example, it set up in Princeton a reasonable copy of the Round Table Group's chief Oxford headquarters, All Souls College. This copy, called the Institute for Advanced Study, and best known, perhaps, as the refuge of Einstein, Oppenheimer, John von Neumann, and George F. Kennan, was organized by Abraham Flexner of the Carnegie Foundation and Rockefeller's General Education Board after he had experienced the delights of All Souls while serving as Rhodes Memorial Lecturer at Oxford. The plans were largely drawn by Tom Jones, one of the Round Table's most active intriguers and foundation administrators.

The American branch of this "English Establishment" exerted much of its influence through five American newspapers (*The New York Times,* New York *Herald Tribune, Christian Science Monitor,* the *Washington Post,* and the lamented *Boston Evening Transcript*). In fact, the editor of the *Christian Science Monitor* was the chief American correspondent (anonymously) of *The Round Table,* and Lord Lothian, the original editor of *The Round Table* and later secretary of the Rhodes Trust (1925–1939) and ambassador to Washington, was a frequent writer in the *Monitor.* It might be mentioned that the existence of this Wall Street, Anglo-American axis is quite obvious once it is pointed out. It is reflected in the fact that such Wall Street luminaries as John W. Davis, Lewis Douglas, Jock Whitney, and Douglas Dillon were appointed to be American ambassadors in London.

This double international network in which the Round Table groups formed the semisecret or secret nuclei of the Institutes of International Affairs was extended into a third network in 1925, organized by the same people for the same motives. Once again the mastermind was Lionel Curtis, and the earlier Round Table Groups and Institutes of International Affairs were used as nuclei for the new network. However, this new organization for Pacific affairs was extended to ten countries, while the Round Table Groups existed only in seven. The new additions, ultimately China, Japan, France, the Netherlands, and Soviet Russia, had Pacific councils set up from scratch. In Canada, Australia, and New Zealand, Pacific councils, interlocked and dominated by the Institutes of International Affairs, were set up. In England, Chatham House served as the English center for both nets, while in the United States the two were parallel creations (not subordinate) of the Wall Street allies of the Morgan

Bank. The financing came from the same international banking groups and their subsidiary commercial and industrial firms. In England, Chatham House was financed for both networks by the contributions of Sir Abe Bailey, the Astor family, and additional funds largely acquired by the persuasive powers of Lionel Curtis. The financial difficulties of the IPR Councils in the British Dominions in the depression of 1929–1935 resulted in a very revealing effort to save money, when the local Institute of International Affairs absorbed the local Pacific Council, both of which were, in a way, expensive and needless fronts for the local Round Table groups.

The chief aims of this elaborate, semisecret organization were largely commendable: to coordinate the international activities and outlooks of all the English-speaking world into one (which would largely, it is true, be that of the London group); to work to maintain the peace; to help backward, colonial, and underdeveloped areas to advance toward stability, law and order, and prosperity along lines somewhat similar to those taught at Oxford and the University of London (especially the School of Economics and the Schools of African and Oriental Studies).

These organizations and their financial backers were in no sense reactionary or Fascistic persons, as Communist propaganda would like to depict them. Quite the contrary. They were gracious and cultured gentlemen of somewhat limited social experience who were much concerned with the freedom of expression of minorities and the rule of law for all, who constantly thought in terms of Anglo-American solidarity, of political partition and federation, and who were convinced that they could gracefully civilize the Boers of South Africa, the Irish, the Arabs, and the Hindus, and who are largely responsible for the partitions of Ireland, Palestine, and India, as well as the federations of South Africa, Central Africa, and the West Indies. Their desire to win over the opposition by cooperation worked with Smuts but failed with Hertzog, worked with Gandhi but failed with Menon, worked with Stresemann but failed with Hitler, and has shown little chance of working with any Soviet leader. If their failures now loom larger than their successes, this should not be allowed to conceal the high motives with which they attempted both.

It was this group of people, whose wealth and influence so exceeded their experience and understanding, who provided much of the framework of influence which the Communist sympathizers and fellow travelers took over in the United States in the 1930's. It must be recognized that the power that these energetic Left-wingers exercised was never their own power or Communist power but was ultimately the power of the international financial coterie, and, once the anger and suspicions of the American people were aroused, as they were by 1950, it was a fairly simple matter to get rid of the Red sympathizers. Before this could be done, however, a congressional committee, following backward to their source the threads which led from admitted Communists like Whittaker

Chambers, through Alger Hiss, and the Carnegie Endowment to Thomas
Lamont and the Morgan Bank, fell into the whole complicated network
of the interlocking tax-exempt foundations. The Eighty-third Congress
in July 1953 set up a Special Committee to Investigate Tax-Exempt
Foundations with Representative B. Carroll Reece, of Tennessee, as
chairman. It soon became clear that people of immense wealth would
be unhappy if the investigation went too far and that the "most respected" newspapers in the country, closely allied with these men of
wealth, would not get excited enough about any relevations to make the
publicity worth while, in terms of votes or campaign contributions. An
interesting report showing the Left-wing associations of the interlocking
nexus of tax-exempt foundations was issued in 1954 rather quietly. Four
years later, the Reece committee's general counsel, René A. Wormser,
wrote a shocked, but not shocking, book on the subject called *Foundations: Their Power and Influence.*

One of the most interesting members of this Anglo-American power
structure was Jerome D. Greene (1874–1959). Born in Japan of missionary parents, Greene graduated from Harvard's college and law school by
1899 and became secretary to Harvard's president and corporation in
1901–1910. This gave him contacts with Wall Street which made him
general manager of the Rockefeller Institute (1910–1912), assistant to
John D. Rockefeller in philanthropic work for two years, then trustee
to the Rockefeller Institute, to the Rockefeller Foundation, and to the
Rockefeller General Education Board until 1939. For fifteen years
(1917–1932) he was with the Boston investment banking firm of Lee,
Higginson, and Company, most of the period as its chief officer, as well
as with its London branch. As executive secretary of the American section of the Allied Maritime Transport Council, stationed in London in
1918, he lived in Toynbee Hall, the world's first settlement house, which
had been founded by Alfred Milner and his friends in 1884. This brought
him in contact with the Round Table Group in England, a contact which
was strengthened in 1919 when he was secretary to the Reparations Commission at the Paris Peace Conference. Accordingly, on his return to the
United States he was one of the early figures in the establishment of the
Council on Foreign Relations, which served as the New York branch
of Lionel Curtis's Institute of International Affairs.

As an investment banker, Greene is chiefly remembered for his sales
of millions of dollars of the fraudulent securities of the Swedish match
king, Ivar Kreuger. That Greene offered these to the American investing
public in good faith is evident from the fact that he put a substantial
part of his own fortune in the same investments. As a consequence,
Kreuger's suicide in Paris in April 1932 left Greene with little money and
no job. He wrote to Lionel Curtis, asking for help, and was given, for
two years, a professorship of international relations at Aberystwyth,
Wales. The Round Table Group controlled that professorship from its

founding by David Davies in 1919, in spite of the fact that Davies, who was made a peer in 1932, had broken with the Round Table because of its subversion of the League of Nations and European collective security.

On his return to America in 1934, Greene also returned to his secretaryship of the Harvard Corporation and became, for the remainder of his life, practically a symbol of Yankee Boston, as trustee and officer of the Boston Symphony Orchestra, the Gardner Museum in Fenway Court, the New England Conservatory of Music, the American Academy in Rome, the Brookings Institution, the Rockefeller Foundation, and the General Education Board (only until 1939). He was also director of the Harvard Tercentenary Celebration in 1934–1937.

Greene is of much greater significance in indicating the real influences within the Institute of Pacific Relations than any Communists or fellow travelers. He wrote the constitution for the IPR in 1926, was for years the chief conduit for Wall Street funds and influence into the organization, was treasurer of the American Council for three years, and chairman for three more, as well as chairman of the International Council for four years.

Jerome Greene is a symbol of much more than the Wall Street influence in the IPR. He is also a symbol of the relationship between the financial circles of London and those of the eastern United States which reflects one of the most powerful influences in twentieth-century American and world history. The two ends of this English-speaking axis have sometimes been called, perhaps facetiously, the English and American Establishments. There is, however, a considerable degree of truth behind the joke, a truth which reflects a very real power structure. It is this power structure which the Radical Right in the United States has been attacking for years in the belief that they are attacking the Communists. This is particularly true when these attacks are directed, as they so frequently are at "Harvard Socialism," or at "Left-wing newspapers" like *The New York Times* and the *Washington Post*, or at foundations and their dependent establishments, such as the Institute of International Education.

These misdirected attacks by the Radical Right did much to confuse the American people in the period 1948–1955, and left consequences which were still significant a decade later. By the end of 1953, most of these attacks had run their course. The American people, thoroughly bewildered at widespread charges of twenty years of treason and subversion, had rejected the Democrats and put into the White House the Republican Party's traditional favorite, a war hero, Dwight D. Eisenhower. At the time, two events, one public and one secret, were still in process. The public one was the Korean War of 1950–1953; the secret one was the race for the thermonuclear bomb.

XVIII

NUCLEAR RIVALRY
AND THE COLD WAR:
THE RACE FOR
THE H-BOMB, 1950-1957

"Joe I" and the American Nuclear Debate, 1949-1954

I N May 1947, at one of the earliest meetings of the Atomic Energy
Commission, the members discussed a suggestion made by one of the
commissioners, the Wall Street investment banker Lewis L. Strauss.
Four months later, at the request of the commission, the air force was
ordered to begin a continuous monitoring of the upper atmosphere to
test for radioactive particles which would indicate if a nuclear explosion
had taken place anywhere in the world. The monitoring service was
tested on our own nuclear explosions in the Marshall Islands early in
1948, and continued thereafter on funds from AEC.

Late in August 1949, a B-29, modified for this service, returned to its
base in the Far East and found that the photographic plates it had been
carrying to a great height were covered with streaks. As the local scientists examined these, they became convinced that the plane had passed
through a heavily radioactive cloud, which must have originated farther
west on the mainland of Asia. Code messages to Washington sent similar
planes over the United States to collect raindrops and high-flying dust
particles. These soon revealed the bad news: a highly efficient plutonium
bomb ("Joe I") had been exploded over Soviet Asia in August. President
Truman, on September 23, 1949, made a public announcement: "Within
recent weeks an atomic explosion occurred in the USSR."

The news of "Joe I" brought to crisis level, and merged together,
two conflicts which had been going on, more or less behind the scenes,
in the American strategic community. One of these conflicts was among
the scientists over the possibility of making a "super" bomb by fusing
hydrogen; the other conflict, involving billions of dollars in defense
contracts and the lives of millions of people, was the struggle among
the armed services over American strategic-defense policies.

Discussion over "Super" had been going on for years, but only intermittently and among a few advanced scientists. In 1927 a young Austrian,
Fritz Houtermans, studying physics at Göttingen, took a walk with Lord
Rutherford's assistant, Geoffrey Atkinson. Houtermans suggested that
the energy of the sun came from the fusion of four hydrogen atoms to
make a single helium atom. They talked about the problem and told a

959

Russian fellow student, George Gamow, who returned to the Soviet Union shortly afterward. In 1933 Houtermans fled from Hitler's anti-Semitic laws to Russia. During Stalin's purges he was imprisoned as a foreign spy and tortured to extract a confession. In 1940, when Stalin was allied with Hitler, Houtermans's wrecked but still living body was turned over to the Germans to receive new indignities from the Gestapo.

In 1933 Gamow fled from Russia and was given a professorship at the George Washington University in the American capital. In 1935 Gamow invited the Hungarian refugee scientist Edward Teller to join him at George Washington. They worked together and talked a good deal about the problem of hydrogen fusion. After listening to them, another refugee, Hans Bethe, winner of the Enrico Fermi award in 1961, then at Cornell, worked out the now accepted equations for nuclear fusion on the sun. Bethe's equations assumed that Carbon-12, by the addition of hydrogen nuclei (protons), one at a time, was raised through Nitrogen-13, N-14, Oxygen-15, and N-15 which then added a final proton and split into C-12 and Helium-4. The carbon thus acted as a catalyst for the fusion of hydrogen to form helium.

Teller, a restless man, fertile with suggestions, but incapable of sustained cooperation with others, went to Columbia University in 1941, to Chicago in 1942, to Berkeley, California, in the summer of 1942, and to Los Alamos in the spring of 1943. He was obsessed with the idea of a fusion bomb and was greatly encouraged by Oppenheimer who obtained special security clearance for him and invited him both to California in 1942 and to Los Alamos in 1943. In both places he worked on the H-bomb, although it was generally known (as suggested by Fermi) that no H-bomb was possible until there was an A-bomb to ignite it.

Hydrogen nuclei (protons), carrying the same (positive) electrical charges, repel each other so strongly that they cannot be pushed together to fuse into helium unless they are raised to tremendous collision speeds by being heated to hundreds of millions of degrees of temperature. Only an A-bomb could produce such heat. In 1942 Fermi suggested that such fusion could be achieved at a somewhat lower temperature by using heavy hydrogen (deuterium). This is an isotope of hydrogen which is twice as heavy as ordinary hydrogen, since its nucleus consists of two unit particles instead of one. Its discovery, for which Harold Urey won the Nobel Prize in 1934, showed that it existed in nature, chiefly in the form of heavy water (D_2O compared to ordinary water H_2O), in the proportion of about one part of deuterium for every 5,000 of ordinary hydrogen.

Shortly afterward, it was calculated that it might be possible to make an even heavier isotope of hydrogen of triple weight (tritium) with a nucleus of three particles. These could be fused to make helium at an even lower temperature. However, it would be so expensive to make tritium that each bomb would cost billions of dollars. By the end of 1942, it seemed clear that the most feasible way to make a bomb would be to use both deuterium and tritium. Collisions of these at over 100 million degrees of temperature should give helium atoms and enormous energy. At that point the project was put on the shelf, and work concentrated on making the A-bomb, which had to be obtained first.

After the war ended, the outstanding scientists gradually returned to their peacetime teaching and research, so that the AEC laboratories, including Los Alamos, quieted down. The superpatriots subsequently criticized the scientists for this, arguing that the latter should have stayed on the job with AEC to develop better weapons than the Russians. This is nonsense, and is most nonsensical when it is implied that the scientists' reluctance for weapon development was based on Soviet sympathies. The fact is that America's whole future depended on getting scientists back to the universities to train new scientists, a job which had been neglected for five years. Moreover, there was another and potent influence working against weapons development in the nuclear area. This was the air force.

The air force could keep its monopoly of atomic weapons only as long as these remained in the large, ungainly shape they had first had in 1945. Accordingly, the air force, through General Brereton's participation on an AEC committee at the end of 1947, was able to block AEC development of smaller, tactical atom bombs. Only three years later, when these were being developed in spite of its opposition, did the air force try to recapture its privileged nuclear monopoly by beginning to insist on development of the H-bomb. This shift brought it into alliance with Teller who had been vainly advocating the H-bomb all the time since 1942.

Ironically enough, once this alliance had been made, sympathizers and allies of both the air force and of Teller conveniently forgot the former's earlier opposition to nuclear weapons development and began to question the loyalty of others who had opposed development of the H-bomb, including those "official scientists" who had done so *because* they realized it would jeopardize the development of tactical A-bombs. Because he cooperated in this attack on Oppenheimer, Teller's prestige among scientists (but not among congressmen and journalists) was almost irreparably damaged.

The turn toward the H-bomb began in 1949, even before "Joe I," largely because of the agitations of Teller and his supporters in the California Radiation Laboratory led by E. O. Lawrence and Luis Alvarez. At the same time, Soviet pressure, especially in Berlin, made it increasingly clear that our nuclear weapons system must be reviewed. Teller at once insisted, "H-bomb!" but the official scientists, led by Oppenheimer, suggested development of a wide panoply of nuclear weapons in all sizes and utilities. In general, the *Bulletin of Atomic Scientists* (BAS) group were reluctant to work for either change. Until 1950, however, the development of smaller A-bombs was prevented by the air-force veto of 1947. As a result, the only testing of A-bombs in the five-year period from Bikini in 1946 to April 1951 was a test at Eniwetok in the spring of 1948 which sought to secure *larger* bombs by more effective use of nuclear material. At these 1948 tests four bombs were exploded, reaching a size of over 100 kilotons, or almost six times the blast of the 1945 bombs on Japan. This lack of testing from 1948 to 1951, for which the air force was responsible, was later attributed by air-force supporters to Oppenheimer's Communist sympathies!

"Joe I" brought this stalemate to a crisis. The question of proceeding toward an H-bomb was submitted to the Advisory Committee (GAC) of the AEC in October, and this group, including Oppenheimer, Conant, Fermi, Lee DuBridge (president of California Institute of Technology), I. I. Rabi of Columbia (Nobel Prize, 1944), and three businessmen, voted *unanimously* against a crash program to make an H-bomb. Glenn Seaborg (Nobel Prize, 1951), who was absent, was noncommittal. The most vigorous opposition came from Conant. In general, the opposition felt that concentration on an all-out effort to make an H-bomb, whose feasibility was very dubious, would be a poor response to "Joe I" and that a better response would lie in: (1) complete reform of American ground forces, including universal military training; (2) reorganization of the defenses of Western Europe, including Germany; and (3) a drive to make a large and varied assortment of A-bombs, especially by decreasing their size for tactical use.

Teller was chagrined at this decision, a view which was shared by Senator Brien McMahon of the joint congressional committee and by the air force. Teller had been visiting about the country, in his impetuous way, even before this decision, seeking to build up support for "Super" and to recruit scientists, with special attention to Bethe (who opposed the effort to make an H-bomb and finally joined the effort, the following year, because he hoped to prove it was impossible).

The GAC's unanimous vote against a crash program for the H-bomb in October 1949 was based on a number of considerations, which still seem valid: (1) The scientists feared that the use of the Hanford reactors to make tritium from lithium, instead of continuing to make plutonium from uranium, would jeopardize the development of tactical A-bombs, especially as the manufacture of a pound of tritium would cost the loss of 80 pounds of plutonium; (2) they felt that the threat of our nuclear retaliation was not a sufficient guarantee against nibbling by Soviet ground forces and wanted our ground forces and those of our European supporters reorganized, expanded, and equipped with tactical atomic weapons; (3) they felt that the atom bomb was sufficiently large for any possible target in Soviet industrial plants or Russian cities and that for such targets the hydrogen bomb was not really necessary; (4) they felt that the advantages of adding the H-bomb to the world's arsenals, in terms of cost, was so slight that the Russians would not try to make it if we abstained from doing so; (5) they felt that the scientific manpower needed to develop the H-bomb could be obtained only from the A-bomb plants or from teaching, and was, for the immediate future, more valuable in these two places; (6) they doubted if any H-bomb would be made small enough to be carried in a plane, and, accordingly, thought it unwise to sacrifice possible strengthening of our defense response where it was urgently needed (on land) for a possibly unobtainable increment of power to our defense response in an area (strategic bombing) where it was not urgently needed, especially as it was not yet established that we would make any nuclear response at all to a minor or moderate Soviet aggression.

These considerations, which so deeply disturbed Conant, Oppenheimer, Lilienthal, and others, were ignored by Teller and his allies, who continued to agitate for a crash program for "Super." The strong support which Teller found in the air force, from the joint congressional committee under Senator McMahon, and from William Liscum Borden, executive director of the joint committee, eventually led President Truman to reverse the GAC. On January 31, 1950, the President gave a decision which has frequently been misrepresented: he ordered the AEC to proceed with its efforts to make the H-bomb and at the same time to continue its work for more varied A-weapons, within the framework of a new over-all survey of American strategic plans which was simultaneously ordered from the National Security Council. This triple order, which is usually misrepresented as the single order for a crash H-bomb effort, required new nuclear reactors.

The order to make an H-bomb was easier to issue than to carry out, because no one knew how to make it. It must be clearly understood that the H-bomb, as tested in November 1952 and subsequently developed, *was not* based on the lines being followed by Teller in 1946–1951. The true sequence of events has been concealed under enormous waves of false propaganda which have tried to show that Teller's development of the H-bomb was held up because the Truman Administration was deeply infiltrated with Communists and fellow travelers. This propaganda came from neo-isolationist, Republican, and air-force sources which formed a tacit alliance to discredit the Democratic administrations of 1933-1953—"Twenty Years of Treason," as they called it.

The chronology here is of some importance. Klaus Fuchs confessed to atomic espionage in England on January 27th; President Truman ordered work on the H-bomb four days later; and McCarthy made his first accusations at Wheeling nine days after that.

One of the reasons the GAC had opposed working on the H-bomb was that such work would jeopardize the production of plutonium and would not overcome the unbalance in our defenses between strategic and tactical forces. On February 24th the Joint Chiefs of Staff demanded that Truman's order to the AEC "to continue" work on the H-bomb be changed into a "crash program." About the same time, the White House ordered the reevaluation of our strategic position by the National Security Council; this led eventually to NSC 68. And, finally, the AEC initiated steps to obtain new nuclear reactors. Work on these, begun in 1951, included a tritium production plant on the Savannah River and two U-235 gaseous-diffusion plants at Portsmouth, Ohio, and Paducah, Kentucky. This gave five great nuclear centers, of which the three diffusion plants used 5.8 million kilowatts of electricity, about half the total output of the TVA, and sufficient for the ordinary needs of 32 million persons. In 1960 this electricity cost over a quarter of a billion dollars, and the total cost of nuclear explosives was running at $2 billion a year.

The method pursued to achieve a thermonuclear explosion up to June 1951, by fusing tritium and deuterium into helium, was possible *as a scientific experiment*, and was achieved at the beautiful atoll of Eniwetok in April 1951. But this method could not be used for a bomb, since the whole mechanism had to be enclosed in a complex refrigerator the size of a small house. The problem of the bomb was to get the hydrogen isotope particles close enough together so that they would fuse. This could be done at the almost unobtainable temperatures over 400 million degrees. It could be done at lower temperatures if the particles were already close together, as they would be when very cold. As hydrogen gets colder, it liquefies at $-423°$ below zero Fahrenheit, but it is very difficult to keep it that cold. It can be kept at the temperature of liquid air, $-414°$ F., by immersing it in this, but at that temperature, $9°$ higher than its own vaporizing point, hydrogen will stay liquid only if it is under pressure of about 2,700 pounds per square inch.

The successful hydrogen fusion at Eniwetok in April, 1951, was achieved with a very small quantity of tritium and deuterium held at these fantastic conditions, then suddenly exposed to the 100-million-degree blast of an exploding A-bomb. The additional energy released by the fusing hydrogen was so small that it was not noticeable to eyewitnesses, but could be inferred from the electronic recording apparatus. Thus it would be a mistake to call this explosion, known as Operation Greenhouse, an H-bomb. As the AEC would say, it was "a thermonuclear device."

The successful way to the thermonuclear bomb emerged from a suggestion made to Teller in February 1951 by a brilliant young Polish mathematician, Stanislaw Ulam. Teller presented the idea, as developed by himself and his assistant Frederic de Hoffman, to a meeting of the GAC held at the Institute for Advanced Study on June 19-20, 1951. Everyone present realized that the problem was solved. As Oppenheimer said, "It was sweet." Briefly, the idea was to merge the two separate operations of making tritium out of lithium and fusing the tritium with deuterium into a single operation as a bomb. The feasibility of this new plan was tested in a successful thermonuclear explosion (called "Mike") as part of the tests of Operation Ivy at Eniwetok on November 1, 1952. This produced a blast equal to about 10 million tons of TNT, creating a fireball 3½ miles wide, whose heat was felt 30 miles away, and which completely destroyed the small islet on which it occurred, leaving a hole in the lagoon 175 feet deep and a mile wide. But this was not a bomb, since the mechanism weighed 65 tons and filled a cubical box 25 feet on each edge.

The great significance of the thermonuclear bomb was that, unlike the A-bomb, it could be made of limitless power. An A-bomb explosion was measured in thousands of tons of TNT (kilotons) and could be made up to a few hundred kilotons in power. The thermonuclear bomb had to be measured in millions of tons of TNT (megatons) and had no limit on its size.

The world's third thermonuclear explosion was a shocker, exploded by the Russians on August 12, 1953, and revealed to the world by American atmosphere-testing devices. It may have been dropped from a plane; if so, the Russians were far in advance of us, since we did not achieve a droppable bomb until May 21, 1956. In that interval we exploded, at Bikini on March 1, 1954, our first real thermonuclear bomb. It was a horrifying device, a triple-stage fission-fusion-fission bomb which spread death-dealing radioactive contamination over more than 8,000 square miles of the Pacific and injurious radiation over much of the world.

This first American thermonuclear *bomb* had a trigger of two A-bombs exploded simultaneously to detonate a second stage consisting of Lithium-6 deuteride. This latter was a compound of a lithium isotope of mass 6 (which makes up about one-fifteenth of natural lithium and has a nucleus of three protons with three neutrons) and of heavy Hydrogen-2. This compound, a white crystalline substance, was surrounded with a shiny sphere of almost a ton of metallic natural uranium. The neutrons from the A-bomb trigger, blasting through the lithium deuterium crystals, split the Lithium-6 into helium and tritium (Hydrogen-3); in a tremendous explosion, the latter then fused with the deuterium to make helium, at the same time emitting a great shower of extra neutrons which split the surrounding natural uranium in a superatomic fission holocaust. The whole process occurred almost instantaneously, with a shattering blast equal to 18,000,000 tons of TNT. With the blast was released a vast quantity of deadly radioactive isotopes, including the dangerous

Strontium-90, which, like calcium, is readily absorbed into human bones, where its deadly radiations may easily engender cancer.

The test of this inhuman weapon (called "Bravo") was announced to the world by the AEC as the test of an H-bomb (it was really a U-bomb, or a "fission-fusion-fission bomb"), and for almost a year (until February 15, 1955) its real nature was concealed by the AEC, apparently at the insistence of the new Republican chairman, Lewis L. Strauss. Secrecy from Strauss left the world with two mistaken ideas: (1) that the successful thermonuclear bomb was simply an H-bomb and (2) that it was, accordingly, made on the lines Teller had been following in 1945–1951. From these errors partisan inference could conclude that our delay in achieving an H-bomb resulted from the restraints placed on Teller's work during the Truman Administration. This, of course, was not believed by the atomic scientists, but seemed convincing to many well-informed persons from the strange fact that William L. Laurence, science editor of *The New York Times*, spread these two mistaken ideas.

As the best-known scientific journalist in America, Laurence's stories were accepted as true by the ordinary well-informed public (though not by scientists). Laurence, the only newspaper reporter allowed to see the test at Alamagordo or the nuclear explosion on Japan, wrote a book on the H-bomb, which he called *The Hell Bomb*, in 1950. It was full of misleading ideas, forgivable at that date, but totally erroneous in following years, when the book continued to be read. It stated that the H-bomb would be exploded by direct fusion of deuterium and tritium, a method which it attributed to Teller. Years later, in *The New York Times*, Laurence still insisted that the test of March, 1954, was not a fission-fusion-fission (F-F-F-bomb) but was simply a fission-fusion H-bomb and not a U-bomb. This version of "Bravo" apparently originated with Strauss, who denied that "Bravo" was a U-bomb, and explained the surprisingly large noxious fallout as a consequence of irradiation of the coral reef on which the bomb exploded. This story entrenched in the public mind that Teller was the "Father of the H-bomb," that he had been held back to the injury of American security by Soviet sympathizers during the Truman Administration, and that there was some basis for the AEC condemnation of Oppenheimer as a security risk in June 1954. Behind much of this was the air force, allied to Teller, Laurence, and Strauss, and very opposed to Oppenheimer. This opposition arose because of Oppenheimer's work for diversification of weapons (which was regarded by the air force as a treasonable diversion of both money and nuclear materials from it to the other services) and for his efforts to get smaller nuclear warheads. These latter paved the way for long-range missiles, for tactical nuclear weapons, and for the Polaris nuclear submarine which supplanted the air force manned bombers and, by the middle 1960's, threatened to shift America's primary deterrence of Soviet aggression from SAC to the navy.

It should be recorded that Teller had little to do with the actual making of the successful thermonuclear bomb. As usual, he was very restless and felt hampered at Los Alamos in 1951 and spent most of his time lobbying with the air force and the Radiation Laboratory trying to get a new second-weapons laboratory of his own. To free himself for this activity, he left Los Alamos in November 1951. When the AEC refused to establish a second laboratory, Teller went to the air force and obtained its support for a second-weapons laboratory, the so-called Livermore Laboratory attached to E. O. Lawrence's Radiation Laboratory at Berkeley, California. This was established in July 1952. All the thermonuclear tests and the final H-bomb which we have mentioned were achievements of Los Alamos, whose operations, under Norris Bradbury, Teller disapproved. Teller himself was present at none of the tests of the lithium bomb, and his Livermore Laboratory did not participate in the tests.

None of this was in fact as it was built up in public opinion in the period 1951–1955. The public record on these matters was rectified in 1955 by Teller, by Laurence, and by the AEC, but by that time Oppenheimer had been condemned, the Republicans were in office, and the story of subversion in the American government had become an established American myth, along with the thermonuclear bomb as a hydrogen bomb and Teller as its father.

These myths were, of course, not believed by the nuclear scientists, a fact that helped to intensify the suspicion the radical Right held for them and for all educated people. The truth about "Bravo" had been revealed to the nuclear scientists of the world, including the Russians, almost immediately after the test and in a most dramatic fashion.

Shortly after the "Bravo" blast at Bikini, a small Japanese fishing boat, *The Lucky Dragon*, was caught in the edge of the lethal radiations from the test. It was, indeed a lucky *Dragon* for only one of the crew subsequently died, although the rest were sick for months. The vessel was ninety miles east of the blast, but, had it been only ten miles farther south, all the crew would have died horrible deaths. Two weeks after the blast, when the doomed vessel reached Japan, Professor Kenjiro Kimura, the first discoverer of Uranium-237, found this rare isotope in the fallout ash all over *The Lucky Dragon*. The U-237 could have come only from fission of U-239. This discovery, published in Japanese in August 1954, revealed that "Bravo" had been a gigantic U-bomb whose deadly nature resided more in its radioactive fallout than in its heat and blast.

Under the tight blanket of the secrecy of Strauss, the scientists who knew asked themselves: Why did the AEC make such a "dirty" bomb? Why was it all kept such a secret? The answer now seems clear: the Soviet H-bomb explosion of August 1953 showed that the Russians were ahead of us in the H-bomb race. This the AEC could not publicly admit. This disadvantage had to be overcome as rapidly as possible, and the best way to do so was to shift from blast warfare to radioactivity warfare. The movement in this direction, which was fortunately only temporary (1953–1956), was intensified by the early, and very secret, stages of the missile race. Late in 1952, immediately following the test of "Mike," John von Neumann headed a committee which recommended an intensified effort to develop a long-range missile (ICBM). At that time the American effort in missiles was restricted very largely to variations of the German V-2 weapon and to lesser rockets such as Aerobee and Wac Corporal. The new effort soon showed that longer range would be easier to achieve than greater accuracy and that it would be very difficult to build a missile which could be depended upon to hit within ten miles of target. At such a distance, blast, even at ten megatons, would do little damage, and if such targets were to be knocked out, this would have to be done by a spreading cloud of radioactive fallout and not by the blast. Hence the U-bomb.

The U-bomb, concealed from public view by secrecy and by misleading statements from AEC, usually from Strauss, remained the weapon of last resort in the American arsenal throughout the Dulles era. The launching of the first "Polaris" submarine in January 1954, six weeks before "Bravo," did not change this situation. The first American test of an airdrop lithium bomb in May 1956 was a delayed fall from a B-52 jet bomber at 55,000 feet; it exploded at 15,000 feet in a four-mile-wide fireball, but was almost an equal distance off its target.

To prepare public opinion to accept use of the U-bomb, if it became necessary, Strauss sponsored a study of radioactive fallout whose conclusion was prejudged by calling it "Project Sunshine." By selective release of some evidence and strict secrecy of other information, the Strauss group tried to establish in public opinion that there was no real danger to anyone from nuclear fallout even in all-out nuclear war. This gave rise to a controversy between the scientists of the BAS group, led by Ralph E. Lapp, and the Eisenhower Administration, led by Strauss, on the nature and danger of fallout and of nuclear warfare in general.

As we shall see in a moment, the Eisenhower government through Dulles's doctrine of "massive retaliation," enunciated in January 1954, was so deeply committed to nuclear warfare that it could not permit the growth of a public opinion which would refuse to accept the use of nuclear weapons because of objections to the danger of fallout to neutrals and noncombatants. In this struggle Strauss, Dulles, and Teller were supported by the air force, which feared and resented the efforts of the Oppenheimer group to shift the defense expenditures over a much wider range than that of massive retaliation. They were particularly alarmed by the efforts of Oppenheimer, Lee DuBridge, and others to spend money on antiair defenses. By 1953 this struggle became so intense that the supporters of the air force and of massive retaliation decided they must destroy the public image and public career of Oppenheimer, to influence public opinion and to deter other scientists of his view from opposition to the new Republican–air-force party line.

The end of the American nuclear monopoly in late 1950 made necessary a reopening of the strategic debate which had been stabilized on the Truman doctrine of "containment" in 1947. "Containment" strategy was based on a strategic balance between Soviet mass armies and the American nuclear monopoly, in which each of these would deter use of the other, thus establishing an umbrella under which the United States could use its economic power to win the Cold War. The strategic balance had been established as the "Truman Doctrine" early in 1947 and had been followed by the containment weapon, in aid to Greece and Turkey and, above all, by the Marshall Plan. This policy in the years 1947–1950 won numerous victories for the West, all along the Soviet-bloc periphery and especially in West Germany and in Japan, both of which became solidly attached to the West. The major failure, justified as inevitable in terms of the magnitude of the problem and the resources available, was the loss of China to the Soviet bloc, but this was generally accepted by the supporters of containment on the double ground that the available resources must go to Europe (as more important than China) and that China would never be a strong or dependable satellite of Russia.

This doctrine of containment, by depriving each side of its strongest weapon (the Soviet mass army and the American SAC force) tended to neutralize these and forced each side into supplementary strategic plans. On the Soviet side, these new plans involved the use of nibbling tactics by its satellites. On the American side, these new plans involved the development of a balanced and flexible defensive posture based on all services and weapons.

The new Soviet plans required a diversion of American aims from the Soviet Union itself to its periphery and to its satellites. They also involved keeping aggression below the level which would trigger a SAC retaliation. This level was much higher for a satellite state than for the Soviet Union itself. In fact, while almost any military aggression by the USSR might trigger a SAC nuclear strike in return, almost no aggression by a satellite (especially a lesser satellite) would do so. The areas in which such indirect adventures by the USSR might take place were obvious: the Near East and the Far East. In both of these areas the ineptness of American policy made the Soviet task fairly easy.

The American response to this shift in Soviet strategy appeared, not as a response to an overt manifestation of Soviet policy, but as a response to "Joe I." Moreover, it was not a Defense Department or JCS response, but was sponsored and pushed through by the policy planning staff of the State Department under Paul Nitze. It arose from the needs of NATO as a defensive force against Russia, and advocated a policy very similar to that desired by Oppenheimer and the GAC (increased emphasis on a balanced defense with strengthened ground forces, including those of our allies, and rapid development of tactical nuclear weapons and a tactical air-force role). This effort, which would have required an increase in the defense budget from the 1950 figure of $13 billion to about $35 billion, was accepted in April 1950 by the National Security Council as directive NSC 68, but with a cost figure of only $18 billion a year. The dominant thought of NSC 68 was the expectation of a strategic nuclear stalemate between the United States and the USSR by 1954 and the necessity of preparing for methods of defense, other than massive bombing, to resist Soviet aggression. Naturally, this directive was abhorrent to the "Big Bomber Boys." The extraordinary thing is that their resistance was successful, and NSC 68 was replaced by "massive retaliation" and a new directive, the so-called NSC 162, in October 1953, in spite of all the lessons of the Korean War of 1950–1953, which the air force and the Eisenhower Administration jointly ignored.

The Korean War and Its Aftermath, 1950-1954

The emphasis by the American armed forces on nuclear retaliation as their chief response to Communist aggression anywhere in the world made it necessary to draw a defense perimeter over which such aggression would trigger retaliation from us. Such a boundary had been established in Europe by the military occupation forces and NATO, but, at the end of 1949, was still unspecified in the Far East because of the recent victory of the Communists in China. At the insistence of the military leaders, especially General MacArthur, that perimeter was drawn to exclude Korea, Formosa, and mainland China; accordingly, all American forces had been evacuated from South Korea in June 1949. In March of that year, MacArthur publicly stated, "Our defense line runs through the chain of islands fringing the coast of Asia. It starts from the Philippines and continues through the Ryukyu archipelago which includes its broad main bastion, Okinawa. Then it bends back through Japan and the Aleutian Island chain to Alaska."

The MacArthur defense perimeter in the Far East was accepted by Secretary of State Acheson in a speech on January 12, 1950, but not at all in the sense in which partisan Republicans attacked it later. Acheson specifically stated that America's guarantee was given only to areas east of that line but that American power might be used to the west of it where independent nations must first seek their security on their own initiative and the organized security system of the United Nations. To Acheson, therefore, the boundary was not between areas we would defend and those we would not defend, but between those we would defend unilaterally and those we would defend collectively.

However, it seems clear that in private, by the end of 1949, all parts of the Administration in Washington looked forward to the fall of Formosa, the complete disappearance of Chiang Kai-shek, the recognition of Red China and its admission to the United Nations, as preliminaries to an intensive diplomatic effort to exploit the split between Soviet Russia and Communist China which was regarded as inevitable. This vision of Chinese "Titoism" never became public policy, but on October 12, 1949, after the JCS under Eisenhower voted that Formosa was not of sufficient strategic importance to warrant its occupation by American troops, the three defense departments and the Department of State agreed unanimously that Formosa would be conquered by Red China by the end of 1950.

Whatever merits there may have been in our Far Eastern defense perimeter and its implications for Formosa, it clearly left Korea in an ambiguous position. The Soviet Union interpreted this ambiguity to mean that the United States would allow South Korea to be conquered by North Korea, just as Red China, about the same time, assumed that the United States would permit it to conquer Formosa. Instead, when Russia, through its satellite, North Korea, sought to take Korea before Red China had taken Formosa, this gave rise to an American counteraction which prevented either aggressor from getting its aim.

There can be little doubt that the United States, along with the rest of the world, underestimated the almost insanely aggressive nature of Red China. From 1949 onward, this newly established regime tried to bite every friendly hand which tried to lead it into the community of established nations. It made it perfectly clear to all its neighbors in Asia that its policies would be based on hatred for any country which did not break with the United States and line up with the Soviet Union. Even India, which leaned over backward to be friendly, was upbraided almost daily in extravagant insults of which one of the more moderate was a charge that Nehru was "the running dog of British-American imperialists." When Great Britain offered diplomatic recognition in January 1950, it was rebuffed.

Nor was this aggressive behavior only verbal. In spite of the devastation and economic dislocation of the Civil War, Red Chinese plans for aggression continued. The general level of Chinese production in 1949 was about half what it had been in 1942, and the country clearly needed an interval to recuperate, but the budget for 1950 allotted 40 percent of its funds for the armed services, imposed a tax of 20 percent on peasant agricultural incomes, and anticipated a deficit of nearly 20 percent to be covered by printing paper money. Its declared immediate plans included the conquest of Hainan Island, Formosa, and Tibet. Hainan was conquered in April 1950, and the buildup against Formosa continued for at least two months more. About 20,000 Koreans in the Chinese forces were detached and returned to North Korea, where they joined the armed forces of the People's Republic of Korea (PRK, that is, North Korea Communist Republic). This may have been done at Russia's request.

On June 25, 1950, after a two-hour artillery bombardment, 60,000 North Koreans, led by a hundred Soviet tanks, crossed the 38th parallel and flung themselves on 90,000 lightly armed and already disspirited South Korean troops. The latter, lacking tanks, planes, or heavy artillery, reeled backward to the south and did not stop until August 6th, when they finally made a stand before Pusan in the southeast corner of the Korean Peninsula. In this retreat the ROK troops suffered 50,000 casualties in the first month.

For forty-eight hours after the Korean attack, the world hesitated, awaiting America's reaction. On June 26, 1950, the fifth birthday of the United Nations, many feared a "Munich," leading to the collapse of the whole United Nations security system at its first major challenge. Truman's reaction, however, was decisive. He immediately committed American air and sea forces in the area south of 38°, and demanded a UN condemnation of the aggression. Thus, for the first time in history, a world organization voted to use collective force to stop armed aggression. This was possible because the North Korean attack occurred at a time when the Soviet delegation was absent from the United Nations Security Council, boycotting it in protest at the presence of the delegation from Nationalist China. Accordingly, the much-used Soviet veto was unavailable. On June 27, 1950, the Security Council, with Yugoslavia casting the only opposing vote, condemned the aggression and asked its members to give assistance to South Korea. On the same day President Truman ordered American forces into action and sent the United States Seventh Fleet to neutralize the Formosa Strait, where the Red Chinese armies were still poised for their invasion of Formosa. This rapid response won general approval within the United States, even from those who later condemned and opposed it. One of these was Senator Taft, who prefaced his temporary approval by charging that all the troubles in the Far East arose from the Democrats' "sympathetic acceptance of Communism" and that the North Korean attack was in response to the invitation contained in Acheson's speech of January 12th: "Is it any wonder that the Korean Communists took us at the word given by the Secretary of State?" He demanded Acheson's immediate resignation, a cry which continued, almost uninterruptedly, over the next two and a half years.

The President's order for ground forces to rescue the South Koreans was not easy to carry out. Air-force success in its budget struggles with the other services and the general budget cutting by the Republican Eightieth Congress (January 1947–January 1949) had left the ground forces with only ten army and two Marine Corps divisions, all seriously undermanned. The four occupation divisions in the Far East, which had to respond to the Korean attack, had a total of only 25 infantry battalions, instead of the 36 allotted. These, and other units, had to be brought up to strength by calling up reservists. Nevertheless, one division from Japan reached Korea by July 9th, a second by July 12th, and a third on July 18th.

The intervention of American forces in Korea was undoubtedly a great shock to the Communists, especially as the North Korean attack was a Soviet operation, while the American landing directly threatened the security of Red China. Coordination between the two Communist Powers was far from perfect and was certainly slow. The Red Chinese had no desire to see American forces reestablished on the Asiatic mainland or in occupation of all Korea up to the Chinese boundary along the Yalu River; on the other hand, they had no desire to get into a war with the United States to prevent this undesired consequence of what was really a Moscow operation, especially as Soviet support was very remote, at the farther end of a long single-track railway across Siberia. Nevertheless, the Red Chinese suspended their attack on Formosa and, in the course of July, assembled several hundred thousand troops in northeast China, considerably withdrawn from the Yalu.

For weeks the successful advance of the North Koreans gave the Chinese hope that they need do nothing. The South Koreans were quickly hurled down to the southeastern corner of the country at Pusan, and for several weeks were on the verge of being pushed into the sea. Their line held, however, and American forces began to assemble in the protected beachhead.

The United States was as eager as the Chinese to avoid a direct clash between the two countries, because such a clash could easily build up into a major war in the Far East, leaving Russia free to do its will in Europe. Washington was fearful that Chiang Kai-shek, since he could not reconquer China himself and hoped America would do it for him, might seek to precipitate such a war by making an attack from Formosa on mainland China. There was also a strong chance that MacArthur might encourage or allow Chiang to do so because that haughty general agreed with Chiang that Europe was of no importance and that the Far East should be the primary, almost the only, area of operations for American foreign policy. He had bitterly opposed the "Germany First" strategy throughout World War II and had begrudged men or supplies sent there on the grounds that these diversions delayed his triumphant return to the Philippines. As the war drew to its close, he had said: "Europe is a dying system. It is worn out and run down and will become an economic and industrial hegemony of Soviet Russia. . . . The lands touching the Pacific with their billions of inhabitants will determine the course of history for the next ten thousand years."

These views were shared by the Right-wing isolationist groups of the Republican Party with whom MacArthur had been in close touch for much of his life and to whom he owed some of his success. In American politics these groups had power to do considerable damage because of their influence on the Republican congressional party and the fact that the bipartisan foreign policy under Senator Arthur Vandenberg of Michigan, which operated elsewhere in the world, did not exist in regard to the Far East. The danger of any Chiang-MacArthur cooperation to build the Korean action up into a major war was intensified by the fact that this would be opposed by the United Nations and by our allies, neither of whom was considered important by the neo-isolationists or by MacArthur, but whom the Truman Administration refused to alienate unnecessarily because they were essential, as bases, in the containment of Russia.

In the first two weeks of August, another American division and parts of other units, including a Marine Corps brigade, landed at Pusan. By the middle of the month, that enclave was entrenched, and a counter-offensive to drive the North Korean forces back to the 38th parallel was being prepared. At that point MacArthur made a brilliant suggestion: To avoid the hard push up the peninsula, he proposed landing two American divisions at Inchon, halfway up the west side of Korea, fifty miles south of the 38th parallel and only 25 miles from Seoul, the capital. Everything was adverse to the plan, unless there was complete tactical surprise. Fortunately, this was achieved, a rather unexpected event in the East. Marine units landed at Inchon from the sea on September 15th and found little opposition. On September 22nd they captured Seoul and, six days later, were joined by the main United Nations offensive driving up the peninsula from Pusan. About half the PRK forces were captured in the bag, while the rest fled northward across the 38th parallel into North Korea. That frontier was reached by the UN forces as the month ended.

The Red Chinese decision to intervene in North Korea was made about the third week in August and began on October 15th, nine days after American troops crossed the 38th parallel into North Korea. Such an intervention was almost inevitable, as Red China could hardly be expected to allow the buffer North Korean state to be destroyed and American troops to occupy the line of the Yalu without taking some steps to protect its own security. China would have welcomed the restoration of the boundary along the 38th parallel, which Russia had so carelessly destroyed by instigating the PRK attack in June. By October they feared that the United States was about to use the Korean area as a base for a general war on China. In such a war, the Chinese expected to become the target of A-bombs, but believed that they could survive if they could wipe out the United Nations Korean base for ground operations. Accordingly, as soon as it became clear that American forces would continue past the 38th parallel to the Yalu, the Chinese intervened, not to restore the 38th parallel frontier, but to clear the United Nations forces from Asia completely.

The Chinese intervention in Korea, which began on October 15, 1950, was a much greater surprise than Inchon, and gave rise to one of the most bitter controversies in American political history, the so-called Truman-MacArthur controversy. The dispute arose from the fact that MacArthur did not accept his government's strategic and political plans, and systematically sought to undermine and redirect them, while in constant communication with the press and with the leaders of the opposition political party for this purpose.

The Truman Administration, after the victory at Inchon, did not intend to stop at the 38th parallel, and hoped to reunite the country under the Seoul government. It is probable that this alone triggered the Chinese intervention, but, to reduce that possibility, Washington set certain restrictions on MacArthur's actions which he soon sought to evade. Washington and Tokyo both knew that the Chinese had about 300,000 troops ready for action in Manchuria north of the Yalu and that neither Russia nor China was attempting to reequip the shattered North Korean forces. To discourage any Chinese intervention, the White House forbade any attack by Chiang on the Chinese coast, any naval blockade of China itself (Korea, of course, was blockaded), or any attack on China or Siberia north of the Yalu, or the use of non-Korean troops in the immediate vicinity of the Yalu as the conquest of North Korea was completed.

On October 9, 1950, two of MacArthur's planes attacked a Russian air base sixty-two miles inside Russian territory and only eighteen miles from Vladivostok. To make certain that MacArthur understood the reasons for these restrictions, President Truman the next day instructed MacArthur to meet him at Wake Island on October 15th. The two leaders had a lengthy discussion, in which these restrictions were reiterated, but within two months of his return to Japan, MacArthur recommenced his almost daily interviews and letters agitating against these limits.

At Wake Island, General MacArthur assured President Truman that any Chinese intervention into Korea would be most unlikely, and, in any case, would be on a scale which could be handled. Even as he spoke, the first Chinese units were already crossing the Yalu River from Manchuria into North Korea. These engaged in combat on October 26th, and by October 30th some had been captured. MacArthur continued to deny that any significant Chinese intervention was present or likely, and tried to discourage it by a vigorous attack northward against the North Korean remnants. Because of lack of American troops for an attack across the width of the peninsula, he divided his forces into two separate attacks on either side of the peninsula with no direct liaison between the two where a considerable gap was left. Moreover, MacArthur on October 24th canceled the restrictions on use of non-Korean forces close to the Chinese and Russian borders. His special communiqué of November 5th which opened his northward offensive spoke of it as one which would for "all practical purposes end the war" and bring the United Nations forces "home by Christmas."

Until November 26th the MacArthur offensive rolled northward against only moderate resistance, but, just as it reached the Yalu frontier at some points, a gigantic Chinese offensive of 33 divisions counter-attacked into the gap between the two UN wings.

MacArthur's communiqué of November 28th spoke of the Chinese attack as a "new war," which "has shattered the high hopes we entertained that the intervention of the Chinese was only of a token nature on a volunteer and individual basis. . . ." At once he began an intensive propaganda campaign both to obtain his earlier aims for direct attacks on coastal China and air attacks on interior points and to rewrite the history of the preceding month so that his own actions would seem to be premeditated and skilled ripostes to Chinese plans. In fact, his public statement of November 28th was in sharp contrast with his private message to Washington almost four weeks earlier which estimated the Chinese forces across the Yalu as half a million men in 56 regular army divisions supported by 370,000 district security forces. In the face of such knowledge, no excuse can be found for MacArthur's use of a divided command with a central gap to attack toward such a force.

The Chinese attack in MacArthur's mind reduced the American situation in the Far East to a simple choice between two extreme alternatives: either all-out war on China, and possibly Russia, to destroy world Communism once for all or the immediate evacuation of our forces from Korea. The former would have given the Soviet Union a free hand in Europe; the latter would have made it impossible for us to obtain resistance against Communist nibbling from any small states or even from our greater allies elsewhere in the world and would have destroyed our prestige in Asia and Africa. A rapid visit by Generals J. Lawton Collins and Hoyt S. Vandenberg to Korea in January 12–17, 1951, convinced them that the middle alternative, which was still Washington's policy, namely, to maintain the independence of South Korea, was still possible.

Rather than accept this alternative, MacArthur intensified his press barrage against the Administration, as well as his numerous messages to isolationist Republican politicians in Washington. A directive of December

6th which ordered him to clear his public statements on foreign and military policy with the respective departments was violated, for some months, with impunity. The congressional elections of 1950 had been disastrous to Administration supporters and had been successful for isolationists of both parties, with the Administration's majority in both Houses cut almost to nothing.

Senator Taft, now unchallenged leader of the isolationist bloc, argued that Governor Dewey's "internationalist" approach had lost the presidential election of 1948 and that his own wholesale opposition to the Administration on an isolationist basis had been victorious in 1950 and would win the Presidency (apparently for himself) in 1952. On this basis a powerful attack was built up against Secretary of State Acheson, against NATO and other American commitments in Europe, and against foreign aid or any efforts to extend America's ground forces. Truman's efforts to send four divisions to Europe and to make General Eisenhower Supreme Commander of NATO were violently opposed, by Taft (who had voted against ratification of NATO) and by Senator Wherry, the Republican floor leader. Every effort was made to reduce the defense of the United States to a simple matter of control of the air and the oceans without need for overseas forces or overseas allies. All this, of course, was simply a refusal to face twentieth-century conditions by men with nineteenth-century ideas, and gave great support to MacArthur's insubordination.

This insubordination and the general's alliance with the Republican opposition in the Congress was brought to a head on April 5, 1951, when the House Republican Leader, Joseph Martin, read to the Congress a letter from MacArthur which was a broad-gauged propagandist attack on the Truman Administration's policies in the Far East. Truman used this as an excuse to remove MacArthur, although his real reason was the general's sabotage of American and British efforts to negotiate an end of the war along the 38th parallel.

Five days after the MacArthur-Martin letter had been read in Congress, Truman removed the general from all his commands in the Far East. This was used by the isolationist opposition for a great triumphal homecoming for MacArthur. The Republican leaders spoke publicly of impeaching the President; Senator Nixon wanted congressional censure of the President and restoration of MacArthur to his commands, since his removal was "appeasement of World Communism." McCarthy said the President had made the decision while he was drunk, while Senator William Jenner said from the Senate floor: "This country today is in the hands of a secret inner coterie which is directed by agents of the Soviet Union. We must cut this whole cancerous conspiracy out of our Government at once. Our only choice is to impeach President Truman and find out who is the secret invisible government which has so cleverly led our country down the road to destruction." Sentiments similar to these were frequent, both in public and in private, for the next few years.

MacArthur's return to the United States after an absence of almost fifteen years was built up into an amazing display of popular hysteria. On landing at San Francisco he was greeted by half a million people in one of the greatest traffic jams in the city's history. At Washington's airport, after midnight on April 19th, the crowds broke out of control. That afternoon, before a joint session of Congress and over a nationwide television broadcast, he made a speech which ranged from old-fashioned eloquence to pure ham. It ended on pathos: "Old soldiers never die, they just fade away. And like the old soldier of that ballad, I now close my military career and just fade away—an old soldier who tried to do his duty as God gave him the light to see that duty. Good-by." This was followed by a parade in Washington before 250,000 spectators, but the real climax was reached in New York, the following day, when, for six and a half hours, more than seven million people, spread over a nineteen-mile parade route, cheered themselves hoarse over the general. This was twice the crowd which had seen Eisenhower's return from Europe after the defeat of Germany in 1945.

The general did not fade away immediately. By May he was back in Washington as star witness for the prosecution in a congressional investigation into the country's Far East policies. Only an infinitesimal fraction of those who had cheered the general so heartily two weeks before paid any attention to the hearings. This was unfortunate. MacArthur seriously maintained that his policies could lead to the total defeat of Communist China, without any increase in ground forces, simply by naval and economic blockade of China, by air attack on Chinese industry, and by "lifting the wraps" off Chiang Kai-shek. On this basis he promised immediate victory with a minimum of risk and casualties. The Administration's policy, he insisted, was not victory but "to go on indecisively fighting with no mission for the troops except to resist and fight . . . a continued and indefinite extension of bloodshed."

Subsequent testimony from others, including the country's leading military experts and the Joint Chiefs of Staff, showed the unsubstantial nature of this vision of Utopia. They rejected MacArthur's ideas as unrealistic and impossible: the bombing of Manchuria alone would take twice as many bombers as SAC had available; bombing of Chinese industry would not deprive the Chinese of military supplies, as their arsenals were in the Soviet Union; an economic and naval blockade could not seriously injure a country as self-sufficient as China, with an open land frontier, and could not be effective at all unless active military combat on the ground increased consumption rates; efforts to adopt these policies would alienate the United States from its allies and the United Nations and would jeopardize the whole anti-Soviet position in Europe.

Few Americans followed the arguments to this point, but MacArthur had given the opposition a new war cry: "In war there is no substitute for victory." This slogan, in which neither war nor victory was defined, was used as a weapon by the neo-isolationists, partisan Republicans, and Radical Right for more than a decade, although by 1960 it had been shortened to the charge that the Democrats favored a "No-win policy." After a decade of reiteration, many persons seriously believed that it was impossible to stop Communism without all-out nuclear war and that continued survival, instead of mutual destruction, could not possibly be regarded as winning! Peace had become appeasement.

These neo-isolationist policies had no relationship to reality, but they exerted great pressure on the last two years of the Truman Administration, driving it toward an increasingly unrealistic course. In 1951 Senator Taft was advocating a three-fold program of reduced military preparedness, reduced government expenditures, and a more aggressive foreign policy in the Far East. This combination could be supported only by assuming a number of things which were not true. One of these was that Chiang Kai-shek's regime on Formosa was still a great Power and that Red China, on the other hand, was on the verge of collapse and was, indeed, so weakened that Chiang would be enthusiastically welcomed back if he merely landed on the mainland. This unrealistic version of the present could be sustained only by an equally unrealistic version of the past, that the Red victory in China was the inevitable consequence of opposition to Chiang by the Democratic Administrations of Roosevelt and Truman and that this opposition was caused by the existence within the Administrations of Communists and Communist sympathizers from the top down. Since almost all experts, including scientists, area and subject experts, and military men, did not accept this version, either of the past or the present, all experts were regarded as suspect and insulted or ignored. In fact, educated or thoughtful men were generally rejected. Instead, emphasis was placed on "practical men," defined as those who "had met a payroll or carried a precinct." This admitted to the charmed circle businessmen and politicians of local stature (like Senator Wherry).

On the whole, the neo-isolationist discontent was a revolt of the ignorant against the informed or educated, of the nineteenth century against the insoluble problems of the twentieth, of the Midwest of Tom Sawyer against the cosmopolitan East of J. P. Morgan and Company, of old Siwash against Harvard, of the *Chicago Tribune* against the *Washington Post* or *The New York Times*, of simple absolutes against complex relativisms, of immediate final solutions against long-range partial alleviations, of frontier activism against European thought, a rejection, out of hand, of all the complexities of life which had arisen since 1915 in favor of a nostalgic return to the simplicities of 1905, and above all a desire to get back to the inexpensive, thoughtless, and irresponsible international security of 1880.

This neurotic impulse swept over the United States in a great wave in the years 1948–1955, supported by hundreds of thousands of self-seeking individuals, especially peddlers of publicity and propaganda, and financed no longer by the relatively tied-up funds of declining Wall Street international finance, but by its successors, the freely available winnings of self-financing industrial profits from such new industrial activities as air power, electronics, chemicals, light metals, or natural gas, which, although utterly dependent on government spending or government-protected exploitation of limited natural resources (such as uranium or oil), pretended to themselves and their listeners that their affluence was entirely due to their own cleverness. At the head of this list were the new millionaires, led by the Texas and southwest oil and natural-gas plungers, whose fortunes were based on tricky tax provisions and government-subsidized transportation systems.

This shift occurred on all levels from changing tastes in newspaper comic strips (from "Mutt and Jeff" or "Bringing Up Father" to "Steve Canyon" or "Little Orphan Annie"), to profound changes in the power nexus of the "American Establishment." It was evident in the decline of J. P. Morgan itself, from its deeply anonymous status as a partnership (founded in 1861) to its transformation into an incorporated public company in 1940 and its final disappearance by absorption into its chief banking subsidiary, the Guaranty Trust Company, in 1959. Incorporation reflected the need to escape the incidence of the inheritance tax, while its final disappearance was based on the relative decrease in large security flotations in contrast to the great increase in industrial self-financing (best represented by du Pont and its long-time subsidiary General Motors, or by Ford).

The less obvious implications of this shift were illustrated in a story which passed through Ivy League circles in 1948 in connection with the choice of a new president for Columbia University. This, of all universities, had been the one closest to J. P. Morgan and Company, and its president, Nicholas Murray Butler, was Morgan's chief spokesman from ivied halls. He had been chosen under Morgan influence, but the events of 1930–1948 which so weakened Morgan in the economic system also weakened his influence on the board of trustees of Columbia, until it became evident that Morgan did not have the votes to elect a successor. However, Morgan (that is, Tom Lamont) did have the votes to preserve the *status quo* and, accordingly, President Butler was kept in his position until he was long past his physical ability to carry on its functions. Finally, he had to retire. Even then Lamont and his allies were able to prevent choice of a successor, and postponed it, making the university treasurer acting-president, in the hope that a favorable change in the board of trustees might make it possible for Morgan, once again, to name a Columbia president.

Fate decreed otherwise, for Lamont died in 1948 and, shortly afterward, a committee of trustees under Thomas Watson of International Business Machines was empowered to seek a new president. This was not an area in which the genius of IBM was at his most effective. While on a business trip to Washington, he confided his problem to a friend who helpfully suggested, "Have you thought of Eisenhower?" By this he meant Milton Eisenhower, then president of Penn State, later president of Johns Hopkins; Watson, who apparently did not think immediately of this lesser-known member of the Eisenhower family, thanked his friend, and began the steps which soon made Dwight Eisenhower, for two unhappy years, president of Columbia.

In the face of the public opinion of 1950–1952, the Truman Administration had to make some concessions to the power of neo-isolationism. The loyalty program to ferret out subversives was established in the government; during the MacArthur hearings of May 1951, Dean Acheson promised that, under no circumstances, would Red China be accepted into the community of nations; aid and support to Chiang was increased; and John Foster Dulles was brought into the State Department. None of these changes helped the Truman Administration's popularity, as was clearly shown in the election of 1952, but they had major repercussions on history. One of these was Dulles's success in obtaining a peace treaty for Japan (September 8, 1951).

Dulles, like the Columbia presidency, was a former Morgan satellite which had been lost, about the same time and for the same reasons. As a partner in Sullivan and Cromwell, one of the Wall Street legal firms closely associated with Morgan, Dulles operated very much in the Morgan vineyard until the late 1940's. An early advocate of bipartisanship in foreign affairs (a Wall Street specialty), he was first brought into Democratic State Department circles, largely under Morgan sponsorship, in 1945, as adviser to Secretary of State Stettinius at the San Francisco Conference. These associations continued, at various meetings and conferences, mostly at the United Nations and at the four postwar Foreign Ministers' conferences of 1945–1949.

But in 1948 a change occurred when Dulles's naturally exaggerated personal ambition got out of hand at the same time that he drifted out of the Wall Street constellations with which his whole career had been associated. Apparently he decided he could get further on his own, especially by adapting himself to the swelling tide of neo-isolationism. The marks of this change were his appointment to the United States Senate by Governor Dewey of New York in July 1949 and his resignation from Sullivan and Cromwell at that time. In the election of November 1949, Dulles was defeated for the full senatorial term by ex-Governor Herbert

Lehman, also of a Wall Street background. In the campaign Dulles tried to portray Lehman as having Communist inclinations and went so far as to say that the election of Lehman would permit the Communists to "chalk up another victory in their struggle to get into office here."

In retirement after this electoral defeat, Dulles continued his movement toward isolationism and unilateralism, a process which was completed by his article "A Policy of Boldness" in *Life* magazine May 19, 1952, and in his subsequent efforts to keep President Eisenhower from standing up against McCarthyism. This movement was marked by increasing neglect of Europe and opposition to our chief allies there and increasing concern with the Far East and the curative powers of strategic nuclear bombing.

The Japanese peace treaty was one of the last constructive achievements of Dulles and was reached without support of the Soviet Union, which refused to sign it. Communist China was also excluded. The treaty's chief aim was to end the Pacific war within a larger security structure which bound the previous enemies into a mutual security system. It had three parts: the peace treaty with Japan, which accepted its loss of the already detached areas and islands; the ANZUS Treaty, which allied Australia, New Zealand, and the United States; and a bilateral mutual defense pact between Japan and the United States.

The neo-isolationist surge in American public opinion so paralyzed the freedom of action of the Truman Administration that it was unable to negotiate any settlement of the war in Korea. Every effort at negotiation gave rise to howls of "appeasement" or "treason." Moreover, the Communists, while willing to negotiate, showed no eagerness to make an agreement, with the result that negotiations crawled along for two years in the isolated military quarters at Panmunjon in Korea. The Kremlin was quite willing to keep America's men, money, and attention tied down in Korea, and could find each day an additional argument to throw as an obstacle into the negotiations. Most of these obstacles were concerned with the disposition of prisoners of war, thousands of whom did not want to return to Communist territory, while only twenty-one captured Americans were unwilling to return to the United States. Simply by insisting that all prisoners must be forced to return, the Communists could extend the negotiations indefinitely in time and thus postpone the day when the United States might be free to turn its men and resources to other areas closer to the Soviet Union and thus more dangerous to it, such as Europe.

Only the death of Stalin in March 1953 broke this stalemate. As soon as the first confusion over this issue had passed temporarily, it became possible to make a Korean truce, an achievement helped by the accession of a new Republican administration in Washington in January. The truce was signed on July 27, 1953, after 37 months of war in which the

United States had lost 25,000 dead, 115,000 other casualties, and about $22 billion in costs.

The Korean War had a totally different impact on the scientists, the Democratic leaders, the army, some of the navy, the new group of strategic intellectuals and non-middle-class educated persons in general than it had on the neo-isolationists, the Republican leaders, the air force, Big Business, and the newly forming Radical Right publicists. To the latter groups it was a totally unnecessary and frustrating experience, resulting from the incompetence, or treason, of their opponents, an aberration and throwback to World War I which must never be permitted to reoccur. To the former alignment, however, the limited war in Korea was an inevitable consequence of nuclear stalemate, arising from the very nature of Communist aggression and of the revolutionary discontents of the buffer fringe, and would be a constantly threatening possibility in the future, either in Korea itself or in a dozen other places along the edges of the Communist bloc. Accordingly, this motley alignment, led by its scientists and liberals, began to work to strengthen America's ability to face any new challenge similar to Korea. In a military sense, this inevitably led to efforts to increase the ability of Europe and America to wage limited war, whatever the cost. The Right, as the defenders of material comforts, were unwilling to engage in such an effort, on the basis of cost alone, and soon convinced themselves that it was unnecessary.

The tactical experience of Korea showed clearly that we had neither the weapons nor the training for limited war and that the air force's claims for the effectiveness of its strategic weapons were as unrealistic as they had been since Douhet. Even the tactical air units had been ineffective, chiefly because they were designed and used in a separate service dominated by "Big Bomber" generals. Some of the most effective work had been done by tools, such as helicopters, which the air force refused to study or order.

To remedy this weakness, the army's specialist on airborne warfare, General James M. Gavin, was sent with a team of scientists to Korea in the autumn of 1950. At the time General Gavin, longtime officer of the heroic 82nd Airborne Division, was much worried at the air force's efforts to monopolize all the air and all nuclear weapons, at its resentment at possession of aviation by the navy and marines, and at its refusal to provide effective tactical support from the air for ground forces or to buy the equipment needed to provide proper airborne mobility, both of men and supplies, for ground troops. The team of scientists who went to the Far East with General Gavin in September-November 1950, included C. C. Lauritsen, professor of physics at the California Institute of Technology, who had developed the whole array of navy and air-force rockets in World War II and had been Oppenheimer's assistant at Los Alamos during the last year of the war; Dr. William B. Shockley of Bell Telephone Laboratories, developer of the transistor, who won the Nobel Prize in 1956; and Dr. Edward Bowles of MIT, our chief expert on military applications of radar in World War II.

From their discussions emerged a series of scientific research projects in 1951–1952 which had a profound effect on American defense capabilities. Project Vista, with President Lee DuBridge of Caltech as chairman and Lauritsen as his deputy, made an over-all study of defense problems for the Department of Defense. In general it sought to reach a well-rounded, diverse defense establishment which could respond effectively to any degree of aggression and do it on land, sea, or air. One of its chief efforts was to get tactical air power for the ground forces and to counteract the massed Soviet Army in Europe by development of tactical nuclear weapons, as well as nuclear warheads to be carried on rockets of 50- to 300-mile range, so that the forcible dispersion of Russian infantry to avoid annihilation would sharply reduce its offensive impact. These weapons could also be used to get "all-weather" tactical bombing support under army control to replace the fair-weather air-force tactical bombing which had proved so ineffective in Korea.

The *Vista Report,* which was submitted to the secretaries of the forces in February 1952, made at least a dozen suggestions of which at least ten were eventually carried out, despite the fact that the report was never accepted. The reason for its rejection was the violent opposition of the air force, which disliked most of it but really exploded when they found, in Chapter 5, that it recommended dividing nuclear materials among the three services. The air force flatly refused to yield up any fissionable materials to the other services. At first it insisted that there was not enough. When months of argument proved there was plenty, the air force simply tripled its requirements. When the air force discovered that Oppenheimer had written the introductory section of Chapter 5, his fate was sealed. Stories about his unreliability were passed about, and eventually it was said that he had somehow rewritten Chapter 5 and inserted it without the committee members knowing what he was doing.

Project Charles and its sequel Project Lincoln were equally objectionable to the air force, although they had been instigated by it. "Charles" suggested that a permanent research laboratory should be established to study the technical problems of air defense. Accordingly, in September 1951, the Lincoln Laboratory was set up at MIT. This eventually had a staff of 1,600 on an annual budget of $20 million. Its special summer Project Lincoln in 1951 included many of the scientists, such as DuBridge, Lauritsen, Zacharias, and Oppenheimer of Project Vista; it estimated that American defense against a Soviet air attack was woefully weak and could not expect to knock down more than 20 percent of the attacking planes, a rate far too low to be acceptable in nuclear warfare. Setting a 70 percent "kill-rate" as a minimum aspiration, Project Lincoln recommended establishment of a Distant Early Warning radar detection net across Canada and Greenland (the so-called "DEW Line"), much improved fighter and missile interception in deep air defense (DAD), and the development of an elaborate, integrated, automatic air-defense communications system.

The cost of this program, billions of dollars, made it less than welcome to the air force. To combat it, air-force supporters spread rumors that a clique of scientists which they called "ZORC" (Zacharias, Oppenheimer, Rabi, and Charles Lauritsen) were out to destroy SAC by devising, or pretending to devise, a near-perfect air defense for the United States. Thus DEW DAD, according to SAC supporters, would be America's Maginot Line behind which the country would lie helplessly bankrupt from its cost of $100 billion. The air force, from its control over the Lincoln Laboratory's budget, was successful in forcing MIT to suppress the DEW DAD report; at least, it was never published. But part of the story, including the horror story about ZORC, was published in the May 1953 issue of *Fortune* magazine, and some of the rest came out in the 1954 hearing on Oppenheimer's security.

The third significant effort in the scientists' campaign for American survival in the early 1950's was known as Project East River. It was also instigated by the air force, early in 1952, and studied the problem of civil defense through a scientific team headed by Lloyd Berkner of Associated Universities. It advocated a fantastically expensive program of air-raid warnings, civilian defense shelters, and radar decentralization, but little was ever done about it. Since such a defensive system would undoubtedly save scores of millions of lives in any all-out nuclear war, and would permit the United States to withstand a Soviet "first strike," the failure to follow up these recommendations is clearly attributable to the cost, a sum which many felt we could not afford and which the air force was convinced could be far better spent on building up the offensive power of SAC. Some of it did go for this purpose.

The air force, which had 48 wings (of which 18 were in SAC) in June 1950, when the Korean War began, had 95 wings in July 1952, as the presidential campaign began, and had 110 wings (of which 42 wings were in SAC) at the end of 1953 in the last Truman budget. During these years, covering the last four budgets of the Truman period, expenditures on national security increased from $13 billion in 1949-1950 to over $50 billion in 1952-1953. A fair amount of this increase went for the changes recommended by the scientists, such as the DEW Line, increase in army ground forces from 10 to 20 divisions, and increased air transportation. As a consequence, American power relative to Soviet power reached its highest point in the postwar period about the end of 1953. It then lost ground until its recovery in the missile race of 1958-1963. The lines of the earlier buildup, as recommended by the various scientific defense projects of 1950–1952, were summed up in a general survey for the incoming Eisenhower Administration in NSC 141. This document did not replace, but supplemented, more intensive efforts in air defense, civil defense, and in military assistance in the Near East and Far East.

The Eisenhower Team, 1952-1956

The last two years of the Truman Administration were marked by waves of partisan propaganda which quite concealed the major improvements being made in the American defense posture. The American people were irritated and puzzled by the stalemate in Korea exactly as the Soviets intended them to be. Disruption of the lives of individuals in a war which was not a war, in which nothing seemed to be achieved except unnecessary casualties, and which disrupted the pleasures of the postwar economic boom with military service, shortages, restrictions, and cost-of-living inflation could not help but breed discontent. The Republican–Dixiecrat alliance in the Congress made it impossible to deal with domestic problems in any decisive way or with foreign problems outside the independent authority of the presidential office. And through it all the mobilized wealth of the country, in alliance with most of the press, kept up a constant barrage of "Communists in Washington," "twenty years of treason," or "corruption of the Missouri gang" in the Truman Administration, and created a general picture of incompetence and bungling shot through with subversion. In creating this picture the leaders of the Republican Party totally committed themselves to the myths of the neo-isolationists and of the Radical Right.

In June 1951, Senator McCarthy delivered in the Senate a speech of 60,000 words attacking General Marshall as a man "steeped in falsehood," who has "recourse to the lie whenever it suits his convenience," one of the architects of America's foreign policy made by "men high in this Government [who] are concerting to deliver us to disaster . . . a conspiracy of infamy so black that when it is finally exposed, its principals shall be forever deserving of the maledictions of all honest men. . . ."

When Truman tried to defend his subordinates, an action which Dulles resolutely refused to do when he became Secretary of State in 1953, Senator Taft attacked the President for this combination of human decency with the established legal privileges of the English-speaking world: he was wrong, according to Taft, to "assume the innocence of all the persons mentioned in the State Department. . . . Whether Senator McCarthy has legal evidence, whether he has overstated or understated his case, is of lesser importance. The question is whether the communist influence in the State Department still exists." Following the tendencies of the day, Taft reversed his previous support of the Korean War, calling it an "unnecessary war," an "utterly useless war," a war "begun by President Truman without the slightest authority from Congress or the people."

A semiofficial version of the Republican position appeared in John Foster Dulles's article "A Policy of Boldness," which was published in *Life* on May 19, 1952. This advocated rejection of "containment" in favor of "liberation," to be achieved on a smaller budget and with reduction of the armed forces leading to a conclusive victory in the near future. All concessions to reality were rejected out of hand: containment itself was damned as fragmentary reactions to Soviet pressure, as negative, endless, and partial, as "treadmill policies which, at best, might perhaps keep us in the same place until we drop exhausted." In place of these, Dulles offered liberation and massive retaliation. These two were not expressly linked together since, apparently, the former (applied chiefly to eastern Europe) would be achieved simply by making clear that the United States wanted it. At least, Dulles believed it would come when American policy made "it publicly known that it wants and expects liberation to occur." The disastrous consequence of this nonsense appeared in 1956 when East Germany and Hungary rose against the Russians and were crushed by Soviet tanks without Dulles raising a hand to help. The threat of instant massive retaliation as the sole weapon by which the United States would get Russia to adopt more acceptable policies was equally unrealistic. No one, not even Dulles, dared to use it in the face of the Soviet Union's capability for retaliation. Nuclear blackmail is bad, but nuclear blackmail in which the blackmailer has no intention or opportunity to inflict his penalty is pointless and dangerous—unless, perhaps, such threats help to win elections.

It helped win an election for Eisenhower in 1952. The candidate had no particular assets except a bland and amiable disposition combined with his reputation as a victorious general. He also had a weakness, one which is frequently found in his profession, the conviction that anyone who has become a millionaire, even by inheritance, is an authoritative person on almost any subject. With Eisenhower as candidate, combined with Richard Nixon, the ruthless enemy of internal subversion, as a running mate, and using a campaign in which the powers of Madison Avenue publicity mobilized all the forces of American discontent behind the neo-isolationist program, victory in November, 1952, was assured. The *coup de grâce* was given to the Democratic candidate, Governor Adlai Stevenson of Illinois, darling of the academic intellectuals, when Eisenhower adopted Emmet Hughes's suggestion that he promise, if elected, to go to Korea to make peace.

Although not himself a neo-isolationist or a reactionary, Eisenhower had few deep personal convictions, and was eager to be President. When his advisers told him that he must collaborate with the Radical Right, he went all the way, even to the extent of condoning Senator McCarthy's attack on General Marshall. This occurred when Eisenhower, under McCarthy's pressure, removed from a Wisconsin speech a favorable reference to Marshall.

Once elected, the new President reintroduced the Republican conception of the Presidency which had been used in 1921–1933. This conception saw the President as a kind of titular chairman of the board who neither acted himself directly nor intervened indirectly in the actions of his delegated assistants. Fully aware of his own limitations of both knowledge and energy, Eisenhower allotted the functions of government to his Cabinet members ("eight millionaires and a plumber," according to one writer) and expected to be consulted himself only in unsettled disputes or major policy changes.

Over-all government operations were divided into two parts, with John Foster Dulles, as secretary of state, in charge of foreign affairs, and ex-Governor Sherman Adams of New Hampshire (in place of Taft, who died in 1953) as assistant President in charge of domestic matters. Apart from these, the real tone of the Administration was provided by three businessmen: George Humphrey, a Taft Republican and president of the great holding company of M. A. Hanna and Company, was secretary of the treasury and the most influential member of the Cabinet; Charles Wilson, president of General Motors, was secretary of defense; and Joseph M. Dodge, a Detroit banker with extensive government experience, was director of the budget, the only man in the government who could, with impunity, do or undo Acts of Congress. The chief aim of the Administration, and almost the sole aim of these three, was to reduce government spending, and subsequently business taxes, by the greatest amount that would not jeopardize reelection in 1956. Dulles and Adams had to work within the financial framework thus provided.

Within this framework foreign policy was boxed, even more narrowly, between the realities of the country's world position and the constant hounding of the neo-isolationist groups in Congress who had been roused to a pitch of unholy expectation by the encouragement they had received from Eisenhower and Nixon during the electoral campaign of 1952. In that campaign they had discovered that Eisenhower could be pushed. They now concluded that their pushing from without, combined with the pulling of Dulles and Nixon from within, could overthrow the foreign-policy lines established by the Truman Administration in the preceding six years and create a new policy more in accord with their mistaken ideas of the nature of the world. Opposed to this change were the old defenders of the Atlantic System, the remnants of former Wall Street influence, the Ivy League colleges, the foundations, the newspaper spokesmen of this point of view (*The New York Times* and *Herald Tribune, Christian Science Monitor*, and *Washington Post*) led by Walter Lippmann, and the unrepentant scientists and "eggheads" straggling behind Adlai Stevenson.

Eisenhower as President can be summed up in one word: amiability. He not only liked people; he was also eager to be liked, and was, indeed, likable. If he gave the impression that he had no firmly held convictions, that was because of two other qualities: he was relaxed, fully willing to live and let live, in an easygoing tolerance of anything which did not disturb his own peace of mind. He was quick-tempered but not a fighter. He had convictions, none of them very firm, but he was not prepared to sacrifice his own rest and relaxation for them, except for brief occasions. His span of attention was neither long nor intense. As a consequence, he was a wonderful companion, but not a leader.

In all this, the President was the antithesis of his secretary of state. John Foster Dulles was a tireless and energetic fighter, full of convictions, most of which he saw in black-and-white terms. He rarely rested and had little time for any relaxation because the world was full of evil forces with which he must wage constant battle. Tolerance and the right to be neutral were to him largely words which had little real meaning in his tightly wound neurological system. To Dulles it was a real effort not to equate opposition with evil. As he hurried throughout the world, traveling 226,645 miles in his first three years in office, in pursuit of Communism, he was like John Wesley, two centuries earlier, racing through England in pursuit of sin, both men fully convinced that they were doing the work of God. Eisenhower, who saw the world as a place almost without evil, once told an adviser, "You and I can argue issues all day and it won't affect our friendship, but the minute I question your motives you will never forgive me." This lesson would have been lost on the secretary of state, for Dulles, almost alone in a world full of sin, was always seeking the reason behind the event, the motive behind the action, and was obligated by his own alignment with righteousness to denounce the reason and the motive when he had discovered them.

It must be evident from this that Eisenhower and Dulles, in spite of their close cooperation and almost unruffled personal relations, were very dissimilar, both in personality and in outlook. Dulles was considerably to the right of Eisenhower, and the Republican congressional party was far to the right of Dulles. As a result, the two were under constant pressure from the party's isolationist leaders in Congress and from the party's big financial supporters to go further toward neo-isolationism and the Right than either Dulles or Eisenhower considered safe. To avoid this, the Administration had to do two basically contradictory things: to make verbal concessions to the Right and to find its congressional legislative support among the Democrats. In 1953 alone, according to the *Congressional Quarterly Almanac*, the "Democrats saved the President . . . fifty-eight times" by their votes in Congress.

Some examples of this skirmishing, in what was locally known as the "Battle of the Potomac," form a necessary background to the development of international affairs in Eisenhower's eight years.

The Republican platform of July 1952 had promised to "repudiate all commitments contained in secret understandings such as those of Yalta which aid Communist enslavements." In his first speech as secretary, Dulles spoke of the liberation of satellite peoples, and told them, "You can count upon us." The Republicans in Congress from then on kept demanding support of these two promises, beginning with a resolution to repudiate Yalta and Potsdam. The Administration naturally had to oppose this congressional desire to take campaign talk seriously, since any repudiation of past agreements could be done by Russia more easily than by us and could jeopardize most of our advanced positions in Europe, beginning with Berlin and Vienna. Eventually the resolution was dropped.

A somewhat similar struggle arose over the Bricker and the substitute Dirksen Amendments to the Constitution. These would have forbidden the Federal government to make any foreign treaties which could not be carried out by powers granted to the Federal government elsewhere in the Constitution. This would have greatly hampered the State Department in making agreements, such as those with Canada to protect migrating game birds, since power to do so was not granted elsewhere in the Constitution. The Amendment was finally defeated by the Administration after a bitter struggle with Republicans in the Congress, and only by the support of Democrats.

The Administration condoned or suffered through all kinds of Rightwing attacks, many of them supported by members of the Cabinet. Some government employees were harassed for years, even suspended without pay for months or years, before final clearance of unfounded charges. Wolf Ladejinsky, the country's greatest authority on East Asian agriculture and a known anti-Communist writer, had been responsible for much of MacArthur's success in occupied Japan as the author of a land-reform program which increased agricultural production and largely eliminated agrarian discontent, so that Communism in Japan, quite opposite to China, ceased to be a rural phenomenon and was, indeed, largely restricted to student groups in cities. Cleared by the State Department to return to Japan, he was suddenly declared a security risk and suspended by Secretary of Agriculture Benson.

Attorney General Herbert Brownell, Jr., confided to a businessmen's luncheon in Chicago that President Truman, knowing that Harry Dexter White was a Russian spy, had promoted him from assistant secretary of the treasury to executive director of the United States Mission to the International Monetary Fund in 1946. Chairman Harold Velde of the House Committee on Un-American Activities at once issued a subpoena to the ex-President to testify before the committee. The summons was ignored. In the resulting controversy Senator McCarthy attacked the Administration over a nationwide broadcast for its failure to force all nations, beginning with Britain, to cease their trade with Red China by threatening to cut off our economic aid. We should say, "If you continue to ship to Red China . . . you will not get one cent of American money." The fact that our allies provided us, at great danger to themselves, with military bases on their own soil from which our strategic pressure on the Soviet Union was maintained meant nothing to the total irresponsibility of the Radical Right. McCarthy's attacks on the United States Information Agency overseas libraries as centers for diffusion of Leftist books led to the burning of hundreds of books in these libraries and eventually to attacks on works like *Tom Sawyer* and *Robin Hood* as subversive, because they did not picture middle-class Middle West American customs (Robin Hood stole from the rich and gave to the poor, clearly a Communist tactic).

Such harassments of the new Administration were almost constant, especially from the Right, which was confident it had won the election of 1952 and should be obeyed as a consequence. On April 30th, in Cabinet, Taft blasted the Administration for its inability to cut more than $5 billion or $6 billion out of the defense budget. The foreign aid "mutual-security" budget of $7.6 billion left by Truman was cut by Chairman John Tabor of the House Appropriations Committee to $4.4 billion in spite of Eisenhower's request for $5.5 billion. Chairman C. W. Reed of the House Ways and Means Committee, despite Eisenhower's appeal, knocked out the new Truman taxes of 1951 on July 1, 1953, six months before they would have ended anyway.

Under Right-wing attacks such as these, Eisenhower was largely disillusioned with his job by the summer of 1953 and spent much time over the next two years considering how he might get rid of the dominant Republican Right and form a new, middle-of-the-road Eisenhower Party. The impracticality of this became apparent to him long before the election of 1956.

These attacks from the Right were much less disturbing to Dulles than they were to the President. The Secretary of State was clear in his own mind on what his aims in foreign policy should be. These aims were largely acceptable to the neo-isolationists and congressional Republicans. Basic to these ideas was his conception of "massive retaliation."

This was publicly announced in his speech of January 12, 1954, before the Council of Foreign Relations, but had been forecast in his article in *Life* almost two years earlier. "Massive retaliation" here meant nuclear reprisal by strategic bombing. It was conceived as an alternative to limited war and was intended to be a deterrent to Soviet instigation of such local limited wars. The points at which it would be applied or the degree of aggression necessary to trigger it were both left ambiguous, in the hope that the threat would deter aggression in all areas and on all levels. Dulles was really rejecting the whole idea of limited war, and saw local defense only as a trigger mechanism for tripping massive retaliation. In this view he was at one with most of the Eisenhower Administration. Secretary Wilson, for example, said, "We can no longer afford to fight limited war." Of course, he was thinking in monetary terms. General Gavin, who heard this statement, replied, "If we cannot afford to fight limited wars, then we cannot afford to survive, for that is the only kind of war we can afford to fight." He was thinking of the cost in terms of human lives.

As a corollary to the idea of massive retaliation as deterrence, Dulles had the additional idea of local defense, and especially local alliances, as triggers. Combined with this was his refusal to accept anything but a two-bloc world, by his resolute refusal to recognize any right to anyone to be neutral. On June 9, 1956, in a speech at Iowa State College, he said that America had made bilateral treaties with forty-two countries and that these agreements "abolish, as between the parties, the principle of neutrality, which pretends that a nation can best gain safety for itself by being indifferent to the fate of others. This has increasingly become an obsolete conception, and, except under very exceptional circumstances, it is an immoral and shortsighted conception." Thus the Secretary of State indicated his readiness to abandon the nonaligned countries to the Soviet bloc, and gave Stalin's successors in the Kremlin a tactical opportunity they were already exploiting. At the same time, as we shall see in a moment, Dulles's treatment of our chief allies was generally so autocratic and even contemptuous that they were soon alienated, especially France, which did not have the "special relationship" with us which kept Great Britain at our side through any slights.

The reason for these actions by Dulles was that he was really an isolationist, convinced that American defense rested wholly on American strength, and, accordingly, he did not regard his treaty partners as allies at all, but rather as a part of an elaborate network of triggers surrounding the Soviet Union. The chief portions of this network were three regional pacts: NATO, the Baghdad Pact (later called CENTRO, or Central Treaty Organization), and SEATO (or Southeast Asian Treaty Organization). NATO included the United States, Canada, and thirteen other states from Iceland to Turkey (by May 1955).

The Baghdad Pact of 1955 was largely a Dulles creation but did not include the United States. Its members were Britain, Turkey, Iran, Iraq, and Pakistan. It was renamed Central Treaty Organization in 1959 when Iraq withdrew and the United States signed bilateral alliances with all its members.

The third pact, SEATO, signed in 1954, had eight members (United States, Britain, France, New Zealand, Australia, Philippines, Thailand, and Pakistan). With Turkey acting as a link between NATO and CENTRO, and Pakistan in a similar role between CENTRO and SEATO, the three pacts were intended to enclose the Soviet bloc in an unbroken perimeter of paper barriers which would deter a Communist movement outward anywhere, by serving as a trigger for American retaliation. Otherwise, CENTRO and SEATO had little military or political merit, and created more problems than they solved.

Dulles was not primarily concerned about the military strength of these pacts or about the military contribution any of these countries could make to a war on the Soviet Union. Above all, he was not concerned with any contribution of a military character the United States could make to the defense of these pacts or areas in any nonnuclear war. Moreover, as triggers, Dulles was not much concerned with the character of the regimes involved or with their military strength. Some mountainous country or tropical jungle of Asia was, for his purposes, about as significant as England or France.

Since England and France were already alienated by the whole idea of massive retaliation, which could so easily, by some independent American act, deluge them with Soviet nuclear bombs, they were even further alienated by Dulles's almost total lack of concern for the fact that they were more cultured and more civilized than other members of Dulles's pacts, that they shared our common Western traditions (of which, indeed, they were the creators), and could contribute more to their own defense with conventional weapons than could some Moslem or pagan areas of Asia. It is no wonder that Dulles, with his unilateralism, his lack of concern for cultural kinship, his readiness to sacrifice all European states in response to a trigger mechanism in some remote and backward jungle, his almost total unconcern with the possible contribution of limited and conventional warfare to save any areas from Communism, it is no wonder, indeed, that Dulles alienated the United States from its natural associates in Western Europe to a degree hitherto unknown in the twentieth century.

At the same time, Dulles alienated himself domestically from all his older associations within American life, and from the forces of rationalization and science which were increasingly a force there. Like Eisenhower, Dulles had an unusual conception of his office; indeed, it was much more unusual than was Eisenhower's. Dulles refused to take any responsibility for the internal functioning of the State Department. His concern was, he thought, only with the high policy of international politics on a world basis as the eyes, ears, and probably the mind of the President. Accordingly, instead of the usual under secretary of state, Dulles appointed two: General Walter Bedell Smith to the regular post, and Donald B. Lourie, president of Quaker Oats Company, as a second one in charge of all departmental administration. Under Lourie he named a McCarthyite, R. W. Scott McLeod, as State Department security officer. In this way the full disruptive force of McCarthyism was brought into the inner fortress, that is, into the personnel security files of the department against which McCarthy and his associates had directed their most blasting assaults. Nor was that all. In his first week in office Dulles announced his policies to the department, and informed its employees that he expected "competence, discipline, and positive loyalty." There is nothing objectionable in these three qualities except that Senator McCarthy had temporarily made "positive loyalty" his own criterion of condemnation.

This beginning became worse. Dulles made no effort to protect his subordinates from the attacks made upon the department or on them individually. His justification for this attitude soon destroyed the morale of much of the department and especially of the Foreign Service. Dulles felt that once an employee became the target of a public attack as unreliable, the question of his guilt or innocence became definitely secondary to the question of whether his value to the department had not been destroyed simply by the fact that he had become a subject of controversy. If so, he should be released from service, even if innocent. This point of view, which was almost an invitation to the McCarthyites to increase their attacks, was never, however, applied to Dulles himself when he became, in a short time, a figure of controversy. The real damage to the Department arose from the elimination of some of its most knowledgeable members. The Radical Right, having eliminated almost everyone who knew anything about the Far East, especially those who knew the Chinese language, now, under Dulles, shifted their target to those who knew anything about Russia, especially the language. In this way, George Kennan was eliminated, and Charles Bohlen narrowly escaped. Paul Nitze resigned in disgust. Some of those eliminated found refuge in Ivy League academic posts.

The chief victim of these purges was Robert Oppenheimer. The attack on the "father of the A-bomb" began in the summer of 1953, as soon as Lewis Strauss succeeded Gordon Dean as chairman of the AEC. On July 7th, at the request of Strauss, the AEC ordered that classified documents in Oppenheimer's possession in Princeton be taken from him. On November 7, 1953, W. L. Borden, who had earlier left the Joint Congressional Committee for private employment with Westinghouse Electric, wrote a letter to J. Edgar Hoover of the FBI: "The purpose of this letter is to state my own exhaustively considered opinion, based upon years of study of the available classified evidence, that more probably than not J. Robert Oppenheimer is an agent of the Soviet Union." This charge was supported by a biased rehash of all the derogatory stories about Oppenheimer which had been known when Oppenheimer was appointed to Los Alamos by General Groves in 1943. Much of the letter was made up of wild charges which no responsible person has ever been willing to defend: "He has been instrumental in securing recruits for the Communist Party," and "He was in frequent contact with Soviet espionage agents." According to Borden, "The central problem is not whether J. Robert Oppenheimer was ever a Communist; for the existing evidence makes abundantly clear that he was. . . . The central problem is assessing the degree of likelihood that he in fact did what a communist in his circumstances, at Berkeley, would logically have done during the crucial 1939-1942 period—that is, whether he became an actual espionage and policy instrument of the Soviets."

On the basis of this letter and at the direct order of President Eisenhower, Chairman Strauss suspended Oppenheimer's security clearance and thus his access to classified information without which scientific work for defense is impossible. The news was given to Oppenheimer by Strauss on December 21, 1953, four days after he received an honorary degree from Oxford University. As provided by law, Oppenheimer appealed the AEC decision to an *ad hoc* investigation committee of three men, one of whom was a scientist. The hearings, from April 12 to May 6, 1954, allowed Oppenheimer to have counsel who were permitted to cross-examine witnesses, but the conduct of the hearings was most unsatisfactory.

The older assumption, which had been practiced regularly in American history and continued, fairly generally, in the Truman Administration, was that any person had a right to be employed by the government unless something adverse could be proved against him. The chief adverse something, in scientific work, would be disloyalty. In the course of the years 1951–1953, these concepts were changing and were formally modified by President Eisenhower's Security Order 10450 of April, 1953. The first change was that public employment no longer was a right but became a privilege; the second was that disloyalty was no longer the chief criterion, but security was; and the third change was that the government no longer had to prove anything derogatory, but merely needed to have a doubt that a person's employment was consistent with the security of the country.

Taken together, these three modifications placed the burden of proof on the employee rather than on the accuser and made the area of proof so wide that it could hardly be met. The government has to prove nothing; it merely must have a doubt, and that doubt need have nothing to do with loyalty or with the employee's work, but may simply be about his discretion, his drinking habits, his truthfulness, or any other personal characteristics of an adverse kind whether these operate in the area of his work or not. The task of an employee seeking to dispel the doubt that he may drink one too many cocktails before dinner, or that he may gossip, or even talk in his sleep is formidable. For example, one of the AEC commissioners who sat in judgment on Oppenheimer fell asleep in a railroad car on June 11, 1954, with the transcript of the case on his lap, and awoke later to find it gone. This was why the transcript was immediately printed and released on June 16th, in spite of the assurances to its forty witnesses throughout its pages that it would be kept secret. A case might be made that an AEC commissioner who lost classified materials by falling asleep while reading them in public was a "security risk." He would have some difficulty removing that doubt.

The shifting of the burden of proof from the board to the accused and the use of an investigatory tribunal rather than the more familiar technique (to English-speaking peoples) of an adversary trial made the hearings even less satisfactory. For the accused, faced with the need to establish the truth in order to dispel any doubts of the members of the tribunal, could hardly establish the truth when he had access only to those documents which had been selected by the counsel for the AEC. In this case the AEC counsel, a one-time United States Attorney for the District of Columbia, conducted the hearings as if he were the prosecutor in an adversary trial. He was allowed to use secret data, from which evidence was pulled at short or no notice, while Oppenheimer's counsel was excluded from access to classified documents for security reasons.

After hearing forty witnesses through 3,000 pages of typed testimony and perusing an equal quantity of file documents, the board voted 2 to 1 (the scientist member dissenting) to recommend continued suspension of Oppenheimer's clearance. They concluded that Oppenheimer was loyal and that he was discreet. It would seem, on the face of it, that a person who filled these two qualifications must be secure, but two members of the board had doubts.

These hearings have endless interest to the historian of recent American history because they provide one of the few glimpses we have behind the scenes into the decision-making processes of our recent government. As far as Oppenheimer is concerned, they show that the animosity against him largely originated with the air force and its close or recent associates. The attack on Oppenheimer came chiefly from the former air-force pilot Borden, from a long-term air-force employee, David T. Griggs, and from Edward Teller and his close associates L. W. Alvarez and W. M. Latimer. There was obvious personal resentment against Oppenheimer by this group, and cross-examination showed that the majority of them had no personal knowledge of Oppenheimer's work in the matter under discussion. This appeared most clearly when they tried to maintain that Oppenheimer opposed or obstructed the H-bomb effort *after* Truman's directive to make it had been issued or that he tried to persuade other scientists not to work on the project. The evidence from persons in a position to have personal knowledge of this matter showed that this charge was not true, and the board rejected it. It is clear from the testimony that the real basis for these men's resentment against Oppenheimer was air-force resentment of Project Vista and its sequels, especially at Oppenheimer's efforts to provide the American defense forces with a full arsenal of diverse weapons, including tactical nuclear weapons, so that the country would not be forced to rely solely or mainly on strategic nuclear bombing to play its role in world politics.

This point was put very well by Professor Walter G. Whitman of MIT, who was a member of GAC from 1950—and had been chairman of the Research and Development Board of the Department of Defense in 1951–1953. He said: "Dr. Oppenheimer was trying to point out the wide variety of military uses of the bomb, the small bomb as well as the large bomb. He was doing it in a climate where many folks felt that only strategic bombing was a field for the atomic weapon. . . . I should say he, more than any other man, served to educate the military to the potentialities of the atomic weapon for other than strategic bombing purposes, its use possibly in tactical situations or in bombing 500 miles back. He was constantly emphasizing that the bomb would be more available and that one of the problems was going to be its deliverability, meaning that the smaller you could make your bomb in size perhaps you would not have to have a great big strategic bomber to carry it, you could carry it in a medium bomber or you could carry it even in a fighter plane. In my judgment, his advice and his arguments for a gamut of atomic weapons, extending even over to the use of the atomic weapon in air defense of the United States, has been more productive than any other one individual. You see, he had the opportunity to not only advise in the Atomic Energy Commission, but advise in the military services of the Department of Defense. The idea of a range of weapons suitable for a multiplicity of military purposes was a key to the campaign which he felt should be pressed and with which I agreed. . . . The Strategic Air Command had thought of the atomic weapon as solely restricted to its own use. I think that there was some definite resentment at the implication that this was not just the Strategic Air Command's weapon."

On the basis of the recommendation of the Hearing Board, the AEC voted 4 to 1 (with the scientist Henry D. Smyth dissenting) not to restore Oppenheimer's clearance. On June 29, 1955, the great scientist's career in government was ended. But his work had been a success. In the interval before the achievement of the thermonuclear bomb in 1955, atomic weapons had been made so plentiful and diverse that they were available for tactical weapons to defend Europe and in sizes small enough to serve as warheads on American missiles of limited boosting power.

The motivations of the Eisenhower Administration were emotional and complex, and represent a sharp reaction against the forces of rationalization and science which we have discussed. They seem to have been based on three narrowing circles of outlook. Broadest of all was a violent neurotic rebellion of harassed middle-class persons against a longtime challenge to middle-class values arising from depression, war, insecurity, science, foreigners, and minority groups of all kinds. This broad problem will be discussed elsewhere. A second, and narrower, circle of outlook was the basic Republican opposition to all kinds of collective action, including collective security, social welfare, and national security. The third was the obsession of business wealth in the country with the wickedness of unbalanced budgets and high taxes.

The Republican opposition to collective action was, of course, of long standing. It is not generally recognized that it appears frequently as an opposition to national security expenditures, especially to defense expenditures for men rather than for equipment, but often for both. Such opposition by Republicans was generally true in the whole period following 1945, and is clearly shown in their votes in Congress. These votes, however, can be understood only in terms of the whole situation.

This situation involves at least three levels: public opinion, Congress, and the Administration and, in each of these, the two parties. In studying these we have available the information of public-opinion polls, voting records, and formal statements. From these records it is clear that public opinion always supported large defense forces and did not object to higher taxes or government spending to sustain them. Moreover, this support was stronger from persons of lower educational and income levels, although generally found on all levels. In sharp contrast to this, public opinion gave much less support to foreign aid, and such support was less on lower educational or income levels and was reflected in far greater opposition to taxation or government spending for economic foreign aid than for defense forces. These statements are based on the file of public-opinion polls at the Public Opinion Research Center at Williams College, as studied by Professor Samuel P. Huntington of Harvard University. This study shows that public-opinion support for stronger armed forces for the whole period 1945–1960 was usually of the order of two to one, and reflected changes in international tensions to a surprisingly limited degree.

In Congress, over the same fifteen years, there was quite a different situation. There we find, just as existed in the decade before Pearl Harbor, strong Democratic support for armed strength and a strong world role for the United States, and fairly consistent Republican opposition both to defense expenditures and to American involvement in world affairs. On the contrary, the congressional Republican Party members, in both periods, were more concerned with what they called "fiscal responsibility" (meaning balanced budgets, reduced government spending, and reduced taxes) than it was with defense or world affairs. Thus the Democratic Party in Congress was much closer in behavior to public opinion than the Republican congressional party was.

Professor Huntington has illuminated this difference by an analysis of congressional voting records over the period 1945–1960. He has examined votes on 79 controversial defense issues in Congress over the 15-year period and found that a majority of Democrats voted pro-defense on 74 of the 79 issues, while a majority of Republicans voted pro-defense on only 39 of the 79 issues. On all these issues, Democratic senators voted 78.8 percent pro-defense and Republican senators voted only 43 percent pro-defense, while Democratic representatives voted 78.4 percent pro-defense and Republican representatives voted 53.8 percent pro-defense. Moreover, the Republican votes in both Houses were less pro-defense in the Eisenhower period than in the Truman period, the Senate Republican pro-defense votes falling from 47.1 to 33 percent with the change in Administration, and the House Republican pro-defense votes falling from 54.8 to 50.4 percent. Moreover, analysis of these votes, on a sectional basis, shows that the Republican pro-defense votes were concentrated in the Northeast and on the Pacific Coast, while the Democratic pro-defense votes were spaced relatively evenly around the country.

·When we shift from the Congress to the Administration, we see that the Democratic Administration, while still pro-defense, was less so than Democratic congressmen, but that the Republican Administration, while not pro-defense, was somewhat more favorable to defense than Republican congressmen.

This situation can be explained in terms of three forces acting upon politicians: (1) the need for votes, (2) the need for campaign contributions, and (3) awareness of world conditions. On the Democratic side, public opinion, which means votes, works from the people to congressmen, while awareness of world conditions works from outside upon the Administration and through it to Congress. The lobbying of special-interest groups and the need for campaign contributions is less significant than the other two forces, but do make the Administration somewhat less pro-defense (because more pro-balanced budget) than Congress.

On the Republican side the influence of special interests is much greater simply because the Republican Party is the party of middle-class and business interests. In fact, the influence of lobbying by special interests is so great that it makes both the Republican Congress and the Republican Administration relatively immune to the need for defense, with the immunity less general in the Administration than in the Congress because the former is compelled, by its position, to pay some attention to world conditions. The Republican congressmen, on the other hand, are relatively immune both to public opinion and the pressure of world conditions, being shielded from the former by the influence of special-interest lobbyists and shielded from the latter by the Administration.

The history of the Eisenhower Administration in defense and strategic matters is largely the story of how its sincere efforts to respond to Big Business demands for balanced budgets and tax reductions were frustrated by the constant challenge of world conditions demanding an intensified defense effort. A significant element in this story is the efforts of the Administration to conceal these frustrations by the manipulation of public opinion by propaganda, especially by propaganda which tried to make it appear much more aggressive against Communism than it actually was. It really reversed Theodore Roosevelt's dictum into "Speak roughly and carry a small stick." The rough speaking was done by Dulles; the small stick was the Republican defense effort; when the smallness of the stick made it necessary to suspend Dulles's bluster briefly, Eisenhower charmed the country, if not the world, with a few words of sweet reasonableness.

The characteristics of the Eisenhower Administration were set immediately after the election. His hurried visit to Korea was little more than a propaganda stunt, required by his campaign promise, and contributed little if anything to the eventual truce in Korea. En route home he had a conference with Dulles, Charles Wilson, General Bradley of JCS, and Admiral Arthur W. Radford (Commander in Chief, Pacific) on the cruiser *Helena* at Wake Island. There, a month before inauguration, he set the pattern of his Administration—fiscal conservatism: "A prodigal outlay of borrowed money on military equipment could in the end, by generating inflation, disastrously weaken the economy and thus defeat the purpose it was meant to serve." Subsequently this point of view was often supported by a favorite quotation of the Radical Right—a quotation attributed to Lenin, although he never said it, that capitalist states could be destroyed by making them spend themselves bankrupt. (The Radical Right had a great love for ambiguous Lenin quotations; another favorite was, "For world communism the road to Paris lies through Peking and Calcutta.")

Another example of the tone of the Eisenhower Administration was given on January 20, 1953. In his inaugural speech the new President announced that he was unleashing Chiang Kai-shek against Red China. Although "unleashing" was not the word used, this was the chief implication of the statement. All the implications were wrong: (*a*) that the Seventh Fleet was patrolling the Formosa Straits to protect Red China against Chiang, (*b*) that Chiang had the strength seriously to threaten China, and (*c*) that the previous situation reflected the "soft" sympathies of Truman's State Department. The validity of the latter's policy in the area was fully supported over the next eight years, as Chinese threats to Formosa again and again required American support to protect Chiang and, eventually in 1955, fear that Chiang might try to recover China by precipitating a general war between China and the United States led the Eisenhower Administration to "re-leash" him, quietly, once again.

This is very much the whole story of Dulles's foreign policy: eventual quiet adoption of the Truman line under cover of loud verbal denunciations of it. The chief real change appeared in a slight reduction in America's defense capabilities, especially in coping with local war by means of conventional weapons, at a time when the Soviet Union's capabilities for waging all types of wars were increasing.

When Eisenhower came to office he found the budget already set by Truman for Fiscal Year 1954 (FY 1954) at $78.6 billion, of which $46.3 billion was military. The latter item was a slight cut from military FY 1953 of over $50 billion. On March 4, 1953, the NSC cut Eisenhower's new FY 1954 budget by $5.1 billion. When the Joint Chiefs (JCS) protested that any cuts would seriously endanger national security, they were ignored. The chief reduction was made in the air force, from $16.8 to $11.7 billion—this at the very time when Dulles was establishing "massive retaliation." The Truman air-force target of 143 wings by 1956 was reduced to 120 wings. An Eisenhower supporter, Admiral Arthur Radford, was made chairman of the reorganized JCS, and the defense changes were given the ambiguous name of the "New Look." The NSC was ordered to prepare a new strategic survey, which ultimately emerged as NSC 162. The pressure they were under may be gathered from the fact that Humphrey and Dodge wanted the FY 1954 defense expenditures cut to $36 billion.

In the meantime, the new JCS, meeting on the secretary of the navy's yacht *Sequoia*, in August, came up with its own suggestions: increased reliance on SAC in retaliatory power, withdrawal of some American forces from overseas positions, increased reliance upon local forces for local defense, with America's contribution restricted to sea and air power; a strengthened reserve pool at home, and improved continental air defense. These views were incorporated in NSC 162 in October 1953, and accepted by the President on October 30th. The chief modification was abandonment of the hope that any significant future war would be fought without nuclear weapons. Shortly afterward, military expenditures were set on a "long-haul" basis at not over $34 billion for FY 1957 and subsequent years. This compares with an average of $43 billion a year over the last four Truman budgets. As a matter of fact, defense spending did decrease fairly steadily, averaging $37.4 billion over the six years 1955–1960. One consequence of this was that there was no general tax increase passed by Congress in the 1950's after January 1951, but this expenditure represented a considerable reduction in real defense expenditures, since the six-year period, covering the Soviet missile challenge, was also a period of rising prices in which money bought less.

The "New Look," like "massive retaliation," was based on a series of erroneous conceptions of which two were paramount: (1) that nuclear weapons were cheaper than conventional weapons and would require less manpower and (2) that strategic weapons could deter all kinds of Communist aggression.

Even on the strategic level nuclear weapons were not cheaper than conventional weapons nor did they use less manpower, and, once they were introduced into tactical levels of combat as well, costs rose astronomically. Really, costs were irrelevant, as long as they were essential, as they indeed were and would continue to be until there was either (1) relaxation between the United States and Russia or (2) one or more substantial new Powers grew up on the land mass of Eurasia.

The costs of modern weapons arose from their intrinsic costs to some extent but also from their rapid rate of obsolescence and the gigantic costs of development. Each of the strategic B-52 bombers cost $8 million, almost ten times the cost of the B-29's of 1945. Bases and costs of skilled manpower rose proportionately, especially when the rise of Soviet retaliatory power made necessary drastic dispersal of SAC bases and a great increase in the constant airborne alert. Moreover, whatever the cost, deliveries of B-52's were slow, only 41 by New Year's 1956, with a production rate of about one a week (with about 25 percent rejected by the air force) after that. This compared with Soviet production of their equivalent planes, the "Bison" and the "Bear" (TU-95) of over five a week in 1956. The display of at least ten "Bisons" in the Red Square "flyover" on May Day 1955 was a considerable shock to the "New Look," but a year later Eisenhower was ready to take it in stride: "It is vital that we get what we believe we need; that does not necessarily mean more than somebody else." Five days later, he introduced a new concept: "Enough is certainly aplenty."

The gradual obsolescence of the manned bomber and the use of nuclear missiles, especially ICBM's, raised the cost of nuclear retaliation. The Minute Man ICBM, of which we needed hundreds, cost over a million dollars each, with tens of millions more for manning and maintenance, while the nuclear submarine with its 16 Polaris missiles ran over $120 million each. Moreover, all these strategic weapons were obsolescent almost as soon as they were operational.

The costs of conventional forces, armed as they must be with nuclear tactical weapons, also soar. The "New Look's" assumption that introduction of the latter types would reduce the need for manpower was quite mistaken. The necessary manpower increases, and, because of a higher degree of training and skill, is more expensive. The introduction of nuclear tactical weapons, which the Russians obtained almost as soon as we did, required that ground forces be widely dispersed and provided with great mobility in small groups (both by air and ground vehicles). This required more men and more money.

The "New Look" curtailment of money was also reflected in men. All services except the air force were cut, so that the total figure for military manpower, at 3.7 million in December 1952, was almost 2.5 million six years later. The army was cut by one-third, from 1,481,000 representing 20 divisions to below a million in 14 divisions. In this way, army expenditures were cut almost in half, from $16,242 million in FY 1953 to $8,702 million in FY 1956. Protests against this by men like Army Chief of Staff General Matthew Ridgway were answered with the bland assertion that these smaller forces had greater fighting power, "a bigger bang for a buck." In 1955, however, when Eisenhower returned from the first, relatively successful, "Summit Conference" with Khrushchev in Geneva, filled with determination to achieve his $33 billion defense-expenditure level in FY 1956 instead of FY 1957 as originally planned, even Dulles and Wilson objected. One reason for the objection was that price inflation of several percent a year had already reduced the amount of defensive strength being obtained without getting within several billions of the budgeting goal.

This dispute over the primacy of fiscal or defense considerations reached a turning point in 1955-1956 in a series of controversies and minor shifts of position by the Administration. These shifts of position were concessions to aroused public opinion and were not a consequence of any real change of ideas within the Administration, as can be seen from the fact that other budget-cutting drives occurred in 1957 and, to a lesser extent, in 1959, both in the face of growing evidence of Soviet capabilities, growing evidence of Soviet unfriendly intentions, increasingly irritated relationships with our European allies, a steady attrition of support from the Administration to the opposition, and an increasingly restive American public opinion.

The Administration's new strategy found relatively little support in military circles except in the air force and in Admiral Radford, who had been made chairman of JCS, in succession to General Bradley, in August 1953, chiefly because he was an Asia First supporter. General Ridgway opposed the Administration's military policies, from his position as army chief of staff, by his testimony before congressional committees. After his retirement in June 1955, he declared in his memoirs that the military budget "was not based so much on military requirements, or on what the economy of the country could stand, as on political considerations."

Six months later, Trevor Gardner resigned as civilian head of Research and Development for the air force with blasts at Secretary Wilson for hampering research on guided missiles and for general obstructionism, even in strategic retaliation, with the single exception of the B-47 medium-range jet bomber (whose use was completely dependent on air bases in allied countries). Gardner's colleague, the well-known scientist and Assistant Secretary of Defense for Research and Development Dr. Clifford C. Furnas also resigned in disgust in February 1957. He was followed by others, notably by General Gavin in 1958.

Most of these later protests arose from Secretary Wilson's opposition to the development of missile weapons and will be mentioned later, but the obstructionism was fairly general. In 1951, as a consequence of Korea, the army demanded tactical airlift equipment for at least two divisions and strategic airlift for one division. More than five years later, Secretary Wilson stated that airlift capacity was adequate when there was still none for even a single division. When his military adviser tried to point out the underrating of our ground forces in view of our obligations to NATO, the secretary replied that we had no commitment to NATO. In November 1954, three years before "Sputnik," a journalist asked Wilson for comment on the possibility that the Russians might beat the United States in the satellite race; the secretary replied, "I wouldn't care if they did." Two years later, in 1956, Furnas made the same warning, and received the secretary's reply, "So what?" The culmination of all this was Wilson's orders of November and December 1956, which crippled the army's ability to use contemporary tactics by restricting it to missiles of less than 200 miles' range, and forbidding it to use planes of over five thousand pounds or helicopters of over ten thousand pounds' weight. As one chief staff said of Wilson, "He was the most uninformed man, and the most determined to remain so, that has ever been secretary."

Unfortunately, President Eisenhower, who prided himself on ceasing to be a military man when he became a politician, invariably supported Wilson even in his most mistaken decisions.

The Rise of Khrushchev, 1953-1958

The United States was saved from the consequences of this shortsighted and ignorant policy by two factors: (a) the Soviet Union had no intention of risking any direct clash with the United States, and (b) the Soviet Union during most of this period was in the midst of an intense internal struggle which made it impossible for it to follow any course of sustained aggression.

At the end of the war, Stalin's rule in Russia was as firmly established as it had ever been. He was head of the government as well as leader of the Communist Party, with the army completely subordinate to his will. The army played only a small role in the domestic politics of the country, but Stalin had shown his power over it in the Great Purge of 1937 when he had destroyed at least 5,000 of its officers on falsified charges of disloyalty. The survivors were under close scrutiny both from secret police units established, for security reasons, throughout its organization and from the party commissars attached to its major units. The secret police, under the Ministry of State Security, was a state within a state, with its own armed forces, including armored divisions and completely autonomous air units. It controlled millions of prisoners and slave laborers, large industrial enterprises, and wide territories (chiefly in northern Asia). Stalin was exempt from the authority of these secret police and, at the same time, had his own secret police powers within the party organization, because the party statutes of 1934 (prepared by Lazar Kaganovich) had given him an independent police apparatus for use within the party; this was controlled from his personal secretariat under Lieutenant General A. N. Poskrebyshev.

The party, like the police, had units (originally called "cells") in almost every industrial enterprise, in many collective farms, in residential neighborhoods, and rose thence, in a hierarchy of cities, regions, provinces, and nations, parallel to the governmental system.

Stalin nullified possible opposition by encouraging division and rivalry not only among the diverse hierarchies of power radiating downward from his own position in government, in party, army, police, and economic life, but also within each hierarchy, by encouraging the ambitious to seek to rise, step by step, through vacancies created by his periodic purges. These purges not only opened the way upward for younger and more ruthless men, but served as justifications for Stalin's growing paranoia.

Within the party the purges of 1924-1929 had eliminated, usually by death, most of the "Old Bolsheviks" (those who had been party members before the 1917 Revolution). In 1929-1934, using a new and younger group, Stalin had killed 10,000,000 Russians (his own estimate) in the drive to establish collective farms. The second great purge of 1934-1939 had killed off a large part of the Stalinists who had assisted Stalin's rise to power and about 5,000 officers of the armed forces. The third great purge, which was shaping up at the end of 1952, was intended to eliminate the rest of the Stalinists who had come to positions of power, in succession to the Old Bolsheviks, in 1929-1935. They were already a dwindling group, from Stalin's insatiable thirst for blood, as can be seen by examining the fate of the members of the Seventeenth Party Congress of 1934, the congress which first raised Khrushchev and Lavrenti Beria to the Central Committee. Of the 1,966 delegates to that Seventeenth Congress, 1,108 were arrested for "antirevolutionary crimes" in sequel to the assassination of S. M. Kirov (party leader in Leningrad), which Stalin himself had arranged in December 1934. Of the 139 members and alternates elected to the Central Committee by that congress of 1934, 98 (or 70 percent) were arrested and shot. Among the survivors were Kaganovich, Vyacheslav Molotov, Georgi Malenkov, Beria, Anastas Mikoyan, K. Voroshilov, and Khrushchev. The new purge of 1953 was apparently aimed at some or most of these survivors.

This terror was made worse by the fact that it did not originate only from Stalin, although it undoubtedly required his acquiescence to proceed very far. Such acquiescence could often be obtained by his top subordinates, for the autocrat undoubtedly appreciated those who were prepared to demonstrate their complete ruthlessness in his service. At the end of the war, Khrushchev, although not yet near the top of the pile, had shown more bloodthirsty ruthlessness combined with more groveling obsequiousness to Stalin than anyone else in Russia.

At the war's end the top trio in the gang were Stalin, Malenkov, and Andrei Zhdanov. The last pair hated each other. Malenkov in 1945–1946 was the most active figure in the government, especially as chairman of the Committee for the Rehabilitation of Liberated Areas, and chairman of the committee in charge of dismantling German industry for reparations. Large-scale bungling in the administration of reparations gave Zhdanov the opportunity he wished. Through Mikoyan, he instigated an attack on Malenkov's handling of reparations, and recommended that dismantling be replaced by the setting up of Soviet-owned corporations to take over German industry in Germany to make goods for the Soviet Union. As a consequence of this failure, Malenkov (with his associates) was demoted from several of his posts for about a year (June 1947–June 1948). Immediately after his rehabilitation, Zhdanov died mysteriously, and his chief supporters were arrested and shot (the so-called "Leningrad Case").

In the meantime, Khrushchev was deeply involved in the effort to restore the collective farms, which had suffered great attrition during the war, and the more difficult task of bringing them under party control. In view of the ruthless way in which the collective farms had been established in 1928–1934, it was not surprising that neither the farms nor the party were popular with the peasants. Both were quietly sabotaged in ways which could neither be observed nor prevented, especially as party members and the secret police were both rare in rural districts. Evidence for such sabotage could be seen in the constant failure of the agricultural section of the economy to fulfill quotas or expectations, in the fact that the peasants produced four times as much (in yield per unit areas) on their small personal plots of ground as they did on the wide acreage of the collective farms, and in the fact that farm animals in 1953 were well below the figures for 1928 (while cows were 13 percent fewer than in 1916), despite a population increase of 25 percent from 1928 to 1953. Moreover, in the confusion of the war, at least 15 million acres of land belonging to the collective farms had been diverted to peasants' private plots, while millions of peasants on the collective farms were living in inefficient semi-idleness.

Early in 1950 Khrushchev returned from twelve years of party butchery in the Ukraine and took over the agricultural problem. His solution, totally unworkable, was to move more vigorously in the Stalinist direction of increased centralization. He wished to merge the collective farms into increasingly large units and to work the peasants in increasingly large "work brigades," in order to bring them under the control of the few Communist Party members to be found in the countryside. A party cell required three members as a minimum, and in 1950 a substantial fraction of the existing collective farms had no party cells at all, while the majority had cells of less than six members each.

In two years, by merging collective farms, Khrushchev reduced the total number of such units from 252,000 to 94,800, but 18,000 still had no party cells, while only 5,000 had cells with over 25 members. Khrushchev wanted to carry the process of concentration even further by destroying the existing villages and centralizing the peasants in large urban settlements (so-called "agro-towns"). In such towns they would be remote from their small private plots, would not spend so much time on them, and would be escorted in large gangs out to work each day on the collective fields. This fantastic scheme was blocked by Beria and Molotov in 1951.

Another scheme, which may have been associated with Khrushchev, was vetoed by Stalin in 1952. This would have distributed the personnel and machinery of the rural Machine Tractor Stations (MTS) among the collective farms, thus, at one strike, increasing the locally available party members from their personnel to build up rural party cells and making available, at short notice, necessary farm machinery. This suggestion was blocked by Stalin as a step backward from Socialism. In its place, he suggested that the peasant's incentive to work on his private plot to produce for sale in the private market be destroyed at one blow by forbidding the peasant access to any market, or even to money, by forcing him to dispose of all his surplus produce, on a barter basis, to the state.

On the whole, Khrushchev's achievements as agricultural leader were far from successful, but this did not injure his reputation with Stalin, who recognized his personal devotion and energy and saw that his efforts were directed toward increasing party control in the countryside rather than the desirable, but clearly less important, goal of increased production. As a mark of this favor, at the Nineteenth Party Congress in October 1952, Khrushchev presented the report on the new party rules and saw one of his supporters, A. B. Aristov, take over charge of all personnel appointments in the wide-spaced party network. Both of these developments were at the expense of Malenkov, the nominal head for party matters, but the latter was more than compensated by the privilege of taking Stalin's place as the chief party speaker (in an eight-hour speech) at the congress.

As this congress of October 1952 assembled and dispersed, Stalin was already laying the groundwork for his third great purge of the party. No one, except perhaps Beria, could guess who was a target for elimination, but the rumors and hints from Stalin's personal secretariat made it appear that every one of the Old Guard of Stalinists should fear the worst. From October 1952 onward, these chief associates of Stalin lived in mounting terror. Like gangsters of the Capone era, they did not dare go to their homes at night, ventured nowhere without personal bodyguards, and carried weapons on their persons. Beria remained dominant until November 1952, because Moscow was garrisoned by secret police divisions, the Kremlin guard was entirely in his control, and no one else was allowed to bring weapons into that enclave.

Stalin moved with his customary skill, steadily dispersing and diluting the authority of the Old Guard: the number of ministries was increased, the Politburo ceased to meet, its ten members were dissolved into a large Presidium of thirty-six, and the Old Guard were shifted from operating ministries to posts without portfolios: Molotov from Foreign Affairs, Kaganovich from Heavy Industry, Nikolai Bulganin from Defense, Mikoyan from Trade. The last of these shifts, in November 1952, was the replacement of Beria as minister of state security by S. D. Ignatiev. By that time, Poskrebyshev and his assistant, Mikhail Ryumin, were already preparing the frame-up of Beria. This was the so-called "doctor's plot," a fabrication which pretended that Zhdanov and other leaders had been poisoned by a group of Kremlin doctors, mostly Jewish, who were, with Beria's knowledge, about to carry out a similar elimination of other leaders, including high military officers. Under torture so severe that two of the nine doctors died, the rest gave confessions.

At this point, just when the purge was to begin, Stalin died, possibly from a series of strokes, on March 5, 1953. Within six hours, the physician in charge of Stalin's last few days; Stalin's son, Vasily, who commanded the air force of the Moscow Military District; Poskrebyshev; and the commanders of the Kremlin, the city, and the local military district all disappeared. Beria was recalled from semi-exile to lead the merged ministries of Interior and State Security, and the administrative changes since October 1952 were undone: the large Presidium was replaced by the previous smaller Politburo of ten men; the number of ministers was reduced from 55 to 25; and the inner Cabinet was cut from fourteen to five. Most significantly, the Old Guard, which Stalin had been slowly moving away from the levers of power, were, at his death, quickly moved back to the center. Malenkov was made secretary of the party and premier of the government with five deputy premiers: Beria, Molotov, Bulganin, Kaganovich, and Mikoyan. Each of these was restored to his previous ministry, while Voroshilov became chairman of the Presidium of the Supreme Soviet. Marshal Zhukov was recalled from rural exile to be first deputy to Bulganin in the Defense Ministry, and Khrushchev, with no major post, was made chairman of Stalin's funeral obsequies. Under his care, the deceased autocrat's body was placed, with the reverence becoming a demigod, alongside that of Lenin, in the shrine overlooking Red Square. Then, "at Premier Malenkov's request," Khrushchev took over one of his two posts, that of secretary of the party. It was a fateful change.

During Stalin's rule, the autocrat had held both chief positions, in the state and in the party. Now, a week after the despot's death, the universal distaste for any revival of his power compelled Malenkov to yield up one of the positions to Khrushchev. We do not know why he decided to keep the premiership and give up the secretaryship of the party. Indeed, we do not know if he had any choice, but it may have seemed from the evidence of Stalin's later years that the premiership was a more significant post than the secretary's. It was not; certainly it was not in the hands of a tactician such as Khrushchev. During the next five years, in a struggle for power whose details are still concealed, Khrushchev rose from the secretary's post to be supreme autocrat, eliminating in the process all other possible claimants to power. The process by which he succeeded Stalin was almost a repetition of that by which Stalin had succeeded Lenin. In each case, the ultimately successful contender was the least prominent of a group of contenders; in each case this victor used the post of secretary of the party as the chief weapon in his upward rise; in each case, this rise was achieved by a series of chess moves in which the most powerful rival contenders were eliminated, one by one, in a series of shifts, beginning with the most dangerous (in one case Trotsky, in the later case Beria). And in both, this whole process was done under a pretense of "collective leadership."

Immediately after Stalin's death, the "collective leadership" was headed by a triumvirate of Malenkov, Beria, and Molotov. Malenkov supported a policy of relaxation, with increased emphasis on production of consumers' goods and rising standards of living, as well as increased efforts to avoid any international crisis which might lead to war; Beria supported a "thaw" in internal matters, with large-scale amnesties for political prisoners as well as rehabilitation of those already liquidated, at home and in the satellite states; Molotov continued to insist on the "hard" policies associated with Stalin, full emphasis on heavy industry, no relaxation of the domestic tyranny, and continued pressure in the Cold War with the West.

Wild rumors, especially among the satellites, and some relaxation, at Beria's behest, in East Germany gave rise to false hopes among the workers there. On June 16, 1953, these workers rose up against the Communist government in East Berlin. After a day of hesitation, these uprisings were crushed with the full power of the Soviet occupation armored divisions. Using this event as an excuse, the leaders in the Kremlin suddenly arrested Beria and shot him with six of his aides (either immediately or in December, depending on the version of these events).

The overthrow of the master of terror was supported by the regular army, whose chief leaders were present in the next room, armed with smuggled machine guns, when the showdown between Beria and his colleagues occurred in the Kremlin conference room. Beria apparently suspected nothing, and set down his briefcase, in which he had a pistol hidden. During the conference, while one leader distracted his attention another removed the pistol from the briefcase. Beria was then told he was under arrest. He dived for his briefcase, found his pistol gone, and looked up into the muzzle of his own gun. He was at once turned over to the army officers in the next room. These had already moved four divisions of their forces into Moscow to replace the usual secret police forces guarding the city. This use of the army to settle the personal struggle in the Kremlin is the chief factor which was different in Khrushchev's rise to power from the earlier rise to power of Stalin in 1924–1929. There can be little doubt that the introduction of this new factor was due to Khrushchev and that his secret speech denouncing Stalin in February 1956 was part of his payoff to the armed forces for their role in the process.

The overthrow of Beria was followed by an extensive curtailment of the secret police and its powers. Most of the latter went to the Interior Ministry, while its forces were subjected to separate control, and its system of secret courts was abolished. Many of its prisoners were released, and there was considerable relaxation of the censorship, especially in literature. Some of the powers of the police were taken over by the party.

In February 1954, a large conference of agricultural leaders in Moscow was thunderstruck by a suggestion from Khrushchev for a radical new approach to the chronic agricultural shortages. This "virgin-lands" scheme advocated opening for cultivation in Asia large areas of grassland which had never been cultivated before. Khrushchev's plan was detailed and dazzlingly attractive. It entailed use of over 100,000 tractors and great hordes of manpower to cultivate grain on 6 million new acres in 1954 and an additional 25 million acres in 1955. The scheme, carried out in an atmosphere of heated discussion, was not supervised by Khrushchev. Its requirements in machinery and equipment were so great that it represented a sharp restriction on Malenkov's shift of emphasis from heavy industry to consumer goods, while Khrushchev's refusal to supervise it placed the responsibility for its success at Malenkov's door. At the same time, Malenkov's public advocacy of a "thaw" in Soviet-American relations was equally weakened by the secret Soviet drive to perfect the H-bomb.

While the undermining of Malenkov was thus in process in 1954, Khrushchev began to undermine Molotov in the foreign field by organizing a series of spectacular foreign visits without the foreign secretary. One of the first of these, in September 1954, took Bulganin, Khrushchev, Mikoyan, and others to Peking to celebrate the fifth birthday of Red China. During the visit Khrushchev apparently made a personal alliance with Mao Tse-tung as well as a complicated commercial treaty which offered Soviet finance, equipment, and specialized skills for an all-out industrialization of China (the so-called "great leap forward").

These events made it possible for Khrushchev to organize a campaign against Malenkov during the winter of 1954-1955. Ostensibly this was based on Malenkov's desire to relax the intense emphasis on heavy industrialization, but, in fact, Malenkov's lack of aggressiveness in foreign policy was equally significant. In combination the two issues created pressure which Malenkov could not resist. On February 8, 1955, his resignation was read to the Supreme Soviet. He assumed responsibility for the unsatisfactory state of Soviet agriculture, and relinquished the post of premier, although remaining on in the Central Committee in the new post of minister of power stations. The new premier was Bulganin, who released his previous post of defense minister to his deputy, Marshal Zhukov, hero of World War II.

These struggles within the Kremlin are based on persons, not on issues, since the latter are used chiefly as weapons in the struggle. In the shift from Malenkov to Bulganin, the critical issues were the chronic agricultural problem and the choice between Stalin's policy of relentless industrialization, regardless of the cost to peasants and workers, and a new policy of increased consumers' goods. In this last issue the needs of defense brought Khrushchev support from Marshal Zhukov, the armed forces, and the "Stalinists," such as Molotov and Kaganovich. Zhukov was rewarded with a ministry and a seat in the Presidium, the only army officer ever to have the latter.

The gradual elimination of Molotov found Khrushchev on the opposite side of the Stalinist versus anti-Stalinist debate, as champion of a "thaw" in the Cold War. This involved a rejection of Stalin's doctrine of the inevitable enmity of nonsatellite countries and the inevitable onset of imperialist war from capitalist aggression. In this struggle Khrushchev found support in Bulganin, Mikoyan, and probably Zhukov. The new policy was established while Molotov was still foreign minister through a series of elaborate state visits by Bulganin and Khrushchev ("B and K," as they were called) to foreign countries. The most significant of these visits, because it marked a sharp reversal both of Stalin and of Molotov, was a six-day visit to Tito in Yugoslavia in May 1955. This acceptance of Titoism is of great importance because it showed Russia in an apologetic role for a major past error and because it reversed Stalin's rule that all Communist parties everywhere must follow the Kremlin's leadership.

The "Belgrade Declaration" admitted that different countries could "walk different roads to Socialism" and that such "differences in the concrete application of Socialism are the exclusive concern of individual countries." Khrushchev and Tito both knew that this statement was playing with fire. The former's motives are obscure; it was probably done simply as a challenge to Molotov's whole past record; Tito unquestionably hoped the dynamite would explode sufficiently to blow the East European satellites out of Soviet control. With his customary shrewdness Khrushchev did not sign the Belgrade Declaration himself, but had Bulganin, the new premier, do it, thus protecting himself from direct responsibility if anything went wrong.

This declaration was not the only stick of dynamite which Khrushchev was juggling as he returned from Yugoslavia. En route home he stopped off in Bucharest and Sofia. In the latter capital he placed the fuse in another, even larger, stick of dynamite, by a secret denunciation of Stalin personally as a bloodthirsty tyrant.

Back in Moscow in early July, Molotov made an uncompromising attack on the Belgrade Declaration, denouncing it as encouragement to the satellites to pursue independent policies, a consequence which all agreed would be totally unacceptable to anyone in the Kremlin, but Khrushchev won over the majority by arguing that the loyalty of the satellites, and especially their vital economic cooperation, could be ensured better by a loose leash than by a club. He scorned Molotov's opposition to an agreement with Tito by contrasting it with Molotov's agreement of August 1939 with Ribbentrop. The solidity of the satellites was to be preserved by the Warsaw Pact of May 14, 1955, which established a twenty-year alliance of the Soviet Union, Albania, Bulgaria, Czechoslovakia, Hungary, Poland, Romania, and East Germany. This was the Communist riposte to NATO, which the newly sovereign West German state had joined, as a fifteenth member, five days earlier (May 9, 1955).

Straight from his arguments with Molotov in the Central Committee,

Khrushchev dashed off with Bulganin, Molotov, and Zhukov to the 1955 "Summit Meeting" in Geneva. There he kept quietly in the background, while his companions discussed the fate of Germany with President Eisenhower, Dulles, Eden, and Premier Faure of France.

The 1955 Summit Conference at Geneva on July 18-24 was Anthony Eden's contribution to the "thaw." Dulles participated most reluctantly, but there had been increasingly unfavorable comment on his inflexible attitude toward the Russians, and he felt compelled to yield to Eden's insistence in order to help Eden's Conservative Party in the British General Elections of May, 1955. Once these were successfully passed, the meeting had to be carried out, but Dulles had no hopes of its success. He contributed little in this direction himself when he insisted that disarmament must be discussed before German reunion. Outsiders, trying to interpret the Russian attitude toward the "thaw" on the basis of no reliable information, placed much greater hopes in the Summit Meeting than Dulles did, chiefly because of the surprising Soviet shift which had produced the Austrian Peace Treaty of May 15, 1955, with its subsequent evacuation of Austria by Russian troops. The Austrian treaty restored the country's frontiers of January 1938 and promised free navigation of the Danube, while prohibiting any union with Germany and binding Austria to neutrality.

The neutralization of Austria gave rise, in 1955, to a good deal of vague talk about "disengagement" in Europe. The idea, however defined, had considerable attraction in Europe, even for experienced diplomats like Eden. Nothing very definite could be agreed upon as making up "disengagement," but everyone was eager for anything which would reduce the threat of war, and the Germans especially had longing thoughts of a neutralized and united country. France, which was deeply involved at the time in Indochina and in the Muslim countries, particularly Algeria, was eager for any relaxation in Europe which would allow a breathing spell to devote to its colonial problems. To help the discussion along, the Russians spoke favorably about disarmament, Europe for the Europeans, and German reunion. When details of these suggestions appeared, however, they usually justified completely Dulles's skepticism. Disarmament, for example, meant to the Russians total renunciation of nuclear weapons and drastic cuts in ground forces, a combination which would make the United States very weak against Russia while leaving Russia still dominant in Europe. Sometimes this result was sought more directly: withdrawal of both the United States and the Soviet Union from Europe, the former to North America, thousands of miles away, and the latter merely to the Russian frontiers. Another Russian suggestion was to replace NATO with a European security pact which would include only European states.

The Soviet suggestions for Germany were equally tricky and show clearly their fear to subject their East German satellite to a popular election and their real reluctance to see Germany united. They demanded unification first and elections later, while the United States reversed the order. The merging of the two existing German governments, followed by a peace treaty along the lines of the Austrian treaty, would have given the Russians what they wanted in Europe, a Germany freed from Western troops ruled by a coalition government, which would allow elections when it judged best.

The Americans wanted elections first to establish an acceptable central German government with which a final peace could be made. The creation of two sovereign German states in 1954 made any settlement remote because the Kremlin insisted that its East German satellite regime, which was not recognized by the United States, must be a party to any settlement and thus be recognized by the United States. This same point became a permanent obstacle also to any agreement to unify Berlin, since the United States was willing to negotiate with Russia but not with East Germany. Eden's own contribution to these discussions was that a demilitarized zone be established along the line of physical contact between East and West in Europe with international inspection of armed forces in Germany.

Suddenly, on the fourth day of the conference, President Eisenhower made a speech which jolted the delegates, and even more the world, out of their casual attention. This was his "open-skies" plan, which never came to anything but which gave the United States a propaganda advantage the Soviet Union could not overcome. It had two parts: the two super-Powers "to give to each other a complete blueprint of our military establishments, from beginning to end, from one end of our countries to the other"; and "Next, to provide within our countries facilities for aerial photography to the other country." Nothing could be more repugnant to the ingrained Soviet love of secrecy except full inspection of the country on the ground, but nothing could more clearly show the world that the United States was as frank and honest as its President's own face: neither had anything to hide.

Nothing significant was achieved at the Geneva Conference, but the discussions were conducted in an unprecedented atmosphere of friendly cooperation which came to be known as the "Geneva spirit," and continued for several years. In fact, it was never completely overcome even when matters were at their worst in the weeks following the U-2 incident of May 1960 and the Cuban crisis of October 1962. This was because the Soviet Union, having emerged from the isolation imposed on it by Stalin's mania, never returned to it completely but continued to cooperate with non-Communist countries in scientific interchange, athletic events, and social intercourse. From 1955 onward, speakers of Russian and of English were in cooperation somewhere on some project. The most amazing of these projects was the International Geophysical Year of 1957–1958, in which scientists of sixty-six countries cooperated over eighteen months to wring from the physical universe of earth, sea, and sun some of its secrets.

Returned to Moscow from Geneva, Khrushchev abandoned his unwonted quiet and resumed his stalking of Molotov. In September 1955, the harassed foreign minister had to make a public confession of error, admitting that he did not know what point the Soviet Union had reached in its progress along the road to Socialism. In February he had told the Supreme Soviet that the foundations of the Socialist society had been built. It now appeared that the society itself was built. Such a mistake, regarded as picayune in the outside world, could inflict almost irreparable damage on a Soviet leader if publicly confessed, as this was. It was a clear indication to other such leaders that Molotov was on the way out.

During all this, Khrushchev had held no office in the Soviet government, and had functioned only as party leader, but what he did in that capacity was of vital significance. Systematically he replaced party functionaries on all levels, moving upward those he could depend on and eliminating those he could not trust to support him personally. The other rival leaders in the government knew what was going on, but ignored it, since they made the one basic error which could not be remedied: they believed that the government was the ruling structure in the Soviet Union, while Khrushchev, quietly at his work within the party structure, looked forward to the day on which he would demonstrate their error.

In February 1956, in what is unquestionably one of the most significant events in the history of Communism, Khrushchev lighted one of his sticks of dynamite. The subsequent explosion is still echoing, and the resulting wound to international Communism still bleeds freely.

Khrushchev's preparation for a Party congress was as careful as Stalin's had ever been: it was to be a sounding board for coordinating party policy by speeches to his hand-picked subordinates. In July 1955 the congress was called for February 14, 1956. At the same time, two Khrushchev agents were added to the Presidium, Mikhail Suslov and Igor Kirichenko, and three Khrushchev agents were added to the party secretariat: Averky Aristov, Ivan Belyaev, and Dmitri Shepilov. The last, who was editor of *Pravda*, the party newspaper, gave the speech on foreign policy at the congress, although Molotov was still foreign minister and was not replaced by Shepilov until August. Aristov soon took over the role Poskrebyshev had previously played for Stalin, in charge of loyalty purges within the party.

The Twentieth Party Congress met for eleven days, February 14–25, 1956, within the Kremlin walls. Its 1,436 hand-picked delegates formed the oldest congress which had ever assembled, with 24 percent over fifty years of age, compared to 15.3 percent over fifty at the Nineteenth Congress, and only 1.8 percent over fifty at the Eighteenth Congress of February 1941. These men were fully prepared to support whatever was told them, but none could have anticipated the shocking revelations they would hear.

It all began in a rather routine fashion. The first speech, of 50,000 words, delivered by Khrushchev over seven hours (one hour less than Malenkov's parallel speech in October 1952), was full of factual details. It was notable only for its frequent reference to the urgent need for co-existence with the West and its infrequent use of the name "Stalin." The emphasis on co-existence was part of the campaign against Molotov, and, as is usual in Communist speeches, was filled with references, by volume and page, to the writings of Lenin. Most of these references proved, on examination, to be embedded in a context expounding the inevitable clash between Communism and Capitalism. The delegates, fully trained in such dialectic, had no difficulty in seeing the point: co-existence was merely a temporary tactic in the larger framework of inevitable struggle. Similar references were made to the possibility of peaceful, rather than revolutionary, change from capitalism to Socialism in single countries. In this case, examples were given: the Baltic States, the East European satellites, and China! The reference to Lenin (Volume XXXIII, pages 57–58) made perfectly clear that the "peaceful road to "Socialism" could be followed only where a small capitalist state was overrun by a powerful Communist neighbor.

The chief surprise of the general sessions of the party congress was the speech from that old party chameleon, Anastas Mikoyan. It openly criticized Stalin for his disregard of party democracy and his "cult of personality" which insisted on personal adulation and on the constant rewriting of party records and Russian history so that Stalin would always appear as the infallible and clairvoyant leader.

The real explosion came at a secret all-night session on July 24–25 from which all foreign delegates were excluded; those who listened were warned to take no notes or records. In a speech of 30,000 words Khrushchev made a horrifying attack on Stalin as a bloodthirsty and demented tyrant who had destroyed tens of thousands of loyal party members on falsified evidence, or no evidence at all, merely to satisfy his own insatiable thirst for power. All the charges which had been made by anti-Communists and anti-Stalinists in the 1930's were repeated and driven home with specific details, dates, and names. The full nightmare of the Soviet system was revealed, not as an attribute of the system (which it was), but as a personal idiosyncrasy of Stalin himself; not as the chief feature of Communism from 1917 (which it was), but only as its chief feature since 1934; and nothing was said of the full collaboration in the process of terror provided to Stalin by the surviving members of the Politburo led by Khrushchev himself.

But all the rest, which the fellow travelers throughout the world had been denying for a generation, poured out: the enormous slave-labor camps, the murder of innocent persons by tens of thousands, the wholesale violation of law, the use of fiendishly planned torture to exact confessions for acts never done or to involve persons who were completely innocent, the ruthless elimination of whole classes and of whole nations (such as the army officers, the kulaks, and the Kalmuck, Chechen, Ingush, and Balkar minority groups). The servility of writers, artists, and everyone else, including all party members, to the tyrant was revealed, along with the total failure of his agricultural schemes, his cowardice and incompetence in the war, his insignificance in the early history of the party, and his constant rewriting of history to conceal these things.

A few passages from this speech will indicate its tone:

"Stalin's negative characteristics, which in Lenin's time, were only beginning, changed in his last years in a grave abuse of power which caused untold harm to the Party. . . . Stalin acted not through persuasion, explanation, and patient cooperation with people, but by imposing his ideas and by demanding complete submission to his opinion. Whoever opposed this or tried to argue his own point of view was doomed to be purged and to subsequent moral and physical annihilation. . . . Stalin originated the concept 'enemy of the people,' a term which made it unnecessary to prove the ideological errors of the victim; it made it possible to use the cruelest repression and utmost illegality against anyone who disagreed in any way with Stalin, against those who were only suspected or had been subjects of rumors. This concept 'enemy of the people' eliminated any possibility of ideological fight or of rebuttal. Usually the only evidence used, against all the rules of modern legal science, was the confession of the accused, and, as subsequent investigation showed, such 'confessions' were obtained by physical pressure on the accused. . . . The formula 'enemy of the people' was specifically introduced for the purpose of physically annihilating these persons. . . . He abandoned the method of ideological struggle for administrative violence, mass repressions, and terror. . . . Lenin used such methods only against actual class enemies and not against those who blunder or err and whom it is possible to lead through theory and even retain as leaders. . . . Stalin so elevated himself above the party and above the state that he ceased to consider either the Central Committee or the party. . . . The number of arrests based on charges of counterrevolutionary crimes increased tenfold from 1936 to 1937. . . . When the cases of some of these so-called 'spies' and 'saboteurs' were examined, it was found that all their cases were fabricated. Confessions of guilt of many were gained by cruel and inhuman tortures. . . . Comrade Rudzutak, candidate member of the Politburo, party member from 1905, who spent ten years in a czarist hard-labor camp, completely retracted in court the confession which had been forced from him. . . . This retraction was ignored, in spite of the fact that Rudzutak had been chief of the party Central Control Commission established by Lenin to ensure party unity. . . . He was not even called before the Central Committee's Politburo because Stalin refused to talk to him. Sentence was pronounced in a trial of twenty minutes, and he was shot. After careful reexamination of the case in 1955, it was established that the accusation against Rudzutak was false and based on falsified evidence. . . . The way in which the NKVD manufactured fictitious 'anti-Soviet centers and blocs' can be seen in the case of Comrade Rozenblum, party member from 1906, who was arrested in 1937 by the Leningrad NKVD. . . . He was subjected to terrible torture during which he was ordered to confess false information about himself and other persons. He was then brought to the office of Zakovsky, who offered him freedom on condition that he make before the court a false confession fabricated in 1937 by the NKVD concerning 'sabotage, espionage, and subversion in a terroristic center in Leningrad.' With unbelievable cynicism, Zakovsky told about the method for the creation of fabricated, 'anti-Soviet plots.' . . . 'You yourself,' said Zakovsky, 'will not need to invent anything. The NKVD will prepare for you an outline for every branch of the center; you will have to study it carefully and to remember well all questions and answers which the court may ask. . . . Your future will depend on how the trial goes and on its results. If you manage to endure it, you will save your head, and we will feed and clothe you at the government's expense until your death.' . . . The NKVD prepared lists of persons whose cases were before the Military Tribunal and whose sentences were prepared in advance. Yezhov would send these lists to Stalin personally for his approval of the punishments. In 1937–1938 such lists of many thousands of party, government, Communist Youth, army, and economic workers were sent to Stalin. He approved those lists. . . . Stalin was a very distrustful man, morbidly suspicious; we knew this from our work with him. He would look at a man and say, 'Why are your eyes so shifty today?' or, 'Why are you turning so much today and why do you avoid looking at me directly?' This sickly suspicion created in him distrust of eminent party workers he had known for years. Everywhere and in everything he saw 'enemies,' 'two-facers,' and 'spies.' . . . How is it possible that a person confesses to crimes which he has not committed? Only in one way—by application of physical pressure, tortures, bringing him to a state of unconsciousness, deprivation of his judgment, taking away of his human dignity. In this way were 'confessions' obtained. . . . Only a few days before the present congress we called to the Central Committee Presidium and interrogated

the investigative judge Rodos, who in his time investigated and interrogated Kossior, Chubar, and Kosaryev. He is a vile person, with the
brain of a bird, and morally completely degenerate. And it was this man
who was deciding the fate of prominent party workers. . . . He told us,
'I was told that Kossior and Chubar were people's enemies and for that
reason, I, as investigative judge, had to make them confess that they are
enemies. . . . I thought that I was executing the orders of the party."

The "secret speech" also destroyed Stalin's reputation as a military
genius:

"During the war and afterward, Stalin said that the tragedy experienced
by the nation in the early days of the war resulted from the unexpected
attack by the Germans. But, Comrades, this is completely untrue. . . . By
April 3, 1941, Churchill through his ambassador to the USSR, Cripps,
personally warned Stalin that the Germans were regrouping their armed
units to attack the Soviet Union. . . . Churchill stressed this repeatedly
in his dispatches of April 18 and in the following days. Stalin took no
heed of these warnings. Moreover, he warned that no credence be given
to information of this sort in order not to provoke the beginning of
military operations. Information of this kind on German invasion of
Soviet territory was coming in from our own military and diplomatic
sources. . . . Despite these particularly grave warnings, the necessary
steps were not taken to prepare the country properly for defense and
to prevent it from being caught unawares. Did we have time and resources for such preparation? Yes, we did. Our industry was fully capable of supplying everything the Soviet Army needed. . . . Had our industry been mobilized properly and in time to supply the Army, our
wartime losses would have been decidedly smaller. . . . On the eve of the
invasion, a German citizen crossed our border and stated that the German armies had orders to start their offensive on the night of June 22 at
3:00 A.M. Stalin was informed of this immediately, but even this was
ignored. As you see, everything was ignored. . . . The result was that in
the first hours and days the enemy destroyed in our border regions a
large part of our air force, artillery, and other equipment; he annihilated
large numbers of our soldiers and disorganized our military leadership;
consequently we could not prevent the enemy from marching deep into
the country. Very grievous consequences, especially at the beginning of
the war, followed Stalin's destruction of many military commanders and
political workers during 1937–1941, because of his suspiciousness and
false accusations. . . . During that time the leaders who had gained military
experience in Spain and in the Far East were almost completely liquidated. . . . After the first severe disaster and defeats at the front, Stalin
thought that this was the end. He said, 'All that which Lenin created

we have lost forever.' After this, Stalin for a long time actually did not direct the military operations and ceased to do anything whatever. . . . Therefore, the danger which hung over our Fatherland in the first period of the war was largely due to the faulty methods of directing the nation and the party by Stalin himself. Later the nervousness and hysteria which Stalin showed, interfering with actual military operations, caused our army serious damage. He was very far from any understanding of the real situation which was developing on the front. This was natural, for, in the whole war, he never visited any section of the front or any liberated city. . . . When a very serious situation developed for our army in the Kharkov region in 1942, we decided to give up an operation seeking to encircle Kharkov to avoid fatal consequences if the operation continued. . . . Contrary to sense, Stalin rejected our suggestion and issued orders to continue the operation. . . . I telephoned to Stalin at his villa, but he refused to answer the phone, and Malenkov was on the receiver. . . . I stated for a second time that I wanted to speak to Stalin personally about the grave situation at the front. But Stalin did not consider it convenient to raise the phone and insisted that I must speak to him through Malenkov, although he was only a few steps away. After listening in this fashion to our plea, Stalin said, 'Let everything remain as it is!' What was the result of this? The worst that we had expected. The Germans surrounded our army concentrations and we lost hundreds of thousands of our soldiers. This is Stalin's military genius and what it cost us. . . . After this party congress we shall have to reevaluate our military operations and present them in their true light. . . . After our great victory which cost us so much, Stalin began to belittle many of the commanders who contributed to the victory, because Stalin excluded every possibility that victories at the front should be credited to anyone but himself. . . . He began to tell all kinds of nonsense about Zhukov. . . . He popularized himself as a great leader and tried to inculcate in the people the idea that all victories won in the war were due to the courage, daring, and genius of Stalin and no one else. . . . Let us take, for instance, our historical and military films and some written works; they make us feel sick. Their real purpose is the propagation of the theme of Stalin as a military genius. Remember the film *The Fall of Berlin*. Here only Stalin acts; he issues orders in a hall in which there are many empty chairs, and only one man approaches him and reports to him—that is Poskrebyshev, his loyal shieldbearer. Where is the military command? Where is the Politburo? Where is the government? What are they doing? There is nothing about them in the film. Stalin acts for everybody; he pays no attention to them; he asks no one for advice. Where are the military who bear the burden of the war? They are not in the film; with Stalin in, there is no room for them. . . . You see to what Stalin's delusions of grandeur led. He had completely lost consciousness of reality. . . . One characteristic example of Stalin's self-glorification and of his lack of elementary modesty was his *Short Biography* published in 1948. It is an expression of most dissolute flattery, making a man into a god, transforming him into an infallible sage, 'the greatest leader and most sublime strategist of all times and nations.' No other words could be found to raise Stalin to the heavens. We need not give examples of the loathsome adulation filling this book. They were all approved and edited by Stalin personally, and some of them were added in his own handwriting to the draft of the book. . . . He added, 'Although he performed his task of leader of the party and the people with consummate skill and enjoyed the unreserved support of the whole Soviet people, Stalin never allowed his work to be marred by the slightest hint of vanity, conceit, or self-adulation.' . . . I'll cite one more insertion made by Stalin: 'The advanced Soviet science of war received further development at Comrade Stalin's hands. He elaborated the theory of the permanently operating factors that decided the issue of wars. . . . Comrade Stalin's genius enabled him to divine the enemy's plans and defeat them. The battles in which Comrade Stalin directed the Soviet armies are brilliant examples of operational military skill.'

"All those who interested themselves even a little in the national situation saw the difficult situation in agriculture, but Stalin never even noticed it. Did we tell Stalin about this? Yes, we told him, but he did not support us. Why? Because Stalin never traveled anywhere, did not meet city or farm workers; he did not know the actual situation in the provinces. He knew the country and agriculture only from films. And these films had dressed up and beautified the existing situation in agriculture. They so pictured collective farm life that the tables were bending from the weight of turkeys and geese. Stalin thought it was actually so. . . . Stalin proposed that the taxes paid by the collective farms and by their workers should be raised by 40 billion rubles; according to him the peasants are well off, and the collective farm worker would need sell only one more chicken to pay his tax in full. Imagine what this meant. Certainly, 40 billion rubles is a sum greater than everything the collective farmers obtained for all the products they sold to the state. In 1952, for instance, the collective farms and their workers received 26,280 million rubles for all their products sold to the government. . . . The proposal was not based on an actual assessment of the situation but on the fantastic ideas of a person divorced from reality."

It was inconceivable that this extraordinary speech could be kept a secret, in spite of all the warnings at its delivery that it must be. Versions of it, some of them softened, were sent out by the Kremlin to foreign party leaders. One of these found its way to the United States government and was published on June 2, 1956. There is not the slightest doubt that the speech is authentic and that almost everything it says is true. But the mystery remains: Why did the Kremlin leaders decide to speak thus of a situation which every student of the subject knew, at least partially, but which could still be denied so long as it was not admitted? One factor in the making of the speech was undoubtedly the determination of the army to clear itself of the unjust accusations made against its officers in 1937–1941 and against the effort to attribute the disasters of 1941–1942 to professional incompetence. Just as the German generals after 1945 wanted to blame their defeats on Hitler, so the Russian generals, with much greater justification, wanted to blame their early defeats on Stalin. But there undoubtedly must have been other causes of which we are not yet aware.

The anti-Stalin speech, like the admission of error in the alienation from Tito, inevitably had an injurious influence on Communism throughout the world, especially in the satellite Powers, and ultimately became the ideological basis for the splitting of these Powers into Stalinist and anti-Stalinist groupings led by Red China and the Soviet Union.

Certain points about this speech are noteworthy. In the first place, all the criticism of Stalin is directed at his actions subsequent to 1934; these are criticized, not because they were vile in themselves, but because they were injurious to the party and to loyal party members. Throughout this speech, as in everything else he did in this period, Khrushchev was working to strengthen the party. Moreover, by directing his criticism at Stalin personally, he exculpated himself and the other Bolshevik survivors who were fully as guilty as Stalin was—guilty not merely because they acquiesced in Stalin's atrocities from fear, as Khrushchev admitted in the speech, but because they fully cooperated with him.

A study of Khrushchev's own life shows that he supported Stalin's atrocities fully at the time, often anticipated them, benefited personally from them, and egged Stalin on to greater ones. In fact, even as Khrushchev in his speech condemned Stalin's acts which caused the deaths of thousands in the party, he defended Stalin's acts which caused the deaths of millions in the country. The fault was not merely with Stalin; it was with the system; and, even wider than that, it was with Russia. Any system of human life which is based on autocracy and authority, as Russian life has always been, will turn up sadistic monsters, as Russia has throughout its history, again and again. And the more completely total and irresponsible power is concentrated in one man's hands, the more frequently will a monster of sadism be produced.

The very structure of Russian life on the authoritarian lines it had always possessed drove Khrushchev, as it had driven Stalin thirty years before, to concentrate all power in his own hands. Neither man could relax halfway to power for fear that someone else would continue on, seeking the peak of power. The basis of the whole system was fear and, like all neurotic drives in a neurotic system, such fear could not be overcome even by achievement of total power. That is why it grows into paranoia as it did with Ivan the Terrible, Peter the Great, Paul I, Stalin, and others.

During all the struggle for power within the Kremlin, foreign affairs were still actively pursued by the Soviet leaders. The chief event was a change in direction from Europe to Asia which took place in the spring of 1955. The Austrian treaty, the reconciliation with Tito, the stalemate over the German problem, the Warsaw Pact, and the "Geneva spirit" were all parts of a plan to put Europe "on ice" in order to shift attention to Southeast Asia, to India, and to the Near East. This new direction was opened by beginning arms shipments to Colonel Gamal Nasser of Egypt in the spring of 1955 and reached its peak in the so-called Suez Crisis of October 1956. A similar effort in India, seeking to win its support for the Soviet bloc, began with the state visit to India and Burma by Bulganin and Khrushchev in November 1955. This new direction and its consequences will be described in a moment, but it must be recognized that the continuing struggle for control within the Kremlin and the satellite states ran parallel with the growing crisis in the Near East and that both reached the critical stage at the same time in October 1956.

The struggle between the Stalinists and the anti-Stalinists within the satellite states and the discontent of the inhabitants with both groups kept public affairs agitated along the whole zone of satellite areas from the Baltic to the Balkans. Khrushchev's "secret speech" increased this agitation. Pressure on Khrushchev inside the Kremlin to reverse his professed policy of de-Stalinization grew. Khrushchev struck back. On June 2, 1956, the same day that Tito arrived for a state visit to Moscow, Molotov was removed as foreign minister and replaced by Khrushchev's agent, Shepilov, the editor of *Pravda*. But the satellite turmoil continued.

This turmoil, which agitated eastern Europe for many years, may be regarded as a series of clashes between Stalinism and Titoism. Neither of these is an extreme pole of dualistic opposition but rather two positions on a number of scales, concerned rather with methods than with goals. Both have as a goal the creation of powerful and prosperous Communist systems, but they do not agree on methods, or rather on the relative mixture of methods to be used to reach their goal. Each sees industrialization as necessary to such a goal, but Tito is, perhaps necessarily, more willing to use foreign investment and foreign technical guidance, if these are free from any political control.

Stalinism in general distrusts all foreign help as spying. Relying on domestic capital accumulation, and determined to raise it speedily, Stalinism puts severe pressures on the peasantry and thus emphasizes collective farms under political pressure, while Titoism is prepared to make much more use of private agriculture and of economic incentives for food production. This entails a slower rate of industrialization and more emphasis on improved standards of living. There are also other, more pervasive, differences. Stalinism insists on uniformity and centralized authority, while Titoism is more willing to allow diversity and collegial control. This, in their terms, is the distinction between a "monolithic block" and "collective leadership"; when the "monolithic bloc" is subject to criticism, it is called the "cult of personality."

In the satellites, for historical reasons, there are other sharp distinctions between Stalinism and Titoism. The former favors Russian domination, while the latter favors local nationalism. As a consequence, in 1945–1960, the former favored those local leaders who had spent the prewar and war periods in exile in the Soviet Union, while the latter favored the underground fighters who had stayed at home in the Left-wing resistance groups. And, finally, the Stalinists upheld their road to Socialism as the only road, while the Titoists contended there were many roads to Socialism. As might be expected, political oppression and the rule of the monolithic party was associated with the one point of view, while a greater readiness to allow diversity of outlook and coalition regimes marked the other.

There is no doubt that Stalin intended to establish a fully Stalinist system as just described in eastern Europe, "the Zone," as Seton-Watson calls it. But this could not be done immediately in the chaos of war's ending. Accordingly, a period of real coalition regimes was established, based on the association of all groups and parties which had resisted Nazism. Most of these groups were made up of peasants, workers, and intellectuals led by a combination of exiles back from Russia and hardened resistance fighters. One of the chief acts of these coalition regimes, in most countries, was agrarian reform, that is, the division of former large estates into the hands of peasant owners.

Within a few years, and in most cases by 1948, this coalition was broken down and replaced by narrow Stalinist control, governed by a typical Stalinist tyranny. This was achieved by getting the significant government posts into the hands of hard-core Stalinists, usually the former Moscow exiles, and forcing other groups out of the coalition. In this process, the presence of Soviet troops was often the vital factor. Along with this went a social, economic, and propagandist campaign to split the farmers by calling the more affluent, better educated, or more obstinate ones "agrarian reactionaries" and "enemies of the people." These were liquidated, frequently by death. The chief index showing that this stage had been reached was usually a reversal of the agricultural policy from agrarian reform to collectivization similar to that achieved in Russia in 1930–1934.

As one consequence of this change, each satellite found its welfare, especially in economics, subordinated to that of the Soviet Union. This was reflected in numerous economic and commercial agreements which set up conditions of commercial exchange and joint-owned public corporations able to milk the satellite countries for Russia's benefit. Some of this was based on reparations. As examples of this exploitation, we might mention that the joint corporations in East Germany drained from that area goods worth a billion Reichsmarks a year in terms of 1936 prices in the 1946–1948 period. The Soviet-Polish coal agreement of 1945 bound Poland to sell coal to Russia at one-tenth the price obtainable elsewhere. In all, it has been estimated that the Soviet Union extracted goods worth $20 billion out of eastern Europe in 1945–1946.

By 1952, eastern Europe, with the notable exception of Yugoslavia, was being organized, as a colony of the Soviet Union, along Stalinist lines. The bitter attacks on Tito arose from Tito's refusal to accept this and from the challenge which the existence of his different system offered to Stalin's control. Tito was able to resist because he was outside the zone of Soviet military occupation and had built up a military and bureaucratic hierarchy loyal to him, while inside that zone these hierarchies had been constructed under Soviet guidance and were loyal to Stalin rather than to the local leaders. The one exception, Albania, sided with Stalin because it feared Yugoslavia, just as Tito feared the Soviet Union, as a too powerful neighbor.

In 1951–1952 the incipient purge in the Soviet Union was extended to the satellites where its anti-Semitic overtones were even more evident. Rudolf Slansky, leader of the Czech Communist Party, was tried and executed in spite of his abject subservience to Stalin, while Anna Pauker was removed from her offices in Romania. This drove Tito closer to the Western camp and led Tito's friend Milovan Djilas to recognize that the problem of Stalinism was not personal but institutional, caused by the structure of the system, a disease fatal to any real social welfare; he called this disease "bureaucratic degeneration." When Djilas went further, at the end of 1953, and recognized that the real issue was between freedom and absolutism, a choice for all the Zone between the West and the East, he broke with Tito because his criticism clearly applied to Tito's authoritarian bureaucracy as well. Many persons in the satellites, even the young who had lifelong indoctrination in the authoritarian outlook, reached similar conclusions and were like tinder to any anti-Soviet spark.

The sparks were provided by Khrushchev, with his continued curtailment of the secret police, his acceptance of Titoism, and, above all, his "secret speech." Few recognized that Khrushchev was basically an ultra-Stalinist himself, fully committed to foreign aggression, to ultraindustrialization, and to ruthless discipline of the working masses, especially the peasants. His tactical shifts were taken as indicators of a moderate personality, while, in fact, Khrushchev was as extreme as Stalin and more reckless.

As part of the thaw in eastern Europe there was a considerable shift from Stalinism. Hundreds of thousands of political prisoners were either released or given reduced sentences, and party leaders who had been purged were restored to the party. Some who had been executed were posthumously rehabilitated. That key indicator, pressure to build up collective farms, was reversed. In Hungary in a single year (May 1953 to May 1954) the acreage under collective farming decreased one-third, while the number of peasants on such farms fell 45 percent. This was fairly typical of the Zone as a whole.

This general shift undoubtedly encouraged resistance to Soviet domination, a feeling which was greatly increased in 1956 by three other factors: (1) the growing impoverishment of the Zone from Soviet exploitation, from the poor crops and food shortages of 1956, and from the equally grave fuel shortages (both coal and petroleum); (2) the shift of Soviet attention from Europe to Asia; (3) the unexpected reaction to the "secret speech." The consequences of these disturbing influences were general in the Zone, but the specific cases of Poland and Hungary hold great interest, because they worked in such totally different ways.

The chief difference, of course, was the great strength of the Polish leaders and people, going back to their terrible experiences at the hands of both Russians and Germans and their memories of the extraordinary feats of the underground resistance. Soviet reactions to Polish demands for liberalizing the regime were undoubtedly influenced by a reluctance to meet that resistance again. However, the chief difference lay in the related fact that the leaders of the Polish Communist Party led the demand for liberalization and maintained a united front while doing so, while the Hungary movement was resisted by the party leaders and could be split by personal ambitions.

The crisis began in both countries in the last week of June 1956. A stoppage of work at the Polish railway factory in Poznan grew into a mass demonstration against the Communist regime. Shots were fired, and eventually over 50 were killed and 323 arrested. Polish Party Secretary Ochab made concessions to the opposition and attributed the episode to "social roots . . . the existence of serious disturbances between the party and the various sections of the working class." This was rejected three days later by Bulganin during a sudden and unexpected visit of the Kremlin leaders to Warsaw; their version attributed the troubles to foreign capitalist agitators. Ochab continued his concessions and, on August 4th, readmitted to the party the popular Vladislov Gomulka, a strong nationalist Communist who had been removed and imprisoned at Stalin's orders in 1951.

Because the continued worsening of economic conditions in the late summer of 1956 made it impossible for the Polish Communists to offer the people any substantial economic concessions, they continued the political relaxation, which alarmed the Kremlin. The trials of those arrested in the June disturbances were fair and punishments lenient, amid growing nationalist enthusiasm. On October 15th Moscow learned of a Polish decision to convene the Polish Central Committee on October 18th to elect a new Politburo which would not include Soviet Marshal K. K. Rokossovsky, defense minister of Poland since the days of Stalin, and would make Gomulka party secretary. After a hurried meeting of the Soviet Presidium on October 18th, Soviet troops and naval contingents began to converge on Poland, and Khrushchev, Molotov, Kaganovich, and Mikoyan burst into the Polish Central Committee session of October 19th just as it began. The presence of that rigid Stalinist Molotov, who had been dismissed as foreign secretary in June, was significant of the precarious decline of Khrushchev's position in the Kremlin.

Khrushchev, however, acted as Soviet spokesman at the session in the Belvedere Palace. He was violent and bellicose, calling Gomulka a "traitor" and threatening dire consequences if the old Politburo, including Rokossovsky, was not reinstated. Ochab, still Polish secretary, was firm, and ordered the immediate halt of Soviet troop advances, or all negotiations would be ended and the Poles would take the consequences. This meant resistance to the Russians by the tough, well-armed Polish Security Corps. Khrushchev stopped his troop movements, the Russians withdrew, and the session of the Polish Central Committee finished its work, electing a new non-Soviet Politburo which excluded Rokossovsky and made Gomulka secretary. The latter in the course of the discussions with Khrushchev had indicated that his liberalization would extend only to domestic affairs and would not injure Polish-Soviet "friendship" or the Warsaw Pact. In his speech to the committee, Gomulka sought to reconcile nationalist Communism with Polish-Soviet friendship, and made a severe attack on the "cult of personality" with its hideous atrocities under the Stalinist regime. Rokossovsky resigned as defense minister and returned to Russia with more than thirty other Soviet high military officers in November.

Khrushchev publicly yielded in the Polish crisis on October 23rd when he issued a statement that he saw no obstacles to relations between the two countries from the committee's actions and that the Soviet troops would be withdrawn to their bases. On the same day, he was taking steps to crush the parallel crisis in Hungary.

The troubles in the Magyar state in the summer of 1956 took the same forms as in Poland, but instead of being directed by the Communist party secretary, they were directed against him. They appeared as agitations against the indefatigable Stalinist Mátyás Rákosi and in favor of the mild Imre Nagy, who had been premier in 1953-1955 as Malenkov's choice and had been removed at Khrushchev's order. On July 18th Khrushchev tried to deflate these agitations by ordering some minor reforms and replacing Rákosi as party secretary by his deputy, the uncouth and obstinate Stalinist Erno Gero. This simply intensified the agitations, which rose to a crescendo in September, chiefly from the meetings and resolutions of students, workers, and literary groups. Some of their demands were successful, including, on October 19th, abolition of the compulsory study of the Russian language.

On October 22nd a meeting of about 4,000 students discussing changes in university life became diverted to political agitations and drew up "Sixteen Points" which they tried to force Radio Budapest to broadcast. Omission of some of the points, demanding a new economic policy, the withdrawal of Soviet troops, free elections, freedom of the press, and reform of the Communist Party, led to a mass demonstration on October 23rd. When Gero refused their demands, the students began to riot, smashing to pieces the huge statue of Stalin in the center of the city. The security police killed several demonstrators, but when the regular Hungarian troops were called to restore order they joined the agitators.

By that time Soviet troops began to move from fifty miles away, and arrived in the capital by 2:00 A.M. on October 24th; Mikoyan had preceded them. It soon became clear that the Soviet tanks could not control the situation, because they could be blocked by overturned streetcars or other obstacles and could not subdue rioters in strong buildings: Mikoyan dismissed Gero and put in, as party secretary, János Kádár, until then a known opponent of the Stalinist group. By that time, October 25th, the revolt had spread through Hungary under the passive eyes of the Soviet troops. On the following day, Nagy, still in touch with Mikoyan, formed a new government and negotiated a cease-fire. The Russian forces withdrew from Budapest, and negotiations were opened between their officers and the Nagy government for their withdrawal from the country. By that time the whole Communist system in Hungary had collapsed; unofficial elected groups had seized power throughout the country; the secret police and the party had disintegrated; a revolutionary council had taken control of the Hungarian Army, and Colonel Pál Maleter, a leader of the revolt, had been made a major general and minister of defense. Most significant of all, the one-party system had been ended, and members of the revived non-Communist parties had joined the Cabinet. On October 31st the official Soviet news agency, Tass, announced that the Kremlin was ready to recognize the new government and negotiate withdrawal of all Soviet troops from the country.

However, as October ended, large Soviet forces had begun to invade Hungary, crossing into the country on numerous temporary combat bridges. On November 1st Kádár, who had pretended to be one of Nagy's closest supporters, fled from Budapest to the Soviet headquarters at Szolnok. There he set up a new government under Soviet control. The same day Nagy called to the United Nations, appealing for help and announcing Hungary's withdrawal from the Warsaw Pact and its resumption of neutrality.

In the meantime, the Soviet invasion was in full operation, overrunning the country and smashing into Budapest before dawn on November 4th. Most of the resistance was overwhelmed that day. As it collapsed, the Nagy government and their families took refuge in the Yugoslav Embassy. The Yugoslavs, including Tito, were obviously confused by Kádár's change of sides, and accepted his promise of safe-conduct to their homes for Nagy and his associates. However, when these people left the security of the embassy on November 22nd, they were seized by Soviet forces and deported to prisons outside Hungary. By that date the flight of refugees from Hungary was in flood, despite efforts by the Kádár government to prevent it. Many were killed as they tried to pass the frontiers, but thousands escaped to the West, where many of them were able to continue their studies in a new way of life. The costs of the uprising were catastrophic. On the Hungarian side there were about 2,800 killed, 13,000 wounded, and 4,000 buildings destroyed, but tens of thousands were in exile or in hiding, the country was shattered, and lay, as a conquered country, under the armed forces of its oppressor.

The unanticipated consequences of Khrushchev's de-Stalinization efforts in eastern Europe were bound to injure Khrushchev in the Kremlin power struggle. Indeed, they brought him to the brink of final disaster early in 1957. As usual, the shifts of power were indicated by changes in personnel. Kaganovich, who had been removed from the government on June 5, 1956, was restored as minister of building materials on September 22nd; Shepilov, who had been Khrushchev's appointee as foreign minister in June, lost his other post as secretary to the Central Committee on Christmas Day 1956. Above all, on November 22nd, Molotov was made minister of state control, a post which had budgetary functions in all parts of the state-controlled economy and could have been built up into a state power, in opposition to Khrushchev's party power, in the economic system. Moreover, de-Stalinization ceased after July 1956, and even Khrushchev found it necessary to praise the old ogre. On December 23rd *Pravda* denied that there had ever been any Stalinism in the Soviet Union. Eight days later, Khrushchev said, "We can state with contrition that we are all Stalinists in fact." On January 17, 1957, at the Chinese Embassy in Moscow, he said, "Stalinism, like Stalin himself, is inseparable from Communism. . . . In the fight against the enemies of our class, Stalin defended the cause of Marxism-Leninism."

For Khrushchev, as for all the Soviet leaders, the great issue was to prevent Titoism from spreading into the Soviet Union and, if possible, to curtail its spread among the satellites. Every effort was made to prevent knowledge of the "Polish October" and the Hungarian revolt from reaching the Soviet people, and the attacks on Tito and Yugoslavia were resumed. Tito struck back on November 11th with the charge that Stalin had taken the domestic and foreign policies of the Soviet Union to dead ends and that his errors were not personal ones but intrinsic in the Soviet system of monolithic authoritarianism. He was refuted in *Pravda*, a week later.

The Hungarian invasion destroyed much of the appeal of Communism to the Leftists of Western Europe and the world; this had already been left in shreds by the "secret speech." Even in the Soviet Union, university students and intellectuals disapproved of the Soviet invasion of Hungary. Many literary works written during the de-Stalinization phase in the spring were published the following winter, when the tide had turned again. Khrushchev struck hard at these groups and continued to do so for several years, with the result that the alienation of Russian intellectuals from Khrushchev became established. This was reflected in the expulsion from the universities later in 1956 of hundreds of students who refused to applaud the Soviet attack on Hungary. The official Soviet line was that most disturbances of this kind arose from the activities of foreign agitators of capitalist aggressors.

Simultaneously with the Soviet political and intellectual reaction after June 1956, came a series of efforts to alienate the economic stringency: wages were raised, taxes reduced on the poorest payers, social benefits were extended, and the labor unions were urged to protect them; numerous projects in heavy industry under the Five-Year Plan were slowed up and their resources diverted to consumer goods. Most significant of all, there was a sharp increase in the influence of state officials and a corresponding decrease in that of party officials.

This reversal was fully evident in the Central Committee session of late December 1956, but the following meeting, in February 1957, showed Khrushchev in an aggressive counterattack. This took the form of suggestions for a drastic reorganization of Soviet economic life toward a more decentralized system. Undoubtedly this plan had considerable merit, but in Khrushchev's eyes it had an additional advantage, since it would remove much of economic life from the influence of the central state ministries and leave it open to increased influence from local party groups. He proposed the division of the Soviet Union into several dozen economic regions, each under an economic council, or *sovnarkhozy*, of diverse groups, and the devolution to these groups of the economic functions of the majority of the economic ministries in Moscow. These ministries would be abolished, along with the State Commission for Current Planning (GEK) and Molotov's Ministry of State Control. This would leave only the long-range economic planning agency (Gosplan) and a few economic ministries at the center, with annual planning and most execution left to the regional or lower groupings.

This plan had real merits which can hardly be covered here. Clearly, the growing complexity of the Soviet economy, over a widely diverse terrain and people, could not be operated efficiently by uniform regulations from the center. Moreover, each economic ministry, because of the constant shortages of resources, materials, and labor, sought to build up, within itself, its own sources of supply and also had a constant urge to hoard equipment and parts, even when they were not needed by it and were urgently needed by enterprises of a different ministry in the next street or district. This hampered expansion and also resulted in very expensive cross-hauling of the freight of one ministry from remote areas at the very time that a different ministry might be hauling similar resources in the opposite direction. The serious overworking of the Soviet railway system, a constant weakness in the economy, was intensified by such needless hauling.

In spite of its merits, the anti-K group in the Presidium was unwilling to adopt this reform because it would drastically weaken centralized state control and strengthen localized party control in the Soviet economy. The state hierarchy of Soviets had fallen into decay, partly because of Stalin's use of the party and secret police, partly as a means to avoid use of the fraudulently democratic Soviet constitution and of its federalist features. As a consequence, the state hierarchy lacked effective or flexible control down through its levels, while the party hierarchy had these well developed. Much of the state's power locally was exercised through the economic ministries, which Khrushchev now wished to abolish. And because of his control of the party and through it of the party press, headed by *Pravda,* Khrushchev could keep up a steady drum of propaganda for his economic reorganization. Every local figure was for it, and it appeared to other rival leaders as an antistate move. Khrushchev, on the other hand, could make the opposition seem "antiparty," with all the treasonable overtones Stalin had given to that expression.

The economic reorganization law was passed on May 10, 1957, abolishing twenty-five economic ministries (retaining nineteen) and devolving their functions to twenty-nine regional *sovnarkhozy;* the State Economic Commission (GEK) was also abolished, leaving, as the only central economic control, the State Committee for Long-Term Planning under Yosif Kuzmin (a Khrushchev party official), who simultaneously became first deputy prime minister of the Soviet Union. Shepilov was restored to the secretaryship of the Central Committee, which he had lost in December. These changes were pushed through by an alliance of the party, the army, and all the forces of localism, both economic and state. Khrushchev had won a great victory, which could make the party dominant in economic life.

Having failed to block Khrushchev's economic plans, his rivals in the Presidium were reduced to a last resort: they had to get rid of the man himself. On June 18th, at a meeting of the Presidium, the motion was made to remove Khrushchev as first party secretary. The discussion grew violent, with Malenkov and Molotov attacking and Khrushchev defending himself. He was accused of practicing a "cult of personality" of his own, of ideological aberrations which threatened the solidarity of Communism, and of economic mismanagement. It soon became clear that the vote was 7–4 against him, with Mikoyan, Kirichenko, and Suslov his only supporters. He was offered the reduced position of minister of agriculture.

Khrushchev refused to accept the result, denying that the Presidium had authority to remove a first secretary and appealing to the Central Committee. The members of this larger group joined in the discussion as they arrived, while Khrushchev's supporters sought to delay a final vote until his men could come in from their party posts in the provinces. Marshal Zhukov provided army planes to bring in the more distant and more reliable ones. The discussion became bitter, especially when Zhukov threatened to produce documentary evidence that Malenkov, Molotov, and Kaganovich had been deeply involved in the bloody purges of 1937. Madame Furtseva, who was, like Zhukov, an alternate member of the Presidium, filibustered with a speech of six hours. Surprisingly, Khrushchev's agent Shepilov spoke against him, but M. A. Suslov, the head of the security police and the most cold-blooded killer left in the Soviet Union, shifted to Khrushchev's side. Eventually there were 309 members present, with 215 wanting the floor, over 60 actually making speeches.

When the vote was finally taken, Khrushchev's loyal supporters in the party hierarchy voted for him solidly, and his removal, already voted by the Presidium, was reversed. Khrushchev at once counterattacked. He moved and carried the expulsion from the Presidium of Malenkov, Molotov, Kaganovich, and Shepilov for "antiparty activities." Then came the election of a new Presidium, from which Pervukhim and Saburov, the two strongest supporters of a centralized, state-controlled economy, were also removed. Pervukhim became an alternate member, but Saburov was dropped completely. The new Presidium had fifteen full members instead of the previous eleven, and nine alternate members instead of six. The old alternate members, Zhukov, Furtseva, L. I. Brezhnyov, and N. M. Shvernik, who had supported Khrushchev, were moved up to be full members, joining the holdovers Khrushchev, Bulganin, Kirichenko, Mikoyan, Suslov, and Voroshilov, while five loyal agents of Khrushchev, led by Aristov and F. R. Kozlov, were added.

This change of July 23, 1957, was Khrushchev's most smashing personal victory and the most significant event in Russia's internal history after the death of Stalin. It led Khrushchev to a position of political power more complete (except for the ambiguous position of the army) than Stalin's had been, although it was clear that Khrushchev would never be allowed to abuse his power the way Stalin had done.

Khrushchev did not rest on his oars. During the summer of 1957 he made notable concessions to the peasants (especially the ending of compulsory deliveries from the products of their personal plots), slammed down the lid on freedom of writers and artists with a strict cultural directive of August 28th, pushed vigorously both the "virgin lands" scheme and the decentralization of industry, and worked to curtail the growing autonomy of the armed forces. On October 27th, while Zhukov was in Albania, he was removed from the Ministry of Defense and, at the same time, was dropped from the Central Committee because of unsatisfactory cooperation with the party's political work in the army. The next few months saw a twofold advance of party influence, on a lesser scale into the army and on a greater scale, both directly and through the intermediary of the revived trade unions, into the new regional economic councils.

The final cap of Khrushchev's rise to power came in the spring of 1958. Following the elections and assembly of the new Supreme Soviet on March 28th, Bulganin resigned as premier and was replaced by Khrushchev. In the autumn, Bulganin, who had cooperated so well with the new autocrat's rise to power, was expelled from the Presidium and condemned as an enemy of the party. This left Khrushchev as complete ruler of the Soviet Union, head of both state and party, as Stalin had been, but resting his power more on the latter than on the former.

In the five years following Stalin's death, military strategy in the Soviet Union underwent a major debate almost as confused as the simultaneous debate going on in the United States during Eisenhower's Presidency. On the whole, the range of theories of war, both strategic and tactical, was much less in the Soviet Union than in the United States, and changes have been much slower. But the basic issues were the same.

The orthodox military ideas of the Russians, like everything else, had been stated by Stalin and were not allowed to change, under the impact of new ideas or of new weapons, until after his death. Thus Stalin orthodoxy regarded war as a struggle between whole societies, each with its distinctive way of life, and judged that the outcome would be determined by what was called the "permanently operating factors." These factors emphasized the characteristics of the society, such as industrial strength, morale, level of training, and reserve forces. Other, "accidental," factors, such as weather, surprise, ability of individual commanders (even Napoleon), or the outcome of single battles, were regarded as of little significance. Accordingly, the Russians had no faith in lightning wars or strategic bombing or in new or, above all, "absolute" weapons. To them, victory was achieved by *destruction of the enemy's armed forces* by a series of blows and conflicts over a long time, during which the permanent factors, especially the forces of industrial strength and national morale, would be decisive. They regarded attacks on the enemy's population, cities, or industry as wasted effort, except where these could be directly linked to a battle. And each battle would be determined by a balance of forces from all branches of the defense services persistently concentrating on the enemy forces over extensive time and space.

In this outlook there was no place for the nuclear bomb, for strategic air attack, or for twenty-four-hour wars, and, accordingly, the American possession of the A-bomb was largely ignored. Protests against its use, and the desire to outlaw it, were undoubtedly based on the fact that it was an American monopoly, but the Russian objection to city-bombing or to strategic terror of the V-2 kind as ineffective and a waste of resources was undoubtedly sincere.

Soviet efforts to get the A-bomb and the H-bomb and to build up a fleet of TU-4's were partly a desire to possess what the enemy had, partly based on a desire to deter our use of SAC against Russia, and partly derived from Stalin's astonishment at the damage our strategic bombers had inflicted on Berlin. But none of these had much influence on Soviet military thinking.

A change in strategic thinking arose in 1954 as a consequence of a debate among Soviet military leaders over the role of surprise in military victory. The possibility of a sudden American nuclear attack on Russia from the air had to be examined. As a consequence of this dispute, the role of surprise was considerably increased, although there was no general feeling that it could be decisive or even that wars might be shortened as a result of nuclear weapons. To this day the Soviet leaders still believe that victory will go to their country after a long war of mass forces using a balance of all arms and weapons. But they now include in this balance of weapons nuclear arms at all stages and ranges. However, they do not believe, as many Americans do, that strategic bombing can be decisive. It is simply an additional arm added on to the older arsenal, and will be used in war against military objectives primarily because wars are fought with the military sectors of a society.

As a consequence of these views, the Soviet Union has no idea of being able to achieve military victory over the United States, simply because they have no method of occupying the territory of the United States at any stage in a war. They hope to defeat the United States as a society by nonviolent means: propaganda, subversion, economic collapse, and diplomatic isolation. If the rivalry with the United States comes to the violent stage, they have every hope that the Soviet Union itself will not be directly involved, but can wear the United States down by fighting through third parties, as in Korea. The Russians generally reject the idea of mutual annihilation or the total destruction *of all civilization* in war, and insist that any war, however severe, will leave some remnant of the Soviet Union surviving as victor on the field. They accept the possibility of limited war, in a geographical sense, but have little hope of any war limited to nonnuclear weapons, because this would be, they feel, to their advantage and, accordingly, not acceptable to us. Thus they are unlikely to use nuclear weapons *first*, although fully prepared to resort to them once they are used by an enemy.

One confusing consequence of the Soviet discussion of the role of surprise in war was an effort to distinguish between "preventive" and "preemptive" war. Because the generals, planners, and staff theorists were convinced that the West must be aggressive because of the "contradictions" of the capitalist economic system, they were convinced that they were in danger of a surprise attack by SAC. Their weakness in this aspect of war made it unlikely that their retaliatory strike would be of decisive significance, so they developed a theory of preemptive strike; this said that they would countersurprise our surprise attack by beating us to the punch with a nuclear attack of their own. Such a "preemptive strike" would be justified only on the basis of conclusive evidence that we were about to launch a surprise attack, since our retaliatory strike after their preemptive strike would still be very damaging to them. The problem arises, however, as to how they can ever be sure that we are about to attack them, and, failing that, how does such a "preemptive" war differ from a "preventive" war, which the Soviet abjures because it is unnecessary to them?

Soviet military thinkers have been very reluctant to accept any theories of nuclear deterrence or of limited war under an umbrella of nuclear deterrence. Since war is a struggle to the death by antipathetical societies, such societies will, in war, use any weapons they have. Accordingly, the Soviet Union believes that any *general* war involving the United States and themselves would be a nuclear war in which their ground forces, with tactical air support and nuclear weapons of all sizes and ranges, would fight its way overland, against nuclear armed enemies, to occupy most of Europe and possibly Asia.

They believe that there are three defenses against tactical nuclear weapons: (1) dispersal of their own forces as widely as possible until the last moment before assault; (2) contact as rapidly and as closely as possible with the enemy in order to deter the enemy from use of nuclear weapons which would also destroy its own forces; and (3) protection of as many of their troops as possible under cover, usually in tanks. The first two of these place great emphasis on rapid mobility of troops, and the third helps to provide this. Accordingly, the Russians anticipate the use of many if not entirely armored forces in overrunning Europe and very extensive use of air transport of troops (with conventional planes, gliders, and helicopters). Such mobility will allow Europe to be overrun rapidly, creating a situation which, they feel, will make a victory for the West impossible, while our strategic attack on the Soviet Union itself will be reduced and eventually ended by strong defensive measures and retaliation.

However, such a war, which would jeopardize the Communist way of life by threatening the Soviet Union, its only accurate embodiment, is regarded by the Soviet leaders as highly undesirable, and to be avoided at almost any cost, while they, in a period of almost endless Cold War, can seek to destroy "capitalist society" by nonviolent means or by local violence of third parties. This theory of "nibbling" the capitalist world to death is combined with a tactic which would resist "capitalist imperialism" by encouraging "anticolonialism." Such a change called forth, on the part of the United States, a defensive tactic which shifted from Dulles's insistence that the "uncommitted nations" must join the West to the more moderate aim of keeping them from becoming Communist.

This shift in aims, in reference to the "uncommitted nations," occurred both in the Soviet Union and in the United States and is of major importance in creating the contemporary world. Stalin and Dulles saw the world largely in black-and-white terms: who was not with them was obviously against them. Accordingly, the world must be either slave or free, each man applying the former adjective to his opponent's side and the more favorable, latter term, to his own group. They were enemies, but they agreed basically that the world must be a two-Power system. This meant that each was aggressive in terms of the "uncommitted nations" because each insisted these must either join his own side or be regarded (and treated) as an enemy.

The great change which occurred in the middle 1950's was that both of the super-Powers had to recognize that most of the "uncommitted nations" were too weak, too backward, and too independent to be forced to be either capitalist or Communist. They had to be something different, something of their own. This view was forced upon the super-Powers, with perhaps greater difficulty in Washington than in the Kremlin, but it was an aspect of reality which had to be recognized. From it came the acceptance of neutralism and the rise of the Buffer Fringe.

This shift was a double one. On the one hand it meant that the super-Powers' attitudes toward the Buffer Fringe shifted from a basically offensive one to a basically defensive one, shifted from an effort to get them to join one's own side to an effort to keep them from joining the opponent's side. And at the same time, it marked the first beginnings of true wisdom and true hope for the world's future in the recognition that there are more than two alternative fashions for organizing a functioning economic, social, and political system. In the long run, this recognition will be a victory for the West, for the West has always, in its real nature, recognized that reality is diverse and is pluralist, while it has been the Russian way to insist that reality is dualistic with each extreme necessarily monistic and uniform. The acceptance of diversity and of pluralism, by the inevitable failure of both capitalism and Communism in the Buffer Fringe, has forced the West to accept and apply its own, often-unrecognized, traditions.

Moreover, the forcing of this recognition upon both the Soviet Union and the West, in respect to the Buffer Fringe, may have the consequence, in time, of forcing each of these to accept it in respect to their internal systems. Here again this would mark a great victory for the West, because the acceptance of diversity and pluralism is part of the tradition of the West and is not acceptable to Russia (whose traditions have always been basically dualistic, seeing reality as a contrast between an unattainable ideal of perfection and a horrible, sinful morass of ordinary living—the imperfections of the latter being acceptable as a necessary consequence of the unattainability of the former, with both extremes being uniform and one). Such an acceptance will reduce the tension of the Cold War by allowing each polar super-Power to develop features of a mixed system which will make them approach each other in their characteristics of organization, a development which is, of course, already apparent to any unbiased observer.

The shift from dualism to pluralism and from uniformity to diversity was forced upon the Soviet Union in its most critical form by the rise of Titoism. This, of course, was chiefly evident in Europe, where conditions of industrial development make it more reasonable for the Kremlin leaders to expect the Soviet example to be followed slavishly by non-capitalist states. The same lesson should, however, have been learned, even earlier, in Asia, because there it became evident to many observers that most nations were neither able nor willing to follow either the Soviet Union or the United States. This observation, however, was impossible under Stalin because his false theories of the nature of both capitalism and imperialism made him regard the two as identical and thus to regard colonial areas as being parts of the capitalist system.

As a consequence of these intellectual errors, the Kremlin under Stalin was prepared to see the fringes of Asia either continuing as colonial areas or breaking away from European domination to become Communist zones, but it did not see the possibility of them becoming non-Communist and noncolonial independent states. This meant that where Stalin intervened in certain areas of Asia he intervened on behalf of the microscopic Communist parties and rebuffed the local native, nationalist, anticolonialist groups. Khrushchev, as we shall see, did the opposite.

Stalin's policy was quite bankrupt even before his death, and it was thus fairly easy for his successors to abandon it and to adopt a more feasible policy of Communist cooperation with local anticolonial (and thus largely anti-Western) forces to detach them, as new, independent, but still non-Communist, nations from the West. The Soviet assistance to such new nations was largely economic, although the limited productivity of the Soviet Union's own economic system, especially in food, made any substantial foreign aid to neutral nations a considerable burden on the Soviet Union itself. For this reason much of the burden of such foreign aid was pushed onto the Soviet satellite states, especially Czechoslovakia.

This shift in the Soviet attitude toward neutralism was helped by Dulles's refusal to accept the existence of neutralism. His rebuffs tended to drive those areas which wanted to be neutral into the arms of Russia, because the new nations of the developing Buffer Fringe valued their independence above all else. The Russian acceptance of neutralism may be dated about 1954, while Dulles still felt strongly adverse to neutralism four or even five years later. This gave the Soviet Union a chronological advantage which served in some small degree to compensate for its many disadvantages in the basic struggle to win the favor of the neutrals.

While these changes were occurring, the strategic debate in the Soviet Union continued. In this subject also, the fact that the Soviet Union was straining its economic resources was of great importance. The demands of the unsuccessful Soviet agricultural program made it necessary to put more and more manpower into agriculture at the very time that the demands of the defense effort and the civilian economy (and the rampant waste and inefficiency in the Soviet system) were increasing the demands for manpower in industry. Moreover, the heavy casualties of the period 1928–1945 from purges and warfare had reduced the population figures and the birthrate to such a degree that the Soviet population figures, even in 1970, would be tens of millions below normal. The only source from which such demands for manpower could be met was in the conventionally armed units of the Soviet defense forces.

As a consequence of these conditions, the Soviet defense strategy debate from 1955 onward took a form somewhat parallel to that going on in the United States; that is, some of the political leaders, including Khrushchev, began to force upon the Soviet military leaders a shift in emphasis from mass conventional forces toward greater reliance upon strategic bombers and missiles. Khrushchev's version of the Eisenhower "New Look," in which the latter's "Bigger bang for a buck" was played by a Soviet version of "More rubble for a ruble," was adopted by Soviet Chief of Staff Marshal Sokolovsky and, less vigorously, by Defense Minister Marshal Malinovsky. The former's view was stated in a widely read book, *Military Strategy*, published in Moscow in September 1962,* but it is quite clear that the military leaders were prepared to yield, slowly, to Khrushchev and other political leaders. The net result seems likely to be a mixed one, somewhat similar to the similar struggle in the United

* Edited by V. D. Sokolovsky and published by Frederick A. Praeger, New York, 1963.

States. The chief difference is that Soviet production and wealth is so much less than that of the United States that all such critical decisions must be made within much narrower parameters.

In spite of these limitations of resources and demonstrations of inexperience and lack of competence parallel to that of the United States, the impact of the super-Powers was tremendous, especially in eastern and southern Asia and in the Near East.

The Cold War in Eastern and Southern Asia, 1950-1957

THE FAR EAST

In the Far East, as a consequence of the Yalta Conference, the Soviet government decided that the chief feature of its policy in the postwar period would be public collaboration with the Nationalist government of Chiang Kai-shek. This non-Communist area was to be held within limits by Soviet control, through local Communist groups, of various peripheral areas of which the chief would be Korea, Outer Mongolia, Sinkiang, possibly Manchuria, and some portions of Southeast Asia. Soviet control of Korea was envisaged as a threat to Japan as much as a buffer on Nationalist China.

This Soviet attitude toward China was reflected in the Sino-Soviet Treaty of August 14, 1945, which obtained Chiang's consent to the concessions which had been made, on his behalf, by Churchill and Roosevelt at Yalta. The most significant section of the agreement was in Molotov's note of the same day which promised that the Soviet Union's moral and material support "be entirely given to the National government as the central government of China" and promised to end any Soviet support of the Chinese Communists in Sinkiang, since it "has no intention of interfering in the internal affairs of China." As implementation of this agreement, Stalin summoned the Chinese Communists to Moscow, told them that "the uprising in China had no prospects and that the Chinese comrades should seek a *modus vivendi* with Chiang Kai-shek, that they should join the Chiang government and dissolve their army." The Chinese Communists agreed, but returned to China to continue their struggle against the Nationalist government. Only when that struggle was achieving its final success, four years later, did Stalin accept a Communist regime in China and seek to bring it under his influence by means of the Red Chinese–Soviet treaty of February 14, 1950.

The lack of Soviet support for the Chinese Communists in the period of their final victory does not mean that the Russians were completely loyal to their commitments with Chiang Kai-shek. They fully expected him to remain the ruler of China, but they wished to hem him in so that he would find it difficult to cooperate with the United States in any anti-Soviet policy in eastern Asia. Accordingly, they not only expected the Communists to remain dominant in Sinkiang; they were also eager to see them take over an additional zone or buffer belt in northwestern China and in Manchuria. For this reason, the Soviet forces, in violation of the treaty of 1945, yielded parts of Manchuria to Communist rather than to Nationalist Chinese forces as they withdrew from that province.

Stalin's real concern in the Far East was with Japan, which he feared might become an aggressive and militarized agent of the United States. He wished to participate in the military administration of Japan but was excluded by the imperious MacArthur. There can be little doubt that the Kremlin under Stalin was much more concerned with getting a Communist Japan than a Communist China, and hoped to see the former reduced to economic and social chaos as a step on the way to a Communist Party victory there. All these hopes were frustrated. The growing prosperity of Japan, and especially the success of Ladejinsky's agrarian reforms, steadily reduced the influence of Communism, with the result that the Communist Party of Japan obtained less than 3 percent of the vote in the parliamentary elections of October 1952 and lost all of its twenty-two seats in the Diet.

As protection against such an eventuality, Stalin insisted on the total demilitarization of Japan, the breakup of the industrial complexes like Mitsui, and possession or domination of surrounding areas such as south Sakhalin Island, the Kuriles, and Korea. The decartelization of Japan was never seriously considered by the MacArthur regime, and the demilitarization, although guaranteed by the new Japanese constitution, was abandoned by MacArthur in the name of Japanese defense needs, beginning in December 1950.

These defeats in Japan made it all the more urgent that Stalin get control of all of Korea, but here again he met a resounding defeat which largely destroyed Soviet prestige in the Far East. The vital event in this process was the need for Soviet-dominated North Korea to call for Red Chinese help to bail it out of the dangerous situation to which the Moscow-encouraged attack on South Korea had brought it.

SOUTHEAST ASIA

Stalin's disappointments in the Far East were also extended to Southeast Asia. This area forms the triangle between the great land masses of India, China, and Australia. It is a jumble of islands and peninsulas occupied by a jumble of peoples of diverse origins and cultures. The indigenous peoples with their animistic religions have been subjected to cultural, religious, and political intrusions of very diverse characteristics. The chief of these intrusions have been those from India and China, a somewhat later Muslim influence from the West, and finally, in recent centuries, the political and commercial influence of Europe and America. For generations there has been persistent Chinese immigration from the north.

By 1939 there was only one independent state in southeast Asia: Siam (Thailand), left as a buffer between the British areas of Burma and the Malay States to the west and French Indochina in the eastern portion of the Malay Peninsula. Southward of the peninsula, in a great sweep eastward to New Guinea, were the multitudinous islands of Indonesia, ruled by the Netherlands from Batavia on the island of Java. To the north of these islands were the Philippines, still under American administration in 1939. Between Java and the Philippines, the great mass of the island of Borneo had a fringe of British dependencies (Sarawak, Brunei, and North Borneo) along its northern coast, while, far to the east, the eastern half of Timor was under Portuguese administration. Thus all Southeast Asia, except Thailand, was under the colonial domination of five Western states in 1939.

The interest of these imperial Powers in Southeast Asia was chiefly strategic and economic. Strategically, these lands lay athwart the waters joining the Pacific with the Indian Ocean, a situation symbolized by the great British naval base of Singapore, at the southern tip of the Malay Peninsula, between Sumatra and Borneo. Economically these areas produced substantial qualities of tin, rubber, petroleum, bauxite, and other products. More significant, perhaps, from the Chinese point of view, many parts of the Malay Peninsula were fertile, were substantially underpopulated, and exported great quantities of rice (especially from Burma).

Western prestige in Malaysia was irretrievably damaged by the Japanese conquests of the Philippines, the Dutch Indies, and Malaya in 1942, so that the reestablishment of the colonial Powers after the Japanese collapse in 1945 was very difficult. Burma and the Philippines were granted their independence by Great Britain and the United States, respectively, soon after the war's end. French Indochina emerged from the Japanese occupation as the three states of Vietnam, Laos, and Cambodia, each claiming independence, while Java claimed sovereignty over the whole Netherlands East Indies as a newly independent state of Indonesia. Efforts by the European Powers to restore their prewar rule led to violent clashes with the supporters of independence. These struggles were brief and successful in Burma and Indonesia, but were very protracted in Indochina. Burma became an independent state in 1948, followed by Indochina in 1949, by Malaya in 1957, and by Singapore (under a special relationship) in 1959. Controversy and intermittent fighting between

Indonesia and the Dutch over western New Guinea continued until 1962, when American pressure persuaded the Netherlands to yield, but left Indonesia, led by Achmed Sukarno, unfriendly to the West.

In all these areas, native nationalists were inclined to the political Left, if for no other reason than the fact that the difficulties of capital accumulation and investment to finance economic improvements could be achieved only under state control. But such independent Socialism merged into other points of view which were clearly Communist. In some cases, such Communism may have been ideological, but in most cases it involved little more than the desire to play off the Soviet Union or Red China against the Western imperialist Powers.

The Communists of Southeast Asia were thus Communists of convenience and tactical maneuver, and originally received little support from the Soviet Union because of Stalin's well-known reluctance to engage in political adventures in areas where he could not dominate the armed forces. But in February 1948, the new Cominform sponsored a Southeast Asia youth conference at Calcutta where armed resistance to colonialism was demanded. A Communist revolt in the Philippines had already begun and was joined, in the course of 1948, by similar uprisings in Burma, Indonesia, and Malaya. Most of these revolts took the form of agrarian agitations and armed raids by Communist guerrilla jungle fighters. Since these guerrillas operated on a hit-and-run basis and had to live off the local peasantry, their exploitation of peasant life eventually made them decreasingly welcome to this very group for whom they pretended to be fighting. In the Philippines the Hukbalahap rebels were smashed in 1953 by the energetic and efficient government of President Ramón Magsaysay. In Indonesia, Sukarno repressed the insurrection and executed its leaders. In Malaya, where the Communists were almost entirely from the Chinese minority, these rebels were systematically hunted down and destroyed by British troops in long-drawn jungle combat. In Burma, the long Chinese frontier provided a refuge for the rebels, and they were not eliminated until 1960.

The real problem was Indochina. There the situation was complex, the French Army was uncompromising, and Communist leadership was skillful. As a result, the struggle there became part of the Cold War and contributed to a world crisis. The Malay Peninsula as a whole is dominated by a series of mountain ranges, with their intervening rivers, running southward from Chinese Yunnan. These rivers fan out, in the south, into fertile alluvial deltas which have attracted invaders of Mongolian type from the less-hospitable north throughout history. Even today they produce surplus food for undemanding peoples. From west to east the chief rivers are the Irrawaddy, the Salween, the Menam, the Mekong, and the Red River. Following this geographical pattern, political units have tended to fall into similar north-south strips with Burma and south-thrusting Malaya in the west, Thailand in the center, Laos and

Cambodia in the Mekong drainage, and Tonkin with Annam in the east.

Indochina brought considerable wealth to France, so that in the late 1930's the Banque de l'Indochine spawned in France an influential political group, who played a major role in the defeatism of 1940 and the subsequent collaboration. After the Japanese withdrawal in 1945, the Paris government was reluctant to see this wealth, chiefly from the tin mines, fall into the hands of Japanese-sponsored native groups, and, by 1949, decided to use force to recover the area.

Opposed to the French effort was Ho Chi Minh, a member of the French Communist Party since its founding in 1920, who had subsequently studied in Moscow and had been leader of the anticolonial agitations of the Indochinese Communist Party since 1931. Ho had set up a coalition government under his Viet Minh Party and proclaimed independence for Vietnam (chiefly Tonkin and Annam) in 1945, while French troops, in a surprise coup, seized Saigon in the south. Unfortunately for Ho, he obtained no support from the Kremlin. The French Communist Party was at that time a major element in the French coalition government, with its leader, Maurice Thorez, holding the office of vice-premier. Stalin had no wish to jeopardize the Communist chances to take over France by his support for a remote and minor Communist like Ho Chi Minh. In fact, Thorez signed the order for military action against Ho's Republic of Vietnam. At first Ho sought support from the United States and from Chiang Kai-shek, but, after the establishment of Red China in 1949, he turned to that new Communist state for help. Mao's government was the first state to give Vietnam diplomatic recognition (January 1950), and at once began to send military supplies and guidance to Ho Chi Minh. Since the United States was granting extensive aid to France, the struggle in Vietnam thus became a struggle, through surrogates, between the United States and Red China. In world opinion this made the United States a defender of European imperialism against anticolonial native nationalism.

During this turmoil, independent neutralist governments came into existence in the interior, with Laos to the north and Cambodia to the south. Both states accepted aid from whoever would give it, and both were ruled by an unstable balance of pro-Communists, neutralists, and pro-Westerners. The balance was doubly unstable because all three groups had armed supporters. On the whole, the neutralist group was the largest, and the pro-Western was the smallest, but the latter could obtain support from America's wealth. The decisive influence in the 1950's, however, was that the Communists, following the death of Stalin, were prepared to accept and support neutralism years before Dulles could get himself to condone it, a situation which gave considerable advantages to the extreme Left.

The intensity of the struggle in Vietnam increased fairly steadily in the years following 1947. The creation of the Cominform and the subsequent Communist withdrawal from the coalition governments of Europe, including France, freed the Kremlin to support anticolonial movements in Europe's overseas territories. At the same time, the reestablished French Army was left with a wounded pride which became, in some cases, a neurotic drive to wipe out the stains of 1940–1942 by subsequent victories in colonial wars. The growing aggression of Communist China and Dulles's fantasies about liberation all contributed to build the Indochina confusion into a flaming crisis. The final step came from the Korean truce of 1953 which freed Red China's hands for more vigorous action in the southeast. The defeat of the Communist risings of 1948 elsewhere in Malaysia turned the new Chinese activities full into Indochina, which had an open frontier for passage of Chinese Communist supplies and advisers.

This intensification of Chinese-supported Communist activities in Vietnam in 1953-1954 was quite contrary to the desires of the Kremlin, which was just entering the post-Stalin "thaw" and already moving toward the "Geneva spirit" of 1955. At the same time, the readiness of Dulles and the French Army to force a showdown in Vietnam was equally unacceptable to the British and to many persons in divided France. Out of these confusions came, on February 18, 1954, a Soviet suggestion for a conference on Indochina to be held at Geneva in April.

By the early months of 1954, the Communist guerrillas were in control of most of northern Indochina, were threatening Laos, and were plaguing the villages of Cochin-China as far south as Saigon. About 200,000 French troops and 300,000 Vietnamese militia were tied in knots by about 335,000 Viet Minh soldiers and guerrillas. France was being bled to death, both literally and financially, with little to show for it, but the French Army was obstinate in its refusal to accept another defeat.

The French strong point at Dien Bien Phu was invested by Viet Minh on March 13, 1954, and by the end of the month its outer defenses were crumbling. The French chief of staff, General Ely, flew to Washington and found Dulles willing to risk an all-out war with Red China by authorizing direct American intervention in Indochina. As usual, Dulles thought that wonders could be achieved by an air strike alone against the besiegers of Dien Bien Phu, where the conflict increased in intensity daily. For a few days the United States, at Dulles's prodding, tottered "on the brink of war." Dulles proposed "a united action policy" which he described in these terms: "If Britain would join the U.S. and France would agree to stand firm, . . . the three Western states could combine with friendly Asian nations to oppose Communist forces on the ground just as the U.N. stepped in against the North Korean aggression in 1950 . . . and if the Chinese Communists intervene openly, their staging bases in south China [will] be destroyed by U.S. air power. . . ."

President Eisenhower agreed, but his calls to Churchill and Eden found the British government opposed to the adventure. The foreign secretary hastened to point out that the Sino-Soviet Treaty of 1950 bound Russia to come to the assistance of China if it were attacked by the United States as Dulles contemplated. Discussion at Geneva, said Eden, must precede any such drastic action.

Few international conferences have taken place amid such external turmoil as the Far Eastern Geneva Conference of April 25–July 20, 1954. During it, two American aircraft carriers, loaded with atomic weapons, were cruising the South China Sea, awaiting orders from Washington to hurl their deadly bombs at the Communist forces besieging the 15,000 exhausted troops trapped in Dien Bien Phu. In Washington, Admiral Radford was vigorously advocating such aggressive action on a generally reluctant government. In Paris, public outrage was rising over Indochina where the French had expended 19,000 lives and $8 billion without improving matters a particle. At Geneva, delegates from nineteen nations were talking and stalling to gain as much as possible without open warfare. The fall of Dien Bien Phu on May 7th opened a vigorous debate in the French Assembly and led to the fall of Premier Joseph Laniel's government, the eighteenth time a Cabinet had been overturned since the end of World War II in 1945. The new prime minister, Pierre Mendès-France, promised a cease-fire in Indochina or his own retirement within thirty days. He barely made the deadline.

The Indochinese settlement of July 20, 1954 was basically a compromise, some of whose elements did not appear in the agreement itself. A Communist North Vietnam state, with its capital at Hanoi (Tonkin), was recognized north of the 17th parallel of latitude, and the rest of Indochina was left in three states which remained associated with the French Union (Laos, Cambodia, and South Vietnam).

The new state system of Southeast Asia was brought within the Dulles network of trip-wire pacts on September 8, 1954, when eight nations of the area signed an agreement at Manila establishing a Southeast Asia Treaty Organization (SEATO). The eight (United States, Britain, France, Australia, New Zealand, Pakistan, Thailand, and the Philippines) made no specific commitments, but set up a council, to meet at Bangkok and operate on a unanimous basis for economic, social, and military cooperation in the area. By special protocol they extended their protection to Laos, South Vietnam, and Cambodia.

The Geneva agreement, in effect, was to neutralize the states of Indochina, but neutrality was apparently not acceptable to the Dulles brothers, and any possible stability in the area was soon destroyed by their activities, especially through the Central Intelligence Agency (CIA) seeking to subvert the neutrality of Laos and South Vietnam. This was done by channeling millions in American funds to Right-wing army officers, building up large (and totally unreliable) military forces led by these Rightist generals, rigging elections, and, when it seemed necessary, backing reactionary *coups d'état*. These techniques might have been justified, in the eyes of the CIA, if they had been successful, but, on the contrary, they alienated the mass of the natives in the area, brought numerous recruits to the Left, gave justification for Communist intervention from North Vietnam, disgusted our allies in Britain and France, as well as many of our friends in Burma, India, and elsewhere, and by 1962 had almost destroyed the American image and the American position in the area.

In Laos the chief political figure was Prince Souvanna Phouma, leader of the neutralist group, who tried to keep a balance between the Communist-supported Pathet Lao on his Left and the American-subsidized politicians and militarists led by General Phoumi Nosavan on his Right. American aid was about $40 million a year, of which about $36 million went to the army. This was used, under American influence, as an antineutralist rather than an anti-Leftist influence culminating in a bungled army attack on two Pathet Lao battalions in May 1959, and openly rigged elections in which all the Assembly seats were won by Right-wing candidates in April 1960. In August 1960, an open revolt in behalf of the neutralist Souvanna Phouma by Captain Kong Le gave rise to a Right-wing revolution led by General Phoumi Nosavan. This drove the neutralists into the arms of the Pathet Lao and to seek direct Soviet intervention. The SEATO Council refused to support the American position, the Laotian Army was reluctant to fight, and the American military mission was soon involved in the confused fighting directly.

The American bungle in Laos was repeated, with variations, elsewhere in southern and southeastern Asia. In South Vietnam, American aid, largely military, amounted to about two-thirds of the country's budget, and by 1962, when it was running at about $400 million a year, it had reached a total of $2 billion. Such aid, which provided little benefit for the people, corrupted the government, weakened the swollen defense forces, and set up a chasm between rulers and people which drove the best of the latter Leftward, in spite of the exploitative violence of the Communist guerrillas. A plebiscite in 1955 was so rigged that the American-supported Right-wing candidate won over 98 percent of the vote. The election of 1960 was similarly managed, except in Saigon, the capital, where many people refused to vote. As might have been expected, denial of a fair ballot led to efforts to assassinate the American-supported President, Ngo Dinh Diem, and gave rise to widespread discontent which made it possible for the Communist guerrillas to operate throughout the country. The American-sponsored military response drove casualties to a high sustained figure by 1962 and was uprooting the peasantry throughout the country in an effort to establish fortified villages which the British had introduced, with success, in Malaya.

These errors of American policy, which were repeated in other places, arose very largely from two factors: (1) American ignorance of local conditions which were passed over in the American animosity against Russia and China, and (2) American insistence on using military force to overcome local neutralism which the mass of Asiatic peoples wanted. The ignorance of local conditions was well shown in the American bungling in Cambodia and in Pakistan.

In Cambodia a neutralist regime was primarily concerned with maintaining its independence between its two hereditary enemies, the Thai to the west and the Vietnamese to the east. The American militarization of both Thailand and South Vietnam was used by these countries to increase pressure on Cambodia, which, in spite of its pro-Western desires, was driven to seek support for its independence from China and Russia. This opened a wedge by which Communist pressure from North Vietnam could move across Laos and southward into Cambodia, between Thailand and South Vietnam, a possibility which would never have arisen if United States aid had not been used to corrupt and to militarize the two exterior states in the trio. At the same time, North Vietnam, with a greater population than South Vietnam (16 million to 14 million in 1960), has a deficiency of food, while South Vietnam, like all the delta areas, is a zone of rice surplus and thus a shining target for North Vietnamese aggression, especially when the agricultural collapse of Communist China made any food supply from the north almost hopeless.

In the west, where Burma is also an area of rice surplus, with much of the population dependent upon the export of this commodity at a remunerative price, this factor alone was sufficient to tie Burma into the Communist bloc. The collapse of the world price of rice at the end of the Korean War left Burma with an unsellable surplus of almost two million tons. Within the next three years (1954–1957) Burma signed barter agreements with Red China and Soviet Europe by which Burma got rid of over a third of its surplus each year in return for Communist goods and technical assistance. These returns were so poor in quality, high in price, and poorly shipped and handled that Burma refused to renew the agreements in 1958.

SOUTHERN ASIA

Farther west, in southern Asia (the correctly called Middle East, extending from the Persian Gulf to Burma) American bungling also opened many opportunities for Soviet penetration which the Communists generally failed to exploit with sufficient skill to earn any significant rewards.

The American error in southern Asia can be expressed very simply:

the key to that area was India; the United States acted as if it were Pakistan. The reason for this was equally simple, but should have been sternly resisted, and might have been except for Dulles. India was determined to be neutral; Pakistan was willing to be an ally of the United States. Dulles tried to make Pakistan the key because he preferred any kind of ally, even a weak one, to a neutral, however strong. But the choice undermined any possible stability in the area and opened it to Soviet penetration.

From the broadest point of view the situation was this: The rivalry between the two super-Powers could be balanced and its tensions reduced only by the coming into existence of another Great Power on the land mass of Eurasia. There were three possibilities of this: a federated and prosperous western Europe, India, or China. The first was essential; one of the others was highly desirable; and possibly all three might be achievable, but in no case was it essential, or even desirable, for the new Great Power to be allied with the United States. A strong and prosperous neutral in at least two of the three positions would box in the Soviet Union and force it to seek its needs in an intensive rather than extensive expansion, and in an economic rather than a military direction. A Soviet Union which was not boxed in would expand outward extensively, and by military means as much as any others. It would seek its needs, as it had done in eastern Europe in 1945–1948, by bringing more resources, including manpower, under its control as satellite areas.

If the Soviet Union were boxed in by allies of the United States, it would feel threatened by the United States, and would seek security by more intensive exploitation of its resources in a military direction, with a natural increase in world tension. If, on the other hand, the Soviet Union were boxed in by at least two great neutral Powers, it could be kept from extensive expansion by (1) the initial strength of such great Powers and (2) the possibility that these Powers would ally with the United States if the Soviet Union put pressure on them. On the other hand, in such a situation, the Soviet Union would be likely to turn to intensive expansion within these boundaries in economic and social directions, not only from the demand within the Soviet Union but also because of its own increased feeling of security from the existence of buffer Powers between the United States and itself.

Some solution such as this had been directly seen by Marshall and Acheson in regard to China in 1948–1950 but had been destroyed by the aggressive Stalinism of Mao's China and the errors leading to the Korean War. In the west the possibility had been destroyed by the immediacy of Soviet pressure which had shifted American emphasis from European Union to American alliance with Europe and from economic revival there to NATO. And in southern Asia the possibility had been lost by Stalin's early pressure on Iran which led Dulles to regard Pakistan instead of India as the key to the area.

The necessity for choice between these two arose from the partition of India before independence in 1947. In India, as in Palestine and earlier in Ireland, partition before independence received a strong impetus from the Round Table Group, and in all three cases it led to horrors of violence. The cause, in all, was the same: lines which seem to divide different peoples on the map often do not do so on the ground, because peoples are intermingled with each other, there are always third or even fourth groups which belong to neither, and their positions are often marked by separation in levels in a social hierarchy rather than by separation side by side in geography.

In India's case, the partition was a butchery rather than a surgical process. Imposed by the British, it cut off two areas in northwestern and northeastern India to form a new Muslim state of Pakistan (cutting right through the Sikhs in the process). The founders of the two states, Gandhi in India and Jinnah in Pakistan, both died in 1948, the former assassinated by a Hindu religious fanatic, so that the two new nations began under new leaders. In the postpartition confusion, minorities on the wrong side of the lines sought to flee, as refugees, to India or Pakistan, while the Sikhs sought to establish a new homeland for themselves by exterminating the Muslims in East Punjab. In a few weeks, at least 200,000 were killed and twelve million were forced to flee as refugees, in most cases with almost no possessions. An additional problem arose from the Indian princely states. Most of these joined the dominion enclosing their territory, but two acute problems arose: in Hyderabad, where a Muslim prince ruled over a Hindu majority, and in Kashmir, where a Hindu prince ruled over a Muslim majority. Hyderabad was settled when Indian troops invaded and took over the area, but Kashmir, on the border of Pakistan itself, could not be settled in such a summary fashion without precipitating war between the two dominions. Fighting broke out, but was eventually suppressed by a United Nations cease-fire team. At this writing, Kashmir still remains a cause of enmity and controversy unjoined to either state.

The death of Jinnah in 1948 left Pakistan, which was so largely his creation, in confusion. Its two sections were separated from each other by 1,100 miles of India territory, its boundaries were irrational, its economic foundations were torn to shreds by the partition, raw materials were left separated from their processing plants in India, irrigation canals separated from their reservoirs, herds separated from their pasturage, ports cut off from hinterland, and traders from their markets. Pakistan looked with yearning on Kashmir, but at the same time feared the greater size and population of India; forced by its insecurity to regard the army as the chief representation of the state, it built its unifying ideology on Islam at a time when belief in Muhammad's teachings was dwindling everywhere. It had no recognized capital city, but began administration from Karachi, and could not agree on a constitution until February 1956. By that time Pakistan was filled with corruption and unrest. Its first Five-Year Plan for economic development was breaking down, foreign exchange was lacking, and inflation with food-hoarding threatened. The Five-Year Plan (1955–1960) failed to make any improvement in living conditions, since its disappointing 2-percent-a-year increase in production was absorbed by an increase of similar size in population. In October 1958, martial law was established and the commander in chief, General Muhammad Ayub Khan, became president and quasi-dictator as martial-law administrator.

In the next four years (October 1958–June 1962), under military rule, Pakistan was put on a more hopeful course. A sweeping land-reform program restricted owners to 500 acres of irrigated, or 1,000 acres of nonirrigated, land, with the surplus distributed to existing tenants or other peasants. Former landlords received compensation for lost lands in long-term bonds. Extensive efforts were made to establish cooperative villages copied from those of Yugoslavia, and to reduce the birthrate. The second Five-Year Plan (1960–1965) got off to a good start with extensive foreign aid, including that of the World Bank, the United States, a European consortium, and increasing help from the Soviet Union. In March 1962 a new constitution with a strong presidency (reserved for three years to Ayub Khan) was announced, martial law ended, and elections were held. But the precarious international position of the country, going back to its original rejection of neutrality, continued.

This rejection of neutrality was based on a mixture of resentment toward India and Afghanistan, a vague feeling of fellowship with other Muslim states of the Near East, and a basic instability of political life. These impelled Pakistan toward a more dynamic foreign policy than India and led it to involvement in the Dulles network of treaties, including SEATO and CENTRO.

This network of treaties in Dulles's eyes was aimed at the Soviet Union, but in Karachi it was much more likely to be viewed in terms of Pakistan's enmities with Afghanistan and India. This, in turn, tended to increase Soviet influence in Kabul and in Delhi. The Kremlin made vigorous protests against the Pakistan-Turkish Treaty of Cooperation of April 1954, the Pakistan-Iraqi alliance of January 1955, the United States–Pakistan negotiations for military cooperation of 1954–1955, and, above all, against the Baghdad Pact of November 1955. The growing militarization of Pakistan, not only from its domestic instability but from the advent of American arms, led to a growing Indian concentration of its military forces in the west. This in turn was interpreted in Pakistan as a threat to Kashmir, and drove tension upward. At the same time,

Afghanistan, whose independence of Russian influence had been guaranteed by the British position in India for over a century, found itself, at the British withdrawal, exposed to increasing pressure both from the Soviet Union and from Pakistan. The nature of these pressures may be seen in the fact that a concession to France to explore Afghanistan for oil in 1952 had to be canceled because of Russian protests. On the other hand, American military aid to Pakistan was protested by Kabul, and led it to accept Soviet aid agreements in 1954.

Afghanistan was a multinational, or rather multitribal, state in which the chief group was the Pushtu. The creation of Pakistan in 1948 left almost half of this language group in Pakistan, and Afghanistan at once began to agitate for self-determination for the Pushtu. Success in this endeavor would create a new Pushtunistan state which would absorb much of western Pakistan and would extend from Soviet Central Asia to the Arabian Sea. The Russians naturally supported these claims, to retaliate against Pakistan cooperation with the United States and to open a Russian outlet to the southern ocean. In counterretaliation, in 1955, Pakistan tightened its control over its Pushtu areas and closed the Afghan border, stopping all Afghan commerce to the south and leaving Afghanistan almost completely dependent on Soviet outlets. This opened the way to a great increase in Communist influence, including that of Soviet satellites, in Afghanistan. These relations were sealed by a state visit of Khrushchev and Bulganin to Kabul in November 1955. From this came a Soviet loan of $100 million (of which $40 million for arms) at 2 percent interest over thirty years. Large amounts of Soviet arms and hundreds of Czech technicians began to move into Afghanistan.

For the Soviet Union the critical area in Asia was that on either side of the Caspian Sea. That was the only frontier where no buffer state stood between the Western bloc and the Soviet Union itself. This was a consequence of Stalin's aggressive threats to Iran and Turkey in 1946, which had driven them into alliance with the West, but it went far back in history to the old Russian ambitions to reach the Persian Gulf and the Aegean Sea. Because of the danger to the Soviet Union in that area, especially to the Soviet oil fields of the Caucasus, the Kremlin was for a long time reluctant to bypass the Turkish-Iran-Pakistan barrier to seek to intervene in the troubled conditions of the Arab Near East. Those conditions obviously provided ample opportunities for Soviet economic, ideological, and political disturbances which could be injurious to the West, especially to western Europe, which was so dependent upon Middle East petroleum supplies. Stalin never was willing to intervene in any area which could not be directly accessible to Soviet troops, and, once his territorial ambitions in northeast Turkey and northwest Iran were defeated in 1946-1947, he left the whole Near East relatively alone.

This condition continued almost unchanged, in spite of domestic disturbances of a major character in Iran and among the Arab States, particularly Egypt. It was not until the summer of 1955 that the new Khrushchev effort to exploit the troubles of the Near East in order to build up local nationalism against the West was made possible by the growing instability of conditions in the area and was called forth by Dulles's persistent efforts to organize the area on an anti-Soviet basis. Thus in this area, as in southeastern and southern Asia earlier, the American insistence on the noncommitted nations adopting anti-Soviet lines opened the way for the Soviet to pose as the friend of such nations by supporting their neutralism.

In Iran and Turkey already burned by Soviet fire, this effort was a failure, but south of this barrier the situation in the Arab world was, from Moscow's point of view, far more promising. There is little doubt that the Soviet decision to upset the apple cart in the Near East by selling arms to the Arab States was a reprisal for Dulles's long-drawn efforts to get the northern tier of Near Eastern states (Turkey, Iran, and Pakistan) into the Western bloc.

These efforts began as far back as May 25, 1950, when the Western Powers offered to sell arms to the Near Eastern states themselves, if the recipients would guarantee not to use such arms for aggression. Fortunately, nothing came from this foolish offer, because the Arab states refused to promise not to use any arms against Israel. In fact, they were very definite that they would do just that as soon as they could untangle their own intra-Arab squabbles. In the interval, Iran and Egypt had domestic disturbances which created severe international repercussions.

Until recent years Iran remained a fairly typical underdeveloped Muslim country, but with distinctive features of its own from the fact that it was not an Arab but an Indo-European country and had an ancient heroic cultural tradition of Persian origin which was distinctly different from the Arab traditions of the Near East. It shared, however, the tribal, patriarchal, pastoral, and poverty-stricken nature of the Near East, and was included in a common geographic pattern by semi-aridity, emphasis on animal husbandry, survival of nomadic life, and the fact that its chief natural resource was oil.

Although most of Iran's inhabitants are Muslim, only about one in ten speaks Arabic as his primary language, while over half speak Persian. The rest speak a variety of dialects of which about a fifth are Turkic. Only about one person in seven is literate, usually in Persian, using Arabic script. Most persons know more than one language, and it is not uncommon to speak one language in the family, write a different language, and pray in a third.

At the end of World War II about 80 percent of the population were peasants, in spite of the fact that geographic and social conditions made agriculture a most difficult way of life. Only about one-tenth of the land was tilled (and only half of that at any one time), while another tenth was used for grazing. The rest, amounting to four-fifths, was almost entirely useless, being either mountainous or arid. Moreover, the peasants who tilled the land were much oppressed by heavy rents to absentee landlords who also controlled, as separate rights, essential access to water. Only about a seventh of the land was owned by the peasants who worked it, and that was either more remote or of poorer quality. These burdens on the land were often so heavy that peasants retained little more than a fifth of what they produced. In consequence many peasants had to supplement their incomes by work as laborers, as small traders, or by village handicrafts. Generally the rigid categories of economic activities in which we think did not exist in Iran, so that most people had a variety of activities as peasants, herdsmen, traders, government employees, laborers, and soldiers moving seasonally or intermittently from one activity to another. Even the landlords were, as often as not, government employees, moneylenders, traders, or all combined.

This fluidity of economic functions was more than canceled out by social rigidity. Family and personal relationships were rigid and hierarchical, and the former were often tribal in nature. The whole of Iranian life was imprinted with leader-follower characteristics of a very personal character, with loyalty and honor two of the outstanding features of all human relationships. Where these did not operate, human relationships were precarious and filled with suspicion, so that many of the patterns of life which form the modern world, such as political or public relationships and impersonal business relationships, were very weak, and, without stable principles, fell readily into nepotism and corruption.

This "leadership" principle in Iranian social life supported a privileged ruling group, or elite, which dominated the country. Made up of landowners and gentry, with substantial interests in business (especially government contracts), it was also the chief source of high government officials and of army officers. The members of this elite, mostly resident in Tehran, have, in most cases, powerful local interests of an economic, family, and social kind in various provinces and are usually the leaders of these districts. Between this elite and the peasantry is a small middle class of businessmen, professional persons, bureaucrats, and educated people who generally differ from the elite because they are less wealthy, have few if any personal followers, and, lacking personal support in land or family, are much less likely to be associated with local districts. This middle class is the principal source of nationalist feeling; one of the chief features of recent Persian life has been the way in which the shah has shifted the basis of his support from the elite landed group to this growing middle class and to those whose social position is based on know-how and training rather than on wealth and family. Chief roles in this shift have been played by the army and the agrarian question.

A century ago, political power in Iran was concentrated in the hands of the autocratic shah supported by the interlocking elite of landlords and army officers. At that time the shah, in fact, was not Persian, but Turkic, the Qajar dynasty of 1796–1925. It was a period in which Persia was a zone of political conflict between the imperialism of czarist Russia and that of Victorian Britain. On two occasions, in 1907 and again in 1942, these two Powers made agreements setting up spheres of influence in Iran. Since these agreements were reached because of their common enmity toward Germany, it was almost inevitable that these agreements would break down and rivalry be resumed on the defeat of Germany in 1918 and again in 1945. It was almost equally inevitable that Iran should seek support from some outside Power against the joint or parallel Anglo-Russian pressure, as it did from Germany before 1914, before 1941, and from the United States since 1946.

Iran's ability to resist any outside pressure was reduced by the general weakness and confusion of its own governmental system. This was a personal royal autocracy resting upon a feudalized substructure of tribal chiefs, great landlords, and religious leaders, even after the establishment of a constitutional government and a National Assembly (the Majlis) in 1906. The strong role played by personal influence, especially that of the shah, prevents the formation of real political parties or the functioning of the governmental structure as a system of principles, laws, conventions, and established relationships.

In the days of his autocratic power, before 1914, the shah sought to raise funds for his personal use by selling concessions and monopolies to foreign groups. Most of these, such as those on tobacco or sugar, were exploitative of the Iranian peoples and were very unpopular. Of these concessions the most significant was one granted in 1901 to William Knox D'Arcy for the exclusive right to exploit all stages of the petroleum business in all Iran except the five provinces bordering on Russia. The control of this concession shuffled from one corporate entity to another until, in 1909, it came into possession of the new Anglo-Persian Oil Company. This company established the world's largest refinery at Abadan on the Persian Gulf and, by 1914, signed an agreement with the British government which made it the chief source of fuel for the British Navy. It gradually extended its activities, through a myriad of subsidiary corporations, throughout the world and simultaneously came to be controlled, through secret stock ownership, by the British government.

At the end of World War I, Iran was a battleground between Russian and British armed forces. By 1920 the withdrawal of British forces and the Bolshevization of Russia left the anti-Bolshevik Russian Cossack

Brigade as the only significant military force in the country. The chief Iranian officer in that force, Reza Pahlavi, in the course of 1921-1925, gradually took over control of the government and eventually deposed the incompetent, twenty-eight-year-old Shah Ahmad.

Reza Shah Pahlavi followed the pattern of modernization established by Kemal Atatürk in Turkey but was constantly hampered by inadequate financial resources, by the underdeveloped economic system, and by the backward social development of the area. Nevertheless, he did a great deal of uncoordinated modernization, especially in education, law, and communications. His chief aim was to break down tribalism and localism and to establish national loyalty to a unified Iran. To this end he defeated the autonomous tribes, settled nomadic groups in villages, shifted provincial boundaries to break up local loyalties, created a national civil service and police force, established a national registration with identity cards for all, and used universal conscription to mingle various groups in a national army. One of his chief efforts, to improve communications and transportation, culminated in the Trans-Iranian Railway from the Persian Gulf to the Caspian Sea, built in eleven years (1929-1940) at a cost of about $150 million. Roads were constructed where only local paths had existed before, and some effort was made to establish industries to provide work for a new urban class.

All these projects required money, which was very difficult to find in a country of limited natural resources. The chief resource, oil, was tied up completely in the concession held by the Anglo-Persian Oil Company (later called Anglo-Iranian or AIOC), with the inevitable result that it became the target of the Iranian nationalist desire for additional development funds. In this struggle the older elite of Iranian life, including the shah, the army, and the landlords would have been satisfied with a renegotiated deal with AIOC yielding additional funds to Iran, but the newer urban groups of professional and commercial origin combined with the religious agitators to demand the complete removal of foreign economic influence by nationalization of the petroleum industry.

In this division within Iran, control of the situation gradually moved from the older elite to the newer nationalist groups for a variety of reasons. The years of the world depression, the financial crisis, and the Second World War greatly intensified all the objectionable features of the AIOC system and, at the same time, seemed to show that no new agreement with the company could remedy these objections. Such a new agreement had been made in 1933, but the situation became worse (from the Iranian nationalist point of view). Accordingly, when the government in 1950 tried to obtain a new supplemental agreement, nationalist feeling rose quickly against it and demanded complete nationalization of the oil business instead. In June 1950, the shah put in as prime minister his man, General Ali Razmara, formerly chief of the General Staff, to force through the supplemental agreement. Opposing groups introduced nationalization bills in opposition to the government.

Gradually the nationalization forces began to coalesce about a strange figure, Dr. Muhammad Mossadegh of an old, wealthy, landed family which had served the Qajar dynasty as ministers of finance since the eighteenth century. Mossadegh was a Westernizer with an earned doctorate in economics from a Swiss university, a man of great personal courage and few personal ambitions or desires, who was convinced that national independence could be established and the obvious corruption of Iranian political life eliminated only by the recovery of Iranian control of its own economic life by nationalization of AIOC. Politically he was a moderate, but his strong emotional appeal to Iranian nationalism encouraged extremist reactions among his followers.

Long and fruitless discussions between AIOC and the Iranian government, with constant interference by the British government led to stalemate. The company insisted that its status was based on a contractual agreement which could not be modified without its consent, while the British government maintained that the agreement was a matter of international public law, like a treaty, which it had a right to enforce. The Iranian government declared that it had the right as a sovereign state to nationalize an Iranian corporation operating under its law on its territory, subject only to adequate compensation and assumption of its contractual obligations.

The Iranian nationalist arguments against the company were numerous and detailed:

1. It had promised to train Iranians for all positions possible, but instead had used these only in menial tasks, trained few natives, and employed many foreigners.

2. It had reduced its payments to Iran, which were based on its profits, by reducing the amount of its profits by bookkeeping tricks. For example, it sold oil at very low prices to wholly owned subsidiaries outside Iran or to the British Navy, allowing the former to resell at world prices so that AIOC made small profits, while the subsidiaries made very large profits not subject to Iranian royalty obligations. Iran believed that the profits of such wholly owned subsidiaries were really part of AIOC and should fall under the consolidated balance sheet of AIOC and thus make payments to Iran, but as late as 1950 AIOC admitted that the accounts of 59 such dummy corporations were not included in the AIOC accounts.

3. AIOC generally refused to pay Iranian taxes, especially income tax, but paid such taxes to Britain; at the same time, it calculated the Iranian profit royalties *after* such taxes, so that the higher British taxes went, the less the Iranian payment became. In effect, thus, Iran paid income

tax to Britain. In 1933 AIOC paid £305,418 in British taxation and £274,412 in Iranian taxes; in 1948 the two figures were £28,310,353 and £1,369,328.

4. The payment to Iran was also reduced by putting profits into reserves or into company investments outside Iran, often in subsidiaries, and calculating the Iranian share only on the profits distributed as dividends. Thus in 1947, when profits were really £40.5 million, almost £14.9 million went to British income tax, £11.5 million went to reserves, over £7.1 million went to stockholders (of which £3.3 million to the British government), and only £7.1 million to Iran. If the payment to Iran had been calculated before taxes and reserves, it would have been at least £6 million more that year.

5. Moreover, AIOC was exempt from Iranian customs tariffs on goods necessary to its operation brought into the country. Since it considered everything it brought in, whatever it was, to be necessary, it deprived Iran of about £6 million a year by this.

6. The company paid only a very small portion of the social costs of its operations in Persia, drawing many persons to arid and uninhabited portions of the country and then providing very little of the costs of housing, education, or health.

7. The AIOC, as a member of the international petroleum cartel, reduced its oil production in Iran and thus reduced Iran's royalties.

8. The AIOC continued to calculate its payments to Iran in gold at £8.10s. per ounce for years after the world gold price had risen to £13 an ounce, while the American corporation, Aramco, in Saudi Arabia raised its gold price on demand.

9. The AIOC's monopoly on oil export from Iran prevented development of other Iranian oil fields in areas outside the AIOC concession.

As a consequence of all these activities, the Iranian nationalists of 1952 felt angered to think that Iran had given up 300 million tons of oil over fifty years and received £105 million, while Britain had invested only £20 million and obtained about £800 million in profits.

The Iranian opposition to nationalization was broken in March 1951, when the prime minister, Ali Razmara, and his minister of education were assassinated within a space of two weeks. The nationalization law was passed the following month and, at the same time, at the request of the Majlis, the shah appointed Mossadegh prime minister to carry it out. This was done with considerable turmoil, which included strikes by AIOC workers against mistimed British wage cuts, anti-British street riots, and the arrival of British gunboats at the head of the Persian Gulf. Rather than give up the enterprise or operate it for the Iranian government, AIOC began to curtail operations and ship home its engineers. On May 25, 1951, it appealed to the International Court of Justice in spite of Iranian protests that the case was a domestic one, not international. Only on July 22, 1952, did the court's decision uphold Iran's contention by refusing jurisdiction.

At first the United States, and especially its ambassador in Tehran, supported the Iranian position. It feared that British recalcitrance would drive Iran toward Russia, and was especially alarmed at the possibility of any landing of British forces, since this would allow the Soviet Union to invade the North Iranian provinces as provided in the Soviet-Iran Treaty of 1921. However, it soon became evident that the Soviet Union, while supporting Iran's position, was not going to interfere. The American position then became increasingly pro-British and anti-Mossadegh. This was intensified by the shift in administration from Truman to Eisenhower early in 1953, and by the pressures on the American government by the international petroleum cartel. At the same time, the American oil companies, which had briefly hoped that they might replace AIOC in the Persian area, decided that their united front with AIOC in the world cartel was more valuable to them.

This world oil cartel had developed from a tripartite agreement signed on September 17, 1928 by Royal Dutch-Shell, Anglo-Iranian, and Standard Oil. The three signers were Sir Henri Deterding of Shell, Sir John (later Lord) Cadman of AIOC, and Walter C. Teagle of Esso. These agreed to manage oil prices on the world market by charging an agreed fixed price plus freight costs, and to store surplus oil which might weaken the fixed price level. By 1949 the cartel had as members the seven greatest oil companies of the world (Anglo-Iranian, Royal Dutch-Shell, Esso, Calso, Socony-Vacuum, Gulf, and Texaco). Excluding the United States domestic market, the Soviet Union, and Mexico, it controlled 92 percent of the world's reserves of oil, 88 percent of the world's production, 77 percent of the world's refining capacity, and 70 percent of the world's tonnage in ocean tankers.

As soon as Britain lost its case in the International Court of Justice and it became clear that Iran would go ahead with its nationalization, Britain put into effect a series of reprisals against Iran which rapidly crippled the country. Iranian funds in Britain were blocked; its purchases in British-controlled markets were interrupted; and its efforts to sell oil abroad were frustrated by a combination of the British Navy and the world oil cartel (which closed its sales and distribution facilities to Iranian oil). These cut off a substantial portion of the Iranian government's revenues and forced a drastic curtailment of government expenditures.

To deal with this situation, especially to cut the military budget, Mossadegh, in July 1952, asked for full powers from the Assembly. He was refused and resigned, but the Ahmad Ghavam government which replaced him lasted only six days, resigning under pressure of pro-Mossadegh street riots. Back in office, Mossadegh obtained dicta-torial power for six months. He broke off diplomatic relations with the British, closed down nine British consular offices, deported various British economic and cultural groups, and dismissed both the Senate and the Iranian Supreme Court, which were beginning to question his actions.

By that time (summer, 1953) almost irresistible forces were building up against Mossadegh, since lack of Soviet interference gave the West full freedom of action. The British, the AIOC, the world petroleum cartel, the American government, and the older Iranian elite led by the shah combined to crush Mossadegh. The chief effort came from the American supersecret intelligence agency (CIA) under the personal direction of its director, Allen W. Dulles, brother of the secretary of state. Dulles, as a former director of the Schroeder Bank in New York, was an old associate of Frank C. Tiarks, a partner in the Schroeder Bank in London since 1902, and a director of the Bank of England in 1912–1945, as well as Lazard Brothers Bank, and the AIOC. It will be recalled that the Schroeder Bank in Cologne helped to arrange Hitler's accession to power as chancellor in January 1933.

Managing Mossadegh's fall in August, 1953, was considerably easier, since he left his defense wide open by an attack on the prerogatives of the Iranian Army, apparently in the belief that the army would be prevented from moving against him by his influence over the mobs in the streets of Tehran. But throughout the Near East, street mobs are easily roused and directed by those who are willing to pay, and Dulles had the unlimited secret funds of the CIA. From these he gave $10 million to Colonel H. Norman Schwartzkopf, former head of the New Jersey State Police, who was in charge of training the Imperial Iranian Gendarmerie, and this was judiciously applied in ways which changed the mobs' tune considerably from July to August 1953. The whole operation was directed by Dulles himself from Switzerland where he was visited by Schwartzkopf, the American ambassador to Tehran, Loy Henderson, and messengers from the shah in the second week of August 1953.

Mossadegh purged the army of opposition elements without complete success in the spring of 1953, going so far as to arrest the chief of staff on March 1st. In July he sought to bypass the Assembly and demon-strate his irresistible popular support by having all his supporters resign from the Majlis (thus paralyzing its operations), and held a plebiscite in August to approve his policies. The official vote in the plebiscite was about two million approvals against twelve hundred disapprovals, but Mossadegh's days were numbered. On August 13th the shah precipitated the planned anti-Mossadegh coup by naming General Fazlollah Zahedi as prime minister, and sent a messenger dismissing Mossadegh. The latter refused to yield, and called his supporters into the streets, where they rioted against the shah, who fled with his family to Rome. Two days later, anti-Mossadegh mobs, supported by the army, defeated Mossadegh's supporters in Tehran, killing several hundred. Mossadegh was forced out of office and replaced by General Zahedi. The shah returned from Italy on August 22nd.

The fall of Mossadegh ended the period of confusions which had ensued since the forced abdication of Reza Shah in 1941. From 1953 on, the shah and the army, backed by the conservative elite, controlled the country and the docile Majlis. Two weeks after the shah's counter-coup, the United States gave Iran an emergency grant of $45 million, increased its annual economic aid payment to $23 million, and began to pay $5 million a month in Mutual Security Funds. These payments reached a total of a quarter of a billion dollars over five years. In return Iran became a firm member of the Western bloc, joined the Baghdad Pact (Central Treaty Organization) in 1955, and provided a close base for surreptitious actions (such as U-2 overflights) against the Soviet Union. The Communist-controlled Tudeh Party, the only political party in Iran with the established doctrine and organized structure of such a party in the Western sense, had been officially banned in 1949 but had supported Mossadegh from underground, where it was relentlessly pursued after 1953.

By 1960 the shah felt his position sufficiently strong to try to pursue a policy of his own, and began to shift his alignment from the older elite group of landlords and army toward the more progressive groups of urban middle-class professional peoples which had supported Mossadegh. The chief evidence of this was an effort to adopt, more or less as his personal policy, a program of agrarian reform which sought to restrict each landlord's holdings to a single village, taking all excess lands over for government payments spread over ten years and granting the lands to the peasants who worked them in return for payments spread over fifteen years. The shah's own estates were among the first to be distributed, but by the end of 1962 over five thousand other villages had also been granted to their peasants.

In the meantime the oil dispute was settled by a compromise in October 1954. The exploitation and marketing of Iran's oil was taken over by a consortium of existing petroleum companies from the world cartel and some American "independents," with a 40 percent interest held by AIOC itself. The previous disputes were compromised without too much difficulty once it was recognized that both sides had a common interest in preserving the world structure of managed oil prices in order to ensure substantial incomes to both. The incomes to Iran were considerably increased, averaging about $250 million or more a year.

THE NEAR EAST

The oil crisis in Iran was limited in scope and duration. Neither of these can be said of the great and continuing crisis experienced by the Arabic Near East in the twentieth century. The crisis of these countries was a crisis of the system itself, the collapse of Islamic civilization culminating in the disappearance of the Ottoman Empire which ruled over it in its later stages. The Near East today is the wreckage of that civilization, and as such presents problems far greater than the simple one of inadequate natural resources. Rather, the problem is a triple one of resources, of creating a workable and viable social organization, and of developing patterns of belief, outlook, and feelings which have some constructive value for human survival.

In this colossal problem the influence of the Soviet Union, or of the Western Powers, or even of the Cold War conflict itself are relatively minor matters which could be reduced to much less significance if the peoples of the area could get themselves organized, both externally and internally, into some viable arrangement of living patterns. The same problem is being faced throughout the broad band of countries from Indonesia and Japan, across China and India, throughout Africa, to Latin America; but almost nowhere is the problem more acute, and apparently more hopeless, than in the Near East. This arises from the area's strategic importance between Asia, Africa, and Europe, its nearness to the Soviet Union, its central position in the air routes and the water communications of the world (symbolized by the Suez Canal), and its great significance in the world's petroleum supplies.

The broadest aspects of the Near East's problems must be reserved to a later discussion dealing with the general problems of the Buffer Fringe and the underdeveloped areas. At the moment we must concentrate on the two most acute and immediate problems of the area. These are Israel and Egypt.

These two problems are working within a background of five significant factors. First is the continuing Soviet-American rivalry, which benefits no one in the Near East. Second is the sordid and grinding poverty of Near Eastern life, a poverty made up, in almost equal parts, of poor natural resources (especially water shortages), wasteful and irrational social organization, and hopelessly uncooperative and spiteful personality patterns. Third is the shifting but perpetual dynastic and political rivalries of the area among the Arab countries themselves. Fourth is the almost incredibly misdirected interferences from the Western Powers, especially the United States. And fifth is the dominant role played by the armed forces in Near Eastern life.

Of these five background factors, only the last requires any amplification here. Wherever a modern state structure appears in an impoverished environment, the possession of arms is restricted to a small group and tends to bring control of the whole society under the influence of those who possess the arms. This problem becomes particularly acute in areas where other countervailing factors, such as religion, family influence, or traditional organizations are weak and where the social values of the society place a high esteem on military prowess or violence. The Arabs had always been warlike; by adopting Islam in the seventh century, they acquired a religion which intensified this tendency. This was clearly shown in the Saracen conquests of the Near East, North Africa, and southwestern Europe within a century of Muhammad's death. Certain restraints, however, were placed upon this militarism by other factors, such as the religious elements in Islam and the powerful influence of family and tribal loyalties. By the twentieth century the steady dwindling of these alternative influences and finally the total disintegration of Islamic society left militarism in a much more dominant position. This situation is evident wherever Arabic influence spread, including North Africa, Spain, and Latin America, so that today the army is the chief political force all the way from the Persian Gulf to Peru. We have already seen the chief example of this in Spain.

The situation is roughly the same throughout the Arabic Near East. This dominance by the armed forces would not be so objectionable were it not that their leaders are (1) ignorant, (2) selfish, (3) outstanding obstacles to any progressive reorganization of the community, especially by their diversion of the limited wealth available for social or economic investment, and (4) are so lacking in military morale or competence that they provide almost no protection for the areas which they are presumably supposed to defend. Certainly any area needs some organized force of arms-bearing persons to maintain public order and to protect the area from external interference, but the incompetence of the existing armed forces from Kuwait to Bolivia is so great that a superior degree of public order and defense could have been achieved with a greater degree of stability from a simple gendarmerie equipped with motorcars and hand guns than from the expensive arrays of complicated and misused equipment which have been provided for, or forced upon, the armies of this great area from the United States, the West European Powers, or, (since 1955) the Communist bloc.

Although parliamentary regimes, in imitation of Britain and France, had been established throughout the Near East, as in much of the world, they never functioned as democratic or even constitutional systems because of the lack of organized political parties and of any traditions of civil and personal rights. Political parties remained largely personal followings or blocs, and political power, based on the arbitrary autocracy of Semitic patriarchal family life, was also personal, and never took on the impersonal characteristics associated with Western rule of law and consitutional practices. The weakness of any conception of rules, and of the material benefits which help rules to survive, made it impossible for the Near East to grasp the conventions associated with cooperation in opposition found in the Western two-party system, parliamentary practices, and sports.

The whole range of human and universal relations of the Arabs was monistic, personal, and extralegal, in contrast to that of the West, which was pluralistic, impersonal, and subject to rules. As a result, constitutional and two-party politics were incomprehensible to the Near East, and the parliamentary system, where it existed, was only a facade for an autocratic system of personal intrigues. It is no accident that two-party politics functioned in the Near East only briefly and in two non-Arabic, if Muslim, countries: Turkey and the Sudan. It is also no accident that in most of the Near East, the chief method for changing a government was by assassination and that such actions usually took place in the most cowardly fashion (to Western eyes) such as shooting in the back.

The growth of militarism in the Near East modified these political practices to some extent but without changing them in any fundamental way. The parliament was ignored or abolished, political groups and blocs were eliminated or outlawed, often being replaced by a single amorphous and meaningless party whose sole purpose was propaganda; and military administration generally replaced civil parliamentary government. Most obviously, perhaps, changes of regime now take place by military coups instead of by rigged elections or by assassinations. Even the Sudan and Turkey had their two-party parliamentary regimes overturned by military *coups d'état* in 1958 and in 1960. Elsewhere factions within the officers' corps have replaced parliamentary political parties as the significant units of political conflict. Thus Iraq had military *coups* in 1936, 1941, 1958, and 1963. Similar events were frequent in Syria, notably in 1949, 1951, 1961, and 1962.

That the poverty, chaos, and disunity of the Arab world was a consequence of organizational and morale factors rather than of such objective obstacles as limited natural resources is clear from the case of Israel. There, in less than eight thousand square miles with no significant resources and hampered by endless external obstacles, the Zionist movement has constructed the strongest, most stable, most progressive, most democratic, and most hopeful state in the Near East. This was possible because of the morale of the Israeli, which was based on outlooks antithetical to the attitudes of the Arabs. The Israeli were full of self-sacrifice, self-discipline, social solidarity, readiness to work, cooperation, and hopes for the future. Their ideology was largely Western, with a devotion to science, democracy, individual respect, technology, and the future which could match or exceed the best periods of the Western past. All these things made them anathema to the Arabs, whose hysterical hatred was not really aimed at the loss of Palestine as a land but at the presence of the Israeli, whose qualities were a refutation of generations of Arab self-deceptions and pretenses.

The precarious balance the British had tried to keep in Palestine between their promises to the Zionists and their efforts to placate the Arabs were destroyed by Hitler's determination to annihilate the Jews of Europe and the conditions of World War II which made it seem that he would be successful. The Jews, their supporters, and allies tried to smuggle in any Jews who could be saved from Europe. Since there was nowhere else they could go, many were smuggled into Palestine. British efforts to prevent this, in fulfillment of their obligations to the Arabs under the League of Nations Mandate, led to a kind of guerrilla warfare between Jews and British, with the Arabs attacking the former intermittently. This problem reached acute form when the conquest of Germany opened the doors for surviving Jews to escape from the horrors of Nazism. In August 1945, President Truman asked British permission to admit 100,000 European Jews into Palestine, but his repeated requests were refused. Ignoring such permission, large-scale efforts were made to smuggle Jewish refugees into Palestine, where they could be cared for by Jewish groups. Many of these were transported under frightful conditions in overcrowded, leaky ships, which were often intercepted by the British, who took their passengers to concentration camps in Cyprus. From such actions came reprisals and counter-reprisals.

The Zionist settlement in Palestine was largely agricultural, the immigrants being settled in close-knit village communities on lands, often semiarid lands, purchased by funds raised by the World Zionist conference or its friends and administered under the Jewish Agency for Palestine. These organizations gave the Zionist groups, over several decades, the political and administrative experience and the patterns of self-sacrifice for a common cause which provided the functioning political structure for the state of Israel as the British mandate for Palestine was ended in 1948. The Zionist communal villages, under constant danger of attack by Arab raiders, developed a mentality somewhat like that of early American frontier settlements amid hostile Indians. Each village developed a force of trained defense fighters, its Haganah, with arms hidden in the village, or in a regional center, for the day in which they must fight for their continued existence. This Haganah organization subsequently became the Army of Israel.

British raids on Zionist centers to arrest illegal immigrants or to seize hidden arms, and Arab attacks upon incautious Zionist settlements, soon led to reprisals and counter-reprisals and to the creation of violent and bitter splinter groups within the Zionist effort. The Jewish Agency did not have absolute control over the Haganah and had decreasingly less over a number of minute reprisal groups of which the chief were the extremist Irgun Zvai Le'umi, with several thousand members, or the terrorist "Stern Gang" of less than two hundred. The latter group had murdered the British high commissioner, Lord Moyne, in November 1944, and later assassinated the United Nations mediator, Count Folke Bernadotte of Sweden, in September 1948.

During the years 1945-1948, the Jewish Agency sought to establish a Jewish state in Palestine, to remove the rigid British restrictions on Jewish immigration and Jewish land purchases, and to obtain an international loan to finance its Jewish settlement policies. These were resisted, not only because of Britain's desires to remain on amicable relations with the Arab states, but also from the obvious lack of sympathy for the Zionist cause within the British government, especially after Churchill's National government was replaced by a Labour Party regime in 1945. The immediate demand for admission of 100,000 Jewish refugees from Europe was rejected by the British, and efforts to smuggle some of these in gave rise to conditions of quasi-warfare between Britain and the Zionist groups. A League of the neighboring Arab states which had been formed under British sponsorship in March 1945 took as its chief aim the destruction of the Zionist plans, and sought to block Jewish immigration or use up Haganah arms by sneak raids on Zionist frontier settlements.

When the Labour government in June 1946 refused the Zionist request for admission of the 100,000 refugees, and, instead, sought to arrest the members of the Jewish Agency, the Irgun Zvai Le'umi in reprisal exploded 500 pounds of TNT under the British headquarters in the east wing of the luxurious King David Hotel in Jerusalem, killing almost a hundred persons. The World Zionist Congress elections of December showed decreasing support for more moderate figures like Dr. Chaim Weizmann and David Ben-Gurion. The former won reelection as president of the World Zionist Movement by a bare majority, and refused to offer his name for reelection as president of the Jewish Agency. This increase in the extremist influence within the Zionist movement made it clear to Britain that peace in Palestine could be maintained only at a great cost which the Labour government was unable and unwilling to pay. Support for the mandate from the United States was unobtainable, since Washington generally tended to favor the Jewish side, while the British, in spite of their valiant efforts to appear impartial, clearly favored the Arabs. Death sentences on Jewish terrorists, first carried out by the British in 1947, merely intensified the violence, with the British armed forces suffering about three casualties a week, one-third fatal.

In April 1947, the British sought to escape from the situation by appealing to the United Nations, which voted in November to partition Palestine into two intertwining Jewish and Arab zones, with an international zone in Jerusalem. The Arab League rejected partition, and its members swore to resist it by force, by a "relentless war," according to a Cairo newspaper. This war opened with Arab riots in Palestine against the UN vote at the very time that the Jews were welcoming it. Arab irregulars began to enter Palestine from Syria and Egypt as the British began to withdraw from their long effort to administer the country.

This British withdrawal from Palestine was but one aspect of the general withdrawal of Britain from its prewar world and imperial position. It was a consequence of the general political weakening of Great Britain, its acute economic and financial position in the postwar period and, above all, by the growing preference of the ordinary British voter for social welfare and higher living standards at home over the remote and impersonal glories of imperial prestige abroad.

On September 26, 1947, the British announced they would withdraw from Palestine and that failure to obtain a United Nations administration or any accepted Arab-Zionist partition would not delay this process. However, the British were determined not to hand over the administration to the only organization available which was capable of handling the job, the Jewish Agency, and as a result simply abandoned or closed down many public services and destroyed or left many essential administrative records. This created a chaotic situation in which the Arab League was unable to rule, the United Nations and Britain were unwilling to rule, and the Jewish Agency was prevented from taking over by the retiring British forces.

At the beginning of April 1948, small forces from Syria, Iraq, and Egypt entered Palestine to support the local Arabs' efforts to prevent the Jewish Agency taking control of the country. They were followed by the Arab Legion of Transjordan, under British officers, which came in as soon as the British mandate ended on May 14, 1948. Although the Zionists were outnumbered and had inferior equipment, their courage, tenacity, and persistence, combined with the mutual rivalries and divisions among the five Arab groups, allowed the Israeli to establish and consolidate a Zionist government in several areas of Palestine. During the interval, financial support from American sympathizers allowed the Zionists to rectify the arms disequilibrium, chiefly by purchases from Czechoslovakia, which had just joined the Iron Curtain bloc in March.

As early as January, many Arab families had begun to flee from Palestine, and by June this became a flood. Many left voluntarily, encouraged by the unrealistic promises of the Arab League to return them as conquerors after the total defeat of Zionism, but a substantial number were uprooted and expelled by Zionist retaliatory actions. Eventually, in spite of the Jewish Agency's promise that Arabs would be welcome to continue to live in Israel if they did not act to subvert the new state, the number of refugees reached an estimated 652,000 persons. Most of these were settled in camps along the frontiers in Jordan and in Egypt and were maintained by international charity administered under the United Nations.

Efforts to resettle these unfortunates within the Arab States of the Near East were blocked by these states, which refused to cooperate in any such recognition of the changed situation in Palestine and which welcomed refugee discontent as an instrument for stirring up hatred of Israel and the West among their own citizens. Large numbers of the refugees eventually left these camps and integrated themselves by their own efforts into the life of the Arab States of the Near East, but birthrates in the camps were so high that the total number in the camps decreased very slowly. In Jordan the refugees who became assimilated were so numerous and so bitter that they came to dominate that precarious state, were a constant threat to the stability of its government, forced it to destroy its friendly relations with Britain, which had founded it, and remained as an explosive threat against Israel.

The new state of Israel was proclaimed by Ben-Gurion on May 14, 1948, and was recognized by President Truman sixteen minutes later, in a race to beat the Soviet Union (whose recognition came on May 17th). Efforts by both to use the United Nations machinery to stop the Israeli-Arab war in Palestine were frustrated by conflicting opinions and especially by British efforts to restrict Israeli acquisition of arms and immigration without placing comparable restrictions on the surrounding Arab States.

A truce imposed by the UN on June 11th was violated by both sides and broke down with a resumption of fighting in July, but by that time the Arab states were squabbling bitterly among themselves, and were increasingly involved in embarrassment because their propaganda falsehoods to their own peoples about their glorious victories over Zionism could not be sustained in the face of the precipitous retreats of their forces under Israeli attacks. Some of the Arab states tried to excuse their defeats as resulting from Transjordanian "treason." Ten days of renewed fighting from July 8–18, 1948, mostly favorable to Israel, were ended by a three-day UN ultimatum threatening sanctions against any state which continued fighting. This curtailment of Israeli successes by United Nations actions and the UN mediator's suggestion that Jerusalem be given to the Arabs led directly to his assassination by Israeli extremists in September.

On September 20th the Grand Mufti of Jerusalem, chief Muslim religious leader of the Levant and a wartime collaborator with the Nazis, proclaimed an "Arab Government of All Palestine," which was at once recognized by all the Arab states except Jordan and was set up at Gaza on Palestine territory occupied by Egypt. Israel in return launched successful and successive week-long attacks on Egypt and Lebanon which were stopped by UN truces on October 31, 1948. Belated recognition of the truth about Egypt's weakness, if not its corruption, led to street riots in Cairo and assassination of the Egyptian prime minister.

British efforts to invoke its 1936 alliance with Egypt to justify British military action against Israel were blocked by Egypt's refusal to allow such a public display of Egypt's helplessness. Five British planes which "attacked" Israel were promptly shot down (January 7, 1949). This led to Britain's *de facto* recognition of Israel on January 29th and the gradual release of Jewish immigrants imprisoned on Cyprus. A series of armistice agreements were negotiated in the spring of 1949. These left various forces in approximately the positions they held, but were accompanied by explicit refusals by the Arab states to make peace with Israel, to recognize its existence, or to allow any steps to be taken to remedy the plight of Arab refugees outside Palestine. To this day these problems remain, with the Arab states still at war with Israel and publicly sworn to exterminate it.

Egypt's defeat in the Israeli war brought to a head persistent Egyptian discontent, especially its hatred for the corrupt and lecherous King Farouk. Egypt's plight, however, was far deeper and more ancient than Israel, and Farouk's blame, in spite of his total failure as a ruler, was less than that of his great-great-grandfather, Muhammad Ali, who had been Khedive of Egypt under the Ottoman sultan in 1811–1848. Until Muhammad Ali's time, Egypt continued its ancient practice of raising a single crop of food from each annual flooding of the Nile Valley. Muhammad Ali, in order to finance his plans to conquer the whole Near East, took over state ownership of all the land and built a great network of irrigation canals which permitted perennial cultivation of the land with two to four crops a year. He also established state monopolies of industrial enterprises to equip his armed forces.

Muhammad Ali's successors, especially his grandson, Ismail, ended state ownership of land and industry, allowing both to fall into private hands where they retained much of their monopolistic character. At the same time, they burdened the country with enormous debts to European bankers for public-works projects of irrigation, railroads, and the Suez Canal. In the same period, the demand for Egyptian long-lint cotton became so great during the world cotton shortage caused by the American Civil War that it became the favorite crop of the landlord class and the chief source of foreign exchange to pay off Egypt's debts. But this meant that Egypt's prosperity became linked to the uncontrolled fluctuations of prices on the Liverpool cotton market.

The results of all this were to create the Egypt of 1936, the first year of Farouk's reign. Irrigation, with its perpetual-motion farming, greatly increased the output of food, and allowed an increase in population from 3.2 million in 1821 to 6.8 million in 1892 to 12.5 million in 1914. At the same time European science, by its control of epidemic diseases, reduced the infant mortality rate. The rise in population began to outstrip the increase in food supply by a wide margin, especially when the small group of large landowners insisted that the land be used for exported cotton rather than for home-consumed food.

In 1914, production of cereals was 3.5 million tons for 12.5 million Egyptians; by 1940 there was only 4 million tons for 17 million persons. The output of food continued to crawl upward, following the great leaps in population. By 1960 the population was increasing at the rate of one person a minute, over half a million a year, and had already passed 26 million. Moreover, as a result of perennial irrigation, the population of 1940 was much less healthy than that of 1840, since it was infected with debilitating, chronic, water-borne, infectious diseases like malaria, bilharzia, ancylostomiasis, and irritating eye infections.

Moreover, unlike the ancient cultivation based on annual flooding which replaced the fertility of the soil, the perennial irrigation of today requires artificial fertilizers (which the harassed peasant cannot afford) to retain the productivity of the soil. Thus by 1950 an enormously increased population, worn down by anemia and malnutrition, was crowded in a narrow valley under the greatest population density in the world, with neither land nor work for idle millions, their miserable fates entirely in the hands of the small ruling elite of landlords, commercial monopolists, and political exploiters of world economic changes.

Until 1952 monopolization of land, although less complete than in other Near Eastern countries, was nevertheless extreme, since 3 percent of the landowners held 55 percent of the agricultural land and 28 percent of the owners held 87 percent of the land. The remaining 72 percent of landowners with 13 percent of the land were too poor to exploit their plots effectively since they could not afford fertilizer, choice seed, or adequate tools, and in most cases had to supplement their work on the land by other activities or by renting plots from other owners.

Since the great owners did not work their lands themselves, most Egyptian soil was worked by renters and sharecroppers, often removed from the real owner by a series of intermediaries and subleasers. In addition, of course, millions without land of their own had to work for about five American cents an hour on the lands of others, and a third group eked out an existence entirely from rented land in which the rents were equal to about three-quarters of the net yield. The burden of population on the land (about 1,500 persons per square mile compared to about 200 in France) left everyone drastically underemployed, with at least half the rural population merely sitting around in the dust or napping all day. Because children were more healthy than their diseased-sapped parents, they were more energetic and often were skillful and could be obtained for wages less than half that of men (about twenty American cents for a day of ten or twelve hours in 1956), much of the agricultural work, especially in cotton, was done by children.

The pressure of population, the productivity of the land from multiple cropping (average annual yields about twice those in Europe), and monopolized landownership drove land prices and rents upward just as they drove wages downward. This gave rise to a steady increase of renting and sharecropping before 1952. By 1948 the cash rental of land per acre was about 30 percent higher than the average net income per acre. Thus the situation in the rural economy was explosive.

These problems reached this critical level under the shield of the artificial prosperity of Egypt during the war. As the chief base for the Allied war effort in the Near East and the center of the British resistance to Rommel's Afrika Korps, Allied supplies and money had poured into Egypt and provided wages and a higher standard of living for all. Moreover, high wartime prices for cotton had created a temporary boom. By 1947 all this collapsed, and hundreds of thousands who had been supported by British spending during the war were wandering the alleys of Cairo without money, work, or hope.

In sharp contrast with the poverty of millions, about 400 families had made immense fortunes from the land since 1850. In 1952, when 250 acres brought its owner an income of about $20,000 a year, the royal family had close to 200,000 acres, and the few hundred landlord families held over a million acres. Little of these incomes was devoted to any constructive purpose, although few of their possessors lived such dissolute and wasteful existences as Farouk.

These economic discontents were capped by political unrest. Egypt had been granted its independence by Great Britain in 1922, but the latter continued to interfere in the governing of the country by peremptory notes or even ultimatums (as in 1924 and 1938). Submission by the monarchy or the government to such pressure roused great animosity in the Assembly, which was generally dominated by the irresponsible nationalist party, the Wafd (led successively by Saad Zaghlul and Mustafa Nahas). Relations with Britain were finally regulated by a treaty in 1936 which established a twenty-year alliance, granted Britain continued possession of the naval base at Alexandria until 1944, and allowed it to keep a force of 10,000 men in the Canal Zone. Other British forces were withdrawn, and the disputed question of conflicting British and Egyptian rights in the Sudan were compromised to allow limited Egyptian migration and limited use of Egyptian troops in that area.

The most significant result of the Anglo-Egyptian Treaty of 1936 was a double one. By providing for withdrawal of British troops from Egypt proper, it made it necessary for Egypt to establish its own army; at the same time, it established two political issues (British troops in the Suez Canal Zone and incomplete Egyptian control of the Sudan) on which that new army could agitate. Most significant of all, Mustafa Nahas's decree of 1936 establishing the Military Academy to train officers for the new army opened this career to any Egyptian, independent of class or economic status. This created the opening by which ambitious and relatively poor young men could work their way upward in power and wealth. It was the first essential step toward the Nasser government of the 1960's and, for the first time in thousands of years, made it possible for Egypt to be ruled by Egyptians (the Muhammad Ali dynasty of 1811–1952 was of Albanian origin). The first class of the Military Academy to graduate after the Treaty of 1936 was the class of 1938, whose members, led by Nasser, made the revolution of 1952. Most of the leaders of that revolt were either the sons or grandsons of poor peasants. The chief aims of their revolt were agrarian reform, elimination of waste, inefficiency, and corruption from the Egyptian government, and the completion of independence by the withdrawal of British influence from the Canal Zone and, if possible, the Sudan.

The revolt moved forward under the impetus of increasing shame and hatred for the Farouk monarchy. In this process two chief steps were the British ultimatum of 1942 and the defeat by Israel in 1948, since these opened an unbridgeable gap between the dynasty and the officers' group.

The conspiracies of the class of 1938 began almost immediately upon their graduation from the Military Academy, when Gamal Abdel Nasser joined a group which exchanged secret oaths to reform Egypt by expelling the British. By 1939 most of this group were in contact with the "Muslim Brotherhood," a secret band of fanatics founded in 1929 to establish (by assassination and violence, if necessary) a political regime founded on purely Muslim principles. Many of both groups were involved in the anti-British and pro-Nazi agitations throughout the Near East of 1938–1942. These centered around the fanatical Mufti of Jerusalem and culminated in the pro-Nazi revolt of Rashid Ali al-Kilani in Iraq, during Hitler's conquest of Crete in April 1941. Britain used force to overthrow the new pro-Hitler government in Iraq, but the anti-British agitations continued throughout the Arab world. When they became acute in Egypt in February 1942, the British ambassador, accompanied by British tanks, visited King Farouk in the Abdin Palace and gave him a choice between cooperation with Britain or deposition. The king yielded at once, but many of the younger officers were outraged at this affront to Egyptian dignity, and Lieutenant Colonel Muhammad Naguib resigned his commission in protest at an army which was "unable to protect its king."

Ten years later, when Farouk's disgraceful behavior had alienated most of the army and disquieted much of the world, this same Naguib, by then a heroic general who had been wounded three times in the war of 1948 with Israel, was the nominal head of the revolt.

This revolt was engineered by a small group of five officers whose real leader was Nasser, although the latter, who had been conspiring against one thing or another since his schooldays, was virtually unknown to the police until the revolt had already started.

Like most revolts, that of 1952 started from an event which had little to do with the conspirators' plans. In October 1951, Mustafa Nahas, who had signed the Anglo-Egyptian Treaty of 1936, enacted a law to abrogate it. Shortly afterward, guerrilla attacks on the British military installations in the Canal Zone drove the British forces to seek to disarm the Egyptian police nearby. In the resulting fight about fifty Egyptians were killed and a hundred wounded. The next day (January 26, 1952) riots in Cairo burned down about four hundred buildings, including the famous Shepheard's Hotel, the center of British tourist life in Egypt. Damage ran to over $60 million, but the real destruction was to the Egyptian political system.

Police and army both refused to fire upon the incendiaries of January 26th. Farouk, who had no wish to alienate the British, dismissed Prime Minister Nahas for the Cabinet's inadequate efforts to suppress the disturbances. But no successor could be found capable of winning the confidence of the diverse groups who sought to exploit the miseries of Egypt.

On the night of July 22nd, eight young officers seized control of the army headquarters, the radio stations, and the government, and forced Farouk to make General Naguib head of the army. Only two soldiers were killed in the process. Four days later, with tanks surrounding the palace, Farouk was forced to abdicate and was sent into exile.

The new revolution had neither doctrine nor program, and continued to improvise year after year. A civilian prime minister was replaced by General Naguib on September 7th, and he was replaced by Nasser on February 25, 1954. Most decrees, with the exception of the Agrarian Law of 1952 and its subsequent revisions, were concerned with the officers' junta's efforts to consolidate itself in power. Opposition groups from all parts of the political spectrum were arrested, usually imprisoned without trial, and sometimes tortured. Some were tried and executed. All political parties were dissolved and their assets confiscated "for the people." A rather vague pro-junta party, called the National Liberation Rally, was established to support the new regime, but without any real program. The Communists, the Muslim Brotherhood, and striking labor unions were persecuted, and most of the wealthy elite were cut down in wealth and influence.

The source of these authoritarian moves was Nasser, even in the period when Naguib was both president of the republic (June 1953 to November 1954) and prime minister (September 1952 to February 1954). Nasser, who replaced Naguib as prime minister in February 1954, replaced him as president as well in November of that year. The general issue on which they broke was Nasser's autocracy, but the specific issue was his outlawing of the Muslim Brotherhood. Nasser won out in the struggle because he was concerned only with the reality of power and was prepared to cooperate with any group, to adopt any program, or to sacrifice any friend if doing so would strengthen his control of Egypt. Originally his personal sympathies were with the peasant masses and with the West, and there is no evidence that he was possessed of the pleasure-loving indolent characteristics which weaken so many ambitious Arabs. He continued to regard himself as a man of the people, but his insatiable thirst was for personal power.

The Agrarian Law of September 1952 determined much of the subsequent political and economic policy of the regime. It sought to alleviate the plight of the peasant and to force the landlord group, the center of Egyptian wealth, to shift their holdings from land to investment in industry and commerce. This was expected to create jobs for the numerous unemployed of the cities and to increase the Egyptian sector in trade, which was still largely in foreign hands. The original law set a maximum of landownership of 315 acres for each family, with 210 for the head of the family and a quarter as much for each of the first two children. Land beyond this amount had to be sold to the peasants who were actually working it, at a price seventy times the annual land tax, in plots of 2 to 5 acres. If not sold thus in six weeks, the surplus was taken by the state in return for thirty-year 3 percent bonds and was then sold to the peasants on long-term payments by the state. Since the peasants' cultivation, whether as laborer, renter, or sharecropper, had previously been strictly regulated by the owner, this regulatory function was, under the new law, taken over by cooperative societies which were made compulsory in each district. These societies also act as purchasing, marketing, and training cooperatives. The law also enacted a reduction in rents for peasants who rented land. Several years later the maximum limit for landownership was reduced to 52.5 acres per person.

The agrarian reform undoubtedly helped the peasants who obtained ownership of plots or those whose rents were reduced, but it did nothing about the landless laborers or the growing mass of persons with no economic role who were multiplying so rapidly from the population explosion. The older landlord class, even on a fifty-acre maximum, was adequately provided for, but the method of compensation for their confiscated lands did not give them the free capital which it had been hoped would expand industry and trade. Moreover, few had sufficient confidence in the economic future of Egypt or the regime itself to put much of their current incomes into such activities, especially as the Nasser government took over many of the largest and most prosperous industrial enterprises. As a result, the government itself had increasingly to create new enterprises from government funds, and the system, although committed to a "mixed economy," increasingly had to move toward Socialism.

It was clear from the beginning that the only remedy for the population explosion was additional land, and it was equally clear that this could be achieved only if the waters of the Nile were spread widely and more effectively over the uncultivated periphery of the Nile Valley. For this purpose the Nasser government proposed a High Dam three miles south of Aswan between the First Cataract of the Nile and the Sudan frontier. The project was technically feasible but enormously expensive, and involved complex political problems.

The proposed dam, three miles long and 120 yards high, would back up a reservoir of about 130 billion cubic meters of water, much of it in Sudan territory, and displacing 60,000 inhabitants as well as submerging many archaeological treasures. The project, originally estimated to cost over a billion dollars, would increase Egypt's farm lands by about 30 percent, or two million acres, and, by equalizing the flow of the Nile throughout the year, would steady the country's whole system of agricultural production. If the flow of water from the reservoir were harnessed to generate electricity, it could yield 10,000 million kilowatt-hours, but this would drive the total cost up to about $4 billion over fifteen years. Such a project could not possibly be financed by Egypt itself, and could not be built without previous agreement with the Sudan. Such an agreement must modify an earlier compromise of 1929 which gave Egypt 48,000 million cubic meters of water and the Sudan only 4,000 million cubic meters out of the total Nile flow of 84,000 million cubic meters, leaving 32,000 million cubic meters which previously flowed to the sea to be divided from the new High Dam reservoir.

From the beginning it should have been clear to Nasser that his regime would be a success only if he found a solution to Egypt's economic plight and that the most substantial contribution to such a solution would come from the High Dam. Such a dam could be built only with the financial assistance of the West, since the Soviet bloc lacked the free resources or the psychological outlook to do the job, and a dam of that size, seventeen times the mass of the pyramid of Cheops, could not be built by Egypt's own resources soon enough to alleviate Egypt's economy. If Nasser had concentrated on this problem and determined to retain relations with the United States sufficiently amicable to obtain the necessary American aid, some progressive solution of the problems of Egypt and the Near East might have been possible.

However, Nasser allowed himself to be distracted by all kinds of emotional upheavals of an unconstructive kind. He maintained a constant state of hatred and tension toward Israel; he insisted on heavy armaments Egypt neither needed nor could afford and which Egyptians lacked the skill and the morale to use; he kept Egyptians and the whole Arab world in an uproar by his incendiary speeches and actions and his continual political intrigues and interventions in a fantastic and needless effort to make himself the leader of Arab political movements all the way from Morocco and Lake Chad to the Persian Gulf and Alexandretta; and he insisted on demonstrating his independence of the West by constant attacks and insults directed at the United States.

The United States, in the Dulles era, contributed to this confusion by its mistaken idea that the Soviet Union was actively engaging in efforts to take over the Near East and by Dulles's efforts to force all the countries of the area into a single defensive pact, like the Baghdad Pact. Dulles's contribution to the confusions of the Near East, as elsewhere, was that he refused to see that the problems of primary concern to the local peoples were local problems and that these were merely worsened by his insistence that the only problem in any area was the Cold War between the West and the Soviet Union.

When the United States rejected Nasser's tentative requests for heavy weapons, Nasser went to the Soviet bloc with his demands and obtained a large part of his requests (far beyond his real needs) but on a barter arrangement which tied up the Egyptian cotton crop for years in the future and removed this major prop of Egypt's economy out of the economic picture. Without cotton to sell for foreign exchange, Nasser could not hope to ameliorate Egypt's immediate economic problems. At the same time, while filling the air with denunciations of the United States and threats to Israel, Nasser opened his discussions for the financial assistance necessary to construct the High Dam. When the International Bank, as well as the American government, agreed to contribute to the project in principle but insisted on certain necessary precautions, such as the right to scrutinize the accounts, Nasser tried to blackmail them by playing off the United States against Soviet Russia by circulating stories of Soviet offers to build the project.

In the meantime, Nasser was engaged in intensive intrigues against the three Arab dynasties of Iraq, Jordan, and Saudi Arabia, all of whom were linked with the West. To increase their local popular support these dynasties had to adopt policies more independent of the West, or even anti-Western, in order to avoid the subversive influence on their subjects of Nasser's wild talk about independence from the West. Most of these anti-Western actions took the form of anti-British actions. One of the chief of these was the dismissal by King Hussein of Jordan of General Sir John Glubb (so-called "Glubb Pasha"), who had trained and commanded the Jordanian "Arab Legion" for many years. This dismissal, in March 1956, left Jordan in a state of semidissolution and in grave danger of being partitioned by its Arab neighbors (Iraq, Egypt, Arabia), since the Arab Legion was one of the chief supports of the dynasty. It also gravely jeopardized British influence in Jordan.

To counteract this, the British tried to shift Iraqi troops from Iraq, where the government of Nuri al Said was still friendly to Britain, to Jordan where they could be used to support King Hussein and perhaps be used to prevent the anticipated pro-Nasser and anti-British outcome of the Jordan election of October 1956. For the same reason, the British prime minister, Sir Anthony Eden, adopted an increasingly anti-Israeli attitude, which culminated late in 1955 when he suggested that the Israeli frontier be redrawn to give some disputed areas to Jordan. Since Israel was already under great threat from both Egypt and Jordan, it continued to rearm in 1956, and made perfectly clear that it would oppose in any way it could any union of the Arab states and especially any move to unite the Iraq and Jordan armed forces or to put them under Egyptian command.

In this tense situation Dulles suddenly upset the balance by withdrawing the United States offer of financial aid for the Aswan Dam. This decision of July 19, 1956, was answered on July 26th, fourth anniversary of the expulsion of King Farouk, by Nasser with the sudden nationalization of the Suez Canal Company so that its profits could be used by Egypt to finance the High Dam.

July to October 1956 was a period of mounting crisis in the Near East as all the principal states concerned mishandled the difficult situation with gross incompetence.

There can be no doubt that Egypt had the right to nationalize an Egyptian corporation such as the Suez Canal Company, and the only concern of the outside world was the twofold on that the owners of record be adequately compensated and that the transit operations through the Canal be efficiently conducted for all shipping. From the beginning the British took their stand on other grounds, maintaining, incorrectly, that the company was not an Egyptian corporation but an international organization, that the Egyptians could not operate it at all, and that Britain would use force, if necessary, to prevent Nasser from obtaining control of the Canal. France supported Britain, chiefly because it wished to strike at Nasser for his assistance to the anti-French rebels (the FLN) in Algeria. Israel supported these two, while following a completely independent policy, because it was increasingly convinced that its survival as a state depended on its ability to break out of the growing encirclement of the Arab states.

Dulles, having precipitated the crisis, sought to placate both sides, refusing to support Britain's arguments yet unwilling to abandon it in public. Accordingly, as usual, Dulles spent most of his efforts trying to find some verbal formula which would gloss over the differences. Though he refused to support Britain and France for fear this would drive Nasser toward Moscow, he was unable to support the Arab states because he needed France and Britain in the American struggle with the Soviet Union. As a result, his ambivalent and changeable actions and statements alienated both sides.

While the controversy raged, in public, in secret conferences, and at the United Nations, the Canal continued to operate with about a third of the dues (including those of American ships) being paid to the new Egyptian Canal authority and the rest going to the old company. The British insisted that the Egyptians were incapable of operating the Canal, and to prove the point recalled all British-controlled pilots and technical operators on September 15, 1956, and at the same time challenged the effectiveness of the new administration by presenting a large number of English and French ships for passage. This attempt was based on biased information accepted by Whitehall from the old Suez Company. It proved, in fact, to be wide of the mark, for the remaining "Egyptian" pilots successfully conducted fifty ships through the Canal in one day. Substitute pilots were obtained at very high wages by advertising throughout the world.

The solution of this technical problem left only the second problem—compensation to the former owners. Because Egypt had the funds to make payment, the practical and legal crisis should have been ended. But Britain and France were still determined to force Egypt to accept some type of international control of the Canal, and many in both countries were determined to humiliate Nasser and bring about his downfall in order to end his intriguing against the two former imperial Powers in the Arab world, especially in the oil-rich Near East and in Algeria. For this reason the two old allies continued to press for an international Canal authority and to prepare their own armed forces in the Near East to compel internationalization. While conferences were still going on, in the United Nations and elsewhere, the showdown was precipitated, somewhat earlier than London and perhaps Paris had expected, by Israel.

During the Suez crisis, the quite separate problem of Israel had become more intense, with increasingly frequent Arab raids on Israel and more violent Israeli reprisals. The situation was made more complex by French support and rearmament for Israel, in the face of continued British support for Jordan and Iraq. Israel felt certain that a complete victory for Nasser in the Canal crisis would encourage him to organize a general Arab attack on Israel. Nasser's troublemaking proclivities, even during the Canal crisis, were revealed when the French captured an Egyptian ship smuggling seventy tons of arms to the Algerian rebels on October 18th. Two days before, a secret Anglo-French conference in Paris discussed the situation and probably decided that the two Great Powers would intervene by an attack on Egypt, under the pretext of restoring order, if an Arab-Israeli war began. They probably expected this movement some time in November, and were not fully ready when it began on October 29th.

The Jordan election of October 21, 1956, was a victory for the anti-Western, pro-Nasser activist parties pledged to revise the Anglo-Jordan alliance. Two days later, Egyptian and Syrian military missions arrived in Jordan and at once set up a joint Egyptian-Jordanian-Syrian military command with an Egyptian designated as commander in chief for any future hostilities with Israel. On the same day began the Soviet armed intervention in Hungary to repress the Budapest insurrection. On the following day Egyptian raiders began to penetrate into Israel, and Israel's mobilization began. Four days later, on the 29th, Israel attacked Egypt, and at once began a spectacular advance across the Sinai Desert toward the Suez Canal and Cairo.

The nine-day Israeli Sinai campaign was a brilliant military success. Individual Egyptians and small units often fought fiercely, but the command was incompetent, morale was almost totally absent, and training was equally bad. Whole units fled like sheep, and much of the newly acquired heavy equipment was abandoned unused. On October 30th a joint Anglo-French ultimatum was sent to Israel and Egypt, ordering them to stop all warlike action, to withdraw their forces at least ten miles from the Canal, and to permit a temporary occupation of three Canal points, Port Said, Ismailia, and Suez, by Anglo-French forces. Israel accepted the ultimatum until it was clear that Egypt would not. The latter was attacked by British planes shortly after the ultimatum expired on October 31st, but Allied paratroops did not drop before November 5th, and the seaborne Anglo-French invasion of Egypt did not begin until November 6th.

The United States Department of State was wild with rage at what it regarded as British perfidy and Anglo-Israeli collusion to engage in war outside the Western alliance and collective security system (actions which had always seemed acceptable to Dulles if applied by the United States to the Formosa Strait or other areas of primary American concern). On October 30th Dulles tried to force through the Security Council of the United Nations a resolution condemning Israel and asking all United Nations members to cut off military, economic, or financial assistance to Israel. This was killed by Anglo-French vetoes, 7–2. Britain, the Commonwealth, and the London Cabinet itself were badly split, while world opinion was strongly against the use of force by any state. In London two ministers resigned, and others threatened to do so.

On November 2nd the Assembly of the United Nations, by its largest majority to date, accepted, by a vote of 64–5, a Dulles resolution calling for an immediate cease-fire in the Near East. Egypt and Israel accepted on November 5th, while the Anglo-French forces stopped their advance the following day, twenty-three miles south of Port Said. The Israel forces were already across Sinai. Of more permanent significance, the petroleum pipelines and pumping stations bringing oil to Levantine seaports across Syria were destroyed, and a number of blockships sunk by Egypt in the Canal had cut off all Near Eastern oil supplies to western Europe by the direct routes. Most important of all, the parallel American-Soviet threats to France and England and the simultaneous Soviet attack on Hungary had made permanent splits in the two great super-Power blocs and had given a greatly increased impetus to the growth of an independent third bloc between them. This development of an increasingly independent Buffer Fringe between the two disintegrating super-Power blocs became the outstanding feature of the next seven years of world history under the awesome canopy of the Soviet-American missile and space race (1956–1963).

Liquidation of the Suez crisis was not completed until the end of 1958, but in the interval the continued confusions of the whole Near East almost totally concealed the process of liquidation. Much of this confusion arose from inept handling by the Western Powers of the very real problems of the area. These problems were four in number: (1) the economic poverty of the area, especially the food crisis in Egypt; (2) the Israel issue; (3) the decline of British power leading to political instability; and (4) the challenge to the French position in Muslim North Africa, especially in Algeria. The decline in British and French influence was a consequence of World War II and especially of the decisions of the British and French peoples to devote their wealth to social welfare rather than to efforts to retain their imperial positions. This left a power vacuum, as the Arab states were obviously unable to maintain order in the area or even to govern themselves, and neither the United States nor the Soviet Union was willing to move into the almost insoluble problem of maintaining political stability in the area or to allow the other super-Power to make the effort to do so. Britain made feeble efforts to retain its influence in Jordan, Iraq, southern Arabia, and the Persian Gulf. In the case of Jordan and Iraq, at least, this was not worth the effort, and was doomed to failure, as became clear with the expulsion of Glubb Pasha in March 1956, and the overthrow of the Iraqi monarchy and of Nuri al Said in July 1958.

American policy in the Near East was based on a series of assumptions which were so remote from the truth that no successful policy could be based on them. These were: (1) that the Near East was an area in which the Soviet Union had plans for immediate penetration and subversion in order to communize it; (2) that the Arab world was a unified bloc, with significant intrinsic power of its own, which would join the Soviet bloc (or at least contribute to increase its strength) if not constantly placated by concessions; (3) that no policy of neutralism of the Near East was feasible or acceptable to the West; (4) that the public opinion of the masses of Arab peoples was of some significance in the formulation of policy in the Arab states; and (5) that the arming of the Arab states would contribute to their ability to resist Soviet penetration and to the political stability of the area.

All five of these assumptions were untrue. The Soviet Union had no significant plans to communize, to subvert, or to penetrate the Near East after 1948, and was eager to see it become a stable and neutral area in order to deprive the United States of any excuse to intervene there. Moreover, the Arab states were neither united nor strong, but were diverse, filled with mutual hatreds and petty jealousies, and almost totally incapable of acting as a bloc even when their primary interests were threatened. In fact, their only common interests were hatred of Israel, desire to be independent and neutral, and the desire for economic handouts (without any accompanying political commitments) from anyone who would give them. The public opinion of the Arab peoples, described in the previous sentence, was of little influence in the face of the concentration of local political power in the hands of the local armed forces, which were, with perhaps the exception of Nasser himself, corruptible. Efforts to arm these forces against a nonexistent Soviet armed threat contributed nothing to their ability to defend the area itself, and merely increased their corruption, their economic burden on the people, and the political instability of the area by increasing their abilities to threaten each other or Israel.

Dulles's policies in the Near East were consistently the opposite of what they should have been. No possible alliance or rearming of the Arab states could have contributed anything to the area's ability to resist Communism, nor could the Arab states have contributed anything but headaches to the Kremlin if Washington's policies had "driven them into the arms of Russia." Over-all defense of the area should have been based on Ethiopia, Israel, and Turkey; the Arab states should have been given the independence, neutrality, and economic aid they wanted. The latter should have concentrated on the Aswan Dam and a Jordan Valley Authority (similar to TVA) for the mutual benefit of Jordan, Israel, and Syria, in return for the Arab states' acceptance of (1) a peace treaty with Israel and (2) resettlement of the Arab refugees from the Israeli war on the new agricultural lands provided by the Jordan Valley project. And, finally, the United States should have declared unilaterally that it would use any force necessary to prevent any Soviet intrusion into the Near East or any attack on the independence of Israel. As a supplementary, but probably unachievable, project the United States should have sought a pooling of the enormous oil revenues of the whole Near East to provide funds for the economic reconstruction of the area as a whole within the framework of an Arab economic community based on free trade and free immigration within the Arab world.

Instead of some such progressive solution of the Near East problem and the Suez crisis, the United States, acting through the United Nations, sought to restore the basically precarious *status quo ante bellum* without any guarantees. The real difficulty was Israel, which refused for several months to yield up the areas it had occupied without obtaining in return some solution of its grievances. These grievances were: (1) the refusal of the Arab states to make a peace treaty or to accept the existence of Israel by ending the 1948 war, (2) the Arab economic, social, and political blockade of Israel, which included boycotts of all world business firms which did business with Israel, (3) the denial of the Suez Canal to Israeli ships or identifiable Israeli goods since 1948, (4) constant harassment of Israeli shipping or fishing on the Gulf of Aqaba and the Jordan River, and (5) the use of the Gaza Strip, non-Egyptian territory occupied by Egypt under the 1948 armistice, as a basis for guerrilla raids on Israel.

Eventually American pressure and world public opinion acting through the United Nations forced Israel to give up the territory it had captured, including the Gaza Strip and the Gulf of Aqaba shores, without any significant guarantees. A UN Emergency Force (UNEF) was sent to supervise the evacuation of Egyptian territory and the Gaza Strip, under pressure of severe economic and financial threats of an unofficial nature from Washington. The effectiveness of such threats rested on the fact that the whole Israeli economy was dependent on the flow of private funds from the United States, while the British attack on Egypt had been abandoned very largely as a consequence of the drain on British dollar and gold reserves, which fell $420 million in September–November 1956.

The American threats of sanctions against its own friends and allies over Egypt at the very time when it was doing nothing to impose sanctions for the Soviet attack on Hungary, and its refusal to cooperate with the Soviet Union in stabilizing the Near East because of Hungary, presented a strange picture of political fantasy as 1956 ended. One of the methods of pressure used by the United States against the Western Powers was support of Egypt's refusal to allow any clearance of the Suez Canal until the withdrawal of troops from Egypt. This, of course, intensified the shortage of Near Eastern fuel oil in Europe as winter deepened. The evacuation of Anglo-French forces on December 22, 1956, and of Israeli forces on March 8, 1957, permitted clearing of the Canal and the reimposition of Egyptian blockade pressures on Israel. In the interval the American position, ignoring all the real problems of the area, was stated in the form of the so-called Eisenhower Doctrine in January 1957. Regarding the problem solely in terms of military opposition to Communism, this doctrine attacked the Soviet Union and threatened to use the armed forces of the United States to defend any "freedom-loving nations of the area . . . requesting such aid against overt armed aggression from any nation controlled by international communism. . . ."

In reply to this unconstructive promise the Soviet Union, in February 1957, suggested a joint effort by four Powers (Russia, the United States, Britain, and France) to reorganize the Near East on the basis of six principles: (1) peaceful settlement of all disputes there, (2) noninterference in internal affairs, (3) renunciation of all efforts to incorporate Near Eastern countries into military blocs of the Great Powers, (4) removal of foreign military bases from the area and the troops based on them, (5) a reciprocal ban on arms deliveries, and (6) promotion of economic development without political or military entanglements.

This promising Soviet offer, which might have been negotiated into some settlement of the Near East's real problems, was rebuffed by the United States; instead, the Eisenhower Doctrine, in spite of the clear lack of any overt Communist threat, was used against Egypt and Syria in regard to Jordan and Lebanon.

The Jordan monarchy was completely dependent upon the army, which was, in turn, completely dependent upon the financial subsidy from Britain. This subsidy (amounting to £12 million a year) was ended by the new Parliament elected in October 1956. Syria and Saudi Arabia, which already had troops on Jordanian soil, joined with Egypt to continue the subsidy. To escape from growing Egyptian and Soviet influence, King Hussein dismissed his prime minister and sought aid from Washington. Rioting from opposition groups led to martial law, a $10 million grant under the Eisenhower Doctrine, and movement of the American Sixth Fleet to the Levant to support Hussein (April 1957).

The rivalry between Saudi Arabia and Egypt for influence in the other Arab countries was marked by an Egypt-Syria economic union in September 1957, a $112 million loan to Syria from the Soviet bloc, and (in February 1958) the union of these two countries into a United Arab Republic. Iraq and Jordan responded to this with a very ephemeral Arab Federation. By the spring of 1958, Nasser was engaged in controversies with all his neighboring states except Syria. A military coup by pro-Nasser officers in Iraq in July abolished the monarchy and assassinated Nuri al Said and his chief supporters and threatened to overthrow the insecure government of President Chemoun of Lebanon. To prevent this, American forces were landed in Lebanon in the same week (July 15–17) in which a United Nations commission on the spot reported a total lack of evidence of any outside forces trying to subvert Lebanon. On the following day, Hussein of Jordan asked, and obtained, a British parachute brigade to protect his position.

Once again Khrushchev appealed for a Great Power conference (this time to include India) on the Near East, but was met by a series of evasions and legalistic obstacles from Washington. The United States refused to act outside the United Nations, and the suggestion finally ended in a series of recriminatory letters in August. A special session of the United Nations Assembly sent Secretary General Dag Hammarskjöld on a mission to the Near East which was able to evacuate the troops from Lebanon and Jordan by November 1958.

This turmoil in the Muslim states continued during the subsequent period of Soviet-American missile rivalry (1956–1963). The United Arab Republic of Egypt and Syria, established in February 1958, was broken by Syria after a military coup had overturned the Syrian government in September 1961. Another Syrian military revolt early in 1963 announced its reestablishment, but internal opposition, chiefly from the Ba'ath Party, prevented this. In Iraq the military revolt of July 1958, led by General Abdul Karim Qassim, remained in power on a relatively pro-Communist and anti-Nasser basis until it was overthrown in a bloody military upheaval on February 8-9, 1963.

XIX

THE NEW ERA,
1957-1964

The Growth of Nuclear Stalemate

THE SHIFTING POWER BALANCE

THE DENOUEMENT OF THE COLD WAR, 1957–1963

The Disintegrating Superblocs

LATIN AMERICA: A RACE BETWEEN DISASTER AND REFORM

THE FAR EAST

The Japanese Miracle

Communist China

The Eclipse of Colonialism

The Growth of Nuclear Stalemate

THE decade from 1953 to 1963 was the most critical in modern history. Man's ability to get through it successfully was a tribute to his good luck and good sense. The avoidance of nuclear war and the extraordinary burst of economic prosperity in the advanced industrial nations during that decade were balanced by the continued growth of acute social disorganization and the even more acute growth of ideological confusions. Nevertheless, man survived, and, by 1963, was at the opening of a new era, based very largely on the relaxaton of the Cold War between the United States and the Soviet Union and on the opportunities to do something about the lagging social and intellectual problems provided by the combination of political relaxation and economic prosperity.

The decade as a whole fell into two parts, divided about 1956. The first three years were marked by the continued "Race for the H-Bomb," and covered the period from the early thermonuclear explosions in 1953 to the achievement of a fusion bomb that could be dropped from an airplane in 1956. The next seven years were filled with the missile race, and reached their culmination and denouement in the year from the Cuban missile crisis of October–November 1962 to the death of President Kennedy in November 1963.

Closely related to this division based on weapons development was the somewhat delayed division of the decade into two parts by a change in American strategic policy. Here the dividing point was about 1960, and is marked by the shift from the strategy of "massive retaliation," associated with the name of John Foster Dulles, to the strategy of "graduated deterrence," associated with the new Democratic Administration of President Kennedy. The shift in 1960, however, was only incidentally associated with the presidential election of that year and the subsequent shift of Administration in the White House. The real change in 1960 was brought about, as we shall see, by the full achievement, at that time, of intercontinental thermonuclear striking ability by the two great Superpowers. The "balance of terror" thus achieved by 1960 led directly to the missile crisis of 1962 and the thermonuclear stalemate of 1963. And these developments led to major changes in the political and ideological structures of all areas of the world, changes that are still going on.

THE SHIFTING POWER BALANCE

As we have seen, the whole period of 1953 to 1960, in the area of defense, was dominated by the so-called "New Look," the Republican effort to reduce the cost of the American defense effort by shifting from "containment" to massive retaliation. This involved a reduction in the American defense budget from an average of $43 billion a year over the last four Truman budgets (1949-1953) to an average of $37.4 a year over the six Eisenhower budgets of 1954-1960. In this process American military manpower was reduced from 3.7 million men to 2.5 million over the six years January, 1953-January, 1959. Foreign economic aid was decreasingly emphasized.

In this fashion, the effort to deter Soviet aggression was based more completely on the threat of American nuclear attack by SAC bombers on the Soviet homeland and less on American readiness to meet Soviet forces on the ground or to win third Powers to our side by economic or other aid. Dulles, who saw the world in black-and-white terms, refused to recognize the right of anyone to be neutral, and tried to force all states to join the American side in the Cold War or be condemned to exterior darkness.

Having thus divided the world into two blocs, he sought to set up between them a continuous circuit of paper barriers along the land frontiers of the Soviet bloc from the Baltic Sea, across Europe and Asia, to the Far East. The chief portions in the barrier were the North Atlantic Treaty Organization (NATO) in Europe (1949), the Central Treaty Organization (1955) in the Near and Middle East (CENTRO), and the South-East Asia Treaty Organization (SEATO) in the Far East (1954). In theory, the paper barrier was made continuous by the presence of Turkey in both NATO and CENTRO and of Pakistan in both CENTRO and SEATO.

Dulles cared little about the military strength, economic prosperity, or political democracy of the states forming this paper ring around the Soviet bloc, since their chief function was to form a paper barrier so that any movement outward by Russia or its satellites, by breaking the paper, would trigger the trip-wire circuit that hurled America's nuclear retaliatory power on the Soviet homeland. In theory this strategic policy meant that any outward movement by the Soviet Union, or by one of its satellite states, in some remote jungle or on some barren mountaintop of central Asia, might lead to all-out nuclear war, initiated by the United States, which would totally destroy European civilization as we know it. For, until 1960, the ability of either of the Superpowers to strike directly at the other from its own soil was very limited, and, accordingly, the two Superpowers had to strike *from* or strike *at* bases in Europe or the Far East.

This change, which took place over the period 1956–1962, is of major significance, since it meant that the Soviet Union and the United States became capable of striking directly at each other and did not have to involve third Powers in their disputes immediately. From the weapons point of view, it represented, on the American side, three changes: (1) the shift in manned bombing planes from the long-range B-47's to the intercontinental-range B-52's and B-58's; (2) the shift in missiles from the intermediate-range ballistic missiles (IRBM's), such as Thor or Jupiter, which had to be based in Turkey, Italy, or Britain in order to reach the Soviet Union, to intercontinental ballistic missiles (ICBM's), such as the Minuteman or Atlas, which could hit the Soviet Union from launching sites in the United States; and (3) the advent, about 1960, of the nuclear-propelled Polaris submarines, whose sixteen nuclear-armed missiles could strike the Soviet Union from submerged positions in the seas bordering the Eurasian land mass.

This American capability to strike the Soviet homeland from North America was not achieved so quickly or so completely on the Russian side, even by the time the nuclear stalemate had been reached in 1963. As a result, the Soviet Union could strike at the United States only by striking at its bases or its allies in NATO or in the Far East. At first, in the 1950's, such a Soviet counterstrike would have been largely by the Soviet ground forces invading westward across central Europe, but by the late 1950's, as the Soviet strategic striking forces were strengthened by its acquisition of strategic bombing planes like the Tu-16 and of IRBM's, this Soviet counterstrike to America's massive retaliation would have resulted in the nuclear destruction and radioactive pollution of much of Europe. The gradual shift of American retaliatory power from intermediate range to intercontinental range (in 1962) reduced the Soviet pressure on Europe by reducing the importance of America's European bases. This had many significant implications for all the nations of Europe, both Communist and Western.

The key to the missile race rested on the fact that the United States and the Soviet Union took opposite routes in their efforts to obtain nuclear-armed rockets. One basic problem was how to combine the American A-bomb of 1945 with the German V-2 rocket. Since the A-bomb was an egg-shaped object 5 feet wide and 10 feet long, which weighed 9,000 pounds, and the V-2 could carry a warhead of only 1,700 pounds 200 miles, the problem was not easy. The Soviet government sought to close the gap between rocket power and nuclear payload by working toward a more powerful rocket, while the American scientists, over the opposition of the Air Force and the aviation industry, sought to close the gap by getting smaller bombs. The result of the race was that the Soviet Union in 1957–1962 had very large boosters which gave it a lead in the race to propel objects into space or into ballistic orbits around the earth, but these were very expensive, could not be made in large numbers, and were very awkward to install or to move. The United States, on the other hand, soon found it had bombs in all sizes down to small ones capable of being used as tactical weapons by troops in ground combat and able to be moved about on jeeps.

As a consequence of the American decision to reduce the size of the bomb (a decision for which the great scientist Robert Oppenheimer was largely responsible), by the early 1960's the United States was producing large numbers of warheads in a great variety of sizes, capable of being delivered by all kinds of vehicles from tactical rockets and cannons, up through Polaris missiles, airplanes of all sizes, and rockets of all ranges, up to city-destroying bombs carried by gigantic SAC bombers or ICBM's.

Apparently the Soviet success in obtaining the A-bomb in 1949, in dropping an H-bomb in 1953, and in startling the world with its powerful rocket boosters in 1957 not only alarmed the United States but also lulled the Kremlin itself into the mistaken idea that it was ahead of the United States in the development of missile nuclear weapons. This so-called "missile gap" was a mistaken idea, for the vast expansion of American production of nuclear materials begun in 1950, combined with the simultaneous reduction in the sizes of nuclear warheads, by 1959 was bringing the United States into a condition of "nuclear plenty" and of "overkill capacity" that posed a grim problem for the Soviet Union. It was, strangely enough, just at that time (end of 1957) that two American studies (the Gaither Report and the Special Studies Project of the Rockefeller Brothers Fund) suggested the existence of a missile gap or inferiority in missile capacity of the United States compared to the Soviet Union. This judgment, apparently based on overemphasis on the *size* of Soviet rocket boosters, played a chief role in the American presidential campaign of 1960 and in the ebullient self-confidence of Khrushchev and his associates in 1957–1961.

The reality of the situation apparently was not recognized in Moscow until 1961, when it penetrated with a cold shock of fear through the deceptive festivities of self-congratulations that had begun with the success of Sputnik I (October 1957) and the successful moon shot, Lunik II (of September 1959).

In this pleasant period of self-deception, intensified by the American presidential campaign's unrealistic discussion of the missile gap in 1960, the Kremlin entered upon an unofficial international suspension of nuclear-bomb testing (the Test Moratorium) from October 31, 1958 to October 23, 1961. Suddenly, in 1961, the Soviet authorities recognized that they had fallen far behind the United States, both in number and in variety of nuclear weapons, because their existing nuclear bombs were too large for many purposes, especially for accurate and numerous long-range ICBM's. Accordingly, in October 1961, the Soviet Union broke the test moratorium of three years by resuming nuclear testing, but, to conceal the purpose of the tests in seeking smaller bombs, they aimed their publicity on the tests at the fact that they exploded the largest bomb ever used, a 58-megaton fusion thermonuclear monstrosity.

After these tests, it soon became clear to the Soviet Union that the American lead in ICBM's could not be overcome by the Soviet Union, in view of its limited industrial capacity and the other urgent demands on that capacity, in any period of time that had strategic meaning. Accordingly, Moscow, probably at the instigation of the Red Army itself, decided to remedy its weakness in ICBM's by seeking to move some of its numerous ICBM's within range of the United States by secretly installing them in Castro's Cuba.

This decision, if we have analyzed it correctly, showed once again the way in which the Soviet defense strategy moved in a direction opposite to that which was influencing American defense decisions. Just at the time (summer 1962) that the Soviet Union was deciding to remedy its weakness in ICBM's by trying to install IRBM's in a third Power close to the United States, the latter was deciding that its supply of ICBM's was increasing so rapidly that it would close down its IRBM bases in third countries close to the Soviet Union (such as Turkey). This American decision was already beginning to be carried out when the Cuban missile crisis broke in October 1962.

The Cuban missile crisis was a turning point in Soviet-American relations, similar in some ways to the Fashoda crisis of 1898 between France and England. It showed both sides that neither wanted a war and that their interests were not antithetical on all points. Thus it signaled the suspension of the Cold War and of the all-out insane armaments race between them. It showed that the United States had missile superiority sufficient to veto any major Soviet aggression, while the Soviet Union had sufficient missile power, in combination with the generally non-aggressive American attitude, to discourage the United States from using its missile superiority to make any aggression on the Soviet Union. Thus was established a nuclear or power stalemate of nuclear vetoes between the United States and the Soviet Union that secured each against the other.

This American-Soviet stalemate, by inhibiting the use of the power of each, permitted third Powers to escape, to a considerable extent, from the need to have power sufficient to back up their actions. This meant that third states could undertake actions which their own power could not in itself justify or enforce. That is to say that the Superpower stale-

mate allowed third states a freedom of action beyond their own intrinsic powers. Thus Indonesia could attack Malaya; China could attack
India; Pakistan, although allied to the United States, could be cozy with
Red China; Cyprus could defy Turkey; Egypt could attack Yemen;
France could defy the United States; Romania could flirt with Peking;
and Britain or Spain could trade with Castro's Cuba, without the Super-
powers feeling free to use their own real strengths to obtain what they
wanted, since most of these strengths were neutralized opposing each
other.

One significant consequence of this situation was the almost total collapse of the system of international law that had been formulated in the
seventeenth century by the work of writers like Grotius. That system of
international law had regarded the state as the embodiment of sovereignty,
an organization of political power on a territorial basis. The criteria
for the existence of such a sovereign state had been its ability to defend
its boundaries against external aggression and to maintain law and public
order among its inhabitants inside those boundaries. By 1964, as a consequence of the power stalemate of the Cold War, dozens of "states"
(such as the Congo) which could perform neither of these actions were
recognized as states by the Superpowers and their allies, and achieved
this recognition in international law by being admitted to the United
Nations. This development culminated over fifty years of destruction of
the old established distinctions of international law such as the distinctions between war and peace (destroyed by the Cold War, which was
neither), between belligerents and neutrals (destroyed by British economic warfare in World War I), or between civilians and combatants
(destroyed by submarine warfare and city bombing). Nuclear stalemate
in the Cold War context made it possible for political organizations with
almost none of the traditional characteristics of a state not only to be
recognized as states but to act in irresponsible ways and to survive on
economic subsidies won from one bloc by threatening to join (or
merely to accept subsidies from) the other bloc.

As a consequence of this situation, all the realities of international affairs
by 1964 had become covered with thick layers of law, theories, practices,
and agreements that had no relationship to reality at all. Today, the pressure of the realities beneath that layer to break through it and emerge
into the daylight where they can be generally recognized has reached a
critical point. As part of that process of increasing sanity (which the
recognition of reality always is), the future of disarmament became more
hopeful than it had been in decades, although the chances of reaching
any substantial disarmament agreements remain slight. This means that
disarmament is more likely to appear in the form of nuclear disengagement and tacit adoption of parallel actions than in the form of explicit
agreements or signed documents.

The amount of myth and false theories that must be pushed aside to permit even the highest peaks of reality to emerge is very large. In the United Nations alone, it involves such points as the recognition of the Congo as a "state," the belief that Taiwan is a Great Power worthy of one of the four permanent, veto-wielding seats on the Security Council, or the pretense that Red China, in spite of its possesssion of all the traditional attributes of statehood, does not exist.

Part of this return to reality is embodied in the growing recognition that there are more situations in which the United States and the Soviet Union have parallel interests than there are in which their interests are antithetical. Certainly they have a common interest in avoiding nuclear war, in preventing the spread of nuclear weapons to additional states, in not poisoning the atmosphere with radioactive fallout from nuclear testing, in slowing up weapons development, technological rivalry, and the space race in order to direct more resources to domestic problems of poverty, social disorganization, and education; or in refraining from outbidding each other in grants of arms and aid to unreliable, ungrateful, unstable, and inefficient neutralist regimes.

One first clear evidence of recognition of this common interest was the peaceful settlement of the Cuban missile crisis, but the first formal agreement based on it was the official Test Ban Treaty of August 1963. This treaty not only aimed to maintain the stalemate between the two Superpowers to the degree that it might be jeopardized by their future testing; it also sought to hamper the spread of nuclear weapons to additional powers by this restriction. Both Superpowers and many neutrals feared that nuclear explosives would get into the control of Red China or other irresponsible hands.

By the late 1960's, considerations such as these revealed that there were considerable areas of common interests among the states of the world covering all three groups of the so-called Free World, the Communist bloc, and the neutrals. The net result was the almost total disappearance of the world as seen by John Foster Dulles only a decade before. The two-power world of Dulles was being replaced by a multi-bloc world in which the two Superpowers, instead of being antithetical on all points, were finding large areas in which their interests were closer to each other than they were to those of some of the other, newer blocs, especially that growing up around Red China. Moreover, as we shall see, in some ways the aims, methods, and structures of the two Superpowers were converging on increasingly parallel courses. Most obviously repugnant to Dulles would have been the rise of neutralism, evident not only in the increasing numbers and independence of the neutral states, but in the disintegration of both the old Superpower blocs as these weakened and dissolved, and former members of these, such as France in the West and Romania in the East, adopted increasingly neutralist policies.

As one obvious consequence of this, the paper groupings and barriers Dulles had so painfully constructed in the 1950's were under liquidation as one of the chief tasks of the 1960's. This was evident, with increasing obviousness, in NATO, the Organization of American States (OAS), CENTRO, and SEATO. Less obviously, except in the Far East, the same disintegrative process has been going on within the Soviet bloc, at first with Yugoslavia in 1948 and then with Red China (1960), Albania, Romania, and others. This whole process of growing neutralism, diversity, and the disintegration of the Superblocs, followed by the increasing emphasis of all groups on the problems of poverty, social disorganization. and spiritual nihilism, was possible only because of the growth of nuclear stalemate, and must, throughout, be recognized as occurring under the umbrella of thermonuclear terror and the danger from new, equally horrible biological weapons.

THE DENOUEMENT OF THE COLD WAR, 1957–1963

Two revealing events in the late summer of 1957 offer conflicting evidence on the nature of the Soviet system. On August 26th the Kremlin claimed its first successful test of an ICBM. A month later it announced that the sixth Five-Year Plan had been scrapped and would be replaced by a new Seven-Year Plan for 1959–1965.

The meaning of this second announcement was difficult to evaluate, but it showed the regime's increasing difficulty in carrying out its grandiose economic projects, a difficulty that arose from the failures of the Soviet agricultural system. The state and collective farms used such quantities of equipment and manpower, and gave such limited production in return, that they became the chief limiting factor in the Soviet efforts to raise standards of living, to maintain the size and power of the defense forces, to win over third states by economic and technical assistance, and to lead the United States in the conquest of outer space. The output of food from the small private plots of the Soviet peasantry, which were presumably worked only in their owners' spare time, produced four or five times the output per acre of the state and collective farms. This was, of course, an indication of the success of private enterprise as a spur in the productive process, a fact which was specifically recognized by Khrushchev in a series of speeches early in 1964.

But in 1957–1959 this meaning of the change in the Soviet economic plan was unrecognized, or at least disputable, and the world's attention became riveted instead on the Soviet success with its rocket boosters. From October 1957, over a period of five years, the Russians showed the way in outer space to the United States. In the newspapers and consequent world opinion, the margin of the Soviet superiority seemed much greater than it was in fact. On October 4th Sputnik I, weighing

184 pounds, was shot into an orbit around our earth; a month later, Sputnik II, weighing 1,120 pounds and containing a living dog, also went into successful orbit. But on December 6th a much publicized effort by the United States, in Project Vanguard, failed in its attempt to place a small sphere of 3¼ pounds into orbit. On the last day of January 1958, the first American spacecraft, Explorer I, weighing 31 pounds, successfully was shot into orbit around our earth, but it was followed by another failure of Vanguard and a failure of Explorer II in the next two months.

In the spring of 1958, our success with Explorer III (31 pounds) and another failure with Vanguard were followed by the successful Sputnik III (2,925 pounds). The two years 1958 and 1959 saw many American failures in space (20 in all) mingled with 16 successful efforts (mostly in 1959). In January 1959, the Soviet government put Lunik I (3,245 pounds) in orbit around the sun five months after our first lunar probe had failed. In September 1959, Lunik II hit the surface of the moon, and a month later Lunik III passed around the moon, photographing its hidden side. In 1960 and 1961 the United States launched numerous successful space vehicles that gathered valuable scientific information. One of these, in January 1959, made the first broadcast from space, relaying messages from American ground stations, but in April and August 1961 Soviet vehicles successfully sent the first human beings into space: Vostok I was recovered after a single orbit, and Vostok II, after 18 successful trips around the globe, was recovered the next day. These first space travelers, Major Yuri Gagarin and Major Gherman S. Titov, returned safely to Soviet soil, descending to earth in remarkable demonstrations of the Soviet success in controlling their space vehicles. The first American astronauts, Captain Alan B. Shepard, Jr., who made a suborbital flight of 117 miles in May 1961, and Colonel John H. Glenn, who orbited the earth three times in February 1962, were recovered by landing in the ocean. In October, United States Navy Commander Walter M. Schirra made a similar landing after a smooth countdown and blast-off at Cape Canaveral (now called Cape Kennedy) and six orbits around the earth. These American achievements were seen on television by millions of viewers and roused considerable praise throughout the world at the courage of the American government in permitting live broadcasts of what could have turned into humiliating fiascos.

The Soviet fiascos in space developments, if any occurred, were well concealed, while their successes continued to astound the world at the end of 1962. In August of that year, the Russians in less than twenty-four hours blasted off Vostok III and Vostok IV, each with a human passenger, brought them within four miles of each other in space, and landed them together, six minutes and 124 miles apart, after several days in space, most of it in a weightless condition. This achievement was remarkable for its exhibition of control of the whole process, since the two vehicles were in almost identical orbits, almost came together in space, and broke all previous records for time and distance in space. Major A. G. Nikolayev circled the earth 64 times, covered 1,625,000 miles, and was weightless for almost four days, during which he worked, ate, slept, and moved about in his capsule. His companion cosmonaut, Lieutenant Colonel P. R. Popovich, made 48 orbits around the earth and was weightless for almost three days. These achievements in the Soviet space program were repeated in June 1963 by similar dual flights of Valentina Tereshkova, the first woman in space, who made 48 orbits, and Lieutenant Colonel Valery Bykovsky, who completed 81 orbits.

The impact of these Soviet "space spectaculars" on world opinion was tremendous. To many neutrals, and even to some in the Western nations, their exploits seemed to indicate that the Soviet Union had moved to first place in ability to apply science to technological development. Only gradually, and never completely, did realization spread that the Soviet Union, by announcing only its successes and concealing its failures, gave a misleading appearance of success. In time, it also began to appear that, while the Soviet Union unquestionably had tremendous boosters and an almost unbelievable accuracy in firing them, the United States space effort included a greater number of attempts, in much greater variety and size, and yielded immensely larger amounts of scientific information. By 1963–1964, when the space rivalry had entered upon a race to place men on the moon, and both sides were beginning to have doubts about the wisdom of this (or at least the wisdom of racing to it), it became clearer that the American space effort was larger, sounder, and more fruitful to science than the amazing and earlier exploits of the Soviet Union. But no such process of revaluation could change the fact that the first men in space were Russians, Yuri Gagarin and Gherman S. Titov, in 1961.

The Soviet successes in space had a triple impact on the United States, with the final result that the whole movement of American life was turned in a new direction. The psychological impact was the least important in spite of its force. More significant was the influence on American education and economic development.

The economic impact of Sputnik and Vostok was such as to direct immense resources, through government spending, toward research in science and technology. By 1964, after six years of its existence, the National Aeronautics and Space Administration (NASA) had settled down to an annual budget of over five billion dollars a year. Sums as large were directed by government sources into research and development in science, medicine, and technology. As a consequence, the whole pattern of American education was changed and so was the relationship between government and education, as well as between the public and education. The educational system was brought into the tempestuous atmosphere of the frantic American marketplace and was being ransacked from the highest levels down to high school and even below for talented, trained, or merely eager people. As the demands for such people grew and their remunerations and opportunities increased, the substantial minority who were not talented, trained, or eager found fewer and fewer opportunities to make a living and began to sink downward toward a steadily growing lower class of social outcasts and underprivileged, the socially self-perpetuating group of the impoverished.

At the same time, within the Soviet Union, similar revolutionary changes were taking place, as millions were called from rural and depressed urban areas to educational opportunities and upward advancement in technological skills and social rewards. The Socialist pretenses of equal rewards were gradually abandoned, with increased emphasis on individual enterprise, advancing hierarchies of wealth and power, and disparate compensations for ambition, application, talent, and adaptability. On the whole, as we shall see, there was a development of Soviet and American ways of life not only in convergence toward each other, but, in a sense, away from life in most other nations.

During this period of convergence of the Soviet and American ways toward more highly developed scientific and technological systems, there was, simultaneously, a superficial sharpening of their political struggle and a less obvious opening of numerous bridges of cooperation between them. Such bridges appeared first in those areas of scientific and educational life where they were developing away from the majority of other nations. It appeared in such a remarkable example of international cooperation as the International Geophysical Year (July 1957 to the end of 1958) and, more specifically, in the Soviet-American agreements on cultural and educational changes, such as that for 1958–1959 signed in January 1958. These brought scientists, teachers, musical performers, industrialists, and even tourists from one country to the other.

In November 1958, two unconnected events began the process that led in four years to the Cuban missile crisis and the relaxation of the Cold War. On November 27th, Khrushchev, filled with self-confidence and truculence, sent a note to the Western Powers demanding settlement of the Berlin problem, under threat that the Soviet Union, at the end of six months, would itself sign a peace treaty with the East German government, would withdraw its own forces from the area, and hand over its rights in Berlin (including control of the Allied access routes into the city) to the East German government. Because the Western Powers did not recognize the East German regime, this action would not only force such recognition but would force them to negotiate with East Germany over rights, based on victory and agreement with the Soviet Union, which were not negotiable, particularly with it.

When Khrushchev sent this "ultimatum" on November 27, 1958, NATO had only twenty-one divisions, one-third of them West German, to defend its position in Europe. But the next day, America's Atlas ICBM, for the first time, shot full range of 6,325 miles.

While the six months of Khrushchev's "ultimatum" were ticking off, the two hostile camps began to disintegrate internally, in western Europe and in the Far East.

In the Far East, the first year of Red China's Five-Year Plan, the so-called "Great Leap Forward," began to collapse within six months of its beginning. Apparently to cover this up, the Chinese government began to adopt a very aggressive attitude toward the Nationalist Chinese government on Formosa (Taiwan), and prepared to mount an all-out assault on its forces on the Chinese territorial islands of Matsu and Quemoy, which were still under Chiang Kai-shek's control. The strong support Dulles gave to Chiang, including reinforcement by an American naval carrier task force, and his psychological readiness to go to "the brink of war," spread down to all parts of the world. The Red Chinese threat gradually petered out, and they made extensive demands on Moscow for military, technical, and financial assistance. About the same time, France made demands on the United States to prevent any possibility of Europe becoming involved in a nuclear war arising from unilateral American actions in the Far East, or elsewhere, in which France had not been consulted. These two demands, from Peking and Paris, soon showed the disintegrative features developing within the two Superblocs.

Red China's demands for assistance from Moscow could not be met, for the simple reason that the Kremlin could not fill the demands of the Soviet Union itself, caught as it was in a three-way vise of a faltering agricultural system, the increasing demands of the Russians themselves for improved standards of living, and the needs of the missile and space races with the United States. Accordingly, the Chinese-Soviet technical-assistance agreement of February 1959 offered only five billion rubles over the next six years, approximately half the amount that had been provided during the previous six years. Within six months, Red China began aggressions against its inaccessible borders with India and was making increasingly unfavorable comments about Khrushchev's doctrines of "peaceful coexistence with capitalism" and the "inevitable victory of Socialism without war."

In this same six months, the United States was having growing difficulties with France within NATO. In September 1958, De Gaulle asked that a tripartite directorate be established of the United States, Britain, and France to provide consultation on a global basis wider than the European limited control exercised through NATO. This demand was very well founded, since America's actions in Quemoy or in the landing of American marines in Lebanon (in July 1958) might have led to war with the Soviet Union and a Soviet attack on western Europe over an area and issue in which France had not been involved or consulted.

De Gaulle's request was rejected. As soon as the imperious general had been inaugurated as the first President of the Fifth French Republic (January, 1959), he took steps to extricate France from some of the French commitments to NATO: The French Mediterranean fleet was removed from NATO control, the use of France as a base for nuclear weapons, either from planes or missiles, was refused, and French participation in a unified European air defense system was denied.

In two-day talks in Paris, December 19–20, 1959, the two Presidents, Eisenhower and De Gaulle, went over the ground again and reached a stalemate: Eisenhower rejected De Gaulle's suggestion for a three-Power global policy directorate, and De Gaulle rejected Eisenhower's desire for an integrated air and naval defense system for Europe.

While these positions were developing, a significant turning point in Soviet-American relations appeared during Khrushchev's visit to the United States, September 15–17, 1959. The Kremlin leader was full of his usual talk of the inevitable future victory of Socialism and the need for peaceful co-existence until that time. He welcomed competition in economic or technological affairs, in athletic or cultural matters, but he ruled out the need for war or the legitimacy of aggression by either side. At first he refused to be impressed with the wealth and power of America, implying that it was not surprising to him and that the Soviet Union could do it better at some future date. But gradually a very important change occurred. In spite of himself, he was impressed. He ceased to pretend to himself that the things he saw were some special exhibits set up, regardless of cost, to delude him. Gradually the incredible truth dawned in his mind: many Americans actually lived like this, in what the ordinary Russian would regard as unbelievable luxury. The real revelation came when he visited farms in Iowa, saw the equipment and way of life of these successful American farmers, and found out the economic statistics of American agriculture at its best. For years afterward he talked of these matters, and, as recently as April 1964, he told the Hungarians about it and advised them to emulate the American farmers.

Khrushchev's journey was notable in other ways. At Camp David with President Eisenhower, he revoked his six-month time limit for settling the German question, on the ground that the consideration of the problem by the Foreign Ministers Conference of the summer of 1959 had suspended the urgency of the problem. At the meeting of the General Assembly of the United Nations in September, Khrushchev won considerable support for his suggestion that the Soviet Union was willing to reach complete disarmament supervised by mutual controls, including aerial photography.

During his visit, Soviet Foreign Minister Gromyko provided a curious glimpse into the intricacies of the Soviet system. At Camp David he tried to make a deal binding each party to limit its propaganda radio broadcasts to the other to three hours a day, with the unstated implication that Moscow might stop jamming the Voice of America if this agreement was reached. Although our broadcasts in Russian, at that time, were only three hours a day, we refused the offer by saying that we wished to increase, not reduce, the flow of information. Gromyko left the impression that the jamming was an expense and burden on the Soviet system. At any rate, in June 1963, with the relaxation of the Cold War, jamming was stopped by the Russians without any agreement.

The weakening of the Soviet position, which the Kremlin recognized in regard to missiles in 1961, also appeared to them in other fields, and was fully apparent to anyone who wished to look at the comparative prosperity of the two Superblocs. Nowhere did this comparison stand out more clearly than in divided Germany, and nowhere could the Kremlin accept it less readily.

In the 1950's and early 1960's, the contrast between the (East) German Democratic Republic and the (West) German Federal Republic were as between night and day. The West, with about 55 million persons, was booming, while the East, with less than 17 million, was grim and depressed. The West German economic miracle was based, as we have said, on low wages, hard work, and vigorous pursuit of profits by private enterprises little hampered by the government or labor unions. It was, in fact, the closest example of traditional nineteenth-century laissez faire that the mid-twentieth century had to offer. The government, under the influence of Minister of Economics (later Chancellor) Ludwig Erhard, operated in terms of what they called "a socially conscious free market economy" (soziale Marktwirtschaft), but the play of free economic forces was to be found in lack of interference by the government and competitive wage rates rather than in price competition among industrial producers. The fluctuations of the business cycle were dampered down by the government's fiscal policy, and it was said that possible inequities in the distribution of the national product could be remedied by a progressive income tax mild enough not to interfere with incentives. Otherwise, taxes were drawn to encourage industry to plow its profits back into the business rather than to raise wages. This policy and the national tendencies of the German outlook favored production of capital goods over consumer goods and for the export market rather than for domestic use. After 1945, labor unions, which had been closely associated with political activities and with agitations for drastic economic and social reforms before the Nazi regime enslaved them, sought to avoid politics and to concentrate on wages and work conditions (as do unions in the United States); but these activities in Germany had traditionally been the concern of other agencies (such as works councils), and they could hardly be much influenced by unions in a period of surplus labor and low prices such as prevailed in Germany in the 1950's.

This surplus of labor in West Germany came from the influx of 13 million refugees into the area, chiefly from East Germany and Czechoslovakia. Once the boom started, the demand for labor was so great that refugees continued to be welcomed, and at least two-thirds of a million non-German, unskilled workers were imported from Italy, Greece, Spain, and elsewhere in southern Europe. The docility and eagerness to work of these peoples kept wages low, profits high, and the boom going through the 1950's and into the 1960's. As late as 1960 only 38,000 man-days of labor were lost by strikes and lockouts in West Germany, compared to almost half a million in the Netherlands, 3 million in the United Kingdom, and 19 million in the United States in that year.

Some of the consequences of this system, besides the most obvious one of booming prosperity, were that the structure of monopolized industry with great rewards for the upper classes, with lesser rewards and little social mobility for workers, continued in the 1950's as it had been in Germany since its industrialization began. In 1958 eight great "trusts" still controlled 75 percent of crude steel production, 80 percent of raw iron, 60 percent of rolled steel, and 36 percent of coal output. The number of millionaires (in marks) more than doubled in four years in the middle 1950's. Yet less than half of the eligible workers were in unions, union membership went up only 20 percent, while the working force increased 67 percent after 1949, and only an insignificant part (5 percent) of university students came from the working class compared to a rate five times as high in Great Britain.

To the outside world, and to most Germans, especially East Germans, the inner nature and structure of the West German "economic miracle" was of little significance. What did matter was that the average West German had steady work at adequate wages and limitless hope for the future. The 10 percent increase each year in the West German gross national product was something that could not be denied or belittled.

Among those who had no desire to ignore it or to belittle it, but, on the contrary, were eager to participate in it, were the East Germans. They continued to flee westward from poverty and despotism to plenty and freedom. Every effort made by the Communist regime to stem that flow merely served to increase it. The more police who were sent to guard the frontier between East and West Germany, the more police there were to flee westward with the others.

The reasons for these flights to the West were clear enough. East Germany has been a Stalinized regime under an unpopular tyrant who is sustained by twenty-two Russian divisions because he is willing to administer East Germany as an economic colony of the Soviet Empire. In spite of Khrushchev's denunciations of Stalinism, he supported a Stalinist regime under Walter Ulbricht, the Communist dictator of East

Germany, because that type of regime extracted the largest booty from its territory for the Kremlin.

This pressure became worse on East Germany just after 1959, when the attractions of West Germany became greater, and the endless demands on Soviet resources for missiles, space spectaculars, improved standards of living, and a disintegrating agricultural system were increasing. To fulfill these demands, East Germany scrapped its unfinished second Five-Year Plan in 1959 and switched to a Seven-Year Plan synchronized to the Soviet Union's new Seven-Year Plan for 1959–1965. As part of that plan, came a forced collectivization of the half of East German agriculture that still remained in private hands. In three months, February–April 1960, almost a million farmers were forced into less than 20,000 collective farms by methods of violence and social pressure similar to those Stalin had used thirty years earlier in Russia. And the consequences were, in an economic sense, very similar: agricultural production collapsed. Shortages of food were soon followed by other shortages, especially of coal. As might be imagined, the East German winters of 1961–1963 became grim nightmares. The Seven-Year Plan of 1959 proved almost at once to be unfulfillable, and was replaced by a new and more modest one for 1964–1970. But the area's subordination to Russia was hardly eased at all.

East Germany, like the rest of Moscow's European satellites, is organized into a unified system of industrial specialization and economic exploitation, the Comecon (Council of Mutual Economic Assistance), the Soviet's version of a common market, set up in opposition to the Marshall Plan in 1949. As a consequence, 80 percent of East Germany's exports go to Communist countries, and it became the Soviet Union's largest customer, supplying 20 percent of its total imports. Generally, this exchange took the form of Russian raw materials exchanged for German industrial goods, especially machinery, chemicals, optical products, and scientific instruments. But the failure of the whole system may be seen in the fact that East Germany, whose prewar industrial capacity was about as large as West Germany's, by 1960 was producing only one-fourth the industrial output of West Germany.

The Communist solution to these difficulties was to increase the tyranny, but this simply forced more East Germans to flee westward. To prevent this, and to prevent, if possible, Communist knowledge of the great successes of the capitalist system to the west of them, the East German authorities on August 13, 1961, clamped down a rigid "death strip" along the East German–West German frontier, and hastily built a wall along the line dividing East Berlin from West Berlin. For months this wall was strengthened and heightened, surrounded and surmounted by barbed wire and watchtowers, with the buildings and concealing places along its length cleared away. Nevertheless, 20,000 persons risked death, injury, and prison and successfully escaped over the wall in its first twelve months. Since then the figure has fallen to 10,000 to 13,000 a year with about 8 to 10 percent made up of those who were supposed to be guarding it.

In contrast with this, the West German economic miracle that made that country the third largest importer and the second largest exporter in the world, with freedom and prosperity, was more than Khrushchev could stand. West Berlin, which shared in the freedom and prosperity of the West, in spite of the fact that it was surrounded by the grim penury of East Germany, was even more objectionable to Khrushchev, because it was a glaring exhibition of the success of the West and the failure of the East. As Khrushchev himself said, West Berlin was "a bone stuck in my throat."

There can be little doubt that Khrushchev's talk about "peaceful co-existence" and "the inevitable triumph of Socialism by competition without war" was sincere. He was convinced that the Soviet Union, as the sole earthly representative of a Communist regime, must be preserved at any cost. He, with his associates, since the testing of the first successful Soviet thermonuclear explosion in August, 1953, have recognized that a thermonuclear war would destroy *all* civilized living, including the victor's. The Red Army at times, and Red China always, objected to this, with the argument that enough would survive to permit reconstruction of a socialistic way of life, but Khrushchev was not persuaded. On this basis, he sincerely wished to divert the Communist-capitalist struggle into non-violent areas. Thus he was sincere in his disarmament suggestions and negotiations, but since he distrusted the Western Powers just as thoroughly as they distrusted him, any advance along the road to disarmament was almost hopeless. The Soviet position sought limitation of nuclear arms and long-range vehicles, and was much less willing to accept limits on conventional arms or ground forces. This is equivalent to saying that he wished to limit the United States and was reluctant to limit the Soviet Union. Only after 1959, with the increased strain on the Soviet Union's economic manpower, was there any readiness to curtail infantry forces. At the same time, the almost insane secrecy of the Russian system made the Kremlin reluctant to accept any effective kind of inspection of disarmament, which was almost automatically regarded by them as espionage. The United States was even less eager than the Kremlin to reach any effective disarmament agreement, since, unlike the Soviet Union, most of the pressures from American economic and business circles were in favor of the continuation of large defense spending, the source of a major segment of America's employment opportunities and industrial profits. Only at the beginning of 1964, when President Johnson astutely sought to combine reduced military expenditures with reduced taxes and a large-scale attack on American domestic poverty to expand demands in the consumers' markets, did it become possible to dissipate some of the opposition to reduced arms expenditures from the military-industrial complex.

Accordingly, the Soviet disarmament proposals of April 30, 1957 were discussed month after month, and year after year, with minimal progress. By 1959 it was quite clear that the Kremlin's chief aim was to prevent Germany and Red China from getting nuclear weapons. Accordingly, they concentrated on efforts to direct the disarmament discussions toward restrictions on nuclear testing and on nuclear-free zones in central Europe and in Asia. The nuclear-free zone in central Europe, which fitted in well with a British-favored policy of "disengagement" in that area, was known as the Repacki Plan, after its nominal proponent, but reappeared, in various versions, for many years.

There can be little doubt that a central role in Soviet foreign policy was played by the Kremlin's not unjustified fear of Germany, and its almost neurotic opposition to a unification of Germany that was not under Soviet control, or to the acquisition by West Germany of nuclear weapons. A stalemate on this subject was ensured by America's refusal to accept the *status quo* of a divided Germany because of our devotion to the Adenauer regime, and our fear that West Germany, rebuffed by us on the issue of reunification, might prefer reunity to prosperity or democracy and make a deal with the Soviet Union to achieve such unity. This we could not accept because of our conviction that German infantry forces were necessary to the West European defense system if there was to be any hope of defending Europe against Soviet ground forces on any level of combat below all-out thermonuclear warfare.

For these reasons, the United States committed itself repeatedly to the Adenauer regime to work for the unification of Germany on democratic lines. Moreover, in 1957, an Eisenhower commitment to Adenauer, subsequently expanded into a formal Declaration of Berlin by the three Western Powers (July 29, 1957), stated that any comprehensive disarmament agreement with the Soviet Union "must necessarily presuppose a prior solution of the problem of German re-unification."

A series of bitter disappointments during the four years 1958–1962 led the Kremlin to the desperate decision to move part of its IRBM's to Cuba. Three factors may have played significant roles in this reckless decision. In the first place, the inability of the Soviet Union in 1961 to overtake the American lead in ICBM's made it seem necessary for the Kremlin to seek to remedy some of its deficiency in these long-range weapons by deployment closer to the United States of some of its larger supply of IRBM's. Moreover, increasing evidence that the Soviet Union could not compete successfully with the United States in such nonviolent areas as agricultural production, raising standards of living, or aid and technical assistance to neutral nations made it seem necessary that the Soviet Union seek some method of increasing its military and political pressure on the United States that would, at the same time, give a boost to its prestige throughout the world among neutral or sympathetic states. Finally, the growing recognition that the Soviet chances were dwindling for reaching the kind of settlement it wanted in West Germany or West Berlin undoubtedly led many in the Kremlin to conclude that a successful emplacement of Soviet missiles in Cuba, even if there were no real intention of using them, could lead to a compromise settlement under which these missiles would be removed from Cuba in return for a Berlin settlement more favorable to the Soviet desires.

Whatever the reason for the Soviet missile buildup in Cuba, once begun, in August 1962, it proceeded with amazing speed. The White House was suspicious by the beginning of September, and on the 24th of that month President Kennedy obtained from the Congress permission to call up 150,000 reservists, but aerial photography did not show missile placements until October 15th. Soviet high altitude AA rockets (SA-2's) had been identified in Cuba in August, and Ilyushin-28 jet bombers in September.

The week of October 14–21 was one of steadily increasing crisis within the United States government, although no public announcement was made before the President's speech of Monday, October 22, 1962. This speech established a "quarantine on all offensive equipment under shipment to Cuba," demanded dismantling of the missile sites, and withdrawal of Soviet forces under threat of stronger action by the United States, and announced that "any missile launched from Cuba against any nation shall be regarded as an attack by the Soviet Union on the United States, requiring full retaliation."

The effects of this speech were explosive. To the world it began six days of crisis in which the two Superpowers hung on the brink of nuclear war. In reality the situation was quite different. The crisis, in fact, was an almost perfect example of a diplomatic crisis and of how such a crisis should be handled.

The pattern for a classic diplomatic crisis has three stages: (1) confrontation; (2) recognition; and (3) settlement. The confrontation consists of a dispute, that is, a power challenge in some area of conflict; Stage 2 is recognition by both sides of the realities of the power relationship between them (always much easier when only two states are involved); and Stage 3 is a yielding by the weaker of the two accompanied by an effort by the stronger to cover that retreat by refusing to inflict a humiliation or obvious triumph over the weaker. As Metternich said, "A diplomat is a man who never allows himself the pleasure of a triumph," and does so simply because it is to the interest of the stronger that an opponent who recognizes the victor's strength and is reasonable in yielding to it not be overthrown or replaced by another ruler who is too ignorant or too unreasonable to do so. The crisis of October 1962 was conducted along these lines in a masterly fashion by President Kennedy, except for a few minor blemishes caused by some of his subordinates.

The power situation throughout the missile crisis was overwhelmingly in favor of the United States (by at least a 4 to 1 ratio). The Kremlin could do nothing to defend Cuba if we attacked it, since its missiles and jet bombers there were not yet ready. Moreover, the Kremlin could expect devastation of the Soviet Union itself, if it pushed the Cuban project. It was a mark of Kennedy's masterful analysis here that he ignored Cuba and made the crisis a simple USSR-USA confrontation. In doing so, he placed the issue on a pure power basis, and made rubbish of the clutter of unrealities accumulated on the American foreign policy scene since 1945: NATO, our allies elsewhere, the United Nations, and the Organization of American States were not consulted before decision and action; they were informed afterward (chiefly on October 23). When informed and asked to back the White House, they could neither decide nor act.

The dominant fact in the whole situation was the overwhelming character of America's power and the fact that this was known both to the White House and to the Kremlin, but was largely unknown, and certainly unpublicized, to the world. Around the Soviet Union's border were 144 Polaris, 103 Atlas, 159 Thor, Jupiter, and Titan missiles; 1,600 long-range bombers, many of them constantly in the air with nuclear bombs. When the President's speech began the public crisis, five divisions of the United States Army Strategic Reserve, totaling about 100,000 men, plus 100,000 air force and an equal number of naval and marine personnel had been mobilized or alerted, the First Armored Division had been flown from Texas to the east coast, 90 naval vessels, including 8 carriers, were on patrol to blockade, a Cuban invasion command had been assembled in Florida, and 2,700 relatives of military personnel had been evacuated from Guantanamo.

Under such pressure Khrushchev wilted (it might almost be said that he panicked) on Friday, October 26th. Only eight days before, on October 18th, Soviet Foreign Minister Gromyko had made a personal visit to the White House and, without mentioning the Soviet activities in Cuba, had threatened Mr. Kennedy: The Soviet Union was unable to postpone any longer the conclusion of a peace treaty with the (East) German Democratic Republic, yielding to it control over the access routes to Berlin. The President had listened and dismissed the foreign minister without saying anything about the missile buildup in Cuba, which was already under discussion within his government. But a week later the world could think of nothing else except the missile buildup and the American response.

As Washington waited for the Kremlin's reaction to the President's speech, work on the missile sites continued, Soviet vessels were approaching the American naval patrol around Cuba, and the American government was approaching its allies, the UN, and the OAS. Before the public crisis began on Monday, the Administration recognized that its blockade was illegal, that the United States itself had once fought a war for free navigation of the seas, and that we recognized blockade only in connection with a declared war. As a concession to this, the American action was called a "quarantine" not a "blockade." The chief point of concern was: Would the Soviet accept it or would their vessels precipitate war by trying to break through? The test came on Thursday, October 25th, at the end of three days of confused activity in other corners of the stage.

On Tuesday, October 23rd, as the United States took its case to the UN and the OAS, reactions came from its allies and world opinion. Both reactions were adverse, but most states made it clear that they would not oppose the American action. Although the British government, like the rest of our allies, supported the American action, public opinion in England, including *The Guardian, The Times,* and the leaders of the Labour Party, flung back at us the criticism the Eisenhower Administration had made of the British attack on Suez six years earlier: ignoring the United Nations, deceiving and bypassing one's allies, resorting to violent rather than peaceful procedures in international disputes, and risking nuclear war before negotiations have been exhausted. Pakistan and India, unable to agree on anything else, were united in their criticism of Kennedy's irresponsible exposure of the world to the risk of war. Sweden flatly rejected the blockade.

In these same days, the twenty other Latin American states voted to support the American blockade of Cuba, and Argentina offered to provide ships to participate in it, but several states indicated that they would not support an American invasion of Cuba if the blockade failed to enforce removal of the missiles.

The United Nations, as might be expected, was not so successful in reaching any agreement. Three resolutions were introduced, submitted by the United States, the Soviet Union, and the forty neutrals (out of 105 member states), but it was impossible to obtain the necessary two-thirds vote for any one of them, and none came to a vote.

In the meantime, for two days the important question hung unanswered: What would the Soviet ships do when they reached the blockade? The first, a tanker, was challenged by an American destroyer on Thursday, was acknowledged, and gave the necessary information that it was carrying no arms to Cuba. Within a few hours, it became clear that twelve of twenty-five Soviet ships en route to Cuba were turning back. The Kremlin had backed down.

The following night (Friday, October 26, 1962) the White House received a long and confused letter from Khrushchev. Its tone clearly showed his personal panic, and, to save his reputation, it was not released to the public. The next morning the Soviet Foreign Office published a quite different text, suggesting that a deal be made dismantling both the American missile sites in Turkey and the Soviet missile sites in Cuba. To those inside both governments, this was recognized as a Soviet surrender, since they knew that the Turkish sites were obsolete and were already scheduled to be dismantled within a few months. Although this would have amounted to giving something for nothing on the Russian side, it was rejected by the White House because it would have represented to the world a surrender of Turkey, our ally on the Soviet border, because the Kremlin had succeeded in establishing a direct threat on our border. Instead, the White House replied to Khrushchev's unpublished first note, extracting from it an offer to remove the Russian missiles if we would lift the blockade and promise not to invade Cuba.

This acceptance was sent off to Moscow on Saturday night, while our mobilization for an attack on the Soviet missile sites if their construction continued went on. On Sunday morning, by radio from Moscow, Khrushchev's acceptance was announced: the work on the missile sites was ordered stopped and they would be dismantled, with UN observation to verify the fact; in return the President would promise not to attack Cuba or allow our allies to do so. This led directly to the removal and deportation of the missiles and Ilyushin bombers over the next few weeks. The Soviet soldiers and technicians left much more slowly and never completely. Inspection of the sites was prevented by Castro, who was wild with anger at the way he had been brushed aside and finally sold out by the Kremlin. As a result of this failure, the American promise not to invade Cuba was also not given.

The missile crisis, by stripping the Soviet-American rivalry down to its essential feature as a crude power rivalry, cleared up a number of ambiguities and opened a new era in twentieth-century history. It showed (1) that the power balance between the two Superpowers was clearly in America's favor; (2) that the United States government, in spite of Khrushchev's doubts, had the will power to face and begin atomic war if necessary; (3) that no one really wanted thermonuclear war and that Khrushchev was prepared to go to any reasonable point to avoid it; and (4) that deterrence actually does deter and, accordingly, that a *modus vivendi* might ultimately be achieved between the two Superpowers.

The Disintegrating Superblocs

The chief consequence of the nuclear stalemate was that it made possible a greatly increased diversity in the world. The mutual cancellation of the strength of the two Superpowers made a situation in which states with little or no power were able to play significant roles on the world stage. At the same time, the Superpowers were not even in a position to press their desires on the members of their own blocs, and the neutrals could act with growing neutrality or even growing irresponsibility. Examples of such behavior could be seen in France, Pakistan, or Red China among the members of the two blocs, or in the Congo or the Arab states among the neutrals. Accordingly, the next divisions of our subject must be concerned with the disintegration of the Superblocs and the growth of neutralism.

LATIN AMERICA: A RACE BETWEEN DISASTER AND REFORM

As time remorselessly moves forward through the second half of the twentieth century, a major problem for the United States is the fate of Latin America, that gigantic portion of the Western Hemisphere that is south of the Rio Grande. It is not an area that can continue to be ignored, because it is neither small nor remote, and its problems are both urgent and explosive. Yet, until 1960, it was ignored.

The Latin America that demanded attention in 1960 was twice the size of the United States (7.5 million square miles compared to 3.6 million square miles), with a population about 10 percent larger (200 million persons compared to our 180 million in 1960). Brazil, which spoke Portuguese rather than Spanish, had almost half the total area with more than a third the total population (75 million in 1960). In 1960 Brazil reached the end of a decade of economic and population expansion during which its economy was growing at about 7 percent a year while its population was growing over 2.5 percent a year, both close to the fastest rates in the world. (The population increase of Asia was about 1.8 percent a year, Russia and the United States were less, while Europe was only 0.7 percent a year.) Brazil's rate of economic growth fell to about 3 percent a year after 1960, while its population explosion became worse, apparently trying to catch up with the Brazilian cost of living, which rose 40 percent in 1961, 50 percent in 1962, and 70 percent in 1963.

Except for its fantastic price inflation, Brazil's problems were fairly typical of those faced by all of Latin America. These problems might be boiled down to four basic issues: (1) falling death rates, combined with continued high birthrates, are producing a population explosion unaccompanied by any comparable increase in the food supply; (2) the social disorganization resulting from such population increase, combined with a flooding of people from rural areas into urban slums, is reflected in disruption of family life, spreading crime and immorality, totally inadequate education and other social services, and growing despair; (3) the ideological patterns of Latin America, which were always unconstructive, are being replaced by newer, equally unconstructive but explosively violent, doctrines; and (4) there is simultaneously an unnecessary spreading of modern weapons and a growing disequilibrium between the control of such arms and the disintegrating social structure and the increasing social and political pressures just mentioned.

Some of the more obvious consequences of these four problems might be mentioned here.

Latin America is not only poverty-ridden, but the distribution of wealth and income is so unequal that the most ostentatious luxury exists for a small group side by side with the most degrading poverty for the overwhelming majority, with a growing but very small group in between. The average yearly per capita income for all of Latin America was about $253 in 1960, ranging from $800 in Venezuela to $95 in Paraguay and $70 in Haiti. The distribution is so unequal, however, that four-fifths of the population of Latin America get about $53 a year, while a mere 100 families own 9/10 of the native-owned wealth of the whole area and only 30 families own 72 percent of that wealth. This disequilibrium is seen most clearly in landholding, on which more than half the population, because of the area's economic backwardness, is dependent. Agrarian reform (land redistribution), which seems attractive to many but is really no solution so long as the peasants lack capital and technical know-how, has been carried out, to some extent, in a few countries (such as Mexico or Bolivia), but, in Latin America generally, landholding is still very unequal. In Brazil, for example, half of all land is owned by 2.6 percent of the landowners, while 22.5 percent of all the land is held by only ½ percent of the owners. In Latin America as a whole, at least two-thirds of the land is owned by 10 percent of the families. Such inequality attracts a good deal of criticism, especially by North American "reformers," but in itself it would be good and not bad if the wealthy owners felt any desire or obligation to make the land produce more, but the greatest bane of Latin American life, as it is in Spain also, is the self-indulgence of the rich that allows them to waste their large incomes in luxury and extravagances without any feeling of obligation to improve (or even to utilize fully) the resources they control. We shall return in a moment to the disastrous ideological patterns that lie behind this attitude.

Almost equally indicative of an unhealthy society is the age distribution within that society and the failure to provide education and health protection. About half of Latin America's population is unproductive and a social burden on the other half because it falls into the two groups of the young (below 15 years) or the old (over 65 years). This compares with only 26 percent of the population in these dependent groups in the United States. Such a distribution, in a healthy society, would require very considerable direction of resources into such social services as education, health protection, and retirement security. All such services in Latin America are painfully inadequate. About two-thirds of Latin Americans are illiterate, and those who may be classified as literate have very inadequate schooling. The average Latin American has had less than two years of schooling, but, like all averages, this one is misleading, since it covers both Paraguay (where very few children ever get near a school) and Castro's Cuba (where, we are told, illiteracy has been wiped out and all children of school age up to 15 are supposed to be in school). Leaving out these two countries, we find that in 1961 in 18 other Latin American countries only 38 percent of the population had finished two years of school, while only 7 percent had finished primary school, and one out of a hundred had attended a university.

The inadequacy of health protection in Latin America is as startling as the inadequacy of education, but may not, in a wider frame, be so objectionable. For if health were better protected, more people would survive, and the problems of scarce food and scarce jobs would have reached the explosive point long ago. Unfortunately, this problem of health and death rates has a very great impact on humanitarian North American observers, with the consequence that a considerable portion of the funds for development provided by the Alliance for Progress since 1961 are aimed at reducing these evils of disease and death. Since this effort is bound to be more successful than the much smaller funds aimed at increasing the food supply, the net consequence of these efforts will be to give Latin America more and hungrier people.

As things stood in 1960, infant mortality varied between 20 and 35 percent in different countries. Even in the Latin American country with the lowest death rate for the first year of life (Uruguay with 25 deaths per thousand births), the rate is ten times as high as in the United States (2.6 per thousand), while in Latin America as a whole it was 56 per thousand, rising to about 90 per thousand in Guatemala. The expectation of life for a new baby in all Latin America is only two-thirds that in the United States (44 years compared to 66 years), but in some areas, such as northeast Brazil, men are worn out from malnutrition and disease at age 30.

While such conditions may rouse North Americans to outrage or humanitarian sympathy, no solution of Latin America's problems can be found by emotion or sentimentality. The problems of Latin America are not based on lack of anything, but on structural weaknesses. Solutions will not rest on anything that can be done to or for individual people but on the arrangements of peoples. Even the greatest evil of the area, the selfish and mistaken outlook of the dominant social groups, cannot be changed by persuading individuals but must be changed by modifying the patterns of social relationships that are creating such outlooks. The key to the salvation of Latin America, and much of the rest of the world, rests on that word: "patterns." Latin America has the resources, the manpower, the capital accumulation, even perhaps the know-how to provide a viable and progressive society. What it lacks are constructive patterns—patterns of power, of social life, and, above all, of outlook—that will mobilize its resources in constructive rather than destructive directions.

Failure to recognize that Latin America's weaknesses are not based on lack of substance but on lack of constructive patterns is one of the two chief reasons why the future of Latin America looks so discouraging. The other reason is failure to recognize that the chief problem in planning Latin America's future is that of establishing a constructive sequence of priorities. In fact, these two problems: obtaining constructive patterns and obtaining a constructive sequence of priorities, are the keys to salvation of all the underdeveloped and backward areas of the globe. We might sum up this general situation by saying that the salvation of our poor, harassed globe depends on structure and sequence (or on patterns and priorities).

In applying these two paradigms to Latin American development, we shall find that the problem of priorities is much easier to solve than the problem of patterns. Obviously, the birthrate must decrease before any vigorous efforts are made to reduce the death rate. Or the food supply must be increased faster than the population. And some provision must be made to provide peasants with capital and know-how before the great landed estates are divided up among them. Equally urgent is the caution that some provision for capital accumulation and its investment in better methods of production must be made *before* the present accumulation of excess incomes in the hands of the existing oligarchies is destroyed by redistribution of the incomes of the rich (who could invest it) to the poor (who could only consume it). It should be obvious (but unfortunately is not) that a more productive organization of resources should have priority over any effort to raise standards of living. And it should be equally obvious that Latin America's own resources (including its own capital accumulation and its own know-how) should be devoted to this effort before the responsibility for Latin American economic development is placed on the resources of North Americans or other outsiders.

This last point might be amplified. We hear a great deal about Latin America's need for American capital and American know-how, when in fact the need for these is much less than the need for utilization of Latin America's own capital and know-how. The wealth and income of Latin America, in absolute quantities, is so great and it is so inequitably controlled and distributed that there is an enormous accumulation of incomes, far beyond their consumption needs, in the hands of a small percentage of Latin Americans. Much of these excess incomes are wasted, hoarded, or merely used for wasteful competition in ostentatious social display. This, as we shall see, is largely due to the deficiencies of Latin American personalities and character. The contrast, from this point of view, between England in the eighteenth and nineteenth centuries and Latin America in the nineteenth and twentieth centuries is very instructive. In both cases there was such a drastic inequity in the distribution of national incomes that the masses of the people were in abject poverty and probably getting poorer. But in England there were groups benefiting from this inequality who eschewed all self-indulgence, luxury, or ostentatious display of wealth, and systematically invested their growing incomes in creating new and more efficient patterns of utilization of resources. This is in sharp contrast to the situation in Latin America where such excess wealth, in the aggregate, is much greater than that being accumulated, a century or more ago, in England, but is very largely wasted and surely is not being used to create more productive patterns for utilization of resources, except in rare cases.

The solution to this problem is not, as we have said, to redistribute incomes in Latin America, but to change the patterns of character and of personality formation so that excess incomes will be used constructively and not wasted (nor simply redistributed and consumed).

A similar situation exists in regard to foreign exchange. Alternately our compassion is stirred and our anger aroused by American reformers and Latin agitators at the iniquities of the colonial character of Latin America's position in the world economy. This simply means that Latin America exports raw materials, minerals, and agricultural products (generally unprocessed goods), and imports processed, manufactured goods. Since the prices of unprocessed goods are generally more competitive, and therefore more fluctuating, than those of manufactured goods, the so-called "terms of trade" tend to run either favorably for or very unfavorably against Latin America. In the latter case, which has been generally prevalent for the last few years, the prices Latin America has to pay on the world's markets have tended to rise, while the prices that it gets for its own goods have tended to fall. As European economists would say, "The blades of the scissors have opened." American farmers, who speak of the "terms of parity," have been suffering the same way in the American domestic market.

Now, this is perfectly true. The Latin American economy is largely a colonial one (like Australia, New Zealand, West Africa, or Montana). In fact, in Latin America, in recent years, at least half the value of American aid has been wiped away by the worsening of Latin America's terms of trade, which made it necessary for it to pay more and more foreign moneys for its imports at the same time that it got less and less foreign moneys for its exports. But the fact remains that this reduction in the supply of foreign exchange available for Latin America's purchases of advanced equipment overseas has been made much worse by the fact that wealthy Latin Americans buy up much of the available supply of such foreign exchange for self-indulgent and nonconstructive spending abroad or simply to hoard their incomes in politically safer areas in New York, London, or Switzerland. Estimates of the total of such Latin American hoards abroad range between one billion and two billion dollars.

The solution to this problem must be found in more responsible, more public-spirited, and more constructive patterns of outlook, of money flows, and of political and social security.

A similar solution must be found for some of the social deficiencies of Latin America, such as inadequate education, housing, and social stability. Widespread tax evasion by the rich; bribery and corruption in public life; and brutality and selfishness in social life can be reduced and largely eliminated in Latin America by changing patterns in Latin American life and utilization of resources without much need for funds, sermons, or demonstrations from foreigners (least of all Americans).

This is not an argument for a reduction in American aid or in American concern for Latin America. It is a plea for recognition, by all concerned, that the problems of Latin America, and the possible solutions to these problems, rest on questions of structure and sequence and not on questions of resources, wealth, or even know-how.

The connection of that last word "know-how" to the whole problem may not be sufficiently clear. We Americans have such pride in our technological achievements that we often seem to feel that we "know how" to do almost everything, but this know-how really exists on two levels. One level is concerned with general attitudes such as objectivity, rationality, recognition of the value of social consensus, and such, while the other level is concerned with technological achievement in any specific situation. The former level has a great deal to contribute to the Latin American situation, while the latter level (the engineering level, so to speak) has much less to contribute to Latin America than most people believe. For example, American agricultural techniques, which are so fantastically successful in the temperate seasonal climate and well-watered and alluvial soils of North America, are frequently quite unadapted to the tropical, less seasonal climate, and semiarid, leached soils of South America. The solution to the Latin American problem of food production is not necessarily to apply North American techniques to the problem, but to discover techniques, different from our own, that will work under Latin American conditions. This situation, applied here to agriculture, is even more true of social and ideological problems.

The problem of finding constructive patterns for Latin America is much more difficult than the problem of finding constructive priorities. One reason for this is that the unconstructive patterns that now prevail in Latin America are deeply entrenched as a result of centuries and even millennia of persistent background. In fact, the Latin American patterns that must be changed because today they are leading to social and cultural disruption are not really Latin American in origin, or even Iberian for that matter, but are Near Eastern, and go back, for some of their aspects, for two thousand or more years. As a general statement, we might say that the Latin American cultural pattern (including personality patterns and general outlook) is Arabic, while its social pattern is that of Asiatic despotism. The pattern as a whole is so prevalent today, not only in Latin America, but in Spain, Sicily, southern Italy, the Near East, and in various other areas of the Mediterranean world (such as Egypt), that we might well call it the "Pakistani-Peruvian axis." For convenience of analysis we shall divide it into "Asiatic despotism" and the "Arabic outlook."

We have already indicated the nature of Asiatic despotism in connection with traditional China, the old Ottoman Empire, and czarist Russia. It goes back to the archaic Bronze Age empires, which first appeared in Mesopotamia, Egypt, the Indus Valley, and northern China before 1000 B.C. Basically such an Asiatic despotism is a two-class society in which a lower class, consisting of at least nine-tenths of the population, supports an upper, ruling class consisting of several interlocking groups. These ruling groups are a governing bureaucracy of scribes and priests associated with army leaders, landlords, and moneylenders. Such an upper class accumulated great quantities of wealth as taxes, rents, interest on loans, fees for services, or simply as financial extortions. The social consequences were either progressive or reactionary, depending on whether this accumulated wealth in the possession of the ruling class was invested in more productive utilization of resources or was simply hoarded and wasted. The essential character of such an Asiatic despotism rests on the fact that the ruling class has legal claims on the working masses, and possesses the power (from its control of arms and the political structure) to enforce these claims. A modified Asiatic despotism is one aspect of the social structures all along the Pakistani-Peruvian axis.

The other aspect of the Pakistani-Peruvian axis rests on its Arabic outlook. The Arabs, like other Semites who emerged from the Arabian desert at various times to infiltrate the neighboring Asiatic despotic cultures of urban civilizations, were, originally, nomadic, tribal peoples. Their political structure was practically identical with their social structure and was based on blood relationships and not on territorial jurisdiction. They were warlike, patriarchal, extremist, violent, intolerant, and xenophobic. Like most tribal peoples, their political structure was totalitarian in the sense that all values, all needs, and all meaningful human experience was contained within the tribe. Persons outside the tribal structure had no value or significance, and there were no obligations or meaning associated in contacts with them. In fact, they were hardly regarded as human beings at all. Moreover, within the tribe, social significance became more intense as blood relationships became closer, moving inward from the tribes through clans to the patriarchal extended family. The sharp contrast between such a point of view and that associated with Christian society as we know it can be seen in the fact that such Semitic tribalism was endogamous, while the rule of Christian marriage is exogamous. The rules, in fact, were directly antithetical, since Arabic marriage favors unions of first cousins, while Christian marriage has consistently opposed marriage of first (or even second) cousins. In traditional Arabic society any girl was bound to marry her father's brother's son if he and his father wanted her, and she was usually not free to marry someone else until he had rejected her (sometimes after years of waiting).

In such traditional Arabic society, the extended family, not the individual, was the basic social unit; all property was controlled by the patriarchal head of such a family and, accordingly, most decisions were in his hands. His control of the marriage of his male descendants was ensured by the fact that a price had to be paid for a bride to her family, and this would require the patriarch's consent.

Such a patriarchal family arose from the fact that marriage was patrilocal, the young couple residing with the groom's father so long as he lived, while he continued to live with the groom's paternal grandfather until the latter's death. Such a death of the head of an extended family freed his sons to become heads of similar extended families that would remain intact, frequently for three or more generations, until the head of the family dies in his turn. Within such a family each male remains subject to the indulgent, if erratic, control of his father and the indulgent, and subservient care of his mother and unmarried sisters, while his wife is under the despotic control of her mother-in-law until her production of sons and the elimination of her elders by death will make her a despot, in turn, over her daughters-in-law.

This Arabic emphasis on the extended family as the basic social reality meant that larger social units came into existence simply by linking a number of related extended families together under the nominal leadership of the patriarch who, by general consensus, had the best qualities of leadership, dignity, and social prestige. But such unions, being personal and essentially temporary, could be severed at any time. The personal character of such unions and the patriarchal nature of the basic family units tended to make all political relationships personal and temporary, reflections of the desires or whims of the leader and not the consequence or reflection of any basic social relationship. This tended to prevent the development of any advanced conception of he state, law, and the community (as achieved, for example, by the once tribal Greeks and Romans). Within the family, rules were personal, patriarchal, and often arbitrary and changeable, arising from the will and often from the whims of the patriarch. This prevented the development of any advanced ideas of reciprocal common interests whose interrelationships, by establishing a higher social structure, created, at the same time, rules superior to the individual, rules of an impersonal and permanent character in which law created authority and not, as in the Arabic system, authority created law (or at least temporary rules). To this day the shattered cultures along the whole Pakistani-Peruvian axis have a very weak grasp of the nature of a community or of any obligation to such a community, and regard law and politics as simply personal relationships whose chief justification is the power and position of the individual who issues the orders. The state, as a structure of force more remote and therefore less personal than the immediate family, is regarded as an alien and exploitative personal system to be avoided and evaded simply because it is more remote (even if of similar character) than the individual's immediate family.

This biological and patriarchal character of all significant social relationships in Arab life is reflected in the familiar feature of male dominance. Only the male is important. The female is inferior, even subhuman, and becomes significant only by producing males (the one thing, apparently, that the dominant male cannot do for himself). Because of the strong patrilocal character of Arab marriage, a new wife is not only subjected sexually to her husband; she is also subjected socially and personally to his family, including his brothers, and, above all, his mother (who has gained this position of domination over other females in the house by having produced male children). Sex is regarded almost solely as simply a physiological relationship with little emphasis on the religious, emotional, or even social aspects. Love, meaning concern for the personality or developing potentialities of the sexual partner, plays little role in Arabic sexual relationships. The purpose of such relationships in the eyes of the average Arab is to relieve his own sexual desire or to generate sons.

Such sons are brought up in an atmosphere of whimsical, arbitrary, personal rules where they are regarded as superior beings by their mother and sisters and, inevitably, by their father and themselves, simply on the basis of their maleness. Usually they are spoiled, undisciplined, self-indulgent, and unprincipled. Their whims are commands, their urges are laws. They are exposed to a dual standard of sexual morality in which any female is a legitimate target of their sexual desires, but the girl they marry is expected to be a paragon of chaste virginity. The original basis for this emphasis on a bride's virginity rested on the emphasis on blood descent and was intended to be a guarantee of the paternity of children. The wife, as a child-producing mechanism, had to produce the children of one known genetic line and no other.

This emphasis on the virginity of any girl who could be regarded as acceptable as a wife was carried to extremes. The loss of a girl's virginity was regarded as an unbearable dishonor by the girl's family, and any girl who brought such dishonor on a family was regarded as worthy of death at the hands of her father and brothers. Once she is married, the right to punish such a transgression is transferred to her husband.

To any well-bred girl, her premarital virginity and the reservation of sexual access to her husband's control after marriage ("her honor") have pecuniary value. Since she has no value in herself as a person, apart from "her honor," and has little value as a worker of any sort, her virginity before marriage has a value in money equal to the expense of keeping her for much of her life since, indeed, this is exactly what it was worth in money. As a virgin she could expect the man who obtained her in marriage to regard that asset as equivalent to his reciprocal obligation to support her as a wife. As a matter of fact, her virginity was worth much less than that, for in traditional Arabic society, if she displeased her husband, even if she merely crossed one of his whims, he could set her aside by divorce, a process very easy for him, with little delay or obligation, but impossible to achieve on her part, no matter how eagerly she might desire it. Moreover, once her virginity was gone, she had little value as a wife or a person, unless she had mothered a son, and could be passed along from man to man, either in marriage or otherwise, with little social obligation on anyone's part. As a result of such easy divorce, and the narrow physiological basis on which sexual relationships are based, plus the lack of value of a woman once her virginity is gone, Arab marriage is very fragile, with divorce and broken marriage about twice as frequent as in the United States. Even the production of sons does not ensure the permanence of the marriage, since the sons belong to the father whatever the cause of the marriage disruption. As a result of these conditions, marriage of several wives in sequence, a phenomenon we associate with Hollywood, is much more typical of the Arabic world and is very much more frequent than the polygamous marriage, which, while permitted under Islam, is quite rare. Not more than 5 percent of married men in the Near East today have more than one wife at the same time, because of the expense, but the number who remain in monogamous union till death is almost equally small.

As might be expected in such a society, Arabic boys grow up egocentric, self-indulgent, undisciplined, immature, spoiled, subject to waves of emotionalism, whims, passion, and pettiness. The consequence of this for the whole Pakistani-Peruvian axis will be seen in a moment.

Another aspect of Arabic society is its scorn of honest, steady manual work, especially agricultural work. This is a consequence of the fusion of at least three ancient influences. First, the archaic bureaucratic structure of Asiatic despotism, in which peasants supported warriors and scribes, regarded manual workers, especially tillers of the soil, as the lowest layer of society, and regarded the acquisition of literacy and military prowess as the chief roads to escape from physical drudgery. Second, the fact that Classical Antiquity, whose influence on the subsequent Islamic Civilization was very great, was based on slavery, and came to regard agricultural (or other manual) work as fit for slaves, also contributed to this idea. Third, the Bedouin tradition of pastoral, warlike nomads scorned tillers of the soil as weak and routine persons of no real spirit or character, fit to be conquered or walked on but not to be respected. The combination of these three formed the lack of respect for manual work that is so characteristic of the Pakistani-Peruvian axis.

Somewhat similar to this lack of respect for manual work are a number of other characteristics of traditionl Arab life that have also spread the length of the Pakistani-Peruvian axis. The chief source of many of these is the Bedouin outlook, which originally reflected the attitudes of a relatively small group of the Islamic culture but which, because they were a superior, conquering group, came to be copied by others in the society, even by the despised agricultural workers. These attitudes include lack of respect for the soil, for vegetation, for most animals, and for outsiders. These attitudes, which are singularly ill-fitted for the geographic and climatic conditions of the whole Pakistani-Peruvian area, are to be seen constantly in the everyday life of that area as erosion, destruction of vegetation and wild life, personal cruelty and callousness to most living things, including one's fellow men, and a general harshness and indifference to God's creation. This final attitude, which well reflects the geographic conditions of the area, which seem as harsh and indifferent as man himself, is met by those men who must face it in their daily life as a resigned submission to fate and to the inhumanity of man to man.

Interestingly enough, these attitudes have successfully survived the efforts of the three great religions of ethical monotheism, native to the area, to change these attitudes. The ethical sides of Judaism, Christianity, and Islam sought to counteract harshness, egocentricity, tribalism, cruelty, scorn of work and of one's fellow creatures, but these efforts, on the whole, have met with little success throughout the length of the Pakistani-Peruvian axis. Of the three, Christianity, possibly because it set the highest standards of the three, has fallen furthest from achieving its aims. Love, humility, brotherhood, cooperation, the sanctity of work, the fellowship of the community, the image of man as a fellow creature made in the image of God, respect for women as personalities and partners of men, mutual helpmates on the road to spiritual salvation, and the vision of our universe, with all its diversity, complexity, and multitude of creatures, as a reflection of the power and goodness of God—these basic aspects of Christ's teachings are almost totally lacking throughout the Pakistani-Peruvian axis and most notably absent on the "Christian" portion of that axis from Sicily, or even the Aegean Sea, westward to Baja California and Tierra del Fuego. Throughout the whole axis, human actions are not motivated by these "Christian virtues" but by the more ancient Arabic personality traits, which became vices and sins in the Christian outlook: harshness, envy, lust, greed, selfishness, cruelty, and hatred.

Islam, the third in historical sequence of the ethical monotheistic religions of the Near East, was very successful in establishing its monotheism, but had only very moderate success in spreading its version of Jewish and Christian ethics to the Arabs. These moderate successes were counterbalanced by other, incidental consequences of Muhammad's personal life and of the way in which Islam spread to make the Muslim religion more rigid, absolute, uncompromising, self-centered, and dogmatic.

The failure of Christianity in the areas west from Sicily was even greater, and was increased by the spread of Arab outlooks and influence to that area, and especially to Spain. The old French proverb which says that "Africa begins at the Pyrenees" does not, of course, mean by "Africa" that Black Africa which exists south of the deserts, but means the world of the Arabs which spread, in the eighth century, across Africa from Sinai to Morocco.

To this day the Arab influence is evident in southern Italy, northern Africa and, above all, in Spain. It appears in the obvious things such as architecture, music, the dance, and literature, but most prominently it appears in outlook, attitudes, motivations, and value systems. Spain and Latin America, despite centuries of nominal Christianity, are Arabic areas.

No statement is more hateful to Spaniards and Latin Americans than that. But once it is made, and once the evidence on which it was based is examined in an objective way, it becomes almost irrefutable. In Spain, the Arab conquest of 711, which was not finally ejected until 1492, served to spread Arab personality traits, in spite of the obvious antagonism between Muslim and Christian. In fact, the antagonism helped to build up those very traits that I have called Arabic: intolerance, self-esteem, hatred, militarization, cruelty, dogmatism, rigidity, harshness, suspicion of outsiders, and the rest of it. The Arab traits that were not engendered by this antagonism were built up by emulation—the tendency of a conquered people to copy their conquerors, no matter how much they profess to hate them, simply because they are a superior social class. From this emulation came the Spanish and Latin American attitudes toward sex, family structure, and child-rearing that are the distinctive features of Spanish-speaking life today and that make Spanish-speaking areas so ambiguously part of Western Civilization in spite of their nominal allegiance to such an essential Western trait as Christianity. For the West, even as it nominally ceases to be Christian, and most obviously in those areas which have, at least nominally, drifted furthest from Christianity, still has many of the basic Christian traits of love, humility, social concern, humanitarianism, brotherly care, and future preference, however detached these traits may have become from the Christian idea of deity or of individual salvation in a spiritual eternity.

In Latin America the Mediterranean version of Arabized life again found its traits preserved, and sometimes reinforced, by the historical process. In Latin America non-Spanish influences, chiefly Indian, Negro, and North American, can be observed in such things as music, dances, superstitions, agricultural crops and diet (largely Indian), or in transportation, communications, and weapons (largely European); but the basic structures of family and social life, of ideological patterns and values are, to this day, largely those of the Arabic end of the Pakistani-Peruvian axis.

The Iberian conquest of Latin America, not as an area of settlement but as an area of exploitation, and the Spanish attitude toward the Indians and Negro slaves as instruments in that exploitative process, the development of plantation colonialism, and of mineral extraction, intensified the exploitative, ransacking, extensive attitude toward resources and peoples which the Mediterranean area had obtained from the Romans and the Saracens. None of these activities became permanent community traits for those involved in them, even for the underlings who operated as part of the exploitative way of life, but remained temporary, get-rich-quick methods of mercenary gain for persons who regarded themselves as strangers whose roots were elsewhere, or nowhere. The Spanish oligarchy in the colonial period saw its roots in Spain itself, and this attitude, widened somewhat to include Paris, London, the Riviera, or New York, has remained the attitude of the ruling oligarchy after the wars of liberation broke the formal links with Spain or Portugal. In the same way, and for these reasons, the colonial economy, and colonialism in financial, educational, cultural, and commercial life, has continued after it ceased in the narrowly political sphere. To this day, the characteristics we have listed as Arabic dominate Latin America: no real concern for the soil, the area, for workers, one's fellow men, or the community as a whole; the dominance of family connection and of masculine dominance with its dual standard of sexual morality, its cult of virility, its selfishness, self-indulgence, lack of self-discipline or of concern for others; and the whole Mediterranean view of politics as a system of exploitative, personal relationships of an arbitrary and corrupt character combining extortion, bribery, tax evasion, and total divorce from community spirit or personal responsibility for the welfare of others or of the nation.

This picture of Latin America and its problems will be resented and criticized by many as exaggerated, one-sided, or even as mistaken. Naturally, in view of its brevity, it is oversimplified, as all brief expositions must be. And equally naturally all its statements do not apply to all groups, all areas, all classes, or all individuals. There are numerous exceptions to large portions of this picture, but they are *exceptions* and are explicable as such. And there are obviously different degrees of emphasis among various groups, backgrounds, and periods. These again are explicable. Those Latin Americans who are close to the Negro traditions of Africa and of slavery put more emphasis on present preference and sociability than they do on domination, harshness, and cruelty. Again those Latin Americans who are close to the Indian tradition put more emphasis on resignation to fate and indigenous superstitions than they do on male dominance and proving their sexual virility (called *machismo*, a key concept in Latin American outlook and behavior). Above all, the scores of millions of Latin Americans who are on a poverty level at, or even below, subsistence have many of the characteristics of social and psychological disintegration that we associate with extreme poverty everywhere, even in the United States, and are to that degree unable to carry on the traditions of Latin American life—or any traditions. As such, they emphasize, interestingly enough, the traits of male dominance and egocentric selfishness rather than the companion traits, in the Arab tradition, of female chastity or family solidarity.

In general, we might say that the Latin American tradition we have identified as a modified Arabic tradition with Asiatic despotic overtones is more typical of the oligarchic, Spanish upper classes than it is of the Negro, Indian, or poverty-racked urban poor. And this is of the greatest significance. For this shows that the means and the method for the reform of Latin American society rest in the same group of that society. Such reform can come about only when the surpluses that accumulate in the hands of the Latin American oligarchy are used to establish more progressive utilization of Latin American resources. By the word "reform" we mean that the power pattern, the economic and social pattern, and the ideological pattern be reorganized in more constructive configurations rather than on the destructive patterns in which they now exist. And of these three, the patterns of ideology—that is, of outlook and value systems—are most in need of change. Of course, in any society it is precisely this pattern of outlook and values that is most difficult to modify. In most societies this remains unchanged—repeated in slogans, war cries, and religious incantations long after the behavioral and structural patterns have changed completely. But in Latin America there is this ray of hope. A more constructive ideological pattern is already familiar, at least in words, to Latin America: Christianity.

The whole system is full of paradox and contradiction. The real obstacle to progress and hope in Latin America rests in the oligarchy, not so much because it controls the levers of power and wealth but because it is absorbed in the destructive Latin American ideology. But the real hope in the area rests in the same oligarchy, because it controls wealth and power, and also because there is no hope at all unless it changes its ideology. The ideology it could adopt is one that places emphasis on self-discipline, service to others, love, and equality, but these virtues, almost wholly lacking in practice in Latin America, are the very ones that are, in words, embodied in the Christian religion to which the oligarchy of Latin America nominally belongs. In a word, Latin America would be on the road to reform if it practiced what it preached, that is, if it tried to be Christian. Of course, we cannot really say that the solution lies in practice of what one preaches, the Christian virtues, because Latin American religion, like everything else, is largely corrupt and, as a consequence, no longer preaches the Christian virtues. The upper clergy have been generally allied to the oligarchy; the lower clergy are as poverty-stricken and almost as ignorant as their fellow poor in lay society. Moreover, both levels of clergy have come to accept the outlook and values of the society in which they live. The message of Christ itself, a positive message of action, has been lost in the negative messages of the Catholic clergy reacting within a corrupt society drenched in the non-Christian outlook that dominates the oligarchy as a whole.

Only in recent years has there been much change in this situation. In most of Latin America, the Church's failure is recorded in the fact that the great mass of Latin American people, especially those below the level of the oligarchy itself, ignore it or reject it, just as they do in Spain. And especially the dominant males have rejected it, except as a social necessity, or an antirevolutionary force, or as a refuge for their martyr-obsessed women. But the advent of Pope John XXIII has had a profound influence on the Church by recalling it from its interests and crass power relationships to the content of Christ's message. The degree to which this can change the clergy's negative injunctions against adultery, Communism, and criminal acts into positive exhortations to acts of social benefit, help, and love is problematical. And even more dubious is the question if it is not going to be too little and too late. This is, indeed, the great question with which all talk of reform in Latin America must end: "Is there still time?"

There was time enough in 1940, when the demands of war in Europe began to push away the acute problems and controversies that had arisen from the world depression, the rise of Fascism, and the Spanish Civil War of the 1930's. World War II, by increasing the demand for Latin America's mineral and agricultural products, pushed starvation and controversy away from the immediate present and into the more remote future. Unfortunately, nothing constructive was done with the time thus gained, and, almost equally tragic, little constructive use was made of the wealth brought to Latin America by the demands of war elsewhere on the globe. Latin America boomed: the rich became richer; the poor had more children. A few poor, or at least not rich, became rich, or at least richer. But nothing was done to modify the basic pattern of Latin American power, wealth, and outlook.

The wars of independence that ended Latin America's political connection with Spain and Portugal did not destroy the power of the upper-class oligarchies or change their outlooks, except to make them somewhat more local. It was about a century, say from 1830 to 1930, before the oligarchic alliance of army, landlords, bankers, and upper clergy was seriously challenged in their exploitation of their peasant subjects or the natural resources of their local areas.

This challenge, which first appeared in Mexico in 1910, was a consequence of the commercialization and, much later, the incipient industrialization of Latin American society. The same influences, reinforced by other developments, such as growing literacy, population increase, and the introduction of new ideas of European and North American origin, served to weaken the union of the older oligarchic groups so that the solidarity of the military with the other three groups was much reduced.

This process of commercialization and incipient industrialization of Latin American society was largely a consequence of foreign investments, which introduced railroads, tram lines, faster communications, large-scale mining, some processing of raw materials, the introduction of electricity, waterworks, telephones, and other public utilities, and the beginnings of efforts to produce supplies for these new activities. These efforts served to create two new and quite divergent social classes which began to fill the gap between the older rural dichotomy of oligarchy and peasantry. The new classes, both largely urban, were labor and bourgeoisie. Both were infected by the class-struggle ideologies of European Socialist groups, so that the new laboring masses sought to be unionized and radical. Both groups were much more political than the old peasant class had ever been. A chief consequence of the whole development was the urbanization and radicalization of Latin American society.

From the political point of view, these developments made the power relationships of Latin America much more complex and unpredictable. For one thing, the army was no longer completely dependent on the landlord groups for support, but found, on the contrary, that its urban bases were under pressure of local labor-union controls of its supplies, while its relations with the bourgeois groups were much more ambiguous than its relations with the landlord group had been previously. At the same time, the influence of the clergy was generally weakened by the influx of anticlerical ideas of European origin into both the new urban groups and, to a much smaller extent, to the peasants.

These changes have not occurred in all areas of Latin America. Indeed, many areas remain much as they were in 1880. But in Mexico, Argentina, and Brazil the process has gone far enough to modify the whole social pattern, while in some lesser areas like Bolivia, Uruguay, Costa Rica and, above all, Cuba, drastic changes have been occurring.

In Mexico the revolution has continued for more than half a century. During at least half of that period, the chief problem was the control of militarism, a task that must be done in all of Latin America. In its early days, the Mexican Revolution was distracted from constructive change by a number of destructive efforts. For example, its attacks on foreign capital led to more damage than good by curtailing foreign investment and foreign technological skills. At the same time, its emphasis on agrarian reform distracted attention from the real agricultural problem to the pseudoproblem of landownership; the real problem is that of increasing agricultural production, regardless of agrarian arrangements. These three early problems have been to some extent overcome. The Mexican Army is now largely professionalized and relatively nonpolitical and responsive to civilian controls. For more than a generation now, the army has not overthrown a government. At the same time, political stability has been increased by the depersonalization of political life, by circulation of leadership within one dominant party, by the establishment of some political principles, including the very significant one of no reelection of the president, and by the use of political power to encourage some progressive tendencies, such as more public funds for education than for defense, encouragement of improved communications and transport, of foreign investment, and of balanced economic development. Many acute problems remain, such as an exploding population, acute poverty, and a very low level of social welfare, but things have been moving, and in a hopeful direction. During the two decades before 1962, the gross national product rose over 6 percent a year, while industrial production rose more than 400 percent in that period. The political system itself is corrupt, with most elections jobbed by the dominant Institutional Revolutionary Party, but at least the outlook for the average Mexican today is more hopeful than it was for his father a generation ago or than it is for his contemporaries in much of the rest of Latin America. The problems of life have not been solved in Mexico, but valuable time has been won.

Efforts of other countries to follow in Mexico's footsteps have been less successful and even disastrous. In Argentina patterns of life have become less constructive during the last generation, despite the fact that Argentina has been less burdened with population and more endowed with resources than other countries in Latin America. But lack of moral principles and excess self-indulgence has betrayed all efforts to obtain better patterns of life. This was evident in the career of Juan D. Perón, an army officer who came to power by a *coup d'état* in 1943 and sought to base that control on an alliance of the military with the workers. He built up a strong labor movement, but his concern with maintaining his own power, his lack of any over-all plan, and his basically unprincipled outlook led to a disintegration of his movement and his overthrow by his own military forces in 1955. The waste of resources by inefficiency and corruption under Perón has left Argentina disorganized and divided, with real power increasingly in the hands of the armed forces (if they could agree on anything) and with many people looking backward with regret to the more affluent days of Perón.

The disintegration of Argentina, which lacked the basic problems that have haunted most Latin American countries, helps to demonstrate the significant role played in Latin American backwardness by unconstructive patterns, especially patterns of outlook. Argentina did not have such problems as excess population, lack of capital, poor and unbalanced resources, extreme poverty, social disorganization, or illiteracy (which is below 10 percent), but the argumentative and divisive nature of social attitudes is as prevalent in Argentina as elsewhere on the Pakistani-Peruvian axis, and is the consequence along the whole length of that axis of the egocentric and undisciplined way in which sons are brought up by their mothers. In all societies, individuals have traits in which they differ from other individuals and traits in which they share. A highly civilized people like the English, by training of the young of all classes (until very recently) have tended to produce adults who emphasize the qualities they share, and play down the qualities in which they differ, even in activities such as games, politics, or competitive business where opposition is part of the rules. In Latin America the opposite is true, as each person tries to emphasize his individuality by finding more and more features of his life (often artificial ones) that distinguish or oppose him to others.

In Argentina, as elsewhere along the Pakistani-Peruvian axis (especially in Spain), this tendency has fragmented social life and led to extremism.

Even groups that seem to have the most obvious common interests in Argentina, such as the armed forces or the urban middle classes, are hopelessly split, and fluctuate from position to position. It is the splitting of these groups, especially of the middle classes, that has given such influence in Argentina to the labor unions on the Left or the landlord group on the Right. The middle classes in Argentina have been split into two political parties that refuse to cooperate. Together they could poll at least half the total vote in any election, but instead each obtains a quarter or less of the total vote and, refusing to join each other, must seek a majority by coalition with smaller, extremist parties.

The failure of Latin America to find solutions to its most urgent real problems are, thus, much more fundamental than the clichés of political controversy, the complexion of governments, or the presence or absence of "revolutionaries." The words Left, Center, or Right mean little in terms of solutions to Latin America's problems, since disorganization, corruption, violence, and fraud are endemic in all. Bolivia, which has had a revolutionary government of peasants and tin miners since 1952, is in a mess, and Nicaragua, which has been under control of a military-dominated oligarchy for almost thirty years, is in a similar mess. So long as any real solutions of Latin America's problems depend upon the slow building up of constructive patterns, including ideological patterns, no solution will be found in shifting power or property from one group to another, even if the beneficent group in such transfers is much larger. This failure of social and economic revolutions to achieve more constructive patterns is evident in Bolivia, Guatemala, and Cuba.

Bolivia's problems always seemed hopeless. In three unsuccessful wars with Chile, Brazil, and Paraguay from 1879 to 1935, it lost territory to its neighbors, including its only outlet to the sea. Its population of less than three million in 1950 (3.6 million a decade later) was crowded on its bleak western plateau, over 12,000 feet up, while its subtropical eastern lowlands were inhabited by only a few wild Indians. These lowlands and its mineral resources, source of 95 percent of its foreign exchange (mostly from tin), were Bolivia's chief assets before the revolution of 1952, but the former were unused, while the tin earnings went chiefly to swell the foreign holdings of three greedy groups, Patiño and Aramayo (both Bolivian) and Hochschild (Argentine). Until the revolution, the Bolivians, mostly of Indian descent, who were treated as second-class persons working as semislaves in the mines or as serfs on the large estates, had a per capita annual income of about $100, one-fifth that of Argentina, and the lowest but two of the twenty-one Latin American countries. As might be expected, the majority were illiterate, sullen, and discouraged.

The poor Bolivian performance in the Chaco War with Paraguay in 1932–1935 gave rise to national feeling even among the Indians, and inspired a group of academic intellectuals, led by Victor Paz Estenssoro, to found a new political party, the National Revolutionary Movement (MNR). Many of the younger officers and the Indian enlisted men sympathized with the movement, and it won the largest vote of any party (45 percent) in the election of 1951. The older officers prevented the MNR from participating in the new government, but their junta split and was overthrown by an uprising in April 1952. Paz Estenssoro returned from exile to become president, with Juan Lechin, leader of the revolutionary tin miners' union, as his chief aid.

Within a year, pressure from the tin miners and from the peasants (*campesinos*) forced the new regime to nationalize the mines and to break up many of the large estates into small peasant holdings. Production of metals and of food both collapsed, the miners demanding more pay and shorter hours for less and less work, driving Bolivian costs of production above the world market price for tin, thus wiping out a major part of the country's foreign-exchange earnings. These fell from $150,-770,000 (96 percent from metals) in 1951 to $63,240,000 (86 percent from metals) in 1958. To make matters worse, as Bolivian costs of tin rose, the world price of tin collapsed in 1957 when the Soviet Union, for the first time, came into the world markets with low-priced tin. In these same years, Bolivia's production of food for the market, which had never been sufficient, was reduced by the transformation of large estates producing for market into small farms producing for subsistence. The nationalization of the railways used to export Bolivia's metals proved as disastrous as the nationalization of the mines, and by 1961 only eighteen of sixty main-line locomotives were still functioning. As might be expected under such a regime, price inflation drove the value of Bolivia's monetary unit down from an official rate of 190 to the dollar in 1954 to an open market rate of 12,000 to the dollar in 1958.

These problems could hardly be handled, even by a government that knew better, because of the popular pressures in a democratic country to live beyond the country's income. Fortunately, the final collapse did not occur, despite continued troubles from Juan Lechin's miners, because of the courageous efforts of Hernán Siles (President in 1956–1960, but unable to succeed himself constitutionally) and assistance from the United States (this increased from $4,853,000 in 1953 to $32,120,000 in 1958). Siles sought to encourage both workers and peasants to seek production increases as a preliminary to increased consumption, a monetary stabilization plan, freezing of wages even while prices were still rising, encouragement of peasants to join in larger groupings with increased emphasis on production for market rather than for subsistence, efforts to bring some of the fertile eastern lowlands into agricultural production, and largely unsuccessful efforts to stop the drastic fall in industrial productivity in order to obtain some goods that could be offered to the peasants in return for their increased production of food. To reduce political pressures from the miners, 10,000 of their total working force of 36,000 were relocated in a new sugar industry in Santa Cruz. But the problem remained critical. Manufactured goods fell from $55.7 million in 1955 to about $40 million in value in 1962, while agricultural goods for sale fell from $132.6 million to $118.7 million in 1959–1961.

The struggle still goes on, showing, if any proof were needed, that radical reforms for sharing the wealth of the few among the many poor is not an easy, or feasible, method for settling Latin America's material problems. However, one asset from this Bolivian experiment does not appear in the statistics or on the balance sheets. Bolivia's intelligent and hard-working Indians, once hopelessly dull, morose, and sullen, are now bright, hopeful, and self-reliant. Even their clothing is gradually shifting from the older funereal black to brighter colors and variety.

Few contrasts could be more dramatic than that between the Bolivian revolutionary government (in which a moderate regime was pushed toward radicalism by popular pressures, and survived, year after year, with American assistance) and the Guatemala revolution where a Communist-inspired regime tried to lead a rather inert population in the direction of increasing radicalism but was overthrown by direct American action within three years (1951–1954).

Guatemala is one of the "banana republics." This perishable fruit, with a world production of 26 billion pounds a year, forms 40 percent of the world's trade in fresh fruit, with almost 70 percent of the world's total produced in Latin America and almost 57 percent of all the world's banana exports going to North America. The retail value of Latin America's part of the world's trade in bananas is several billion dollars a year, but Latin America gets less than 7 percent of that value. One reason for this is the existence of the United Fruit Company, which owns two million acres of plantations in six Latin American countries, with 1,500 miles of railroad, 66 ships, seaports, and communications networks. This corporation handles about a third of the world's banana sales and about two-thirds of the American sales. It controls 60 percent of the banana exports of the six banana republics (Guatemala, Honduras, Costa Rica, Ecuador, Colombia, Panama) and accounts for over 40 percent of the foreign-exchange earnings in three of the six countries. It pays about $145 million a year into the six countries, and claims to earn about $26 million profits on its $159 million investment each year, but this profit figure of about 16.6 percent a year is undoubtedly far below the true figure. A United States suit against United Fruit in 1954–1958 claimed that the latter controlled 85 percent of the land suitable for banana cultivation in five countries, and ordered it to get rid of most of its subsidiary transportation, distribution, and land operations by 1970. At the time, about 95 percent of the land held by United Fruit was uncultivated. The antitrust consent decree, even if carried out, will not materially reduce

United Fruit influence in Central America, since its relations with its subsidiaries can merely be shifted from ownership to contractual arrangements.

Guatemala, like Bolivia, has a population that consists largely of impoverished Indians and mixed bloods (mestizos). From 1931 to 1944 these were ruled by the dictator Jorge Ubico, the last of a long line of corrupt and ruthless tyrants. When he retired to die in New Orleans in 1944, free elections chose Juan José Arevalo (1945–1950) and Jacobo Arbenz Guzmán (1950–1954) as presidents. Reform was long overdue, and these two administrations tried to provide it, becoming increasingly anti-American and pro-Communist over their nine-year rule. When they began, civil or political rights were almost totally unknown, and 142 persons (including corporations) owned 98 percent of the arable land. Free speech and press, legalized unions, and free elections preceded the work of reform, but opposition from the United States began as soon as it became clear that the Land Reform Act of June 1952 would be applied to the United Fruit Company. This act called for redistribution of uncultivated holdings above a fixed acreage or lands of absentee owners, with compensation from twenty-year, 3 percent bonds, equal to the declared tax value of the lands. About 400,000 acres of United Fruit lands fell under this law and were distributed by the Arbenz Guzmán government to 180,000 peasants. This and other evidence was declared to be Communist penetration of the Americas, and John Foster Dulles, in a brief visit to the OAS meeting at Caracas in 1954, forced through a declaration condemning Guatemala. The Secretary of State left the execution of this condemnation to his brother, Allen Dulles, Director of the Central Intelligence Agency, which soon found an American-trained and American-financed Guatemalan Colonel, Carlos Castillo Armas, who was prepared to lead a revolt against Arbenz. With American money and equipment, and even some American "volunteers" to fly "surplus" American planes, Armas mounted an attack of Guatemalan exiles from bases in two adjacent dictatorships, Honduras and Nicaragua. Both these countries are horrible examples of everything a Latin American government should not be, corrupt, tyrannical, cruel, and reactionary, but they won the favor of the United States Department of State by echoing American foreign policy at every turn. Nicaragua, often a target of American intervention in the past, was decayed, dirty, and diseased under the twenty-year tyranny of Anastasio Somoza (1936–1956). His assassination in 1956 handed the country over to be looted by his two sons, one of whom became President while the other served as Commander of the oversized National Guard. In 1963 the presidency was transferred to a Somoza stooge, René Schick.

From these despotic bases, the CIA-directed assault of Colonel Armas overthrew Arbenz Guzmán in 1954 and established in Guatemala a regime similar to that of the Somozas. All civil and political freedoms were over-thrown, the land reforms were undone, and corruption reigned. When Armas was assassinated in 1957 and a moderate elected as his successor, the army annulled those elections and held new ones in which one of their own, General Miguel Ydígoras Fuentes, was "elected." He liquidated what remained of Guatemala's Socialist experiments by granting these enterprises, at very reasonable prices, to his friends, while collecting his own pay of $1,094,000 a year. Discontent from his associates led to a conservative army revolt against Ydígoras in November 1960, but American pressure secured his position. The United States at the time could not afford a change of regime in Guatemala, since that country was already deeply involved, as the chief aggressive base for the Cuban exiles' attack on Cuba, at the Bay of Pigs, in April 1962.

As we all know, the CIA success in attacking "Communist" Guatemala from dictatorial Nicaragua in 1954 was not repeated in its more elaborate attack on "Communist" Cuba from dictatorial Guatemala in 1962. In fact, the Bay of Pigs must stand as the most shameful event in United States history since the end of World War II. But before we tell that story we must examine its background in Cuba's recent history, a story that well exemplifies the tragedy of Cuba.

The causes of the Cuban disaster are as complex as most historical events, but, if we oversimplify, we may organize them in terms of two intersecting factors: (1) the personality deficiencies of the Cubans themselves, such as their lack of rationality and self-discipline, their emotionalism and corruptibility, and (2) the ignorance and ineptitude of the American State Department, which seems incapable of dealing with Latin America in terms of the real problems of the area, but instead insists on treating it in terms of America's vision of the world, which is to say in terms of American political preconceptions and economic interests.

Cuba is more Spanish than much of Latin America, and obtained its independence from Spain only in 1898, two generations later than the rest of Latin America. Then, for over thirty years, until the abrogation of the Platt amendment in 1934, Cuba was under American occupation (1898-1902) or the threat of direct American intervention. During that period the island fell under American economic domination by American investments on the island and by becoming deeply involved in the American market, especially for its sugar crop. In the same period, a local oligarchy of Cubans was built up, including an exploitative landlord group that had not existed previously.

With the establishment of the Good Neighbor Policy in 1933 and the ending of the threat of American direct intervention, it became possible for the Cubans to overthrow the tyrannical and bloody rule of General Gerardo Machado which had lasted for eight years (1925-1933). The opportunity to begin a series of urgently needed and widely demanded social reforms under Machado's successor, Ramón Grau San Martín, was lost when the United States refused to recognize or to assist the new regime. As a result, a ruthless Cuban army sergeant, Fulgencio Batista, was able to overthrow Grau San Martín and begin a ten-year rule of the island (1934–1944) through civilian puppets, chosen in fraudulent elections, and then directly as president himself. When Grau San Martín was elected president in 1944, he abandoned his earlier reformist ideas and became the first of a series of increasingly corrupt elected regimes over the next eight years. The fourth such election, scheduled for 1953, was prevented when Batista seized power once again, in March 1952.

The next seven years were filled by Batista's efforts to hold his position by violence and corruption against the rising tide of discontent against his rule. One of the earliest episodes in that tide was an attempted revolt by a handful of youths, led by twenty-six-year-old Fidel Castro, in eastern Cuba on July 26, 1953.

The failure of the rising of July 26th gave Castro two years of imprisonment and more than a year of exile, but at the end of 1956 he landed with a handful of men on the coast of Cuba to begin guerrilla operations against the government. Batista's regime was so corrupt and violent that many of the local powers of Cuba, including segments of the army and much of the middle class, were either neutral or favorable to Castro's operations. The necessary arms and financial support came from these groups, although the core of the movement was made up of peasants and workers led by young, middle-class university graduates.

This Castro uprising was not typical of the revolutionary coups that had been familiar in Cuba and throughout Latin America in an earlier day, because of Castro's fanatical thirst for power, his ruthless willingness to destroy property or lives in order to weaken the Batista regime, and his double method of operation, from within Cuba rather than from abroad and from a rural base, the peasants, rather than the usual urban base, the army, used by most Latin American rebels.

By destroying sugar plantations and utilities, Castro's rebels weakened the economic and communications basis of the Batista government. The steady attrition of the regime's popular and military support made it possible for Castro's forces to advance across Cuba, and, on New Year's Day of 1959, he marched into Havana. Within two weeks, an additional and very ominous difference in this revolution appeared: the supporters of the Batista regime and dissident elements in Castro's movement began to be executed by firing squads.

For a year Castro's government carried on a reformist policy administered by his original supporters, the July 26th group of young, middle-class, university graduates. These reforms were aimed at satisfying the more obvious demands of the dispossessed groups who had provided the mass basis for Castro's movement. Military barracks were converted into schools; the militia was permanently established to replace the regular army; rural health centers were set up; a full-scale attack was made on illiteracy; new schools were constructed; urban rents were cut by half; utility rates were slashed; taxes were imposed on the upper classes; the beaches, once reserved for the rich, were opened to all; and a drastic land reform was launched. These actions were not integrated into any viable economic program, but they did spread a sense of well-being in the countryside, although they curtailed the building boom in the cities (especially Havana), largely rooted in American investment, and they instigated a flight of the rich from the island to refuge in the United States.

Beneath this early and temporary bloom of well-being, many ominous signs appeared. Castro soon showed that he was a tactician of revolution, not a strategist of reconstruction. He not only proclaimed permanent revolution in Cuba, but at once sought to export it to the rest of Latin America. Arms and guerrilla fighters were sent, and lost, in unsuccessful efforts to invade Panama, Nicaragua, Haiti, and the Dominican Republic. Failure of these turned him to methods of more subtle penetration, largely worked by propaganda and the arming and training of small subversive underground groups, especially in areas where democratic or progressive regimes seemed to be developing (as in Venezuela under Betancourt or Colombia under Alberto Lleras Camargo). At the same time, an unsuccessful effort was made to persuade all Latin America to form an anti-Yankee front.

Although the United States, in October 1959, had promised to follow a policy of nonintervention toward Cuba, these changes within the island, and especially the long visit there of Soviet Deputy Premier Anastas Mikoyan in February 1960, forced a reconsideration of this policy. The Mikoyan agreement promised Cuba petroleum, arms, and other needs for its sugar, although the price equivalent allowed for the sugar was only 4 cents a pound at a time when the American price was 6 cents; by June 1963, when world sugar prices reached 13 cents, the USSR raised its price for Cuban sugar to 6 cents. This trade agreement was followed by establishment of diplomatic relations with the Soviet Union in May and with Red China later in the year. The Soviet embassy in Havana became a source of Communist subversion for all of Latin America almost at once, while in September Khrushchev and Castro jointly dominated the annual session of the General Assembly of the United Nations in New York.

As part of the trade agreement with Russia, Castro obtained Soviet crude petroleum for Cuban sugar. When he insisted that American-owned refineries in Cuba process this oil, they refused and were at once seized by Castro. The United States struck back by reducing the Cuban sugar quota in the American market, which led, step by step, to Castro's sweeping nationalization of foreign-owned factories on the island. The United States retaliated by establishing a series of embargoes on Cuban exports to the United States. These controversies led Castro into an economic trap similar to that into which Nasser had fallen with Egypt's cotton. Each nationalist revolutionary leader committed his chief foreign-exchange-earning product (sugar or cotton) to the Soviet Union as payment for Communist (often Czech) arms. This tied these countries to the Soviet Union and deprived them of the chance to use their one source of foreign money for equipment so urgently needed for economic improvement. By December 1960, when American diplomatic relations with Cuba were broken off, the Cuban economic decline had begun, and soon reached a point where standards of living were at least a third below the Batista level, except for some previously submerged groups.

At the end of 1960, the Eisenhower Administration decided to use force to remove Castro. This decision was a major error and led to a totally shameful fiasco. The error apparently arose in the Central Intelligence Agency and was based on a complete misjudgment of the apparent ease with which that agency had overthrown the Arbenz regime in Guatemala in 1954 by organizing a raid of exiles, armed and financed by the CIA, into Guatemala from Nicaragua. The CIA analyzed this apparently successful coup quite incorrectly, since it assumed that Arbenz had been overthrown by the raiding exiles, when he had really been destroyed by his own army, which used the raid as an excuse and occasion to get rid of him. But on this mistaken basis, the CIA in 1960 decided to get rid of Castro by a similar raid of Cuban exiles from Guatemala.

This decision was worse than a crime; it was stupid. A unilateral, violent attack on a neighboring state with which we were not at war, in an area where we were committed to multilateral and peaceful procedures for settling disputes, was a repudiation of all our idealistic talk about the rights of small nations and our devotion to peaceful procedures that we had been pontificating around the world since 1914. It was a violation of our commitment to nonintervention in the Americas and specifically in Cuba. In sequence to our CIA intervention in Guatemala, it strengthened the Latin American picture of the United States as indifferent to Latin America's growing demand for social reform and national independence and as hostile to these when they conflicted with its own drives for wealth and power. Moreover, the attack on Cuba was ill-advised at a time when Castro's prestige at home was rapidly dwindling and when opposition was rising to his chaotic rule throughout the island. And, finally, the whole operation, patterned on Hitler's operations to subvert Austria and Czechoslovakia in 1938, was bungled as Hitler could never have bungled anything. The project was very much of a Dulles brothers' job, and its execution was largely in the hands of the Central Intelligence Agency, which organized the expeditionary force from Cuban exiles, financed and armed them, and supervised their training in Guatemala and elsewhere.

The plan of the invasion of Cuba seems to have been drawn on typical Hitler lines: the expeditionary force was to establish a beachhead in Cuba, set up a government on the island, be recognized by the United States as the actual government of Cuba, and ask Washington for aid to restore order in the rest of the island which it did not yet control. The Joint Chiefs of Staff approved of the plan, and President Kennedy was persuaded to accept it, after his inauguration, because of the CIA's argument that something must be done to remove Castro before his newly acquired Soviet armaments became operational. The President was assured that if matters were allowed to go on as they were, Castro would be strengthened in power (which was untrue) and that the invasion would be a success because the Cuban people, led by the anti-Castro underground, would rise against him as soon as they heard of the landing.

Whatever truth there was in this last contention, the CIA handling of the invasion made it impossible, because the CIA refused to use either the anti-Castro underground in Cuba or the Cuban refugees in the United States (except as volunteers to be targets in the invasion attempt), and kept all planning and control of the invasion in its own hands. The executive committee of Cuban refugees in the United States, mostly representatives of the older ruling groups in Cuba, were eager to restore the inequitable economic and social system that had existed before Castro. They were alienated from the most vigorous anti-Castro groups in the Cuban underground, who had no desire to turn back the clock to the Machado-Batista era but wanted to free the social and economic reform movement from Castro, the Communists, and the antidemocratic and totalitarian forces that had taken control of it. The CIA would not cooperate with the anti-Castro underground because it was opposed to their wish for social and economic reform, and it would not use the Miami refugee committee because it doubted either their discretion or fighting spirit. Accordingly, the CIA launched the invasion without notifying the Cuban underground and kept the refugee committee locked up without communication for the week of the attack. Then the attack itself was bungled, since it was aimed at an inappropriate spot, without eliminating Castro's air power, and without provision for fighting it, and with the logistics for the whole tactical operation of the invasion at an unbelievable level of incompetence.

As a result of these errors, the 1,500 men landed at the Bay of Pigs in southern Cuba on April 17, 1961 were destroyed in seventy-two hours by Castro's speedily mobilized and well-armed militia. At the same time, Castro's police destroyed any possible simultaneous rising of the underground by arresting thousands of suspects. To do the wrong thing is bad, but to do it incompetently is unforgivable.

The blow to American prestige from the Bay of Pigs was almost irretrievable. On the other hand, it greatly strengthened Castro's prestige, in Latin America more than in Cuba itself, and made it possible for him to bind the Kremlin to his cause so tightly that it could neither reduce its support nor control his policies. This in turn permitted him to survive a deepening wave of passive resistance and sabotage within Cuba itself, chiefly from the peasants. And, finally, as we shall see, this made it possible for him to recapture control of the Cuban revolutionary movement for himself and the Fidelistas from the Cuban Communists. This last point was in March, 1962, but the others began in 1961.

Until the Bay of Pigs fiasco, the Soviet commitment to Castro had been considerable but not irretrievable. Soviet armaments began to arrive as early as July 1960, and in the first year exceeded 30,000 tons valued at 50 million dollars. As payment, the Communist bloc's portion of Cuba's export trade rose from 2 percent to 75 percent. Within a year of the failure at the Bay of Pigs, Sino-Soviet military support for Castro doubled. It also changed its quality to late model antiaircraft missiles, long-range missiles capable of carrying nuclear warheads, and even Soviet combat troops. By the time these changes became evident to Washington in October 1962, the Soviet military buildup in Cuba had cost over 700 million dollars.

Before this Soviet military buildup in Cuba reached its stage of most rapid acceleration in July–October 1962, a number of significant changes occurred in Cuba itself. Two of these were the growth of Cuban resistance to the Castro regime and Castro's acceptance and sudden reversal of a Communist usurpation of his power within Cuba.

Castro's efforts to take Cuba into the Communist bloc began almost as soon as he took Havana in January 1959. His refusal to allow post-revolutionary elections to confirm his victory, a traditional Latin American tactic, and his outlawing of the traditional political parties (but not the Communists, PSP, which had secretly cooperated with Batista for years) left him in an ideological and political vacuum. Soon the closing down of all opposition newspapers, but the continued publication of the Communist paper, *Hoy*, showed that only this group would fill that vacuum. And finally the small group of Old Communists in Cuba were allowed to take over control of the administrative system and, within months, had a reasonable facsimile of the Kremlin's arrangements operating from Havana. They took control of the Rebel Militia, especially G-2, its Intelligence branch; President Manuel Urrutia was removed for an anti-Communist speech and replaced by a fellow-traveller, Osvaldo Dorticós Torrado. A struggle between the Communists and the Fidelistas of the 26th of July Movement for control of the Confederation of Cuban Labor Unions was settled by Castro himself in favor of the Communists. A chief Communist leader, Carlos Rafael Rodríguez, professor of economics at the University of Havana, led a student revolt that gave the

Communists control of the university. All political movements were merged into the Integrated Revolutionary Organizations (ORI), whose leadership was practically identical with the Old Communist leadership. This group set up Communist-type cells in farms, factories, and government offices. Anibal Escalante, secretary of the Communist Party, became organizational secretary to ORI. The Military Secret Police, G-2, was transformed into a Ministry of the Interior, based on the Kremlin's MVD, with a Communist, Ramiro Valdes, at its head. The lands that had been distributed or seized by peasants were "nationalized" by local Communist groups, and many of the cooperative farms that had risen from these became collective farms. In all significant governmental posts, Fidelistas were replaced, or circumvented, by Communists. Control of the economy was taken from Major Ernesto "Che" Guevara and given to Professor Rodríguez, who became president of the Agrarian Reform Institute, and drew up the economic development plans for the years following 1961. Thus within a few months, the ORI became a real government, making most of the significant daily decisions, and Escalante was exercising more power than Castro. The latter, still the darling of the masses, spent much of his time rousing them to frenzy with his speechmaking and marching.

The chief resistance to this Communization of Cuba came from the peasants, by curtailing production and by sabotage. Smaller farmers produced enough for their families but no more, in resistance to government-fixed prices and the compulsion to sell all their marketable produce to the National Institute of Agrarian Reform. Farmers refused to labor on the collective or state farms and occasionally set fire to the canebrakes on these. A good part of the coffee crop of 1961 was lost because the workers refused to harvest it. Similar resistance arose with the sugar and other crops. Drastic food rationing had to be established in March 1962. The 1962 coffee crop was sabotaged, and coffee rationing had to be established in February 1963. Most critical was the sugar crop, source of four-fifths of Cuba's foreign exchange. Efforts to harvest the crop with the militia, students, or city workers failed, and by 1962 the crop harvested had fallen to about half of the pre-Castro figure. At the same time, the ending of almost all trade ties with the United States, which had been a principal source of Cuban food, left Cuba dependent on countries like the Communist bloc, which had difficulties feeding themselves. The food ration fell to ¾ pound of meat a week per person, and 5 eggs with 2 ounces of butter a month. The food shortage was soon followed by shortages of manufactured goods, as the exodus of technicians, lack of spare parts, and bureaucratic confusions disorganized industrial production.

The economic collapse in no way discouraged Castro's efforts to establish a socialist regime, but the Communist Party's curtailment of his personal power led to a strong counteraction in March 1962. On May Day 1961, Castro had proclaimed that Cuba would be a socialist state, and, in a two-day speech on December 1–2, 1961, he had announced his own "Marxist-Leninist" beliefs. This ended the earlier arguments, disseminated by American Establishment circles led by *The New York Times,* that Castro was simply a progressive reformer. But despite his statements, he was not in any way a convinced Communist or a convinced anything else, but was a power-hungry and emotionally unstable individual, filled with hatred of authority himself, and restless unless he had constant change and megalomaniac satisfactions. His tactical skill, especially in foreign affairs, is remarkable, and shows similarity to Hitler's. His allegiance to Communism had nothing to do with ideological conviction or devotion to the Kremlin, but arose from his recognition that Russia was the only Power in a position to counterbalance the United States and was, to him, preferable to the United States both because of its greater distance and because its ideological pretenses would never allow it to permit an admitted Communist state like Cuba to be attacked by the United States. Thus Castro sought to get the Soviet Union more deeply committed to Cuba so that it could not disentangle itself whatever Castro did but must protect him from the United States, even when he openly disregarded its advice. In the same way, Castro was willing to build up his indebtedness to the Soviet Union because the Communist commitment would not allow the Kremlin to do anything drastic to collect such a debt. For these reasons, Castro wished to join the Warsaw Pact, but this at least Moscow was able to prevent. At the same time, Castro recognized that his own adoption of the Communist ideology would not weaken him in Latin America, where the impoverished masses care nothing about ideologies, and the middle classes, especially the youth and university students, like Communism as an ideology, although it has little influence on their own actions or political behavior.

Although the Communist takeover in Cuba began in 1960, it was not until February 1962 that Castro began to realize what had happened. Within a month, particularly during the week of March 16–22, he eliminated the Communists from most positions of significant power. The Rodríguez economic plan of November 1961 was denounced; the ORI system was purged; his brother, Raúl Castro, was made vice-premier; Escalante was forced into exile; the militia and bureaucracy were recaptured by the Fidelistas; and on March 26th Fidel himself gave a five-hour speech narrating what had happened. Pravda did not accept the change until April 11th.

This acceptance of the reestablishment of Fidelism by both the Kremlin and the Cuban Communist Party, largely because they had no alternative, was followed by their full-scale support of the Castro regime in political and economic policies. On May 31st it was announced that Moscow would provide 600,000 tons of food in the balance of 1962 to stave off the Cuban economic collapse, and later Moscow released claims on some Cuban sugar so that it could be sold in the world market for hard currencies. Above all, the Soviet Union appeared to accept Castro's argument that another American military assault on Cuba was in preparation.

The United States, Castro, and Moscow all must have known that no effort was likely to be made to repeat the American invasion of Cuba, but Castro made the charge because he wanted Soviet weapons, and the Kremlin pretended to believe it for reasons that are still doubtful. It is possible that the Russians hoped that the Soviet IRBM's in Cuba would help to slow up the increasing American lead over the Soviet Union in the missile race. It is also possible that they hoped that such missiles, once established, might be bargained away in return for a Soviet-favored solution to the Berlin question.

The increasing American aerial patrols over Cuba, which detected the Russian missile buildup on the island, were used by Cuba and the Soviet Union as evidence of the approaching American attack. By September, still unknown to the public, the crisis began to form, and in October it was in full progress, with the consequences already described.

The ending of the Cuban missile crisis at the end of 1962 may have opened a new era in the world's history, but it left Latin America still floundering in the same old problems, which became more complicated and insoluble with each passing day. As we have said, these problems can be solved only by obtaining more constructive patterns in the proper priority sequence. On the whole, the role of the United States in Latin America has not been such as to help either patterns or priorities, largely because our concern has been with what seems to be useful or better for us rather than with what would be most helpful to them.

From the point of view of Latin America's real interests, basic priorities might include five things: (1) more constructive psychological patterns; (2) increased political stability; (3) a greatly reduced birthrate, with emphasis on the quality rather than on the quantity of population; (4) a large increase in the food supply and in the most fundamental needs of human life, such as housing; (5) increased emphasis on light industry, especially processing and semiprocessing of local raw materials; and (6) continued improvements in transportation and communications. This combination of advances could provide rising standards of living and jobs for everyone. In moving in this direction much greater use should be made of local resources, including local capital and local skills, especially those of the present upper classes. This last point will become feasible only if the first two points begin to develop: a better outlook, especially in the upper classes, and a sufficiently stabilized political system so that duress can be put upon those classes to force them to use both their lives and their resources in a more constructive way. This will be possible only if the armed forces of Latin America (and of the whole Pakistani-Peruvian axis) move much more rapidly in a direction they have been moving in already, but too slowly: the direction of increased concern for stronger, more honest, more constructive, and more widely distributed improvements in conditions of living among their own people.

This point of view has already shown itself along the Pakistani-Peruvian axis, in military circles in Pakistan, Egypt, Argentina, and elsewhere; in the royal entourage in Iran; among university youth in much of Latin America. But in all these circles, despite the enthusiasm and energy that make it possible for them to overthrow corrupt and tyrannical regimes, it soon becomes clear that they have little idea what to do once they get into power. As a result, they fall under the personal influence of unstable and ignorant men, the Nassers, the Peróns, and the Castros, who fall back on emotionally charged programs of hatreds and spectacular displays of unconstructive nationalism that waste time and use up resources while the real problems of the whole enormous area go unsolved.

A heavy responsibility rests on the United States for this widespread failure to find solutions to problems all the way from Pakistan to Peru. The basic reason for this is that our policies in this great area have been based on efforts to find solutions to our own problems rather than theirs: to make profits, to increase supplies of necessary raw materials, to fight Hitler, to keep out Communism, and in recent years to fight the Cold War and prevent the spread of neutralism. The net result of our actions has been that we are now more hated than the Soviet Union, and neutralism reveals itself as clearly as it dares through the whole area.

This is, perhaps, more obvious on the Pakistan end of the axis than on the Peruvian end, but is true from one end to the other. Dulles's insistence on arming the Middle and Near East and seeking to line the area up into a military bulwark against the Soviet Union destroyed the precarious political stability of the area, intensified local rivalries and animosities (as between India and Pakistan or between Egypt and Israel), led to large-scale waste of resources and energies on armament rivalries, divided the armed forces into cliques whose rivalries increased the frequency of military coups, and often entrenched in power reactionary and unprogressive minorities.

The sad thing about all this is that it was so unnecessary. There never was a moment in which the arms of this axis (excluding Turkey and Israel) contributed anything significant to keeping the Soviet Union out of it. Even less so in Latin America. On the contrary, the Dulles efforts to bring both areas into the Cold War in a military way by treaties and armaments have succeeded only in bringing Soviet influences and Communism in by methods of subversion, propaganda, and economic penetration that cannot be excluded by military agreements and armaments.

And at no time did these military agreements and armaments provide any real strength to keep Russia out as a military threat, for at all times that task rested on the deterrent power of the United States and the Western alliance. The sole consequence of the Dulles efforts to do the wrong thing along the Pakistani-Peruvian axis has been to increase what he was seeking to reduce: local political instability, increased Communist and Soviet influence, neutralism, and hatred of the United States.

Although the Dulles period, because it was a crucial period, shows most clearly the failures of American foreign policy in Latin America, the situation was the same, both before and since Dulles, with a possible brief exception in the first administration of Franklin Roosevelt. Otherwise, American policy in Latin America has been determined by American needs and desires and not by the problems of Latin Americans. A brief survey of these policies will show this clearly.

There are four chief periods in United States policy toward Latin America in the twentieth century. The first, a period of investment and interventionism, lasted until 1933 and was basically a period of commercial imperialism. American money came to Latin America as investments, seeking profits out of the exploitation of the area's most obvious local resources, mineral or agricultural, such as copper, bananas, and petroleum, or as markets for American goods. There was little respect for the people themselves or for their way of life, and intervention by American military and diplomatic forces was always close at hand as a protection for American profits and investments.

The Good Neighbor Policy, announced by President Roosevelt in 1933, reduced intervention while retaining investment. It was partly a consequence of the idealism and progressive nature of the New Deal itself, but was equally based on the fact that the need of Latin America for American investment funds and for the American market, especially in the depressed conditions of 1933, made it so amenable to our economic and commercial influence that there was little need for our use of diplomatic intimidation or the Marines.

The third and fourth stages in America's Latin American policy, from 1940 to the present, have been concerned with our efforts to involve the area in our foreign policy (not theirs), that is, in the effort to get them as deeply involved as possible in the struggle against Hitler and Japan and, since 1947, in the struggle against the Soviet Union. Both of these efforts have been mistakes (with the possible exception of our relations with Brazil and Mexico in the period following 1940) because the states of Latin America, however dutifully they may have lined up in the Hot War against Hitler or the Cold War against Soviet Russia, contributed little more to victory in these struggles than they would have contributed if they had not been pressured by us to line up at all.

This four-stage chronology of American policy toward Latin America ignores completely the significant change that has occurred in the history of Latin America itself during the twentieth century, chiefly in the 1950's. This is the shift in emphasis in Latin American history, especially in the history of political disturbances and governmental changes from the superficial *coups d'état* that were prevalent in the nineteenth and early twentieth centuries to the profound economic and social upheavals that first appeared in Mexico in 1910 and were followed in the 1950's by the revolutions in Bolivia, Cuba, and elsewhere. The failure in coincidence between the stages of the history of American policy and the stages of the history of Latin America itself is a fair measure of the irrelevance and futility of our policy. That this failure continued into the 1960's was clear in Washington's joy at the military coup that ejected the left-of-center João Goulart government from Brazil in April 1964, for that government, however misdirected and incompetent, at least recognized that there were urgent social and economic problems in Brazil demanding treatment.

No real recognition that such problems existed was achieved in Washington until Castro's revolution in Cuba forced the realization. As a consequence the Alliance for Progress should be regarded as the North American reaction to Castro rather than its reaction to Latin America's real problems. This helps to explain why the achievement of the Alliance for Progress has been so limited.

In its early announcement, by President Kennedy during his second month in office, the projected Alliance for Progress seemed more hopeful than any earlier United States reaction to Latin America's problems had been. It accepted the idea of central economic planning for the Latin American nations and the role of state intervention in investment and economic life, both of which had been rejected by the Eisenhower Administration. To these it added two other basic assumptions: that Latin America be required to take steps to help itself and not merely expect grants from the United States and, also, that social improvements, such as better housing, increased literacy, and improved social amenities, be regarded as intrinsic parts of, or even prerequisites to, purely economic expansion, and not be considered, as hitherto, to be incidental consequences of such expansion.

The formal agreement for the Alliance for Progress was signed by all members of the Organization of American States except Cuba, at Punta del Este, Uruguay, on August 17, 1961. Its aims and attitudes were admirable, but required implementation and organizational features that were not covered in the Charter itself and have largely remained deficient since. Its preamble said, in part, "We, the American Republics, hereby proclaim our decision to unite in a common effort to bring our people accelerated economic progress and broader social justice within the framework of personal dignity and personal liberty. Almost two hundred years ago we began in this Hemisphere the long struggle for freedom which now inspires people in all parts of the world. . . . Now we must give a new meaning to that revolutionary heritage. For America stands at a turning point in history. The men and women of our Hemisphere are reaching for the better life which today's skills have placed within their grasp. They are determined for themselves and their children to have decent and ever more abundant lives, to gain access to knowledge and equal opportunity for all, to end those conditions which benefit the few at the expense of the needs and dignity of the many."

These were fine words, and the specific detail to fulfill them was generally recognized. The latter included "a substantial and sustained growth of per capita incomes at a rate designed to attain, at the earliest possible date, levels of income capable of assuring self-sustaining development, and sufficient to make Latin American income levels constantly larger in relation to the levels of the more industrialized nations. . . . In evaluating the degree of relative development, account will be taken not only of average levels of real income and gross product per capita, but also of indices of infant mortality, illiteracy, and per capita daily caloric intake." The minimum desirable rate of economic growth was stated to be 2.5 percent per capita per year. It was, perhaps unrealistically, stated that economic progress should be made "available to all citizens of all economic and social groups through a more equitable distribution of national income, raising more rapidly the income and standard of living of the needier sectors of the population, at the same time that a higher proportion of the national product is devoted to investment." This aim to redistribute income and achieve simultaneously higher consumption *and* higher investment is, of course, impossible except in the most advanced industrial societies that have already reached such levels of consumption of material goods that further increases in consumption increase problems rather than solve them. To add to this rather confused idea of the process of economic development, the Charter immediately added, "Special attention should be given to the establishment and development of capital-goods industries."

Other desirable goals listed in the Charter included "replacing latifundia and dwarf-holdings by an equitable system of land tenure," "to maintain stable price levels, avoiding inflation or deflation and the consequent social hardships and maldistribution of resources," "to strengthen existing agreements on economic integration," and "to develop cooperative programs designed to prevent the harmful effects of excessive fluctuations in the foreign exchange earnings derived from exports of primary products. . . ." Among the social goals were "to eliminate adult illiteracy and by 1970 to assure, as a minimum, access to six years of primary education for each school age child in Latin America," "to increase life expectancy at birth by a minimum of five years, and to increase the

ability to learn and produce, by improving individual and public health
. . . to provide adequate potable water supply and drainage to not less
than 70 percent of the urban and 50 percent of the rural population; to
reduce the mortality rate of children less than five years of age to at
least one-half of the present rate; to control the more serious transmittible
diseases, according to their importance as a cause of sickness and
death . . . ," and so on.

The methods of achieving these desirable goals were only incidentally
established in the Charter. The participating Latin American countries
were required to formulate, within eighteen months, long-term development programs that would include improved human resources through
education and training, a reform of tax structures (including adequate
taxation of large incomes and real estate), laws to encourage investment
both foreign and domestic, and improved methods of distribution to
provide more competitive markets. The drawing of such programs in
areas that lacked adequate statistical information and had few trained
economists was a considerable obstacle to carrying out the Charter, and
only a handful of programs were approved in the first three years of the
Alliance.

As part of the Charter the United States offered "to provide assistance
under the Alliance" amounting to $20 billion, of which half was to
come from the government and half from private sources, over a ten-
year period. Nothing was said in the Charter as to the nature of this assistance, but the government's share has been generally in the form of
credits, the least helpful type of such foreign assistance, and the amount
of such assistance has not, as might appear at first glance, amounted to
$2 billion a year in new moneys, since private American investments in
Latin America already amounted to many hundreds of millions a year
and aid from the United States government was almost equally large, so
that the total of *additional* assistance promised by the Alliance was
roughly about two-thirds of a billion dollars or less each year.

It would be possible to state the achievement of the Alliance for
Progress in terms of hundreds of thousands of housing units, schools,
new hospitals, roads, additional drinking water, and experimental or
demonstration farms, but such lists, however large the numbers, indicate
little about the success of the Alliance. On the whole, it cannot be said
that the Alliance has failed; but, even more emphatically, it cannot be
said that it has been a success. Its achievement has been ameliorative
rather than structural, and this alone indicates that it has not been a success. For unless there are structural reforms in Latin American society,
its economic development will not become self-sustaining or even manage
to keep up with the growth of population on the basis of income per
capita.

The failure of the Alliance for Progress to achieve what it was touted to achieve has many causes, but the chief is undoubtedly that it was not intended primarily to be a method for achieving a better life for Latin Americans but was intended to be a means of implementing American policy in the Cold War. This became clearly evident at the second Punta del Este Conference of January 22-31, 1962, where Washington's exclusive control over the granting of funds for the Alliance was used as a club to force the Latin American states to exclude Cuba from the Organization of American States. The original plan was to cut off Cuba's trade with all Western Hemisphere countries and to break off diplomatic relations as well. A two-thirds vote by countries was needed to make the recommendations official; it was obtained only by the minimum margin (14 votes out of the 21 members) and only after the most intense American "diplomatic" pressure and bribery involving the granting and withholding of American aid to the Alliance. Even at that, six countries, representing 75 percent of Latin America's area and 70 percent of its population, refused to vote for the American motions. These six were Brazil, Mexico, Argentina, Chile, Bolivia, and Ecuador.

Much of the weakness of the Alliance for Progress arises from its failure to work for structural reforms that will change the patterns of Latin American life in more constructive directions. The aid, as we have said, is entirely under the control of the United States; it generally takes the form, not of money which can be used to buy the best goods in the cheapest market, but as credits which can be used only in the United States. Much of these credits goes either to fill gaps in the budgets or the foreign-exchange balances of Latin American countries, which provides a maximum of leverage in getting these governments to follow America's lead in world affairs but provides little or no benefit to the impoverished peoples of the hemisphere. Moreover, the grants, which provide dollars to these countries, are often counterbalanced by contrary influences, such as increased tariffs or other restrictions on the flow of Latin American goods to the United States, or decreases in the prices of Latin American primary products, or (what leads to the same results) increases in the export prices of American industrial goods.

A decrease of a cent or two in the price that the United States pays for coffee can wipe out all the funds that it provides for the coffee-producing countries under the Alliance for Progress. For example, from 1959 to 1960 the price that the United States paid for its coffee fell from an average of 39¢ a pound to 34¢ a pound. This decrease of a nickel a pound would represent a decrease in the total amount the United States paid for coffee, from one year to the next, of more than $150 million for the 30 billion pounds bought in 1960. Similarly, a decrease of one cent per pound on Chile's copper means a loss of about $11,000,000 a year. On the other hand, an increase in the prices of American television sets of one dollar each costs Latin American buyers about $15,000,000.

When both occur together, so that the prices of what Latin America sells are falling while the prices that it has to pay for American goods are increasing, as has been generally true during recent years, it means that most of the funds that Washington extends to Latin America under the Alliance for Progress are evaporating before they can be used, in terms of the total amount of dollars available for Latin American purchases of goods and equipment needed to modernize the Latin American production system.

There are many other aspects of this situation that help to explain the weak achievement of the Alliance for Progress. The tax-reform projects designed to force the rich to pay a fair share of taxes and to encourage them to invest rather than simply to hoard their surplus funds have come to almost nothing. But the possibility that something of this nature might be done has caused large volumes of funds to flee from Latin America to seek shelter abroad. It is possible that the total of such Latin American funds hiding abroad may amount to as much as $20 billion, the same amount the United States promised to provide over the whole ten years of the Alliance's projected life. While we have no accurate figures on these sums, an official report gives $4 billion as the amount of Latin American money on deposit in the United States at the end of 1961.

All of these considerations make it clear that problems of our neighbors in the Western Hemisphere are still rising more rapidly than they are being solved, a condition equally true in southern Asia, southeast Asia, and the Near East. In all of these, failure to find some answers to the problems that are rising can only lead to neutralism, eventual hatred of the Western world, and violent explosions by disappointed peoples that achieve nothing constructive either for them or for us. There are those who say that all these disappointments are inevitable because the problems of the backward areas are basically insoluble. To these skeptics we need only say: Look at the Far East, where, in vivid contrast, we can see the outstanding case where the problem of development has been solved and the most frightening example of what may happen when it is not solved.

THE FAR EAST

From the opening of the Far East to Western trade and influence, largely at the insistence of American traders, China was the recipient of American favor and protection, while Japan was regarded with suspicion and rivalry. The culmination of this process was in World War II, when China was an ally and Japan was our enemy. In fact, as Pearl Harbor showed, American intervention in the war arose over its efforts to protect China from Japanese aggression. Yet, in the postwar period, this relationship was reversed. Japan now represents the greatest success and China the greatest failure of America's postwar foreign policy. Our policies are often praised or blamed for these discordant results, but they should not be, for it could easily be argued that we were hardly aware of what we were doing in either case, and the outcomes were the consequence of forces quite beyond our control. This almost certainly is correct in China, but the amazing success story that is to be seen in contemporary Japan may well be attributed to successful American policies in combination with the peculiar social and personality patterns of the Japanese people.

The Japanese Miracle

The word "miracle" has been applied to a number of postwar events, such as the economic upsurge in West Germany, but it is nowhere more applicable than in Japan. For Japan is the only major area outside Europe, except the United States itself, which has reached that stage in economic development which W. W. Rostow called "takeoff." That is, it has reached a point in development where the process continues by its own momentum, accumulating and investing its own capital, with increasing production of food from a constantly dwindling farm population, a shift in diet from emphasis on "energy foods" to emphasis on "protective foods," and a shift in industrial activity from products requiring unskilled labor in a low capital-to-labor ratio toward products requiring highly skilled labor in a high capital-to-labor ratio. The Soviet Union itself has not yet reached this point in development, so that Japan is now the only fully advanced industrial nation in Asia and has, as a consequence, taken on characteristics that are familiar to us from Western European and American experience but are totally unknown elsewhere in Asia, Latin America, or Africa. As a consequence, Japan is, for these still backward areas, a more helpful model of economic development than either the United States or Western Europe, since these two earlier examples of development did not have to face some of the problems, such as lack of resources and heavy population pressure on the land, which Japan was able to overcome. Thus a Peace Corps of missionaries for development techniques would be more helpful from Japan than the present American Peace Corps of recently graduated college students, on the ground of technical experience if not on the ground of humanitarian motivation.

The key to the Japanese "takeoff" rests, as it must, on the relationship between population growth and food supply.

Japan, whose population growth from 44 million in 1900 to 93 million in 1960 once made it a prime example of an "overpopulated" country, now has the demographic pattern of a Western industrial society. It has one of the world's lowest birth and death rates and a life expectancy of sixty-five years for males and seventy for females, with an increasing percentage of older persons. The birthrate and death rate per 1,000 were both cut in half from 1946 to 1961, the former from 34.6 to 16.9 and the latter from 15.3 to 7.4. By 1963 Japan had the lowest death rate in the world (about 7 per 1,000). As a result of these factors, the population increase of Japan, which was once over 1,700,000 a year, is now about 900,000 yearly and in 1959 fell to 780,000. It is expected that Japan's population may reach a peak of about 107 million by 1990 and then begin to decrease, falling below 100 million again by 2010.

This changing population picture in Japan owes nothing to the American military occupation and rests, very largely, on the strong, self-disciplined, "inscrutable" Japanese character. Of this we know very little. There have been a number of studies of the Japanese personality, the best known of which, by Ruth Benedict and Geoffrey Gorer, are based on no real personal knowledge and on impressionistic evidence. The truth is that the Japanese personality seems to have an "achieving" pattern, but at present we know very little about it. At any rate, the Japanese solution of their population explosion rests very largely on aspects of their personality structure. Abortion plays a much greater role in their population control than would be acceptable to many persons in our Western culture.

Unlike their population control, the recent Japanese success in producing food owes a great deal to the American occupation. This Japanese agrarian reform is one of the remarkable economic transformations of this century.

With 650 persons per square mile, compared to 50 in the United States and 25 in the Soviet Union, Japan has only two-tenths of an acre of arable land per person, and most farms are merely gardens of less than two acres. By 1940 about 70 percent of Japanese farmers were paying rent for land and almost 30 percent were landless. Rents were high, and agrarian discontent became one of the chief pressures behind Japanese aggression in the 1930's. At that time, the land was extensively exploited in the Asiatic fashion, by applying larger amounts of hand labor to it. Much of it was terraced; more than half of it was irrigated; there was intensive application of fertilizers, including human waste, and the chief emphasis was on energy-yielding food, mostly rice.

The reorganization of Japanese agriculture was largely due to the American Military Occupation (SCAP), and was so successful that the index of agricultural production increased 40 percent in the decade 1951–1961. This revolution rested on two supports: the agrarian reform and technological advances.

The agrarian reform redistributed the ownership of land by the government taking all individual land holdings beyond 7.5 acres, all rented land over 2.5 acres, and the land of absentee owners. The former holders were paid for these lands with long-term bonds. In turn, peasants without land or with less than the maximum permitted amount of 7.5 acres were allowed to buy land from the state on a long-term, low-interest-rate basis. Cash rents for land were also lowered.

As a result of this program, Japan became a land of peasant owners, with about 90 percent of the cultivated soil worked by its owners. The peasants were helped in making the transfer because the early period of the Occupation was one of food shortages, inflation, and an active black market with high prices. These profits also helped finance the beginnings of the new revolution in agricultural technology.

This drastic change in farming methods in Japan was toward the American method of farm development, using less and less hand labor and greater amounts of capital, especially in farm machinery and fertilizers. Today all kinds of power and mechanical equipment, such as threshers, pumps, lifts, sprayers, and such, are common in Japan. Most spectacular has been the spreading of hand tractors or power cultivators of 3 to 7 horsepower, something like American rototillers. These have increased from 7,000 in use in 1947 to 85,000 in 1955, and to almost a million by 1962. These can be used with special attachments as plows, cultivators, pumps, sprayers, saws, and draft vehicles, and have helped to eliminate draft farm animals and to reduce heavy human labor. Since a farmer can do as much work, especially plowing, with this piece of equipment, in one day as used to require ten days' work using animal power, he has a longer growing season, can extend the practice of double cropping, and has much more time for other work.

Two aspects of this agricultural revolution deserve special mention. Japan, like the United States, is now shifting its diet from energy foods, like rice, toward protective foods, like meat, milk, fruit, and green vegetables. And Japan, also like the United States, has now broken free from the older alternative of *either* high output per acre *or* high output per unit of labor, and has now reached the stage where both are rising together. In the ten years of this agricultural revolution (1951–1961) rice production went up 30 percent, but dairy cattle increased ten times, meat products about three times, fruit production almost doubled, and the number of persons engaged in farming has fallen rapidly, by better than 10 percent, or more than 1.5 million persons, in the five years 1956–1961. As a result, the percentage of the working population engaged in farming is now about 28 percent, and has a steadily increasing portion of older persons and of females, as the younger males stream steadily to the city, seeking jobs in industry.

Of course, this transformation in agriculture could never have occurred if there had not been taking place equally drastic changes in industry. These industrial changes, including a high rate of investment, rapid technological change, and excellent demand for industrial products, provided a plentiful supply of jobs and an increased demand for food and other agricultural products by city dwellers. These conditions acted like a magnet to attract a growing flood of farm products and energetic young peasants to the cities.

The contrast between the structure and distribution of Japan's population and that of other Asiatic nations shows clearly that Japan is no longer a backward, underdeveloped, or colonial area from any point of view. The marks of such a backward society are usually a high birthrate and death rate, a largely young, rural population, with the great majority in agriculture, and mostly illiterate. In Japan, all of these characteristics are untrue. Birth and death rates are very low; the population is aging rapidly, is almost totally literate, has below 29 percent in agriculture, and has over 60 percent resident in areas classified as urban. Moreover, the revolution in Japanese industrial development has shifted the country out of its previous colonial orientation in economic organization and commerce.

Before the war, Japan lived by exporting labor, largely unskilled labor. It did this by importing raw materials, working them up by largely unskilled labor into products of light industry, chiefly textiles, and exporting these products for more raw materials and food. Today the Japanese need for imported food is decreasing and is shifting away from its previous food needs, notably rice, to foods of more protective character, such as proteins. At the same time, its raw material imports are slowly shifting from those used in light industry, such as raw cotton, to those used in highly skilled industrial lines, such as electronics, where few other nations can compete. This inevitably means that Japan's trade has been shifting from Asia and other backward areas, where it exchanged cotton textiles for rice, to the United States and Europe where it exchanges cameras, radios, tape recorders, and optical supplies for metals, manufactured goods, or materials for advanced industry. Its needs for petroleum, iron ore, and other bulk raw materials are tending to shift to colonial areas, so that its petroleum now comes from the Persian Gulf instead of the United States, and its iron ore comes increasingly from India.

The social impact of economic changes such as these is far-reaching. The cities are growing rapidly, while many rural areas are losing population as their peoples flock to urban areas. By 1961, 44 percent of the total population was clustered in 1 percent of the country's total area. Tokyo, with 7 million people in 1940, was down to 3 million in 1945, and passed 10 million in 1961. Other cities grew steadily but at a slower rate, and by the present day are agglomerating into four megalopolitan areas. Tens of millions of commuters swarm into these to work each day, and the traffic problem, especially in Tokyo, has become almost insoluble.

As might be expected, such rapid material advance and profound social change has given rise to all kinds of social problems. Family discipline has weakened, and the older Japanese morality and outlooks are now widely rejected. Marxism and existentialism vie for the allegiance of the educated, while the less esoterically informed are satisfied with the pursuit of material success and personal pleasures. The gap between these two groups is considerable, and much of the stability, both political and social, in Japanese society today seems to rise from the self-satisfaction of the new middle class and the eagerness of many peasants and workers to get into that class and enjoy its benefits. These benefits increasingly provide a life like that in American suburbia, with television, baseball, bulldozers, picture windows, neon-lighted department stores, mass advertising, instant foods, and weekly slick magazines. The speed with which this has come about is almost beyond belief. Commercial television began in Japan in 1953; five years later, 16 percent of urban houses had a set, but by 1961, 72 percent had sets; electric washing machines increased from 29 percent of urban houses in 1958 to 55 percent three years later. This salaried middle class is the key to the rapid achievement and political stability of Japan. Ambitious, hard-working, loyal, reliable, very adaptable to bureaucratic organization, scientific training, and rationalizing processes, they are suspicious of ideologies or extremist doctrines of any kind, and form one of the world's most amazing peoples.

These general attitudes have given Japan the appearance of successful adaptation to democratic political life as determined by the SCAP-imposed constitution of 1947. As a matter of fact, the Japanese are basically uneasy about individualism, democracy, mass society, and the speed of their economic change, but few have much of an urge to rock the boat, and those old enough to remember the years of tension and war from 1931 to 1944 have no preference for them. There are discontented groups, including the ultranationalists on the extreme Right and the various Socialist, Communist, and student groups on the Left. Both of these extremes, especially the former, operate in an atmosphere of considerable unreality. The really notable feature of Japanese political ideology is the way in which SCAP's agrarian reform has driven Communism out of the rural areas and restricted it to the cities, chiefly to student groups.

The foundations of the present political system in Japan were established by SCAP in the early years of the Occupation. In the early months of peace, 5,000,000 Japanese military were demobilized and 3,000,000 civilians were repatriated from overseas areas. When Japanese prisoners of war were eventually returned, about 375,000 in the hands of the Russians were never accounted for. More than 4,200 Japanese were convicted of war crimes, over 700 were executed, and about 2,500 were sentenced to life imprisonment. An additional 220,000 persons were permanently excluded from public life, and about 1,300 nationalist and extremist organizations were banned. The Shinto religion was separated from the state, forbidden to propagate militaristic or ultranationalist doctrines, and Emperor Hirohito was forced to issue a public statement denying that he was divine.

A Japanese "Bill of Rights" protecting the rights of individuals and political freedoms, on a much more extensive basis than we have in the United States, was issued in 1945. The centralized police control in the Home Ministry was abolished, and police powers were curbed. A new civil code established freedom from family domination for all and equality for females.

The Constitution itself, issued by SCAP in 1946, provided that a prime minister be chosen by the 467 members of the House of Representatives, who themselves were chosen by universal adult suffrage. These were elected from 118 electoral constituencies, each represented by from three to five members, although the voter could cast his ballot for only one candidate. This ensured representation for minority views and made it difficult to obtain a majority in the House without coalitions of parties. However, the parties have tended to coalesce into two wings around the conservative Liberal Democrats and the Socialist Party. Except for the period April 1947–October 1948, when the Socialists controlled the government during a period of extreme labor unrest and violence, control has been in the hands of the Liberal Democratic Party and its allied groups. These have generally won almost two-thirds of the seats in elections over the last ten years (since 1955), while the Socialists have had difficulty in obtaining one-third of the seats.

The chief differences between the two parliamentary groups revolve around foreign affairs, with the Liberal Democrats committed to a pro-Western policy in strong alliance with the United States and rather isolated from Asia. The Socialist group wishes to weaken the American connection and resume Japan's traditional position as a leading Asiatic Power. The economic orientation of Japan and its booming prosperity have made the task of the Socialists a difficult one.

The different views of the two parties in domestic politics are reflected in a controversy over the Constitution. This document, in Article Nine, renounces war and forbids maintaining an army, navy, or air force. Despite this, in July 1950, General MacArthur ordered formation of a defense force, and the United States insisted on this at the time of the Peace Treaty with Japan, the following year. The Mutual Defense Alliance with the United States, signed in March 1954, bound Japan to maintain a defense force of 275,000 men. Since this force is unconstitutional, the Socialists have sought vigorously to keep their parliamentary representation at over one-third of the seats, to prevent an amendment removing Article Nine. All amendments require a two-thirds vote of the Parliament plus a majority in a national referendum. However, even in 1963, when the Socialists made a desperate effort to obtain one-third of the seats (156), they fell 12 seats short of the necessary number. They have received little help from the Communists, whose parliamentary representatives rose to a peak of 35 seats in the disturbed period of 1949, but they alienated the Japanese by their addiction to violence and have elected only a handful of members since 1950 (none in October 1952, following the May Day riots of that year and only 3 in 1960, increased to 5 in 1963).

On the whole, Japan in the twentieth century has been an extraordinary country, and this characterization does not decrease with the passing years. It is a bulwark of strength to the Western bloc, not because of its military power, which is insignificant, or even as an American military base in the Far East, but because it, like West Germany, is an example of the freedom and prosperity associated with being an American "satellite," in sharp contrast with the unhappy plight of the Soviet satellite states. Above all, Japan, for the neutrals and the backward areas of the world, is a living proof that it is possible to advance from backwardness and slavery to prosperity and freedom.

Communist China

Nothing could be more different from the experience of Japan than that of Japan's greatest neighbor, mainland China. On Taiwan, the Nationalist Government of China has combined a typical Chiang Kaishek political despotism with an economic program, including agrarian reform, somewhat similar to Japan's, but Red China, as far as we can discern, has passed through one great crisis after another in a desperate and tyrannical effort to follow the Stalinist model of Soviet Russia's experience. Like the Soviet Union, Red China may be able to organize itself into a powerful and expanding society, but the problems in China are much greater and more intractable than they were in Russia.

For one thing, China's huge population has been placing heavy pressure on limited resources, while Russia has always been an underpopulated country with enormous untapped resources capable of extensive exploitation. Under the czar, Russia produced great surpluses, especially of food, which were exported abroad. In a sense the Communist problem in Russia was to reestablish these surpluses (which had been destroyed in the Civil War period of 1917–1921) and divert them, along with surplus peasants, to the city to provide capital and labor for the industrialization process. In China there was no surplus food, so that the problem, from the beginning, was how to increase the production of food, not how to reestablish it and rechannel it. Moreover, in Russia, a centralized despotic state capable of enforcing these changes was part of the country's past experience; the direct authority of the state in the form of the recruiting officer, the tax collector, and the priest had impinged on the lowest peasant, at least since the abolition of serfdom, and on most of the society for over a thousand years. In China, as we have seen, the state's authority was remote and separated from the peasants by many layers of semiautonomous gentry. In China the authority that impinged on the peasant was social rather than political; the enveloping influence of his family and clan formed the real social unit of the society, which was structured on these units and not on the individual, as in Russia or the West.

Moreover, in China, the authority that impinged on the ordinary individual was not only social; it was static. Based on custom and tradition rather than on law or political power, its whole tendency was to resist change. In Russia, on the other hand, the absence of such a binding social nexus, the fact that the basic social and metaphysical reality there was the individual, the fact that the state's power impinged on that individual and that that power, for centuries, had been seeking change (as it had under Peter or Catherine, under Alexander I and II), all these things assisted the establishment of a Communist dictatorship in the Soviet Union. Moreover, almost constant internal migration in Russia from its earliest days, and the constant threat and reality of war and invasion, gave Russia an ability to accept changing personal conditions. This was in the sharpest possible contrast with Chinese conditions, where the heaviest obligation on each family was to maintain its fixed ancestral shrines, an obligation that tied the family to its traditional village.

Nowhere was the contrast between Russian and Chinese conditions more emphatic than in religion and general outlook. The Chinese were pragmatic, while the Russians were dualistic, and the West was pluralistic. In both the West and in Russia, belief in personal salvation in the hereafter and the need to work or to suffer for such future reward had given the prevailing outlooks a powerful impression of "future preference." Moreover, in Russia the close association of Church and State, and the teaching of the former that the latter was an essential element in reality and that submission to the czar's authority was part of the process of future salvation, prepared the way for the future Communist system. The dualistic and messianic outlook of Russia prepared Russian minds to accept any kind of uncompromising, intolerant, and painful authority as the only mechanism by which man could be shifted from this level of materialistic deprivation to the other level of salvationist future reward, since man, by his own power, could not cross the metaphysical gap, the no-man's land of almost unbridgeable distance, between the two levels of Russian dualism. In the West, man could, by his own activity, contribute to his rise to a high level of value and reward because, to the West, reality was not dualistic but pluralistic, with an infinite variety of steps and paths formed by the mutual interpenetration of spirit and matter in all the intermediate levels between their two extremes.

China had none of this. There all reality was on the same mundane level; human activity sought to survive, that is, to retain the existing situation, by pragmatic adaptation and flexible response to shifting pressures. In China both philosophy and religion were largely ethics, and this ethics was both pragmatic and conservative. In such an environment the messianic, salvationist, dynamic, future-oriented, state-dominated, abstract, and doctrinaire nature of Marxist-Leninism was utterly alien.

Nevertheless, Marxist-Leninism came to China and took control of it. This could not have occurred if the Old China had not been almost totally destroyed by the intrusion of the West, by the destruction of Chinese confidence in their way of life in the face of Western power, wealth, and ideology, and by the sixty years of turmoil and war extending from the Japanese attack on China of 1894 to the final Communist pacification in 1954.

Of course, no people lose their culture completely, no matter how it may disintegrate, and many of the fragments of Chinese cultural patterns continue to persist. One obvious example of this is in foreign policy, where China's patterns were remote from those of the traditional sovereign states, equals in international law, found in modern Europe. The Chinese system was always very ethnocentric in that they not only saw themselves as the center of the world, but saw themselves as the only civilized unit in their world picture in a planetary arrangement in which lesser peoples encircled them and lived in increasingly dark barbarism, depending on their distance from Peking. In the traditional view of China by the Chinese, there was, outside the three planetary rings of China itself (the imperial system, the provincial gentry, and the Chinese peasantry), increasingly remote peoples who were dependent upon China for cultural guidance, civilized example, and economic stimulation and were, in many cases (such as Indochina, Tibet, Mongolia, or Korea), in a tribute-paying relationship. This whole relationship, which was quite alien to Europe's idea in the nineteenth century of the balanced powers of equally sovereign states, was, on the contrary, very similar to the modern Communist idea of satellite states.

It seems likely that the Chinese, in spite of the many good reasons they had to be resentful of the Russians, were willing to be a satellite to the Russian sun until about 1955, when they became increasingly impatient with Khrushchev's efforts to relax the Cold War.

These relationships can be seen most clearly in military assistance and economic aid. The Chinese Communists triumphed over Chiang

Kai-shek in the civil war with only limited Soviet assistance, since Stalin apparently wanted China to be controlled by a Nationalist coalition government in which the Communists would participate. Stalin wanted China weak rather than Communist, and all his actions seem to have been consistent with this aim. The Russians allowed some of the captured Japanese military equipment to go to the Communists in 1945, but this was small in amount compared to that which the Communists obtained by capture or purchase from the Nationalist forces, and the Soviet Union gave no military aid to the Communists during the last four years of the civil war (1945–1949).

The Sino-Soviet Alliance of February 1950 was accompanied by an economic development loan of $300 million and was followed by the arrival in China of a Soviet military mission of about 3,000 men, but all military aid was sold to China, and at high prices. These arms, which were entirely of obsolescent types, cost about two billion dollars over seven years, 1950–1957. No effort was made toward coordination of military exercises or training, in spite of the alliance of 1950; there was no coordination of air or sea defenses, and China was not brought into the Warsaw Pact. Moreover, the Soviet Union, by its exclusive control of the North Korean Army, built it up, launched it into the Korean War, and thus eventually dragged Red China into a war on which they had not been consulted and had no wish to be involved, but were compelled, in defense of their own security, to intervene. Early in 1955, the Soviet Union gave China some moderate help in starting a Chinese military industrial base, chiefly in the assemblage of light planes, tanks, and naval vessels, but the development of American and Soviet thermonuclear capacity and missiles left China even further behind. In November 1957, Mao Tse-tung took a delegation to Moscow and made a formal request for nuclear warheads, but was rebuffed. As a result, by 1958 Red China was embarked on the long and difficult task of seeking to make an atomic bomb of its own. This seemed such an impossible job that, almost at once, Mao began to issue public statements belittling nuclear weapons and promising that the enormous numbers of China's militia would be able to survive any nuclear attack. The Quemoy crisis of August–September 1958 showed how little support the Soviet Union would give Red China on that issue and showed equally how divided the two countries were and how averse the Soviet Union was to China's approach "to the brink of war" in the Far East.

The defensive power of Red China remains very great, chiefly because of its large population and the great distances in which it can maneuver, but its offensive power, except over the minor states on its borders, is small. Military strength in the Far East is still in the hands of the Soviet Union, which has no intention of allowing it to be used in that part of the world, except in the unlikely event that the United States made an all-out assault on Red China. Even in that remote case, the Soviet Union's contribution would be limited, and its real strength would continue to be aimed at Europe, to be used there rather than in the Far East. Nonetheless, China's power in world politics does not rest on its own military strength but on the nuclear stalemate of the Soviet Union and the United States, both of whom are immensely more powerful in a strategic sense than anyone else in the Far East.

Under cover of that nuclear stalemate and the high restraint of both Superpowers in the use of nuclear weapons, Red China is in a position to engage in local wars, "national liberation movements," and "anti-imperialist" guerrilla activities all around its own borders, except along the frontier it has with the Soviet Union itself. These guerrilla adventures by Red China are correlated with domestic policy rather than with foreign policy, as the Quemoy crisis of summer 1958 was related to the "Great Leap Forward" of that year.

In this correlation of China's domestic and foreign policies, a major role will be played by China's most critical problem: the population–food-production balance.

This problem is probably more acute in China than in any similarly large area in the world. The Communist census of 1953 showed a Chinese population of almost 583 million, considerably more than had been expected. By 1962 this figure may have reached 700 million. With a birthrate of 17 per 1,000, China's natural increase was about 2 percent, and gave the country about one-quarter of the world's total population. Only about one-tenth of the land was arable, providing about 270 million acres, or less than an acre of cultivated land for every two persons. There has been some small success in increasing the area of cultivated lands, but obviously the problem can be solved only by slowing up the increase in population and by increasing the yields of crops per unit area of land. There seems to have been little success in either of these over the past decade or so. However, the centralized control of the Peking government over the Chinese people is so strong that it could probably bring the population explosion under control fairly quickly if a decision was made to do so. This would probably be achieved by supplying every woman with a birth-control pill at the noon meal each day, since that meal, for the majority of Chinese, is usually taken in a communal eating place where the process could be controlled as the authorities wished. The exclusive control of the state over information and public opinion, and its ability to mobilize local social pressures, increase its ability to carry out this policy.

This steadily growing crisis was brought abruptly to the acute stage by the "Great Leap Forward" in 1958, the first year of the Second Five-Year Plan. The earlier Five-Year Plan of 1953–1957 was based on the similar plan of the Soviet Union. It concentrated on investment in heavy industry, with little attention to consumers' goods or agriculture. About $3.5 billion a year, probably 20 percent of national income, was allotted to investment, with another 16 percent assigned to the armed forces. If we can believe China's own figures, the plan was a success, with output of coal, electricity, cement, and machine tools doubled and production of steel tripled. Total production of these commodities still left China largely unindustrialized, but by 1957 the government controlled 70 percent of all industry, 85 percent of retail trade, and almost all banking, foreign, and wholesale trade.

In the First Five-Year Plan, China was almost totally lacking in trained personnel, and was dependent for these, as well as for necessary equipment, on foreign sources. These could be found only within the Soviet bloc, but were not provided freely and had to be paid for, with settlement of accounts and new yearly agreements on an annual basis. The severity of the Soviet's terms on aid to China were in sharp contrast to its more generous behavior toward some of China's lesser neighbors and must have had an adverse influence on China's attitude toward Moscow even from the beginning. However, the necessary help could not be obtained elsewhere, and the achievement of the First Chinese Five-Year Plan rested on this assistance. In addition to the loan of $300 million in 1950, the Soviet Union in 1953–1956 agreed to sell China $2 billion in equipment, and sent several thousand technical advisers to help build 211 major industrial projects.

On this basis, the First Five-Year Plan achieved an annual rate of increase in production of at least 6 percent. The effort was financed very largely by accumulation of surplus agricultural commodities from China's hard-pressed peasantry and exchange of these for petroleum, machinery, and other commodities needed for the industrialization of China. Since these came largely from the Soviet Union and the European Communist satellites, 80 percent of China's trade was with the Communist bloc at the end of this First Five-Year Plan.

It is possible that this process could have continued, but it is even more likely that the faster rate of increase of population in comparison with the rise in food production may have indicated that the process could not continue. In any case, the powers in Peking decided to do something about it. Although it is not completely clear what they decided to do, and even less clear why they decided to do it, the consequence was a disaster. The "Great Leap Forward" of 1958 became a great stumble. This was the third stage in the agrarian reorganization of China.

The first stage in agrarian reform had been the "elimination of landlordism" in 1950–1952. Previous to the Land Reform Law of June 1950, 10 percent of families owned 53 percent of the farm land, while

32 percent owned 78 percent of the land. This left over two-thirds of such families (58 percent) with only 22 percent of the land. The landlords were eliminated with great brutality in a series of spectacular public trials in which landlords were accused of every crime in the book. At least three million were executed and several times that number were imprisoned, according to the official figures, but the total of both groups may have been much higher. The land thus obtained was distributed to poor peasant families, with each obtaining about one-third of an acre.

The second stage in the agrarian reform (1955) sought to establish cooperative farming. In effect it took away from the peasants the lands they had just obtained. The argument for forming collectives was persuasive; most peasant holdings were too small to work effectively, since abundant fertilizers, new crops and methods, specialized tools, and efficient land management could not be used on the average peasant farm of half an acre. To permit such improvements in farm practices, the peasants were forced into cooperatives. By the end of 1956, 83 percent of the peasants, or 125 million families, had joined into 750 thousand cooperatives.

The third stage of agrarian reform, constituting the basic feature of the "Great Leap Forward," merged the 750 thousand collective farms into about 26,000 agrarian communes of about 5,000 families each. This was a social rather than simply an agrarian revolution, since its aims included the destruction of the family household and the peasant village. All activities of the members, including child rearing, education, entertainment, social life, the militia, and all economic and intellectual life came under the control of the commune. In some areas the previous villages were destroyed and the peasants were housed in dormitories, with communal kitchens and mess halls, nurseries for the children, and separation of these children under the communes' control in isolation from their parents at an early age. One purpose of this drastic change was to release large numbers of women from domestic activities so that they could labor in fields or factories. In the first year of the "Great Leap Forward," 90 million peasant women were relieved of their domestic duties and became available to work for the state. In many cases, factories and craft centers were established in the communes to use this labor, manufacturing goods not only for the commune but for sale in the outside market.

One of the chief aims of this total reorganization of rural life was to make available, for savings and investment, surpluses of agricultural income from the rural sector of Chinese society in order to build up the industrial sector. The regime estimated that it could reverse the previous division of agricultural incomes, under which 70 percent was consumed by the agricultural population and only 30 percent was available to the nonagricultural sectors of Chinese society. At the same time, it was expected that the communes would totally shatter the resistant social structure of Chinese society, leaving isolated individuals to face the power of the state. Finally, it was expected that these isolated individuals could be mobilized along military lines to carry out agricultural duties in squads and platoons assigned to specific fields and tasks.

This last expectation, at least, was mistaken. "The Great Leap Forward" did not increase agricultural output but on the contrary reduced it drastically, despite the extravagant estimates of increases in production that were issued by officials toward the end of the first year. Officially, the agricultural disasters of 1958–1962 were attributed to unfavorable climate conditions, including unprecedented droughts, floods, storms, and insect pests, but the reversal of the "Great Leap's" plans and priorities in 1960–1961 shows that the Chinese themselves recognized the organizational element as contributing to their farming problems. It is undoubtedly true that adverse climate also contributed to the difficulties, and it may well be true that such climate conditions in the nineteenth century might have resulted in far greater want and famine than did actually occur in 1958–1962, for the Communist government was not involved in corruption, self-enrichment, and calculated inefficiency as earlier Chinese governments were, and had both greater power and greater desire to operate a fair rationing system, but the fact remains that in China, as in other Communist states, including the Soviet Union and Yugoslavia, the inability of a communized agricultural system to produce sufficient food surpluses to support a thoroughly communized industrial system at a high rate of expansion is now confirmed. On the other hand, the need for all these Communist regimes to purchase grain from the bulging agricultural surpluses of the Western countries, including Australia, Canada, the United States, and even Europe, confirms the fact that there is something in the Western pattern of living (but not necessarily in its economic organization) which does provide a bountiful agricultural system.

The details of the Chinese agricultural fiasco are not yet clear. It would appear that the Chinese diet (in which at least three-quarters of food is carbohydrates, and statistically recorded as "grain" even when it may be potatoes) requires a basic survival diet of at least 2,000 calories a day, with at least 1,500 calories from "grain." For a population of 700 million this requires a *minimum* crop of 180 million metric tons of "grain" a year, a figure that leaves nothing for reserves or for the inevitable inefficiencies of maldistribution through the inadequate Chinese transportation system. Moreover, this crop must increase each year to provide for the annual population increase of 2 percent (which gave 14 million more mouths in 1962).

The official estimates for the 1958 grain crop were originally set at over 300 million tons, but in 1959 and later, this was revised to less than 250 million tons. It was probably less than 200 million. The crop for 1959 was even less (perhaps 190 million tons), while that for 1960 may have been 150 million tons. These three adverse years undoubtedly used up all China's grain reserves, and the Chinese purchases of grain in the world's markets, beginning with about 10 million tons in 1961, may have been to rebuild some reserves rather than to provide a minimal increase for the average hungry Chinaman. It seems clear that the "average diet" of urban Chinese over these three harsh years may have fallen as low as 1,400 calories a day, at least 600 below the level that permits steady effective work.

The impact of the Chinese food crisis of 1958–1962 extended into all aspects of Chinese life and policy, including foreign affairs. This process was intensified from the fact that the "Great Leap Forward," from the beginning, involved much more than the reorganization of China's agriculture. It also included a considerable decentralization of economic management of China as a whole, from centralized technical experts to local party and working leaders; there was a considerable increase in the influence of the Communist Party in contrast to the state bureaucracy, and there was the general shift from emphasis on heavy industrial investment to more short-range economic objectives. It seems likely that there was also a change in economic accounting from emphasis on output to emphasis on the profits accumulation of individual enterprises.

Some of these changes were undoubtedly steps in the right direction, but they were lost to view under the general failure of agricultural production in 1958–1961. This failure reacted on industrial production by curtailing both investment and labor, so that output from this sector of the economy may have fallen by half. At the same time, China's reduced ability to export raw materials and agricultural products (simply because they could not be spared) and the need to make bulk purchases of food, especially grain, in Australia, Canada, or elsewhere, brought China face to face with a great shortage of foreign exchange and made it almost impossible for China to purchase necessary equipment abroad. China received little help from the Soviet Union during these difficult years. The repayment of loans to Russia continued and was, if anything, speeded up in spite of the terrible burden they placed on the Chinese economy. Soviet imports from China were 793 million rubles in 1958 and 990 million in 1959, but fell to 496 million in 1961; Soviet exports to China, which were 859 million rubles in 1959, were down to 331 million in 1961. As a result, Sino-Soviet trade as a whole had a total balance favorable to China (in the sense that China received more than it gave to Russia) of 984 million rubles over six years,

1950–1955, but had a total balance unfavorable to China of —750 million rubles over six years, 1956–1961. The Soviet Union advanced no development credits to China in these difficult years (as it was doing to Mongolia, North Korea, and North Vietnam at the time), but collected payment on China's debts to it exactly as if no Chinese food crisis were occurring. The Soviet Union exported 6.8 million tons of grain to other countries in 1960 and 7.5 million tons in 1961, but none to China. On the contrary, China's debt obligations made it necessary for it to ship over $250 million in agricultural exports to Russia in 1960 at the same time that it was paying out over $300 million of hard-earned foreign exchange for grain from Western countries. The Soviet attitude was: Business is business; an agreement is an agreement; and the economic development of the Soviet Union itself cannot be sacrificed for the sake of a heretical member of the Communist bloc. In 1961 the Soviet Union made some minor concessions to China's difficulties, including release of 500,000 tons of Cuban sugar to China from the total due to Russia, to be repaid in sugar later, and the sale of 300,000 tons of Soviet grain to China (only about 5 percent of China's foreign grain purchases that year). The withdrawal of almost all Soviet technical and military advisers in China during the summer of 1960 could not be defended solely on the basis of "good business practice," and marked one of the major steps on the continued deterioration of Sino-Soviet relations. It also established the almost complete dependence of China on its own resources, supplemented by whatever it could get wherever it could get it, for building up its economic system. As one symbol of that changed situation, it might be noted that trade with the Communist bloc had, at its peak, accounted for over 80 percent of China's total foreign trade, but by 1962 it had fallen below 50 percent.

The food crisis in Red China is, apparently, chronic, as it is, to a lesser degree, in all Communist countries. For example, in May 1962, not a year in which the crisis was generally acute, 70,000 hungry Chinese pushed across the barricaded border of China into the booming British colony of Hong Kong during the month. This intrusion was apparently caused by some local food maldistribution within China. It is not clear why the Chinese border guards permitted this worldwide revelation of its agricultural failure, although it might have been part of an effort to overwhelm and suffocate Hong Kong's booming prosperity, which must be as unacceptable on China's border as the prosperity of West Germany or West Berlin is to Communist East Germany.

Although the Soviet Union did not take advantage of China's food crisis in 1958–1962 to wage direct economic warfare on its fellow Communist regime, its businesslike indifference to all appeals of fellowship or even humanitarian considerations undoubtedly intensified the alienation of the two countries, which had begun much earlier and on quite different grounds.

This alienation of the world's two greatest areas of Communist rule began in the earliest days of the Red Chinese regime and was bound to become an open schism sooner or later. From the simple fact of balance of power, the one political event the Soviet Union had to fear was the appearance of a new Superpower adjacent to the Soviet Union on the land mass of Eurasia. The only possibilities for such a development would be a unified western Europe or a powerful China, with India as a much more remote and unlikely possibility.

In the second place, Communist China's needs for technical and economic assistance were inevitably so great that they directly compete with the Soviet Union's need for its own resources for its own development. Whatever China obtained of this nature from Russia could hardly fail, in the long run, to become a source of bitter feelings.

In the third place, from the beginning, a fissure between the two was inevitable, because, to the Soviet Union, Europe was the primary area of concern, while to China the Far East was primary. Each Power inevitably felt that the other should support it in its primary area and ease off pressures in the area of its own primary concern, an assumption about as unrealistic as any could be. Thus Red China resented the Soviet Union's attempts to work up crises over Berlin as deeply as Moscow resented Peking's efforts to work up crises over Taiwan. As we shall see in a moment, China's aggressive foreign policy in the Far East extended far beyond Taiwan, to all of the border areas that had once been tributary to Peking.

A fourth source of discord arose from the fact that the two Communist Powers were at quite different stages on the road to Socialism. The basic question in the allotment of economic resources in any state is concerned with the division of such resources among the three sectors of (1) governmental, especially defense; (2) investment in capital equipment; and (3) consumers' goods for rising standards of living. In Stalin's day the Soviet Union placed major emphasis on (1) and (2) at the expense of (3), but under Khrushchev there have been increasing pressures to shift the allotment of resources toward (3). Red China, which is at least forty years behind the Soviet Union in the development process, must emphasize the first two sectors, and can obtain the resources to do this only from curtailed consumption. Thus it must look at its problems from a point of view much closer to Stalin than to Khrushchev, a difference that led to alienation when Khrushchev began to attack Stalinism in 1956.

Closely related to this fourth source of friction was a fifth, the monolithic quality of the Marxist-Leninist states. By 1960 the Soviet Union's experiences in Europe, especially with Yugoslavia, Hungary, and Poland, clearly demonstrated that Communist states had their individual characteristics and rhythms of development and could not all be ruled from one center. This necessity by 1960 was being hailed in Moscow under the name "Socialist polycentrism," but was unacceptable in Peking under any name. At first Peking wanted the monolithic solidarity for which it yearned to be operated from Moscow after discussion by all Communist states, but by 1960 it was clear that if a Communist monolith were to be created it would have to be done by Peking itself.

A sixth source of alienation between Moscow and Peking is rather difficult to document but may well be more important than the others. It is concerned with a growing recognition, by China if not by the Soviet Union, that the Kremlin was being driven, under a multitude of pressures, toward a policy of peaceful co-existence with the United States, not as a temporary tactical maneuver (which would have been acceptable to China) but as a semipermanent policy. Part of this policy involved the Soviet attitude toward the fundamental theories of Marxist-Leninism, especially on the Leninist side. These theories had envisioned the advanced capitalist states as approaching a condition of economic collapse from "the internal contraditions of capitalism itself." According to the theory, this crisis would be reflected in two aspects: the continued impoverishment of the working class in advanced industrial countries, with consequent growth of the violence of the class struggle in such countries and increasing violence of the imperialist aggressions of such countries toward each other in struggles to control more backward areas as markets for the industrial products that the continued impoverishment of their own workers made impossible to sell in the domestic market. The falseness of these theories was fully evident in the rising standards of living of the advanced industrial countries, and especially in the ones, such as West Germany or the United States, which were most capitalistic in their orientation; it was also evident in the willingness of Britain, the United States, and others to see the end of colonialism in Asia and Africa.

This evidence of the errors of Marxist-Leninist theories was increasingly clear to the Kremlin, although it could not be admitted, but it was quite unclear to Peking, whose leaders were almost totally ignorant of the conditions of the non-Communist world. None of the chief Chinese leaders had any firsthand knowledge of the outside world and, indeed, had in most cases never been outside China at all, except for a couple of quick visits to the Soviet Union late in life. As a consequence, the Chinese Communist leaders were ignorant, dogmatic, doctrinaire, and rigid.

These attitudes appeared clearly within China in the fading of the "Hundred Flowers Campaign" of 1957. In theory the Communist system, after the elimination of Trotsky, accepted free discussion of goals and means until a decision on these had been reached by the party machinery, when discussion must stop and the decision be carried out with full loyalty. This procedure had never been observed under the tyrannical rule of the Kremlin and was even less likely to be followed in

Peking. In 1956, however, Mao Tse-tung announced a new policy of free criticism of the regime: as he said, "Let a hundred flowers bloom and a hundred schools of thought contend." This was a period of ideological confusion in the world Communist movement, which looked back on the struggle in the Kremlin to establish Stalin's successor, was still reeling from Khrushchev's anti-Stalin speech at the Twentieth Party Congress, and late in 1956 was called upon to face revolts against the Kremlin in Budapest and Warsaw. Although Chou En-lai, the foreign minister of Red China, rushed to Europe to extend his country's support to Khrushchev in this power struggle, ideological confusion was everywhere within the Communist world, and Mao was undoubtedly concerned about the solid basis for his own power and the problem of establishing a rule of succession in Peking.

In February 1957, Mao gave a speech to a large conference on the subject of "The Correct Handling of Contradictions Among the People." It was not published until June, but in the interval gave rise to the "Hundred Flowers" controversy. In his speech Mao invited criticism and free discussion *within the structure of the existing Communist state system.* He promised immunity to the critics, so long as their criticism contributed to the unity of Red China. These restrictive phrases were widely ignored and, in a few weeks, widespread and often fundamental criticisms of the regime were being voiced in meetings, the press, and especially in educational institutions. Three evils that Mao had mentioned—"bureaucracy, dogmatism, and sectarianism"—were being freely denounced, with the Communist Party cadres the chief targets. Some critics suggested that the proper solution to these problems was to permit the establishment of a legal opposition party within some kind of parliamentary system. The general consensus of the complaints was aimed at the lack of freedom to speak out, to move about, to disagree, or to publish.

On June 8th the government's counterattack began, at first relatively moderately but with increasing insistence. The principle of free criticism was not revoked, but the publication of Mao's February speech on June 17th set the limits that had presumably always been in effect. Within a year there had been a considerable shake-up of party and state personnel, many discontented persons (revealed by their criticism) had been removed or disciplined in various ways, and "all Rightists had been eliminated." The chief punishment was public denunciation and personal criticism of these discontented, but undoubtedly punishment, in many cases, went much further than that.

One sequel to the "Hundred Flowers" criticism was a reorganization of the upper ranks of the party and government and the provision of a succession to Mao.

Mao Tse-tung, son of a peasant who became wealthy on speculation and moneylending, was born in 1893 in Hunan Province. His father, a domestic tyrant and local miser, had less than four acres, but used the labor of his three sons and a hired hand to work them. He gave his sons a basic education, but his personal despotism drove his whole family into alliance against him. Young Mao's early life thus was one of severe discipline, constant domestic strife, and secret dreams of rebellion. By paying for a substitute worker in his own stead on the family land, he was able to get away to study for five years in Hunan Normal School (finished 1918). There he read deeply in Chinese history, especially military history, and formed a discussion group on large social questions. Becoming an employee of the library of Peking National University, he continued his reading, discussion, and self-education, and in 1920 was one of the eleven original founders of the Chinese Communist Party (CCP).

Until 1935, Mao's position in the CCP was that of a dissident, and he was, more than once, reprimanded and demoted, or removed from party positions. His chief difficulty was that he refused to accept the party's official view, insisted on by Russian-trained Communist leaders, that the revolution must be based on urban industrial workers, the "real proletariat." Instead Mao envisioned the party as a tightly disciplined group that could be raised to power on the revolutionary activities of the great mass of impoverished and discontented peasantry. Closely related to this idea were two others that were equally unorthodox: (1) the role of rural guerrilla warfare in wearing down and ultimately defeating a "reactionary government" and (2) a fundamental emphasis on the distinction between "imperialist" and "colonial" nations. This last point made it possible for Mao to regard the backward and undeveloped colonial areas as possible areas of revolutionary activity, where, as in China, the exploited peasants could provide the revolutionary impetus and could defend their revolutionary achievements by guerrilla warfare. The more orthodox Communist line was that a revolution could be carried out only by an urban proletariat that could be found only in an advanced industrial area, and that such an industrial base was essential to provide the modern military equipment needed to defend the revolutionary achievement against the counterattacks of aggressive, capitalist countries. In a sense Mao was much closer to the realities of modern politics and to the experience of Soviet Russia itself, since it is perfectly clear that no advanced industrial nation will go Communist and that the movement must make its advances in underdeveloped areas if it is to be successful anywhere. Since the objections to Mao's position came from the center of world Communist theory in Moscow, Mao distinguished between the Russian and the Chinese experience by calling Russia an "ex-imperialist" country and China an "ex-colonial country." In fact, however, they both became Communist while still backward countries, and did so as a consequence of invasion and defeat of the established government in a foreign war. Thus Mao's interpretation, while possibly erroneous in its belief that the revolutionary regime comes to power by guerrilla warefare supported by discontented peasantry, may well be correct, based on the Russian precedent, that Communist regimes are more likely to come to power in backward states and will survive there if they are able to use the state's despotic power to direct the utilization of economic resources toward investment to provide a high rate of economic development, as Soviet Rusisa has done.

Red China, like Soviet Russia, is governed under a parallel structure of the party and the government in which successive layers of assemblies and committees build up from the local level to the central authority. Until 1959, Mao held the chairmanship at the peak of both party and government. As a first step toward establishing a succession that would not repeat the desperate intrigue and violence that had occurred in the Kremlin following Stalin's death, he resigned from the chairmanship of the republic in favor of Liu Shao-chi, but retained his position as chairman of the Central Committee of the party. The third man in the system, Chou En-lai, is a member of the seven-man Standing Committee that controls the party, has been premier of the government since 1949, and was also foreign minister in 1949–1958.

While the structure of the governmental system of Red China is very similar to that of Soviet Russia, its spirit seems quite different. This is reflected in two ways. In Russia the Old Bolsheviks of the early days of the party were all eliminated, mostly by violent death, in the internecine power struggles which went on behind the grim walls of the Kremlin, while the Politburo throughout maintained a monolithic, impassive face to the outside world. In Red China most of the party leaders of today are still those who came together to engage in the earliest revolutionary struggles of the party in the 1920's. Moreover, they have, over the past forty years, often differed and even engaged in violent struggles and controversies with each other, but always were able to continue to work together, and to patch up their differences. The real distinction here is that the Kremlin has always insisted on presenting to the outside world a picture of itself as united and infallible. This is why Khrushchev's speech at the Twentieth Party Congress, attacking Stalin, was such a shock to the world. But the Chinese party leadership has never hesitated to admit that it has often been divided and fallible. Even Mao has changed his ideas and admitted his errors. Moreover, this, apparently, can be done without any need to punish or to liquidate the fallible comrades.

The key to this rather significant difference in the tone of Communist government in Moscow and Peking may be found in two basic distinctions: a difference of outlook and a difference of procedure. In Russia the ancient doctrinaire and rigidly ideologistic tone associated with the traditional Russian outlook and the traditional Russian religious system, both going back to their roots in Greek rationalism and Zoroastrian religion, established patterns of ideology that have continued under materialistic and atheistic Communism. Such attitudes are foreign to the traditions of Chinese pragmatism. Moreover, the origins of Chinese Communist organization in discussion groups in which all those present recognized their own ignorance and the inadequacy of their information on social facts, as well as on Marxist dogma, has continued in the practice of almost endless party meetings on all levels, filled with discussion, debate, and individual examination of one's own position and attitudes. As one remarkable consequence of these differences between China and the Soviet Union, there are at least half a dozen legal, minor political parties in Red China today. These not only exist and are permitted to participate in the governing process in a very minor way, but they are subject to no real efforts at forcible suppression, although they are subject to persistent, rather gentle, efforts at conversion. Such efforts would, of course, change to ruthless reprisal, if these tamed minor parties made any real effort to change or destroy the position of the Communist Party itself.

These differences between Communism in China and the Soviet Union may be explained most readily in terms of the different traditions of the two countries. The same applies to their different foreign policies, to which we have already referred.

The foreign policy of Red China has a number of diverse aims that hold quite distinct status on any list of Chinese priorities. Naturally, in first place is to avoid any foreign-policy action that might jeopardize the Communist regime in China. In second place is the desire to restore the traditional international position of old imperial China as a self-sufficient, isolated giant surrounded by subordinate tributary states; in this case the tribute consists of ideological loyalty to the Chinese Communist position. In third place is the Chinese desire to restore a unified ideological bloc on a world-wide basis supporting the true (Chinese) version of Marxist-Leninism. This version is not completely orthodox in traditional Marxist-Leninist terms, since it expects Communist regimes to rise in backward and ex-colonial countries rather than in advanced industrial countries, and expects these events to be precipitated and carried through by discontented peasants under intellectual leaders rather than by the industrial proletariat. On the other hand, this version is certainly closer to the facts of present-day politics, and on many points, such as the inevitability of revolution, the necessary imperialist aggression of advanced capitalist states, and the role of war as the midwife of Communism, is closer to Leninism than the ideas actually held in the Kremlin.

The argument as to which version of Communist ideology, the Chinese or the Russian, is closer to Marxist-Leninist orthodoxy is singularly unrewarding, since both sides claim the advantage here, and the ideology itself, however interpreted, is so remote from the facts of economic-social development in advanced countries that no real virtue can exist in being orthodox. The chief fact is that the Chinese version is potentially a much greater source of trouble to the outside world than Khrushchev's ideas of peaceful competition and noninevitable war. The Chinese version is dangerous simply because it threatens the West in an area where it is particularly vulnerable and where it has shown no great competence, that is, among the underdeveloped nations.

However, Chinese aggression in the period since 1954 has not been based on this third priority in its foreign-policy schedule but on its second priority, which seeks to create a belt of satellite subordinate states around the Chinese borders. The year 1954 may be taken as the initial date in this effort, because at that time the Peking government published a map of China that showed the Chinese border pushed deeply into Tibet, India, and southeast Asia. As early as the end of 1949, the Red Chinese had commenced a moderate intervention in Vietnam, but their most successful effort to restore the traditional Chinese satellite system was in Tibet.

China's suzerainty in Tibet has been generally recognized by the outside world, even in the years when China was rent by civil wars and banditry. By the treaty of May 23, 1957, Tibet itself accepted this status without recognizing that the status of "suzerainty" could become one of direct subordination, under Chinese pressure. This pressure began at once, and reached an acute stage in March 1959, when the Chinese authorities sought to arrest the Dalai Lama, head of the theocratic Tibetan government. The anti-Chinese revolt that resulted was crushed in two weeks, and the Dalai Lama fled to India.

During this period Chinese pressure continued into southeastern Asia, in Burma, which desperately tried to maintain a neutralist course, and especially in the successor states of former Indochina. The subsequent division of Vietnam, the struggle for Laos, and the valiant efforts of Cambodia to follow Burma's path to neutralism have already been mentioned. For years, guerrilla operations in South Vietnam and Laos have permitted an increased Chinese intervention in the area and have made increasing demands on American wealth and power to oppose it.

No solution to the problem of southeast Asia can be based on the belief that its troubles arise wholly, or even largely, from Communism or from Chinese aggression. For centuries, the central portion of the Malaysian peninsula, consisting of Laos and Cambodia along the Mekong River, has been under pressure from the Thai peoples to the west and the Vietnamese to the east. From at least the seventeenth century, the area we regard as Laos was divided into three or more petty kingdoms that were unable to unite in resistance to their more imperialist neighbors. The French hegemony in all of Indochina, from the nineteenth century to the Japanese invasion in 1942, suspended this process, but it would have been resumed in any case with the collapse of the French colonial sys-

tem there in 1954. So too, the southward movement of the Chinese, attracted by the rich rice lands of the Malayan river deltas, would have occurred in any case, even if Communism had never been invented. The
Communist issue simply added another, very acute, issue to a complex
situation.

As we have seen, French expenditure of $7 billion and about 100,000
lives during an eight-year struggle ended at Geneva in 1954. The Geneva
agreements opened the way to a succession of troubles in Laos by recognizing the Leftist Pathet Lao as the government of two provinces, and
recommending that it be admitted to a coalition government after a
proved cease-fire and free elections. The most vital clause provided that
all foreign military forces, except a French training group, be withdrawn
from Laos. An International Control Commission representing India,
Poland, and Canada was to supervise these provisions.

These agreements settled nothing. The elections of December 1955
brought the premiership to Prince Souvanna Phouma; he was a neutralist
and brother of Souphannouvong, a Communist fellow traveler and
founder of Pathet Lao. The two brothers brought Pathet Lao into the
government, but it did not give up its military bases in the two provinces
it dominated. The withdrawal of other miltary forces greatly increased
the potential power of Pathet Lao. When the latter showed increased
strength in subsequent elections in May 1958, the anti-Communist group
combined in August to oust Souvanna Phouma and put in as premier
the pro-Western Phoui Sananikone. This government in turn was ejected
and replaced by a Right-wing military junta led by General Phoumi
Nosavan in January 1960; but within seven months a new coup, this
time from the Left, and led by Kong Le, changed the regime and brought
Souvanna Phouma back to office. Four months later, in December 1960,
Nosavan once again replaced Phouma by military force. The Communist
countries refused to recognize this change, continued to recognize Souvanna Phouma, and increased their supplies to the guerrilla Pathet Lao
by Soviet airlift. In March 1961, England and France, acting through
the SEATO conference in Bangkok, vetoed any direct American or
SEATO intervention in Laos.

At the suggestion of Soviet Russia, the Geneva Conference was reassembled in 1962 and drew up two complicated agreements whose chief
consequence was to revive the agreements of 1954 within a more neutralized frame: coalition government, elimination of all foreign military
forces, neutrality, and a reactivation of the International Control Commission. The resulting troika coalition of Leftists, Neutrals, and Rightists
served to paralyze the country, while the Pathet Lao guerrillas, using
Communist North Vietman as a base, threatened to secure control of the
whole country. This effort broke out into open warfare in the Plaine
des Jarres in April 1963. The growing success of these attacks over the

next few years greatly agitated Washington, where officials generally felt that the fall of Laos, because of its central position, might well lead to a succession of Communist take-overs, in Cambodia, South Vietnam, Thailand, and Burma, leaving India wide open to a Red Chinese intrusion directly across these collaborating areas into the Indian plains. Some substance was lent to this fear from the fact that Red China spent the years 1955–1958 constructing a number of military roads that linked Sinkiang to Tibet, with offshoots southward toward the Malay Peninsula. This fear became intensified in 1962–1964 as a consequence of the Communist take-over in Burma, the American fiascoes in Vietnam, and the direct Chinese attack on India.

The strange thing about Burma was that the increase in Communist power was brought about by the army, which was increasingly dissatisfied by the ineffectual and corrupt government of the democratic U Nu. The latter, who was personally sincere, idealistic, and honest, represented the Burmese desire for peace, democracy, and unity from World War II on. By October 1958, however, his subordinates in the government had paralyzed the government with bickering and corruption. When the ruling Anti-Fascist Party split, U Nu judged it impossible to carry out the approaching elections, and yielded control of the country to a caretaker military government that promised to restore unity, honesty, and adequate administration, and supervise the elections.

By February 1960, the military leaders judged their task to be achieved, and held the new elections. U Nu's section of the Anti-Fascist Party won a sweeping victory, and he returned to office. The restored premier made valiant efforts to establish national unity, to raise the level of public spirit and cooperation, and to placate the various groups that divided the country, but was no more successful in restraining partisan conflict and corruption in 1960–1962 than he had been in the period before October 1958. Accordingly, in March 1962, another military coup, led by General Ne Win, ousted U Nu, suspended the constitution, and ruled through a junta of seventeen officers. Soon an effort was made to merge all political groups into a single national political party with a socialist program. The Communists were treated with increasing leniency, while leaders of democratic groups continued to languish in prison. Students and other dissident groups were violently suppressed, and civil liberties were generally curtailed. Suddenly, in February 1963, a completely socialist regime was established by the nationalization of most property rights under increasing Communist influence.

Although Burma has sought to hold a neutralist course in foreign affairs, it has been drifting toward the Red Chinese camp. Late in 1960 a protracted frontier dispute between the two nations was ended by an agreement that was generally favorable to Burma, and a few months later, in 1961, the two countries signed an economic agreement that brought

Burma a loan of $84 million and technical cooperation from China. Like everything in Burma, this was implemented in a lackadaisical fashion, and the Burmese economic situation has deteriorated steadily since World War II. Part of this has been due to increased difficulty in marketing Burma's chief exports, rice and lumber, but the chief problem has been the steady increase in population, which has reduced the per capita income by about a third, although national income as a whole has increased about a seventh since independence was won in 1948.

While Burma on the western edge of the Malay Peninsula thus drifted toward Communism, Vietnam on the eastern edge moved in the same direction with violent struggles. The Geneva agreement of 1954 had recognized the Communist government of North Vietnam, dividing the country at the 17th parallel, but this imaginary line across jungle terrain could not keep discontent or Communist guerrillas out of South Vietnam so long as the American-supported southern government carried on its tasks with corruption, favoritism, and arbitrary despotism. These growing characteristics of the Vietnam government centered around the antics of the Diem family. The nominal leader of the family was President Ngo Dinh Diem, although the fanatical spirit of it was his brother's wife, Madame Nhu. The brother, Ngo Dinh Nhu, was the actual power in the government, residing in the palace, and heading up a semisecret political organization that controlled all military and civil appointments. Madame Nhu's father, Tran Van Chuong, who resigned from his post as Vietnam Ambassador to the United States as a protest against the arbitrary nature of the Diem family government, summed up his daughter's career as "a very sad case of power madness." The same authority spoke of President Diem as "a devoted Roman Catholic with the mind of a medieval inquisitor." On the Diem family team were three other brothers, including the Catholic Archbishop of Vietnam, the country's ambassador in London, and the political boss of central Vietnam, who had his own police force.

The Diem family tyranny came to grief from its inability to keep in touch with reality and to establish some sensible conception of what was important. While the country was in its relentless struggle with the Vietcong Communist guerrillas who lurked in jungle areas, striking without warning at peasant villages that submitted to the established government or did not cooperate with the rebels, the Diem family was engaged in such pointless tasks as crushing Saigon high school agitations by secret police raids or efforts to persecute the overwhelming Buddhist majority and to extend favors to the Roman Catholics who were less than 10 percent of the population.

When Diem became president in 1955, after the deposition of the pro-French Emperor Bao Dai, the country had just received 800,000 refugees from North Vietnam which the Geneva Conference of 1954 had yielded to Ho Chi Minh's Communists. The overwhelming majority of these refugees were Roman Catholics, and their arrival raised the Catholic population of South Vietnam to over a million in a total population of about 14 million. Nevertheless, President Diem made these Catholics the chief basis of his power, chiefly by recruiting the refugees into various police forces dominated by the Diem family. By 1955 these were already beginning to persecute the Buddhist majority, at first by harassing their religious festivals and parades but later with brutal assaults on their meetings. An attempted *coup d'état* by army units which attacked the Royal Palace in November 1960 was crushed. From that date on, the Diem rule became increasingly arbitrary.

In the middle of all this disturbance, American aid tried to revive the country's economy, and American military assistance tried to curtail the depredations of the Communist guerrillas. The two together amounted to about $200 million a year, although economic aid alone was originally twice this figure. The intensity of the guerrilla attacks steadily increased, following President Diem's reelection, with 88 percent of the vote, in April 1961. As these attacks slowly increased, the American intervention was also stepped up, and gradually began to shift from a purely advisory and training role to increasingly direct participation in the conflict. From 1961 onward, American casualties averaged about one dead a week, year after year. The Communist guerrilla casualties were reported to be about 500 per week, but this did not seem to diminish their total numbers or relax their attacks, even in periods when their casualties were heavy.

These guerrilla attacks consisted of rather purposeless destruction of peasant homes and villages, apparently designed to convince the natives of the impotence of the government and the advisability of cooperating with the rebels. To stop these depredations, the government undertook the gigantic task of organizing the peasants into "agrovilles," or "strategic hamlets," which were to be strongly defended residential centers entirely enclosed behind barricades. The process, it was said, would also improve the economic and social welfare of the people to give them a greater incentive to resist the rebels. There was considerable doubt about the effectiveness of the reform aspect of this process and some doubt about the defense possibilities of the scheme as a whole. The American advisers preferred stalking-patrols to seek out the guerrillas rather than static defenses, stressed the need for night rather than only daytime counteractions, and the use of the rifle instead of large-scale reliance on air power and artillery. Moreover, most observers felt that very little of America's economic aid ever reached the village level but, instead, was lost on much higher levels, beginning with the royal palace itself. By the summer of 1963, guerrillas were staging successful attacks on the strategic hamlets, and the need for a more active policy became acute. Unfortunately, just at that time, the domestic crisis in Vietnam also was becoming acute.

This final crisis in the story of the Diem family and its henchmen arose from religious persecution of the Buddhists under the guise of maintaining political order. Restrictions on Buddhist ceremonies led to Buddhist protests, and these in turn led to violent police action. The Buddhists struck back in a typically Asiatic fashion, which because it was Asiatic proved to be very effective in the Asiatic context: individuals or small groups of Buddhists committed suicide in some crowded public place near a governmental center. The favorite mode of suicide was to drench the victim's long yellow robes with gasoline and ignite these with a match as he knelt in a public square or street. The calloused reaction of the Diem family, especially of Madame Nhu, shocked the world, and outraged feeling rose rapidly in the summer of 1963. When thirty-five university professors and a number of public officials (including the father of Madame Nhu) resigned, the police attacked Buddhist shrines, arresting hundreds of their priests. Student agitations led to the closing of Saigon University and of all public and private schools, with the arrest of many students. A United Nations fact-finding commission was isolated by Diem police. On November 1, 1963, an American-encouraged military coup, led by General Duong Van Minh, overthrew the Diem family, killing several of its members. A new government, with a Buddhist premier, calmed down the domestic crisis, but by 1964 showed itself no more able to suppress guerrilla activities than its predecessor had been.

The Red Chinese intervention in southeast Asia, except perhaps in Burma, was generally indirect and through intermediaries. Elsewhere in southern and eastern Asia, this was not true. But in all areas, from 1960 onward, it was evident that the increase in Chinese influence was not so much at the expense of the United States as it was at the expense of the Soviet Union. In North Vietnam and Burma, the Chinese influence was direct before 1960, but after that date it grew stronger in Laos, South Vietnam, and Siam, while Cambodia vainly sought to obtain a guarantee of its neutrality from all concerned. In North Korea the change was dramatic, since the dominant Soviet influence there was replaced by open Chinese influence in 1961. A similar process could be observed in southern Asia, especially in Pakistan, and even in India.

The Chinese invasion and crushing of Tibet in March 1959 revealed that they had constructed a military road from Sinkiang to Lhasa. The Dalai Lama, in exile in India, accused the Chinese of genocide, and it seemed clear that a third of a million Chinese had moved into southern Tibet after resistance was crushed. Many Tibetans were compelled to work on a 1,500-mile railroad from China to Lhasa and on a road system toward the borders of India, Nepal, Sikkim, and Bhutan. Thousands of Tibetan refugees crowded into these countries, while others were machine-gunned by the Chinese as they fled. Many Buddhist shrines and lamasaries were destroyed.

By October 1962, Chinese-Indian border incidents, on territory claimed by both, erupted into open war. The consequences were startling: Indian forces collapsed almost at once and were revealed to be almost wholly lacking in supplies, training, and fighting spirit. As the responsible official concerned, the minister of defense and vice-premier, Krishna Menon, a close adviser of Nehru, an open sympathizer with the Soviet Union, and a skilled and sardonic baiter of the West, was removed from power. India's appeal for aid was answered by the United States with five million dollars' worth of weapons by November 10th, but the Soviet Union found itself in the cruel dilemma of either abandoning its long efforts to win over India or contributing to a war on its nominal ally, China. It abandoned the former by suspending arms shipments already committed. Most ominous of all, by the end of November 1962, the Indian military collapse was so complete that it became clear that China could achieve in three months what Japan had sought to achieve without success, throughout World War II: a breakthrough with ground forces onto the Indian plain.

Such a breakthrough was, apparently, not China's aim. Its chief concern seems to have been to secure control of the Aksai Chin area, where the territories of China, India, and the Soviet Union converge. Chinese domination of this inaccessible area and improvements of Chinese communications there is a threat to the Soviet Union rather than to India, which has generally ignored the area. The Chinese desire to hold the region may be part of a scheme to relieve Soviet pressure on the Chinese borders farther east, near Mongolia.

In any case, the Chinese resort to war on India must have been a consequence of very complex motivations, and surely gave rise to complicated consequences. It was aimed at the Soviet Union and at the United States rather than at India, but did serve to discredit all concerned, to demonstrate the power and vigor of the new China, and to cut down drastically the Indian way (as contrasted with the Chinese way) as a model for other underdeveloped Asiatic nations.

One notable consequence of the Chinese attack on India was that it served to pull Pakistan further out of the Western camp toward the Communist side of neutralism. Pakistan as a member both of CENTRO and SEATO had a vital position in John Foster Dulles's line of paper barriers surrounding the Soviet heartland, but in Pakistani eyes the controversy with India over Kashmir was of more immediate and more intense appeal. The Chinese humiliation of India was received with ill-concealed pleasure in Pakistan, although the Chinese were also intruding on some areas claimed by Pakistan. These disputes were settled by a frontier treaty with China in May 1962, and the Muslim state showed increased confidence that its claims against India over Kashmir would obtain Chinese support.

During all these events the divisions between the Soviet Union and Red China became increasingly public and increasingly bitter. As usual in Communist controversies, they were enveloped in complicated ideological disputes. By 1962 the Chinese had reached the point where they were accusing Khrushchev of betraying the revolution and the whole Communist movement from a combination of increasingly bourgeois obsession with Russian standards of living and a cowardly fear of American missile power. Thus they accused the Soviet Union of betraying international Communism in accepting "polycentrism" (especially in Yugoslavia) and of weakness in accepting "peaceful co-existence" (as in the Cuban missile crisis). Khrushchev alternated between striking back at the Chinese criticism and seeking to stifle them in order to avoid a complete ideological split of the world Communist movement. The Chinese were adamant, and continued to work toward such a split, seeking to win over to their side the Communist movement and Communist parties throughout the world, especially in the more backward countries where the Chinese experience often seemed more relevant. By 1964 the split within the Communist movement seemed unbridgeable.

The Eclipse of Colonialism

One of the most profound and most rapid changes of the postwar period has been the disintegration of the prewar colonial empires, beginning with the Dutch in the Netherlands Indies and ending with the Portuguese in Africa and elsewhere. We have no need to go into any detailed narration of the events that accompanied this process in specific areas, but the movement as a whole is of such great importance that it must be analyzed.

When World War II began in 1939, a quarter of the human race, six hundred million people, mostly with nonwhite skins, were colonial subjects of European states. Almost all of these, with the exception of those under Portuguese rule, won independence in the twenty years following the Japanese surrender in 1945.

Except in a few areas, such as the Dutch Indies, French Indochina, and British Malaya, which had been under Japanese occupation during the war, the anticolonial movement was not significant until a decade or more after the war's end. In many places, especially in Africa, the movement toward independence was of little importance until 1956. Nevertheless, the war may be regarded as the trigger for the whole process, since the early defeats suffered by the Netherlands, France, and Britain, especially when they were inflicted by an Asiatic people, the Japanese, gave a deadly blow to the prestige of European rulers. The war also mobilized many natives into military activities, during which they learned to use arms and were often moved to unfamiliar areas where they discovered that the subordination of natives to Europeans, and especially the subjection of dark-skinned peoples to whites, was not an immutable law of nature.

These events also showed many native peoples that their tribal divisions were but local and parochial concerns and that they could, and must, learn to cooperate with other persons of different tribes, different languages, and even different religions, to face common problems that could be overcome only by cooperative efforts. In many cases, the great demand and high prices for native products during the war gave native peoples, for the first time, a realization that the contrast of European affluence and native poverty was not an eternal and unchangeable dichotomy. Accordingly, such peoples were unwilling to accept the decreasing demand, falling prices, and declining standards of living of the postwar period, and determined to take political action to obtain independent control of their own economic situations. Moreover, just at that time, the Communist argument that colonial impoverishment and European affluence arose from the exploitation of colonial peoples by imperialist Powers began to spread in Asia and Africa, brought back from imperial cities like London and Paris where small groups of natives, in search of education, had come in contact with Communist propagandists.

Except for this last point, these factors were closely associated with the war and its outcome. But there were other influences of a much longer duration. The acquisition of European languages that permitted native peoples to surmount the linguistic isolation of their tribal differences had begun in the nineteenth century, but by the 1950's had become a more widespread phenomenon, especially among those natives who were most unwilling to fall back into tribal apathy and an inferior status. Many natives, in one way or another, had acquired a smattering or more of European education, and with this, even when it entailed a respect and affection for European culture, they had picked up much of the basic libertarian outlook endemic in European politics. In fact, in British colonial areas, educated natives had been systematically inculcated with English theories of political resistance and self-rule which went back to Magna Carta and the Glorious Revolution. Thus the myths of English history became part of the solvent of the British imperial structure.

Another factor, which had been going on for a considerable time in 1956, was the process of detribalization associated with the growth of cities and the development of commercial and craft activities that brought many diverse subjects of colonialism together in urban districts or trade unions outside the stabilizing nexus of their previous tribal associations or of their peasant communities. Better educated and more energetic individuals among these natives took advantage of this situation to organize groups and parties to agitate for a larger share in the political control of their own affairs and eventual independence.

In spite of the pressure and even the power of these changes in the colonial situation on the side of the subject peoples, there were at least equally significant, and largely unrecognized, changes on the side of their imperial rulers. For it must be recognized that in very few cases did native peoples achieve independence as a consequence of a successful revolt by force. On the contrary, in case after case, independence was granted, after a relatively moderate agitation, by a former ruling power which showed a certain relief to be rid of its colonial burden. This indicates a profound change in attitudes toward colonies within the imperialist countries. The significance of this change can hardly be denied; the real question is concerned with its causes.

Before 1940 the possession of colonial territories was of little direct concern to most persons in the imperial homeland. They knew that their country had colonies and ruled over peoples quite different from themselves, and this was regarded, rather generally, as probably a good thing, a source of pride to most citizens and probably of some material advantage to the country as a whole. The costs of holding colonial areas were not generally recognized and were usually felt to be minor and incidental. But in the postwar period these costs very rapidly became major and direct charges, quite unacceptable to the ordinary citizen, when the postwar period and increased anticolonial agitations required heavy taxation and compulsory military service to regain or to retain such colonial areas. Once this was recognized, the former rather vague satisfaction with colonial possessions soon disappeared, and there was a rapidly spreading conviction that colonies were not worth it. The burden of taxes and military service in remote areas was regarded as part of the war, to be ended, as completely as possible, with the war itself, not to be continued indefinitely into the postwar period.

Another closely related change occurred in economic aspirations. The citizens of the European colonial Powers had survived six years of hardships in the war itself and, in most cases, a decade or more of economic hardships in the prewar depression. The war demonstrated that such economic hardships had been needless. The massive economic mobilization for the war showed clearly that there could be an equally massive postwar mobilization of resources for prosperity. The ordinary European was determined to obtain the rising standards of living and welfare security that he had been denied in the depression and war, and he had no stomach to be denied these any longer in order to hold in subjection native peoples who wanted independence. Thus the former beneficiaries and upholders of empire, usually restricted to an upper-class minority or specialized interest groups, found that these interests no longer would be supported by the majority of their own citizens.

In some cases independence was achieved after a period of violence, rioting, and guerrilla warfare, although in no case did these actions, however extensive, become a matching of force between the colonial area and the imperial Power. In no case could these powers be matched, since the latter was overwhelmingly larger. In most cases, a more or less token display of force by the colonial peoples showed that they could be subdued only by an expenditure of resources and inconveniences which the ruling Power decided it did not care to make. The existence of the Soviet bloc and the appearance of the Cold War, with its almost irresistible demands for expenditures of resources, helped to tip the decision toward independence. Moreover, the opinion of the United States was favorable to independence for subject peoples in a rather doctrinaire and naïve anticolonialism, rooted in the American revolutionary tradition, without regard for the very great benefits the native peoples had obtained from their European rulers.

Resistance to the decolonizing process was strong only in exceptional cases, such as in the French Army and in the Portuguese ruling groups. In Portugal the despotic character of the regime made it possible for the adherents of the colonial system to sustain the policy of resistance to independence, but the role of the French Army, especially in Indochina and Algeria, was almost unique.

This unique quality in the Algerian crisis rested on three factors: (1) Algeria, which had been held by France since 1830, was constitutionally part of France, and its problem was part of the domestic history of the metropolitan country, since 30 of the 626 members of the French Assembly represented Algeria; (2) in Algeria there was a large group of European settlers (about 12 percent of the total population) who could not be turned over to an independent Arab majority, whom they had treated as inferiors for years; and (3) the French Army, after a series of defeats from 1940 to Indochina in 1954, resolved not to be defeated in Algeria and was prepared to overthrow by civil war any French cabinet that wished to grant independence to that area. Bitterness in Algeria was intensified by many other issues, including drastic religious, economic, social, and intellectual contrasts between the European settlers and the Algerian majority. The latter, for example, as a result of French medical skills, had one of the world's major population explosions, while the settlers owned most of the land and almost all the local economic activities.

The bitterness of the Algerian struggle almost exceeded belief, as the extremists on each side adopted intransigent positions and sought to eliminate by assassination the more moderate of their own groups. Both sides resorted to strikes and riots in the cities, guerrilla operations and farm burnings in rural areas, and assassination in France itself. By 1960 indiscriminate bombings and reprisals against innocent peoples were alienating increasing numbers of persons from the extremes toward more moderate positions nearer the center, although the extremists as they decreased in numbers became more violent in action. In 1958 the crisis brought General de Gaulle back to office in France from retirement, largely because his supreme self-confidence and ambiguous position on the chief issues of controversy gave grounds for belief that he could find some solution to the crisis, or at least could maintain domestic order. This change ended the Fourth French Republic and brought into existence a new regime, the Fifth Republic, whose constitutional provisions were custom made to De Gaulle's type of despotic ambiguity (October 1958).

It took almost four years more before agreement was reached between the Algerian rebels and the De Gaulle regime on a settlement of the Algerian dispute (March 18, 1962). Even then, sporadic violence continued for months. The final cost of the Algerian crisis, over seven years, has been estimated at 250,000 lives and $20 billion.

The intensity of this conflict and the socialistic policies of the new Algerian government of Muhammad Ben Bella provided an unattractive future to the previously superior European settlers, and many of these left the country to seek residence elsewhere, chiefly in France although only a small portion of them were of French origin. The erratic instability and demagogy associated with so many newly independent states was displayed by Ben Bella during his visit to the Western Hemisphere in October 1962. Although he came to seek economic concessions and was given an especially warm welcome by President Kennedy, a few days later he visited Castro in Cuba and made a scathing attack on United States policy, demanding American evacuation of the Guantánamo Bay Naval Base. The following month, on his return home, Ben Bella nationalized mines, power, foreign trade, and much of the lands of European settlers. At the same time, the Communist Party was outlawed and hundreds of "enemies" of the regime were arrested.

A number of newly independent states followed what we might call the Nasser pattern of postcolonial policy. This involved a large amount of verbal attack on the United States and the European ex-colonial powers, a rather ambivalent but generally favorable attitude toward the Soviet bloc, and a less public effort to obtain Western aid or economic concessions to compensate for the basic inability of the Soviet bloc to provide such aid. With this double policy, there frequently went a rather aggressive attitude toward neighbors with which the new state had real or fancied grievances, which were played up at critical moments as a cover for the inability of the new regimes to cope with the postliberation economic and social problems of their own peoples. In many cases, such as Sukarno of Indonesia, Nasser, Kwame Nkrumah of Ghana, and

Castro, these leaders sought to exercise the qualities of personal popularity and superhuman personification of popular aspirations that we call "charismatic leadership."

None of these policies or attitudes was much help in coping with the very real problems that have faced the newly independent nations with growing urgency. The enthusiasm that greeted independence and the acceptance by the world of that status through admission to the United Nations was followed, in most cases, by a postindependence reaction as the scope and almost insoluble nature of each country's problems had to be recognized.

The nature of these problems must be evident from what has already been said. At a minimum they could be divided into three or four groupings concerned with the patterns of power, of wealth, of social relationships, and of outlook.

In the European tradition, power has tended to rest on some kind of synthesis of military (force), economic (material rewards), and ideological elements and on some kind of political structure (such as the parliamentary system) in which the opposition was incorporated into the constitutional system. In most colonial or backward areas, power has tended to rest on other aspects of the total social structure, notably on religion or on social pressures derived from kinship and tribal groupings or from stable social patterns in villages or residential patterns. There has been a tendency toward conformity and even uniformity; opposition groups and diversity have tended to be encapsulated into exogamous social groupings like the castes of India.

In these traditional societies, except where the English tradition was successfully established, there has been a reluctance to accept majority rule or the organized oppositional structure of the parliamentary system because of the native desire for a unified social context. Instead of decision by majority rule, which was often unacceptable to native peoples because it seemed to force an alienated situation on the minority, native peoples in many areas preferred to reach decisions by what could be called "reaching a consensus." This method, exemplified in the American Indian "powwow" or in American business conferences, achieved agreement and decision, usually unanimously, by comment from each person present in sequence until consensus was reached. The difficulty of using this method in the large assemblies of newly independent governments often led to other mechanisms for achieving unanimity, such as a constitutional provision that any political party that captured a majority of the vote should have all the seats. To the Western European such a rule seems to be a scandalous refusal to listen to minority opinion; to natives it often seems a most necessary mechanism for preserving solidarity. Really it is a mechanism for keeping diverse opinions behind the scene, out of public view, and force the reconciliation of differences to take place in some concealed area of backstage intrigue and discussion rather than out in the public arena of the national assembly. The latter body becomes a mechanism for publicly demonstrating national solidarity or for proclaiming public policy, rather than an area of conflict as it had become in the western European parliamentary system.

This tendency to seek a public display of uniformity and national solidarity through political and constitutional processes was evident in Hitler's Third Reich, as it has been in other recent European authoritarian states, including the Soviet Union, and has also appeared in the more traditionally free governments of western Europe and the United States.

The European tradition to seek a settlement of disputes or differences by force or in battle was evident in the feudal tradition, in the electoral and parliamentary systems, in the contentious (rather than investigatory) nature of English legal procedure, and in the European, and especially English, obsession with sports and athletic contests. It is part of the warlike tradition of Europe that gave it the weapons development and political power to dominate the world.

Such an emphasis on force as a prime factor in human life is rarer in colonial areas, especially in those where peasant traditions are strong and pastoral traditions are weak (such as India, southeast Asia, China, and much of Negro Africa). In these areas force often appeared in a ritual or symbolic way, so that the outcome of a battle was settled by the infliction of a single casualty, which was taken to indicate a religious or magical settlement of the dispute, making further conflict unnecessary.

This reluctance to the use of force in social life in many colonial areas has raised the problem of how the areas claimed by these new nations can be defended, either against their more aggressive neighbors or against more militant tribes or groups within their own population. In many areas, notably in Africa, the existing boundaries of the new nations have no relationship to any power structure or to any existing factual realities at all. As colonies these areas' boundaries reflected, to some extent, the power relationships of their imperial countries in Europe, but now that independence has been achieved, the boundaries reflect nothing. In many cases the existing boundary, drawn as a straight line on the map, cuts through the center of tribal areas, the only existing local political reality.

The lack of a military tradition in many ex-colonial areas makes defense a difficult problem, as was shown in the Indian defensive weakness during the Red Chinese attack of 1962. In many areas, natives are eager to become soldiers, because of the salaries and benefits associated with the role, but they do not regard fighting as part of that role. In many cases, they become pressure groups seeking additional benefits and may become a considerable burden on the new nation's budget and a threat to the stability of the state itself while providing little or no protection to the state against possible outside enemies.

The economic problems of the new nations are already clear. In most cases they center upon the imbalance between a rapidly growing population and a limited food supply, with the accessory problem of finding employment for such additional population in their underdeveloped economic status. Technical knowledge is limited, and large-scale illiteracy hampers the spread of such knowledge, if it exists. But in most cases it does not exist, for it must be emphasized that the technical knowledge built up in Europe and America under quite different geographic and social conditions is often not applicable to colonial areas. This was made brutally clear in the so-called "ground-nut scheme" in British East Africa in the early postwar period, which sought to grow peanuts over a vast acreage, using American methods of tractor cultivation; it led to disastrous results, with monetary losses of many hundreds of millions of dollars. Any technology must fit into the natural and social ecology of the situation. The conditions of most ex-colonial areas are so different from those of western Europe and North America that our methods should be applied only with the greatest caution. American methods in particular are usually based on scarce and high-cost labor combined with plentiful and cheap material costs to provide labor-saving but material-wasteful methods of production requiring large savings and heavy investment of capital. Almost all ex-colonial areas have an oversupply of cheap and unskilled labor with limited material and land resources and are in no position to raise or utilize heavy capital investments. As a consequence, quite different technological organizations must be devised for these areas.

The social consequences of decolonization are, in some ways, similar to those that have appeared recently in the poorer areas of Western cities. This has been called "anomie" (the shattering of stable social relationships), and arises from rapid social change rather than from decolonization. It gives rise to isolation of individuals, destruction of established social values and of stability, personal irresponsibility, shattered family relationships, irresponsible sexual and parental relationships, crime, juvenile delinquency, a greatly increased incidence of all social diseases (including alcoholism, use of narcotics, and neuroses), and personal isolation, loneliness, and susceptibility to mass hysterias. The crowding of large numbers of recently detribalized individuals into rapidly growing African cities has shown these consequences, as, indeed, they have been shown in many American cities, such as New York or Chicago, where recently deruralized peoples are exposed to somewhat similar conditions of anomie.

Some of the more intractable difficulties of newly decolonized areas are psychological, especially as these difficulties are hard to identify and often provide almost insuperable obstacles to development programs, especially to those directed along Western lines. It is, for example, not usually recognized that the whole economic expansion of Western society rests upon a number of psychological attitudes that are prerequisites to the system as we have it but are not often stated explicitly. Two of these may be identified as (1) future preference and (2) infinitely expandable material demand. In a sense these are contradictory, since the former implies that Western economic man will make almost any sacrifice in the present for the sake of some hypothetical benefit in the future, while the latter implies almost insatiable material demand in the present. Nonetheless, both are essential features of the overwhelming Western economic system.

Future preference came out of the Christian outlook of the West and especially from the Puritan tradition, which was prepared to accept almost any kind of sacrifice and self-discipline in the temporal world for the sake of future eternal salvation. The process of secularization of Western society since the seventeenth century shifted that future benefit from eternity to this temporal world but did not otherwise disturb the pattern of future preference and self-discipline. In fact, these became the chief psychological attributes of the middle class that made the Industrial Revolution and the great economic expansion of the West. They made people willing to undergo long periods of sacrifice for personal training and to restrict their enjoyment of income for the sake of higher training and for capital accumulation. This made it possible to develop an advanced technology with massive shifting of economic resources from consumption to forming capital equipment. On this basis Quakers, Puritans, and Jews built the early railroad systems, and English Non-Conformists combined with Scottish Presbyterians to build the early iron industry and steam-engine factories. Other advances were based on these.

The mass production of this new industrial system was able to continue and to accelerate to the fantastic rate of the twentieth century because Western man placed no limits on his ambition to create a secularized earthly paradise. Today the average middle-class family of suburbia has a schedule of future material demands which is limitless: a second car is essential, often followed by a third; an elaborate reconstruction of the basement provides a recreation room, which must be followed in short order by an elaborate patio with outdoor cooking equipment and a swimming pool; almost immediately comes the need for an outboard motorboat and trailer to carry it, followed by the need for a summer residence by the water and a larger boat. And so it goes, in an endless expansion of insatiable demands spurred on by skilled advertising, the whole keeping the wheels of industry turning, and the purchasing power of the community racing around in an accelerating cycle.

Without these two psychological assumptions, the Western economy would break down or would never have started. At present, future preference may be breaking down, and infinitely expanding material demand may soon follow it in the weakening process. If so, the American economy will collapse, unless it finds new psychological foundations.

The connection of all this with ex-colonial areas lies in the fact that without these two attitudes it will be very difficult for underdeveloped nations to follow along the Western path of development. This does not mean that no "achieving" society can be constructed without these two attitudes. Not at all. Many different attitudes, in proper arrangement, might be made the basis for an "achieving" society, but it would probably not be along the Western lines of individual initiative and private enterprise. Religious feeling or national pride or many other attitudes could become the basis for achievement and economic expansion, as they were in ancient Mesopotamia and Egypt or in medieval Europe, but such other bases for achievement would be unlikely to provide a system using private savings as its method of capital accumulation or personal ambition as its motivation for acquisition of highly developed technological training and skills, as in our economy.

The ordinary African is very remote from either future preference or infinitely expandable material demands. He generally has preference for the present, and his demands are often nonmaterial and even noneconomic, such as his desire for leisure or for social approval. The African has a fair recognition of the immediate past, a dominant concern for the present, and little concern for the future. Accordingly, his conception of time is totally different from that of the average Western man. The latter sees the present only as a moving point of no dimension that separates the past from the future. The African sees time as a wide gamut of the present with a moderate dimensioned past and almost no future. This outlook is reflected in the structure of the Bantu languages, which do not emphasize the tense distinctions of past, present, and future, as we do, but instead emphasize categories of condition, including a basic distinction in the verb between completed and incompleted actions that places the present and the future (both concerned with unfinished actions) in the same category. We do this occasionally in English when we use the present tense in a future sense by saying, "He is coming tomorrow," but this rare use of the present to indicate the future does not blur our conception of the future the way constant use of such a construction does in Bantu.

In addition to his present preference, the Bantu has a list of priorities, in his conception of a higher standard of living, which contains many noneconomic goals. A fairly typical list of such priorities might run thus: food, sex dalliance, joking with one's friends, a bicycle, music and dancing, a radio, leisure to go fishing. Any list such as this, with its high priority for noneconomic and basically leisure activities, does not provide the constantly expanding material demands that are the motivating force in the West's economic expansion. Nor is the African's strongly socialized personality, which shares all its successes and wants with others and constantly yearns for the social approval obtained by sharing income with kinfolk and friends, capable of supporting any economy of private selfishness and individual capital accumulation that became the basis for the industrial expansion of the West.

These remarks about the differences in African outlooks and our own could be applied also to differences in the material bases for economic expansion, as we have already indicated. It is perfectly true that the obstacles we have mentioned do not apply to all Africans or to all parts of Africa, but in general it can be said that most Western methods and organizations do not fit the non-Western context of the newly independent countries and that these differ so greatly from one another, or even in some cases (such as India) within a single nation, that the direct application of Western methods to these new areas is inadvisable. Such Western methods might work if native peoples could acquire some of the more basic attitudes that have been the foundation of Western progress. For example, the victory of the West in World War II was attributed to our capacity for rationalization and for scientific method. These in turn rest on the most basic features of the Western outlook and traditions, on the way in which our cognitive system categorizes the world, and the value system we apply to this structure of categories. But our cognitive system is derived from our past heritage, such as our Hebrew ethical system, the Christian heritage (which strangely enough made us accept the reality and the value of the temporal world at the same time that it placed our final goal, achievable through behavior in the world of the flesh, in the eternal world of the spirit), and the lessons of Greek rationalism with its insistence on dealing with the world in a quite artificial system of two-valued logic based on the principle of identity and the law of contradiction. Non-Western peoples who do not find in their own system of cognition any acceptance of the rules of identity or of contradiction do not see reality in terms of two-valued logic, and must make an almost impossible effort to adopt the West's natural tendency to rationalize problems. On this basis, they find it difficult either to rationalize their own emotional positions and thus to control or direct them, or to rationalize (which is to isolate and analyze) their problems and thus to seek solutions for them. Africans, for example, unless they have been thoroughly Westernized, do not make the sharp distinctions we do between the living and the dead, between animate and nonanimate objects, between deity and man, and many other distinctions which our long submission to Greek logic have made almost inevitable to us.

In view of the similarity of the problem faced by the newly independent nations, it may seem curious that they have not shown a greater tendency to cooperate with each other or to attempt to form some kind of common front toward the world. The chief effort to do this has been in the form of a number of meetings of so-called "uncommitted nations" of which the chief was held at Bandung, Indonesia, in 1955, and a number of efforts to move toward some kind of Pan-African system. On the whole, however, this effort toward cooperation has been blocked by three influences: (1) the sensitivity of newly independent nations to preserve this independence intact as long as possible, even to the degree that particularist local interests and rivalries are dominant over common interests; (2) the fact that all these nations need economic aid and technical assistance from the advanced countries, and are, on the whole, in competition with each other to get it; and (3) the tendency of many of the newly independent areas (such as Indonesia or Egypt) to adopt pro-Soviet attitudes in the Cold War leading to efforts by the Soviet Union to infringe upon their basically neutralist policies to persuade them to make a commitment to the Communist side in the Cold War.

In many ways the problems of independence have a distinctly different character in Africa from Asia. In Asia, as is traditional along the Pakistani-Peruvian axis, the structure of societies has been one in which a coalition of army, bureaucracy, landlords, and moneylenders have exploited a great mass of peasants by extortion of taxes, rents, low wages, and high interest rates in a system of such persistence that its basic structure goes back to the Bronze Age empires before 1000 B.C.

In Africa the situation has been quite different, and has generally been in constant flux. This results from a number of influences, of which one is that Africa has been underpopulated and has not developed the kind of land monopolization that supported Asiatic despotism. The dominant social units of African society have been kinship groups: extended families, lineages, clans, and tribes with landownership (generally of little importance) vested in these and often with a fairly wide division between ownership and rights of usufruct. Moreover, land use in Africa has generally been a fallow system, often of the "slash-and-burn" type, in which land is cropped for a few years and then abandoned for an extended period to recover its fertility. Thus agriculture has been on a shifting basis, and peasant life in Africa has been almost as mobile as pastoral activities are, without the permanent localism that is associated with rural villages in Eurasia. Moreover, in Africa tillage of the soil, usually by digging stick rather than by plow, has tended to be carried on by women, usually wives, and the relationship of the agricultural worker to any exploiter has been a matrimonial or family relationship rather than a relationship that was basically economic, as in Eurasia's serfdom, hired laborer, or plantation slavery.

All these features of the basic relationships between men and the land in Africa have restricted the growth of the kind of agrarian superstructure associated with Asiatic despotisms, and left instead a very amorphous and fluctuating system in which no complex exploitative system could be screwed down on the masses of the people because these people were too free to move elsewhere. As a result of this, the kinship groups that are the chief feature of rural Africa are constantly mobile, and even today can tell how their common ancestor, a few generations back, arrived in their residence from some other vague place.

This mobile and transitory character of native African life has been increased by two other historical features of Africa's past: the pastoral intrusions and slave raiding.

The pastoral intrusions arose from the movement into and across Africa of warlike peoples who lived from herds of cattle or horses and imposed their loose rule upon the more peaceful peasant natives. These pastoral intruders have been of two kinds. The first were Bantu cattle herders who derived their way of life from other peoples in northeastern Africa and moved generally south and southwest towa'd Natal and Angola. These include such savage fighting peoples as the Zulus or the Matabeles of Rhodesia.

The second pastoral group has been made up of Arabic or at least Islamized intruders, also from northeastern Africa, who have moved, generally westward across Africa, with horses. These generally followed the grasslands of the Sudan, between the desert and the tropical forest, and are found today as dominant and warlike upper classes in many areas such as northern Nigeria. Both groups of pastoral intruders brought in distinctive social and cultural contributions, including new religious ideas, and have enserfed numbers of the African peasants, as groups of villages or tribes rather than as individuals.

The second major force that has traditionally disrupted African life and prevented it from developing any elaborate social hierarchies or long residence linked to specific areas has been the practice of slave raiding, which goes back to ancient Egypt, was carried on by both kinds of pastoral intruders, and culminated in the devastation of much of Africa in the massive slave-trade raids of the middle nineteenth century, such as were witnessed by Dr. Livingston.

The establishment of European colonial rule over Africa, chiefly after 1880, eventually abolished the slave trade and greatly reduced the influence of the pastoral intruders. But this did not decrease the mobility and transitory characteristic of African life, since any increase in rural stability was more than overbalanced by the extension of commerce and of craft manufactures which led to a drastic growth of towns and the shattering of many of the kinship structures such as lineages and tribes. In fact, one of the most obvious problems brought to Africa by European influence has been the detachment of atomized individuals from the social nexus, based on blood and marriage, that previously guided their lives and determined their systems of values and obligations.

Each imperial power imposed its own patterns on the people under its colonial domination, most obviously in the introduction of its own language. These different patterns and languages remain as dominant forces after independence is achieved, serving to link together the areas with the same colonial past and to separate those with a different colonial experience. In fact, the division of Africa into separate French-speaking, English-speaking, and Portuguese-speaking areas (with all that these differences imply) is now one of the chief obstacles to the creation of any major Pan-African unity.

In very general terms we might say that the British impact on its African territories was largely political, the French was cultural, the Belgian was economic, and the Portuguese was religious.

The obsession of the upper classes of Britain with government and politics was reflected in their colonial policies, which emphasized the introduction of law and order, introduced political and legal systems based on English models, and educated the minority of native peoples who obtained education in the politically dominated training provided for the English upper classes (most educated natives studied political science and law). To this day ex-British colonial areas show this pattern.

The French in Africa talked of their "mission civilisatrice," by which they meant, at a minimum, to offer native peoples the French language with a smattering of French culture. Many natives fell in love with this culture, and with Paris, so that when liberation came they did not, as did the British-trained natives, become obsessed with the spirit of political opposition, but rather showed a desire to continue the extension of French cultural life, especially literature, along with political independence. Today some of the best poetry written in the French language comes from Africans.

The Belgians in the Congo rejected any effort to extend political or cultural life to their native peoples, but instead sought to provide them with skills as trained laborers and to build up a prosperous economic basis for a high native standard of living while at the same time allowing them to get no glimpse of European life, the outside world, political training, or cultural and intellectual ideas. As a result, when independence came to the Congo in 1960, that vast area had one of the highest native standards of living in tropical Africa but had fewer natives who had attended a university or had even traveled abroad than any French or British territory.

The Portuguese were concerned with conversion of natives to Christianity and with little else, believing that their control of their areas could be maintained best if all other kinds of change were kept minimal. They practiced racial equality and were willing to admit to Portuguese citizenship any native who was individually successful in obtaining a Portuguese education, but on the whole they did not encourage even this kind of development.

The background of the whole process of African decolonization was built up in the wartime and early postwar periods, but the trigger on the chain reaction of the decolonization process was the defeat of the Anglo-French effort at Suez because of America and Soviet pressure in October 1956. As might, perhaps, be expected, the process began in a British colony, the Gold Coast, now called Ghana.

The independence of Ghana was a personal achievement of Dr. Kwame Nkrumah, who returned to Accra from an educational process in Pennsylvania and the London School of Economics. The year before, in 1946, the Gold Coast obtained the first British African Legislative Assembly that was allowed a majority of Africans. Nkrumah's agitations, including the founding of a new political party, the Convention People's Party, under his own control, earned him a two-year jail sentence. While he was still in jail, his party won 34 of the 38 seats in the Assembly in the election of 1951; therefore he was released from confinement to take control of the administration. With good will on both sides, a transition period of six years gave Ghana its independence, under Nkrumah's rule, in March 1957.

Within a year of independence, Nkrumah faced the typical problems of postcolonialism that we have mentioned: a rapid fall in cocoa prices upon which Ghana's international trade position depended; disease in the cocoa trees, which required destruction of thousands of trees over the violent protests of their peasant owners; dissension between the pagan, commercial, coastal area, in which the Convention People's Party was based, and the more pastoral, Islamic, remote interior.

Nkrumah soon showed his readiness to handle all problems with ruthless decision. The "sick" cocoa trees were cut down; political opponents were silenced in one way or another; Nkrumah was ballyhooed as the father of all Africans, the unique genius of the African revolution, the mystic symbol of all black men's hopes. A Five-Year Plan for economic development (1959–1964) promised to spend over 92 million dollars. In 1960 the previous British-granted constitution was replaced by a new republican constitution that was amended almost at once by a clause allowing Nkrumah to rule without parliament whenever necessary. The leader's Pan-African hopes were reflected in a clause that permitted "the surrender of the whole or part of the sovereignty of Ghana" to a union of African states. By the end of the same year, political party designations were abolished in Parliament, and the Preventive Detention Act (which allowed Nkrumah to imprison his enemies without charge) was used to arrest the chief members of the political opposition. Ghana embarked on an economic war with the Union of South Africa in protest against the latter's extreme segregation of the races and on a somewhat weaker system of economic reprisals against France in retaliation for its nuclear-explosion tests in the Sahara. Vigorous activities at the United Nations, in African affairs (chiefly in opposition to any Pan-African movement that would not be dominated by Nkrumah), in balancing the two sides of the Cold War while seeking economic aid from both, in establishing a Ghana shipping line defiantly called the "Black Star Line," and in constructing a gigantic hydroelectric and aluminum manufacturing complex on the Volta River, kept Nkrumah's name in the world's press.

Nigeria, the largest territory in the British colonial empire, larger than any European state and four times the size of the United Kingdom, with 35 million inhabitants, did not become free until 1960. The delay was caused by the internal divisions within the territory. These were not unexpected, for the territory was an artificial creation, cut out of the African wild by Lord Lugard just before World War I. It consisted of three regions—North, West, and East—which had no central assembly until 1946, and continued to have diverse interests and attitudes. Each region had a separate government with a joint federal government at Lagos. The Northern Region is Muhammadan, patriarchal, underdeveloped, poor, ignorant, and feudal, ruled by an aristocratic upper group of emirs descended from pastoral conquerors. The Western Region is small but rich and thickly populated with progressive agriculturalists, chiefly Yoruba. The Eastern Region, dominated by the Ibo peoples, tends to dominate the whole federation. There are tribal and religious differences between the three, since the south is pagan, and government of the federation must be by coalition of two regions against the third. American-educated Dr. Nnamdi Azikiwe (known as "Zik") was the first governor-general, functioning as president and the dominant political figure from the Eastern Region, while the prime minister was Sir Abubakar Tafawa Balewa, a Muslim from the Northern Region. The Opposition was led by Chief Obafemi Awolowo of the Western Region. This rather precarious balance of forces was stabilized by the strength of the English-speaking tradition of moderation and rule of law, both much more securely established in Nigeria than in Ghana, and by the industrious, alert, and balanced character of Nigeria's chief tribal groups. The economy was also better balanced than that of many African states, with a productive agriculture as well as varied mineral resources.

The key to Africa's future may rest with the success of former French Africa, since this group seems to provide a nucleus on which the more moderate forces on the continent may congregate. The chief difficulty from which they suffer is that most are arid and all are poor (compared to the Congo or Nigeria).

The impact of war was much more significant in French Africa than in British Africa, because of the defeat of France and the fact that the supporters of De Gaulle's resistance, rather than of Pétain's pseudo-Fascism, controlled these territories during much of the war. Such control could be sustained only with the support of the African population, which was loyally given, although few rewards came in return for more than a decade after the war. Then freedom came swiftly, in sequence to the military disasters in Indochina in 1954 and the rising disaster in Algeria, rather than from the events or struggles in Black Africa itself.

The first effort was not toward independence but toward closer union with France, by incorporating the African territories in an elaborate federal structure, the French Union, which gave the Africans representation and even cabinet posts in Paris. One of the incidental consequences of this largely transitory structure was that the neutralism of the African end of the structure tended to spread to the metropolitan end in Paris. At the same time, American support of independence for colonial areas, at a time when Paris was seeking to strengthen its African connections, was one more in a series of American actions that drove France, and especially De Gaulle, toward a neutral position for Paris itself.

The French Union was still in process of being established in 1958, after having lost Indochina in 1954, Morocco and Tunis in 1956, when the Fourth French Republic disintegrated beneath the strain of the Algerian crisis, and De Gaulle came in with his constitution for the Fifth Republic. This provided a federal system by which essential powers were reserved to the central authority and other powers devolved upon the "autonomous" member states. The key "Community" functions reserved to France included foreign affairs, defense, currency, common economic and financial policy, control of strategic materials, and (with certain exceptions) higher education, justice, external transportation and communications.

' The new constitution was presented to the overseas areas of France with the opportunity to accept or reject it, but with little expectation that any area would reject it because of their need for French economic air and other expenditures of federal funds. Sékou Touré, of Guinea, however, persuaded his area to vote against ratification and was, in retaliation by De Gaulle, instantly ejected from the French Community, and its political and financial support (about $20 million a year) was stopped. The newly independent and outcast area sought support in Moscow, spreading panic in other capitals at this opening of the African scene to Soviet penetration. For about five years, Guinea sought an alternative to the French system, established an authoritarian one-party Leftish regime, signed an act of "union" with Ghana (a meaningless agreement that brought Touré a $28 million loan from Nkrumah), and welcomed Soviet aid and Communist technicians to Conakry. Guinea recognized East Germany, welcomed influences from Red China, accepted American offers of counteraid, and nationalized all schools, churches, and many French-owned business enterprises. For a while, a possible union of Ghana, Guinea, and the Mali Republic (former French Sudan), signed in 1961, threatened to form a "Union of African States," but this hope faded, along with the anticipation of any substantial Soviet aid or assistance, and Guinea, by 1963, was in process of working its way back into the French African system.

The Guinea exodus from the French Community in 1958, regretted by both sides within a few years, opened the way to independence for all French Africa. Senegal and the Sudanese Republic, linked together briefly as the Mali Republic, obtained freedom in April 1960, and started a flood of declarations of independence led by Madagascar (Malgache Republic). This political disintegration of the French areas in Africa raised at once two acute problems: (1) What would be their relationship with France, a connection that had brought French Africa over two billion dollars in French development funds in the 1947–1958 period? and (2) What arrangements could be made between the newly independent states to prevent the Balkanization of Africa, with its resulting inability to handle problems of transportation, communications, public health, river development, and such, which transcend small local areas?

To answer the first question, a French constitutional law of June 1960 changed the French Community to a contractual association. Fourteen French African states signed a multitude of individual agreements with France that recognized their full sovereignty on the international scene but established "cooperation" with France over a wide range of economic, financial, cultural, and political relationships. Thus by voluntary agreement, French control along the general lines of the existing *status quo* was preserved.

The effort to prevent Balkanization by some sort of federal arrangement for the French African areas was prevented by the objections of Ivory Coast and of Gabon. The former was the wealthiest of the eight French Western African states, while Gabon was the richest of the four French Equatorial African states. This opposition broke up the Mali union of Senegal and Soudan in 1960, and the latter, taking the name Mali to itself, drifted off toward cooperation with Guinea. This disintegration of French Africa was stopped only because of growing anxiety at the efforts of Ghana's Nkrumah to form an opposed Pan-African bloc of a Leftish tinge. This effort gave rise to the "Union of Independent African States" and the "All-African Peoples' Conferences."

The Union of Independent African States arose from the Pan-African dreams of the late George Padmore and was organized by him for Nkrumah. Its first meeting, at Accra in April 1958, had representatives of the eight states then independent in Africa (Ethiopia, Ghana, Liberia, Libya, Morocco, Sudan, Tunisia, and the United Arab Republic). They demanded an end to French military operations in Algeria and immediate independence for all African territories. Three subsequent meetings in 1959–1960 advanced no further, except to attack the establishment of racial segregation ("apartheid") in South Africa, and Nigeria blocked efforts to take immediate steps toward a United States of Africa in June 1960.

The All-African People's Conferences, also sponsored by Nkrumah, were great mass conventions of labor unions, youth groups, political parties, and other organizations from all Africa, including nonindependent areas. They achieved little beyond the usual denunciations of colonialism, apartheid, and the Algerian war. Three of these conferences were held at Accra, Tunis, and Conakry in 1958–1960.

In opposition to these Ghana-inspired movements, in late 1960, Dr. Félix Houphouet-Boigny, the political leader of Ivory Coast, one-time French cabinet minister and French spokesman at the United Nations, took steps to organize a French-centered union of African states. Called the "Brazzaville Twelve," after their second meeting at Brazzaville, French Congo, in December 1960, these formed a loose organization for cooperation and parallel action in Africa, the United Nations, and the world. In the United Nations they established a bloc to vote as a unit from October 1960. At the same time, they began to work closely as a group with a number of technical, economic, educational, and research organizations that had grown up under the United Nations, or with international sponsorship to deal with African problems. Of the large number of these, we need mention only the Commission for Technical Cooperation in Africa South of the Sahara (head office in London) and its advisory council, the Scientific Council for Africa South of the Sahara (head office in Belgian Congo), the Foundation for Mutual Assistance in Africa South of the Sahara (office in Accra).

As we have said, the Ghana-Guinea Union of May 1959 was expanded, with the accession of Mali in July 1961, into the pompously named Union of African States (UAS). At Brazzaville, in December 1960, six French territories of West Africa and four of Equatorial Africa joined with the Cameroons Federation and the Malgache Republic to form the "Brazzaville Twelve" (officially entitled Union of African and Malagasy States, or UAMS). At a conference at Casablanca in January 1961, the UAS moved a step further by forming rather tenuous links with Morocco, the United Arab Republic, and the provisional government of Algeria. Four months later, at Monrovia, the UAMS formed a more stable and homogeneous grouping of twenty, by adding to the Brazzaville group Liberia, Nigeria, Togo, Sierra Leone, Ethiopia, Somalia, Libya (which had previously been at Casablanca), and Tunisia. This represented a considerable victory over the UAS group, and was the result of several influences: a number of African leaders, led by President Tubman of Liberia, objected to Nkrumah's efforts to introduce the Cold War into Africa and to his extravagant propaganda, controversy, and cult of personality within the African context; moreover, the Casablanca grouping was paralyzed by the rivalry between Nkrumah and Nasser and by the non-African orientation of the Muslim North Africa members, who constantly sought to drag the African states into non-African issues, such as the Arab hatred of Israel.

The UAMS group has eschewed these issues, has sought to avoid controversy and propaganda, and has played down the anti-imperialist, anti-Portuguese, anti-South African issues which rouse such enthusiasm but achieve so little in mass assemblies of Africans. The UAMS also, unlike the UAS group, has rejected any efforts to interfere in the domestic affairs of its African members and neighbors. Instead it has tended to work quietly on rather technical questions and has been satisfied with moderate agreements. Its chief meetings, usually twice a year, have assembled the chiefs of the member states, with a different host city on each occasion. Agreements reached at these high level conferences are then generally implemented by subsequent meetings of specialized or technical experts. The Union's concerns have been economic and social rather than political or ideological, and its approach to its problems has been generally conciliatory, tolerant, empirical, relatively democratic, pro-Western, and, above all, tentative. Most of its achievements have resulted from months of careful testing of the ground and have usually been considered at several of its "summit" conferences. Its charter of Union, for example, was not signed until the fourth conference, at Tananarive, in September 1961. Its mechanisms of operation, beyond the semiannual meetings of chiefs of state, consists of a secretariat and secretary-general at Cotonou, Dahomey; a Defense Union consisting of a council of the twelve defense ministers and a general staff and military secretariat at Ouagadougou, Volta; the Organization of African-Malgache Economic Cooperation stationed at Yaounde, Cameroon; an African-Malgache Union of Posts and Telecommunications consisting of the twelve ministers concerned with these and a central office at Brazzaville; a joint "Air Afrique" airline, associated with "Air France"; and other, similar, organizations concerned with development, shipping, research, and other activities. Several agreements have been signed establishing judicial, financial, and commercial cooperation. The whole system has an independent budget financed by a fixed percentage grant from each state's budget to the common fund. The whole relationship has formed the chief element of stability in African problems, has retained its close contacts with France, and has formed the core of a moderate group among the growing multitude of neutrals at the United Nations. Its possible implications for the future political organization of Africa, if not for a wider area, will be considered in the next chapter.

XX

TRAGEDY AND HOPE:
THE FUTURE
IN PERSPECTIVE

The Unfolding of Time

The United States and the Middle-Class Crisis

European Ambiguities

Conclusion

I N an age of change and competing doubts, there is one thing of
which we can be certain: the world is changing and will continue
to change. But there is no consensus on the direction of such change.
Human beings are basically conservative, in the sense that they expect
and wish to continue to jog along in the same old patterns. Accordingly,
they tend to regard most changes as regrettable, although one might get
the impression, in a bustling and dynamic place like the United States,
that men preferred change to stability.

It is perfectly true that Americans now have change built into the pattern of their lives, so that saving and investment and, in general, the flows
of claims on wealth (what most of us call "money") now go in directions
that make constant change almost inevitable. Summer has hardly arrived
before summer dresses have been sold out, autumn clothing is beginning
to arrive on the dealers' racks, and extensive plans are already in process
to make next summer's clothing (which goes on sale in the southern
resorts in winter) quite different. This year's cars are not yet available for
sale when the manufacturers are planning changed versions for next year's
models. And urban commercial buildings are still new when plans for
remodeling, or even total replacement, are already stirring in someone's
mind.

In such an age the sensible man can only reconcile himself to the fact:
change is inevitable. But few men—average or exceptional—feel any
competency in deciding the direction that change will take. Forecasting
can be attempted only by extrapolating recent changes into the future,
but this is a risky business, since there is never any certainty that present
directions will be maintained.

In attempting this risky procedure, we shall continued to divide society into six aspects, falling into the three major areas of the patterns of
power, rewards, and outlooks. The area of power is largely, but not exclusively, concerned with military and political arrangements; the area
of rewards is similarly concerned with economic and social arrangements;
and the area of outlooks is concerned with patterns that might be termed
religious and intellectual. Naturally, all these are different, and even dras-

tically different, from one society to another, and even, to a lesser extent, between countries, and areas within countries. For the sake of simplicity, we shall be concerned, in this chapter, with these patterns in Europe and the United States, although, as usual, we shall not hesitate to make comparisons with other cultures, especially with the Soviet Union.

The Unfolding of Time

The political conditions of the latter half of the twentieth century will continue to be dominated by the weapons situation, for, while politics consists of much more than weapons, the nature, organization, and control of weapons is the most significant of the numerous factors that determine what happens in political life. Surely weapons will continue to be expensive and complex. This means that they will increasingly be the tools of professionalized, if not mercenary, forces. All of past history shows that the shift from a mass army of citizen-soldiers to a smaller army of professional fighters leads, in the long run, to a decline of democracy. When weapons are cheap and easy to obtain and to use, almost any man may obtain them, and the organized structure of the society, such as the state, can obtain no better weapons than the ordinary, industrious, private citizen. This very rare historical condition existed about 1880, but is now only a dim memory, since the weapons obtainable by the state today are far beyond the pocketbook, understanding, or competence of the ordinary citizen.

When weapons are of the "amateur" type of 1880, as they were in Greece in the fifth century B.C., they are widely possessed by citizens, power is similarly dispersed, and no minority can compel the majority to yield to its will. With such an "amateur weapons system" (if other conditions are not totally unfavorable), we are likely to find majority rule and a relatively democratic political system. But, on the contrary, when a period can be dominated by complex and expensive weapons that only a few persons can afford to possess or can learn to use, we have a situation where the minority who control such "specialist" weapons can dominate the majority who lack them. In such a society, sooner or later, an authoritarian political system that reflects the inequality in control of weapons will be established.

At the present time, there seems to be little reason to doubt that the specialist weapons of today will continue to dominate the military picture into the foreseeable future. If so, there is little reason to doubt that authoritarian rather than democratic political regimes will dominate the world into the same foreseeable future. To be sure, traditions and other factors may keep democratic systems, or at least democratic forms, in many areas, such as the United States or England. To us, brought up as we were on a democratic ideology, this may seem very tragic, but a number of perhaps redeeming features in this situation may well be considered.

For one, our society, Western Civilization, is almost fifteen hundred years old, and was democratic in political action for less than two hundred of these years (or even half of that, in strict truth). A period that is not democratic in its political structure is not necessarily bad, and may well be one in which people can live a rich and full social or intellectual life whose value may be even more significant than a democratic political or military structure. Of equal significance is the fact that a period with a professionalized army may well be, as it was in the eighteenth century, a period of limited warfare seeking limited political aims, if for no other reason than that professionalized forces are less willing to kill and be killed for remote and total objectives.

The amateur weapons of the late nineteenth century made possible the mass citizen armies that fought the American Civil War and both of this century's world wars. Such mass armies could not be offered financial rewards for risking their lives, but they could be offered idealistic, extreme, and total goals that would inspire them to a willingness to die, and to kill: ending slavery, making a world safe for democracy, ending tyranny, spreading, or at least saving, "the American way of life," offered such goals. But they led to a total warfare, seeking total victory and unconditional surrender. As a result, each combatant country came to feel that its way of life, or at least its regime, was at stake in the conflict, and could hardly be expected to survive defeat. Thus they felt compulsion to fight yet more tenaciously. The result was ruthless wars of extermination such as World War II.

With a continued professionalization of the armed services, caused by the increasing complexity of weapons, we may look forward with some assurance to less and less demand for total wars using total weapons of mass destruction to achieve unconditional surrender and unlimited goals. The rather naïve American idea that war aims involve the destruction of the enemy's regime and the imposition on the defeated people of a democratic system with a prosperous economy (such as they have never previously known) will undoubtedly be replaced by the idea that the enemy regime must be maintained, perhaps in a modified form, so that we have some government with whom we can negotiate in order to obtain our more limited aims (which caused the conflict) and thus to lower the level of conflict as rapidly as possible consistent with the achievement of our aims. The nature of such "controlled conflict" will be described in a moment.

The movement toward professionalization of the armed forces and the resulting lowering of the intensity of conflict is part of a much larger process deriving from the nuclear and Superpower stalemate between the Soviet Union and the United States. The danger of nuclear destruction will continue and become, if anything, more horrifying, but will, for this very reason, become a more remote and less likely probability. In the late 1960's the United States will have about 1,700 vehicles (missiles and SAC planes) targeted on the Soviet bloc; by the 1970's this will rise to about 2,400. Moreover, by 1970, 650 of these will be Polaris missiles on our 41 nuclear submarines, which cannot be found and eliminated by any Soviet missile counterstrike, once they are submerged at sea. The great value of the Polaris over its land-based rivals, such as Minuteman, is that the Soviet Union knows where the latter are and can countertarget on them. This means that the MM's must be fired out of their silos before the Soviet warheads, seeking them out to destroy them, can arrive fifteen minutes after takeoff. Such a precarious position encourages nervous anticipation and possibility of precipitate action, capable of beginning a war no one really wants. Thus, on an enormously greater scale, we have something like the von Schlieffen Plan that made it necessary for Germany to attack France in 1914 when there was no real issue justifying resort to war between them. The Polaris missiles at sea, since they cannot be found and counterforced, can be delayed, without need to strike first or even to strike second in immediate retaliation, but can be held off for hours, days, and weeks, compelling the Soviet to negotiate even after the original Soviet strike has devastated America's cities. Thus the Soviet Union cannot win in a nuclear exchange, even if they make the first strike.

The reverse is also true. In the mid-1960's the Soviet Union has vehicles able to deliver up to six hundred or seven hundred nuclear warheads on the United States and perhaps seven hundred or eight hundred on our European allies. Their warheads are larger than ours (with up to 100-megaton ICBM's, while our largest are 9 MT). In spite of the fact that their missile sites are poorly organized, with missiles, fuel, crews, and warheads widely scattered, so that they are at least twelve hours from takeoff even in their fourth stage of readiness, the inaccuracy of our counterforce missiles is so great that we could not eliminate all their missiles, even if we made a first strike with no warning. It would require only about 200 Soviet warheads to devastate our cities totally, and an American strike at Soviet missile bases delivered without warning would leave almost that number not eliminated; these would be free to make a retaliatory strike at us. Moreover, the Soviets have several dozen Polaris-type submarines that can fire four missiles each from surfaced positions. Many of these would survive an American unannounced first strike.

All this means that we are as much deterred by the Soviet missile threat as they must be by our much greater threat. Such deterrence has nothing to do with the relative size of the numbers of missiles possessed by two countries. It rests on whether an unannounced first strike would leave surviving enough missiles for a retaliatory strike capable of inflicting unacceptable damage. This is now the situation on both sides, and the existence of Polaris-type missiles makes it impossible to avoid this by striving for greater numbers of missiles, for larger warheads able to obliterate wide areas, or for greater accuracy that would increase the statistical possibility of eliminating enemy missiles on first strike. Thus no one will wish to make such a strike. Possibly for this reason, about a year after the Cuban missile crisis, the Soviet Union ceased to work on new missile bases and accepted its permanent inferiority to the United States. But the mutual veto on the use of missiles, the nuclear stalemate, remained.

This stalemate between the two Superpowers on the use of nuclear weapons also extended to their use of lesser, nonnuclear, weapons, so that the nuclear stalemate became a Superpower stalemate. This meant that much of the power of the Soviet Union and the United States, and not merely their nuclear power, was neutralized to a considerable degree, since each feared to use its nonnuclear powers for fear they might escalate into nuclear conflict. This meant that the use of nuclear tactical weapons and the use even of conventional tactical weapons were inhibited to an undetermined degree by the presence of nuclear strategic weapons no one wanted to see used. The costs of using nuclear tactical weapons are so great that it is very doubtful if they are worth the cost. For example, the Western Powers lack the conventional forces to stop any intrusion of the great masses of Soviet ground forces if these began to drive westward in an attempt to conquer Germany. The West is committed to oppose such an effort. Since it is very doubtful that the NATO forces could oppose this successfully by using only conventional weapons, there would be great pressure to use the nuclear tactical weapons that NATO forces in Europe possess. It has been estimated that the chief targets of such nuclear tactical weapons would be bridges and similar narrow passages, in an effort to close these to Soviet advances. But it seems clear that if these passages were closed and the bridges destroyed, the advance of the Soviet armies (in armored and mechanized divisions) would be held up only a few weeks at most, and up to 50 million Germans would be killed from the blast and side effects of the use of nuclear weapons. At such a cost, the Germans would probably prefer not to be defended.

In fact, it appears increasingly likely that fewer and fewer advanced people will regard large-scale war as an effective method of getting anything. What could a people obtain through war that they could not obtain with greater certainty and less effort in some other way? Indeed, the very idea of winning a general war is now almost unimaginable. We do not even know what we mean by "win." Whatever Germany, Japan, and Italy sought from World War II, they would surely not have obtained by winning; yet they obtained the most significant parts of it by losing. Glory, power, and wealth may all be obtained with less effort and greater certainty by nonwarlike methods. As science and technology advance, making war more horrible, they also make it possible to achieve any aims at which war might be directed by other, nonviolent, methods.

The relationships between political organizations (to us, states) are chiefly political relations, based on power and concerned with influencing the policies of other such entities. We have tended to see such relationships in dichotomies, especially the sharp contrast between violent and nonviolent methods of war and peace. In fact, however, methods of influencing policy form a spectrum without any significant real discontinuities, and range from all-out nuclear warfare at the upper end, down through tactical nuclear weapons and conventional weapons, then through various levels of nonviolent political, social, and economic pressures, to levels of peaceful persuasion and reciprocal favors, to economic grants and even gifts.

When Khrushchev renounced the use of both nuclear war and conventional violence, and promised to defeat the West by peaceful competition, he was dividing the spectrum into three levels, but in fact it is a continuous spectrum with 100-megaton bombs at the upper end and Olympic Games, International Geophysical Years, and foreign economic aid at the other end. When Khrushchev made his statement, he was convinced that the Soviet Union could outperform the United States on the level of peaceful competition because it could, in his opinion, overcome the American lead in the race for economic development and that, as a result, the Socialist way of life would become the model for emulation by the uncommitted nations. The failures of Socialist agricultural production in Russia, Cuba, China, and elsewhere, and the great triumphs of non-Socialist economies in Japan, Europe, and the United States, soon revealed, even to Khrushchev's supporters, that the Soviet chances of triumphing over the West by peaceful competition were very small. Conceivably this might force the Kremlin to raise its anti-American activities to a higher level of conflict, even to the level of violence, although probably through surrogates and satellites and in third-party areas (such as southeast Asia, Africa, or Latin America).

To prevent such a raising of the level of Soviet-American conflict, it might be worth while for the West to consider the possibility of yielding the Kremlin some victories on the lower, nonviolent, levels, especially if this could be achieved at little cost to us. It might also be worth while for us to consider what must be Russia's real goals. Obviously preservation of the Communist regime must have a higher level of desirability to Moscow than Castro's success in Cuba or the Kremlin's control of Budapest. Thus to the Politburo, now as earlier under Stalin, continued control in the Kremlin has a higher priority than world revolution. The West can help Russia's rulers get what they really want (their own domestic power), and at small cost, in return for what they can want only secondarily (the expansion of Communism). Thus, like Stalin, they can be forced back to "Socialism in one country." With rising domestic demand for higher standards of living in Russia, and growing evidence that these are more likely to be obtained under a non-Socialist or mixed economy, they could be forced back to "non-Socialism in one country," if this strengthened their own control in the Kremlin, as it well might do.

In fact, some such process is already under way. The Soviet Union has always been more conservative and less extremist in international matters than it appeared or sounded. Much of Khrushchev's truculence, even abroad, was for domestic rather than for foreign consumption. A recent study of 29 crisis situations in foreign affairs involving the Soviet Union in the 1945–1963 period shows that they were aggressive in only four, were cautious in eleven, and were more cautious than aggressive in fourteen. The four aggressive ones were concerned with Berlin, Hungary, the U-2 incident, and Cuba. The study showed that only 8 of the 29 crises were initiated by the Soviet Union, while 11 were initiated by the United States. The general conclusion of the study was that Soviet policy would grow increasingly conservative, since they were primarily concerned with state building and retaining what they have already achieved.

The chief uncertainty of continuing this process arises from the problem of political succession in the Kremlin, a major unpredictable factor. Here the chances are two out of three that the trend would continue in Soviet policy, since the one case of a successor who would reverse the more conservative policy is outbalanced by the two cases of a successor who would retain it or of a disputed succession that would make an active Soviet foreign policy difficult. The fact remains that there are in the Soviet Union no institutional safeguards *for any policy*, just as there are none for the succession. But it is clear that pressures to continue a more moderate foreign policy will be strong, under any successor, now that the Russians are increasingly convinced that their present achievements are worth keeping, as the pressures for domestic improvements continue, and as their future hopes and expectations along these lines become more clearly envisaged.

In this way the Superpower neutralization (and the included nuclear stalemate) will continue into the future. From this flow three consequences:

1. Movement of Soviet-Western rivalry down to lower, less violent, levels of conflict and competition.

2. Continued disintegration of the two Superblocs, from the inability of the chief Power in each to bring force against its allies because of the

need to accept growing diversity within each bloc in order to retain as much as possible the appearance of unity within the bloc. This process is well illustrated by Moscow's difficulties with China, Albania, and now Romania, or by Washington's troubles with De Gaulle or with its Latin American allies.

3. A growing independence of the neutrals and uncommitted nations because of their ability to act freely in the troubled waters stirred up by the Soviet-American confrontation.

These changes, rooted in weapon developments and technological changes, have less obvious political implications. Policy and politics are concerned with methods of influencing the behavior of others to obtain cooperation, consent or, at least, acquiescence. In our Western world, power has been based to a significant extent on force (that is, weapons), and to a lesser degree on economic rewards and ideological appeal. In other cultures, such as in Africa, politics has been based to a considerable extent on other considerations, such as kinship, social reciprocity, and religion. Changes in weapons within the Western states system have brought about changes in political patterns and organization that threaten to cause profound changes in political life and probably in the Western states system.

For many centuries, from the ninth century to the twentieth, the increasing offensive power of Western weapons systems has made it possible to compel obedience over wider and wider areas and over larger numbers of peoples. Accordingly, political organizations (such as the state) have been able to rule over larger areas, and thus have become larger in size and fewer in numbers in our Western world. In this way, the political development of Europe over the last millennium has seen thousands of feudal areas coalesce into hundreds of principalities, and these into scores of dynastic monarchies, and, finally, into a dozen or more national states. The national state, its size measured in hundreds of miles, was based, to a considerable extent, on the fact that the weapons system of the nineteenth century, founded on citizen soldiers with handguns and moved (or supplied) by railroads and wagons, could apply force over hundreds of miles. This, in many cases, proved to be approximately the same size as the European linguistic and cultural groupings of peoples; and, accordingly, it became easy to base the popular appeal for allegiance to the state structure upon nationalism (that is, upon this common language and cultural tradition). Languages and cultures covering lesser areas than those that could be ruled over by the existing nineteenth-century system of weapons and transport, such as the Welsh, the Bretons, the Provençals, the Basques, Catalonians, Sicilians, Ukrainians, and others, by failing to become centers for one of these dominant weapons-organized structures, went into political eclipse.

As the technology of weapons, transportation, communications, and propaganda continued to develop, it became possible to compel obedience over areas measured in thousands (rather than hundreds) of miles and thus over distances greater than those occupied by existing linguistic and cultural groups. It thus became necessary to appeal for allegiance to the state on grounds wider than nationalism. This gave rise, in the 1930's and 1940's, to the idea of continental blocs and the ideololgical state (replacing the national state). Embraced by Hitler and the Japanese, and (much less consciously) by the United States and Britain, this growing pattern of political organization and appeal to allegiance was smashed in World War II. But during that war technological developments increased the area over which obedience could be compelled and consent obtained. By 1950, Dulles and others talked of a two-Power world, as if consent could be obtained by only two Powers, and as if each were hemispherical in scope. They were not. For, while the area of power organizations had expanded, they had not become hemispherical, and new counterbalancing factors had appeared that threatened to reverse the whole process.

Instead of power in the 1950's being concentrated in two centers, each hemispherical in scope and able to compel obedience over distances of 10,000 miles, the Superpowers could compel obedience over distances in the range of 6,000 to 8,000 miles, leaving a considerable zone between them. In addition the neutralization of their real power in their Superpower confrontation made this zone between more obvious, and weakened their ability to obtain obedience to extreme demands even within 6,000 miles of their power centers (which were situated, let us say, in Omaha and Kuibyshev). In this power gap between the less than hemispherical Superpowers appeared the neutrals of the Buffer Fringe.

But there was more to the situation than this geographical limitation. The nature of power was also changing, although few noticed this. The role of force in politics had been effective to the degree that it was able to influence the minds and wills of men. But the new weapons, in seeking increased range, had become weapons of mass destruction rather than instruments of persuasion. If the victims of such weapons are killed, they can neither obey nor consent. Thus the new weapons have become instruments, not of political power, but of destruction of all power organizations. This explains the growing reluctance by all concerned to use them. Furthermore their range and areas of impact make them most ineffective against individual men and especially against the minds of individual men. And, finally, in an ideological state it is the minds of men that must be the principal targets. Any organization is coordinated both by patterned relationships and by ideology and morale. If the former become increasingly threatened by weapons of destruction, the organization can survive by becoming decentralized, with less emphasis on organizational relationships and more emphasis on morale and outlook. They thus become increasingly amorphous and invulnerable to modern weapons of destruction. The peoples of Africa are, for this reason among others, not susceptible to compulsion by megaton bombs. And Western peoples or Soviet peoples can become less susceptible by becoming Africanized.

This process has not gone very far yet, but it is already observable, especially among the younger generation of the United States, Europe, and the Soviet Union. To the young in all three of these areas there is a growing, if quiet, skepticism of any general abstract appeal to allegiance and loyalty, and a growing concern with concrete, interpersonal relationships with local groups of friends and intimates.

There is still another element in this complex picture. This is also related to weapons. The past history of weapons over thousands of years shows that the reason political units have grown larger in certain periods has been because of the increased power of the offensive in the dominant weapons systems, and that periods in which defensive weapons became dominant have been those in which political units remained small in area or even became smaller. The growing power of castles in the period about 1100 B.C. or about A.D. 900 made political power so decentralized and made power units so small that all power became private power, and the state disappeared as a common form of political organization. Thus arose the so-called "Dark Ages" about 1000 B.C. or A.D. 1000.

We do not expect any such extreme growth of defensive power in the future, but *any increase* in defensive weapon power would stop the growth in size of power areas and would, in time, reverse this tendency. There would be thus a proliferation in numbers and a decrease in size of such power units, a tendency already evident, in the past twenty years, in the great increase in the number of United Nations member states. No drastic increase in the defensive power of existing weapons can yet be demonstrated in any conclusive way, but the rising ability of guerrilla forces to maintain their functional autonomy shows definite limits on the offensive power of contemporary weapons. Any drastic increase in the ability of guerrilla forces to function would indicate such an increase in the defensive power of existing weapons, and this, in turn, would indicate an ability to resist centralized authorities and thus an ability to maintain and defend small-group freedoms.

Such a rise in the strength of defensive weapons, with a consequent decentralization of political power, would require a number of other changes, such as a decentralization of economic production. This probably seems very unlikely to us who live in the frantic economic expansion of the electronic revolution and the space race, but it is at least conceivable. Such a change would require a plentiful, dispersed source of industrial energy and the use of plentiful and widely scattered materials for industrial fabrication. These do not seem to be completely unlikely possibilities. For example, a shift from our present use of fossil fuels as a chief energy source to the use of the sun's energy directly in many small local energy accumulators might provide a plentiful supply of decentralized energy. More remote might be use of the tides, or of differential ocean temperatures, or even of the winds. Possibly some development in the use of nuclear energy, or, above all, some method for cheap separation of the oxygen and hydrogen in ordinary water that could release energy, perhaps through fuel cells, as they recombine.

Such a decentralized energy source, if developed, could be used to build up a decentralized industrial system using cellulose or silicon as raw materials to produce an economy of plastics and glass products (including fiber glass). These two raw materials found in vegetation and sand are among the most common substances in the world. On such a basis, with the proper development of guerrilla weapon tactics, the costs of enforcing centralized orders in local areas might rise so high that a considerable process of political decentralization and local autonomies (including local liberties) could arise, thus reversing the process of political centralization that has continued in the Western tradition for about a thousand years.

In this process, a significant role might be played by the appearance of a major, nonnuclear, deterrence. This already exists, but is not publicly discussed because it presents such a threat to the existing world political structure. It rests in the existence of biological and chemical weapons (BCW) that can be just as devastating as nuclear weapons and do not require a rich or elaborate industrial system for their manufacture or use. Thus they might be more readily available or usable by the less advanced industrial nations, but are not being researched by such nations to any considerable degree because they might also be more effective as weapons against such backward nations. At the same time, the more advanced nations also hesitate to publicize the existence of such weapons because there is no assurance that they might not, while being readily available to backward nations, still be relatively effective against advanced nations.

Much of the significance of this relationship can be seen in regard to Red China. This potential enemy has already exploded some kind of a nuclear device and will have a nuclear weapon in the next few years, but this offers little potential danger to us since they will have no effective long-range delivery vehicle. On the other hand, their threat with this against our allies, such as Japan or the Philippines, or their ability even now with their mass armies to threaten our interests in India, Southeast Asia, or Korea, is potentially high. Against such a threat, our nuclear missiles are relatively weak, because China is too dispersed and decentralized to offer vital targets. On the other hand, China's vulnerability to the threat of biological warfare is very large. This explains their hysterical attacks on American "germ warfare" during the Korean War. The word puts them into a panic, and rightly so, since they are critically vulnerable to such weapons used by us. The virus for wheat rust and rice blast, in varieties especially virulent on Chinese-type plants, can be produced in large amounts relatively easily at costs well below $40 a pound. Spread on the fields at the proper time in the annual growing cycle, these would destroy up to 75 percent of these crops. And there is no effective defense. In consequence the Chinese food intake would be cut from about 2,200 calories per person a day, not much above the subsistence level, to about 1,300 calories a day. If the Chinese permitted this, they would have few people strong enough to work at the defense effort, either in the combat areas or in industrial plants. If they tried to keep the food intake of more indispensable defenders up by strict rationing, leaving nothing for many children, old people, and women, they would suffer about 50 million deaths from malnutrition within a year. The armed forces, still largely of peasant origin, would not allow a rationing system that doomed their families in the villages, and would turn against the regime, especially if an American offer to feed the Chinese on American surplus food after a Chinese surrender were broadcast to the Chinese people.

The danger of such weapons becoming common, or even becoming commonly known, among the people of the world, including the less developed nations, is very great, opening an opportunity to all kinds of political blackmail or even to merely irresponsible threats. The parallel danger from new weapons of chemical warfare are even more horrifying. One of the nerve gases now currently available in the United States is so potent that a small drop of it on an individual's unbroken skin can cause death in a few seconds. Moreover, many of these BCW weapons are cheap to make, and easier to make than to control. Most can be made in any well-equipped kitchen or ordinary laboratory, with the chief restriction arising from the difficult safety precautions. But if the latter could be handled, and if delivery systems (which in some cases need be no more than men walking by fields or urban reservoirs) could be obtained, the deterrent effect of BCW weapons might be much greater than that of nuclear weapons now is, and would be much less predictable and forseeable, since they would not be restricted, as the nuclear threat is, to heavily industrialized nations. This might well contribute toward the decentralization of power already mentioned.

Another significant element in this complex picture is the convergence toward parallel paths of the United States and the Soviet Union. This is, of course, something that rabid partisans of either side will refuse to recognize. It arises from three directions: (1) there is an absolute convergence of interests between the two states, as will be indicated in a moment; (2) the structures of the two countries are, to some extent, changing in similar ways; and (3) as the only Superpowers able to inflict or receive instant annihilation, these two countries, to some extent, stand apart from other states and in a class together. The last point is almost obvious, since it must be clear that only these two are prepared to engage in a race to the moon or have an almost insatiable demand for mathematicians or space scientists, or are looked to by impoverished neutrals as obligated to provide economic assistance to the latters' ambitions.

The converging of interests of the two Superpowers arises largely from the other two factors. These common interests include a wide variety of items, such as restricting the proliferation of nuclear weapons to additional states, establishing restrictions on the economic demands of neutral nations, especially by refusing to allow one Superpower to be bid against the other; the ending of nuclear testing, the slowing up of the space race, the approaching domination of the United Nations by the growing majority of small and backward countries, the increasing aggressiveness of Red China, the unification of Germany, the acceleration of the population explosion in backward areas, and many others.

Along with this convergence of interests is the growing parallelism of structure: (1) In spite of the great difference in the theories and the appearances of political life in the two countries, each is increasingly reaching its most fundamental decisions, not through party politics or by decision in a political assembly, but by the shifting pressures of great lobbying blocs acting upon each other by largely hidden contacts carried on behind the scenes. (2) These pressures are chiefly concerned with the allotment of economic resources, through fiscal and budgetary mechanisms, among three competing sectors of the economy concerned with consumption, governmental expenditures (chiefly defense), and capital investment. (3) Socially, both societies are undergoing a similar circulation of elites in which education is the chief doorway to social advancement and is crowded with applicants from the lower (but not lowest) stratum of society (equivalent to the petty bourgeoisie or lower middle classes) but is receiving relatively fewer successful applicants from the upper (but not uppermost) group whose parents are already established in the prevalent structure. (4) In both countries trained experts and technicians, as a consequence of this educational process, are replacing political figures or other social groups, especially political specialists. In both, the military leaders, although qualified for supreme influence by their possession of power, are held at secondary levels by personal manipulations. (5) In both countries there is a growing intellectual skepticism toward authority, accepted ideologies, and established slogans, replaced by a rising emphasis upon the need for satisfactory small-group, interpersonal relations.

As a result of all the complex interrelationships of weapons and politics that we have mentioned up to this point, it seems very likely that the international relations of the future will shift from the world we have known, in which war was epidemic and total, to one in which conflict is endemic and controlled. The ending of total warfare means the ending of war for unlimited aims (unconditional surrender, total victory, destruction' of the opponent's regime and social system), fought with weapons of total destruction and a total mobilization of resources, including men, to a condition of constant, flexible, controlled conflict with limited, specific, and shifting aims, sought by limited application of diverse pressures applied against any other state whose behavior we wish to influence.

Such controlled conflict would involve a number of changes in our attitudes and behavior:

1. No declarations of war and no breaking off of diplomatic relations with the adversary, but, instead, continuous communication with him, whatever level of intensity the conflict may reach.

2. Acceptance of the idea that conflict with an adversary in respect to some areas, activities, units, or weapons does not necessarily involve conflict with him in other areas, activities, units, or weapons.

3. Military considerations, and the use of force generally, will always be subordinate to political considerations, and will operate as part of policy in the whole policy context.

4. Armed forces must be fully professionalized, trained and psychologically prepared to do any task to the degree and level they are ordered by the established political authorities, without desire or independent effort to carry combat to a level of intensity not in keeping with existing policy and political considerations.

5. There must be full ability at all times to escalate or to descalate the level of warfare as seems necessary in terms of the policy context, and to signal the decision to do either to the adversary as a guide to his responses.

6. Ability to descalate to the level of termination of violence and warfare must be possible, both in psychological and procedural terms, even with continuance of conflict on lower, nonforce, levels such as economic or ideological conflict.

7. There must exist a full panoply of weapons and of economic, political, social, and intellectual pressures that can be used in conflict with any diverse states to secure the specific and limited goals that would become the real aims of international policy in a period of controlled conflict.

8. Among the methods we must be prepared to use in such a period must be diplomatic or tacit agreement with any other state, including the Soviet Union or Red China, to seek parallel or joint aims in the world. This will be possible if all aims are limited to specific goals, which each state will recognize are not fatal to his general position and

regime, and by which one specific aim can be traded against another, even tacitly. This will become possible for the double reason that professionalization of the fighting forces and the growing productiveness of the Superpower economies will not require either the total psychological mobilization or the almost total economic mobilization necessary in World War II.

9. All this means a blurring of the distinction between war and peace, with the situation at all times one of closely controlled conflict. In this way endemic conflict is accepted in order to avoid, if possible, epidemic total war. The change will become possible because the ultimate policy of all states will become the preservation of their way of life and existing regime, with the largest possible freedom of action. These aims can be retained under controlled conflict but will be lost by all concerned in total war.

In spite of this shift in the whole pattern of international power relations, the Soviet Union will remain for a long time the chief adversary of the United States, a situation for which there is no real solution until a new, *and independent*, Superpower rises on the land mass of Eurasia, preferably in a unified Western Europe. The fundamental differences between the United States and the Soviet Union will remain for a long time. They are critical, and include the following: (1) a basic difference in outlook in which the outlook of the West is based on diversity, relativism, pluralism, and social consensus, while the Russian outlook is based on a narrow range of competing opinions and little diversity of knowledge, and is monolithic, intolerant, rigid, unified, absolute, and authoritarian; (2) the difference in stages of economic development, in which they are looking forward, with eager anticipation, to an affluent future, while we have already experienced an affluent society and are increasingly disillusioned with it; (3) the fact that the American economy is unique, because it is the only economy that no longer operates in terms of scarce resources. It may be inside a framework of scarce resources, but this framework is so much wider than the other limiting features of the system (notably its fiscal and financial arrangements) that the system itself does not operate within any limits established by that wider framework.

The third distinction may be seen in the fact that, in other economies, when additional demands are presented to the economy, less resources are available for alternative uses. But in the American system, as it now stands, additional new demands usually lead to increased resources becoming available for alternative purposes, notable consumption. Thus, if the Soviet Union embraced a substantial increase in space activity, the resources available for raising Russian levels of consumption would be reduced, while in America, any increases in the space budget makes levels of consumption also rise. It does this, in the latter case, because increased space expenditures provide purchasing power for consumption that makes available previously unused resources out of the unused American productive capacity.

This unusued productive capacity exists in the American economy because the structure of our economic system is such that it channels flows of funds into the production of addi..... capacity (investment) without any conscious planning process or any real desire by anyone to increase our productive capacity. It does this because certain institutions in our system (such as insurance, retirement funds, social security payments, undistributed corporate profits, and such) and certain individuals who personally profit by the flow of funds not theirs into investment continue to operate to increase investment even when they have no real desire to increase productive capacity (and, indeed, many decry it). In the Soviet Union, on the contrary, resources are allotted to the increase of productive capacity by a conscious planning process and at the cost of reducing the resources available in their system for consumption or for the government (largely defense).

Thus the meaning of the word "costs" and the limitations on ability to mobilize economic resources are entirely different in our system from the Soviet system and most others. In the Soviet economy "costs" are real costs, measurable in terms of the allotment of scarce resources that could have been used otherwise. In the American system "costs" are fiscal or financial limitations that have little connection with the use of scarce resources or even with the use of available (and therefore not scarce) resources. The reason for this is that in the American economy, the fiscal or financial limit is lower than the limit established by real resources and, therefore, since the financial limits act as the restraint on our economic activities, we do not get to the point where our activities encounter the restraints imposed by the limits of real resources (except rarely and briefly in terms of technically trained manpower, which is our most limited resource).

These differences between the Soviet and the American economies are: (1) the latter has built-in, involuntary, institutionalized investment, which the former lacks, and (2) the latter has fiscal restraints at a much lower level of economic activity, which the Soviet system also lacks. Thus greater activity in defense in the USSR entails real costs since it puts pressure on the ceiling established by limited real resources, while greater activity in the American defense or space effort releases money into the system, which presses upward on the artificial financial ceiling, pressing it upward closer to the higher, and remote, ceiling established by the real resources limit of the American economy. This makes available the unused productive capacity that exists in our system between the financial ceiling and the real resources ceiling; it not only makes these unused resources available for the governmental sector of the economy from which the expenditure was directly made but also makes available portions of these released resources for consumption and additional capital investment. For this reason, government expenditures in the United States for things like defense or space may entail no real costs at all in terms of the economy as a whole. In fact, if the volume of unused capacity brought into use by expenditure for these things (that is, defense, and so on) is greater than the resources necessary to satisfy the need for which the expenditure was made, the volume of unused resources made available for consumption or investment will be greater than the volume of resources used in the governmental expenditure, and this additional government effort will cost nothing at all in real terms, but will entail *negative* real costs. (Our wealth will be increased by making the effort.)

The basis for this strange, and virtually unique, situation is to be found in the large amount of unused productive capacity in the United States, even in our most productive years. In the second quarter of 1962, our productive system was running at a very high level of prosperity, yet it was functioning about 12 percent below capacity, which represented a loss of $73 billion annually. In this way, in the whole period from the beginning of 1953 to the middle of 1962, our productive system operated at $387 billion below capacity. Thus, if the system had operated near capacity, our defense effort over the nine years would have cost us almost nothing, in terms of loss of goods or capacity.

This unique character in the American economy rests on the fact that the utilization of resources follows flow lines in the economy that are not everywhere reflected by corresponding flow lines of claims on wealth (that is, money). In general, in our economy the lines of flow of claims on wealth are such that they provide a very large volume of savings and a rather large volume of investment, even when no one really wants new productive capacity; they also provide an inadequate flow of consumer purchasing power, in terms of the flows, or potential flows, of consumers' goods; but they provide very limited, sharply scrutinized, and often misdirected flows of funds for the use of resources to fulfill the needs of the governmental sector of our trisectored economy. As a result, we have our economy of distorted resource-utilization patterns, with overinvestment in many areas, overstuffed consumers in one place and impoverished consumers in another place, a drastic undersupply of social services, and widespread social needs for which public funds are lacking. In the Soviet Union, money flows follow fairly well the flows of real goods and resources, but, as a result, pressures are directly on resources. These pressures mean that saving and investment conflict directly with consumption and government services (including defense), putting the government under severe direct strains, as the demands for higher standards of living cannot be satisfied except by curtailing investment, defense, space, or other government expenditures.

Many countries of the world, especially the backward ones, are worse off than the Soviet Union, because their efforts to increase consumers' goods may well require investment based on savings that must be accumulated at the expense of consumption. In many areas, as we have seen in Asia, the Mediterranean, and Latin America, savings are accumulated by structural monetary flows, but there are no institutional flows toward investment, little incentive or motivation for investment, and the economy lags in all three sectors.

As a chief consequence of these conditions, the contrast between the "have" nations and the "have-not" nations will become even wider. This would be of little great importance to the rest of the world were it not that the peoples of the backward areas, riding the "crisis of rising expectations," are increasingly unwilling to be ground down in poverty as their predecessors were. At the same time, the Superpower stalemate increases the abilities of these nations to be neutral, to exercise influence out of all relationship to their actual powers, and to act, sometimes, in an irresponsible fashion. These areas will be the chief sources of real trouble in the future, for clashes between the United States and the Soviet Union (or even Red China) are unlikely to arise from direct conflicts of interests, but may well arise from conflicts over neutrals.

These neutrals and other peoples of backward areas have acute problems. Solutions of these problems do exist, but the underdeveloped nations are unlikely to find them. As we have indicated elsewhere, their chief problems are three: (1) the relationship between population explosion and limited food supplies; (2) problems of political stability, especially the relationship between political aims and quite diverse weapons-control patterns; and (3) the problem of obtaining constructive rather than destructive patterns of outlook. The United States and the Soviet Union have a common interest in seeing that these problems find solutions. In general, these underdeveloped nations cannot follow American patterns, and are attracted to the Soviet system despite its heavy costs in loss of personal freedoms. We do not have either the knowledge or influence that would make it possible for us to direct their steps along more desirable routes such as that followed by Japan.

One development in political life during the next generation or so that will be difficult to document is concerned with the very nature of the modern sovereign state. Like so much of our cultural heritage from the seventeenth century, such as international law and puritanism, this may now be in the process of a change so profound as to modify its very nature. As understood in western Europe over the last three centuries, the state was the organization of sovereign power on a territorial basis. "Sovereign" meant that the state (or ruler) had supreme legal authority to do just about anything regarded as public, and this authority impinged directly on the subject (or citizen) without any intermediaries or buffer corporations, and did this in a dualistic power antithesis typical of the Greek two-valued logic that was applied to almost everything in the seventeenth century. As part of this sovereign system, it was assumed that rights of property and of permanent association were not natural or eternal, but flowed from grants of sovereign power. Thus property in land required the state's recognition in the form of a document or deed, and no corporation could exist except at the charter of the sovereign or with his tacit consent. Moreover, all citizens on the territory were subject to the same sovereign power. The latter consisted, as it still largely does in our tradition, of a mixture of force (military), economic rewards, and ideological uniformity. This view of public authority is by no means universal in the world, and shows strong ir lications that it may be changing in the West. Corporations exist and have the earliest mark of divinity (immortality), and have become, as they were in the nonsovereign Middle Ages, refuges where individuals may function shielded from the reach of the sovereign state. The once almost universal equivalence between residence and citizenship may be weakening. If the ideological state continues to develop its likely characteristics, persons of different ideologies and thus of different allegiances may become intermingled on the same territory. The number of refugees and resident aliens is now increasing in most countries.

Moreover, the incorporation of such a wide variety of peoples with such diverse traditions into the United Nations is also contributing to this process. We have seen that traditional China did not exercise power on the vast majority of its subjects (the peasants) in terms of force, rewards, or even ideology, but did so by social pressures through the intermediary of the family and the gentry. Similarly in Africa, power has been quite different in its character than it was in the traditional European state, and was based rather on kinship, social reciprocity, and religion. When African natives met to settle political disputes in battle, this was not, as in Europe, a clash of military force to settle the issue; rather it was an opportunity for spiritual entities to indicate their decisions in the case. As soon as a few casualties appeared on one side, this was taken as an indication that the spirits concerned had made a decision adverse to that side, and, accordingly, the victims' associates broke and ran, leaving the field to the other side. Like the medieval judicial trial by battle or by ordeal, this was not an effort to settle a dispute by force, but the attempt to give a spiritual entity an opportunity to reveal its decision.

It may seem farfetched to expect our state to succumb to the introduction of religious, magical, or spiritual influences such as this, but there can be little doubt that social pressures such as used to exercise influence in China will become more influential in our power structures in the future.

It seems likely also that there will be a certain revival of the use of intermediaries in removing or weakening the impact of sovereign power on ordinary individuals. This implies a growth of federalism in the structure of political power. On the whole, the history of federalism has not been a happy one. Even in the United States, the most significant example of a successful federalist structure in modern history, the federalist principle has yielded ground to unitary government for 150 years or so. Moreover, in our own time a number of efforts, chiefly British, to set up federal unions have failed. Thus the Central African Federation of the Rhodesias and Nyasaland broke up after a few years, and the West Indies Federation was even less viable. Recently the Malaysian Federation of the Malay States, Singapore, North Borneo, and Sarawak has been threatened with destruction by Indonesia, itself once a federal system that has now largely yielded to unitary developments.

Nevertheless, the federal principle seems likely to grow as a method by which certain functions of government are allotted to one structure while other functions go to a narrower or wider structure. This tendency seems likely to arise from a number of influences of which the chief might be: (1) the inability of many of the new, small states to carry on all the functions of government independently and alone, and their consequent efforts to carry out some of them cooperatively; (2) the tendency for these new states to look to the United Nations to perform some of the most significant functions of government, such as defense of frontiers or maintaining public order; for example, Tanganyika recently disbanded its armed forces and entrusted its defense and public order to a Nigerian force under United Nations control; (3) the need for economic cooperation over wider areas than the boundaries of most states in order to obtain the necessary diversity of resources within a single economic system, a need that will continue to encourage the establishment of customs unions and economic blocs, of which the European Common Market is the outstanding example; similar unions are projected for Central America and other areas.

The most interesting example of this process may be seen in the slow growth of some kind of multilevel federal structure covering much of tropical Africa. This arose from the disintegration of the French colonial system in Black Africa in 1956-1960 and was known as the Brazzaville Twelve at first (from December in 1960), but is now much expanded to include non-French areas under the name Union of African and Malagasy States. This Union shows a tendency to become one of the middle layers in a multilevel political hierarchy. In this hierarchy, the top level is held by the United Nations and its associated functional bodies, such as the World Health Organization, UNESCO, the Food and Agricultural Organization, the ILO, the International Monetary Fund, the World Bank, the International Court of Justice, and others. On the second level are various organizations that have Pan-European or Third Bloc overtones such as the European Common Market or its now stalemated political counterpart, along with Euratom, the European Coal and Iron Community, and some others. The De Gaulle veto on the continued development of these has suspended their growth and also any tendency for them to coalesce with a number of older French Community organizations.

On the third, fourth, and fifth levels is a rather confused mass of organizations of which the third consists of those which are Pan-African in scope, the fourth are those allied with the UAMS, and the fifth are the relatively viable Brazzaville Twelve projects. On the third level are such organizations as the Economic Commission for Africa South of the Sahara, the Technical Cooperation Commission for Africa, the Scientific Council for Africa, two African commissions of the World Conference of Organizations of the Teaching Professions, the African Trade Union Confederation (set up at Dakar in 1962), and a number of others. On the fifth level are a whole series of organizations associated with the Brazzaville Twelve, its semiannual "summit conferences" of heads of state, its Secretary General and Secretariat, its Defense Union, its Organization for Economic Cooperation, and others. On the fourth level are similar organizations, including an Assembly of Heads of States, a Council of Members, and a Secretariat-General set up for the UAMS at Lagos in January 1962. Possibly these third, fourth, and fifth levels will coalesce and eliminate some reduplication as memberships become firmer.

On the sixth level are a number of local unions of states, such as those for local river controls, customs unions, and such. And on the seventh level are the individual states which in theory (like the states of the United States) will continue to hold full sovereignty. But when two-third votes on higher levels can make binding decisions on member states, or when states intend to vote as a bloc in the United Nations, or when states have reduced their military and police forces so that they are dependent on forces from higher levels to defend their territories or to maintain order, or when states look to higher levels for funds for investment or to restore their annual foreign-exchange imbalances, the realities of sovereign power become dispersed and some areas of the world begin to look more like the Germanies of the late medieval period than like the nationalist sovereign states of the nineteenth century. How far this process will go we cannot foretell, but the possibility of such developments should not be excluded by us just because they have not been experienced by us in recent generations.

This is more than enough on the power patterns in our near future. we must now turn to a much briefer discussion of the patterns of economic and social life. There we see a most extraordinary contrast. While the economic life of Western society has been increasingly successful in satisfying our material needs, the social aspect has become increasingly frustrating. There was a time, not long ago, when the chief aims of most Western men was for greater material goods and for rising standards of living. This was achieved at great social costs, by the attrition or even destruction of much of social life, including the sense of community fellowship, leisure, and social amenities. Looking backward, we are fully aware of these costs in the original factory towns and urban slums, but looking about us today we are often not aware of the great, often intangible, costs of middle-class living in suburbia or in the dormitory environs that surround European cities: the destruction of social companionship and solidarity, the narrowing influence of exposure to persons from a restricted age group or from a narrow segment of social class, the horrors of commuting, the incessant need for constant driving about to satisfy the ordinary needs of the family for groceries, medical care, entertainment, religion, or social experience, the prohibitive cost and inconvenience of upkeep and repairs and, in general, the whole way of life of the suburban "rat race," including the large-scale need for providing artificial activities for children.

Rebellion against this rat race has already begun, not from the lower middle class who are just entering it and still aspire to it, but from the established middle class who have, as they say, "had it." On the whole, the efforts to find a way out while still retaining a high standard of material living have not been successful, and the real rebellion is coming, as we shall see later, from their children. These have expanded the usual adolescent revolt against parental dominance and authority into a large-scale rejection of parental values. One form that this revolt has taken has been to modify the meaning of the expression "high standard of living" to include a whole series of desires and values that are not material and thus were excluded from the nineteenth-century bourgeois understanding of the expression "standard of living." Among these are two we have already listed as disconcerting elements in the Africans' understanding of standard of living: small group interpersonal relationships and sex play. These changes, as we shall see, have come to represent a challenge to the whole middle-class outlook.

The social costs of the contemporary economic system are staggering. On the whole, they have been widely discussed and are generally recognized. As economic enterprises have become larger and more tightly integrated into one another, the freedom, individualism, and initiative traditionally associated with the modern economy (in contrast with the medieval rural economy) have had to be sacrificed. The self-reliant individual has gradually changed into the conformist "organization man." Routine has displaced risk, and subordination to abstractions has replaced the struggle with diverse concrete problems. The constantly narrowing range of possibilities for self-expression has given rise to deep frustrations with their concomitant growth of irrational compensating customs, such as the obsession with speed; vicarious combativeness, especially in sports; the use of alcohol, tobacco, narcotics, and sex as stimulants, diversions, and sedatives; and the rapid appearance and disappearance of fads in dress, social customs, and leisure activities.

Most crucial have been the demands of the modern industrial and business system, because of advancing technology, for more highly trained manpower. Such training requires a degree of ambition, self-discipline, and future-preference that many persons lack or refuse to provide, with the result that a growing lowest social class of the social outcasts (the *Lumpenproletariat*) has reappeared. This group of rejects from our bourgeois industrial society provide one of our most intractable future problems, because they are gathered in urban slums, have political influence, and are socially dangerous.

In the United States, where these people congregate in the largest cities and are often Negroes or Latin Americans, they are regarded as a racial or economic problem, but they are really an educational and social problem for which economic or racial solutions would help little. This group is most numerous in the more advanced industrial areas and now forms more than twenty percent of the American population. Since they are a self-perpetuating group and have many children, they are increasing in numbers faster than the rest of the population. Their self-perpetuating characteristic as a group is not based on biological differences but on sociological factors, chiefly on the fact that disorganized, undisciplined, present-preference parents living under chaotic economic and social conditions are most unlikely to train their children in the organized, disciplined, future-preference and orderly habits the modern economic system requires in its workers, so that the children, like their parents, grow up as unemployables. This is not a condition that can be cured by providing more jobs, even if the jobs are in the proper areas, because the jobs require characteristics these victims of anomie do not possess and are unlikely to acquire.

All this leads to one of the most significant of current changes, the changes in attitudes and outlooks. At this point we shall not discuss the middle-class outlook and its challenges, which are the central aspect of this subject in the United States, but shall restrict ourselves to an equally large subject, the changes in the outlook of Western society as a whole, especially in Europe.

The intellectual and religious aspects of any society, including all those things I call "pattern of outlook," change at least as rapidly as the more material aspects of the society, and are generally less noticed. Among these the most significant, and the least noticed, are the categories into which any society divides its experiences in order to think about them or to talk about them and the values the society, often in unconscious consensus, places upon these categories. In every society there are certain groups, perhaps an intellectual elite, who think new thoughts, new at least in comparison with what went just before. In time, some of these thoughts spread and become familiar, until it may seem that everybody is thinking them. Of course, everybody is not, because in every society there are three other groups: the large group who do not think at all, the substantial group who are not aware of anything new and who retain the same outlook for years and even generations, and the small group who are always opposed to the consensus simply because opposition has become an end in itself.

In spite of these complexities, we can still look at the past and see a sequence of prevalent outlooks, often with rather confused periods of transition in between. Over the past two centuries, there have been five such stages: the Enlightenment in 1730–1790, the Romantic Movement in 1790–1850, the Age of Scientific Materialism in 1850–1895, the Period of Irrational Activism of 1895–1945, and our new Age of Inclusive Diversity since 1945.

These changing patterns of outlooks arise because men are complicated creatures trying to operate in a complex universe. Both man and universe are dynamic, or changeable in time, and the chief additional complexity is that both are changing in a continuum of abstraction, as well as in the more familiar continuum of space-time. The continuum of abstraction simply means that the reality in which man and the universe function exists in five dimensions; of these the dimension of abstraction covers a range from the most concrete and material end of reality to, at the opposite extreme, the most abstract and spiritual end of reality, with every possible gradation between these two ends along the intervening dimensions that determine reality, including the three dimensions of space, the fourth of time, and this fifth dimension of abstraction. This means that man is concrete and material at one end of his person, is abstract and spiritual at the other end, and covers all the gradations between, with a large central zone concerned with his chaos of emotional experiences and feelings.

In order to think about himself or the universe with the more abstract and rational end of his being, man has to categorize and to conceptualize both his own nature and the nature of reality, while, in order to act and to feel on the less abstract end of his being, he must function more directly, outside the limits of categories, without the buffer of concepts. Thus man might look at his own being as divided into three levels of body, emotions, and reason. The body, functioning directly in space-time-abstraction, is much concerned with concrete situations, individual and unique events, at a specific time and place. The middle levels of his being are concerned with himself and his reactions to reality in terms of feelings and emotions as determined by endocrine and neurological reactions. The upper levels of his being are concerned with his neurological analysis and manipulation of conceptualized abstractions. The three corresponding operations of his being are sensual, emotional or intuitive, and rational. The sequence of intellectual history is concerned with the sequence of styles or fads that have been prevalent, one after another, as to what emphasis or combinations of man's three levels of operations would be used in his efforts to experience life and to cope with the universe.

In the most general terms, we might say that primitive man emphasized an empirical approach to these problems with use of man's sensual equipment and chief emphasis on specific concrete situations; archaic man (say from 5000 B.C. to about 500 B.C. in Eurasia) emphasized man's emotional and intuitive equipment with emphasis on symbols, ritual, myth, and magical actions; Classical man (say from 500 B.C. to A.D. 500) emphasized man's rational equipment and regarded man's concepts as the major portion of reality. But Western man, since A.D. 500, has sought to find some combination of all three parts of his equipment that will provide satisfactory explanation and successful operation in terms both of man's nature and of the universe. The combinations he has tried provide the changing sequence of intellectual history.

The Age of Enlightenment, following on the successes of the Age of Newton (which had discovered a rational and mechanical explanation of the material universe), tried to apply the same techniques to man and society, and came up with a static, mechanical, and rationalist conception of both. The inadequacy of this view of man, already rejected by poets and literary figures in the mid-eighteenth century, led to its general rejection as inadequate because of the excesses of the French Revolution. The following Romantic period, accordingly, adopted a much more irrational picture of man, of society, and of the universe. As a consequence, emphasis shifted from the earlier rational, mechanical, and static views to irrational and dynamic views of man and society.

This period of Romanticism (about 1790–1850) was marked by poets of "storm and stress," the Gothic revival, and a growing emphasis on history as the correct key to understanding man and society. The period, associated with Hegel, Hugo, and Heine, culminated in Karl Marx's *Communist Manifesto* (1848), which found the key to man's social position in past struggles.

The third generation of the nineteenth century (1850–1895) was in an age of science and rationalism whose typical figures were Darwin and Bismarck. While emphasizing the empirical and rational aspects of science, it tried to apply these to biology and to history in terms of a scientific materialism that could explain biology and change as Newton's science had explained mechanics. By the end of the century, man was frustrated and disillusioned with scientific method and materialism and with emphasis on the nonhuman world and was turning once again to the problems of man and society with a conviction that these problems could be handled only by nonrational methods and by the clash of contending forces, since the problems themselves were too complex, too dynamic, too irrational to be settled by science or even by human thought.

The result was a new period, the Age of Irrational Activism. It began with men, like Henri Bergson and Sigmund Freud, who emphasized the nonrational nature of the universe and of man, quickly shifted Darwin's doctrines of struggle and survival from nonhuman nature to human society, and rejected rationalism as slow, superficial, and an inhibition on both action and survival. As Bergson said in his *Creative Evolution* (1907): "The intellect is characterized by a natural inability to comprehend life. Instinct, on the contrary, is molded on the very form of life."

This period felt that man, and nature, and human society were all basically irrational. Reason, regarded as a late and rather superficial accretion in the process of human evolution, was considered inadequate to plumb the real nature of man's problems, and was regarded as an inhibitor on the full intensity of his actions, an obstacle to the survival of himself as an individual and of his group (the nation). Any effort to apply reason or science, based on rational analysis and evaluation, would be a slow and frustrating effort: slow because the process of human rationality is always slow, frustrating because it cannot plumb into the real depths and nature of man's experience, and because it can always turn up as many and as good reasons for any course of action as it can for the opposite course of action. The effort to do this was dangerous, because as the thinker poised in indecision, the man of action struck, eliminated the thinker from the scene, and survived to determine the future on the basis of continued action. To the theorist of these views, the thinker would always be divided, hesitant, and weak, while the man of action would be unified, decisive, and strong.

This point of view, nourished on Marx and Heinrich von Treitschke, justified class conflicts and national warfare, and formed the background for the cult of violence that was reflected in the political assassinations of 1898–1914 and the imperialist aggressions that began with Japan, Italy, and Britain in China, Ethiopia, and South Africa in 1894–1899. The explicit justification of this view could be found in Georges Sorel *Réflexions sur la Violence* (1908) or in the political events of the summer of 1914. From that fateful summer, for more than forty years, higher levels of violence became the solution of all problems, whether it was the question of winning a war, Stalin's efforts to industrialize Russia, Hitler's efforts to settle the "Jewish problem," Rupert Brooke's effort to find meaning in life, Japan's desire to find a solution to economic depression, the English-speaking nations' search for security, Italy's search for glory, or Franco's desire to preserve the *status quo* in Spain. The culmination of the process in total irrationalism and total violence was Nazism, "The Revolution of Nihilism."

Expressed explicitly this cult of Irrational Activism was based on the belief that the universe was dynamic and largely nonrational. As such, any effort to deal with it by rational means will be futile and superficial. Moreover, rationalism, by paralyzing man's ability to act decisively, will expose him to destruction in a world whose chief features include struggle and conflict. Men came to believe that only violence had survival value. The resulting cult of violence permeated all human life. By mid-century, the popular press, literature, the cinema, sports, and all major human concerns had embraced this cult of violence. The books of Mickey Spillane or Raymond Chandler sold millions to satisfy this need. Humphrey Bogart became the most popular film hero because he courted women with a blow to the jaw.

On a somewhat more profound level, the Nazi Party mobilized popular support with a program of "Blood and Soil" (*Blut und Boden*), while the Fascists in Italy covered every wall with their slogan, "Believe! Obey! Fight!" In neither was there any expectation that men should think or analyze.

On the highest philosophic levels, the new attitude was justified. Bergson appealed to intuition, and Hitler used it. Other philosophers vied with one another to demonstrate that the old mechanism of abstract, rational thought must be rejected as irrelevant, superficial, or meaningless. The semanticists rejected logic by rejecting the idea of general categories or even of definition of terms. According to them, because everything is constantly changing, no term can remain fixed without at once becoming irrelevant. The meaning of any word depended on the context in which it was used; since this was different every time it was used, the meaning, consisting of a series of connotations based on all previous uses of the term, is different at each use. Every individual who uses a term is simply the culmination of all his past experiences that make him what he is; since experience never stops, he is a different person every time he uses a term, and it has a different meaning for him. On this basis the Italian playwright Luigi Pirandello (1867–1936) wrote a series of works to show the constantly changing nature of personality, which is also a reflection of the context in which it operates, so that each person who meets someone knows him as a different personality.

The most widely read of twentieth-century philosophers, the existentialists, reflected this same attitude, although they could agree on almost nothing. In general they were skeptical of any general principles about reality, but recognized that reality did exist for each individual as the concrete instant of time, place, and context in which he acted. Thus he must act. In order to act he must make a decision, a commitment, to something that would give him a basis from which to act. By acting he experiences reality, and to that extent knows and demonstrates, at least to himself, that there is a reality.

All these ideas, reflecting the disjointed malaise of the century, permeated the outlook of the period and left it hungry for meaning, for identity, for some structure or purpose in human experience. Insanity, neurosis, suicide, and all kinds of irrational obsessions and reactions filled increasing roles in human life. Most of these were not even recognized as being irrational or obsessive. Speed, alcohol, sex, coffee, and tobacco screened man off from living, injuring his health, stultifying his capacity to think, to observe, or to enjoy life, without his realizing that these were the shields he adopted to conceal from himself the fact that he was no longer really capable of living, because he no longer knew what life was and could see no meaning or purpose in it. As his capacity to live or to experience life dwindled, he sought to reach it by seeking more vigorous experiences that might penetrate the barriers surrounding him. The result was mounting sensationalism. In time, nothing made much impression unless it was concerned with shocking violence, perversion, or distortion.

Along with this, ability to communicate dwindled. The old idea of communication as an exchange of concepts represented by symbols was junked. Instead, symbols had quite different connotations for everyone concerned simply because everyone had a different past experience. A symbol might have meaning for two persons but it did not have the same meaning. Soon it was regarded as proper that words represent only the writer's meaning and need have no meaning at all for the reader. Thus appeared private poetry, personal prose, and meaningless art in which the symbols used have ceased to be symbols because they do not reflect any common background of experience that could indicate their meaning as shared communication or experience. These productions, the fads of the day, were acclaimed by many as works of genius. Those who questioned them and asked their meaning were airily waved aside as unforgivable philistines; they were told that no one any longer sought "meaning" in literature or art but rather sought "experiences." Thus to look at a meaningless painting became an experience. These fads followed one another, reflecting the same old pretenses, but under different names. Thus "Dada" following World War I eventually led to the "Absurd" following World War II.

But even as this process continued, twenty years after Hiroshima, deep within the social context of the day, new outlooks were rising that made the views associated with Irrational Activism increasingly irrelevant. One of these we have already mentioned. The victory of rational analysis, operational research, and organized scientific attitudes over irrationality, will, intuition, and violence in World War II reversed the trend. Nothing succeeds like success, and no success is greater than ability to survive and find solutions to critical problems involving existence itself. The West in World War II and in the postwar period, in spite of the hysterical protests of the extremists, showed once again that it was able to overcome aggression, narrow intolerance, hatred, tribalism, totalitarianism, selfishness, arrogance, imposed uniformity, and all the evils the West had recognized as evils throughout its history. It not only won the war: it solved the great economic crisis, prevented the extension of tyranny while still avoiding World War III, and did all this in a typical Western way by fumbling cooperatively down a road paved with good intentions. The final result was a triumph of incalculable magnitude for the Outlook of the West.

The Outlook of the West is that broad middle way about which the fads and foibles of the West oscillate. It is what is implied by what the West says it believes, not at one moment but over the long succession of moments that form the history of the West. From that succession of moments it is clear that the West believes in diversity rather than in uniformity, in pluralism rather than in monism or dualism, in inclusion rather than exclusion, in liberty rather than in authority, in truth rather than in power, in conversion rather than in annihilation, in the individual rather than in the organization, in reconciliation rather than in triumph, in heterogeneity rather than in homogeneity, in relativisms rather than in absolutes, and in approximations rather than in final answers. The West believes that man and the universe are both complex and that the apparently discordant parts of each can be put into a reasonably workable arrangement with a little good will, patience, and experimentation. In man the West sees body, emotions, and reason as all equally real and necessary, and is prepared to entertain discussion about their relative interrelationships but is not prepared to listen for long to any intolerant insistence that any one of these has a final answer.

The West has no faith in final answers today. It believes that all answers are unfinal because everything is imperfect, although possibly getting better and thus advancing toward a perfection the West is prepared to admit may be present in some remote and almost unattainable future. Similarly in the universe, the West is prepared to recognize that there are material aspects, less material aspects, immaterial aspects, and spiritual aspects, although it is not prepared to admit that anyone yet has a final answer on the relationships of these. Similarly the West is prepared to admit that society and groups are necessary, while the individual is important, but it is not prepared to admit that either can stand alone or be made the ultimate value to the sacrifice of the other.

Where rationalists insist on polarizing the continua of human experience into antithetical pairs of opposing categories, the West has constantly rejected the implied need for rejection of one or the other, by embracing "Both." This catholic attitude goes back to the earliest days of Western society when its outlook was being created in the religious controversies of the preceding Classical Civilization. Among these controversies were the following: (1) Was Christ Man or God? (2) Was salvation to be secured by God's grace or by man's good works? (3) Was the material world real and good or was spirituality real and good? (4) Was the body worthy of salvation or was the soul only to be saved? (5) Was the truth found only by God's revelation or was it to be found by man's experience (history)? (6) Should man work to save himself or to save others? (7) Does man owe allegiance to God or to Caesar? (8) Should man's behavior be guided by reason or by observation? (9) Can man be saved inside the Church or outside it? In each case, with vigorous partisans clamoring on both sides (and in many cases still clamoring), the answer, reached as a consensus built up by long discussion, was *Both*. In fact a correct definition of the Christian tradition might well be expressed in that one word "Both." Throughout its long history, controversy over religion in Western society has been based on a disturbance of the arrangement or balance within that "Both."

From this religious basis established on "Both" as early as the Councils of Nicaea (325) and Chalcedon (451), the outlook of the West developed and spread with the growth of the new Christian Civilization of the West to replace the dying Classical Civilization. And today, when the Civilization of the West seems as if it too may be dying, we may reassure ourselves by recalling that our civilization has saved itself before by turning back to its tradition of Inclusive Diversity. This apparently is what has been happening since 1940. It was Inclusive Diversity that created the nuclear bomb in World War II, and it may well be Inclusive Diversity that will save the West in the postwar world.

Any outlook or society that finds its truth in Inclusive Diversity or in "Both" obviously faces a problem of relationships. If man finds the truth by using body, emotions, and reason, these diverse talents must be placed in some workable arrangement with one another. So too must service to God and to Caesar or to self and to fellow man.

In an age like ours, in which all these relationships have become disrupted and discordant, such relationships can be reestablished by discussion and testing, but in this process each discussant must rely on his experience. The great body of such experience, however, will not be found among living discussants, whose whole lives have been passed in a culture in which these relationships were discordant, but in the experiences of those whose lives were lived in earlier ages before the relationship in question became discordant. This gives rise to the typical Western solution of relying on experience and, at the same time, helps the society to link up with its traditions (the most therapeutic action in which any society can engage).

From this examination of the tradition of the West, we can formulate the pattern of outlook on which this tradition is based. It has six parts:

1. There is a truth, a reality. (Thus the West rejects skepticism, solipsism, and nihilism.)

2. No person, group, or organization has the whole picture of the truth. (Thus there is no absolute or final authority.)

3. Every person of goodwill has some aspect of the truth, some vision of it from the angle of his own experience. (Thus each has something to contribute.)

4. Through discussion, the aspects of the truth held by many can be pooled and arranged to form a consensus closer to the truth than any of the sources that contributed to it.

5. This consensus is a temporary approximation of the truth, which is no sooner made than new experiences and additional information make it possible for it to be reformulated in a *closer* approximation of the truth by continued discussion.

6. Thus Western man's picture of the truth advances, by successive approximations, closer and closer to the whole truth without ever reaching it.

This methodology of the West is basic to the success, power, and wealth of Western Civilization. It is reflected in all successful aspects of Western life, from the earliest beginnings to the present. It has been attacked and challenged by all kinds of conflicting methods and outlooks, by all kinds of alternative attitudes based on narrowness and rigidity, but it has reappeared, again and again, as the chief source of strength of that amazing cultural growth of which we are a part.

This method has basically been the method of operation in Western religious history, despite the many lapses of Western religion into authoritarian, absolute, rigid, and partial affirmations. The many problems, previously listed, that faced the Church at the time of the Council of Nicaea were settled by this Western method. Throughout Western religious history, in spite of the frequent outbursts by dissident groups insisting that the truth was available—total, explicit, final, and authoritative—in God's revelation, Western religious thought has continued to believe that revelation itself is never final, total, complete, or literal, but is a continuous symbolic process that must be interpreted and reinterpreted by discussion.

The method of the West, even in religion, has been this: The truth unfolds in time by a cooperative process of discussion that creates a temporary consensus which we hope will form successive approximations growing closer and closer to the final truth, to be reached only in some final stage of eternity. In the Christian tradition the stages in this unfolding process for each individual are numerous; they include: (1) man's intuitive sense of natural law and morality, (2) the Old Testament, (3) the New Testament, (4) the long series of Church councils and ecclesiastical promulgations that will continue indefinitely into the future, (5) for each individual a continued process of knowledge in eternity after death, and, finally, (6) the Beatific Vision. Until this final stage, all versions of the truth, even when their factual content is based on divine revelation, must be understood and interpreted by community discussion in terms of past experiences and traditions.

This version of the religious tradition of the West as an example of the Western outlook as a whole may seem to many to be contradicted by the narrow intolerance, rigid bigotry, and relentless persecutions that have disfigured so much of the religious history of the West. This is true, and is a clear indication that individuals and groups can fall far short of their own traditions, can lose these for long periods, and can even devote their lives to fighting against them. But the traditions of the West, certainly the most remarkable any civilization has had, always seem to come back and march on to other victories. Even in our day, in Vatican Council II we can see what outsiders may regard as surprising efforts to apply Western traditions to an organization which, to most outsiders, and even, perhaps, to most insiders, must appear as one of the most authoritarian organizations ever created. But the tradition is there, however buried or forgotten, and the realization of this has made Vatican Council II a symbol of hope, even to non-Catholics and even to those who realize it will not do half the things that are crying urgently to be done.

Before we leave this subject, concerned with an area (religion) and an organization (the Roman Catholic Church) where we might expect the tradition of the West to be weak or even absent, we might comment on one other issue. The rigidity of Western religious thought that often seems to be unappreciative of the Western tradition (although fundamentally it is not) is often explained by the role divine revelation plays in Western religion. The Word of God may seem to many a rigid and inflexible element repugnant to the flexible and tentative outlook I have identified as the tradition of the West. But, on an early page of the new version of Thomas Aquinas now appearing in English in sixty volumes, we read this typical Western comment on the role of revelation in religious truth: "Revelation is not oracular. . . . Propositions do not descend on us from heaven ready made, but are . . . more a draft of work in progress than a final and completed document, for faith itself, though rooted in immutable truth is not crowning knowledge, and its elaboration in teaching, namely theology, is still more bound up with discourses progressively manifesting fresh truths or fresh aspects of the truth to the mind. So the individual Christian and the Christian community grow in understanding; indeed, they must if, like other living organisms, they are to survive by adaptation to a changing environment of history, ideas, and social pressures." *

* The Summa Theologiae of Saint Thomas Aquinas; Latin Text and English Translation, Vol. 1 New York, McGraw-Hill, 1964), p. 102.

To the West, in spite of all its aberrations, the greatest sin, from Lucifer to Hitler, has been pride, especially in the form of intellectual arrogance; and the greatest virtue has been humility, especially in the intellectual form which concedes that opinions are always subject to modification by new experiences, new evidence, and the opinions of our fellow men.

These procedures that I have identified as Western, and have illustrated from the rather unpromising field of religion, are to be found in all aspects of Western life. The most triumphant of these aspects is science, whose method is a perfect example of the Western tradition. The scientist goes eagerly to work each day because he has the humility to know that he does not have any final answers and must work to modify and improve the answers he has. He publishes his opinions and research reports, or exposes these in scientific gatherings, so that they may be subjected to the criticism of his colleagues and thus gradually play a role in formulating the constantly unfolding consensus that is science. That is what science is, "a consensus unfolding in time by a cooperative effort, in which each works diligently seeking the truth and submits his work to the discussion and critique of his fellows to make a new, slightly improved, temporary consensus."

Because this is the tradition of the West, the West is liberal. Most historians see liberalism as a political outlook and practice found in the nineteenth century. But nineteenth-century liberalism was simply a temporary organizational manifestation of what has always been the underlying Western outlook. That organizational manifestation is now largely dead, killed as much by twentieth-century liberals as by conservatives or reactionaries. It was killed because liberals took applications of that manifestation of the Western outlook and made these applications· rigid, ultimate, and inflexible goals. The liberal of 1880 was anticlerical, antimilitarist, and antistate because these were, to his immediate experience, authoritarian forces that sought to prevent the operation of the Western way. The same liberal was for freedom of assembly, of speech, and of the press because these were necessary to form the consensus that is so much a part of the Western process of operation.

But by 1900 or so, these dislikes and likes became ends in themselves. The liberal was prepared to force people to associate with those they could not bear, in the name of freedom of assembly, or he was, in the name of freedom of speech, prepared to force people to listen. His anticlericalism became an effort to prevent people from getting religion, and his antimilitarism took the form of opposing funds for legitimate defense. Most amazing, his earlier opposition to the use of private economic power to restrict individual freedoms took the form of an effort to increase the authority of the state against private economic power and wealth in themselves. Thus the liberal of 1880 and the liberal of 1940 had reversed themselves on the role and power of the state, the earlier seeking to curtail it, the latter seeking to increase it. In the process, the upholder of the former liberal idea that the power of the state should be curtailed came to be called a conservative. This simply added to the intellectual confusion of the mid-twentieth century, which arose from the Irrational Activist reluctance to define any terms, a disinclination that has now penetrated deeply into all intellectual and academic life.

In this connection we might say that the whole recent controversy between conservatism and liberalism is utterly wrongheaded and ignorant. Since the true role of conservatism must be to conserve the tradition of our society, and since that tradition is a liberal tradition, the two should be closely allied in their aim at common goals. So long as liberals and conservatives have as their primary goals to defend interests and to belabor each other for partisan reasons, they cannot do this. When they decide to look at the realities beneath the controversies, they might begin with a little book that appeared many years ago (1902) from the hand of a member of the chief family in the English Conservative Party over the past century. The book is *Conservatism* by Lord Hugh Cecil. This volume defines conservatism very much as I have defined liberalism and the Outlook of the West as tentative, flexible, undogmatic, communal, and moderate. Its fundamental assumption is that men are imperfect creatures, will probably get further by working together than by blind opposition, and that, since undoubtedly each is wrong to some extent, any extreme or drastic action is inadvisable. Conservatism of this type was, indeed, closer to what I have called liberalism than the liberals of 1880 were, since the conservatives of this type were perfectly willing to use the Church or the army or the state to carry out their moderate and tentative projects, and were prepared to use the state to curtail arbitrary private economic power, which the liberals of the day were unwilling to do (since they embraced a doctrinaire belief in the limitation of state power).

All this is of significance because it is concerned with the fact that there is an age-old Western tradition, much battered and destroyed in recent generations, that has sent up new, living shoots of vigorous growth since 1945. These new shoots have appeared even in those areas where the orthodox nineteenth-century liberals looked to find only enemies—in the Church and in the armed forces. The operation of what I have called the liberal tradition of the West is evident in all religious thought of recent years, even in that of Roman Catholicism. It is almost equally evident in military life, where the practice of consulting diverse, and even outside, opinion to reach tentative decisions is increasingly obvious. Recently I attended a conference of the United States Navy Special Projects Office where a diverse group tried to reach some consensus about the form of naval weapons systems twelve years in the future. The agenda, as set up for seven weeks, provided for thirty-three successive approximations narrowing in on the desired consensus. This was listed on the agenda as "Final Approximation and Crystallization of Dissent." The recognition that the final goal was still approximate, and the equal role provided for disagreement within this consensus, show clearly how the tradition of the West operates today within the armed forces of the West.

This return to the tradition of the West is evident in many aspects of life beyond those mentioned here. Strangely enough, the return of which we speak is much more evident in the United States than it is in Europe, and, accordingly, some of the most significant examples of it will be mentioned in the following section, which is concerned with the United States.

The reason for this, apparently, is that Europeans, after their very difficult experiences of depression and war, are now overly eager for the mundane benefits made possible by advancing technology and are, as a result, increasingly selfish and materialistic, while Americans, having tasted the fleshpots of affluence, are increasingly unselfish, community-conscious, and nonmaterial in their attitudes. A careful look, however, will show that the movement is present on both sides of the Atlantic, and appears perhaps most obviously in a growing concern with one's fellow men, a kind of practical Christianity, and a spreading evidence of charity and love in the old Christian meaning of these terms. There seems to be, especially among the younger generation, a growing emphasis on fellowship and interpersonal relations and an increasing skepticism toward abstract power, high-blown slogans, old war cries, and authority. There is a reaching out to one another, seeking to understand, to help, to comfort. There is a growing tolerance of differences, an amused attitude of live and let live; and, above all, there is an avid discussion of values and priorities that include more spiritual items than a generation ago. There is an almost universal rejection of authority, of rigid formulas, and of final or total answers. In a word, there is a fumbling effort to rediscover the tradition of the West by a generation that has been largely cut off from that tradition.

We have said that this tradition is one of Inclusive Diversity in which one of the chief problems is how elements that seem discordant, but are recognized as real and necessary, may be fitted together. The solution to this problem, which rests in the tradition itself, is to be found in the idea of hierarchy: diverse elements are discordant only because they are out of place. Once the proper arrangement is found, discord is replaced by concord. Once, long ago, a young person said to me, "Dirt is only misplaced matter"—a typically Western attitude. Today young persons spend increasing time in argument and thought on how diverse things, all of which seem necessary, can be arranged in a hierarchy of importance or priority: military service, preparation for a vocation, love and marriage, personal development, desire to help others—all these compete for energy, time, and attention. In what order should they be arranged? This is quite different from the successful young man of yesteryear who had one clearly perceived goal—to prepare for a career in moneymaking. The road to that career was marked by materialism, selfishness, and pride, all attitudes of low favor in the outlook of the West, not because they are absolutely wrong but because they indicate a failure to see the place of things in the general structure of the universe. Even pride, either in Lucifer or in Soames Forsyte, is a failure to realize one's own position in the whole picture. And today, especially in America, increasing numbers of people are trying to see the whole picture.

The United States
and the Middle-Class Crisis

The character of any society is determined less by what it is actually like than by the picture it has of itself and of what it aspires to be. From this point of view, American society of the 1920's was largely middle class. Its values and aspirations were middle class, and power or influence within it was in the hands of middle-class people. On the whole, this was regarded as proper, except by iconoclastic writers who gained fortune and reputation simply by satirizing or criticizing middle-class customs.

To be sure, even the most vigorous defenders of bourgeois America did not pretend that all Americans were middle class: only the more important ones were. But they did see the country as organized in middle-class terms, and they looked forward to a not remote future in which everyone would be middle class, except for a small, shiftless minority of no importance. To these defenders, and probably also to the shiftless minority, American society was regarded as a ladder of opportunity up which anyone could work his way, on rungs of increased affluence, to the supreme positions of wealth and power near the top. Wealth, power, prestige, and respect were all obtained by the same standard, based on money. This in turn was based on a pervasive emotional insecurity that sought relief in the ownership and control of material possessions. The basis for this may be seen most clearly in the origins of this bourgeois middle class.

A thousand years ago, Europe had a two-class society in which a small upper class of nobles and upper clergy were supported by a great mass of peasants. The nobles defended this world, and the clergy opened the way to the next world, while the peasants provided the food and other material needs for the whole society. All three had security in their social relationships in that they occupied positions of social status that satisfied their psychic needs for companionship, economic security, a forseeable future, and purpose of their efforts. Members of both classes had little anxiety about loss of these things by any likely outcome of events, and all thus had emotional security.

In the course of the medieval period, chiefly in the twelfth and thirteenth centuries, this simple two-class society was modified by the intruison of a small, but distinctly different, new class between them. Because this new class was between, we call it *middle* class, just as we call it "bourgeois" (after *bourg* meaning town) from the fact that it resided in towns, a new kind of social aggregate. The two older, established, classes were almost completely rural and intimately associated with the land, economically, socially, and spiritually. The permanence of the land and the intimate connection of the land with the most basic of human needs, especially food, amplified the emotional security associated with the older classes.

The new middle class of bourgeoisie who grew up between the two older classes had none of these things. They were commercial peoples concerned with exchange of goods, mostly luxury goods, in a society where all their prospective customers already had the basic necessities of life provided by their status. The new middle class had no status in a society based on status; they had no security or permanence in a society that placed the highest value on these qualities. They had no law (since medieval law was largely past customs, and their activities were not customary ones) in a society that highly valued law. The flow of the necessities of life, notably food, to the new town dwellers was precarious, so that some of their earliest and most emphatic actions were taken to ensure the flow of such goods from the surrounding country to the town. All the things the bourgeois did were new things; all were precarious, and insecure; and their whole lives were lived without the status, permanence, and security the society of the day most highly valued. The risks (and rewards) of commercial enterprise, well reflected in the fluctuating fortunes of figures such as Antonio in *The Merchant of Venice*, were extreme. A single venture could ruin a merchant or make him rich. This insecurity was increased by the fact that the prevalent religion of the day disapproved of what he was doing, seeking profits or taking interest, and could see no way of providing religious services to town dwellers because of the intimate association of the ecclesiastical system with the existing arrangement of rural landholding.

For these and other reasons psychic insecurity became the keynote of the new middle-class outlook. It still is. The only remedy for this

TRAGEDY AND HOPE

insecurity of the middle class seemed to it to be the accumulation of more possessions that could be a demonstration to the world of the individual's importance and power. In this way, for the middle class, the general goal of medieval man to seek future salvation in the hereafter was secularized to an effort to seek future security in this world by acquisition of wealth and its accompanying power and social prestige. But the social prestige from wealth was most available among fellow bourgeoisie, rather than among nobles or peasants. Thus the opinions of one's fellow bourgeoisie, by wealth and by conformity to bourgeois values, became the motivating drives of the middle classes, creating what has been called the "acquisitive society."

In that society prudence, discretion, conformity, moderation (except in acquisition), decorum, frugality, became the marks of a sound man. Credit became more important than intrinsic personal qualities, and credit was based on the appearances of things, especially the appearances of the external material accessories of life. The facts of a man's personal qualities—such as kindness, affection, thoughtfulness, generosity, personal insight, and such, were increasingly irrelevant or even adverse to the middle-class evaluation of a man. Instead, the middle-class evaluation rested rather on nonpersonal attributes and on external accessories. Where personal qualities were admired, they were those that contributed to acquisition (often qualities opposed to the established values of the Christian outlook, such as love, charity, generosity, gentleness, or unselfishness). These middle-class qualities included decisiveness, selfishness, impersonality, ruthless energy, and insatiable ambition.

As the middle classes and their commercialization of all human relationships spread through Western society in the centuries from the twelfth to the twentieth, they largely modified and, to some extent, reversed the values of Western society earlier. In some cases, the old values, such as future preference or self-discipline, remained, but were redirected. Future preference ceased to be transcendental in its aim, and became secularized. Self-discipline ceased to seek spirituality by restraining sensuality, and instead sought material acquisition. In general, the new middle-class outlook had a considerable religious basis, but it was the religion of the medieval heresies and of puritanism rather than the religion of Roman Christianity.

This complex outlook that we call middle class or bourgeois is, of course, the chief basis of our world today. Western society is the richest and most powerful society that has ever existed largely because it has been impelled forward along these lines, beyond the rational degree necessary to satisfy human needs, by the irrational drive for achievement in terms of material ambitions. To be sure, Western society always had other kinds of people, and the majority of the people in Western society probably had other outlooks and values, but it was middle-class urgency that pushed modern developments in the direction they took. There were always in our society dreamers and truth-seekers and tinkerers. They, as poets, scientists, and engineers, thought up innovations which the middle classes adopted and exploited if they seemed likely to be profit-producing. Middle-class self-discipline and future preference provided the savings and investment without which any innovation—no matter how appealing in theory—would be set aside and neglected. But the innovations that could attract middle-class approval (and exploitation) were the ones that made our world today so different from the world of our grandparents and ancestors.

This middle-class character was imposed most strongly on the United States. In order to identify it and to discuss a very complex pattern of outlooks and values, we shall try to summarize it. At its basis is psychic insecurity founded on lack of secure social status. The cure for such insecurity became insatiable material acquisition. From this flowed a large number of attributes of which we shall list only five: future preference, self-discipline, social conformity, infinitely expandable material demand, and a general emphasis on externalized, impersonal values.

Those who have this outlook are middle class; those who lack it are something else. Thus middle-class status is a matter of outlook and not a matter of occupation or status. There can be middle-class clergy or teachers or scientists. Indeed, in the United States, most of these three groups are middle class, although their theoretical devotion to truth rather than to profit, or to others rather than to self, might seem to imply that they should not be middle class. And, indeed, they should not be; for the urge to seek truth or to help others are not really compatible with the middle-class values. But in our culture the latter have been so influential and pervasive, and the economic power of middle-class leaders has been so great, that many people whose occupations, on the face of it, should make them other than middle class, none the less have adopted major parts of the middle-class outlook and seek material success in religion or teaching or science.

The middle-class outlook, born in the Netherlands and northern Italy and other places in the medieval period, has been passed on by being inculcated to children as the proper attitude for them to emulate. It could pass on from generation to generation, and from century to century, as long as parents continued to believe it themselves and disciplined their children to accept it. The minority of children who did not accept it were "disowned" and fell out of the middle classes. What is even more important, they were, until recently, pitied and rejected by their families. In this way, those who accepted the outlook marched on in the steadily swelling ranks of the triumphant middle classes. Until the twentieth century.

For more than half a century, from before World War I, the middle-class outlook has been under relentless attack, often by its most ardent members, who heedlessly, and unknowingly, have undermined and destroyed many of the basic social customs that preserved it through earlier generations. Many of these changes occurred from changes in childrearing practices, and many arose from the very success of the middle-class way of life, which achieved material affluence that tended to weaken the older emphasis on self-discipline, saving, future preference, and the rest of it.

One of the chief changes, fundamental to the survival of the middle-class outlook, was a change in our society's basic conception of human nature. This had two parts to it. The traditional Christian attitude toward human personality was that human nature was essentially good and that it was formed and modified by social pressures and training. The "goodness" of human nature was based on the belief that it was a kind of weaker copy of God's nature, lacking many of God's qualities (in degree rather than in kind), but none the less perfectible, and perfectible largely by its own efforts with God's guidance. The Christian view of the universe as a hierarchy of beings, with man about two-thirds of the way up, saw these beings, especially man, as fundamentally free creatures able to move, at their own volition toward God or away from him, and guided or attracted in the correct direction for realization of their potentialities by God's presence at the top of the Universe, a presence which, like the north magnetic pole, attracted men, as compasses, upward toward fuller realization and knowledge of God who was the fulfillment of all good. Thus the effort came from free men, the guidance came from God's grace, and ultimately the motive power came from God's attractiveness.

In this Western point of view, evil and sin were negative qualities; they arose from the absence of good, not from the presence of evil. Thus sin was the failure to do the right thing, not doing the wrong thing (except indirectly and secondarily). In this view the devil, Lucifer, was not the epitome of positive wickedness, but was one of the highest of the angels, close to God in his rational nature, who fell because he failed to keep his perspective and believed that he was as good as God.

In this Christian outlook, the chief task was to train men so that they would use their intrinsic freedom to do the right thing by following God's guidance.

Opposed to this Western view of the world and the nature of man, there was, from the beginning, another opposed view of both which received its most explicit formulation by the Persian Zoroaster in the seventh century B.C. and came into the Western tradition as a minor, heretical, theme. It came in through the Persian influence on the Hebrews, especially during the Babylonian Captivity of the Jews, in the sixth century B.C., and it came in, more fully, through the Greek rationalist tradition from Pythagoras to Plato. This latter tradition encircled the early Christian religion, giving rise to many of the controversies that were settled in the early Church councils and continuing on in the many heresies that extended through history from the Arians, the Manichaeans, Luther, Calvin, and the Jansenists.

The chief avenue by which these ideas, which were constantly rejected by the endless discussions formulating the doctrine of the West, continued to survive was through the influence of St. Augustine. From this dissident minority point of view came seventeenth-century Puritanism. The general distinction of this point of view from Zoroaster to William Golding (in *Lord of the Flies*) is that the world and the flesh are *positive* evils and that man, in at least this physical part of his nature, is essentially evil. As a consequence he must be disciplined totally to prevent him from destroying himself and the world. In this view the devil is a force, or being, of positive malevolence, and man, by himself, is incapable of any good and is, accordingly, not free. He can be saved in eternity by God's grace *alone,* and he can get through this temporal world only by being subjected to a regime of total despotism. The direction and nature of the despotism is not regarded as important, since the really important thing is that man's innate destructiveness be controlled.

Nothing could be more sharply contrasted than these two points of view, the orthodox and the puritanical. The contrasts can be summed up thus:

Orthodox	Puritan
Evil is absence of Good.	Evil is positive entity.
Man is basically good.	Man is basically evil.
Man is free.	Man is a slave of his nature.
Man can contribute to his salvation by good works.	Man can be saved only by God.
Self-discipline is necessary to guide or direct.	Discipline must be external and total.
Truth is found from experience and revelation, interpreted by tradition.	Truth is found by rational deduction from revelation.

The puritan point of view, which had been struggling to take over Western Civilization for its first thousand years or more, almost did so in the seventeenth century. It was represented to varying degrees in the work and agitations of Luther, Calvin, Thomas Hobbes, Cornelius Jansen (*Augustinus,* 1640), Antoine Arnauld (1612–1694), Blaise Pascal, and others. In general this point of view believed that the truth was to be found by rational deduction from a few basic revealed truths, in the way that Euclid's geometry and Descartes's analytical geometry were based on rational deduction from a few self-evident axioms. The result was a largely deterministic human situation, in sharp contrast with the orthodox point of view, still represented in the Anglican and Roman churches, which saw man as largely free in a universe whose rules were to be found most readily by tradition and the general consensus. The Puritan point of view tended to support political despotism and to seek a one-class uniform society, while the older view put much greater emphasis on traditional pluralism and saw society as a unity of diversities. The newer idea led directly to mercantilism, which regarded political-economic life as a struggle to the death in a world where there was not sufficient wealth or space for different groups. To them wealth was limited to a fixed amount in the world as a whole, and one man's gain was someone else's loss. That meant that the basic struggles of this world were irreconcilable and must be fought to a finish. This was part of the Puritan belief that nature was evil and that a state of nature was a jungle of violent conflicts.

Some of these ideas changed, others were retained, and a few were rearranged and modified in the following periods of the Enlightenment, the Romantic movement, and scientific materialism. All three of these returned to the older idea that man and nature were essentially good, and to this restored belief in the Garden of Eden they joined a basically optimistic belief in man's ability to deal with his problems and to guide his own destiny. Society and its conventions came to be regarded as evil, and the guidance of traditions was generally rejected by the late Enlightenment and the early Romantics, although the excesses of the French Revolution drove many of the later Romantics back to rely on history and traditions because of their growing feeling of the inadequacy of human reason. One large change in all three periods was the Community of Interests, which rejected mercantilism's insistence on limited wealth and the basic incompatibility of interests for the more optimistic belief that all parties could somehow adjust their interests within a community in which all would benefit mutually. The application of Darwinism to human society changed this idea again, toward the end of the nineteenth century, and provided the ideological justification for the wars of extermination of Nazism and Fascism. Only after the middle of the twentieth century did a gradual reappearance of the old Christian ideas of love and charity modify this view, replacing it with the older idea that diverse human interests are basically reconcilable.

All this shifting of ideas, many of them unstated, or even unconscious, assumptions, and the gradual growth of affluence helped to destroy middle-class motivations and values. American society had been largely, but not entirely, middle class. Above the middle class, which dominated the country in the first half of the twentieth century, were a small group of aristocrats. Below were the petty bourgeoisie, who had middle-class aspirations, but were generally more insecure and often bitter because they did not obtain middle-class rewards. Below these two middle classes were two lower classes: the workers and the *Lumpenproletariat* or socially disorganized, who had very little in common with each other.

Outside this hierarchical structure of five groups in three classes (aristocrat, middle, and lower) were two other groupings that were not really part of the hierarchical structure. On the left were the intellectuals and on the right were the religious. These held in common the idea that the truth, to them, was more important than interests; but they differed greatly from the fact that the religious believed that they knew what the truth was, while the intellectuals were still seeking it.

This whole arrangement was much more like a planetary arrangement of social-economic groupings than it was like the middle-class vision of society as a ladder of opportunity. The ladder really included only the middle classes with the workers below. The planetary view, becoming increasingly widespread, saw the middle classes in the center with the other five surrounding these. Social movement was possible in circular as well as in vertical directions (as the older ladder view of society believed), so that sons of workers could rise into the middle classes or move right into the religious, left into the intelligentsia, or even fall downward into the declassed dregs. So too, in theory, the children (or more likely the grandchildren) of the upper middle class could move upward into the aristocracy, which could also be approached from the intellectuals or the religious.

Strangely enough, the non-middle classes had more characteristics in common with each other than they did with the middle classes in their midst. The chief reason for this was that all other groups had value systems different from the middle classes and, above all, placed no emphasis on display of material affluence as proof of social status. From this came a number of somewhat similar qualities and attitudes that often gave the non-middle-class groups more in common and easier social intercourse than any of them had with the middle classes. For example, all placed much more emphasis on real personal qualities and much less on such things as clothing, residence, academic background, or kind of transportation used (all of which were important in determining middle-class reactions to people). In a sense all were more sincere, personally more secure (not the *Lumpenproletariat*), and less hypocritical than the middle class, and accordingly were much more inclined to judge any new acquaintance on his merits. Moreover, the middle classes, in order to provide their children with middle-class advantages, had few children, while the other groups placed little restriction on family size (except for some intellectuals). Thus aristocrats, religious, workers, the declassed, and many intellectuals had large families, while only the uppermost and most securely established middle-class families, as part of the transition to aristocracy, had larger families.

Ideas of morality also tended to set the middle classes off from most of the others. The latter tended to regard morality in terms of honesty and integrity of character, while the middle classes based it on actions, especially sexual actions. Even the religious based sin to some extent on purpose, attitude, and mental context of the act rather than on the act itself, and did not restrict morality as narrowly to sexual behavior as did the middle classes. However, the middle-class influence has been so pervasive in the modern world that many of the other groups fell under its influence to the extent that the word "morality," by the early twentieth century, came to mean sex. The Jansenist influence in American Roman Catholicism, for example, is so strong that sins concerning sex are widely regarded by Catholics as the worst of sins, in spite of the fact that Catholic doctrine continues to regard pride as the worst sin and sexual sins as much less important (as Dante did). At any rate, sex was generally regarded with greater indulgence by aristocrats, workers, intellectuals, or the declassed than by the middle classes or the more puritanical religious.

In America, as elsewhere, aristocracy represents money and position grown old, and is organized in terms of families rather than of individuals. Traditionally it was made up of those whose families had had money, position, and social prestige for so long that they never had to think about these and, *above all*, never had to impress any other person with the fact that they had them. They accepted these attributes of family membership as a right and an obligation. Since they had no idea that these could be lost, they had a basic psychological security, similar to that of the religious and workers. Thus like these other two, they were self-assured, natural, but distant. Their manners were gracious but impersonal. Their chief characteristic was the assumption that their family position had obligations. This *noblesse oblige* led them to participate in school sports (even if they lacked obvious talent), to serve their university (usually a family tradition) in any helpful way (such as fund raising), to serve their church in a similar way, and to offer their services to their local community, their state, and their country as an obligation. They often scandalized their middle-class acquaintances by their unconventionality and social informality, greeting workers, recent immigrants, or even outcasts by their given names, arriving at evening meetings in tweeds, or traveling in cheap, small cars to formal weddings.

The kind of a car a person drove was, until very recently, one of the best guides to middle-class status, since a car to the middle classes was a status symbol, while to the other classes it was a means of getting somewhere. Oversized Oldsmobiles, Cadillacs, and Lincoln Continentals are still middle-class cars, but in recent years, with the weakening of the middle-class outlook, almost anyone might be found driving a Volks-wagen. Another good evidence of class may be seen in the treatment given to servants (or those who work in one's home): the lower classes treat these as equals, the middle classes treat them as inferiors, while aristocrats treat them as equals or even superiors.

On the whole, the number of aristocratic families in the United States is very few, with a couple in each of the older states, especially New England, and in the older areas of the South such as Charleston or Natchez, Mississippi, with the chief concentrations in the small towns around Boston and in the Hudson River Valley. Mrs. Eleanor Roosevelt would be an example. A somewhat larger group of semiaristocrats con-sist of those like the Lodges, Rockefellers, or Kennedys who are not yet completely aristocratic either because they are not, in generations, far enough removed from money-making, or because of the persistence of a commercial or business tradition in the family. But these are aristocrats in the sense that they have accepted a family obligation of service to the community. The significance of this aristocratic tradition may be seen in Massachusetts politics; there two decades ago, the governorship and both senatorial seats were held by a Bradford, a Saltonstall, and a Lodge, while in 1964 two of these positions were held by Endicott Peabody and Leverett Saltonstall.

The working class in the United States is much smaller than we might assume, since most American workers are seeking to rise socially, to help their children to rise socially, and are considerably concerned with status symbols. Such people, even if laborers, are not working class, but are rather petty bourgeoisie. The real working class are rather relaxed, have present rather than future preference, generally worry very little about their status in the eyes of the world, enjoy their ordinary lives, including food, sex, and leisure, and have little desire to change their jobs or positions. They are generally relaxed, have a taste for broad humor, are natural, direct, and friendly, without large basic insecurities of personality. The world depression, by destroying their jobs and eco-nomic security, much reduced this group, which was always propor-tionately smaller in America, the land of aspiration for everyone, than in Europe.

The second most numerous group in the United States is the petty bourgeoisie, including millions of persons who regard themselves as middle class and are under all the middle-class anxieties and pressures, but often earn less money than unionized laborers. As a result of these things, they are often very insecure, envious, filled with hatreds, and are generally the chief recruits for any Radical Right, Fascist, or hate cam-paigns against any group that is different or which refuses to conform to middle-class values. Made up of clerks, shopkeepers, and vast num-bers of office workers in business, government, finance, and education, these tend to regard their white-collar status as the chief value in life, and live in an atmosphere of envy, pettiness, insecurity, and frustration. They form the major portion of the Republican Party's supporters in the towns of America, as they did for the Nazis in Germany thirty years ago.

In general, the political alignments in the United States have been influenced even more by these class and psychological considerations than they have been by income, economic, or occupational considerations. The Republican Party has been the party of the middle classes and the Democratic Party has been the party of the rest. In general, aristocrats have tended to move toward the Democrats, while semiaristocrats often remain Republican (with their middle-class parents or grandparents), except where historical circumstance (chiefly in New England, the Middle West, and the South, where Civil War memories remained green) operated. This meant that the Republican Party, whose nineteenth century superiority had been based on the division of farmers into South and West over the slave issue, became an established majority party in the twentieth century, but became, once again, a minority party, because of the disintegration of their middle-class support following 1945.

Even in the period of middle-class dominance, the Republicans had lost control of the Federal government because of the narrowly plutocratic control of the party that split it in 1912 and alienated most of the rest of the country in 1932. Twenty years later, in 1952, the country looked solidly middle class, but, in fact, by that date middle-class morale was almost totally destroyed, the middle classes themselves were in disintegration, and the majority of Americans were becoming less middle class in outlook. This change is one of the most significant transformations of the twentieth century. The future of the United States, of Western Civilization, and of the world depends on what kind of outlook replaces the dissolving middle-class ideology in the next generation.

The weakening of this middle-class ideology was a chief cause of the panic of the middle classes, and especially of the petty bourgeoisie, in the Eisenhower era. The general himself was repelled by the Radical Right, whose impetus had been a chief element (but far from the most important element) in his election, although the lower-middle-class groups had preferred Senator Taft as their leader. Eisenhower, however, had been preferred by the Eastern Establishment of old Wall Street, Ivy League, semiaristocratic Anglophiles whose real strength rested in their control of eastern financial endowments, operating from foundations, academic halls, and other tax-exempt refuges.

As we have said, this Eastern Establishment was really above parties and was much more concerned with policies than with party victories. They had been the dominant element in both parties since 1900, and practiced the political techniques of William C. Whitney and J. P.

Morgan. They were, as we have said, Anglophile, cosmopolitan, Ivy League, internationalist, astonishingly liberal, patrons of the arts, and relatively humanitarian. All these things made them anathema to the lower-middle-class and petty-bourgeois groups, chiefly in small towns and in the Middle West, who supplied the votes in Republican electoral victories, but found it so difficult to control nominations (especially in presidential elections) because the big money necessary for nominating in a Republican National Convention was allied to Wall Street and to the Eastern Establishment. The ability of the latter to nominate Eisenhower over Taft in 1952 was a bitter pill to the radical bourgeoisie, and was not coated sufficiently by the naming of Nixon, a man much closer to their hearts, for the vice-presidential post. The split between these two wings of the Republican Party, and Eisenhower's preference for the upper bourgeois rather than for the petty-bourgeois wing, paralyzed both of his administrations and was the significant element in Kennedy's narrow victory over Nixon in 1960 and in Johnson's much more decisive victory over Goldwater in 1964.

Kennedy, despite his Irish Catholicism, was an Establishment figure. This did not arise from his semiaristocratic attitudes or his Harvard connections (which were always tenuous, since Irish Catholicism is not yet completely acceptable at Harvard). These helped, but John Kennedy's introduction to the Establishment arose from his support of Britain, in opposition to his father, in the critical days at the American Embassy in London in 1938–1940. His acceptance into the English Establishment opened its American branch as well. The former was indicated by a number of events, such as sister Kathleen's marriage to the Marquis of Hartington and the shifting of Caroline's nursery school from the White House to the British Embassy after her father's assassination. (The ambassador, Ormsby-Gore, fifth Baron Harlech, was the son of an old associate of Lord Milner and Leo Amery, when they were the active core of the British-American Atlantic Establishment.) Another indication of this connection was the large number of Oxford-trained men appointed to office by President Kennedy.

The period since 1950 has seen the beginnings of a revolutionary change in American politics. This change is not so closely related to the changes in American economic life as it is to the transformation in social life. But without the changes in economic life, the social influences could not have operated. What has been happening has been a disintegration of the middle class and a corresponding increase in significance by the petty bourgeoisie at the same time that the economic influence of the older Wall Street financial groups has been weakening and been challenged by new wealth springing up outside the eastern cities, notably in the Southwest and Far West. These new sources of wealth have been based very largely on government action and government spending but have, none the less, adopted a petty-bourgeois outlook rather than the semiaristocratic outlook that pervades the Eastern Establishment. This new wealth, based on petroleum, natural gas, ruthless exploitation of national resources, the aviation industry, military bases in the South and West, and finally on space with all its attendant activities, has centered in Texas and southern California. Its existence, for the first time, made it possible for the petty-bourgeois outlook to make itself felt in the political nomination process instead of in the unrewarding effort to influence politics by voting for a Republican candidate nominated under Eastern Establishment influence.

In these terms the political struggle in the United States has shifted in two ways, or even three. This struggle, in the minds of the ill informed, had always been viewed as a struggle between Republicans and Democrats at the ballot box in November. Wall Street, long ago, however, had seen that the real struggle was in the nominating conventions the preceding summer. This realization was forced upon the petty-bourgeois supporters of Republican candidates by their antipathy for Willkie, Dewey, Eisenhower, and other Wall Street interventionists and their inability to nominate their congressional favorites, like Senators Knowland, Bricker, and Taft, at national party conventions. Just as these disgruntled voters reached this conclusion, with Taft's failure in 1952, the new wealth appeared in the political picture, sharing the petty bourgeoisie's suspicions of the East, big cities, Ivy League universities, foreigners, intellectuals, workers, and aristocrats. By the 1964 election, the major political issue in the country was the financial struggle behind the scenes between the old wealth, civilized and cultured in foundations, and the new wealth, virile and uninformed, arising from the flowing profits of government-dependent corporations in the Southwest and West.

At issue here was the whole future face of America, for the older wealth stood for values and aims close to the Western traditions of diversity, tolerance, human rights and values, freedom, and the rest of it, while the newer wealth stood for the narrow and fear-racked aims of petty-bourgeois insecurity and egocentricity. The nominal issues between them, such as that between internationalism and unilateral isolationism (which its supporters preferred to rename "nationalism"), were less fundamental than they seemed, for the real issue was the control of the Federal government's tremendous power to influence the future of America by spending of government funds. The petty bourgeois and new-wealth groups wanted to continue that spending into the industrial-military complex, such as defense and space, while the older wealth and nonbourgeois groups wanted to direct it toward social diversity and social amelioration for the aged and the young, for education, for social outcasts, and for protecting national resources for future use.

The outcome of this struggle, which still goes on, is one in which civilized people can afford to be optimistic. For the newer wealth is unbelievably ignorant and misinformed. In their growing concern to control political nominations, they ignored the even greater need to win elections. They did not realize that the disintegration of the middle classes, chiefly from the abandonment of the middle-class outlook, was creating an American electorate that would never elect any candidate the newer wealth would care to nominate. As part of this lack of vision, the new wealth and its petty-bourgeois supporters ignored the well-established principle that a national candidate must have a national appeal and that this is obtained best by a candidate close to the center.

In American politics we have several parties included under the blanket words "Democratic" and "Republican." In oversimplified terms, as I have said, the Republicans were the party of the middle classes, and the Democrats were the party of the fringes. Both of these were subdivided, each with a Congressional and a National Party wing. The Republican Congressional Party (representing localism) was much farther to the Right than the National Republican Party, and as such was closer to the petty-bourgeois than to the upper-middle-class outlook. The Democratic Congressional Party was much more clearly of the fringes and minorities (and thus often further to the Left) than the Democratic National Party. The party machinery in each case was in Congressional Party control during the intervals between the quadrennial presidential elections, but, in order to win these elections, each had to call into existence, in presidential election years, its shadowy National Party. This meant that the Republicans had to appear to move to the Left, closer to the Center, while the Democrats had also to move from the fringes toward the Center, usually by moving to the Right. As a result, the National parties and their presidential candidates, with the Eastern Establishment assiduously fostering the process behind the scenes, moved closer together and nearly met in the center with almost identical candidates and platforms, although the process was concealed, as much as possible, by the revival of obsolescent or meaningless war cries and slogans (often going back to the Civil War). As soon as the presidential election was over, the two National parties vanished, and party controls fell back into the hands of the Congressional parties, leaving the newly elected President in a precarious position between the two Congressional parties, neither of which was very close to the brief National coalition that had elected him.

The chief problem of American political life for a long time has been how to make the two Congressional parties more national and international. The argument that the two parties should represent opposed ideals and policies, one, perhaps, of the Right and the other of the Left, is a foolish idea acceptable only to doctrinaire and academic thinkers. Instead, the two parties should be almost identical, so that the American people can "throw the rascals out" at any election without leading to any profound or extensive shifts in policy. The policies that are vital and necessary for America are no longer subjects of significant disagreement, but are disputable only in details of procedure, priority, or method: we must remain strong, continue to function as a great world Power in cooperation with other Powers, avoid high-level war, keep the economy moving without significant slump, help other countries do the same, provide the basic social necessities for all our citizens, open up opportunities for social shifts for those willing to work to achieve them, and defend the basic Western outlook of diversity, pluralism, cooperation, and the rest of it, as already described. These things any national American party hoping to win a presidential election must accept. But either party in office becomes in time corrupt, tired, unenterprising, and vigorless. Then it should be possible to replace it, every four years if necessary, by the other party, which will be none of these things but will still pursue, with new vigor, approximately the same basic policies.

The capture of the Republican National Party by the extremist elements of the Republican Congressional Party in 1964, and their effort to elect Barry Goldwater to the Presidency with the petty-bourgeois extremists alone, was only a temporary aberration on the American political scene, and arose from the fact that President Johnson had preempted all the issues (which are, as we have said, now acceptable to the overwhelming majority) and had occupied the whole broad center of the American political spectrum, so that it was hardly worth while for the Republicans to run a real contestant against him in the same area. Thus Goldwater was able to take control of the Republican National Party by default.

The virulence behind the Goldwater campaign, however, had nothing to do with default or lack of intensity. Quite the contrary. His most ardent supporters were of the extremist petty-bourgeois mentality driven to near hysteria by the disintegration of the middle classes and the steady rise in prominence of everything they considered anathema: Catholics, Negroes, immigrants, intellectuals, aristocrats (and near aristocrats), scientists, and educated men generally, people from big cities or from the East, cosmopolitans and internationalists and, above all, liberals who accept diversity as a virtue.

This disintegration of the middle classes had a variety of causes, some of them intrinsic, many of them accidental, a few of them obvious, but many of them going deeply into the very depths of social existence.

All these causes acted to destroy the middle classes by acting to destroy the middle-class outlook. And this outlook was destroyed, not by adult middle-class persons abandoning it, but by a failure or inability of parents to pass it on to their children. Moreover, this failure was largely restricted to the middle class itself and not to the petty bourgeoisie (lower middle class), which, if anything, was clinging to its particular version of the middle-class outlook more tenaciously and was passing it on to its offspring in an even more intensified form.

What I am saying here is that the disintegration of the middle class arose from a failure to transfer its outlook to its children. This failure was thus a failure of education, and may seem, at first glance, to be all the more surprising, since our education system has been, consciously or unconsciously, organized as a mechanism for indoctrination of the young in middle-class ideology. In fact, rather surprisingly, it would appear that our educational system, unlike those of continental Europe, has been more concerned with indoctrination of middle-class outlook than with teaching patriotism or nationalism. As a reflection of this, it has been more concerned with instilling attitudes and behavior than with intellectual training. In view of the fact that the American ideals of the 1920's were as much middle class as patriotic, with the so-called "American way of life" identified rather with the American economic and social system than with the American political system, and the fact that a majority of schoolchildren were not from middle-class families, it is not surprising that the educational system was devoted to training in the middle-class outlook. Children of racial, religious, national, and class minorities all passed through the same system and received the middle-class formative process, with, it must be recognized, incomplete success in many cases. This refers to the public schools, but the Roman Catholic school system, especially on its upper levels, was doing the same things. The large number of Catholic men's colleges in the country, especially those operated by the Jesuits, had as their basic, if often unrecognized, aim the desire to transform the sons of working class, and often of immigrant, origins into middle-class people in professional occupations (chiefly law, medicine, business, and teaching).

On the whole, this system was, until recently, a success, but is now becoming less and less successful in turning out middle-class people, especially from its upper educational levels. This failure can be attributed rather to the context within which the educational system has operated than to a failure of the system itself. As we shall see in a moment, this failure occurred chiefly within the middle-class family, a not unexpected situation, since outlook is still determined rather by reaction to family conditions than by submission to a formal educational process.

Much of the disintegration of the middle-class outlook can be traced to a weakening of its chief aspects, such as future preference, intense self-discipline, and, to a lesser degree, to a decreasing emphasis on infinitely expandable material demand and on the importance of middle-class status symbols. Only a few of the factors that have influenced these changes can be mentioned here.

The chief external factor in the destruction of the middle-class outlook has been the relentless attack upon it in literature and drama through most of the twentieth century. In fact, it is difficult to find works that defended this outlook or even assumed it to be true, as was frequent in the nineteenth century. Not that such works did not exist in recent years; they have existed in great numbers, and have been avidly welcomed by the petty bourgeoisie and by some middle-class housewives. Lending libraries and women's magazines of the 1910's, 1920's, and 1930's were full of them, but, by the 1950's they were largely restricted to television soap dramas. Even those writers who explicitly accepted the middle-class ideology, like Booth Tarkington, Ben Ames Williams, Sloan Wilson, or John O'Hara, tended to portray middle-class life as a horror of false values, hypocrisy, meaningless effort, and insecurity. In *Alice Adams,* for example, Tarkington portrayed a lower-middle-class girl, filled with hypocrisy and materialistic values, desperately seeking a husband who would provide her with the higher social status for which she yearned.

In the earlier period, even down to 1940, literature's attack on the middle-class outlook was direct and brutal, from such works as Upton Sinclair's *The Jungle* or Frank Norris's *The Pit,* both dealing with the total corruption of personal integrity in the meatpacking and wheat markets. These early assaults were aimed at the commercialization of life under bourgeois influence and were fundamentally reformist in outlook because they assumed that the evils of the system could somehow be removed, perhaps by state intervention. By the 1920's the attack was much more total, and saw the problem in moral terms so fundamental that no remedial action was possible. Only complete rejection of middle-class values could remove the corruption of human life seen by Sinclair Lewis in *Babbitt* or *Main Street.*

After 1940, writers tended less and less to attack the bourgeois way of life; that job had been done. Instead they described situations, characters, and actions that were simply nonbourgeois: violence, social irresponsibility, sexual laxity and perversion, miscegenation, human weakness in relation to alcohol, narcotics, or sex, or domestic and business relationships conducted along completely nonbourgeois lines. Ernest Hemingway, William Faulkner, Erskine Caldwell, John Dos Passos, and a host of lesser writers, many of them embracing the cult of violence, showed the trend. A very popular work like *The Lost Weekend* could represent the whole group. A few, like Hemingway, found a new moral outlook to replace the middle-class ideology they had abandoned. In Hemingway's case he shook the dust of upper-middle-class Oak Park, Illinois, off his feet and immersed himself in the tragic sense of life of Spain with its constant demand upon men to demonstrate their virility by incidental activity with women and unflinching courage in facing death. To Hemingway this could be achieved in the bullring, in African big-game hunting, in war or, in a more symbolic way, in prizefighting or crime. The significant point here is that Hemingway's embrace of the outlook of the Pakistani-Peruvian axis as a token of his rejection of his middle-class background was always recognized by him as a pretense, and, when his virility, in the crudest sense, was gone, he blew out his brains.

The literary assault on the bourgeois outlook was directed at all the aspects of it that we have mentioned, at future preference, at self-discipline, at the emphasis on materialistic acquisition, at status symbols. The attack on future preference appeared as a demonstration that the future is never reached. Its argument was that the individual who constantly postpones living from the present (with living taken to mean real personal relationships with individuals) to a hypothetical future eventually finds that the years have gone by, death is approaching, he has not yet lived, and is, in most cases, no longer able to do so. If the central figure in such a work has achieved his materialist ambitions, the implication is that these achievements, which looked so attractive from a distance, are but encumbrances to the real values of personal living when achieved. This theme, which goes back at least to Charles Dickens's *A Christmas Carol* or to George Eliot's *Silas Marner*, continued to be presented into the twentieth century. It often took the form, in more recent times, of a rejection of a man's whole life achievement by his sons, his wife, or himself.

The more recent form of this attack on future preference has appeared in the existentialist novel and the theater of the absurd. Existentialism, by its belief that reality and life consist only of the specific, concrete personal experience of a given place and moment, ignores the context of each event and thus isolates it. But an event without context has no cause, meaning, or consequence; it is absurd, as anything is which has no relationship to any context. And such an event, with neither past nor future, can have no connection with tradition or with future preference. This point of view came to saturate twentieth-century literature so that the original rejection of future preference was expanded into total rejection of time, which was portrayed as simply a mechanism for enslaving man and depriving him of the opportunity to experience life. The writings of Thomas Wolfe and, on a higher level, of the early Dos Passos, were devoted to this theme. The bourgeois time clock became a tomb or prison that alienated man from life and left him a cipher, like the appropriately named Mr. Zero in Elmer Rice's play *The Adding Machine* (1923).

A similar attack was made on self-discipline. The philosophic basis for this attack was found in an oversimplified Freudianism that regarded all suppression of human impulse as leading to frustration and psychic distortions that made subsequent life unattainable. Thus novel after novel or play after play portrayed the wickedness of the suppression of good, healthy, natural impulse and the salutary consequences of self-indulgence, especially in sex. Adultery and other manifestations of undisciplined sexuality were described in increasingly clinical detail and were generally associated with excessive drinking or other evasions of personal responsibility, as in Hemingway's *A Farewell to Arms* and *The Sun Also Rises* or in John Steinbeck's love affair with personal irresponsibility in *Cannery Row* or *Tortilla Flat*. The total rejection of middle-class values, including time, self-discipline, and material achievement, in favor of a cult of personal violence was to be found in a multitude of literary works from James M. Cain and Raymond Chandler to the more recent antics of James Bond. The result has been a total reversal of middle-class values by presenting as interesting or admirable simple negation of these values by aimless, shiftless, and totally irresponsible people.

A similar reversal of values has flooded the market with novels filled with pointless clinical descriptions, presented in obscene language and in fictional form, of swamps of perversions ranging from homosexuality, incest, sadism, and masochism, to cannibalism, necrophilia, and coprophagia. These performances, as the critic Edmund Fuller has said, represent not so much a loss of values as a loss of any conception of the nature of man. Instead of seeing man the way the tradition of the Greeks and of the West regarded him, as a creature midway between animal and God, "a little lower than the angels," and thus capable of an infinite variety of experience, these twentieth-century writers have completed the revolt against the middle classes by moving downward from the late nineteenth century's view of man as simply a higher animal to their own view of man as lower than any animal would naturally descend. From this has emerged the Puritan view of man (but without the Puritan view of God) as a creature of total depravity in a deterministic universe without hope of any redemption.

This point of view, which, in the period 1550–1650, justified despotism in a Puritan context, now may be used, with petty-bourgeois support, to justify a new despotism to preserve, by force instead of conviction, petty-bourgeois values in a system of compulsory conformity. George Orwell's *1984* has given us the picture of this system as Hitler's Germany showed us its practical operation. But in view of the present upsurge of nonbourgeois social groups and social pressures, this possibility becomes decreasingly likely, and Barry Goldwater's defeat in the presidential election of 1964 moved the possibility so far into the future that the steady change in social conditions makes it remote indeed.

The destruction of the middle classes by the destruction of the middle-class outlook was brought about to a much greater degree by internal than by external forces. And the most significant of these influences have been operating within the middle-class family. One of the most obvious of these has been the growing affluence of American society, which removed the pressure of want from the childbearing process. The child who grows up in affluence is more difficult to instill with the frustrations and drives that were so basic in the middle-class outlook. For generations, even in fairly rich families, this indoctrination had continued because of continued emphasis on thrift and restraints on consumption. By 1937 the world depression showed that the basic economic problems were not saving and investment, but distribution and consumption. Thus there appeared a growing readiness to consume, spurred on by new sales techniques, installment selling, and the extension of credit from the productive side to the consumption side of the economic process. As a result, an entirely new phenomenon appeared in middle-class families, the practice of living up to, or even beyond, their incomes—an unthinkable scandal in any nineteenth-century bourgeois family. One incentive in this direction was the increased emphasis, within the middle-class ideology, upon the elements of status and ostentatious display of wealth as status symbols rather than on the elements of frugality and prudence. Thus affluence weakened both future preference and self-denying self-discipline training.

Somewhat related to this was the influence of the depression of 1929–1933. The generation that was entering manhood at that time (having been born in the period 1905–1915) felt that their efforts to fulfill their middle-class ambitions had involved them in intensive hardships and suffering, such as working while going to college, doing without leisure, cultural expansion, and travel, and by the 1950's these were determined that their children must never have it as hard as they had had it. They rarely saw that their efforts to make things easy for their children in the 1950's as a reaction against the hardships they had suffered themselves in the 1930's were removing from their children's training process the difficulties that had helped to make them achieving men and successful middle-class persons and that their efforts to do this were weakening the moral fiber of their children.

Another element in this process was a change in the educational philosophy of America and a somewhat similar change in the country's ideas on the whole process of child training. Early generations had continued to cling to the vestiges of the Puritan outlook to the degree that they insisted that children must be trained under strict discipline, including corporal punishment. This seventeenth-century idea, by 1920, was being replaced in American family ideology by an idea of the nineteenth century that child maturation is an innate process not subject to modification by outside training. In educational theory this erroneous idea went back to the *Emile* of Jean-Jacques Rousseau (1762), which idealized the state of nature as equivalent to the Garden of Eden, and believed that education must consist in leaving a youth completely free so that his innate goodness could emerge and reveal itself. This idea was developed, intensified, and given a pseudoscientific foundation by advances in biology and genetics in the late nineteenth century. By 1910 or so, childrearing and educational theories had accepted the idea that man was a biological organism, like any animal, that his personality was a consequence of hereditary traits, and that each child had within him a rigid assortment of inherited talents and a natural rate of maturation in the development of these talents. These ideas were incorporated in a series of slogans of which two were: "Every child is different," and "He'll do it when he's ready."

From all this came a wholesale ending of discipline, both in the home and in school, and the advent of "permissive education," with all that it entailed. Children were encouraged to have opinions and to speak out on matters of which they were totally ignorant; acquisition of information and intellectual training were shoved into the background; and restrictions of time, place, and movement in schools and homes were reduced to a minimum. Every emphasis was placed on "spontaneity"; and fixed schedules of time periods or subject matter to be covered were belittled. All this greatly weakened the disciplinary influence of the educational process, leaving the new generation much less disciplined, less organized, and less aware of time than their parents. Naturally this disintegrative process was less evident among the children of the petty bourgeois than in the middle class itself. These influences in themselves would have contributed much to the weakening of the middle-class outlook among the rising generation, but other, much more profound, influences were also operating. To examine these we must look inside the middle-class family structure.

In marriage, as in so many other things, Western Civilization has been subjected to quite antithetical theories; these we might call the Western and the Romantic theories of love and marriage. The Romantic theory of these things was that each man or woman had a unique personality consisting of inborn traits, accumulated by inheritance from a unique combination of ancestors. This is, of course, the same theory that was used to justify permissive education. In Romantic love, however, the theory went on to assume, simply as a matter of faith, that for each man or woman there existed in a world a person of the opposite sex whose personality traits would just fit into those of his or her destined mate. The only problem was to find that mate. It was assumed that this would be done, at first sight, when an almost instantaneous flash of recognition would reveal to both that they had found the one possible life's partner.

The idea of love at first sight as a flash of recognition was closely related to the Manichaean and Puritan religious idea that God's truth came to men in a similar flash of illumination (an idea that goes back, like so many of these ideas, to Plato's theory of knowledge as reminiscence). In its most extreme form, this Romantic theory of love assumed that each of the destined lovers was only part of a person, the two parts fitting together instantly on meeting into a single personality. Associated with this were a number of other ideas, including the idea that marriages were "made in heaven," that such a Romantic marriage was totally satisfying to the partners, and that such a marriage should be "eternal."

These ideas of Romantic love and marriage were much more acceptable to women than to men (for reasons we have not time to analyze) and were embraced by the middle class, but not, to any great extent, by other classes. The theory, like so much of the middle-class outlook, originated among the medieval heresies, such as Manichaeism (as the Swiss writer Denis de Rougemont has shown), and was thus from the same tradition that saw the rise of the bourgeois outlook in the Middle Ages and its reinforcement by the closely associated Puritan movement of modern times. The Romantic theory of love was spread through the middle class by incidental factors, such as that the bourgeoisie were the only social class that read much, and Romantic love was basically a literary convention in its propagation whatever it may have been in its origins. It made no real impression on the other social classes in European society, such as the peasants, the nobility, or the urban working craftsmen.

Strangely enough, Romantic love, accepted as a theory and ideal by the bourgeoisie, had little influence on middle-class marriages in practice, since these were usually based on middle-class values of economic security and material status rather than on love. More accurately, middle-class marriages were based on these material considerations in fact, while everyone concerned pretended that they were based on Romantic love. Any subsequent recognition of this clash between fact and theory often gave a severe jolt and has sometimes been a subject for literary examination, as in the first volume of John Galsworthy's *The Forsyte Saga*.

Opposed to this Romantic theory of love and marriage, and almost equally opposed to the bourgeois practice of "sensible" marriage, was what we may call the Western idea of love and marriage. This assumes that personalities are dynamic and flexible things formed largely by experiences in the past. Love and marriage between such personalities are, like everything in the Western outlook, diverse, imperfect, adjustable, creative, cooperative, and changeable. The Western idea assumes that a couple come together for many reasons (sex, loneliness, common interests, similar background, economic and social cooperation, reciprocal admiration of character traits, and other reasons). It further assumes that their whole relationship will be a slow process of getting to know each other and of mutual adjustment—a process that may never end. The need for constant adjustment shows the Western recognition that nothing, even love, is final or perfect. This is also shown by recognition that love and marriage are never total and all-absorbing, that each partner remains an independent personality with the right to an independent life. (This is found throughout the Western tradition and goes back to the Christian belief that each person is a separate soul with its own, ultimately separate, fate.)

Thus there appeared in Western society at least three kinds of marriage, which we may call Romantic, bourgeois, and Western. The last, without being much discussed (except in modern books on love and marriage), is probably the most numerous of the three, and the other two, if they prove successful, do so by gradually developing into this third kind. Romantic marriage, based on the "shock of recognition," has in fact come to be based very largely on sexual attraction, since this is the chief form that love at first sight can take. Such marriages often fail, since even sex requires practice and mutual adjustment and is too momentary a human relationship to sustain a permanent union unless many other common interests accumulate around it. Even when this occurs and the marriage becomes a success, in the sense that it persists, it is never total, and the Romantic delusion that marriage should be totally absorbing of the time, attention, and energies of its partners, still expected by many women brought up on the Romantic idea, merely means that the marriage becomes an enslaving relationship to the husbands and a source of disappointment and frustration to the wives.

Middle-class marriage, in fact, was not romantic, for, in the middle class, marriage, like everything else, was subject to the middle-class system of values. Within that value system, middle-class persons chose a marriage partner who would assist in achieving middle-class goals of status and achievement. A woman, with her parents' approval, chose a husband who showed promise of being a good provider and a steady, reliable, social achiever, who would be able to give her a material status at least as high as that provided by her own parents. A man chose as a wife one who showed promise of being a help in his upward struggle, one able to act as hostess to his aspirant activities and to provide the domestic decorum and social graces expected of a successful business or professional man.

Such a marriage was based, from both sides, on status factors rather than on personal factors. The fact that a man was a Yale graduate, was trained for a profession, had a position with a good firm, drove an expensive car, could order dinner with assurance in an expensive restaurant, and had already applied for membership in a golf or country club were not reasons for loving him as a person, since they were simply the accessories of his status. Yet middle-class persons married for reasons such as these and, at the same time, convinced themselves and their friends that they were marrying for Romantic love (based on the fact that they were, in addition to their mutual social acceptability, sexually attracted).

For a time the new marriage could keep up these pretenses, especially as the elements of sex and novelty in the relationship helped conceal the contrast between theory and fact and that the marriage was basically an external and superficial relationship. But this fact remained, and in time unconscious frustrations and dissatisfactions began to operate. Often these did not reach the conscious level, especially a few generations ago, but today the question is posed by every women's magazine, "Is your marriage a success?" But unconsciously, long before this, realization had been growing that the marriage relationship was not based on love, which must be a recognition and appreciation of *personal qualities*, not of status accessories. Without personal feeling based on such personal qualities, the relationship was really not a personal relationship and was really not based on love, even when the partners, with the usual lack of introspection associated with middle-class minds, still insisted that it was based on love. The consequences of such unconscious recognition of the real lack of love in the bourgeois marital relationship, in a society that never stopped reiterating in song, cinema, magazine, and book the absolute necessity of love for human happiness and "fulfillment," will be examined in a moment.

Three generations ago the bourgeois wife rarely became aware of her frustrations. She was largely confined to her home, was kept too busy with children and housework to find much time for meditation on her situation or for comparison with other wives or the outside world generally. Brought up in a male-dominated family, she was prepared to accept a similar situation in her own life. This means that her outside contacts and her general picture of the world came to her through the screen of her husband's vision of these things.

The decrease in the number of children in middle-class families and the spread of labor-saving devices, from vacuum cleaners to frozen foods, gave the bourgeois wife increasing leisure in the 1920's and 1930's. Enterprising editors like Edwin Bok filled that leisure with new slick women's magazines (like the *Ladies' Home Journal*). Popular novels and, to a lesser extent, the early movies, dramatic matinees, and spreading women's clubs allowed women to build up a vision of a fantasy world of romantic love and carefree, middle-class housewives with dazzling homes and well-behaved and well-scrubbed children. By 1925 the average bourgeois housewife was becoming increasingly frustrated because her own life was not that pictured in the women's magazines. Her increasing leisure gave her time to think about it, and her more frequent contact with other wives encouraged her to raise her voice in criticism of her husband whose financial inability to provide her with the life she came to regard as her due seemed to her to justify her desire to nag him onward to greater effort in pursuit of money. To him this became nagging; to her it was only an occasional reminder of the expectations under which she had entered upon the marriage relationship.

While this was going on, the outside world was also changing. Women became "emancipated" as a consequence of World War I, with considerable urging onward from the women's magazines. Shorter skirts and shorter hair became symbols of this process, but even more significant was the appearance in the outside world of a great increase in the number of jobs that could be done best, or only, by women. As part of this process, there took place considerable changes in bourgeois morality, the ending of chaperonage, greater freedom between the sexes, and the acceptance of divorce as morally possible in bourgeois life (a custom that came in from the stage and cinema).

As part of this whole process, there occurred a dramatic event of great social significance. This was the reversal in longevity expectations of men and women in adult life. A century ago (to be sure, in a largely rural context), a twenty-year-old man could expect to live longer than a twenty-year-old wife. In fact, such a man might well bury two or three wives, usually from the mortality associated with childbirth or other female problems. Today, a twenty-year-old man has little expectation of living as long as a twenty-year-old woman. To make matters worse, a twenty-year-old woman a century ago married a man considerably older than herself, at least in the middle classes, simply because future preference required that a man be established economically before he began to raise a family.

Today, from a series of causes, such as the extension of the female expectation of life faster than the male expectation, the increased practice of birth control, coeducation (which brings the sexes into contact at the same age), weakening of future preference and of the middle-class outlook generally, which leads to marriages by couples of about the same age, husbands now generally die before their wives. Recognition of this, the increased independence of women, adaptation to taxes and other legal nuisances, has given rise to joint financial accounts, to property being put in the wife's name, and to greatly increased insurance benefits for wives. Gradually the wealth of the country became female-owned, even if still largely male-controlled.

But this had subtle results; it made women more independent and more outspoken. Bourgeois men gradually came to live under a regime of persistent nagging to become "better providers." To many men, work became a refuge and a relief from domestic revelations of the inadequacy of their performance as economic achievers. This growth of overwork, of constant tension, of frustration of emotional life and of leisure began to make more and more men increasingly willing to accept death as the only method of achieving rest. Bourgeois men literally began to kill themselves, by unconscious psychic suicide, from overwork, neurotic over-indulgence in alcohol, smoking, work, and violent leisure, and the middle class slowly increased its proportion of materially endowed widows.

One notable change in this whole process was a shift, over the past century, from the male-dominated family to a female-dominated family. The locality in which the young couple set up their home had an increasing tendency to be matrilocal rather than patrilocal. In increasing numbers of cases, where the young couple married before the groom's educationɪl process was finished, they even lived with her family (but very rarely with his family). Increasingly part of the burden of housework was shifted to the husband: washing dishes, buying groceries, even tending the children. In 1840 a child could cry at night and would invariably be tended by its mother, while the father slept peacefully on, totally unaware of what was going on. By 1960, if a child cried at night, the chances were as likely as not that the mother would hear nothing while the father took over the necessary activities. If this were questioned by anyone, the mother's retort was pointed: "I take care of baby all day; I don't see why he can't take care of it at night!"

Closely related to this confusion, or even reversal, of the social roles of the sexes was decreasing sexual differentiation in child-rearing practices. As recently as the 1920's girl babies were reared differently from boys. They were dressed differently, treated differently, permitted to do different things, and admonished about different dangers. By 1960, children, regardless of sex, were all being brought up the same. Indeed, with short cropped hair and playsuits on both, it became impossible to be sure which was which. This led to a decrease in the personality differences of men and women, with males becoming more submissive and females more aggressive.

This tendency was accelerated by new techniques of education, especially in the first twelve years of life. The neurological maturation of girls was faster than that of boys, especially in regard to coordination, such as in feeding oneself, talking, dressing oneself, toilet-training, learning to read, and general adjustment to school. The shift from home to school in the early grades was adjusted to by girls more easily than by boys, partly because girls were more self-assured and gregarious. By the age of ten or twelve, girls were developed physically, neurologically, emotionally, and socially about two years in advance of boys. All this tended to make boys less self-assured, indecisive, weak, and dependent. The steady increase in the percentage of women teachers in the lower grades worked in the same direction, since women teachers favored girls and praised those attitudes and techniques that were more natural to girls. New methods, such as the whole-word method of teaching reading or the use of true-and-false or multiple-choice examinations, were also better adapted to female than to masculine talents. Less and less emphasis was placed on critical judgment, while more and more was placed on intuitive or subjective decisions. In this environment girls did better, and boys felt inferior or decided that school was a place for girls and not for boys. The growing aggressiveness of girls pushed these hesitant boys aside and intensified the problem. As consequences of this, boys had twice as many "nonreaders" as girls, several times as many stutterers, and many times as many teen-age bedwetters.

While the outside world was decreasing its differential treatment of children on a sexual basis by treating boys and girls more and more alike (and that treatment was better adapted to girls than to boys) within the middle-class home, the growing emotional frustrations of the mother were leading to an increasing distinction on a sexual basis in her emotional treatment of her children.

The earliest feeling of sensual reassurance and comfort any child experiences is against the body of its mother. To a boy baby this is a heterosexual relationship, while to the girl it is a relationship with the same sex. In most cases the little girl avoids any undesirable persistence of this homosexual tendency by shifting her admiration and attention to some available male, usually her father. Thus by the age of six or eight, a daughter has become "Daddy's girl," awaiting his return from work to communicate the news of the day, getting his slippers and newspaper, and hoping that he will read her a story or share her viewing of a favorite television program before she must go to bed. By the age of twelve, in a normal girl, this interest in male creatures has begun to shift to some boy in her class at school. With a boy baby the transference is later and less gradual. The undesirable aspects of his love for his mother are avoided by the powerful social pressures of the incest taboo, but this merely means that the sexual element in his concern for the opposite sex is suppressed and is undeveloped. Thus there is a natural, we might almost say biological, tendency in our society for the sexual development of the boy to be delayed and for the girl to be free from this retarding influence.

In the American middle-class family of today, these influences have been extraordinarily exaggerated. Because the middle-class marriage is based on social rather than personal attraction, the emotional relation of the wife to her husband is insecure, and the more her husband buries himself in his work, hobbies, or outside interests, the more insecure and unsatisfactory it becomes for his wife. Part of the wife's unused emotional energy begins to be expended in her love for her son. At the same time, because of the emotional insecurity in the mother's relationship with her husband, the daughter may come to be regarded as an emotional rival for the husband's affection. This resentment of the daughter is most likely to occur when there is some other cause of disturbance in the mother's psychology, especially if this cause is associated with her relationship to her own father. For example, as female domination becomes, generation by generation, a more distinctive feature of American family life, the daughter's shift of attention to her father becomes less complete, and, by adolescence, she tends to pity him rather than to admire him and may become relatively ambivalent in her feelings toward both her father and mother, sometimes hating the latter for dominating her father and despising his weakness in allowing it. In such a case, the whole development of which we speak is accelerated and intensified in the next generation, and the daughter's relatively ambivalent feelings toward her parents are repeated in her relatively ambivalent feelings toward her husband. This serves to intensify both her emotional smothering and overprotection of her son and her tendency toward emotional rejection of her daughter as a potential danger to the relatively precarious emotional relationship between husband and wife.

As a consequence of this situation, the frustrated wife has a tendency to cling to her son by keeping him dependent and immature as long as possible and to seek to hasten the maturing of her daughter in order to edge her out of the family circle as soon as possible. The chief consequence of this is the increasingly late maturity, the weakness, undersexuality, and dependence of American boys and American men of middle-class origins and the increasingly early maturing, aggressiveness, oversexuality, and independence of American middle-class girls. The mother's alienation of the daughter (which often reaches an acute condition of mutual hatred) may begin in childhood or even at birth (especially if the girl baby is beautiful, is not nursed by the mother, and is welcomed with excessive joy by the husband). It usually becomes acute when the daughter reaches puberty and may become very acute if the mother, about the same time, is approaching her menopause (which she often mistakenly feels will reduce her attraction as a woman to her husband).

During this whole period, the mother's rejection of her daughter appears chiefly in her efforts to force her to grow up rapidly, and leads to premature exposure of the daughter to such modern monstrosities as preteen "mixed parties," training bras, access to overly "sophisticated" movies, books, and conversations, and the practice of leaving daughters unchaperoned in the house with boy classmates, on the early high school or even junior high school level. Such experiences and the increasingly frequent clashes of temperament between mother and daughter lead a surprisingly large percentage of middle-class girls to move from the home before the age of twenty. And whether she leaves or not, sexual and emotional maturity comes to the American middle-class girl earlier and earlier, not only in comparison with the middle-class boy but even in absolute terms. We are told, for example, that the onset of puberty among American girls (an event which can be dated exactly by the first menstrual period) has been occurring at an earlier age by about nine months for each passing decade. As a result, this milestone is reached by American girls today up to three years earlier than with American girls of the early twentieth century.

Over the same period, the American middle-class boy has been moving in the opposite direction, although the physiological element cannot be documented. Indeed, it need not be. More significant is the changing relationship between the arrival of sexual awareness and of emotional readiness to accept sex. There can be no doubt that the American child today, especially in a middle-class family, becomes aware of sex much earlier than he did a generation or two ago, and long before he is emotionally ready to face the fact of his own sexuality. In the nineteenth century three things came fairly close together in the fifteen to seventeen age bracket: (1) sexual awareness; (2) emotional readiness for sex; and (3) the ending of education and the opportunity to seek economic independence from parents. Today sexual awareness comes very early for all, perhaps around the age of ten. Emotional readiness to face the fact of one's own sexuality comes earlier and earlier for the girl today, but later and later for the boy, chiefly because the middle-class mother forces independence and recognition of the fact that she is a woman upon her daughter but forces dependence and blindness to the fact that he is a man upon her son. And the date for the ending of education and seeking economic independence from parents gets somewhat later for girls but immensely later for men (a process that becomes increasingly extravagant).

One result of this is that the much greater (sometimes indefinitely postponed) delay for a boy of emotional readiness after sexual awareness leaves the boy emotionally desexed for so long that it affects his sexuality and emotional maturity adversely and to an increasingly advanced age. But the opposite is true for a girl, because of the shorter and decreasing lag of her emotional readiness after her sexual awareness. Lolita, who is not as rare as the readers of that novel wanted to imagine, becomes increasingly frequent, and cannot be satisfied by boys of her own age; consequently she seeks for many reasons, including financial resources and greater emotional maturity, her sex companions among older men.

On the other hand, the position of the middle-class boy becomes even more complex and pitiful, since he not only must face the fluctuating chronology of these developments to a greater degree but must free himself from his emotional dependence on his mother with little help from anyone. If his father tries to help (and he is the only one who is likely to try to do so), and insists that his son become a responsible and independent human being, the mother fights like a tigress to defend her son's continued immaturity and dependence, accusing the husband of cruelty, of hatred for his son, and of jealousy of his son's feeling for the mother. She does not hesitate to use the weapons that she has. They are many and powerful, including a "reluctant" and ambiguous "revelation" to the son that his father hates him. Any effort by the father to argue that true love must seek to help the son advance in maturity and independence, and that insistence that he avoid or postpone these advances might well be regarded as hatred rather than love, are usually blocked with ease. At this stage in the family history, emotional frustrations and confusions are generally at so high a level that it is fairly easy for mother and son to agree that black is white. "Momism" is usually triumphant for a more or less extended period, while normal adolescent rebellion becomes a wholesale rejection of the father and only much later a delayed effort at achieving emotional detachment from the mother.

The point of all this is that normal adolescent rebellion has become, in America today, a radical and wholesale rejection of parental values, including middle-class values, because of the protracted emotional warfare which now goes on in the middle-class home with teen-age children. The chief damage in the situation lies in the pervasive destruction of the adolescent middle-class boy and his alienation from the achieving aspects of middle-class culture. The middle-class girl, chiefly because she still tries to please her father, may continue to be a considerable success as an achiever, especially in academic life where her earlier successes make continuance of the process fairly easy. But the middle-class boy who rejects the achieving aspects of middle-class life often does so in academic matters that seem to him to be an alien and feminine world from the beginning. His rejection of this world and his unconscious yearning for academic failure arise from a series of emotional influences: (1) a desire to strike back at his father; (2) a desire to free himself from dependence on his mother and thus to escape from the feminine atmosphere of much academic life; and (3) a desire to escape from the endless academic road, going to age twenty-three or later, which modern technical and social complexities require for access to positions leading to high middle-class success. The lengthening of the interval of time between sexual awareness and the ending of education, from about two years in the 1880's to at least ten or twelve years in the 1960's, has set up such tensions and strains in the bourgeois American family that they threaten to destroy the family and are already in the process of destroying much of the middle-class outlook that was once so distinctive of the American way of life.

From this has emerged an almost total breakdown of communication between teen-agers and their parents' generation. Generally the adolescents do not tell their parents their most acute problems; they do not appeal to parents or adults but to each other for help in facing such problems (except where emotionally starved girls appeal to men teachers); and, when any effort is made to talk across the gap between the generations, words may pass but communication does not. Behind this protective barrier a new teen-age culture has grown up. Its chief characteristic is rejection of parental values and of middle-class culture. In many ways this new culture is like that of African tribes: its tastes in music and the dance, its emphasis on sex play, its increasingly scanty clothing, its emphasis on group solidarity, the high value it puts on interpersonal relations (especially talking and social drinking), its almost total rejection of future preference and its constant efforts to free itself from the tyranny of time. Teen-age solidarity and sociality and especially the solidarity of their groups and subgroups are amazingly African in attitudes, as they gather nightly, or at least on weekends, to drink "cokes," talk interminably in the midst of throbbing music, preferably in semidarkness, with couples drifting off for sex play in the corners as a kind of social diversion, and a complete emancipation from time. Usually they have their own language, with vocabulary and constructions so strange that parents find them almost incomprehensible. This Africanization of American society is gradually spreading with the passing years to higher age levels in our culture and is having profound and damaging effects on the transfer of middle-class values to the rising generation. A myriad of symbolic acts, over the last twenty years, have served to demonstrate the solidarity of teen culture and its rejection of middle-class values. Many of these involve dress and "dating customs," both major issues in the Adolescent-Parental Cold War.

In the days of Horatio Alger, the marks of youthful middle-class aspiration were such obvious symbols as well-polished shoes, a necktie and suit coat, a clean-shaved face and well-cut hair, and punctuality. For almost a generation now, teen culture has rejected the necktie and suit coat. Well-polished shoes gave way to dirty saddle shoes, and these in turn to "loafers" and thong sandals. Shaving became irregular, especially when schools were not in session; haircuts were postponed endlessly, with much parental-adolescent bickering. Fewer and fewer young people carried watches, even when they lived, as on a college campus, in fairly scheduled lives.

"Dating," as part of adolescent rebellion, became less and less formalized. The formal middle-class dance of a generation ago, arranged weeks ahead and with a dance program, became almost obsolete. Everything has to be totally "casual" or today's youth rejects it. By 1947 a dance program (listing the dances in numbered order with the girl's partner for each written down) was obsolete. "Going steady," which meant dancing only with the boy who invited her, became established, a complete rejection of the middle-class dance whose purpose was to provide the girl with a maximum number of different partners in order to widen her acquaintance with matrimonial possibilities.

"Going steady," like much of adolescent culture of the "jive" era, was derived from the gangster circles of south Chicago and was first introduced to middle-class knowledge through George Raft movies of the 1930's. It was satirized in a now forgotten popular song of the 1920's called "I Want to Dance with the Guy What Brung Me." But by 1947 it was the way of life of much of adolescent America. As a consequence, teen-age couples at high school dances "sat out" most of the evening in bored silence or chatted in a desultory fashion with friends of the same sex. The "jive" language of the period also had a south-Chicago origin and has been traced back, to a large extent, to a saloon run by a certain local oracle called "Hep" early in the twentieth century.

Fortunately, "going steady" was only a brief, if drastic, challenge to parental attitudes, and was soon replaced by tribal gregariousness and tolerant sexual broad-mindedness, which might be called "clique going," since it involved social solidarity (sometimes sexual promiscuity) within a small group, usually of ten or less. This became, to their adults, the "teen-age gang," which still thrives, but never in a very formal way in middle-class circles as it does in lower-class ones. Two casualties of this process are sexual jealousy and sexual privacy, both of which have largely disappeared among many upper-middle-class young people. In some groups sex has become a purely physiological act, somewhat like eating or sleeping. In others, sexual experience is restricted to loved ones, but since these youths love many persons (or even love everyone) this is much less of a restriction than it might seem to a middle-class mind. Generally a sharp distinction is made between "loving someone" (which justifies sex) and being "in love" with someone (which justifies monogamous behavior).

But there is widespread tolerance and endless discussion of all these issues. This discussion, like most of the adolescents' endless talk, never reaches any decisions but leaves the question open or decides that "it all depends on how you look at it." As part of such discussions, there is complete casual frankness as to who has had or is having sexual experiences with whom. Widely permeated with an existentialist outlook, the adolescent society regards each sexual experience as an isolated, contextless act, with no necessary cause or consequence, except the momentary merging of two lonelinesses in an act of togetherness. Among middle-class youth it is accompanied by an atmosphere of compassion or pity rather than of passion or even love (the way Holden Caulfield might experience sex). Among lower-class persons it is much more likely to be physiologically inspired and associated with passion or roughness. This often attracts middle-class girls who become dissatisfied with the weakness and undersexuality of middle-class boys. But petty-bourgeois youth, as befits the final defenders of middle-class conventionality and hypocrisy, still tend to approach sex with secrecy and even guilt.

Because of the breakdown of communication between the generations of middle-class families, parents know little of this side of teen-age culture, at least so far as their own children are concerned. They usually know much more about the behavior of their friends' children, because they are more likely to catch glimpses of the behavior of the latter in unguarded moments. On the whole, middle-class parents today are surprisingly (and secretly) tolerant about the behavior of their daughters so long as they do not create a public scandal by "getting into trouble." Mothers usually feel that their sons are too young and should wait for sexual experience, while fathers sometimes secretly think it might do their son's immaturity some good. When middle-class children get into trouble, or any kind of a scrape, their only large anxiety is to prevent their parents from finding out. Petty-bourgeois parents, as the last defense of middle-class conventionality, generally disapprove of any illicit sexual experiences by any of their children. Naturally there are great variations in all these things, with religion as the chief varying factor and variety of local customs in secondary significance. However, even in religious circles, the behavior of the young is not at all what their adults expect or believe. For example, the number of Roman Catholic young people who have premarital, or even casual, sexual experiences is much larger than the number who are willing to eat meat on Friday.

One reason for the spreading of these relaxed ideas on behavior is the devastating honesty of the younger generation, especially about themselves. This seems to be based on their gregarious garrulity. An earlier generation had its share of illicit actions of various kinds, but they kept these a secret and regarded each as an aberrant action that was psychologically excluded from their accepted social patterns and would not, therefore, be repeated. This view continued, no matter how often it was repeated. But the younger generation of today has accepted the existentialist idea, "I am what I do." The adolescent tells his group what he did, and they usually agree that this is the way he is, however surprising it is. Their whole attitude is pragmatic, almost experimental: "This is what happened. This is the way things are. This is the way I am." They are engaged in a search for themselves as individuals, something they were called upon to do in the early grades of school, thanks to the misconceptions of John Dewey, and they are quite alien to any theory that the self is a creature of trained patterns and is not a creature of discovered secrets. Now, in the 1960's, this opinion of man's nature is changing and, as a consequence of George Orwell, mishmash conceptions of brainwashing, and the revival of Pavlovian psychology through the work of men like Professor B. F. Skinner of Harvard, the idea of personality as something trained under discipline to a desired pattern is being revived. With this revival of a basically Puritanical idea of human nature reappears the usual Puritan errors on the nature of evil and acceptance of the theory of the evil of human nature (as preached in William Golding's *Lord of the Flies*).

The new outlook emerging from all this is complex, tentative, and full of inconsistencies, but it will surely play an increasing role in our history as the younger generation grows older, abandoning many of the ideas they now hold, with increasing responsibility; but at the same time the new outlook will force very great modifications in the American point of view as a whole.

This new outlook of the rising generation of the middle class has a negative and a positive side. Its negative side can be seen in its large-scale unconcern for the basic values of the middle-class outlook, its rejection of self-discipline, of future preference, of infinitely expandable material living standards, and of material symbols of middle-class status. In general this negative attitude appears in many of the activities we have described and above all in a profound rejection of abstractions, slogans, clichés, and conventions. These are treated with tolerant irony tinged with contempt. The targets of these attitudes are the general values of the petty bourgeoisie and of middle-class parents: position in society, "what people think," "self-respect," "keeping up with the Joneses," "the American Way of Life," "virtue," "making money," "destroying our country's enemies," virginity, respect for established organizations (including their elders, the clergy, political leaders, or big businessmen), and such.

The shift from a destructive or negative to a positive view of the new American outlook is, to some extent, chronological; it may be seen in the former popularity of Elvis Presley and the newer enthusiasm for Joan Baez (or folk singers generally). There is also a social distinction here to some extent, as Elvis remains, to a fair degree, popular with the lower classes, while Joan is a middle-class (or even college-level) favorite. But the contrast in outlook between the two is what is significant. Joan is gentle, compassionate, unemphatic, totally honest, concerned about people as individuals, free of pretenses (singing quietly in a simple dress and bare feet), full of love and fundamental human decency, and committed to these.

The rejection of acquisitiveness and even of sensuality may be seen in the change in tastes in movies, especially in the popularity of foreign films directed by men like Ingmar Bergman and Federico Fellini. The latter's *La Dolce Vita* (1961), a smash hit in the United States, was a portrayal of the meaningless disillusionment of material success and of sensuality in contrast with the power and mystery of nature (symbolized by a giant fish pulled from the sea and left to die by thoughtless men and the direct honesty and innocence of a child watching the scene).

This rejection of material things and of sensuality is, in some strange way, leading the younger generation to some kind of increased spirituality. Property and food mean very little to them. They share almost everything, give to others when they have very little for themselves, expect reciprocal sharing but not repayment, and feel free to "borrow" in this way without permission. Three meals a day is out; in fact, meals are almost out. They eat very little and irregularly, in sharp contrast to the middle classes early in the century who overate, as many mature middle-class persons still do. The petty bourgeoisie and lower classes still tend to overeat or to be neurotic snackers, but middle-class youth is almost monastic in its eating. Food just is not important, unless it is an occasion for a crowd to gather. Much of this decrease in emphasis on food is a consequence of their rejection of the discipline of time.

Everything in their lives is irregular (including their natural bodily processes). They usually get up too late to eat breakfast, snack somewhere along the day, refuse to carry watches, and often have no idea what day of the week it is.

This new outlook is basically existentialist in its emphasis on direct, momentary personal experience, especially with other people. It emphasizes people, and finds the highest good of life in interpersonal relations, handled generally with compassion and irony. The two chief concerns of life are "caring" and "helping." "Caring," which they usually call "love," means a general acceptance of the fact that people matter and are subjects of concern. This love is diffuse and often quite impersonal, not aimed at a particular individual or friend but at anyone, at persons in general, and especially at persons one does not know at all, as an act of recognition, almost of expiation, that we are all helpless children together. The whole idea is very close to Christ's message, "Love one another," and has given rise to the younger generation's passionate concern with remote peoples, the American Negroes, and the outcast poor. It is reflected in the tremendous enthusiasm among the young for the Peace Corps, civil rights, and racial equality, and the attack on poverty, all of which have much greater support among middle-class young people than can be measured even by the surprisingly large numbers who actively do something.

This desire to do something is what I call "helping." It is a strange and largely symbolic kind of helping, since there is with it a fairly widespread feeling that nothing that the helper can do will make any notable dent in the colossal problem; none the less, there is an obligation to do something, not only as a symbolic act but also as an almost masochistic rejection of the middle-class past. The younger generation who support the Peace Corps, the attack on poverty, and the drive for Negro rights have an almost irresistible compulsion to do these things as a demonstration of their rejection of their parents' value system, and as some restitution for the adults' neglect of these urgent problems. But the real motivation behind the urge "to help" is closely related with the urge "to care"; it consists simply of a desire to show another human being that he is not alone. There is little concern for human perfectibility or social progress such as accompanied middle-class humanitarianism in the nineteenth century.

Both of these urges are existentialist. They give rise to isolated acts that have no significant context. Thus an act of loving or helping has no sequence of causes leading up to it or of consequences flowing from it. It stands alone as an isolated experience of togetherness and of brief human sharing. This failure or lack of context for each experience means a failure or lack of meaning, for meaning and significance arise from context; that is, from the relationship of the particular experience to the whole picture. But today's youth has no concern for the whole picture; they have rejected the past and have very little faith in the future. Their rejection of intellect and their lack of faith in human reason gives them no hope that any meaning can be found for any experience, so each experience becomes an end in itself, isolated from every other experience.

This skepticism about meaning, closely allied with their rejection of organizations and of abstractions, is also closely related with a failure of responsibility. Since consequences are divorced from the act or experience itself, the youth is not bound by any relationship between the two. The result is a large-scale irresponsibility. If a young person makes an appointment, he may or may not keep it. He may come very late or not at all. In any case, he feels no shame at failure to carry out what he had said he would do. In fact, the young people of today constantly speak of what they are going to do—after lunch, tonight, tomorrow, next week—but they rarely do what they say. To them it was always very tentative, a hope rather than a statement, and binding on no one. If the young fail to do what they say, they are neither embarrassed nor apologetic, and hardly think it necessary to explain or even mention it. Their basic position is that everyone concerned had the same freedom to come or not, and if you showed up while they did not, this does not give you any right to complain because you also had the same right to stay away as they had.

The other great weakness of the younger generation is their lack of self-discipline. They are as episodic in their interests and ambitions as they are in their actions. They can almost kill themselves with overwork for something that catches their fancy, usually something associated with their group or with "caring" and "helping," but in general they have little tenacity of application or self-discipline in action.

They lack imagination also, an almost inevitable consequence of an outlook that concentrates on experiences without context. Their experiences are necessarily limited and personal and are never fitted into a larger picture or linked with the past or the future. As a result they find it almost impossible to picture anything different from what it is, or even to see what it is from any long-range perspective. This means that their outlooks, in spite of their wide exposure to different situations through the mass media or by personal travel, are very narrow. They lack the desire to obtain experience vicariously from reading, and the vicarious experiences that they get from talk (usually with their fellows) are rarely much different from their own experiences. As a result, their lives, while erratic, are strangely dull and homogeneous. Even their sexual experiences are routine, and any efforts to escape this by experimenting with homosexuality, alcohol, drugs, extraracial partners, or other unnecessary fringe accessories generally leave it dull and routine.

Efforts by middle-class parents to prevent their children from developing along these non-middle-class lines are generally futile. An effort to use parental discipline to enforce conformity to middle-class values or behavior means that the child will quote all the many cases in the neighborhood where the children are not being disciplined. He is encouraged in his resistance to parental discipline by its large-scale failure all around him. Moreover, if his parents insist on conformity, he has an invincible weapon to use against them: academic failure. This weapon is used by boys rather than by girls, partly because it is a weapon for the weak, and involves doing nothing rather than doing something, but also because the school seems to most middle-class boys an alien place and an essential element in their general adolescent feeling of homelessness. Girls who are pressured by their parents to conform resist by sexual delinquencies more often than boys, and in extreme cases get pregnant or have sexual experiences with Negro boys. From this whole context of adolescent resistance to parental pressures to conform to middle-class behavior flows a major portion of middle-class adolescent delinquency, which is quite distinct in its origin from the delinquency of the lowest, outcast class in the slums. It involves all kinds of activities from earliest efforts to smoke or drink, through speeding, car stealing, and vandalism of property, to major crimes and perversions. It is quite different in origin and usually in character from the delinquencies of the uprooted, which are either crimes for personal benefits (such as thievery and mugging) or crimes of social resentment (such as slashing tires and convertible tops or smashing school windows). Some activities, of course, such as automobile stealing, appear among both.

These remarks, it must be emphasized, apply to the middle class, and are not intended to apply to the other classes in American society. The aristocrats, for example, have considerable success in passing along their outlook to their children, partly because it is presented as a class or family attitude, and not as a parental or personal attitude, partly because their friends and close associates are also aristocrats or semi-aristocrats, and rejection of their point of view tends to leave an aristocratic adolescent much more personally isolated than rejection of his parents' view leaves a middle-class adolescent (indeed, the latter finds group togetherness only if he *does* reject his parents), partly because there is much more segregation of the sexes among aristocrats than in the middle class, but chiefly because the aristocrats use a separate school system, including disciplined boarding schools. The use of the latter, the key to the long persistence of the aristocratic tradition in England, makes it possible for outsiders to discipline adolescents without disrupting the family. Among the middle class, effort to discipline adolescents is largely in the hands of parents, but the effort to do so tends to disrupt the family by setting husband against wife and children against parents. As a result, discipline is usually held back to retain at least the semblance of family solidarity as viewed from the outside world (which is what really counts with middle-class people). But the aristocratic private boarding school, modeled on those of England in accord with the basic Anglophilism of the American aristocracy, is sexually segregated from females, tough, sports-orientated, usually High Episcopal (almost Anglican), and disciplines its charges with the importance of the group, their duty to the group, and the painfulness of the ultimate punishment, which is alienation from the group. As a consequence of this, any resentment the aristocratic adolescent may have is aimed at his masters, not at his home and parents, and home comes to represent a relatively desirable place to which he is admitted occasionally as a reward for long weeks on the firing line at school. Such a boy is removed from the smothering influence of "momism," grows up relatively shy of girls, has more than his share of homosexual experiences (to which he may succumb completely), but, on the whole, usually grows up to be a very energetic, constructive, stable, and self-sacrificing citizen, prepared to inflict the same training process on his own sons.

Unfortunately for the aristocrat who wishes to expose his son to the same training process as that which molded his own outlook, he finds this a difficult thing to do because the organizations that helped form him outside the family, the Episcopal Church (or its local equivalent), the boarding school, the Ivy League university, and the once-sheltered summer resort have all changed and are being invaded by a large number of nonaristocratic intruders who change the atmosphere of the whole place.

This change in atmosphere is hard to define to anyone who has not experienced it personally. Fundamentally it is a distinction between playing the game and playing to win. The aristocrat plays for the sake of the game or the team or the school. He plays whether he is much good or not, because he feels that he is contributing to a community effort even if he is on the scrubs rather than a star or starting player. The newer recruits to former aristocratic educational institutions play for more personal reasons, with much greater intensity, even fanaticism, and play to excel and to distinguish themselves from others.

One reason for the accessibility of formerly aristocratic organizations to people of nonaristocratic origin has already been noted, but probably was discounted by the reader. That is my statement that the American Establishment, which is so aristocratic and Anglophile in its foundation, came to accept the liberal ideology. The Episcopal Church, exclusive boarding schools, and Ivy League universities (like Eton and Oxford) decided that they must open their door to the "more able" of the nonaristocratic classes. Accordingly, they established scholarships, recruited for these in lower schools they had never thought of before, and made efforts to have their admission requirements and examinations fit the past experiences of nonaristocratic applicants. By the end of the 1920's, Philips Exeter Academy was welcoming on scholarships the sons of laboring immigrants with polysyllabic names, and by the 1950's Episcopal clergymen were making calls on "likely-looking" Negro families.

As a consequence of this, the sons of aristocrats found themselves being squeezed out of the formative institutions that had previously trained their fathers and, at the same time, discovered that these institutions were themselves changing their character and becoming dominated by petty-bourgeois rather than by aristocratic values. At the alumni reunions of June 1964, the President of Harvard was asked in an open forum what the questioner should do with his son, recently rejected for admission to Harvard in spite of the fact that the son was descended from the *Mayflower* voyagers by eleven consecutive generations of Harvard men. To this tragic question President Pusey replied: "I don't know what we can do about your son. We can't send him back, because the *Mayflower* isn't running any more." Despite this facetious retort, which may have been called forth by the inebriate condition of the questioner, the fact remains that the aristocratic outlook has a great deal to contribute to any organization fortunate enough to share it. Among other things, it has kept Harvard (where aristocratic control continued almost to the present day) at the top or close to the top of the American educational hierarchy decade after decade.

The sincere effort, by aristocrats and democrats alike, to make the social ladder in America a ladder of opportunity rather than a ladder of privilege has opened the way to a surge of petty-bourgeois recruits over the faltering bodies of the disintegrating middle class.

The petty bourgeois are rising in American society along the channels established in the great American hierarchies of business, the armed forces, academic life, the professions, finance, and politics. They are doing this not because they have imagination, broad vision, judgment, moderation, versatility, or group loyalties but because they have neurotic drives of personal ambition and competitiveness, great insecurities and resentments, narrow specialization, and fanatical application to the task before each of them. Their fathers, earning $100 a week as bank clerks or insurance agents while unionized bricklayers were getting $120 a week when they cared to work, embraced the middle-class ideology with tenacity as the chief means (along with their "white collared" clothing) of distinguishing themselves from the unionized labor they feared or hated. Their wives, whom they had married because they held the same outlook, looked forward eagerly to seeing their sons become the kind of material success the father had failed to reach. The family accepted a common outlook that believed specialization and hard work, either in business or in a profession, would win this material success.

The steps up that ladder of success were clearly marked—to be the outstanding boy student and graduate in school, to win entrance to and graduation from "the best" university possible (naturally an Ivy League one), and then the final years of specialized application in a professional school.

Many of these eager workers headed for medicine, because to them medicine, despite the ten years of necessary preparation, meant up to $40,000 a year income by age fifty. As a consequence, the medical profession in the United States ceased, very largely, to be a profession of fatherly confessors and unprofessing humanitarians and became one of the largest groups of hardheaded petty-bourgeois hustlers in the United States, and their professional association became the most ruthlessly materialistic lobbying association of any professional group. Similar persons with lesser opportunities were shunted off the more advantageous rungs of the ladder into second-best schools and third-rate universities. All flocked into the professions, even to teaching (which, on the face of it, might have expected that its practitioners would have some allegiance to the truth and to helping the young to realize their less materialistic potentialities), where they quickly abandoned the classroom for the more remunerative tasks of educational administration. And, of course, the great mass of these eager beavers went into science or business, preferably into the largest corporations, where they looked with fishy-eyed anticipation at those rich, if remote, plums of vice-presidencies, in General Motors, Ford, General Dynamics, or International Business Machines.

The success of these petty-bourgeois recruits in America's organizational structure rested on their ability to adapt their lives to the screening processes the middle classes had set up covering access to the middle-class organizational structures. The petty bourgeoisie, as the last fanatical defenders of the middle-class outlook, had, in excess degree, the qualities of self-discipline and future preference the middle classes had established as the unstated assumptions behind their screens of aptitude testing, intelligence evaluation, motivational research, and potential-success measurements. Above all, the American public school system, permeated with the unstated assumptions of middle-class values, was ideally suited to demonstrate petty-bourgeois "success quotients." These successive barriers in the middle-class screening process were almost insurmountable to the working class and the outcast, became very difficult to the new generation of middle-class children, who rejected their parents' value system, but were ideally adapted to the petty-bourgeois anxiety neuroses.

By 1960, however, big business, government civil service, and the Ivy League universities were becoming disillusioned with these petty-bourgeois recruits. The difficulty was that these new recruits were rigid, unimaginative, narrow and, above all, illiberal at a time when liberalism (in the sense of reaching tentative and approximate decisions through flexible community interaction) was coming to be regarded as the proper approach to large organization problems. In his farewell report the Chairman of Harvard's Admissions Committee, Wilbur Bender, summed up the problem this way:

"The student who ranks first in his class may be genuinely brilliant or he may be a compulsive worker or the instrument of domineering parents' ambitions or a conformist or a self-centered careerist who has shrewdly calculated his teachers' prejudices and expectations and discovered how to regurgitate efficiently what they want. Or he may have focused narrowly on grade-getting as compensation for his inadequacies in other areas, because he lacks other interests or talents or lacks passion and warmth or normal healthy instincts or is afraid of life. The top high school student is often, frankly, a pretty dull and bloodless, or peculiar fellow. The adolescent with wide-ranging curiosity and stubborn independence, with a vivid imagination and desire to explore fascinating bypaths, to follow his own interests, to contemplate, to read the unrequired books, the boy filled with sheer love of life and exuberance, may well seem to his teachers troublesome, undisciplined, a rebel, may not conform to their stereotype, and may not get the top grades and the highest rank in class. He may not even score at the highest level in the standard multiple choice admissions tests, which may well reward the glib, facile mind at the expense of the questioning, independent, or slower but more powerful, more subtle, and more interesting and original mind."

These remarks bring us close to one of the major problems in American culture today. We need a culture that will produce people eager to do things, but we need even more a culture that will make it possible to decide what to do. This is the old division of means and goals. Decisions about goals require values, meaning, context, perspective. They can be set, even tentatively and approximately, only by people who have some inkling of the whole picture. The middle-class culture of our past ignored the whole picture and destroyed our ability to see it by its emphasis on specialization. Just as mass production came to be based on specialization, so human preparation for making decisions about goals also became based on specialization. The free elective system in higher education was associated with choice of a major field of specialization, and all the talk about liberal arts, outside electives, general education, or required distribution were largely futile. They were futile because no general view of the whole picture could be made simply by attaching together a number of specialist views of narrow fields, for the simple reason that each specialist field looks entirely different, presenting different problems and requiring different techniques, when it is placed in the general picture. This simple fact still has not been realized in those circles that talk most about broadening outlooks. This was clearly shown in the influential Harvard Report on General Education (1945). As one reviewer of this document said, "It cost $40,000 to produce and a better answer could have been found by buying one of the books of Sir Richard Livingstone for $2.75." This remark is equally mistaken on the opposite side, a fact that shows that the solution can be found only by all parties freeing themselves from their preconceptions by getting as familiar as possible with the diverse special areas in a skeptical way.

Means are almost as difficult as ends. In fact, personal responsibility, self-discipline, some sense of time value and future preference, and, above all, an ability to distinguish what is important from what is merely necessary must be found, simply as valuable attributes of human beings as human beings. Neither America nor the world can be saved by a wholesale re-creation of African social realities here in consequence of our rejection of the middle-class outlook that brought us this far. Here we must discriminate. We have an achieving society because we have an achieving outlook in our society. And that achieving outlook has been, over the last few centuries, the middle-class outlook. But there are other achieving outlooks. An achieving society could be constructed on the aristocratic outlook, on the scientific outlook (pursuit of truth), on a religious basis, and probably on a large number of other outlooks. There is no need to go back to the middle-class outlook, which really killed itself by successfully achieving what it set out to do. But parts of it we need, and above all we need an achieving outlook. It might be pleasant just to give up, live in the present, enjoying existential personal experiences, living like lotus-eaters from our amazing productive system, without personal responsibility, self-discipline, or thought of the future. But this is impossible, because the productive system would itself collapse, and our external enemies would soon destroy us.

We must have an achieving society and an achieving outlook. These will inevitably contain parts of the middle-class outlook, but these parts will unquestionably be fitted together to serve quite different purposes. Future preference and self-discipline were originally necessary in our society so that people would restrict consumption and accumulate savings that could be spent to provide investment in capital equipment. Now we no longer need these qualities for this purpose, since flows of income in our economy provide these on an institutional basis, but we still need these qualities so that young people will be willing to undergo the years of hard work and training that will prepare them to work in our complex technological society. We must get away from the older crass materialism and egocentric selfish individualism, and pick up some of the younger generation's concern for the community and their fellowmen. The unconventionality of this younger group may make them more able to provide the new outlook and innovation every society requires, but they cannot do this if they lack imagination or perspective.

Above all, we must bring meaning back into human experience. This, like establishing an achieving outlook, can be done by going backward in our Western tradition to the period before we had any bourgeois outlook. For our society had both meaning and purpose long before it had any middle class. Indeed, these are intrinsic elements in our society. In fact, the middle-class outlook obtained its meaning and purpose from the society where it grew up; it did not give meaning and purpose to the society. And capitalism, along with the middle-class outlook, became meaningless and purposeless when it so absorbed men's time and energies that men lost touch with the meaning and purpose of the society in which capitalism was a brief and partial aspect. But as a consequence of the influence of capitalism and of the middle classes, the tradition was broken, and the link between the meaning and purpose of our society as it was before the middle-class revolution is no longer connected with the search for meaning and purpose by the new post-middle-class generation. This can be seen even in those groups like the Christian clergy who insisted that they were still clinging to the basic Christian tradition of our society. They were doing no such thing, but instead were usually offering us meaningless verbiage or unrealistic abstractions that had little to do with our desire to experience and live in a Christian way here and now.

Unfortunately, very few people, even highly regarded experts on the subject, have any very clear idea of what is the tradition of the West or how it is based on the fundamental need of Western Civilization to reconcile its intellectual outlook with the basic facts of the Christian experience. The reality of the world, time, and the flesh forced, bit by bit, abandonment of the Greek rationalistic dualism (as in Plato) that opposed spirit and matter and made knowledge exclusively a concern of the former, achieved by internal illumination. This point of view that gave final absolute knowledge (and thus justified despotism) was replaced in the period 1100–1350 by the medieval point of view that derived knowledge from the tentative and partial information obtained through sensual experience from which man derived conceptual universals that fitted the real individual cases encountered in human experience only approximately. Aquinas, who said, "Nothing exists in the intelligence which was not first present in the senses," also said, "We cannot shift from the ideal to the actual." On this epistemological basis was established the root foundations of both modern science and modern liberalism, with a very considerable boost to both from the Franciscan nominalists of the century following Aquinas.

The Classical world had constantly fallen into intellectual error because it never solved the epistemological problem of the relationship between the theories and concepts in men's minds and the individual objects of sensual experience. The medieval period made a detailed examination of this problem, but its answer was ignored when post-Renaissance thinkers broke the tradition in philosophy because they felt it necessary to break the tradition in religion. From Descartes onward, this epistemological problem was ignored or considered in a childish way, as if the medieval thinkers had never examined it. Today it remains as the great philosophic problem of our age. Irrational Activism, semanticism, and existentialism flourish because the present century has no answer to the epistemological problem. In fact, most contemporary thinkers do not even recognize that there is a problem. But Bergson's rejection of intelligence and his advocacy of intuition was based, like the Irrational Activism whence it sprang, on recognition of the fact that the space-time continuum in which man generally operates is nonrational. The whole existential movement was based on the same idea.

Semanticism tried to solve the problem, in a similiar fashion, by bringing the infinitely varied and dynamic quality of actuality into the human mind by insisting that the meaning of each word must follow the dynamics of the world by changing every time it is used. All these movements tried to reject logic and rationality from the human thinking process because they are not found in space-time actuality. But the tradition of the West, as clearly established in the Christian religion and in medieval philosophy, was that man must use rationality to the degree it is possible in handling a universe whose ultimate nature is well beyond man's present rational capability to grasp. This is the conclusion that the success of the West in World War II forces the West and the world to recognize once again. And in recognizing it, we must return to the tradition, so carelessly discarded in the fifteen century, which had shown the relationship between thought and action.

Alfred Korzybski argued (in *Science and Sanity*) that mental health depended on successful action and that successful action depended on an adequate relationship between the irrational nature of the objective world and the vision of the world that the actor has subjectively in his head. Korzybski's solution, like most other thinkers over the last two generations, has been to bring the irrationality of the world into man's thinking processes. This solution of the problem is now bankrupt, totally destroyed at Hiroshima and Berlin in 1945. The alternative solution lies in the tradition of the West. It must be found, and the link with our past must be restored so that the tradition may resume the process of growth that was interrupted so long ago.

Korzybski, Bergson, and the rest of them are quite correct—most of man's experience takes place in an irrational actuality of space-time. But we now know that man must deal with his experience through subjective processes that are both rational and logical (using rules of thought explicitly understood by all concerned); and the necessary adjustments between the conclusions reached by thought and the confused irrationalities of experience must be made in the process of shifting from thought to action, and not in the thinking process itself. Only thus will the West achieve successful thought, successful action, and the sanity that is the link between these two.

As a result of this rupture of tradition, the thinkers of today are fumbling in an effort to find a meaning that will satisfy them. This is as true of the contemporary babbling philosophers as it is of the younger generation who fumblingly try to express Christ's message of love and help without any apparent realization that Christ's message is available in writing and that generations of thinkers debated its implications centuries ago. The meaning the present generation is seeking can be found in our own past. Part of it, concerned with loving and helping, can be found in Christ by going back to the age before his message was overwhelmed in ritualism and bureaucracy. Part of it can be found in the basic philosophic outlook of the West as seen in medieval philosophy and the scientific method that grew out of it.

The problem of meaning today is the problem of how the diverse and superficially self-contradictory experiences of men can be put into a consistent picture that will provide contemporary man with a convincing basis from which to live and to act. This can be achieved only by a hierarchy that distinguishes what is necessary from what is important, as the medieval outlook did. But any modern explanation based on hierarchy must accept dynamicism as an all-pervasive element in the system, as the medieval hierarchy so signally failed to do. The effort of Teilhard de Chardin to do this has won enormous interest in recent years, but its impact has been much blunted by the fact that his presentation contained, in reciprocal relationship, a deficiency of courage and a surplus of deliberate ambiguity.

However, the real problem does not rest so much in theory as in practice. The real value of any society rests in its ability to develop mature and responsible individuals prepared to stand on their own feet, make decisions, and be prepared to accept the consequences of their decisions and actions without whining or self-justification. This was the ideal that the Christian tradition established long ago, and in consequence of its existence, our Western society, whatever its deficiencies, has done better than any other society that has ever existed. If it has done less well recently than earlier in its career (a disputable point of view), this weakness can be remedied only by some reform in its methods of childrearing that will increase its supply of mature and responsible adults.

Once this process had been established, the adults thus produced can be relied upon to adopt from our Western heritage of the past a modified ideology that will fit the needs of the present as well as the traditions of the past. And if Western culture can do that, either in America or in Europe, it need fear no enemies from within or from without.

European Ambiguities

The problems facing Europe cannot be presented in a simple outline such as we have offered for those of the United States. Europe is too diverse, on a national or even regional basis; its long history has left too many influential survivals as exceptions to any simple analysis; and its class lines are more complicated and much more rigid than in America. Nonetheless, it is probably true to say that America has passed Europe in the evolution of our Western Civilization and that Europeans in general are concerned with problems, notably the problems of material acquisition, which were dominant in the United States almost a generation ago. However, because of the diversity of Europe, any statements we make about this situation would almost certainly have more exceptions than confirming examples, in Europe as a whole.

The general picture we might draw is of a continent deprived, for at least one full generation (1914–1950), of political, economic, social, and psychological security; in consequence, that area came to regard these things as major aims in its personal behavior patterns. So many European families were deprived of even the necessary materials of living that they are today, to varying degrees, obsessed with the desire for these, now that it seems possible to get them. For this reason, the chief impression the visiting American brings back from Europe is one of grasping materialism and exaggerated individualism. This is a spirit akin to America of the 1920's rather than of the 1950's. It is found, with a variety of emphasis, among the peasants, the workers, and even the aristocracy, as well as among the bourgeoisie and petty bourgeoisie, where we expect it. It is combined with an antagonism between classes and groups that is rare in America (except among the petty bourgeoisie). The middle-class adolescent revolt is rarer and much harsher in Europe, shot through with elements of hatred, where in America it is shot through with elements of indiscriminate loving. And in Europe the selfishness and general bitchiness of middle-class girls is much greater than in the United States, probably because the stronger male-dominant tradition of Europe leaves them less freedom, less self-esteem, and lower personal evaluation. As an example of the diversity of Europe, we should say that this last remark is more true of southern Europe than of northern Europe, and largely untrue of England. In fact, most generalizations about Europe do not apply to England at all.

In the European search for security the two dominant aims have been security against a Soviet attack and nuclear war and security against economic collapse such as occurred in the 1930's and opened the way to Nazism and World War II. The disorganization of Europe in the immediate postwar period allowed the United States to play a dominant role in both of these aims. However, by the later 1950's, as fear of war and depression subsided, it became possible for Europe to adopt a more independent attitude. At the same time, the personal influence of President de Gaulle gave this new independence anti-American overtones, which, however justified by the general's personal experiences with incompetent American foreign policies, none the less were injurious to the solidarity and prosperity of Europe.

As long as American influence was dominant, the security of Europe was based primarily on America's strategic nuclear power, supplemented in an ambiguous way by the fifteen-nation NATO Treaty, which included both the United States and Canada. On the economic side, European prosperity was based, for many years, on American economic aid. Both of these influences were exercised to develop, as an ultimate goal, an integrated western Europe that would include Britain and be closely allied to North America.

As we have already seen, these efforts gradually bogged down in a complicated morass of partly integrated systems on a functional, rather than a federative, basis and by 1965 were stalemated over a number of unresolved inconsistencies of approach. These problems will be analyzed in a moment, but before we do so we should point out that a new Europe is clearly being formed on lines that have little in common with the Europe of prewar days. That earlier Europe was based on the social and ideological patterns of the past, and continued to reflect them, even when the real forces of military and economic technology were creating quite different relationships. Moreover, these older patterns were quite rigid and doctrinaire. In most of Europe they showed sharp, almost irreconcilable, divisions into three political groupings that we might designate as conservative, liberal, and Socialist. These represented, in order, the social forces of the eighteenth century, of the mid-nineteenth century, and of the early twentieth century. The conservatives stood for an alliance of all the forces of the period before the French Revolution of 1789: the agrarian and landed interests, the old nobility and monarchy, the clerical interests, and the old army. The liberals stood for the bourgeois interests of the commercial, financial, and industrial revolutions; they were concerned with maintaining the dominant position of property, were usually rigid supporters of laissez faire, were opposed to influence based on birth or land, were opposed to extension of state authority, and were usually anticlerical and antimilitarist. The Socialists represented the interests and ideas of the working masses of the cities. They were in favor of democracy and individual political equality, and wanted the activities of the state to be extended to regulate economic life for the benefit of the ordinary man. The Socialists were generally opposed to the same social groups and older interests as the liberals, but added to these enemies the bourgeoisie also. In general, these three diverse groupings were rigid, and put more emphasis on the things that divided them than on matters of common concern. Their hatreds were more dominant than their common interests.

These divisions of Europe along lines of selfish interests, old slogans, doctrinaire hatreds, and misconceived rivalries made possible the rise of Fascism and the disasters of World War II. Out of these disasters, in the turmoil and violence of the Resistance, there began to appear the lineaments of a new Europe. This new Europe was much more pragmatic, and thus less doctrinaire; it was much more cooperative and less competitive; it was much more receptive to diversity, partial solutions, and the need for mutual dependence than the period before 1939 had been. On the whole this new spirit, found among the leaders rather than among the masses, was much closer to what we have defined as the tradition of the West than the Europe of 1900 had been.

It must be recognized that this new Europe had its roots in the Resistance, and, as such, had traces of those elements of self-sacrifice, human solidarity, personal integrity, and flexible improvisation that appeared so unexpectedly among the hardened Resistance fighters. We might say that many of the elements of outlook and leadership of the new postwar Europe emerged from underground, and were unnoticed by those who had not been in active contact with the underground. Thus they were not observed by the leaders in Washington and in London, even by De Gaulle, and, above all, were unreported by Allen Dulles, who was supposed to be observing the underground for the OSS from Switzerland.

Supporters of this new outlook were determined to break free from the nationalistic hatreds of the prewar period and to emphasize instead Europe as a cultural entity of diverse nationalities. Above all, they were insistent on the urgent need to heal the terrible breach, running through the heart of Europe, between France and Germany. They were eager to establish some kind of liaison between religion and Socialism, by way of Christian charity and social welfare, in order to repudiate the unnatural nineteenth-century alliance between the clergy and capitalism. They were determined to use the power of the state to settle the common problems of man, unhampered by doctrinaire liberalism and laissez faire. And they recognized the joint role of capital and labor in any productive process, although they had no way of measuring or of dividing the rewards of each from that process. In two words this new outlook was determined to make Europe more "unified" and more "spiritual."

This new outlook was unable to influence the fate of Europe for at least a decade after the ending of World War II in 1945 because of the urgent material need to repair the devastation of the war, the overwhelming threat to Europe from the Soviet Union and from doctrinaire Communism, and because of the dependence of Europe, both for reconstruction and defense, on the United States and Britain, both of whom ignored the new forces stirring on the Continent. By 1955, however, as these urgent problems receded into the background and Europe became increasingly able to stand on its own feet, the new structure began to become visible, indicated by the cooperation of Christian Socialists and Social Democrats in the constructive process and by the continued decline of the forces of the extreme Right and the extreme Left.

It was the new spirit, rooted in the Resistance and the tacit agreement of the Christian Socialist and Social Democratic political groups, that made it possible to work toward European unity and to use this unity as the foundation for a rich and independent Europe. The task is still only partly done; it may, indeed, never be completed, for nothing is more persistent than the old established institutions and outlooks that stand as barriers along the way.

The central problem of Europe remains today, as it has for a century, the problem of Germany. And today, as before, this problem cannot be solved without Britain. But such a solution requires that Britain accept the fact that it is, since the invention of the airplane and the rocket, a European, and not a world, or even an Atlantic, Power. This the leaders of Britain and the American branch of the British Establishment have been unwilling to accept. As a consequence, Britain remains aloof from the Continent, committed to the "Atlantic Community" and to the Commonwealth of Nations, and, accordingly, the political unification of Western Europe stands suspended, part way to fulfillment, while the German problem, still capable of triggering the destruction of Western society, remains unsolved.

Briefly the problem is this: no one concerned—the Soviet Union, the United States, or Europe itself—can permit Germany to be unified again in the foreseeable future. A united Germany would be a force of instability and danger to everyone, including the Germans, because it would be the most powerful nation in Europe and, balanced between East and West, might at any time fall into collaboration with one of these to the intense danger of the other; or, if the Russian-American antithesis remained irreparable, a united Germany could put extreme pressures on its lesser neighbors between the two Superpowers. The peace and stability of Europe thus require the permanent division of Germany, something on which the Soviet Union is adamant to the point of resorting to force to retain it, although the official policy of the United States is still committed to a reunification of Germany, partly in the belief that the loyalty of West Germany to the Atlantic Alliance can be retained only if the United States remains explicitly committed to a future reacquisition of

East Germany by West Germany. In fact, the eagerness of the latter to acquire the former is dwindling, although very slowly, since the east is now so poor that it could bring little but poverty to West Germany's booming prosperity.

This separation of the Germanys can be made permanent only if each is incorporated, as fully as possible, into a larger, and distinct, political system. But the smaller countries of Europe, particularly the Netherlands and Belgium, do not wish to be united with Germany in any federated system that includes only one other large Power, such as France (or even France and Italy), since an alignment of West Germany and France in such a federation could dominate the small states completely. Accordingly, the small states want Britain, as a democratic counterweight to Germany, within any West European federal structure. But De Gaulle, as he made evident in January 1963, will accept Britain into a West European federation only if Britain becomes clearly a European Power and renounces its special relationship of close collaboration with the United States and if it is also willing to subordinate its position as leader of the British Commonwealth of Nations to its membership in the European system. The abandonment of its "special relationship" with the United States and with the Commonwealth, the two major concerns of the English Establishment for more than forty years, was too heavy a price to pay for membership in the European Economic Community and would have been an unacceptable reversal of established policy in return for something that Britain sought without great enthusiasm.

The integration of Western Europe began in 1948 as a consequence of the growth of Soviet aggression that culminated in the Prague coup and the Berlin blockade. The United States had offered Marshall Plan aid with the provision that the European recovery be constructed on a cooperative basis. This led to the Convention for European Economic Cooperation (OEEC) signed in April 1948 and the Hague Congress for European union held the following month. The OEEC, which eventually had eighteen countries as members and in 1961 was reorganized as the Organization for Economic Cooperation and Development (OECD), sought to administer American aid and further economic cooperation between sovereign states. The Hague meeting of May 1948, with Winston Churchill and Konrad Adenauer as its chief figures, called for a united Europe, and took a very minor step in that direction by establishing a purely advisory consultative body of ten (later fifteen) states, the Council of Europe, as a parliamentary assembly at Strasbourg.

These steps were clearly inadequate. In 1950 Robert Schuman, then French foreign minister and later prime minister, who had been a German subject during World War I, suggested that a first step be taken toward a federation of Europe by putting the entire coal and steel production of France and Germany under a common High Authority. The real attraction of this project was that it would so integrate this basic industry that it would make any war between France and Germany "physically impossible." One element in this project was to reconcile the anti-Germans to the economic rehabilitation of Germany which the continued Soviet aggressions made increasingly necessary. It would also provide a solution to the Franco-German disagreement over the final disposition of the Saar. From this came the European Coal and Steel Community. This was a truly revolutionary organization, since it had sovereign powers, including the authority to raise funds outside any existing state's power. This treaty, which came into force in July 1952, brought the steel and coal industries of six countries (France, West Germany, Italy, and Benelux) under a single High Authority of nine members. This "supranational" body had the right to control prices, channel investment, raise funds, allocate coal and steel during shortages, and fix production in times of surplus. Its power to raise funds for its own use by taxing each ton produced made it independent of governments. Moreover, its decisions were binding, and could be reached by majority vote without the unanimity required in most international organizations of sovereign states.

The ECSC was a rudimentary government, since the High Authority was subject to the control of a Common Assembly, elected by the parliaments of the member states, which could force the Authority to resign by a two-thirds vote of censure, and it had a Court of Justice to settle disputes. Most significantly, the ECSC Assembly became a genuine parliament with political party blocs—Christian-Democrats, Socialists, and liberals—sitting together independent of national origins.

By 1958 the ECSC had abolished internal barriers to trade in oil and steel among the Six (such trade increased by 157 percent during the first five years) and had set up a common tariff against imports of coal and steel into the Six. Production of steel increased 65 percent during the five years, and the process of using ECSC funds to modernize the coal industry and to close down exhausted mines (moving hundreds of thousands of miners out of mining and into other employment) had begun.

When the Korean War began in 1950, the United States demanded formation of twelve German divisions to strengthen NATO in Europe. The French, who feared any rebirth of German militarism, drew up an elaborate scheme for a European Defense Community (EDC) that would merge the German recruits into a European army under joint European control. Like ECSC, the European Defense Community was to be a supranational agency that would eventually take its place, along with the ECSC, within a European government. The general pattern of this supergovernment was established in the EDC project itself, with a bicameral European parliament and a president to preside over a European Cabinet Council. Unfortunately for these plans, the Left and the Right in the

French Assembly joined together to reject the EDC treaty (August 1954). The Left was opposed to EDC because any union of Europe would reduce Soviet influence on the Continent, while the Right, led by the Gaullists, were unwilling to see German armed forces reestablished without any guarantee that Britain and the United States would retain forces within Europe to balance the new German forces. Failure of Britain to recognize explicitly its inevitable commitment to European defense early in 1954 allowed EDC to die.

A symbolic, but ineffectual, step was made to calm these French fears in September 1954, when Sir Anthony Eden instigated a Western European Union (WEU) of seven states (the Six plus Britain) as a consultative group to oversee German rearmament. As part of this agreement the British promised to keep four divisions in Europe until the year 2000 if necessary, but within three years one of these divisions was pulled out and the other three fell substantially below full strength.

As a result of this agreement and a number of other factors, including recognition that the rearmament of Germany was inevitable, the French Assembly in December 1954 ratified the Paris Treaties that legalized the changes in Germany's status that France most feared. Western Germany regained its sovereign independence, obtained the right to have a national army (although without nuclear weapons), and became an equal member of NATO.

Having thus accepted much of what they did not want (an armed and sovereign Germany), it became clear to many Frenchmen that they must make a strenuous effort to get some of the things they did want (chiefly the merging of Germany into a West European system that would prevent the new German power from being used in a nationalistic aggression). Accordingly, the Six met again, at Messina in June 1955. There they decided that the next step toward West European integration must be economic rather than political. From this flowed the Rome Treaty of March 1957, which established the European Economic Community, better known as the Common Market, as well as the European Atomic Community for joint exploitation of nuclear energy for peaceful purposes (Euratom). Both agreements went into effect at the beginning of 1958.

The EEC Treaty, with 572 articles over almost 400 pages, like the treaties establishing ECSC and Euratom, looked forward to eventual political union in Europe, and sought economic integration as an essential step on the way. The project originated with the head of the French economic planning commission, Jean Monnet, whose ideas were pushed along by the energy of Foreign Minister Paul-Henri Spaak of Belgium. Within the three large nations, agreement was obtained by the efforts of the leaders of the respective Christian-Democratic parties: Adenauer, Schuman, and Alcide de Gasperi. The Catholic religious background of all three was a significant factor in their willingness to turn from nationalistic to international economic methods, while Spaak's Socialist prestige helped to reconcile the moderate Left to the scheme. The slowing up of the process of economic recovery that had begun with the Marshall Plan in 1949 helped to win widespread acceptance of the new effort for joint economic expansion.

Briefly the Rome Treaty established the methods and time schedule by which the signatory countries, as well as other nations that might wish to join, could integrate their economies into a single, more expansive, system. Tariffs and other restrictions on trade between them were to be abolished by stages and replaced by a common tariff against the outside world. At the same time, investment was to be directed so as to integrate their joint economy as a whole, with special attention to the industrialization of backward and underdeveloped regions such as southern Italy. Special consideration was given to agriculture, largely detaching it from the market economy to cushion the integrative process while improving the standards of living and social protection of the farming population. As part of the integrative process there was to be free movement of persons, services, and capital within the Community, with gradual development of Community citizenship for workers. This whole process was to be achieved by stages over many years. The agricultural agreement, for example, was implemented by an elaborate agreement that was signed after 140 hours of almost continuous negotiation in January 1962. By the middle of that year the internal tariffs among members had been reduced in three stages to half their 1958 levels.

The institutional organization for carrying on this process was similar to that set up for the ECSC and the abortive EDC: a European Parliamentary Assembly of supranational party blocs of Christian-Democrats, Socialists, and liberals sitting and voting together irrespective of national origins; a Council of Ministers representing the member governments directly; an executive High Commission of nine that is enjoined by law to "exercise their functions in complete independence" of their national governments; a Court of Justice with powers to interpret the treaty and settle disputes; two advisory groups (the Monetary Committee and the Social and Economic Committee); a European Investment Bank to channel funds for integrative and development purposes within the Community; the Overseas Development Fund to do the same for former colonial territories now associated indirectly with the ECC; a European Social Fund for industrial retraining and unemployment compensation; and finally the two associated Communities (ECSC and Euratom). These last two were integrated with ECC from the fact that the Parliamentary Assembly, the Court of Justice, and the Council of Ministers are shared by all three communities.

These organizations have some of the aspects of sovereignty from the fact that their decisions do not have to be unanimous, are binding on states and on citizens who have not agreed to them, and can be financed by funds that may be levied without current consent of the persons being taxed. On the whole, the supranational aspects of these institutions will be strengthened in the future from provisions in the treaties themselves. All this is very relevant to the remarks in the last chapter on the disintegration of the modern, unified sovereign state and the redistribution of its powers to multilevel hierarchical structures remotely resembling the structure of the Holy Roman Empire in the late medieval period.

The impact of these tentative steps toward an integrative Europe has been spectacular, especially in the economic sphere. In general, the economic expansion of Western Europe, especially its industrial expansion, has been at rates far higher than those of Communist-dominated eastern Europe, with the EEC rates higher than those of non-EEC Western European countries, and considerably higher than those of either Britain or the United States. By 1960 the 300 million people of Western Europe had per capita incomes over a third higher than the 260 million persons in the same area had in 1938–1939. Industrial production more than doubled over the same time span, while agricultural production was a third larger with a smaller working force. This optimistic picture was even brighter for the Six of the EEC, whose general economic growth rate was considerably over 6 percent a year during the 1950's. This was more than double the rate of growth in the United States, which was not much different from that in Britain. If these rates are maintained, it has been estimated that the income per head in the EEC would increase from about a third of the income per head in the United States in 1960 to more than half the United States income per head in 1970.

The reasons for this relative boom in the EEC (and in Western Europe generally) in comparison with the slower economic dynamics of the English-speaking countries are of some importance. It does not seem to rest, as might appear at first glance, on a contrast between directed planning and laissez faire, because, within the EEC, the French economy is fairly rigorously planned and the West German economy is surprisingly free, yet both have had high rates of growth. The West German conditions, however, have been misleading and have arisen very largely from artificially low wage levels and thus low costs of production, especially on articles for export into the international competitive market, such as Volkswagens. These low labor costs arose from the large number of East European refugees seeking work in Germany, a condition that will be of decreasing importance in the future.

The conditions of economic growth in the EEC has been based on steady demand, high rates of investment, and liberal fiscal and financial policies. In 1961, for example, the rate of net investment in Britain was about 9 percent compared to the West German rate of about 17 percent. The high demand that spurred on this process arose from fiscal policies, but also from the large new market of about 100 million persons provided in EEC.

In Britain and in the United States (with Canada) fiscal policies were much more conservative, with demand somewhat dampened down by efforts to balance budgets, to control inflation, and to influence both adverse balances of international payments and the flows of domestic credit by conservative financial policies (notably, high interest rates). Moreover, in both countries, there was a good deal of unproductive expenditure either in misjudged enterprises and inefficient production or in defense and other nonproductive areas. As a consequence, not only have growth rates been low in the English-speaking countries but unemployment rates have been high. In 1960, for example, the United States unemployment rate was 5.4 percent and the Canadian 6.9 percent, while that of France was 1.3 percent and of West Germany only 0.9 percent.

This sharp contrast between the prosperity of the EEC and the languishing economy of Britain eventually brought the latter to a recognition of the advantages of membership in the European system. But the decision was too late, based on wrong motives, and was eventually nullified by the imperious De Gaulle, who, like an elephant, never forgets an injury. Governments in London paid lip service to European unity and to British cooperation with it, but whenever an opportunity offered to take a real step toward European union, Britain balked. In the immediate postwar period, this reluctance was attributed to the rather provincial and doctrinaire Socialist outlook of the British Labour Party, but the situation did not improve when Winston Churchill returned to office in 1951. The general British outlook was that British participation in a united Europe was precluded by Britain's rather intangible and sentimental commitments to the Commonwealth and to the United States (that is, to the "English-speaking idea") and that a unification of Europe without Britain would be a threat to British markets on the Continent. This decision by Britain was copied by the Scandinavian and Baltic countries (Denmark and Finland), whose trade alliance with England went back to the creation of the "Sterling Bloc" in 1932. In a similar way Britain refused to cooperate in the ECSC or EDC.

This reluctance in London was a great tragedy, excluding Britain from the European growth toward economic prosperity, making it difficult or impossible for the European effort toward integration to make decisions that would have hastened the whole integrative process, and leaving Britain emphasizing Commonwealth and American relationships that were less and less prepared to give due weight to British ideas and power. In a sense Britain was making commitments to areas that were not prepared to make reciprocal commitments to Britain and would, if the occasion arose, leave Britain out on a limb. This, indeed, is exactly what happened in October 1956, when the United States threatened to throw its power

and prestige against Britain's efforts in the Suez fiasco. And throughout
the period, the chief Commonwealth countries, notably South Africa
and Canada, made it perfectly clear that they were not willing to make
any notable sacrifices for Britain's prosperity, and were reluctant to follow London's lead in many of the world's political issues of the period.

In fact, even with Commonwealth preference and all the intangibles
that link the Commonwealth together, Britain's trade and financial links
with the Commonwealth are decreasing in importance, and the links of
both with outsiders are increasing. For example, Nigeria and Ghana
doubled their exports to EEC over the 1955–1959 period, while their
exports to Britain decreased by 15 percent. On the whole, in recent years,
the countries associated with the sterling area have found that association
one of decreasing satisfaction. This is reflected in matters other than market conditions. Sterling itself has been subject to periodic crises since the
war ended. The reason is obvious, for the United Kingdom tries to handle
$12.3 billion in imports and $10.9 billion in floating short-term debts on
a base of reserves of no more than $3 billion (in 1961), while, at the same
time, the EEC, with $16 billion in reserves, had only $2 billion in short-
term debts and handled $23.2 billion in imports. As a result of all this,
London is decreasingly attractive as a source of investment capital, while
the EEC becomes increasingly prominent in that activity. And as a source
of development funds for backward areas, the United Kingdom has ceased
to be of major significance. In 1960, for example, the United States
provided $3,781 million and EEC provided $2,626 million, compared to
the United Kingdom's $857 million and the rest of the OECD countries'
$469 million. In fact Germany's $616 million was almost comparable to
Britain's $857 million, with both far less than France's $1,287 million.
Thus the Six provide about a third of the world's financial assistance
to underdeveloped countries, while Britain provides only one-ninth.

Considerations such as these help to indicate that the Commonwealth
attachment to the United Kingdom is based rather on the intangibles of
traditions and old patterns than on the solid advantages of today's economic and financial situation. The merging of the United Kingdom into
the EEC would still give a fair jolt to economic life both in England and
in the Commonwealth, but the slack would be taken up very rapidly. In
fact, the rising demand for goods of higher quality in Japan will probably
draw much of the export trade of New Zealand and Australia in butter,
meat, or even wool from their older English-speaking markets even without Britain joining the Common Market.

The reluctance of the English leadership to face these changing conditions, like their refusal to face the causes of Britain's economic lassi-
tude, contributed much to confuse the situation that Europe, and especially EEC, reached by the mid-1960's. In December 1956, in a vain
effort to sidetrack European integration, British Foreign Secretary Selwyn

Lloyd produced a "Grand Design," a pompous name for an undigested scheme to dump an assortment of European consultative bodies into the Common Assembly of the Coal and Steel Community. This idea was generally recognized as sabotage, and sank without a ripple.

The next British effort was for a Free Trade Area; this was a scheme to permit British goods to enter the Common Market without Britain joining it. This was necessary, in British eyes, because the joint external tariff of the ECC was to be higher than the tariffs of four of the Six had previously been, and would reduce British sales in those countries. The Free Trade Area plan was for an all-Europe free-trade zone embracing the Six along with all those who did not wish to join the EEC. That means that the Free Trade Area would abolish mutual trade barriers but would not establish a common external tariff. This British suggestion, made in November 1956, was regarded within EEC as another effort at sabotage, or, at best, a typical British attempt to have the advantages of both worlds by combining the abolition of European tariffs on British goods with continued British preference for Commonwealth foodstuffs. The lower prices on the latter (compared to food prices within the Six) would permit Britain to have lower wage costs and thus lower industrial prices to give British industry a competitive advantage in the unprotected Common Market.

When France, with West German support, broke off the Free Trade Area negotiations in December 1958, the British were left out of the EEC, which began to function in the ruins of the Free Trade Area. Britain reacted by forming the European Free Trade Association (EFTA) of Britain, Sweden, Norway, Denmark, Austria, Switzerland, Portugal, and (later) Finland.

This EFTA provided for mutual tariff reductions of member states by steps to complete abolition by 1970, but the process added only 38 million persons to the existing British market of 52 million, and promised small prospect of any substantial increase in sales because the tariffs of most of these countries were already low on British goods. This could not compare with the EEC market of 170 million customers, but British public opinion, even in the 1960's, could not bring itself to accept the reorientation of outlook required to view itself as a European state necessary to make it possible to accept the economic integration that could make this great market available to British industry. For this, the semislump of 1960–1961 was needed, and only in July 1961 did the British government announce its readiness to start the complex negotiations needed for its joining the Common Market. By that late date, De Gaulle was well established in power in France, and was prepared to impose his own peculiar point of view on the negotiations.

The French economic resurgence, which the British so belatedly asked to join, was in no sense a consequence of De Gaulle's policies, nor were they synchronized, except accidentally, with the advent of De Gaulle and his Fifth French Republic on May 13, 1958. The basis for the French economic boom was laid under the Fourth French Republic, and De Gaulle simply profited from it. It might be said that the economic expansion, and its continuation after 1958, was based on those factors of the French system which the new De Gaulle regime left relatively unchanged—an educational structure accessible to anyone willing to work hard at his studies, the high quality of upper-level technical education, the close alliance between the administrative bureaucracy and the industrial system, and the ease with which highly educated technicians can pass from one to the other; by the readiness of the French mind to accept a rational, over-all view of life and its problems (this contributed considerably to the success of French economic planning), and by the whole concept of individual opportunity and careers open to talent within a structured social arrangement. All these go back to the Napoleonic period of French history and were, thus, well adapted to De Gaulle's personal inclinations. The fact that they are all quite alien to the English way of life also helps to explain the relative failure of the British economy in the Plan Era.

The Fifth Republic was obviously tailored to De Gaulle's personal inclinations, but it was also adapted to the bureaucratic substructure that had continued, as a semi-alien basis, to underlie the French political system in the bourgeois era. Worded in another way, we might say that the shift of the Western world over the last three decades from a bourgeois to a technocratic pattern was well adapted to the subterranean bureaucratic basis that had survived in France, more or less unobserved, during the century in which property was obviously triumphant. The bureaucracy Louis XIV and Napoleon had built up had been directed toward totalitarian power and national glory; the age of property (roughly 1836–1936) had sought to establish the influence of wealth unhampered by bureaucracy, and one of its chief aims had been to keep the bureaucratic structure, the centralized French tradition of administration, and the forces of French rationalism outside the sphere of economics and moneymaking. The economic depression of the 1930's and the defeat of 1940, both directly caused by the selfish interests and the narrow outlook (especially the narrow and selfish financial outlook) of the French bourgeoisie, made it clear that some new system was needed in France, just as the experience of the Resistance made it clear that some new system was needed in Europe. It was, in view of the French rationalist and bureaucratic tradition, almost inevitable that the new domestic system would be a more integrated, more rational, and more bureaucratic one than that of the bourgeois era, although it is not so clear what this new system will establish as its goal. This, indeed, is the prob lem facing France today, a problem concerned with goals rather than with methods, since there is now a broad consensus (including the bourgeoisie) prepared to accept a rationalized, planned, bureaucratized society dominated by a pervasive fiscalism, a kind of neomercantilism, but there is no consensus on what goals this new organization should seek.

Only a very small group of Frenchmen share De Gaulle's idea that the new system of France, the Fifth Republic, should make national power and glory its primary aim. A larger, and surprisingly influential, group, best represented by Monnet, wishes to work for the kind of rational humanism or unified diversity that this volume has used as its chief criterion for judging historical change. This group hopes, by the proper organization of men and resources, to increase the production of wealth and to reduce the conflicts of power sufficiently to remove these distracting matters from the center of human concern so that, once prosperity and peace have been relatively secured, men will find the time and energy to turn to their more important ends of personality development, artistic expression, and intellectual exploration. This point of view, based on a significant distinction between what is necessary and what is important, hopes to find the opportunity to turn to important matters once the necessary ones have achieved a level of minimal satisfactions.

The Frenchmen of a third group, which includes the major part of the population, have little concern with the goals of De Gaulle and even less with those of Monnet but are concerned with an almost repulsive pursuit of material affluence, something of which they had long heard but never considered achievable before. Today, for the first time, such affluence seems achievable to the great mass of Frenchmen as it does to the great mass of West Germans, to many English, and to increasing number of Italians. Americans and Swedes, who are already disillusioned with the fruits of affluence, must be indulgent to these recent arrivals in the materialist rat race. The chief political aim of this large group is for political stability free from partisan upheavals, an end that De Gaulle and the Fifth Republic seem more capable of securing than the unstable, multipartied Fourth Republic.

Much of the ambiguity about De Gaulle rests on a failure of historical synchronisms. This can be seen in regard to the three aspects of (a) political ideology, (b) economic management, and (c) the relationship between these two. In the 1920's, all three of these were antipathetic to De Gaulle's outlook, since forty years ago the three were: (a) a democratic, nationalist, sovereign, independent state pursuing the goal of national self-interest; (b) a capitalistic economy; and (c) a laissez-faire relationship of no government in business. De Gaulle's ideas are rather those of Louis XIV, that is: (a) a sovereign, independent, authoritarian state pursuing the goal of national glory; (b) a mixed economy of a corporative sort; and (c) political domination of economic life. The point of view of the "new Europeans" on these matters was: (a) a democratic, co-operative political structure of shared and divided powers on a European basis, seeking peace and stability in an interlocking organizational structure rising through European, Atlantic-Western, and worldwide levels; (b) a mixed economy; and (c) a planned, state-directed drive toward increased affluence. De Gaulle cares only for (a) and has little interest in (b) or (c) so long as they provide him with a rate of economic expansion capable of supporting his ambitions in (a). The mass of French people care little about De Gaulle's ambitions in (a) so long as they obtain political stability that will allow them to seek the affluence they wish from (c); while the technicians, concerned largely with (b), are prepared to let De Gaulle seek glory in (a) and the people seek affluence in (c) so long as both leave them alone to manage the proper mixture of the economy they desire in (b). Thus France, by this most extraordinary mixture of cross-purposes, is led into the future by a man whose ideas in all three areas are almost completely obsolete.

It is easy for English-speaking persons to condemn De Gaulle. Many of them consider his obsolescent ideas a danger to Europe and to the world. Indeed, they are, but this does not mean that they do not have some basis in De Gaulle's personal experience and in the recent history of France itself. The general was determined to restore the power and prestige of France as an independent state within a context of national states similar to that in which France had suffered the blows to its prestige in 1919–1945. To him these defeats were almost personal psychic injuries that could be repaired only by new French triumphs in the same nationalistic context and not by successes in an entirely different context such as that of an integrated Europe. Obsessed by the pursuit of the glory of France in the nationalistic era in which his own character had been formed and personally piqued by the rebuffs he had received in his own career, the rejection of his military advice by his superiors in the 1920's and 1930's, the defeats of France in the diplomatic and military arenas in the period 1936–1940, the rebuffs administered by the United States Department of State and the White House to his efforts to make himself the leader of the Free French in 1940–1943, and finally the general belittling, as he saw it, to his ideas and dignity during the liberation— all these served to make his outlook more remote, more rigid, and more opinionated until he came to regard himself as the God-given leader for a revived France and came to regard the English-speaking nations as the chief obstacles in his path to this end.

The culmination of De Gaulle's irritation with the United States came during the five years 1953–1958, during which he was retired from public life and had to watch, in helpless impotence, John Foster Dulles's studied belittling of France's role in world affairs. The American Secretary of State's unilateralism and "brinkmanship," his emphasis on the Far East and his ignoring of Europe, his refusal to consult with his NATO allies, and his lack of sympathy for the French position in Indochina, Algeria, and Europe itself—all this drove De Gaulle into an icy antipathy for American policy and a conviction that the interests of France could be protected only by France itself and could be furthered as well by collaboration with the Soviet Union as by alliance with the United States.

De Gaulle was especially irritated by the American lack of concern for French and European interests in nuclear-weapons policy. Dulles's willingness to go to war with the Communist Powers over Asiatic questions (such as the Chinese offshore islands or the Formosa Strait) without consultation with its European allies, when the most immediate consequence of any Soviet-American war would be a Russian attack on Europe and the exposure of France to a threat of nuclear attack over an issue on which Paris had not even been consulted gave De Gaulle (perfectly justifiably) profound irritation.

When the disruption of French political life over the Algerian dispute brought De Gaulle back to public life as premier in June 1958, he took steps to end this situation. What he wanted was a "Western troika," that is, a tripartite consultation of the United States, the United Kingdom, and France on all world disputes that could involve NATO in war in Europe. In this way he hoped to prevent in the future such events as Dulles's unilateral cancellation of the American offer of credits for the Aswan Dam that had led to the Suez crisis of 1956. This suggestion by De Gaulle was rebuffed, and led by logical steps to his decision to disentangle France from its NATO obligations and to establish an independent French nuclear *force de frappe*.

According to De Gaulle's line of thought, Washington not only ignored French interests and ideas on a worldwide basis, but involved it, without consultation, in the risk of war in Europe. The general also argued that the growth of nuclear stalemate between the United States and the Soviet Union left Europe unprotected so long as it based its security on an American threat of nuclear war with the Soviet Union. Washington, he felt, would not reply to a Soviet aggression in Europe by any nuclear attack on the Soviet Union when it realized that the Soviet counterreply to such an attack would be the nuclear devastation of American cities by Soviet missiles. Why, according to De Gaulle, would the United States destroy its own cities in retaliation for a Soviet aggression, at any level, on Europe? This opened the whole problem of "nuclear credibility," with De Gaulle at such a high level of skepticism of American good faith that he saw little credibility and thus little deterrent value in the American threat to use nuclear weapons against the Soviet Union to defend France. According to De Gaulle, the only secure French defense must be based on France's own military power, which must, inevitably, be nuclear power.

At first glance, the idea of modest French nuclear armaments serving as deterrence to the mighty Soviet threat to Europe, either conventional or nuclear, seems even less credible. But De Gaulle was one of the first to recognize, as a feasible policy, an idea that was subsequently adopted by the Soviet Union itself. This was the idea that a nuclear deterrence does not require the possession of overwhelming nuclear power or even the nuclear superiority in which Washington long believed, but may be based on the capacity to inflict *unacceptable* nuclear damage. In De Gaulle's mind, the explosion of French hydrogen bombs over three or four major Soviet cities, including Moscow, would constitute unacceptable damage in the Kremlin's eyes and would thus provide effective deterrence against a Soviet aggression in Europe (or at least against France) without any need for France to rely on any uncertain American response.

To provide for such a French threat of nuclear response to Soviet aggression, De Gaulle's regime accepted the great economic and financial burden of obtaining a *force de frappe*. In its first stage, to be achieved by 1966, this would consist of 62 Mirage IV supersonic manned jet bombing planes to carry France's first-generation, 60-kiloton plutonium bombs. By the end of 1964, when twenty of these planes were operational, they were being produced at a rate of one a month and were being matched by the production of one bomb a month from the atomic pile at Marcoule. By 1966 the power of the bomb is expected to increase to its maximum size of about 300 kilotons.

The Mirage IV, as vehicle for the French nuclear threat, will be replaced by twenty-five land-based missiles fired from underground silos. These will be operational about 1969, and will shift their warheads from A-bombs to H-bombs some time in the early 1970's. The third generation of French nuclear weapons will probably be Polaris-type nuclear submarines to become operational some time in the 1970's. If these can be speeded up and the Mirage IV could be retained, it is possible that the brief transition stage of land-based missiles might be skipped completely. The total nuclear submarine fleet will probably not exceed three vessels, even in the late 1970's.

These plans do not seem impressive in comparison with the nuclear armament of the two Superpowers, but they are expected to make France an independent nuclear Power and allow it to exercise an independent nuclear deterrence. However, if countermeasures, such as the development of an anti-missile missile, become more successful, the additional penetration devices needed to allow the French nuclear threat to be credible may raise the financial cost of the whole effort to a level that would put a very severe strain on the French budget. In that case, France must either give up the effort or try to persuade the European Community to do it as a joint effort. (This might re-activate the West European Union or fall to the largest fragment of a divided NATO.) But in this case, France, despite De Gaulle, will have to accept some kind of European political union.

All of this points up the fact that the future political and military structure of Europe revolves about two quite separate problems: (1) Will it be a united Europe or a Europe of national states? (as De Gaulle wants), and (2) Will it be aligned with the United States or will it be an independent neutralist factor in the Cold War? The United States wants Europe to be united and allied; De Gaulle wants it to be disunited and independent; the Kremlin wants it disunited and neutral; London's policy, until 1960, was to see it disunited and allied to the Atlantic system. It seems likely, for reasons already given, that Europe's interests and those of the world as a whole might be served best if Europe could be united and independent. Moreover, in view of the conflicting forces involved, it seems very likely that Europe, after a considerable delay caused by De Gaulle, will finally emerge as united and independent.

Thus the future of Europe, like that of France itself, depended, in the mid-1960's, on De Gaulle's continuance in office. This was ensured, at least until the next presidential election in 1965, unless interrupted by death, by the fact that no alternative to De Gaulle could be seen clearly even by his opponents. In the early 1960's, the political pattern of France was dominated by four factors: (1) the terrorism of the extreme Right, led by the Secret Army Organization (OAS), which resisted the Algerian settlement even after it was completed in 1962 and made several efforts to assassinate De Gaulle; (2) the disorganization and discontent of the older political leaders as De Gaulle continued to change French politics to a simple administrative structure with himself as an almost monarchical figure standing as a symbol of France above political considerations; (3) the steady, if not always enthusiastic, support of De Gaulle by the passive mass of Frenchmen who saw the general as a center of solidity in the middle of a sea of confusions; and (4) the unpredictable and despotic control of the political initiative by De Gaulle himself.

The chief discontents came in 1960 and 1961 from those groups in the population, notably farmers, civil servants, and university students, who found that they were sharing in the economic boom less than others or were being squeezed by its dynamics. The price inflation of about 50 percent in the decade following 1953 injured government employees, whose salaries did not rise as rapidly as prices; university students were also squeezed by the inflation but were squeezed much more literally in housing, eating accommodations, and classroom space by a great increase in enrollments which was not sufficiently prepared for by government efforts to increase facilities. And the peasants, encouraged by government technocrats to modernize their methods, found that increased production led to lower farm prices and decreased incomes for themselves.

In view of the authoritarian character of the De Gaulle regime, these discontents tended to become extralegal agitations. There were sporadic strikes, protest parades, and even riots of these groups to call public attention to their grievances. Farmers were particularly violent when agricultural prices decreased and industrial prices continued to inch upward. The Gaullist government hoped to remedy the situation by reducing the costs of distribution through middlemen and thus provide French farmers with an increasing share of the reduced price of produce to the consumer, but on the whole the incredibly inefficient distribution of French farm produce, which forced most produce, regardless of source or destination, to pass through the Parisian markets, was too difficult a problem even for De Gaulle's experts, at least in any time interval that mattered. To obtain concessions, the farmers rioted, often on a large scale, such as an outburst of 35,000 of them at Amiens in February 1960. They blocked national automobile routes with their tractors, spread unsold or unremuneratively priced farm produce over the roads or city streets, and responded with violence when efforts were made to disperse them.

Through this whole period, De Gaulle's conduct of the government, through his handpicked prime ministers, made a shambles of the Fifth Republic constitution, which had been tailored to his specifications. Since a government could not be overthrown by defeat of a bill but only by a specific vote of censure, and this latter would lead to a general election in which all of De Gaulle's prestige could be used against those who had voted for the censure, the ordinary deputy's love of office and reluctance to wage an expensive and risky electoral campaign made it possible for De Gaulle's premiers to obtain almost any law he desired. The older political leaders were very restive under this system but could mobilize no organized opposition to it, because no one could see any real alternative to De Gaulle.

A significant example of De Gaulle's high-handed operations may be seen in the way he forced through the bill to create an independent French nuclear force without allowing the Assembly to debate the issue or to vote on the bill itself (November–December 1960). This was done under Article 49 of the constitution, which allows the government to pass a bill on its own responsibility without consideration by the Assembly unless a vote of censure is passed by a majority (277) of all the deputies. By use of this article, the three readings of the Nuclear Arms bill were replaced by three motions of censure that obtained no more than 215 votes. There seems to have been a clear majority, both in the Assembly and in the country as a whole, against the nuclear force, but few were willing to risk the fall of the government with no acceptable alternative in sight, and even fewer were willing to precipitate a general election.

As might be expected in such a system, the danger of assassination as a method for changing a government increased greatly, but De Gaulle continued on his imperturbable course in spite of a number of attempts on his life. One of the chief dangers to the Gaullist regime came from the discontent of the highest officers in the armed forces, but the mutiny and revolt of several army contingents in Algeria in April 1961 showed fairly clearly that this opposition movement was largely restricted to the highest officers, and De Gaulle was able to eliminate them and thus to reduce them, like the rest of his opponents, to angry impotence or to assassination efforts. De Gaulle's success in retiring from public life the only surviving Marshal of France, Alphonse Juin, clinched his superiority over the army.

Equally successful, and typical of De Gaulle's actions, were his constant appeals to public opinion, by television or on personal regional tours, or by local elections or plebiscites, against the disunited opposition, especially against the traditional political party leaders. A successful example of these techniques occurred in 1962 when De Gaulle decided to change the method of electing the president (or reelecting himself) from the constitutional method of choice by an electoral college of 80,000 "notables" to election by popular vote. To bypass the Senate, which was constitutionally entitled to vote on such matters and would unquestionably reject the change, De Gaulle announced that the amendment would be submitted to a popular referendum of the whole electorate. This method of changing the constitution by referendum was denounced as unconstitutional by all the political parties except his own, and was declared illegal by the Council of State.

Gaston Monnerville, president of the senate, who would become president of France if De Gaulle died, denounced the referendum as illegal, and accused De Gaulle of "malfeasance." When De Gaulle's rage at Monnerville became evident, the Senate reelected Monnerville as its presiding officer with only three dissenting votes. The Assembly, in an overnight session, October 4–5, 1962, passed a vote of censure with 280 votes. By the referendum on the constitutional change, on October 28, 1962, De Gaulle achieved his purpose with almost 62 percent of the votes registering "ayes" (this was only 46 percent of the registered votes because of the 23 percent nonvoting) in spite of the fact that his proposal was opposed by all political parties except his own. The following month, November 1962, in the general election made necessary by the vote of censure, De Gaulle's bloc won 234 seats out of 480, with an additional 41 seats committed to his support. The Right was practically wiped out in the election, although the Communists increased slightly to 41 seats.

This pattern of personal and rather arbitrary rule, opposed by the older ruling groups but sustained by the ordinary Frenchman whenever De Gaulle asked for such support, has continued to be the pattern of De Gaulle's political system, and will undoubtedly continue unless he meets some unforeseen sharp diplomatic defeat or a domestic economic collapse. Both of these are unlikely at the present time.

While French political life passed through these stages of superficial drama and fundamental boredom, British political life wallowed in a malaise of mediocrity. No groups were actually discontented, and certainly none was enthusiastic about the situation in Britain over the 1957–1964 period leading up to the General Election of October 1964. The Conservative Government came to office in 1951, was returned in the elections of. 1955, and returned again in the elections of October 1959. Anthony Eden served a brief and rather unsuccessful prime ministership from the retirement of Winston Churchill in April 1955 until his own retirement in favor of Harold Macmillan in January 1957. The latter's term of office had no spectacular failures such as Eden had experienced in the Suez Crisis of October 1956, but on the whole there were also no great successes.

Macmillan sought to avoid issues if possible, to strengthen contacts with the United States and the Commonwealth by personal diplomacy, to follow Washington's policy as closely as possible without appearing openly obsequious, and to hold a fairly tight rein over the Conservative Party and the House of Commons. An endless series of nasty little problems were met and somehow disposed of, to be followed by the rise of similar problems without any significant changes of course or speed. Abroad, the chief problems arose from the demands of various areas within the Commonwealth for self-government and the intrusion of the racial issue into these disputes, especially in Central Africa, East Africa, British Guiana, and Malaya. The chief problems at home were equally endless and were concerned with the continual weakness of the pound sterling on the foreign exchange market and the social problems associated with the British economic expansion, such as increased vehicular traffic, spreading juvenile and adolescent delinquency, an apparent decline in the level of adult moral behavior, and the growing attacks, especially in industry and finance, on the economic bases of the older Establishment.

In general, there was a slow spreading disillusionment with the structure of English society, especially with the continued dominance by the old established families of political and economic life. This was especially notable among the middle and lower middle classes, while the lower class was, apparently, less antagonistic because of the continued relative prosperity and, above all, from the weakening of what might be called the Labour Party ideology of class conflict.

In spite of a weakening of class antagonisms, there was a spreading rejection of the established class structure of England as it had existed for about a century. The good manners of the lower and middle classes, which had made visits to England such a pleasure, have slowly worsened, since they have come to be regarded as a mark of acceptance of the rigid class structure of the country, something that is decreasing in all classes. This shift is evident even in legislation, such as an Act of 1963, permitting peers to give up their titles in order to run for office in the House of Commons. It is, perhaps, most threatening in the animosity expressed by some of the new class of very rich who reject the established social prestige of the older aristocratic families.

This last point is of some importance, for it may mark the end of a very significant period of English history. In this history the English social structure was retained because of its flexibility rather than its rigidity. Access to higher social levels had never been closed to those with the energy and luck to work upward. These climbers invariably became strong defenders of the class structure, buying country houses, sending their children to boarding schools, and adopting the accent and other distinctive idiosyncrasies of the English upper classes. This "aping of their betters" on all levels preserved the English class structure and provided the relatively frictionless character of English social life. Frictions have now appeared at the very time that class antagonisms have been weakened. The reason for this has been the slow spreading in Britain of a kind of individualistic and nominalistic outlook that had been prevalent in much of the Western world for several generations but had been played down in Britain, until the last decade or so, by the pressures to conform on those who wished to rise socially and even on those who wished to remain in their same social level. As a result, traditionally in England, individualists have been eccentrics, that is, persons so well established that their social positions could not be changed notably by their personal behavior. This is now changing.

Increasingly, those who wish to remain in their social status and, most significantly, a surprising number of those who are rising in the economic, academic, and political hierarchies feel called upon to reject in an explicit fashion the established class structure. This began with the writings of Labour Party intellectuals early in the century; but it has now become so widespread that rising young men today still continue to rise without conforming to the established behaviorial patterns of their aspirant levels. One reason for this, of course, is that control of the ladders to success are no longer so closely held. In the old days, the merchant bankers of London, EC2, controlled fairly well the funds that were needed for almost any enterprise to become a substantial success. Today much larger funds are available from many diverse sources, from abroad, from government sources, from insurance and pension funds, from profits of other enterprises, and from other sources. These are no longer held under closely associated controls and are much more impersonal and professionalized in their disposal, so that, on the whole, an energetic man (or a group with a good idea) can get access to larger funds today and can do so without anyone much caring if he accepts the established social precedents.

At the same time, on lower levels, young men working their way upward, although not, perhaps, to "the top," no longer conform in dress and behavior to the expected patterns of respectability of their social aspirations, but often show a more or less open defiance of these. The most obvious, and in a way most frightening, examples of this are to be found in the open defiance of all respectability by adolescents and post-adolescents of various social levels, but chiefly low ones, who have rioted by the thousands at various seaside resorts on long weekends in recent years.

These most obvious examples of rebellion against English conformity are, however, not nearly so significant as the less obvious, but much more significant, rejections of the established system by men whose training and positions would lead us to expect that they would be firm supporters of it. This includes men like the following: (1) John Grigg, who disclaimed his title of Lord Altrincham in 1963, was educated at Eton and New College, was in the Grenadier Guards, edited the *National Review* (which had been acquired from Lady Milner), and was close to the Establishment from his father's long-time associations with the Milner Group, the *Times*, the Round Table, and his intimate friendship with Lord Brand; the son shocked the Court by his open criticism of the Queen's social associations as undemocratic; and his weekly articles for the *Guardian* advocated, among other things, abolition of a hereditary House of Lords; or (2) Goronwy Rees of New College and All Souls who had denounced the English amateur tradition in government and business as a "cult of incompetence," and demanded, to replace it, a system of training and recruitment that will provide a British managerial class marked by professional competence rather than by what he regards as "frivolity"; or (3) John Vaizey, one-time Scholar of Queens College, Cambridge and now Fellow of Worcester College, Oxford, who denounces the whole English educational system as inadequate and misguided and would replace it with something more like the French openly competitive system of free education.

One, perhaps surprising, voice in this criticism, aimed at attitudes rather than class structure, has been that of Prince Philip. He has tried, with only moderate success, to introduce scientists, technicians, and managerial types into Court circles (at least occasionally), but these circles continue, as in the past, to be dominated by the old rural upper-class interests of horses, hunting, and parlor games. At the same time, by a series of calculated indiscretions, His Royal Highness has sought to encourage the change of attitude that so many feel is essential to the continued survival of Britain in an era of advanced technology. Samples of his statements continue to be quoted, especially in circles that disapprove of them. In February 1961, the Prince said, "If anyone has a new idea in this country, there are twice as many people who advocate putting a man with a red flag in front of it," and eighteen months later, in a speech on Britain's inability to remain competitive in the world's export markets, he said, ". . . we are suffering a national defeat comparable to any lost military campaign, and, what is more, a self-inflicted one. . . . The bastions of the smug and the stick-in-the-mud can only be toppled by persistent undermining. . . ." These criticisms of complacency, now a chronic disease of the British upper classes, have had relatively small influence, at least in those circles where they are most needed and where they are discreetly regarded as "unfortunate remarks."

However, the volume of such criticism, especially on relatively high levels of the established hierarchies, has been growing, and must eventually force significant changes of outlook and behavior. They are more effective evidence of the breakdown of established outlooks than more spectacular events, like the antics of juvenile rioters or even the sinful lives of Cabinet ministers exposed in the popular press for the whole world to see, as was done of the war minister's encounters with a teenage prostitute whom he met (of all places) at Lady Astor's "Cliveden" estate. It seems possible, however, that any constructive change in England will be so long delayed that it may be anticipated by waves of unconstructive change, especially the rapid spread of frantic materialism, self-indulgence, and undisciplined individualism. That this should occur in the country that offered the world of the twentieth century its finest examples of self-disciplined response to the calls of social duty would, indeed, be a profound tragedy.

It would seem that Britain, perhaps more than any other European country except Sweden, is passing through a critical phase where it does not know what it wants or what it should seek. The patterns of outlook and behavior that brought it to world leadership by 1880 were going to seed by 1938. There was sufficient vitality still left in them to bring forth the magnificent effort of 1940–1945, but since 1945 it has become clear that the old patterns are not adapted to success in the contemporary world of technocracy, operations research, rationalization, and mass mobilization of resources. The British method of operating through a small elite, coordinated by leisurely personal contact and shared outlooks, and trained in the humanities, cannot handle the problems of the late twentieth century. Britain has the quality to do this, for, as we have seen, operations research, jet engines, radar, and many of the technological advances that helped create the contemporary world originated in Britain; but these things must be available on a mass basis for any country wishing to retain a position of substantial world leadership today, and they cannot be made available in Britain on a quantity basis by any continuation of the patterns of training and recruitment used by Britain in the nineteenth century.

There are those who say in all sincerity that there is no need for Britain to seek to retain a position of leadership that would require it to destroy everything that made the country distinctive. These people are prepared to abandon world leadership, international influence, and economic expansion for the sake of preserving the late nineteenth-century patterns of life and society. But pressures from outside as well as from within make this impossible. Lycurgus renounced social change in prehistoric Sparta only by militarizing the society. Britain certainly cannot refuse to change and at the same time hope to retain the leisurely, semiaristocratic, informally improvising social structure of its recent past. The outside world is not prepared to allow this, and, above all, the mass of British people will not allow it. In fact, the reluctance of the Conservative Party under Macmillan to face up to this problem has pushed a large number of British voters, reluctantly, toward the Labour Party. As a result, Labour won the election of October 1964 by a bare majority of the House of Commons.

It is widely agreed that Britain's problems in facing the contemporary world fall under two headings: (a) a rather complacent lack of enterprise and (b) an educational system that is not adapted to the contemporary world. The lack of enterprise is rooted in the self-satisfied attitude of the established elite, especially in their rather unimaginative attitude toward industry and business. For example, at the time that the Volkswagen was sweeping the American small-car import markets, the British Motor Corporation had in the Morris Minor a car that was slightly inferior in a few points, superior on several important points, and sold for several hundred dollars less, yet no real effort was made by the British firm to fight for a share of the American market.

Critics of contemporary England tend to concentrate their fire on the educational system, which, despite great changes, remains inadequate, in the sense that large numbers of young people are not being trained for the tasks that have to be done, especially for teaching itself. To be sure, Britain has provided about three billion dollars on new educational buildings since the war, with about a hundred thousand more teachers, an extension in the school-leaving age of about eighteen months, and a sixfold increase in opportunities for higher education (with new universities being established in provincial towns almost yearly); but the subjects studied, the methods used, and the attitudes toward these are not directed toward the needs of the future world; no real coordination or ready access is provided between the educational system and the world of action, and access to either by the ordinary Englishman remains restricted by social and economic barriers.

Instead of the gradual elimination of those who are unwilling to study, such as operates in theory in France and to a lesser extent in the United States, Britain still has barriers at ages eleven and eighteen that shunt the major part of the country's young people into terminating and specialized curricula, and do so on largely irrelevant criteria, such as ability to pay or social background. A survey of more than four thousand children, reported by Thomas Pakenham in *The Observer*, concluded that "the 11-plus examination and our selective educational system itself are seriously biased in favour of middle-class children and against virtually all those from poorer families." Using I.Q. tests that are themselves biased in favor of middle-class children, the survey showed that of all eight-year-old children with I.Q.'s of 105, only 12 percent of lower-class children were subsequently able to get to grammar schools, while 46 percent of those from the middle class could get to grammar schools (and thus get access to a curriculum preparing for college). Of eight-year-olds with I.Q.'s of 111, 30 percent from the lower class but 60 percent of a higher social background subsequently reached grammar school. And of those exceptional children with I.Q.'s above 126, about 82 percent of both social levels get to grammar school.

These figures are taken from a recent volume, edited by Arthur Koestler, entitled *Suicide of a Nation?* (Hutchinson, 1963). The significance of the volume does not rest so much in what it says as in the fact that a team of writers, including Koestler, Hugh Seton-Watson, Malcolm Muggeridge, Cyril Connolly, Austen Albu, M.P., Henry Fairlie, John Mander, Michael Shanks, and others, could contribute to a volume with the rhetorical title borne by this one. Several of these writers apply to the ruling groups of contemporary Britain the designation that Gilbert Murray, more than a generation ago, taught their elders to use with reference to ancient Athens: "a failure of nerve." There may indeed be a failure of nerve in both historical cases, but there is equally evident a failure of imagination and of energy. For the Britain that won glory in World War II had many opportunities to do great things in the postwar period but failed to do so because its leaders were unwilling to grasp the opportunity.

On the whole, the two contending political parties in Britain continue to offer the mass of English voters opposing visions that have no real appeal to the great majority of English, and, at the same time, show an obvious disinclination to take drastic action to realize these visions, probably because party leaders know that their views are repugnant to the majority.

These two opposed visions offer, on the one hand, the nostalgic yearnings of the Conservatives for the world of 1908 and, on the other side, the state Socialism and unilateral disarmament of the Labour Party doctrinaires. Neither of these has much to contribute to the real problems facing Britain in the last half of the twentieth century, which is why the mass of British voters, who can detect irrelevance even when they themselves have no clear knowledge of what is relevant, have little enthusiasm for either. The Conservative standpatters were challenged by a number of vigorous and able veterans of World War II, such as Iain Macleod, Peter Thorneycroft, Quintin Hogg (Lord Hailsham), Reginald Maudling, Enoch Powell, Ted Heath, and others. These were essentially empiricists, but they wanted Conservatism to make an active attack on Britain's problems and to make their party more appealing to the great mass of Englishmen by associating it with vigor and a social conscience.

In one way or another, Macmillan was able to sidetrack all of these, to derail the traditional leader of the older aristocratic Conservative families, Lord Salisbury, and to block other significant contenders for control of the party such as R. A. Butler. In fact, Macmillan's eagerness to avoid decisions or activity in matters concerned with the welfare of the country was exceeded only by his activity in consolidating his own personal power in the party. In some ways, notably in his insatiable yearning for power, his skill in concealing this fact, and his evident lack of any very rigid principles on other matters, Macmillan recalled his predecessor, Baldwin. Both had the same pose as typical country squires and both had Oxford University closer to their hearts than any other public issue. But where Baldwin was lethargic and relatively sensitive, Macmillan was active and secretly ruthless, quite willing, apparently, to disrupt the Establishment or the party itself to further his personal position and his surprisingly narrow social interests. This was seen in his last-minute, successful, campaign against Sir Oliver Franks for the honorary position of Chancellor of Oxford University in 1960 and in the way in which, operating from a hospital bed in 1963, he pushed aside all other claimants to be his successor as prime minister to put into that office the fourteenth Earl of Home, Alexander Frederick Douglas-Home. This disregard of tradition, of the lines of expected procedure, of the claims of past service and cooperation, and, above all, of the expectations of public opinion in order to raise a man whose chief claim seemed to many to be based on long lineage was a fair commentary on Macmillan's attitude toward his office and his party. Its influence on the morale of the party itself cannot be assessed, but it cannot have been a good one.

The Labour Party was similarly divided, and similarly fell under the control of a man whose will to power was stronger than any ideology or party principles. On the whole the party was split between leaders of labor-union origin and intellectuals from jobs in university teaching. At the same time, it was split beween those who still saw some merit in the old theories of class struggles and imperialist wars and felt that the solutions to both was to be found in nationalization of industry and drastic, if not unilateral, disarmament (at least in regard to nuclear weapons). The postwar world, in Britain as elsewhere, violated all the anticipations of Socialist Party theories. The former Socialist Utopia, the Soviet Union, became the archenemy, and the United States, previously regarded as the epitome of capitalist corruption, became a combination of St. George and Santa Claus; the postwar experience with nationalization disillusioned all but the most doctrinaire of Socialists, and the majority of voters, once they had obtained the basic elements of social welfare, medical care, and social insurance in the immediate postwar period, showed a strange preference for moderate or even Conservative leaders rather than for the advocates of Left-wing policies.

As a consequence of these experiences, the Labour Party tended to split into a major wing that sought to win votes and office by appeals to moderation and a minor wing that sought to repeat the older war cries for seeking working-class benefits through class legislation and nationalization. The disappearance from the scene of the prewar Labour Party leaders, such as Clement Atlee, Ernest Bevin, and Hugh Dalton, made Hugh Gaitskell leader of the party and of its moderate wing. By 1956 Gaitskell was being challenged from the Left by Frank Cousins, a former miner, who was backed by a million votes in the Transport and General Workers Union. At the Party Conference of 1960 Gaitskell was defeated on four resolutions favoring unilateral disarmament and rejecting British cooperation with NATO, which were passed over his objections. Gaitskell was able to reverse these votes in 1961, but could not wipe from the public mind the impression that the party might not be completely reliable in support of Britain's role in the defense of the West against Communist aggressions. While still concerned with this task, Gaitskell died early in 1963, and was succeeded as party leader by Harold Wilson, whose brilliant record as student and teacher did not hamper his work as a skilled and tireless manipulator of intraparty political influence.

From 1959 onward, a small but steady sagging in popular support for the Conservatives was evident. The party delayed calling a new election until the very end of the five-year term of the Parliament's life in the vain hope that some success, or at least some decisive improvement in Britain's economic condition, might provide the margin for an unprecedented fourth consecutive electoral victory. By late 1960 it was clear that some decisive step must be taken to regain popular support.

Macmillan was driven, still with reluctance, to seek membership for Britain in the booming European Economic Community. Application was made in August 1961, opening many months of onerous negotiations. During this period De Gaulle made a spectacular state visit to West Germany, spoke of the national glories of Germany, and persuaded Chancellor Adenauer to sign a special treaty of Franco-German friendship, whose real meaning was ambiguous to all concerned, except that it seemed to exclude both the great English-speaking Powers from the inner European circle. The latter two reaffirmed their solidarity—in what looked to some like British inferiority to Washington—in a conference between Macmillan and President Kennedy in the Bahamas in December 1962.

The Nassau Conference sought to iron out various Anglo-American differences, to agree on steps that might avert De Gaulle's steady weakening of NATO, and, on Macmillan's part, to show the British electorate the Conservative leader's close relations with President Kennedy. The meeting confirmed an American decision to abandon the "Skybolt," an air-to-ground missile on which the British had constructed much of their nuclear defense, and proposed to strengthen NATO by establishing a "multinational force." The latter project hoped to establish NATO's strategic nuclear force in a fleet of surface naval vessels, armed with Polaris-type missiles and operated by mixed crews from all the NATO Powers. These mixed crews would prevent France from continuing its divisive policies within the NATO military array, increase the cohesion of Europe, give its nuclear strategy at least an appearance of independence from the United States, and provide the groundwork for some kind of European Defense Community, including Britain, if France split NATO completely.

De Gaulle's answer to this weak and symbolic gesture of Anglo-American cooperation was decisive. Within less than a month, in January 1963, he rejected the British seventeen-month-old application to join the EEC. This resounding defeat to Macmillan and the United States was delivered in typical De Gaulle fashion. In superb disregard of the established EEC procedures for dealing with applications for membership, De Gaulle, at a personal press conference, announced that France would oppose the British request, on the grounds that it was a belated effort to get into a system that the British had earlier sought to impede with their rival Outer Seven Free Trade Area and that Britain was not yet ready for admission to any purely European system since, as he said, "Britain, in effect, is insular, maritime, and linked by her trade, her markets, and her suppliers to a great variety of countries, many of them distant . . . [so that] the nature, structure, and circumstances of Britain differ profoundly from those of continental states." If Britain were admitted to EEC, according to De Gaulle, she would at once seek to bring in all the other members of OECD, and "in the end there would appear a colossal Atlantic community under American dominance and leadership which would completely swallow up the European Community."

The other five EEC nations, with Britain and the United States, opposed De Gaulle's efforts to break off the Brussels talks on the British application for membership, but on January 29, 1963, the French vetoed continuance of the discussion, and the British application was, in effect, rejected.

The De Gaulle veto suspended indefinitely the movement toward Europe's political unity. At the same time, De Gaulle rejected the Anglo-American suggestion for a multinational nuclear force within NATO. On January 22, 1963, with President Adenauer of West Germany, he signed the French-German Treaty of friendship and consultation, providing periodic conferences of the two countries on foreign policy, defense, and cultural matters. Before the end of the month, over strong Labour Party opposition, the British Parliament approved the Anglo-American Nassau Pact and heard Prime Minister Macmillan announce his government's determination to build an independent nuclear force of four or five British-built Polaris submarines by purchasing the necessary equipment from the United States.

In this way, the movement for European unity was suspended and the Continent remained "at sixes and sevens." This condition of stalemate was protracted for almost two years, through 1963 and 1964, by extensive governmental changes and important national elections. In February 1963, the Conservative government of Prime Minister Diefenbaker of Canada was overthrown on a no-confidence vote based on charges that he had failed in vigor in supplying warheads for Canada's section of the North American defense system. He was replaced by a Liberal government headed by Lester B. Pearson. In the same month, in England the death of the Labour Party leader Gaitskell brought to the head of that opposition group a relatively unknown Left-wing intellectual and former university instructor, Harold Wilson, who had often supported Aneurin Bevan against Gaitskell's more moderate views. In June of 1963 the whole movement for Christian religious reunion and reform of the Catholic Church was suspended by the death of the very popular Pope John XXIII and installation of his successor as Pope Paul VII. In October one of the semipermanent fixtures of the European postwar political scene disappeared when the eighty-seven-year-old Chancellor Konrad Adenauer resigned after a fourteen-year term; he was replaced in the chancellorship by Economic Minister Ludwig Erhard, who was widely regarded as the chief architect of Germany's spectacular economic recovery. Three days after Adenauer's resignation, Harold Macmillan, on grounds of ill health, resigned as prime minister and was able to impose on his party as his successor the ex-Earl of Home, renamed Sir Alec Douglas-Home. Thus the

British General Election of October 1964 was fought with new leaders on both sides.

A few weeks after the shift of government in London, a more significant change of government took place in Rome as part of a long-term shift to the Left in the Italian political balance. Essentially the dominant Christian-Democratic group broke free, to some extent, from its reactionary Right wing and from the need to seek support on the Right by detaching the Left-wing Socialists from their long and uncomfortable alliance with the Communists by bringing this group into the government and leaving the Communists almost completely isolated on the Left. Aldo Moro, political secretary of the Christian Democratic Party, became premier of the new arrangement in December 1963, with Pietro Nenni, of the Left-wing Socialists, as deputy premier. In theory the coalition rested on an agreement to seek to extend the benefits of the Italian prosperity boom to the less affluent workers' groups who had been relatively neglected in the hysterical pursuit of profits by more affluent entrepreneurs under the preceding governments.

The Italian Cabinet shift was still in process when President Kennedy was assassinated by an unstable political fanatic in Dallas, Texas, on November 22, 1963. This, in view of the power and influence of the American Presidency, was the most significant governmental change for many years. After an unprecedented display of worldwide mourning, the new President, Lyndon B. Johnson, of Texas, took control of the American Presidency's global responsibilities and national obligations with only eleven months in which to establish his position as a candidate in the presidential election of 1964.

As a consequence of these changes, the removal from office of Khrushchev in October 1964, and the death that year of Jawaharlal Nehru, who had been prime minister of India from the achievement of independence in 1947, the governments of all major countries except France and Red China underwent significant shifts of personnel in a period of about fifteen months. This gave rise to a "pause" in world history for almost all of 1963–1964, during which each country placed increased emphasis on its domestic problems, especially on the demands of its citizens for increased prosperity, civil rights, and social security. Since the same tendency became evident also in France and Red China where the previous leaders continued in power, the last two years covered by this book were years of hesitation, decreased world tension, and confused plans for future courses.

Conclusion

Tragedy and Hope? The tragedy of the period covered by this book is obvious, but the hope may seem dubious to many. Only the passage of time will show if the hope I seem to see in the future is actually there or is the result of misobservation and self-deception.

The historian has difficulty distinguishing the features of the present, and generally prefers to restrict his studies to the past, where the evidence is more freely available and where perspective helps him to interpret the evidence. Thus the historian speaks with decreasing assurance about the nature and significance of events as they approach his own day. The time covered by this book seems to this historian to fall into three periods: the nineteenth century from about 1814 to about 1895; the twentieth century, which did not begin until after World War II, perhaps as late as 1950; and a long period of transition from 1895 to 1950. The nature of our experiences in the first two of these periods is clear enough, while the character of the third, in which we have been for only half a generation, is much less clear.

A few things do seem evident, notably that the twentieth century now forming is utterly different from the nineteenth century and that the age of transition between the two was one of the most awful periods in all human history. Some, looking back on the nineteenth century across the horrors of the age of transition, may regard it with nostalgia or even envy. But the nineteenth century was, however hopeful in its general processes, a period of materialism, selfishness, false values, hypocrisy, and secret vices. It was the working of these underlying evils that eventually destroyed the century's hopeful qualities and emerged in all their nakedness to become dominant in 1914. Nothing is more revealing of the nature of the nineteenth century than the misguided complacency and optimism of 1913 and early 1914 and the misconceptions with which the world's leaders went to war in August of 1914.

The events of the following thirty years, from 1914 to 1945, showed the real nature of the preceding generation, its ignorance, complacency, and false values. Two terrible wars sandwiching a world economic depression revealed man's real inability to control his life by the nineteenth century's techniques of laissez faire, materialism, competition, selfishness, nationalism, violence, and imperialism. These characteristics of late nineteenth-century life culminated in World War II in which more than 50 million persons, 23 million of them in uniform, the rest civilians, were killed, most of them by horrible deaths.

The hope of the twentieth century rests on its recognition that war and depression are man-made, and needless. They can be avoided in the future by turning from the nineteenth-century characteristics just mentioned and going back to other characteristics that our Western society has always regarded as virtues: generosity, compassion, cooperation, rationality, and foresight, and finding an increased role in human life for love, spirituality, charity, and self-discipline. We now know fairly well how to control the increase in population, how to produce wealth and reduce poverty or disease; we may, in the near future, know how to postpone senility and death; it certainly should be clear to those who have their eyes open that violence, extermination, and despotism do not solve problems for anyone and that victory and conquest are delusions as long as they are merely physical and materialistic. Some things we clearly do not yet know, including the most important of all, which is how to bring up children to form them into mature, responsible adults, but on the whole we do know now, as we have already shown, that we can avoid continuing the horrors of 1914–1945, and on that basis alone we may be optimistic over our ability to go back to the tradition of our Western society and to resume its development along its old patterns of Inclusive Diversity.

Index